PICTORIAL ENGLISH DICTIONARY

A TO Z

COVENT
GARDEN
BOOKS

A DORLING KINDERSLEY BOOK

First published in Great Britain in 1997
by Dorling Kindersley Limited.
9 Henrietta Street, London, WC2E 8PS

2 4 6 8 10 9 7 5 3 1

Copyright © 1997 Dorling Kindersley Limited, London
Reprinted 1997

This edition published in 1999 for Covent Garden Books

A CIP catalogue record for this book is available
from the British Library.

This edition revised by Dorling Kindersley

ISBN 1-85605-501-9

Printed and bound in Italy by LegoPrint

LIST OF ABBREVIATIONS

a(s)	adjective(s)	*fem*	feminine	*phot*	photography
abbr	abbreviation	*fig*	figurative(ly)	*phr v(s)*	phrasal verb(s)
adv(s)	adverb(s)	*fml*	formal	*pl*	plural
anat	anatomy	*geog*	geography	*polit*	politics
ar	archaic	*geol*	geology	*poss*	possessive
arch	architecture	*geom*	geometry	*pp*	past participle
astron	astronomy	*Ger*	German	*prep*	preposition
Aust	Australian	*Gk*	Greek	*pron(s)*	pronoun(s)
aut	cars, motoring	*gram*	grammar	*pr p*	present participle
aux	auxiliary	*her*	heraldry	*psyc*	psychology
avia	aviation	*hist*	historical	*pt*	past tense
bio	biology	*hort*	horticulture	*rad*	radio
bot	botany	*idm*	idiom	*reflex*	reflexive
Brit	British	*interj*	interjection	*sb('s)*	somebody('s)
cap	capital (initial)	*interrog*	interrogative	*Scot*	Scottish
chem	chemistry	*It*	Italian	*sing*	singular
coll	colloquial	*Lat*	Latin	*sl*	slang
comm	commerce	*leg*	legal	*Sp*	Spanish
comp	comparative	*ling*	linguistics	*sth*	something
comput	computers	*lit*	literary	*sup*	superlative
conj	conjunction	*masc*	masculine	*telecom*	telecommunications
dated	old-fashioned	*math*	mathematics	*[TM]*	Trademark
dem	demonstrative	*mech*	mechanics	*TV*	television
det(s)	determiner(s)	*med*	medicine	*US*	American
dram	drama, theatre	*met*	meteorology	*usu*	usually
eccl	ecclesiastical	*mil*	military	*v(s)*	verb(s)
econ	economics	*mus*	music		
eg	for example	*myth*	mythology		
elec	electrical, electronics	*n(s)*	noun(s)		
esp	especially	*naut*	nautical		

a, an *indefinite article* one.

A1 *a* first-rate.

AA *abbr* 1 Alcoholics Anonymous 2 Automobile Association.

aardvark *n* S African ant-eating mammal.

AB *abbr* 1 *Brit* able seaman 2 *US* Bachelor of Arts.

aback *adv* **be taken aback** be startled.

abacus *n* **-uses.** counting-frame with beads strung on parallel wires.

abaft *adv, prep* at or towards the stern of ship; behind.

abalone *n* mollusc; shell lined with mother-of-pearl.

abandon *v* 1 desert; forsake 2 give up altogether; *ns* **abandon, -ment** freedom from inhibition; *a* **-ed** 1 deserted 2 unrestrained; depraved.

abase *v* humiliate; *n* **abasement.**

abashed *a* ashamed; embarrassed; *n* **abashment.**

abate *v* make or become less intense; *n* **abatement.**

abattoir *n* slaughter-house.

abbess *n* head of convent or nunnery.

abbey *n* 1 (dwelling place of a) community of monks or nuns 2 church formerly attached to such a building.

abbot *n* head of abbey or monastery.

abbreviate *v* shorten; *n* **abbreviation.**

ABC[1] *n* 1 the alphabet as learnt by children 2 basic facts of a subject.

ABC[2] *abbr* 1 American Broadcasting Company 2 Australian Broadcasting Commission.

abdicate *v* give up (power, position, responsibility); *n* **abdication.**

abdomen *n* belly; *a* **abdominal.**

abduct *v* carry off unlawfully, kidnap; *n* **abduction.**

abeam *adv* at right angles to the length of a ship or aircraft.

aberration *n* deviating from what is normal; mental disorder; *a* **aberrant.**

abet *v* help or take part in a wrong doing; *n* **abettor.**

abeyance *n* temporary suspension.

abhor *v* detest, loathe; *a* **abhorrent;** *n* **abhorrence.**

abide *v* **abides, abiding, abode** or **abided** 1 tolerate; endure 2 dwell; remain; **abide by** be faithful to; *a* **abiding** lasting.

ability *n* power to do something; skill.

abject *a* miserable, cast down, servile; *adv* **abjectly;** *n* **abjectness.**

abjure *v* renounce on oath; *ns* **abjurer, abjuration.**

ablaut *n ling* systematic vowel mutation (*eg* in verb forms *sing, sang, sung*).

ablaze *a* 1 burning fiercely 2 very bright.

able *a* having the power or skill to do a thing; clever; talented; *adv* **ably;** *n* **ability.**

able-bodied *a* strong and fit.

able(-bodied) seaman *n Brit navy* ordinary trained seaman.

ablution *n* ceremonial washing; **perform one's ablutions** wash oneself.

ABM *abbr* antiballistic missile.

abnegate *v* deny oneself; renounce; *n* **abnegation.**

abnormal *a* out of ordinary; deviating from normal; *adv* **-ly;** *n* **-ity.**

aboard adv in or on a ship, train, aeroplane etc.

abode n home; dwelling place; pt, pp of **abide**.

abolish v do away with, wipe out; ns **abolition; abolitionist** one who favours abolition.

Abominable Snowman n yeti.

abominate v detest, loathe; a **abominable**; adv **abominably**; n **abomination** object of disgust.

Aboriginal n native inhabitant of Australia; a relating to the native inhabitants of Australia.

abort v 1 (to cause) to miscarry (of a foetus) 2 to end prematurely (of a mission or plan); n **abortion** 1 miscarriage 2 failed project 3 deformed thing; a **abortive** unsuccessful.

abound v be plentiful, well-supplied; a **abounding**.

about prep 1 concerning; on the subject of 2 around; adv 1 nearby; all around 2 nearly; **just about** very nearly; **be about to** be going to.

about-turn n Brit (US **about-face**) change to opposite direction, opinion or policy.

above prep over; higher than; more than; adv, a overhead; n **the above**, something mentioned before (in business letters).

above-board a open and honest.

abracadabra n magic formula; spell; gibberish.

abrade v rub or wear off; n, a **abrasive**; n **abrasion** place where skin is scraped off, sore so caused.

abreast adv, a side by side; on a line with.

abridge v shorten, condense; n **abridg(e)ment**.

abroad adv in another country; outdoors; at large.

abrogate v repeal; annul; n **abrogation**.

abrupt a 1 gruff 2 sudden; adv -ly; n -ness.

abscess n inflamed swelling containing pus.

abscond v run away secretly, esp to escape law.

abseil v make controlled rapid descent of steep rock face by means of rope.

absent a not present; inattentive; v **absent oneself** (**from**) stay away; adv **absently**; ns **absence**; **absentee** one who is not present, habitually absent; **absenteeism**.

absent-minded n inattentive; forgetful; adv -ly; n -ness.

absinthe n wormwood; green alcoholic liqueur flavoured with this.

absolute a 1 unlimited 2 independent of other factors 3 undiluted; pure; adv **absolutely**; n **absoluteness**.

absolute pitch n ability to identify exact musical pitch.

absolutism n (principle of) government with unlimited power.

absolve v pronounce free from sin; release from obligation;

pardon; n **absolution**.

absorb v take in; soak up; swallow up; a **absorbing** engrossing; ns **absorbent, absorption**.

abstain v 1 refrain from (esp alcohol or food) 2 refuse to vote; n **abstainer**; a **abstinent** refraining from food etc; ns **abstinence** self-denial, **abstention** (case of) not using a right to vote.

abstemious a temperate; not given to excess, esp in food and drink; adv **abstemiously**; n **abstemiousness**.

abstract a withdrawn from reality; n summary; v steal; take away; a **abstracted** absent-minded; n **abstraction**; advs **abstractedly, abstractly**.

abstruse a difficult to understand; obscure; adv -ly; n -ness.

absurd a unreasonable; ridiculous; adv **absurdly**; ns **absurdity, absurdness**.

ABTA abbr Association of British Travel Agents.

abundance n plenty; a **abundant**; adv **abundantly**.

abuse v 1 misuse 2 betray trust 3 insult; ns **abuse**; **abusiveness**; a **abusive**; (adv -ly).

abut v to be adjacent to.

abysm n abyss; a fig **abysmal** very bad; adv -ly.

abyss n bottomless pit.

AC abbr alternating current.

a/c abbr account.

acacia n tree or shrub with yellow or white flowers.

academy n 1 place of higher education 2 society for advancement of learning; n **academician**; a **academic** scholarly; adv **academically**.

Acadia n French-speaking areas of the Atlantic provinces of Canada.

ACAS abbr Advisory Conciliation and Arbitration Service.

accede v 1 succeed to 2 give consent or support 3 comply with; n **accedence**.

accelerate v increase speed; ns **accelerator** device for increasing speed in machines etc; **acceleration**.

accent n stress or emphasis; mark used to indicate sound of vowel; manner of pronunciation; v stress; accentuate; n **accentuation**.

accept v receive; take; admit; believe in; agree to; a **-able**; ns **-ability**, **acceptance**.

access n means of approach; right of entry; v comput retrieve or input (information); a **-ible** easy to reach, approach; ns **-ibility**, **accession** coming to throne, office.

accessory n 1 additional equipment; 2 a **accessory** additional 3 n leg person who helps to commit a crime.

access time n comput time taken to obtain stored information.

accidence n part of grammar dealing with the variable forms of words.

accident n 1 unexpected events 2 mishap; a **accidental**; adv **-ally**.

accident-prone a liable to accidents more often than most people.

acclaim n loud applause; welcome; approval; v applaud; n **acclamation**; a **acclamatory**.

acclimatize v adapt to a new climate; n **acclimatization**.

acclivity n upward slope of a hill.

accolade n 1 light stroke with a sword used in bestowing knighthood 2 any supreme reward.

accommodate n 1 fit 2 lodge 3 help by act of kindness; a **accommodating** obliging; n **accommodation** lodgings.

accompany v 1 go with; escort 2 play music supporting (a soloist); ns **accompanist**, **accompaniment**.

accomplice n 1 partner in crime 2 confederate.

accomplish v finish; bring to successful conclusion; a **accomplished** 1 finished 2 talented; n **accomplishment**.

accord v 1 be in harmony; agree 2 bestow; a **according** (**according as** conj depending on whether; **according to** prep 1 as stated by 2 following); n **accordance** agreement; adv **accordingly** therefore.

accordion n musical instrument with bellows, keys and metal reeds.

accost v 1 speak first to.

account n 1 record of money owed or paid 2 record of money or credit transactions 3 report; description 4 credit (**buy sth on account**) 5 reason (**on no account** for no reason) 6 consideration (**take into account, take account of**); prep **on account of** because of; v **account** regard; consider; phr v **account for 1** make a detailed record of **2** explain.

accountant n professional person appointed to keep or inspect financial accounts; n **accountancy**; a **accountable** answerable; adv **accountably**.

accoutrements n pl US **accouterments** equipment, esp a soldier's.

accredited a officially recognized or having the power to act in a certain capacity.

accretion n 1 growth; increase 2 something added.

accrue v increase, esp interest on invested money.

accumulate v amass; increase in mass or number; ns **accumulation**; **accumulator** apparatus for storing electrical or hydraulic energy; a **accumulative**.

accurate a exact in detail; precise; adv **-ly**; ns **accuracy**, **accurateness**.

accurse v curse; a **accursed** (**accurst**) under a curse; ill-fated; detestable; adv **accursedly**.

accuse v bring charge against;

blame; *ns* **accuser**, **accusation**; *adv* **accusingly**.

accustom *v* make familiar; get used to; *a* **accustomed**.

ace *n* 1 single spot on dice or cards 2 highest 3 best.

acerbate *v* 1 make sour or bitter 2 irritate; *a* **acerbic** sharp; bitter; *n* **acerbity**.

acetate *n* salt of acetic acid.

acetic *a* pertaining to vinegar; *n* **a. acid** organic acid giving vinegar characteristic taste.

acetone *n* inflammable liquid used as a solvent.

acetylene *n* inflammable gas formed by the action of water on calcium carbonate.

ache *v* suffer dull, continuous pain, physically or emotionally; *n* dull, continuous pain.

achieve *v* finish; gain; win; *n* -ment.

Achilles' heel *n* weakness; vulnerable point.

Achilles' tendon *n* sinew joining the calf muscles to the heelbone.

achromatic *a* colourless.

acid *n* sour substance with ph of less than 7; usually having corrosive effect; *a* 1 sour and sharp to taste 2 sharp-tempered; *ns* **acidity**, **acidness**; *adv* **acidly**.

acid house *n* electronically edited dance music of the late 1980's.

acidosis *n* an acid condition of the blood.

acid rain *n* rain polluted by industrial smoke and harmful to crops.

acid test *n* test that shows the real value of sth.

acidulous *a* sharp; bitter.

acknowledge *v* admit; recognize as true; indicate receipt of; *n* **acknowledg(e)ment** recognition of; *a* **acknowledgeable**.

acme *n* 1 highest point; summit 2 perfection.

acne *n* skin disease common in adolescence and characterized by pimples on the face and neck.

acolyte *n* 1 priest's attendant 2 any devoted assistant.

aconite *n* 1 poisonous plant with blue or yellow flower 2 drug obtained from such plants.

acorn *n* the fruit of the oak tree.

acoustic *a* 1 connected with hearing or sound 2 *mus* (of instruments) not electric; *adv* **acoustically**; *n* **acoustics** theory of sound.

acquaint *v* inform; make aware of; *idm* **be acquainted (with)** have some knowledge (of); *ns* **acquaintance** 1 slight knowledge 2 person slightly known; **acquaintanceship**.

acquiesce *v* agree passively or tacitly; *n* **acquiescence**; *a* **acquiescent**.

acquire *v* get or gain possession of; *n* **acquisition** 1 act of gaining 2 object gained; *a* **acquisitive** desirous of gain; *n* **acquisitiveness**.

acquit *v* -quitting, -quitted.

declare not guilty (of offence); *idm* **acquit oneself** behave correctly; *n* **acquittal** release by court.

acre *n* measure of land 4046 sq m (4840 sq. yds); *n* **acreage** area in acres.

acrid *a* bitter; caustic; *n* **acridity**; *adv* **-ly**.

acrimony *n* bitterness of manner of speech; *a* **acrimonious**; *adv* **-ly**.

acrobat *n* highly skilled gymnast; *n* **acrobatics**; *a* **acrobatic**; (*adv* **-ally**).

acronym *n* name or word formed by the initial letters of other words *eg* NATO, UNICEF, OPEC.

across *adv*, *prep* 1 on the other side (of) 2 from one side to the other side (of).

across-the-board *a* affecting all members, groups or types.

acrostic *n* verse or puzzle in which first and/or last letters, reading across and down, make words.

acrylic *n* type of synthetic material.

act *v* 1 do something 2 *dram* perform 3 (of drugs) have effect 4 behave; *phr v* **act up** cause trouble; *n* 1 thing done 2 main section of play or opera 3 item in circus or variety show 4 legislative measure 5 *idm* **put on an act** pretend; *ns* **actor**, *fem* **actress** one who acts (stage, TV or film).

act of God *n* unforeseeable event, *esp* disaster.

acting *n* *dram* performing; *a*

functioning temporarily as.

actinium *n* a radio-active element.

action *n* 1 act 2 movement 3 effect 4 *dram* main events 5 *sport* exciting play 6 battle 7 lawsuit; *a* **actionable** giving cause for legal action.

active *a* in action; quick; lively; *adv* **-ly**; *v* **activate** make active; set in motion.

activist *n* one taking active part in politics.

activity *n* 1 liveliness 2 busy action 3 occupation, *esp* of leisure.

actual *a* 1 existing 2 real; true; *adv* **-ly** 1 in fact 2 surprisingly; *n* **actuality** reality.

actuary *n* expert who calculates insurance risks; *a* **actuarial**.

actuate *v* 1 cause sth to work or begin 2 cause sb to act.

acuity *n* sharpness of perception.

acumen *n* ability to judge well.

acupuncture *n* treatment of pain or disease by sticking needles into the patient's body.

acute *a* 1 sharp 2 severe; agonizing; *adv* **-ly**; *n* **-ness**.

ad *n coll* advertisement.

AD *abbr* anno Domini (*Lat* = in the year of the Lord).

adage *n* old saying; proverb.

adagio *a, adv mus* slow(ly); *n* slow movement.

adamant *a* stubbornly determined; *adv* **-ly**; *n* very hard stone; *a* **adamantine**.

Adam's apple *n coll* lump at

front of throat, prominent in men; thyroid cartilage.

adapt *v* 1 modify; make fit for new use 2 become adjusted to new circumstances; *a* **adaptable**; *ns* **adaptability; adaptation; adaptor** 1 person who adapts (also **adapter**) 2 device for linking pieces of equipment, *esp* electrical plugs.

ADC *abbr* 1 aide-de-camp 2 analogue-digital converter.

add *v* 1 put sth together with sth 2 combine numbers and find the sum total 3 say further; *ns* **addition;** *a* **additive** something added; *a* **additional;** *adv* **-ly;** *phr vs* **add to** increase; **add up** 1 calculate sum of 2 make sense; **add up to** 1 amount to 2 indicate.

addendum *n* **-denda.** *Lat a* thing to be added.

adder *n* small venomous snake of viper family.

addict *n* 1 person unable to stop taking drugs, alcohol, etc 2 person with a passionate interest; *a* **addicted (to)** 1 dependent (on) 2 keenly interested (in); *n* **addiction;** *a* **addictive** habit-forming.

addled *a* 1 (of brains) confused 2 (of eggs) rotten.

address *n* 1 identification of residence or place of work 2 speech to an audience 3 *comput* details about storage location of data; *v* 1 speak to 2 write on a letter, parcel, etc details of its destination;

n **addressee** person to whom one is writing; *phr v* **address oneself to** turn one's attention to.

adduce *v* cite as proof.

adenoids *n pl* mass of tissue at back of nose, near throat.

adept *a* expert; *n* skilled person; expert; *adv* **adeptly**.

adequate *a* 1 sufficient 2 good enough; *adv* **-ly;** *n* **adequacy.**

adhere *v* stick or remain stuck; *phr v* **adhere to** remain loyal to; *n* **adherence** state of adhering; *n* **adherent** loyal supporter.

adhesive *n a* (substance) which causes things to be stuck together; *n* **adhesion** 1 being stuck together 2 loyalty to sth.

ad hoc *a, adv Lat* 1 for this purpose 2 not prepared in advance.

adieu *interj, n* goodbye; *pl* **adieus** or **adieux.**

ad infinitum *adv Lat* without limit.

adipose *a* fatty; *n* **adiposity.**

adjacent *a* lying near to; adjoining; *a* **adjoining** neighbouring.

adjective *n* word used to qualify a noun; *a* **adjectival.**

adjoin *v* be next to; *a* **adjoining** neighbouring.

adjourn *v* put off, postpone; *n* **-ment.**

adjudge *v* 1 decide by law 2 grant or award.

adjudicate *v* judge; pronounce judgment on; act as a judge; *ns* **adjudicator, adjudication.**

adjunct *n* thing added, but less

important.

adjust v 1 fit; arrange; a **-able**; n **-ment**.

ad lib a, adv Lat unprepared; v improvise.

adman n coll person who works in advertising.

administer v 1 manage 2 dispense; give out; ns **administrator**, **administration**; a **administrative**.

admirable a worthy of esteem; adv **admirably**.

admiral n high-ranking naval officer; n **admiralty** board that controls naval affairs.

admire v view with pleasure or respect ns **admirer**, **admiration**.

admissible a allowable; adv **-ibly**; n **admissibility**.

admission n 1 being allowed to enter 2 entrance fee 3 acknowledgement of fact; confession.

admit v 1 let in 2 acknowledge; confess; n **admittance** right of entry; adv **admittedly** granted.

admonish v warn; reprove; n **admonition**; a **admonitory**.

ad nauseam adv Lat to a sickening extent; excessively.

ado n fuss; bother; trouble; bustle.

adolescence n state of growing up; a, n **adolescent** boy, girl growing up.

adopt v 1 take and bring up as one's own child 2 accept formally; n **adoption**; a **adopted**; n **adoptability**.

adore v worship; regard with lavish affection, love; n **adoration**; a **adorable**; adv **-ably**.

adorn v beautify; embellish; n **adornment** decoration.

ADP abbr automatic data processing.

adrenal a near kidney; n **adrenalin** hormone produced by adrenal glands.

adrift a, adv 1 loose on water 2 without purpose.

adroit a dexterous; adv **-ly**; n **-ness**.

adult a, n grown-up; mature (person).

adulterate v corrupt; make impure; n **adulteration**.

adultery n sexual infidelity in marriage; n **adulterer**, fem **adulteress**; a **adulterous**.

adumbrate v foreshadow; n **-ation**.

advance v 1 move forward 2 lend money 3 promote; n 1 forward move; progress 2 money paid before due 3 loan 4 increase in amount; a early; before the due time; idm **in advance** beforehand; idm **make advances** to try to establish a relationship with; a **advanced** 1 beyond; intermediate 2 far on in life 3 modern in outlook; n **advancement** promotion.

advantage n favourable condition; a **advantageous**; adv **advantageously**.

advent n coming, esp of Christ; four weeks preceding Christmas; n **Adventism** belief in Millennium.

adventitious a accidental; casual.

adventure n exciting incident; hazardous exploit; n **adventurer** one who lives by his wits; a **adventurous**; adv **-ly**.

adverb n word qualifying verb, adjective or another adverb; a **adverbial**.

adversary n 1 enemy 2 opponent.

adverse a unfavourable; adv **-ly**; n **adversity** unfavourable event or circumstances.

advertise v 1 make known publicly 2 praise in order to sell; ns **advertisement** (also coll **ad**, **advert**), **advertiser**, **advertising**.

advert to phr v fml draw attention to.

advice n counsel; guidance; information.

advise v give advice to; inform of; n **adviser**; adv **advisedly** expedient; a **advisable**, **advisory**.

advocate v speak in favour of; recommend; n 1 person who speaks in support 2 defence lawyer; Scot barrister; n **advocacy** giving of support.

adze n curved bladed tool for cutting wood surface.

aegis n patronage; protection; auspices.

aeon, **eon** n a great age of time; eternity.

aerate v expose to air; charge with gas; n **aeration**.

aerial a of, in, like air; n antenna, rod or wire for

receiving or sending electromagnetic waves.

aerobatics n spectacular display by aircraft; a **aerobatic**.

aerobics n system of exercise to increase oxygen in the blood; a **aerobic**.

aerodrome n airfield.

aerodynamics n branch of physics dealing with forces exerted by moving air or gases; science of flight; a **aerodynamic**; adv **-ally**.

aerogram(me) n air mail letter.

aeronaut n flyer of balloon or aircraft; n **aeronautics** science of air navigation; as **aeronautic, aeronautical**.

aeroplane n aircraft.

aerosol n (container of) pressurized liquid for releasing as a spray.

aerospace n (technology related to) earth's atmosphere and space beyond.

aesthetics n study of beauty, esp in art; a **aesthetic**; adv **-ally**; n **aesthete** one who claims to have a special appreciation of art and beauty.

afar adv far away; **from afar** from a great distance.

affable a friendly; polite; adv **-ably**; n **affability**.

affair n 1 thing (to be) done 2 event or series of events 3 extramarital sexual relationship; pl **affairs** business matters.

affect v act upon; influence; work on (feelings); ns

affectation show; **affection** love; a **affectionate** (adv **-ly**).

affiance v betroth.

affidavit n leg, Lat written statement made under oath.

affiliate v accept persons, societies as members of institution; n **affiliation**.

affinity n kinship (by marriage); chemical attraction; relations between, implying common origin.

affirm v declare positively; confirm; n **affirmation**; n, a **affirmative**; adv **-ly**.

affirmative action n US positive discrimination.

affix v fix; fasten; n addition esp to word.

afflict v cause to suffer; a **afflicted**; n **affliction**.

affluence n wealth; a **affluent**; (adv **-ly**); n **affluent**, tributary stream.

afford v 1 have means for 2 supply; furnish; yield.

afforest v plant trees on; n **-ation**.

affray n fight.

affront v insult; offend; n impudent or defiant act.

aficionado n enthusiast for a particular activity.

afield adv **far afield** far away, esp from home.

afire a, adv on fire; burning.

aflame a, adv in flames; on fire.

afloat a, adv floating; in circulation.

afoot a 1 on foot 2 happening.

aforesaid a mentioned before.

afraid a frightened; timid; feeling fear.

afresh adv again; anew; once more.

Afrikaans n official language of S Africa.

Afro a, n (in a) loose bushy hairstyle, similar to that of some black people.

Afro- prefix of Africa.

after prep 1 later than 2 following 3 as a result of 4 in pursuit of 5 in the style of 6 despite; idm **after all** 1 despite everything 2 one must not forget; conj 1 later than 2 although; adv 1 later 2 behind.

afterbirth n placenta and foetal membranes expelled from womb after birth.

afterburner n 1 device giving extra thrust to jet engine 2 device to reduce danger of exhaust fumes.

aftercare n treatment or services offered to a person after medical treatment.

afterglow n 1 glow left after light has faded, eg after sunset 2 warm and happy feeling after an exciting experience.

aftermath n period following an event.

afternoon n period of day between noon and evening.

aftershave n lotion for use on face after shaving.

afterthought n 1 later idea 2 sth added later.

afterwards adv later on.

afters n Brit coll dessert.

again adv 1 once more 2 as

1 1

before **3** likewise.

against *prep* close to; opposite; in anticipation of.

agate *n* a semiprecious stone.

age *n* length of time, thing or person has existed; historical period; closing years of life; *v* grow old; *a* **aged; ageless** timeless.

ageism, agism *n* discrimination because of age; *a, n* **ageist, agist.**

agency *n* place or business providing service; *idm* **through the agency of** through the action of.

agenda *a* list of things to be discussed at meeting.

agent *n* **1** one who acts for person or company **2** natural force.

agent provocateur *n Fr* person used to tempt criminals or rebels to act illegally in order to arrest them.

agglomerate *v* (of volcanic rock) (cause to) form a mass; *a, n* fused (into a) mass; *n* **agglomeration.**

agglutinate *v* glue together; *n* **-ation.**

aggrandize *v* make greater in power, rank or wealth; *n* **aggrandizement.**

aggravate *v* **1** make worse **2** annoy; *a* **aggravating** annoying; *n* **aggravation.**

aggregate *n* entire sum; *v* collect; *n* **aggregation.**

aggressive *a* rude; offensive; *adv* **-ly;** *ns* **aggression; aggressor.**

aggrieve *v* hurt; cause distress to; *a* **aggrieved.**

aggro *n Brit coll* behaviour intended to provoke violence.

aghast *a* struck with horror or amazement.

agile *a* active; nimble; *adv* **agilely;** *n* **agility.**

agitate *v* disturb; shake violently; stir up unrest; *ns* **agitation, agitator.**

aglow *a, adv* glowing; in a glow.

AGM *abbr* annual general meeting.

agnostic *n* one believing that nothing can be known concerning God; *n* **agnosticism** theory of this belief.

ago *adv* gone by; in the past.

agog *a, adv* excited; eagerly anticipating.

agonize *v* suffer great anxiety; *a* **agonizing** unbearably painful; *a* **agonized** expressing agony.

agony *n* anguish of mind or body.

agony aunt *n Brit coll* person who gives advice on personal problems of readers who write letters to a newspaper or magazine column (**agony column**).

agoraphobia *n* morbid fear of open spaces; *a* **agoraphobic.**

agrarian *a* relating to land.

agree *v* consent (to); settle; concede (that); *as* **agreed; agreeable** pleasant; *adv* **agreeably;** *n* **agreement.**

agribusiness *n* range of enterprises concerned with processing, distribution and

support of farm products.

agriculture *n* art and theory of farming; *a* **agricultural** (*adv* **-ly**).

agronomy *n* science of controlling soil for crops.

aground *a, adv* grounded; beached; stranded (on shore).

ague *n* fever, as with malaria.

ah *interj* exclamation of satisfaction, surprise, happiness, pain, etc.

ahead *adv* **1** in front; in advance **2** forward.

ahoy *interj* call used in hailing (a ship).

AI *abbr* **1** artificial intelligence **2** artificial insemination.

AID *abbr* artificial insemination by donor.

aid *v* help in any way; *n* **1** support **2** money loan.

aide *n* assistant.

aide-de-camp *n* officer assisting a general.

aide-mémoire *n Fr* document used to aid memory.

AIDS, Aids *abbr* Acquired Immune Deficiency Syndrome.

ail *v* be out of health; *a* **-ing;** *n* **-ment.**

aileron *n* flap on airplane wing.

aim *v* point weapon; direct energy towards; *n* **1** action of aiming **2** purpose; *a* **aimless** (*adv* **-ly;** *n* **-ness**).

ain't *v coll* **1** am/is/are not **2** has/have not.

air *n* **1** gaseous substance around the earth **2** manner **3** tune; *pl* **airs** affected

manner; *as* **airy, airless**; *adv*
airily; *n* **airing** exposure to
air; outing in open air; *idms*
in the air a matter of
rumour; **on the air**
broadcasting; **off the air** not
broadcasting; *v* **air 1**
ventilate 2 dry 3 make
known (one's views).

airbase *n* military airport.

airborne *a* 1 flying 2 moving
in the air.

air-brake *n* brake worked by
compressed air.

air-brush *n* device used for
spraying paint or ink.

airbus *n* aircraft making short
to medium flights at
frequent regular intervals.

air-condition *v* treat air to
ensure purity and even
temperature; *n* **-ing**.

air-cooled *a* cooled, *esp*
engines, by currents of air.

aircraft *n* any kind of flying
machine.

aircraft-carrier *n* ship designed
to carry aircraft.

airfield *n* place where aircraft
land or take off.

air force *n* airborne branch of
armed forces.

air-gun *n* gun discharged by
compressed air.

air hostess *n* stewardess on
passenger aircraft.

airily *adv* in a carefree manner.

airlane *n* specified route for
aircraft.

air letter *n* sheet of paper that
folds and seals to form a
cheap light-weight letter to
send by air.

airlift *n* transport of people or

supplies, *esp* to or from a
place of difficult access.

airline *n* company operating
aircraft on regular route; **air-
liner** aircraft used by airline.

airlock *n* 1 airtight
compartment 2 airbubble
stopping flow of liquid in
pipe.

airmail *n* mail carried by
aircraft.

airman *n* a member of the
crew of an aircraft.

airplane *n* **aeroplane**.

air-pocket *n* current causing
aircraft to drop suddenly.

airport *n* aerodrome for
transport of passengers etc.

air raid *n* raid by aircraft
dropping bombs.

airship *n* flying machine.

airspace *n* atmosphere above a
country, regarded as its legal
property.

air-strip *n* narrow runway for
use by aircraft.

airtight *a* impermeable to air.

air-to-air *a* from one aircraft in
flight to another.

airway *n* airline.

airworthy *a* fit or safe to fly; *n*
airworthiness.

aisle *n* passageway between
seats or pews.

ajar *a* partly open.

akimbo *adv* with hands on hips
and elbows bent.

akin *a* 1 related by blood 2
alike; similar.

alabaster *n* smooth, white
stone for making ornaments;
a of or like this.

à la carte *adv Fr* ordering
separate items (on a menu).

alack *interj* expressing dismay,
regret, sorrow.

alacrity *n* speed; briskness;
eagerness.

à la mode *adv Fr* in fashion.

alarm *n* 1 call to arms 2
warning of danger; *v* fill
with fear; *a* **alarming**;
adv **-ly**; *n* **alarmist**.

alas *interj* expressing dismay,
grief, sorrow.

albatross *n* large seabird of the
petrel type.

albeit *conj* even though;
notwithstanding.

albino *n* person or animal with
white skin and hair, and
pink eyes due to lack of
pigment; *pl* **albinos**.

album *n* 1 book of blank pages
for stamps, photographs etc
2 long playing record with
several tracks.

alchemy *n* medieval chemistry;
n **alchemist**.

alcohol *n* pure spirit of wine;
intoxicating liquor; *a*
alcoholic; *ns* **alcoholism**
disease due to excessive
drinking of alcohol;
alcoholic one so addicted.

alcopop *n* soft drink with
added alcohol.

alcove *n* recess in room or
garden; artificial bower.

alderman *n* senior councillor
in borough or city.

ale *n* kind of beer.

alert *a* ready in body and
mind; *n* **alertness**.

A-level *n Brit* advanced level
(examination).

alfalfa *n* kind of plant used for
fodder.

alfresco adv, a in the open air.

algae n sing **algae**. lowly organized plants, as seaweed etc.

algal bloom n sudden excessive growth of algae.

algebra n branch of mathematics using symbols for numbers and quantities ; a **algebraic**; adv **-ally**.

algorithm n way of solving problems step by step.

alias adv aliases. otherwise; n false name.

alibi n alibis. proof of being elsewhere when crime was committed.

alien a 1 foreign 2 repugnant; n; v **alienate** estrange; ns **alienation**; **alienist** specialist in mental disease.

alight a lit; v dismount; come to rest.

align v bring into line; n **alignment**.

alike a similar; adv to same degree.

aliment n food; a **alimentary** of food channel in body.

alimentary canal n passage from mouth to anus along which food passes and is digested.

alimony n allowance to wife after legal separation.

alive a living; aware; alert; sensitive; swarming.

alkali n potash; substance neutralizing acid; a **alkaline**.

all a whole of; full number of; total; n everything, everyone; one's whole property; adv entirely; idms **all along** since the start; **all**

but almost; **all in 1** inclusive **2** exhausted; **all out** with maximum effort; **all there** sane; quick-thinking; **all up** ended in failure.

Allah n (Muslim name for) God.

allay v ease; soothe; make more bearable.

all clear n **1** signal of no danger **2** permission to go ahead.

allege v state as fact; a **alleged**; n **allegation**.

allegiance n loyalty.

allegory n story with moral; a **allegorical**.

allegretto n mus fast movement, but slower than allegro; adv at this speed.

allergy n abnormal sensitiveness to any substance; a **allergic**.

alleviate v lighten; relieve (pain); n **alleviation**.

alley n alleys. narrow passage between houses.

alliance n treaty between countries **1** joining together by people, nations or organisations.

alligator n reptile of crocodile family.

alliteration n recurrence of same stressed sounds in verse or prose; a **alliterative**.

allocate v grant; assign (to); n **-ation**.

allot v **-lotting, -lotted**. assign as lot; n **allotment 1** share **2** plot of land.

allow v permit; grant; n **allowance**.

alloy n mixture of two or more

metals.

all right a **1** safe **2** acceptable; adv **1** agreed **2** for certain.

all-round a with wide range of skills, esp in sport.

allspice n pungent W Indian spice.

all-star a with many famous actors.

all-time a surpassing all at any time.

allude v; phr v **allude refer to**; n **allusion**; a **allusive**.

allure v attract; a **alluring**; ns **allure, allurement**.

alluvium n soil deposited by water; a **alluvial**.

ally v combine, join by treaty; n person or state acting in support of another; pl **allies**.

alma mater n Lat school or university where one is/was educated.

almanac, almanack n calendar of months and days.

almighty a omnipotent; n **the Almighty** God.

almond n kernel of fruit of almond-tree.

almoner n official distributor of alms.

almost adv very nearly; not quite.

alms n money given in charity to poor; **almshouse** endowed home for poor and aged people.

aloe n desert plant; (**bitter**) **aloes** juice from its leaves.

alone a, adv single; apart from others; unsupported.

along prep beside whole or part of length of; adv lengthwise; **alongside** at side of.

aloof *adv* apart; *a* haughty; *n* -ness.

aloud *adv* in an audible voice; loudly.

alp *n* mountain pasture; *a* **alpine**; *n* **alpinist** climber.

alpaca *n* S American llama with soft wool.

alpha *n* 1 first letter of Greek alphabet 2 *Brit* highest academic grade.

alphabet *n* 1 set of letters used in written language 2 the ABC; *a* **alphabetical** (*adv* -ly).

alphanumeric *a* made up of both letters and numbers.

alpine *a* of the mountains, *esp* the Alps.

already *adv* before this; by this time.

Alsatian *n* large wolf-like dog, used as guard dog.

also *adv*, *conj* besides; in addition; as well.

also-ran *n* unsuccessful participant in contest.

altar *n* 1 Communion table 2 slab used for sacrifices.

alter *v* change; *a* alterable; *n* -ation.

altercation *n fml* angry dispute.

alter ego *n Lat* other self.

alternate *v* occur by turns; *n* **alternating** electricity reversing direction of flow regularly; *a* **alternate** every second; *adv* -ly.
  alternative *n* other possible (choice).

alternative medicine *n* forms of treatment offered instead of conventional medicine.

although *conj* even though; notwithstanding.

altitude *n* height above sea level.

alto *n* person with singing voice between soprano and tenor.

altogether *adv* completely; wholly; in the main.

altruism *n* unselfishness; *a* **altruistic**; *n* **altruist**.

alum *n* mineral salt; crystalline substance used as astringent.

aluminium *n* very light white metal.

alumnus *n Lat* graduate of university; *pl* **alumni**; *fem* **alumna**; *pl* **alumnae**.

alveolus *n* **alveoli**. small cavity; *a* **alveolate**.

always *adv* at all times; invariably.

Alzheimer's disease *n* serious disorder of the brain resulting in premature senility.

am *1st person sing present tense* of BE.

am, AM *abbr* ante meridiem (before noon).

AM *abbr rad* amplitude modulation.

amalgam *n* mixture, *esp* used in dentistry; *v* **amalgamate** unite; *n* **amalgamation**.

amass *v* heap together; pile up.

amateur *n Fr* person following pursuit for love of it, not to make money; *a* **amateurish** not well done.

amaze *v* astound; *n* -ment *a* **amazing**.

Amazon *n* legendary female warrior.

ambassador *n* diplomat representing his country at foreign court; *fem* **ambassadress**.

amber *n* hard yellow fossil resin.

ambergris *n* secretion of spermwhale used in making perfume.

ambidextrous *a* able to use both hands equally.

ambient *a* entirely surrounding; *n* **ambience**.

ambiguous *a* not clear in meaning; *adv* -ly; *n* **ambiguity**.

ambit *n* full scope; compass; extent.

ambition *n* strong desire for success; *a* **ambitious**.

ambivalent *a* undecided; unclear; *n* **ambivalence**.

amble *v* move at easy pace, *esp* horse; walk easily.

ambulance *n* vehicle for carrying sick and wounded.

ambulatory *a* connected with walking.

ambush *n* surprise attack; *v* waylay.

ameba *US* = amoeba.

ameliorate *v* improve; *n* -ation; *a* -ative.

amen *interj* 'So be it'; *n* word of assent.

amenable *a* tractable; submissive; *adv* -ably; *n* -ability.

amend *v* improve; correct; *ns* **amendment, amends** reparation.

amenity *n* desirable feature; pleasantness.

amethyst *n* purple kind of

quartz; its colour.

amiable *a* kindly; lovable; *adv* **-bly**; *n* **amiability**.

amicable *a* friendly; *adv* **-ably**; *n* **amiability**.

amid(st) *prep* in middle of; among.

amidships *adv* in middle of ship.

amigo *n Sp* friend.

amino acid *n* any of several organic acids in proteins.

amiss *adv* wrongly; *a* faulty.

amity *n* friendship.

ammeter *n* meter for measuring ampere units.

ammo *n coll* ammunition.

ammonia *n* pungent, colourless gas; *a* **ammoniac**.

ammonite *n* type of fossil shell.

ammunition *n* gunpowder, bullets, shells, etc.

amnesia *n* loss of memory.

amnesty *n* pardon given to offenders against State.

amniocentesis *n* sampling of amniotic fluid to test for abnormality in a developing foetus.

amniotic fluid *n* fluid surrounding developing foetus.

amoeba *n* microscopic one-celled animal.

amok, amuck *adv* in a frenzy; *v* **run amok** get out of control.

among, amongst *prep* in midst of; by joint or mutual action of.

amoral *a* without morals; *n* amorality.

amorous *a* prone to love; *adv* **-ly**.

amorphous *a* formless.

amortize *v* pay off a debt gradually.

amount *n* sum total; quantity; *phr v* **amount to** add up to.

amour *n Fr* love affair (usually secret); lover.

amp *abbr* ampere.

ampere *n* electric unit of force; *n* **amperage**.

ampersand *n* the sign & (meaning 'and').

amphetamine *n* stimulant drug.

amphibian *n* animal or vehicle able to live or operate on land and in water; *a* **amphibious**.

amphitheatre *n* arena surrounded by tiered seats.

amphora *n* Greek or Roman jar; *pl* **amphorae**.

ample *a* plenty; large; *adv* **amply**; *n* **ampleness**.

amplify *v* **-fying, -fied**. make louder; *ns* **amplifier, amplification**.

ampoule *n* glass tube holding dose of drug.

amputate *v* cut off part of body; *n* **amputation**.

amulet *n* talisman; charm *esp* hung round neck.

amuse *v* provoke mirth or interest; divert; *n* **-ment**; *a* **amusing** (*adv* **-ly**).

an *see* **a**.

anabaptist *n* advocate of adult (re)baptism.

anabolic steroid *n* synthetic hormone used to promote development of muscle and bone.

anabolism *n* building up process of metabolism.

anachronism *n* thing or event placed in the wrong context of time.

anaemia *n* lack of red corpuscles in blood; *a* **anaemic**.

anaesthesia *n* insensibility caused by drugs or disease; *ns* **anaesthetic; anaesthetist** one who gives anaesthetic.

anagram *n* word made by rearranging letters in another word; *a* **anagrammatic**; *adv* **-ally**.

anal *a* of the anus.

analgesia *n* absence of pain; *a* **analgesic** pain killing.

analogy *n* similarity; *a* **analogous**; *adv* **analogically**.

analyse *v gram* examine minutely structure of sentence; break down into smallest parts; *a* **analytical** (*adv* **-ly**); *ns* **analysis, analyst**.

anarchy *n* no supreme power in State; lawlessness; *n* **anarchism** practice of anarchy; *n* **anarchist**.

anathema *n* curse; hateful thing; *v* **-ematize**.

anatomy *n* science of structure of body; *a* **anatomical**; *v* **anatomize** dissect; *n* **anatomist**.

ANC *abbr* African National Congress.

ancestor *n* forebear; *a* **ancestral**; *n* **ancestry** lineage.

anchor *n* mass of iron, securing ships to sea-bed; *v* fasten by anchor; *n* **anchorage** place for anchoring.

anchovy n small fish of the herring type.

ancient a belonging to distant past; very old.

ancillary a subordinate; auxiliary.

and conj word joining words, phrases; also; as well as.

andante adv (music played) slowly.

androgynous a with characteristics of male and female.

android n robot of human appearance.

anecdote n trivial story of isolated event; a anecdotal.

anemia n US = anaemia.

anemometer n gauge for speed and force of wind.

anemone n wind-flower; sea-anemone small sea creature.

aneroid a dry; containing no fluid.

anesthesia, anesthetic, anesthetize US = anaesthesia, anaesthetic, anaesthetize.

anew adv again; afresh.

angel n celestial being; old gold coin; a angelic.

angelica n herb used in cookery; its candied stalk.

anger n wrath; rage; v provoke to anger.

angina n heart spasm; quinsy.

angle v to fish; ns angling, angler.

angle space between two lines that meet; corner; a angular.

Anglican a member of the Church of England.

anglicize v give English form to (a foreign word).

Anglo- prefix of England.

anglophile n, a (a person) loving English people and way of life; n anglophilia.

anglophobe n, a (person) hating English people and way of life; n -phobia.

Anglo-Saxon n (language of) inhabitant of England from 5th century until Norman invasion (1066) also a.

angora n type of rabbit, cat or goat; fabric made from this goat's hair.

angostura n bitter aromatic bark used as flavouring.

angry a full of anger; tempestuous 2 (of a wound or rash) inflamed; adv angrily.

angst n state of acute anxiety about the world, anguish.

anguish n acute pain of body or mind.

angular a 1 with sharp corners 2 not vertical or horizontal; slanting n angularity.

animadversion n depreciatory reference to.

animal n living creature with power of voluntary motion; a of animal nature; sensual.

animate v give life to; a living; n animation; a animated lively (adv -ly).

animism n belief that natural objects have souls.

animosity n enmity; hatred.

aniseed n aromatic seed used for flavouring.

ankle n the joint between foot and leg.

anklet n ornament or support for the ankle.

annals n yearly chronicle of events.

annex v join to; steal; n annexation.

annexe n supplementary building.

annihilate v destroy utterly; n annihilation.

anniversary n yearly celebration of an event.

annotate v make explanatory notes on; n annotation.

announce v declare; ns -ment, announcer.

annoy v vex; irritate; a -ing; n -ance.

annual a yearly; n plant living for year only; yearly publication of book; adv annually.

annuity n fixed sum paid yearly; n annuitant.

annul v -nulling, -nulled. cancel; nullify; n -ment.

annular a ring-shaped.

annunciation n announcement, esp of Incarnation made to Virgin Mary; v annunciate.

anode n positive electric pole.

anodyne n drug which relieves or soothes pain.

anoint v pour oil upon; esp by use of consecrated oil in religious ceremony; n -ment; a anointed.

anomaly n irregularity; a anomalous.

anon adv soon; presently.

anonymous a not named; adv -ly; abbr anon; n anonymity.

anopheles n malaria-carrying mosquito.

anorak n warm, hooded jacket (rain- and wind-proof).

anorexia n 1 complete loss of appetite for food 2 also **anorexia nervosa** chronic and dangerous form of this; a **anorexic**.

another a 1 additional 2 different; pron one more.

answer v give reply to; a **answerable** responsible.

answering machine n machine for answering a telephone and taking messages.

ant n industrious small insect.

antacid n substance that counteracts acid.

antagonist n adversary; opponent; v **antagonize** render hostile; n **antagonism**; a **antagonistic**.

antarctic a belonging to south polar regions.

ante- prefix Lat before.

antecedent a prior to; n pl -s line of descent.

antechamber n waiting-room outside main room.

antedate v happen earlier than.

antediluvian a 1 of the age before the Flood 2 old-fashioned.

antelope n deer-like animal allied to goat.

antenatal a occurring before birth.

antenna n **antennae**. 1 feeler of insect 2 radio aerial.

anterior a before; earlier; more to the front.

anthem n sacred words set to music; song of praise.

anthology n collection of poems, stories, etc.

anthracite n hard slow-burning smokeless coal.

anthrax n pustular disease attacking animals and human beings.

anthropoid a like a man; n manlike creature.

anthropology n science of man; a **anthropological**; n **anthropologist**.

anthropomorphic a resembling a human being.

anti- prefix Gk 1 against 2 the reverse of (ant- before vowel).

antiballistic a against missiles.

antibiotic a destroying growth, esp of bacteria; n such a substance.

antibody n natural antidote to infection produced in blood.

antic n playful, comic gesture pl -s playful or ridiculous behaviour.

Antichrist n one hostile to Christ and His teaching.

anticipate v take action in advance; n **anticipation**; a **anticipatory**.

anticlerical a opposed to influence of clergy, esp in political affairs.

anticlimax n disappointing turn to an exciting situation; a **anticlimactic**.

anticyclone n state of high atmospheric pressure, tending to produce fine weather; a **anticyclonic**.

antidote n chemical that counteracts effects of poison.

antifreeze n chemical added to water to prevent it freezing in winter.

antigen n substance causing body to make antibodies.

antihero n main character of book, play etc lacking the traditional virtues of a hero.

antihistamine n type of drug used to treat allergies.

antimony n brittle silver-white metallic element.

antipathy n dislike; repugnance; a **antipathetic**.

antiperspirant n substance applied to the body to prevent sweating.

antipodes n places on opposite sides of earth.

antiquary, antiquarian n one who collects antiques; a **antiquated** old-fashioned.

antique a old; n relic of past age; ns **antiquity** remote past; **antiquities** ancient museum pieces.

antirrhinum n the snapdragon plant.

anti-Semite n hater of Jews; n **anti-Semitism**.

antiseptic n substance for preventing infection; n **antisepsis** method of preventing infection.

antisocial a 1 going against the conventions of society 2 avoiding the company of others; unsociable.

antithesis n **antitheses**. contrast (of ideas).

antitoxin n substance that neutralizes poison.

antler n a branched horn of deer.

antonym n word of opposite

meaning to another.

anus n opening at lower end of alimentary canal.

anvil n block of iron on which blacksmith works.

anxious a 1 worried 2 eager to do (something); adv **-ly**; n **anxiety**.

any a, pron some; every; prons **anybody**, **anyone**, **anyway**, **anywhere**.

aob abbr any other business.

aorta n main artery of human body; a **aortic**.

apace adv at a quick pace; swiftly.

apart adv separately; aside; a separate.

apartheid n segregation of races practised in S Africa 1948–1992.

apartment n room; flat; set of rooms.

apathy n indifference; a **apathetic**.

ape n monkey esp tailless kind; v mimic; n **aping**.

aperitif n drink taken as an appetizer.

aperture n hole; opening, esp that into a camera.

APEX abbr 1 Brit Association of Professional, Executive, Clerical and Computer Staff.

apex n tip; top; peak; pl **apexes**, **apices**.

aphasia n loss of power of speech.

aphelion n point of orbit farthest from the sun.

aphid n small insect such as a greenfly that feeds on sap of plants.

aphorism n maxim; short pithy saying.

aphrodisiac a exciting sexual desire; n such a drug.

apiarist n bee-keeper; **apiary** beehive; **apiculture**.

apiece advto or for each; each by itself.

aplomb n self-possession.

Apocalypse n Book of Revelation; prophetic vision.

Apocrypha n noncanonical parts of the Bible.

apocryphal a not genuine; fictitious.

apogee n point in heavenly body's orbit farthest from earth; culmination.

apology n expression of regret; v **apologize**; a **apologetic** (adv **-ally**).

apostle n one sent out to preach; reformer; a **apostolic**.

apostrophe n exclamatory address to person present or absent; a mark (') showing omission of letter(s) or the possessive form.

apostrophize v (in poem or speech) address or pretend to address.

apothecary n old name for druggist, pharmicist.

apotheosis n deification of human being.

appal v **-palling**, **-palled**. horrify; a **appalling**; (adv **-ly**).

apparatus n equipment; instruments for specific use.

apparent a visible; adv **apparently** seemingly.

apparition n supernatural visual impression; ghost.

appeal v seek higher judgment; ask earnestly; attract; n act of appealing; a **appealing** attractive; (adv **-ly**) earnestly.

appear v 1 become visible 2 present oneself; seem; n **appearance** bearing; look.

appease v soothe; pacify; satisfy; n **appeasement**.

appellant n one appealing to higher court; n **appellation** a name or title.

append v add; attach; n **appendage**.

appendix n **appendixes**, **appendices**. addition to book; anat vermiform appendix tube leading out of caecum.

appendicitis n inflammation of vermiform appendix.

apperception n self-consciousness.

appertain v be appropriate or relate (to).

appetite n enjoyment of food; desire; n **appetizer** anything giving relish for a meal; a **appetizing**.

applaud v express approval by clapping hands; n **applause**.

apple n firm, fleshy fruit with pips.

appliance n device; gadget; machine.

appliqué n Fr one material cut out and applied to surface of another, as in embroidery etc.

apply v **-plying**, **-plied.** 1 put on; bring into contact 2 administer 3 have relevance; *phr vs* **apply for** request; **apply oneself (to)** devote oneself (to); *a* **applied** put to practical use; *n* **application** act of applying; something applied; close attention; **applicant** person applying; *a* **applicable** relevant, suitable.

appoint *v* fix; ordain; select for office; equip; *n* -**ment** 1 act of appointing 2 assignation.

apportion *v* share out; allot; *n* -**ment**.

apposite *a* apt; pointed; *n* **apposition**.

appraise *v* assess price or value of; *ns* **appraisal**, **appraisement**.

appreciate *v* 1 estimate highly 2 be sensible of 3 increase value; *n* -**ation**; *a* -**iative** grateful (*adv* -**ly**); *a* **appreciable** noticeable; (*adv* -**ably**).

apprehend *v* 1 arrest 2 understand 3 dread; *n* **apprehension**; *a* **apprehensive**; (*adv* -**ly**).

apprentice *n* one learning a trade or craft and bound by indentures; *n* **apprenticeship**.

apprise *v* inform.

appro *n* **on appro** *Brit coll* on approval.

approach *v* 1 come near 2 make advances to; *n* drawing near; *a* -**able** willing to be consulted.

approbation *n* commendation; approval; *a* **approbatory**.

appropriate *v* take for oneself;

filch; *a* suitable to; *adv* -**ly**; *n* **appropriation** funds granted for special purpose.

approve *v* sanction; commend; *n* **approval**; *as* **approved**, **approving**; *adv* **approvingly**.

approx *abbr* approximately.

approximate *a* very near; about correct; *v* make or come close to; *adv* -**ly**; *n* **approximation**.

appurtenance *n* adjunct; accessory.

après-ski *n*, *a Fr* (of or for) leisure time after skiing.

apricot *n* 1 orange-red fruit allied to peach 2 its colour.

April *n* 4th month of year.

a priori *a*, *adv* by deductive reasoning.

apron *n* garment to protect clothes; part of theatre stage in front of curtain.

apropos *a* appropriate; *adv* with reference to.

apt *a* fit; likely; skilled; *adv* **aptly**; *ns* **aptness**; **aptitude** fitness; capacity.

Aqualung *n* underwater breathing apparatus.

aquamarine *n* bluish-green stone; colour.

aquaplane *v* ride on board towed by motorboat; *n* such a board.

aquarium *n* tank where water plants and fish are kept; *pl* **aquaria**, **aquariums**.

Aquarius *n* 11th sign of the zodiac (the Water-bearer); *a*, *n* **Aquarian**.

aquatic *a* living in water; taking place in or on water.

aquatint *n* etching process

producting print like water-colour; print made by this process.

aqueduct *n* artificial conduit for water; bridge-like part of a structure supporting conduit.

aqueous *a* watery.

aquiline *a* eagle-like; (nose) curved as an eagle's beak.

Arab *n* member of a group of people who originated in Arabia but now live throughout Middle East and N Africa; horse; *a* **Arabian**; *n* **Arabic** language of Arabs.

arabesque *n* 1 fanciful pattern of leaves, scrolls etc in Arabian decoration 2 posture in ballet.

Arabic numeral *n* any of the numerals 0, 1, 2, 3, 4, 5, 6, 7, 8, 9.

arable *a* suitable for tilling, cultivation.

arachnid *n* one of the genus including spiders.

arbiter *n* person recognized as able to make a decisive judgement.

arbitrage *n* buying and reselling elsewhere so as to profit from difference of prices in different places.

arbitrary *a* 1 based on impulse or chance 2 dictatorial; *a* **arbitrarily**; *n* **arbitrariness**.

arbitrate *v* make judgement or settle a dispute between others; *ns* **arbitrator**; **arbitration**.

arbor *n* main support or spindle of machine.

arborist *n* person caring for

welfare of trees.

arc n 1 part of circumference of circle 2 luminous glow made by electricity crossing gap between electrodes; n **arc lamp** lamp which works in this way.

arc welding n welding by means of electrical arc.

arcade n covered pedestrian passageway lined with shops or market stalls.

arcane a secret; mysterious.

arch- prefix chief.

arch a coy; prep chief; adv -ly; n -ness.

arch n curved structure acting as support; curve itself; v build arch over; form an arch.

archaeology n study of prehistoric cultures; a -ological; n -ologist.

archaic a out of date; adv -ally.

archangel n chief angel.

archbishop n chief bishop; n **archbishopric** office of archbishop.

archdeacon n priest next below bishop in rank.

archer n one shooting with bow and arrows; n **archery**.

archetype n prototype; a **archetypal**.

archipelago n archipelagoes. sea containing many islands; group of such islands.

architecture n art and science of building; a **architectural** (adv -ly); n **architect** one who designs buildings.

archives n place where records are kept; records themselves; n **archivist** keeper of archives.

archway n way or passage under an arch.

arctic a of or near region of the N Pole.

ardent a fiery; eager; adv -ly; n **ardour**.

arduous a difficult; strenuous; adv -ly.

are n 100 square metres.

area n region; surface measured in sq units; scope.

arena n place of combat or conflict; pl **arenas**.

aren't contracted form of 1 are not 2 am not.

argent n silver; white colour in heraldry.

argil n kind of clay used by potters.

argot n slang.

argue v dispute; prove; debate; ns **argument** discussion in which reasons are given; as **arguable, argumentative**.

aria n vocal solo in operas and oratorios.

arid a dry; parched; barren; adv aridly; n **aridity**.

Aries n 1st sign of the zodiac (the Ram); a, n **Arien**.

aright adv rightly; without error.

arise v arising, arose, arisen. ascend; occur.

aristocracy n ruling class; nobility; n **aristocrat**; a **aristocratic** (adv -ally).

arithmetic n science of numbers; n **arithmetician**; a **arithmetical**; adv -ally.

arithmetic progression n series of numbers where difference between successive numbers is constant.

ark n flat bottomed boat; Jewish chest containing Tablets of the Law; coffer.

arm[1] n 1 upper limb of human body 2 anything extending from main body (arm of tree, chair etc.).

arm[2] n weapon; branch of military forces; v supply with weapons; prepare for battle.

armada n fleet of warships, esp Spanish.

armadillo n S American burrowing mammal.

armament n force equipped for war; pl war equipment.

armchair n chair with armrests.

armistice n truce pending a formal peace treaty.

armlet n cloth band for the arm.

armorial a relating to heraldic arms.

armour n protective covering for the body in battle; protective plating of ship or vehicle; a **armoured**; ns **armoury; armourer** one who makes or repairs armour.

armpit n hollow under the arm below the shoulder.

arms n pl 1 weapons 2 coat of arms; idm **be up in arms** protest strongly.

army n 1 military force that operates on land 2 large group of people or animals.

arnica n genus of plants; drug used for sprains etc.

aroma n pleasant smell; a **aromatic** fragrant, spicy.

aromatherapy n the use of scented plant oils in massage; n **aromatherapist**.

arose pt of **arise**.

around prep 1 in a circle round 2 at or to various places within 3 (at) about; approximately; adv 1 here and there 2 somewhere nearby 3 turning in a circle 4 on all sides; phr v **get around** travel widely; idm **have been around** have had experience of the world.

arouse v 1 awaken 2 stimulate; excite; n **arousal**.

arpeggio n notes of a chord played in quick succession.

arr abbr 1 arrival; arrives 2 mus arranged by.

arrack n strong alcoholic drink from rice.

arraign v accuse; indict on criminal charge; n **arraignment** act of indictment.

arrange v put in order; fix; adapt (novel, music); n **arrangement**.

arrant a unmitigated; out-and-out; adv **arrantly**.

array v 1 dress 2 draw up; n 1 troops 2 impressive display.

arrears n debt not paid; work not done.

arrest v 1 seize by legal authority 2 gain (attention) 3 stop 4 stay (judgment); a **arresting** striking; n **arrest**.

arrive v 1 reach destination 2 achieve fame; n **arrival**.

arrogant a haughty; proud; n **arrogance**; adv **-ly**.

arrogate v claim as one's own; n **arrogation**.

arrow n feathered rod with sharp point shot from bow.

arrowroot n W Indian plant with starchy roots.

arsenal n place where weapons and ammunition are made or stored.

arsenic n metallic poison.

arson n deliberate setting on fire of property.

art n 1 creative skill and its application 2 craft or trade 3 cunning; pl humanities as opposed to sciences.

Art Deco n, a (in) the utilitarian, geometrical style of interior design, jewellery, architecture etc popular in the 1930s.

artefact see **artifact**.

arteriosclerosis n disease where hardening of the walls of the arteries impedes circulation of the blood.

artery n blood-vessel conveying blood from the heart; main line of communicaton; a **arterial**.

artesian well n well sending up constant supply of water under pressure.

artful a cunning; crafty; adv **-ly**.

arthritis n painful inflammation of joints; a **arthritic**.

artic abbr articulated lorry.

artichoke n plant with edible roots or flower base.

article n item; short piece of writing; clause in legal document; in grammar, words the, a, an; v bind to trade or profession; a **articled**.

articulate a 1 formed with joints 2 expressive; having the power of speech; v 1 join 2 utter distinctly; adv **-ly**; ns **articulateness** ability to communicate; **articulation**.

artifact, artefact n any object made by human skill.

artifice n ingenuity; trickery.

artificial a not natural; adv **-ly**; n **artificiality** insincerity.

artificial insemination n injection of semen into the womb by artificial means to cause conception.

artificial intelligence n (study of) capacity for machines to simulate human intelligence.

artificial respiration n method of making a person or animal breathe when natural breathing has stopped.

artillery n guns of various types; branch of army which uses heavy guns.

artisan n skilled manual worker.

artist n 1 person who practises any fine art, esp painting 2 very skilful worker or performer, a **artistic** (adv **-ally**) n **artistry**.

artiste n professional entertainer, esp singer, dancer.

artless a naive; sincere; simple.

Art Nouveau n Fr late 19th century decorative art style based on curves, with leaf and flower motifs.

arty *a coll* a showy enthusiasm for art; affecting an artistic style.

arty-crafty *a coll* 1 affecting the look of simple handmade craftware.

arum *n* kind of lily; wild lily or 'Lord and Ladies'.

as *adv, conj* 1 when 2 because 3 equally, in the capacity of 4 in the manner of; like.

ASA *abbr* 1 Advertising Standards Authority 2 (of film speeds) American Standards Association.

asafoetida *n* gum resin with nauseous smell.

asap *abbr* as soon as possible.

asbestos *n* fibrous fireproof mineral substance.

ascend *v* go up; rise to higher rank; slope upwards; climb; *ns* **ascent; ascendancy** domination; **ascension**.

ascertain *v* find out; get to know for certain.

ascetic *a* self-denying; austere; *n* hermit; *adv* **-ally**; *n* **asceticism**.

ASCII *abbr comput* American Standard Code for Information Interchange.

ascorbic acid *n* vitamin C.

ascribe *v* attribute (to); *a* **ascribable**.

aseptic *a* free from pus-forming bacteria; *n* **asepsis**.

asexual *a* 1 without sex 2 having no interest in sex.

ASH *abbr* Action on Smoking and Health.

ash *n* grey powdery residue of

anything burnt; *pl* **ashes** cremated human remains; **the Ashes** symbol of victory in cricket series between Australia and England; *n* tree of olive family; *as* **ashen, ashy**.

ashamed *a* troubled by sense of guilt or shame.

ash can *n* US = Brit dustbin.

ashore *a, adv* on shore; to shore; on land.

ashtray *n* receptacle for tobacco ash.

Ash Wednesday *n* 1st day of Lent.

Asian *a, n* native of Asia; *a* **Asiatic**.

aside *adv* on, to or at one side; apart; *n* phrase spoken in an undertone.

asinine *a* like an ass; stupid; *n* **asininity**.

ask *v* seek answer to; request; invite.

askance *adv* with sideways glance; with suspicion.

askew *a adv* sideways; out of the straight.

aslant *adv* on the slant; obliquely.

asleep *adv a* 1 into or in a state of sleep 2 numb.

AS level *n* advanced supplementary level (examination).

asp *n* small poisonous snake.

asparagus *n* plant whose shoots are eaten as vegetable.

aspect *n* appearance; expression; view; look.

aspen *n* poplar tree with tremulous leaves.

asperity *n* harshness; severity; roughness.

aspersion *n* derogatory, damaging remark.

asphalt *n* bituminous substance for surfacing roads.

asphyxiate *v* cause or undergo suffocation; *ns* **asphyxia, asphyxiation**.

aspic *n* savoury jelly.

aspidistra *n* indoor plant with green glossy leaves.

aspirate *n* breathed sound, usually expressed by letter h; *v* pronounce with breath; draw off (fluid etc) from cavity, by means of **aspirator**; *a* **aspirated**.

aspire *v* seek eagerly; *a* **aspiring**; *n* **aspiration** 1 strong desire 2 act of breathing 3 pronunciation of an aspirate.

aspirin *n* drug used for relief of pain.

ass *n* 1 member of horse family 2 stupid person.

assail *v* attack; *a* **assailable**; *n* **assailant**.

assassin *n* treacherous (*usu* political) murderer; *v* **assassinate** (*n* **-ation**).

assault *n* sudden attack; *v* make an assault.

assay *n* testing purity of metals; *v* test or analyse (metals); *n* **assayer**.

assemble *v* collect; fit together; *ns* **assembler; assembly** 1 gathering of persons 2 collection of parts.

assembly line *n* sequence of machines and workers for

assembling parts in a factory.

assent v agree; concur; n compliance, agreement.

assert v state strongly; declare; n **assertion**; a **assertive** aggressively confident; adv **-ly**.

assess v estimate and fix amount of (fine or tax); estimate value; a **assessable**; ns **assessment, assessor**.

asset n thing of value belonging to person, business etc; pl all such property.

asset-stripping n buying assets from a company in financial difficulties and selling them at a profit.

asseverate v state emphatically; n **asseveration**.

assiduity n diligence; perseverance; a **assiduous** (adv **-ly**; n **-ness**).

assign v make over; allot; fix; ascribe; a **assignable**; ns **assignment** allotted task; **assignee; assignation** secret meeting.

assimilate v absorb physically or mentally, make similar; a **assimilable**; n **assimilation**.

assist v help; aid; attend; ns **assistant, assistance**.

assizes n periodical sessions of judges held to try criminal and civil cases.

associate v join; connect; combine; n partner; member of a society; a linked in function; n **association** union of persons for common purposes.

assonance n rhyming of vowel sounds; a **assonant**.

assort v separate into sorts or classes; a **assorted**; n **assortment** mixed kinds.

assuage v soothe; quench; n **-ment**.

assume v put on; take upon oneself; adopt; n **assumption**.

assure v make sure; state positively; a **assured** confident; adv **assuredly** certainly; n **assurance** pledge; confidence; insurance.

assurgent a rising, ascending.

asterisk n symbol (*) used by printers.

asteroid n small planet; a starshaped.

asthma n chronic or acute condition of the lungs.

astigmatism n defect in eye causing faulty vision; as **astigmatic**; adv **astigmatically**.

astir a, adv in motion; in state of excitement.

astonish v fill with wonder; amaze; a **astonishing**; adv **astonishingly**; n **astonishment**.

astound v strike with amazement or alarm; a **astounding**; adv **astoundingly**.

astraddle a, adv straddling; astride.

astrakhan n curly pelt of unborn Astrakhan lamb.

astral a of stars; **astral body** ghost.

astray a, adv off right path; of

mental error; of moral lapse.

astride adv with one leg on each side.

astringent n drug or other agent causing contraction (of tissues, cut blood vessels); n **astringency**.

astro- prefix of the stars and outer space.

astrolabe n early instrument for measuring altitude of stars, planets, etc above the horizon.

astrology n psuedo-science of prediction of events by stars; n **astrologer**; a **astrological**.

astronaut n traveller in space.

astronomy n science of heavenly bodies; n **astronomer**; a **astronomical** 1 of astronomy 2 unusually large in number or quantity.

astrophysics n study of physics and chemistry of stars.

astute a shrewd; wily; adv **astutely**; n **astuteness**.

asunder adv apart; into parts; a separated.

asylum n sanctuary; place for care of insane.

asymmetry n irregularity; absence of symmetry; adv **asymmetrically**.

at prep expressing general position in space or time; idm **be at it** be busy doing sth.

atavism n resemblance to remote ancestor; reversion to earlier type; a **atavistic**.

ate pt of **eat**.

atheism n belief that there is no God; n **atheist**; a **atheistic**.

athirst *a* thirsty; eagerly desiring.

athlete *n* one skilled in physical exercises; *a* **athletic;** (*adv* **-ally);** *n* **athletics.**

Atlantic *a* relating to the Atlantic Ocean.

atlas *n* **1** book of maps **2** top vertebra of neck.

atmosphere *n* **1** gaseous envelope surrounding earth or any heavenly body **2** any moral or mental influence; *a* **atmospheric;** (*adv* **-ally);** *n* **atmospherics** disturbances in radio reception.

atoll *n* coral island; belt of coral reefs surrounding lagoon.

atom *n* smallest particle of an element; *v* **atomize** reduce to atoms; *ns* **atomization; atomizer** device for changing liquids into fine spray.

atomic *a* pertaining to atoms. *Hence:* **a. bomb; a. energy; a. reactor; a. warfare; a. weight.**

atomic number *n* number of protons in nucleus of atom.

atomize *v* reduce to fine particles of spray; *n* **atomizer.**

atonal *a mus* without any sense of key; *n* **atonality.**

atone *v* make amends; expiate; *n* **atonement.**

atop *adv*, *prep* at the top (of).

atrium *n* **1** enclosed court of public building **2** one of two upper chambers of the heart.

atrocious *a* abominable;

wicked; evil; *adv* **-ly;** *ns* **-ness; atrocity** brutal deed.

atrophy *n pl* **-atrohies.** wasting away of body; weakening of mental or moral power; *v* **-phying, -phied.** (cause to) waste away; *a* **atrophied.**

atropine *n* poison obtained from belladonna.

attach *v* **1** fasten; affix **2** seize legally; *a* **attached;** *n* **attachment.**

attaché *n Fr* member of diplomatic staff; **attaché-case** small case for carrying documents.

attack *v* **1** assault; assail **2** work upon; *n* **attacker.**

attain *v* **1** accomplish; achieve; *a* **attainable;** *ns* **attainment, attainability.**

attainder *n* loss of civil rights through judicial sentence; disgrace; dishonour.

attaint *n* disgrace; stain; *v* dishonour.

attar *n* perfume distilled from flower petals.

attempt *v* try; endeavour; *n* an effort, try.

attend *v* **1** give heed (to) **2** be present **3** escort; *n* **attendance 1** act of being present **2** those present; *a, n* **attendant;** *a* attentive; (*adv* **-ly,** *ns* **-ness);** **attention.**

attenuate *v* make thin; *a* **attenuated;** *n* **attenuation.**

attest *v* **1** testify **2** put (someone) on oath; *n* **attestation.**

attic *n* small room under roof

of house; a garret.

attire *v* dress; put robes on; *n* dress; clothing.

attitude *n* posture; disposition; *v* **attitudinize** adopt affected gestures.

attorney *n* lawyer; one acting for another in legal matters; **attorney general** chief legal officer.

attract *v* draw towards; allure; *n* **attraction;** *a* **attractive;** (*adv* **-ly);** *n* **-ness.**

attribute *n* characteristic quality of thing or person; *v* ascribe (to); *a* **attributable;** *n* **attribution.**

attrition *n* act of wearing away by friction.

attune *v* **1** bring into harmony **2** help to get used to.

atypical *a* not representative; *adv* **-ly.**

aubergine *n* **1** fruit of egg-plant **2** deep purple colour.

aubretia *n* small perennial trailing rock plant.

auburn *a* reddish- or golden-brown.

auction *n* public sale in which articles are sold to highest bidder; *v* sell by auction; *n* **auctioneer.**

audacious *a* bold; impudent; *adv* **audaciously;** *ns* **audaciousness, audacity.**

audible *a* able to be heard; *adv* **audibly;** *n* **audibility.**

audience *n* **1** assemblage of persons present or looking on **2** interview or formal hearing.

audio *a* of sound signals.

audio- *prefix* of, for or using

sound.

audiometer n instrument measuring power of hearing.

audio-visual a combining sound and vision.

audit v official scrutinizing of accounts; n **auditor**.

audition n 1 sense of hearing 2 test-hearing for singer, actor, etc; v conduct such a test.

auditorium n pl **-ums, -ia.** building in which an audience gathers.

auditory a of the sense of hearing.

au fait a Fr well informed.

auger n tool for boring holes in wood.

augment v cause to increase; n **augmentation**.

augur n soothsayer; v predict; n **augury** an omen.

August n the eighth month of the year.

auk n type of sea bird.

auld lang syne Scot traditional song of friendship and good times long ago, often sing on New Year's Eve.

aunt n mother's or father's sister; uncle's wife.

au pair n Fr young person, usu foreign, living in a family home and helping with housework or care of children.

aura n mysterious emanation surrounding living things.

aural a of the ear; adv **aurally.**

aureola, aureole n sun's corona; celestial crown or halo.

auricle n external ear of animals; upper chamber of heart; a **auricular.**

auricula n primrose-like flower.

aurora n the dawn; **a. borealis** Northern Lights; **a. australis** similar lights in S Polar sky.

auspices npl 1 omens 2 patronage; a **auspicious** favourable; (adv **-ly).**

Aussie n, a coll Australian.

austere a 1 stern 2 ascetic; adv **-ly;** n **austerity.**

austral a of or coming from the south; southerly.

Australasian a of Australia, N Zealand and adjacent islands; native of Australasia.

Austro- prefix of Austria.

authentic a genuine; reliable; adv **-ally;** n **authenticity;** v **authenticate** prove real or genuine.

author n writer of book, play, poem, etc; originator; fem **authoress;** n **authorship.**

authoritarian n, a (person) expecting complete obedience from others; n **authoritarianism.**

authority n 1 right to command; natural power 2 expert 3 controlling body; a **authoritative,** adv **-ly;** v **authorize** give authority or approval to.

autism n psychological disorder, esp in children, where one is unable to relate to or communicate with others; a, n **autistic.**

auto- prefix 1 self 2 car; motor.

autobiography n life of person written by himself; a **autobiographic(al);** n **autobiographer.**

autocrat n absolute monarch; n **autocracy;** a **autocratic;** adv **autocratically.**

Autocue [TM] n text displayed on screen for TV performers.

autoeroticism n sexual arousal from one's own body a **autoerotic.**

autograph n person's own signature; v write one's signature (in); a **autographic.**

autogyro n aircraft designed for vertical ascent and descent by means of horizontal propeller.

auto-harmony n prefabricated harmony in a musical synthesizer.

autoimmune a (of a disease) caused by antibodies produced against substances naturally present in the body.

automat n food-dispenser operated by coins in slots.

automate v cause to work by automation.

automatic a working by itself; behaving mechanically; adv **-ally.**

automatic pilot n device that automatically maintains an aircraft's course; also called **autopilot.**

automation n control of industrial processes by electronic and other means.

automaton n automatons machine that performs human actions; n

automatism mechanical action.

automobile n motor-driven passenger vehicle.

autonomy n self-government; as **autonomic, autonomous**; n **autonomist** one who supports autonomy.

autopsy n examination of dead body by dissection.

auto-rhythm n prefabricated rhythm in a musical synthesizer.

auto-suggestion n suggestion coming from within oneself.

autumn n third season of the year; a **autumnal**.

auxiliary a helping; additional; supplementary; n verb helping to make up tense, mood etc of another.

AV abbr 1 audio-visual 2 Authorized Version.

avail v be of use; benefit; a **available** at hand; capable of being used; n **availability**.

avalanche n mass of snow, ice rushing down a mountain.

avant-garde a favouring progressive ideas, esp in art and literature; n group of people promoting such ideas.

avarice n greed; cupidity; a **avaricious**; adv **-ly**.

avenge v inflict retribution for a wrong; take revenge for injury on behalf of someone; n **avenger**.

avenue n 1 way of approach 2 roadway bordered by trees 3 wide street in a town.

aver v **averring, averred.** affirm positively.

average n mean proportion; a mean, ordinary; v estimate average of or average rate of.

averse a opposed; unwilling; n **aversion** 1 antipathy; dislike 2 thing or person disliked.

aversion therapy n method of curing addiction by instilling unpleasant associations in the mind.

avert v turn aside; prevent.

aviary n large cage for keeping birds; n **aviarist, aviculture**.

aviation n art of flying aircraft; everything connected with flying; v **aviate** fly an aircraft; n **aviator** a pilot.

avid a eager; greedy; adv **avidly**; n **avidity**.

avionics n science of electronics applied to aviation.

avocado n pl **-dos**. pear-shaped tropical fruit.

avocation n occupation; minor pursuit; hobby.

avoid v shun; keep away from; refrain from; a **avoidable**; adv **avoidably**; n **avoidance**.

avoirdupois n 1 system of weights used in UK and USA 2 coll excessive weight of person.

avow v own publicly to; admit openly; a **avowed**; adv **avowedly** admittedly; n **avowal** confession.

avuncular a of or like an uncle.

await v wait for; expect; be ready for.

awake v rouse from sleep or inaction; pt **awoke**; pp **awoken**; a no longer

sleeping; vigilant; n **awakening; idm** a rude **awakening** the shattering of an illusion.

award v grant after due judgment; n something awarded after judgment; prize.

aware a conscious; cognizant; knowing; n **-ness**.

awash a just above or level with surface of water.

away adv at or to a distance; absent.

awe n fear with respect; solemn wonder; v fill with awe; a **awesome** causing awe.

awe-inspiring n causing feelings of awe and wonder.

awe-struck a filled with awe.

awful a appalling; very bad; adv **awfully** very.

awhile adv for a short time.

awkward a 1 clumsy; ungainly 2 difficult to manage; disconcerting 3 ill at ease; embarrassment; adv **-ly**; n **-ness**.

awl n small pointed tool for piercing holes.

awning n canvas sheet stretched on frame-work used as protection from sun.

awoke pt **awoken** pp of awake.

AWOL abbr absent without leave.

awry a crooked; twisted; adv wrong; askew.

axe n chopping tool with wooden handle and iron head.

axiom n obvious truth; principle accepted without

question; *a* axiomatic;
adv -ally.

axis *n* **axes** imaginary line
about which a body may
rotate real or imaginary line
dividing figure into two
equal parts; *a* **axial**;
adv **axially**.

axle, axle tree *n* rod or bar
connecting two wheels and
on which wheel revolves.

ay, aye *adv, n ar* 1 always 2
yes.

ayatollah *n* Shiite Muslim
religious leader.

azalea *n* flowering shrub of
rhododendron family.

azimuth *n* distance of a star in
angular degrees from N or S
point of meridian; *a*
azimuthal.

Aztec *n* American Indian
people ruling Mexico before
Spanish conquest.

azure *a* blue like the sky; *n* the
colour sky-blue.

B

BA *abbr* Bachelor of Arts.

baa *n* the bleat of a sheep; *v* bleat.

babble *v* 1 talk indistinctly 2 reveal (secrets); *n* 1 foolish talk 2 murmur of stream; *n* **babbler**; *a* **babbling**.

babe *n* baby; inexperienced person.

baboon *n* kind of large ape.

baby *n* young child or animal; infant *a* **babyish** childish; *n* **babyhood**.

baby boom *n* time of increase in birth rate; **baby boomer** *n* person born in the late 1940s

baby-sit *v* mind children when parents are out; *ns* **baby-sitter, baby-sitting**.

baccarat *n* gambling card game.

bachelor *n* 1 unmarried man 2 holder of first university degree; *ns* **bachelor-girl** unmarried girl, **bachelorhood**.

bacillus *n* minute plant organism either harmful or harmless; bacterium; *pl* **bacilli**; *a* **bacilliform**.

back *n* 1 part opposite the front 2 (part of body containing) the spine; *v* 1 move backwards 2 support; *a* 1 situated behind 2 of the past 3 overdue *adv* 1 away from the front 2 in or to an earlier condition 3 in return; *idm* **the back of beyond** isolated place without social or cultural activity; *idm* **be on sb's back** hinder or annoy sb; *phr v* **back down** US **back off** yield; **back up** 1 support 2 b. **-up** *comput* make a spare copy; *n* backup.

back-bencher *n* Brit MP without ministerial status; *n* **back-benches** seats in House of Commons for such MPs.

backbiting *n* malicious gossip; *n* backbiter.

backbone *n* spine, vertebrae; courage, firmness.

backbreaking *a* exhausting.

backchat *n* answering back in a cheeky manner.

backdrop *n* 1 backcloth 2 natural background.

backdate *v* make applicable from an earlier date.

backer *n* one who supports another, *esp* with money; one who bets on a horse, or sporting event.

backfire *n, v* 1 *aut* (emit) loud explosion due to premature ignition of fuel 2 (of plans) go wrong.

backgammon *n* a board game played with draughtsmen and dice.

background *n* part of picture behind chief figures 2 a person's past history; *n, a* inconspicuous (position).

backhand *n* 1 shot played with back of hand towards opponent 2 side from which such a shot is played *a* **backhanded** 1 played on the backhand 2 (of personal remarks) equivocal *n* **backhander** 1 remark of this kind 2 *coll* small bribe.

backing *n* 1 anything used to cover back of object 2 support, aid 3 act of one who backs 4 *mus* accompaniment.

backlash *n* 1 sudden sharp recoil 2 hostile *esp* political reaction.

backlog *n* accumulation of unfinished business.

back-of-beyond *n coll* place

remote from civilisation.

back-pack US = rucksack; v hike with backpack ns **backpacker, backpacking**.

back passage n rectum.

backpedal v 1 pedal backwards 2 reverse in action, policy or decision.

back projection n projection from behind a translucent screen to create an illusion of movement in front.

back-room boy n Brit person with scientific or other expertise, that the general public is unaware of.

back seat n rear seat; idm take a back seat accept a less important role; n **back-seat driver** passenger who tries to tell the driver how to drive.

back-slapping a jovial and noisy.

backside n rear part of person or animal, rump.

backslide v relapse into bad habits; n **backslider**.

backspace n, v (key to) move typewriter carriage back.

backstage a, adv 1 behind the stage 2 in private.

backstreet a unofficial; illicit.

backstroke n swimming on the back.

back-to-backs n Brit closely built terraced housing.

backtrack v 1 go back over same path 2 reverse an earlier action or statement.

backup n 1 person or thing that supports or reinforces another 2 accumulation from a stoppage

3 alternative kept in reserve.

backward, backwards adv towards rear; with back first; a 1 turned back 2 retarded mentally 3 shy.

backwash n waves caused by passage of vessel.

backwater n small creek containing stagnant water; coll an isolated place.

backwoods n forest region beyond cleared land; fig culturally remote.

bacon n back and sides of pig, salted and smoked.

bacterium n one-celled plant organism; pl **bacteria**; a **bacterial**; n **bacteriology** study of bacteria; a **-ological**; n **-ologist**.

bad a evil; faulty; rotten; ill; adv **-ly**; n **-ness**.

bad blood n resentment.

bad debt n debt that cannot be paid.

baddy n coll villain.

bade v pt of **bid**.

badge n emblem of office, token of membership.

badger n nocturnal burrowing animal; v bait, tease.

badly-off a not having enough, esp of money; comp **worse-off**, sup **worst-off**.

badminton n game played with shuttlecock and racquets.

bad-mouth v sl, esp US malign.

baffle v confuse; puzzle; n plate to divert flow of liquid, gas, or sound waves; n **bafflement**; a **baffling**.

BAFTA abbr British Association of Film and Television Arts.

bag n 1 pouch; sack 2 day's take of game; v **bagging, bagged** capture; acquire; n **bagful**; a **baggy** loosely hanging; n **bagginess**.

bagatelle n trifle; game where players roll small metal balls into holes.

bagel n hard, ringlike roll.

baggage n 1 army equipment 2 luggage.

bagpipes n pl musical wind instrument.

baguette n long thin loaf of bread made esp. in France.

bail n 1 sum paid as security for person's reappearance in court 2 cricket one of two small sticks laid across top of wicket; v release on bail; **bail (out)** scoop water out.

bailey n outer wall of castle; court enclosed by it.

bailiff n sheriff's officer; land agent or steward.

bailiwick n 1 district of bailiff's jurisdiction 2 person's area of expertise or authority.

bairn n esp Scot child, baby.

bait n anything used to lure prey; v put bait on; torment; give food to (esp horses); n **baiting**.

bake v cook or harden by means of heat; ns **baker; bakery; baking powder** powder used instead of yeast n **baker's dozen** thirteen.

balaclava n close-fitting woollen hood, covering ears and neck.

balance n 1 weighing

instrument 2 equilibrium 3 remainder 4 difference between credit and debit sides of an account 5 regulating mechanism in clock or watch; v weigh; be equal in weight to; adjust; be in state of equilibrium; n **balance-sheet** statement of accounts.

balance of payments n difference between money imported and money exported over a given period.

balance of power n 1 situation where rival powers gain no advantage by making war 2 power of minor political party to influence affairs by alliance with others.

balance of trade n difference in value between goods imported and goods exported.

balcony n projecting platform outside window protected by railing; tier of seats above circle (in theatre).

bald a having no natural covering esp of hair; bare; plain; adv **baldly**; n **baldness**.

balderdash n rubbish, nonsense.

baldric n ornamented belt worn over shoulder to carry sword, bugle, etc.

bale n bundle of goods, hay etc bound with cord or wire; v **1** make into a bale **bale** v 2 see bail (out); phr v **bale out** jump from aircraft

by parachute in emergency.

baleful a evil, malicious; adv **-ly**; n **-ness**.

balk, baulk n hindrance; heavy, squared beam; division on billiard table; v avoid; hinder; jib, esp of horse.

ball[1] n 1 roundish body of any size 2 bullet or shot; v form into a ball; idm **on the ball** alert and aware of new ideas; idm **play ball** coll cooperate.

ball[2] n social gathering for dancing; n **ballroom**; idm **have a ball** coll enjoy oneself.

ballad n traditional story in song; simple song.

ballade n 1 poem with three eight-lined stanzas and a short conclusion 2 mus romantic piece, usu for piano.

ballast n heavy material placed in ship's hold or balloon, to steady it; v steady with ballast.

ball-bearings n steel balls used to relieve friction on bearings.

ball-cock n device for regulating level of liquid.

ballerina n a female ballet dancer.

ballet n action or story expressed by dancing, miming etc; **balletomane** ballet lover.

ballistics n science of projectiles and means of their propulsion; a **ballistic**.

balloon n gas or hot air-filled

bag that rises in air; inflatable rubber bag; v inflate; billow out in wind; n **balloonist**.

ballot n printed sheet used in voting; act of voting; v vote by ballot n **ballot box 1** box for deposit of voting slips 2 system of democratic elections.

ballpark n 1 US baseball field 2 coll approximate range of figures.

ballpoint n, a (pen) that dispenses ink by a rollerball.

ballroom n large room for dancing.

balm n 1 aromatic resin 2 fragrant garden herb 3 healing ointment; a **balmy**; adv **balmily**; n **balminess**.

baloney n stupid talk; nonsense also **boloney**.

balsa n tropical tree whose wood is extremely light.

balsam n 1 aromatic resin 2 anything healing, soothing or restorative.

baluster n small post supporting a hand-rail; n **balustrade** set of balusters.

bamboo n giant grass with hard, hollow, jointed stem.

bamboozle v trick, puzzle or confuse.

ban n prohibition; denunciation; v **banning, banned.** forbid; exclude.

banal a trite, trivial ordinary; n **banality**.

banana n tropical fruit tree; its fruit; n **banana skin** coll unforeseen cause of embarrassment.

band *n* 1 tie or ligament of any material 2 flat strip applied on another object 3 body of persons united for common purpose, *esp* company of musicians; *v* unite; gather together; tie, fasten with a band.

bandage *n* strip of cloth etc used to bind up wounds; to apply a bandage to.

Band-aid [TM] US type of sticking plaster.

bandanna *n* large brightly coloured handkerchief.

B and B *abbr* (place providing) bed and breakfast.

bandbox *n* light-weight box for hats.

bandeau *n* Fr 1 band keeping hair in place 2 band inside hat.

bandit *n* outlaw, robber or brigand.

band-saw *n* endless steel saw running over wheels.

bandstand *n* covered platform for band playing outdoors.

bandwagon *n* idm **climb/jump on the bandwagon** join in a successful or popular enterprise.

bandy *v* -**dying, -died.** pass to and fro; *idm* **bandy words** quarrel, *a* **bandy-legged** bow-legged.

bane *n* source of evil; curse, ruin; *a* **baneful**; *adv;* -**ly;** *n* -**ness.**

bang[1] *n* sudden loud noise; sharp blow; *v* thump; beat, shut noisily; explode.

bang[2] *n* hair cut to form fringe.

bangle *n* ornamental bracelet for arm or ankle.

bang-on *adv sl* exactly right.

banish *v* drive into exile; (of mental action) dismiss; *n* **banishment.**

banister *n* rail and supports along a stairway.

banjo *n pl* -**jos,** or -**joes.** musical instrument of guitar family.

bank[1] *n* heap or mound of earth; edge of river etc; *v* 1 pile up 2 put aircraft at angle when turning.

bank[2] *n* 1 commercial concern engaged in keeping, lending and exchanging money 2 place where sth is stored; *v* deposit money in bank; have an account with bank; *phr v* **bank on** rely on; *ns* **banker, banking.**

bank card *n* cheque guarantee card.

bank holiday *n* 1 Brit official public holiday that falls on a weekday 2 US weekday when banks are closed.

bank rate *n* minimum interest rate fixed by central banks.

bankroll *n, v esp* US (act as sb's) source of finance.

bankrupt *n, a* an insolvent person; *v* make bankrupt; *n* **bankruptcy.**

banner *n* flag as symbol of country, regiment etc.

bannock *n* flat cake made of oatmeal or barley meal.

banns *n* announcement in church of intended marriage.

banquet *n* Fr ceremonial or

official feast; *n* **banqueter.**

banshee *n* fairy whose wail supposedly warns of death.

bantam *n* 1 breed of small fowl 2 light-weight boxer.

banter *n* good-natured chaff; *v;* *a* **bantering.**

Bantu *n* 1 group of black communities native to central and S Africa 2 languages spoken by them; *a* **Bantu.**

banyan *n* Indian fig-tree, *also* **banian.**

baobab *n* African tree with gourd-like fruit.

baptism *n* ceremony of admitting person to Christian church by immersing in or sprinkling with water; *v* **baptize** name; *a* **baptismal;** *n* **baptist(e)ry** part of church where baptism is administered; *idm* **baptism of fire** 1 first taste of warfare 2 first ordeal of a gruelling kind.

Baptist *n, a* (member of Protestant church) believing in baptism by full immersion.

bar *n* 1 rod of solid material 2 sandbank at mouth of river 3 rail in courtroom 4 legal profession 5 counter in a public house 6 obstruction 7 musical unit 8 non-material obstacle; *v* fasten with (bar); rule out *prep* except; *idm* **bar none** without exception.

barb *n* backward-curving point on arrow, fish-hook, harpoon, etc; *as* **barbed, barbate.**

barbarian n uncivilized person; ns **barbarism, barbarity, barbarousness;** a **barbaric;** adv **barbarously.**

barbecue n outdoor feast; grid for roasting meat over charcoal fire; v cook in such manner.

barber n one who cuts hair, shaves or trims beards.

barbican n outer defence of castle or fortress.

barbiturates n pl group of drugs used to induce sleep or ease pain; a **barbituric.**

bard n Celtic poet or minstrel; a **bardic.**

bare a naked; simple; empty; scanty; v reveal; adv **-ly;** n **-ness;** a **bare-faced** shameless; idm **the bare bones** only the basic essentials.

bargain n 1 agreement; pact 2 something obtained at small price; v make agreement; discuss or argue about terms.

barge n broad flat-bottomed boat; state or pleasure boat; n **bargee** person in charge of a barge; v force way clumsily.

baritone n, a voice ranging between tenor and bass.

barium n heavy, white metallic element; **barium meal** n chemical taken internally to enable the digestive tract to be X-rayed.

bark¹ n outside covering of trees; v strip bark from; scrape skin off.

bark², **barque** n three-masted sailing ship; small ship; ns

barkentine, barquentine small bark.

bark³ n sharp cry or noise made by dog or fox; v speak sharply; n **barker** tout who induces people at a fair or circus to see show.

barley n cereal plant; its seed or grain.

barm n yeast; leaven; a **barmy** 1 frothy 2 coll dimwitted.

barmaid n woman who serves drinks in a bar; n **barman** man who does this.

bar mitzvah n (ceremony for) Jewish boy of 13, taking on adult religious responsibilities.

barn n building for storing hay, grain etc; ns **barn-dance** lively rustic dance; **barnyard; barn-owl.**

barnacle n species of goose; type of shell-fish that cling to rocks, ship's bottom, etc.

barney n coll brawl or quarrel.

baro- prefix weight, pressure, esp of atmosphere.

barometer n instrument for recording atmospheric pressure; a **barometric;** adv **barometrically;** ns **barograph** type of barometer.

baron n lowest rank in peerage; fem **baroness;** n **barony;** a **baronial;** n **b. of beef** double sirloin.

baronet n lowest hereditary title; n **baronetcy.**

baroque a grotesque, fantastical; n style of music, architecture or art.

barrack n (usually pl) building

in which soldiers live; v jeer derisively at in public; n **barracking.**

barracuda n large edible fierce fish.

barrage n 1 barrier placed in river 2 continuous gunfire to cover movement of troops.

barrel n 1 cylindrical vessel or cask with bulging sides; measure of capacity 2 metal tube of gun; v pack, stow in barrel; idm **over a barrel** helpless; at one's mercy.

barren a sterile; bare; bleak; n **-ness.**

barricade n makeshift barrier; v block with barricade.

barrier n anything obstructing passage or advance.

barrister n advocate in higher courts of law.

barrow¹ n burial mound of earth or stones; tumulus.

barrow² n small wheeled handcart.

barter n, v trade by exchange of goods.

basalt n dark-coloured volcanic rock; a **balsaltic.**

bascule n mechanism working on see-saw principle.

base¹ n 1 bottom; starting point 2 word-stem 3 main ingredient; as **basal, basic, baseless;** n **basement** floor below ground level; idm **not get to first base** coll make an unsuccessful start; phr v **base sth on/upon sth** use sth as a starting point.

base² a 1 low; mean; vicious; vile 2 (of metal) counterfeit; n **-ness;** adv **-ly.**

baseball n American ball-game similar to rounders.

baseline n sport line at the back end of a court.

base rate n standard interest rate at a bank.

bases n pl of **basis**.

bash n a heavy blow; v strike violently.

bashful a shy, modest; adv **-ly**; n **-ness**.

basic a fundamental; essential adv **-ally** n pl **basics** basic principles.

BASIC, Basic n comput simple programming language.

basil n aromatic plant of mint family.

basilica n church with double colonnade and apse.

basilisk n 1 fabulous lizard whose breath and glance were fatal 2 kind of crested lizard.

basin n 1 hollow vessel 2 region drain by river 3 dock; land-locked harbour.

basis n base, foundation or principle; pl bases.

bask v luxuriate in (sun etc).

basket n 1 container made of woven rushes or canes 2 banking group of currencies ns **basketwork; basket-ball** kind of ball game **basket case** n sl, esp US badly incapacitated person.

basket ball n US 1 ball game played with two teams of five players on a rectangular court 2 the ball used.

Basque n member of race living in W Pyrenees.

bass[1] n voice of deep quality;

lower part of musical register; a low in tone.

bass[2] n common perch; **sea-bass** edible sea fish like salmon.

basset n type of hound with short legs.

bassoon n woodwind instrument with bass tone.

bast n fibrous strips from trees used for mats, ropes.

baste v **basting**. moisten (roasting meat) with melted fat, etc; tack loosely; thrash.

bastion n projecting part of fortification; bulwark.

bat[1] n small nocturnal mammal which flits about.

bat[2] n 1 wooden implement used in ball-games 2 **batting, batted**. blow; v strike with bat; ns **batsman; batting;** idm **off one's own bat** on one's own initiative; idm **not bat an eyelid** be unperturbed.

batch n whole product of one baking; set of things of the same kind.

bate v diminish; abate; moderate; a bated; idm **with bated breath** too anxious to breathe.

bath n act of washing; vessel to wash in; pl place where baths may be taken.

bath chair n wheel chair for an invalid.

bathe v apply water to; swim; ns **bather, bathing.**

bathos n fall from sublime to ridiculous; a **bathetic.**

bathrobe n 1 loose garment worn before and after

having a bath 2 US dressing gown.

bathroom n 1 room with bath 2 US lavatory.

bathysphere n large metal sphere used for deep-sea observation.

batik n method of dyeing cloth using wax on parts not to be dyed; cloth dyed in this way.

batiste n a fine cotton muslin.

batman n servant to an officer.

bat mitzvah n (ceremony for) Jewish girl of 13, paralleling the **bar mitzvah.**

baton n stick esp of orchestral conductor.

bats a coll insane.

batsman n cricket player who bats.

battalion n Army unit of about 1000 men.

batten n narrow strip of wood; v secure with battens.

batten v grow fat; phr v **batten on** thrive at the expense of.

batter v beat heavily with repeated violent blows; n 1 mixture of flour, milk and eggs beaten together 2 baseball player who bats.

battery n 1 physical assault 2 artillery unit 3 group of cells for storing electrical energy 4 set of hen coops designed for quick production of eggs.

battle n fight between armies, fleets or aircraft; v fight, struggle; ns **battlefield** place of battle; **battleship** heavily armed and armoured warship.

battering-ram n beam of wood with metal end formerly used in war for breaking down doors and walls.

battleaxe (US **-ax**) n 1 heavy axe used as weapon 2 *coll* hostile, domineering woman.

battlements n pl defensive wall(s) of a castle with openings for firing weapons through.

batty a *coll* crazy.

bauble n flashy jewellery; gewgaw; trifle.

baud n unit of measure for speed of a signal or data transfer, *esp* in computer modems.

bauxite n clay from which aluminium is obtained.

bawd n prostitute; procuress; a **bawdy** lewd n **bawdiness**.

bawl v shout, cry loudly; n loud cry.

bay[1] n kind of laurel.

bay[2] n 1 inlet of sea 2 division of building 3 recess in a room; **sick-bay** sick quarters.

bay[3] n deep bark of hound, *esp* in pursuit; v howl.

bay[4] *idm* **hold/keep at bay** keep at a safe distance.

bay[5] n, a (horse of) reddish brown (colour).

bayonet n dagger-like blade fixed to rifle; v wound with bayonet.

bayou n arm of a river.

bay rum n fragrant liquid for cosmetics and medicines.

bay window n projecting window area of house.

bazaar n 1 Oriental market 2 sale in aid of charity.

bazooka n portable anti-tank gun.

BB *abbr* 1 Boy's Brigade 2 (of black pencils) very soft.

BBC *abbr* British Broadcasting Corporation.

BC *abbr* before the birth of Christ.

be v exist; have quality, feeling or state; *pt* **was, were;** *pp* **been;** *pr p* **being.**

beach n sea-shore *esp* if sand; v run (a boat) on shore; n **beach buggy** motor vehicle for use on beach n **beachcomber** beach-haunting tramp; n **beach-head** position established by invading troops.

beacon n signal light or fire on hill, tower, etc.

bead n 1 small ball of glass, wood, etc with hole through it, used to form necklace, rosary 2 small drop of moisture; *as* **beaded; beady** round, bright; n **beading** moulded strip of wood, stone etc on furniture or wall as decoration.

beadle n mace-bearer; minor parish or church officer.

beagle n small hound used in hunting.

beak n 1 bill of bird 2 *sl* magistrate 3 *sl* headmaster.

beaker n large cup or mug; glass vessel kept by chemists.

be-all and end-all n only important thing.

beam n 1 thick piece of

timber; bar of balance 2 shaft of light radio wave 3 extreme breadth of ship; v shine, emit or radiate.

bean n leguminous plant; its kidney-shaped seed; *idm* **not have a bean** *coll* be penniless.

beanbag n 1 small bag of dried beans used for games of throwing 2 large cushion for use as an informal seat.

beano n a feast; jollification

bear[1] n 1 heavy, clumsy, fur-clad mammal 2 rude, bad-tempered person; a **bearish**; n **-ness**.

bear[2] v 1 support, carry 2 endure 3 bring forth, give birth to; *pt* **bore;** *pp* **borne (born** in most contexts relating to birth); n **bearer** carrier; *phr vs* **bear down** 1 overcome 2 press down hard; **bear down on/upon** approach fast in a hostile manner; **bear on/upon** be relevant to; **bear out** confirm; **bear up** persevere with courage; **bear with** tolerate patiently; a **bearable;** adv **-ably.**

beard n 1 growth of hair on man's cheeks and chin 2 gills of oyster; v confront face to face; *as* **bearded, beardless.**

bearing n 1 behaviour 2 meaning 3 direction 4 heraldic emblem 5 part of machine where moving parts revolve.

bearskin 1 pelt of bear 2 tall black fur hat worn by

guardsmen.

beast *n* 1 four-footed animal; 2 brutal person; *a* **beastly** brutal; *n* **beastliness**.

beat *v* 1 hit repeatedly 2 conquer 3 mark (time) by strokes; 4 pulsate; *pt* **beat**; *pp* **beaten**; *n* 1 blow 2 throb 3 regular route; *a* **beaten** 1 shaped by beating 2 defeated 3 mixed by beating; *n* **beater** on who rouses game; *idm* **beat about the bush** talk indirectly without saying what one means; *idm* **Beat it!** *sl* Go away!; *idm* **beat time** mark tempo of music by regular movements.

beatify *v lit* make happy, blessed; *a* **beatific** *adv* **-ally;** *n* **beatitude** supreme bliss.

beatnik *n* type of young person in late 1950s who rejected normal social conventions.

beau *n* boyfriend.

Beaufort Scale *n* number scale indicating wind speeds.

beaujolais *n* table wine, *usu* red, from Beaujolais area of France.

beautician *n* person who gives beauty treatment.

beauty *n* 1 loveliness; charm; grace 2 lovely woman *a* **beautiful;** *v* **beautify** make beautiful *n* **beauty spot** 1 beautiful place 2 mole or artificial dark spot on a woman's face.

beaver *n* water-loving rodent; its fur; *v* work hard.

becalmed *a* (of a ship) deprived of wind.

became *pt of* **become**.

because *conj prep* for the reason that **because of** on account of.

beck *n* 1 small stream 2 nod, sign of command; *idm* **at one's beck and call** ready to carry out one's every order or request.

beckon *v* signal or call by a gesture.

become *v* **-coming, -came, -come.** come to be; suit; *a* **becoming** proper, enhancing appearance of *adv* **-ly.**

BEd *abbr* Bachelor of Education.

bed *n* 1 thing to sleep on 2 piece of ground 3 foundation; 4 mineral stratum 5 bottom of sea or river; *v* **bedding, bedded.** plant out; place on foundations.

bedbug *n* wingless bloodsucking insect found in beds.

bedding *n* 1 bedclothes and mattress 2 straw or litter for sleeping on 3 foundation 4 *geol* stratification.

bedfellow *n* 1 person sharing bed 2 close companion.

bedeck *v* decorate, adorn.

bedevil *v* confuse, harass, bewitch; *n* **bedevilment.**

bedizen *v* dress in a cheap, gaudy way.

bedlam *n* lunatic asylum; noisy scene or uproar.

bed of roses *n* idyllic, carefree state.

Bedouin *n sing or pl* nomadic Arab(s).

bedpan *n* container used as toilet by person ill in bed.

bedraggle *v* drag through mire; *a* **bedraggled.**

bedridden *a* confined to bed, *esp* permanently ill.

bedrock *n* 1 solid rock 2 basic principles.

bedside manner *n* doctor's way of talking tactfully.

bed-sitter *n* room used as both bedroom and living-room.

bedsore *n* raw spot on skin from lying too long in bed.

bedspread *n* cover for bed, *usu* decorative.

bedstead *n* frame of bed on which mattress rests.

bed-wetting *n* urinating during sleep in bed.

bee *n* four-winged insect, producing honey; *ns* **bee eater** small brightly coloured bird; **bee hive; beeswax;** *idm* **a bee in one's bonnet** an obsession; *idm* **the bee's knees** superior person or thing.

beech *n* species of tree; its wood, **beech-mast** nuts.

beef *n* flesh of ox, cow, considered as food; *pl* **beeves;** *a* **beefy** sturdy; *n* **Beefeater** Yeoman of the Guard.

beefcake *n sl* (photographs of) strong muscular men.

beeline *idm* **make a beeline for** go directly towards.

been *pp of* be.

beep *v, n* (make) noise of or as of a car horn.

beer *n* alcoholic drink make

from malted hops, yeast, etc; *a beery*.

beeswax *n* wax taken from honeycomb.

beet *n* edible red vegetable root (beetroot); white root used in sugar manufacture.

beetle[1] *n* insect with biting mouth parts; heavy wooden mallet.

beetle[2] *v* overhang; *a* **beetling**; *n* **beetle-brow** heavy projecting brow.

befall *v* happen to; *pt* **befell** *pp* **befallen**.

befit *v* **befitted**. be worthy of; fitting; *a* **befitting**, *adv* **befittingly**.

before *prep* 1 front of 2 preceeding in time, rank; *adv* in front; sooner; *conj* rather than sooner; *a*, **beforehand** in advance, ahead of time.

befriend *v* be a friend to; help.

befuddle *v* confuse; make hazy.

beg *v* **begging, begged. 1** entreat 2 live by receiving alms; *n* **beggar** person who begs; *a* **beggarly** *idm* **beg the question** assume that an answer or proof has been given when it has not; *idm* **go begging** be unwanted.

beget *v* **-getting, -get** *or* **-got.** produce; father; *pt* **begot, begat**; *pp* **begotten;** *n* **begetter**.

begin *v* **-ginning, -gan, -gun.** commence, start; originate; *ns* **beginner** novice; **beginning**.

begone *interj* go away!

begonia *n* colourful tropical plant.

begrime *v* soil with dirt or smoke.

begrudge *v* envy (a person something); be stingy in giving.

beguile *v* 1 deceive; cheat 2 amuse; charm; *n* **beguiler** deceiver, seducer; *a* **beguiling**.

behalf *idm* **on behalf of** in the name of.

behave *v* conduct (oneself); act with decorum; *n* **behaviour** conduct, manners.

behaviourism *n* belief that all human action could be related to stimulus and response *n, a* **behaviourist**.

behead *v* cut the head off.

behest *n* order; command.

behind *prep* at back of; in support of; inferior to; *adv* in arrears; *idm* **be behindhand** *idm* be late.

behold *v* to look at, see; *pt, pp* **beheld**; *n* **beholder**; *a* **beholden** under an obligation.

beige *n a* (of) light yellowish-brown (colour).

being *n* 1 existence 2 human creature 3 essence, nature.

belabour *v* beat heartily; thrash.

belated *a* unduly deferred; *adv* **-ly.**

belay *v* make fast or secure (a rope).

belch *v* 1 release wind through mouth 2 pour out under force; *n* 1 release of wind 2 spurt of flame, smoke etc.

beleaguer *v* besiege.

belfry *n* bell-tower.

belie *v* **-lying, -lied.** give lie to; misrepresent.

believe *v* accept as true; place trust in; have faith; *ns* **believer, belief;** *as* **believable, believing.**

Belisha beacon *n* flashing orange light at a pedestrian crossing.

belittle *v* make little of; disparage; *n* **-ment.**

bell *n* 1 hollow cup-shaped object giving musical sound when struck 2 cry of stag in rut; *v* roar, bellow.

belladonna *n* deadly nightshade; poisonous drug.

bell-bottoms *n pl* flared trousers.

belle *n* beautiful young woman.

belles-lettres *n pl* Fr essays that are purely literary.

bellicose *a* war-like; quarrelsome; *n* **bellicosity.**

belligerent *a* waging war; aggressive; *adv* **-ly;** *n* **belligerence.**

bellow *v* roar, cry out; *n* roar of a bull etc; any deep cry or shout.

bellows *n* apparatus for producing draughts of air.

belly *n* lower part of body beneath diaphragm, abdomen; *v* swell out, bulge.

bellyache *v* grumble frequently, without justification.

belly-button *n coll* navel.

belly-dance *n* erotic type of dance by woman from the

Middle East n belly-dancer.

belong v be owned; be part or member; n **belongings** possesions.

beloved a, n (one who is) greatly loved.

below prep lower than; a, adv beneath.

belt n 1 band of leather or other fabric worn round waist 2 zone 3 endless band used in driving machinery; v 1 encircle 2 sl thrash; a **belted**; idm **below the belt** coll unfair(ly); idm **under one's belt** coll already acquired; phr vs **belt along** coll drive at top speed; **belt out** coll sing or emit very loudly; **belt up** sl be quiet.

bemoan v lament; sorrow for.

bemuse v daze, confuse, stupefy.

bench n long seat, work-table; judge's magistrates' seat in court; coll magistrates' judges.

benchmark n 1 mark used by land surveyors 2 standard example for making comparison.

bend n 1 curve 2 type of know; v twist; turn 1 curve 2 submit; pt, pp **bent**; idm **round the bend** coll insane; n pl **the bends** coll decompression sickness suffered by deep-sea divers who surface too quickly.

beneath adv below; prep underneath.

benediction n blessing; blessing at end of church service.

benefactor n person who gives help or money fem **benefactress**; n **benefaction**.

beneficent a doing good; n **beneficence.**

benefit n favour; profit; v - **fited** or **-fitted.** do or receive good; pt, pp benefited; ns **benefaction** good deed; **benefactor**; a **beneficial** useful; improving; (adv **-ly**) ns **benefice** church living; **beneficiary** one benefiting from will, etc.

benevolence n kindliness; generosity; a **benevolent.**

benighted a 1 overtaken by darkness 2 ignorant.

benign a 1 kindly; gentle; gracious 2 (of diseases) not malignant; adv - **ly** n **benignity.**

benison n blessing.

bent[1] pt, pp of bend idm **bent on** determined on; a 1 distorted 2 Brit sl dishonest.

bent[2] n 1 inclination; aptitude 2 stiff coarse grass.

benumb v make numb.

benzedrine n drug used as stimulant and nasal spray.

benzene n aromatic liquid obtained from coal-tar.

benzine n colourless inflammable solvent from petroleum.

bequeath v give or leave by will; n **bequest**.

berate v scold; rebuke.

bereave v to deprive by death; rob fig of immaterial things; pp, pt **bereaved** (but pp

bereft in fig sense); n - **ment.**

beret n small, soft, flat cap.

berg n iceberg.

bergamot n (oil from) pear-shaped Asian fruit.

beri-beri n disease caused by lack of vitamin B.

berk n Brit sl idiot.

berry n small fleshy fruit containing seeds but no stone; a **berried**.

berserk a mad; wild; frenzied.

berth n 1 space for anchoring ship in dock 2 sleeping-place on ship or train; v moor a ship; idm **give sb a wide berth** keep well away from sb.

beryl n green mineral.

beseech v implore, beg; a **beseeching** adv **-ly**; pt, pp **besought.**

beset v -**setting**, pt -**set.** surround; assail; a **besetting.**

beside prep at side of; adv, prep **besides** other than; in addition to.

besiege v beset with armed forces; n **besieger**.

besmirch v soil, smear.

besotted a 1 drunk 2 infatuated 3 foolish.

bespatter v spatter; **besotted** a 1 foolish 2 drunk.

bespeak v arrange in advance; claim; pt **bespoke**; pp **bespoken**; made to order.

bespectacled a wearing spectacles.

best a, adv (sup of **good**, **well**) most excellent(ly); v beat (someone); get the better of.

bestial *a* coarse; brutish; *n* **bestiality**.

bestir *v* -stirred. stir up, rouse to action.

best man *n* bridegroom's attendant.

bestow *v* give, stow away; *n* **bestowal**.

bestride *v* put one's legs on each side of (something); *pt* **bestrode**; *pp* **bestridden**.

bet *v* betting, bet or betted. wager; *n* stake given; *n* **better** one who bets.

betake *v idm* -takes, -taking, -took, -taken. **betake oneself to** *fml* go to.

bete-noire *n Fr* person or thing one hates most.

bethink oneself *v ar* remind oneself; think again.

betide *v* happen to; befall.

betimes *adv* in good time; early.

betoken *v* indicate, signify.

betray *v* act falsely towards; reveal secret improperly; *ns* **betrayal, betrayer**.

betroth *v* promise, engage in marriage; *ns* **betrothal, betrothed**.

better *a, adv* (*comp of* **good, well**) (in a) superior or improved (way); *v, n* **betterment**.

between *prep, adv* separated by.

betwixt *prep, adv* between.

bevel *n* 1 sloping edge 2 joiner's tool; *v* **bevelled**. form angle.

beverage *n* drink (other than water).

bevy *n* group of girls or women; flock of larks, quails.

bewail *v* 1 mourn over 2 complain over.

beware *v* be on one's guard (against).

bewilder *v* perplex, confuse; *as* **bewildered, bewildering** (*adv* -ly); *n* -**ment**.

bewitch *v* cast a spell over; fascinate; *a* **bewitching**.

beyond *prep, adv* 1 to or on the other side (of) 2 exceeding; past the limit of 3 apart from; *idm* be **beyond sb** to be too hard for sb to understand.

bi- *prefix* two.

bias *n* 1 slant; prejudice 2 tendency; *v* influence unfairly; *pt, pp* bias(s)ed; *pr p* bias(s)ing; *a* biased prejudiced in **bias binding** strip of material to bind edges.

bib *n* garment placed under child's chin to protect its clothes; *v* tipple; *n* **bibber** tippler.

Bible *n* sacred book of Jews and Christians; *idm* **one's bible** authoritative book on any subject; *a* **biblical**.

bibliography *n* study of books; list of books on a particular subject; *a* **bibliographical**; *n* **bibliographer**.

bibulous *a* given to drinking alcoholic drinks.

bicameral *a* having two parliamentary chambers.

bicarbonate of soda *n* sodium bicarbonate, used as a medicine or as a raising

agent in baking.

bicentenary *n a* (celebrating) the 200th anniversary *also US* **bicentennial**.

biceps *n* muscle with double attachment, *esp* of upper arm.

bicker *v* quarrel; wrangle; *n* **bickering**.

bicycle *n* two-wheeled vehicle propelled by foot pedals; *v* ride this vehicle.

bid *v* command, invite; *pt* **bade**; *pp* **bidden**; offer, try; *pt, pp* **bid**; *n* 1 offer to give certain price 2 attempt 3 (in card-games) a call *ns* **bidder, bidding**.

bide *v* wait; remain; dwell.

bidet *n* low basin for washing anal area and genitals.

biennial *a* happening every two years; *n* plant lasting two years; *adv* -**ly**.

bier *n* wooden frame on which a coffin is carried.

biff *n* sharp blow with fist; *v* strike such a blow.

bifocals *n* spectacles with double lenses to correct both distant and reading vision; *a* **bifocal**.

bifurcate *v* divide into two branches.

big *a* -**gger**, -**ggest**. possessing great size, bulk etc.

bigamist *n* one who marries another whilst still married; *n* **bigamy**; *a* **bigamous**; *adv* -**ly**.

big bang *n* explosion of matter from which the universe is believed to have originated *n* **the big-bang theory**.

big dipper n Brit roller-coaster; US **the Great Bear** astron the Plough.

big end n aut end of connecting rod joining crankshaft.

big game n large wild animals, esp when hunted.

bighead n coll conceited person.

bight n 1 loop in rope 2 a wide bay.

big noise, big shot n very influential person.

bigot n narrow-minded, intolerant person; a **bigoted**; n **bigotry**.

big time n coll top level in business, esp entertainment.

big top n circus tent.

bijou n Fr (of house, flat etc.) small, elegant.

bigwig n coll important person.

bike n, v coll bicycle.

bikini n small two-piece bathing costume for women.

bilateral a having two sides; adv -**ly**.

bilberry n moorland shrub, or its bluish berries.

bile n 1 secretion of liver, aiding digestion 2 ill-humour.

bilious a 1 sick; sickly; 2 yellowish n -**ness**.

bilge n 1 space in ship's bottom into which filth and seawater drain 2 dirt collecting there 3 coll stupid talk or writing.

bilingual a of or using two languages.

bilk v cheat, defraud, elude payment of (debt).

bill, billhook n curved chopping tool.

bill[1] n 1 bird's beak 2 point of anchor; idm **bill and coo** kiss and cuddle.

bill[2] n 1 draft of proposed legislation 2 statement of money due 3 written programme of events 4 poster 5 bank-note; idm **foot the bill** pay the cost.

billabong n Aust 1 stagnant backwater pool 2 dry channel or bed of stream.

billboard n large outdoor advertisment.

billet[1] n soldier's quarters; v provide lodgings.

billet[2] n faggot; block of wood.

billet-doux n love letter.

billiards n game played with cue and balls on cloth-covered table with pockets.

billion n a million millions; US a thousand millions.

billow n large swelling wave; v swell out; a **billowy**, **billowing**.

billy, billy-can n can used as camp kettle.

billy goat n male goat.

bin n 1 container for corn, coal, waste etc 2 rack for storing wine bottles.

binary a dual; involving two.

bind v 1 tie round; make fast 2 pledge (oneself) 3 fasten sheets of book into cover; pt, pp **bound**; ns **binder** bookbinder; thing that binds; **binding** book-covering; phr v **bind sb over** leg order sb.

bindweed n climbing plant;

convolvulus.

binge n spree; drinking bout.

bingo n gambling game with random numbers.

binnacle n box for compass in ship.

binocular a using both eyes at once; n **binoculars** field or opera glasses.

binomial n algebraic expression having two terms.

bio- prefix = life.

biochemistry n chemistry of living organisms.

biodata n US curriculum vitae.

biodegradable a capable of being decomposed by nature.

biography n story of person's life written by sb else; study of such writings; n **biographer**; a **biographical**.

biology n study of living organisms; n **biologist**; a **biological** (adv -**ly**).

bionic a 1 of bionics 2 having superhuman power.

bionics n 1 study of biological functions applicable to development of electronic equipment 2 use of mechanical parts to replace damaged living organs.

biopic n life of a famous person in film.

biopsy n analysis of body tissue and fluid to test for disease.

bioscope n apparatus for projecting motion pictures.

biosphere n the part of the Earth's service and atmosphere that supports life.

biotechnology n use of living cells in industry.

bipartisan a representing two parties or sides.

bipartite a in two parts; shared by two parties.

biped n a two-footed animal.

biplane n aircraft with two pairs of wings.

birch n 1 tree with thin, smooth bark; wood of this tree 2 birch rod used for caning; v to flog.

bird n feathered biped that lays eggs.

bird brain n coll stupid person; a **bird-brained.**

birdie n, v golf score (of) one under par; n coll bird.

birdlime n sticky material spread to snare birds.

bird of paradise n songbird of New Guinea with bright plumage.

bird's eye view n view from above.

biretta n square black cap worn by RC priests.

Biro [TM] ballpoint.

birth n bearing of offspring; act of being born; parentage; n **birth-right** patrimony.

birth control n contraception.

birthday n anniversary of the day one was born.

birthmark n distinguishing mark on skin from birth.

birth rate η number of births over a given period.

birth sign n sign of zodiac under which one is born.

biscuit n thin crisp cake made of eggs, flour etc.

bisect v divide into two parts;

a **bisectional**; ns **bisection; bisector** divider of angle into two equal parts.

bisexual a of both sexes; sexually attracted to both sexes.

bishop n clergyman of high rank in Christian church; n **bishopric** his diocese or office.

bismuth n metallic element used as medical drug.

bison n large wild ox, American buffalo.

bistro n Fr small wine shop or restaurant.

bit n 1 small portion; fragment 2 tool for boring 3 metal mouth-piece of bridle 4 comput smallest unit of information; v fit in (horse's mouth).

bitch n female dog or wolf, vixen.

bite v biting, bit. 1 use teeth upon 2 act on by friction 3 pierce; a biting (adv -ly) scathingly; n **bite** 1 nip with teeth 2 wound (by teeth) 3 sting 4 taking of bait; idm **bite off more than one can chew** try sth beyond one's ability; idm **bite the bullet** cope with a painful situation; idm **bite the dust** coll 1 fall down dead 2 be defeated.

bit part n dram small speaking part.

bitter a of sharp taste; opposite of sweet; ranking; piercing; adv -ly; n -ness n **bitter** light beer.

bitters n liquor with bitter

vegetable ingredients.

bittern n marsh bird noted for deep, booming cry.

bittersweet n woody nightshade; a fig pleasant but sad.

bitty a made of many bits, without coherence.

bitumen n asphalt; natural mineral pitch; a **bituminous**.

bivalve n mollusc with double-hinged shell, as oyster.

bivouac n temporary rest spot for troops.

bizarre a unusual, odd, fantastic.

blab v reveal secrets; n **blabber** or **blabbermouth** coll indiscreet talkative person.

black n 1 darkest colour 2 people of African or Caribbean origins 3 darkness; a 1 sombre 2 wicked 3 sullen; v **black, blacken** make black; denigrate; n **-ness**; ns **blackball** vote against; ns **blackberry** bramble; **blackbird** song-bird; **blacking** black polish.

black belt n (person of) top grade in judo or karate.

black box n automatic flight recorder in aircraft.

blackcurrant n bush with small edible black berries; fruit of this.

Black Death n 14th century epidemic of bubonic plague.

black economy n unofficial business enterprises that avoid assessment for tax purposes.

blackguard n scoundrel,

worthless person; v revile; a **blackguardly**.

blackhead n small black pimple.

black hole n area in outer space from which light or matter cannot escape.

black ice n invisible ice on a road surface.

blackjack n 1 US type of cosh 2 the game pontoon.

blackleg n one who works during strike.

black list n list of people in disfavour or due for punishment; v **blacklist**.

black magic n magic invoking the powers of evil.

blackmail n, v 1 attempt to extort money by threatening to reveal a guilty secret 2 use threats to induce sb to act in a certain way; n **blackmailer**.

Black Maria n coll police van for carrying prisoners.

black market n illegal trading of goods; n **black marketeer.**

blackout n failure of electricity; temporary loss of consciousness.

black power n movement to promote political power for black people.

black pudding n dark sausage of pig's blood, suet, etc.

black sheep n disreputable member of family.

blacksmith n a smith who forges iron.

black spot n place where accidents tend to occur.

blackthorn n thorntree, which bears sloes.

black-tie a when dinner jackets should be worn.

black widow n very poisonous type of spider.

bladder n sac in body for holding secreted liquids; any tough, inflated, membraneous bag; n **bladderwrack** seaweed with strings of air capsules.

blade n cutting edge of knife etc; flat of oar; bat, propeller, etc; long thin leaf of grass, corn etc; a **bladed**.

blame v censure; find fault with; hold responsible; n culpability; a **blameless** adv -**ly**; a **blameworthy**.

blanch v make white; scald; grow pale.

blancmange n sweet dish based on cornflour.

bland a gentle; mild; urbane; n -ness.

blandish v flatter; coax; n -ment.

blank n empty space; cartridge without shot; a 1 without writing, print expression or features 2 (of verse) unrhymed 3 (of denial or refusal) total adv -**ly**; idm **draw a blank** get a negative result.

blank cheque n US blank check 1 signed cheque with the amount left blank 2 authority to make all decisions.

blanket n soft woollen cloth used for bedcover, horse-rug etc; v cover with (as with blanket); idm **wet blanket** pessimist.

blare v utter loudly, like a trumpet; n harsh noise.

blarney n flattery; v cajole, speak, coaxingly.

blasé a Fr dulled by pleasure, bored, cynical.

blaspheme v speak profanely of; talk irreverently ns **blasphemer, blasphemy;** a **blasphemous** (adv -ly).

blast n sudden strong gust of wind; explosion; v scorch; shatter by explosion; phr v **blast off** be launched by firing of rockets; n **blast-off**.

blasted a 1 ravaged by wind or fire 2 coll annoying.

blast furnace n furnace for melting iron ore.

blatant a noisy, vulgarly obvious; adv **blatantly** n **blatancy**.

blather v talk foolishly; n stupid; foolish talk.

blaze[1] n burst of flame or intense light; outburst of rage etc; v burst into flame; shine brilliantly; idm **blaze a trail** act as a pioneer.

blaze[2] n mark tree by cutting bark; white mark on face of animal; v mark (tree or trail) by cutting bark.

blazer n light flannel sports jacket.

blazon n coat of arms; v paint shield with arms; proclaim widely.

bleach v whiten, esp of cloth; n **bleaching**.

bleak a bare, desolate; cheerless; n **bleakness**.

blear a watery, dim; v dim, blur; a **bleary**.

bleat n cry of sheep, goat; v cry feebly; n, a **bleating**.

bleed v draw blood from; extort money from; lose blood; pt, pp **bled**; ns **bleeder** unpleasant person; **bleeding** a losing blood; sl extremely; idm **bleed sb dry/white** take all sb's money.

bleep n, v (emit a) short high-pitched electronic sound, esp as a warning signal; n **bleeper**.

blemish n physical, moral defect; flaw; v mar; deface.

blend v mix together; n mixture; mingling; pt, pp **blended**.

bless v pronounce benediction; make holy; make happy; n **blessing**; a **blessed**; n **-ness**.

blight n disease or insect pest attacking plants; v spoil.

blighter n Brit coll 1 fellow 2 despicable person.

blimey interj Brit coll expressing surprise.

blimp n 1 small non-rigid airship 2 pompous reactionary; a **blimpish**.

blind a 1 sightless 2 lacking foresight 3 reckless 4 closed at one end; n 1 window shade 2 artifice; v make blind; adv **-ly**; n **-ness**; a, n **blinding**; v **blindfold** put something over the eyes of; idm **turn a blind eye** pretend not to notice; idm **blind sb with science** impress or confuse sb by display of specialist knowledge.

blind alley n 1 cul-de-sac 2 course of action which seems good but leads nowhere.

blind date n coll meeting arranged between two people who have never met, usu a man and a woman.

blinders n US = blinkers.

blind spot n 1 part of retina not sensitive to light 2 area not visible to motorist 3 subject on which one is ignorant.

blindworm n legless lizard; slow-worm.

blink v flap eyelids rapidly; flicker; fig attempt to evade; n wink; twinkle; idm **on the blink** not working properly.

blinkers n pl small flaps preventing horse from seeing sideways; a **blinkered** narrow-minded.

blip n 1 spot of light on radar screen 2 short sharp sound.

bliss n perfect enjoyment, happiness; a **blissful**; adv **blissfully**; n **blissfulness**.

blister n 1 bubble-like swelling full of liquid under the skin 2 swelling on surface of paint; v form blisters; a **blistering** 1 (of heat) extreme 2 (of criticism) severe.

blithe a carefree; adv **-ly**; a **blithesome**.

blitz n sudden attack.

blizzard n blinding snowstorm with high wind.

bloat v swell a **bloated**; n **bloater** smoked herring.

blob n spot; drop of liquid.

bloc n political or national alliance of interests.

block n 1 lump of wood 2 mould 3 plate used in letter-press printing 4 group of buildings 5 obstruction 6 large quantity; v 1 stop 2 shape, esp blocks; ns **blockhead** stupid person; **blockage** obstruction.

blockade v stop access by seige; n closure of port etc.

block and tackle n device for lifting with pulleys.

blockbuster n 1 powerful bomb 2 any successful commercial promotion.

block letters n capital letters.

bloke(e) sl man.

blond(e) a a fair-coloured; n person with fair hair and complexion.

blood n 1 red fluid circulating through body 2 kinship 3 life itself; adv **-ily**; ns **-iness**; **bloodbath** massacre; as **bloodless**; **bloodcurdling** terrifying; **bloodshot** suffused with blood; **bloody** 1 blood-stained; murderous 2 sl taboo intensifier expressing any positive or negative attitude; idm **in cold blood** without emotion.

blood brother n man pledged to another like brothers.

blood count n (counting of) number of white corpuscles in a blood sample.

bloodhound n a hunting dog; detective.

blood letting 1 killing 2 removal of blood for medical reasons.

blood pressure n pressure

exerted by the blood on the walls of the blood vessels, linked to the strength of the heart and the state of the blood vessels.

bloodmobile n mobile vehicle for taking blood donations.

blood pressure n force of blood on inner walls of blood vessels.

bloodshed n the shedding of blood.

blood sport n killing of wildlife for sport.

bloodstock n thoroughbred horses.

blood-stone n opaque green stone with red flecks.

bloodthirsty a ferocious, savage, cruel.

Bloody Mary n cocktail of tomato juice with vodka.

bloody-minded a obstructive on purpose; n -ness.

bloom n 1 blossom; 2 prime of life 3 thin film on certain fruits; v flower; prosper; n **bloomer** coll mistake; a **blooming** 1 flowering 2 coll euphemism for taboo bloody.

bloomers n pl short baggy trousers gathered at the knee for women.

blossom n flower; v come into bloom.

blot n spot; disgrace; v blotted. stain, smudge, obliterate; idm **blot one's copybook** spoil a good reputation; phr v **blot out** hide; obliterate.

blotter n paper for blotting or protecting n **blotting paper** absorbent paper to dry up ink.

blotch n discoloured patch on skin, etc; a **blotchy**.

blotto a coll very drunk.

blouse n loose kind of shirt.

blow v produce current or gust of air; expel from lungs into trumpet etc; pt **blew**; pp **blown**; n 1 blast 2 hard knock 3 sudden set-back; a **blown** 1 winded 2 putrefying; idm **blow one's own trumpet/horn** praise oneself; idm **blow one's top/stack** coll lose one's temper; idm **blow sb's mind** sl give sb an exhilarating shock; a **mind-blowing**; idm **blow the whistle on** coll expose in order to put an end to (sth illicit); phr vs **blow over** pass; **blow up** 1 fill with air 2 enlarge 3 explode; destroy; be destroyed 4 begin with sudden force 5 reprimand; ns **blow-fly** meat fly; **blowhole** nostril of whale; breathing hole in ice.

blow-by-blow a related in detail chronologically.

blower n 1 device that blows currents of air 2 Brit coll telephone.

blowlamp, blowtorch n burner for removing old paint.

blown pp of **blow**.

blow-out n 1 burst tyre 2 melted fuse 3 escape of gas or oil 4 coll feast.

blubber n fat of whales; v weep.

bludgeon n short heavy club; v strike with this.

blue n 1 colour of unclouded

sky 2 pigment 3 University sportsman 4 unhappy 5 indecent; v make or treat with blue; idm **out of the blue** unexpectedly; n pl **the blues** 1 coll mental depression 2 melancholy type of jazz; a **bluish**; ns **bluebell** wild hyacinth; **blueberry** bilberry; **bluebottle** meat-fly; **bluejacket** sailor; **blueprint** copy of plan; **bluestocking** scholarly woman.

blue baby n baby with blue skin due to heart defect.

blue-blooded a of aristocratic descent.

blue-chip n, a (industrial share) regarded as safe to invest in.

blue-collar a concerned with manual work.

blue-eyed boy n coll sb's favourite who does no wrong.

bluegrass n 1 type of N American grass 2 type of country music from Kentucky.

blue moon idm **once in a blue moon** coll hardly ever.

blue murder idm **scream blue murder** protest noisily.

Blue Peter n flag flown when ship is leaving harbour.

blue-sky a US (of idea) having no pratical application.

blue tit n small bird with blue top and yellow breast.

bluff[1] n steep headland, bank; a 1 having steep perpendicular front 2 hearty; outspoken; adv -ly.

bluff[2] v deceive; n deception; idm **bluff it out** survive by continued pretence; idm **call sb's bluff** challenge sb to carry out threat.

bluish a fairly blue.

blunder n mistake; v make such; stumble; flounder; n **blunderer**; a **blundering**; adv **blunderingly**.

blunt a having rough edge or point; outspoken; v dull edge of; adv **bluntly**; n **bluntness**.

blur n, v **blurred**. smear; blot.

blurb n brief description of book's contents.

blurt out phr v utter hastily or indiscreetly.

blush v grow red; n flush; n, a **blushing**.

bluster v (wind) blow boisterously; rage; scold; n noise; empty threats; n **blusterer**; a **blustery**.

BM abbr 1 Bachelor of Medicine 2 British Museum.

BMA abbr British Medical Association.

BMX n strong bicycle designed for use on rough ground.

BO abbr coll unpleasant body odour.

boa n 1 non-poisonous snake that kills by crushing 2 fur of feather neck wrap.

boar n male pig; wild hog.

board n 1 plank 2 thick, stiff, compressed paper 3 table 4 official body 5 slab of covered wood or card on which games (chess, etc.) are played; pl the stage; v provide with meals; n **boarder** one who pays for food, lodging; child living at school in term; idm **above board** open and honest; idm **across the board** involving all members of groups; idm **go by the board** be ignored; idm **on board** on a ship or aircraft; idm **sweep the board** win everything; idm **take on board** recognize (a problem); assume (a responsibility).

boarding-school n school with living accommodation.

boardroom n room for meetings of company directors.

boast v praise oneself; claim proudly; n **boaster**; a **boastful**; adv -**ly** n -**ness**.

boat n generic term for all water craft; ns **boathouse**; **boating**; **boatswain, bosun** ship's officer.

boater n hard flat-topped straw hat.

boathook n long pole with hook for pulling boats.

bob n 1 quick up-and-down movement; clumsy curtsey 2 short haircut; v **bobbed**. move jerkily up and down.

bobbin n spool on which thread is wound.

bobble n small decorative ball, usu woollen, esp on a hat; n **bobble-hat**.

bobby n sl Brit policeman.

bobby socks, bobby sox n pl US short socks for girls.

bobcat n American lynx, wild cat.

bobsled n sledge steered by wheel on movable front portion, also **bobsleigh**.

bode v portend; a **boding** foretelling.

bodice n part of woman's dress above the waist.

bodice ripper n coll romantic novel containing sex and violence.

bodkin n large-eyed blunt needle.

body n 1 physical organism of living creatures 2 corpse 3 main part 4 mass 5 trunk 6 group of people; v give shape to; a **bodiless**; a, adv **bodily**.

bodyblow n 1 boxing blow to the body 2 severe setback.

bodyguard n person or persons guarding someone.

body language n indication (usu subconscious) of one's thoughts and feelings by one's posture and movements.

body popping n mechanical style of dancing of 1980s.

bodysnatcher n (formerly) stealer of corpses.

body stocking n close-fitting garment covering body.

body warmer n sleeveless quilted coat.

body wax n car shampoo containing protective wax.

boffin n coll scientific or technical expert.

bog n marsh; swamp; sl latrine; v become stuck in bog etc; a **boggy**; idm **bogged down** coll stuck; unable to progress.

boggle v 1 bungle 2 shrink from; n **boggler**.

bogie n wheeled frame-work beneath front of locomotive or railway coach.

bogus a not genuine, sham.

boil[1] v bubble with heat; cook in boiling water; phr v **boil down to** be no more than; n **boiler** vessel or tank for heating or boiling.

boil[2] n inflamed swelling, filled with pus.

boiler suit n overalls.

boisterous a rough, turbulent; adv **boisterously**; n **boisterousness**.

bold a daring; shameless; clear, prominent; adv **boldly**; n **boldness**.

bole n trunk or stem of a tree.

bolero n lively Spanish dance; loose short jacket.

bollard n mooring post for ship on dockside.

bolshie, bolshy a coll uncooperative.

bolster n long cushion; v support; a **bolstered**.

bolt n 1 metal rod used to bar door etc 2 thunderbolt 3 heavy arrow; v 1 secure with bolt 2 gulp food 3 run away; idm **bolt upright** erect and unbending.

bolthole n place to escape to.

bomb n metal shell filled with explosive, etc; v attack with bombs; n **bomber** bomb-carrying aircraft; idm **spend/cost a bomb** coll spend/cost a lot of money.

bombard v attack with shells, missiles, words; direct rays from radio-active substance at; ns **bombardment**;

bombardier artillery NCO.

bombast n pompous, empty, insincere talk; a **bombastic**; adv **-ally**.

bombshell n unpleasant shock.

bona fide a Lat in good faith.

bonanza n rich vein of ore; unexpected wealth.

bonbon n Fr sweetmeat.

bond[1] n 1 binding force 2 state of being firmly joined; n **bonding** 3 written promise, esp to repay money.

bond[2] n 1 shackle; 2 covenant; pl **bonds** ropes or chains for holding sb prisoner; v 1 bind 2 store goods until payment of duty; a **bonded** held in bond.

bondage n servitude, slavery; n **bondsman** slave.

bone n substance of which skeleton of vertebrates is made; any part of skeleton; v take out bones; as **bony, boneless, bone-dry**; idm **cut to the bone** reduce to the bare minimum; idm **feel in one's bones** feel instinctively; idm **have a bone to pick** have reason to quarrel; idm **make no bones (about)** not hesitate (about); idm **near the bone** rather tactless; likely to offend; phr v **bone up on** coll find out quickly what needs to be known about.

bonehead n coll stupid person.

bonfire n open-air fire for festive occasions, or to burn rubbish.

bongo n **bongos**. small drum played by hand.

bonhomie n hearty friendliness.

bonk v, n coll hit (not very hard).

bonkers a sl crazy.

bon mot n Fr witty saying.

bonnet n 1 head covering 2 covering over motor engine.

bonny a handsome; comely; adv **bonnily**.

bonsai n dwarf tree or shrub.

bonus n sum paid beyond what is due; premium; pl **bonuses**.

boo interj used to indicate disapproval, to startle; v make this sound.

boob n coll stupid error; dunce; v make mistake.

boo-boo n 1 mistake 2 minor injury.

booby n 1 dunce 2 seabird; ns **booby prize** award for lowest score; **booby trap** device to catch the unwary; practical joke.

book n 1 sheets of paper bound together in cover to form a volume 2 literary composition 3 list of bets in race; v reserve in advance; enter in book; idm **a closed book** unfamiliar subject; idm **by the book** strictly according to the rules; idm **throw the book at sb** remind sb forcefully of correct procedure; phr v **book in** register one's name; a **bookish**; scholarly; ns **booklet** small book; **bookkeeper, bookkeeping** keeping of accounts.

book club n club selling books cheaply by mail order.

bookend n device to stop books falling over on a shelf.

bookmaker n professional betting man, *also* **bookie**.

bookmark n sth left inside a book to mark a place.

bookstall n stall where books and magazines are sold.

book token n voucher exchangeable for a book or books.

bookworm n one devoted to study of reading.

boom n 1 long pole keeping bottom of sail extended 2 barrier across harbour 3 hollow roar 4 sudden prosperity; v 1 make hollow roar 2 rise in prices, birth rate.

boomerang n wooden object returning to thrower.

boom market n *comm* time when shares are rising rapidly in value.

boon n blessing; favour.

boondocks n US 1 backwoods 2 remote rural area.

boor n lout; ill-bred person; a **boorish** (adv -ly; n -ness).

boost v raise; augment; praise; n **booster** device for raising power or voltage.

boot[1] n 1 foot and ankle covering 2 space for luggage in car (US **trunk**); v kick; idm **give sb the boot** coll dismiss from employment; idm **put the boot in** coll 1 kick sb 2 be ruthless; phr v **boot out** coll expel

forcefully.

boot[2] n benefit; profit; v avail; a **bootless**; adv **to boot** in addition.

booth n temporary stall in market etc.

bootlegger n one engaged in traffic in illicit liquor; v, a **bootleg**; n **bootlegging**.

bootless a ar useless.

booty n spoils of war; plunder.

booze n, v sl drink; n **boozer** sl 1 pub 2 one who drinks; a **boozy**; n **booze up** drinking orgy.

bop n, v dance to pop music, *also* **bebop**.

borage n plant used for flavouring.

borax n white crystalline salt used as antiseptic, etc, a **boracic**.

bordello n brothel.

border n 1 edge; frontier 2 flower bed; v line; verge (on).

borderline n, a (on the) dividing line between two categories.

bore v 1 make hole in 2 weary by being dull; n 1 hole bored 2 dull person 3 high tidal wave in river; a, pr p **boring**; n **boredom** state of being bored.

born v be born come into the world; a **born** natural.

born-again a converted, esp evangelical Christian.

borne pp of **bear**.

boron n non-metallic element used to harden steel.

borough n 1 town or city with municipal corporation 2 one

with privileges granted by royal charter.

borrow v obtain on loan; adopt; use another's material; ns **borrower**, **borrowing**.

borstal n Brit reform school for young offenders.

bosh n coll empty talk; rubbish.

bosom n human breast; seat of emotions; n **bosom friend** very close friend.

boss n 1 head man; overseer; v direct; **bossy** arrogant; n **bossiness** 2 any projecting part; ornamental stud.

botany n science of plant life; n **botanist**; as **botanic**, **botanical**; adv **-ly**; v **botanize**.

botch v patch roughly; bungle; n clumsy piece of work.

both a, pron the two; conj, adv as well.

bother v worry; feel anxiety; n fuss a **bothersome**.

bottle n glass container for liquids; its contents; v put into bottles; n **bottler**; idm **be on/hit the bottle** drink too much alcohol; idm **have a lot of/no bottle** Brit sl have/lack courage; phr v **bottle out** Brit sl lose courage; idm **bottle up** suppress (feelings).

bottle bank n large bin for bottles for recycling.

bottleneck n narrow passage; condition hindering free circulation.

bottom n lowest part of anything; bed of sea, river, lake etc; human rump; a lowest; a -less; idm at bottom basically; phr v bottom out comm reach lowest level before recovering.

bottom line n essential fact or factor.

botulism n form of food poisoning.

boudoir n private room for women.

bougainvillaea n climbing shrub with red or purple bracts.

bough n limb of tree.

bought pt, pp of buy.

bouillon n clear soup.

boulder n large rounded mass of rock or stone.

boulevard n broad avenue.

bounce v rebound, as ball, on striking anything; spring; n bouncer chucker-out; a bouncing robust.

bound[1] v move with sudden spring; n leap; spring.

bound[2] pt, pp of bind; idm bound to certain to; idm bound up in busy with.

bound[3] v set limit to, restrict; n that which limits, confines; idm out of bounds beyond permitted area; a boundless adv -ly; n boundary something fixing limit, area etc.

bound[4] a bound for, -bound on the way to.

bounty n generous gift; as bountiful; bounteous liberal; advs bountifully, bounteously plentiful.

bouquet n 1 bunch of flowers 2 aroma of wine.

bourbon n Fr type of whisky.

bourgeois n, a Fr middle-class; n bourgeoisie.

bourn(e) n 1 rivulet 2 limit 3 realm.

bout n 1 spell 2 turn 3 trial; contest.

boutique n small shop selling fashionable clothes.

bovine a 1 pertaining to ox or cow 2 patient; stolid.

bovver n Brit sl aggression.

bow[1] n inclination of head or body in respect; v make bow 2 submit; yield; defeat; phr v bow out resign; phr v bow to yield to, n, a (at) front end of ship.

bow[2] n 1 weapon for shooting arrows 2 implement for playing violin etc 3 bend; curve; v use bow.

bowdlerize v expurgate (a book).

bowels n intestines.

bower n leafy grove; n bower bird Australian bird.

bowl[1] n hollow dish; drinking cup.

bowl[2] n wooden ball; v roll ball; phr v bowl over 1 knock down 2 astound; ns bowls game played on bowling green; bowling alley indoor area for bowls etc; bowler one who bowls; hard round felt hat.

bow-legs n pl legs curving outwards at the knee a bow-legged.

bowman n archer.

bow-tie n small tie with double loop.

bow window n curved window.

box[1] n hardwood tree 2 case 3 private compartment in theatre 4 sentry's shelter 5 carriage driver's seat 6 ruled-off space; idm (on) the box (coll on) television; v put in box.

box[2] v strike with fist or hand; n such a blow to head; n boxer one who fights with fists as sport (boxing).

boxcar n enclosed railroad freight car.

Boxing Day n first weekday after Christmas Day.

box number n number used for receiving replies to advertisements in newspapers and magazines.

box office n kiosk in cinema, theatre, etc where tickets are sold.

boxroom n small storage room in a house.

boy n male child, youth; a boyish; n boyhood.

boycott v 1 ban 2 stop dealing with.

boyfriend n 1 male sweetheart 2 male friend.

bozo n US sl stupid man.

BP abbr British Petroleum.

BR abbr British Rail.

bra n coll brassiere.

brace n 1 support 2 pair 3 device for holding bit; pl support for trousers; v support; a bracing invigorating.

bracelet n wrist band or ornament.

bracken n coarse common fern.

bracket n projecting support;

pl symbols [], (), enclosing word, etc; *v* join, associate.

brackish *a* (of water) salty; *n* **-ness**.

bract *n* small leaf at base of flower.

brad *n* thin flat nail; **bradawl** boring tool.

brag *v* **bragging, bragged.** boast; *n* 1 boast 2 cardgame; *n* **braggart** boaster.

Brahman, Brahmin *n* member of highest Hindu caste.

braid *n* plait of hair; band of fabric; *v* plait.

braille *n* system of printing for use by the blind.

brain *n* soft mass of nervous substance within skull; *pl* intelligence; *v* dash out brains of; hit on head; *as* **brainy, brainless;** *v* **brainwave** sudden bright idea; *v* **brain-wash** indoctrinate.

brainchild *n* original idea.

brain-drain *n* loss of skilled people emigrating to work in other countries.

brainstorm *n* Brit brief madness; US brilliant idea; *n* **brainstorming** way of tackling a problem by rapid interchange of ideas by a group.

braise *v* cook by simmering in closed pan.

brake *n* 1 device for checking wheel's motion 2 thicket 3 kind of waggon; *v* apply brake to, slow down.

bramble *n* prickly shrub, blackberry.

bran *n* husks remaining after grain is ground.

branch *n* limb of tree; any offshoot from main stem; *a* secondary; *v* produce branches; *n, a* **branching**; *phr v* **branch out** extend one's range.

brand *n* trade-mark; identifying mark; particular type of goods; burning stick; *v* mark with brand.

brandish *v* flourish, wave.

brand-new *a* completely new.

brandy *n* strong spirit distilled from wine.

brandy snap *n* crisp biscuit rolled into a cylinder.

brash *a* 1 impudently self-assertive 2 loud; *adv* **-ly**; *n* **-ness**.

brass *n* alloy of copper and zinc; *as* of brass; *a* **brassy** strident; *n* *coll* the **brass** high-ranking.

brassed off *a* Brit *sl* fed up.

brasserie *n* Fr restaurant for quick meals and drinks.

brass hat *n* Brit *sl* senior army officer.

brassiere *n* Fr undergarment supporting woman's breasts.

brat *n* uncomplimentary name for a child.

bravado *n* show of boldness or bluster.

brave *a* courageous; fine; *n* N American Indian warrior; *v* face with courage; *adv* **bravely**; *n* **bravery**.

bravo *interj* well done!

brawl *n, v* quarrel; fight.

brawn *n* 1 muscle; strength 2 pickled cut-up pork; *a* **brawny** strong.

bray *v* cry, as donkey.

braze *v* cover with brass; join with solder; *a* **brazen** shameless; *v* adopt defiant manner; *adv* **brazenly**.

brazier *n* 1 iron basket for holding hot coals 2 brass-worker.

breach *n* break; violation of law, contract; *v* make an opening in.

bread *n* 1 food made from flour, water, yeast and baked 2 food in general 3 livelihood 4 *sl* money; *n* **bread-fruit** fruit resembling bread when roasted; *idm* **bread and butter** way of earning a living; *a* **bread-and-butter** basic.

breadbasket *n* 1 main grain-producing area 2 stomach.

breadline *idm* **on the breadline** very poor.

breadth *n* distance across, width.

bread-winner *n* person supporting family with earnings.

break *v* **breaking, broke, broken.** 1 smash; destroy 2 tame 3 make bankrupt 4 interrupt; *n* 1 breach; fracture 2 interruption 3 lucky change; *a* **breakable**; *idm* **break new ground** begin sth new; *idm* **break the back of** do the most difficult part of; *idm* **break the ice** initiate social contact; *idm* **break wind** release air from bowels; *phr v* **break down** 1 reduce/be reduced to pieces 2 analyse

3 fail to work 4 lose control of emotions; idm **break even** make neither profit nor loss; phr vs **break out** start suddenly; **break out in** manifest (visible signs of disease); **break up** 1 divide 2 end a relationship 3 collapse 4 begin school holidays.

breakage n act of breaking; thing broken.

breakaway n, a (person or group) deserting main body of an organisation.

break-dance n acrobatic style of dance; v perform this.

breaker n wave that breaks near the shore.

break-even n point where income equals outgoings.

breakfast n first meal of day.

breakdown n 1 failure to operate 2 nervous collapse 3 statistical analysis.

breakneck a fast and reckless.

breakthrough n important discovery leading to progress.

breakwater n barrier that offers protection from waves.

bream n fish of carp family.

breast n bosom; mammary gland; v face boldly; idm **make a clean breast** confess everything; ns **breastplate** armour to cover breast; **breastwork** defensive wall.

breastbone n sternum.

breast stroke n style of swimming using a sideways sweep of both arms simultaneously.

breath n air drawn into or expelled from lungs; slight breeze; fragrance; idm **take one's breath away** astonish one; idm **under one's breath** inaudibly; v **breathe** inhale and exhale air; live; utter gently; blow lightly; idm **breathe down sb's neck** follow sb very closely; idm **breath one's last** die; n **breather** short rest; a **breath-taking** very exciting; ns **breathing**; a **breathless**; n -ness.

breathalyse, -lyze n measure amount of alcohol drunk by motorist; n **breathalyser, -lyzer** apparatus for this.

breech n hind end of anything; buttocks; pl **breeches** trousers; idm **breeches buoy** device for rescuing at sea.

breech birth, breech delivery n birth with baby's feet or buttocks emerging first.

breed v bear; offspring; rear; nourish; give rise to; pt, pp **bred**; n strain; kind; ns **breeder; breeding** manners.

breeze n gentle wind; a **breezy** airy; jolly; adv **breezily**.

breeze-block n light brick of cinders, sand and cement.

bren gun n light machine gun.

brethren lit pl of **brother**.

breve n mus note equal in length to four minims.

brevet n promotion without a pay increase.

breviary n book of daily prayers used by Roman Catholics.

brevity n briefness; conciseness.

brew v 1 make beer, tea etc 2 contrive 3 be afoot; n act or product of brewing; ns **brewing, brewer, brewery**.

briar, brier n thorny shrub; wild rose; bramble.

bribe n money, favour given to influence person; v influence thus; n **bribery**.

bric-a-brac n curios; knick-knacks.

brick n oblong block of baked clay used in building; v build with bricks; idm **drop a brick** make a gaffe; n **bricklayer**.

brickbat n 1 brick fragment 2 caustic criticism.

brickwork n assembled bricks.

bridal a of a bride or wedding.

bride n newly-married woman; **bridegroom** newly-married man; **bridesmaid** girl attendant on bride.

bridge[1] n card-game.

bridge[2] n 1 structure allowing access over river, railway, etc 2 part of ship used by captain and navigating officer 3 wooden strut under strings of violin etc 4 upper part of nose; v build bridge over; n **bridging loan** credit for business.

bridgework n partial denture fixed to other teeth.

bridle n head harness of horse; curb; v 1 fit with bridle 2 check 3 show disdain etc.

bridle path n path for horse riding.

Brie n soft white French cheese.

brief *a* lasting short time; concise; *n* synopsis of law case; *v* give final instructions to; *adv* **briefly**.

briefcase *n* flat case for business documents.

briefs *n pl* short pants or knickers.

brier *n* 1 thorny shrub 2 tobacco pipe.

brig *n* two-masted, square-rigged vessel.

brigade *n* military unit; organised body of people.

brigadier *n* officer commanding a brigade.

brigand *n* bandit; outlaw.

brigantine *n* square-rigged sailing vessel with two masts.

bright *a* shining; lively; vivid; intelligent; *adv* **-ly**; *adv* **-ness**; *v* **brighten** 1 make bright 2 become fine.

bright spark *n* Brit coll intelligent person.

brill *n* flat sea-fish similar to turbot.

brilliance *n* 1 splendour; radiance 2 outstanding talent; *a* **brilliant**; *adv* **-ly**.

brilliantine *n* hair oil for men.

brim *n* rim, edge (of cup, hat, etc); *v* full to rim; *as* **brimming, brimful, brimless**.

brimstone *n* sulphur.

brindle *n* streaked colouring or an animal with such coloring; **brindled** *a* a light brown colour with darker streaks.

brine *n* salt water used for pickling meat; *a* **briny**.

bring *v* cause to come; fetch; carry; cause *pt*, *pp* **brought**; *phr vs* **bring about** cause to happen; **bring forth** give birth; **bring forward** 1 introduce; propose 2 put at an earlier time; **bring off** 1 manage successfully 2 *sl taboo* give an orgasm to; **bring on** 1 put on show 2 cause; **bring over/round** convert to another opinion; **bring round/to** restore to consciousness; **bring up** 1 rear (children) 2 mention 3 vomit.

brink *n* edge (of chasm, precipice etc).

brinkmanship *n* art of taking political position as far as safety will allow.

brioche *n* Fr small light bun made with yeast and eggs.

briquette *n* Fr small block of compressed coal dust used as fuel.

brisk *a* lively, energetic, bracing; *adv* **-ly**.

brisket *n* joint of beef cut from breast.

brisling *n* small sardine-like fish.

bristle *n* short, stiff hair; *v* 1 stand on end, as bristles 2 show indignation; *a* **bristly**.

Brit *n* coll British person.

britches *see* breeches.

British *a* of Britain.

Briton *n* inhabitant of Britain.

brittle *a* easily broken; *n* **brittleness**.

broach *n* boring tool; roasting spit; *v* pierce (cask); open, begin (a subject).

broad *a* wide, large; general; coarse; of marked accent; *v* **broaden** make wider; *a* **broadminded** tolerant; *adv* **broadly**; *n pl* the **Broads** stretches of water in Norfolk; *ns* **broad bean** large flat edible bean; plant bearing it; **broadcloth** woollen cloth.

broadcast *v* scatter (seed) widely; spread abroad; transmit (radio, television); *pt*, *pp* **broadcast**; *n* such a transmission.

Broad Church *n* group favouring liberal attitude to doctrinal matters in C of E.

broadsheet *n* 1 large sheet printed on one side only 2 large format newspaper.

broadside *n* 1 naval firing of all guns on one side 2 fierce verbal attack.

brocade *n* stiff silk fabric with raised design.

broccoli *n* hardy type of cauliflower.

brochure *n* pamphlet; printed folder.

brogue *n* 1 stout rough shoe; 2 accent, *esp* Irish.

broil *n* noisy quarrel; *v* grill on open fire; **broiler** *n* quickly-reared chicken sold ready for broiling; *a* **broiling** *coll* very hot.

broke *pt* of break; *a* coll having no money.

broken *pp* of break.

brokenhearted *n* overcome by grief.

broker *n* one buying for another on commission; *n*

brokerage his commission or business.

brolly n Brit coll umbrella.

bromide n a sedative drug.

bronchitis n inflammation of bronchial tubes; a **bronchial**.

bronco n half-tamed horse.

brontosaurus n large herbivorous dinosaur.

bronze n alloy of copper and tin; its colour; v make or become bronze; a **bronze** sun-tanned; covered with bronze.

brooch n ornamental clasp or pin.

brood n young of animals esp birds; v sit on eggs; ponder anxiously; a **broody** inclined to brood.

brook n small stream; v endure, tolerate.

broom n 1 flowering shrub 2 sweeping brush; n **broomstick**.

broth n thin meat soup.

brothel n house used by prostitutes.

brother n 1 son of same parents 2 member of religious order, trade union etc; pl **brothers, brethren**; a **brotherly**; ns **brotherhood** group united by common interest; **brother-in-law** brother of husband/wife.

brought pt, pp of bring.

brow n 1 eyebrow; forehead 2 top of hill etc.

browbeat v bully.

brown n colour made by mixing black, red and yellow; a tanned; v make or become brown; **brown study** reverie.

browned off a coll esp Brit fed up.

brownie n 1 fairy, elf 2 junior Girl Guide 3 small square chocolate cake.

Brownie point n notional mark of credit for good deed.

browse v feed (as animal) on grass, leaves etc; glance through book.

bruise n injury that discolours flesh; contusion; v inflict this; n **bruiser** prizefighter.

brunch n breakfast and lunch combined.

brunette n woman with dark hair.

brunt n chief stress, strain of attack.

brush n 1 implement for sweeping, painting, dressing hair etc 2 tail of fox 3 skirmish 4 small shrubs 5 electrical device 6 light touch; v 1 sweep 2 use brush 3 touch lightly; phr vs **brush up (on)** revive knowledge of; **brush sb off** ignore the attentions of sb; ns **brush-off** snub; **brushwood** broken branches or twigs.

brusque a abrupt, curt; n **brusqueness**.

Brussels sprout n (brassica with) edible bud like small cabbage.

brute n 1 lower animal 2 cruel person; as **brutal** cruel and violent; (adv -ly n -ity); **brutish**; as of an animal; unrefined (adv -ly n - ness).

BS abbr 1 British Standard 2 Brit Bachelor of Surgery 3 US Bachelor of Science.

BSc abbr Brit Bachelor of Science.

B-side n flip side.

BSB abbr British Sky Broadcasting (also **BSKYB**).

BSE abbr bovine spongiform encephalopathy; fatal disease of cattle that attacks the central nervous system.

BST abbr 1 British Summertime 2 British Sky Television.

Btv abbr Baronet.

BT abbr British Telecom.

BTU abbr Board of Trade Unit.

bubble n globule of gas, air; plan lacking solidity; v form bubbles; make bubbling sound.

bubble jet printing n fine high quality printing; **bubble jet printer** machine that produces this.

bubo n suppurating swelling of gland in armpit, groin; a **bubonic (plague)**.

buccaneer n pirate; n **buccaneering**.

buck n 1 male deer, rabbit etc 2 dandy 3 sudden spring 4 US sl dollar; v leap suddenly; **buck up** phr v 1 try to improve 2 make more cheerful; n **buckskin** soft leather.

bucket n vessel for carrying water etc; pail; scoop in dredger; n **bucketful**.

bucket-shop n Brit coll unregistered firm selling airline tickets at bargain prices.

buckle n 1 clasp with catch for fastening 2 bulge; warp; v fasten with buckle warp; phr v **buckle (down) (to)** begin in earnest.

buckler n shield.

buckram n stiff cotton textile.

buckshee a, adv Brit sl free; gratis.

buckshot n medium-sized lead shot.

buckskin n skin of a buck.

bucktooth n projecting tooth or teeth.

buckwheat n dark cereal grain.

bucolic a rustic; rural.

bud n growth from which leaf of flower will develop; v **budding, budded.** put forth buds; graft; idm **nip in the bud** stop from developing.

Buddhism n religion based on teachings of Buddha; n, a **buddhist.**

buddleia n. purple and yellow flowering shrub.

buddy n coll friend; chum.

budge v move position.

budgerigar n small parakeet, lovebird.

budget n estimated financial schedule; v plan spending.

buff n 1 soft leather 2 pale yellow colour 3 bare skin; v polish.

buffer n 1 something that protects against or lessens the force of an impact 2 polishing device.

buffers n spring-loaded steel pads attached to railway rolling stock and ends of track to cushion impact.

buffalo n -oes kind of ox; American bison.

buffet[1] n, v slap; cuff.

buffet[2] n 1 side board 2 refreshment bar.

buffoon n clown; n **buffoonery.**

bug n small parasitic insect; n, v **bugging, bugged.** (install) hidden device for spying; a **bugged.**

bugbear n source of real or fancied fear.

buggy n 1 light carriage 2 small motor vehicle 3 also **baby buggy** baby carriage.

bugle n 1 kind of small trumpet 2 glass bead; ns **bugler, bugle-call.**

build v **building, built.** construct; n form; ns **builder, building.**

building society n business organisation that arranges long-term loans for the purchase of housing and pays interest to investors.

buildup n 1 steady increase 2 publicity campaign.

built-in a 1 constructed as part of 2 inherent.

built-up a with many buildings.

bulb n 1 globular, modified leafbud, usu underground; 2 electric lamp; a **bulbous.**

bulge n rounded swelling; v swell; as **bulgy, bulging.**

bulk n 1 volume 2 cargo; idm **in bulk** in large quantities; idm **the bulk of** the larger part of; idm **bulk large** be very prominent a **bulky** voluminous; n **bulkiness.**

bulkhead n. aeroplane or ship partition.

bull[1] n 1 male of ox family etc 2 speculator in rising stock values; ns **bullock** castrated bull; **bull's-eye** centre of target.

bull[2] n official papal enactment.

bulldog n 1 powerful dog with protruding lower jaw 2 University proctor's attendant.

bulldozer n powerful tractor for moving earth; v **bulldoze** overcome opposition by brutal force.

bullet n metal ball or missile fired from gun.

bulletin n brief official statement.

bullfinch n songbird, of which male has pink breast.

bullfrog n large frog with loud croak.

bullheaded a blindly obstinate.

bulimia n eating disorder in which bouts of over-eating are followed by self-induced vomiting.

bullion n gold or silver before being coined.

bullish a 1 like a bull 2 showing promise of success in stock market 3 optimistic.

bullock n castrated bull.

bull's-eye n 1 centre of target 2 hard peppermint sweet.

bully n -lies. overbearing, cruel ruffian; v -lying, -lied, intimidate.

bully beef n corned beef.

bully boy n thug, *esp* one paid to intimidate people.

bulrush n large rush of sedge family.

bulwark n 1 rampart 2 defence 3 ship's side above deck 4 breakwater.

bum n 1 US tramp 2 loafer; v cadge; *phr v* **bum around** *coll* spend time or travel aimlessly.

bumble v speak incoherently; *phr v* **bumble about/along** act in a disorganised way; a **bumbling**; n **bumbledom** fussy officialdom.

bumble-bee n large wild humming bee.

bump n 1 blow; collision 2 swelling due to blow; protuberance; v collide with; strike; jolt; *phr vs* **bump off** kill; **bump up** increase; n **bumper** 1 motor-car fender 2 full glass; a plentiful.

bumph, bumf n *Brit coll* (excess of) paperwork.

bumpkin n country yokel, rustic.

bumptious a arrogant; offensively self-assertive; *adv* **-ly**; n **-ness**.

bun n small cake; small round bunch of hair.

bunch n, v cluster (of things growing, or tied together).

bundle n number of things tied or rolled together; v 1 tie in a bundle 2 hustle (someone) away.

bung n 1 cork, wooden stopper, *esp* for cask 2 *coll* bribe, *esp* in football; v insert bung; *coll* put sth somewhere carelessly; *phr v* **bung up** block up.

bungalow n one-storied house.

bungle v botch; blunder; n something botched; confusion; n **bungler**; a **bungling**.

bunion n inflamed swelling, *esp* on big toe.

bunk[1] n sleeping-berth; *coll* escape.

bunk[2], **bunkum** n empty talk, nonsense.

bunker n 1 large bin, *esp* for fuel 2 military dugout 3 hazard on golf course.

bunny n (child's word for) rabbit.

Bunsen burner n type of gas burner.

bunting n 1 small bird allied to finch 2 coloured flags used for decoration, *esp* of streets, ships etc.

buoy n floating object anchored in water to mark channel, rocks etc; life-buoy; v mark with buoy; *phr v* **buoy up** keep afloat; sustain morally; a **buoyant**; *adv* **buoyantly**; n **buoyancy**.

bur, burr n seed-case covered with hooked spines.

burble v make gentle gurgling sound; babble.

burden n load; something difficult to bear; v load; encumber; a **-some**.

burdock n weed with purple flowers encased by bristles.

bureau n -eaux, or -eaus. *Fr* 1 writing table 2 information office 3 government department.

bureaucracy n government by state officials; n **bureaucrat**; a **bureaucratic**.

burgeon v to bud.

burger n *coll* = hamburger.

burgess n dweller in borough, with full municipal rights.

burgh n Scottish variant spelling of borough.

burgher n *ar* citizen of a town.

burglar n one who breaks into house to steal; n **burglary**; v **burgle**.

burial n burying; funeral; n **burial-ground**.

burlesque n derisive imitation; v ridicule; a mocking.

burly a of sturdy build; n **burliness**.

burn[1] v 1 injure or destroy by fire 2 use as fuel 3 be on fire 4 be consumed by fire 5 yearn; *pt, pp* **burnt, burned**; n mark caused by heat; a **burning**; n **burner**; *idm* **burn one's boats** or **bridges** do sth that makes it impossible to turn back; *idm* **burn the candle at both ends** work overtime and risk complete exhaustion.

burn[2] n brook; stream.

burnish v polish; n **burnisher**.

burnous n hooded cloak worn by Arabs.

burnout n mechanical failure through overheating or exhaustion of fuel.

burn-up n spell of fast reckless driving.

burp v, n belch.

burr n 1 hard stone 2 rough edge or line made by etching-tool on metal.

burrow n hole scooped in ground by animal, *esp* rabbit, fox etc; v make hole; dig, search.

bursar n treasurer, *esp* of college; n **bursary** grant.

burst v **bursting, burst.** explode; open out; erupt; puncture; n explosion; n, a **burst** sudden spurt.

bury v **burying, buried.** inter; conceal; n, a **burial**.

bus[1] n omnibus, large passenger motor vehicle.

bus[2], **busbar** n *comput* group of electrical conductors for carrying data.

busby n fur hat worn by certain British regiments.

bush[1] n 1 shrub; thicket 2 wild country; a **bushy**; n **bushiness**.

bush[2] n metal lining for circular hole; v fit bush.

bushbaby n small African lemur with large eyes.

bushed a *coll* exhausted.

bushel n dry measure equal to eight gallons.

bush telegraph n unofficial dissemination of news.

business n 1 occupation, profession, trade etc 2 affair; a **businesslike** efficient; ns **businessman, businesswoman, business card, business studies**; *idm* **like nobody's business** very fast or effectively.

busk v *Brit* earn money by playing music in the street ns **busker, busking**.

busman's holiday n holiday spent doing normal work.

bust n upper part of human body; sculpture of such part or **busted** n **buster**; a **bust, busted** *coll* broken; *idm* **go bust** fail; go bankrupt.

bustard n large, swift-running bird.

buster US way of addressing a man.

bustle n noisy movement; v move quickly, fussily.

bust-up n 1 violent quarrel 2 end of relationship.

busy a **busier, busiest.** at work; fully occupied; v **busying, busied.** occupy (oneself); *adv* **busily**; ns **busyness; busybody** meddling officious person.

busy lizzie n potplant with many small flowers.

but *adv* only just; without; *prep* except; *conj* on the contrary; yet; unless; **all but** almost.

butane n inflammable gaseous compound.

butch a *coll* 1 (of women) masculine in appearance and behaviour 2 (of men) aggressively masculine.

butcher n 1 tradesman dealing in meat 2 brutal murderer; v kill for food, or indiscriminately.

butler n head man-servant of a household.

butt n 1 barrel 2 end; stub 3 US *coll* buttocks 4 figure of fun; v 1 align end to end 2 push with head or horns; *phr*

v **butt in** interrupt.

butter n solidified fat obtained from cream by churning; v spread with butter; *phr* v **butter up** flatter.

buttercup n yellow cup-shaped wild flower.

butterfingers n person who tends to drop things.

butterfly n 1 four-winged insect, usually brightly coloured 2 flighty person; *pl* **butterflies** nervousness.

buttermilk n liquid left when butter has been made.

butterscotch n kind of hard toffee.

buttery n place for storing wines, liquors etc.

buttocks n the rump.

button n small flat disc for fastening clothing etc; small knob; v fasten with button; *idm* **buttoned up 1** fixed 2 inhibited.

buttonhole n 1 slit in lapel 2 worn in this; v detain and force sb to hear what one has to say.

buttress n support giving extra strength to anything; v support, prop.

buxom a robust, plump, rosy, comely; n **buxomness**.

buy v obtain by paying; bribe; *pt, pp* **bought**; n **buyer**.

buyer's market n time when low demand leads to low prices.

buy-out n giving control of a company by acquiring majority of shares.

buzz n low humming noise, as of bee; v make such sound;

murmur; *n* **buzzer** mechanical device that buzzes; *phr v* **buzz off** *coll* go away fast.

buzzword *n* specialist expression that has become fashionable to use.

buzzard *n* large bird of prey.

BW *abbr* biological warfare.

B/W *abbr* black and white.

by *prep* **1** near; close to **2** through; over **3** not later than **4** expressing agency; *adv* **1** at hand **2** aside **3** past; *idm* **by and by** eventually; *idm* **by and large** generally; everything considered.

by- *prefix* near; secondary; indirect; subsidiary; apart from. *Where the meaning may be deduced easily from the simple word, the compounds are not given here.*

bye *n* **1** free entry into next round of contest **2** cricket run scored without the ball touching the bat; *interj* also **bye-bye** *coll* goodbye.

by-election *n* election held by itself, not during General Election.

bygone *a* past, gone by; *n pl* **bygones** the past.

by law *n* local law or regulation.

bypass *n* **1** route avoiding busy area **2** *med* alternative passage for blood during surgical operation; *v* **1** go round **2** avoid consulting sb *ns* **bypass surgery, bypass valve.**

byplay *n* action of secondary importance.

by-product *n* subsidiary product or result.

bystander *n* one standing near; onlooker.

byte *n comput* unit of information (= 8 bits).

byway *n* quiet road or path.

byword *n* **1** typical example **2** proverb.

Byzantine *a* **1** of Byzantium **2** of art or architecture of the Byzantine Empire **3** (of politics) complex and inscrutable.

cab n 1 taxi 2 driver's shelter on engine, lorry or bus.

cabal n intrigue; secret plot.

cabaret n Fr entertainment in restaurant or night-club.

cabbage n green edible vegetable.

cabby n coll taxi driver.

caber n pole tossed in contest in Highland games.

cabin n small room on ship, esp for sleeping; hut.

cabin cruiser n motor boat with sleeping berths.

cabinet n 1 case or set of drawers 2 body of ministers governing country.

cable n 1 thick strong rope or line 2 telephone, telegraph line 3 message sent by cable; v send cable.

cable car n mountain car suspended on cable.

cable television n satellite TV system with multiple channels.

caboodle idm the whole

caboodle coll a lot, whole.

caboose n 1 ship's galley 2 US guard's van.

cabriolet n 1 one-horse carriage 2 motor-car with folding top.

cacao n plant from seeds of which cocoa and chocolate are made.

cache n secret store or hiding place.

cachet n Fr mark of excellence, authenticity.

cack-handed a Brit clumsy.

cackle n 1 noise made by hen, goose 2 shrill chatter; v make such noise.

cacophony n harsh discordant sound.

cactus n, pl -tuses, -ti. prickly plant with fleshy stem.

CAD abbr computer-aided design.

cad n ill-bred vulgar person.

cadaverous a looking like corpse; pale, gaunt.

cadenza n mus virtuoso passage for soloist at climax of concerto movement.

caddie, caddy n golfer's attendant.

caddy n small box for tea.

cadence n rhythm in poetry; rise and fall of voice in speaking.

cadet n student training for commissioned rank.

cadge v beg; sponge on others; n **cadger**.

cadmium n white metallic element.

cadre n permanent nucleus of military unit.

caesarian section n surgical operation to deliver baby when normal birth is impossible.

café n Fr restaurant serving light meals; n **cafeteria** self-service cafe.

caffeine n alkaloid stimulant, obtained from coffee and tea plants.

caftan, kaftan n long, loose robe, as worn by Arabs.

cage n structure for confining animals, etc; v to confine to cage; a **cagey** wary.

cagoule n light waterproof hooded jacket.

cahoots idm, esp US **in cahoots with** conspiring with.

cairn n 1 pile of stones built as monument etc 2 small terrier.

cajole v flatter with ulterior motive; n **cajolery**.

Cajun n 1 Lousiana inhabitant descended from Acadian immigrants 2 food particular to these people.

cake n 1 kind of sweet dough, baked in tin 2 hard mass; v to form hard mass, as of clay etc.

CAL abbr computer-assisted learning.

calamine n pink lotion to soothe sore skin.

calamity n terrible, disastrous event; a **calamitous**.

calcareous a made of lime.

calcium n metallic element, base of lime.

calculate v 1 reckon, esp by arithmetic 2 fit for particular purpose; a **calculating** able to make calculations; scheming; ns **calculation, calculator; calculus** branch of mathematics dealing with rates of variation.

calendar n almanac; system for fixing beginning and end of year; list of official dates.

calender n rolling machine for smoothing, polishing paper etc; v smooth so.

calf[1] n young of cow and various other mammals; its leather; pl **calves**; v **calve** give birth to calf.

calf[2] n fleshy back of leg below knee; pl **calves**.

calf love n immature infatuation of adolescent.

calibre n diameter of bore of gun; quality of mind or character; v **calibrate**; n **calibration**.

calico n cloth made of cotton.

call v 1 name; describe as 2 speak loudly (to); summon 3 visit briefly or regularly 4 telephone 5 rouse; wake 6 convene; ns **caller; calling** 1 shouting 2 profession; phr vs **call by/in** visit briefly when nearby; **call for** 1 collect 2 require 3 merit; **call off** 1 cancel (event) tell to stop threatening; **call on/upon** 1 visit 2 invite to speak 3 appeal to for help; **call out** 1 shout aloud 2 order to help 3 order to go on strike; **call up** 1 Brit recruit 2 telephone; idm **a close call** narrow escape; idm **on call** available for work if needed.

call-box n telephone kiosk.

call-girl n prostitute contactable by telephone.

calligraphy n handwriting; beautiful writing; n **calligrapher**.

call-in n = **phone-in**.

cal(l)iper n 1 instrument for measuring 2 leg brace.

callisthenics n exercises to develop strength and grace.

callous a hard-hearted; unfeeling; hardened (of skin); adv **-ly**; n **-ness**.

callow a undeveloped; inexperienced.

call-up n (order for) recruitment.

callus n lump of hard skin.

calm n windlessness; stillness; a quiet; peaceful; v become still, tranquil; adv **-ly**; n **-ness**.

calorie n unit of heat; esp in relation to value of food; a **calorific** heat making.

calumny n false accusation;

slander.

calve v give birth to calf.

calves pl of **calf**.

calypso n type of West Indian song.

calyx n cup of leaves surrounding flower petals.

CAM abbr computer-aided manufacture.

cam n projection on shaft controlling desired movement; n **camshaft** device in engine to lift valves.

camaraderie n comradeship.

camber n slight convexity on road, ship's deck, etc; curvature of aircraft wing.

cambric n fine white linen cloth.

camcorder n video camera with recorder.

came pt of **come**.

camel n large, ruminant, humped animal.

camellia n shrub with white, red or pink flowers.

cameo n gem carved in relief on contrasting background.

camera n photographic apparatus; idm **in camera** privately; n **cameraman**.

camiknickers n combined camisole and knickers.

camisole n woman's sleeveless undergarment.

camomile n plant with aromatic flowers, used medicinally.

camouflage v disguise appearance of objects, esp from enemy; n deception.

camp n 1 temporary shelter for travellers 2 place where

tents or huts are erected for troops 3 faction or party; *a sl* effeminate; too ornate; dandified; *v* build, lodge in camp; *ns* **camping, camper; camp-bed** narrow folding bed; **camp-chair** portable folding chair; **camp-follower 1** non-combatant accompanying an army 2 non-committed hanger-on to a political group.

campaign *n* **1** series of military operations **2** action to achieve particular purpose; *v* serve in, organize campaign.

campanile *n* lofty detached tower in which bells are rung.

campanologist *n* one who studies or peals bells; *n* **campanology.**

camphor *n* aromatic volatile white substance; *a* **camphorated** impregnated with camphor.

campus *n* chief grounds of college, university, school.

can [1] *v aux* be able, be allowed to; *pt* **could;** *pp* **been able.**

can [2] *n* tin vessel used for holding food for preserving; *v* preserve in can; *idm* **carry the can** be held responsible.

canal *n* **1** artificial waterway **2** duct in living body.

canapé *n Fr* small savoury appetizer on biscuit, toast, etc.

canard *n* rumour; hoax.

canary *n* yellow song-bird.

canasta *n* card game similar to rummy.

cancan *n* high-kicking dance

by women in long skirts.

cancel *v* delete; cross out; abolish; suppress; *phr v* **cancel out** balance each other; *n* **cancellation.**

cancer *n* malignant tumour or growth in body; *a* **cancerous.**

candelabrum *n* branching ornamental candle holder (*pl* **candelabra**), *also* **candelabra** (*pl* **candelabras**).

candid *a* frank, honest, outspoken; *adv* **candidly;** *ns* **candidness, candour.**

candida *n* yeastlike parasitic fungus that causes thrush.

candidate *n* **1** person standing for election **2** person taking examination; *n* **candidature.**

candle *n* stick of wax with wick, for giving light; *ns* **candle-light; candle-power** unit of measure of light; **candlestick** candle holder.

candour (*US* **candor**) *n* frankness.

candy *n* crystallized sugar; *v* preserve, become encrusted with sugar; *a* **candied.**

candy floss *n* light fluffy sweet of sugar on a stick.

cane *n* hard stem of bamboo etc; walking stick; *v* beat with stick; *n* **caning.**

canine *a* of, related to dog.

canister *n* box, usually of tin.

canker *n* **1** ulcerous sore; **2** disease in trees; **3** *fig* moral corruption; *a* **cankered** spiteful.

cannabis *n* **1** hemp **2** drug extracted from this.

canned *a* put into cans or

sealed jars **2** *coll* recorded in advance.

canneloni *n It* pasta tubes with stuffing of meat or vegetable.

cannery *n* factory where food is canned.

cannibal *n* human who eats human flesh; *n* **cannibalism;** *v* **cannibalize** use (machine product, artefact, etc) to reassemble in new form; *n* -**ization;** *a* **cannibalistic.**

cannon *n* **1** large mounted gun **2** stroke in billiards; *pl* **cannon, cannons;** *v* make cannon in billiards collide; *n* **cannonade** discharge of artillery; *n* **cannon fodder** troops regarded as expendable in war.

cannot *v* can not.

canny *a* cautious; shrewd; wary.

canoe *n* light boat propelled by paddling; *pl* **canoes;** *n* **canoeist.**

canon *n* **1** rule, law, *esp* of church **2** ecclesiastical dignitary **3** list of saints; *v* **canonize** declare officially to have been a saint.

canopy *n* overhead covering.

can't *v coll* cannot

cant *n* **1** insincere speech; **2** jargon; *v* use cant; *adv* **canting.**

cant *v* slope, lean to one side; slant; *a* **canted.**

cantaloupe(e) *n* type of melon.

cantankerous *a* ill-natured; touchy; quarrelsome.

cantata *n* choral composition.

canteen *n* **1** restaurant (in

factory, school, etc) 2 *Brit* set of cutlery 3 camper's water flask.

canter *n* easy hand-gallop; *v* ride at such pace.

canticle *n* chant with biblical text.

cantilever *n* girder etc securely fixed at one end, free hanging at other; *n* **cantilever bridge** centre part supported by cantilever arms.

canto *n* chief division of long poem.

canton *n* state in Swiss Republic.

cantor *n* synagogue or church singer.

canvas *n* strong coarse hempen cloth used for sails or painting pictures on; *idm* **under canvas** in tents.

canvass *v* solicit votes; discuss; *n* **canvasser** one soliciting votes.

canyon *n* deep gorge between cliffs.

cap *n* 1 brimless head-covering 2 military headdress; 3 sign of membership of sports team 4 lid; *v* 1 put cap on 2 confer University degree on.

capable *a* able; competent; having capacity; power; *n* **capability**; *adv* **capably**.

capacity *n* power of holding, absorbing (material or non-material things); *a* **capacious** 1 spacious 2 receptive; *n* **capacitor** *elec* condensor.

caparison *n* (formerly) decoration for horses; *v*

adorn.

cape *n* 1 sleeveless cloak 2 headland; promontory.

caper *v* skip about; frisk; *n* leaping about; *pl* silly pranks.

capillary *a* hair-like; *n* very narrow blood vessel.

capital *n* 1 chief city 2 large-sized letter 3 head of column 4 accumulated wealth; *a* 1 punishable by death 2 vital 3 excellent 4 leading; *adv* **-ly**; *ns* **capitalism** system of individual ownership of wealth; **capitalist**; *phr v* **capitalize on** take advantage of.

capital gain *n* profit from the sale of an asset, such as real estate or bonds.

capital punishment *n leg* punishment by death.

capitation *n* tax payable by or on each person.

capitol *n* building used by a legislature, *esp* Congress.

capitulate *v* surrender; cease to contend; *n* **-lation**.

capon *n* castrated fowl, *esp* when prepared for table.

cappuccino *n* Italian coffee made with hot, frothy milk.

caprice *n* whim; sudden fancy; *a* **capricious**; *n* **-ness**.

capsicum *n* pepper plant with hot-tasting seeds.

capsize *v* overturn; *esp* of boats.

capstan *n* 1 rotating post for winding ship's anchor 2 shaft that winds tape on tape-recorder.

capsule *n* 1 seed-container (of

plant) 2 part of spaceship in which astronaut travels 3 small, gelatine case containing drug or medicine.

captain *n* 1 naval or military officer 2 leader of team or side; *v* act as leader of side or team.

caption *n* title of picture, etc; heading.

captious *a* fond of finding fault; critical.

captivate *n* enchant; fascinate; charm; *pr p*, *a* **captivating** delightful, alluring.

captive *n* person held as prisoner; *a* unable to escape; *n* **captivity**.

capture *v* take prisoner; catch; *n* act of taking; *n* **captor**.

car *n* 1 motor-car 2 railway carriage 3 wheeled vehicle; *n* **car-boot sale** sale of second-hand goods from car boots on a specially hired site.

carafe *n* bottle, usually glass, for water, wine.

caramel *n* sweetmeat; burnt sugar for flavouring.

carapace *n* shell (of tortoise, crustacean).

carat *n* measure (of weight of diamonds, etc; of purity of gold).

caravan *n* covered vehicle, used as home, by Gipsies, holiday-makers; party of merchants, etc crossing desert; *n* **caravanserai** Eastern inn accommodating caravans.

caraway *n* aromatic seed used

for flavouring.

carbide n compound of calcium, producing acetylene gas.

carbine n short rifle used by mounted troops.

carbohydrate n energy-giving food containing sugar or starch.

carbolic a derived from carbon; n **carbolic acid** used as disinfectant.

carbon n non-metallic element occurring as graphite, diamond etc; as **carbonic, carbonaceous** like coal.

carboniferous coal-producing; v **carbonize** impregnate with carbon; n **carbon paper** coated one side with carbon, for duplicating typed or written matter.

carbonated a fizzy; containing carbon dioxide.

carbon dioxide n gas formed by burning of carbon or by breathing of animals.

carbon monoxide n poisonous gas emitted in exhaust fumes of petrol engines.

Carborundum [TM] compound of carbon and silicon used for polishing and grinding.

carboy n large glass vessel covered by wicker-work.

carbuncle n 1 inflamed boil, tumour 2 deep-red gem.

carburettor n device for mixing petrol vapour and air, forming explosive mixture, in internal combustion engines.

carcass, carcase n dead body;

skeleton or framework (of ship, building).

carcinogen n any substance likely to cause cancer; a **carcinogenic**.

carcinoma n type of cancer.

card[1] v comb wool or cotton; n comb for cleansing wool etc.

card[2] n thin pasteboard also **cardboard** visiting-card; playing-card; post-card; idm **get one's cards** be dismissed from work; idm **lay/put one's cards on the table** speak frankly about one's plans; idm **on the cards** quite possible; idm **play one's cards right** adopt the right plan of action.

cardamon n (seed of Indian plant used as) spice.

cardiac a concerning heart; n **cardiograph** record of heart action.

cardigan n knitted woollen or cotton jacket.

cardinal a of chief importance; n prince of RC Church, next in rank to Pope; ns **cardinal numbers** 1,2,3 etc; **cardinal points** NSE and W.

care n 1 grief 2 concern 3 charge; v feel anxiety; idm **have a care/take care** be careful; phr v **care for** 1 like 2 look after; a **careful** (adv **-ly**); a **careless** (adv **-ly**).

careen v expose keel of ship for cleaning or repair.

career n 1 rapid course 2 mode of living 3 occupation; v rush wildly.

carefree a free from anxiety.

caress n mark of affection, –

kiss, embrace etc; v fondle, embrace.

caret n mark (λ) used to show insertion of letter, word.

caretaker n person employed to look after a building.

cargo n freight or load of ship etc.

caribou n N American reindeer.

caricature n grotesque, laughable drawing or imitation of person; v represent in caricature.

caries n decay, esp of bones, teeth.

carillon n peal or chime of bells; melody played thereon.

carmine n crimson-red colour, obtained from cochineal.

carnage n severe slaughter; massacre.

carnal a pertaining to flesh; sensual; adv **-ly**; n **carnality**.

carnation n cultivated variety of clove pink.

carnival n organized festivities; revelry.

carnivore n flesh-eating mammal; pl **carnivora**; a **carnivorous** of animals and also some plants.

carob n kind of bean used as substitute for chocolate.

carol n joyful song, esp Christmas hymn; v sing.

carom v hit and rebound; n rebound.

carouse n drinking bout; v drink deeply; n **carousal** noisy drinking bout.

carousel n US merry-go-round.

carp[1] n fresh-water fish.

carp[2] v find fault unreasonably; a **carping** captious.

carpel n female reproductive organ of a flowering plant.

carpenter n wood worker in house-building etc; n **carpentry** craft of carpenter.

carpet n fabric for covering floor etc; v cover with carpet.

carpet-bagger n political opportunist from outside trying to get elected.

car pool n 1 group of drivers with shared transport 2 Brit fleet of cars for use by business employees.

carriage n 1 railway coach 2 transportation of anything 3 cost of carriage 4 deportment; bearing 5 vehicle.

carriageway n Brit part of road used by moving vehicles.

carrier n 1 person or thing that carries 2 one that passes a disease to others 3 = **aircraft-carrier**.

carrier pigeon n pigeon used to carry messages.

carrion n rotten flesh; putrefying animal carcass.

carrot n edible reddish-orange root; a **carroty** reddish, esp of hair.

carry v 1 transport 2 bear, support weight of anything 3 mil capture 4 retain (in memory); n range of projectile from gun.

carry-on n Brit coll fuss.

cart n two- or four-wheeled vehicle, usually horse-drawn; v carry; ns **carter**; **carthorse** strong horse **cart-track** rough road.

carte blanche n complete control or authority.

cartel n 1 written agreement for exchange of prisoners-of-war 2 agreement between manufacturers, fixing prices etc.

cartilage n strong, elastic tissue; gristle.

cartography n art of making maps, charts; n **cartographer**.

carton n box made of cardboard, corrugated board.

cartoon n sketch or design for work of art; topical drawing in newspaper, etc; n **cartoonist**.

cartridge n metal case containing charge for gun; n **cartridge paper** strong drawing-paper.

cartwheel n 1 wheel of cart 2 sideways somersault.

carve v 1 cut and shape wood, stone, etc; engrave 2 cut in slices or pieces (meat); ns **carving** piece of carved work; n **carver** 1 person who carves 2 carving knife 3 Brit dining-room chair with arms **carving-knife** long knife for carving meat.

cascade n small waterfall; something resembling this; v fall in cascades.

case[1] n 1 condition 2 state of affairs 3 grammatical relationship 4 instance 5 law-suit 6 med patient; idm

in any case whatever happens; idm **in case of 1** in the event of 2 as a precaution against.

case[2] n box; chest; protective covering, wrapping; v put in case.

casein n main protein of milk; basis of cheese.

case-hardened n (of steel) having a toughened surface.

casement n window side-hung on hinges.

case-study n extended study of an individual or group.

casework n social work, studying family or personal problems.

cash n 1 coins and notes 2 any sort of money; v exchange for notes and coins; idm **cash in on** profit from (sth enjoyed by others); ns **cashier** one in charge of cash; **cash-register** till.

cash-and-carry n shop where goods are paid for in cash and taken away by the customer.

cash card n card enabling bank-account holders to get cash from a machine at any time.

cash crop n crop grown in order to sell.

cashew n small kidney-shaped edible nut.

cash flow n movement of money in business; idm **cash-flow problem** lack of funds.

cashier v dismiss from the service; deprive of rank.

cashmere n soft material woven from goat's hair.

cashpoint n cash dispensing machine.

cash register n machine in a shop for recording purchases with a drawer for safe-keeping of money.

casing n protective covering, *eg* for machinery.

casino n public room with gambling facilities.

cask n barrel, mainly used for liquids.

casket n 1 small box, plain or ornamented, for jewels, trinkets etc; 2 coffin *US*.

cassata n *It* ice cream made with bits of fruit and nuts.

casserole n fireproof dish for cooking and serving food; food cooked in this way.

cassette n plastic or metal container for film or tape.

cassock n long vestment, usually black, worn by clergy etc.

cast v 1 throw down, off 2 shed (snake-skin) 3 reckon up (accounts) 4 mould (metal etc) 5 hurl 6 assign parts in a play; *pt, pp* **cast**; *idm* **cast an eye over** look quickly over to check; *phr vs* **cast about/around (for)** try to find quickly; **cast aside/away** abandon; **cast off** 1 untie a boat 2 finish off a piece of knitting; n 1 throw 2 impression taken of something 3 actors in a play; *a* formed by moulding metal; n **casting** piece of metal shaped by casting.

castanets n *mus* instrument of two wooden shells clicked rapidly together in the hand.

castaway n person adrift after a shipwreck.

caste n division of Indian society; exclusive social class.

castellated a with battlements.

caster sugar n fine-grained white sugar.

castigate v chastise; punish severely; scold bitterly; n **castigation**.

casting vote n deciding vote when there is a tie.

cast iron n hard brittle type of iron *a* **cast-iron** 1 of cast iron 2 tough; unbreakable.

castle n fortress; stronghold; piece in chess (rook); *a* **castellated** like a castle, having turrets etc.

castor, caster n 1 vessel with perforated top for sprinkling pepper, sugar etc 2 small wheel on swivel fixed to leg of chair etc.

castor-oil n laxative oil made from seeds of castor-oil plant.

castrate v remove testicles; geld; emasculate; expurgate (book etc); n **castration**.

casual a accidental; careless; occasional; *adv* **casually**; n **casualty** victim of accident, battle; *pl* **casualties** number killed, wounded in war.

casuistry n specious reasoning; application of ethical rules and principles; n **casuist**.

CAT *abbr* 1 College of Advanced Technology 2 computer-aided technology 3 computer-aided tomography.

cat n 1 small, deomsticated, carnivorous quadruped; any animal of genus *Felix* 2 spiteful woman 3 whip with nine lashes; *idm* **a cat-and-dog life** a life full of strife; *idm* **play cat-and mouse with** keep in cruel suspense; *idm* **let the cat out of the bag** carelessly reveal a secret; *idm* **the cat's whiskers** the best person, thing; n **cat's-eye** 1 semi-precious stone 2 reflective glass in roadway.

catabolism n destructive metabolism.

cataclysm n violent upheaval, social or physical; *as* **-al, -ic**.

catacomb n subterranean cemetery.

catalepsy n trace-like state in which the body is rigid *a* **cataleptic**.

catalogue n list of objects, names, etc arranged in order; v make such list.

catalyst n 1 substance causing chemical change without itself changing 2 person, thing facilitating change.

catalytic converter n *aut* device for converting harmful exhaust fumes into carbon dioxide.

catamaran n raft of logs lashed together; twin-hulled sailing boat.

catapult n elastic sling fixed on forked stick for shooting pellets, stones; apparatus assisting aircraft to take off, *esp* from ship.

cataract n 1 large, high

waterfall 2 disease of eye.

catarrh n inflammation of mucous membrane, *esp* of nose; *a* **-al**.

catastrophe n disaster; sudden irrevocable calamity; *a* **catastrophic**.

catcall n jeer.

catch v 1 get hold of; seize 2 grasp (of mind) 3 be infected by (disease); become entangled 4 be in time for 5 overtake; *pt, pp* **caught** n 1 act of catching, *esp* something caught 3 mechanical device to secure lock; *idm* **catch fire** begin burning; *idm* **catch it** be in trouble; *idm* **catch sb's eye** get sb's attention; *phr vs* **catch on** 1 understand 2 become fashionable; **catch out** show up as ignorant or in the wrong; **catch up** 1 make up for lost time 2 draw level with; *idm* **caught up in** deeply involved in; **catcher** one who catches; *as* **catchpenny** worthless; showy; **catchy** attractive; easy to remember (of tune).

catch-22 n bureaucratic regulation giving hope of escape from an intolerable situation, but also containing a clause that makes escape impossible; **catch-22 situation** situation governed by such a regulation.

catching a infectious.

catchment area n 1 *geog* area which feeds river, lake, etc with rainwater 2 area served

by a particular school, hospital, etc.

catch-phrase n widely-used saying, *usu* copied from a famous person.

catchword n word or phrase placed to attract attention.

catechize v teach by question and answer; examine by searching questions; n **catechism** form of instruction *esp* religious.

categorize v divide into classes.

category n class; division; mode of grouping; *a* **categorical** absolute; positive.

cater v provide food, pleasure for; n **caterer**.

caterpillar n 1 larva of butterfly, moth 2 endless belt of plates, on vehicle, used instead of wheels.

caterwaul v, n (make) howling voice of a cat.

catfish n *US* freshwater fish.

catgut n cord from animal intestines used for strings of musical instruments, tennis rackets, etc.

catharsis n 1 release of strong emotions, *esp* through drama, art, etc or by talking 2 *med* emptying of bowels; *pl* **catharses** a **cathartic**.

cathedral n chief church of diocese; *a* belonging to, containing such.

catheter n tube introduced into one of passages of body, to draw off fluid, or to dilate.

cathode n negative electrode; **cathode rays** negative

discharge.

catholic a 1 universal 2 of whole body of Christians 3 of Roman Catholic Church; ns **Catholic** a Roman Catholic; **Catholicism**.

catkin n furry flower of willow, birch, etc.

catnap n short sleep.

catnip n plant with scented leaves.

cat's paw n person used cynically by another; dupe.

CAT-scanner n type of body scanner used in hospitals.

catsuit n close-fitting garment from neck to feet.

catsup n *US* = ketchup

cattery n home for cats.

cattle n bovine animals; human beings (disparaging).

catty a spiteful; *adv* **cattily**; n **cattiness**.

catwalk n long narrow raised footpath.

Caucasian n, a (member) of the white races of mankind.

caucus n inner group of people controlling political policy.

caudal a of the tail.

caught *pt* of **catch**.

cauldron, caldron n large metal pot or boiler.

cauliflower n white, fleshy, edible flower-head, variety of cabbage.

caulk, calk v make seam (of ship) watertight, by packing in oakum, tow and pitch; n **caulking, calking**.

cause n force producing effect; motive; reason; lawsuit; v bring about; effect.

causeway n raised path across

wet, marshy ground.

caustic *a* 1 corrosive; burning 2 satirical; *n* corrosive substance; *adv* **-ally**.

cauterize *v* sear, burn with hot iron or caustic; *ns* **cautery, cauterization.**

caution *n* carefulness; warning; *v* warn; *a* **cautious;** *n* **-ness;** *a* **cautionary** serving as warning.

cavalcade *n* procession of riders, carriages etc.

cavalier *n* horseman; *a* careless; thoughtless; *n* **cavalry** horse soldiers.

cave *n* hollow in earth with lateral extension; den; *n* **cavern** deep cave; *a* **cavernous;** *n* **cavity** hole; *phr v* **cave in** 1 collapse 2 give up; *n* **cave-man** primitive man.

caveat *n leg* warning.

cavern *n* cave; see cave.

caviar(e) *n* delicacy of salted sturgeon roe.

cavil *v* quibble; raise frivolous objections to.

cavity *n* hole, *esp* in a tooth; *n* **cavity wall** double wall with vertical air space between to give insulation.

cavort *v* prance about noisily.

cavy *n* small rodent, as guinea-pig.

caw *n* call of rook, crow; *v* utter such cry.

cayenne *n* ground red pepper.

cayman *n* variety of alligator.

CBE *abbr* Companion of the British Empire.

CBI *abbr* Confederation of British Industry.

CB radio *abbr* Citizens' Band radio.

cc *abbr* cubic centimetre(s).

CCTV *abbr* closed circuit television.

CD *abbr* 1 civil defence 2 compact disc.

CD-I *abbr* Compact Disc Interactive.

CD-ROM *n comput* compact on which large quantities of information can be stored.

CDT *abbr* Craft Design and Technology.

cease *v* desist from; discontinue; *a* **-less.**

cease-fire *n* truce.

cedar *n* large coniferous evergreen tree.

cede *v* 1 yield; surrender 2 grant; admit.

Ceefax [TM] BBC teletext service.

ceiling *n* 1 lining of upper surface of room 2 extreme height attainable by aircraft 3 upper limit of prices, wages etc.

celandine *n* wild flower, resembling buttercup.

celebrate *v* 1 observe with proper rites 2 do honour to (by ceremony); 3 *coll* have a good time; *ns* **celebrant** priest; **celebration; celebrity** famous person; fame; *a* **celebrated** well-known.

celerity *n* swiftness, rapidity.

celery *n* vegetable with long, juicy edible stalks.

celestial *a* pertaining to sky; divine, heavenly.

celibacy *n* unmarried state; abstinence from sexual

relations; *n* **celibate.**

cell *n* 1 small room, in monastery, prison etc 2 biological basic unit 3 compartment in honeycomb 4 component of galvanic battery.

cellar *n* underground part of house; stock of wine; *ns* **coalcellar, wine cellar.**

cello *n mus* stringed instrument of violin type held between the knees; *pl* **cellos;** *n* **cellist.**

Cellophane [TM] transparent foil for wrapping.

cell phone *n* mobile telephone used on cellular network.

cellular *a* 1 of living cells 2 porous 3 *telecom* based on communications network; *ns* **c. handset** mobile phone, **c. operator, c. subscriber.**

cellulite *n* type of body fat that causes dimpling of the skin.

celluloid *n* inflammable plastic material.

cellulose *n* carbohydrate cell-walls of plants; raw material used in plastics; *v* varnish with nitrocellulose lacquer.

Celsius *a* = centigrade.

Celtic *a* of the Celts.

cement *n* 1 powdery substance which, mixed with water, sets hard 2 liquid adhesive; *v* cover with, join by cement; *fig* unite closely.

cemetery *n* burial-ground, other than churchyard.

cenotaph *n* monument raised in memory of one whose body is not therein.

censor *n* 1 one authorized to

prevent publication of books, plays etc 2 official, *esp* in wartime, empowered to open all written communications and suppress any harmful to safety of nation; *v* subject to censorship; *n* **censorship**; *a* **censorious** disapproving; severely critical.

censure *v* criticize adversely; blame; *n* reproof.

census *n* official periodic counting of population of a state.

cent *n* hundredth part of dollar; **per cent** in every hundred.

centaur *n* mythical creature half man, half horse.

centenary *n* hundredth anniversary; *a* celebration of this; *n* **centenarian** one who is 100 years old; **centennial** occurring every 100 years.

center *n*, *a* US = **centre**.

centi- *prefix* one hundred.

centigrade *a* having 100 equal parts; *esp* **c. thermometer** freezing point 0 and boiling point 100.

centigramme *n* measure of weight, hundredth part of a gramme.

centimetre *n* measure of length, hundredth part of metre.

centipede *n* long, crawling insect with many feet.

central *a* 1 at the centre 2 most important; *adv* **-ly**; *v* **centralize** put under central control; (*ns* **-ization,** **-izationism** policy of central

control; *n*, *a* **-izationist**);

central heating *n* heating system from a central boiler through pipes and radiators.

central reservation *n Brit* strip dividing carriageways on motorway or dual carriageway.

centre *n* 1 middle point 2 axis 3 point in body on which certain activity depends.

centreboard *n* retractable keel of sailing-boat.

centrefold *n* (picture filling) centre pages of magazine.

centre of gravity *n* point of balance.

centrifugal *a* moving away from the centre; *n* **c. force** tendency for objects to fly outwards from circular motion; *n* **centrifuge** machine using this force to separate substances.

centripetal *n* moving towards the centre.

centrist *n*, *v* (person) avoiding political extremes.

centurian *n* Roman officer commanding 100 men.

century *n* 1 100 years 2 100 things of same kind, collectively.

ceramic *a* pertaining to pottery; *n pl* **ceramics** art of making pottery etc. of clay.

cereal *a* pertaining to edible grain; *n* grain itself.

cerebral *a* pertaining to brain; *n* **cerebral palsy** disability caused by damage to the brain before or after birth; *n* **cerebration** working of brain.

ceremony *n* act of reverence; public observance of solemn event; *n*, *a* **ceremonial;** *a* **ceremonious.**

cerise *n*, *a* pinkish red (colour).

cert *abbr* 1 certificate 2 *coll* certainty.

certain *a* definite; inevitable; of some amount; unerring; *adv* **-ly**; *ns* **certainty, certitude** mental conviction.

certify *v* 1 assure 2 attest in written document; *a* **certifiable** *esp* of insanity; *n* **certificate** written declaration.

certitude *n* sureness.

cervical *a* of the cervix; *n* **cervical cancer.**

cervix *n*., *pl*. **cervixes,** **cervices** narrow part of womb joined to vagina.

cesarean *a* = **caesarean.**

cessation *n* stopping; pause; ceasing.

cess-pit *n* cavity in ground, used for draining sewage from house etc.

CFC *abbr* chlorofluorocarbon.

Chablis *n* French dry white burgundy wine.

chafe *v* 1 rub against 2 become sore from friction 3 become restive; *n* **chafing dish** dish for keeping food hot.

chaff *n* 1 husk of grain 2 chopped straw 3 teasing.

chaffinch *n* small wild bird.

chagrin *n* mortification; disappointment.

chain *n* 1 series of connected metal links 2 connected

series of things, visible or
non-material; v confine;
restrain. *Makes many
compounds eg* c.-drive,
c.-letter, c.-reaction.

chain-letter n letter sent to
several people who are asked
to send copies to others in
turn, *usu* with a request for
money.

chain-reaction n sequence of
events each leading to
further events.

chain-smoke n smoke
continuously; n **chain-
smoker**.

chainstore n one of a group of
shops owned by one firm.

chair n 1 single seat with back
and four legs 2 professorship;
seat of authority etc; v 1
carry person in triumph 2
preside at.

chairperson n chairman or
chairwoman in charge of a
meeting or head of a board
of directors.

chaise longue n long seat for
reclining with single
backrest and armrest.

chalet n small wooden Swiss
house; wooden cabin.

chalice n 1 drinking cup 2
Communion-cup.

chalk n soft limestone; crayon;
v mark with chalk; a **chalky**;
phr v **chalk up** 1 write with
chalk 2 record success 3
charge sb's account, *eg* for
drinks in a pub.

challenge n summons to fight;
dispute; objection taken; v
call in question; summon to
fight; n **challenger**.

chamber n 1 room; apartment
2 body of persons composing
legislative assembly; n pl 1
lawyer's office 2 lodgings; ns
chamberlain court official;
chambermaid housemaid at
hotel; **chambermusic** music
suitable for room or small
hall, with few instruments.

chamber-pot n bedside
receptacle for urine.

chameleon n small lizard able
to change colour; a
inconstant.

chamfer n bevel; groove; v
make bevel or groove.

chamois n Fr goat-like animal;
n **chamois-leather** soft
pliable leather.

champ[1] v (of horses) chew
noisily; *idm* **champ at the bit**
show signs of impatience
and restlessness.

champ[2] n coll champion.

champagne n French white
sparkling wine from
Champagne region.

champion n upholder of cause;
one who excels (in sport,
shows or exhibitions); v act
as champion.

chance n 1 opportunity;
possibility 2 unforeseen
fortune 3 risk; a **chancy**
hazardous.

chancel n east part of
Christian church, where
altar stands.

chancellor n 1 chief judge 2
head of University 3 chief
finance minister.

chancery n division of High
Court of Justice.

chandelier n branched support

for lights, hanging from
ceiling.

chandler n one making,
dealing in candles; n **ships'
chandler** dealer in stores
and provisions for ships.

change v 1 exchange; alter,
substitute 2 interchange
(train etc) 3 put on different
clothes; v 1 alteration 2
small money; *as* **-able**
variable, fickle; **-less**
constant; n **changeling** child
secretly substituted for
another.

channel n 1 river bed; body of
water joining two seas; deep
passage in shallow water 2
groove 3 that through
which liquid flows more 4 *fig*
means of communication 5
frequency band for
transmission of TV, radio; v
form, supply through
channel.

chant n song, sacred hymn; v
sing; utter in musical
monotone; ns **chanter** 1
singer 2 pipe of bag-pipes,
producing notes; **chanty,
shanty** sailor's song.

chaos n confusion; utter
disorder; muddle; a **chaotic**.

chap v. **chapped.** split, become
sore from exposure to cold
etc; n 1 crack in skin 2 coll
man, boy; a chapped one.

chapatti n Indian flatcake of
unleavened bread.

chapel n 1 private church;
place of worship for
nonconformists to C. of E.;
cathedral antechamber with
small altar 2 section of a

trade union in the print industry.

chaperon *n* older lady accompanying younger one in public or on social occasion; *v* act in this way.

chaplain *n* clergyman attached to institution, armed forces, or private household.

chaplet *n* **1** wreath for the head **2** prayer beads.

chapter *n* **1** main division of book **2** stage in history **3** governing body of cathedral; **chapter house** room where chapter meets, attached to cathedral.

chapter of accidents *n Brit* series of unlucky events.

char[1] *v* scorch, burn; *a* **charred**.

char[2] *v* do housework for hourly, daily payment.

char[3] *n* small fish of salmon or trout family.

character *n* **1** mark; symbol; letter **2** essential nature **3** personality (in play, book etc) **4** testimonial of ability, habits; *a* **characteristic**; *v* **characterize** describe (*n* -ization); *a* **characterless**.

charade *n Fr* form of riddle, when each syllable of word is acted.

charcoal *n* form of carbon, made from charred wood.

charge *v* **1** load **2** restore electricity to battery **3** cost **4** attack **5** accuse **6** entrust; *n* **1** cost **2** accusation **3** command **4** amount of electricity in battery; *idm* **in charge of** responsible for; *a*

chargeable.

charge card *n* shopper's credit account card.

chargé d'affaires *n Fr* diplomat representing government in absence of ambassador.

charge hand *n Brit* worker with responsibility grade below a foreman.

charger *n* cavalry horse.

charge-sheet *n Brit* police record of charges made.

chariot *n* ancient two-wheeled car for fighting, state occasions, racing; *n* **charioteer**.

charisma *n* power to inspire devotion; *a* **charismatic**.

charity *n* love; benevolence (of mind); liberality; *a* **charitable**.

charlady *n* charwoman.

charlatan *n* imposter; quack.

Charleston *n* popular dance of the 1920s.

charlie *n Brit coll* foolish person.

charm *n* magic spell; fascination; small object worn on person; *v* attract; bewitch; enchant; *n* **charmer** fascinating person; *a* **charming**.

charnel-house *n* vault where bodies or bones are stored.

chart *n* map, *esp* for navigational use; graph; *v* make map, graph.

charter *n* document granting rights etc; *v* let or hire; *a* **chartered** licensed, privileged; *n* **charter-party** contract made between ship owner and skipper.

Chartreuse [TM] *n* green or yellow liqueur made from herbs and flowers; the colour of this.

charwoman *n Brit* woman working as a cleaner.

chary *a* careful; parsimonious; *n* **chariness**; *adv* **charily**.

chase *v* pursue; drive away; *n* hunting; pursuit; *n* **chaser** drink taken after stronger one.

chase *v* engrave ornamentally.

chasm *n* deep abyss; fissure.

chasse *n ballet* gliding step.

chassis *n* framework, wheels and machinery of motor vehicle; undercarriage of aircraft.

chaste *a* pure; continent; *adv* **chastely**; *n* **chastity**.

chasten *v* punish in order to correct; *a* **chastened** subdued.

chastise *v* punish by beating; *n* **chastisement**.

chasuble *n* loose overgarment worn by priest.

chat *n* easy, informal talk; *v* talk idly; *phr v* **chat up** talk to get better acquainted; *a* **chatty**; *n* **chatter** rapid, trivial talk; *v* talk idly; rattle teeth; *ns* **chatterer**, **chattering**, **chatterbox** incessant chatterer.

château *n* -s *or* -x. *Fr* castle or large country house.

chatline *n* telephone line offering conversation, advice or entertainment for a special fee.

chat show *n* radio or TV show where guests or members of audience take part in discussion with host or hostess.

chattel n movable property; pl goods, possessions.

chauffeur n Fr driver of motorcar, usually paid; fem **chauffeuse**.

chauvinism n perverted, blind patriotism.

cheap a of low price, relative to value; inferior; adv -ly; n -ness; v cheapen.

cheapskate n miser.

cheat v swindle; defraud; practise trickery; n swindler; trickster.

check v 1 retard; restrain; stop 2 verify; n 1 call in chess 2 control 3 ticket (cloakroom) 4 pattern in squares; ns **checkmate** final winning move in chess; defeat; **checkout** pay desk in supermarket; **checkpoint** place where documents, vehicles, etc are inspected, eg at a frontier.

checkered a US = chequered.

checkers n US = draughts.

check-up n full examination, esp medical.

Cheddar n firm smooth, yellow cheese.

cheek n 1 side of face below eye 2 impudence; pertness; v address impudently; a **cheeky**.

cheer n 1 state of mind 2 rich food and drink 3 applause; v 1 applaud vocally 2 encourage; a **cheerful**; n -ness; a **cheery**; adv **cheerily**; **cheerless**; n -ness.

cheerleader n person who leads cheering at sports event.

cheese n consolidated milk curd used as food; ns **cheesecake** 1 sweet flan with cream cheese 2 coll provocative pictures of scantily dressed women.

cheeseburger n hamburger topped with melted cheese.

cheesecloth n light, thin cotton fabric.

cheesed off a Brit sl fed up.

cheeseparing n a miserly.

cheetah n fast-running predator of the cat family with spotted skin.

chef n professional cook; chief cook in restaurant.

chef d'oeuvre n masterpiece; pl **chefs d'oeuvre**.

chemise n woman's loose-fitting undergarment or dress.

chemist n 1 person who sells medical supplies; pharmacist = US **druggist** 2 specialist in chemistry.

chemistry n natural science dealing with composition, reaction of substances; n **chemist**; n, a **chemical**.

chemotherapy n treatment of disease, esp cancer, by use of chemicals.

chenille n tufted cord of silk or worsted.

cheque n paper form for withdrawing money from bank; n **cheque book**.

cheque card n card which guarantees payment of cheques up to a specified value.

chequer n pattern of squares, as chess board; v mark in squares; a **chequered** 1 having squares of alternating colour 2 with alternating good and bad fortune.

cherish v hold dear; take care of; keep in mind.

cheroot n kind of cigar, open at both ends.

cherry n edible small-stoned fruit either red, black, or white; tree bearing this fruit; a red.

cherub n heavenly being, rosy-faced child; beautiful, innocent child; pl **cherubim**, **cherubs**; a **cherubic**.

chess n game of skill, played with 32 chessmen, on chequered board; ns **chessmen**, **chess-board**.

chest n 1 coffer; larger box 2 upper front of body; idm get sth off one's chest make a confession.

chesterfield n heavy padded sofa studded with buttons.

chestnut n 1 tree bearing nuts (sweet c. edible; horse c. inedible) 2 reddish-brown colour 3 hoary joke.

chevron n Fr V-shaped stripe(s) indicating rank, worn on uniform.

chew v masticate; phr v **chew over** coll think carefully about.

chewing gum n flavoured substance for chewing, usu made of chicle.

Chianti n dry red or white Italian wine.

chic n smartness; style;

elegance; *a* smart, elegant.

chicane *n* trick; *bridge* hand with no trumps; obstacle in motor race; *v* quibble; *n* **chicanery** verbal trickery.

chichi *a* affected in style.

chick *n* 1 newly hatched bird 2 affectionate name for child; *n* **chicken** young bird, *esp* hen; *phr v* **chicken-out (of sth)** refuse to do sth out of fear; *n* **chicken-feed** 1 food for poultry 2 *coll* paltry amount, *esp* of money; *a* **chicken-hearted** timid; *n* **chicken-pox** mild contagious disease, chiefly of children.

chickadee *n* small grey N American bird.

chick-pea *n* (Asiatic plant with) yellow pea-like seed.

chicory *n* blanched salad vegetable.

chide *v* reprove, scold; *pt* **chid**; *pp* **chidden**; *a*, *n* **chiding**.

chief *n* leader; head; *a* principal, foremost; *adv* **chiefly**; *n* **chieftain** head, *esp* of Highland Clan.

chiff-chaff *n* bird of warbler species.

chiffon *n Fr* thin gauze-like material.

chignon *n Fr* woman's hair worn in a roll or knot at the back.

chihuahua *n* tiny dog with smooth hair.

chilblain *n* painful swelling on feet, hands, or ears, due to cold.

child *n* young human being; *pl* **children**; *a* **childish**

pertaining to child; foolish; silly; *ns* **childhood** period of life to puberty; **childbirth**, **childbed** state of giving birth to child; *as* **childless**, **childlike**; *n* **child's play** simple task.

chill *n* coldness; illness due to cold; *a* frigid (of manner); discouraging; *v* chill or become cold; *as* **chilled**, **chilly** unwelcoming; *n* **chilliness** coldness of sensation or manner.

chilli *n* (powder from dried) pod of hot red pepper.

chilli con carne *n* Mexican meat stew with kidney beans and chillies or chilli powder.

chime *n* set of bells; musical sequence produced by such; *phr v* **chime in** break into a conversation.

chimera *n* 1 fabulous monster 2 illusory hope, dream.

chimney *n* 1 outlet for smoke 2 narrow cleft in rock.

chimpanzee *n* arboreal ape, related to gorilla.

chin *n* part of jaw below mouth.

china *n* fine porcelain ware; *a* made of this.

chinchilla *n* (soft grey fur of) small squirrel-like animal; (similar fur of) rabbit or cat.

chine *n* 1 narrow ravine 2 backbone; *v* to chop backbone (joint of meat).

chink[1] *n* slit; cleft.

chink[2] *n* tinkling, metallic sound; *v* make such sound.

chinless *a Brit coll* weak; cowardly.

chintz *n* printed cotton fabric; used in upholstery.

chip *n* small piece of substance cut, broken off; *v.* **chipping**, **chipped**. cut chips off; *idm* **a chip off the old block** just like one's father or mother; *idm* **have a chip on one's shoulder** *coll* maintain a resentful attitude because one feels badly treated in the past; *idm* **when the chips are down** *coll* at a critical moment; *phr v* **chip in** *coll* 1 interrupt 2 contribute money.

chipmunk *n* small striped squirrel-like mammal.

chipolata *n esp Brit* small sausage.

chipper *a US* cheerful.

chippy *n coll* 1 *Brit* fish and chip shop 2 carpenter.

chiropody *n* care of feet; *n* **chiropodist**.

chiropractor *n* person who treats disease by massage and manipulation of joints.

chirp, chirrup *v* utter short piping note (of birds); *n* this sound.

chisel *n* cutting tool, for stone, etc; *v* to use chisel.

chit[1] *n* short note; memo; *n* **chitchat** gossip.

chit[2] *n* small slightly-built girl.

chivalry *n* 1 body of knights 2 courtesy 3 courage; *a* **chivalrous** having knightly qualities.

chive *n* herb with leaves mildly onion-flavoured leaves; *pl* these chopped finely for flavouring food.

chlorine n non-metallic element; poison gas; ns **chloral** hypnotic; **chloride** bleaching agent; v **chlorinate** purify water.

chlorofluorocarbon n compound gas containing chlorine, fluorine, and carbon, used as a refrigerant and a propellant gas in aerosols and believed to be harmful to the ozone layer.

chloroform n volatile liquid used as anaesthetic; v to make insensible with this.

chlorophyll n green colouring matter in plants.

chocaholic n coll person addicted to eating chocolate.

chock n wooden wedge; v make secure, prevent rolling; a, adv **chockfull**, **chock-a-block** coll packed tight.

chocoholic n person addicted to or very fond of chocolate.

chocolate n sweetmeat made from ground cacao beans; n **hot chocolate** drink of this; a dark brown colour.

choice n 1 act of choosing 2 something specially selected; a of high excellence.

choir n group of singers, esp in church; chancel; n **chorister** singer; a **choral**.

choke v smother; obstruct; throttle; stifle; phr v **choke back** suppress (bad feelings).

choler n anger; wrath; a **choleric** irascible.

cholera n infectious disease of bile, often fatal.

cholesterol n fatty substance, believed in excess to cause hardening of the arteries.

chomp v chew noisily.

choose v select; prefer; pt **chose**; pp **chosen**.

choosy n fussy; hard to please.

chop v chopping, chopped. cut with knife etc; make quick blow; n piece of lamb, pork with rib-bone; n **chopper 1** tool for chopping 2 coll helicopter; a **choppy** rough (sea).

chopsticks n pair of sticks designed for taking food to the mouth in East Asian countries.

chop suey n Chinese dish of slivers of meat with rice and vegetables.

choral a of a choir; sung by a choir.

chorale n 1 type of hymn 2 group of singers.

chord n blending of notes in harmony.

chore n tedious job of work.

choreography n art of ballet dancing, or arranging dances; n **choreographer**.

chorister n member of choir, esp choirboy.

chortle n, v (utter) loud chuckle of enjoyment.

chorus n group of singers; refrain of song; n **chorale** hymn for congregational use.

chose pt, **chosen** pp of CHOOSE.

choux pastry n Fr light thin pastry made with egg.

chow n 1 type of dog with thick fur 2 sl food.

chowder n US thick soup of fish and vegetables.

chow mein n Chinese dish served on fried noodles.

christen v 1 make a member of the Christian church by baptism 2 name at official ceremony, esp a ship 3 use for the first time n **christening**.

Christendom n all Christian people in the world.

Christian n followers of Christ; a pertaining to Christians; **C. name** baptismal name; **C. Science** belief in healing by prayers; ns **Christianity** teaching of Christ.

Christmas n 1 feast day (December 25th) celebrating the nativity of Jesus Christ 2 period of days before and after this (also **Christmas-time/-tide**).

chromatic a relating to colour; mus scale ascending or descending by semitones.

chrome n 1 chromium 2 yellow pigment.

chromium n brittle metallic element, used for plating.

chromosome n tiny rods carrying genes in living cells.

chronic a long-lasting (of disease); sl tedious, bad.

chronic fatigue syndrome n illness characterized by extreme fatigue and muscle weakness.

chronicle n record of events in order of time; v register (events, dates); n chronicler.

chronology n table or list of dates; a **chronological** in order of time.

chronometer n watch for measuring time exactly.

chrysalis n., pl. **chrysalises** sheath enclosing insect larva during resting stage.

chrysanthemum n hardy plant with large flowers in bright colours.

chub n river fish of carp family.

chubby a fat; stumpy; plump; n **chubbiness**.

chuck v throw; phr vs **c. out** eject forcibly; **c. up** give up; n 1 throw 2 pat (under chin) 3 part of drill holding bit 4 cut of beef from neck.

chuckle v laugh softly; n low laugh of satisfaction.

chum n close friend.

chump n 1 block of wood 2 thick end of meat 3 sl idiot.

chunk n thick piece broken off; coll large part of a written piece; a **chunky** thick; bulky.

chunnel n coll tunnel under the English Channel.

church n 1 place of Christian worship 2 whole body of Christians; clergy; ns **churchwarden** officer representing parish; long clay pipe; **churchyard**.

churlish a 1 boorish 2 ungracious; selfish; mean.

churn n vessel for making butter; v shake liquid violently; phr v **churn out** coll produce in great quantity but not quality.

chute n inclined slope for sending down logs, water, any heavy thing.

chutney n hot sweet-tasting pickle or relish.

chutzpah n coll nerve; impudence.

CIA abbr Central Intelligence Agency.

cicada n large grasshopper-like insect.

cicatrix n cicatrices Fr or Lat scar.

CID abbr Criminal Investigation Department.

cider n drink made of fermented apple juice.

cigar n solid roll of tobacco leaves for smoking.

cigarette n finely cut tobacco, rolled in thin paper.

C-in-C abbr Commander-in-Chief.

cinch n coll 1 easy task 2 sure thing.

cinder n remains of burnt-out coal; a **cindery**.

cine- prefix indicating a relationship to cinematography, e.g. **c.-camera, c.-film, c.-projector**, etc.

cinema n place where cine-films are shown.

cinematography n art of producing moving pictures on film; a **cinematographic** projecting film.

cinnamon n bark of Ceylon laurel, used as spice; a of yellowish-brown colour.

cipher, cypher n 1 symbol 0; zero 2 person of no importance 3 monogram 4

secret way of writing.

circa prep (of dates) around.

circle n 1 perfectly round plane figure 2 group of people united by common interest 3 ring; v move round; surround; n **circlet** small circular band, esp round the head.

circuit n 1 distance round 2 series of places where Assizes are held 3 path of electric curent; a **circuitous** indirect.

circular a 1 forming or moving in a circle 2 letter circulated to many people.

circulate v 1 (cause) to move round a closed system 2 move round freely 3 inform by circular letter; n **circulation** 1 flow through a system 2 passing of money 3 number of people receiving a publication.

circumcise v cut off foreskin; n **circumcision**.

circumference n boundary of a circle.

circumlocution n elaborate way of saying sth simple.

circumnavigate v sail round.

circumscribe v limit; restrict.

circumspect a decorous; prudent; cautious.

circumstance n event; fact; pl financial condition; pomp; a **circumstantial** accidental; incidental; indirect.

circumvent v outwit; frustrate; n **-vention**.

circus n 1 entertainment with, clowns, animals etc 2 round open space in city.

cirrhosis n disease of liver.

cirrus n high fleecy cloud.

CIS abbr Commonwealth of Independent States (territories from former Soviet Union).

cissy = sissy

cistern n 1 water-tank 2 natural reservoir.

citadel n fortress protecting a town.

cite 1 summon 2 quote an authority; n **citation**.

citizen n one living in city or town; n **-ship**.

citizens' band n range of radio frequencies useable by the public for private communication.

citron n fruit like lemon or lime, less acid; a **citric** of acid of lemon etc; n **citric acid** weak acid found in many fruits, esp citrus.

citrus fruit n pl citrons, lemons, oranges etc.

city n large-sized town.

civet n cat-like mammal (also **civet cat**); secretion from this animal used in making perfumes.

civic a of a city or citizens; n **civics** study of rights and responsibilities of citizens; US study of government.

civil a 1 relating to citizens of same State 2 non-military 3 affable; polite 4 not criminal; ns **civility** politeness; **civilian** non-military person; v **civilize** bring from barbarism; n **civilization**; a **civilized**.

civil engineering n building of public works.

civil service n government departments (except military and legal); people employed there; n **civil servant**.

civil war n war between citizens of one country.

civvies n sl civilian clothes.

cl abbr centilitre.

cladding n protective covering, esp of outside walls.

claim v assert; apply for as right; n demand for, assertion of just title to something; n **claimant**.

clairvoyant n person having second sight; n **clairvoyance**.

clam phr v **clam up** coll refuse to speak.

clambake n US 1 picnic by the sea 2 informal party.

clamber v climb clumsily or laboriously.

clammy a moist and cold to touch; sticky; n **clamminess**.

clamour n loud outcry; noise; a **-ous**.

clamp n 1 tool for holding things together 2 heap of potatoes, etc straw covered for winter storage; v fasten with clamp; phr v **clamp down on** suppress.

clamp-down n imposing of restrictions.

clan n tribe; group of families under chief, having common ancestor; a **clannish**; ns **-ness**; **clansman**.

clandestine a guiltily secret;

surreptitious.

clang n loud, metallic ring; v make sound; ns **clanger** Brit coll tactless mistake; **clangour** repeated ringing; din.

clank n sharp metallic sound; v to make such sound.

clap v. **clapping, clapped.** strike together, with noise; applaud with hands; n sharp noise; sudden burst of thunder; ns **clapper** tongue of bell.

clap-board n, a US (faced with) weather board.

clapped-out a Brit coll exhausted; worn out.

clapper-board n film hinged board used to mark the start of each take.

clap-trap empty talk; idm **like the clappers** Brit coll flat out.

claque n hired applauders.

claret n red wines of Bordeaux.

clarify v. **-fying, -fied.** purify; make clear; ns **clarification, clarity**.

clarinet n woodwind musical instrument.

clarion n kind of trumpet; a ringing; ns **clarionet, clarinet** wood-wind instrument.

clash v 1 come together suddenly 2 disagree; n metallic sound; conflict.

clasp n hook, bolt for fastening; v fasten; embrace; grasp; n **clasp-knife**.

class n any division, kind, sort; rank; category; v **classify** arrange methodically in classes; n **classification**; a

classifiable; classless a not having divisions of social class.

classified a (of information) limited to authorized persons.

classic a 1 of highest merit 2 of ancient Greek and Roman culture; n work of art or literature, regarded as model of excellence; pl Greek or Latin language; a **classical** possessing excellence, esp of music.

clatter n series of dull, hard noises; rattle; noisy talk; v make clatter.

clause n short sentence, part of main one; article in treaty, will, contract, etc.

claustrophobia n morbid fear of enclosed spaces.

clavichord n early predecessor of piano.

clavicle n collar-bone; a **clavicular**.

claw n sharp nails or talons of animals and birds; v seize, scratch with claws.

clay n sticky earth; human body; a **clayey**; n **clay-pigeon** clay disc used in shooting contest.

claymore n big sword once used by Scottish Highlanders.

clean a 1 free from dirt 2 pure 3 shapely 4 neat; v render clean; adv **cleanly**; ns **cleaner, cleanness, cleanliness**; v **cleanse** remove impurity from.

clean-cut a neat and presentable; clear in outline.

clean sweep n 1 removal of the unnecessary 2 victory.

clear a 1 audible 2 bright 3 distinct 4 unimpeded 5 free from doubt 6 transparent; idm **in the clear** 1 out of danger 2 known to be innocent 3 with a net profit; phr vs **clear off/out** go away; **clear up** 1 elucidate 2 tidy; adv **clearly**; v make, become clear; acquit; disentangle; ns **clearance** 1 act of clearing 2 riddance of surplus stock 3 certificate that ship has discharged port dues 4 clear space between two objects; **clearness; clearing** land cleared of trees; **clearing-house**, where documents, etc are sorted; as **clear-headed, clear-sighted** discerning.

clearway n Brit stretch of road where vehicles may not stop except in an emergency.

cleavage n 1 division 2 hollow between a woman's breasts seen above neckline of dress.

cleave v split; divide by force; pt **clove, cleft**; pp **cloven, cleft**; phr v **cleave to** 1 stick fast to 2 fml remain steadfastly loyal to; ns **cleft** split, fissure; **cleaver** chopper.

clef n sign of pitch of stave in music.

cleft stick idm **be (caught) in a cleft stick** be trapped in a problematic situation.

cleft palate n genetic defect of fissure in the roof of the mouth.

clematis n climbing, flowering plant.

clemency n (of weather) mildness, warmth; fig gentleness, leniency; a **clement**.

clench v make firm; close (fist); set closely together.

clerestory n upper rows of windows in church.

clergy n body of ordained minister in Christian churchs; ns **clergyman**; **cleric** any person in Holy Orders; a **clerical** of clergy.

clerk n official in government corporation service; office subordinate; a **clerical** pertaining to office work.

clever a intelligent; adroit; dexterous; adv **-ly**; n **-ness**.

cliché n hackneyed phrase; catchword

click v 1 make slight, sharp sound; 2 coll become instantly friendly or popular 3 be understood; n thin, rapid, sharp sound.

client n customer of professional man or tradesman; n **clientele**; whole body of clients.

cliff n steep rock-face esp facing sea.

cliffhanger n serial story, film, etc where each episode ends in great suspense.

climacteric n critical phase in humanlife; menopause.

climate n weather conditions of a country etc; a **climatic**.

climax n culminating point; point of greatest tension in film, story etc; v to reach this.

climb v ascend by effort; creep up; n **climber**; phr v **climb down** admit one was wrong.

clinch v 1 make fast 2 decide; n grip, lock (boxing) 2 coll amorous embrace; n **clincher** decisive argument.

cling v stick to; remain near to; pt, pp **clung**.

cling-film n transparent plastic film for wrapping food to keep it fresh.

clinic n practical teaching of medicine, surgery; place for medical examination, treatment; a **clinical** 1 of the treatment of patients 2 efficient and objective; without feeling (adv **-ly** from clinical observation); n **clinical thermometer** used to take temperature of patient.

clink n slight tinkling sound; v make or cause this sound; n sl prison.

clinker n refuse of coal or coke.

clinker-built n (of boats) made with planks overlapping.

clip v **clipping, clipped.** cut with shears or scissors.

clip n 1 device of metal, plastic, etc for fastening 2 short extract from film or video; n **clipboard** board with clip for holding papers.

clip joint n sl nightclub, restaurant, etc overcharging its customers.

clipper n fast sailing ship, air-liner; pl small shears.

clippings n pl 1 extracts cut

from newspaper 2 ends of hair left after clipping hair or beard.

clique n Fr exclusive set; select and snobbish group.

clitoris n small erectile part of female genitals.

Cllr abbr councillor.

cloak n outer sleeveless garment; disguise; v cover; hide; n **cloakroom** place where coats, hats, luggage etc may be left.

clobber[1] v attack violently 2 overwhelm.

clobber[2] n Brit coll clothes or equipment.

cloche n Fr bell-shaped protective glass for plants.

clock n device for measuring time, not intended for wearing; idm **around the clock** day and night; idm **put the clock back** return to old ways and ideas; idm **watch the clock** think about the time for finishing work; idm **work against the clock** try to complete a job within a given time; v **clock in, out** record automatically arrival, departure from work; phr v **clock up** 1 record the time taken 2 manage to score.

clockwise adv in the direction of a clock's hands.

clockwork idm like **clockwork** smoothly and easily.

clod n lump of earth; fig stupid person; n **clod-hopper** oaf.

clog n wooden-soled shoe; v **clogging, clogged.** hinder, cause to jam.

cloister n covered arcade, esp

in monastery, college; v confine; seclude; a **cloistered.**

clone n animal or plant produced asexually from the cells of another.

close a 1 near 2 dense 3 careful 4 sultry, heavy of (weather); n precinct of cathedral; adv **-ly**; n **-ness**; idm **close on** nearly; idm **close to home** near to the (unpalatable) truth; idm **(sail) close to the wind** operate in a risky, almost illegal way; a **closefisted** mean; n **close-up** film shot taken near subject.

close v 1 shut; conclude 2 come together; n end.

close call n narrow escape.

close-cropped a (of hair) very short.

closed-circuit television n system transmitting within an institution to a limited audience.

closed shop n place where employees must join a specified trade union.

close-fisted a stingy.

close-hauled a naut with sails set for sailing close to the wind.

close-knit, closely knit a (of people) united by shared beliefs, interests, etc.

close shave n narrow escape.

closet n small, private room; cupboard; a **closeted** private.

closure n closing.

clot n coagulated, partially solidified mass, esp of blood; v **clotting, clotted.**

coagulate; cause to clot.

cloth n woven fabric; pl **clothes** garments; bed-coverings; **n clothing; clothe** to dress; pt, pp **clothed, clad;** n **clothier.**

clothes horse n frame on which clothes are hung to dry; US coll person keen on fashion in clothes.

cloud n mass of condensed water vapour in sky; mass of smoke; dust in air; v make dark; dim; become cloudy; as **cloudy, cloudless, clouded;** idm **under a cloud** under suspicion.

cloudburst n sudden heavy downpour of rain.

clout n piece of rough cloth; blow, esp on head.

clove n dried flower bud, used for flavouring.

clove hitch n double loop securing rope to a pole.

cloven pp of **cleave.**

clover n plant, trefoil grown as fodder; idm coll **in clover** living in luxury.

cloverleaf n motorway intersection with links in four directirons pl **clover-leaves.**

clown n jester; buffoon in circus or pantomine; v play the fool; n **clowning.**

cloy n satiate, glut with sweetness or pleasure.

club n 1 thick wooden stick 2 stick for golf 3 group of people associated for benefit or pleasure 4 black trefoil on playing card; v **clubbing, clubbed.** beat with club; phr

v **club together** unite for common purpose.

club foot n congenitally deformed foot.

cluck n noise made by hen; v make such noise.

clue n guide to solution of mystery, crime; as **clueless** utterly helpless, stupid; **clued up** coll well-informed.

clump n compact mass; group of trees, plants; clout; v mass together; strike.

clumsy a ungainly; unwieldly; adv **clumsily;** n **clumsiness.**

clung pt, pp of **cling.**

cluster n bunch; group; v come together; grow in clusters.

clutch v grasp suddenly; n 1 set of eggs hatched at one time 2 device permitting gradual engagement of mechanism; idm **in sb's clutches** under sb's control.

clutter n things left untidily; v make untidy.

cm abbr centimetre.

CNAA abbr Council for National Academic Awards.

CND abbr Campaign for Nuclear Disarmament.

CNN abbr Cable News Network.

co abbr company.

CO abbr commanding officer.

c/o abbr 1 care of 2 carried over.

coach n railway carriage; passenger bus; horse-drawn carriage; instructor; tutor; v tutor; n **coachman.**

coagulate v clot; form moss; curdle; n **coagulation.**

coal n combustible carbonised

vegetable matter, used as fuel; v take in, supply with coal; n **coalfield.**

coalesce v unite; intermingle; ns **coalescence, coalition** alliance, esp political.

coal-face n part of coal-mine where coal is cut.

coarse a rough; common; crude; gross; adv **-ly;** n **-ness.**

coarse-fish n Brit freshwater fish, excluding trout and salmon v **coarse-fishing**

coast n edge of land at seashore; v 1 sail along coast 2 slide down 3 free wheel; idm **the coast is clear** coll one is safe from observation.

coaster n 1 small mat or tray for glasses, bottles, etc 2 ship which sails along the coast.

coast guard n official employed to enforce maritime law, prevent smuggling, and save lives at sea.

coat n 1 outer garment with sleeves 2 natural covering of animals 3 layer of paint, etc applied to surface; v cover with coat; n **coat of arms** heraldic device.

coat hanger n shaped piece of wood, wire or plastic with hook for hanging coats.

coax v persuade by flattery; wheedle; cajole.

coaxial a having a common axis; n **coaxial cable** wire for simultaneous long distance transmittal and reception for radio or television signals.

cob n 1 thick-set, stocky horse 2 male swan 3 building

material 4 cobnut 5 head of maize.

cobalt n metallic element; dark blue colour.

cobble n round stone; v pave with cobbles; mend roughly; repair shoes; n **cobbler** shoe mender.

cobblers n Brit sl nonsense.

COBOL n high-level computer language.

cobra n venomous hooded snake.

cobweb n spider's web, single thread of this.

Coca-Cola [TM] n sweet carbonated drink.

cocaine n drug used as local anaesthetic, or taken as stimulant.

coccyx n **coccyxes** or **coccyges** anat small bone at base of spine.

cochineal n red dye made from dried insects.

cock[1] n 1 male bird 2 leader 3 stop valve to regulate flow of liquids 4 hammer of gun; v set cock of gun; set, turn up jauntily; idm **cock a snook at** Brit coll make rude gesture to; show disrespect for; phr v **cockerel** young cock.

cock[2] n pile of hay; v put hay into cocks.

cockade n hat badge, rosette of ribbon.

cock-a-hoop a in high spirits.

cock-and-bull story n absurd story, esp used as an excuse for sth.

cockatoo n crested parrot.

cockchafter n large, nocturnal winged beetle.

cocker n small spaniel.

cock-eyed a coll 1 crooked 2 squinting 3 impractical.

cockle n edible bivalve; weed; small boat.

Cockney n native of London; London dialect.

cockpit n small space in aircraft for pilot.

cockroach n insect, blackbeetle.

cocksure, cocky a conceitedly self-confident.

cocktail n 1 mixed alcoholic drink 2 mixture of fruits or seafoods 3 coll mixture of dangerous substances.

cock-up n Brit coll bungling.

coco, coconut n tropical palm, with edible nut.

cocoa n fine powder made from cacao beans; drink.

cocoon n sheath of silk, silk-like thread enclosing chrysalis.

cocopeat n fibrous substance obtained from coconuts.

COD abbr cash on delivery.

cod n large edible sea fish; n **codling** young cod.

coda n final passage of a musical movement, following the last formal section.

coddle v pamper, cosset.

code n 1 cypher used in sending (secret) messages 2 symbols used in computers 3 accepted social customs 4 set of laws; ns **codification; coding** translation into code; v **codify** put into code or systematic form.

codeine n alkaloid narcotic

derived from opium.

codex n -dices. book of ancient texts.

codger n coll old man.

codicil n addition to will.

codify v (of laws, rules) arrange systematically; n **codification**.

codpiece n bag covering front opening of breeches.

codswallop n Brit coll nonsense.

coed n US female student in mixed college.

coeducation n education of boys and girls together; a -**ational**.

coefficient n joint agent or factor.

coerce v constrain; force; a **coercive**; n **coercion** compulsion.

coeval a of same age or date.

coexist v exist, live together; n **co-existence**.

coffee n 1 evergreen shrub; ground roasted coffee-beans; drink made from this 2 light brown colour.

coffer n chest; money-box.

coffer-dam n enclosure erected in water and pumped dry to allow building or other work to be done safely.

coffin n case for dead body.

cog n tooth-like projection on wheel; idm coll **cog in a machine** person playing a small but vital part in a large organization; n **cogwheel**.

cogent a impelling; urgent; clear, forceful; n **cogency**.

cogitate v ponder; think

deeply; n **-ation**.

cognac n Fr high quality French brandy.

cognate n related; from common stock; origin.

cognition n process of acquiring knowledge; a **cognitive**.

cognizance n knowledge; fact of being aware; idm **take cognizance of** notice; a **cognizant**.

cognomen n appellation; surname.

cognoscenti n pl It connoisseurs.

cohabit n live together, esp as man and wife.

cohere v stick together; be consistent; a **coherent** intelligible; sticking together; n **cohesion** state of union; a **cohesive**.

cohort n body of troops, army.

COHSE abbr Confederation of Health Service Employees.

coif n (formerly) close-fitting cap worn by women.

coiffeur n Fr hair-dresser.

coil n 1 series of spiral loops 2 IUD v wind in rings, spiral folds.

coin n piece of money; v mint; invent new word etc; idms **coin money, coin it (in)** make a lot of money quickly; ns **coinage** money of country; **coiner** maker of counterfeit coins.

coincide v happen at same time; correspond exactly; a **coinciding**; n **coincidence**.

coition, coitus n sexual intercourse.

coke n 1 substance left when gas and tar have been extracted from coal 2 coll Coca-Cola.

coir n fibre from coconut husk, used for making ropes, matting, etc.

cola n soft drink containing cola nut extract.

colander n strainer used in cooking.

cold a 1 without heat 2 unmoved; frigid; n 1 lack of heat 2 acute nasal catarrh; idm **get cold feet** coll lose one's nerve; idm **give/get the cold shoulder** rebuff/be rebuffed; idm **out in the cold** rejected; isolated. n **coldness**; ns **c. feet** fear sl; **c. shoulder** rebuff; **c. storage** refrigeration.

cold-blooded a 1 bio with varying blood temperature 2 cruel.

cold comfort n little or no consolation.

cold cream n skin-cleansing and softening ointment.

cold-hearted a cruel; indifferent; adv **-ly**.

cold-storage n 1 preservation of food by refrigeration 2 setting aside of a plan or idea until a later date.

cold turkey n sl sick feeling of a drug addict when deprived of the drug.

cold war n state of continued hostility without military action.

coleslaw n salad of shredded cabbage, carrot, etc with salad dressing.

coley n edible fish with white or grey flesh.

colic n acute pain in bowels.

coliseum n large stadium.

collaborate v work together; esp in literature, art; ns **-ator**, **-ation**.

collage n picture made by pasting various materials on a flat surface.

collapse v fall down or in; fail; n 1 **break down (of health)** 2 falling away; a **collapsible** capable of being folded, packed up.

collar n band on garment, round neck; v capture; sl seize hold of; n **collar-bone** clavicle.

collate v 1 compare critically 2 place printed sheets in order; n **collation** light repast.

collateral a accompanying; from common ancestor; n additional security for loan.

colleague n associate in work or profession.

collect v gather, come together; accumulate; as **collected** not distracted; gathered; **collective** viewed as whole; ns **collection** group of articles of same nature; **collector**.

collect n prayer.

collectible n object collected; a able to be collected.

collectivism n principal of communal control of production, etc.

college n institution of higher learning; self governing body of persons; a **collegiate**.

collide v crash into; strike forcefully together; n **collision**.

collie n type of sheep-dog.

collier n coal-miner; coaling ship; n **colliery** coal-mine.

collocate v ling (of words) occur regularly together; n **-ation**.

colloquial a used in common speech; n **colloquy** conference.

collusion n conspiracy (to deceive) esp in legal matters; a **collusive**.

collywobbles n coll 1 stomach pain 2 nervousness.

cologne n perfume made of plant oils and alcohol.

colon n part of large intestine; punctuation mark (:).

colonel n commander of regiment.

colonialism n policy of extending national authority over foreign territorites; n **colonialist**.

colonic a relating to the colon; n **colonic irrigation** irrigation of colon for cleansing purposes.

colonnade n row of columns.

colony n body of people in new country, who remain subject to fatherland; area so settled; community who form a racial, cultural or national minority; ns **colonist, colonial**; v **colonize**; n **colonization**.

colophon n publisher's device, imprint.

color US = colour.

colossus n huge statue;

strikingly large person or thing; a **colossal**.

colour n 1 hue; tint 2 paint; pigment 3 fig pretext 4 semblance; pl 1 badge, ribbons symbolic of party, school etc 2 flag of ship, regiment; v 1 paint 2 exaggerate 3 influence 4 blush; a **coloured** non-white.

colour-bar n legal discrimination between people of different colour (US **color-line**).

colour-blind a unable to distinguish certain colours.

colour supplement n free colour magazine supplied with (esp Sunday) newspaper.

colt n young male horse.

columbine n flower of buttercup family.

column n vertical pillar or support; vertical division of page; military formation; a **columnar**; n **columnist** journalist.

coma n deep unconsciousness; a **comatose**.

comb n toothed instrument for dressing hair, cleaning wool; cock's crest; v apply comb to.

combat v oppose; fight; n **combatant**.

combine v join together; mix; ns **combination** union; **combine** syndicate.

combine harvester n machine which reaps and threshes grain.

combo n mus small group, esp

jazz players.

combustion n process of burning; a **combustible**.

come v move towards; arrive; occur; happen; be derived from; pt **came**; pp **come**; prp **coming**; idm **how come?** how did it happen? idm **come what may** whatever happens; phr vs **come about** happen; **come across** 1 (of ideas) be received 2 find by chance; **come along** 1 appear 2 accompany sb 3 make progress; **come apart** separate; disintegrate; **come at** attack; **come by** 1 pass near 2 acquire; **come down** fall; idm **come down in the world** suffer decline in standard of living; phr vs **come down on** criticize; punish; **come down to** be no more than; **come down with** fall ill with; **come forward** offer help or information; **come in** become fashionable; **come in for** be exposed to; **come into** inherit; **come off** 1 become detached 2 succeed; idm **come off it!** coll expressing disbelief; phr vs **come on** progress; **come out** 1 appear 2 be removed 3 go on strike 4 prove to be 5 be clearly reproduced 6 be a debutante 7 sl declare oneself homosexual; **come out against** declare opposition to; **come out in** discover (eg a rash) on one's skin; **come out with** say unexpectedly;

come over 1 move across **2** pay a visit **3** communicate; **come round/to** regain consciousness; **come round to 1** be converted to **2** eventually find time to; **come up with** devise; produce.

comeback n **1** recovery **2** retort; complaint **3** redress.

comedy n **1** humour **2** light-hearted amusing play; **comedian** comic actor; fem **comedienne**.

comely a attractive; handsome; n **comeliness**.

comer n **all comers** anyone who wants to accept a challenge

comet n luminous heavenly body, with gaseous tail.

come-uppance n deserved punishment.

comfit n ar sweet containing fruit or nut.

comfort v reassure; console; n well-being; bodily ease; consolation; a **comfortable**.

comfortably off a having adequate money for comfort.

comfy a coll comfortable and cosy.

comic a laughable; funny; n comedian; comic paper; a **comical**.

comic strip n = strip cartoon.

comity n courtesy, urbanity of manners.

comma a punctuation mark (,), separating words, phrases etc.

command v order; be in authority; n peremptory order; power to control,

govern, dominate; ns **commandant, commander, commandment; v commandeer;** v appropriate.

command module n control area in a spacecraft.

commando n unit of shock troops; member of such unit.

command performance n special performance for head of state.

commemorate v celebrate solemnly; n **-ation;** a **-ative.**

commence v begin; start; n **-ment.**

commend v entrust; praises; a **commendable;** n **commendation.**

commensurate a proportionate; in accordance.

comment n remark; annotation; v explain; express view; ns **commentary** series of critical remarks; **commentator** radio or TV reporter.

commerce n dealings; business trading; a **commercial;** v **commercialize** make business of; n **-ization.**

commercial traveller n person travelling to sell goods for a firm by taking orders.

commie n, a coll communist.

commiserate v express sympathy; condole; n **-ation.**

commissar n head of a Soviet government department.

commissariat n department for supplies of food and transport.

commission n **1** warrant giving

authority, esp to officer in armed forces **2** body appointed to hold enquiry **3** authority to act as agent, agent's percentage; v authorize; give order for; idm **out of commission 1** not in service **2** out of order; ns **commissioner** member of commission; one empowered to act by warrant; **commissionaire** uniformed door-keeper or attendant.

commit v **-mitting, -mitted. 1** entrust **2** send for trial **3** perpetrate (crime); ns **committal, commitment;** idm **commit oneself 1** make or decision or promise **2** give a firm opinion.

committee n group appointed to consider particular activity.

commode n **1** chest of drawers **2** seat to accommodate chamberpot.

commodity n article of commerce; useful object.

commodore n naval officer; courtesy title; eg president of yacht club, etc.

common n tract of public land; a **1** shared by two or more **2** usual; ordinary **3** vulgar; pls common people of realm; adv **-ly;** n **commoner** person not of nobility; a **commonplace** ordinary; trite; n **commonwealth** democratic state.

common law n unwritten law; a **common-law.**

common market n the EEC.

common-or-garden a coll

ordinary.

common room n room which members of a specialised group can use.

commotion n agitation; tumult; upset.

commune[1] n 1 smallest unit of local government (eg in France) 2 community sharing possessions, living and working together.

commune[2] v share thoughts and feelings; a **communal** for common use; n **Holy Communion** sacrament of Eucharist.

communicate v 1 impart; transmit; exchange information 2 receive Holy Communion; a **communicable**; n **-ation**; a **communicative** talkative.

communiqué n Fr official communication.

communism n extreme form of socialism; a, n **communist**.

community n body of people sharing locality, religion etc; fellowship; **community service** n Brit punishment for criminals that involves doing work within the community.

commutator n device for altering direction of electric current; v **commutate** alter in this way.

commute v exchange; travel daily by season ticket; n **commuter** daily traveller to work.

compact[1] n agreement; contract.

compact[2] a neatly packed into small space; n small case holding face powder.

compact disc n recording disc from which sounds are reproduced by laser.

companion n comrade, associate; one of matching pair; a **companionable**; n **companionship**.

companion-way n staircase on a ship.

company n gathering of guests; companionship; group of business associates; group of actors; unit of regiment; ship's crew.

company secretary senior official of business firm who handles legal matters.

compare v observe similarity of one thing with another; be like; as **comparable**; (adv **-ably**); **comparative** (adv **-ly**) relative; n **comparison**.

compartment n part divided off by partition, esp in railway carriage.

compartmentalize v separate into distinct categories; n **-ization**.

compass n boundary; extent; range; instrument showing N and directions from it; pl instrument drawing circles.

compassion n sympathy; pity; a **compassionate**; adv **-ly**.

compatible a able to co-exist; agreeing; n **compatibility**.

compatriot n fellow-countryman.

compel v enforce; bring about by force; a **compelling** 1 very interesting 2 urgent; n **compulsion**.

compendium n 1 full information in concise form; a **compendious**; 2 box of games.

compensate v make amends; reward; make up for; a **compensatory**; n **compensation**.

compete v contend with; vie with; a **competitive**; ns **competition, competitor**.

competence, competency n 1 ability, efficiency 2 sufficiency; esp of money; a **competent**.

compile v collect together from various sources, eg as a book; ns **compiler, compilation**.

complacent a self-satisfied; adv **-ly**; ns **complacence, complacency**.

complain v grumble; find fault with; bring charge; ns **complaint** expression of discontent; ailment; **complainant** leg plaintiff.

complement n that which completes; full allowance; a **complementary**.

complete a entire; finished; v make whole; adv **-ly**; ns **-ness; n completion**.

complex a complicated; involved; n psychological obsession; n **complexity**.

complexion n colour, texture of face; disposition.

compliance n obedience; a **compliant**.

complicate v to make difficult, involved; n **-ation**.

complicity n partnership in crime etc.

compliment n expression of esteem, praise, regard; v pay compliment to; a **-ary**.

compline n last service of the day (Catholic church).

comply v **-plying, -plied.** agree; consent; yield.

component n constituent part; a forming part.

comport v **comport oneself** behave oneself; n **-ment**.

compose v 1 create musical form, literary work 2 set up type 3 settle; make up; a **composed** calm; ns **composer** one who composes, esp music; **composition**; **compositor** typesetter; **composure** calmness.

composite n, a (thing) made of several elements.

compost n mixture of manure, soil, rotten vegetable matter.

compote n Fr fruit in syrup.

compound v mix together; compromise; condone (an offence); a not simple; composite; n 1 mixture; compound substance 2 enclosure.

compound interest n interest on both capital and accumulated interest.

comprehend v take in; comprise; understand; n **comprehension**; a **comprehensive** taking in wide range of objects; a **comprehensible**.

compress v press together; concentrate; make smaller; n wet pad put on inflamed part; n **compression**.

comprise v include; contain; pr p **comprising**.

compromise v make concession; incur risk, suspicion; n middle course.

compulsion n 1 strong urge to do sth 2 sth which forces action; a **compulsive**; (adv **-ly**).

compulsory a required by law or rules; adv **compulsorily**.

compunction n regret for wrong done; remorse.

compute v calculate, reckon; n **computation**.

computer n electronic machine for storing, classifying and reproducing information and relaying instructions; v **computerize**; n **-ization**.

comrade n friend; companion; associate; n **-ship**.

con v **conning, conned.** 1 examine carefully; 2 learn by heart; 3 sl swindle.

concave n hollow; curved inwardly; n **concavity**.

conceal v keep secret; hide; n **-ment**.

concede v surrender; admit truth of; allow; n **concession** that which is conceded.

conceit n vanity; a **conceited** holding exaggerated opinion of one's own importance.

conceive v 1 think of; imagine 2 become pregnant; a **conceivable**.

concentrate v direct to single centre; increase strength; fix efforts on one point, object; n **concentration**.

concentration camp n prison

for political prisoners.

concentric a having common centre.

concept n idea; mental picture; a **conceptual**; v **-ualize**.

conception n 1 beginning of pregnancy 2 plan; planning 3 understanding.

concern v relate to; be worried; affect; n business; affair; a **concerned** interested; anxious; idm **concerned with** connected with; prep **concerning** regarding; about.

concert n 1 harmony; agreement 2 mus entertainment; idm **at concert pitch** in a state of readiness; a **concerted** planned in common; ns **concerto** musical composition for solo instrument with orchestra; **concertina** musical instrument.

concert grand n large piano for concerts.

concertmaster n US leader of orchestra.

concession n 1 yielding after argument 2 reduced price; (a **concessionary**) 3 special permission n **concessionaire** person granted such permission.

conch n large spiral shell.

conchie n sl conscientious objector.

concierge n (esp in France) resident caretaker.

conciliate v pacify; win over; ns **conciliation, conciliator**; a **conciliatory**.

concise *a* brief; terse; *adv* **-ly**; *n* **-ness**.

conclave *n* secret, private assembly, *esp* for election of pope.

conclude *v* 1 end; finish 2 arrange 3 infer; *n* **conclusion**; *a* **conclusive** decisive.

concoct *v* invent; make up (story, new dish etc); *n* **concoction**.

concomitant *a* accompanying; simultaneous; *adv* **-ly**; *n* **concomitance**.

concord *n* agreement; harmony; *a* **-ant**; *n* **concordance** index (words).

concordat *n* agreement between the pope and a government.

concourse *n* crowd; broad open space *esp* in airport buildings.

concrete *n* mixture of sand and cement; *a* 1 of concrete 2 actual; *v* cover with concrete; *adv* **concretely**.

concubine *n* woman living with a man but not married to him 2 secondary wife in polygamous societies *usu* of lower social rank.

concupiscence *n* sexual desire; lust; *a* **-scent**.

concur *v* **-curring, -curred.** agree; coincide; *a* **concurrent**; *n* **-rence**.

concuss *v* shake violently; injure brain by blow on head; *n* **concussion**.

condemn *v* 1 censure 2 declare unfit for use 3 find guilty; *n* **-ation**.

condemned cell *n* cell of person condemned to death.

condense *v* 1 abridge 2 concentrate 3 reduce gas etc to liquid; *ns* **condensation, condenser** device for storing electricity.

condescend *v* deign; patronise; be affable; *a* **-ing**; *n* **condescension**.

condign *a* *esp* of *punishment* fitting, deserved.

condiment *n* spicy, pungent seasoning for food.

condition *n* 1 state of being 2 rank 3 stipulation; *n* determine state or condition; train; make healthy; *a* **conditional** subject to conditions.

condole *v* offer sympathy; grieve with; *n* **condolence**.

condom *n* contraceptive sheath.

condominium *n* *US* block of flats, each owned by occupier (*coll* **condo**).

condone *v* overlook; find excuses for; *n* **condonation**.

condor *n* large S American vulture.

conduce *v* help; tend to produce; *a* **conducive**.

conduct *v* 1 lead 2 manage 3 transmit (heat, electricity); *idm* **conduct oneself** behave; *n* behaviour; *ns* **conductor** 1 guide 2 fare-collector on bus etc 3 director of orchestra 4 substance capable of transmitting (electricity etc); **conductivity**.

conduit *n* channel or pipe for conveying fluids, or

protecting electric cables.

cone *n* 1 solid body with circular base and tapering to apex 2 fruit of conifers 3 storm warning; *a* **conic, conical**.

confection *n* sweetmeat, preserve; *ns* **confectioner** dealer in sweets, cakes, etc; **confectionery** sweetmeats.

confederate *n* accomplice; *v* ally with; *ns* **-ation, confederacy**.

confer *v* **-ferring, -ferred.** grant; discuss; *ns* **-ment** act of bestowing; **conference** meeting to discuss.

confess *v* admit; declare sins orally; *ns* **confession; confessional** priest's box; **confessor** priest hearing confession.

confetti *n* small pieces of coloured paper thrown at wedding etc.

confidant *n* *Fr* person in whom one confides one's private affairs and thoughts; *fem* **confidante**.

confide *v* trust in; tell, as secret; *as* **confident, confidential, confiding** trusting.

confidence *n* 1 trust 2 self-assurance 3 secret; *idm* **in confidence** as a secret; *a* **confidential**; *adv* **-ly**.

confidence trick *n* swindle in which the swindler first gains the victim's confidence; *coll* **con trick**.

configuration *n* 1 figure, form 2 relative aspect of planets.

confine *v* imprison; limit; keep

in (bed, house); n -ment 1 imprisonment 2 childbirth; n pl confines boundaries.

confirm v make firm; ratify; administer confirmation; n confirmation rite to confirm vows made at baptism; corroboration; a confirmed habitual.

confiscate v seize; appropriate, esp by authority; n -ation.

conflagration n a great fire.

conflict n fight; variance; clash (of option); v contend; be incompatible.

confluence n 1 uniting of streams etc 2 crowd; a confluent.

conform v comply; submit; be in agreement; ns -ation, adaptation; formation; conformity.

confound v confuse; perplex; dismay.

confounded a 1 bewildered 2 damned.

confront v bring face to face; meet boldly, in opposition; n -ation.

Confucian n, a (follower) of Confucius.

confuse v mix up; bewilder; n confusion.

confute v disprove; convict of error; n confutation.

conga n Latin American dance performed in a long line.

congeal v freeze, solidify.

congenial a having same nature, tastes etc; suited to.

congenital a born with, esp defects, diseases etc.

conger n large salt-water eel.

congest v overcrowd; impede

flow of; fill to excess; a congested overcharged (with blood); n congestion.

conglomerate v gather, collect into mass; n -ation jumble of things.

congratulate v wish joy; express pleasure at; n -ation; a -atory.

congregate v assemble; n -ation gathering of persons, esp for worship; a -ational.

congress n formal assembly; legislative body; a congressional; n congressman member of US Congress.

congruent a 1 of identical shape 2 congruous; n -ence.

conical a cone-shaped.

conifer n cone-bearing tree, shrub, pine, fir; a coniferous.

conjecture v guess; surmise; n guess-work; a conjectural.

conjoin v unite; combine; a conjoint.

conjugal a pertaining to marriage; between husband and wife.

conjugate v inflect verb in various moods, tenses etc; n -ation.

conjunction n 1 part of speech, as and, but; 2 simultaneous occurrence; a conjunctive done jointly.

conjunctivitis n inflammation of the conjunctiva, the membrane covering the front of the eye and the inside of the eyelid.

conjure v 1 ask earnestly 2 perform tricks by sleight-of-

hand; cast spells; ns conjuration solemn spell; conjurer, -or, conjuring.

conk n sl nose.

conker n coll fruit of horse-chestnut; pl children's game with this on string.

conk out phr v coll 1 (of machine) break down 2 (of person) collapse exhausted or die.

connect v unite (with); join together; associate (mentally); as connective, connected.

connection, connexion n 1 linking; relationship 2 transfer from one transport to another 3 person of influence to whom one is related by family, business or social life; idm in connection with regarding.

conning-tower n armoured control station on war-ship, submarine etc.

connive v acquiesce in wrong-doing of another; n connivance tacit agreement.

connoisseur n Fr expert in artistic matters.

connote v imply in addition to primary meaning; n connotation.

conquer v overpower; subjugate; prevail; ns conqueror, conquest.

consanguinity n relationship by blood; kinship.

conscience n sense of right and wrong; a conscientious thorough; n -ness.

conscience clause n clause allowing conscientious

objector to be exempt on moral grounds.

conscience money n sum paid to relieve sense of guilt.

conscious a in possession of one's senses; awake; n **-ness** awareness.

conscript v enrol by compulsion for military service; n one so enrolled; n **conscription**.

consecrate v render holy; set apart as sacred; n **-ation**.

consecutive a following in regular order; expressing consequence.

consensus n general agreement.

consent v agree to; permit; n acquiescence; permission; a **consentient**.

consequence n outcome; logical result; importance; as **consequent, consequential** pompous; adv **consequently** therefore.

conservatoire n school of music, drama.

conservatory n 1 conservative 2 greenhouse joined to main house.

conserve v protect; preserve, esp from change, waste, etc; ns **conservancy** board responsible for preservation of nature, rivers, trees, etc; **conservation; conservative** moderate political party; a **conservative** opposed to change.

consider n 1 think about 2 regard as 3 take into account; a **considering** in view of; n **consideration** 1

thought; reflection 2 concern 3 fact worth remembering 4 payment; idm **take into consideration** keep in mind when judging; a **considerate** thoughtful for others; careful.

consign v commit; entrust; send goods; ns **consignor, consignee, consignment** goods consigned

consist in phr v be a matter of (doing certain things).

consist of phr v be composed of.

consistent a agreeing with; n **consistence, consistency** degree of density; relevance.

console v comfort; make up for; as **consolable, consolatory**; n **consolation**.

console n 1 ornamental bracket supporting shelf etc; 2 large cabinet for radio, TV etc 3 control panel (usu for electrical machinery) 4 organ keydesk.

consolidate v make, become solid, firm; combine; n **-ation**, n pl **consols** abbr Consolidated Annuities, British Government stock giving low rate of interest.

consommé n Fr clear meat soup.

consonant n letter other than vowel; a agreeing; consistent; n **consonance** harmony, esp of sounds.

consort n 1 husband, wife, esp of monarch 2 ship accompanying another; phr v **consort with** associate with.

consortium n **-s** or **consortia**. temporary association of (commercial, education, etc) institutions for a common purpose.

conspectus n survey.

conspicuous a outstanding; remarkable; plainly visible; n **-ness**.

conspire v plot; join another in secret, usu for unlawful purpose; ns **conspiracy, conspirator;** a **conspiratorial**.

constable n policeman; warden of fortress; high officer of State; **Chief C.** head of police in city or county; n **constabulary** police force.

constant a 1 continuous; unvarying 2 steadfast; faithful; n math unvarying term, factor; n **constancy** steadfastness.

constellation n group of fixed stars.

consternation n surprise and alarm; dismay.

constipation n inactivity of bowels; v **constipate** make bowels sluggish.

constituent a component; entitled to elect; n essential part; voter in constituency; n **constituency** place represented in Parliament; body of voters.

constitute v make into; set up; give form to; n **constitution** structure; natural state of body, mind etc; principles of government; a **constitutional** pertaining to constitution; (n walk taken for the health *adv* **-ly**).

constrain *v* bring force to bear on person; *n* **constraint** compulsion; embarrassment.

constrict *v* contract; compress; cramp; *ns* **constrictor, constriction;** *a* **constrictive**.

construct *v* build; form; put together; *ns* **constructor, construction;** *a* **constructive**.

construe *v* 1 translate 2 analyse grammatically 3 deduce.

consubstantiation *n* doctrine that after consecration blood and wine become the body and blood of Christ.

consul *n* official appointed by State, living in foreign country and protecting nationals and business interests there; *a* **consular;** *ns* **consulate, consulship**.

consult *v* seek advice from; confer with; *ns* **consultant, consultation;** *a* **consultative** advisory.

consume *v* 1 destroy by fire; waste, etc 2 use up; devour; drink up; *ns* **consumer** buyer, user of commodity.

consumer durable *n* manufactured article of fairly long life, *eg* car, washing machine.

consumer goods *n pl* goods produced for the general public to buy and use.

consumerism *n* movement to defend consumer interests.

consummate *v* complete; finish; *a* complete, of greatest perfection; *n*

consummation completion, *esp* physical, of marriage.

consumption *n* 1 using of food or resources 2 amount used 3 TB; *a* **consumptive** suffering from TB.

cont *abbr* continued.

contact *n* being in touch; close proximity; *v* get in touch with; *n* **c. lens** lens resting directly on eyeball.

contagion *n* spreading of disease by contact; disease, physical or moral, spread so; *a* **contagious**.

contain *v* hold; compromise; enclose; restrain (oneself); *n* **container** box, jar, etc holding something.

contaminate *v* pollute; defile; make impure; *n* **-ation** pollution.

contemplate *v* gaze on; consider; intend; meditate; *n* **-ation;** *a* **-ative**.

contemporary *a* living; existing, made at same time; *n* one having same age, or living during same age as another; *a* **contemporaneous**.

contempt *n* act of despising, scorn; **c of court** disregard for, disobedience to court of law; *as* **-ible** (*adv* **-ibly**), contemptuous (*adv* **-ly**).

contend *v* struggle; fight; assert; *n* **contention** controversy; disputed point; *a* **contentious** quarrelsome.

content *a* satisfied; *n* holding capacity; real meaning; *pl* that which is inside; list of topics in book; *v* satisfy;

n **-ment** satisfaction; *a* **contented** satisfied, pleased.

contest *v* dispute; fight for; *n* 1 strife 2 competition; *n* **contestant**.

context *n* parts of book, speech, etc, which come immediately before and after passage, words, etc and which fix meaning.

contiguous *a* touching; adjoining; *n* **contiguity**.

continence *n* self-restraint; *a* **continent**.

continent *n* one of the great unbroken land areas of earth; *a* **-al** (*n* inhabitant of Europe).

continental drift *n geol* theory that continents once belonged to a single land mass and then separated.

continental shelf *n* shallow part of sea-bed close to continental land mass.

contingency *n* possibility, chance occurrence; *a* **contingent** possible, dependent on; *n* quota, *esp* of troops.

continue *v* go on; persist; prolong; resume; remain; *a* **continual;** *ns* **continuance, continuation** resumption; sequel; *a* **continuous** unceasing; *n* **continuity** unbroken succession.

continuo *n* instrumental accompaniment giving bass part in Baroque music.

continuum *n* **-s** or **continua**. thing without breaks or sudden changes.

contort *v* distort; twist out of

shape; ns **contortion, contortionist** acrobat.

contour n outline; shape of figure, mountain, etc.

contra- prefix 1 against 2 opposite to 3 mus of lower pitch.

contraband n smuggled goods; illicit trading.

contrabass n mus double bass.

contraception n birth-control; n, a **contraceptive** (that) which prevents conception.

contract n solemn, binding agreement; v 1 enter into agreement 2 become smaller 3 incur 4 catch (disease); as **contractual, contracted** shortened; drawn together; ns **contraction, contractor** one making contract, esp builder.

contradict v deny; be opposed to; argue; a **contradictory**; n **contradiction**.

contraflow n arrangement during road repairs when traffic on one side of dual carriageway or motorway has to use lane/lanes on opposite side.

contralto n female voice of deep tone; singer with such a voice.

contraption n contrivance; eccentric device.

contrapuntal a mus of or involving counterpoint.

contrary n exact opposite, of object, fact, quality; a different; against; perverse; advs **contrarily, contrariwise** conversely; **contrariness** perversity.

contrast v compare, show difference; n striking difference.

contravene v infringe; disobey (law); n **contravention**.

contretemps n unlucky, embarrassing incident; mishap.

contribute v give to common fund; write for the press; have share in producing result; ns **contributor contribution** donation; a **contributory**.

contrite a penitent; sorrowful for sin; n **contrition** remorse.

contrive v 1 invent; devise; scheme 2 manage; n **contrivance** device; artful scheme.

control v -trolling, -trolled. 1 restrain; regulate 2 test 3 command; n 1 restraint 2 domination 3 standard for testing; pl s instruments guiding machine; a **controllable**; n **controller** person regulating expenditure.

controversy n dispute; argument; debate; a **controversial** liable to provoke controversy.

contumacy n stubborn, perverse resistance; a **contumacious**.

contumely n 1 contemptuous insolence of speech or manner 2 disgrace.

contusion n bruise without breaking skin.

conundrum n riddle; difficult problem.

conurbation n large urban area formed by expansion of smaller towns close together.

convalesce v regain health gradually; n **convalescence** state of recovering health; n, a **convalescent** (person) recovering from illness; a **convalescing**.

convection n transference of heat by liquids or gases; n **convector** circulator of warm air.

convene v summon; convoke; ns **convener** official, esp of Trade Union, who convenes meeting; **convention 1** formal assembly 2 custom, usage; a dictated by convention.

convenient a suitable; handy; n **convenience 1** personal comfort; ease 2 lavatory.

convenience food n food sold ready to eat with minimal preparation, but storable for a time if required.

convent n community of monks or nuns; building occupied by community.

converge v meet at given point; a **convergent**; n **convergence, convergency**.

converse v talk with someone; n **conversation**; as -al ready to talk; **conversant** familiar with, informed concerning.

converse a contrary; opposite; reversed; n the opposite.

convert v change, transmute a thing; cause to alter religious, moral beliefs; ns **convert** one who is converted; **conversion 1** change of state 2 misappropriation of property; *a* **convertible** capable of being converted.

convex *a* curving outwards; reverse of concave; *n* **convexity**.

convey *n* 1 carry 2 impart 3 transmit; *leg* make over by deed; *ns* **conveyance** deed by which title to property is transferred; **conveyancer** lawyer dealing with conveyance of property; **conveyancing** his business.

conveyor belt *n* continuous belt for transferring items from one area of factory, airport etc to another.

convict *v* prove, find guilty of crime; *ns* **convict** criminal serving sentence of imprisonment; **conviction** act of convicting; assured belief.

convince *v* persuade, arouse belief in, by argument or proof; *a* **convincing** compelling belief.

convivial *a* festive; sociable; *n* **conviviality**.

convoke *n* call together; summon to assemble; *n* **convocation** assembly, *esp* of clergy, university graduates.

convolution *n* spiral fold, coil, whorl; *a* **convoluted**.

convoy *n* escort and protect; *n* **convoy** group of ships, vehicles etc being convoyed; protecting force.

convulse *v* agitate violently; cause sudden violent muscular spasms; *a* **convulsive**; *n pl* **convulsions**

hysterical fits of emotion; spasms.

cony, coney *n* rabbit; fur made of rabbit skins.

coo *v* utter soft murmuring sound (of doves); speak softly and caressingly; *n* such sound.

cook *n* one who prepares food for eating; *v* prepare food for tables, *esp* by heat; *idm* **cook the books** falsify the accounts; *idm* **cook sb's goose** spoil sb's plans; *ns* **cooker** 1 stove for cooking 2 fruit suitable for cooking; **cookery** art of cooking; **cook-house** camp kitchen.

cookie *n* US 1 biscuit 2 person.

cool *a* pleasantly cold; *fig* calm; casual; not ardent; *v* make, become cool; *idm* **keep one's cool** remain calm; *ns* **coolness** 1 state of being cool 2 absence of cordiality; **cooler** 1 vessel in which anything is made or kept cool 2 *sl* prison; *adv* **coolly**.

coolant *n* liquid for keeping engine cool.

coomb, combe *n* deep, narrow valley.

coop *n* wooden cage or pen for hens; *v* shut up in coop; confine.

cooper *n* one who makes barrels and casks; *n* **cooperage** work, workshop of cooper.

co-operate *v* act together for common aim; *ns* **co-operation** working together; **co-operative** profit sharing

concern (*a* working together; helpful).

co-opt *v* choose as extra member; *n* **co-option**.

co-ordinate *a* having equal rank, order etc; *v* adjust, cause to harmonize; *n* **co-ordination**.

coot *n* small black water bird of rail family.

cop *v sl* copping, copped. catch; *idm* **cop it** be punished; *phr v* cop out (of) *coll* avoid taking responsibility; *n sl* 1 policeman 2 arrest.

cope *n* ceremonial clerical vestment; covering; *n* **coping** protective covering course of wall.

cope *v* handle successfully, contend with efficiently.

copier *n* machine that makes copies.

copious *a* plentiful, abundant, profuse, full; *adv* copiously.

cop-out *n coll* evasion through fear.

copper *n* reddish, ductile, malleable metal; washing vessel for clothes; *sl* policeman; *v* cover with copper; *ns* **copper plate** one used for etching, print from this; copybook style of writing.

coppice, copse *n* thicket, wood of small trees.

copra *n* dried, coconut kernels.

copula *n ling* link verb between subject and complement.

copulate *v* join, unite sexually; *n* **-ation**; *a* **copulative**.

copy *n* 1 imitation;

reproduction 2 single specimen of book etc 3 written material for press 4 example to be copied; v copying, copied. imitate; follow pattern; ns copyhold leg form of land tenure; copyright legal exclusive right to reproduce book, music, work of art etc; copy-writer one who writes text of advertisements.

copy-book n book for copying model handwriting; a perfect.

copycat n coll person who copies other people's ideas.

coquette n Fr female flirt; a coquettish engagingly enticing; n coquetry.

cor anglais n mus instrument like oboe, lower in pitch.

coracle n light boat made of wicker covered with hide etc.

coral n hard red or white substance made by marine polyps and which forms reefs etc; a made of coral; a coralline coral (red) in colour.

corbel n stone or wood support projecting from wall.

cord n 1 stout cord or thin rope 2 ribbed cloth; v bind with cord; n cordage cords or ropes, esp rigging of ship.

cordial a hearty, friendly, sincere; n stimulating, warming drink; n cordiality.

cordless teleport n type of mobile telephone.

cordon n 1 line of troops or police 2 ribbon of an Order

3 fruit tree pruned to single stem.

cordon bleu a, n Fr (cooking) of highest standard.

cords n pl coll corduroy trousers.

corduroy n ribbed cotton material, with pile like velvet.

core n 1 innermost, central part 2 seed-case of some fruits; idm to the core completely; thoroughly; v take out core; n corer implement for removing cores.

co-respondent n person charged with adultery with petitioner's husband/wife in divorce case.

corgi n breed of small Welsh dog.

coriander n plant with aromatic seeds used as flavouring.

Corinthian a of Corinth; n ornate type of Greek column.

cork n bark of cork oak; piece used as stopper for bottle etc; v stop up with a cork; a corked (of wine) tasting of decayed cork; ns corkscrew tool for extracting corks; corkage charge made by inn-keepers for serving wine not bought in the house.

corm n solid fleshy underground stem.

cormorant n large seabird.

corn¹ n 1 grain; seed of cereals 2 music or writing that is banal and sentimental; ns corn-chandler retailer of

corn; corn-crake landrail; cornflour finely ground maize, rice flour; cornflower blue-flowered wild plant of cornfields; corn syrup sweet syrup derived from corn.

corn² n hardened, thickened skin causing pain, usually on toe.

cornea n transparent protective membrane over front of eyeball; a corneal.

corncob n woody core of an ear of corn in which the grains are embedded.

corned beef n processed tinned beef.

cornelian n reddish or white semi-precious stone.

corner n meeting place of two converging lines; hidden remote place; angle formed by meeting walls, sides (of box etc); v 1 force into difficult position 2 buy up all available stocks of; a cornered; n corner-stone fig something indispensable; basis.

cornet n trumpet having valves; cone shaped wafer holding ice-cream.

cornflakes n breakfast cereal of crisp flakes from corn.

cornflour n finely ground flour from maize or rice.

cornice n carved moulding round top of building or room.

cornish pasty n small pie with vegetables, esp potato, and meat.

cornucopia n symbolic horn of plenty; fig abundance,

overflowing supply.

corny a sl (of jokes, stories) unoriginal; banal.

corolla n cup-like form made by petals of flowers.

corollary n additional inference; result.

corona n luminous circle around heavenly body.

coronary a like a crown; anat relating to arteries supplying heart muscle; **c. thrombosis** formation of clot in coronary artery.

coronation n act or ceremony of crowning a sovereign.

coroner n leg officer holding inquiry as to cause of any unnatural death, or into ownership of treasure-trove.

coronet n small crown.

corporal[1] n NCO ranking below sergeant.

corporal[2] a of the human body.

corporation n 1 group of persons regarded as a unit; legally formed business company; civic or municipal authority; 2 sl large protruding stomach.

corporeal a bodily; physical; tangible.

corps n largest tactical military unit; any organised group of persons.

corpse n dead body, usually human.

corpulent a stout; obese; fat; n **corpulence**.

corpus n **corpora. 1** body **2** principal of estate, fund **3** all extant writings on a subject.

corpuscle n minute body or organism, esp red and white constituent particles of blood.

correct v put right; punish; adjust; neutralize; ns **-tion, -ness;** a **-ive**.

correlate v bring into mutual relation; n either of two reciprocally related things; n **-ation;** a **-lative**.

correspond v agree with; be equal to; write letters to; ns **correspondent, correspondence 1** similarity **2** exchange of letters; a **corresponding**.

corridor n 1 passage in building, railway coach, etc **2** strip of land (or air route) passing through state to which it does not belong.

corroborate v confirm; make more certain; n **corroboration;** a **corroborative**.

corrode v eat into; wear away gradually, esp by chemical action; a **corrosive;** n **corrosion**.

corrugate v form wrinkles or folds; bend into ridges; a **-ated;** n **-ation**.

corrupt a rotten, putrid; depraved; bribable; (of texts) not genuine; v make corrupt; pervert; a **-ible;** n **-tion**.

corset n close-fitting undergarment worn for support; stays.

corslet, corselet n body armour.

cortège n Fr ceremonial procession, esp funeral cortège.

cortex n bark; outer covering; pl **cortices**.

cortisone n drug used in treatment of rheumatoid arthritis.

corundum n hard mineral used in grinding and polishing.

coruscate v sparkle, scintillate; n **-ation**.

cos n long-leaved lettuce.

cosh n small bludgeon; v strike with cosh.

cosine n sine of complement of angle.

cosmetic n preparation for beautifying hair, complexion, skin; a **cosmetic**.

cosmic a relating to universe and laws governing it; ns **cosmogony** theory of universe and its creation; **cosmography** mapping of universe; **cosmology** science of universe; **cosmos** n the whole universe; **cosmic rays** shortest electro-magnetic rays from outer space.

cosmonaut n astronaut, space traveller.

cosmopolitan n citizen of the world; a of all parts of world; free from national prejudice.

Cossack n member of S Russian tribe of horsemen.

cosset v pamper, fondle, pet.

cost n 1 price of purchase 2 expenditure of time, energy, labour; pl **costs** expenses of law suit; idm **at all costs** whatever happens; idm **at cost** without making any profit; idm **to one's cost** to one's disadvantage; v 1 cause expenditure of **2** cause loss of **3** estimate cost of production; *pt, pp* **cost**; *a* costly expensive; valuable; *n* **costliness**.

costal *a* pertaining to ribs or side of body.

co-star *n* famous actor/actress in the same film as another such actor/actress; *v* appear in this way.

cost-effective *a* profitable enough to justify the investment of capital; *adv* **-ly**; *n* **-ness**.

coster, coster monger *n* seller of fruit and vegetables from a barrow.

costive *a* constipated; *fig* sluggish.

costume *n* mode of dress, *esp* if peculiar to nation, period etc; theatrical clothes; *n* **costumier** dress-maker; *n* **costume jewellery** artificial jewellery

cosy *a* warm; snug; comfortable; *adv* **cosily**; *n* **cosiness**.

cot *n* light bed; swing bed on ship; child's bed; *n* **cot death** the sudden death of an infant from no apparent illness.

coterie *n Fr* set, group of people with similar tastes etc; social clique.

coterminous *a fml* having the same limit or boundary.

cottage *n* small house, *esp* in the country; *n* **cottager** dweller in cottage.

cottage cheese *n* soft cheese from skimmed milk.

cottage industry *n* small business where goods are produced at home or by a small group of people.

cottage pie *n* = **shepherd's pie**.

cotton *n* plant; downy covering of its seeds; thread, fabric made from this down; *a* made of cotton; *idm* **cotton on** understand; realize; *idm* **cotton to** *US coll* take a liking to.

cottonmouth *n* venomous snake of southeastern US swamps (also **water moccasin**).

cotyledon *n* primary leaf of seed embryo.

couch *n* sofa, long seat for reclining on; *v* **1** express (in words) **2** crouch; lie down.

couchette *n Fr* train seat convertible into a bed.

couch-grass *n* coarse grass, with creeping roots.

couch potato *n* inactive person who spends a lot of time watching television.

cougar *n* puma.

cough *v* expel air noisily, violently from lungs; *n* act of coughing, usually caused by irritation of lungs or throat; *idm* **cough up** *Brit coll* pay reluctantly.

could *pt or conditional* of CAN.

coulomb *n* unit of measure for electrical charge.

council *n* deliberative or executive assembly; *n* **council tax** tax levied by local authorities; *n* **councillor** member of council.

counsel *n* **1** guidance; advice **2** barrister; *v* advise; recommend; *n* **counsellor 1** adviser **2** barrister.

count[1] *v* **1** enumerate **2** reckon total number **3** include **4** possess value; *phr v* **count on/upon** depend on; *n* **leg** each charge in indictment; act of reckoning; *idm* **out for the count** asleep; unconscious *a* **countless**; *n* **countdown** counting down to zero in timing firing of missile; *n* **counting-house** office where accounts are kept.

count[2] *n* foreign title corresponding to British earl; *fem* **countess**.

countenance *n* facial expression; favour; *v* approve; tolerate.

counter[1] *n* **1** table in bank, shop across which money is paid, goods sold **2** small disc used in scoring in card or other games.

counter[2] *a, adv* opposite; contrary; *v* oppose; *boxing, fencing* parry; *n* parry.

counter- *prefix* makes compounds meaning opposite, retaliatory, neutralizing. *Such compounds are not given, where the meaning may be deduced from the simple word.*

counteract *v* stop or reduce the effect of.

counterblast *n, v* reply to criticism in strong terms.

counterclockwise *a US* anticlockwise.

counterfeit a forged, spurious; v imitate with intent to deceive; n **counterfeiter**.

counterfoil n part of cheque, receipt etc, kept by issuer as record.

countermand v cancel a previous order.

counterpane n bedspread, quilt.

counterpart n person or thing exactly resembling another; duplicate.

counterpoint n harmonious, simultaneous combination of two or more melodies.

counterpoise n weight balancing another, equilibrium.

counterproductive a achieving opposite of desired effect.

countersign n password given in reply to another; v fig ratify.

countersink v sink head of screw, etc level with surface of material being used.

counter tenor n mus adult male alto.

countervailing a fml compensating.

countess n woman with rank of count or earl; wife of count or earl.

countless a innumerable.

country n 1 land with definite boundaries, distinctive name, occupied by one nation 2 land of birth 3 rural areas; idm **go to the country** Brit dissolve Parliament for a general election; a **countrified** rustic in appearance and manners; ns **countryman** one living in country; compatriot; **countryside** rural area.

country-and-western n (also **country music**) popular style derived from folk music of S and W states in US.

country cousin n person unused to living in a city.

country seat n large country house, estate.

county n division of a country; a shire.

coup n Fr successful move or gamble.

coup d'état sudden overthrowing of government.

coup de grace n finishing touch.

coupé n Fr closed two-seater motor car.

couple n two objects or persons; leash for two hounds; pair; brace; v 1 join; unite; link together 2 (of animals) mate 3 associate (in mind); ns **coupling** link connecting railway carriages; **couplet** two lines of rhyming verse.

coupon n negotiable ticket, voucher, etc; entry form for pools, competitions etc; voucher exchangeable for goods.

courage n bravery; ability to face danger, pain etc. without fear; a **courageous**; adv -ly; n -ness.

courgette n Fr (also Brit) small green marrow (US zucchini).

courier n express messenger;

person conducting travellers on tour.

course n 1 line followed by moving object 2 passage of time 3 mode of action 4 part of meal served at one time 5 area of land used for racing, golf etc 6 channel (water) 7 series of lectures, lessons 8 continuous layer of bricks, etc at same level in building; v hunt, esp with greyhounds; n **courser** swift horse; idm **of course** certainly; idm **take its course** develop as normal, as expected.

court n 1 open space, paved yard enclosed by buildings or walls 2 space marked out, for playing games like tennis 3 household of sovereign 4 place of justice where trials are held 5 body with judicial powers; v woo; seek favour of; n **courtier** attendant at royal court; a **courtly** elegant, refined; n **courtliness**; ns **court-card** king, queen or knave in cards; **court-martial**, pl **courts-martial** court of officers trying military or naval offences; **courtroom**, **courthouse** room, place where courts of law are held; **courtship** wooing.

courtesy n politeness, considerateness, civility; idm **by courtesy of** 1 with the permission of 2 through the kindness of n **courtesy title** Brit title given by custom with no legal significance; a **courteous** polite, urbane; n

courtesy title one held by favour, not by right.

courtesan n prostitute associating with upperclass men, esp royalty.

couscous n semolina dish, served with sauce.

cousin n son or daughter of uncle or aunt; any kinsman.

cove n small sheltered bay, or inlet.

coven n group of witches.

covenant n formal agreement, contract; v grant, promise to covenant.

Coventry idm **send sb to Coventry** punish sb by not speaking to him/her.

cover v 1 place, spread over 2 include 3 shield 4 report on 5 point gun at 6 protect financially, by insurance; conceal; n 1 anything which covers 2 individual table setting; n **coverlet** counterpane.

cover charge n fixed charge in a restaurant added to cost of actual food.

covering letter n explanatory letter sent, eg with a parcel.

covert n place, esp thicket sheltering game; a veiled; implied.

cover-up n concealment of illegal activity or a mistake.

covet v coveting, coveted. desire ardently, esp property of another; a **covetous**; n - ness.

covey n brood of partridges; set.

cow[1] n adult female of bovine and various other animals.

cow[2] v frighten; overawe; intimidate.

coward n one lacking courage; a **cowardly** fearful; n **cowardice**.

cowboy n 1 man, usu on horseback, who grazes cattle in US 2 Brit dishonest or incompetent workman or trader.

cower v shrink fearfully from; cringe; crouch.

cowl n hooded cloak worn by monk; hood-shaped top for chimney or ventilator; n **cowling** casing round aero-engine.

cow-pat, cow-cake n patch of cow dung on the ground.

cow-pox n disease of cows, source of vaccine immunizing from small-pox.

cowrie n small shell used as money in parts of S Asia and Africa.

cowslip n wild plant of primrose family.

cox, coxswain n one steering boat; (naval) petty officer in charge of ship's boat; v **cox** act as cox.

coy a affecting shyness; demure; n **coyness**.

coyote n N American prairie wolf.

coxcomb n dandy.

cozen v act deceitfully; beguile.

cozy a US = cosy.

cp abbr 1 candlepower 2 compare.

CPR n cardiopulmonary resuscitation, a lifesaving techique to restart action of the heart and lungs.

CPU abbr central processing unit.

crab n edible shell-fish, with 8 legs and two pincers; v find fault with; a **crabbed** bitter; bad-tempered; cramped (handwriting); n **crab** small sour wild apple.

crab apple n wild apple-tree; its sharp-tasting fruit.

crabby a bad tempered.

crack n 1 break with sharp noise 2 split partially 3 make sharp noise, (whip etc; 4 (of voice) become hoarse 5 make (joke); n 1 fissure 2 sharp blow 3 report of gun; ns **cracker** firework; brittle biscuit; **crackle** sound of small cracks; **crackling** crisp, browned skin of roast pork; **cracksman** burglar.

crack-brained a crazy.

crack-down n rigorous campaign to control criminal activity.

cracked a coll insane.

crackers Brit coll crazy.

crackpot n coll eccentric person.

crack-up n coll 1 disintegration 2 nervous breakdown.

cradle n baby's bed or cot; supported framework; v rock, lay to rest as in cradle; nurse.

craft n 1 cunning 2 manual dexterity 3 members of skilled trade, guild 4 boat; ns **craftsman, craftsmanship;** a **crafty** subtly cunning; adv **craftily**.

crag n rough, steep mass of rock; a **craggy** rugged.

cram v **cramming, crammed.** stuff, pack tightly into; eat greedily; coach intensively for exams; n **crammer** tutor who crams pupils for exams.

cramp n sudden painful muscular spasm; tool with tightening screw to hold wood, masonry together; v hamper, confine, restrict 3 idm **cramp sb's style** impede sb's performance.

crampon n iron spike on climbing boots.

cran n measure for herrings, 37 1/2 gallons.

cranberry n small red berry, used in cooking.

crane n 1 slender wading bird with long neck 2 machine for raising heavy weights; v stretch out one's neck.

cranium n skull; a **cranial**.

crank n 1 bar with right angle bend for turning things 2 eccentricity of manner or thought (person with) 3 fad; v wind, turn; start up engine by hand; a **cranky** 1 shaky 2 cross 3 crazy; n **crankshaft** main shaft of engine.

cranny n chink, narrow opening; a **crannied**.

crape n thin wrinkled black material used for mourning.

craps n US gambling game with dice a crap.

crash v 1 fall violently with loud noise 2 fig collapse; be ruined 3 (of vehicles) to have collision, smash; n

loud noise caused by impact or fall; fig ruin.

crash-dive v (of aircraft, submarine) dive suddenly.

crash-land v avia land in an emergency, with probable damage; n **crash-landing**.

crass a grossly obtuse, stupid.

crate n wooden or wicker packing case; v pack in crate.

crater n bowl-shaped hole in ground; mouth of volcano.

cravat n necktie.

crave v 1 beg; entreat 2 have strong desire for; n **craving** longing.

craven a cowardly; faint-hearted; n coward.

craw n bird's crop.

crawl v 1 creeping movement 2 stroke in swimming; v 1 advance on hands and knees 2 creep 3 fig abase oneself.

crayfish, crawfish n fresh water edible shell-fish like lobster.

crayon n stick of charcoal or coloured chalk; v draw with crayons.

craze n popular fashion; exaggerated fondness; v become mad; as **crazed** insane; marked with surface cracks; **crazy** 1 mentally deranged 2 rickety, shaky (of structure) 3 coll madly eager for.

crazy paving n Brit paved area with slabs of irregular shape.

CRE abbr Commission for Racial Equality.

creak n grating, squeaking

noise; v make such sound.

cream n 1 fat part of milk 2 best of anything; v 1 skim cream from milk 2 form into a cream; phr v **cream off** take best of; a **creamy** like cream; n **creamery** place where milk is bottled, butter and cheese are made, or dairy produce is sold.

cream of tartar n white powder of tartaric acid used in baking powder.

crease n wrinkle; ridge made by folding; line marking position of batsman or bowler in cricket; v make creases; become wrinkled.

create v make; bring into existence; sl make a fuss; ns **creator; creature** 1 living being 2 servile dependant; **creation;** a **creative;** n **-tivity.**

creature comforts n things which assist bodily comfort.

creche n public day nursery.

credence n belief.

credentials n pl letters of introduction, esp of ambassador; testimonials.

credible a trustworthy; worthy of belief; n **credibility.**

credibility gap n difference between what is said and what people believe to be true.

credit n 1 belief 2 integrity 3 prestige gained by merit 4 sum in person's bank account; idm **on credit** allowing person to have goods for later payment; idm **to one's credit** worthily; v believe; attribute; place on credit side of account; *a* **-able** adding honour to *adv* **-ably**; *n* **creditor** one to whom money is due.

credit card *n* card which permits buying of goods without cash.

credulous *a* easily deceived; gullible; *adv* **-ly**; *n* **credulity**.

creed *n* set of principles; formally phrased confession of faith.

creek *n* narrow inlet on sea coast; arm of river.

creel *n* angler's wicker basket.

creep *v* move stealthily, slowly; crawl; *bot* grow along ground or wall; *fig* squirm with fear; cringe; *pt, pp* **crept**; *n* **creeper** creeping or climbing plant; *a* **creepy** eerie; feeling fear; *n* **creepiness**.

creepy-crawly *n coll* crawling creature, insect, spider.

cremation *n* burning (corpse) to ashes; *v* **cremate**; *n* **crematorium** place where cremation takes place.

crème de menthe *n Fr* peppermint liqueur.

crenellated *a* having battlements; *n* **-ation**.

creole *n* hybrid of two languages, established as main language of a community; *n* **Creole** descendant of European settlers in West Indies or southern US.

creosote *n* oily antiseptic distilled from wood- or coal-tar, used for preserving wood.

crepe *n Fr* fabric resembling crape; *n* **crepe-de-chine** fine silk; *n* **crepe rubber** washed rubber.

crepe paper *n* thin, wrinkled paper for decorating and wrapping.

crepitate *v* crackle, creak, rattle; *n* **crepitation**.

crept *pt* of **creep**.

crepuscular *a* of the twilight.

crescendo *a, adv n* gradual increase in loudness, *esp* of music.

crescent *n* 1 shape of new moon 2 curved row of houses.

cress *n* various edible pungent leaved plants.

crest *n* 1 tuft or ridge on animal's head 2 top of mountain, wave etc 3 device on coat of arms; *a* **crest-fallen** dejected, disappointed.

cretaceous *a* a chalky.

cretin *n* mentally or physically deformed; *sl* idiot.

cretonne *n Fr* strong cotton cloth, printed with design.

crevasse *n Fr* deep cleft in glacier.

crevice *n* small chink, fissure.

crew *n* ship's aircraft's company; gang (of workmen, people).

crew cut *n* very short hair cut for men.

crew neck *n* plain round neckline, *esp* for pullover.

crib *n* 1 fodder-rack; manger 2 child's bed 3 copy; plagiarism; *v* **cribbing**, **cribbed**. 1 copy closely 2

confine closely.

cribbage *n* card game for two, three or four players.

crick *n* painful spasm of back or neck muscles.

cricket[1] *n* chirping insect.

cricket[2] *n* game played by teams of eleven a side, with wickets, bats and ball; *idm* **not cricket** *Brit* not fair or honourable.

cried *pt* of **cry**.

cries *3rd sing present of* **cry**.

crikey *interj Brit coll* expressing surprise.

crime *n* grave violation of law; any evil act; *mil* offence against regulations; *a, n* **criminal**; *n* **criminology** study of crime and criminals.

crimp *v* press into tiny pleats; curl (hair); *n* **crimping-iron** implement for crimping hair, or fabric.

Crimplene [TM] crease-resistant material.

crimson *n* deep, slightly bluish red colour; *a* of this colour; *v* turn crimson; blush.

cringe *v* cower; fawn; shrink from.

crinkle *v* wrinkle; rumple; *n* undulation.

cripple *n* lame, disabled or maimed person; *v* maim; impair.

crisis *n* decisive movement; turning-point, *esp* in illness; time of acute danger or difficulty; *pl* **crises**.

crisp *a* dry and brittle; curly *esp* hair; *fig* brisk; bracing.

crisscross *a, adv, v* form(ing) network of lines.

criterion n standard of judgment; test; pl **criteria**.

critic n 1 professional reviewer of plays, books, art etc 2 fault-finder; a **critical** 1 relating to crisis; crucial 2 discerning; censorious; v **criticize** pass judgment on; censure; ns **criticism**, **critique** 1 art of criticism 2 critical analysis, eg of writers work.

croak v 1 emit hoarse, dismal cry, as frog, raven 2 grumble 3 sl die; n sound itself; a, n **croaking**.

crochet n Fr kind of fancywork done with small hooked needle; v make such work.

crock n 1 earthenware pot; broken piece of this 2 old worn-out person, horse; n **crockery** domestic china and earthenware articles.

crocodile n large amphibious reptile; n pl **crocodile tears** insincere show of grief.

crocus n -ses. small spring-flowering plant.

croft n small farm or piece of arable land; n **crofter** one who owns and works croft.

croissant n Fr flaky crescent-shaped pastry.

cromlech n prehistoric structure of flat stone resting on two upright ones.

crone n hideous, withered old woman.

crony n old friend, close companion.

crook n 1 shepherd's staff; long hooked stick 2 coll criminal

3 bend; sharp turn; v bend sharply; a **crooked** 1 bent; winding 2 dishonest 3 deformed; (adv -ly; n -ness).

croon v sing softly, sentimentally; ns **crooner**; **crooning**.

crop n 1 season's produce or yield of any cultivated plant 2 pouch in gullet of birds 3 stock of whip 4 closely cut hair; v **cropping**, **cropped**. 1 reap, gather 2 clip hair 3 graze; idm **come a cropper** 1 fall 2 fail; phr **crop up** occur.

croquet n game played on lawn, with mallets, balls and hoops.

croquette n Fr fried ball of meat, fish potato etc.

crosier, crozier n pastoral staff of bishop.

cross n 1 upright stake with transverse bar, used for execution; 2 the Cross, on which Christ died; symbol of Christian faith 3 mark made by intersecting lines 4 mixture of breeds; mongrel, hybrid etc 5 affliction; v 1 place or lay across 2 traverse 3 interbreed 4 thwart; obstruct; idm **cross oneself** make the sign of the cross; idm **cross one's mind** occur to one; phr v **cross off/out** delete; a 1 transverse 2 contrary 3 bad-tempered 4 intersecting; advs **crossways**, **crosswise**, **crossly**.

cross- prefix: makes compounds meaning opposing; crossing; transverse, across. Such compounds are not given

where the meaning may be deduced from the simple word.

cross-benches n pl seats in Parliament for MPs independent of main official parties n **cross-bencher** such an MP.

crossbill n bird with crossed mandibles.

crossbow n small powerful bow fired from the shoulder by pulling a trigger.

crossbred a of mixed breed; n **cross-breed**.

crosscheck v check again by another method.

cross-country a 1 proceeding over fields, through woods, etc., rather than on a road or track 2 from one end of the country to another; n sport of **cross-country** running.

cross-dressing n transvestism.

cross-examine v interrogate closely.

cross-eyed a squinting.

cross-fertilize v 1 fertilize a plant with pollen from a different plant 2 stimulate progress in one field of study with ideas from another; n **-ization**.

cross-grained a perverse.

crosspatch n cross, peevish person.

crosspiece n bar, usu horizontal, linking other parts of structure.

crossply n, a (tyre) of material with cords lying crosswise.

cross-reference n note referring to another place in

a book or article.

crossroads n 1 place where two roads intersect 2 decisive point in time.

cross-section n 1 (image of) surface formed by cutting across, *usu* at right angles 2 representative sample.

cross-talk n 1 *Brit* fast witty dialogue 2 interference in radio, telephone communication from other voices.

crossword n puzzle built up of intersecting words, in numbered squares with some letters in common.

crotch n 1 forked stick; 2 fork of tree or branch 3 where legs fork from body.

crotchet n note in music, half time value of minim; *a* **crotchety** faddy, peevish.

crouch v stoop low; cringe; lie close to ground.

croup n 1 throat disease of children. 2 hind-quarters of horse.

croupier n one presiding at gaming table, who rakes in and pays out money.

crouton n *Fr* cube toasted/fried bread served in soup.

crow[1] n large black bird of raven family; *idm* **as the crow flies** in a straight line.

crow[2] v utter cry of cock; triumph (vocally); *pt* **crowed, crew** (of birds only); *pp* **crowed**.

crowbar n heavy iron bar for levering.

crowd n large number of people or things close

together; throng; v cram into small place; press forward in mass; *phr* v **crowd out** exclude for lack of time, space; *a* **crowded** filled by crowd; too full.

crown n 1 royal head-dress 2 wreath worn on head 3 sovereignty; supreme power 4 summit; head 5 top of hat; 6 *fig* highest achievement; 7 foreign coins; v place crown on; make king; *idm* **to crown it all** on top of everything else.

crow's feet n pl wrinkles at outer corner of the eye.

crow's nest n lookout platform high up on ship's mast.

crozier = **crosier.**

crucial a 1 critical; decisive 2 severe.

crucible n melting-pot, for use in great heat.

cruciform a in the shape of a cross.

crucify v -**fying, -fied. 1** put to death by nailing or binding to cross; 2 *coll* torment; humiliate by ridicule; ns **crucifixion; crucifix** figure of Christ on the Cross.

crude a 1 raw; not prepared for use; in natural state 2 blunt; rude; n **crudity.**

cruel a 1 willing to cause physical or mental pain; pitiless 2 painful; n **cruelty.**

cruet n stand holding containers for condiments.

cruise v travel at leisurely speed, *esp* ship, car etc; n sea voyage for pleasure; n **cruiser** ship that cruises; fast

warship.

cruise missile n computer-guided missile flying at low altitude.

crumb n very small particle, scrap, *esp* of bread or cake; v cover with crumbs.

crumble v break into crumbs; decay; disintegrate.

crummy a *sl* inferior; worthless.

crumpet n thin, unsweetened doughy cake, usually toasted.

crumple v make creases or folds; fall into wrinkles; *a* **crumpled.**

crunch v chew, crush noisily with teeth; tread heavily on gravel etc; n sound made by crunching; *idm* **the (final) crunch** the final disaster.

crupper n 1 hind quarters of horse 2 strap passing under tail, holding saddle in place.

crusade n 1 holy war with religious object *esp* to free Holy Land 2 campaign against social abuse or evil; n **crusader.**

cruse n small pot or jar for liquids.

crush v compress violently; squeeze, press out of shape; pulverize; *fig* subdue forcibly; n act of crushing; *idm* **a crush (on sb)** *coll* strong but brief adolescent infatuation (with sb).

crust n hard outer part; dry piece of bread; hard covering of anything; v form crust; *a* **crusty** crust-like; *fig* harsh, irritable.

crustacean n animal having hard crust-like shell, eg lobster, crab, etc.

crutch n staff with cross piece to go under arm, to help lame to walk; support; crotch.

crux n knotty point; important or critical point; puzzle.

cry n 1 loud call 2 weep 3 slogan 4 characteristic call of animal; *idm* **a far cry from** quite different from; v **crying, cried.** make such sound; announce; weep; *idm* **for crying out loud** *coll* expressing protest.

cryogenics n study or use of extremely low temperatures; a cryogenic.

crypt n underground vault, *esp* of church; a **cryptic** secret, mystic.

crypto- *prefix* hidden; ns **cryptogram** written cypher; **cryptography** art of cypher writing, decoding.

cryptogam n plant reproducing without seed; a -gamous.

crystal n clear transparent quartz; solidified inorganic substance of geometrical form; fine, hard glassware; as **crystalline, crystalloid;** v **crystallize** form crystals; become clear; ns **crystallization; crystallography** science of structure and formation of crystals.

crystal ball n glass sphere used by fortune tellers.

crystal-gazing n 1 looking into a crystal ball 2 trying to predict future events.

CS gas n gas causing tears and painful breathing, used to control riots.

cub n young fox, bear, etc; v bring forth cubs; n **cubbing** hunting of foxcubs.

cubby, cubby-hole n snug place; small storage place.

cube n 1 regular geometric solid with six equal square faces; anything cube shaped; 2 *math* third power; v calculate cube of; as **cubic, cubical.**

cubicle n small, enclosed part in larger room, sleeping car, etc.

cubism n painting and sculpture style reducing natural forms to geometric shapes; n a cubist.

cubit n ancient measure of length.

cuckold n man whose wife is unfaithful.

cuckoo n migratory bird, with characteristic call, which lays eggs in another bird's nest.

cucumber n long fleshy green fruit of plant of gourd family, used in salads.

cud n partially digested food brought up by ruminants, to chew at leisure; *idm* **chew the cud** ponder, reflect on.

cuddle v hug; nestle; be close to; n a hug.

cudgel n stout, short thick stick; v beat with cudgel.

cue[1] n word serving as signal to another to act or speak; *fig* hint, lead.

cue[2] n long tapering rod used in billiards.

cuff[1] n wrist-band of garment; end of sleeve.

cuff[2] v hit with fist or hand; n such a blow.

cuisine n quality, style of cooking.

cul-de-sac n *Fr* blind alley; passage with one open end.

culinary a connected with cooking or the kitchen.

cull v 1 gather 2 pluck (flowers) 3 select 4 kill selectively; n something picked out.

cullender = **collander.**

culminate in *phr* v end in; reach its climax in; n -ation.

culpable a worthy of blame; guilty; n **culpability.**

culprit n one guilty of crime, offender.

cult n system of religious belief; devotion to person or cause; fashion.

cultivate v till, work land; grow (crops); improve; seek acquaintance of; ns -ation, -ator.

cultivated a educated and well-mannered.

culture n rearing of animals, plants; high intellectual development; artificial rearing, *esp* of bacteria; elegance of manners; as **cultured** refined; **cultural** pertaining to culture.

culvert n channel carrying water under road etc.

cum *prep* together with.

cumber v hinder, hamper; as **cumbersome** clumsy, unwieldy; **cumbrous.**

cumin n aromatic seed used as flavouring.

cummerbund n broad sash round waist.

cumulative a increasing in force, value etc by successive additions.

cumulus n cloud formation of rounded, heaped up masses.

cuneiform a wedge-shaped, esp of form of ancient writing.

cunning n skill dexterity; (of mental qualities) slyness; a having such qualities; wily; artful; adv **-ly.**

cup n 1 small drinking vessel with handle 2 contents of cup 3 trophy in shape of cup, usually silver 4 drink made of wine mixed with other ingredients; v **cupping, cupped.** bleed surgically; ns **cupful, cupboard** small closet with shelves for china, etc.

cupboard love n Brit show of love with selfish motive.

cup final n Brit match to decide winner of knock-out competition, esp in football.

cupid n figure of winged boy with bow and arrow, representing love.

cupidity n avarice; greed; covetousness.

cupola n small dome.

cupreous, cupric, cuprous a of, containing or like copper.

cur n mongrel dog; esp snappy one; low ill-bred fellow.

curable a able to be cured.

curaçao n orange-flavoured liqueur.

curate n rector's or vicar's assistant; v act as curator; n **curacy** his office.

curative n, a (substance) effecting a cure.

curator n person in charge of a museum collection.

curb n 1 restricting chain, strap fastened to horse's bit 2 fig check; restraint 3 edging of pavement; kerb; v restrain, subdue.

curd n thick substance separated from milk by acid action; v **curdle** turn into curd; coagulate; fig **c. the blood** terrify; a **curdy.**

cure v 1 restore to health; heal 2 preserve (food) by salting; n remedy, treatment restoring health.

cure-all n cure for anything; panacea.

curet(te) n surgical scraper; n **curettage** use of this.

curfew n regulation requiring all persons to be indoors by stated hour.

curia n papal court and government.

curie n unit of radioactivity.

curio n **-s.** small, esp unusual, collector's item.

curiosity n 1 inquisitiveness 2 strange, interesting object; a **curious** 1 eager to know; prying 2 puzzling 3 rare; adv **-ly.**

curl n coiled lock of hair; ringlet; spiral or similar shape; a **curly;** v twist, roll

or press into spirals; play at curling; n **curling** game like bowls, played on ice.

curlew n wading bird of snipe family.

currant n small dried grape; edible fruit of various shrubs.

current a 1 in general use; 2 up-to-date 3 generally known; n 1 flow of body of water, air 2 movement of electricity; n **currency** state of being current; money in circulation.

curriculum n **-la** or **-lums** course of study at a school, college, etc.

curriculum vitae n (document with) details of one's qualifications and professional experience.

curry[1] v **-rying, -ried.** rub down (horse) with comb; dress (leather).

curry[2] n **-ries.** highly spiced, hot flavoured dish of meat, fish etc; v make into a curry; idm **curry favour with** try to influence by flattery, bribery, etc; n **curry powder** mixture of turmeric and other spices.

curse v call down divine wrath or vengeance; swear (at); afflict; n words used to curse; profane oath, imprecation; bane; coll menstrual period; a **cursed** wicked; afflicted by a curse; n **cursedness** perversity.

cursive a in a flowing style (of hand writing).

cursor n mark on a computer

screen that shows where you are working.

cursory *a* brief; not careful or detailed.

curt *a* short, abrupt, rudely brief; *n* **curtness**; *v* **curtail** cut short; reduce; *n* **curtailment**.

curtain *n* sheet of material hung to screen window, door etc; screen separating stage and audience; anything which screens, covers; *v* cover with a curtain; *idm* **(be) curtains for (sb)** (be) the end or a disaster (for sb).

curtain call *n* reappearance of actor(s) to acknowledge applause at end of play, opera, etc.

curtain-raiser *n* **1** short piece before main play **2** any preliminary event.

curtsey, curtsy *n* movement of respect, bending, of knees made by women; *v* make such gesture.

curvaceous *a* (of woman) with shapely figure.

curve *n* line of which no part is straight, rounded bend; *v* impart a curve to; *n* **curvature** act of curving, being curved.

cushion *n* pillow, soft pad to lie, sit or rest upon; any resilient support; lining round inner side of billiard table; *v* protect with cushion.

cushy *a sl* easy; light; profitable.

cusp *n* horn of crescent; *a* **cuspidal** ending in point.

cuspidor *n* spittoon.

custard *n* dessert made of milk, eggs, sugar, baked or boiled.

custard pie *n* plate of wet sloppy stuff thrown at sb in slap-stick comedy.

cute *a* pretty; charming; cheeky.

custody *n* safe-keeping; guardianship; imprisonment; *n* **custodian** keeper, curator.

custom *n* habit; business patronage; practice; *pls* duties on imports; place where these are collected (*also* **custom house**); *a* **customary** usual; *n* **customer** buyer.

custom-built *n* made to customer's own specifications.

customize *v* adapt to customer's requirements.

cut *v* **1** wound, separate, gash with sharp instrument **2** shape, trim, carve by cutting **3** mow; reap **4** abridge **5** ignore (person) **6** strike sharply **7** intersect; *pt, pp* **cut**; *idm* **cut both ways** have both pros and cons; *idm* **cut corners** sacrifice perfection in interests of speed and economy; *idm* **cut it fine** allow the minimum amount of time for sth; *idm* **cut no ice** have no influence; *idm* **cut one's losses** abandon (an enterprise) to avoid further loss; *phr vs* **cut across 1** take a short route across **2** not correspond to; **cut back 1** prune **2** reduce; **cut down 1** fell **2** reduce (*idm* **cut**

down to size 1 make humble **2** make more realistic); **cut in 1** interrupt **2** move too close in front of another vehicle; **cut off 1** separate **2** disconnect **3** suddenly move off in a new direction **4** deprive of inheritance **5** *sl* kill (*idm* **be cut off in one's prime** die young); *idm* **cut out for** well suited to; *idm* **a cut above** somewhat superior to; *n* **cutting 1** act of cutting **2** thing cut off, *esp* excavation through high ground, for railway, road etc **3** slip cut from plant; *a* sarcastic; bitter; *a* **cut-throat** merciless; *n* type of razor; fierce ruffian.

cut-and-dried *a* arranged and settled.

cut and thrust *n* **1** attack and counter-attack **2** very competitive atmosphere.

cutaneous *a* of skin.

cutaway *n* **1** tailcoat **2** drawing showing internal details, *eg* of machine **3** film, TV shot giving view of simultaneous event in a different place.

cut-back *n* reduction.

cut glass *n* glass with decorative carved patterns.

cuticle *n* outer layer of skin; skin at base of nails.

cutlass *n* short, broad-bladed sword.

cutler *n* one who makes, mends, sells knives and cutting instruments; *n* **cutlery** such implements.

cutlet *n* small meat chop.

cut-off n 1 stopping point 2 device to control flow.

cut price a cheap.

CUTS abbr Computer Users' Tape System.

cutter n 1 person who cuts 2 sailing boat 3 small fast boat 4 esp pl cutting tool.

cutthroat a 1 murderous 2 fiercely competitive; n very sharp razor.

cutting edge a 1 sharp edge 2 incisiveness of speech or writing 3 key area of technological advance.

cuttle, cuttle-fish n marine mollusc which squirts out inky fluid.

cv abbr curriculum vitae.

cwt abbr hundredweight.

cyanide n prussic acid.

cyanosis n blueness of skin.

cybernetics n study of automatic communication and control, esp in relation to computers.

cyberpunk n style of science fiction set in a world of advanced computer technology.

cyberspace n the environment through which electronic information and pictures travel when they are sent from one computer to another.

cyclamate n artificial sweetener.

cyclamen n plant with pink, white, red or purple flowers and turned-back petals.

cycle n 1 period of time during which there is regular orderly series of events 2 great period of time; 3 group of poems, connected with central theme 4 coll bicycle; v 1 recur in cycles 2 ride bicycle; a **cyclic, cyclical**; ns **cyclist** bicycle rider; **cyclometer** device for measuring distance travelled by wheel.

cyclone n rotating winds surrounding regions of low pressure; a **cyclonic**.

cyclostyle v produce multiple copies from a stencil; n machine which does this.

cyclotron n machine for accelerating atomic particles in nuclear research.

cygnet n young swan.

cylinder n solid or hollow roller-shaped body; piston chamber of engine; a **cylindrical**.

cymbal n musical percussion instrument, one of two brass plates struck to make clashing sound.

cynic n sceptical, mocking person; a **cynical** sneering; thinking worst of people; n **cynicism** being a cynic.

cynosure n centre of attraction.

cypress n dark evergreen coniferous tree.

Cyrillic alphabet n alphabet used in written Russian and some other Slavonic languages.

cyst n med abnormal sac containing pus, fluid; a **cystic** of bladder; n **cystitis** inflammation of the bladder.

cystic fibrosis n hereditary disease that affects the respiratory and digestive systems.

cytology n study of plant and animal cells.

czar n **tsar** former emperor of Russia.

DA *abbr* US district attorney.

dab *v* **dabbing, dabbed.** touch lightly; *n* **1** slight tap **2** small flat fish.

dabble *v* **1** dip in and out of water **2** engage in half-heartedly (study, etc); *n* **dabbler.**

dabchick *n* small water-bird.

dab hand *n* Brit coll expert.

dace *n* small river-fish.

dachshund *n* type of long-bodied, short-legged dog.

dad, daddy *n* childish word for father.

daddy-long-legs *n* crane-fly.

dado *n* border or panelling on wall of room.

daemon *n* **1** (in Greek myth) demigod **2** spirit that inspires.

daffodil *n* spring-flowering bulb; narcissus.

daft *n* foolish, feeble-minded.

dagger *n* short two-edged blade for stabbing; *idm* **look daggers at** glare at.

daguerreotype *n* early type of photograph.

dahlia *n* type of autumn-flowering plant.

Dáil *n* lower house of parliament in Irish Republic.

daily *a, adv* every day *n* **1** newspaper published on weekdays **2** Brit coll (*also* **daily help**) person who helps to clean the house daily; *idm* **daily bread 1** daily food **2** coll livelihood.

dainty *a* delicate; elegant; refined; *n* delicacy (food); *n* **daintiness.**

dairy *n* place where milk and its products are dealt with or sold; *n* **dairy cattle** cows kept to produce milk.

dais *n* raised platform.

daisy *n* type of common wild flower.

daisy wheel *n, a* (having high-quality printing from) rapidly rotating wheel with choice of typeface.

Dalai Lama *n* Tibetan spiritual leader.

dale *n* valley, *esp* in N England; *n* **dalesman.**

dally *v* **dallying, dallied.** linger; delay; *phr v* **dally with 1** think about **2** flirt with; *n* **dalliance.**

Dalmatian *n* large white dog, with black spots.

dam[1] *n* barrier arresting water flow; water so obstructed; *v* **damming, damned.** hold back by dam.

dam[2] *n* mother of animals usually domestic livestock.

damage *n* harm, injury, hurt to persons, property etc; *pl* money claimed, or paid as compensation for injury libel etc; *v* harm, injure.

damask *n* silk, linen material with pattern woven into it; colour of damask rose; rosy-pink; *v* **damascene** decorate metal with inlaid gold or silver.

dame *n* lady; *cap* title of lady member of Order of British Empire.

damn *v* condemn to eternal punishment; curse; *interj* oath; *a, adv* **damned;** *coll* used as intensifier; *idm* **I'll be damned** expressing surprise or frustration; *a* **damnable;** *n* **damnation;** *idm* **in damnation** expressing anger; *idm* **do one's damndest** coll do the most one can.

damp *n* moisture; noxious gas in coal-mines; *a* slightly wet;

v make damp *fig* discourage;
(of plants) to wither off from
mildew, *idm* **damp down**
suppress *v* **dampen** become
damp; depress; *n* **damper**
anything that discourages;
plate in flue to regulate
draught.

**damp course, damp-proof
course** *n* layer of waterproof
material preventing rising
damp in a builing.

damsel *n* young girl.

damson *n* small, purple, very
sour plum.

dance *v* move, leap with
rhythmic sequence of steps,
usually to music; *n* social
gathering organized for
dancing; form of dance; *ns*
dancer; dancing art and
practice of the dance.

dandelion *n* common yellow
wild flower.

dander *idm* **get one's dander
up** *coll* make sb angry.

dandle *v* move (child) up and
down in one's arms, on one's
knee.

dandruff *n* small scales of dead
skin on scalp, scurf.

dandy *n* fop; extravagantly
fashionable man.

Dane *n* native of Denmark.

danger *n* menace; exposure to
peril, risk of death; *a*
dangerous (*adv* -**ly**).

dangle *v* hang, sway loosely;
show as enticement *idm*
keep sb dangling keep sb in
suspense.

Danish *n* the language of
Denmark.

dank *a* disagreeably damp; *n*

dankness.

daphne *a* flowering shrub

dapper *a* neat and smart in
appearance; trim.

dapple *v* mark with spots of
different colour; *a* **dappled**,
variegated.

dare *v* have courage for;
venture to; challenge; *pt*
dared, durst; *pp* **dared;** *pr p*
daring.

dare-devil *n, a* (person)
behaving in a foolishly
reckless way.

daren't *contracted form of* dare
not.

daresay *idm* **I daresay** *or* **I dare
say** probably; it may be true
(that).

daring *a* bold; *n* audacity.

dark *a* 1 without light; (of
colour, complexion) deep in
shade 2 secret 3 evil; *idm* **in
the dark** without
information; *v* **darken** make,
or become darker; *as*
darkish; darkling growing
dim; *n* **darkness**, absence of
light.

Dark Ages *n* period between
the end of the Roman
Empire and the
Renaissance.

dark horse *n* person whose
talents remain hidden.

darkroom *n* enclosed place for
developing and printing
film.

darling *n* dearly loved person;
term of endearment.

darn *v* repair hole with
interlacing stitches; *n* part so
mended; *n* **darning**.

darn *interj* milder form of

damn.

dart *n* 1 light pointed missile 2
sudden rapid forward
movement 3 tapering seam
in garment; *pl* indoor game
played with target and small
darts; *v* shoot out or forward
quickly, swiftly.

Darwinian *a* of evolution (as
stated by Charles Darwin).

dash *v* 1 fling with violence 2
rush furiously 3 sprinkle; *n* 1
rush 2 small quantity (of
liquid) 3 short line (-) used
to denote a pause; *a* **dashing**
spirited; eager.

dashboard *n* instrument panel
inside car, in front of driver.

dastard *n* despicable coward; *a*
dastardly mean.

DAT *abbr* Digital Audio Tape.

data bank *n comput* centre
with large supply of data.

database *n comput* large store
of data for reference.

data processing *n comput*
operating on data to analyse,
solve problems, etc.

data *n pl* known facts from
which conclusion can be
drawn; *sing* **datum**.

date[1] *n* 1 particular day in the
calendar 2 arrangement to
meet 3 person with whom
one has a social
engagement; *idm* **out of date**
1 old fashioned 2 no longer
valid; *idm* **to date** until now;
idm **up to date** 1 modern 2
completed to schedule 3
well informed; *phr vs* **date
from/back to** be applicable
from; *a* **dated** 1 marked with
the date 2 old fashioned; *a*

dateless never becoming dated.

date[2] *n* sweet, single stoned fruit of date palm.

date palm *n* tree with an edible fruit; *n* date.

dative *n* case of noun or pronoun expressing indirect object.

daub *v* smear; coat; plaster; paint roughly; *n* unskilful painting; smear.

daughter *n* female child or offspring; *a* **daughterly**; *n* **daughter-in-law** son's wife.

daunt *v* inspire with fear, dismay; discourage; *a* **dauntless** intrepid; fearless.

dauphin *n* former title of eldest son of French king.

davit *n* small crane for raising and lowering boats.

Davy Jones's locker *n* coll the bottom of the sea.

daw *n* kind of crow; jackdaw.

dawdle *v* linger; loiter; waste time; *n* **dawdler**.

dawn *v* begin to grow light; *phr v* **dawn on** gradually become evident to; *n* daybreak; *n* **dawning** the dawn; *fig* beginning.

day *n* period between sunrise and sunset; 24 hours; specified day; *pl* epoch, period of time; *idm* **call it a day** (agree) to stop working; *idm* **carry/win the day** be successful; *idm* **make sb's day** make sb happy; *ns* **day care** Brit daytime care for children, old people; **day-book** for recording day sales; **day-break** dawn; **day-dream**

reverie; **daylight** natural light *(idm* **beat/knock/scare the living daylights out of** hit/scare sb very badly); **daytime** hours between sunrise and sunset.

daylight saving *n* in summer adjusting clocks to make nightfall appear later.

day release course *n* Brit course attended by workers by arrangement with employers.

day-to-day *a* 1 everyday 2 one day at a time.

daze *v* stupefy, confuse, usually by blow, shock; *a* **dazed**.

dazzle *v* confuse vision; blind by brilliant light; daze by hope of success.

dB *abbr* decibel.

DBE *abbr* Dame Commander of the order of the British Empire.

DBS *abbr* direct broadcasting (by) satellite.

DBX *abbr* Dolby noise reduction.

DC *abbr* 1 *mus* da capo 2 *elec* direct current 3 District of Columbia 4 detective constable.

D-day *n* 1 6th June 1944, when allies invaded Normandy 2 any day when an important plan is to be launched.

DD *abbr* direct debit.

DDT *n* type of insecticide.

DE, DoE *abbr* Department of Employment.

de- *prefix; forms compounds expressing down, off, away, deficiency, negation. Where*

the meaning may be deduced from the simple word, the compounds are not given here.

deacon *n* ordained person, lower order than priest; *fem* **deaconess** woman appointed to help in church work.

dead *a* no longer living; obsolete (of language); complete; lifeless; extinguished; numbed; *n coll* dead persons; *v* **deaden** reduce force of; muffle; benumb; *a* **deadly** fatal; implacable; *ns* **deadliness**.

dead-and-alive *a coll* lifeless; boring.

dead beat *a coll* exhausted *n* **dead-beat** *coll* idle person with no desire for improvement; drop-out.

dead centre *n* exact centre.

dead cert *n coll* 1 absolute certainty 2 certain winner.

dead duck *n coll* abandoned scheme; one sure to fail.

dead end *n* impasse; *a* **dead-end** without prospects.

dead heat *n* race where two runners reach finish simultaneously.

deadline *n* time limit for finishing a job.

deadlock *n* situation in dispute when neither opposing party will give way, so progress is impossible *a* **deadlocked**.

dead loss *n coll* useless person or situation.

deadly nightshade *n* plant with very poisonous black berries (*also* belladonna).

dead man's handle *n* safety handle for stopping electric train automatically when released.

deadpan a expressionless; without sign of emotion.

dead reckoning n calculation of position without mechanical aids.

dead ringer n coll person closely resembling another.

dead set a positively determined.

dead weight n heavy lifeless mass.

dead wood n 1 useless things 2 ineffectual people.

deaf a without whole or partial hearing; inattentive; v **deafen** make deaf; n pl **the deaf** deaf persons; n **-ness**; a **deafening**; n **deaf-mute** person who is deaf and cannot speak.

deal¹ v 1 give, hand out 2 distribute, esp playing cards; pt, pp **dealt**; phr vs **deal in** 1 buy and sell 2 indulge in; **deal with** 1 trade with 2 handle; n business transaction; act of dealing cards etc; idm **a good/great deal** a lot; ns **dealer**; dealing trading; n pl **dealings (with)** relations (with), esp business.

deal² n Brit timber from fir or pine tree.

dean n head of chapter of cathedral; head of university faculty; ns **rural dean** one with powers over group of parishes; **deanery** office or house of dean.

dear 1 a precious; beloved 2 costly; expensive 3 polite

form of address in letter; n lovable person; adv **dear, dearly**, at high price; n **dearness**.

dearth n scarcity; want; (esp of food) famine.

death n end of life; annihilation; state of being dead; idm **at death's door** (seeming to be) very ill and about to die; idm **do/flog to death** coll play or perform so frequently that people become bored; idm **like death warmed up** coll looking very ill or tired; idm **put to death** execute; idm **sick to death (of)** coll absolutely fed up with; n **d. duty** tax due on estate of person at death; a **deathless, immortal**; a, adv **deathly**, like death.

death duty n Brit tax on property after death.

death row n US place where condemned prisoner awaits execution.

death's head n human skull (symbolizing death).

deathwatch beetle n beetle whose larva eats wood, causing damage to buildings.

débâcle n Fr rout; sudden and overwhelming disaster.

debar v **-barring, -barred.** prevent; exclude; prohibit.

debark v disembark; put, go ashore.

debase v lower in value, esp of coinage; render base (dignity, morals); n **-ment**.

debate v discuss; argue; consider; n formal public

discussion; a **debatable** questionable, n **debater**.

debauch v corrupt; lead astray; seduce; orgy; licentious bout; ns **debauchee, debauchery**.

debenture n certificate of stock held, bond of company or corporation.

debility n weakness, feebleness of health; v **debilitate** make weak.

debit n entry in account, of sum owing; v charge as due.

debit card n payment card with which goods are paid for directly from a bank account.

debonair a genial; affable; cheerful; sprightly.

debouch v come out into a wider space.

debrief v question sb in detail about a mission, task or enterprise after completion n **debriefing**.

debris n broken remains rubbish loose rock fragments.

debt n something owed; liability; n **debtor**.

debug v 1 remove hidden microphones from (eg house) 2 identify and remove faults from machine, computer program, etc.

debunk v expose as false or exaggerated.

début n Fr first appearance in public; n fem **debutante** girl making her debut in Society.

dec-, deca- prefix, ten, tenfold; eg **decametre** 10 metres. *Where the meaning may be* *deduced from the simple word the compounds are not given here.*

decade n period of ten years.

decadent a deteriorating; declining in morals; n **decadence**.

decaffeinate v remove caffeine from.

decagon n plane figure with ten sides.

decahedron n solid with ten faces.

decalcify v remove lime from, as teeth, bones etc.

Decalogue n Ten Commandments.

decamp v 1 break camp 2 run away; abscond.

decant v pour off gently, leaving sediment; n **decanter** stoppered glass vessel for decanted wine.

decapitate v cut off head; behead; n -**ation**.

decarbonize v remove carbon from; n **decarbonization**.

decathlon n athletic contest for the best overall result in ten events.

decay v 1 rot 2 lose vigour, power etc.; decline; n **decomposition**; rotting; gradual breaking up; a **decayed**.

decease v die; n death; n **deceased** the dead person.

deceive v 1 mislead 2 delude oneself 3 cheat; ns **deceiver**; **deceit** act iof deceiving; fraud; sham; a **deceitful**, misleading; giving false idea; (adv -ly n -**ness**).

decelerate v decrease speed

n -**ation**.

December n twelfth month of year.

decennial a 1 ten yearly 2 lasting ten years; n tenth anniversary.

decent a seemly; respectable; modest; n **decency**.

decentralize v remove from central control n -**ization**.

deception n 1 deceiving; being deceived 2 trick; a **deceptive**; adv -**ly**.

deci- prefix one tenth.

decibel n unit of measure of loudness of sounds.

decide v determine; settle; make up one's mind; a **decided** determined; definite; n **decision**; a **decisive**; adv -**ly**.

deciduous a (of trees, shrubs etc) shedding leaves annually.

decimal a based on number ten; n decimal fraction; v **decimalize** reduce to decimal fractions or system; n -**ization** process of converting to decimals.

decimate v kill every tenth man, or large proportion of anything; n **decimation**.

decipher v 1 decode 2 make out meaning of; a -**able**.

decision n 1 conclusion 2 ability to decide a decisive; adv -**ly**; n -**ness**.

decisive a 1 determining 2 resolute; adv **decisively**.

deck n 1 horizontal flooring of ship, bus, etc. 2 pack of cards; v 1 cover with deck 2 adorn; decorate.

deck chair n folding portable seat for reclining on a beach.

declaim v speak or read as to an audience; n **declamation**; a **declamatory**.

declare v 1 state 2 announce formally 3 admit one's interest, liability 4 cricket end innings prematurely; n **declaration**.

declination n phys deviation of compass from true north.

decline v 1 slope downwards 2 deteriorate 3 refuse 4 give inflections of nouns etc; n gradual loss of vigour; wasting disease; ns **declination** deviation; **declension** act of declining; inflection of nouns etc.

declivity n downward slope.

declutch v (of engine etc) disengage clutch.

decoct v boil down, extract essence by boiling, n **decoction**.

decode v translate from cipher or code.

decoke v aut coll = **decarbonize**.

décolleté a Fr with a low neckline.

decolonize v make politically independent; n -**ization**.

decommission v take out of service or dismantle.

decompose v decay; break into constituent parts; n **decomposition** state of being decomposed.

decompress v reduce air pressure (on); n -**ion**.

decongestant n, a (medicant)

relieving congestion, *eg* of nose, chest.

decontaminate *v* free from contamination; *n* **-ation**.

décor *n Fr* decorative scheme of room, stage set, etc.

decorate *v* adorn by additions; paint, paper a room; invest with badge, medal etc., showing honour to; *ns* **-ation; -ator** tradesman who paints and papers rooms etc.; *a* **-ative**.

decorous *a* seemly; sober; decent; *n* **decorum** propriety.

decoy *v* lure into danger; *n* thing or person used as a lure or bait.

decrease *v* lessen; grow, make smaller; *n* lessening.

decree *n* decision; formal order; edict; *v* order, command by decree.

decree absolute *n leg* final divorce order.

decree nisi *n leg Lat* provisional divorce order.

decrepit *a* old; feeble; tottery; *n* **decrepitude**.

decriminalize *v* declare no longer illegal; *n* **-ization**.

decry *v* disparage, cry down; *pt, pp* **decried;** *pr p* **decrying.**

dedicate *v* devote solemnly; inscribe (book etc.) to a person; *n* **-ation**.

deduce *v* infer; draw as conclusion from given facts; *n* **deduction** conclusion reached; *a* **deductive** by a deduction.

deduct *v* subtract, take away; *n* **deduction** amount

subtracted.

deed *n* 1 action; 2 legal document.

deed poll *n leg* document registering a change of name.

deem *v* believe; consider; regard; *n* **deemster** a justice of Isle of Man.

deep *a* 1 extending far down, in; of, at given depth 2 hard to fathom 3 engrossed (in study etc.) 4 dark (of colour) 5 low-pitched (of sound etc.) 6 cunning; *n* deep water, sea; *idm* **go off the deep end** *coll* react angrily; *idm* **(get) in (to) deep water** (get in(to) difficulties; *idm* **thrown in at the deep end** *coll* presented with all possible problems from the start; *v* **deepen;** *ns* **-ness** quality of being deep **depth** distance from surface; *as* **deep-rooted** firmly fixed; **deep-seated** not superficial.

deep-freeze *v* freeze (food) quickly to ensure longer preservation *pt* **deep-froze;** *pp* **deep-frozen;** *n* **freezer.**

deep-fry *n* fry in deep pan of oil or fat.

deer *n* family of ruminants, with deciduous antlers; *pl* **deer;** *ns* **deer-hound; deer-stalker; 1** one who hunts deer **2** kind of hat.

deface *v* disfigure; mar; obliterate; *n* **-ment**.

de facto *a, adv Lat* in fact (whether legally or not).

defalcation *n* misappropriation

of property, funds etc.; embezzlement.

defame *v* speak evil of; *n* **-ation;** *a* **-atory**.

default *v leg* fail to appear; fail to pay, or act; *n* absence; deficiency; *n* **defaulter; in default of** in absence of.

defeat *v* conquer; frustrate; *n* conquest; frustration; *n* **defeatism** acceptance of defeat; pessimism; *a, n* **-ist**.

defecate *v* remove impurities; void excrement; *n* **defecation**.

defect *n* fault; blemish; shortcoming; *v* desert ones country, duty; *ns* **defector** one who defects; **defection;** *a* **defective** faulty; imperfect.

defend *v* guard; ward off attack; *leg* oppose, fight case; uphold; *ns* **defence; defender;** *a* **defensive** protecting; *n* attitude of defence; *a* **defensible** justified; *n* **-ibility**.

defer *v* **-ferring, -ferred.** delay, put off; *n* **-ment**.

defer *v* **-ferring, -ferred.** yield to another's wishes; *n* **deference** respect, consideration for; *a* **deferential**.

defiant *see* **defy**.

deficiency *n* shortage; lack; *a* **deficient** lacking, incomplete in something; *n* **deficit** excess of liabilities over assets.

defile *v* pollute; corrupt; desecrate; **defilement**.

defile *v* march in file; *n* narrow valley or pass.

define v 1 show clearly 2 fix limits of 3 state meaning; as **definable; definite** exact; clear; certain; **definitive** decisive; n **definition** exact description.

definite article n the word 'the'.

deflate v 1 let out air, gas from 2 reduce inflated currency; n **-ation**; a **-ationary**.

deflect v change course of; deviate; ns **deflection** or **deflexion; deflector** device causing deflection.

deflower v ar deprive (maiden) of virginity.

deforest v clear land of trees; n **-ation**.

defoliant n chemical which destroys leaves; v **defoliate**; (n **-action**).

deform v spoil shape, beauty of; disfigure; ns **-ation; -ity**.

defraud v cheat; swindle; deprive of lawful rights.

defray v bear cost of.

defrock v banish from priesthood.

defrost v remove frost or ice from; unfreeze.

deft a skilful; neat; competent; n **-ness**.

defunct a dead, deceased.

defuse v 1 remove fuse; render (bomb, etc) harmless; 2 make (situation) less dangerous.

defy v **-fying, -fied**. challenge; resist; flout; disobey openly; a **defiant;** insolently disobedient; n **defiance**.

degenerate v decline from higher to lower state or condition; a lower in quality; depraved; n degenerate person, thing; ns **-ation; degeneracy**.

degrade v reduce in rank, status, quality; debase; humiliate; a **degraded;** n **degradation** act of degrading; state of misery, squalor.

degree n 1 unit of measurement 2 grade in any series 3 extent of progress, skill 4 amount 5 university rank.

dehumanize v 1 make inhumane 2 make mechanical; n **-ization**.

dehydrate v remove water from; n **-ration**.

de-ice v free from ice; n **de-icer**.

deify v **-fying, -fied**. look on, worship as god; n **deification**.

deign v condescend to do; think fit.

deism n reasoned belief in God's existence n **deist;** a **-istic**.

deity n a god, divinity; **the Deity** God.

déjà vu n Fr 1 sense that a new event has been experienced before 2 coll sense of boredom with familiar situation.

deject v depress, dispirit; a **dejected;** n **dejection**.

de jure a, adv Lat by legal right.

dekko n have a dekko Brit coll dated have a look.

delay v 1 retard 2 keep back 3 linger, n act of delaying; tardiness.

delectable a delightful, enjoyable; n **delectation** pleasure.

delegate v 1 send as representative 2 entrust with duties etc; n representative; ns **-ation; delegacy** body of delegates.

delete v erase; remove; obliterate; n **deletion**.

deleterious a harmful, injurious.

deliberate v 1 discuss; 2 study closely; a 1 studied 2 intentional 3 unhurried; n **-ation** careful reflection on.

delicatessen n shop selling specially imported foods, eg cheese, cooked meats; coll **deli**.

delicate a 1 sensitive 2 difficult situation 3 dainty 4 not robust; finely made 5 easily injured; n **delicacy** 1 fineness; refinement 2 weakness (of health) 3 tasty food.

delicious a agreable to sense, esp taste; delightful.

delight n great pleasure; v charm; give, take great pleasure; a **delighted** very pleased; a **delightful** pleasing; fascinating.

delimit v define limits; n **-ation**.

delineate v depict; describe; ns **-ator, -ation**.

delinquent n, a (person) committing illegal acts n **delinquency**.

deliquesce v become liquid;

a **-escent**; *n* **-escence**.

delirious *a* 1 subject to delirium 2 *coll* excited and happy; *adv* **-ly**; *n* **delirium** mental disturbance due to illness, *esp* fever causing wildness of speech.

delirium tremens *n* (also **DTs**) delirium caused by taking too much alcohol.

deliver *v* 1 set free; hand over 2 utter (sermon etc) 3 aim (blow etc) 4 assist at childbirth; *ns* **delivery**; **deliverer**; **deliverance** rescue.

dell *n* small wooded hollow.

delouse *v* rid of lice.

delphinium *n* genus of plants, including larkspur.

delta *n* 1 alluvial land at river mouth 2 Greek letter.

delude *v* deceive; mislead; *n* **delusion**; *a* **delusive**.

deluge *v* inundate; flood; overwhelm; *n* flood; torrent (of words etc); downpour.

deluxe *a* luxurious.

delve *v* dig; burrow; *fig* look deeply into.

demagnetize *v* deprive of magnetic power.

demagogue *n* political agitator.

demand *v* 1 require 2 ask as by right; *n* 1 urgent claim 2 need 3 call for specific commodity.

demarcation *n* boundary line; limit; distinction.

demean *v* behave; conduct oneself; *n* **demeanour** bearing; deportment.

demean *v* **demean oneself** lower, degrade oneself *a*

demeaning.

demeanour *n* bearing; conduct.

demented *a* insane; crazy; wild; *n* **dementia** form of insanity.

demerara *n* kind of brown sugar.

demerit *n* *fml* fault; defect.

demesne *n* landed property; estate.

demi- *prefix: forms compounds with meaning half, partial. Where the meaning may be deduced from the simple word, the compounds are not given here.*

demigod *n* heroic character.

demijohn *n* large narrow-necked bottle with wicker covering.

demilitarize *v* free from military equipment; *n* **-ization**.

demi-monde *n* any social group not considered to be wholly respectable.

demise *v* convey by lease; leave as legacy; *n* 1 conveyance by will etc 2 death.

demitasse *n* small coffee cup.

demo *n* trial product offered to attract buyers; *v* demo.

demobilize *v* disband, discharge forces; *n* **-ization**.

democracy *n* rule by the people; state so governed; *a* **-cratic**; *n* **-crat** supporter of democracy.

demographic *a* statistics on population; *adv* **demographically**; *n* **demography**; *adv* **demographically**; *n*

demography.

demolish *v* pull down; destroy, break up; *n* **demolition**.

demon *n* 1 devil; evil spirit 2 wicked, cruel person; *as* **demonaic** possessed by demon; **demonic** inspired by demon.

demonetize *v* deprive currency of value; *n* **-ization**.

demonstrate *v* prove by reasoning; show by example; show feelings; *as* **demonstrable** proved; **-ative** conclusive; showing clearly; *ns* **-ation** 1 proof 2 exhibition of method 3 expression of force, public feeling; **-ator** one who demonstrates.

demoralize *v* lower morale of; dishearten, discourage; *n* **-ization**.

demote *v* reduce in order, rank, etc.; *n* **demotion**.

demotic *a* of the ordinary people; in popular use.

demur *v* hesitate; raise objections to.

demure *a* modest; affecting coyness, gravity.

den *n* lair of wild animals; cage; small room, study.

denationalize *v* remove from state control; *n* **-ization**.

denature *v* alter natural quality of; adulterate.

dene *n* small valley.

denial *n* negation; refusal.

denier *n* 1 unit of weight showing fineness of silk 2 nylon yarn.

denigrate *v* sneer at; defame; *n* **-ation**.

denim n coarse cotton, cloth.

denizen n inhabitant.

denominate v name; designate; ns **-ation** name of particular class, religion etc.; **-ator** divisor in vulgar fractions.

denote v mark, indicate by sign, symbol; mean.

denouement n Fr final situation (in play, book etc.); climax.

denounce v accuse publicly; repudiate (treaty); n **denunciation**; a **denunciatory**.

dense a crowded; thick; compact; fig stupid; ns **-ness**, **density**, specific gravity; fig stupidity.

dent n slight hollow made by blow etc.; v make, mark with dent.

dental a pertaining to teeth or dentistry; a **dentate** toothed.

dental floss n soft thread for cleaning teeth.

dentifrice n fml toothpaste or powder.

dentine n hard substance of tooth beneath enamel coat.

dentist n surgeon who cares for teeth; **dentistry** art of dentist; **dentition** teething; **denture** (s) set of false teeth.

denude v make bare; strip; n **-ation** erosion of soil by natural forces.

denunciation n denouncing; being denounced.

deny v declare untrue; refuse (request); disown; abstain from; n **denial**.

deodorize v make bare; strip; remove smell

from; ns **ization**; **-izer**; **deodorant**.

deontology n branch of ethics dealing with moral duty; a **-ological**; n **-ologist**.

Deo volente interj Lat God willing.

deoxidize v remove oxygen from; n **-ization**.

depart v go away; leave; die; deviate; ns **-ment** branch; part; division; **department store** large shop selling variety of goods; a **departmental**; n **departure** starting out; leaving.

depend v 1 hang 2 rely on 3 be contingent on; a **dependable** reliable; ns **dependant** person relying on another for support; a **dependent**; ns **dependence**; **dependency** subordinate territory.

depict v describe verbally; represent pictorially.

depilatory n substance able to remove hair; n **depilation** act of removing hair.

deplete v empty out; exhaust; n **depletion**.

deplore v 1 lament 2 regret 3 disapprove; a **deplorable** lamentable; disastrous.

deploy v extend; open out (troops etc); n **deployment**.

deponent n one who makes statement on oath; v **depone**.

depopulate v drive out, destroy population; n **depopulation** decline in population.

deport v 1 banish 2 expel 3 behave oneself; ns **deportee** person deported;

deportation expulsion from state; **deportment** carriage, behaviour.

depose v 1 remove from office 2 dethrone 3 testify, n **deposition**.

deposit v 1 entrust for safe keeping 2 leave (as sediment) 3 set down; n 1 sediment 2 money deposited at bank or given as pledge of good faith; ns **depositor**; **depository** place where things are deposited; storehouse.

depot n storehouse; regimental HQ; bus garage.

deprave v pervert; corrupt; n **depravity** viciousness; moral corruption.

deprecate v express disapproval of; a **deprecative**; **-atory**; n **-cation**.

depreciate v 1 lower value of 2 fig disparage 3 lose quality (by wear); n **-ation** reduction in value (by wear and tear); allowance made for this in valuations; a **-atory**.

depredation n plundering; laying waste; n **depredator** one who robs, despoils.

depress n press down; make dejected; weaken; n **depression** 1 concavity 2 despondence 3 low atmospheric pressure 4 slump in trade; a, n **depressant** sedative.

deprive v take away from; dispossess; n **deprivation**.

depth n degree of deepness;

idm **in/out of one's depth 1**
able/unable to touch bottom
with head above water **2**
able/unable to cope or
understand; *pl* **depths**
deepest part or feeling.

depute *v* appoint as agent,
substitute; delegate; *ns*
deputy substitute, delegate;
deputation body of persons
acting as deputies; *v*
deputize act for another.

derail *v* leave or cause to leave
rails; *n* **-ment**.

derange *v* upset; disturb; drive
mad; *n* **-ment** mental
disorder.

derby *n* **1** the Derby horse race
at Epsom **2** *US* annual horse
race **3** *sport* important
contest, *esp* between local
teams.

deregulate *v* free from legal
control; *n* **-ation**.

derelict *a* deserted; worthless;
neglected; *n* thing forsaken
esp ship; *n* **dereliction**
neglect of duty.

deride *v* mock at; ridicule; *n*
derision; *a* **derisive**; *adv* **-ly**;
a **derisory** mocking,
ironical.

de rigueur *a* required by
custom.

derive *v* get from; trace origin
of; spring from; *ns*
derivation; **derivative**; *a*
derivative.

derm, derma *n* inner layer of
skin; *as* **dermal**; *ns*
dermatitis inflammation of
skin; **dermatology** study of
skin and its diseases;
-ologist.

dermis *n anat* layer of skin
below surface.

derogate *v* detract (from);
disparage; *n* **derogation**; *a*
derogatory disparaging,
taking away merit.

derrick *n* crane, stationary or
movable; latticed tower over
oil well.

derring-do *n ar* heroic deeds.

derringer *n* short large-calibre
pistol.

derv *n* diesel fuel.

dervish *n* Muslim monk vowed
to poverty.

DES *abbr* Department of
Education and Science.

desalinate *v* remove salt from;
n **-ation**; *n* **desalination
plant**.

descant *n* song accompanying
plainsong; talk at length.

descend *v* **1** move, come down
2 stoop **3** lower oneself **4** be
derived **5** pass by
inheritance; **descend** *idm* **be
descended from** have as
ancestor(s) *n* **descendant**;
phr v **descend on/upon 1**
visit unexpectedly **2** attack
without warning; *ns*
descendant offspring.

descent *n* **1** downward
movement **2** downward
slope **3** ancestry; family
origins.

describe *v* give account of;
depict in words; mark out,
trace form or line of; *a*
descriptive; *n* **description**
account; kind, species.

descry *v* **-crying, -cried.** make
out; discern.

desecrate *v* profane; *ns* **-ation,**

-ator.

desegregate *v* abolish racial
segregation in; *n* **-ation**.

deselect *n Brit* reject (existing
MP) as candidate in next
election.

desert *v* forsake; abandon; *mil*
abscond from service; *ns*
deserter, desertion.

desert *n* barren, uninhabited
tract; *a* uninhabited, lonely.

deserts *n pl* what is deserved.

deserve *v* be worthy of; merit;
a **deserved**; *adv* **-ly**; *a*
deserving worthy of.

deshabille *n* partial undress.

desiccate *v* dry completely; *a*
desiccated; *n* **-ation**.

desideratum *n* acknowledged
want.

design *v* **1** plan out; intend **2**
make, invent, pattern; *n* **1**
purpose, intention **2**
decorative pattern; *pl*
designs *idm* **have designs
(up)on** be planning to get or
win by unscrupulous means;
n **designer** one who makes
artistic designs *a* **1** made by
a notable designer **2** *coll*
appearing fashionable; *a*
designing artful, scheming.

designate *v* indicate; nominate
for office; specify; *a*
nominated but not installed;
n **-ation** distinctive name.

desire long for; yearn for;
request; *n* strong longing;
wish, hope; something
desired; *a* **desirable** worth
having; *n* **desirability**; *a*
desirous wishful.

desist *v* stop, cease.

desk *n* table or other piece of

furniture used for reading or writing on.

desktop publishing n design and production of publications using a computer.

desolate a waste, dismal; forsaken; lonely, forlorn; v lay waste; make lonely, sad.

despair v lose hope; n hopelessness.

despatch, dispatch v 1 send off 2 kill 3 finish off speedily; n 1 sending off 2 official report, message 3 speed.

desperado n dated dangerous criminal.

desperate a beyond hope; driven to extremity; frantic; ns **desperation, desperado** adventurer; violent ruffian.

despise v look down on; feel contempt; a **despicable** contemptible; adv **-ably** mean.

despite n spite; hatred; malice; prep in spite of.

despoil v plunder; strip of; n **despoliation**.

despond v lose hope, courage; be dejected a **despondent**; n **despondency**.

despot n tyrant, oppressor; n **despotism** tyranny.

dessert n fruit, sweet served at end of meal.

dessert spoon n medium-sized spoon.

destination n place where sb/sth is going, being sent.

destine v determine future of; intend; n **destiny** pre-ordained fate.

destined a 1 fated 2 intended.

destitute a extremely poor; lacking; penniless; n **destitution**.

destroy v ruin; demolish; n **destroyer** one that destroys; type of fast warship; as **destructible; destructive** ruinous; mischievous; n **destruction**.

desultory a rambling; aimless; disconnected.

detach v unfasten; disconnect; a **-ed**; separate; impartial; aloof; n **-ment 1** separation 2 unconcern 3 number of troops etc. detached for special duty; a **-able**.

detail v deal with item by item; select for duty; n small part; item.

detain v hinder; withold; retain in custody; n **detention** forced delay; keeping in custody.

detainee n person detained, esp by police.

detect v discover; find out; ns **detection; detective** police investigator of crime; **detector** one who detects; rad frequency changer.

détente n Fr reduction of international political tension.

detention n being kept in a place against your will, esp. as a pupil in school.

deter v **-terring, terred.** hinder; discourage; a, n **deterrent.**

detergent a cleansing; n cleansing, purifying substance.

deteriorate v become worse;

depreciate; n **-ation**.

determine v decide; resolve; set limit to, fix; as **determined** resolute; **determinate** fixed; n **-ation** resolution.

determinant n that which decides or controls result.

determiner n ling word which identifies a noun and stands before other adjectives, eg the, this, that; **determinism** n belief that all is decided in life and cannot be changed; n **determinist;** a **-istic**.

deterrent n, a (thing) which deters.

detest v hate, abhor, loathe; a **-able;** n **-ation**.

dethrone v remove from throne, depose; n **-ment**.

detonate v explode (bomb etc.); ns **-ator; -ation**, violent explosion.

detour n going round; alternative route.

detoxify v remove poison from, also **detoxificate;** n **detoxification**.

detract (from) v take away from; disparage; n **detraction**.

detrain v set down, alight from train.

detriment n harm; loss; injury; a **-al** damaging.

detritus n rock debris; n **detrition** wearing down by friction.

deuce n 1 die or playing card with two spots 2 score 40-all, in tennis; a **deuced** excessive.

deus ex machina n Lat person

whose sudden intervention solves an otherwise insoluble problem.

Deutschmark n main unit of German currency.

devaluate v reduce in value; v devalue; n devaluation.

devalue v reduce in value, esp currency; n **devaluation**.

devastate v lay waste, make desolate; n -**ation**.

develop v grow; unfold; elaborate; cause to appear esp image on photographic plate; exploit building site; ns -**er**; -**ment**.

developing country n poor country trying to improve economy and living conditions.

development a **developmental** involved in development; adv -**ly**.

deviance n change from normality; a, n **deviant** (person) showing deviance.

deviate v turn aside; diverge; ns -**ator**; -**ation**; a **devious** rambling; crooked; fig shifty.

device n 1 tool or gadget 2 trick 3 lit special use of words 4 her emblem; pl idm **leave sb to his/her own devices** let sb solve a problem in his/her own way.

devil n Spirit of evil, Satan; wicked, evil person; a **devilish** sl very; ns **devilry** cruel behaviour; **devilment** mischievous prank; v **devil** 1 grill with hot spices 2 do hack work for another.

devil-may-care a reckless.

devil's advocate n person

challenging a proposal or idea simply in order to test its validity.

devious a 1 not direct 2 cunningly dishonest; n -**ness**.

devise v 1 invent; contrive; plan 2 leave by will.

devoid (of) a lacking, without.

devolution n transfer of power to others.

devolve v transfer; delegate; phr v **devolve (up)on** fall upon; leg pass by succession.

devote v set apart, dedicate; addict oneself to; a **devotee** one fervidly devoted; **devotion** strong affection; adherence; pl religious observances; a **devotional**.

devoted a 1 zealous 2 dedicated.

devour v eat voraciously; consume; fig read eagerly, absorb; n **devourer**.

devout a pious; devoted, earnest.

dew n condensed moisture from air, falling on earth; v wet with, or as dew; n **dewiness**; a **dewy**; n **dewpond** ancient artificial pond.

dexterity n adroitness, manual and mental; deftness; manual skill; a **dexterous** skilful; easy; a **dexter** on right-hand side; her on spectator's left.

dextrose n starch sugar, glucose.

DF abbr Defender of the Faith.

DFC abbr Distinguished Flying Cross.

DFM abbr Distinguished Flying Medal.

DI abbr Detective Inspector.

di- prefix 1 double 2 composed of two atoms.

dia- prefix forms compounds with meaning through, across, apart. Where the meaning may be deduced from the simple word, the compounds are not given here.

diabetes n disease characterised by excess sugar in urine; a, n **diabetic**.

diabolic(al) a devilish, fiendish; sl very bad, unpleasant.

diaconal a of a deacon(ess).

diacritic a distinctive; n mark showing phonetic value.

diadem n fillet, crown.

diaeresis n sign (¨) placed over second vowel of two, to indicate separate pronunciation.

diagnose v identify disease from symptoms; n **diagnosis**; a **diagnostic**.

diagonal a oblique; n line from corner to corner; adv -**ly**.

diagram n plan, chart; geometric illustration of theorem; a **diagrammatic**; adv -**ly**.

dial n 1 face of clock 2 graduated face of gauge, meter, compass etc 3 disc on automatic telephone 4 sl human face; v use telephone.

dialect n regional form of language.

dialectics n pl art of logical discussion and disputation.

dialogue n conversation; its representation in writing, in drama, books etc.

dialysis n med process for purifying blood.

diamanté n, a (material) studded with tiny sparkling stones.

diameter n straight line passing from side to side, through centre of solid or geometric figure; length of such line; unit of magnifying power of lenses; a **diametrical** opposite (adv -ally).

diamond n 1 hard, brilliant precious stone of crystalized carbon 2 suit of cards 3 rhombus; a made of, set with diamonds.

diamond jubilee n 60th anniversary celebration.

diamond wedding n 60th anniversary of marriage.

dianthus n genus of plants, including pinks, etc.

diapason n 1 range, compass of voice, instrument 2 organ stop.

diaper n 1 linen cloth woven with diamond pattern 2 baby's nappy.

diaphanous a transparent, translucent.

diaphragm n 1 muscular wall between thorax and abdomen 2 device controlling transmission of light, sound etc. 3 vibrating disc producing sound waves 4 contraceptive device for women.

diarrhoea n excessive,

irritable laxity of bowels.

diary n daily record, esp of personal events or thoughts; book used for keeping such record; n **diarist**.

Diaspora n exile and dispersal of Jews to other countries.

diastole n dilation of heart muscle.

diathermy n electro-medical treatment with high frequency current.

diatonic a mus using regular major or minor scales.

diatribe n vituperative attack; abusive criticism.

dibber, dibble n pointed tool for making holes in ground, for seeds or plants; v **dibble** use a dibble.

dice n pl (sing **die**) 1 cubes marked on each side (1-6 spots), used in game of chance 2 small cubes of meat, vegetables etc.; v 1 to gamble with dice 2 cut into small cubes; idm **dice with death** coll risk one's life; a **dicey** not certain; risky.

dichotomy n division into two parts.

dick n US dated sl policeman.

dickens idm **what the dickens** coll giving force to what is said.

dicker v haggle, bargain, chaffer.

dicky n open seat at back of car; sl false shirt-front; a weak.

dickybird n (word used to children for) bird; idm **not a dickybird** coll not a word.

Dictaphone [TM] small

recording machine for dictating messages.

dictate v 1 speak or read aloud for another to transcribe 2 command 3 prescribe; impose arbitrarily; n order, command; ns **dictation; dictator** despot, absolute ruler; **dictatorship;** a **dictatorial** overbearing, imperious.

diction n choice and use of word.

dictionary n book listing words alphabetically, with their meanings etc.; reference books with details of subject arranged alphabetically.

dictum n **dicta**. formal statement; maxim.

didactic a intended to instruct; dictatorial.

diddle v cheat, swindle.

didgeridoo n Australian wind instrument of bamboo.

didn't contracted form of did not.

die[1] v **dying, died.** expire; cease; grow weaker; wither; idm **be dying for/to** want urgently; idm **die hard** resist change; take long to disappear; phr vs **die away** fade until no longer noticeable; **die down** subside; **die off** die one by one; **die out** become extinct; n **diehard** one who resists change to the end.

die[2] idm **the die is cast** an irreversible decision has been made.

diesel a of oil-burning internal

combustion engine.

diet[1] n usual food; planned feeding, for medical reasons; v follow prescribed diet, esp to lose weight; a **dietary**; n pl **dietetics** science of diet; n **dietician, dietitian** expert in nutrition and dietary requirements.

diet[2] n international or parliamentary assembly, conference.

differ v disagree; be unlike; quarrel; n **difference** disagreement; dissimilarity; remainder left after subtraction a **different** unlike; separate, distinct; a **differential** relating to, showing difference in outward circumstances; n math having small quantitative differences; **d. gear** one enabling rear wheels to revolve at different speeds, when cornering; v **differentiate** discriminate; become different.

differential calculus n branch of mathematics concerned with rates of change, etc.

difficult a not easy; needing great physical or mental effort; hard to please; n **difficulty** obstacle; objection; pl **difficulties** in trouble esp financial.

diffident a shy; self-effacing; timid; n **diffidence**.

diffract v break up light into bands of colour or dark and light; n **diffraction**.

diffuse v scatter, spread

around; radiate; a 1 not localized 2 verbose; ns **diffusion;** act of diffusing; dissemination; **diffuser;** a **diffusive** tending to diffuse.

dig v **digging, dug.** 1 turn over and break up (earth) 2 make hole (in earth, sand, etc) 3 coll understand 4 prod; idm **dig sb in the ribs** give sb a hard nudge; idm **dig into one's pocket(s)** provide money reluctantly; phr vs **dig in** 1 settle securely into a place or activity 2 coll begin eating; **dig up** 1 unearth 2 reveal 3 invent; n **dig** 1 act of digging 2 prod 3 gibe; idm **get a dig (in) at** tease or criticize.

digest v 1 convert food in digestive tract for assimilation into blood 2 summarize, condense 3 absorb mentally; n classified summary; magazine containing condensed versions of books, etc.; as **digestive; digestible;** n **digestion.**

digit n 1 any figure 1 to 9 2 finger or toe; a **digital** numerical; adv **-ly;** v **digitalize** express in digital form.

digital computer n computer with data stored in digital form through electronic circuits.

digital piano n keyboard instrument with sound produced artificially by digital electronic means.

digital recording n recording made by converting sound into electrical pulses using binary digits.

digitalis n genus of plants including foxglove; drug made from foxglove.

dignify v do honour to; exalt; ennoble; n **dignity** stateliness; serenity; high office, rank; a **dignified** stately; serene; n **dignitary** holder of high office esp in church.

digress v depart from main subject esp in talking, writing, etc.; wander, ramble; n **-ion.**

digs n coll lodgings.

dihedral a having two plane faces.

dike, dyke n ditch; embankment or causeway to prevent flooding.

diktat n unreasonable command.

dilapidate v fall or allow to fall into disrepair; deteriorate; a **dilapidated** fallen into disrepair; (of persons) shabby, down-at-heel; n -ation.

dilate v expand; swell; write, speak at length; n **dil(at)ation.**

dilatory a causing delay; slow; belated; n **dilatoriness.**

dilemma n choice of evils; quandary.

dilettante n It one with superficial knowledge of fine arts; a unprofessional.

diligent a painstaking; industrious; n **diligence.**

dill n herb of carrot family, used medicinally and for flavouring.

dilly dally v coll delay.

dilute v weaken, thin down fluid by adding another fluid; a **diluted**; n, a **diluent**; n **dilution**.

diluvium n deposit left flood or glacier; as **diluvial**; **diluvian**.

dim a **dimmer**, **dimmest**. 1 faint; not bright 2 unintelligent; adv **-ly**; n **-ness** **dimming**, **dimmed**. make or become dim; idm **take a dim view** disapprove.

dime n (in U.S.A.) ten-cent coin.

dimension n length, breadth, thickness; extent; size; algebra number of factors in a term; a **dimensional**.

diminish v lessen; reduce; n **diminution**; a **diminutive** tiny.

diminished responsibility n leg mental state where one cannot be held fully responsible for actions.

diminishing returns n state where more effort or investment leads to reduction in profits.

diminuendo n mus gradual decrease in loudness.

dimity n corded cotton fabric.

dimmer n device to vary brightness of light (also d. **switch**).

dimple n small depression in surface of skin, esp of cheek; v make dimples.

dimwit n coll stupid person; a **dimwitted**.

DIN n 1 phot logarithmic expression of film speed 2 elec type of plug or socket used for audio, video connections.

din n loud continuous noise; clamour; v **dinning**, **dinned**. make din; phr v **din sth into sb** tell sb sth repeatedly to make it fully understood.

dine v take, give dinner to; phr vs **dine out** eat away from home; **dine out on** enjoy popularity from (a story, piece of news) ns **diningroom**; **diner** one who dines; **dining-car** on train; **diner** n 1 person dining 2 dining car 3 US eating house.

ding v make ringing sound; n **dingdong** 1 sound of bell 2 coll equally balanced, hard-fought fight.

dinghy n small boat (usu with sails).

dingle n dell; small valley.

dingo n Australian wild dog.

dingy a dull; dirty; shabby; n **dinginess**.

dining car n railway coach with meals served by waiters.

dinkum a Aust genuine.

dinky a Brit coll tiny and attractive; US coll small and insignificant.

dinner n main meal of the day, eaten in the middle of the day or in the evening.

dinosaur n gigantic, extinct reptile.

dint n dent, mark; **by dint of** by force of.

diocese n district under jurisdiction of bishop; a **diocesan**.

diode n elec semiconductor coverting alternating to direct current.

dioxide n oxide having two parts of oxygen to one of metal.

dip v **dipping**, **dipped**. put, plunge quickly into liquid; lower and raise rapidly; sink, drop suddenly; geol slope down; v phr **dip into** glance at briefly; n act of dipping; hollow; n **dipper** ladle, etc.; kind of bird.

diphtheria n serious, infectious disease of throat.

diphthong n two vowel sounds pronounced as one syllable.

diploma n document attesting holder's proficiency; one granting honour, privilege; state documents.

diplomacy n art of management of international relations; tactful skill in dealing with people, situations etc.; n **diplomat** professional employed in diplomacy; **-matist** tactful person; a **-matic** (adv **-ally**).

dipolar a having two poles; n **dipole** type of aerial.

dipsomania n morbid and irresistible craving for alcohol.

dipstick n marked rod for measuring level of liquid.

dire a dreadful; terrible.

direct v 1 guide; control 2 address (letter) 3 show way

4 focus (aim) 5 order with authority; *a* straight; frank; without intermediary; *n* **direction** 1 guiding 2 command 3 course taken by moving object; *pl* **directions** instruction; **director** one who controls; member of board managing company; **directorate** board of directors; **directory** book listing names and addresses, telephone numbers etc.

direct debit *n comm* system of regular payments by which payee can call for sums to be transferred direct from payer's bank account.

direct mail *n* publicity material sent to many people.

directive *n* official order.

direct object *n ling* noun, noun phrase, pronoun or noun clause following a transitive verb.

direct speech *n* actual words spoken.

dirge *n* lament for dead; mournful song.

dirigible *n* airship capable of being steered; *a* steerable.

dirk *n* short dagger.

dirndl *n* 1 Austrian peasant dress with close bodice and full gathered skirt 2 skirt of this type.

dirt *n* 1 earth; soil 2 filth; grime 3 excrement 4 *coll* obscenity 5 *coll* malicious gossip; *idm* **eat dirt** *coll* accept insults without protest; *idm* **dirt cheap** *coll* very cheap; *a* **dirty** 1 not clean 2 causing dirt 3 foul;

obscene; indecent 4 unfair 5 (of weather) rough 6 (of colour) dingy; *adv* **dirtily;** *n* **dirtiness;** *idm* **dirty old man** *coll* older man taking unhealthy interest in sex, *esp* in adolescent girls; *idm* **dirty great** *sl* very great; **dirt-track** *n* rough cinder track for motor-cycle races.

dirty work *n* 1 unpleasant manual work 2 *coll* illegal or dishonest activity; *idm* **do sb's dirty work** consent to act immorally, illegally on sb else's orders.

dis- *prefix expressing* separation; negation *or* reversal; deprivation; *eg* **disable** make unfit; **disorder** lack of order; **dispossess** deprive of possession. *Where the meaning may be deduced from the simple word, the compounds are not given here.*

disability *n* handicap; incapacity.

disabuse *v* undeceive, free from illusion.

disadvantage *n* unfavourable condition or situation; *as* **disadvantaged; disadvantageous.**

disaffection *n* disloyalty; *a* **disaffected** discontented, seditious.

disaffiliate *a* sever links with; *n* **-ation.**

disagree *v* differ; quarrel; *phr v* **disagree with** (of health) not to suit; *n* **-ment** difference of opinion, dispute; *a* **-able** bad tempered; distasteful;

adv **-ably.**

disallow *v* refuse to sanction; prohibit.

disappear *v* vanish; *n* **disappearance.**

disappoint *v* fail to fulfil the desires or hopes of; *n* **-ment;** *as* **disappointed** (*adv* -ly); **disappointing** (*adv* -ly).

disapprove (of) *v* show, express unfavourable attitude (to); *a* **disapproving** *n* **disapproval.**

disarm *v* deprive of weapons; conciliate; reduce armaments; *n* **disarmament.**

disarrange *v* make untidy.

disarray *v* throw into confusion; disturb.

disaster *n* sudden great misfortune; calamity; *a* **disastrous.**

disavow *v* repudiate; deny belief in; *n* **disavowel.**

disband *v* scatter, disperse; break up (organized body, etc).

disbar *v* expel from the Bar (of barristers).

disbelief *n* lack of belief; *v* **disbelieve** *a* **disbelieving.**

disburse *v* give, pay out, spend money; *n* **disbursement.**

disc, disk *n* round thin object; gramophone record; *n* **disc jockey** *sl* radio announcer of programme of recorded popular music.

discard *v* throw aside as valueless; reject; cast off.

discern *v* make out; distinguish (by senses or with mind); *as* **discerning,** shrewd; **discriminating; discernible**

that can be clearly seen; n **discernment**, insight; keen judgment.

discharge v 1 fire (gun etc) 2 emit 3 unload (ship) 4 dismiss 5 release; n 1 act of discharging 2 release 3 matter discharged or emitted 4 payment.

disciple n follower, one who learns from another, *esp* one of Jesus' twelve Apostles.

discipline n systematic training in obedience, self-control and orderliness; maintenance of order and control; v control; train mentally, morally, physically; n **disciplinarian** one who enforces strict discipline; a **disciplinary**.

disclaim v repudiate, disown; n **disclaimer**; *leg* renunciation of right, title etc.

disclose v reveal, bring to light; make known; n **disclosure**, revelation.

disco n 1 party with dancing to recorded pop music 2 club or place where disco dancing occurs 3 type of music for this dancing (*also* **disco music**).

discography n list of recordings on disc.

discolour v alter, change colour of; stain; n **discoloration**.

discombobulate v US coll confuse.

discomfit v disconcert; defeat; n **discomfiture**.

discomfort n 1 lack of comfort 2 embarrassment.

discompose v disturb calmness of, agitate; n **discomposure**.

disconcert v discompose, embarrass.

disconnect v 1 detach 2 deprive of service *eg* telephone; a **-ed** 1 detached 2 incoherent; n **disconnection**.

disconsolate a forlorn; sad; unhappy.

discord n 1 disagreement; strife 2 harsh sound; a **-ant**; n **-ance**.

discothèque n Fr disco.

discount n sum deducted from debt, for prompt or cash settlement; v 1 pay or receive money in advance in payment (for bill of exchange etc not yet due) 2 depreciate 3 allow for exaggeration.

discountenance v disapprove; discourage.

discourage v dishearten; advise against; try to prevent; n **-ment**.

discourse n speech; lecture; conversation; v lecture; preach; converse.

discourteous a impolite; adv **-ly**.

discover v find out, *esp* something unknown before; ns **discovery; discoverer**.

discredit v 1 spoil the good reputation of 2 create doubts about 3 not believe; a **-able** shameful; adv **-ably**.

discreet a careful, prudent, circumspect; ns **-ness**.

discrepancy n inconsistency; contradiction; a **discrepant**.

discrete a clearly separate.

discretion n 1 tact 2 ability to judge well; idm **at sb's discretion** according to sb's own decision; idm **the age/years of discretion** maturity; a **discretionary** allowing freedom of decision.

discriminate v make a distinction; idm **discriminate against/in favour of sb** treat sb worse/better than other people; as **discriminating** showing good judgement; **discriminatory** discriminating against; n **discrimination**.

discursive a dealing with wide range of subjects; rambling.

discus n heavy disc thrown in contest of strength.

discuss v debate fully; argue in detail, n **discussion**.

disdain v treat with contempt, scorn; n scorn; aloofness; a **disdainful**.

disease n illness; ailment; a **diseased** suffering from or impaired by disease.

disembark v go, put ashore from ship; n **-ation**.

disembodied a not seeming to belong to a body.

disembody v free from the body.

disembroil v free from entanglement.

disenchant v disillusion; n **-ment**.

disengage v release, set free; a **disengaged** free, at leisure.

disestablish v deprive of established status; n **-ment**.

disfavour n idm **fall into disfavour** go out of favour.

disfigure v mar; render unsightly; ns **-ment** defect; blemish; **disfiguration**.

disfranchise v deprive of rights of citizenship, of right to vote.

disfrock v = defrock.

disgorge v give up; eject from throat.

disgrace v bring shame on; dismiss from favour; n shame, disrepute; dishonour; a **-ful** shameful.

disgruntled a displeased; sulky; in bad temper.

disguise v change appearance of; conceal identity of; n deceptive appearance; misrepresentation.

disgust n strong aversion; repugnance; v fill with loathing; nauseate; a **-ing** repulsive, sickening.

dish n shallow vessel with rim, for holding, cooking food; contents of dish; v **1** serve in dish **2** sl upset, spoil; idm **dish out** coll give away lavishly; idm **dish it out** sl attack with words or blows; phr v **dish up** coll **1** serve up (food) **2** concoct (ideas, etc).

deshabille = deshabille.

dishcloth n cloth used for washing dishes, wiping tables and kitchen surfaces.

dishearten v make despondent, depress; a **-ing**.

dishevelled a (of hair) ruffled, untidy; unkempt in appearance.

dishonest n not honest; deceitful; adv **-ly**; n **dishonesty**.

dishonour n (US **dishonor**) disgrace; v **1** bring disgrace to **2** (of bank) refuse to cash cheque a **-able**; adv **-ably**.

dishwasher n person or machine that washes dishes.

dishwater n water left from washing up.

disillusion v make aware of unpleasant truth; as **disillusioned, disillusioning**; n **-ment**.

disincentive n thing which discourages.

disinclined a rather unwilling.

disinfect v destroy infection; remove harmful germs etc; v **-ant** substance that disinfects.

disinfest v rid of vermin, bugs, etc.

disinformation n false information deliberately given to mislead.

disingenuous a fml pretending to know very little; adv **-ly**.

disinherit v deprive of right to inherit.

disintegrate v split up, resolve into parts, elements; fall to pieces; n **-ation**.

disinterested a without selfish motives; impartial.

disinvestment n selling of investments.

disjoint v dismember; separate at joints; a **disjointed** dismembered; (of speech, thought) incoherent; disconnected.

disk n **1** comput disc carrying data **2** US = **disc**.

disk drive n comput device for transferring data between disk and computer memory.

diskette n comput small disk.

dislocate v put out of joint; displace; fig disorganize; confuse; n **-ation**.

dislodge v remove from resting-place; drive out (enemy); n **-ment**.

disloyal a not loyal; adv **-ly**; n **disloyalty**.

dismal a depressing; gloomy, cheerless.

dismantle v strip of equipment, furnishings etc; remove (defences); n **dismantling**.

dismay v alarm, frighten; n apprehension, consternation.

dismember v tear limb from limb; divide up; n **-ment**.

dismiss v **1** send away **2** expel from office **3** banish from mind **4** leg reject (case); n **dismissal**; a **dismissive**; adv **-ly**.

dismount v **1** get or throw down from saddle **2** remove from mounting.

disobedient a not obedient; adv **-ly**; n **disobedience**; v **disobey**.

disoblige v refuse to cooperate a disobliging.

disorder n lack of order; a **-ly 1** untidy **2** lacking self-control; n **-liness**.

disorderly house n leg brothel.

disorient(ate) v take away sense of direction; n **-ation**.

disown v refuse to

acknowledge.

disparage v belittle; throw doubt upon; n **-ment**; a **disparaging**; adv **-ly**.

disparate a essentially different; unequal; n **disparity** inequality; incongruity.

dispassionate a calm; unbiased.

dispatch see **despatch**.

dispatch-box n container for official documents; **the Dispatch Box** Brit box in centre of House of Commons at which Ministers deliver speeches.

dispel v **-pelling, -pelled.** drive away; cause to vanish.

dispense v 1 give out 2 make up medicine 3 grant exemption (from rule etc.); phr v **dispense with** do without; ns **dispenser**; **dispensary** place where medicine is made up; **dispensation** divine decree; eccles relaxation of law; a **dispensable**.

disperse v drive away; scatter; a **dispersed**; ns **dispersion**; **dispersal**.

dispirit v deject, cast down; discourage; a **dispirited**.

displace v move out of place; oust; a **displaced** out of place; n **-ment** displacing; volume of liquid or gas displaced by solid in it.

displaced person n refugee.

display v show; exhibit; make obvious; n parade; showing off; exhibition.

displease v annoy; offend;

cause dissatisfaction; n **displeasure**; anger, indignation.

disport v play; amuse oneself; frolic.

disposable a 1 available 2 to be used once and discarded; n article of this kind.

dispose v 1 arrange 2 make willing 3 adjust 4 determine; phr vs **dispose of 1** get rid of 2 deal with; **dispose sb to** make sb willing to; n **disposal** removal; idm **at one's disposal** available to one for use or for help; n **disposition** plan; temperament; ordering.

dispossess v deprive of property; a **-ed**; n **dispossession**.

disproportionate a out of proportion; excessive; n **disproportion**.

disprove v refute; show to be false.

dispute v discuss; question validity of; oppose; wrangle; n argument; controversy; **beyond d.** finally decided; n **disputation** verbal argument.

disqualify v make ineligible; debar; incapacitate; n **disqualification**.

disquiet v make anxious, apprehensive, restless; n **disquietude**.

disregard v ignore; n lack of concern.

disrepair n bad condition resulting from negligence.

disreputable a of bad repute; adv **-ably**; n **disrepute**.

disrespect n lack of respect; v show this; a **-ful**; adv **-fully**.

disrobe v undress; take off official robes.

disrupt v upset; cause disorder to; a **-ive**; adv **-ively**; n **disruption**.

dissatisfy v fail to satisfy; a **dissatisfied**; n **dissatisfaction**.

dissect v 1 anat, bot cut up for examination 2 divide in pieces 3 criticize in detail; ns **dissection**; **dissector**.

dissemble v conceal feelings, motives etc; deceive; act hypocritically n **-r**.

disseminate v spread abroad; scatter as seed; ns **-ation**; **-or**.

dissension n discord.

dissent v disagree; withhold assent; n **Dissenter** Nonconformist, person disagreeing with views of established C of E.

dissertation n formal discourse or treatise.

disservice n harm or injury.

dissident a not in agreement; n **dissidence** disagreement.

dissimilar a unlike; n **dissimilarity**.

dissimulate v conceal one's feelings; dissemble; n **dissimulation**.

dissipate v 1 scatter; dispel 2 squander 3 engage in dissolute occupations; n **dissipation 1** dispersion 2 intemperance; extravagance; a **dissipated 1** dispelled 2 debauched.

dissociate v separate; sever,

repudiate connection with;
n **dissociation**.

dissoluble a able to be
dissolved, broken up.

dissolute a lax in morals,
conduct; debauched; adv **-ly**;
n **-ness**.

dissolve v 1 liquefy; melt 2
become faint 3 break up 4
terminate; annul; a
dissoluble capable of being
dissolved; ns **dissolvent** that
which dissolves; **dissolution**
act or process of dissolving;
breaking up (esp of
Parliament).

dissonant a discordant; at
variance; n **dissonance**.

dissuade v persuade against;
advise against; n **dissuasion**.

dissymmetry n lack of
symmetry; symmetry in
reverse; a **dissymmetrical**.

distance n 1 space between
two things 2 remoteness 3
aloofness; idm **go the
distance** persevere to the
end; idm **keep one's distance
1** remain at a safe distance 2
avoid being too friendly; idm
keep sb at a distance
prevent sb being too
friendly; v put, keep far
away; outstrip; idm **distance
oneself (from)** avoid being
involved (in); a **distant** far
off; faint; haughty, reserved.

distaste n aversion; dislike;
a **-ful** unpleasant; repellent.

distemper n contagious disease
of dogs; thick paint used for
internal walls; v paint with
distemper.

distend v inflate; become

blown out.

distil v **-tilling, -tilled.**
evaporate liquid and
condense it again; refine by
this method; trickle; ns
distillation; distiller one
who distils, esp alcoholic
spirit; **distillery** place where
distillation is carried on.

distinct a 1 separate 2 easily
seen; definite; ns
distinctness; distinction
difference; high standing or
special quality; mark of
favour; a **distinctive**
characteristic.

distinguish v 1 discern; mark
difference in 2 make
honoured; a **-ed** famous;
celebrated.

distort v spoil shape of;
misrepresent; n **distortion**.

distract v 1 divert (thoughts)
2 perplex 3 drive mad; n
distraction 1 amusement 2
madness; a **distraught**
agitated; driven mad.

distrain v leg seize goods to
enforce payments; n
distraint legal seizure.

distrait a absent-minded;
preoccupied.

distraught a extremely
distressed.

distress n grief; physical
exhaustion; danger; extreme
poverty; v afflict, cause
mental or bodily pain to; as
distressed poor; **distressing**
painful.

distribute v deal, share out;
disperse; a **distributive**
involving distribution;
ns **-ution; -uter, -utor;**

switch distributing
electricity in motor-car
engine.

district n region; area; locality.

distrust n doubt; suspicion;
lack of confidence in; v feel
distrust.

disturb v alter normal state,
position of; unsettle;
disorder; alarm; ns **-ance;
-er**.

disunite v become, cause to
separate; n **disunion**.

disused a no longer used; n
disuse; idm **fallen into
disuse** disused.

disyllabic a having two
syllables.

ditch n narrow trench cut in
earth, used for drainage or
defence; v 1 make, repair
ditches 2 sl drive car into
ditch; throw away.

dither v waver; tremble;
hesitate nervously.

ditto n the same, as already
said or written.

ditty n short simple song.

diuretic a med causing increase
in flow of urine.

diurnal a daily; lasting a day;
of the day.

diva n prima donna.

divan n 1 low backless couch,
bed 2 oriental council.

dive v plunge esp head first
into water; descend
suddenly; phr v **dive into**
become quickly involved in;
n 1 act of diving 2 sl low-
class bar; idm **take a dive** coll
deliberately lose a match for
dishonest gain; n **diver** one
who dives; water bird of

diving habits.

diverge v branch off set course; separate; n **divergence**; **diversion** turning aside or away; alternative route; a **divergent**.

diversify v make different; give variety to; a **diverse** dissimilar; varied; ns **diversification**; **diversity**.

diversion n 1 rerouting of traffic 2 entertainment 3 distraction of attention; a **diversionary**.

divert v 1 turn aside 2 distract; amuse; n **diversion** entertainment; a **diverting**.

divertimento n -**menti**. mus light chamber music.

divest v deprive (of clothing, of power); idm **divest oneself** get rid of.

divide v 1 split into two or more parts 2 share out 3 separate for voting (of Parliament) 4 find out number of times one number is contained in another; ns **dividend** 1 number divided by another 2 profit on money invested; share of profits etc; idm **pay dividends** bring great reward; pl **dividers** measuring compasses; as **divisible** capable of division; **divisional** pertaining to a division.

divine a pertaining to God; god-like; sacred; n theologian; priest; n **divinity** 1 god 2 theology 3 quality of being divine; v predict; discover by intuition; ns

diviner 1 soothsayer 2 one who finds hidden water, metal; **divining rod** twig used in discovering water.

Divine Office n formal prayers led by RC priests.

divine right n right to power said to be given by God.

division n 1 dividing into parts; sharing 2 one such part 3 thing which divides 4 dividing of one number by another 5 disagreement 6 parliamentary voting; a -**al**.

divisive a causing disagreement; adv -**ly**; n -**ness**.

divisor n math denominator; number dividing another number.

divorce v dissolve marriage; separate; n legal dissolution of marriage; separation; n **divorcee** divorced spouse.

divot n small piece of turf.

divulge v make known, reveal (secret etc.); ns **divulgement; divulgence**.

dixie n Brit large camp cooking pot.

Dixie n southern states in USA.

Dixieland n 1 Dixie 2 style of jazz originating from New Orleans.

DIY abbr do-it-yourself.

dizzy a giddy; suffering from vertigo; confused; v make dizzy; n **dizziness**.

DJ abbr 1 disc jockey 2 Brit dinner jacket.

djinn n genie.

DM abbr Deutschmark.

DMS abbr Diploma in

Management Studies.

DNA abbr chem **deoxyribonucleic acid** (acid carrying genetic information in living cells).

D-notice n Brit notice prohibiting publication of certain classified information.

do v pt did pp done. 1 perform; complete 2 study 3 make 4 be enough 5 coll visit as a tourist 6 coll swindle 7 coll punish; beat; idm **do well by** be generous to; phr vs **do away with** 1 abolish 2 kill; **do down** 1 cheat 2 undermine pride 3 slander; **do for** coll 1 clean house for 2 ruin; **do in** coll 1 kill 2 exhaust 3 wreck; **do sb out** of cheat sb of; **do over** sl attack; beat up; **do up** 1 fasten; wrap up 2 make repairs; improvements to; **do with** idm **can/could do with** need(s); idm **have/be to do with** be connected with; idm **what to do** with how to treat or use; phr v **do without** manage without; idm **do's and don'ts** things which must or must not be done.

DOA abbr dead on arrival.

dob abbr date of birth.

doc n coll doctor.

docile a tractable; amenable to training and discipline; n **docility**.

dock[1] n coarse, large-leaved weed.

dock[2] n artificial basin where ships are loaded, repaired; v

enter, put into dock; ns
dockyard series of docks,
warehouses, etc.; **docker**
dock labourer.

dock³ n enclosure in court, for
accused.

dock⁴ v cut short, *esp* animal's
tail; deduct part of.

docket n 1 label; ticket 2 list
of contents, cases for trial.

Doc Martens [TM] type of
ankle boots with thick soles.

doctor n 1 holder of highest
degree in any faculty of
University 2 medical
practitioner; v 1 give
medical treatment to 2
repair 3 falsify.

doctorate n highest university
degree.

doctrine n accepted belief;
dogma *esp* of sect; n
doctrinaire narrow-minded,
obstinate (person) seeking
to apply theory, regardless of
consequences.

document n written
information, evidence; v
bring written evidence; n, a
documentary factual
(report, film); n
documentation
documentary proof,
evidence.

dodder v move shakily, feebly;
totter; n -**er**; a -**ing** infirm;
senite.

doddle n coll very easy task.

dodge v 1 swerve from, *esp*
pursuit 2 evade by tricking 3
shirk; n 1 act of dodging 2
coll trick; ingenious plan;
device; n **dodger** trickster;
shirker.

dodgems n pl (*also* **dodgem
cars**) Brit small electric cars
driven to bump or avoid
bumping each other in
fairground amusements.

dodo n dodos, dodoes. extinct
bird, with useless wings.

D.o.E. abbr Department of the
Environment.

doe n female of deer, rabbit,
hare etc.

does 3rd sing pres of **do**.

doesn't contracted form of **does
not**.

doff v take off *esp* hat etc.;
abandon.

dog n 1 domestic quadruped,
related to wolf; 2 male wolf,
fox etc. 3 andiron 4 toothed
grip; v. **dogging, dogged**. to
follow and watch constantly,
to hamper idm **dog's
dinner/breakfast** confused
mess; idm **dog eat dog**
ruthless competition; idm
dog's life miserable life; idm
**(dressed) like a dog's
dinner** coll smartly dressed;
idm **dog in a manger** one
who prevents others from
enjoying what he/she does
not need; pl idm **go to the
dogs** go to ruin; v follow
closely; as **dogged** obstinate;
doggy pertaining to dogs.

dog-collar n 1 collar for dog 2
coll clergyman's stiff white
collar.

dog-eared a with corners of
pages turned down.

dog-end n coll cigarette end.

dogfish n small fish related to
shark.

doggone, doggoned a, adv US

coll used to express surprise
or annoyance.

doggy bag n bag for taking
home uneaten food from
restaurant.

doghouse n kennel; idm **in the
doghouse** in disgrace.

dogleg n sharp bend.

dogma n article of belief; body
of such theories etc.; a
dogmatic relating to
dogma;dictatorial; adv -**ally**;
n **dogmatism**.

do-gooder n coll person who
tries to do good deeds but is
regarded as interfering.

dog-paddle, doggie paddle n
swimming stroke of quick
short movements.

dogrose n wild hedge rose.

dogsbody n Brit person who
does menial jobs for others.

dog tired a coll utterly
exhausted.

doily, doyley n small mat
placed on, under dish.

do-it-yourself n doing one's
own repairs, decorating, etc,
not using professional
workmen.

Dolby [TM] system of noise
reduction for recording.

doldrums n pl 1 low spirits; 2
calm seas near Equator.

dole n charitable gift;
unemployment benefit; v
give out sparingly.

doleful a woeful; sad;
lugubrious.

doll n child's toy, like human
figure; sl sexist any girl; n
dolly child's name for doll.

dollar n unit of coinage in
USA, Canada etc.

dollop n big shapeless lump.

dolmen n prehistoric stone chamber, cromlech.

dolphin n sea-mammal akin to whale, but smaller.

dolt n slow witted, stupid person; a **doltish** stupid.

domain n land, realm held, ruled over; fig sphere of activity or influence.

dome n convex curved roof; cupola; a **domed**.

Domesday (Book) n record made in 1086, of lands, owners, extent, value.

domestic a 1 pertaining to home or family 2 not foreign 3 (of animals) kept by man; n household servant; v **domesticate** tame animals; ns **-ation**; **domesticity**.

domicile n usual dwelling-place; as **domiciliary** of dwelling-place; **domiciled** residing.

dominant a 1 most important 2 overpowering n **dominance**.

dominate v 1 have control over 2 tower above; a **dominating** n **domination**.

domineer v act harshly, arrogantly; tyrannise; bully; a **domineering**.

Dominican n, a (member) of order of friars of St. Dominic.

dominion n 1 supremacy, sovereignty 2 self-governing territory of British Commonwealth.

domino n 1 loose cloak with mask 2 small oblong piece of bone etc. marked with 1-6

dots; pl **dominoes** game using 28 such pieces.

domino effect n sequence of events each resulting in another or others.

don[1] v **donning**, **donned**. put on; assume.

don[2] n 1 Spanish title 2 fellow, tutor of college.

donate v give; ns **donation** gift; **donor**.

done pp of **do** 1 finished 2 Brit socially acceptable.

Don Juan n Sp coll man having reputation for frequent amorous conquests.

donkey n ass; fig stupid person.

doodle v draw, scribble idly; n design so made.

doom n 1 fate; evil destiny 2 formal judgement; v condemn; destined to ruin; idm **doom and gloom** despair; a **doomed** destined to fail or die; n **Doomsday** Day of Judgement.

door n hinged, sliding, revolving structure for closing an entrance; idm **by the back door** secretly and unofficially; idm **shut/close the door** remove every opportunity; n **doorway** opening so closed.

do-or-die a recklessly daring.

doormat n 1 mat for wiping dirt from shoes 2 coll person who lets others treat him/her with disrespect.

doorstepping n canvassing people at their doors.

dope n 1 kind of lacquer 2 sl foolish person; v treat with dope; drug; a **dopey** drugged.

doppelgänger n Ger double of another living person.

Doric a simplest style of Greek architecture.

dormant a inactive; sleeping; hibernating; n **dormancy**.

dormer n vertical window in sloping roof.

dormitory n sleeping room with several beds.

dormouse n small hibernating rodent, like mouse; pl **dormice**.

dormy a golf leading by as many holes as are left to play.

dorsal a pertaining to, on, near the back.

dose a amount of drug etc. taken at one time; v give medicine; n **dosage**.

doss Brit sl, idm **(it's) a bit of a doss** (it's) a job/way of life that requires little or no effort; phr vs **doss about/around** do very little; **doss down** go to sleep; ns **dosser** vagrant; **doss-house** cheap lodging house, esp for vagrants.

dossier n Fr set of documents etc, concerning particular person or subject.

dot[1] n small round mark or spot; idm **on the dot** punctually; v **dotting, dotted**. mark with a dot or dots; idm **dot the i's and cross the t's** complete the final details; **dot sb one (in the eye)** coll punch sb (in the eye); a **dotted** made of dots; idm **sign on the dotted line** make formal written agreement; *idm* **dotted about** scattered; *a* **dotty** *coll* crazy.

dot[2] *n* dowry.

dotage *n* senility.

dote *v* love blindly; be foolish over.

dot matrix *n* method of printing by pattern of tiny dots.

double *a* twice as much; ambiguous; twofold; **1** *n* thing or person exactly like another **2** twice the amount; *v* make, become double; fold in two; *idm* **at the double 1** running **2** fast; *idm* **double as 1** play another role **2** do another job; *phr vs* **double back** return by the same route; **double up 1** bend at the waist **2** share a room; *adv* **doubly** twice as much; *n pl* **doubles** match for opposing pairs; **doubly** in two ways; twice over.

double agent *n* spy acting for two opposing countries.

double bass *n mus* largest instrument of violin family.

double cream *n* very thick cream.

double-cross *n*, *v* swindle; *n* **-er.**

double dealer *n* swindler *n* **double-dealing.**

double-decker *n* **1** bus with two floors **2** two-layered sandwich.

double Dutch *n coll* incomprehensible speech.

double entendre *n* phrase which can have two meanings, one of them sexual.

double glaze *v* fit window with double glass panel for better heat insulation; *n* **double glazing.**

double-jointed *a* having very flexible joints.

double standard *n* moral premise that is applied differently to individuals or groups.

double stopping *n mus* playing on two strings together.

double take *n* delayed exaggerated reaction of surprise.

double-talk *n* misleading ambiguous speech.

double-think *n* ability to accept two contradictory principles or ideas at the same time.

double wammy *n* double portion of something, *esp* troublesome (US).

doubt *v* be uncertain; waver; suspect; *n* uncertainty; misgiving; lack of belief; *as* **doubtful**; **doubting**; *adv* **doubtless** assuredly; probably.

douche *n Fr* jet of liquid sprayed on to, into, the body; *v* apply douche to; *fig* damp enthusiasm.

dough *n* flour moistened and kneaded; *sl* money; *a* **doughy.**

doughnut *n* round or ring-shaped cake cooked in fat.

doughty *a* bold, valliant; *n* **doughtiness** valour.

dour *a* stern; grim; obstinate; *adv* **-ly;** *n* **-ness.**

douse *v* **1** dip in water **2** extinguish (light).

dove *n* bird of pigeon family; symbol of peace; *n* **dovecote** house for doves; *n* **dovetail** joints with fan-shaped tenons; *v* **dovetail 1** join by dovetails **2** *fig* fit (facts etc) together neatly.

dowager *n* widow whose title derives from deceased husband.

dowdy *a* unfashionable; illdressed, shabby; *n* **dowdiness.**

dowel *n* wooden, metal or plastic peg for joining sheets of wood, metal or plastic.

dower *n* widow's share of husband's property; dowry; *v* endow.

down[1] *n* fine soft feathers; any fine fluffy substance; *a* **downy** like down.

down[2] *adv* towards lower position, size, quality etc.; *prep* from higher to lower position; along; *idm* **down and out** destitute *n* (**down-and-out**); *idm* **be down to sb** be attributable to sb; *idm* **be/go down with** be/fall ill with; *n* **1** movement downwards **2** depressed state of morale **3** hostile attitude; *idm* **have a down on** show prejudice against; *v* **down tools** strike; *a*, *adv* **downward** descending.

downbeat *a* **1** casual **2** pessimistic.

downcast *a* dejected.

downfall *n* collapse; ruin; defeat.

downgrade v reduce to lower grade; classify as inferior.

downhearted a discouraged.

downhill idm **go downhill 1** move down a slope **2** suffer a decline in health or morale.

Downing Street n **1** home of the British Prime Minister **2** fig the British government.

download v comput transfer (data).

down-market a cheaper; less prestigious.

down payment n first payment of instalment payment plan.

downpour n sudden heavy fall of rain.

downright a **1** frank **2** complete; adv absolutely.

downs n pl rolling grassy hills.

downstream a adv with the current of a stream.

Down's Syndrome n congenital abnormality causing mental retardation (also **mongolism**).

downstage a, adv nearer to the audience.

downtime n comput time when out of use.

down-to-earth a practical; unsophisticated.

downtown a, adv esp US to, in the (main business) centre.

downtrodden a exploited; oppressed.

downturn n decline, esp economic.

dowry n money or property brought by a woman to marriage.

dowse v seek water with diviningrod; n **dowser**.

doxology n short hymn of praise to God.

doyen n senior member of body or profession fem **doyenne**.

doze v sleep lightly; be half asleep; n light sleep.

dozen n set of twelve; **baker's d.** thirteen.

DP abbr **1** data processing **2** displaced person.

DPP Director of Public Prosecutions.

drab a mud-coloured; fig monotonous.

drab n slattern; prostitute.

drachm n unit of weight, dram.

drachma n unit of Greek currency.

draconian a harsh; excessively severe.

draft n **1** body of troops for special duty **2** rough sketch, scheme **3** order for payment; v **1** send on special duty **2** make draft; n **draftsman, draughtsman** one who makes drawings etc. fem **draftswoman, draughtswoman**.

drag v **dragging, dragged. 1** pull along **2** sweep with nets, grappling irons etc **3** lag behind; move slowly; idm **drag one's feet/heels** act slowly and ineffectually on purpose; phr vs **drag in 1** involve unwillingly **2** mention inappropriately; **drag on** continue monotonously; **drag out** prolong needlessly; **drag sth out of sb** force sb to say sth; **drag up** mention (to sb's embarrassment); n **drag 1** sth made to be dragged **2** air resistance **3** sl boring person or situation **4** sl inhaling from a cigarette.

dragee n sugar coated fruit or nut.

dragon n fabulous winged reptile, breathing out fire.

dragon-fly n iridescent long bodied insect.

dragoon n mounted infantryman; v enforce rigidly.

drain v **1** draw off (liquid) gradually **2** exhaust gradually; n **1** pipe; ditch; sewer **2** fig constant strain (on strength, time etc); idm **down the drain** wasted; thrown away.

drainage n (system for) draining of waste water.

draining-board n sloping surface next to sink where dishes, etc can be drained.

drake n male duck.

dram n **1** unit of weight; drachm **2** small drink of liquor.

drama n play for stage, radio, TV, etc; a **dramatic** pertaining to drama; thrilling, exciting; adv **-ally;** n **dramatist** playwright; v **dramatize 1** make into play, drama **2** exaggerate; n **dramatization**.

dramatic irony n effect of ambiguous words when audience understand implications unknown to the characters.

dramatis personae n pl Lat

characters in a play.

drank pt of **drink**.

drape v arrange in folds; cover loosely; n pl **drapes** US curtains; cloth; n **draper** dealer in cloth etc.; **drapery** draper's business, goods etc.; hangings.

drastic a having powerful effect; violent; severe; adv **-ally**.

draught n 1 act of hauling 2 drink 3 depth of water displaced by ship 4 current of air; pls game played on chess board; v to draft; n **draughtsman** one who makes plans etc 2 piece used in draughts; **draughtsmanship**; **draught-horse** strong horse; a **draughty** exposed to currents of air.

draw v 1 drag; haul; pull 2 extract (liquid) 3 win 4 obtain (salary etc.) 5 extend 6 attract 7 sketch with pencil etc; pt **drew**; pp **drawn**; idm **draw a blank** be unsuccessful; idm **draw blood** 1 cause to bleed 2 hurt sb's feelings; idm **draw the line (at)** refuse (to go further); idm **draw a veil over** tactfully forget; phr vs **draw back** be unwilling; **draw in** come to the side of the road; **draw on** (of time) approach; idm **draw on sb's experience/knowledge** make use of what sb knows; n 1 act of drawing 2 tie at end of game; ns **drawing** art of depicting in pencil etc;

drawback disadvantage;

drawer 1 one who draws 2 lidless, sliding box in table etc.

drawbridge n defensive lifting bridge over a moat.

drawing pin n large-headed pin for fixing picture, map, etc on wall.

drawing room n room for entertaining people.

drawl v speak slowly and affectedly; n such manner of speech.

drawn pp of **draw**; a pale and tired.

dray n low sideless cart used for heavy loads.

dread v feel fear, misgiving; n anxiety, fear; a awesome; **dreadful** terrible; n **dreadnought** battleship.

dreadlocks n pl long curled strands of hair, as worn by Rastafarians.

dream n illusion of senses occurring in sleep; fantasy; idm **a dream of** a coll a beautiful, wonderful; idm **like a dream** very smoothly; without a hitch; v have dreams; idm **would not dream of** would never consider; phr v **dream up** invent; imagine; pt, pp **dreamed, dreamt**; ns **dreamer, dreaminess**, as **dreamy** vague; **dreamless**.

dreamboat n coll attractive person.

dreary a gloomy; tedious; dismal; n **dreariness**.

dredge v bring up (mud etc.) from under water; n type of

net, scoop etc.; n **dredger** ship used for dredging.

dredge v sprinkle with flour, sugar etc.; n **dredger**.

dregs n pl sediment; fig lowest, most worthless part.

drench v soak thoroughly; give dose of medicine (to animal); n large dose; a, n **drenching** soaking.

dress v 1 put clothes on 2 arrange for display 3 prepare (food) 4 align (troops) 5 apply dressing to (soil, wound etc.); n frock; formal clothes; ns **dresser** 1 one who dresses (actors etc.) 2 assistant to surgeon 3 kitchen sideboard; **dressing** thing applied (fertilizer, bandage, etc.); a **dressy** smart.

dressage n training of horse to make exact movements; performance of these.

dress-circle n first tier of seats in theatre.

dressing down n reprimand.

dressing gown n loose garment worn at home (over night clothes or underwear).

dress rehearsal n rehearsal in costume before first performance.

drew pt of **draw**.

drey n squirrel's nest.

dribble v trickle; n drop; ns **driblet** small amount.

dribs n in **dribs and drabs** coll in small amounts.

dried pt, pp of **dry**.

drift n 1 deviation from course 2 something driven by wind, water 3 general meaning; v move aimlessly; ns **drifter** fishing vessel using drift-net; **drift-net** one allowed to float with the tide.

drift-wood n wood found floating or washed ashore.

drill[1] n instrument for boring holes; narrow furrow for seeds; v bore hole; sow seed in rows.

drill[2] n regular physical, mental exercise; military training; v perform, cause to perform drill.

drill[3] n coarse cotton twill.

drily = **dryly**.

drink v **drinking, drank, drunk. 1** swallow liquid **2** fig absorb eagerly **3** take alcoholic liquor; n liquid swallowed; beverage esp alcoholic; n **drinker** a **drinkable** fit for drinking.

drip v **dripping, dripped.** trickle, let fall drop by drop; n act of dripping; n **dripping 1** falling in drops **2** fat dripping from roast meat; a **dripping** very wet.

drive v **1** force into movement **2** set in motion and control (vehicle) **3** go, travel in vehicle **4** advance strongly **5** hit with force (ball etc.); idm **be driving at** be trying to say; pt **drove**; pp **drive**; n **1** strong impulse; energy **2** private road to house **3** ride in vehicle; n **driver 1** one who drives **2** golfclub; a **driving** transmitting force, movement.

drive-in n a bank, restaurant, etc., serving people in motorcars; a accommodating people in motorcars.

drivel n talk foolishly; n nonsense.

driveway n path in front of house.

drizzle v rain finely; n very fine rain.

drogue n sea-anchor; wind-indicator.

droll a funny; quaint; n **drollery.**

dromedary n riding camel, having one hump.

drone n **1** male honey bee **2** fig idler **3** low humming sound; v **1** hum **2** speak monotonously.

drongo n **-os** or **-oes.** sl stupid person.

drool v slaver over.

droop v sink; hang down limply; wilt; a **drooping.**

drop n **1** small globule of liquid; minute quantity **2** descent **3** decrease in amount etc; idm **at the drop of a hat** instantly; on demand; v **dropping, dropped. 1** let fall **2** become less **3** give up; abandon **4** let down from vehicle **5** end relationship with **6** leave out of team; phr vs **drop back/behind** go more slowly; **drop in/by/around** pay a brief visit; idm **drop sb in it** coll put sb in an embarrassing position; phr vs **drop off 1** go to sleep **2** let down from vehicle; **drop out** choose not to participate; n pl **drops** liquid medicine taken a few drops at a time;

n **droplet** little drop.

drop-out n **1** person opting out of conventional society **2** person failing to complete academic course.

dropsy n abnormal collection of fluid in tissues, cavities of body; a **dropsical.**

drought n lack of rain; long period without rain.

drove[1] pt of **drive.**

drove[2] n moving herd of cattle; n **drover** driver of, dealer in cattle.

drown v **1** die, kill by suffocation in water **2** fig overwhelm **3** muffle (sound); idm **drown one's sorrows (in drink)** drink alcohol to console oneself.

drowsy a sleepy, lethargic; adv **drowsily;** n **drowsiness;** v **drowse** doze, be half asleep.

drudge n overworked servant; v work like drudge; n **drudgery** hard, wearisome toil.

drug n any vegetable, mineral substance used in medicine; v **drugging, drugged.** give drug (esp narcotic) to; habitually take drugs; n **druggist** pharmaceutical chemist.

drugstore n US pharmacy.

drugget n coarse, woollen floor-covering.

Druid n ancient Celtic priest; official of Welsh Eisteddfod.

drum n **1** percussion instrument **2** various hollow cylindrical objects **3** part of ear; v **drumming, drummed.** play drum; rap continuously;

phr vs **drum sth into sb** say sth repeatedly until it is understood; **drum sb out** dismiss formally with dishonour; **drum up** obtain by sustained effort; *ns* **drummer**; **drum-major** commander of regimental band.

drumstick *n* 1 stick used by drummer 2 lower leg of cooked chicken, turkey, etc.

drunk *a* intoxicated by alcohol; *pp* of **drink**; *n* **drunkard** habitual heavy drinker.

drunken *a* intoxicated; *adv* **-ly**; *n* **-ness**.

dry *v* **drying, dried.** remove or lose moisture; *phr v* **dry out** 1 remove the wetness from 2 treat, be treated against alcoholism; **dry up** 1 dry things after washing up 2 be unable to think what to say next 3 *coll* stop talking; *a* 1 without moisture 2 having low rainfall 3 (of *wine*) not sweet; *adv* drily, dryly without emotion; *ns* **dryness**; **dry-dock**.

dryad *n* wood nymph.

dryly *adv* 1 without emotion 2 ironically (also **drily**).

dryness *n* 1 lack of wetness 2 lack of sweetness 3 lack of emotion 4 ironical tone.

dry-clean *v* clean with chemicals, without washing *ns* **dry-cleaner, dry-cleaning.**

dry goods *n pl* 1 grain, fruit, etc. 2 *US* haberdashery.

dry ice *n* solid carbon-dioxide.

dry rot *n* (fungus causing) decay of wood into powder.

dry run *n coll* = **dummy run.**

dry-shod *n* with feet, shoes dry.

DSC *abbr* Distinguished Service Cross.

DSc *abbr* Doctor of Science.

DSO *abbr* Distinguished Service Order.

DTI *abbr* Department of Trade and Industry.

DTP *abbr* desk top publishing.

DTs *n coll* delirium tremens.

dual *a* of two; double; twofold; *n* **duality.**

dual carriageway *n* main road where opposite streams of traffic are separated by a central reservation.

dub *v* 1 confer knighthood on 2 (of *films*, etc.) re-record sound track, with additions etc.; *n* **dubbing**; **dubbin** grease for water-proofing leather.

dubious *a* doubtful; *n* **-ness.**

ducal *a* of a duke or duchess.

duchess *n* 1 wife of duke 2 female peer with status of duke.

duchy *n* land owned by duke or duchess.

duck *n* 1 flat-billed water bird *esp* female of this 2 score of nought in cricket; *ns* **duckling** young duck; **ducky** *coll* darling.

duck *v* 1 plunge person, thing into liquid 2 bob down (to avoid blow); *n* **ducking.**

duct *n* tube for conveying liquid; ventilating flue; *as* **ductile** malleable; **ductless.**

dud *n* 1 unsuccessful person, thing 2 bad coin, note; *a* useless.

dude *n US sl* 1 city dweller 2 man 3 dandy.

dudgeon *n* state of sullen resentment, anger.

due *a* 1 (of *money*) owing 2 adequate 3 scheduled to arrive; *idm* **due to** resulting from; *adv* (of *direction*) exactly; *n* something owed, deserved; *pls* regular fee, levy.

duel *n* contest (physical or intellectual) between two persons; *v* fight duel; *n* **duellist.**

duet *n* musical work for two performers.

duff *a* *Brit* worthless; *v* *Brit sl* mishit, *esp* in golf; *idm* **duff up** *sl* beat; thrash.

duffel, duffle *n* thick woollen cloth; **d.coat** coat made of this fabric.

duffer *n* stupid, clumsy person.

dug[1] *pt, pp* of **dig.**

dug[2] *n* udder; teat.

dug-out *n* 1 hollowed out canoe 2 underground shelter.

duke *n* holder of highest hereditary rank of peerage; *fem* **duchess**; *ns* **dukedom**; **duchy** small state.

dulcet *a* melodious; sweet-sounding; pleasing.

dulcimer *n* old, harp-like instrument.

dull *a* 1 stupid; tedious 2 lacking clearness, brightness 3 blunted; 4 overcast; *v* make, become dull; *ns* dullard oaf; dullness; adv dully.

duly adv 1 as expected 2 punctually.

dumb a incapable of speech; silent; sl unintelligent; adv -ly; n -ness; n dumbness; n pl dumbbells weights used for exercise; v dumbfound strike dumb with amazement.

dumb-bell n 1 short bar with a ball at each end for weight-lifting 2 US coll stupid person.

dummy n 1 sham object 2 tailor's model; 3 bridge hand exposed on table; a sham; used in pretence.

dummy run n practice attempt, not the real thing.

dump v unload roughly (refuse etc.); n rubbish heap; place for depositing refuse; depot for ammunition, stores etc.; pl idm in the dumps sad.

dumper n vehicle used on building sites (also d.truck).

dumpling n small piece of boiled suet, dough; a dumpy squat and short n dumpiness.

dun¹ a of a dull grey brown colour.

dun² v demand persistently for payment of debt.

dunce n dullard; pupil slow to learn.

dunderhead n stupid person.

dune n wind-driven sand hill.

dung n excrement of animals; manure.

dungarees n pl overalls of coarse cotton fabric.

dungeon n dark, underground prison cell.

dunk v dip bread etc in liquid before eating it.

duo n mus 1 pair of players 2 piece for two players; duet.

duodecimal a twelfth; reckoned by twelves.

duodenum n upper part of small intestine; a duodenal.

duologue n dialogue for two.

dupe v deceive; trick; n victim of duping.

duplex a double; twofold; v duplicate make double; make exact copy; n replica; ns duplication; duplicator copying machine; duplicity double dealing, deception.

durable a long-lasting; n pl durables goods expected to last; ns durability; duration length of existence; prep during throughout; in course of.

durance n ar imprisonment.

duration idm for the duration while sth lasts.

Durex [TM] condom.

duress n imprisonment; restraint; compulsion.

during prep 1 in the course of 2 throughout.

dusk n late twilight; a dusky dark.

dust n powdery particles (of earth etc.) suspended in air; v remove dust; sprinkle with powder etc.; phr v dust off start to use again, after long disuse; ns duster cloth for wiping away dust; dust-bin receptacle for household refuse; a dusty (idm a dusty

answer a curt rejection; idm not so dusty quite good).

dust bowl n area suffering from loss of vegetation through drought.

dustcart n vehicle which collects refuse.

dustjacket n protective paper cover of book.

dustpan n flat container for collecting dust.

dust-up n coll noisy quarrel; brawl.

Dutch a, n pertaining to Holland, its people and language; idm go Dutch (with sb) share the cost.

Dutch cap n contraceptive device.

Dutch courage n coll courage gained by taking alcohol.

Dutch oven n covered pan for cooking slowly.

Dutch uncle n idm talk (to) sb like a Dutch uncle criticize severely.

duty n legal or moral obligation; proper expression of respect; tax on goods; as dutiful showing respect; dutiable liable to customs or other duty.

duvet n light warm quilted bedcover filled with feathers.

dwarf n dwarfs or dwarves. person, animal or plant much below usual size; pl dwarfs; v make look small, overshadow.

dwell v live; reside; phr v dwell on keep thinking, talking about; pt, pp dwelt, dwelled; ns dweller inhabitant;

dwelling abode.

dwindle *v* become smaller, waste away, diminish.

dyad *n* two units considered as one.

dye *v* **dyeing, dyed.** impart colour to; tint; change colour; *n* substance, colouring matter used for dyeing; *n* **dyer** one whose trade is dyeing.

dyed-in-the-wool *a* unchangeable.

dying *pr p* of **die.**

dyke *n* = **dike.**

dynamics *n pl* 1 branch of physics dealing with force as producing changes of motion 2 *pl mus* variations in loudness; *a* **dynamic** 1 pertaining to force in motion 2 forceful; vigorous 3 opposed to static *n* **dynamism.**

dynamite *n* high explosive made with nitro-glycerine; *v* blow up with dynamite.

dynamo *n* **-mos.** machine for converting mechanical energy into electrical energy.

dynasty *n* succession of rulers of same family; *n* **dynast** hereditary ruler; *a* **dynastic.**

dyne *n* unit of force.

dysentery *n* disease of large intestine, akin to diarrhoea.

dyslexia *n* pathological inability to spell or read; word-blindness; *as* **dyslectic, dyslexic.**

dyspepsia *n* indigestion; *a* **dyspeptic.**

E

each *a, pron* every one considered separately; *idm* **each way** (of bets) for a win or a place.

eager *a* keen; impatient to act; *idm* **eager beaver** very keen, hardworking person; *n* **eagerness** keenness.

eagle *n* large bird of prey; *idm* **eagle eye 1** good eyesight **2** close watchfulness; *n* **eaglet** young eagle.

ear[1] *n* **1** organ of hearing **2** sense of tune **3** attention; *idm* **(be) all ears** *coll* (be) listening closely; *idm* **sb's ears are burning** sb not present would be embarrassed if he/she knew what was being said; *idm* **play (it) by ear** improvise; *idm* **up to one's ears (in)** overwhelmed (with).

ear[2] *n* spike, cluster of seeds of cereal.

eardrum *n* membrane of inner ear which vibrates in response to sound waves.

earful *idm* **give sb an earful** *coll* reprimand or attack sb with abusive words.

earl *n* rank in peerage below marquis.

earldom title or territory of earl.

earlobe *n* soft lobe of outer ear.

early *a, adv* **1** near start of period of time **2** before the time stated; *idm* **at the earliest** no sooner.

early bird *n* person who arrives early, gets up early.

earmark *v* note or set aside for a specific purpose.

earn *v* gain by labour, merit, etc; deserve; *idm* **earn a few bob** *coll* earn a little money; *n pl* **earnings** wages; salary; *a* **earnings-related** adjusted according to earnings.

earnest *a* sincere; serious; *idm* **in (deadly/real) earnest** with determination; *adv* **-ly**; *n* **-ness**.

earphones *n pl* headphones.

earpiece *n* **1** protective flap on cap **2** part of spectacles that hooks over the ear.

earplug *n* small piece of soft material fitting inside the ear, the keep out water, noise, etc.

earring *n* item of jewellery worn on lobe of ear.

earshot *n* **within/out of earshot** within/out of range of audibility.

ear-splitting *a* unbearably loud.

earth *n* **1** planet inhabited by man **2** dry land; soil; mould **3** lair of fox etc **4** conductor of electricity to earth; *v* **1** cover with earth **2** connect electric wire with earth; *as* **earthen** made of baked clay; **earthly** belonging to earth; **earthy** like earth.

earth-bound *a* **1** unable to leave the Earth's surface **2** lacking in imagination.

earthen-ware *n* coarse pottery.

earthling *n* inhabitant of earth (in Science Fiction).

earthquake *n* tremor of earth's surface.

earth-shaking, earth-shattering *a* shocking.

earthwork *n* bank of earth built as fortification.

earthworm *n* burrowing worm.

earwig *n* small insect with pincers at rear.

ease *n* comfort; freedom from pain, trouble, exertion, poverty etc.; absence of difficulty; *v* relieve pain, anxiety, strain; *idm* **ill at**

ease awkward; *phr v* **ease off/up** make or become less intense.

easel *n* frame to hold paintings, blackboard etc.

east *n* one of four cardinal points; part of horizon where sun rises; eastern countries; *a* situated in, coming from east; *as* **easterly** from, to east; **eastern** of living in the east; *a; adv* **eastward** towards east.

Easter *n* annual festival commemorating Resurrection.

Easter egg *n* decorated egg or egg-shaped confectionery eaten at Easter.

easy *a* not difficult; **easy-going** casual; *idm* **go easy on 1** use economically **2** treat sympathetically; *idm* **on easy street** with plenty of money; *idm* **of easy virtue** promiscuous.

eat *v* eating, ate, eaten. **1** partake of food **2** consume **3** corrode; *idm* **be eaten up (with)** have an intense feeling (of, *usu* negative emotion); *idm* **eat one's words** admit a bad mistake; *idm* **eat out of sb's hand** do exactly what sb wants without question; *idm* **eat one's heart out** be tortured with jealousy; *a* **eatable**; *ns* **eats** *coll* food.

eating disorder *n* illness characterized by compulsive dieting or over-eating.

eau-de-cologne *n Fr* scented toilet water.

eaves *n pl* projecting edge of roof; *v* **eavesdrop** listen secretly; *n* **eavesdropper**.

ebb *n* going out of tide; *fig* decline; *idm* **at a low ebb** in a poor-state; depressed; *v* flow back; diminish; *n* **ebb-tide**.

ebony *n* hard, black wood; jet black colour.

EBU *abbr* European Broadcasting Union.

ebullient *a* boiling; exuberant; *ns* **ebullience** act of boiling over; exuberance; **ebullition** *fig* sudden outburst.

eccentric *a* odd; unconventional; slightly crazy; **2** *geom* not having same centre; *n* **1** odd, slightly mad person **2** device for converting rotary into to-and-fro movement.

ecclesiastic(al) *a* pertaining to church or clergy; *n* clergyman.

echelon *n* arrangement of troops, planes etc., in steplike formation.

echo *n* **1** sounds reflected back from solid surface **2** imitation; *pl* **echoes**; *v* **-oing, -oed**. reverberate; imitate closely.

echo-sounder *n* device for measuring depth of sea or river bed, etc.

éclair *n Fr* finger-shaped iced cake filled with cream.

éclat *n Fr* applause; striking success.

eclectic *a* selecting from various sources; not exclusive; *n* philosopher

who selects doctrines.

eclipse *n* obscuration of light of sun, moon by another heavenly body; *fig* obscurity; *a* **ecliptic**.

ecliptic *n* apparent annual path of the sun.

ecology *n* study of relation of living things to the environment; *a* **ecological**; *n* **ecologist**.

economy *n* management of affairs of household or State; avoidance of waste; *a* **economic(al)** relating to economics; cheap; *n pl* **economics** scientific study of production and distribution of wealth; *n* **economist** student of economics; *v* **economize** cut down expenses.

ecosystem *n* ecological unit with all forms of life that interact within it.

ECS *abbr* European Communications Satellite.

ecstasy *n* **1** rapture; intense exaltation; **2** stimulant drug; *a* **ecstatic**.

ECT *abbr med* electro-convulsive therapy.

ectoplasm *n* substance said to emanate from body of medium in a spiritualist seance.

ECU *abbr* European Currency Unit; *also n* **ecu**.

ecumenical *a* relating to the universal Christian church or to the matter of Christian unity.

eczema *n* inflammatory disease of skin.

Edam n mild-flavoured Dutch cheese.

eddy n eddies. small whirlpool; spiral current of air etc.; v **eddying, eddied.** move in whirls.

Eden n garden of Eden state of innocent bliss (as known by Adam and Eve before their fall from grace).

edge n 1 boundary; extreme border 2 cutting side of knife etc. 3 acrimony; v 1 **give edge to** move little by little, idm **have the edge on** be (slightly) superior (to); idm **on edge** nervous; a **edgy** adv **edgily**; idm **take the edge off** soften; reduce the effect of; adv **edgeways** sideways; n **edging** border.

edible a suitable, wholesome to eat; n **edibility**.

edict n formal order, decree issued by authority.

edifice n large building; v **edify** benefit morally; n **edification** improvement of mind.

edit v prepare for publication, broadcasting; direct policies of editing; ns **editor; edition** one of several forms in which a book etc. is published; total number of copies published at one time; **editorial** leading article; a **editorial** of editor; n **editorship** positon of editor.

EDP abbr electronic data processing.

educate v train, cultivate mind of; instruct; pay for education of; n **education; as educational; educative; n educator** teacher; **educationalist** expert in educational theory, methods.

Edwardian a of (the reign of) Edward VII.

eel n long snake-like fish.

eerie, eery a strange, uncanny, causing fear; n **eeriness.**

eff and blind v coll use obscene language.

efface v erase; reflex keep oneself in background; n **effacement; a effaceable.**

effect v cause; bring about; n result; impression (mental or physical); idm **in effect** in reality; idm **come into effect** come to operation; idm **take effect** begin to operate; pl property, goods; as **effectual** producing intended effect; **effective** producing result; competent; adv **-ly; n -ness.**

efficient a acting effectively.

effigy n image; representation.

efflorescent a blossoming; n **efflorescence;** v **effloresce.**

effluent n a flowing out; stream flowing out of lake etc.; liquid sewage; ns **effluvium** exhalation, smell esp tainted; pl **effluvia; efflux(ion)** act of flowing out.

effort n mental, physical exertion; attempt; a **effortless;** adv **-ly;** n **-ness.**

effrontery n impudence, audacity.

effulgent a shining, radiant; n **effulgence.**

effusion n profuse, gushing speech, writing; a **effusive** profuse; gushing (adv **-ly,** n **-ness**); v **effuse** pour, gush out.

EFL abbr English as a foreign language.

EFTA abbr European Free Trade Association.

eg abbr Lat exempli gratia (for example).

egalitarian n, a (person) concerned with social equality; n **-ism.**

egg[1] n oval body, containing embryo, reptile, etc; female cell for producing young; idm **have egg on one's face** appear foolish.

egg[2] v incite, urge.

egg-cup n small cup for serving a boiled egg.

egghead n coll intellectual.

eggplant n aubergine.

egg-timer n timing device for boiling an egg.

ego n conscious awareness of self; ns **egoism** selfishness; **egoist;** a **egoistic(al);** ns **egotism** self-conceit; **egotist;** a **egotistical** conceited.

ego-trip n self-centered activity, esp one that boosts one's sense of importance.

efficacy n power; effectiveness; a **efficacious** having desired effect; n **efficiency** confidence; a **efficient** adv **-ly.**

effervesce v 1 bubble up 2 be excited; n **effervescence;** a **effervescent.**

egregious *a* remarkable, in bad sense; *n* **egregiousness**.

egress *n* way out; departure.

egret *n* a type of heron.

eider *n* arctic sea-duck; *n* **eiderdown** soft down of eider; quilt stuffed with this.

eight *n, pron, det, dets* cardinal number, one above seven; *n* crew of 8-oar boat; *as, ns* **eighth** ordinal number; eighth part; **eighteen** eight plus ten; **eighteenth; eighty** eight tens; **eightieth**.

either *a, pron* one of two; *adv, conj* choice of.

ejaculate *v* 1 exclaim 2 eject suddenly; *n* **ejaculation**.

eject *v* fling out; dispossess; emit; *ns* **ejection; ejector**.

ejector seat US **ejection seat** *n avia* seat which ejects pilot clear of plane in emergency.

eke out *v* add to; spin out; lengthen.

elaborate *v* work out in detail; *a* complicated; highly ornamented; *ns* **elaboration, elaborator**.

élan *n Fr* vigour; enthusiasm.

eland *n* large S African antelope.

elapse *v of time* pass.

elastic *a* resuming normal shape after distension; *fig* adaptable; *n* fabric having rubber woven in it; *ns* **elasticity** resilience.

elastic band *n Brit* rubber band.

Elastoplast [TM] adhesive dressing to protect cuts and grazes on the skin while healing.

elated *a* very happy; in high spirits; *adv* **-ly**; *n* **elation** exaltation; high spirits.

elbow *n* joint between forearm and upper arm; *v* push, jostle with elbows.

elbow-grease *n coll* physical hard work, *esp* polishing, cleaning, etc.

elbow room *n coll* enough room to operate in.

elder *a* (*comp of* old) older, senior; *as* **elderly** growing old; (*sup of* old) **eldest** oldest.

elder *n* tree having white flowers and black fruit.

elect *v* choose, select by vote; *a* selected, but not yet in office; *ns* **election; elector; electorate** body of voters; *a* **electoral**; *v* **electioneer** canvass for votes.

Electra complex *n psyc* girl's subconscious sexual desire to replace mother in father's affection.

electric chair *n* (in US) method of executing criminal by electrocution.

electricity *n* form of energy, produced by friction, magnetism etc; supply of electrical current, for lighting etc; *a* **electric(al)**; *v* **electrify** charge with electricity; *fig* startle; *ns* **electrification; electrician** mechanic who works with electricity.

electro- *prefix. Makes compounds with meaning by (or caused by) electricity, eg* **electrocute** *v* kill by

electricity; *n* **electroplate** metal articles coated with silver etc., by electrolysis. *Where the meaning may be deduced from the simple word, the compounds are not given here.*

electrocardiogram *n* tracing of electrical activity of the heart *n* **electrocardiograph** instrument for doing this (*abbr* ECG).

electroconvulsive therapy *n med* use of electric shock in treatment of psychic disorder.

electrode *n* either of a pair of conductors of electric current, *eg* from a battery; terminal.

electroencephalogram *n* tracing of electrical activity in the brain; *n* **electroencephalograph** instrument for doing this (*also* EEG).

electrolysis *n* 1 separation of substance into different elements by electric current 2 destruction of hair roots, tumours, etc; *a* **electrolytic**.

electromagnet *n* iron or steel core with wire wound round that becomes magnetic when electric current is passed through it; *a* **electromagnetic**.

electron *n* particle of matter bearing negative charge, revolving round atom.

electronic *a* related to, operated by movement of electrons, by electric current; *adv* **-ally**.

electronic mail *n* transmission of information between computer terminals.

electronics *n* study of behaviour of electrons and application of this to technology.

electronic organiser *n* small pocket device in which personal information is stored electronically and displayed on a screen when required.

electron microscope *n* very powerful microscope using electrons in place of light rays.

eleemosynary *a* related to charity.

elegant *a* refined; graceful tasteful; *n* **elegance**.

elegy *n* song of mourning; sad poem; *a* **elegiac** mournful.

element *n* basic constituent; natural, suitable environment; *pl* **the elements 1** basic facts of subject **2** (inhabitable) weather; *idm* **in/out of one's element** happy/unhappy with one's surroundings or activity; *as* **elemental** relating to elements; **elementary** simple.

elementary school *n* US state school covering first six to eight years of education.

elephant *n* very large mammal with trunk and ivory tusks; *a* **elephantine** huge; *n* **elephantiasis** skin and limb disease.

elevate *v* lift, raise up (physically or morally); exalt; *ns* **elevator 1** person, thing which elevates **2** grain storehouse **3** lift.

elevation *n* **1** act of lifting, being lifted **2** height above sea level **3** angle above horizon **4** architect's plan of one side of building.

eleven *n, pron, det* cardinal number one above ten; team of eleven players; *a, det* **eleventh** ordinal number of eleven.

elevenses *n Brit coll* mid-morning snack.

eleventh hour *n* the last possible moment.

ELF *abbr rad* extremely low frequency.

elf *n* small woodland sprite; *fig* mischievous child; *pl* **elves**; *a* **elfin** fairy like; roguish.

elicit *v* bring, draw out (information); obtain.

elide *v* omit in pronunciation.

eligible *a* fit, qualified to be chosen; suitable.

eliminate *v* remove; get rid of; exclude; *n* **elimination**.

elite *n* select body of persons; aristocracy.

elitism *n* belief that a society should be ruled by the elite class.

elixir *n* powerful invigorating remedy.

Elizabethan *n, a* culture, people and architecture of the time of Queen Elizabeth I.

elk *n* large deer.

ell *n* measure of length, 1 1/4 yrds (1.43m).

ellipse *n* oval; *a* **elliptic** having

sphere of ellipse.

ellipsis *n* omission of word, usually understood, from sentence.

elm *n* kind of deciduous tree; its wood.

elocution *n* art and manner of speaking; voice management; *a* **elocutionary**; *n* **elocutionist** teacher of elocution.

elongate *v* extend; prolong; *n* **elongation**.

elope *v* run away secretly, with lover, *esp* in order to marry; *n* **elopement**.

eloquence *n* fluency; persuasiveness in speech; *a* **eloquent**.

else *adv* besides; instead; otherwise; *adv* **elsewhere** in, to, another place.

ELT *abbr* English Language Teaching.

elucidate *v* explain, make clear; *n* **elucidation**.

elude *v* dodge, baffle; *n* **elusion**; *a* **elusive** evasive; difficult to catch, to remember.

elves *pl* of **elf**.

em- *prefix* (see **en-**).

em *n* unit of measure of type (printing).

emaciate *v* make, become very thin; *n* **emaciation** abnormal thinness.

E-mail *abbr* electronic mail.

emanate *v* issue forth; originate from; *n* **emanation**.

emancipate *v* set free; *n* **-ation** freedom.

emasculate *v* castrate; weaken; *n* **-ation**.

embalm v preserve corpse from decay, by use of preservatives; n -ment.

embankment n artificial bank carrying road, railway etc, or damming water.

embargo n order prohibiting movement of ships; official ban on trade etc.

embark v put, go on board ship; fig start, engage in; n -ation.

embarrass v hinder; perplex; abash; n -ment.

embassy n 1 staff, official residence, of ambassador 2 deputation 3 mission.

embattled a fortified; prepared for battle.

embed, imbed v -bedding, bedded. implant deeply, firmly; fig fix deeply.

embellish v adorn; improve; n -ment.

ember n (usu pl) glowing, smouldering ashes; cinders.

embezzle v misappropriate money in trust; ns -ment, embezzler.

embitter v make bitter, worse, discontented.

emblazon v adorn with coat-of-arms; extol.

emblem n concrete symbol of idea, quality etc; badge; a emblematic.

embody v give form to; represent; include, n embodiment.

embolism n med blockage of vein/artery by blood clot.

emboss v cover with design in relief.

embrace v hug, clasp in arms; include; n such action.

embrasure n recess for door, window; opening in wall for cannon etc.

embrocation n pain-relieving lotion.

embroider v ornament with needlework; fig add fanciful details (to story etc); n embroidery.

embroil v involve in quarrel, confusion; n -ment.

embryo n -bryos. unborn, not fully developed animal; any rudimentary object, idea etc; idm in embryo undeveloped; a embryonic; n embryology study of embryos.

emend v correct mistake; improve (text); n -ation.

emerald n bright green precious stone; this colour.

emerge v come out; appear; rise to view; become known, apparent; n emergence; a emergent.

emergency n unexpected happening, requiring swift action; crisis.

emeritus n title given to retired professor etc.

emery n hard variety of corundum, used for grinding etc n emery cloth, -paper cloth, paper coated with ground emery.

emetic n, a (medicine) causing vomiting.

emigrate v leave one's country to live in another; ns -ation; emigrant.

eminence n Fr distinction, fame; height, high ground; title of cardinal; a eminent

outstanding; famous.

eminence grise n Fr person who secretly wields great influence.

emit v emitting, emitted. give out; send out; ns emission; emissary one sent on mission.

Emmenthaler n Swiss cheese similar to Gruyère.

Emmy n US award for best TV performance/production.

emollient a softening, soothing; n soothing medicinal substance.

emolument n esp pl salary; profit from employment.

emote v display exaggerated emotion.

emotion n agitation of feelings (joy, fear, hatred, etc); a -al given to, appealing to, the emotions; adv -ally.

emotive a stimulating emotion.

empanel v fml select for panel or jury service.

empathy n ability to identify with another person's feelings; v empathize.

emperor n ruler of an empire.

emphasis n stress; emphatic assertion; special importance; v emphasize; a emphatic positive; stressed; adv -ally.

emphysema n med disease of lungs affecting breathing.

empire n (group of States, under) supreme rule (of an emperor.)

empirical a (of knowledge) based on experience and observation, not theory *adv* -ly; *ns* empiricism, - ist.

emplacement *n* gun platform.

employ *v* use; give work to; occupy (time); *n* employment work, occupation; use of; employee; employer.

emporium *n* -s *or* -ia. large general store; trading centre.

empower *v* authorize; enable.

empress *n* 1 female ruler of empire 2 wife of emperor.

empty *a* -tier, -tiest. containing nothing; unoccupied; pointless, stupid; *v* -tying, -tied. make, become, devoid of contents; *n* emptiness.

empty-headed *a* foolish; devoid of common sense.

empyrean *n* highest heaven; the sky; *a* empyreal.

EMS *abbr* European Monetary System.

EMU *abbr* European Monetary Union.

emu *n* large flightless Australian bird.

emulate *v* try to equal; imitate; *n* -ation rivalry; *as* emulative, emulous eager to imitate.

emulsion *n* globules of one liquid suspended in another; *v* emulsify.

en- *prefix* (em-*before labials b, m, p*) *forms verbs with sense of* on, into, put into, *eg* encash turn into cash. *Where the meaning may be deduced from the simple word, the compounds are not given here.*

en *n* unit measure of type, half

an em (printing).

enable *v* make able; empower; give means to.

enact *v* make into law; act a part.

enamel *n* hard, glossy coating, paint, used to preserve surface; outer coating of tooth; *v* coat with enamel.

enamoured (with) (US enamored) *a* very fond (of).

encamp *v* settle in camp; pitch tents; *n* encampment.

encapsulate *v* 1 enclose in a capsule 2 summarize.

encase *v* cover entirely.

encephalitis *n* inflammation of the brain.

enchant *v* charm; delight; captivate; *ns* -ment; enchanter; *fem* enchantress.

enchilada *n* Mexican dish of tortilla with meat and chilli sauce.

encircle *v* surround; form circle round.

enclave *n* district surrounded by foreign territory.

enclose *v* surround completely; insert; *n* enclosure object enclosed.

encode *v* convert into code.

encomium *n* speech of praise.

encompass *v* surround; encircle.

encore *n* call for repetition (of song etc); repetition; *v* ask for encore.

encounter *v* meet face to face, in hostility; *n* meeting.

encounter group *n* group meeting to increase self-awareness and mutual understanding.

encourage *v* inspire with courage, hope; further a cause; *n* encouragement; *a* encouraging; (*adv* -ly).

encroach *v* usurp (rights etc.); (of sea) advance on; trespass; *n* encroachment.

encrust *v* form, cover with crust; stud thickly with.

encumber *v* burden; hinder; *n* encumbrance.

encyclical *n* Papal letter sent to whole RC Church.

encyclopaedia *n* book, set of books, of classified information on one or all subjects.

end 1 final limit 2 conclusion 3 cessation 4 death 5 purpose 6 result; *v* finish; complete; cease; *idm* in the end finally; *idm* make ends meet cope with financial problems; *idm* no end of *coll* an unlimited amount of; *idm* on end 1 vertically 2 continuously; *idm* put an end to terminate; *phr v* end up finish a journey or one's life.

endear *v* make, cause to be dear; *a* -ing; *n* -ment. affectionate term or word.

endeavour *v* strive; try hard; *n* vigorous effort.

endemic *a* (of disease) regularly occurring in an area.

endgame *n* last stage of game of chess.

endive *n* kind of chicory, used in salads.

endocrine *a, n* (hormone, or secretion) produced by ductless glands.

endogenous *a* originating within an organism.

endorse *v* sanction; ratify; write (name) on back of (document etc.); *n* **-ment**.

endow *v* bestow; provide permanent income for; *n* **-ment**.

endowment mortgage *n* mortgage of which the principal is repaid by maturing of an endowment policy.

endowment policy *n* life assurance with guaranteed sum payable to policy holder on maturity.

endue with *phr v fml* provide with; endow with.

endure *v* last; remain staunch; tolerate; *a* **endurable** bearable; *n* **endurance**.

endways *adv* 1 end to end 2 lengthways (*also* **endwise**).

enema *n* liquid medicine for the bowels.

enemy *n* opponent; hostile person, factor, *a* pertaining to enemy.

energy *n* power; force; vigour; *a* **energetic**; *adv* **-ally**; *v* **energize** stimulate.

enervate *v* weaken; *n* **-ation** weakness.

en famille *adv Fr* with the family; at home.

enfant terrible *n Fr* person whose behaviour seems shocking, unconventional.

enfeeble *v* make feeble, weak.

enfilade *v* to subject a position or formation to fire from a flank.

enfold *v fml* embrace.

enforce *v* demand, insist on; compel by force; *n* **-ment**; *a* **-able**.

enfranchise *v* grant right to vote; set free; *n* **-ment**.

engage *v* 1 bind by promise, contract 2 hire 3 interlock 4 occupy 5 join in battle; *idm* **engage in** take part in; *a* **engaged** 1 occupied; in use 2 promised in marriage to sb; *n* **-ment** *esp* betrothal; *a* **engaged**.

engender *v* cause; arouse, stir up.

engine *n* any machine converting physical force into mechanical energy; *n* **engineer** one skilled in mechanical science; one in charge of engine.

engineering *n* practical application of physics, chemistry, etc.

English *a, n* relating to England; language, people of England.

engrain *v* dye thoroughly; implant (habits etc.) firmly; *a* **engrained** deeply-rooted.

engrave *v* cut (lines etc.) deeply; *fig* fix firmly; *ns* **engraving** print taken from engraved plate; **engraver**.

engross *v* 1 write out in legal form, or in clear formal manner 2 absorb attention; *n* **-ment**.

engulf *v* overwhelm.

enhance *v* add to; heighten; intensify.

enigma *n* riddle; puzzle; baffling person; *a* **enigmatic (al)**; (*adv* **-ally**).

enjoin *v* insist on; order; give directions to.

enjoy *v* 1 have pleasure from 2 have the benefit of; *idm* **enjoy one-self** be happy; *a* **-able**; *adv* **-ably**; *n* **-ment**.

enlarge *v* make, grow larger; *phr v* **enlarge upon** explain in detail; *n* **-ment**.

enlighten *v* free from ignorance, bias etc.; make meaning clear; *n* **-ment**.

enlist *v* enrol in services; obtain (help, sympathy in a cause etc); *n* **-ment** enrolment, *esp* in services.

enliven *v* add liveliness to; cheer up.

en masse *adv Fr* as a whole; all together.

enmesh *v* entangle (as in a net).

enmity *n* hatred; animosity; hostility.

ennoble *v* 1 make more dignified 2 raise to mobility.

ennui *n* boredom; lack of interest.

ENO *abbr* English National Opera.

enormity *n* atrocious crime; gross offence; *a* **enormous** huge; vast; *adv* **-ly**; *n* **-ness**.

enough *a* as much as necessary; sufficient; *n* sufficiency; required amount.

en passant *adv Fr* in passing; by the way.

enquire *see* **inquire**.

enrage *v* infuriate; provoke to rage.

enrapture *v* delight; entrance with joy.

enrich v make rich; add to; n **-ment**.

enrobe v dress, clothe, invest.

enrol v **-rolling, -rolled.** record, register (name) on list etc, esp as member; n **-ment**.

en route adv Fr on the way.

ensconce v place, conceal safely, snugly.

ensemble n parts considered as whole; mus combination of soloists and chorus.

enshrine v place in shrine; fig cherish memory of.

enshroud v cover, hide completely.

ensign n badge of office etc; naval, military flag.

ensilage n green fodder stored in silo.

enslave v reduce to slavery; deprive of liberty; n **-ment**.

ensnare v entangle; catch in trap.

ensue v follow; be consequent on.

en suite adv Fr (of rooms) forming a unit.

ensure v make safe, secure; guarantee.

ENT abbr med ear, nose and throat.

entail v leg restrict succession (of estate etc.) to certain person, and his heirs; n such settlement; v necessitate.

entangle v involve; catch (as in net); entrap; n **entanglement**.

entente n friendly understanding esp between nations.

enter v 1 come, go into 2 put in writing 3 enrol 4 pierce 5 join; n **entrance** going, coming in; opening; door; ns **entrant** one who enters esp contest; **entry** way in; item noted down (in book etc.).

enteric a of, relating to intestines; n typhoid fever; n **enteritis** inflammation of intestines.

enterprise n plan, project, esp daring, difficult venture; ability to take initiative; a **enterprising**.

entertain v 1 give, show hospitality to 2 amuse 3 foster (an idea etc); ns **-er; -ment** amusement.

enthral (l) v **-thralling, -thralled.** captivate; absorb; hold spellbound.

enthrone v put on throne.

enthusiasm n zeal; intense admiration; n **enthusiast** one animated by intense zeal; a **enthusiastic**; adv **-ally**; v **enthuse** express enthusiasm.

entice v attract; allure; tempt; n **-ment**; a **enticing**; adv **-ally**.

entire a whole; complete; perfect; n **entirety**.

entitle v give title to; give right, claim to; n **-ment**.

entity n real thing in itself; being, existence.

entomb v 1 put in tomb 2 imprison underground.

entomology n study of insects; n **entomologist**; a **entomological**.

entourage n surroundings; retainers, associates.

entrails n pl internal organs; intestines; viscera.

entrance v enrapture; carry away with delight.

entrant n person entering race, competition, etc.

entrap v catch; phr v **entrap sb (into doing)** entice sb (to do).

entreat v beg earnestly; beseech; implore; n **entreaty** urgent request.

entrecôte n Fr beefsteak from between ribs.

entrée n Fr dish served between fish and meat.

entrench v establish firmly in position; n **-ment**.

entrepreneur n Fr 1 person organizing commercial venture, esp with risk 2 person acting as intermediary in business for others; a **entrepreneurial**.

entropy n 1 state of disorder 2 tendency of energy, heat to level out evenly.

entrust v give into care of; charge with.

entry n 1 act of entering 2 person who enrols for sth.

entwine v twist together; wind one round the other.

E number n number used to identify additive to food.

enumerate v count; ns **enumeration; enumerator**.

enunciate v utter distinctly; proclaim; state formally n **enunciation**.

envelop v **enveloping, enveloped.** wrap round; fig obscure, conceal; ns **-ment**; **envelope** outer covering, esp of paper for enclosing letters etc; wrapper.

envenom v 1 put poison into 2 fill with hatred.

enviable a to be envied; adv **-ably.**

envious n full of envy; adv **-ly.**

environ v surround; pl **environs** immediate surroundings.

environment n conditions of life; surroundings; a **-mental;** adv **-mentally;** n **-mentalist** person concerned with protecting, improving the environment; a **environmentally friendly** not harmful to the environment.

envisage v visualize; contemplate.

envoy n agent; diplomatic representative.

envy v begrudge another's success, possessions etc.; feel jealous of; n covetousness; jealousy; as **envious** feeling envy; **enviable** exciting envy.

enzyme n chemical ferment.

ep-, eph-, epi-, prefix: forms compounds with meaning on, upon, during; eg **ephemeral** of short duration; **epicarp** outer skin of fruits; **epitaph** memorial inscription upon tomb. Where the meaning may be deduced from the simple word, the compounds are not given here.

epaulet, epaulette n mil shoulder decoration.

épée n Fr thin sharp sword used in fencing; use of this.

ephemeral a of short duration; impermanent.

epic n long, narrative poem; book or film.

epicene a having characteristics of both sexes.

epicentre n area immediately above origin of earthquake.

epicure n person who enjoys good food and drink and has fastidious taste; a **epicurean.**

epidemic a (of disease) prevalent in one community; n such disease.

epidermis n outer skin.

epidural n med anaesthetic injected into spine, esp to counter pain during childbirth.

epiglottis n structure that covers the larynx during swallowing.

epigram n brief, pointed, witty saying, or poem; a **epigrammatic.**

epigraph n inscription on stone etc.

epilepsy n nervous disease, attended by fits and unconsciousness; a, n **epileptic** arising from, or sufferer from epilepsy.

epilogue n concluding lines of play; short speech at end of day.

epiphany n 1 appearance; act of appearing 2 sudden perception or realization.

Epiphany n festival held on January 6 to celebrate the manifestation of Christ to the Magi.

episcopal a pertaining to bishop; n **episcopacy**

government by body of bishops; n, a **-ian** member of episcopal church.

episode n one of series of events; incident in story etc.; a **episodic.**

epistle n letter esp apostolic.

epitaph n memorial inscribed on tomb.

epithet n descriptive adjective, name or phrase.

epitome n person or thing that embodies a quality etc; v **epitomize** abridge.

epoch n period of time, era, esp of great events; a **epochal.**

epoxy n tough synthetic resin, used in glue.

Epsom salts n pl white powder with laxative properties.

equable a steady, uniform; unvarying; n **equability.**

equal a of like amount, degree, value, merit; equable; n one having same rank, qualities etc as another; v be equal to; n **equality** condition of being equal; v **-ize** make, become equal; n **-ization.**

equanimity n tranquillity, calmness of mind; composure.

equate v consider as equal; reduce to common standard; n **equation,** math statement of equality between known and unknown quantities.

equator n imaginary circle dividing earth into two equal parts; a **equatorial.**

equestrian a pertaining to horses, horse-riding; n horseman; fem **equestrienne.**

equi- *prefix* equal(ly).

equidistant *a* equally distant.

equilateral *a* having equal sides.

equilibrium *n* state of perfect balance; *n* **equilibrist** performer of balancing tricks.

equine *a* of or like a horse.

equinox *n* time of year when day and night are of equal length; *a* **equinoctial.**

equip *v* **equipping, equipped.** fit out; provide, supply; *ns* **-ment; equipage** retinue; carriage and horses; requisites.

equipoise *n* 1 balanced state 2 counterbalance.

equitation *n fml* horse-riding.

equity *n* 1 fairness; justice 2 correction of severe, unfair law 3 market value; *n pl* **equities** ordinary shares; *a* **equitable** just, reasonable.

equivalent *a* equal in value, amount, meaning etc.

equivocal *a* ambiguous; doubtful; *v* **equivocate** use words of doubtful meaning to mislead.

ER *abbr* Elizabeth Regina.

era *n* period of time dating from particular point; epoch.

eradicate *v* root out; destroy; abolish; *ns* **eradication, eradicator.**

erase *v* rub out; expunge; *ns* **eraser; erasure.**

ere *prep, conj lit* before; sooner than.

erect *v* set upright; raise; build; *a* upright; *ns* **erection; erector.**

erg *n* unit of work, energy.

ergot *n* fungus disease in cereals; drug from this.

ERM *abbr* Exchange Rate Mechanism.

ermine *n* common stoat, in winter coat; such fur.

erode *v* eat into; corrode; *n* **erosion;** *a* **erosive.**

erogenous *a* producing sexual desire.

erotic *a* pertaining to sexual desire, love; *n* **eroticism** sexual excitement.

erotica *n* erotic literature or art.

err *v* go astray; make mistakes; be wrong; *as* **erratic** irregular; wandering; **erroneous** wrong, mistaken; *ns* **erratum,** *pl* **errata** mistake in printing etc; **error** mistake.

errand *n* short journey undertaken to perform a task; *n* **errand-boy** boy employed to run errands, *esp* in shop.

errant *a* wandering; roving.

erratic *a* unreliable; unsteady; *adv* **-ally.**

erratum *n* **errata** printed error.

erroneous *a* mistaken; incorrect; *adv* **-ly.**

erst, erstwhile *adv* formerly.

eructate *v* belch; *n* **eructation.**

erudite *a* well-read, learned; *n* **erudition** learning.

erupt *v* burst out; become active; *n* **eruption** bursting out, *esp* of volcano.

escalate *v* increase by stages; *n* **escalation.**

escalator *n* moving stairway.

escalope *n* thin slice of meat; cutlet.

escapade *n* daring adventure; prank.

escape *v* get free; issue out; avoid; elude; *n* evasion; leakage (of gas, etc.); *ns* **escapement** mechanical device; balance wheel of watch etc.; **escapade,** wild, mischievous prank; **escapism** avoidance of realities, by indulging in fantasy.

escape velocity *n* minimum speed required for spacecraft to escape earth's gravitational pull.

escapology *n* technique of escape as form of entertainment; *n* **escapologist.**

escarpment *n* steep hillside, inland cliff.

escheat *n* reversion of property to State, in absence of heirs.

eschew *v* shun, avoid.

escort *v* go with, as protector, or as sign of courtesy; *n* person, persons escorting another.

escritoire *n* writing desk or table.

escutcheon *n her* shield bearing coat of arms.

Eskimo *n* member of N American Indian race living in Arctic.

ESL *abbr* English as a Second Language.

esoteric *a* secret; for initiated only.

ESP *abbr* 1 extrasensory perception 2 English for

Special Purposes.

esparto n Spanish, Algerian grass, used in paper-making etc.

especial a remarkable; principal, particular.

Esperanto n artificial, universal language.

espionage n spying; use of spies.

esplanade n levelled terrace *esp* promenade along sea-front.

espouse v marry; support (a cause etc); n **espousal**.

espresso n -os. strong black coffee.

esprit de corps n Fr group loyalty.

esq abbr esquire.

espy v espying, espied. perceive; catch sight of.

esquire n title of respect used on letter, abbreviated to Esq; formerly knight's attendant.

ESRO abbr European Space Research Organization.

essay v try, attempt; ns short treatise; attempt; n **essayist**.

essence n 1 most important quality 2 concentrated extract from plant, etc; idm **in essence** basically; idm of **the essence** vitally important; a **essential**; adv **-ly**.

establish v set up; give firm basis to; prove; n **establishment** act of establishing; household; permanent civil, military force; business; Established Church.

established church n official

national church.

estate n 1 stage, condition of life 2 landed property 3 *leg* possessions.

estate car n car with rear doors and luggage area behind folding seats (*also* **station wagon**).

esteem v respect, consider highly; n respect.

ester n chem compound produced by reaction between alcohol and acid.

estimate v appraise, calculate value of; form opinion of; n computation, in advance, of approx. cost; n **estimation** opinion; esteem; a **estimable** worthy of respect.

estrange v alienate; hurt feelings of; n **estrangement** decrease in affection.

estuary n mouth of river, where tide enters.

ETA abbr estimated time of arrival.

et al abbr coll Lat 1 et alii (and other people) 2 et alia (and other things).

etc abbr etcetera (and the rest).

etch v make designs on metal, by eating away by acid; ns **etcher; etching**.

eternal a everlasting; increasing; n **eternity**.

eternal triangle n situation when two people are both in love with the same person.

ether n highly volatile liquid, used as anaesthetic; the upper air; hypothetical medium supposed to fill all space; a **ethereal** light, airy;

spiritual.

ethical a moral; n pl **ethics** system of morally correct conduct.

ethnic a of race; a **ethnocentric** having strong prejudice about superiority of one's own race, culture, etc; ns **ethnocentrism, ethnocentricity**; n **ethnography** study of races of humanity; a **ethnographic**; n **ethnology** study of different races; a **ethnological**; adv **-ly**; n **ethnologist**.

ethnic cleansing n the mass expulsion or killing of people of certain ethnic groups within an area.

ethos n fml characteristic spirit or ideas.

ethyl alcohol n drinkable form of alcohol.

etiolated a 1 bot pale from lack of light 2 weak, pale and spindly.

etiquette n Fr polite conventional procedure, manners.

etymology n branch of philology dealing with derivation of words; a **etymological**; ns **etymologist, etymon** primitive word form.

EU abbr European Union.

eucalyptus n genus of Australasian trees, yielding pungent, volatile oil.

Eucharist n Holy Communion; consecrated elements.

eugenic a promoting breeding

of fine, healthy stock, *esp* in human race; *n pl* **eugenics** this science.

eulogy *n* praise, written or spoken; *v* **eulogize** praise, extol; *a* **eulogistic**.

eunuch *n* castrated man.

euphemism *n* mild word used in place of unpleasant one; *a* **euphemistic**.

euphony *n* pleasing sound; *as* **euphonic; euphonious** harmonious; *n* **euphonium** bass saxhorn.

euphoria *n* sense of well-being; *a* **euphoric**.

euphuism *n* artificial, affected literary style.

Eurasian *n* person of mixed European and Asiatic blood.

eureka *interj* expressing triumph of discovery.

eurhythmics *n pl* art of rhythmical free movement.

Euro- *prefix* of Europe.

Eurocrat *n* member of EC administration.

Eurocheque *n* cheque cashable in EEC country in the currency of that country.

Eurocurrency *n* currency of any country in Europe held on deposit outside its own country used as source of finance for easy convertibility.

Eurodollar *n* US dollar as part of European holding.

Euromanager *n* manager dealing with firm's European business.

Europartner *n* European firm with whom one has business partnership.

European *n, a* (inhabitant) of Europe.

European Union *n* political and economic organization of European countries.

eustachian tube *n* duct leading from pharynx to middle ear.

euthanasia *n* painless death, as administered to avoid suffering by incurable illness.

evacuate *v* make empty; withdraw from; discharge (contents); *ns* **evacuation; evacuee** person removed from danger zone.

evade *v* escape; avoid; shirk; *n* **evasion** 1 avoidance 2 excuse for not answering properly; *a* **evasive**; *adv* **-ly**; *n* **-ness**.

evaluate *v* find value of; appraise; *n* **-ation**.

evanesce *v* fade away; vanish; *a* **evanescent** transient; *n* **evanescence**.

evangelic, evangelical *a* of, based on the Gospels; *ns* **evangelism** spreading of the Gospel; **evangelist** one of four writers of Gospels; travelling preacher; *v* **evangelize** preach Gospel to.

evaporate *v* turn into vapour; expel moisture, by heating; *n* **-ation**.

eve *n* evening or day before festival or event; *ns* **even** evening; **evensong** evening prayer.

even *a* 1 flat 2 uniform 3 equal 4 balanced 5 divisible by two; *v* 1 make even 2 equalize; *phr v* **even out** 1

become level 2 become evenly balanced; *adv* **evenly** 1 smoothly 2 equally.

even-handed *a* fair; impartial.

evening *n* 1 part of day between afternoon and night 2 entertainment at this time of day 3 later part of sb's life.

evening dress *n* formal clothes worn at evening event.

evensong *n* service of evening prayer in C of E.

event *n* 1 occurrence; incident 2 race; contest; *idm* **at all events/in any event** in any case; *idm* **in that event** if that happens; *idm* **in the event** as it happened; *idm* **in the event of sth** if sth happens; *a* **eventful**.

eventual *a* final; *adv* **eventually**.

eventuality *n* possible event.

eventuate *v fml* turn out.

ever *adv* at any time; in any degree; *idm* **ever so/such** extremely; *adv* **evermore** always.

evergreen *n, a* (tree, shrub) with green leaves all year.

everlasting *a* 1 lasting for ever 2 continual.

every *a* each one of all; *idm* **every other** 1 all the other 2 alternate; *ns* **everybody; everyone; everything;** *a* **everyday** usual; *adv* **everywhere**; in all places.

evict *v* put out of a property; expel by legal process; *n* **eviction**.

evidence *n* 1 supporting fact(s); testimony 2 sign;

indication; *idm* **(be) in evidence** (be) clearly seen.

evident *a* clear; obvious; visible.

evil *a* bad; depraved; ill-omened; *n* evil thing or act; *adv* **evilly**.

evil eye *n* power to harm sb by a look.

evince *v* show; demonstrate.

eviscerate *v* disembowel.

evoke *v* call forth; cause to appear; *n* **evocation**; *a* **evocative**.

evolve *v* develop, open out gradually, naturally; *n* **evolution** course of development of species; (*a* **-ary**).

ewe *n* female sheep.

ewer *n* large water-jug; pitcher.

ex-, e-, ef- *prefix: forms compounds with meaning of out from, from, out of. Such words are not given, where the meaning may be deduced from the simple word.*

ex, excl *abbr* excluding.

exacerbate *v* make worse; irritate; embitter; *n* **-bation**.

exact *a* absolutely correct, accurate; *v* demand; extort; insist on; *a* **-ing** severe; exhausting; *ns* **-itude; -ness** accuracy.

exaggerate *v* over-emphasize; overstate; enlarge; *n* **-ation** overstatement.

exalt *v* raise to higher rank; extol; *n* **exaltation**; elevation; elation.

examine *n* **1** scrutinize **2** investigate **3** question **4** test knowledge of; *ns*

examination; examiner.

example *n* sample; precedent; model; *idm* **make an example of** single out for reward or punishment to encourage others.

exasperate *v* make angry; aggravate; provoke; *n* **-ation**; *a* **-ating** very annoying.

exc *abbr* except.

ex cathedra *a, adv Lat* (made) with authority.

excavate *v* hollow out; dig out; unearth; *ns* **-ation; -ator**.

exceed *v* go beyond (limit etc.); surpass; *adv* **exceedingly** extremely.

excel *v* **-celling, -celled**. surpass, rise above; be very good at; *a* **excellent** very good; *ns* **excellence; excellency** title given to ambassadors etc.

except *v* exclude; object; *prep* omitting; *conj* unless; *n* **-exception** thing excluded; objection (*idm* **take exception to** object to; *a* **-al** *adv* **-ally**; *a* **-able** likely to offend); *prep* **excepting** excluding.

excerpt *n* selected passage, extract from book etc.

excess *n* amount, sum over normal, usual quantity etc.; over indulgence; *a* **-ive** extreme.

exchange *v* give (something), receive (another thing) in return; interchange; *n* act of exchanging; place where brokers, merchants transact business; district telephone office; *a* **-able**; *n* **-ability**.

exchequer *n* treasury; State department dealing with finance, revenue.

excise *v* cut out; remove cut; away; *n* **excision**.

excise *n* duty on goods manufactured, consumed within a country; *n* **exciseman** collector of excise duties.

excite *v* rouse up; agitate; stimulate; *as* **excitable** easily excited; (*adv* **-ly**); *n* **excitability**; *a* **exciting** thrilling; *n* **excitement**.

exclaim *v* cry out suddenly, loudly; *n* **exclamation** interjection (of surprise etc.); **exclamation mark** (US **exclamation point**) mark of punctuation written after an exclamatory remark; *a* **exclamatory**.

exclude *v* shut out; disallow; not include; *n* **exclusion**; *a* **exclusive** excluding; snobbish; unsociable; (*adv* **-ly**).

excommunicate *v* expel from Church, and deprive of privileges; *n* **-ation**.

excoriate *v* flay; graze, abrade skin; *n* **-ation**.

excrement *n* waste matter from bowels; dung; *v* **excrete** discharge waste matter from body; *n* **excretion**; *n, a* **excretory**, (organ) serving to excrete.

excrescence *n* abnormal growth on organism.

excruciating *a* acutely painful; agonizing; *adv* **-ly**.

exculpate *v* vindicate; free

from blame; n **-ation**.

excursion n journey, *esp* pleasure trip; digression.

excuse v 1 exonerate 2 overlook (fault etc); 3 release from obligation; **excuse oneself** apologize; n apology; pretext; a **excusable**.

ex-directory a (of telephone number) not shown in public directory.

exeat n leave of absence.

execrate v detest; loathe; curse; n **execration**; a **execrable** abominable.

execute v 1 perform; carry out 2 kill 3 complete legal instrument; ns **execution**; **executioner** one who carries out capital punishment; a **executive** able to put into effect (n one charged with administrative, executive work); n **executor** (*fem* **executrix**) one appointed to carry out provisions of will.

exemplar n model, example; a **exemplary** worthy, commendable.

exemplify v **-fying, -fied**. serve as example; make official copy of; n **-ification**.

exempt v from duty, obligation; a not liable to; n **exemption**.

exequies n pl funeral rites, ceremonies.

exercise n healthy physical activity; mental exertion; use of (rights etc); *mil* manoeuvres; v take, give exercise to; use; train.

exercise bike n (*also* **exercise cycle**) fixed exercise machine with pedals.

exert v make an effort; put into action; n **exertion** activity, mental or physical.

exeunt *dram* they go out.

ex gratia a *Lat* payment made as a favour.

exhale v breathe out; evaporate; emit; n **exhalation**.

exhaust v drain off; use up; tire out; n waste gas, steam discharged from engine; n **exhaustion** intense fatigue; a **exhaustive** comprehensive; (*adv* **-ly**).

exhibit v show in public; give evidence of; n thing exhibited, *esp* in museum, or as material evidence in court; ns **exhibition** display of works of art etc; grant to student (ns **-ism -ist**); exhibitor one who exhibits *esp* in show.

exhilarate v enliven; cheer; raise spirits of; n **-ation**.

exhort v admonish; beg earnestly; n **-ation**.

exhume v disinter; dig up *esp* corpse; n **-ation**.

exigent a exacting; pressing; urgent; n **exigence, exigency** urgent need; a **exigible** capable of being exacted.

exiguous a too small; scanty.

exile n banishment; one banished; v banish; expel.

exist v live; be; occur; n **-ence**; a **-ent**.

existentialism n *philosophy* theory that man is a free agent responsible for his own actions; a, n **existentialist**; a **existential** 1 relating to existence 2 existentialist; *adv* **existentially**.

exit n 1 act of leaving, going out 2 way out; v leave stage; go out.

exodus n departure *esp* of many people; *cap* second book of Old Testament.

ex officio a, *adv Lat* by virtue of office (not elected).

exogamy n marriage to an outsider.

exonerate v free from blame; exculpate; acquit; n **-ration**.

exorbitant a excessive; immoderate; n **exorbitance**.

exorcise v expel (evil spirit) by religious means; ns **exorcism, -ist**.

exotic a foreign; rare, unusual; n **exoticism**.

expand v spread out; extend; dilate; develop; *phr v* **expand on** explain in more detail; ns **expanse** wide, open tract of land; **expansion -ism, -ist**; a **expansive** effusive.

expatiate on v dilate, enlarge upon.

expatriate v banish; quit one's country; a **-ated**; n expatriated person; n **-ation**.

expect v await; anticipate; look for as due, right; a **expectant** awaiting; ns **expectancy** anxious, eager anticipation; **expectation** that which is expected; future prospects.

expectorate v spit; cough up (phlegm, etc); n **-ation**.

expedient a suitable; advantageous; convenient; n means to an end; device; n **expediency** convenience.

expedite v hasten, speed up (progress of); despatch; n **expedition** journey for set purpose esp military, exploratory; as **expeditionary; expeditious** rapid; prompt.

expel v -**pelling**, -**pelled**. drive out; dismiss; n **expulsion**.

expend v give out; spend; use up; ns **expenditure; expense** cost; disbursement; **expense** n cost; idm **at sb's expense** 1 paid for by sb 2 making mockery of sb; pl **expenses** costs incurred; a **expensive** costly; **expendable** inessential, of little value.

expense account n arrangement for employer to pay expenses incurred by an employee through work.

experience n living through events, emotions etc; knowledge, skill, gained by personal practice, observation etc.; event witnessed, lived through; v undergo, meet with; a **experienced** skilful, competent.

experiment n trial, undertaken to test theory, discover new facts; v make experiments; a -**al**; adv -**ally**.

expert a skilled; dexterous; n one having special knowledge; n **expertise**.

expert system n problem solving computer system.

expiate v atone for; make amends for; n -**ation**.

expire v exhale, die; come to an end; ns **expiration; expiry** conclusion.

explain v make intelligible; interpret; account for; n **explanation;** as **explanatory; explanative**.

expletive a superfluous; n exclamation; oath.

explicable a able to be explained.

explicate n explain.

explicit a clearly stated; unequivocal; adv -**ly**; n -**ness**.

explode v burst violently, with loud report; cause to explode.

exploit n bold, adventurous deed; v make unfair use of, esp to one's own benefit; develop resources of; ns -**ation**; -**er**.

explore v examine closely; travel in strange region and investigate it; probe; ns **exploration; explorer;** a **exploratory**.

explosion n 1 violent release of energy resulting from a chemical or nuclear reaction 2 sudden increase.

explosive n, a (substance) which explodes; adv -**ly**.

exponent n 1 person explaining a belief, showing a skill 2 math figure showing how many times a number is to be multiplied by itself; a **exponential** resulting from such multiplication.

export v send (goods) abroad for trade; ns **exportation; exporter**.

expose v lay bare; leave unprotected; display; reveal; n **exposure;** idm **expose oneself** display one's private parts in public; idm **expose oneself to sth** leave oneself unprotected from sth.

exposé n exposure of wrongdoing.

exposition n 1 setting out; explaining 2 exhibition.

ex post facto a, adv Lat acting retrospectively.

expostulate v remonstrate; protest against; n -**lation**.

expound v explain, set forth; ns **exponent; exposition** explanation; exhibition; a **expository;** n **expositor** interpreter.

express 1 v make known by speech, visual image etc. 2 squeeze out; a **explicit;** of special kind; sent, travelling at fast speed; n fast postal, train service; n **expression** 1 expressing 2 utterance 3 feeling 4 facial aspect; as -**ness; expressive;** adv -**ly;** (n -**ness**).

expressionism n style of art portraying subjective emotions; n, a **expressionist**.

expressway n US motorway.

expropriate v deprive of possession of; n -**ation**.

expulsion n act of expelling.

expunge v wipe out; erase; delete; n **expunction**.

expurgate v remove offensive material from text (of books etc.); n -**ation**.

exquisite a select; extremely beautiful; tasteful; acutely sensitive.

extant a still surviving; still in existence.

extempore a, adv without preparation; a **extemporary**; v **extemporize** improvise; make up speech, song etc, on spur of moment.

extend 1 v stretch out; expand; prolong 2 offer; bestow 3 last; n **extension** stretching out; expansion; addition; a **extensive** widespread; comprehensive; n **extent** area scope; degree.

extenuate v lessen; minimize esp guilt, blame; n **extenuation**; a **extenuating**.

exterior a outside; external; n outward appearance.

exterminate v wipe out; extirpate; destroy; ns **extermination**; **exterminator**.

external a outside; adv **-ly**; v **externalize** give outward expression to; pl **externals** outward appearances.

extinct a 1 having died out; no longer existing 2 inactive (of volcano); n **extinction**; v **extinguish** quench, stifle; n **extinguisher** device for putting out fire.

extirpate v root out; destroy; n **extirpation** total destruction.

extol v **-tolling, -tolled.** laud, praise highly.

extort v obtain money by threats; n **extortion**; n, a **extortionist**; a **extortionate**

unreasonably expensive.

extra a additional; more than usual; n something extra.

extra- prefix: forms compounds with meaning of outside, beyond. Where the meaning may be deduced from the simple word the compounds are not given here.

extract v 1 pull, draw out esp by force 2 select; distil; n thing extracted; ns **extraction**; **extractor**.

extracurricular a not part of course of study.

extradition n surrender of an alleged criminal, by one State to another, under treaty; v **extradite** give, obtain such surrender.

extramarital a (of sexual behaviour) outside marriage.

extramural a outside walls of; associated with, not taking place in University.

extraneous a unrelated to; not essential; foreign.

extraordinary a unusual; exceptional; adv **-arily**.

extrapolate v deduce or guess from known facts or personal observation.

extrasensory perception n ability to acquire information not through the physical senses.

extraterrestrial a (from) beyond the earth.

extraterritorial a outside limits, jurisdiction of country.

extravagant a excessive; wasteful; flamboyant; adv **-ly**; n **extravagance**.

extravaganza n elaborate and costly entertainment.

extreme a 1 remotest 2 of highest degree 3 severe 4 last; final 5 beyond moderate; adv **-ly**; ns **extremist** one holding extreme views (in politics); **extremity** end; great distress, danger; pl **-ies** hands and feet.

extreme unction n sacrament for dying person.

extricate v free from; disentangle; **extrication**.

extrinsic a not belonging to; from outside; adv **-ally**.

extrovert n one whose interests are directed outwards from self; vigorous personality.

extrude v thrust out; expel; n **extrusion**.

exuberant a full of vitality; overflowing; over-abundant.

exude v ooze out; discharge through pores; n **exudation**.

exult v rejoice greatly; triumph; n **exultation**; a **exultant** jubilant.

eye n 1 organ of sight 2 power of observation 3 hole in needle 4 ring for a hook to fit 5 calm spot in centre of storm; idm **an eye for an eye** retaliation (equal to the offence); idm **easy on the eye** good-looking; idm **have an eye for** be capable of judging; idm **in the eyes of** in the opinion of; idm **keep an eye on** watch closely; idm **one in the eye for** coll rejection or defeat for; idm

make eyes at flirt with; *idm*
see eye to eye understand
one another; agree; *idm* **up
to one's eyes in** *coll*
extremely busy with; *idm*
with an eye to 1 keeping in
mind **2** with the intention
of; *v* **eyeing** or **eying, eyed.**
look at; stare at; *ns* **eyeball**
(*idm* **eyeball to eyeball** *coll*
face to face); **eyebrow** ridge
of hair above eye; **eyeglass**
monocle; **eyelash** hair
fringing eyelid; **eyesore**
something offensive to eye;
eye-tooth canine tooth;
eyelet small hole in
material.

eye-catching *a* striking,
attractive. **eye contact** *n*
attracting sb's gaze by
looking into his/her eyes.

eyelid *n* skin covering eyeball.

eye-opener *n* thing, event
revealing surprising new
facts.

eye shadow *n* make-up used
on eyelids.

eyesight *n* power of seeing.

eyesore *n* ugly object, *esp*
spoiling landscape.

eyewash *n coll* deceptive
nonsense.

eyewitness *n* person actually
present at event.

eyot, ait *n* small island in river.

eyrie, eyry *n* eagle's nest.

FA *abbr* 1 Football Association; *n* **FA cup** 2 *Brit sl taboo* fuck-all (nothing at all).

Fabian *n, a* 1 socialist 2 (of tactics) stealthy.

fable *n* short story with moral; myth; fiction; *as* **fabled** legendary; **fabulous** mythical; exaggerated; unbelievable *adv* -**ly**.

fabric *n* structure, framework; woven cloth; *v* **fabricate** *v* 1 manufacture 2 invent falsely; forge *n* **fabrication**.

fabulous *a* 1 incredible 2 legendary 3 *coll* wonderful; *adv* -**ly** extremely.

façade *n Fr* front of building; outward appearance.

face *n* 1 front part of head 2 visual expression 3 *coll* make-up 4 top or front surface 5 dignity; prestige 6 effrontery; *idm* **face to face** close up; in direct contact, opposition; *idm* **in the face**

of (going) against; in spite of; *idm* **on the face of it** judging by appearances; *idm* **to sb's face** openly *v* 1 turn towards 2 meet; oppose 3 cover front of; *phr v* **face up to** 1 meet courageously 2 be realistic about; *a* **faceless** of unknown identity or character.

face card *n US* court card.

facing *n* decorative or protective lining.

face-lift *n* plastic surgery to improve face; *fig* (of building) renovation.

face-pack *n* application to face for refreshing skin.

face-saver *n* thing which saves sb from embarrassment *a* **face-saving**.

facet *n* aspect; side.

facetious *a* not serious; flippant *adv* -**ly** *n* -**ness**.

face value *n* (of money) value shown; *idm* **take sth at its face value** assume sth is

what it seems to be.

facia, fascia *n* 1 flat strip of wood, metal on building 2 part of shopfront, showing name etc 3 stripe.

facial *a* of the face; *n* beauty treatment of face.

facile *a* easily done; fluent; *v* **facilitate** make easier; *n* **facility** ease; dexterity; *pl* **facilities** helpful opportunities.

facsimile *n* exact copy.

fact *n* thing known to be true actual experience; reality; *a* **factual** *adv* -**ly**.

faction[1] *n* group within a political party *a* **factious** 1 caused by faction 2 quarrelsome.

faction[2] *n* TV dramatized version of factual events.

factious *a* causing trouble.

factor *n* contributory force to a result; agent; *n* **factory** building in which goods are manufactured.

factory farm *n* farm with intensive food production.

facts of life *n* 1 facts of sexuality 2 true nature of situation.

faculty *n* aptitude; inherent ability; natural or special function (of mind or body); division of University; collectively, members of such a division.

fad *n* whim; passing craze; pet notion; *n* **faddiness** *as* **faddish, faddy**.

fade *v* 1 (cause to) lose colour 2 disappear gradually 3 become less audible; *phr vs*

fade away die;

fade in/out 1 bring slowly into/out of view **2** make more/less clearly audible.

faeces n excrement; a **faecal**.

fag n **1** Brit sl tedious job **2** sl cigarette **3** (in Public School) junior body servant to senior; a **fagged (out)** exhausted.

fag end n **1** Brit coll cigarette butt **2** coll last (and least interesting) part.

faggot n bundle of sticks for firewood; bundle of steel rods; savoury chopped liver dish.

Fahrenheit a scale of temperature, having boiling point 212°, and freezing point 32°.

fail v **1** be unsuccessful **2** let down; disappoint **3** become weak **4** not function properly; idm **fail to do** neglect to do; idm **without fail** certainly; reliably; n **failing** fault, defect prep without.

fail-safe a designed for extra security in emergency.

failure n **1** lack of success **2** person, thing that fails **3** inability.

faint a feeble; weak; vague; v swoon; n fainting fit.

faint-hearted a cowardly.

fair¹ a **1** market for sale of goods, often with side-shows etc.; trade exhibition.

fair² a **1** just; impartial honest **2** quite good; average **3** not dark **4** good-looking **5** favourable; adv **-ly 1** in an honest way **2** rather; n **-ness** idm **fair and square** honestly; idm **fair dinkum** Aust honestly; idm **fair enough** all right.

fair cop n sl legitimate arrest.

fair copy n corrected copy.

fair game n person, thing considered reasonable to mock or take advantage of.

fairway n **1** navigation channel **2** golf mown part of course between tee and green.

fairy n imaginary being with magic powers; ns **fairyland**; **f. godmother** person who helps sb in trouble; **f. lights** set of coloured lights for decoration, esp at Christmas; **f.-tale 1** story of magic **2** untrue story a magically wonderful.

fait accompli n Fr thing done which cannot be undone.

faith n **1** trust **2** strong belief **3** sincerity; a **faithful** loyal; reliable adv **-ly**; a **faithless -ness**; idm **break/keep faith (with)** break/keep a promise (to); in **f. healing** treatment of disease by prayer.

fake v make imitation of something rare, valuable; touch up; counterfeit; n sham; fabrication; forgery; n **faker**.

fakir n Muslim or Hindu monk.

falcon n bird of prey, esp female trained in hawking; ns **falconer** one who keeps, hunts with, falcons;

falconry hawking.

fall¹ v **1** drop **2** hang loosely **3** become lower **4** occur **5** be killed or wounded **6** be defeated; succumb **7** (of face) become sad **8** enter a specified state; become, pt fell pp fallen; idm **fall flat** collapse; fail; idm **fall foul of** get into trouble with; idm **fall short** be inadequate; phr vs **fall about** laugh uncontrollably; **fall apart** disintegrate; **fall away** disperse; disappear; **fall back** retreat; **fall back on** use as reserve or support; **fall behind** fail to keep up; **fall for 1** be attracted by **2** be deceived by; **fall off** decrease in intensity, quantity or quality; **fall on** attack; **fall out 1** quarrel **2** occur; **fall over oneself** make every effort; **fall through** (of plans) fail; **fall to** begin; **fall under** be classified as; a **fallen** no longer innocent.

fall² n **1** act of falling **2** decline **3** distance downwards; **4 the Fall** Bible loss of human innocence; pl **falls** waterfall.

fallacy n **1** false belief **2** false reasoning; a **fallacious**; adv **-ly**.

fallible a liable to error; n **fallibility**.

falling star n shooting star.

fallopian tube n tube by which egg passes from ovary to womb.

fall-out n **1** radio-active dust

in air following nuclear explosion 2 effects of this.

fallow[1] n land ploughed up, left unsown; a uncultivated.

fallow[2] a of brownish, reddish yellow (of deer).

false a 1 wrong; mistaken 2 deceptive 3 disloyal 4 sham; artificial; ns **-hood** lie; **-ness** disloyalty; **falsity** quality of being false; v **falsify** alter with intent to deceive, misrepresent; n **falsification**.

falsetto n (use by man of) high-pitched head voice as of female.

falsies coll n pl pads used to make breasts look larger.

falter v stumble, be unsteady; stammer; hesitate; a **faltering**.

fame n renown, reputation; a **famed** well-known.

familial a of the family.

familiar a intimate; well known; conversant with; vulgarly cordial; n **familiarity**; v **familiarize** accustom someone to something.

family n 1 group of people related by blood, marriage 2 one's children 3 people with a common ancestor 4 group of related living things 5 group of related languages; a 1 of family members (ns **f. gathering**; **f. planning**; **f. tree** genealogical table) 2 suitable for children (n **f. entertainment**).

Family Credit n Brit welfare payments for poor families.

famine n acute shortage of food; starvation; v **famish** starve.

famous a widely known adv **-ly** coll extremely well.

fan[1] n 1 device causing flow of air; ventilating machine 2 outspread tail feathers of bird; v **fanning, fanned.** cause a rush of air with a fan.

fan[2] n enthusiastic supporter.

fanatic(al) a having violent, unreasoning belief in; n zealot; n **fanaticism**.

fan belt n aut belt connecting engine drive to fan for cooling engine.

fancy n 1 imagination 2 thing imagined 3 desire 4 small cake; idm **take sb's fancy** attract; idm **take a fancy to** become keen on; v 1 like; wish for 2 imagine; idm **fancy oneself** have a high opinion of oneself; n **fancier** one with special knowledge, esp of breeding animals, birds; as **fanciful** 1 imaginary 2 capricious; **fancy** 1 brightly decorated (n **f. cake**) 2 unusual n **f. dress** 3 extravagant (n **f. idea**) 4 specially bred.

fancy-free a not committed to any relationship.

fandango n -os. lively Spanish dance.

fanfare n flourish of trumpets.

fang n long, pointed tooth; poison tooth of snake.

fanlight n small window above main window or door.

fantasia n imaginative composition in free form, esp music (also **fantasy**).

fantasize v have fantasies.

fantasy a 1 imagination 2 wild, unrealistic idea 3 fantasia; a **fantastic** 1 wild and strange 2 impractical 3 coll wonderful adv **-ally**.

fanzine n a magazine produced especially for fans.

FAO abbr 1 for the attention of 2 Food and Agricultural Organization.

far a, adv 1 at a distance 2 very much 3 extreme(ly); idm **as far as** 1 up to and no further 2 to the extent that; idm **by far/far and away** by a great amount; idm **far be it from me to** I certainly would not; idm **far from doing** instead of doing; idm **so far** until now.

farce n Fr ludicrous, boisterous comedy; absurd, futile situation; a **farcical**.

fare n sum charged for conveyance of passenger; passenger; food; v travel; prosper; feed; get on.

Far East n countries of eastern and southern Asia.

farewell n leave-taking; interj good-bye.

far-fetched a unbelievable.

far-flung a located at great distances.

far gone a almost beyond recovery.

farina n flour, meal, ground from corn, nuts, etc; a **farinaceous** mealy.

farm n 1 area of land for growing crops and rearing

animals 2 house and buildings near this; ns **farmer, farming, farmhouse, farmyard; farmhand** farm worker; *phr v* **farm out** delegate; send to be cared for by others.

far-off *a* distant.

far-out *a coll* 1 unconventional 2 very good.

far-reaching *a* having extensive influence.

farrier *n* blacksmith who shoes horses.

farrow *n* litter of pigs; *v* give birth to pigs.

farsighted *a* 1 showing awareness of possible future developments (*also* **far-seeing**) 2 US longsighted.

farther *a, adv* = **further**.

farthest *a, adv* = **furthest**.

farthing *n obsolete Brit* copper coin.

farthingale *n* hooped petticoat.

fascia *n pl* sign above a shop.

fascinate *v* enchant, bewitch; subdue by fixed stare; *n* **fascination**; *a* **fascinating**.

Fascism *n* extreme right-wing dictatorial political system; *n* **Fascist**.

fashion *n* style; latest mode, vogue; method; *idm* **after a fashion** in an inadequate way; *v* form, shape, make; *a* **fashionable** modish; *adv* **-ably.**

fast[1] *a* 1 firmly fixed; sure 2 rapid 3 (of clock) ahead of actual time 4 dissipated; *adv* 1 rapidly 2 fixedly; securely; *idm* **fast asleep**; *v* fasten fix;

secure; attach; seize (upon); *n* **fastness** secure place, stronghold.

fast[2] *v* abstain from food or some kinds of food; *n* act of fasting.

fasten *v* 1 secure; attach 2 become secured; *phr v* **fasten on** seize on and use; *n* **fastener, fastening.**

fast food *n* food that can be cooked easily and eaten quickly or taken away.

fast forward *n* facility on audio or video player for moving quickly ahead.

fastidious *a* difficult to please; critical; discriminating; *n* **fastidiousness.**

fat *a* **fatter, fattest.** 1 plump; obese 2 greasy 3 fertile 4 thick; stumpy; *idm* **a fat chance** *coll* very little chance; *idm* **a fat lot of good** *coll* very little (good); *n* oily, animal substance; best part; *idm* **the fat of the land** the finest food and drink; *n* **fat cat** US rich influential person; *v* **fatten** (*of cattle*) make fat for slaughter; *a* **fatted** fattened; *n* **fatness**; *a* **fatty**; *n* **fat-head** dull, stupid person.

fatal *a* ending in death; destructive; *ns* **fatality** calamity; death by accident; **fatalism** doctrine that all events are preordained; *a, n* **-ist.**

fate *n* supposed power controlling course of all events; destiny; one's

lot, condition; evil fate, doom; *as* **fated** destined; **fateful** fraught with fate; decisive.

father *n* male parent; forefather; originator; title of respect, *esp* of priest etc; *v* beget; care for as father; be author of; *as* **-ly, -less**; *ns* **fatherhood; f.-in-law** wife's, husband's father; **fatherland** native country.

Father Christmas *n* old man with red robe and white beard giving presents to children at Christmas (*also* **Santa Claus**).

father-figure *n* older man who protects and is respected by young people.

fathom *n* measure of depth, 6 ft.; *v* take soundings of; understand; *a* **fathomless** very deep.

fatigue *n Fr* exhaustion; weariness, of body or mind; weakness in metal after repeated stresses; *v* weary, weaken.

fatten *v* make fatter.

fatty *a* 1 like fat; 2 full of fat; *n coll* fat person.

fatuous *a* silly; stupid; futile; *adv* **-ly** *n* **-ness** *n* **fatuity.**

faucet *a* tap for drawing liquid from cask, pipe etc.

fault *n* 1 defect; error 2 fracture in earth's crust 3 offence; *idm* **at fault** to blame; *idm* **find fault (with)** criticize; *idm* **to a fault** excessively; *a* **faulty** *adv* **-ily**; *a* **faultless** *adv* **-ly**, *n* **-ness.**

faun n myth rural deity with horns and goat's feet.

fauna n all animal life of region or period.

faux pas n Fr embarrassing mistake; tactless remark.

favour n 1 act of good will 2 partiality 3 rosette; badge; idm **in favour of** 1 supporting 2 payable to; idm **in sb's favour** to sb's advantage; v 1 approve 2 resemble 3 support; a **favourable** propitious; approving; adv **-ably** n **favourite** favoured person or thing; a preferred; most liked; n **favouritism** undue partiality.

fawn[1] n young deer; a pale, greyish brown.

fawn[2] v (of person) cringe, act servilely towards; (of dogs etc) show affection by grovelling.

fax n message sent along a telephone line then printed on a special machine; v send a message in this way; n **fax machine**.

faze v coll, esp US fluster.

FBI abbr Federal Bureau of Investigation.

FC abbr football club.

fear n dread; anxiety; awe; idm **No fear!** coll certainly not; v be afraid (of); expect (sth bad); idm **not much fear of sth** sth is unlikely to happen; as **fearful** apprehensive; awful; **fearsome** horrible; **fearless** courageous.

feasible a possible; practicable;

n **feasibility**.

feasibility study n preliminary investigation as to whether a project is practicable or not.

feast n 1 religious day of rejoicing 2 lavish repast 3 village fete; idm **feast one's eyes on** enjoy looking at; v give, eat sumptuous banquet.

feat n exceptional deed, act of bravery, skill etc.

feather n one of quilled, soft appendages forming plumage of birds; idm **feather in one's cap** achievement to be proud of; v 1 line, adorn with feathers 2 turn oar; idm **feather one's nest** make oneself rich at someone else's expense; a **feathery** soft light; n **feather-weight** very light person, or thing.

feather-brained a thoughtless and silly.

feature n 1 part of face 2 noticeable or prominent part of anything 3 special article in newspaper etc; v portray; give prominence to; present; a **featureless** without anything distinctive.

feature-length a (of film) full-length.

febrile a feverish.

February n second month of year.

fecal, feces US = faecal, faeces.

feckless a thoughtless, careless, irresponsible.

fecund a fruitful; fertile; prolific; n **fecundity**.

fed pt and pp of **feed**.

federal a relating to States which unite for external affairs, but remain internally independent; n **federate** unite to form federation; n **-ation** federal union, society.

FBI n Federal Bureau of Investigation US centrally controlled police bureau.

fedora n soft felt hat.

fed up a bored; dejected; dissatisfied.

fee n charge for professional and other services; entrance money for examination, etc.

feeble a infirm, weak; ineffectual; frail; adv **feebly**.

feed v give food to; supply with fuel, material; eat; consume; pt, pp **fed**; n fodder; material supplied; ns **feeder** one who feeds; that which supplies; child's bib or bottle; **feed-pipe**; **feed-pump**; **feeding trough**; a **fed up** sl bored.

feedback n 1 information from user back to originator of idea or product 2 elec output from eg amplifier returned as new input.

feeding bottle n bottle with small aperture for feeding liquid to babies or small animals.

feel v feeling, felt. 1 explore by touch 2 experience physically or emotionally 3 give specified sensation 4 be affected by 5 be capable of sensation; idm **feel like**

want; *idm* **feel for** sympathise with; *n* 1 exploration by touch 2 sensation; *idm* **get the feel of** become used to; *idm* **have a feel for** be appreciative of.

feeler *n* antenna by which insect feels things; *idm* **put out feelers** test people's opinions.

feel-good factor *n* general feeling of optimism among the population of a country.

feeling *n* 1 sensation 2 emotion 3 awareness 4 belief 5 sympathy; *a* showing emotion *adv* -ly.

feet *pl of* foot.

feign *v* pretend; assume; simulate.

feint[1] *n* misleading action; pretence.

feint[2] *a* with faintly printed lines.

feisty *a US coll* 1 spirited 2 quarrelsome.

feldspar *n* white or red mineral rock (*also* felspar).

felicity *n* happiness, bliss; contentment; *a* **felicitous** happy; apt; *v* **felicitate** congratulate *n* -ation.

feline *a* of cats; catlike.

fell[1] *v* 1 *pt of* fall 2 cut down.

fell[2] *n* bare rocky hillside or moorland in Northern England.

fell[3] *a* destructive; *idm* **at one fell swoop** suddenly; devastatingly.

feller *n sl* man; fellow.

fellow *n* companion; associate; member (of society, governing body of college etc).

fellowship *n* 1 companionship 2 society 3 position of fellow in university college.

fellow traveller *n* 1 travelling companion 2 sympathiser with but not member of (*esp* Communist) party.

felony *n* grave crime; more heinous than misdemeanour; *n* **felon** criminal guilty of felony; *a* **felonious**.

felt[1] *n* fabric made of compressed wool; *a* made of felt.

felt[2] *pt of* feel.

felt-tip *a, n* (pen) with felt nib.

female *a* 1 of the sex that bears offspring or fruit 2 of women 3 (of mechanical parts) with a hole to accommodate a male part; *n* woman or female animal.

feminine *a* of women; having gender referring to females; *ns* **femininity; feminism** advocacy of complete equality between sexes; *a, n* -ist.

femme fatale *n Fr* woman attractive but dangerous to men.

femur *n* thigh-bone; *a* **femoral**.

fen *n* low, flat, marshy land; *a* **fenny**.

fence *n* 1 hedge; railing; 2 receiver of stolen goods; *idm* **sit on the fence** be non-commital; *v* enclose, protect with fence; fight with sword; avoid direct answer; *ns* **fencer**; swordsman; **fencing** protective fences; art of sword play.

fend *v* keep, ward off; *phr vs* **fend for** look after; protect; **fend off** ward off; push away; *n* **fender** 1 metal surround of fireplace 2 *US aut* wing 3 ball of rope protecting side of boat or ship.

fennel *n* fragrant herb used in cooking.

feral *a* fatal; gloomy; undomesticated; wild.

ferment *v* undergo chemical process involving effervescence; become excited; *n* substance causing fermentation, eg yeast; tumult, commotion; *n* -ation act of fermenting.

fern *n* plant with fronds, feathery or plain; *a* **ferny** abounding in ferns.

ferocious *a* savage, fierce, cruel; *n* **ferocity**.

ferret *n* small, half-tamed animal of weasel family, used for driving rabbits out of holes; *v* hunt with ferret; *fig* search thoroughly.

ferric, ferreous, ferrous *a* of, containing iron; *a* **ferriferous** yielding iron; *n* **ferrite** type of iron ore; **ferro-** *prefix* denoting presence of iron.

Ferris wheel *n* (at fairground) big wheel.

ferrule *n* metal cap protecting end of stick, etc.

ferry *v* -rying, -ried. convey,

cross, over river, channel etc, n **-ies.** boat, raft used for ferrying (*also* **f. boat**); place where ferry is.

fertile *a* capable of producing offspring; fruitful; prolific; abundant; rich in ideas; *n* **fertility;** *v* **fertilize** make fertile; *ns* **-ization, -izer.**

fervent *a* burning, glowing; ardent, intense; *ns* **fervency; fervour;** *a* **fervid** hot; impassioned.

fester *v* suppurate; decay; rankle; *n* ulcer.

festival *n* joyful celebration; series of organized musical, dramatic performances; *a* **festive,** joyous; convivial; *ns* **festivity** gaiety, joyousness; *pl* **festivities** joyful celebration.

festoon *n* chain or garland of flowers, ribbons etc, hung in loops; *v* decorate with festoons.

fetch *v* 1 go for and bring back 2 be sold for 3 *dated* be the cause of; *idm* **fetch and carry** do small menial duties; *phr v* **fetch up** *coll* arrive; *a* **fetching** attractive *adv* **-ly.**

fête *n* festival; fair, usually open-air; *v* honour with festivities.

fetid, foetid *a* stinking.

fetish *n* object worshipped by savages; object of exaggerated devotion; *n* **fetishism** *n,* *a* **-ist.**

fetlock *n* tufted pad at the back of horse's leg, just above hoof.

fetter *n* shackle for feet; *pl* restraint; *v* put in irons; impede; *a* **fettered** restrained.

fettle *n* condition or state; *v* put in order; repair.

fetus = foetus.

feud[1] *n* bitter, long-standing hostility between two persons, clans etc.

feud[2] *n* land held in return for service to overlord.

feudal *a* pertaining to land held as feud; **f. system** medieval system of land tenure; *n* **-ism.**

fever *n* 1 disorder characterized by high temperature 2 extreme nervous excitement; *a* **feverish;** *adv* **-ly;** *n* **-ness.**

few *a,* *n* not many; small number of.

fey *a* 1 fated to die 2 full of whimsical beliefs, unnatural gaiety.

fez *n* felt cap.

ff *abbr* 1 following pages 2 *mus* fortissimo.

fiancé *n* Fr betrothed man; (*fem* **fiancée**).

fiasco *n* total, utter failure.

fib *n* mild untruth; *v* **fibbing, fibbed.** tell fib; *n* **fibber.**

fibre *n* US **fiber;** thread of animal, plant tissue; thread-like substance that can be spun; *a* **fibrous** *ns* **fibreboard** board of compressed wood fibres; **fibreglass** material from glass fibres and resin for bodywork in cars, boats etc (*also* **glass fibre**); **fibre optics** transmission of data

by infra-red signals along thin glass fibre *a* **fibre-optic.**

fibrositis *n* inflammation of fibrous tissue, *esp* muscle.

fibula *n* outer bone of lower leg; *a* **fibular.**

fickle *a* changeable; inconstant; *n* **fickleness.**

fiction *n* 1 literature of the imagination 2 untrue statement; *a* **fictional** *v* **-ize.**

Fid Def *abbr* (on British coins, *also* **FD**) Fidei Defensor (Defender of the Faith).

fiddle *n* 1 violin 2 *sl* wangle; *idm* **as fit as a fiddle** completely healthy; *v* 1 play violin 2 fidget; move restlessly 3 swindle; wangle; *ns* **fiddler, fiddlestick** violin bow; *interj* **fiddlesticks** *dated* nonsense.

fiddling *a* small and trivial.

fiddly *a* awkward to manipulate or do.

fidelity *n* 1 faithfulness 2 exactitude.

fidget *v* move restlessly; be uneasy; fuss; *n* one who fidgets; *pl* nervous restlessness; *a* **fidgety.**

fiduciary *a* of trustee; held in trust.

field *n* 1 area of *usu* enclosed land for crops or pasture 2 area with specified characteristic 3 area of military or sporting activity 4 range of operation 5 academic sphere of interest 6 *sport* all competitors 7 *comput* section of record with specific information; *idm* **play the field** *coll esp* US avoid committing oneself to one partner; *idm* **take the field** *mil*, *sport* prepare for action; *v* 1 deal successfully with difficult questions 2 *sport* select (people to play) 3 *cricket* 1 play against the batting team 2 stop the ball to prevent scoring of runs; *n* **fielder**.

field day *n* 1 day of military operations 2 day for sport or outdoor activity (at college); *idm* **have a field day** enjoy period of exciting activity.

field event *n* athletic contest other than running.

field glasses *n* binoculars.

fieldmarshal *n* high ranking officer in British army.

field-test *n* educational visit, *usu* with project work.

field-work *n* 1 academic work outside class, laboratory; *n* **fieldworker** 2 *mil* temporary fortification.

fiend *n* demon, devil; excessively evil person; *a* **fiendish**, cruel, malevolent.

fierce *a* 1 savage; wild; cruel 2 intense; strong; *n* **fierceness**.

fiery *a* 1 of, resembling fire 2 flaming, glowing 3 choleric; spirited; *n* **fieriness**; *adv* **fierily**.

fiesta *n* festival, *esp* religious one in Spanish speaking countries.

FIFA *abbr* Fédération Internationale de Football Association (International FA Federation).

fife *n* shrill, flute-like instrument.

fifteen, fifth, fifty *see* **five**.

fifth column *n* group in country at war helping enemy secretly.

fifty-fifty *a*, *adv* (shared) equal(ly) between two.

fig[1] *n* soft, sweet pear-shaped fruit, with many seeds, eaten fresh or dried; tree bearing this.

fig[2] *abbr* 1 figurative 2 figure.

fight *v* contend against violently; engage in single combat; manoeuvre troops, etc in battle; oppose (by arguments etc); *pt*, *pp* **fought**; *phr vs* **fight back** 1 retaliate 2 recover from losing situation; **fight off** repel; resist (illness); *ns* **fighter, fighting**; *idm* **a fighting chance** slight but positive chance of success with effort, *n* contest; struggle; *n* **fighter** one who fights; fast aircraft used for fighting.

figment *n* fantasy; something imagined.

figure *n* 1 outer shape; bodily form (*esp* human); appearance 2 statue; ornament 3 diagram 4 numerical symbol 5 *dancing, skating* series of movements 6 *gram* special use of words for effect 7 sum; amount; *v* 1 imagine; depict 2 calculate 3 be conspicuous; *idm* **that figures** *US* it makes sense; *phr vs* **figure on** *US* plan; expect; **figure out** calculate; *a* **figurative** metaphorical; symbolic; pictorial; *n* **figure-**

head 1 figure, bust, under bowsprit of ship 2 nominal leader.

figure of speech *n* figurative expression.

figurine *n* statuette.

filament *n* fine thread or fibre; fine conductor wire in electric light bulb, wireless valve.

filbert *n* type of nut.

filch *v* *coll* steal, pilfer.

file[1] *n* hard steel tool with rough surface, for cutting or smoothing metal etc.; *n* use file on; *n* **filing** action of using file; *pl* particles of metal removed by filing.

file[2] 1 *n* stiff wire, box or folder for storing documents 2 collection of documents so kept for reference; *v* place in or on file; place on record; *phr vs* **file away** classify and store; **file for** *leg* request formally.

file[3] *n* line of persons, objects one behind another; *v* march, move in file.

filet mignon *Fr n* small tender cut of beef.

filial *a* of, concerning son or daughter.

filibuster *n* 1 irregular combatant 2 pirate 3 political obstructionist (also *v*).

filigree *n* ornamental work of fine wires.

filing *n* 1 minute particle of metal filed off, *esp pl* 2 act of classifying, storing documents *n* f. cabinet.

fill *v* 1 make full; occupy

completely 2 become full 3 stop up 4 satisfy 5 appoint sb to (post, office etc); *phr vs* **fill in** 1 complete with details; give information to 2 act in sb else's place; **fill out** 1 become fatter 2 complete in writing; *n* full supply; *ns* **filler** substance for filling holes; **filling** tooth stopping; **filling-station** petrol station; *a* **filling** (of food) satisfying.

fillet *n* 1 head-band 2 piece of boneless meat, fish; *v* slice and remove bones.

fillip *n* exciting or arousing thing.

filly *n* female foal, young mare.

film *n* 1 fine, thin skin or layer 2 thin flexible sensitized strip or roll used in photography, cinematography 3 motion picture 4 haze; *v* cover with film; make, direct, produce motion-picture; *a* **filmy** gauzy, delicate; *n* **filminess**.

film clip *n* short extract from film.

film star *n* famous film actor/actress.

filter *n* 1 cloth, etc used for straining liquids 2 device eliminating some light or electrical frequencies 3 traffic light allowing one lane to bypass the red light; *v* 1 strain liquid; percolate 2 *fig* leak out 3 enter traffic lane gradually; move in direction shown by filter light; *n* **filtration**.

filter tip *n* cigarette with filter

for smoke at one end.

filth *n* 1 nasty, revolting dirt 2 obscenity; *a* **filthy**; *n* **filthiness**.

fin *n* wing-like organ by which fish swim; projecting plane on aircraft etc.

final *a* at the end; decisive, *n* last examination, game or heat of series; **finalist** competitor in final of race, game etc; **finality, finale** end; concluding movement, number of symphony, opera etc.

finance *n* management of (public) money; *pl* money resources of nation, company or individual; *v* supply money for; *a* **financial**; *n* **financier**.

finch *n* small seed-eating birds.

find *v* discover for first time; come upon (lost object, person); provide, equip with; return verdict; learn by experience; *pt, pp* **found**; *n* thing found; valuable or pleasing discovery; *idm* **find one's feet** 1 be able to walk steadily 2 learn how to be independent; *idm* **be found wanting** prove to be incapable; *phr vs* **find against** *leg* give judgement against; **find for** *leg* give judgement in favour of; *ns* **finder**; **finding** *esp pl* 1 things found by official enquiry 2 *leg* decision or verdict.

fine[1] *n* sum exacted as penalty; *v* punish by fine.

fine[2] *a* 1 thin; delicate 2 sharp

3 in minute particles 4 refined 5 not raining 6 showy; striking 7 excellent; finished; *v* 1 refine, purify 2 make thinner; *ns* **fineness**; **finery** elaborate dress; **finesse** subtlety; adroitness; *cards* attempt to take trick with low card, whilst holding higher one (also *v*.)

fine arts *n pl* painting, sculpture, music, etc.

finger *n* one of five (or four, excluding thumb) members at end of hand; anything finger shaped; *v* touch with fingers, handle; *idm* **be all fingers and thumbs** be clumsy with one's hands; *idm* **have a finger in every pie** *coll* be involved in every possible activity; *idm* **keep one's fingers crossed** hope for good luck; *idm* **put one's finger on** identify precisely; *ns* **f.-board** neck of stringed instrument; **f. bowl** bowl for rinsing fingers at table; **f.-nail; fingerprint; f.-stall** protective cover for injured finger; **fingertip** end of finger; **fingering** 1 touching with finger 2 indication in music of which fingers to use.

finicking, finical *a* fussy, over-fastidious; *a* **finicky**.

finis *n* end, *esp* of book.

finish *v* 1 bring to an end; complete 2 cease; put an end to 3 kill 4 make perfect; *phr vs* **finish off** 1 complete; terminate 2 kill; **finish with** 1 have as final item 2 have

no further use for 3 end
relationship with; n end;
final appearance; mode of
finishing; a **finished**
accomplished; perfect; n **-er**.

finite a bounded, having
limits.

Finnish a, n of Finland.

fiord, fjord n narrow inlet of
sea between cliffs, esp in
Norway.

fir n coniferous, evergreen tree
of pine family.

fire n 1 state of burning; thing
burning 2 electric or gas
heater 3 shooting of
weapons 4 passion; idm
catch fire start burning; idm
fire away start asking
questions; idm **hang fire**
make no progress; stagnate;
idm **open/cease fire**
begin/stop shooting; idm **on
fire** burning; idm **under fire**
being shot at; v 1 shoot
(missile or firearm) 2 dismiss
from post 3 inspire; excite 4
bake (pottery) in kiln; ns **f.-
alarm, f.-arm** gun; **fireball,
firebomb; f.-brand** 1 piece
of burning wood 2 agitator;
firebreak land cleared to
prevent spread of fire; **f.-
brigade** body of fire-fighters;
firebug arsonist; **f.-damp**
explosive gas found in coal
mine; **f.-dog** andiron; **f.
drill, f. practice** practice
routine for ensuring safe
escape from fire; **f.-fighter,
f.-fighting, fireguard,
f.irons, fireman** (pl
firemen); **fireplace;
firepower** power of artillery;

f.-raiser arsonist; **f.station**
HQ of fire brigade; **f.storm;
firetrap** unsafe building;
firewood; firework
chemical container,
emitting bright coloured
light or exploding when
ignited (pl **-s** 1 display of
these 2 violent show of
temper 3 brilliant
performance, esp music).

firefly n nocturnal beetle that
produces light.

fireplace n a recess in a wall of
a room for a fire.

fireproof a safe against fire; v
make safe from fire.

fireside n area close to
fireplace; hearth.

firing line n front line of
battle; idm **in the firing line**
exposed to criticism.

firing squad n method of
execution by shooting.

firkin n small cask; measure of
capacity, 8-9 galls.

firm a solid; stable; resolute;
steady; not fluctuating; v
make firm; solidify; n
partnership; business
company.

first a 1 earliest 2 highest; best
3 principal 4 basic;
elementary; adv before all
else, all others; n, pron 1
best person or thing 2 Brit
top class examination result;
ns **f. aid** emergency medical
treatment; **firstborn; f.
cousin** child of uncle or
aunt; **f.floor** Brit floor above
ground floor; US ground
floor; **f. night** premier of
play, opera, etc; **f. person**

form of pronoun used when
speaker refers to
himself/herself; **f.strike**
attack on enemy before they
attack you; as **firstclass,
firsthand** (of information)
direct from source; **f.-hand**
excellent; **f-string** regularly
in team; adv **firstly** as first
point, argument.

firth n estuary; inlet of sea.

fiscal a concerned with public
revenue; n high legal
official.

fish n cold-blooded vertebrate,
with fins, living in water;
flesh of fish used as food; v 1
catch, or try to catch, fish 2
try to get information; ns
fisher; ns **f.farm** place for
breeding of fish; **f.finger**
small piece of fish coated in
breadcrumbs; **fishing;
fishmonger** seller of fish;
fishnet netlike fabric; **f.-
plate** plate for connecting
metal rails; **f.slice** spatula for
turning or serving fish;
fishwife coll loud abusive
woman; a **fishy** 1 of fish 2
coll dubious n **-iness**.

fish-eye lens n wide-angled
lens.

fission n 1 splitting of atomic
nucleus 2 bio dividing of
cells; a **fissile** capable of
splitting.

fissure n cleft, esp in rock.

fist n clenched fist; v strike
with fist.

fistula n narrow, winding ulcer.

fit[1] n sudden sharp attack of
illness; seizure, spasm;
passing whim; idm **by fits**

and starts in an irregular manner; *idm* **have/throw a fit** be deeply shocked, outraged; *a* **fitful** restless; spasmodic *adv* **-ly.**

fit[2] *a* **1** suitable; competent proper **2** strong; vigorous; *v* **fitting, fitted. 1** suit; be adapted to, of correct size **2** supply; furnish **3** be properly adjusted to; *n* that which fits; adjustment; *v phr vs* **fit in** harmonize; **fit sth in** make time, space for sth; **fit in (with)** adapt (to); **fit out** equip; *a* **fitted 1** made to size and shape **2** fixed in position; *ns* **fitness** suitability; good bodily health; **fitter** tailor who fits clothes; mechanic who adjusts machines; **fitment** built-in furniture; **fitting** action of fitting; *pl* furnishings and equipment; *a* **fitting** suitable, proper, seemly.

five *n, pron, det* cardinal number after four; *as, ns, dets* **fifth** ordinal number; a fifth part; **fifteen** five plus ten; **fifteenth; fifty** five tens; **fiftieth;** *n* **fives** ball-game played in walled court.

fix *v* make fast **1** stable, secure **2** arrange **3** determine **4** repair **5** gaze steadily at **6** *sl* get even with **7** *sl* bribe or trick; *ns* **fixation** obsession; **fixative** fixing agent; **fixer** person with ability to arrange events by secret influence or dishonest means; **fixity;** immobility;

fixture 1 sth fixed in a building **2** *sport* event fixed on a certain date.

fizz *v* hiss; splutter; effervesce; *n sl* champagne; noise of fizzing; *v* **fizzle** splutter weakly; *phr v* **fizzle out** become feeble and ineffective.

fjord *n* long, narrow coastal inlet caused by glaciation.

flab *n coll* flabby loose flesh.

flabbergast *v* dumbfound; astonish; disconcert.

flabby *a* hanging loosely; limp; flaccid; *n* **flabbiness.**

flaccid *a* limp; weak, without energy; *n* **flaccidity.**

flag[1] *v* **flagging, flagged.** droop; become feeble.

flag[2] *n* name of various kinds of iris.

flag[3] *n* flat paving-stone; *n* **flagstone.**

flag[4] *n* sheet of bunting, bearing emblem etc, attached to mast etc, used as standard or to signal; *v* signal by flag; *ns* **flag-officer** naval officer entitled to his own flag; **flagship** admiral's ship; **flagstaff** mast pole, for flag.

flag day *n Brit* day when paper flags are sold for charity.

flag of convenience *n* foreign flag used by ship to avoid certain taxes and regulations.

flag-waving *n* noisy expression of patriotic feeling.

flagellate *v* scourge, whip; *n* **-ation.**

flageolet *n* small flute-like

instrument.

flagon *n* vessel for serving wine; large wine bottle.

flagrant *a* scandalous; blatantly evil; *ns* **-ance, ancy.**

flail *n* implement for threshing grain by hand.

flair *n* natural aptitude; instinctive discernment.

flake *n* thin, light scale, layer; light, fleecy particle (of snow); *v* come off in flakes; *a* **flaky** *n* **-iness.**

flamboyance *n* ostentation; showiness; exaggeration of speech, manner; *a* **flamboyant 1** showy **2** *arch* having wave-like tracery.

flame *n* **1** burning gas or vapour; jet of fire **2** ardent passion, imagination; *v* emit flames; blaze; flare.

flamenco *n* (music for) lively Spanish dance.

flaming *a* **1** burning **2** brightly coloured **3** *sl* absolute; damned.

flamingo *n* scarlet-feathered aquatic bird, with long legs and neck.

flammable *n* easily set on fire.

flan *n* round, shallow, open pastry shell.

flange *n* projecting rim, edge, or rib.

flank *n* part of side of body between hip and ribs; side of hill, building, or body of troops; *v* guard, attack flank; be at side of.

flannel *n* soft woollen cloth; cloth for washing; *pl* trousers *esp* casual, sporting; *n*

flannelette cotton imitation flannel.

flap *v* **flapping, flapped.** slap lightly; move (wings) up and down; sway; flutter; *n* act of flapping; flat piece of material partly attached and hanging; *idm* **in a flap** panicky; *n* **flapper** flipper of seal etc; *sl dated* young girl; **flapjack** sweet oatcake.

flare[1] *n* 1 bright, unsteady flame 2 vivid signal light 3 outburst of anger 4 outward spread, curve; *v* blaze up; spread outwards; *a* **flaring** gaudy.

flare[2] *v* be wider at bottom; *n* flare shape; *pl* **-s** flared trousers.

flarepath *n* illuminated runway for aircraft to land.

flare-up *n* outbreak of violent activity.

flash *v* emit sudden bright light; gleam; pass rapidly by; signal by flashing; *n* 1 sudden brief gleam of light 2 moment 3 cloth mark worn on uniform; *idm* **in a flash** instantly; *ns* **flashback** episode going back in time; **flashbulb, flashcube, flashgun; flashlight** 1 device for taking photos in bad light 2 *US* torch; **f.point** 1 temperature at which ignition occurs 2 place or situation where violence is likely to break out; *as* **flash, flashy** showy, tawdry; *n* **flashlight** *US* small electric torch; **flashpoint** temperature at which oil,

spirit, vapour ignites.

flask *n* small, flattened pocket bottle for spirits etc; wine-bottle; small narrow-necked bottle for scientific use.

flat *a* 1 level and smooth; not curved or raised; in a horizontal plane 2 deflated 3 dull; uninteresting; (of pictures) without contrast 4 having lost effervescence 5 *mus* below pitch indicated 6 (of denial) absolute; *idm* **flat and that's flat** *coll* it's decided and cannot be discussed; *idm* **in a flat spin** confused; panicky; *idm* **flat out** at full speed; *n* 1 apartment; *ns* **flatlet** small flat; **flatmate** 2 flat tyre 3 section of stage scenery 4 *usu pl* expanse of level ground 5 flat part of sth 6 *mus* sign indicating a semitone lower; *a* **flat-chested** (*usu* of woman) with small breasts; *n* **f.feet** *a* **flat-footed**; *ns* **flatfish**; **f.race** race with no jumps; **flat rate** unvarying inclusive price; *adv* 1 *mus* below pitch 2 at full extent; level with the ground 3 absolutely; *idm* **fall flat on one's face** fail in a humiliating way; *adv* **-ly** absolutely *n* **-ness** *v* **flatten** 1 make or become flat 2 overwhelm.

flatter *v* praise insincerely; adulate; represent too favourably; congratulate oneself; *ns* **flatterer; flattery.**

flatulence, flatulency *n* wind, gas in stomach or intestines;

a **flatulent** caused by, affected with flatulence; *fig* vapid.

flaunt *v* flourish, wave insolently; make display of.

flautist *n* flute player.

flavour *n* (*US* **flavor**) 1 taste (*also* **flavouring**) 2 special characteristic; *v* give taste to *as* **-ed, -less**; *idm* **flavour of the month** *coll* thing or person now favoured.

flaw *n* defect, blemish; crack; *v* crack, make flaw in; *a* **flawless** perfect; irreproachable.

flax *n* herb, whose fibres are spun into linen thread, seeds produce linseed oil; *a* of, like flax; pale yellow.

flaxen *a* (of hair) pale yellow.

flay *v* strip off skin; criticize savagely.

flea *n* small bloodsucking jumping insect; *idm* **with a flea in one's ear** having been rebuked; *ns* **fleabag** *coll* 1 *Brit* dirty person; mangy animal; 2 *US* dirty hotel; **fleabite** 1 bite of flea 2 very minor inconvenience; *a* **fleabitten** scruffy; **f.-market** street market for cheap second-hand goods; **f.-pit** *coll* dirty old cinema or theatre.

fleck *n* spot; freckle; particle; *v* mark with flecks; dapple.

flee *v* run away; avoid; shun; *pt, pp* **fled**.

fleece *n* sheep's wool; *v* swindle, plunder; *a* **fleecy** soft, woolly; resembling, covered with, fleece.

fleet[1] n number of warships under one command; number of ships, aircraft, cars owned by one company or person; creek, inlet.

fleet[2] a speedy; nimble; swift; v move swiftly, silently; n **fleetness**; a **fleeting** transient; transitory.

flesh n 1 soft tissue of body, beneath skin, covering bones 2 edible animal tissue; meat 3 pulp of vegetable or fruit 4 animal nature of man; sensuality; idm **in the flesh** physically present; in person; n **flesher** butcher; as **fleshly** carnal; **fleshy** pulpy; plump.

fleshpots n pl 1 places to indulge bodily pleasures 2 life of self-indulgence.

flew pt of **fly**.

flex v bend, be bent; n flexible, insulated wire; ns **flexibility** ability to bend; **flexion** act of bending; inflexion; **flexor** muscle bending joint inwards; a **flexible** pliant; adaptable; versatile.

flexitime n system of variable working hours.

flick v tap, flip lightly and jerkily; n sharp light blow.

flicker v flutter; waver; burn, shine unsteadily; n unsteady gleam; or movement.

flick-knife n Brit knife with hidden blade released by pressing button.

flies n pl front opening of trousers.

flight n 1 act of flying; distance flown 2 unit,

formation of aircraft 3 volley of arrows 4 series of stairs, steps 5 act of fleeing; ns **f.deck**, **f.path**; **f.recorder** black box.

flighty a giddy; fickle; frivolous; n **-iness**.

flimsy a thin and fragile; weak and paltry; n thin paper for carbon copy.

flinch v draw back in pain, fear; wince.

fling v throw, hurl; move with haste; lash out; flounce; pt, pp **flung**; n 1 throw 2 vigorous dance 3 bout of dissipation 4 brief amorous relationship.

flint a very hard dark grey quartz; anything hard, obdurate; piece of flint.

flintlock n old type of gun.

flip v flipping, flipped. flick; jerk; make smart light tap; n **flipper** limb or fin for swimming; a **flippant** lacking seriousness; frivolous; n **flippancy** a, adv **flipping** coll nasty.

flip-flop n 1 Brit flat open rubber sandal 2 electronic circuit switching between two states 3 US polit U-turn.

flip-side n second side of record; not main side.

flirt v pay amorous attentions without serious intent; phr v **flirt with sth** 1 pretend to be interested in 2 expose oneself to the risk of; a **flirtatious** adv -ly ns -ness; **flirtation**.

flit v flitting, flitted. pass lightly, rapidly and quietly; sl

move house secretly.

flitch n side of bacon.

float v 1 rest, drift on surface of liquid 2 glide through air 3 start; set going; launch (loan, company etc); n 1 anything that floats, esp supporting something else on liquid 2 low-floored, shallow cart 3 cork on fishing net 4 sum of cash for running expenses.

floating voter n person who may change political views.

flock n lock, tuft of wool; wool, cotton fibres used in waste; a **flocculent** of, resembling wool or flock.

flock n number of animals (esp sheep) or birds, as unit; congregation; v assemble in large numbers; crowd together.

floe n sheet of ice floating on sea.

flog v flogging, flogged. beat hard; thrash with whip or stick; coll sell, esp illicitly; idm **flog a dead horse** coll persist in unprofitable activity.

flood n inundation; overflow of water in usually dry place; rising tide; coll floodlight; v inundate; overflow; overwhelm; ns **f.gate** sluice; **f.tide**.

floodlight n powerful artificial lighting; v illuminate by floodlights; a **floodlit**.

floor n lower surface of room etc; storey; body of a hall etc, idm **go through the floor** coll (or prices) fall

below tolerable level; *idm*
take the floor 1 begin
dancing **2** speak in public; *v*
furnish with floor; knock
down; *coll* confound; *ns*
flooring boards, blocks etc.
forming floor; **f.-show**
cabaret.

floosie, floozie *n* woman of
loose morals; prostitute.

flop *v* **flopping, flopped.** move
limply, heavily; fall clumsily,
noisily; *coll* fail utterly; *adv*
floppily; *n* act, noise of
flopping; *coll* fiasco, failure; *a*
floppy slack; loose, limp;
n **-iness.**

flophouse *n* US cheap hotel.

floppy disk *n comput* plastic
disc for storing data.

flora *n* flowers, plants,
collectively, of particular
areas; classified list of
species; *a* **floral** of flowers; *ns*
florescence season, state of
flowering; **floret** small
flower; **florist** grower of,
dealer in flowers.

florid *a* ruddy.

floss *n* rough silk covering of
cocoon; spun silk; *a* **flossy.**

flotation *n* starting of a new
business company.

flotilla *n* Sp fleet of small ships
or boats.

flotsam *n* floating wreckage or
goods on the sea.

flounce[1] *v* go, move jerkily,
impatiently; *n* such
movement.

flounce[2] *n* ornamental strip,
frill on garment.

flounder[1] *n* kind of flatfish.

flounder[2] *v* **1** stagger, roll

helplessly, *esp* in water, mud;
2 hesitate.

flour *n* finely ground meal, *esp*
of wheat; any very fine, soft
powder; *v* cover with flour.

flourish *v* thrive; be florid in
style, manner; brandish;
sound fanfare; *n* act of
brandishing anything;
fanciful curved line; florid
expression; fanfare.

flout *v* show scorn of; mock at;
defy.

flow *v* **1** (*of water*) glide along;
gush; move along ceaselessly
2 (*of blood*) circulate **3** (*of
fabric*) fall in loose folds, or
masses **4** (*of food, drink etc*)
abound; *n* that which flows;
rising tide; steady, copious
supply.

flow chart *n* diagram showing
how stages of a process
interconnect (also **flow
diagram**).

flower *n* **1** blossom; bloom **2**
choicest, prime part; *v* **1**
produce blooms **2** reach
highest state of
development; **flowerbed**
prepared ground for growing
flowers; **floweret** small
flower; *as* **flowery**
abounding in flowers; florid;
flowered decorated with
floral pattern.

flown *pp* of **fly.**

fl oz *abbr* fluid ounce(s).

flu *n* influenza.

fluctuate *v* rise and fall; vary;
be unstable; *a* **-ating;**
n **-ation.**

flue *n* tube, pipe, shaft
conveying air, smoke etc;

chimney.

fluent *a* flowing; able to, easily,
rapidly; graceful; *n* **fluency.**

fluff *n* soft down, hair; light
soft mass of wool, dust; *v*
make into fluff; *sl* bungle; *a*
fluffy.

fluid *n* liquid; gas; not solid; *a*
flowing easily; *n* **fluidity.**

fluke[1] *n* flat-fish; parasitic
worm.

fluke[2] *n* part of anchor; *pl* tail
of whale.

fluke *n* lucky stroke, shot;
happy chance; *v* make, gain
by fluke.

flummox *v* bewilder; abash;
disconcert.

flung *pt, pp* of **fling.**

flunk *v* US **1** fail **2** mark as
failure.

fluor *n* mineral containing
fluoride; *ns* **fluorine** non-
metallic element; **fluoride**
compound of fluorine;
fluoridation.

fluorescence *n* property
possessed by certain
transparent bodies, of
emitting light rays of
different colour from those
reflected; *a* **fluorescent.**

fluoride *n* chemical protecting
teeth against decay, *v*
fluoridate *n* **-ation.**

flurry *n* **1** sudden gust **2** state
of agitation of mind **3**
death-throes of whale; *v*
bewilder; fluster.

flush *v* fly, start up suddenly, as
when startled; *n* flock of
birds put up.

flush *v* **1** flow suddenly,
copiously **2** redden **3** cleanse

by rush of water 4 elate; exhilarate; n 1 rush of water 2 blush; sudden emotion 3 initial vigour; a 1 full to brim; level with 2 sl having plenty (of money).

flush n cards hand of same suit; run of same suit.

fluster v 1 muddle; fuss; worry 2 be confused.

flute n 1 wind-instrument, with side mouthpiece, and holes stopped by keys or fingers 2 narrow groove; v make grooves in; a fluted grooved, ns fluting; flautist player of flute.

flutter v move wings quickly, nervously; quiver; be excited; throb rapidly but feebly; move, wave (flag) quickly; n 1 act of fluttering 2 nervousness; 3 sl small bet.

fluvial a of rivers.

flux n 1 flowing state, movement 2 morbid discharge of fluid (from body) 3 substance added to help fusion; v fuse (metals) by melting.

fly[1] n two-winged insect; imitation used as fish-bait; idm fly in the ointment nuisance; idm fly on the wall secret observer; idm no flies on sb sb is not easily beaten, fooled; a flyblown tainted, maggoty; n fly-catcher small bird; flyweight boxer weighing 51 kg (112 pounds) or less.

fly[2] v 1 move on wings; control, travel in, aircraft 2 be propelled through air 3

flee from 4 flutter; idm fly in the face of defy; idm fly off the handle lose one's temper; pt flew; pp flown idm fly in the face of defy; idm fly off the handle lose one's temper.

flying saucer n disk-shaped vehicle, thought to come from outer space.

flyleaf n blank page in front or back of book.

flywheel n mechanism that equalizes speed of machinery.

FM abbr radio frequency modulation.

FO abbr 1 Foreign Office 2 flying officer.

foal n young of horse, ass, etc; v bear (foal).

foam n mass of small bubbles, froth, on surface of liquid; v form, emit foam; emit thick saliva, or sweat; as -y, -ing.

fob n small pocket for watch, in waistband.

fob off v fobbing, fobbed. cheat; trick; delude into accepting (worthless article).

focus n point at which converging rays of light, heat, waves of sound, meet; centre of activity or intensity; pl focuses, foci; v adjust; cause to converge; concentrate; a focal pertaining to focus.

fodder n dried food for cattle, horses etc.

foe n enemy.

foetus, fetus n distinctly developed embryo in womb

or egg; a foetal.

fog n thick mass of water vapour, smoke, dust in lower atmosphere; thick mist; v fogging, fogged.1 cover in fog 2 confuse; a foggy; ns fog-bank belt of fog; ns foghorn warning for ships in fog; f. lamp; a fogbound trapped by fog.

fogey, fogy n fussy, slow old-fashioned person.

foible n weakness of character; idiosyncrasy.

foil[1] n 1 thin sheet of metal 2 quick-silver coating behind glass of mirror 3 person, thing enhancing another by contrast.

foil[2] n light sword with button on end, used in fencing; v baulk; frustrate; repel (attack).

foist v palm off; impose fraudulently.

fold[1] v bend over back on itself; double up; wrap round; clasp (in arms etc); n crease made by folding; piece of folded material; hollow in hill; n folder folded printed circular, paper etc; container for documents.

fold[2] n enclosure, pen for sheep; v enclose in fold.

foliage n collectively, leaves of trees etc; a foliate bearing leaves; leaf-like.

folio n -os. 1 sheet of paper folded once 2 large size paper; book made of such sheets 3 page number; v number pages of book.

folk n 1 nation 2 people in general; ns **folk dance** traditional dance; **folklore** traditional beliefs etc.

follicle n small sac; seed-vessel; cocoon; a **follicular**.

follow v 1 go, come after 2 go by, along 3 be later than; come (next) after 4 understand 5 arise; be logical, necessary consequence 6 take interest in; monitor 7 obey; be disciple of; idm **follow suit** do likewise; phr v as **follow through** pursue to the end; **follow up** 1 investigate 2 take further action on; ns **follower**, **f.-through**, **f.-up**; a **following** 1 next 2 (of wind) favourable; n group of supporters.

folly n 1 foolish act 2 rashness 3 useless, fantastic building.

foment v apply holt lotion, poultice to; stir up (trouble etc.); n **fomentation**.

fond a loving, affectionate; over-indulgent; idm **be fond of** have affection /liking for; n **fondness**; v **fondle** caress.

font[1] n bowl for baptismal holy water, in church.

font[2] n US = **fount**.

food n any substance, esp solid, consumed to support life and growth; idm **food for thought** sth which will stimulate thinking; ns **f.-chain** sequence of living beings each eating the next as food; **f.poisoning**, **f.processor**, **foodstuff**, **f.value**; **foodie**, **foody** coll

person obsessed with eating, preparing food.

fool[1] v stupid, silly person; dupe; clown; buffoon; v 1 act with levity 2 dupe; hoax; a **foolish** stupid; absurd; unwise; n **foolery** foolish behaviour; as **foolhardy** rash; foolishly daring (n **-iness**); **fool-proof** infallible; n **foolscap** 1 dunce's cap 2 size of paper.

fool[2] n dish of sieved fruit mixed with cream.

fool's paradise n illusory state of happiness that will not last.

foot n feet. 1 lowest part of leg below ankle 2 bottom end of sock, stocking 3 base; bottom of sth 4 end of bed opposite to head 5 infantry 6 measure of 12 inches 7 metrical unit of verse; pl **feet**; idm **one foot in the door** advantageous position for further manoeuvres; idm **put one's foot down** be insistent; idm **put one's foot in it** coll make a faux pas; idm **ten feet tall** very proud and confident; idm **foot the bill** pay the cost; ns **football**, **footballer**, **football pools** gambling on results of football matches **footbridge** bridge for pedestrians; **footfall** sound of walking; **footfault** tennis step over baseline when serving; **foothill** low hill; **foothold** limited secured position for further progress; **footman** uniformed servant; **footnote**

note at bottom of page; **footpath**, **footprint**, **footstep**; idm **follow in sb's footsteps** imitate sb's actions; ns **footstool**, **footwear**; **footwork** agility with one's feet; v **footslog** walk or march long distance; a **footsore**.

footing n secured position; be on a good footing (with) have a good standing and reputation (with).

footlights n pl floor lights at front of stage.

footloose a free to move or travel.

footnote n note at the bottom of page.

footsie n coll 1 playful touching of feet to arouse sexual interest 2 US secret dealings.

fop n dandy; vain man; a **foppish**.

for prep suitable to; because of; toward; in favour of; instead of; during; at price of; in spite of; in search of; conj because.

for- prefix: forms compounds (mostly verbs implying negative action) with meaning of from, away, against, eg forget, forbid. Also contraction of fore- (see later). Where the meaning may be deduced from the simple word, the compounds are not given here.

forage n food for horses, cattle; v search for forage; rummage about; ns **forager**; **forage cap** military undress cap.

forasmuch as *conj* because, considering that.

foray *n* raid; plundering incursion; *v* raid; ravage.

forbear *v* refrain, abstain from; *pt* **forbore**; *pp* **forborne**; *n* **forbearance**; *a* **forbearing** patient, lenient.

for(e)bear *n* ancestor.

forbid *v* prohibit; prevent; *pt* **forbade**; *pp* **forbidden** *a* **forbidding** threatening; sinister.

force *n* 1 power; mental, moral strength 2 compulsion 3 body of troops, police etc 4 violence; *idm* **in force** operational; *idm* **join forces (with)** unite (with); *v* 1 compel; urge 2 break open 3 cause plants to flower, fruit before natural season 4 produce by effort; *idm* **force sb's hand** make sb act before ready to one's advantage; *as* **forced** produced by special effort or necessity; strained; **forcible** done by force; convincing; **forceful** powerful; impressive.

force-feed *v* make sb eat or drink unwillingly.

force majeure *n Fr* unforeseen circumstance which excuses one from keeping a promise or bargain.

forceps *n* surgical pincers or tweezers.

ford *n* shallow place in river; *v* cross by means of ford.

fore[1] *a, adv* before; in front (of); *comp* **former, further**; *sup* **foremost, first, furthest**; *n* front, forward part; *idm*

come to the fore become prominent, well-known.

fore[2] *interj* golfer's warning call.

fore- *prefix* 1 earlier; before, *eg* **foretell, forewarn** 2 front; leading, *eg* **forecourt, foreman, forearm**.

fore-and-aft *a* along length of ship.

forearm *n* arm between elbow and wrist.

forebode *v* prophesy; portend; *n* **foreboding**, presentiment.

forecast *v* estimate (result) beforehand; *n* prediction of future event.

foreclose *v* take away power of redeeming mortgage; *n* **foreclosure**.

forefather *n* ancestor.

forefinger *n* index finger (next to thumb).

forego *v* **-going, -went, -gone**. foreprecede, go without; *a* **foregone** preceding; already settled.

foregone conclusion *n* certain outcome.

foreground *n* nearest part of picture or view; *idm* **in the foreground** prominent; very noticeable.

forehand *n, a, tennis* (side) where player has palm of hand facing opponent.

forehead *n* part of face between brow and hairline.

foreign *a* 1 of a country other than one's own 2 from outside 3 alien; *idm* **foreign to** strange, unnatural to; *ns* **f.affairs; f.exchange** (dealing in) currencies of

different countries; **F.Office** *Brit* government department handling foreign affairs; **f.national, foreigner** foreign person of other nationality.

forelock *n* front part of hair; *idm* **touch one's forelock** form of salutation, *usu* indicating respect to superior.

foreman *n* 1 leading worker 2 leader of jury; *fem* **forewoman**.

foremost *a* most distinguished; first in position, degree, dignity etc.

forename *n* first name.

forensic *a* pertaining to lawcourts; **f.medicine** medical jurisprudence.

foreplay *n* erotic stimulation prior to intercourse.

forerunner *n* harbinger; precursor.

foresee *v* **-seeing, -saw, -seen**. predict; *a* **foreseeable**.

foreshadow *v* presage; indicate in advance.

foreshore *n* area between limits of high and low tides.

foresight *n* ability to see and plan ahead.

foreskin *n* loose skin covering tip of penis.

forest *n* large tract of land covered with trees; large unenclosed tract of waste land, heath etc; *ns* **forestry** art of managing forests; **forester** 1 one skilled in forestry 2 dweller in forest.

forestall *v* to get ahead of another by anticipation.

forethought *n* prudent thought

for future.

forever *adv* always; *n* eternity.

forewarn *v* warn in advance.

forewent *pt of* forego.

foreword *n* preface.

forfeit *v* lose, as penalty; give up; *n* anything lost as penalty in law or game; *a* confiscated by law; *n* **forfeiture**.

forge *v* 1 soften, shape (metal) by heating 2 imitate deceitfully, counterfeit 3 *fig* hammer out painstakingly; *idm* **forge ahead** progress quickly; *n* smithy; workshop, plant for working red-hot metal; *ns* **forger** counterfeiter; **forgery** fraudulent making or alteration of signature, document etc.

forget *v* -getting, -got, -gotten. cease to remember; accidentally omit; neglect; *a* **forgetful** having bad memory; *n* **forget-me-not** marsh plant with small blue flower.

forgive *v* forgiving, forgave. 1 (offence) pardon 2 (debt); cancel; *n* **forgiveness**.

fork *n* 1 pronged tool, implement for digging, lifting 2 pronged tool for eating 3 junction of two roads, rivers 4 meeting of bough and trunk of tree; *v* 1 dig, lift, toss with fork 2 divide into branches; bifurcate; *idm* **fork out** *coll* pay reluctantly; *a* **forked** dividing with two or more points or branches; *n*

f.lightning.

forklift truck *n* truck with device for lifting heavy weights, crates, etc.

forlorn *a* forsaken; desperate; neglected; **f.hope** very faint hope; *adv* **forlornly**; *n* **forlornness**.

form *n* 1 shape, visible appearance 2 mode of expression; construction 3 type or kind 4 convention, pattern 5 printed formal document with blank spaces to be filled in with information 6 wooden bench; class in school 7 (*also* **forme**) type set and locked in chase 8 (*also* **forme**) hare's lair; *v* 1 shape; create 2 act as 3 develop; educate 4 construct 5 assume shape; *a* **formal** according to rule; orderly; of outward form, lacking reality; stiff; *ns* **formality** 1 propriety 2 *esp pl* conventional procedure 3 ceremony, *esp* one without real meaning or use; **formation** forming; structure; *a* **formative** giving form; tending to shape, develop; *a* **formless** shapeless.

formaldehyde *n* colourless chemical compound; *n* **formalin** solution of formaldehyde used as antiseptic.

format *n* 1 shape of book 2 general plan of sth 3 *comput* arrangement of data; *v* *comput* -**matting**, -**matted**.

prepare with a format; *a* **formatted**.

formation *n* 1 act or instance of forming 2 thing formed 3 pattern of people or vehicles moving together.

former *a* of earlier time; *n* thing or person referred to first; *adv* -**ly** in the past.

Formica [TM] hard laminated heat-resistant plastic sheet.

formidable *a* terrifying; overwhelming; presenting obstacles; huge.

formula *n* 1 set form of words, prescribed for use on particular occasion 2 definition of dogma 3 recipe; prescription 4 method of solving problem; (*pl* **formulae**, **formulas**); *v* **formulate** 1 express in formula 2 reduce to definite terms; *n* **formulation**.

fornication *n* sexual intercourse between unmarried persons; *v* **fornicate**.

forsake *v* abandon; desert; give up; *pt* **forsook**; *pp* **forsaken**.

forswear *v* renounce on oath; perjure oneself; *pt* **forswore**; *pp* **forsworn**.

forsythia *n* shrub with bright yellow flowers.

fort *n* fortress; fortified place, stronghold; *idm* **hold the fort** take care of everything in sb's absence.

forte[1] *n* special ability; strong point.

forte[2] *adv* *mus* loudly; **fortissimo** very loudly.

forth *adv* forwards; onwards; *a*

forthcoming about to appear; *fig* affable; communicative; *adv* **forthwith** at once; immediately.

forthright *a* outspoken;, downright; candid.

fortieth *pron, det* ordinal number of 40.

fortify *v* **-fying, -fied.** strengthen; convert into fortress; *n* **fortification** act of strengthening; *pl* defensive works, walls etc.

fortitude *n* sustained courage, resoluteness in face of pain, danger etc.

fortnight *n* two weeks; *adv* **fortnightly.**

FORTRAN *n comput* high-level progamming language (mathematics, science, etc).

fortress *n* fortified place, stronghold.

fortuitous *a* due to chance; accidental; *n* **fortuity.**

fortune *n* 1 chance; luck; lot in life 2 prosperity; wealth; *a* **fortunate** lucky; *ns* **fortune-hunter** unscrupulous person, trying to obtain wealth, *esp* by marriage; **fortune-teller** one who predicts one's future.

forty *a, n* four tens; **fortieth.**

forty-five *n* pistol of .45 calibre.

forty winks *n coll* daytime nap.

forum *n Lat* 1 public meeting place 2 tribunal; law court.

forward *a* 1 in front of one 2 *fig* advanced; pert; *adv* (*also* **forwards**) towards front; at, in fore part (of ship etc.);

onwards (in direction, time); *n sport* one of players in front line; *v* further; send, post on farther; dispatch; *n* **-ness** pertness.

forwent *pt* of forgo.

fossil *n* petrified remains of prehistoric animal, vegetable organism found preserved in earth or rocks; *fig* antiquated person; *v* **fossilize** petrify; convert into fossil.

foster *v* 1 rear another's child as one's own 2 encourage; cherish; *ns* **foster-child** one not related by blood to foster parents; **f.-mother; f.-father; f.-brother.**

foul *a* 1 dirty and disgusting 2 unpleasant 3 evil 4 obscene (*a* **f.-mouthed**) 5 against the rules; *n, v* act against the rules; *v* 1 make dirty 2 become entangled with; *idm* **foul up** *coll* ruin (life, event, etc) *n* **foul-up**; *n* **f.play** 1 unfair play 2 murder.

found[1] *v* 1 establish; institute 2 endow 3 base; *ns* **foundation** 1 founding 2 substructure of building 3 basis 4 endowed institution (**f.garment** corset; girdle; **f.stone** first stone formally laid of new building); **founder.**

found[2] *v* melt (metal, minerals) and pour into mould; cast; *n* **foundry** place where founding, casting is carried out.

founder *v* (*of ship*) fill with water and sink; (*of horses*)

fall, break down, *esp* through lameness.

fount, font *n* set of printing type of one size and kind.

fount *n* fountain; *fig* source.

fountain *n* artificial, ornamental jet of water; jet of drinking water; *ns* **f.head** source; origin; **f.pen** one with ink reservoir.

four *n, pron, det* cardinal number next after three; *as, ns, dets* **fourth** fourth part; ordinal number; **fourteen** four plus ten; **fourteenth;** *ns* **four-in-hand** vehicle with four horses driven by one person; **four-poster** bed with four posts for curtains; **foursome** game, dance for four persons; *a* **foursquare** firm and steady; *n* **four-stroke** type of internal combustion engine.

four-letter word *n* obscene word, *esp* of four letters.

fourth dimension *n* time.

fourth estate *n* the press.

fowl *n* bird, domestic cock or hen; flesh of birds (as food); *ns* **fowler** hunter of wild birds; **fowling-piece** light gun.

fox *n* 1 reddish bush-tailed animal 2 crafty person; *v* act cunningly; mislead; *ns* **foxglove** plant with long spikes of tubular flowers; **foxhound** hound used for hunting fox; **fox-terrier** small terrier formerly used to drive fox from cover; *a* **foxy** cunning.

foxtrot *n* ballroom dance in

quadruple time.

foyer n large hall, anteroom of theatre.

FPA abbr Family Planning Association.

Fr abbr 1 French 2 eccl Father.

fr abbr franc(s).

fracas n brawl; noisy quarrel.

fraction n numerical quantity less or more than integer; small piece; fragment; a **-al** insignificant; **-ary** fragmentary.

fractious a peevish; fretful; cross.

fracture n 1 breaking, esp of bone 2 break; crack; v break.

fragile a easily broken; brittle; frail; n **fragility**.

fragment n piece broken off; unfinished part; a **-ary** incomplete; n **-ation** separation into fragments.

fragrant a sweet-scented; n **fragrance**.

frail a fragile; not robust (in health); morally weak; n **frailty**.

frame v 1 construct; contrive 2 express in words; 3 coll cause to appear guilty 4 surround with, serve as, frame; n structure; border of wood etc round picture setting; wood and glass structure protecting plants etc; idm **frame of mind** mood; ns **framer**; **frame-up**, false evidence; **framework** substructure, skeleton.

franc n French, Belgian, Swiss etc coin, monetary unit.

franchise n 1 voting rights of citizen 2 right to sell

company's goods or services; v grant such a right.

Franciscan n, a (friar) of Order of St. Francis.

Franco- prefix of France.

Franglais n French full of English expressions and words.

frank a outspoken; sincere; candid; n signature, mark exempting letter from postal charges; v mark letter so; adv **-ly** openly; n **-ness** candour.

frankfurter n German smoked sausage.

frankincense n sweet pungent gum resin used in incense.

frantic a violenty excited, esp with rage, grief, pain; frenzied; adv **-ally, -ly**.

fraternal a pertaining to brother; brotherly; n **fraternity** 1 brotherhood; 2 brotherliness 3 association of men with common interest 4 US male student society; v **fraternize** be on friendly terms; ns **-ization**; **fratricide** crime of killing one's brother; person who kills his/her brother.

fraud n criminal deception, wilful dishonesty; impostor; a **fraudulent**; adv **-ly**; n **-ence**.

fraught a charged; teeming; full of.

fray[1] n noisy fight, brawl; conflict.

fray[2] v make, become ragged (as cloth) by rubbing; wear; ravel edges.

frazzle v fray; wear out; exhaust; n rags and tatters.

freak n abnormal form; monstrosity; whim; caprice; a **-ish**.

freckle n small brownish spot on skin, caused by sun; v mark or become marked with freckles; a **freckled**.

free a 1 not enslaved, confined or restricted 2 open; frank 3 independent 4 exempt 5 gratuitous 6 unattached 7 chem uncombined; idm **free with** generous in giving; idm **make free with** use (sb else's) without permission; adv **-ly**; ns **freedom; freebie** coll free gift; **F.Church** Nonconformist Church; f.**enterprise** system of trade without government control; **f.-fall** falling from plane without parachute open; **freefone** Brit system allowing phone calls to be made without charge to specified numbers; **f.-for-all** general dispute; n, a, adv **freehold** (with) complete ownership of land, building; n **f.house** public house with beer not restricted to one brewery; **f.kick** kick awarded for infringement of rule; **f.lance** (also **freelancer**) self-employed independent worker; **freeman** person given the freedom of the city; **Freemason** member of secret society for mutual help; **Freemasonry, Freepost, f.port; f.rein** freedom of action; **f.speech; f.thinker, f.thinking, f.trade, f.verse**

verse without rhyme, with irregular metre; **freeway** US motorway; **f.will**; as **freehand** drawn without instruments; **free-range** (of eggs) laid under natural conditions; vs **free-load** US coll take advantage of others' generosity; accepting free food, lodging, etc; n **freeloader; freewheel 1** cycle without pedalling **2** act casually, irresponsibly.

freeze v **1** become ice; **2** congeal with cold **3** refrigerate; chill keep (wages, interest etc) fixed at present level **4** fig become rigid **5** pt froze; pp frozen; phr v **freeze out** prevent from taking part; ns **freezer** refrigerator; **freezing point** temperature at which liquids freeze; a **frozen** (food) preserved by freezing; (assets etc) unrealizable.

freight n hire of ship for conveyance of goods; any load of goods for transport, esp ship's cargo; v hire, load (vessel); ns **freighter** cargo vessel; **freightage** charge for transport of goods; **freightliner** fast goods train.

French n, a (the language) of France; pl people of France; ns **F.bean** haricot, kidney bean; **F.chalk**; **F.dressing** salad dressing with oil and vinegar; **F.fries** esp US thin chips; **F.horn** mus brass instrument with coiled tube and valves; **F.kiss** open-mouthed kiss; **F.leave** coll

unofficial leave; **F.letter** coll condom; **F.polish** wood polish of shellac; **F.toast** Brit bread toasted on one side; US bread dipped in egg and fried; **F.window** glazed door to garden or balcony.

frenetic a very busy, frantic.

frenzy n violent excitement; paroxysm of rage, grief etc; a **frenzied**.

frequency n repeated occurrence; elec number of cycles per second of alternating current; **high f., medium f., low f.,** rad rate of vibration of sound waves.

frequent a happening often; numerous; common adv **-ly**; v visit habitually.

fresco n wall-painting on damp plaster.

fresh a **1** new; untainted **2** bracing **3** clean **4** inexperienced **5** sl impudent **6** (of food) not preserved or stale **7** (of water) not salt **8** (of wind) cool; brisk; adv **-ly** with freshness; anew; n **-ness**; v **freshen** make, become fresh; ns **freshnet** freshwater stream flowing into sea; **freshman** undergraduate in the first year.

freshwater a of inland (not salinated) water.

fret[1] v **fretting, fretted.** harass; vex; worry; n worry.

fret[2] n **1** complicated net-like carved work **2** bar on finger board of stringed instrument; v ornament with fret work; ns **f.-saw**

fine-toothed narrow saw used for fret-work; **f.-work** ornamental lace-like carving on wood.

Freudian a pertaining to Sigmund Freud, psychologist, or his theories; n **Freudian slip** error in speech attributed to influence of subconscious thought.

friable a crumbly.

friar n member of mendicant religious order; n **friary** convent of friars.

fricasse n Fr dish of meat, cut in pieces, cooked in rich white sauce; v cook thus.

fricative n, a (consonant) made by air passing through narrow space between teeth, tongue, lips, etc.

friction n rubbing; resistance met when surface of body moves across another; fig antagonism; a **frictional**.

Friday n sixth day of week.

fridge n coll refrigerator.

friend n person for whom one feels affection and respect; companion; helper; associate; member of Society of Friends (Quakers); as **-less; -ly** kind, amiable; ns **-ship** amity; kindly feeling; **-liness** kind attitude of mind.

Friesian n black and white breed of cattle.

frieze n **1** kind of coarse woollen cloth **2** ornamental horizontal band in room or building.

frigate n light warship; sailing warship.

fright n 1 sudden alarm, fear, terror 2 grotesque ugly person; v **frighten** alarm; terrify; a **frightful** shocking; horrible adv **-ly** n **-ness**.

frigid a cold; distant and repellent; devoid of feeling; adv **frigidity**.

frill n pleated, flounced ornamental trimming on edge of dress, curtains etc; pl **-s** affected airs; v make into, adorn with frills; a **frilly**.

fringe n 1 ornamental edging of threads, loops, tassels etc 2 border of hair cut and hanging over forehead 3 outer edge; border; limit; v adorn with, act as fringe.

fringe benefit n benefit from work not part of pay.

Frisbee [TM] saucer-shaped plastic disc for throwing.

frisk v gambol, frolic; a **frisky**; n **-iness**.

fritter n slice of fruit etc, fried in batter.

fritter v waste, dissipate money, time etc.

frivolous a silly; futile; empty-headed; n **frivolity** levity.

frizz v hiss; splutter (as bacon being fried); curl, crisp (hair); a **frizzy** curly.

fro adv (only in phrase) **to and fro** back and forth; up and down.

frock n woman's dress; monk's robe; v invest as priest.

frock coat n (formerly) knee-

length coat for men.

frog n 1 tailless amphibian, developed from tadpole 2 attachment to belt supporting sword 3 ornamental loop and button on clothes; ns **frogman** swimmer equipped and trained for underwater operations; **frog spawn** frog's eggs; **frog in the throat** hoarseness; v **frog-march** carry offender face downwards, four men holding limb each.

frolic a merry; jovial; n merry making; gaiety; v **-icking**, **-icked**. gambol, play pranks; a **frolicsome**.

from prep expressing source, distance, divergence, cause; opposite of **to**; not near to.

front n 1 forward part 2 battle area, forward line 3 promenade by seaside 4 face of building 5 something, person acting as cover for illegal activities 6 forward part of weather change; v face; stand opposite to; idm **in front of** 1 ahead of 2 in the presence of; idm **up front** coll to be paid in advance; **frontage** width of building or plot at front; n, a **frontbench** (occupying) front rows of seats reserved for leading party members in House of Commons, n **-er**; ns **frontier** boundary between states pl **-s** furthest extent; **frontiersman** pioneer of American West; **frontispiece** illustration at

front of book; **front line** most advanced position, a **f.-line**; **f.man** coll 1 leader of organization in touch with public 2 TV presenter; **f.-runner** person with best chance of success.

frost n 1 particles of frozen moisture on earth's or other surface; air temperature causing this 2 sl coolness of manner; v affect with frost; make frosted (with sugar icing etc); a **frosty** freezing; not genial; hoary; n **frostbite** gangrenous injury to tissues, due to exposure to extreme cold; a **frost-bitten**.

froth n light mass of small bubbles; foam; fig futile talk; v cause to emith froth; a **frothy**.

frown v wrinkle forehead; seem gloomy, angry; n contraction of brows.

FRS abbr Fellow of the Royal Society.

frugal a 1 sparing; thrifty 2 inexpensive; n **-ity**.

fruit n 1 edible part of plant containing seed 2 offspring 3 usu pl result of effort; reward a **fruitful** successful adv **-ly** n **-ness**; a **fruitless** vain adv **-ly** n **-ness**; ns **f.bat** tropical fruit-eating bat; **f.cake** 1 cake with dried fruit 2 coll crazy person; **fruiterer** person selling fruit; **f.machine** Brit coin operated gambling machine (also **one-armed bandit**); **f.salad** mixture of fruits in syrup; a **fruity**.

fruition n fulfilment; enjoyment.

frump n plain, dowdy woman; a -**ish**.

frustrate v baffle; circumvent; foil; n -**ation**.

fry[1] n young fishes; **small f. 1** young children **2** insignificant person.

fry[2] v -**ying, -ied.** cook, be cooked in hot fat.

frying pan n **1** shallow pan for frying; idm **out of the frying pan into the fire** coll escaping one disaster to land in something even worse.

fry-up n Brit coll meal of fried food.

ft abbr foot.

FT Index abbr Financial Times Industrial Ordinary Shares Index.

fuchsia n ornamental flowering shrub.

fuddle v make stupid by intoxication; tipple.

fuddy-duddy n, a fussy, old-fashioned (person).

fudge[1] n **1** soft, sugary sweetmeat **2** nonsense.

fudge[2] v coll **1** perform clumsily **2** evade **3** falsify.

fuel n any material used for burning; v **fuelling, fuelled.** provide with, take in fuel.

fug n fustiness; closeness of air; a **fuggy**.

fugitive a fleeing; transient; evanescent; n one fleeing from danger, captivity etc.

fugue n musical contrapuntal composition with recurring themes.

fulcrum n point on which lever moves.

fulfil v -**filling, -filled.** satisfy; comply with; carry out, perform; n -**ment**.

fulgent a shining; radiant; blazing; n **fulgency**.

full a **1** unable to hold more **2** well fed **3** complete; ample **4** maximum **5** (of sound) resonant **6** (of clothes) hanging loosely **7** plump; idm **be full of** think only of; as **f.-blooded** whole-hearted; vigorous; **f.-blown** fully developed; **f.-grown** adult; **f.-length, f.-scale, f.-time;** adv **fully;** as **fully-fashioned** shaped to fit; **fully-fledged 1** with full feathers ready to fly **2** fully trained; ns **fullness** idm **in the fulness of time** in the end; **fullback** field sport defender; **f.house 1** capacity audience **2** poker three of one suit and two of another; **f.moon, f.stop** punctuation at end of sentence; idm **come to a full stop** stop doing, moving altogether.

fuller n tradesman who shrinks, cleanses cloth; v **full** thicken, cleanse, dress, cloth; n **fuller's earth** clay used in fulling.

fulminate v **1** flash; explode; detonate; **2** denounce violently; n highly explosive compound; n -**ation**.

fulsome a excessive.

fumble v grope clumsily with hands; bungle; n.

fume n **1** esp pl pungent smoke; vapour **2** fig anger; v **1** emit fumes **2** fig fret, be angry; v **fumigate** disinfect by fumes ns -**ation, -ator.**

fun n mirth; enjoyment; sport; joking; **make f. of** ridicule; **in f.** as joke.

function n **1** normal action, occupation or purpose; duty **2** official task, ceremony **3** large social gathering **4** math quantity whose value is linked to varying value of another; v work; act; a -**al** having special purpose; med affecting function; n -**ary** official.

fund n permanent stock; sum set apart for special purpose; pl -**s** money resources; v convert into, provide, invest in, permanent fund; n **funding** act, process of creating funded debt.

fundament n buttocks; a **fundamental** basic; essential; adv -**ly** n basic rule; principle ns -**ism, -ist.**

funeral n burial, interment of dead; a relating to funeral; ns **f.director** undertaker; **f.parlour** (US **f.home**) undertaker's premises; as **funereal** mournful; dismal; black; **funerary** of, for funeral.

funfair n esp Brit travelling fair with amusements.

fungus n -**i** plant or allied growth reproducing by spores, eg mushroom, mildew etc; a **fungoid, fungous;** n **fungicide** substance which destroys fungi.

funicular a connected with,

worked by rope.

funk n 1 fear 2 coward; v fear; try to avoid, through fear.

funky a coll 1 with simple style 2 fashionable.

funnel n 1 cone shaped tube for pouring liquids through to container 2 smoke stack of ship, locomotive; v pour off, as through funnel.

funny a 1 amusing 2 strange; idm be **funny with** cause problems (on purpose); adv **funnily**; ns **funniness**; **funny bone** elbow; **f.business** coll trickery; **f.farm** US mental hospital.

fur n 1 short soft hair forming animal coat; dressed skin of animal; pl such skins collectively 2 coating; deposit (on tongue, in kettle etc); v cover, become coated, with fur, n **furrier** dealer in furs; a **furry** of, like fur.

furbish v polish, clean up; burnish.

furcate a branched; forked.

furious a raging; violent; frenzied; savage; vehement; ns **-ness**, **fury**.

furl v roll up and bind securely (sail, umbrella).

furlong n ⅛th mile, 220 yards (approx, 207 m).

furnace n enclosed chamber of brick, metal in which great heat can be generated.

furnish v provide; equip, esp house, office etc with furniture; ns **furnisher** one who sells furniture; **furnishing** act of equipping

house pl **-s** furniture, fittings.

furniture n movable household equipment.

furor n general excitement.

furore n strong public protest.

furrier n person making, selling fur clothing.

furrow n 1 groove made in land by plough 2 deep wrinkle on face etc; v make furrows.

further v forward; promote; adv besides; a, adv (comp of far) more distant; to greater degree, extent; idm **further to** adding to a, adv **furthest** most distant; to greatest degree, extent; n **furtherance** promotion; adv **furthermore** besides; a **furthermost** most distant.

further education Brit post-16+ non-university education.

furtive a stealthy, secret, sly; n **-ness**.

fury n 1 extreme anger; rage 2 avenging goddess.

furze n thick growing, yellow flowered prickly shrub.

fuse n 1 device to explode shells, mines etc 2 soft wire with low melting point, used as safety device in electric circuits; v 1 melt (metal) with heat 2 fit fuse to; a **fusible**; n **fusion** act of melting, blending; fig coalition.

fuselage n body of aircraft.

fusel-oil n mixture of crude alcohols.

fusillade n continuous rapid firing.

fuss n nervous, anxious state of mind; needless bustle; v worry about; make nervous.

fusspot n coll fussy person.

fusty a stale and stuffy; old-fashioned.

futile a vain; useless; ineffectual; n **futility**.

futon n padded quilt used as bed.

future a happening hereafter; of, connected with time to come; n 1 time to come 2 fate 3 tense of verb indicating future; pl **-s** comm goods or shares for later delivery paid for at today's prices, ns **futurity**; **futurism** non-representational art against tradition; a **futuristic**.

fuzz n 1 stiff fluffy hair 2 sl police; a **fuzzy** fluffy; blurred

FYI abbr US for your information.

g *abbr* gram.

gab *n* chatter; talkativeness; *v* **gabble** utter rapidly and indistinctly; *n* rapid, confused speech; jabbering.

gabardine, gaberdine *n* 1 thin, ribbed woollen fabric; rainproof coat of this 2 long, loose gown, *esp* worn by Jews.

gabble *v* speak too fast to be intelligible; *n* such talk.

gable *n* triangular upper part of wall of building enclosed by roof ridges.

gad *v* **gadding, gadded.** wander about aimlessly or seeking pleasure; *n* **gadabout** pleasure-seeker.

gadget *n* ingenious applicance; device, often useless.

Gaelic *n* Celtic speech, *esp* of Scotland; pertaining to Gaels; *n* **Gael** Scottish, Irish Celt.

gaffe *n* blunder; tactlessness.

gaffer *n* aged rustic; foreman.

gag *n* 1 anything thrust into mouth to silence person 2 device for keeping mouth open during operation 3 unscripted remark; *sl* joke; *v* **gagging, gagged.** 1 silence by gag 2 put in jokes, remarks not in script 3 retch.

gaga *a coll* senile.

gage[1] *n* pledge; symbol of challenge to fight; *v* pledge; stake.

gage[2] *US* = **gauge.**

gaggle *n* flock of geese; *v* cackle.

gaiety *n* cheerfulness.

gaily *adv* in a cheerful manner.

gain *v* 1 obtain; secure; win 2 profit 3 improve 4 earn; *n* increase; improvement; *a* **-ful,** yielding gain.

gainsay *v* **gainsaying, gainsaid.** dispute; contradict; deny.

gait *n* manner of walking, running.

gaiter *n* cloth, leather covering for lower leg.

gal *n coll* girl.

gala *n* festivity; fête.

galaxy *n* vast cluster of stars, as Milky Way; *fig* brilliant assembly *a* **galactic.**

gale *n* strong, violent wind.

galena *n* natural lead sulphide.

gall[1] *n* 1 bile, bitter secretion from liver 2 *fig* bitterness 3 effrontery; *ns* **g.-bladder** small bladder, containing bile; **g.-stone** hard stony concretion formed in gall-bladder.

gall[2] *n* 1 sore, *esp* on horse, caused by friction 2 growth on tree, *esp* oak, produced by gall-fly; *v* make sore by rubbing; irritate.

gallant *a* 1 brave; daring 2 chivalrous; attentive to women; *n* **gallantry.**

galleon *n* old three- or four-decked sailing ship.

gallery *n* 1 upper tier of seats in theatre, church etc 2 underground passage in mine 3 long narrow covered passage, open at one side 4 room, building for showing works of art.

galley *n* 1 low, single decked ship with sails and oars 2 ship's cookhouse 3 tray holding composed type 4 galley-proof; *ns* **g.-proof** proof before being made up into pages; **g.-slave** one condemned to row in galley; drudge.

Gallic *a* of, relating to Gaul; French; *n* **Gallicism** French word, idiom used in another language.

gallivant v gad about.

gallon n liquid or dry measure of capacity.

gallop n fastest pace of horse etc; quick ride; v move, ride at gallop; fig hurry.

Gallop poll n survey of public opinion.

gallows n wooden structure used for hanging criminals.

galore adv plentifully; in great abundance.

galosh, golosh n protective overshoe worn in wet weather.

galvanism n electricity produced by chemical action; a **galvanic** fig spasmodic; v **galvanize** electrify by galvanism; coat with metal by galvanizing; n **galvanization**.

gambit n 1 chess opening move, when piece is intentionally sacrificed 2 initial move in action, conversation etc.

gamble v play games of chance for money stakes; place (money) at stake; fig take risk or chance; n act of gambling; risky chance; n **gambler**.

gambol v frolic.

game[1] n pastime; sporting contest; artful trick; jest; v gamble; a plucky; lame; n **gamester** gambler.

game[2] n birds, animals hunted for food, sport; pl **-s** (series of) sporting contests; **game-keeper** man employed to look after game.

gamesmanship n art of winning by distracting one's opponent without breaking any rules.

gamet n mature sexual reproductive cell that joins with another to form a new organism.

gamin n 1 street urchin 2 neglected, impertinent child.

gamma n third letter of Greek alphabet; **g-rays** very short electro-magnetic waves.

gammon n cut of bacon.

gammy a coll crippled, lame.

gamut n whole range, compass of voice, notes etc; fig whole extent, scope.

gamy a strong scented, flavoured like game that has been hanging.

gander n 1 male goose 2 sl look.

gang n group; squad; band of criminals; n **ganger** foreman; phr v **gang up on** conspire against.

gangland n underworld of professional crime.

gangling a awkwardly tall and thin.

ganglion n 1 nerve-centre 2 hard globular swelling, usually on sinew.

gangplank n moveable gangway for boarding, leaving ship.

gangrene n mortification of living tissue, necrosis; a **gangrenous**.

gangster n 1 member of criminal gang; violent, armed criminal.

gangway n passage; road 2 movable bridge from ship to shore 3 way between rows of seats.

ganja n cannabis.

gaol n (also **jail**) place of confinement for criminals.

gap n hole, opening, space; interval.

gape v stare in wonder or amazement; open widely.

garb n clothing, dress.

garbage US n 1 food waste 2 useless information.

garbled a confused, jumbled.

garden n area of ground for growing flowers, fruit, or vegetables; v cultivate a garden; ns **gardener**; **gardening**; **garden centre** place where plants, garden tools, etc are sold.

gargantuan a extremely large.

garish a gaudy; ostentatious.

garland n wreath of flowers, leaves, used as decoration, or sign of victory; v hang, adorn with garlands.

gargle v wash or soothe sore throat with liquid held there by blowing gently.

gargoyle n often grotesque head carved on waterspout on a church.

garlic n bulbous-rooted plant of onion family, used as flavouring.

garment n article of clothing.

garner v store up; accumulate.

garnet n red semi-precious stone.

garnish v decorate, improve appearance of (esp food); n

material for this; n **garniture** ornamentation.

garret n room under roof of house; attic.

garrison n troops defending fortress, town etc; v furnish with, act as garrison.

garrotte v execute by strangling; strangle; n instrument used for execution in Spain; cord so used; n -**er**.

garrulous a talkative; n **garrulity**.

garter n band worn to keep stocking up; cap highest order of knighthood in Britain.

garth n enclosed space; court; yard; garden.

gas n -**es** or -**ses**. 1 one of various vapourous substances 2 air-like fluid 3 coal-gas used for heating, lighting, etc 4 poisonous vapour used in warfare 5 such vapour used as anaesthetic 6 US petrol; v **gassing, gassed**. use gas upon; sl talk nonsense at length; ns **gasholder, gasometer; gasman, g. mask; g. pedal** US aut accelerator; **g. station** US filling station; **gasworks**; as **gaseous; gassy**; n **gassiness**.

gash n deep cut; slash; v cut deeply.

gasket n 1 rope, cord for securing sail 2 tow; jointing, packing material 3 type of washer.

gasolene, gasoline n liquid distilled from petroleum; US

petrol (also **gas**).

gasp v catch breath suddenly, as in surprise or fear; n sudden catching of breath.

gastric a of, relating to stomach; ns **gastritis** inflammation of stomach.

gastroenteritis n inflammation of stomach and bowels.

gastronomy n science of good food; a **gastronomic; (adv - ally).**

gate n 1 hinged frame of wood or metal across opening, path etc 2 sluice 3 way in or out of place 4 total number of spectators at sporting event 5 total amount paid by these for admission; v confine (undergraduate) to college; v **gatecrash** enter uninvited; n -**er**.

gateau n Fr rich, fancy cake; pl **gateaux**.

gateleg table n table with folding top and moveable leg.

gateway n entrance with gate; idm **gateway to** way of reaching or acquiring sth.

gather v 1 bring together; collect 2 acquire 3 infer 4 fester 5 pucker; n **gathering** 1 assembly 2 purulent swelling; **gathers** small pleats in fabric.

gauche a clumsy; tactless; awkward; n **gaucherie**.

gaucho n S American cowboy.

gaudy a showy; garish; vulgarly fine; n -**iness**.

ga(u)ge n 1 standard of measure (diameter of wire, distance between rails,

thickness of sheet metal, etc) 2 instrument for measuring rainfall, force of wind, speed of current, etc 3 device for testing size of tools etc; v measure; fig estimate.

gaunt a lean and haggard; grim and forbidding.

gauntlet a glove with protective cuff; idm **throw down g.** issue challenge; idm **run the g.** run (as punishment) between two rows of hostile men; fig be exposed to hostile attacks, criticism.

gauss n unit of intensity of magnetic field.

gauze n thin, transparent silk or other fabric; light haze; a **gauzy**.

gavel n chairman's, auctioneer's hammer.

gawky a awkward; ungainly; n **gawk** such a person.

gawp v stare at in a stupid way.

gay a 1 dated bright; cheerful 2 homosexual; n homosexual.

gaze v look intently, fixedly.

gazebo n pavilion structure set on a lawn.

gazelle n small, delicately formed antelope.

gazette n official journal giving public notices, government and services appointments, bankruptcies etc; title of newspaper; v publish in gazette; n **gazetter** geographical dictionary.

gazump v Brit raise the price of property after an offer has been accepted; ns -**er, -ing.**

GB *abbr* Great Britain.

GBH *abbr* grievous bodily harm.

GCHQ *abbr* Government Communications Headquarters.

GCSE *abbr* General Certificate of Secondary Education.

GDP *abbr* gross domestic product (country's total annual production figure).

GDR *abbr* (formerly) German Democratic Republic.

gear *n* 1 apparatus; tools 2 harness 3 mechanism transmitting, regulating, or controlling movement 4 gear ratio 5 *sl* clothes; wheel, cog with teeth; *v* provide with, put in gear; *ns* **gear-box, g.-case** case enclosing gear wheels etc; **gearing system of cog-wheels, forming gear; out of g.** disengaged from gear; *fig* inharmonious.

gecko *n* house lizard.

geese *pl* of **goose.**

geezer *n coll* man.

Geiger counter *n* instrument that detects radio-activity.

geisha *n* Japanese singing and dancing girl.

gelatin(e) *n* glutinous substance, obtained by simmering animal tissue, bones etc; *a* **gelatinous** like gelatin, jelly.

geld *v* castrate; *n* **gelding** castrated horse.

gelignite *n* highly explosive form of dynamite.

gem *n* precious stone, *esp* one cut and polished; *v* stud, set with gems.

gen *n coll* correct information.

gendarme *n* French police officer.

gender *n* 1 classification of nouns, pronouns according to sex 2 sex.

gender-bender *n coll* transvestite.

gene *n* carrier of hereditary factor in chromosome.

genealogy *n* line of descent from ancestors; pedigree; study of this; *a* **-logical**; *n* **-logist**.

genera *pl* of **Genus.**

general *a* not specific; relating to whole class, group; usual; lacking details; miscellaneous; not specializing; *n* army rank above colonel; *adv* **generally** 1 usually 2 by most people 3 without looking at details; *ns* **general election** national election; **g. practice** public everyday medical service; **g. practitioner** doctor in this; **g. staff** army officers; **g. strike** *ns* **generalissimo** supreme commander; **generality** undetailed statement; *v* **generalize** draw general conclusions; *ns* **-ization; generalship** skilful leadership.

generate *v* beget; produce; be cause of; *n* **generation** 1 act of generating 2 all persons of approx. same age group 3 all persons in same degree of descent from common ancestor 4 period of approx.

30 years separating birth of parent and child; *a* **generative**; *n* **generator** apparatus for producing electricity.

generation gap *n* lack of understanding between parents and younger generation.

generic *a* pertaining to genus or class.

generous *a* 1 open-handed; magnanimous 2 abundant 3 (of wine) full bodied; *n* **generosity** quality of being generous; liberality.

genesis *n* origin; mode of production; *pl* **geneses**; *n cap* first book of Bible.

genetics *n* branch of biology, dealing with heredity; *a* **genetic**.

genetic engineering *n* artificial change to genetic structure of organism to produce new strain.

genetic fingerprint *n* the genetic information about an individual, used to identify the person or as evidence in court.

genial *a* 1 kindly; amiable; cordial 2 (*of climate*) mild, warm; *n* **-ity**.

genie *n* genii Arabian demon or spirit.

genital *a* relating to animal reproductive organs; *n pls* external reproductive organs.

genitalia *n pl* genitals.

genius *n* 1 exceptional intellectual, artistic ability 2 person having such ability 3 natural aptitude 4 guardian spirit; pl **geniuses**.

genocide n deliberate murder of a people.

genre n 1 kind; style; species 2 painting of rustic life.

gent n coll gentleman; pl **-s** Brit men's toilet.

genteel a unnaturally polite, elegant or affected (usu sarcastic).

gentian n herb usually having vivid blue flowers.

gentile n person who is not Jewish.

gentle a 1 well-born 2 mild; serene 3 soft 4 moderate; docile; ns **gentility** gentle breeding; **gentleman** well-born man; honourable, courteous man; **gentleness** quality of being gentle; kindliness; **gentry** upper-class people, below nobility; **gentleman's agreement** agreement binding by honour (not legally); a **gentlemanly**.

genuflect v bend knee in reverence etc; n **genuflexion** (also **genuflection**).

genuine a 1 true; real 2 sincere; adv **-ly**; n **-ness**.

genus n kind; sort; class; species; group of similar species; pl **genera**.

geo- prefix of the earth.

geocentric a having earth as centre; seen, measured from centre of earth.

geodesic dome n hemispherical structure of polygonal shapes.

geodesy n science of measuring earth and its surface.

geography n 1 science describing earth's physical features, divisions, products, climate, plant and animal life, population etc 2 book on geography; n **geographer**; a **geographic(al)**.

geology n science dealing with earth's crust, its history and structure; n **geologist** a **geologic(al)**; v **geologize** study geology of earth.

geometry n mathematical science dealing with properties and relations of lines, surfaces etc; n **geometrician**; a **geometric(al)** adv **-ally**.

geophysics n science dealing with earth's physics; a **geophysical**.

geopolitics n study of effects of geographic, economic factors on politics; a **geopolitical**.

Geordie n person from NE England.

geostationary a maintaining the same position above the Earth.

geranium n one of genus of flowering plants, as crane's bill; pelargonium (cultivated).

gerbil n small, burrowing rodent often kept as a pet.

geriatrics n pl medical care and treatment of old people; a **geriatric** of old people.

germ n 1 rudimentary form of organism from which new one can develop 2 microbe 3 fig elementary thing; n

germicide substance capable of killing germs.

German n (native, language) of Germany; **g. measles** contagious disease; **German shepherd** large wolflike dog used in police work and as guide for the blind.

germane a relevant; pertinent; appropriate.

germicide n chemical that kills germs.

germinate v begin, cause, to sprout or develop; n **germination**.

gerontology n study of old age.

gerrymander v falsify facts; manipulate for personal politic advantage.

gerund n verbal noun.

Gestapo n Nazi secret police.

gestation n period from conception until birth.

gesticulate v use motions of hands, arms, when speaking, for emphasis; n **gesticulation**.

gesture n 1 movement of limbs, etc to convey meaning 2 something done for effect.

get v getting, got. 1 receive; obtain 2 reach; bring to specified state 3 make happen 4 come to the point of doing 5 move 6 induce 7 become 8 understand; phr **get around to** find time to; **get at** 1 criticize; attack 2 imply; understand; **get away with** avoid being punished for; **get by** survive; manage; **get sb down** depress sb; **get down to** start work on; **get off**

escape punishment; **get off with** *coll* form an amorous relationship with; **get on 1** progress 2 be friendly; **get round 1** avoid 2 persuade; **get up** organize; **get up to** do (mischief).

getaway *n* escape.

getup *n coll* choice of clothes.

geyser *n* natural spout of hot water; device for heating domestic water.

ghastly *a* terrifying; horrible; shocking; pallid.

gherkin *n* small cucumber used in pickles.

ghetto *n* Jewish quarter of city, town; any (*usu* poor) quarter inhabited by one racial or ethnic group.

ghetto blaster *n coll* large portable radio-cassette player.

ghost *n* spirit; wraith; spectre; anything vague, shadowy, *ns* **g. town** deserted town; **g. writer** person writing material for a well-known person, under whose name it will be published; *idm* **(not) the ghost of a** (not) the slightest; **-ly;** *n* **-liness.**

ghoul *n* 1 spirit that feeds on corpses 2 person of morbid interests; *a* **-ish.**

GHQ *abbr* Government Headquarters.

ghyll, gill *n* ravine; gully; chasm.

GI *n US* enlisted soldier.

giant *n* man, animal or plant of abnormally large size; mythical being of enormous size; *fem* **giantess;** *a* huge; *a*

gigantic huge, immense.

gibber *v* talk, chatter incomprehensibly; *n* **gibberish** incoherent speech; meaningless words.

gibbet *n* gallows-post, used for execution by hanging.

gibbon *n* small, long armed ape.

gibbous *a* convex, bulging; humped; (of moon) between half and full.

gibe *v* deride; sneer; utter taunts.

giblets *n pl* edible inner parts of fowl.

giddy *a* 1 dizzy; have feeling of, cause vertigo 2 flighty; *n* **giddiness.**

gift *n* 1 something given; present 2 talent; aptitude 3 act, right of giving; *a* **gifted** talented.

gift-wrap *v* wrap as for presentation; *n* **g-wrapping.**

gig[1] *sl* (booking for) performance of pop-music.

gig[2] 1 ship's boat 2 two-wheeled carriage.

gigabyte *n* one billion bytes.

gigantic *n* enormous.

giggle *v* laugh in suppressed, nervous way; titter.

gigolo *n* young man kept by older woman.

gild *v* gilding, gilded or gilt. coat thinly, with gold; *fig* embellish; *a* gilt gilded; *n* gilt gold leaf or paint.

gilt-edged *a* (of securities) with fixed, guaranteed interest rate.

gill[1] *n* liquid measure, ¼ pint.

gill[2] *n* fish's breathing organ;

flesh under chin and jaws of man.

gimbals *n pl* rings and pivot for keeping compass etc horizontal.

gimlet *n* small tool for boring holes.

gimmick *n sl* trick; gadget; device for attracting publicity.

gimp *n* plaited cord, braid used as trimming.

gin[1] *n* alcoholic liquor distilled from grain, flavoured with juniper berries.

gin[2] *n* 1 snare; trap 2 kind of crane 3 machine separating seeds from cotton.

ginger *n* 1 tropical spicy plant 2 *sl* energy, spirit; *a* sandy red colour; *phr v* **ginger up** *coll* stir up, stimulate; *ns* **g. ale, g. beer; gingerbread** cake flavoured with ginger; **g. group** politically active group; **g. nut** ginger biscuit (*US* **g. snap**), *a* **gingery 1** of, like ginger 2 reddish 3 *fig* testy.

gingerly *a* cautious; *adv* carefully.

gingham *n* cotton cloth, often checked or striped.

gingivitis *n* inflammation of gums.

ginseng *n* root of plant eaten to promote vitality.

Gipsy, Gypsy (also gipsy, gypsy) *n* 1 member of wandering race of Indian origin 2 their language; Romany.

giraffe *n* very tall African ruminant.

gird v girding, girded or girt. encircle with belt, esp at waist; put on (belt etc); attach to (with belt); n **girder** large metal or wooden beam.

girl n female child; young unmarried woman; coll any young(ish) woman; n **-hood**; a **-ish**.

giro n 1 computer-operated banking system 2 Brit (cheque issued as) social security payment.

girth n belly-band of saddle etc; circumference.

gist n essence, main points (of speech etc).

gîte n Fr country house for hire.

give v giving, gave. 1 present; offer 2 pay 3 provide 4 cause; inflict 5 yield 6 utter 7 communicate; idm **not give a damn** not care at all; idm **give and take** show readiness to compromise; n **give-and-take**; idm **give it to sb** 1 attack; criticize 2 admit; **give way (to)** 1 yield (to) 2 be superseded (by) 3 fail to control; phr vs **give away** 1 present 2 sell for no profit 3 betray 4 reveal (secret); **give in** surrender; **give off** emit; **give out** 1 distribute 2 be exhausted; fail; **give over** coll make room by moving; **give up** 1 surrender; abandon 2 treat as lost 3 treat as too difficult; a **given** fixed; n **g. name** US first name; conj **given (that)** granted (that);

idm **be given to** have a tendency towards; n **giver**.

giveaway n 1 revealing act or remark 2 event where prizes are awarded.

gizzard n muscular stomach of birds.

glabrous a smooth; hairless.

glaciation n formation of glaciers.

glacier n slowly moving mass of ice, in mountain valleys; a **glacial** of ice, glaciers, very cold; fig frigid.

glad a happy; joyful; pleased; v **gladden** make glad; cheer; n **-ness**. ns **g. eye** coll seductive look; **g. hand** warm welcome; **g. rags** coll clothes for special occasion.

glade n opening, clearing in wood, forest.

gladiator n in ancient Rome, professional fighter with sword etc in arena.

Gladstone bag n large leather bag.

glamour n mysterious charm; magical illusion; fascination; a **glamorous**; v **glamorize**.

glance n, v (give) quick look; idm **at a glance** instantly; phr v **glance off** strike at angle and ricochet; a **glancing** hitting at an angle.

gland n organ that secretes substance for use in body, and also transforms, excretes; a **glandular**; n **glanders** contagious disease of horses.

glare v 1 emit dazzling light 2 stare angrily; n blinding brightness; a **glaring**

dazzling; flagrant.

glasnost n former Soviet policy of speaking openly.

glass n 1 hard, brittle substance, usu transparent, made by fusion of sand, soda, potash etc 2 drinking vessel of glass 3 its contents 4 mirror 5 barometer 6 telescope 7 optical lens; pl **-es** 1 lenses 2 spectacles; ns **glassblower, glassblowing**; **g. fibre** fibreglass; **glasshouse, glassware, glassworks**; a **glassy**; adv **glassily**; n **-iness**.

glaucoma n disease of the eye.

glaucous a 1 greyish-green 2 bot with waxy, powdery surface.

glaze v 1 put glass into 2 coat with glassy substance 3 become glassy; n glass-like surface; vitreous coating for pottery; glossy coating; n **glazier** one who glazes windows.

gleam v emit beams of light; reflect light; n beam; transient flash of light.

glean v pick up stray ears of corn, scraps; fig gather (facts etc); n **gleaner**.

glebe n land held by incumbent of benefice.

glee n light-hearted mirth; partsong; a **-full**.

glen n narrow valley (usu with woods and stream).

glib a fluent; plausible; smooth-spoken; n **-ness**.

glide v 1 slide, move along smoothly, stealthily 2 fly (aircraft) without use of engine; fly in glider; n 1 action, motion of gliding 2 musical slur 3 glancing stroke (cricket); n **glider** aircraft without engine.

glimmer v flicker, glow faintly; n **-ing** fitful dream; fig faint idea.

glimpse a fleeting view; passing sight; v catch glimpse of.

glint v flash, reflect light faintly; glitter.

glissade n slide (usu on feet) down snow or ice slope; sideward glide in dancing.

glisten v glitter, shine, sparkle.

glitch n elec sudden malfunctioning.

glitter v shine, sparkle intermittently; fig make brilliant show.

glitterati n fashionable, wealthy literary or show-business personalities.

glitz n showy glamour; a **-y**.

gloaming n Scot twilight.

gloat v dwell upon, exult in silently, with malicious joy.

globe n 1 sphere; ball 2 Earth; model of Earth; a **global** 1 worldwide; universal 2 covering whole group, overall; adv **-ly**; ns **globetrotter** extensive traveller; v **g.-trotting**; n **global warming** increase in temperature of the earth's atmosphere believed to be caused by the greenhouse effect.

globule n drop of liquid; a **globular** ball-shaped; n **globulin** protein

constituent of haemoglobin.

glockenspiel n instrument of metal bars struck by hammers, giving bell-like notes.

glomerate v collect into ball, cluster; n **-ation**.

gloom n darkness; melancholy; a **gloomy** 1 dismal; dark 2 pessimistic.

glory n 1 splendour; earthly pomp 2 heavenly bliss; high degree of pride etc; v take delight in; boast; v **glorify** exalt; invest with glory; n **-fication**; a **glorious** sublime; famous; illustrious.

glory-hole n Brit coll room, storage area where things need not be left tidily.

gloss[1] n sheen; polished surface; v put gloss on; phr v **gloss over** conceal (faults); a **glossy**.

gloss[2] n marginal note; explanation; v comment; explain away; n **glossary** explanatory list of words.

glottal stop n sound made by closure of glottis followed by release of air, eg when speaking the word "little".

glottis n opening of larynx; a **glottal**.

glove n covering for hand and fingers; v provide with gloves; idm **hand in g.** very intimate; n **glover** one who sells, makes gloves.

glow v 1 be incandescent; emit steady light without flame 2 be hot with emotion 3 be, look warm; n

incadescence; sense of bodily warmth; ardour; n **g. worm** beetle; a **glowing**.

glower v scowl.

glucose n sugar found in fruits.

glue n adhesive, esp one made from horns, hoofs, etc; v fasten with glue; idm **glued to** unable to turn one's attention from.

glue-sniffing n inhaling fumes of certain glues for intoxicating effect; n **g.-sniffer**.

glum a morose; sullen; moody.

glut v surfeit; satiate; n superabundance.

gluten n protein found in wheat flour; a **-ous**.

glutinous a of nature of glue; adhesive, sticky.

glutton n greedy feeder; insatiable enthusiast (for work, etc); wolverine; a **-ous** greedy; n **gluttony**.

glycerin(e) n sweet, colourless, viscous liquid extracted from fats and oils.

GM abbr George Medal.

GMT abbr Greenwich Mean Time.

gnarl n knot on a tree.

gnarled a knobby; rugged; weather-beaten.

gnash v grind teeth with rage.

gnat n small blood-sucking winged insect.

gnaw v chew, bite steadily at; wear away (by pain, worry etc).

gneiss n crystalline, banded granite-like rock.

gnome n dwarfish earth-goblin.

gnomes of Zurich n pl powerful, esp Swiss bankers.

gnomic a (full) of sayings; seemingly profound.

gnosis n special mystical knowledge; a **gnostic**.

GNP abbr gross national product.

gnu n S African antelope; wildebeest.

go v going, went. 1 move; depart 2 operate; function 3 belong; be appropriate; fit 4 lead to 5 make (noise) 6 become 7 turn out; idm **anything goes** anything is acceptable; idm **go for nothing** be wasted; idm **sth to be going on with** as a temporary measure; phr vs **go about 1** reverse direction 2 approach (task); go ahead proceed; **go along with** agree with; **go back on** change one's mind about; **go down 1** descend 2 be defeated 3 be received; **go down with** fall ill with; **go for 1** attack 2 aim at 3 have a liking for 4 be applicable to; **go in for 1** enter (contest) 2 like 3 practise; **go off 1** depart 2 explode 3 (of food) turn bad 4 cease to like 5 start ringing, sounding 6 succeed; **go over 1** check 2 transfer allegiance; **go through 1** experience 2 succeed 3 search; **go under** fail; become bankrupt; n vitality; idm **it's all go** there's non-stop activity; idm **have a go** try; idm **make a go of sth** make sth succeed; idm **on**

the go very busy; n **goer** active person.

goad n pointed stick for driving cattle; fig incentive; v urge on; fig provoke; incite.

go-ahead a forward-looking; n permission to begin.

goal n 1 score posts in football etc; score so made 2 aim; purpose; destination ns **goalkeeper** defender of goal; **g. kick, g. line g.mouth; g. post** one of two posts supporting crossbar to form goal-mouth; idm **move the goal posts** Brit coll change accepted conditions without consultation.

goat n agile ruminant, often horned and bearded; n **goatee** small pointed beard.

gob n sl mouth; blob of spittle; n **gobbet** morsel of food; v **gobble** eat noisily, greedily; make throaty noise (as turkey); n **gobbler** male turkey-cock.

gobbledygook n jargon; pompous, obscure officialese.

go-between n carrier of messages between people who cannot meet directly.

goblet n drinking vessel without handles.

goblin n malicious ugly sprite.

gobsmacked sl a astounded, astonished, amazed.

god n supernatural being with divine powers; object of worship; idol; cap the Supreme Creator and Ruler; pl coll gallery (theatre); fem

goddess; ns **godfather, -mother, -parent** sponsor at baptism; **godchild** one who is sponsored at baptism; **godhead** godhood, divinity; **godliness** piety; as **God-fearing, godly** pious; **godless** wicked; **godforsaken** desolate, depraved.

gods n pl coll highest seating area in theatre.

godsend n unexpected blessing; lucky chance.

gofer n US assistant who runs menial errands.

go-getter n coll enterprising person.

goggle v (of eyes) bulge; stare stupidly; n wide-eyed stare; n pl protective spectacles; a **g.-eyed** having bulging, staring eyes; n **g.-box** Brit coll TV set.

go-go a US 1 energetic 2 of discos, fast music and dancing.

going n conditions for travel; a thriving; prosperous.

going-over n coll 1 inspection 2 beating.

goings-on n pl mysterious or undesirable activities.

goitre n enlargement of the thyroid gland.

go-kart n small low vehicle for racing.

gold n 1 yellow precious metal 2 objects, esp coins made of this 3 the colour of this; ns **goldfield** area where gold is found; **goldfish**; **g.-digger** woman interested in a man for his money; **g.-dust**; **g.leaf** thin sheet of gold; **g.**

medal, g. medallist, g. mine, g. plate, g. rush, goldsmith; g. standard economic system with money related to value of gold; *a* golden 1 of gold colour or appearance 2 valuable; *ns* age 1 (mythical) time of universal happiness; prosperity 2 period of artistic, literary excellence; g. eagle; g. handshake large sum given to employee on leaving; g. jubilee 50th anniversary celebration; g. mean principle of moderation; g. rule vital principle; G. Syrup [TM] pale refined treacle; g. wedding 50th wedding anniversary.

golf *n* game in which small hard ball is struck by clubs into series of holes, on an open course; *v* play golf; *ns* golfer, golf-course, -links land laid out for golf; g. ball 1 ball for playing golf 2 metal ball with choice of typeface for typewriter; g. club 1 stick for hitting golf ball 2 club with grounds and clubhouse for golf players.

golly *interj coll* to express surprise.

gonad *n* reproductive gland.

gondola *n* Venetian canal-boat; *n* gondolier rower of gondola.

gone *pt of* go.

goner *n coll* person doomed to fail or die.

gong *n* 1 metal disc giving resonant note when struck 2

Brit sl medal, *esp* military.

gonorrhoea *n* venereal disease.

goo *n coll* 1 sticky wet mess 2 sentimentality; *a* -ey; *n* -iness.

good *a comp* better *sup* best 1 right; proper 2 virtuous; pious 3 well-behaved 4 useful; beneficial; valid 5 of positive merit, quality 6 efficient; *idm* good at proficient, clever at; *idm* a good (+quantity) at least; *idm* a good deal a lot; *idm* a good few several; *idm* good for sb indication of congratulating sb; *idm* for good for ever; *idm* make good 1 repair 2 fulfil 3 improve one's ways 4 be a success; *n* 1 what is morally right 2 benefit 3 virtuous people; *pl* 1 wares 2 possessions; *idm* what's the good (of)? what's the use of? *ns* -ness; g. afternoon/day/evening/morning greeting to sb at time specified; G. Book the Bible; G. faith sincerity; honesty; G. Friday Friday before Easter; g. humour cheerfulness (*a* -ed); g. -neighbourliness; g. offices help, mediation to sb in difficulty; G. Samaritan helper of sb in desperate need; goodwill 1 friendship 2 (value estimated for) good reputation of a business firm; goody *esp* adj pl -ies 1 tasty thing to eat 2 good person as hero (*eg* in film); *as* g. hearted, g.-looking, g.-natured, g.-tempered; *a*,

n goody-goody unbearably virtuous.

good-bye *interj*, *n* farewell.

goof *n sl* stupid, awkward person; *a* goofy silly; stupid; *phr v* goof off *US coll* waste time.

googly *n* off-break ball bowled with leg-break action (in cricket).

goon *n sl* foolish person.

goose *n* geese. 1 large web-footed bird 2 *sl* fool 3 tailor's iron; *ns* gooseflesh pimply bristling of skin due to cold, fear etc (*also* goose-pimples); goosestep high-stepping way of marching with stiff legs.

gooseberry *n* 1 thorny shrub, with hairy, sweet edible berries 2 *coll* unwelcome chaperon or third party.

gore[1] *n* blood, shed and clotted; *a* gory.

gore[2] *n* triangular gusset in garment.

gore[3] *v* pierce with horn or tusk.

gorge *n* 1 deep, narrow valley, ravine 2 throat; *v* eat greedily, in excess; *n* gorget throat-armour.

gorgeous *a* wonderful; beautiful.

gorgon *n* 1 mythical snake-haired woman 2 terrifying woman.

Gorgonzola *n* Italian blue cheese.

gorilla *n* largest anthropoid ape.

gormless *a Brit coll* stupid.

gorse *n* spiny yellow-flowered

shrub.

goshawk n large, fierce shortwinged hawk.

gosling n young goose.

go-slow n Brit working slowly as a form of protest.

gospel n 1 one of four books of New Testament; account of life and teaching of Christ 2 fig strongly held principle 3 coll absolute truth.

gossamer n filmy cobweb threads, floating in air, on bushes and grass; any thin filmy material.

gossip n 1 idle talk, esp about others; ill-founded rumour 2 busy-body; v chat casually; spread rumours.

got pt, pp of get.

Gothic a of Goths; n, a arch (of) style of pointed arches 2 (of) German black-letter type face.

gotten US pp of get.

gouache n opaque water-colour paint mixed with gum; picture painted in gouache.

Gouda n type of mild Dutch cheese.

gouge n concave chisel for making grooves; v cut with gouge; phr v gouge out dig out with sharp tool.

goulash n rich stew of meat and vegetables, seasoned with paprika.

gourd n plant of melon, pumpkin class; fleshy fruit of plant; its dried rind used as vessel.

gourmet n connoisseur of food and wine; epicure.

gout n painful, inflammatory

disease of joints esp big toe; a **gouty**.

govern v 1 direct; control; rule 2 determine; influence 3 restrain 4 ling decide (case etc); a **governable**; ns **governor** 1 ruler 2 device regulating speed etc of machine 3 sl father; employer; **governess** private woman teacher; **government** ruling of state; ministry, persons responsible for this; political administrative system; a -**al**.

gown n 1 loose flowing garment 2 woman's dress 3 academic, official robe.

GP abbr general practitioner.

grab v grabbing, grabbed. 1 seize; grasp suddenly 2 snatch eagerly 3 steal; phr v **grab at** attempt to seize; n action of grabbing; idm **up for grabs** coll available to anyone to take; n **g. bag** US lucky dip.

grace n 1 elegant beauty 2 mercy 3 extra time 4 favour; goodwill 5 prayer of thanks for food; idm **have the grace** to be polite enough to; idm **with good/bad grace** willingly/unwillingly; a **graceful** 1 elegant in movement, shape, manner 2 tactful; adv -**fully**; a **graceless** 1 clumsy; 2 rude; boorish; adv -**ly**; n -**ness**; a **gracious** 1 charming; courteous 2 beneficent; adv -**ly**; n -**ness**; v 1 adorn 2 honour.

grade n 1 step 2 degree 3 class;

standard; v classify; arrange in grades; ns **g. crossing** US level crossing; **g. school** elementary school; idm **make the grade** succeed; ns **graduation** arrangement in grades; gradual shading off in colour; **gradient** degree of slope; a **gradual** coming on by degrees; gentle.

graduate v take university degree; mark in degrees, grades; n holder of university degree; n **graduation**.

graffiti n pl writing, drawing on walls.

graft n 1 cutting from one plant fixed to grow on the stem of another 2 skin, bone etc transferred to grow elsewhere on the body 3 use of unfair means, esp bribery from gaining advantage 4 Brit sl hard work n -**er** hard worker.

grail n chalice; Holy Grail.

grain n 1 small, hard particle 2 hard seed esp of cereals 3 smallest unit of weight 4 texture, direction of fibres, (of wood etc) 5 natural disposition; v give imitation wood graining to; n **graining**; a **granular** of, like grains.

gram, gramme n metric unit of weight.

grammar n science dealing with correct use of words, their classes, and structure; book on this; n **grammarian**; a **grammatic(al)** pertaining to, following rules of, grammar; n **grammar school**

type of school.

gramophone n phonograph, instrument for reproducing recorded sounds.

grampus n killer- or spouting-whale; heavy breather.

gran n *Brit coll* grandmother.

granary n grain storehouse.

grand a 1 big; splendid 2 dignified; important 3 *coll* excellent; delightful 4 chief; *idm* **grand old man** person long and deeply respected; n 1 grand piano 2 $1000 or £1000, *pl=sing*; ns **grandchild, granddaughter, grandson** child of daughter/son; **grandad/grandpa** *coll* grandfather; **g.duke**; **grandfather clock** pendulum clock housed in tall case; **g. finale**; **grandma** *coll* grandmother; **g. master** chess champion; **g. opera**; **grandparent, grandfather, grandmother** parent of father/mother; **g. piano** large piano with horizontal strings; **G. Prix** international car race(s); **g. slam** outright victory in all events; **grandstand** tiered seating under cover for spectators; **g. total**.

grandee n nobleman.

grandeur n imposing greatness.

grandiose a imposing; pretentious.

grand jury n panel designated to determine if a law has been broken and prosecution should proceed.

grange n country house, with farm buildings.

granite n very hard granular igneous rock.

granny n *coll* grandmother; ns **g. flat** for old person; **g. knot** insecure variant on reef knot.

grant v assent to; bestow; concede; *idm* **take for granted 1** assume to be true **2** fail to show due appreciation to/for; n gift; money given to maintain student; scholarship allowance.

granule n small grainlike particle; a **granulous, granular; v granulate** reduce to particles; roughen surface; n **granulation** healing formation of grainlike bodies on wound.

grape n fruit of vine; ns **grapefruit** large citrus fruit; **g.-shot** cluster of small iron balls fired from cannon; **grape-sugar** glucose, dextrose, g. **vine** vine on which grapes grow; *idm* **hear on the grape-vine** learn from unofficial but well-informed sources.

graph n diagram showing relative positions, variations (of quantity, temperature etc).

graphic a 1 clear; vivid 2 of visual symbols, writing, drawing; n g. **equalizer** *elec* device for adjusting selected tonal frequencies; *adv* **-ally 1** clearly **2** using graphs; n **graphics 1** drawing by mathematical principles 2

display of information by pictures, etc.

graphology n study of handwriting.

graphite n form of carbon, used in pencils, and as lubricant.

grapnel n hooked anchor for seizing, mooring ship.

grapple n grapnel; close hold, grip; v seize tightly; come to grips; *phr v* **grapple with** struggle with.

grappling iron n grapnel.

grasp v 1 seize, hold firmly; clutch 2 understand; n 1 firm hold, grip 2 comprehension 3 reach; a -ing eager for gain; rapacious.

grass n 1 green herbage of fields, lawns etc 2 pastureland; ns **grasshopper** jumping insect that makes shrill singing noise; **g. roots** *polit* ordinary people; **g. snake**; **g. widow** woman whose husband is often away from home; *idm* **put out to grass 1** leave to graze **2** *coll* force to retire; v sow with grass; *phr v* **grass (on)** *Brit sl* inform police (about other criminals); a **grassy;** n **grassiness.**

grate n fire bars and framework of fireplace; n **grating** open framework of bars.

grate v 1 rub, scrape with rough surface 2 grind into small pieces 3 make harsh noise, by rubbing; *fig* annoy, irritate; n **grater** kitchen utensil; a **grating** rasping;

jarring.

grateful a thankful; feeling gratitude; n **gratefulness**.

gratify v **-fying, -fied.** please; satisfy; content; indulge; ns **gratification, gratitude** feeling of thankfulness, appreciation.

grating n framework of bars across opening allowing passage of air or water, but not larger objects.

gratis a, adv free of charge.

gratitude n gratefulness.

gratuitous a freely given; unwarranted; n **gratuity** gift, esp money, for services rendered.

grave[1] n hole dug in earth for burial; tomb; ns **gravestone, graveyard**.

grave[2] a weighty, serious, solemn; low pitched; n **gravity**.

gravel n small pebbles, coarse sand; shingle; urinary crystals in bladder; v surface (path) with gravel; a **-ly 1** covered with or like gravel **2** (of voice) low and harsh.

gravitate v move by force of gravity; fig be attracted by; n **-tation**.

gravity n **1** force that attracts objects towards one another in space **2** seriousness; importance; phr v **gravitate to/towards** be drawn, attracted to(wards); n **gravitation**; a **-tional**.

gravy[1] n sauce made from juice of roasting meat.

gravy[2] sl esp US money; n **g. train** easy profit with little effort.

gray US **grey**.

grayling n freshwater fish; butterfly.

graze v feed in pastures; n **grazier** one who feeds and fattens cattle.

graze v touch by glancing blow; abrade; n slight abrasion caused by grazing.

grease n soft, melted animal fat; semi-solid oil as lubricant; v apply grease to; a **greasy**; ns **greasiness, grease-gun** lubricating appliance.

greasepaint n theatrical make-up.

grease-proof paper n Brit paper impermeable to grease.

great 1 large; big **2** eminent; important **3** avid **4** coll splendid; ns **great grandparent/grandfather/ grandmother/aunt/uncle** parent of grandparent, etc; **G. Bear** northern constellation (Ursa Major); **G. Britain** England, Wales and Scotland; **greatcoat** military overcoat; **G. Dane** big powerful smooth-haired dog; **G. Lakes** five lakes between USA and Canada; **G. War** First World War (1914-18); adv **-ly**; n **-ness**.

grebe n fresh water diving bird.

Grecian a of ancient Greece.

greedy a gluttonous; fig covetous; longing for; ns **greed** avarice; **greediness** gluttony.

Greece idm coll **it's all Greek to me** it's incomprehensible.

green a **1** of colour between blue and yellow, colour of grass, leaves, etc **2** rich in vegetation n **g. belt** area free from urban development **3** unripe; immature **4** inexperienced; gullible (n **greenhorn**) **5** envious (a **green-eyed** n **g.-eyed monster** jealousy) **6** fertile (n **g. fingers** Brit success in growing plants (US **g. thumb**)) **7** fresh; vigorous **8** concerned with conservation of environment (ns **g. party; greenpeace** non-violent organization that campaigns actively for projection of nature; **g. politics**); idm (give/get) **the green light** (give/get) signal of consent; n **1** green colour; green clothing **2** grassy area **3** member of green party; pl **-s** green vegetables; ns **-ness; greenback** US banknote; **greenery** vegetation; **greenfly** small insect harmful to plants; **greengage** yellowish-green plum; **greengrocer** Brit seller of fruit, vegetables; **greengrocery** his business; n **greenhorn** see above **greenfield site** area of land not previously developed or built on; **greenhouse** building with glass sides and roof for growing plants under protected conditions; **greenhouse effect** gradual warming of earth's atmosphere owing to increased pollution, eg build-up of carbon dioxide; **g.room** room where actors can relax; *a* **greenish**.

greet *v* salute on meeting; welcome; meet; *n* **greeting**.

gregarious *a* living in herds, flocks; sociable; *n* **-ness**.

gremlin *n* imaginary creature supposed to be cause of malfunction in machines.

grenade *a* small bomb thrown by hand; globular fire-extinguisher.

grenadier *n* (formerly) soldier armed with grenades; (now) member of British infantry regiment.

grenadine *n* thin silk fabric; pomegranate syrup; red dye.

grew *pt* of **grow**.

grey *a* **1** of colour between black and white, colour of slate, ash, etc **2** having hair this colour; *ns* **g. area** aspect of situation hard to define, hard to deal with; **greyhound** slim long-legged dog used for racing; **g. matter 1** brain cells **2** *coll* intelligence; *n* grey colour; grey clothes; *a* **greyish**.

grid *n* **1** grating **2** national network of electricity supply **3** luggage carrier on car **4** numbered network of squares on map, as reference.

griddle *n* metal plate for baking over fire.

grief *n* sorrow; distress; woe; *idm* **come to grief** have an accident; fail; *v* **grieve** cause, feel grief; *n* **grievance** cause for complaint; *a* **grievous**

distressing; painful.

griffin, griffon, gryphon *n* mythical animal, part eagle, part lion.

grill *n* gridiron; food cooked on this; *v* cook, be cooked on grill; *sl* interrogate closely; *n* **-ing** severe cross examination; *a* very hot; *n* **grill, g. room** room in restaurant etc where grilled food is served.

grille *n* open, metal framework over opening.

grim *a* stern, forbidding; inflexible; cruel.

grimace *n* facial contortion, expressing ridicule, pain etc; *v* make grimaces.

grime *n* soot; ingrained dirt; squalor; *v* soil; begrime; *a* **grimy**.

grin *v* **grinning, grinned.** show teeth in smile, grimace etc; *n* broad smile; cruel smile.

grind *v* **grinding, ground.** reduce to small pieces or powder by pressure; wear down; make smooth; sharpen; grate; *n* act of grinding; *sl* hard work; *ns* **grindstone** hard sandstone used for grinding; **grinder**.

gringo *n coll* English-speaking foreigner in Latin America.

grip *v* **gripping, gripped.** clutch, hold firmly; hold interest; *n* **1** grasp **2** mastery **3** handle **4** suitcase; *a* **gripping** thrilling.

gripe *v* cause, feel spasms of pain of colic; *sl* complain; *n* spasm of pain in bowels.

grisly *a* horrifying; gruesome;

ghastly.

grist *n* grain for grinding; *idm* **(all) grist to the mill** sth useful, that can be turned to profit.

gristle *n* cartilage, *esp* in cooked meat.

grit *n* **1** small fragments of stone **2** coarse sand **3** *fig* courage; *pls* coarsely ground oats etc; *v* **gritting, gritted. 1** treat surface with grit **2** make grinding sound (with teeth); *v idm* **grit one's teeth** show determination and courage; *a* **gritty** *n* **grittiness**.

grizzly *a* greyish; *n* **g. bear** large N American bear; *a* **grizzled** (of human hair) turning grey.

groan *v* utter deep sound of pain, grief etc; be overburdened; (of wood) creak; *n* sound made in groaning; moan.

grocer *n* dealer in dry and canned goods, household requisites etc; *n* **grocery** grocer's trade; *pl* **groceries** goods sold by grocer.

grog *n* spirit (*usu* rum) with water; *a* **groggy** unsteady; shaky; weak.

groin *n* **1** depression between thigh and abdomen **2** line made by intersection of two vaults **3** *US* **groyne** breakwater on beach, to resist tidal erosion; *v* form groin.

groom *n* servant in charge of horses; officer in royal household; bridegroom; *v* tend, care for (horse); keep one's clothes and person smart; n **groomsman** best man.

groove n narrow channel, furrow, *esp* cut by tool in wood, metal; fixed routine, rut; v cut groove in; *idm* **stuck in a groove** fixed in one's habits; a **groovy** *dated sl* excellent; modern.

grope v 1 feel round blindly, fumble 2 search cautiously.

gross a 1 fat; coarse 2 obscene 3 flagrant 4 total; not net; n 1 the whole 2 twelve dozen; *adv* -**ly**; n -**ness**.

grot n *sl* inferior stuff; a **grotty** *coll* 1 nasty 2 shabby 3 unwell.

grotesque a fantastic; distorted; bizarre; *art* highly decorated with intertwined animal forms and foliage; n.

grotto n cave; artificial cavern; *pl* **grottoes**

grouch v *sl* grumble persistently; n.

ground n 1 surface of earth; area of it 2 soil 3 piece of land for specified use 4 reason; argument 5 area for discussion 6 bottom of sea; *ns* **g. crew, g. floor; groundnut** peanut; **g. plan; g. rule** basic rule; **groundsheet** waterproof sheet for camping; **g. staff, g. stroke** (tennis); **g. swell** 1 heavy slow-moving wave 2 rapid surge of public feeling; **groundwork** work providing for future development; *idm* **get off**

the ground make a successful start; *idm* **prepare the ground for** make possible; *idm* **run into the ground** wear out; *idm* **go/run to ground** hide; *idm* **run sb to ground** find sb in hiding; v 1 touch bottom of sea 2 force to stay on the ground; *phr vs* **ground sb in** give sb basic instruction in; **ground sth on** base *sth* on; a -**ed**; n -**ing** basic instruction; a **groundless** without cause; *adv* -**ly**; *pl* **grounds** 1 land round building; land designated for a purpose 2 solid dregs of coffee after brewing.

group n collective unit of persons, things; class; number of persons sharing views, interests etc; *art* several figures forming one design; v place, form into group.

groupie n *coll* keen fan following pop groups on tour.

group practice n group of doctors working as partners.

grouse[1] n wild game-bird; its edible flesh.

grouse[2] v *sl* grumble; complain; n **grouse**.

grout n, v (fill spaces between tiles, etc with) fine mortar; v cover, fill, with grout; *ns* -**er**, -**ing**.

grove n small wood.

grovel v -**elling**, -**elled**. lie flat; *fig* humble oneself.

grow v develop; become larger; cultivate; flourish; *pt* **grew**;

pp **grown;** *phr vs* **grow on** become increasingly attractive to; **grow out of 1** become too big for **2** cease to enjoy; **grow up 1** become adult **2** arise and develop; a **grown(-up)** adult; **growing pains** n 1 pains in limbs of growing children 2 *fig* problems arising in development of enterprise; n **growth** that which has grown, or is growing.

growl v utter deep rumbling sound of anger; grumble; grouse; n make growling sound.

growth n 1 process of growing; development 2 increase in economic activity 3 *sth* that has grown 4 abnormal formation on or in the body.

grub v **grubbing, grubbed.** dig; uproot; *fig* search arduously; n larva of insect; *sl* food; a **grubby** dirty.

grudge v be reluctant to give or do *sth*; n feeling of resentment; a **grudging**; *adv* -**ly**.

gruel n thin watery oatmeal porridge; a **gruelling** exhausting (n punishment).

gruesome a ghastly; macabre; horrible.

gruff a rough; surly; hoarse; n **gruffness**.

grumble v complain; murmur angrily; rumble; n complaint.

grumpy a bad-tempered; *adv* **grumpily**; n -**iness**.

grungy a *sl* dirty or upkempt.

grunt v utter deep, rough,

nasal sound; make this sound; n deep snort.

Gruyère n hard type of Swiss cheese with large holes.

gryphon n griffin.

G-string n narrow strip of cloth barely concealing genital area.

guarantee n pledge, promise given that conditions of contract will be carried out; manufacturer's undertaking to make good defects in product; v undertake; give guarantee; ns **guaranty** surety; undertaking to be responsible for another's debts; **guarantor** one who gives guaranty.

guard n 1 protector; sentry 2 state of wariness against danger 3 armed escort 4 railway official in charge of train 5 protective device or part; v protect; defend; idm **be off/on one's guard** be unready/ready to cope with danger; phr v **guard against** take care to prevent; forestall; a **guarded** 1 protected 2 wary; adv **-ly**; n **-ness**; ns **guardhouse**, **guardroom** building/room manned by soldiers on guard duty; **guardian** person looking after a child in lieu of parent; **guardianship**.

guava n tropical tree, having egg-shaped fruit.

gubernatorial a of a governor.

gudgeon n small fresh-water carp.

gudgeon n piston pin; socket; bearing.

guer(r)illa n irregular warfare; one engaged in it.

guernsey n thick knitted sweater; cap breed of dairy cows.

guess v conjecture; form opinion without material evidence; suppose ns **guesstimate** coll rough estimate based on a guess; **guesswork** process of guessing.

guest n person enjoying another's hospitality; one staying in hotel etc.

guest-house n small private hotel.

guff n coll nonsense.

guffaw n burst of loud, vulgar laughter.

guide v show way; direct; control; advise; n one who, that which, guides; guide-book; one who leads tourists, hunters etc; ns **guidance** 1 leadership 2 help with personal problems; g.-**book**, g.-**dog**, g.-**lines** advice on policy; a **guided** not independent (ns **g.missile** rocket controlled by radar; **g.tour**, **g.visit**, **g.writing**).

guild n association of people with common trade, profession or aim; n -**hall** meeting place of guild or corporation.

guilder n unit or currency in Netherlands.

guile n deceit; wiliness; as -**ful**, -**less**.

guillotine n machine for beheading; one for paper-

cutting; v use guillotine.

guilt n condition, fact of having committed crime, or sin; culpability; as **guilty** having incurred guilt; **guiltless** innocent; n **guiltiness**.

guinea n obsolete English coin.

guinea-fowl ns domesticated fowl, like pheasant; **guinea-pig** domestic rodent.

guise n disguise; false appearance.

guitar n six-stringed musical instrument; n **guitarist**.

gulag n (formerly) Soviet state labour camp.

gulch n deep ravine or torrent-bed.

gules n her red.

gulf n large, deep, inlet of sea; chasm; fig impassable gap; pl -**s**.

gull n 1 web-footed sea-bird 2 dupe; fool; v deceive; cheat; a -**ible** credulous, easily duped; n -**ibility**.

gullet n passage from mouth to stomach.

gully, gulley n channel worn by water.

gulp v swallow noisily; choke back; n large mouthful.

gum[1] n firm tissue around teeth; n **gumboil** abscess in gum.

gum[2] n 1 sticky viscid substance exuded by certain trees 2 liquid glue 3 chewing-gum; v **gumming**, **gummed**. stick with gum; a **gummy**; n pl **gumboots** rubber boots.

gumdrop n hard jelly-like

sweet.

gumshoe n US sl detective.

gumtree n eucalyptus; idm **up a gumtree** in difficulty.

gumption n shrewdness; common sense; intelligence.

gun n tubular weapon from which missiles are fired; any fire-arm; phr vs **gun down** shoot to kill or wound; **gun for** seek chance to attack; ns **gunboat diplomacy** negotiation with threat of force; **gunfire** (noise of) shooting; **gunman** armed criminal; **gunner** artilleryman; **gunpoint** idm **at gunpoint** with threat of shooting; **gunpowder** explosive powder; **g.-running** secret illegal importation of arms; **g.-runner** person doing this.

gunge n Brit coll messy liquid substance a **gungy**.

gung-ho a coll thoroughly enthusiastic and loyal.

gunwale n upper edge of boat's side.

guppy n tiny tropical fish.

gurgle v flow with, utter, bubbling sound; n **gurgling** sound.

guru n Hindu spiritual teacher.

gush v burst forth; flow out copiously; coll talk effusively; n violent flow; fig effusiveness; n **-er** person who gushes; oil-well not needing pumps.

gusset n triangular section let into garment, to enlarge or strengthen it; **gust** n sudden, brief blast of wind, rain etc;

fig brief, outburst of anger, passion etc; a **gusty**.

gusto n relish; zest; enjoyment.

gut n sing **1** fine thread made from animal guts, used in surgery, violin-strings etc **2** narrow passage; pl **1** bowels; intestines **2** coll courage; stamina; a sl **gutted** disappointed, upset; v **gutting, gutted**. remove guts of; destroy inner contents of (house etc, esp by fire).

gutter n **1** narrow trough under eaves to carry rain water **2** open channel along road **3** fig lowest social class; slums; v form channels in; ns **g.-snipe 1** ragged child **2** ill-bred person; **g. press** newspapers preoccupied with scandal; v (of candle) burn fitfully; n **guttering** system of gutters; **g.-urchin** street urchins.

guttural a pertaining to throat; (of voice) rasping, harsh.

guy[1] n rope, wire, chain used to guide, steady or secure something; v steady with guy.

guy[2] n **1** grotesque effigy of Guy Fawkes burnt on Nov 5th; scarecrow; badly dressed person; **2** coll man; v mock; make fool of.

guzzle v drink, eat greedily and to excess.

gybe v (of boom or sail) swing from side to side; jib.

gym n coll **1** gymnasium **2** gymnastics.

gymkhana n athletics display, esp equestrian events.

gymnasium n hall for physical training and gymnastics; n pl **gymnastics** physical exercises, with or without apparatus; n **gymnast** one skilled in gymnastics.

gym-slip n sleeveless tunic worn by some schoolgirls as part of uniform.

gynaecology n science dealing with functions and diseases of women; a **-logical**; n **-logist**.

gypsum n sulphate of calcium, used for making plaster of Paris.

gypsy n see **gipsy**.

gyrate v revolve; whirl round; n **-ration**; a **-atory** revolving; spinning.

gyro-compass n gyroscope with compass card attached.

gyroscope n fly-wheel capable of rotating about any axis, used to stabilize ships, aircraft etc; a **gyroscopic**.

habeas corpus n leg writ issued requiring prisoner to be produced in court.

haberdasher n retailer of small articles of dress, sewing cotton, pins, etc. n **-shery**.

habiliments n pl Fr clothes.

habit n usual behaviour; bio normal mode of growth; distinctive dress, (esp monk's riding-habit); a **habitual** customary, usual; v **habituate** render familiar with; ns **habitat** natural home of animal; **habitude** usual custom; **habitué** Fr regular visitor.

habitable a able to be inhabited; adv **habitably**.

habitation n place of abode.

hack[1] v cut roughly; chop; kick shins of; cough harshly; coll put up with; n act of hacking n **h.-saw** short saw for cutting metal.

hack[2] n hired horse, esp for riding; over-worked horse; fig badly-paid writer; v ride hack; ride at pace of hack; n **hack-work** literary drudgery.

hacker n person obtaining illegal entry to computer system and using or altering data stored in it.

hacking cough n hard dry persistent cough.

hackles n pl long feathers on cock's neck; hairs on back of animal's neck; idm **make sb's hackles rise/raise sb's hackles** make sb very angry.

hackney n medium-sized ordinary riding horse.

hackneyed a trite; common.

hacksaw n saw for cutting metal.

had pt, pp of **have**.

haddock n edible sea-fish, akin to cod.

Hades n abode of dead; underworld.

hadn't contracted form of had not.

haem-, haema- haemo- prefix of blood.

haematin n pigment found in blood.

haemoglobin n protein substance of red blood corpuscles.

haemophilia n hereditary disease, in which blood fails to clot.

haemorrhage n bleeding; v med to bleed.

haemorrhoids n med piles.

haft n handle; hilt; v fit haft.

hag n ugly old woman; witch.

haggard a gaunt; having worn, wasted look.

haggis n Scottish culinary dish.

haggle v wrangle over price; dispute terms.

hagiology n study of saints or of their lives; n **hagiographer** writer of saint's life.

hail[1] n small lumps of ice falling like rain; v shower down hail; n **hailstone**.

hail[2] interj used in greeting; v greet; accost; **hail from** come from.

hail-fellow-well-met a coll friendly and informal.

hair n fine threadlike growth from skin of animal; mass of such growth on human head; fur of animal; idm **keep your hair on** coll don't lose your temper; idm **let one's hair down** relax; behave in an uninhibited manner; idm **not turn a hair** not show any fear, surprise, etc; idm **by a hair's breadth** (of escape, victory) very narrowly; as **hair-raising**

terrifying; **hairy 1** covered with hair **2** *coll* dangerous; difficult; *ns* **hairiness, hairdresser** one who cuts, sets, tints hair, *esp* women's hair; **hairspring** very fine spring in watch etc.

haircut *n* **1** act of cutting hair **2** style in which hair is cut.

hairdo *n coll* hair style.

hairpiece *n* small wig covering bald patch.

hairpin bend *n* sharp V-shaped corner *esp* on steep road.

hairsplitting *n* fussing about minute unimportant detail.

hairspray *n* liquid spray to hold hair in place.

hair trigger *n* very sensitive trigger on gun.

hake *n* coarse edible sea-fish, related to cod.

halberd *n* long handled spiked battle-axe.

halcyon *n* kingfisher; *a* tranquil, peaceful; **h. days** period of calm weather, about winter solstice.

hale *a* healthy, robust, vigorous, *esp* of the elderly.

half *n* one of two equal parts of sth; 50% *pl* **halves**; *a* **1** consisting of, equal to half (*ns* **h. moon, halfpenny**) **2** partial (*ns* **halflight, h.measures, h.truth**); *idm* **sb's better/other half** sb's husband/wife; *idm* **do things by halves** do things incompletely; *idm* **go half-and-half/halves** share equally; *idm* **not half** *Brit coll* **1** a great deal **2** not at all; *ns* **h.back** *sport* midfield player;

h.board bed and breakfast with one other main meal; **h.brother/sister; h.-life** time taken for radio-activity of substance to reduce by half; **h.-mast** point halfway up flag-mast; **h.nelson** hold in wrestling with opponent's arm bent behind his back; **h.term** short holiday in middle of school term; **h.time** short rest midway through sports match; **h.-wit** stupid person *a* **h.-witted**; *as* **h.-baked** inadequate; **h.-hearted** lacking in enthusiasm; *adv* **-ly**; *a, adv* **h.-price**; *as* **h.size; h.-timbered** with wooden framework filled in with brick, stone, plaster; *a, adv* **h.-way** at the midpoint; *n* **h.-way house 1** midway position **2** compromise **3** rehabilitation centre.

halibut *n* large edible flat sea-fish.

halitosis *n* foul breath.

hall *n* **1** large public room **2** passage, lobby at entrance to building **3** large private house; **hallmark** official mark on gold, silver plate, used by Goldsmith's Hall.

hallelujah *n, interj* praise the Lord!

hallo, hello *interj* cry of surprise; greeting.

hallow *v* make holy; consecrate.

Halloween *n* October 31st, the eve of All Saints Day and celebrated by masquerading.

hallucination *n* fancied perception by senses of some non-existent thing; *v* **hallucinate** affect with hallucinations; *a* **hallucinatory.**

hallucinogen *n* drug causing hallucinations; *a* **-ic.**

halo *n* **haloes** ring of light round sun, moon etc; golden circle, disk around head of figure in picture, symbolizing holiness.

halogen *n chem* any of elements fluorine, chlorine, bromine, astatine forming salts by union with metal; **h.lamp, h.lighting** bright lighting with low energy consumption.

halt[1] *a* lame; *v fig* hesitate; *a* **-ing** stumbling; hesitant.

halt[2] *n* stoppage of movement; small railway station; *v* cause to stop; pause.

halter-neck *n* style of dress with supporting strap round neck and bare back and shoulders.

halve *v* divide in halves; diminish by half; share.

halyard, halliard *n* rope used for raising sail, flags.

ham *n* **1** back of thigh **2** thigh of hog, *esp* smoked and salted **3** amateur radio operator; *a* **h.-fisted, h.-handed** clumsy; *n* **hamstring** tendon at back of knee; tendon behind horse's hock; *v* lame by cutting hamstring.

hamburger *n* fried minced beef and onions in bread

roll.

hamlet n small village.

hammer n 1 long-handled tool with heavy head, for driving in nails, working metal, crushing etc 2 striking part of gun-lock 3 device for striking bell 4 auctioneer's mallet; idm **go at it hammer and tongs** argue violently; idm **come under the hammer** be sold by auction; v strike with, use hammer; knock loudly; phr v **hammer out** solve problem by repeated discussion.

hammerhead shark n shark with broad flat nose.

hammock n canvas or net bed, slung on cords.

hamper[1] n large basket with lid.

hamper[2] v hinder; impede; obstruct.

hamster n rodent with cheek pouches.

hamstring n cordlike tendon in back of leg; v render helpless.

hand n 1 end of arm below wrist 2 style of writing 3 pointer on dial, clock, etc 4 direction; position 5 set of cards held by player; round of cards 6 manual worker 7 assistance 8 measure of four inches (10.16cm); idm **at hand** nearby; idm **hand in hand** 1 holding each other by the hand 2 in collaboration; idm **have a hand in** be involved in; idm **in hand** being dealt with; idm **on hand** ready; idm

off/out of one's hands not one's responsibility; idm **(get) out of hand** (go) out of control; idm **to hand** available; v pass; give; idm **hand it to sb** acknowledge sb's skill, success, courage; phr vs **hand down** bequeath; **hand in** deliver idm **hand in one's notice** resign; **hand on** pass; **hand out** issue; v **hand-out**; phr vs **hand over** give possession of, control of; **hand round** distribute; ns **handbag** woman's light bag; **handball** ball game; **handbill** small printed notice; **handbook** manual; **handbrake, handcart; handcuffs** chain with rings for holding prisoner by the hands (v **handcuff**); ns **handful** 1 amount that the hand can hold 2 small number 3 coll uncontrollable child, animal; **h.grenade, handgun, handhold, h.luggage; hand-me-down** Brit coll used clothing passed to sb else; **handset** telephone receiver; **handstand** upside-down position supported on hands; **handwriting** (style of) writing by hand (a **handwritten**); as **h.made; h.-picked** carefully chosen; **h.-to-hand** involving physical contact; **h.-to-mouth** with barely the means to survive; **hands-on** with much personal involvement.

handicap n disability (physical or mental); disadvantage in time, weight etc; race, contest where handicaps are imposed; v **-capping, -capped.** impose handicap.

handicraft n artistic skill with hands; product of this.

handiwork n 1 work needing skill with hands 2 result of sb's action.

handkerchief n small cloth for wiping nose, face, etc.

handle n part of tool, utensil etc held in hand; v 1 touch, feel with hands 2 control; manage 3 deal in; n **handler** person in control.

handlebars n pl bar held in hands for steering bicycle.

handmaid n personal female servant (also **handmaiden**).

handsome a good-looking; generous; having dignity.

handy a 1 useful 2 skilful with the hands 3 accessible adv **handily**; n **-iness;** n **handyman** person doing minor jobs, repairs.

hang v 1 suspend; be suspended 2 fix, attach to wall pt, pp **hung** 3 execute by hanging from rope round neck pt **hung,** pp **hanged;** idm **hang it** coll damn it; idm **go hang** coll be damned; idm **hang one's head** look ashamed; phr vs **hang about/around** coll loiter; **hang back** show reluctance; **hang on** 1 hold on tight 2 wait; **hang on in** US coll persevere; have faith, courage; **hang onto** coll keep hold of; **hang out** live; stay; **hang up 1** suspend **2** end telephone conversation abruptly; **be hung up on/about** be obsessed about; *n* way in which sth hangs; *idm* **get the hang of** understand; *idm* **not give a hang** *coll* not care; *a* **h.-dog** dejected; guilty; *ns* **hanger** clothes/coat-hanger; **hanger-on** person hoping to cultivate friendship for personal gain (*pl* **hangers-on**); **h.glider** large kite-like frame for flying without engine; **h.gliding** sport of flying with this; **hanging** execution with rope; **hangman** person doing this; **hangings** curtains; **hangover 1** sick feeling the day after taking too much alcohol **2** lasting effect of sth; **hang-up** *sl* sth causing unusual anxiety.

hangar *n* covered shed, *esp* for aircraft.

hank *n* skein, coil, length, *esp* measure of yarn.

hanker *phr v* **hanker after/for** desire strongly; *n* **-ing**.

Hansard *n* official report of proceedings in Parliament.

Hanukkah, Chanukah *n* annual Jewish festival.

hap *n* chance; *a* **-less** unlucky, wretched; **haphazard** random, accidental.

happen *v* take place; chance; *n* **-ing** occurrence; *sl* fantastic, weird event.

happy *a* cheerful; content; fortunate; *adv* **happily**; *n*

happiness; *a* **h.-go-lucky** carefree; easy-going.

happy hour *n* time when drinks are sold more cheaply than usual.

hara-kiri, hari-kari *n* Japanese ritual suicide.

harangue *n* vehement speech; *v* harass through speech.

harass *v* worry, vex, annoy by repeated attack; *n* **-ment**.

harbinger *n* forerunner, precursor, herald.

harbour *n* haven, port; shelter; *v* shelter; conceal; lodge.

hard *a* **1** firm; solid **2** difficult **3** strenuous **4** harsh; severe **5** (of water) not lathering well **6** (of drugs) dangerous, addictive **7** (of lines, colours) too emphatic; *adv* intensively; *idm* **hard at it** working hard; *idm* **hard done by** unfairly treated; *idm* **hard put to it** finding great difficulty; *idm* **hard of hearing** rather deaf; *idm* **hard up** *coll* short of money, etc; *v* **harden** make hard (*phr v* **harden to** make/become less sensitive to); *ns* **-ness**; **hardback** hard-covered book; **hardball** US baseball; **hardboard, h.cash** coins and notes; **h.copy** printed copy; **h.currency** stable currency; **h.disk** *comput* rigid disk with large storage capacity; **h. labour** hard physical work as punishment; **h.landing** landing causing destruction of spacecraft;

h.line unchanging policy; **h.-liner; h.luck** bad luck; **h.sell** pressurized method of selling; **hardship** privation; suffering; **h.shoulder** *Brit* hard area at side of motorway for emergency stopping; **hardware 1** domestic tools, pots and pans **2** *comput* machines **3** weapons; *as* **h.-and-fast** fixed; **h.-bitten** tough; **h.-boiled 1** boiled with yolk is hard **2** cynical; insensitive; **h.-headed** practical; **h.-hitting** ruthless; effective; **h.-nosed** ruthless; **h.-pressed** very busy; **h.-wearing** durable.

hardcore *a* **1** graphic; explicit **2** totally committed.

hardhat *n* **1** worker's helmet **2** working-class conservative.

hare *n* swift rodent, resembling rabbit; *v coll* run wildly; run fast; *a* **h.-brained** rash, flighty; *n* **h.-lip** congenital fissure of human upper lip.

harem *n* women's quarters in Muslim house; seraglio.

haricot *n* French bean, stew of mutton, turnips and beans.

hark *v* listen to; *phr v* **h. back** to revert to (a subject).

harlequin *n* comic character in pantomime; *a* multi-coloured; *n* **harlequinade** pantomime scene; buffoonery.

harlot *n* prostitute; whore.

harm *n* physical or moral damage; injury; *idm* **out of harm's way** safe; *v* hurt;

injure; *a* **harmful**; *adv* **-ly**; *a*
harmless; *adv* **-ly**; *n* **-ness**.

harmony *n* concord;
agreement; melodious
sound, chord; *a* **harmonic** of
harmony; *n* one of
components of complex
musical tone; *n pl* **harmonics**
science, art of musical
harmony; *a* **harmonious** in
harmony; melodious; *n*
harmonica mouth-organ; *v*
harmonize bring into
harmony; reconcile; be in
harmony; *n* **-ization**; *n*
harmonium small organ.

harness *n* straps, usually
leather, and fastenings of
horse; any gear resembling
this; *v* put into harness; *fig*
control, use.

harp *n* musical instrument,
with strings plucked by
hand; *phr v* **harp on** talk of
repeatedly, tediously; *ns*
harpist; **harpsichord**
forerunner of piano.

harpoon *n* barbed spear with
rope attached, for striking
whales and large fish; *v*
strike with harpoon; *ns*
harpooner, h.-gun one used
to fire harpoon.

harpy *n* **1** mythical monster,
half woman, half bird **2**
cruel merciless person.

harrow *n* spiked frame dragged
over ground, to break it up;
v use harrow; *fig* cause
mental distress; *a* **-ing** heart-
rending.

harsh *a* **1** rough to touch **2**
discordant **3** glaring **4**
severe.

hart *n* adult male deer; *n*
hartshorn salvolatile,
formerly distilled from hart's
antlers; *n* **hart's-tongue** fern
with long narrow leaves.

harvest *n* gathering in of
crops; season for this; results
of this; *v* gather in; *ns*
h.festival Christian service
of thanksgiving; **h.home**
meal given by farmers to
farm workers after harvest;
h.moon full moon nearest to
autumn equinox.

has *3rd person sing pres of* **have**.

has-been *n coll* person whose
success, popularity is all in
the past.

hash *n* **1** dish of chopped
cooked meat **2** *coll* mess;
muddle **3** hashish; *v* chop
up; mismanage.

hashish *n* dried hemp, used as
narcotic.

hasn't *contracted form of* has
not.

hasp *n* metal clasp, or hinged
flap for fastening door etc.

hassle *n coll* **1** difficulty **2**
quarrel; *v* **1** harass **2** argue.

hassock *n* tuft of coarse grass;
kneeling cushion.

haste *n* speed; hurry; *v* **hasten**
urge on; hurry; move with
haste; *a* **hasty**; *adv* **-ily**.

hat *n* head-covering, usually
with crown and brim; *idm*
keep under one's hat keep
secret; *idm* **take one's hat
off to** congratulate; *idm*
(get/score) a hat trick *sport*
succeed three times in one
single match; *n* **hatter** one
who makes, sells hats.

hatch[1] *n* trap door covering
opening (in ship's deck;
floor or roof).

hatch[2] *v* incubate; bring forth
(young) from shell; emerge
from egg.

hatch[3] *v* shade in fine lines
(for engraving).

hatchback *n* car with rear door
hinged at top.

hatchet *n* small axe;
tomahawk; *idm* **bury the
hatchet** forget past quarrels;
a **h.-faced** with sharp gaunt
features; *ns* **h.job** *US coll*
malicious attack; **h.man**
person employed to
intimidate opponents, or
one to carry out ruthless
economies in a business.

hate *v* dislike intensely; detest;
n loathing; *n* **hatred**
profound ill-will; *a* **-ful**.

haughty *a* proud; disdainful;
arrogant; *n* **-iness**.

haul *v* drag, pull with effort;
transport; *naut* alter ship's
course; *n* act of hauling;
distance hauled; *fig* booty; *ns*
-age carting, conveying of
goods; charge for this;
haulier carter; man who
hauls coal in mine.

haulm *n* dried stalks; stubble;
straw.

haunch *n* hip, upper thigh and
buttocks; hind quarter.

haunt *v* visit habitually,
frequent; *fig* fill mind of; *n*
habitual resort of human or
animal.

haute couture *n Fr* high
fashion; companies
responsible for this.

haute cuisine n Fr high-class cookery.

have v 1 possess; own (also **have got**) 2 be affected with, subject to; suffer from (also **have got**) 3 accept 4 receive 5 experience 6 obtain 7 give birth to; produce 8 coll defeat 9 coll deceive 10 used as auxiliary verb in present perfect and past perfect tenses; 3rd sing pres **has**, pt, pp **had**; idm **had better** (do/not do) ought to/not to do; idm **have done with** finish; idm **have had it** coll be doomed (to failure, punishment, death); idm **have it in for** sb intend to harass sb, have vengeance on sb; idm **have it out with** sb settle by open discussion; idm **have to** be obliged to; phr vs **have on** mislead for fun; **have up** Brit prosecute; n **have-not** poor person.

haven n harbour; fig refuge; shelter.

haven't contracted form of have not.

haver v hesitate.

haversack n canvas bag for carrying rations, camping equipment etc.

havoc n devastation; destruction.

haw n red fruit of hawthorn; ns **hawthorn** thorny shrub with white, pink or red flowers.

haw v hesitate in speech; n inarticulate sound expressing doubt.

hawk[1] n 1 short-winged long-tailed falcon 2 polit person who favours aggressive tactics; a **hawkish**.

hawk[2] v sell from door to door; fig spread about; **hawker** n itinerant seller of wares.

hawk[3] v clear throat noisily; spit phlegm.

hawse n part of ship's bows where anchor cables pass through holes.

hawser n large rope or small cable.

hay n grass mown and dried for fodder; ns **haycock** heap of hay; **hayseed** grass seed; **haystack** rick of hay; **hay-fever** allergic catarrh of nose and throat.

haywire a infml amiss.

hazard n game of chance, played with dice; chance; risk; danger; v expose to risk; a **hazardous** risky.

haze[1] n mist; vapour; a **hazy** misty; obscured; vague; confused (mental state).

haze[2] v play abusive tricks on.

hazel n tree with edible nuts; light brown colour; a.

HB abbr hard black (of pencils).

H-bomb n hydrogen bomb.

he masc nom pron (3rd pers sing) male person etc just referred to; as prefix **he-** denotes male animal n **he-man** coll virile man.

head n 1 part of body housing brain, eyes, mouth, etc (ns **h.-ache**, **h.-band**, **h.-dress**, **h.-gear**, **h.-rest**, **h.-scarf**); 2 top or front part (ns **headlamp**, **headlight**, **headline**); 3 chief person (ns **h.master/mistress/ teacher**, **headman**, **H. of State**); 4 mind; mental ability 5 individual n **h.count**; 6 elec part of tape-recorder in contact with tape, converting electrical signals into sound 7 froth on top of beer 8 geog cape; headland 9 main division of topic (also **heading**); pl -s side of coin showing head of sb; idm **above/over one's head** too hard to comprehend; idm **bring/come to a head** bring to/reach a vital point; idm **give sb his/her head** let sb act freely; idm **go to sb's head** make sb over-excited; idm **have one's head in the clouds** day-dream; idm **head and shoulders above** much better than; idm **keep one's head** remain calm; idm **keep one's head down** avoid danger, distraction; idm **head over heels** completely; idm **make head or tail of** understand; idm **off one's head** coll mad; v 1 lead 2 be at front, top of list 3 hit with the head; phr vs **head for** go towards; **head off** 1 (cause to) change direction 2 prevent; ns **headbanger** coll uncontrolled person, inclined to violence; **headboard** board at head of bed; **header** 1 act of diving headfirst 2 act of striking ball with head; **h.-hunter** 1 tribal warrior who collects heads 2 person recruiting senior staff; **headland** promontory; **headphone** listening apparatus *usu pl*; **headquarters** central office; **headset** headphones with microphone; **headship** post of head teacher; **h.start** early advantage; **headstone** stone placed at head of grave; **h.waters** streams at source of river; **headway** progress; **headwind** wind in one's face; *as, advs* **headlong 1** head first **2** in haste; **head-on** with the front part in collision; *as* **headstrong** impetuous; self-willed; **heady** intoxicating.

heal *v* make, become sound or healthy; cure; *n* **health** state of well-being; bodily condition; toast drunk wishing one health and prosperity; *ns* **h.centre** *Brit* headquarters for group of doctors, medical services; **h.farm** place where people go to stay for help with diet, exercise, etc; **h.food** natural, organic food; **h.visitor** *Brit* trained nurse visiting sick, elderly people in their homes; *as* **healthful** promoting good health; **healthy** in good health; vigorous; *n* **healthiness**.

heap *n* piled-up mass of things; large number or quantity; *v* amass; form into heap.

hear *v* **hearing, heard.** perceive by ear; listen to; *idm* **won't/wouldn't hear of**

it refuse(s) to even consider it; *phr vs* **hear from** get news from; **hear out** listen patiently to; *leg* try as judge; learn; *ns* **hearer, hearing** sense by which sound is perceived; formal, official listening; **hearsay** rumour.

hearken *v* listen attentively.

hearse *n* funeral vehicle for coffin.

heart *n* muscular organ which pumps blood round the body; *fig* seat of human emotions, affection, courage etc; core; central part; *n idm* **after one's own heart** exactly as one likes; *idm* **at heart** basically; *idm* **by heart** from memory; *idm* **have a heart** *coll* be merciful, sympathetic; *idm* **have one's heart in one's mouth** be terrified; *idm* **no heart for** no appetite for; *idm* **set one's heart on** long for; *idm* **take to heart** feel deeply; *ns* **heartache** sorrow; **h.attack** malfunction of heart; **heartbeat** pumping of heart; **h.-break** anguish *as* **h.breaking; h.-broken; heartburn** indigestion pain; **h.failuire** heart stopping; **heartland** main central area; **h.-lung machine; h.-searching** examining of one's conscience; **h.-strings** deepest feelings of love, pity; **h.-throb** *coll* person arousing strong amorous feeling; *n, a* **h.-to-heart** frank personal (discussion); *v* **hearten;** *v* **hearten** cheer up; *as*

encourage; *as* **heartfelt** sincere; **heartfree** not being in love; **heartless** unfeeling, cruel; *adv* **-ely;** *n* **-ness;** *as* **h.-rending** deeply moving; **heartwarming** giving great pleasure; **hearty 1** cordial; **hearty 1** cordial; jovial **2** (of meals) big; *adv* **heartily** *n* **-iness.**

hearth *n* place where domestic fire is made; *fig* home.

heat *n* **1** hotness; sensation of warmth **2** *fig* strong emotion **3** period of sexual desire in female mammals **4** eliminating round or course in race or contest; *n, ns* **h.barrier** effect of friction on speed of aircraft; **h.rash; h.shield** protective covering on spacecraft; **h.-stroke** sunstroke; **h.wave** spell of very hot weather; *n* **-er** machine for heating; *n* **-ing** means of providing heat; *a* **-ed** angry; excited *adv* **-edly;** *v* make, become hot; *a* **heated** excited, vehement.

heath *n* open, shrubby ground; heather; ling.

heathen *n* one who does not believe in God; barbarous, irreligious person; *a* unenlightened; savage; *a* **heathenish** *fig* barbarous; pagan.

heather *n* plant of heath family, growing on heaths and mountains.

Heath Robinson *a* (of machinery) absurdly elaborate and impractical.

heave *v* lift up; drag along; throw (something heavy);

utter (sigh); (of waves) rise up, swell; retch.

heaven n abode of God; sky; *fig* state of extreme bliss; *a* **h.-sent** very lucky; timely; *a* **-ly** of, from heaven; *sl* delightful, beautiful.

heavy a 1 weighty; difficult to lift 2 serious 3 dull; overcast 4 severe 5 clumsy 6 indigestible 7 sad; gloomy; n 1 *dram* serious or bad character 2 *sl* big man used as bodyguard; ns **h. breathing** suggestive noises made by anonymous caller on telephone; **h. duty** a made to withstand hard work, weather etc; **h. handed** a tactless; clumsy; **h. hearted** a full of sorrow or worry; n **h. heartedness**; **heavy-set** a large-bodied; **h. industry**; **h. metal** loud type of pop music; **h. petting** erotic caressing but not sexual intercourse; **h. water** water in which hydrogen is replaced by deuterium; **heavyweight** 1 heaviest class of boxer 2 very important person; *adv* **heavily**; n **-iness**.

hebdomadal a weekly.

Hebrew n language of the Jewish people.

hecatomb n sacrifice of 100 oxen; *fig* massacre.

heckle v interrupt public speaker with questions; n **heckler**.

hect-, hecto- prefix hundred.

hectare n (area of) 10,000 square metres.

hectic a exciting; rushed; busy.

hector v bully; browbeat; bluster at.

he'd contraction for 1 he had 2 he would.

hedge n shrubs planted closely as fence or boundary; v 1 enclose with plant, hedge 2 *coll* refuse to commit oneself; *idm* **hedge one's bets** protect oneself against loss by backing more than one possibility; ns **hedgehog** small wild spiny mammal; **hedger** man who makes, repairs hedges; **hedgerow** wild hedge.

hedonism n theory that pleasure is the chief good; n **-ist**.

heebie-jeebies n pl coll uneasiness.

heed v take notice; regard carefully; a **-less** careless; reckless.

heel n hind part of foot; part of shoe, boot supporting this; last part; v 1 supply with heel 2 *rugby* pass (ball) out of scrum with heel.

heel v tilt to one side, *esp* of ship; cause to do this; n list.

hefty a weighty; muscular; big and strong.

hegemony n leadership; political control.

heifer n young cow that has not yet calved.

height n vertical dimension; loftiness; culmination; hill; v **-en** make, become higher; augment.

heinous a hateful; atrocious; odious.

heir n one who succeeds to another's rank, property, on the death of the latter; ns **h. apparent** person certain to inherit; **h. presumptive** person who may inherit if no-one is born with superior claim; *fem* **heiress**; n **heirloom** object inherited from ancestors; chattel that goes with real estate.

heist n US sl armed robbery.

helical a spiral.

helicopter n aircraft deriving lift from horizontally rotating rotors.

heliograph n signalling device using reflected rays of sun.

heliport n base for take-off and landing of helicopters.

heliotrope n plant of borage family, with fragrant purple flowers; a colour of flowers; a **-tropic** turning towards sun.

helium n light non-inflammable gaseous element.

hell n abode of damned souls; place, state of intense suffering, misery, cruelty; *fig* gambling den; *idm* **a hell of a** *sl* 1 a dreadful 2 very (*also* a **helluva**); *idm* **like hell** coll 1 very fast; very much 2 not at all; *as* **h.-bent** recklessly determined; **hellish** awful; *adv* **-ly**; n **-ness**; n **hell's angel** member of leather-clad motorcycle gang.

he'll contracted form of he will.

Hellenic a Greek.

hello interj used in greeting or showing surprise.

helm n steering wheel of ship,

tiller; *idm* **at the helm** in control; *n* **-sman** steersman.

helmet *n* protective covering for head.

help *v* 1 aid; assist 2 serve; supply 3 alleviate; be able; *idm* **(not) be able to help (sth) (not)** to avoid (doing sth); *n* **-er**; *as* **-ful; -less** powerless; useless; *n* **helpmate**, comrade, partner, *esp* husband or wife.

helter-skelter *adv* in disorderly haste.

hem *n* edge of cloth turned up and stitched; *v* **hemming, hemmed.** sew thus; confine; *phr v* **hem in** trap; *n* **h.-line** lower edge of dress; *n* **hemstitch** decorative stitch.

hem-, hema-, hemo- *prefixes see* haem-, haema-, haemo-.

hemisphere *n* half a sphere; half of earth's surface; *a* **-spherical.**

hemistich *n* half line of verse.

hemlock *n* plant producing powerful sedative; poison extracted from it.

hemp *n* plant, fibre of which is used for rope; narcotic drug made from it; *a* **hempen.**

hen *n* female domestic fowl, or any bird; *a* **hen-pecked** nagged by wife.

hence *adv* from this; therefore; *advs* **-forth, -forward** from now onwards.

henchman *n* trusty attendant; staunch supporter.

henna *n* Asiatic shrub; red or brown dye for hair made from it.

hepatic *n* pertaining to liver; *n*

hepatitis inflammation of liver.

hepta- *prefix* seven; *n* **heptagon** plane figure with seven sides; **heptateuch** first seven books of Bible.

her *a* object *or poss* case of **she**; *pron* **hers** of her; *pron* **herself.**

herald *n* official who makes public announcements or arranges ceremonies; one charged with care of armorial bearings etc; forerunner, harbinger; *v* announce; usher in; *a* **-ic**; *n* **heraldry** study of use of armorial bearings.

herb *n* plant whose stem dies down annually; one used in medicine, or flavouring; *as* **-aceous** dying down in winter; perennial flowering; **-al** of herbs; *ns* **herbage** grass, pasture; **herbalist** dealer in medicinal herbs; **herbarium** collection of preserved plants.

herbicide *n* substance for killing plants, esp weeds.

herculean *a* requiring extraordinary strength, effort, courage, etc.

herd *n* group, flock of animals, usually of same species, living, feeding together; *fig* rabble; mob; *v* 1 tend (herd) 2 huddle together; *n* **herdsman.**

here *adv* in, towards this place; at this point; *adv* **hereafter** in future; *n* life after death; *adv* **herewith.**

hereabouts *adv* somewhere

near here.

hereby *adv fml* by this means.

heredity *n* passing of bodily, mental characteristics from parent to child; *a* **hereditary** passing by inheritance or heredity; *n* **hereditament** thing that can be inherited.

herein *adv* in this.

hereinafter *adv leg* in the following text.

heresy *n* erroneous religious belief; opinion contrary to orthodox one; *n* **heretic** one guilty of religious heresy; *(a* **-al).**

heritage *n* inheritance; characteristic derived from ancestors; *a* **heritable.**

hermaphrodite *n* human being, animal, plant with both male and female characteristics.

hermetic *a* air-tight; *adv* **-cally** so as to be perfectly closed.

hermit *n* one living in solitude, for prayer, meditation; *fig* recluse; *n* **-age** cell of hermit.

hernia *n* rupture, *esp* abdominal.

hero *n* 1 one noted for valour, noble qualities 2 chief male character in play, book etc 3 demigod; *pl* **heroes;** *fem* **-ine;** *a* **-ic** courageous; larger than life; *adv* **-ally;** *n* **heroic couplet** rhyming pair of iambic pentameters; *n pl* **heroics** bombastic talk, behaviour; *ns* **heroism** courage; **hero worship** excessive admiration of someone.

heroin n narcotic, habit-forming drug, derived from morphine.

heron n long-necked, long-legged wading bird.

herpes n skin disease; shingles.

herring n edible sea-fish; n **h.-bone** pattern of criss-cross lines.

herself reflex or emphatic form of **she**.

hertz n radio unit of frequency.

he's contracted form of 1 **he is** 2 **he was**.

hesitate v pause in doubt; falter; be reluctant; a **hesitant** undecided; ns **hesitancy, hesitation** indecision; speech impediment.

hessian n coarse hempen fabric.

heterodox a unorthodox.

heterogenous a composed of unrelated kinds.

heterosexual a, n (person) feeling sexual attraction towards opposite sex.

het up a coll excited; upset.

heuristic a solving problems by trial and error; adv **-ally**.

hex n US evil spell; v put a **hex on**.

hexagon n plane figure with six sides; a **-al** six-sided.

hexameter n verse of six feet.

hey-day n peak; acme; prime.

hey presto interj announcing a piece of magic.

HGV abbr heavy goods vehicle.

hiatus n gap; break in continuity; slight pause between two vowels.

hibernate v pass winter in torpid state; ns **-ation, -ator**.

hibiscus n rose-mallow; showy flowering plant.

hiccup, hiccough n spasm of diaphragm, with closure of glottis; sound made by this; v utter this sound.

hick n provincial, unsophisticated person.

hickory n N American hardwood tree bearing nuts.

hide[1] n raw or dressed animal skin; n sl **hiding** thrashing; a **hidebound** fig narrow-minded.

hide[2] v **hiding, hid, hidden**. conceal; cover up; keep secret; ns **hide-and-seek** game in which players look for one who is hiding; **hideaway** (also **hidey**) place of escape from other people.

hideous a repulsive; horrible.

hierarchy n rank, order, class of sacred persons; any graded system of officials.

hieroglyph n symbol used in ancient Egyptian picture writing; fig secret writing; a **hieroglyphic**.

hi-fi n, a coll (equipment) for high-fidelity sound reproduction.

higgledy-piggledy a, adv completely disordered; jumbled up.

high a 1 tall (n **h. chair** chair for babies); 2 far above ground (ns **h. jump, h. tide, h. water**) 3 raised; elevated (n **h. table** table for senior members) 4 near the top 5 exalted 6 chief; most important (ns **H. Commissioner, H. Court, h. priest, h. street**) 7 very great (ns **h. speed, h. tension, h. treason**) 8 goods (ns **h. grade, h. life, h. quality**) 9 raised in pitch (**h. note, h. voice**) 10 (of meat) tainted 11 coll intoxicated; drugged; idm **high and dry** deserted; idm **get on one's high horse** behave in an arrogant way; idm **be for the high jump** incur reprimand, punishment; idm **on a high note** with cheerful optimism; idm **in high places** among people of influence; n 1 high point 2 met anticyclone 3 state of excitement; ns **highball** drink of spirits with soda and ice; **h. explosive** (also **HE**); **h.-flier** ambitious person; **h. jinks** coll fun and games; **highlands**; **highlight** 1 important detail 2 part reflecting most light 3 climax (v emphasize); **h. point**; **h. school** secondary school; **h. seas** oceans; **h. spot** coll outstanding event; **h. tea** Brit early evening meal; **h. technology** use of most up-to-date equipment and processes; a **h. tech** (also **hitech**); **h.-water mark** 1 mark left by high tide 2 point of greatest achievement; **highway** main road; **Highway Code** rules for using the roads; **highwayman** (formerly)

person who robs travellers;
as **h.-and-mighty** arrogant;
h. class superior; **h.-falutin**
coll pretentious; **h. fidelity**
reproducing sound almost
perfectly; **h.-flown**
extravagant; **h.-handed** too
authoritative (*adv* **-ly**;
n **-ness**); **h. minded** with
noble thoughts (*adv* **-ly**;
n **-ness**); **h.-rise** multi-
storey; **h.-spirited** lively; *adv*
highly greatly (*a* **h.-strung**
excitable); *n* **highness** title
used in referring to or
addressing members of royal
family.

hijack *v* take over control of
vehicle, *esp* aircraft by force;
stop and rob vehicle; *n*
instance of this; *n* **-er**.

hike *v* tramp; walk through
country; *n* walking
excursion; *n* **hiker**.

hilarity *n* cheerfulness, mirth,
jollity; *a* **hilarious**.

hill *n* small elevation of earth's
surface; small artificial
mound; *n* **hillock** little hill;
a **hilly**.

hilt *n* handle of sword, dagger
idm **up to the hilt**
completely.

him *pron* objective case of **he**;
pron **himself** emphatic form.

hind *n* female of red deer.

hind, hinder *a* at back,
posterior.

hinder *v* impede; obstruct;
prevent; *n* **hindrance**.

hindmost *a* furthest behind.

hindquarters *n*, *pl* back legs
and rump.

hindsight *n* understanding of

past mistakes.

Hindu *n* 1 Ayran non-Muslem
of N India 2 follower of
Hinduism.

hinge *n* joint on which door,
lid etc hangs and turns; *v*
provide hinge; *fig* depend
on.

hint *n* indirect suggestion;
brief advice; *v* give hint of;
make hint.

hinterland *n* district behind
coast, or that served by port.

hip *n* 1 projecting part of
upper thigh 2 fruit of briar
or rose; *a* trendy.

hip bath *n* portable bath.

hip hop *n sl* pop culture started
in the 1980s comprising rap
music, graffite, and break
dancing.

hippie, hippy *n* person
rejecting conventions of
society.

hippodrome *n* arena for
chariot-racing, horse-shows
etc.

hippopotamus *n* large ungainly
amphibious African
mammal.

hire *n* payment for services of
person, or use of thing; *v*
engage for wages; pay for
temporary use; *ns* **hireling**
mercenary person; **h.
purchase** payment by
instalments, with right of
use after first payment.

hirsute *a* hairy.

his *pron*, *a* belonging to him.

Hispanic *a* of Spain, Portugal,
Latin America.

hiss *v* make noise like sound of
prolonged S; express

disapproval, scorn by this
sound; *n* **-ing**.

hist *interj* hush! be silent.

histamine *n* chemical
produced in the body that
can cause allergic reactions.

history *n* systematic record of
past events in existence of
nation, individual, etc; study
of such events; methodical
account of evolution (of
language, art etc); *n*
historian writer of history;
as **historic** famous; epoch-
making; **-ical** based on,
recorded in history; *n*
natural h. zoology; botany.

historiography *n* study of
writing of history; *n* **-pher**;
a **-phic**.

hit *v* 1 strike, knock with blow,
missile 2 injure 3 find by
design or luck 4 reach
target; *pt*, *pp* **hit**; *idm* **hit the
nail on the head** say the
right thing; *phr vs* **hit back**
retaliate; **hit out at/against**
attack vigorously; *n* 1 well
aimed blow 2 *coll* popular
success *ns* **h. list** list of
people against whom action,
esp killing is planned; **h.
man** hired assassin; **h.
parade** list of best-selling
pop songs; *a* **hit-or-miss**
casual.

hitch *v* 1 raise with jerk 2
fasten by hook 3 ride free in
sb else's car (*also* **hitch a lift,
hitchhike**); *phr v* **hitch up**
pull up into place; adjust; *n*
1 temporary problem 2 jerk;
lifting movement 3 quick
fastening with rope; *a*

hitched *sl* married.

hi-tech *a* using high technology.

hither *adv lit*, *ar* to, towards this place; *a* nearer, on this side; *adv* **hitherto** until now, up to this time.

HIV *n* virus in the blood responsible for AIDS; *a* **HIV positive** infected with HIV.

hive *n* box for honey bees to live in; *idm* **hive of industry** busy place; *v* gather, place in hive; *phr v* **hive off** separate from larger group; transfer elsewhere, *esp* to make independent.

hives *n pl* skin eruption; croup.

HM *abbr* His/Her Majesty('s).

HMI *abbr* His/Her Majesty's Inspector.

HMS *abbr* His/Her Majesty's Ship (of Brit Navy).

hoard *n* secret store; hidden treasure; *v* amass, gather and keep hidden.

hoarding *n* temporary wooden fence, *esp* one used for posters.

hoarse *a* husky; rough; harsh; *n* **-ness**.

hoary *a* grey with age; *fig* ancient; greyish-white.

hoax *n* practical joke; mischievous trick; *v* play practical joke on; *n* **-er**.

hob *n* **1** ledge beside grate for keeping things hot **2** peg used as mark in quoits etc.

hobble *v* **1** limp, walk clumsily **2** tie two legs (of horse etc) together to prevent straying; *n* straps, rope used to hobble animal.

hobby *n* favourite leisure occupation; *n* **h.-horse** rocking-horse; *fig* hobby.

hobgoblin *n* mischievous imp; *n* **hob** rustic elf.

hobnail *n* large headed nail for studding boots.

hobnob *v* **-nobbing, -nobbed.** be on familiar terms with.

hobo *n* **hoboes.** *US* tramp; migratory worker.

Hobson's choice *n* situation where no choice is given.

hock[1] *n* joint in middle of hind leg of horse, ox etc; *v* hamstring.

hock[2] *n* German white wine.

hock[3] *v sl* pawn; *idm* **in hock** *sl* **1** pawned **2** in debt **3** in prison.

hockey *n* game played with ball and curved sticks, in field or on ice.

hocus-pocus *n* trickery; conjuror's jargon; nonsense; *v* **hocus** dupe; swindle; stupefy with drugs.

hod *n* small trough on handle for carrying bricks, mortar etc.

hodge-podge *n* mixture; jumble.

hoe *n* tool for breaking soil, weeding etc; *v* hoeing, hoed. use hoe.

hog *n* adult male pig, *esp* castrated one; *fig* greedy, filthy person; *n* **hogshead** large cask; liquid measure, 52 ½ imp. gallons.

Hogmanay *n Scot* New Year's Eve.

hogwash *n coll* nonsense.

hoick *v coll* lift abruptly.

hoi-polloi *n* common people; the masses.

hoist *v* raise with tackle; heave, lift up; *n*.

hoity-toity *a* haughty.

hold[1] *v* holding, held. **1** grasp; keep in hand **2** keep in position **3** occupy **4** maintain (opinion) **5** remain fixed **6** enclose; contain **7** restrain **8** be valid **9** detain **10** celebrate; *v idm* **hold it** stop and wait; *idm* **hold one's own** keep one's position; *idm* **hold water** (of argument, excuse) stand up to testing; be valid *phr vs* **hold against** oppose; **hold forth** talk pompously at length; **hold off** delay; **hold on 1** wait **2** retain one's grip; persevere; **hold out 1** offer **2** endure **3** last; **hold out for** persevere until one gets; **hold over 1** postpone **2** intimidate with; **hold up 1** delay **2** rob with threat of violence (*n* **h.-up**); *phr v* **hold with** approve of; *n* **1** grasp **2** manner of holding; *idm* **a hold on/over** means of control, influence; *ns* **holdall** large travelling bag; **holder 1** person in possession **2** container; **holding 1** land held by tenant **2** property or shares owned.

hold[2] *n* space below deck, for cargo, in ship.

hole *n* cavity; opening; tear, rent; outlet; den, burrow; *v* make, go into hole.

holiday *n* day, time of rest from

work; time of recreation; religious festival; *a* festive.

holier-than-thou *a* self-righteous.

holiness *n* 1 state of being holy 2 *cap* title of pope.

holistic *a* related to the whole; *n* **h. medicine** (*also* **alternative medicine**).

hollandaise *n* rich, egg-based sauce.

holler *v* US shout.

hollow *n* cavity; depression; hole; small valley; *a* not solid; sunken; echoing; *fig* insincere; *v* make hollow; scoop out.

holly *n* evergreen shrub with glossy, prickly leaves and red berries.

hollyhock *n* tall flowering plant.

holm *n* islet, *esp* in river; rich land near river.

holocaust *n* 1 complete destruction by fire 2 *usu cap* **the H.** Nazi mass murder of Jewish people during Second World War.

hologram *n phot* flat image that appears 3-dimensional when lit by laser beam; *n* **holography** science of making holograms; *a* **-phic**; *adv* **-phically**.

holograph *n* document hand-written by signatory.

holster *n* leather case for pistol, hung from belt etc.

holt *n* copse; wooded hill.

holy *a* pertaining to God; sacred, deeply pious; *ns* **H. Ghost** third person of Trinity (*also* **H. Spirit**); **h.**

of holies inner sanctum; **H. Week** week leading to Easter; **H. Writ** 1 the Bible 2 authoritative writing; *n* **holiness** sanctity; title of pope.

homage *n* declaration of allegiance; *fig* honour, respect, devotion.

homburg *n* man's felt hat with curved brim.

home *n* 1 family dwelling-place 2 native place 3 place of rest; asylum; *idm* **at home** 1 comfortable 2 welcoming visitors; *idm* **home and dry** having succeeded without mishap; *phr vs* **home in on** direct one's aim at; **home onto** be guided automatically towards; *a* pertaining to home or country; *ns* **homebody, homebrew, homecoming; H. Counties** area round London; **h. front** (wartime activities of) civilians; **h. economics** study of household management; **h. help, homeland; H. Office** *Brit* government department dealing with law and order; **h. rule** self-government; **h. run** baseball strike enabling batter to complete circuit in one run; **homestead** house with small farm; **h. truth** unpleasant fact that one has to face up to; **h. straight** last part of race; **homework**; *adv* at, to home; *as* **h.-brewed, h.-cured, h.-grown,**

h.-made; homeless; homely 1 simple 2 US plain looking; **homesick** longing for home; (**n -ness**); **homespun** unsophisticated; **homeward** towards home; *adv* **-s.**

homeopathy, homoeopathy *n* treatment of disease with small doses of drugs that would cause symptoms of the disease in a healthy person.

homicide *n* killer, killing of human being; *a* **-idal.**

homily *n* sermon; *fig* tedious lecture.

homing *a* 1 able to find home unaided 2 able to steer automatically to a target or destination.

hominid *n* human or human-like being.

homo-, homoeo- *prefix: forms compounds with meaning same, same kind. Where the meaning may be deduced from the simple word, the compounds are not given here.*

homogeneous *a* belonging to same category; uniform *n* **homgeneity** *v* **homogenize** 1 make homogenous 2 treat (milk) to cause blending of cream with the rest.

homograph *n* word having same spelling as another.

homonym *n* word having same spelling and sound as another but a different sense.

homophobia *n* hatred or fear of homosexuals or homosexuality; *a* **homophobic.**

homophone n word having same sound as another, but different spelling.

Homo sapiens n Lat the human species.

homosexual a attracted to one's own sex; **-lity**.

honest a straightforward, not criminal, sincere; open frank; n **honesty 1** integrity; trustworthiness **2** garden herb, with transparent seed pods.

honey n sweet sticky fluid made from nectar by bees; n **-comb** mass of hexagonal wax cells, made by bees, to store honey or larvae; v pierce with many holes; riddle; ns **-dew** sweet deposit on plants; **-suckle** climbing plant with fragrant flowers; **-moon** holiday spent alone by newly-married couple.

honk n cry of wild goose; similar sound esp of motor horn; v to make this sound.

honky-tonk n, a (of) ragtime piano music.

honour n **1** respect, esteem **2** good reputation; moral dignity, high rank **3** mark of esteem; pl distinction in University exam; v esteem highly; confer honour on; pay (bill, draft etc) when due; as **-able, honorary** given, done as honour; giving services without pay; **honorific** conferring, expressing honour; n **honorarium** voluntary payment for services.

hood n **1** soft covering for head and neck **2** cowl **3** folding roof of car etc **4** chimney-cowl; v cover with hood; v **hoodwink** deceive.

hoodlum n violent petty criminal.

hoof n hoofs or hooves. horny sheath protecting animal's foot.

hoo-ha n coll fuss.

hook n **1** curved piece of metal, wood, plastic or other substance, for holding, hanging, catching or pulling something **2** curved cutting implement **3** blow with bent arm in boxing; v **1** grasp, seize, hold, fasten with hook **2** hit ball to striker's left; idm **off the hook** freed from danger, difficulty a **hooked** shaped like a hook; idm **hooked (on)** coll addicted (to); n **h. worm** parasitic worm.

hookah n Oriental pipe, in which smoke passes through tube and water-bottle.

hook-up n link between electrical circuits, radio or TV stations.

hooky idm **play hooky** US play truant.

hooligan n noisy, destructive (usu young) ruffian.

hoop n circular band of wood, metal esp to bind cask; large ring of wood, bowled along, as toy; v bind with hoop.

hooray interj expressing delight.

hoot n **1** cry of owl **2** sound of motor-horn etc **3** cry of derision; v utter hoots; cause to hoot.

hoover [TM] n vacuum cleaner; v clean with a vacuum cleaner.

hooves pl of hoof.

hop[1] n plant whose flowers are used in making beer; pl dried flower cones; v gather, produce hops; n **hopping** gathering hops.

hop[2] v hopping, hopped. jump on one leg; advance so; idm **hop it** coll go away; idm **on the hop** unprepared n **1** leap **2** informal dance **3** coll short aircraft flight.

hope n confident expectation of something desired; likelihood that something desired will happen; thing, person, action which inspires hope; v entertain hope; desire and expect; a **-ful;** (n young h. promising boy or girl); a **-less.**

hopper n funnel-like device for feeding grain to mill, coal to machine etc; self-discharging dredging barge, or rail truck; that which hops; hop picker.

hopscotch n children's game of jumping into and across marked squares.

horal, horary a pertaining to an hour; hourly; lasting an hour.

horde n band of nomads; destructive gang, rabble.

horizon n circle bounding visible part of earth's surface; line where earth and sky seem to meet; fig limits of interest, mental outlook; *a* -tal parallel with horizon; level; (*adv* -ly).

hormone *n* internal secretion by glands, which stimulates functional activity of organs of body.

hormone replacement therapy *n* hormone treatment for women, *esp* after the menopause.

horn *n* 1 one of hard bony pointed growths on head of cow etc 2 substance of horns; various things made of, or like it 3 wind-instrument 4 warning device on car, lighthouse etc; *as* -ed having horns; **horn-pipe** old wind-instrument; sailors, dance.

hornbill *n* tropical bird with big curved beak.

hornblende *n* mineral found in granite and other igneous rocks.

hornet *n* large species of wasp; *idm* **stir up a hornet's nest** provoke trouble.

horology *n* art of clock-making, or measuring time; *n* **horologer** clock- or watch-maker.

horoscope *n* calculation of positions of heavenly bodies at particular moment, *esp* of person's birth, to predict fortune, character, etc.

horrendous *a* terrible, dreadful.

horror *n* terror; disgust; repulsion; its cause; *as* **horrible** causing horror;

shocking; terrifying; **horrid** frightful, disgusting; *v* **horrify** excite horror in; *a* -ific horrifying.

hors de combat *a* wounded and unable to go on fighting.

hors d'oeuvre *n* Fr light savoury dish served before meal as appetizer.

horse *n* 1 large four-footed domesticated mammal, used for riding on, or draught 2 stallion 3 cavalry 4 frame with legs, for support 5 vaulting-block **horse** *idm* **from the horse's mouth** from the person who knows; *ns* **h.-box** vehicle for horse; **h.-chestnut** tree with inedible shiny brown nuts; **h. laugh** loud coarse laugh; **horseman, horsemanship; horseplay** rough noisy play; **horsepower** unit of engine power (*also* hp); **horseradish** edible root with hot flavour; **h.-race; h. sense** common sense; **horseshoe** U-shaped shoe, symbol of good luck; **h.-trading** *coll* clever bargaining; **horsewhip** *v* beat with whip; **horsewoman;** *a* **horsy** 1 like a horse 2 interested in horses.

hortative, hortatory *a* exhorting; admonitory.

horticulture *n* study of gardening; *a* -tural; *n* -turalist.

hosanna *interj* Hebrew exclamation of praise.

hose *n* flexible tube for carrying water or other liquids; *pl* **hose** socks, stockings; *n* **hosiery** underwear, socks, stockings etc; shop dealing in this; stockings; **hosier.**

hospice *n* 1 house of rest for travellers, *esp* one kept by monks 2 home for terminally ill.

hospitable *a* welcoming to visitors; *adv* -ably.

hospital *n* place where sick and injured are cared for; *v* -ize send, admit to hospital; *n* -ization.

hospitality *n* cheerful, friendly entertainment, feeding and lodging of guests; *a* **hospitable** inviting, generous, friendly.

host[1] *n* one who entertains a guest; hotelkeeper; compere on TV.

host[2] *n* army; great number.

hostage *n* one given or taken as pledge that promises will be kept.

hostel *n* lodging-house for students, workers, young people etc.

hostess *n* 1 female host 2 air hostess 3 woman entertaining men at nightclub 4 female compere on TV.

hostile *a* unfriendly; warlike; *n* **hostility** enmity; (*pl* -ies acts of war).

hot *a* 1 of high temperature; feeling, giving heat 2 pungent 3 *fig* violent 4 lustful 5 *coll* (of news) exciting and fresh **6** *sl* (of stolen goods) sought by police **7** angry; *ns* **h.air** meaningless talk; **h.-air balloon**; **hotbed** place where ideas can develop; **hot-cross bun** spicy bun eaten on Good Friday; **h. dog** frankfurter in long bread roll; **h. gospeller** *coll* enthusiastic, emotional preacher; **hothead** *n* rash person; *a* **hotheaded**; **hothouse** greenhouse; **h. line** direct telephone link between heads of state; **hotplate** surface for cooking; **h. rod** car rebuilt for speed; **h. seat** (*idm* **in the h. s.** responsible for making difficult decisions); **h. spot** dangerous place; **h. stuff** *coll* **1** exciting thing or person **2** skilful person; **h. water** (*idm* **in h.w.** in trouble); **h.-water bottle** receptacle for warming bed; *as* **h.-blooded** passionate; **h.-tempered** irascible.

hotel *n* large, superior inn; *n* **hotelier**.

houmous *see* Hummus.

hound *n* dog hunting by scent; *v* pursue; persecute.

hour *n* sixty minutes; ¼ part of day; fixed point of time; *pl* regular time of work; *adv* **hourly** every hour; *n* **h.-glass** sand-glass which runs out in one hour.

house *n* **1** dwelling designed for human habitation **2** hotel, inn etc **3** business firm **4** legislative assembly

or building used for such **5** family; lineage; *v* provide house for; harbour; *idm* **bring the house down** provoke loud laughter or applause; *idm* **get on like a house on fire** *coll* have a good relationship; *idm* **keep house** look after household affairs; *idm* **keep open house** offer welcome at all times; *idm* **on the house** *coll* paid for by manager; *ns* **h. arrest**, **houseboat**; **housebreaker** burglar, **housebreaking**; **housecoat** woman's long garment worn at home; **household** people living in a house (**household name/word** well known name/word); **householder** head of household; **housekeeper** person employed to look after house; **housekeeping 1** work of running house **2** money for this; **h. lights** theatre auditorium lights; **housemaid** female servant; **houseman** *Brit* trainee doctor; **housemaster**; **housemistress** teacher responsible for school house; **h. of cards 1** structure made of playing cards **2** scheme likely to fail and collapse; **H. of Commons** assembly of elected representatives in UK and Canada; **H. of Lords** assembly of British nobility and bishops; **H. of Representatives** assembly of elected representatives in USA, Australia, New

Zealand; **h.-warming** party given by new occupants; **housewife**; *as* **h.-proud** fussy about appearance of home; **h.-trained** (of animals) trained not to urinate, defecate indoors.

housing *n* **1** living accommodation **2** cover for machinery.

hove *pt*, *pp* of **heave**.

hovel *n* small, shabby dwelling.

hover *v* **1** (of birds) float motionless in air **2** *fig* linger; hesitate; *n* **hovercraft** craft moving along, on cushion of air, over land or water.

how *adv* in what way; by what means; to what degree; *idm* **How come?** why?; *idm* **How do you do?** used as formal greeting.

however *adv* **1** nevertheless **2** in whatever way; to whatever degree **3** by what (possible) means.

howitzer *n* short-barreled canon that fires shells from an angle.

howl *v* utter loud dismal cry; *n* such cry; *n* **howler 1** person, animal or thing that howls **2** *sl* stupid mistake.

HP *abbr* **1** hire purchase **2** horsepower (*also* **hp**).

HQ *abbr* headquarters.

hr, hrs *abbr* hour(s).

HRH *abbr* His/Her Royal Highness.

HRT *abbr* hormone replacement therapy.

hub *n* central part of wheel; *fig* centre of activity or importance.

hubcap n metal cover for centre of car wheel.

hubbub n uproar; riot.

hubby n coll husband.

hubris n excessive pride or self-confidence.

huckleberry n N American shrub; its fruit.

huckster n hawker; pedlar; v haggle; carry on petty trade.

huddle v heap, gather into confused mass; crowd together; n such a crowd.

hue n colour; tint; complexion.

hue and cry n loud outcry; angry pursuit.

huff v 1 bully; hector 2 take offence 3 (draughts) remove opponents piece as forfeit; n sulkiness; a **huffy**; adv -ily.

hug v **hugging, hugged.** embrace warmly; clasp tightly in arms; fig keep close to; n act of hugging.

huge a very great, enormous.

hugger-mugger n 1 secrecy 2 disorder a, adv in disorder.

hula n Hawaiian woman's dance.

hulk n 1 derelect, dismantled ship 2 fig clumsy, unwieldy person; a **hulking** big and clumsy.

hull n 1 body of ship 2 pod, shell of pea; v 1 pierce hull of ship 2 remove hull from pea.

hullabaloo n uproar; din; clamour.

hum v **humming, hummed.** produce low buzzing, droning sound, as bee; utter musical sound with closed lips; n continuous low drone; n **humming-bird** small tropical bird making humming noise with wings.

human a pertaining to mankind; associated with man; adv **humanly** in human manner; a **humane** kind; merciful; (adv -ly); ns **humanism** system of thought dealing with human interests; **humanist** 1 student, advocate of humanism 2 classical scholar; **humanity** human race as whole; kindness of heart; pl **Humanities** classical literary studies; a, n **humanitarian** philanthropist; v **humanize** make, become human, humane.

humanoid a having human characteristics.

humble a lowly; meek; modest; not exalted in rank, position; v abase; put to shame; adv **humbly.**

humbug n 1 hoax; nonsense 2 empty, boastful person 3 peppermint sweetmeat; v deceive; dupe.

humdinger n sl sb or sth superb.

humdrum a commonplace; dull.

humerus n bone of upper arm in man; a **humeral** of shoulder.

humid a moist; damp; n -idity; v -ify.

humiliate v put to shame; lower pride of; abase;

n -ation.

humility n quality of being humble; meekness.

humankind n people collectively.

humming bird n minute tropical bird with long beak.

hummus n Gk puree of chickpeas, tahina etc (also **houmous**).

hummock n knoll; hillock; ridge of ice.

humour n (US humor) 1 mood; state of mind 2 fun; jocular action, saying 3 whim; fancy; v indulge moods; act tactfully; n **humorist, humorist** one who makes jokes; comic writer, artist or actor; a **humorous** laughable, funny; amusing.

hump n 1 rounded lump, bulge or mound 2 sl mental depression; v carry on back; -**back** person with spinal deformity; a -**backed** having hump.

humus n decayed organic matter giving fertility to soil.

hunch v coll premonition; v stoop; draw shoulders up; n -**back** humpback.

hundred n, pron, det cardinal number, ten times ten; a -**th** ordinal number 100th; a, adv **hundredfold**; n **hundredweight** measure of weight = 112 lbs. or ½₀ ton.

hung pt, pp of **hang.**

hunger n desire for food; exhaustion, emaciation due to lack of food; fig craving; phr v **hunger after /for/ long**

for; n **h. strike** refusal of all food, as protest; a **hungry** feeling hunger; starving; adv **hungrily**.

hunk n thick piece

hunt v pursue (animals), often with hounds in order to kill, or catch; pursue (person); search for, track down; n search; local association of persons with their horses, hounds engaged in hunting; ns **huntsman** man in charge of hounds; **hunter**; fem **huntress**.

hurdle n light wooden framework, as temporary fence or to jump over; n **hurdler** one who runs in hurdle races; **h.-race** race in which series of fences or hurdles are leapt.

hurdy-gurdy n small barrel-organ.

hurl v throw violently; hurtle; ns **-ing** Irish or Cornish ball-game; **hurler**.

hurly-burly n noisy activity.

hurricane n violent wind-storm, of 75 mph (120kmph) or more; tropical cyclone; n **h.-lamp** lamp with well-shielded flame.

hurry v **-hurrying, hurried.** move, do quickly; hasten; urge to haste; a **hurried**; adv **-ly**; v,n **h.-scurry** rush.

hurt v **hurting, hurt.** cause pain to; injure, distress; damage; n harm; wound; pain; a showing, feeling pain or offence; a **-ful**.

hurtle v move violently; dash against; whirl.

husband n married man; v manage thriftily; n **ship's h.**, agent managing ship's business for owners.

hush v make, become silent, quiet; phr v **hush up** keep secret; n silence; stillness.

husk n dry covering of certain seeds; v strip husk from; a **husky** dry as husk; hoarse; harsh, rasping; adv **huskily**; n **-iness**.

husky n Eskimo sledge dog.

hussy n pert, ill-mannered girl.

hustings n pl Guildhall Court; electioneering platform; election proceedings.

hustle v hurry; jostle; urge along roughly; n bustle; hurry; n **hustler** one who gets things done.

hut n shed; small wooden building; hovel; n **-ment** encampment of huts.

hutch n box; bin; chest; box-like coop for rabbits etc.

hyacinth n bulbous plant with spikes of fragrant, bell-shaped flowers.

hybrid n animal or plant produced by parents of different species; fig anything derived from mixed origins; a cross-bred; v **-ize** cross-fertilize; interbreed; n **-ization**.

hydra n 1 myth many headed serpent; 2 fig evil that defies destruction 3 freshwater polyp.

hydrangea n shrub with pink, blue or white flowers.

hydrant n pipe from water-main, with attachment for hose.

hydraulic a conveying water; water-powered; n pls science dealing with flow of liquids.

hydr-, hydro- prefix; forms compounds with meaning of water, e.g. **hydroplane** n seaplane. Where the meaning may be deduced from the simple word, such compounds are not given here.

hydrocarbon n organic compound of hydrogen and carbon.

hydrochloric a containing hydrogen and chlorine; n **h. acid**.

hydrodynamics n pl mathematical study of liquids in motion.

hydroelectric a pertaining to electricity generated by water power.

hydrofoil n boat with vanes that lift hull above water to reduce drag and increase speed.

hydrogen n colourless gas combining with oxygen to form water; **h. bomb** highly destructive atom bomb.

hydrometer n measuring device for density of liquids.

hydrophobia n rabies; abnormal fear of water, esp as symptom of this.

hydrotherapy n use of water to treat disease.

hyena n carnivorous dog-like animal with cry like wild laughter.

hygiene n science and principles of maintaining health; cleanliness; a hygienic.

hygrometer n instrument for measuring humidity of atmosphere.

hymen n membrane partly covering entrance to vagina of a virgin.

hymn n song of praise *esp* to God; a, n **-al** (book) of hymns.

hype n exaggerated publicity; *phr v* **hype up** publicize in a wildly exaggerated way a **hyped up 1** over promoted **2** over stimulated (as if) by drugs.

hyper- *prefix: forms compounds with meaning of excessive, above; eg* **hypercritical** *a too critical. Where the meaning may be deduced from the simple word, such compounds are not given here.*

hyperactive n excessively restless; unable to settle down.

hyperbola n curve formed by section of cone when cutting plane makes larger angle with base than side makes.

hyperbole n rhetorical exaggeration.

hypercritical a overly critical.

hypermarket n Brit very big self-service store.

hypertension n med **1** abnormally high blood pressure **2** abnormal emotional tension.

hyphen n mark (-) indicating that two words or syllables are connected; a **-ated**.

hypnosis n induction of sleep; artificially induced state resembling deep sleep; a **hypnotic** inducing sleep; v **hypnotize** affect with hypnosis; ns **hypnotism, -ist**.

hypo-, hyph-, hyp- *prefix: forms compounds with meaning of below, less, under. Such compounds are not given where the meaning may be deduced from the simple word.*

hypo n solution of hyposulphite used in developing film negatives.

hypoallergenic a (of cosmetics) unlikely to cause an allergic reaction on the skin.

hypocaust n underfloor heating system used by Romans.

hypochondria n morbid obsession with one's health; n **-driac** person with this; a **-driacal**.

hypocrisy n pretending to be better morally than one is; n **-crite**, such a person; a **-critical**.

hypodermic a under the skin; n **h. syringe** one used for giving such injection.

hypotenuse n side of right-angled triangle opposite the right angle.

hypothermia n very low body temperature, *esp* in old people.

hypothesis n supposition; unproved theory; pl **-theses**; a **-thetical**.

hysterectomy n surgical removal of uterus; n **hysterotomy** incision into uterus.

hysteria n extreme emotional excitability, and loss of will-power; a **hysteric (al)**; n pl **hysterics** fit of hysteria.

Hz abbr hertz.

I *pron* (1st per sing nom) myself; (*pl* **we**).

iambus *n* metrical foot of one short and one long syllable.

IBA *abbr* Independent Broadcasting Authority.

Iberian *a* of Spain and Portugal.

ibis *n* wading bird with long curved bill.

IBM *abbr comput* International Business Machines.

ICBM *abbr* intercontinental ballistic missile.

ice *n* 1 frozen water 2 ice-cream; *idm* **break the ice** initiate relations; remove embarrassment; *idm* **cut no ice** fail to impress; *idm* **keep on ice** 1 keep chilled 2 (of ideas) hold in reserve; *idm* **skate on thin ice** take unwise risk; *ns* **i.age** very cold pre-historic era on earth; **i.axe**; **iceberg** mass of floating ice at sea (*idm* **the tip of the iceberg** only a

small part of the problem; **icebox, i.-breaker; i.-cap** permanently frozen polar region; **i.cream** frozen confection of flavoured cream, custard etc; **i.hockey; i.lolly** flavoured confection of ice on a stick; **i.-pack** bag of ice for cooling the head or body; **i.-pick** tool for breaking ice; **i. rink** artificial sheet of ice for skating, ice hockey etc; **i.-skate** boot with metal blade for skating on ice (*v* **i.-skate, i.-skating**); *n* **i. water**; *as* **i.-blue, i.-bound, i.-cold**; *v* 1 make cold with ice 2 cover with sugar-icing; *ns* **icicle** long hanging piece of ice formed from dripping water; **icing** (also *US* **frosting**) decorative coating for cake made from icing sugar; *a* **icy**; *adv* **icily**; *n* **iciness**.

ichneumon *n* small Eastern animal, like weasel; *n* **i.fly**

parasitic insect.

ICI *abbr* Imperial Chemical Industries.

icon *n* image; sacred portrait; *n* **iconoclast** *fig* one who attacks established customs and beliefs.

I'd *abbr* 1 **I** had 2 **I** should 3 **I** would.

ID *abbr* identification; identity.

id *n psyc* instinctive impulses of the individual.

idea *n* notion; opinion; plan; thought.

ideal *a* 1 visionary 2 of highest standard; *n* supreme perfection; standard of excellence to be copied; *ns* **idealism** practice of seeking perfection in all things; unrealistic attitude to life; **idealist** 1 one who believes in idealism 2 impractical person; *v* **idealize** exaggerate good qualities of; *n* **-ization**; idealized view.

idée fixe *n* Fr obsession.

identify *v* show, prove, recognize who/what sb/sth is; *idm* **identify with 1** consider sb/sth to be connected with 2 sympathize with; *ns* **identification; identikit** artificial portrait of suspected criminal composed from descriptions by witnesses.

identity *n* 1 individuality 2 absolute sameness; *a* **identical** the very same; impossible to distinguish.

ideograph *n* symbolic

representation of an object, without naming it; n **-graphy** shorthand writing; symbolic writing.

ideogram n symbol to represent idea (as in Chinese).

ideology n set of political, religious, social ideas; a **-logical** (adv **-ly**); ns **-ologist, -ologue** advocate of particular ideology.

Ides n pl (Roman Calendar) 15th March, May, July, October, 13th of other months.

idiocy n stupidity; example of this.

idiom n mode of expression; one peculiar to a language; dialect; a **-atic** character of language; fluent and colloquial.

idiosyncrasy n individual peculiarity of manner, thought, way of speaking etc; a **idiosyncratic** (adv **-ally**).

idiot n imbecile; person of defective intellect; n **idiocy**; a **-otic** utterly foolish, senseless; adv **-ically**.

idle a lazy; not functioning; v 1 waste time 2 (of machine) run at low speed; n **-ness**; adv **idly**; n **idler**.

idol n 1 image representing deity 2 false god 3 person, object of extreme devotion; ns **idolater** worshipper of false gods (fem **idolatress**); **idolatry**; a **idolatrous**; v **idolize** make an idol of; love, admire excessively.

idyll n 1 short, simple poem on homely, pastoral subjects 2 romantic incident, usually rural; a **-ic**.

ie abbr id est Lat that is.

if conj supposing that; even though; whenever; whether.

iffy a coll uncertain.

igloo n Eskimo hut of frozen snow blocks.

igneous a fiery; produced by volcanic action.

ignite v set on fire; be kindled; n **ignition** setting on fire; means of firing of explosive gaseous mixture by electric spark.

ignoble a base; degraded; humiliating; shameful; adv **-bly**.

ignominy n dishonour; degradation; public disgrace; a **-minious** shameful; humiliating.

ignorance n lack of education; inexperience; a **ignorant** uninformed; unaware; n **ignoramus** ignorant person.

ignore v disregard; refuse to consider.

iguana n large, crested S American tree lizard.

ilk a Scot same; **of that ilk** 1 of same name etc 2 coll of that kind.

ill a 1 physically or mentally sick 2 bad; harmful (ns **i.effects, i.feeling, i. health, i.luck, i.repute, i.will**); n harm; evil; pl **-s** misfortunes; adv (esp prefix forming compound as, vs) badly; wrongly; as i. **-assorted** badly matched; i.**-advised**

unwise; i.**-bred**, i.**-considered**, i.**-defined**, i.**-fated**; i.**-gotten** dishonestly acquired; i.**-mannered**, i.**-natured** bad tempered; i.**-omened**, i.**-timed**; vs i.**-treat** (n **-ment**); i.**-use** (n i.**-usage**).

illegal a unlawful; n **-ity**.

illegible a difficult to read; adv **-ibly**; n **-ibility**.

illegitimate a unlawful; not born in wedlock; n **-timacy**.

illicit a prohibited; forbidden.

illiterate a unable to read or write; n **illiteracy**.

illogical a irrational; unsound.

illuminate v make light; adorn with lights; decorate (manuscript) with gold and colours; a **-ating** helpful and revealing; n **-ation**; v **illumine** enlighten.

illusion v deceptive appearance; delusion; n **-ist** conjuror.

illustrate v 1 make clear; explain 2 furnish (book etc) with pictures; ns **-ation**; illustrator.

illustrious a famous, distinguished, glorious.

I'm abbr I am.

im- prefix see **in-**

image n 1 visual representation 2 idea, esp popular opinion about a person, company or commercial product 3 statue or portrait 4 reflection 5 simile 6 counterpart; n **imagery** images; mental pictures.

imagine v form image, idea in

mind; suppose; as **-inative**.

imago n final state of insect, esp of winged one.

imbalance n lack of balance or proportion.

imbecile a mentally deficient; n such a person; n **-ility**.

imbibe v drink in; absorb; drink.

imbue v saturate; dye; phr v fml **imbue (with)** fill (with).

IMF abbr International Monetary Fund.

imitate v copy closely; mimic; n **-tation** act of imitating; copy; counterfeit; a **-tative**; n **-tator**.

immaculate a pure; unsoiled; innocent n **I. Conception** Roman Catholic belief that the mother of Jesus was born without original sin.

immanent a inherent; ever present.

immaterial a not consisting of matter; spiritual; unimportant.

immature a not adult; unripe; adv **-ly**; n **immaturity**.

immeasurable a vast; incalculable.

immediate a 1 happening now or next; nearest in time 2 nearest in space, in relationship; adv **-ly 1** at once **2** with nothing between; conj as soon as; n **immediacy** nearness; urgency.

immemorial a beyond living memory; very ancient.

immense a very great; vast; sl very good; n **immensity**.

immerse v dip, plunge into

liquid; fig engross; n

immersion (i.heater electric water heater).

immigrate v come to foreign country to live; ns **-ation**; **immigrant** (also a) person settling in foreign country.

imminent a impending; threatening; about to happen; adv **-ently**; n **-ence**.

immobile a not moving; fixed; n **-bility**; v **immobilize** render immobile; n **-ization**.

immoderate a excessive; unrestrained.

immoral a morally wrong; corrupt.

immortal a never dying; everlasting; n **-ity**.

immune a free from; exempt from; resistant to (disease); ns **i. system** function of body to combat disease; **immunity;** v **immunize** (n **-ization); immunology** bio study of immunity (a **-logical**; n **-logist**); a **immunosuppressive** bio overriding the immune system (a, n **-essant**).

immure v shut up; enclose; imprison.

immutable a unchangeable.

imp n little devil; mischievous child.

impact n collision; fig strong impression; v press strongly together.

impair v weaken; injure; n **-ment**.

impale v transfix, esp on pointed stake; n **-ment**.

impart v transmit; make known; bestow.

impartial a unprejudiced; just; fair; adv **-ly**; n **-ity**.

impassable a not capable of being crossed over.

impasse n deadlock; blind alley.

impassioned a ardent; passionate.

impassive a without emotion; calm; n **-ivity**.

impatient a intolerant of restraint; irritable; restless; adv **-ly**; n **impatience**.

impeach v indict, charge with crime esp high treason; n **-ment**.

impeccable a faultless; incapable of sin; adv **-ably** n **-bility**.

impecunious a poor; hard up; n **impecuniosity**.

impede v obstruct; delay; n **impediment**; n pl **impedimenta 1** baggage; equipment **2** encumbrances.

impel v **-pelling, -pelled.** drive forward; urge on; force.

impend v overhang; be about to happen; threaten; a **impending** due.

impenetrable n **1** impassable **2** incomprehensible.

imperative a peremptory; urgent; necessary; n imperative mood.

imperfect a faulty; adv **-ly**; n **-ion** blemish.

imperial a of empire or emperor; n **1** type of beard **2** paper size; ns **-ism** belief in colonial empire; **-ist**.

imperil v **-illing, -illed.** endanger.

imperious a dominating;

dictatorial; haughty.

impersonal a 1 not distinctive 2 automatic; without feelings 3 (of verb) without personal subject.

impersonate v pretend to be another; act part of; ns -ation; -ator.

impertinent a irrelevant; impudent, insolent; adv -ly; n impertinence.

imperturbable a calm; not liable to be ruffled; adv -ably.

impervious a not allowing entry; fig insensible to; n -ness.

impetuous a violent; rash and hasty; impulsive; adv -ly; n impetuosity.

impetus n momentum; driving force; fig stimulus.

impinge v fall on, against; infringe.

impious a without piety; ungodly; adv -ly; n -ness.

implacable a inexorable; relentless; n implacability.

implant v insert; fig instil (into mind); n sth implanted in the body by surgery.

implement n tool; utensil; instrument; v carry into effect; complete; n -ation.

implicate v entangle; involve; include; -tion; a implicit 1 hinted at 2 unquestioning; unquestioned; adv -ly.

implore v ask for earnestly; entreat.

imply v -plying, -plied. suggest; insinuate.

impolitic a unwise; tactless.

imponderable a, n (thing) the

importance of which cannot be assessed.

import v bring in (esp goods from abroad); signify, imply; n 1 thing imported 2 consequence; ns -ation; importer.

important a 1 distinguished 2 of consequence; essential 3 pompous; adv (-ly); n importance.

importune v pester with troublesome demands; a importunate; adv -ly; n importunity.

impose v 1 exact (tax etc) 2 foist upon 3 deceive; ns imposition 1 act of imposing 2 tax 3 deception 4 task given as school punishment; imposter deceiver; charlatan; fraudulent person; imposture; impost 1 tax; duty 2 weight carried by race-horse; a imposing impressive.

impossible a not feasible; coll insufferable; adv -ibly; n -ibility.

imposter n person who pretends to be someone else to deceive people.

impotent a powerless; feeble; lacking sexual capacity (esp of males); n impotence.

impound v 1 confiscate 2 confine; enclose in pound.

impoverish v make poor; weaken; n -ment.

imprecation n curse.

impregnable a unassailable; invincible.

impregnate v 1 make pregnant; fertilize 2 saturate;

n -ation.

impress[1] v stamp; fig affect deeply; fix mark on; n impression 1 number of copies of book etc printed at one time 2 effect produced, esp on mind 3 belief; a -able easily influenced; ns impressionism style of painting giving general effect without detail; -ist; a impressive making great effect.

impress[2] v compel to serve in army, navy.

imprest n loan made to individual by the State.

imprint v 1 stamp 2 fix in mind; n mark, stamp made by pressure; publisher's, printer's name etc in book.

imprison v put in prison; confine; n -ment.

impromptu adv, a without preparation; unrehearsed.

improper a 1 incorrect 2 socially unacceptable; indecent; adv -ly; n impropriety.

improve v make, become better; n -ment.

improvident a imprudent; wanting foresight; adv -ly; n -dence.

improvise v compose, do on spur of moment, esp with makeshift materials; n -ation.

impudent a insolent; bold; saucy; adv -ly; n -dence.

impugn v criticize; challenge.

impulse n push; sudden inclination to act; stimulus; n impulsion impetus; a

impulsive rash; acting without thought.

impunity n freedom, safety from penalty; idm **with impunity** without being penalized.

impure a dirty; adulterated; unchaste; n **impurity**.

impute v ascribe to; credit with; n **imputation** reproach; accusation.

in prep **1** contained by **2** during **3** into **4** at end of (time) **5** wearing (clothes) **6** showing manner (eg in a hurry), circumstances (eg in an emergency), condition (eg in ruins); idm **in all** altogether; idm **in that** because; adv **1** inside **2** at home **3** included **4** in/into a certain state **5** available; delivered **6** coll fashionable; idm **be in for** be going to experience; idm **be in on** share, participate in; idm **be in with** be in favour with; idm **have (got) it in for** bear a grudge against; a **1** coll fashionable **2** belonging to an exclusive group; n idm **the ins and outs** complex details.

in- prefix forming as, advs, ns (also **im-** before **b**, **m** or **p** and **il-**, **ir-** before **1** and **r** respectively) **1** not **2** lack of **3** opposite of; eg a **inaccurate** not accurate; n **inaccuracy** lack of accuracy; adv **illegibly** not legibly; n **immodesty** opposite of, lack of modesty. Such words, if not listed, can have their meaning

deduced by removing the prefix; eg **irregular** (not regular) and **irregularity** (lack of regularity) can be understood by looking up **regular, regularity.**

inadvertent a unintentional; adv **-ly**; n **inadvertency**.

inalienable a that cannot be taken away (n **i. right**).

inane a senseless; frivolous; n **inanity** silly remark.

inasmuch conj as seeing that; since.

inaugurate v install in office with ceremony; begin, open esp formally; n **-al**; n **-ation**.

inauspicious a ill-omened; unlucky; unfavourable; adv **-ly**.

inborn, inbred a inherent; natural; n **inbreeding** breeding from closely related stocks.

inbuilt a forming an inherent part of sth.

inc abbr incorporated.

incalculable a beyond calculation; unpredictable; uncertain.

incandescent a luminous with heat; brilliant; n **incandescence**; v **incandesce**.

incantation n magic spell; charm.

incapacitate v render unfit; disable; disqualify; n **incapacity**.

incarcerate v imprison, confine; n **-ation**.

incarnate a embodied in human form; personified; v give bodily form to; n **-ation**.

incendiary n, a (one) who maliciously sets property on fire; inflammatory; n **incendiarism** arson.

incense[1] n fragrant smoke from burning spices etc.

incense[2] v anger, enrage.

incentive n stimulus; motive; a rousing; inciting.

inception n beginning.

incessant a constant; unceasing.

incest n sexual intercourse between close blood relations; a **-uous**.

inch n ¹⁄₁₂th. linear foot; v advance by small degrees.

inchoate a undeveloped; rudimentary.

incident n happening; event; a **-al 1** relatively unimportant (n **i. music** music played as accompaniment) **2** occurring by chance; adv **-ally** by the way; n **incidence** fact of affecting; scope of occurrence.

incinerate v consume by fire; ns **-ation**; **-ator**.

incipient a beginning; in early stages.

incise v cut into; carve; n **incision**; **incisor** cutting tooth; a **incisive** sharp; fig pointed; vigorously clear.

incite v inflame; urge; rouse; n **-ment**.

inclement a (of weather) cold, severe, rough.

incline v **1** slope; lean; bend **2** tend; be disposed; n slope; slant; n **-ination 1** slope **2** bow or nod head **3** tendency; liking.

include v contain; regard as part of whole; n **inclusion**; a **inclusive**.

incognito a passing under assumed name; n **1** such a name **2** person adopting it.

incoherent a rambling, disconnected; lacking cohesion; n **-rence**.

income n money received (esp annually) from investments, salary etc; ns **i. support** state benefit for the unemployed and people on low incomes; **i.tax.**

incoming a coming in; next to take office.

incommode v disturb; trouble; a **-modious** inconvenient.

incommunicado adv not allowed to communicate with anyone.

incomparable a too good to be compared; adv **-ly**.

incompatible a not suited to one another; unable to exist together; adv **-ly** n; **-bility**.

incongruous a inconsistent; unsuitable; n **incongruity**.

inconsequential a unimportant; irrelevant; adv **-ly**.

incontestable a that cannot be disputed; adv **-ly**.

incontinent a unable to control one's bladder; n **-ence**.

incontrovertible a totally indisputable; adv **-ibly**.

inconvenient a causing difficulty or discomfort; adv **-ly**; n **-ence**; v **-ence**.

incorporate v include; blend; form legal corporation; n **-**ration.

incorrigible a impossible to correct or improve; adv **-ibly**; n **-ibility**.

increase v **1** grow, become larger; enlarge **2** multiply; n enlargement; growth; adv **increasingly** more and more.

incredible a unbelievable; coll remarkable.

incredulous a unbelieving; sceptical; n **incredulity**.

increment n addition; increase.

incriminate v accuse; render liable to accusation.

incubate v hatch, sit on eggs; ns **-ation** med period between infection and appearance of symptoms; **-bator** apparatus for artificially hatching eggs, or rearing premature babies.

inculcate v implant, impress on mind; n **-ation**.

incumbent a **1** lying, resting on **2** morally binding; n holder of office; n **incumbency**.

incur v **-curring, -curred**. run into, become liable to (debt etc); n **-sion** attack; invasion; inroad.

incurable a **1** that cannot be cured **2** inveterate.

indebted a owing; under obligation; n **-ness**.

indecent a **1** improper **2** offending against sense of decency, morality; ns **i. assault** leg sexual molesting but not rape; **i. exposure** public display of genitals; adv **-ly**; n **indecency**.

indecorous a fml showing lack of manners, taste; adv **-ly**; n **indecorum**.

indeed adv truly; in fact; certainly.

indefatigable a untiring; unremitting; adv **-ly**.

indefeasible a leg not to be made void, forfeited.

indefensible a untenable; inexcusable.

indefinite a vague; not precise; adv **-ly** for an indefinite period; a **indefinable** vague.

indelible a not capable of being erased or effaced; adv **-ly**; n **indelibility**.

indelicate a lacking in refinement; embarrassing; adv **-ly**; n **indelicacy**.

indemnity n security from loss, injury etc; compensation for loss etc; v **indemnify** compensate.

indent v **1** notch; carve out **2** make official order for; n **1** notch; marginal cut **2** requisition; ns **-ation** dent; **indenture** deed, contract drawn up in duplicate, esp one binding apprentice to employer.

independent a not subordinate; free; financially self-supporting; (adv **-ly**); n one not attached to any political party; ns **independence, independency** self-reliance; independent state.

indescribable a indefinable; vague; adv **-ly**.

index n **1** pointer; indicator **2** forefinger **3** alphabetical list of words, subjects in book 4 *math* exponent; *pl* indexes or *math* indices; *v* provide with index; enter in index; *n* i. finger finger nearest thumb; *a* i.-linked related to cost-of-living index (*n* i.-linked pension).

india-rubber *n* pencil eraser.

Indian *a* of India or N or S American Indians; *ns* I. club bottle-shaped object for juggling; I. corn maize; I. ink thick black ink; I. summer warm spell in autumn.

indicate *v* point out; reveal; imply; *ns* indication sign; suggestion; indicator one who, that which indicates; *a* indicative 1 *ling* stating facts; asking questions of fact 2 i. (of) showing; indicating.

indict *v* accuse formally; *n* -ment; *a* -able.

indifferent *a* 1 uninterested; callous 2 mediocre 3 impartial; *adv* -ly; *n* indifference.

indigenous *a* native; not foreign; natural to a country.

indigestion *n* dyspepsia; inability to digest food.

indignant *a* feeling, expressing righteous anger; *ns* indignation; indignity insult; humiliating treatment.

indigo *n* blue dye got from indigo plant; *a* deep blue.

indirect 1 not straight 2 allusive 3 (*of tax*) imposed on goods, services; *adv* -ly;

ns i. object *ling* person for whom sth is done, to whom sth is given etc; i. question, i. speech report of what is said, not the actual words spoken.

indiscreet *a* not tactful; *adv* -ly; *n* indiscretion 1 lack of tact 2 indiscreet act or remark.

indiscriminate *a* done at random, without careful thought; *adv* -ly.

indisposition *n* 1 slight illness 2 reluctance; *a* indisposed 1 unwell 2 averse.

idium *n* silvery metallic element used in transistors.

individual *n* one particular person, animal or thing; single person; *a* distinct; characteristic of single person, thing; *adv* -ly one by one; *as* -ist, -istic; *ns* -ism, -ist; individuality personality; individual character.

indoctrinate *v* teach; imbue with particular doctrine; *n* -ation.

Indo-European *a* of the family of languages originating in Europe and parts of Asia (*eg* English, French, German, Russian, Greek, Hindi, etc).

indolent *a* lazy; inactive; *adv* -ly; *n* indolence.

indomitable *a* unyielding.

indoor *a* pertaining to inside of houses, etc; domestic; *adv* indoors.

indubitable *a* beyond doubt; *adv* -ably.

induce *v* persuade; bring

about; *n* -ment incentive, motive.

induct *v* install formally; *n* -ion 1 installation 2 transference of electric force without physical contact; *a* -ive; *n* -or.

indulge *v* gratify; give way to; pamper; *n* indulgence favour; gratification of one's desires; (RC) remission of punishment for sins; *a* indulgent.

industrial *a* relating to extraction and refinement of raw materials or production of goods; *n* -ism, -ist; *v* -ize (*n* -ization); *ns* i. action *Brit* action by employees to obtain demands (*eg* striking); i. estate *Brit* factory area; i. relations; i. revolution change in economy from agricultural to industrial base; *a* industrious hard-working; (*adv* -ly); *n* industry 1 hard work 2 manufacturing or production 3 firm that does this.

inebriate *v* intoxicate; *n* -ation drunkenness.

inedible *a* not suitable to be eaten.

ineffable *a* unutterable; inexpressibly great.

ineffectual *a* unsatisfactory; futile.

inefficient *a* unable to work properly; wasteful; incompetent; *n* -ency.

ineligible *a* unqualified; unsuitable; *n* -ibility.

ineluctable *a* *fml* inevitable.

inept a fatuous; absurd; n -itude.

inert a without power of action; slow; inactive; ns -ness; inertia sluggishness; tendency to resist change (ns i. reel reel with tape that resists sudden pull, used for safety belts; i. selling mailing of unsolicited goods with demand for payment).

inestimable a not to be estimated; invaluable.

inevitable a unavoidable; certain to happen; adv -ably; n -ability.

inexorable a relentless.

inexplicable a not able to be explained.

inextricable a impossible to separate, to escape from; adv -ly.

infallible a never mistaken; certain; unerring; adv -ibly; n -ibility.

infamous a disgraceful; notorious; shameful; adv -ly; n infamy.

infant n very young child; legal minor; ns infancy; infanticide murder of child, esp new-born; a infantile.

infantry n foot soldiers; n -man member of this.

infarction n death of body tissue.

infatuate v make foolish; inspire with extreme passion; a infatuated besotted; n -ation.

infect v pass disease to; pollute; affect by example; n -ion; a -ious catching, spreading.

infer v -ferring, -ferred. draw conclusions; deduce; n -ence.

inferior a lower; of less value, quality; n one lower in rank etc; ns -ity; i. complex psyc lack of self-confidence.

infernal a devilish; fiendish; sl confounded; adv -ly.

inferno n -os. very large fire.

infest v swarm in; overrun; n -ation.

infidel n unbeliever; pagan; n infidelity 1 (act of) disloyalty 2 (act of) adultery.

infield n cricket area near the wicket; n -er.

in-fighting n discord between members of group.

infiltrate v filter through; permeate; penetrate by stealth; n -ation.

infinite a boundless; a infinitesimal minute; n infinity unlimited time, quality, space etc; n ling infinitive mood expressing action only, not person, number etc.

infirm a feeble; physically weak; ns -ity; infirmary hospital; sick-quarters.

in flagrante delicto adv leg Lat red-handed.

inflame v set on fire; med make, become red, hot, swollen; fig rouse passion in; a inflammable easily set on fire; excitable; (ns -ability); n inflammation morbid condition of redness, swelling, pain; a inflammatory.

inflate v 1 swell, distend with air, gas 2 increase (currency) in circulation 3 raise (prices) artificially; as inflatable, inflated; n inflation 1 inflating, being inflated with air, etc 2 upward trend in costs and prices; a inflationary.

inflect v 1 bend, curve inwards 2 modify direction of words; n inflection 1 intonation 2 variation in form of words; a inflexible unbending; n -ibility.

inflict v cause to undergo; impose; n infliction punishment; suffering.

inflorescence n arrangement of flowers on stem; flowering.

inflow n flowing in.

influence v affect; sway; persuade; n effect produced; moral power (over); power of influencing important persons; idm under the influence drunk; a -ential.

influenza n infectious virus disease.

influx n flowing in, inflow.

info n coll information.

inform v tell; instruct; bring charge against; phr v inform against/on report to authorities; ns informant giver of information; informer one who informs esp against criminal.

information n facts; knowledge given or obtained (n i. technology use of computers for collection, storage and retrieval of information); a informative.

information superhighway n means of transferring information very quickly via an electronic network.

infra adv below; further down, on; **i. dig** coll beneath one's dignity; n **i. red rays** invisible heat radiation.

infraction n infringement of regulation.

infrastructure n underlying systems and installations that enable an organization or political, social unit to operate.

infrequent a rare; unusual; ns **infrequence; -quency**.

infringe v transgress; disobey; break; ns **-ment, infraction** violation; transgression.

infuriate v enrage; drive to frenzy; a **-ating**.

infuse v steep, soak in liquid; fig permeate; n **infusion** liquid extract so obtained.

ingenious a clever at inventing; cleverly made; n **ingenuity**.

ingenuous a frank; candid; guileless; adv **-ly**; n **-ness**.

ingestion n taking (of food) into stomach.

ingle n fire on hearth; n **i. nook** chimney corner.

inglorious a shameful; adv **-ly**.

ingot n block of cast metal.

ingrained a firmly fixed.

ingrate n fml ungrateful person.

ingratiate v obtain another's good will.

ingredient n component; one part of mixture.

ingress n entry; power, right of entry.

in-group n group giving preference to members.

inhabit v dwell in; occupy; ns **-ant; -ation**.

inhale v breath in; n **inhalation**.

inherent a innate; naturally associated with; adv **-ly**.

inherit v derive from parents, ancestors; succeed as heir; ns **-ance** property inherited; **-or** heir, one who inherits.

inhibit v restrain; hinder; obstruct; n **inhibition** psyc unconscious restraint, or suppression of natural urge; a **inhibitory**.

in-house a within the organization.

inhuman a brutally cruel; n **inhumanity**.

inhumane a unkind; lacking in humanity; adv **-ly**.

inimical a hostile; unfriendly; antagonistic.

inimitable a incapable of being imitated; unrivalled; adv **-ably**.

iniquity n injustice; wickedness, sin; a **iniquitous** unfair, wicked; ad **-ly**; n **-ness**.

initial a occurring at beginning; adv **-ly**; n initial letter; v write, mark with, one's initials; v **initiate 1** originate **2** admit (to society etc); n initiated person; ns **initiation; initiative** first move; enterprise.

inject v introduce, drive in (fluid) by force; fill by this

means; ns **-ion; -or**.

injunction n writ issued to restrain; order; command.

injury n **1** harm; wound **2** moral hurt, insult etc; v **injure** do harm, hurt to; a **injurious**.

injustice n wrong; injury; unjust act.

ink n coloured fluid used for printing and writing; v mark with ink; a **-y**.

inkjet printer n printer in which the characters are produced by tiny jets of ink.

inkling n hint; vague idea; suspicion.

inlaid a **1** embedded in another substance **2** having with inlaid design.

inland n interior of country; a away from sea; adv in, towards inland; n **I. Revenue** Brit department responsible for collection of taxes.

in-laws n relations by marriage other than wife/husband.

inlay v decorate by embedding pieces of substance, in contrasting colour, in groundwork; n inlaid material.

inlet n creek; entrance.

in loco parentis adv Lat acting as parents.

inmate n inhabitant; lodger.

in memoriam adv in memory of.

inmost a deepest; most intimate (also **innermost**); sup of **in**.

inn n public house providing lodging etc, for traveller; n

Inns of Court four legal societies admitting to English Bar.

innards n pl inside parts, eg stomach.

innate a native; instinctive; inborn.

inner a inside; interior; comp of in; n ring next to bull on target in archery; ns **i. city; i. tube** inflatable tube inside outer cover of tyre.

innings n pl cricket period of batting; fig period of active life.

innkeeper n landlord, manager of inn.

innocent a blameless; guileless; not guilty; simple; n guileless child or person; n **innocence**.

innocuous a harmless; inoffensive.

innovate v introduce new methods, changes; ns **-ation, -ator**; as **-active, -atory**.

innuendo n **-does.** hint; insinuation.

innumerable a countless; too many to be counted.

inoculate v introduce (disease etc) into system, as protection; render immune by infecting with specific germ; n **-ation**.

inoffensive a harmless; giving, causing no offence.

inoperable a not suitable for treatment by surgical operation.

inopportune a ill-timed; unseasonable.

inordinate a excessive; extravagant.

inorganic a not result of natural growth; of substances without carbon.

in-patient n patient treated in hospital.

input n 1 action of putting in 2 (of ideas, electric power, computer data, etc) what is put in 3 place on machine where this occurs; v **inputing, inputed** or **input** comput to record data; ns **i. circuit; i. device.**

inquest n legal, judicial inquiry, esp into a death.

inquire v ask (also **enquire**); phr v inquire into investigate; a **inquiring** showing curiosity, desire for knowledge; ns **inquirer; inquiry** 1 question 2 investigation.

inquisition n 1 searching examination 2 ecclesiastical court for suppression of heresy; n **inquisitor**; as **inquisitorial; inquisitive** curious; prying.

inroad n invasion; incursion; idm **make inroads (into)** 1 make advance into new area 2 use up substantial amount of.

insane a mad; crazy; senseless; n **insanity** lunacy; madness.

insanitary a unhealthy; filthy.

insatiable a that cannot be satisfied; adv **-ably.**

inscribe v 1 write, engrave on, in 2 dedicate 3 draw (geometric figure within another); n **inscription.**

inscrutable a enigmatic; impenetrable, mysterious;

adv **-ably**; n **-ability.**

insect n invertebrate animal having six legs and segmented body, usually two or four wings; n **insecticide** substance for killing insects; a **insectivorous** insect-eating.

inseminate v implant; impregnate; n **-ation.**

insensate a unreasoning; inanimate; foolish.

insensible a not feeling; unconscious; unaware.

insert v set in; introduce; ns **insertion; insert** something added, inserted.

in-service a (occurring) as part of one's work time.

inset n picture, diagram etc within the frame of a larger one.

inshore adv, a near shore.

inside a within; adv on the inner side; n inner side; idm **inside out** 1 with the inside part turned outside 2 thoroughly; ns **i. story; i. track; insider** n person within organization; ns **i. dealing** illegal dealing in shares by people with inside knowledge of company concerned (also **i. trading**).

insidious a cunning; treacherous; sly.

insight n discernment; knowledge.

insignia n pl badges of office; distinguishing marks (of honour etc).

insinuating a ingratiating; v **insinuate** hint at; gradually penetrate; n **-ation.**

insipid *a* lacking flavour; dull; *n* **-ity**.

insist *v* emphasize; assert; demand urgently; *a* **-ent**; *n* **-ence**.

in-situ *adv Lat* in the correct place.

insofar as *conj* as far as.

insolent *a* insulting; rude; haughty; *n* **-ence**.

insolvent *a* without funds to pay debts; *n* **insolvency**.

insomnia *n* inability to sleep; sleeplessness.

insouciant *a* indifferent; unconcerned; *n* **-ance**.

inspect *v* examine closely, thoroughly; *ns* **inspection; inspector**.

inspire *v* 1 encourage; give stimulus to 2 create a feeling of; *n* **inspiration** 1 stimulation of ideas 2 sb/sth that inspires 3 sudden bright idea; *a* **inspired** brilliant (*n* **i. guess, i. suggestion**).

install *v* 1 place in office formally; establish 2 put in position for use etc; *n* **-ation**.

instalment *n* 1 one part-payment of debt 2 one part of thing appearing, supplied at intervals.

instance *n* 1 example 2 request; *v* cite; refer to; *a* **instant** 1 urgent; immediate 2 *dated comm* of current month; *n* precise moment; *a* **instantaneous** occurring in an instant; *adv* **instanter** instantly, immediately.

instead *adv* in place of; as alternative to.

instep *n* upper surface of foot

in front of ankle.

instigate *v* incite; urge; stir up; *ns* **instigation; instigator**.

instil *v* **-stilling, -stilled**; implant; infuse; *n* **instilation**.

instinct *n* natural aptitude; impulse; intuition; *a* **instinctive**; (*adv* **-ly**).

institute *v* set up; found; begin; set going; *n* scientific, social, etc society; building occupied by such society; *n* **institution** 1 custom 2 organization 3 act of founding; *a* **-al**; (*adv* **-ally**); *v* **-alize**; (*n* **-alization**).

instruct *v* teach; give orders to; *n* **instruction**; *a* **instructive** informative; *adv* **-ly**; *n* **instructor**.

instrument *n* 1 tool; implement 2 device for producing musical sounds 3 legal document; *a* **instrumental** 1 acting as means, or instrument 2 produced by musical instruments; *adv* **-ly**; *ns* **instrumentality** means; **instrumentation** arrangement of music for particular instruments.

insubordinate *a* rebellious; disobedient; unruly; *n* **insubordination**.

insufficiency *n* inadequacy; lack; *a* **insufficient**; *adv* **-ly**.

insular *a* of, like an island; *fig* narrow-minded; *n* **insularity**.

insulate *v* isolate; prevent passage of electricity, heat or sound by use of non-

conducting material; *ns* **insulation; insulator**.

insulin *n* extract from animal pancreas, used in treating diabetes, etc.

insult *v* abuse; treat with contempt; *n* affront; insolence; *a* **insulting**.

insuperable *a* not to be overcome or surmounted.

insure *v* 1 enter into contract to secure payment in event of loss of (life, health etc) 2 make safe 3 make sure; *ns* **insurance; insurer; insurance-policy** written contract of insurance; *a* **insurable**.

insurgent *a* rebellious; *ns* **-ency; insurrection** rebellion.

insurrection *n* armed revolt.

insusceptible *a* not capable of being moved by feeling; unimpressed; *adv* **-ibly**; *n* **-ibility**.

intact *a* untouched; entire; uninjured.

intaglio *n* design carved, engraved on hard surface; jewel carved so (a cameo).

intake *n* 1 what is taken in 2 air-shaft in mine 3 (in car) air passage to carburettor 4 body of new recruits, members etc.

intangible *a* insubstantial; impalpable; vague; *adv* **-ibly**; *n* **-ibility**.

integer *n* anything complete, entire; whole number; *a* **integral** 1 essential 2 whole; complete; *n* **integral calculus** branch of mathematics; v **integrate 1** make whole; bring into one body **2** abolish segregation; a **integrated** (n **i. circuit** very small electronic circuit, eg silicon chip); ns **-ation** integrating; being integrated; **integrity 1** honesty **2** state of being undivided, unharmed.

integument n **1** outer covering; skin **2** rind; shell.

intellect n faculty of knowing, reasoning; a **-ual** of, exercising intellect; inclined to mental activity (n intellectual person; adv **-lly**).

intelligence n **1** intellect; mental ability; quickness in learning **2** news; information esp military etc; **i. quotient** number indicating level of intelligence; **intelligent** clever; well-informed; n **intelligencer** informant; secret agent; a **intelligible** clear in meaning; (adv **-ibly**; n **-ibility**); n **intelligentsia** cultured, intellectual classes.

intemperate a unrestrained; given to excess; adv **-ly**; n **-erance**.

intend v **1** design; destine **2** mean **3** contemplate.

intense a **1** excessive; extreme **2** violent **3** ardent; eager; v **intensify** increase; deepen; make stronger; ns **intensification; intensity** strength; depth; a **intensive** thorough; concentrated (n **i. care** constant medical

attention for patient in critical condition).

intent a concentrating; earnest; n purpose; motive; idm **to all intents and purposes** virtually; idm **intent on/upon 1** occupied in **2** intending; adv **-ly**; n **-ness**.; ns **intention** aim; meaning; **-ness**; a **intentional**.

inter v **-terring, -terred**; bury; n **-ment**.

inter- prefix Lat among; between; mutual; forms compounds, eg **interaction** acting on each other; **interrelation** relation between things, persons. Such words are not given here where the meaning may be deduced from the simple word.

interact v act upon another; n interaction; a interactive.

interactive a **1** acting on each other **2** comput allowing exchange of information between user and machine during program.

inter alia adv Lat among other things.

intercede v plead for; mediate; ns **-cession; -cessor**.

intercept v hinder; prevent passage of; ns **-ion; -or**; a **-ive**.

interchange v exchange; alternate with; n **1** (act of) interchanging **2** system of linking roads between motorways, other main roads; a **-able**; adv **-ably**.

intercity a providing fast transport between cities; n **1**

such a service **2** such a train, coach etc; n **i. paging** communication system by cellular phone.

intercommunicate v communicate with; (of rooms) open one into another; n **intercom** internal telephone system.

intercontinental ballistic missile n long range missile with usu nuclear warhead (also **ICBM**).

intercourse n **1** mutual dealings, relations **2** coition (also **sexual i.**).

interdependent a mutually dependent; n **-ence**.

interdict n prohibition; exclusion from sacraments and religious rites; v prohibit; restrain; n **-diction**.

interest n **1** concern; intellectual curiosity **2** advantage; benefit **3** finance idm **in sb's interest** to sb's advantage; payment made for use of money; v rouse, hold attention; concern; a **-ing**.

interface n point where two systems meet, interconnect and work together; v connect by interface.

interfere v meddle; hinder; mediate; idm **interfere with 1** hinder **2** cause malfunction by touching **3** assault sexually; n **-ference 1** interfering **2** rad extraneous noise.

interferon n protein in body that inhibits viruses.

intergalactic a between

galaxies.

interim *a* temporary; meantime.

interior *a* inner; internal; inland; *n* inside; inland.

interject *v* interrupt by, break in with (word etc.); *n* **-jection** exclamation.

interlace *v* twist together.

interlard *v* (*of writing, speech*) mix with words, expressions, subject matter of another kind.

interleave *v* insert blank pages among others in book.

interlock *v* lock or fit closely together.

interlocutor *n* person taking part in dialogue; *n* **-locution**.

interloper *n* intruder; meddler in another's affairs.

interlude *n* interval between two acts of play; short entertainment during such interval.

intermediate *a* in the middle; *ns* **-mediary**; **-mediator** mediator.

intermezzo *n* **-s** *or* **intermezzi**. short piece of music, *esp* between acts of an opera.

interminable *a* endless; unduly prolonged.

intermission *n* interval; respite; *a* **-mittent** ceasing at intervals.

intern *v* confine to specified area; *ns* **-ment**; **internee** person interned.

internal *a* inner; interior; *adv* **-ly**; **-ize**; *n* **-ization**; **i. combustion engine** one driven by explosion of air and fuel in cylinder.

international *a* pertaining to relations between nations; *n* 1 game, match between different countries 2 player taking part in such contest; *adv* **-ly**; **-ism**; **-ist**.

Internet *n* international computer network allowing computer users to exchange information.

interplay *n* reciprocal action; interaction.

Interpol *n* international police organization.

interpolate *v* insert (spurious matter) in book etc; *n* **-ation** words etc added by another author.

interpose *v* insert; interrupt; intervene; obstruct.

interpret *v* explain; construe; translate; *ns* **-er**; **-ation**.

interregnum *n* interval between reigns.

interrogate *v* ask searching questions of; *ns* **-ation**; **-ator**; *as* **-ative**; questioning; **-atory**.

interrupt *v* break in on; obstruct; cut off continuity of; *n* **-ruption**.

intersect *v* cut through; cross each other; *n* **-section**.

intersperse *v* scatter among; diversify.

interstice *n* chink; small opening.

interval *n* 1 intervening space or time 2 pause; break 3 *mus* difference of pitch.

intervene *v* come between; interfere; take part in; *n* **-vention**.

interview *n* formal meeting

and conversation; one arranged to test suitability of applicant for position, or to obtain views, opinions of a personality; *v* have interview with; *n* **interviewer**; *n* **interviewee** person interviewed.

intestate *a* not having made a will; *n* **intestacy**.

intestine *n* lower part of alimentary canal, bowel; *a* *fig* internal; domestic; *a* **intestinal**.

intimate[1] *a* 1 inward 2 closely linked 3 familiar 4 having sexual relationship; *n* **-macy**.

intimate[2] *v* make known; hint; *n* **-ation** notice.

intimidate *v* frighten; terrorize; restrain by threats; *n* **-ation**.

into *prep* from outside to inside; to place of, condition of, form of.

intone *v* chant; recite in monotone; *n* **intonation** modulation of voice; sounding of musical notes.

in toto *adv* *Lat* entirely.

intoxicate *v* make drunk; *fig* excite greatly; *ns* **intoxicant** intoxicating liquor; **-ation**.

intransigent *a* obstinately hostile; uncompromising; *n* **-ence**.

intrauterine device *n* contraceptive coil (*also* IUD).

intravenous *a* into a vein; *adv* **-ly**.

intrepid *a* brave; fearless; *n* **-ity**.

intricate *a* involved; entangled; puzzling; *n*

intricacy.

intrigue n secret plot; illicit love affair; v 1 carry on intrigue 2 interest; n **intriguer**.

intrinsic a inherent; real; genuine.

intro- prefix within; into.

introduce v 1 bring into use, notice etc 2 make known formally 3 insert; n **-duction**, a **-ductory** preliminary.

introit n hymn, etc sung as priest approaches altar.

introspection n self-analysis; a **-spective** dwelling on one's own thoughts.

introvert n self-centred, introspective person; v direct, cause to turn inwards; n **-version**.

intrude v thrust in; force in uninvited; ns **intruder**, **intrusion**; a **intrusive**.

intuit v fml sense by intuition; n **intuition** (power of) instant understanding without facial evidence or logical reasoning; a **intuitive**; adv **-ly**.

Inuit n Eskimo.

inundate v flood; swamp; fig overwhelm; n **-vation**.

inure v accustom; harden.

invade v 1 enter with hostile intent 2 fig assail 3 encroach on; ns **invader; invasion**.

invalid[1] a not valid; n **-ity**; v **-ate**.

invalid[2] n, a (person) suffering from ill-health, weakness; v render infirm; remove from active service.

invaluable a priceless; very valuable.

invariable a constant; unchanging; adv **-ly**.

invective n abuse; vituperation.

inveigh v attack violently with words.

inveigle v delude; lure; entice; n **-ment**.

invent v originate; contrive for first time; make up; n **invention** something that is invented; fabrication; ability to invent; a **-ive** originative; resourceful; n **-or**.

inventory n detailed list of stock etc; catalogue.

inverse a reversed; contrary; n 1 inverted state 2 the opposite; n **inversion**.

invert v turn upside down; reverse position of; a **-ed** (ns **i. comma** quotation mark; **i. snob** person claiming not to be a snob and gratuitously finding fault with things of good quality).

invertebrate n animal without backbone; a spineless; fig irresolute.

invest v 1 use money to earn interest 2 mil beseige; phr vs **invest in** buy; **invest with 1** confer (honour) upon 2 deposit money (to earn interest) at; ns **investment 1** act of investing 2 property purchased; **investor**.

investigate v enquire into; examine carefully; ns **-ation; -ator**.

inveterate a persistent; long-established; obstinate.

confirmed.

invidious a giving offence by injustice; likely to arouse ill-will; adv **-ly**; n **-ness**.

invigilate v Brit supervise during test or examination; ns **-ation; -ator**.

invigorate v strengthen; refresh.

invincible a unconquerable; adv **-ibly**; n **-ibility**.

inviolable a unprofaned; not to be dishonoured or violated; a **inviolate** strictly preserved; kept sacred; uninjured.

invisible a not capable of being seen; adv **-ibly**; n **-ibility**.

invite v 1 ask person to come to social gathering etc 2 request 3 attract; provoke; a **inviting** attractive (adv **-ly**); n **invitation 1** act of inviting 2 request to come 3 provocation.

in vitro a Lat in test tube or by artificial means; n **i.v. fertilization**.

invoice n list of goods sent, with prices; v make out invoice.

invoke v appeal to; implore; call on; n **invocation**.

involuntary a unintentional; automatic; instinctive; adv **-arily**.

involuted a 1 complex 2 coiled in on itself.

involve v 1 entangle; complicate 2 implicate; entail 3 imply; a **involute** intricate; spirally curved; n **-ution**.

inward, inwards *adv* 1 towards interior 2 into the mind; *a* **inward** 1 internal 2 spiritual; mental; *n pl* entrails; *adv* **-ly** privately.

iodine *n* non-metallic element used in medicine.

iodize *v* treat with iodine.

ion *n* electrically charged atom; *v* **ionize** charge ions with electricity; *n* **-ization**.

ionosphere *n* layers of earth's atmosphere that reflect radio signals.

iota *n* Greek letter *i*; very small part, jot.

IOU *n* signed acknowledgement of debt.

IPA *abbr* International Phonetic Alphabet.

ipecac *n* root of S American plant, used as emetic.

ipso facto *adv Lat* by the fact itself.

IQ *abbr* intelligence quotient.

ir- *prefix see* in-.

IR *n* information retrieval

IRA *abbr* Irish Republican Army.

Iranian *a, n* (inhabitant) of Iran.

Iraqi *a, n* (inhabitant) of Iraq.

irascible *a* easily provoked to anger; *n* **-ibility**.

irate *a* furiously angry; *adv* **-ly**; *n* **-ness**.

iridescent *a* changing in colour, like rainbow; *n* **iridescence**.

iridium *n* hard silvery metallic element.

iris *n* coloured part of eye, around pupil; tuberous-rooted plant.

Irish *n, a* (language, inhabitant) of Ireland; *ns* **I. coffee** coffee with cream and whisky; **I. stew** stew of meat, potatoes and onions.

irk *v* weary; worry; *a* **irksome** tiresome.

iron *n* 1 very hard metallic element; most common metal used for tools, weapons etc and the raw material of steel 2 appliance for smoothing, pressing cloth etc 3 metal-headed golf-club; *n pls* fetters; *idm* **have several irons in the fire** have alternative plans ready; *a* 1 of iron 2 very strong 3 unyielding 4 hard; *v* smooth (clothes) with an iron; *phr v* **iron out** remove (disagreements, problems); *ns* **I. Age** period after Bronze Age; **I. Curtain** frontier between W Europe and Communist countries of E Europe between Second World War and 1980s; **i. lung** machine to assist breathing; ironmonger; **i. pyrites** fool's gold; **i. rations** emergency food rations; *a* **i.-grey**; *n* **ironing** (**i. board** board for ironing clothes).

irony *n* 1 way of speaking, in which the meaning is the opposite of apparent meaning 2 sarcasm 3 perverseness in a situation occurring in the wrong way or at the wrong time; *n* **dramatic irony ambiguity** in words or fatal course of action, understood by the audience knowing sth as yet unknown to the character(s) in the play; *a* **ironic** of irony.

irradiate *v* treat with light or electromagnetic radiation; *n* **-iation** exposure to therapeutic rays.

irrational *a* without reason or judgement.

irreconcilable *a* 1 that which cannot be brought to an agreement 2 bitterly opposed.

irrefutable *a* indisputable.

irreparable *a* beyond repair; not able to be remedied.

irrespective *a* without regard, reference to; not taking into account.

irrevocable *a* impossible to change later on; *adv* **-ably**.

irrigate *v* water by artificial channels; *n* **-ation**.

irritate *v* 1 annoy; exasperate 2 provoke 3 inflame; make sore; *n* **-ation**; *as* **irritant** causing irritation; **irritable** irascible; easily angered; (of *wounds etc*) inflamed; sore; (*adv* **-ably**; *n* **-ability**).

irruption *n* invasion; sudden violent incursion.

ISBN *abbr* International Standard Book Number.

Islam *n* Muslim religion; *a* **Islamic**.

island *n* 1 piece of land, surrounded by water 2 detached isolated patch, mound; *n* **-er** one who lives on island.

isle *n* island; *n* **islet** small island.

isn't *abbr* is not.

isobar *n* line on map joining places with equal mean atmospheric pressure.

isolate *v* set apart; keep (infected person) away from others; *ns* **-lation**; **-ationism** policy of avoiding involvement in world politics; **-ationist**.

isomer *n chem* compound with same number of atoms, but arranged differently.

isosceles *a* triangle, having two equal sides.

isotherm *n* line on map joining places of same mean temperature.

isotope *n* atom of element having different atomic weight from other atoms in same element; *as* **-topic**.

issue *n* 1 flowing, coming out 2 publication 3 outlet 4 offspring 5 result 6 problem; *v* 1 go out 2 emit 3 publish 4 be derived from 5 distribute.

isthmus *n* narrow strip of land between two seas, connecting two land areas.

it *pron* 3rd pers. neuter; 1 *referring to inanimate objects* that one 2 *coll* the important thing 3 *sl* sex appeal; *a* **its** belonging to it; *pron* **itself** emphatic form.

IT *abbr* information technology.

Italian *a, n* native or language of Italy.

italic *a* of type, with letters sloping up to right; *n pl* this type, used for emphasis; *v* **italicize** print in italics.

itch *v* 1 feel itch 2 have restless desire; *idm* **be itching** *coll* to be longing to; *idm* **have an itching palm** *coll* be greedy for money; *n* 1 itching feeling 2 strong desire; *a* **itchy**; *ns* **i. feet** *coll* desire to travel; **itchiness**.

it'd *abbr* 1 it would 2 it had.

item *n* single detail in list; piece of news; subsection of agenda etc; *adv* likewise; *v* **-ize**; *n* **-ization**.

iterate *v* repeat; *n* **-ation**.

itinerant *a* travelling from place to place; wandering; (*of judges, preachers etc*) on circuit; *n* **itinerary** route; plan for or record of travel; guide book.

it'll *abbr* it will.

ITN *abbr* Independent Television News.

its *poss a* belonging to it.

it's *abbr* it is.

itself *emphatic pron.*

IUD *abbr* intrauterine device.

I've *abbr* I have.

IVF *abbr* in vitro fertilization.

ivory *n* hard white substance from tusks of elephants etc; **i. black** black pigment made from burnt ivory; **i. tower** place where people escape from life's hard realities.

ivy *n* climbing evergreen plant; *a* **I. League** US typical of group of older universities in eastern states.

jab v jabbing, jabbed. poke suddenly, with force; thrust roughly.

jabber v speak rapidly, gabble; chatter.

jabot n frill, ruffle on bodice, shirt-front.

jacaranda n tropical American hard-wood tree.

jacinth n reddish-orange variety of zircon.

jack n 1 device for raising load from below 2 cards knave 3 bowls ball used as mark 4 ship's flag; prefix male; large; phr v **jack up** raise by jack; ns **jackhammer** US pneumatic drill; **j.-in-the-box** box with doll which springs up when lid is released; **j.knife** large pocket knife (v **jackknife** fold suddenly in the middle);

j.-of-all-trades person of varied skills; **jackpot** maximum prize of money.

jackal n wild scavenging animal, allied to a dog.

jackass n male ass; n **laughing j.** large Australian kingfisher.

jackboot n large boot reaching above knee.

jackdaw n small kind of crow.

jacket n 1 short coat 2 outer casing, covering.

jack-knife n large pocket knife.

jackpot n pool in poker-game; money prize increasing in value until won.

Jacobean n of reign of James I; n **Jacobite** adherent of Stuarts after abdication of James II.

Jacuzzi [TM] bath with air-

jets creating constant bubbles.

jade[1] n hard green or white gem stone; colour green.

jade[2] n 1 worn-out horse 2 sl disreputable woman; a **jaded** tired, wearied.

jag n sharp, pointed projection; ragged tear in cloth; a **jagged**.

jaguar n large carnivorous S American mammal.

jail n prison (also **gaol**) n **jailbird** coll prison inmate or former inmate.

jam n 1 fruit preserve 2 crush 3 traffic hold-up; v **jams, jamming, jammed.** 1 block, fill up 2 cease to work n **j. session** unrehearsed music session; as **j.-packed** coll very crowded; **jammy** 1 covered with jam 2 Brit sl easy 3 Brit sl surprisingly lucky.

jamb n side post of door; window-frame.

jamboree n spree; social gathering; Boy Scout rally.

jangle v make harsh, clanging sound; n such sound.

janitor n doorkeeper; caretaker.

January n first month of year.

Japanese n native or language of Japan; a **Japanese.**

jape n joke.

japonica n type of quince tree with red flowers.

jar n round glass, earthenware vessel.

jar v jars, jarring, jarred. 1 be, sound discordant 2 grate upon 3 cause to shake, vibrate; n harsh sound, shock.

jardinière n Fr ornamental trough for plants.

jargon n gibberish; excessively technical language.

jasmin(e), jessamin(e) n fragrant flowering shrub.

jasper n opaque reddish, yellow or brown quartz.

jaundice n morbid state, characterized by yellow tint of eyes and skin; a jaundiced fig jealous; biassed.

jaunt n short pleasure trip; v go on jaunt, n **jaunting-car** Irish two-wheeled cart.

jaunty a care-free; sprightly; swaggering; adv -**ily**; n -**iness**.

javelin n light throwing spear, or shaft.

jaw n two bones, in which teeth are set, and their muscles; pl -**s** 1 animal's mouth 2 gripping part of pliers or similar tool 3 cap coll killer shark; ns **jawbone**; **jawbreaker** 1 word difficult to pronounce 2 hard boiled sweet; v sl talk at length; lecture.

jay n noisy, brightly-coloured bird of crow family.

jay-walk v cross the road without regard for traffic; n **jay-walker**.

jazz n syncopated rhythmical music; phr v **jazz up** make more lively; a **jazzy** with bright colours or vivid patterns.

jealous a envious; grudging; suspicious; distrustful; n

jealousy.

jean n twilled cotton fabric; pl trousers, overalls of this cloth.

jeep n light, open truck, with fourwheel drive.

jeer v mock, scoff at; n taunt, gibe.

Jehovah n God of Old Testament; n **J.'s Witness** member of fundamentalist sect.

jejunum n middle of small intestine.

jell v US gel.

jello n US jelly.

jelly n semi-solid, transparent food made with gelatine, any substance of similar consistency; v **jell** turn to jelly; set; sl take definite form; n **j.-fish** free floating sea-creature; medusa.

jenny n 1 spinning machine 2 female ass.

jeopardy n hazard; peril; danger; v **jeopardize** imperil.

jerboa n small African burrowing rodent; desert rat.

jeremiad n lamentation.

jerk[1] n quick pull, twitch; sudden, sharp movement; v move with jerk; a -**y**; adv -**ily**; n -**iness**.

jerk[2] n stupid and awkward person.

jerkin n close-fitting leather jacket.

jerry-built a hastily, flimsily constructed.

jersey n close-fitting knitted jumper; breed of cow.

jest n joke; v make jokes; n **jester** joker.

Jesuit n member of RC religious order; a jesuitical.

Jesus n founder of Christian religion (also **Jesus Christ**).

jet[1] n hard black mineral, used for ornaments etc; a **j. black**.

jet[2] n 1 stream, spurt of liquid, gas, forced from small opening 2 nozzle 3 aircraft propelled by jet engine; v **jets, jetting, jetted**. gush, give out in jet; ns **jetfoil** hydrofoil; **j. lag** tiredness after long flight by jet plane; **j. set** rich social group who travel frequently across the world (a, n **j.-setting** n **j.-setter**); n **j. stream** strong winds high up; a **j.-propelled** n **j. propulsion**.

jetsam n things thrown overboard to lighten vessel, and washed ashore; v **jettison** throw overboard; fig get rid of; abandon.

jetty n pier; mole; quay.

Jew n member of Hebrew race; n **Jewry** collectively Jews; n **jew's harp** small musical instrument held in mouth.

jewel n precious stone, gem; ornament set with one; precious object; ns **jeweller** dealer in jewels; **jewellery**.

jib n ship's triangular foremost stay-sail; projecting arm of crane etc; v **jibs, jibbing, jibbed**. pull over (sail) to other side; (of horse) balk; phr v **jib at** refuse to do.

jibe n, v gibe.

jiffy bag [TM] n padded envelope.

jig n 1 lively dance 2 template

guiding cutting tool; v jigs, **jigging, jigged.** move jerkily up and down; dance jig.

jiggery-pokery n Brit coll trickery.

jigsaw n machine fretsaw for cutting curved, irregular patterns; n **j. puzzle** picture mounted on wood, etc and cut in irregular pieces, to be re-assembled.

jihad n Islamic holy war.

jilt v reject (lover) after encouraging him.

jingle n 1 light, ringing, tinkling sound, as of small bells 2 verses with simple catchy words; v make, cause to make this sound.

jingo n warmonger; n -**ism** aggressive patriotism.

jink v move with sudden twists and turns; dodge.

jinx n hoodoo; bringer of bad luck.

jitters n pl sl extreme nervousness; panic; a **jittery** nervy; jumpy; n **jitterbug 1** one who dances convulsively 2 one who panics easily.

jive n lively dance performed to jazz and rock and roll, esp in 1940s and 1950s; v dance to this style.

Jnr abbr junior.

job n piece of work; task; employment; matter; affair; ns **j. centre** office assisting the unemployed to find work; **j. lot** coll articles sold together; **jobsharing** dividing fulltime post between two people; v **1**

work at piece-rate 2 hire out 3 act as broker; ns **jobber 1** odd jobman 2 dealer in Stock Exchange securities; **jobbery** corrupt practice in public position.

jock n US athlete; n **jockstrap** sport garment for protection of man's genitals.

jockey n professional rider in horse-racing; v cheat; trick; manoeuvre.

jocose a facetious; playful; jesting n **jocosity**; a **jocular** joking; n -**larity**.

jocund a merry; cheerful; n -**ity**.

jodhpurs n pl riding-breeches.

jog n **jogs, jogging, jogged.** push; nudge; keep moving steadily; fig stimulate memory; n **j.-trot** slow steady trot.

joggle v move jerkily; shake slightly.

John Bull n coll England; English people.

John Doe n US unidentified person or body.

johnny n Brit 1 coll man 2 sl condom.

join v connect; unite; become member of; fasten; phr v **j.-up** enlist; n place of joining; ns -**er** craftsman in wood; -**ery.**

joint n 1 joining place of bones, of pieces of wood etc 2 Brit large piece of meat for roasting 3 sl bar or nightclub 4 sl cigarette with cannabis; a shared; n **j. venture** enterprise by cooperative management.

joist n one of parallel beams, supporting floor or ceiling.

jojoba n desert shrub.

joke n jest; something not meant to be serious; v make jokes; talk jestingly; n **joker** one who jokes; odd card in pack.

jolly a **1** jovial; merry; hearty **2** pleasant; v cajole; persuade by flattery; phr vs **jolly along** coll encourage in a lighthearted way; **jolly up** coll brighten; make more cheerful; n **J. Roger** pirate flag with skull and crossbones; adv coll very; idm **jolly well** coll certainly; ns **jollity, jollification** merrymaking.

jolly-boat n ship's boat.

jolt v shake with sudden jerk; jog; n sudden jerk or bump.

Jonah n person thought to bring bad luck to others with him/her.

Joneses idm keep up with the **Joneses** compete socially by having all the material things one's neighbour has.

josh v US coll tease.

joss n Chinese idol; ns **j.-house** Chinese temple; **j.-stick** incense.

jostle v knock or bump against.

jot n trifle; small amount; v **jots, jotting, jotted.** make brief written note; phr v **jot down** make quick written note of; ns **jotter** notebook or pad; **jotting** (usu pl) brief note: n -**ter** notebook.

joule n unite of electrical energy.

journal n 1 daily record; diary 2 periodical 3 daily newspaper 4 part of axle resting on bearings; ns **journalese** newspaper language full of clichés; **journalism** profession of producing, editing, writing in newspapers etc; **-ist**; a **-istic**.

journey n act of travelling; distance travelled; v travel.

journeyman -**men**. 1 trained employee 2 reliable but not brilliant worker.

joust n encounter between two armed, mounted knights; v take part in tournament; tilt.

jovial a convivial; cheery; hearty; festive; n **-ity**.

jowl n lower part of face, jaw; dewlap of cattle.

joy n great pleasure, gladness; happiness; cause of this; **j.-ride** coll ride taken for fun without owner's permission (v take such a ride; ns **j.-rider, j.-riding**; as **joyful** (adv **-ly** n **-ness**); **joyless** (adv **-ly** n **-ness**); **joyous** (adv **-ly** n **-ness**.).

joystick n control lever of aircraft, or computer.

JP abbr Justice of the Peace.

Jr abbr Junior.

jubilation n rejoicing; a **jubilant** exultant, elated.

jubilee n fiftieth anniversary; festive celebration.

Judaism n Jewish religion, custom.

Judas n traitor.

judder v Brit (of machine)

shake violently; ns **judder, juddering**.

judge n official appointment to preside over court of justice; one who decides a dispute; umpire; arbiter; v try (case) in law court; form opinion, decide on; estimate worth; idm **judge of** person qualified to evaluate; n **judgement, judgment** 1 sentence of court 2 opinion 3 divine retribution (ns **j. day, day of j.** day when God will judge the human race) 4 ability to evaluate.

judicature n administration of justice; body of judges; judicial system; as **judicial** of, befitting court of law, judge; impartial; **judicious** wise, prudent; n **judiciary** body of judges.

judo n Japanese system of unarmed combat.

jug n 1 vessel with handle and lip or spout, for holding liquids; its contents 2 sl prison; v stew in jug (esp hare).

juggernaut n 1 Brit very large articulated lorry 2 powerful, relentless destructive force.

juggle v perform conjuring tricks; fig deceive; ns **jugglery; juggler**.

jugular a of, relating to neck, throat.

juice n 1 liquid part of animal or vegetable tissue; 2 sl petrol; a **juicy** 1 succulent 2 sl spicy; suggestive.

ju-jitsu, ju-jutsu n judo.

ju-ju n W African fetish;

charm, taboo.

juke-box n automatic coin-operated record player.

julep n 1 sweet, soothing, medicated drink 2 iced mint-flavoured alcoholic drink.

Julian a of Julius Caesar, esp of calendar introduced by him.

July n seventh month.

jumble v mix up, confuse together; n disorded heap; **j. sale** charitable sale of second-hand goods.

jumbo a coll enormous; n coll (nickname for) elephant; n **j. jet** very large aircraft.

jump v 1 spring into the air by use of leg muscles 2 move suddenly (in specified direction) 3 pass over (obstacle) by jumping 4 react in surprise 5 (of prices, costs etc) rise steeply 6 malfunction by moving suddenly out of position 7 attack 8 pass illegally (**j. a barrier, a policeman**); go out of turn (**j. the gun, the queue, the (traffic) lights**); idm **jump down sb's throat** coll attack sb verbally without waiting for explanations; idm **jump bail** fail to appear after being released on bail; idm **jump out of one's skin** react with fright; idm **jump to it** coll be quick; phr v **jump at** grab eagerly; n 1 act of jumping 2 sharp rise 3 obstacle to cross; idm **one jump ahead** able to anticipate rivals and hold an advantage; ns

jumper 1 one who jumps **2** pullover; **jumping** (n **j.-off point** starting point); **j.-jet** aircraft with vertical take-off; **j.-lead** *aut* electric lead for connecting two batteries; **j.-start** *aut* way of starting car by pushing when battery is flat; **j. suit** garment combining jacket and trousers in one; *as* **jumped-up** upstart; **jumpy** nervous (n **-iness**).

junction n joining; place, point of union; station where branches of railway meet.

juncture n position of affairs; critical point.

June n sixth month.

jungle n wild, uncultivated land, with thick undergrowth; *fig* confused, tangled mass.

junior a younger; of lower status; n subordinate; one who is younger; *cap US* younger of two men in family with identical names; n **j. school** *Brit* school for children aged 7-11 (following infant school).

juniper n evergreen tree.

junk[1] n **1** old rope **2** *sl* useless articles **3** rubbish **4** salt meat ns **j. food** snack food that is of little nutritional value; **j. mail** mass-printed, mainly advertising matter sent unsolicited by post to people's homes.

junk[2] n large flat-bottomed Chinese sailing vessel.

junket n **1** milk curdled with rennet **2** *coll* pleasure trip for government official financed with public money.

junkie, junky n **1** *sl* heroin addict **2** *coll* any kind of addict (n **TV junkie**).

junta n Spanish or Italian council of state; political faction.

Jupiter n supreme Roman god; the largest planet.

jurisdiction n authority to administer law; area covered by authority; a **juridical** legal; n **jurisprudence** science, knowledge of law; a **jural** of law n **jurist** law graduate; writer on law.

jury n **1** body of persons sworn to return verdict in court of law **2** panel of judges for a contest ns **juror, juryman** member of jury; **jury-box** enclosed place, in court, for jury to occupy.

jury-mast n temporary mast.

just a, adv **1** exactly (*eg* just here, just right, just so) **2** instantly (*eg* just coming) **3** barely; scarcely (*eg* just about, just missed, just in time, only just) **4** only (*eg* just a little, just a minute); n **justice 1** fairness **2** administration of law **3** punishment for crime **4** judge; magistrate (n **J. of the Peace**, *also* **JP**); *idm* do **justice to 1** treat fairly **2** show appreciation of the excellence of; v **justify 1** prove to be right vindicate; exonerate; a **justifiable** (*adv* **-ably**) **2** *printing* space

letters to give lines of equal length; a **justified** (n **j. line**); n **justification**.

jut v **juts, jutting, jutted.** project; stick out.

jute n fibre of Indian plant, used for rope, canvas etc.

juvenile a young; suited to, characteristic of youth; n young person; youth; ns **j. delinquency** criminal activity by young person; **j. delinquent** such a person; n **-ility.**

juxtapose v put side by side; n **-position.**

kaftan n long loose garment with belt (*also* **caftan**).

kaiser n German emperor.

kale, kail n cabbage with curly leaves, cole.

kaleidoscope n tube containing pieces of coloured glass and reflectors, showing varying patterns, when tube is moved; a **-scopic** ever-changing.

kamikaze n (Second World War) Japanese suicide pilot (n **k. attack**).

kangaroo n Australian marsupial with powerful hindlegs; n **k. court** sl irregular, illegal court.

kapok n soft fibre from silk-cotton tree seeds, used to fill cushions etc.

kaput a sl broken; dead.

karaoke n amateur impromptu singing with disco.

karat see **carat**.

karate n Japanese martial art using hands and feet.

karma n fate; destiny; ethical causation.

katabolism n destructive metabolism.

kayak n Eskimo canoe made of stretched sealskin.

KC abbr Brit King's Counsellor (high-ranking lawyer).

kebab n pieces of meat cooked on skewer.

kedgeree n dish of rice, fish and chopped, boiled egg.

keel n ship's lowest longitudinal timbers or plates, on which hull is built; phr v **keel over 1** capsize **2** fall over sideways; v **keelhaul** fig rebuke severely.

keen a sharp; acute; eager; shrewd.

keen n Irish funeral lament; v wail over; lament.

keep v keeps, keeping, kept. **1** hold; retain **2** preserve; maintain; look after; **3** do (specified action) continuously or repeatedly **4** detain; delay **5** fulfil (promise) **6** (of food) remain fresh; idm **keep one's cool/one's head** coll stay calm; idm **keep sb company** be a companion to sb; phr vs **keep back 1** retain **2** not tell about; **keep down** control; **keep in with** stay in favour with; **keep on** continue; **keep on at** nag; n **1** cost of day to day living **2** castle tower; idm **for keeps** coll for ever; ns **-er** guard; guardian; **-ing** care; charge; idm **in keeping with** consistent with; n **keepsake** memento.

keg n small cask.

kelp n large brown seaweed, source of iodine.

kelvin n unit of temperature; **K. scale** international temperature scale.

ken v Scot know; n range of knowledge.

kennel n hut, shelter for dog; fig hovel; pl boarding, training establishment for dogs; v keep, put in kennel.

kept pt, pp of **keep**.

keralin n protein found in nails, claws etc.

kerb n stone edging of pavement; ns **k.-crawling** driving slowly close to kerb in order to find a prostitute; **k.-crawler** man doing this.

kerchief n head-covering; scarf.

kerfuffle n Brit fuss.

kernel n inner, germinating part of nut, or fruit-stone; fig essential, vital part.

kerosene n paraffin oil distilled from petroleum.

kestrel n small migratory falcon or hawk.

ketch n small two-masted fishing vessel.

ketchup n spicy sauce made from tomatoes, etc.

kettle n metal vessel with spout and handle, used for boiling water; idm **a fine kettle of fish** a messy, unpleasant situation.

kettledrum n cauldron-shaped brass or copper drum, having variable musical pitch.

key n 1 metal instrument to fasten/unfasten lock, to wind clockwork mechanism etc 2 lever, button on typewriter, musical instrument 3 clue; explanation 4 essential factor 5 roughness of prepared surface for repainting; 6 mus set of related notes (n **k. signature** written symbols indicating key); idm **in the same key** 1 mus 2 (of speech) in similar style or tone; idm **in key** harmonizing; idm **out of key** discordant; a very important (eg **k. figure, k. issue, k. speech**); v 1 comput type 2 prepare surface for painting; phr vs **key in** type in; **key up** make anxious (a **keyed up** excited); ns **keyboard** finger board of typewriter, piano etc (n **k. skills** ability to type); **keyhole; keynote** 1 first note of musical key 2

dominant factor; **keystone** central wedge-shaped stone of.

keyhole surgery n surgery performed through a very small incision on the body.

kg abbr kilogram.

KGB n (formerly) Soviet secret police.

khaki a dull brownish-fawn, earth coloured; n military uniform n **k. election** election influenced by government's conduct of military operations.

khan n Asiatic ruler in medieval times.

kibbutz n Israeli collective farm settlement.

kibosh n sl rubbish; nonsense; idm **put the kibosh on** put an end to.

kick v 1 strike out with foot 2 recoil 3 resist 4 sl give up (harmful habit); idm **kick one's heels** be idle; idm **kick sb upstairs** give sb an apparent promotion to make him/her less powerful in reality; idm **kick the bucket** die; phr vs **kick off** coll begin; **kick out** dismiss without ceremony; **kick out against** protest strongly about; **kick up** make trouble; n 1 act of kicking 2 recoil of gun, motorbike) 3 coll force; idm **for kicks** sl for a thrill; idm **get/give a kick** coll get/give pleasure; ns **k.-back** coll money given for favours; **k.-off** start, esp of football match; n, v **k.-start** (method used to) start a

motorcycle.

kid n 1 young goat; leather made of its skin 2 coll child; idm **use kid gloves** deal gently with sb; v **kids, kidding, kidded.** sl tease; hoax.

kidnap v **kidnaps, kidnapping, kidnapped.** take sb away by force and demand a ransom in exchange for returning them; n **kidnapper;** n **kidnapping.**

kidney n one of a pair of glandular organs, secreting urine; fig kind; class; n **k. machine** med apparatus to save life of patient with diseased kidneys.

kill v 1 cause to die 2 destroy; neutralize idm **kill time** find way of making time pass easily; idm **kill two birds with one stone** take action that serves two purposes simultaneously; n 1 act of killing 2 thing killed; idm **in at the kill** present at climax of struggle; ns **killer** (n **k. whale**); **killing** (idm **make a killing** have big success with stocks and shares); a coll very funny; adv **-ly**; n **killjoy** person spoiling pleasure for others.

kiln n furnace, oven.

kilo- prefix thousand, as in kilobyte comput 1000 or 1024 bytes; n **kilogram(me)** 1000 grams; **kilometre** 1000 metres; **kilowatt** 1000 watts.

kilohertz n unit of radio frequency.

kilt n short pleated skirt,

usually tartan; *v* tuck up (skirt) in pleats; *a* -ed.

kilter *idm* out of kilter not working.

kimono *n* loose wide-sleeved Japanese robe, with sash; dressing-gown in this style.

kin *n* relatives; *a* related by blood; *n* -dred blood-relationship; *a fig* similar; congenial; *ns* -ship, kinsman; -woman.

kind[1] *n* type; sort; *idm* a kind of *coll* used to express uncertainty a sort of; *idm* in kind (of payment) with goods (not money); *idm* kind of *coll* rather.

kind[2] *a* friendly; considerate to others (*also* kindly) as k.-hearted (*adv* -ly; *n* -ness); *ns* kindness, kindliness; *adv* kindly; *idm* take kindly to be pleased, willing to accept.

kindergarten *n* infant school.

kindle *v* set light to; *fig* excite, stir up; *n* kindling small sticks to start fire.

kindred *a, n* (people to whom one is) related; *a* similar; *n* k. spirit person with similar interests, tastes, ideals.

kinematics *n* science of pure motion; *a* kinematic.

kinetics *n* science of motion in relation to force; *a* kinetic.

king *n* 1 male ruler of nation; monarch 2 card with picture of king 3 piece in game of chess; *a* kingly noble, royal; *n* kingdom 1 state ruled by king; monarchy 2 domain,

sphere, *esp* of nature; *ns* **kingfisher** diving bird with bright plumage; k.-maker; k.-pin 1 swivel-pin 2 *fig* chief person; kingpost main vertical support for roof; *a* k.-size extra large.

kingfisher *n* small brilliantly coloured fish-eating bird.

king-pin *n* 1 swivel pin 2 *fig* chief person.

kink *n* twist, bend in rope, hair etc; *fig* eccentricity; *v* make, put kink in.

kinship *n* relationship.

kinsman *n* relative (*pl* -men) *fem* kinswoman (*pl* -women).

kiosk *n* open pavilion; refreshment, newspaper stall; telephone booth.

kip *n sl* bed; sleep; *v sl* go to bed.

kipper *n* 1 smoked, salted herring 2 salmon at spawning time; *v* cure fish by smoking, salting.

kirk *n Scot, N Eng* church.

kiss *v* 1 caress with lips 2 *billiards* touch lightly; *n* act of kissing 3 a k.-and tell *coll* (of story) creating scandal about well-known person and earning large sum of money; *ns* k. of death *coll* cause of certain disaster; k. of life form of artificial respiration by breathing into patient's mouth.

kit *n* 1 small wooden tub 2 equipment 3 outfit; *v* provide with kit; *n* -bag bag for holding soldier's or traveller's belongings; *phr v*

kit out/up equip.

kitchen *n* place where food is cooked; *n* k.-garden vegetable garden (*n* k.-sink drama realistic drama of working-class life); **kitchenette** small kitchen.

kite *n* 1 bird of prey 2 light framework covered with paper, flown in wind; *ns* k. balloon captive observation balloon; K. mark mark of approval from BSI.

kith and kin *n* family and relations.

kitsch *n* vulgarized, pretentious art or literature with popular or sentimental appeal.

kitten *n* young cat; *a* -ish like kitten; playful.

kittiwake *n* kind of seagull.

kitty *n* 1 pool of money in some gambling games; jointly held fund 2 *bowls* the jack.

kiwi *n* flightless N Zealand bird; *sl* N Zealander.

kiwi fruit *n* oval fruit with green flesh (*also* Chinese gooseeberry).

klaxon *n* loud electric horn.

Kleenex *n* [TM] soft paper handkerchief; *sing or pl*.

kleptomania *n* compulsive impulse to steal; *n, a* -maniac.

klutz *n US sl* idiot.

km *abbr* kilometre.

knack *n* aptitude; talent; habit; trick.

knacker *n* dealer in worn-out horses for slaughter; *v Brit sl* exhaust; *a* -ed.

knapsack n bag carried on back, small rucksack.

knave n rogue; jack, lowest court card; n **knavery** villainy; a **knavish**.

knead v squeeze and press with hands, *esp* to work bread dough; massage.

knee n 1 joint between upper and lower leg 2 part of trousers covering this; *idm* **bring sb to his/her knees** defeat, humiliate sb; v hit with the knee; *as* **k.-deep**; **k.-high**; **k.-jerk** automatic (**k.-jerk reaction**); *ns* **kneecap** flat bone protecting knee-joint; **knees-up** *Brit coll* rowdy party with dancing.

kneel v rest on knees; *pt, pp* **knelt**; n **kneeler** hassock.

knell n sound of tolling bell; omen of doom.

knew *pt of* **know**.

knickerbockers n *pl* loose, baggy breeches; n *pl* **knickers** woman's undergarment.

knick-knack n trifle, trinket.

knife n cutting implement with blade set in handle; n **k.-edge 1** cutting edge **2** any sharp edge; *idm* **on a k.-edge** in a critical situation; v cut, stab with knife.

knight n one who receives non-hereditary honour, carrying title 'Sir'; n **-hood**; v create (man) knight; a **-ly**.

knit v **knits, knitting, knitted** or **knit.** make fabric by fastening loops of wool, etc together with needles; draw

close together, make compact; *ns* **knitter**; **knitting** knitted work (**k. needles**); **knitwear**.

knives *pl of* **knife**.

knob n 1 rounded handle, switch, button etc 2 small lump; a **knobbly** (*US* **knobby**) lumpy.

knock v 1 strike 2 collide with 3 *coll* criticize 4 (of car engine) make tapping noise; *phr vs* **knock about/around 1** loiter 2 batter (a **k.-about** boisterous); **knock back** drink quickly; **knock down** reduce (price) (a **k.-down** bargain); **knock off 1** finish work 2 *coll* subtract 3 *sl* steal 4 *sl* kill 5 *coll* finish quickly; v **knock on** *rugby* knock ball forward; a **k.-on** resulting from a previous action; n **k.-on effect**; v **knock out 1** strike unconscious 2 eliminate; n **knockout 1** act of rendering unconscious (n **k. blow**) 2 contest in which players are gradually eliminated 3 *coll* impressive or attractive person; **knock up 1** *Brit* awaken 2 *Brit* assemble hastily 3 *tennis* practise before actual game (n **k.-up**); n **1** blow 2 tapping noise 3 *coll* slight misfortune; *ns* **-er 1** hinged bar for knocking on door 2 *coll* critic; a **k.-kneed** legs that curve in at the knees.

knoll n small rounded hill, mound.

knot n 1 tightly tied loop of string, rope etc 2 *fig*

difficulty 3 hard lump where branches joint trunk 4 unit of ship's speed 5 one nautical mile an hour; v **knots, knotting, knotted.** tie into, make knot; become entangled; a **knotty** full of knots; *fig* complicated.

know v **knowing, knew, known. 1** be aware of, acquainted with 2 understand 3 be informed of 4 recognize; *idm* **know apart** be able to distinguish; *idm* **know backwards/back to front/inside out** know thoroughly; *idm* **in the know** well-informed; *ns* **k.-all, k.-how**; a **knowing**; *adv* **-ly**; n **-ness**; n **knowledge 1** what is known 2 understanding 3 information; a **knowledgeable** (*adv* **-ably**).

knuckle n 1 bone at finger-joint 2 knee-joint of veal, pork etc; v clench hand, showing knuckles; *phr v* **knuckle under** submit; yield; n **k.-duster** metal guard worn on knuckles to add force to blow.

KO n *coll* knock-out.

koala n small Australian marsupial, living in trees.

kooky a *US coll* crazy; eccentric.

kola n bitter, stimulating extract from kola nut.

Koran n sacred book of Muslims.

Korean a, n (inhabitant, language) of Korea.

kosher a ceremonially fit,

pure, clean, as laid down by Jewish law.

kotow, kowtow *n* in China, humble situation; *v* bow to; *fig* be servile to.

kraal *n* 1 African fenced village 2 cattle enclosure.

kremlin *n* 1 Russian citadel 2 *cap* (seat of) Russian government.

krill *n* tiny crustaceans, food for whales.

Krugerrand *n* S African gold coin.

krypton *n* rare gaseous element.

Kt *abbr* knight.

kudos *n sl* fame; credit.

kulak *n* (formerly) Russian landed peasant opposed to collectivisation.

kung fu *n* Chinese martial art combining skills of judo and karate.

kw *abbr* kilowatt.

lab *abbr* laboratory.

Lab *abbr* Labour Party.

label *n* slip of paper etc attached to object giving information on it; *v* **labels, labelling, labelled. 1** fix label to **2** *fig* classify as.

labial *a* of lips; sound made by lips.

laboratory *n* scientific establishment for research and experiment.

labour *n* **1** hard work; task **2** act of childbirth **3** body of workers (*n* **L. party** political party favouring better social conditions for workers); *v* **1** work hard; toil **2** (of ship) toss in heavy seas **3** perform with difficulty; *idm* **labour the point** emphasize sth unnecessarily; *phr v* **labour under** suffer from; *ns* **-er** manual worker; *a* **-ed** slow; lacking in spontaneity; *a* **l.- intensive** using a lot of manpower; **l.-saving**

economical of effort; *a* **laborious**, industrious; wearisome.

labrador *n* large retriever dog.

laburnum *n* tree with pendulous yellow flowers.

labyrinth *n* maze; network of winding paths.

lace *n* **1** patterned net-like fabric **2** string, cord used as fastening, *esp* for shoes; *v* **1** fasten with laces **2** *coll* add spirits to (coffee etc); *a* **lacy.**

lacerate *v* tear; mangle; *fig* distress; *n* **laceration.**

lachrymal *a* of tears; *as* **lachrymatory**, causing flow of tears; *a* **lachrymose**, tearful.

lack *n* deficiency; absence; need; *v* be short of; want; *a* **lacking** missing; *idm* **be lacking in** be devoid of, short of; *a* **lacklustre** dull; lifeless.

lackadaisical *a* dreamy;

affectedly languid.

lackey *n* servile follower.

laconic *a* brief; using few words; terse; *adv* **-ally.**

lacquer *n* hard glossy varnish; *v* paint with this.

lacrosse *n* ball-game played with long-handled racquet, or crosse.

lactic, lacteal *a* of milk; *n* **lactation**, secreting of milk; period of suckling.

lactose *n* *chem* form of sugar found in milk.

lacuna *n* **1** gap; hiatus **2** empty space, *esp* in book **3** cavity (in bone or tissue).

lad *n* boy; young man; *pl* **the lads** *Brit coll* one's male friends.

ladder *n* **1** climbing device of two poles joined by rungs **2** vertical flaw in stockings; *v* (of stockings etc) cause, develop vertical flaw.

lade *v* load; put cargo into; *pt, pp* **laden** or **laded**; *a* **laden** a heavily loaded.

lading *n* cargo; freight.

ladle *n* long-handled, deep-bowled spoon; *v* serve with ladle.

lady *n* **1** woman of good social standing; **2** *coll* any woman **3** *cap* title of wives of knights, baronets and peers below rank of duke **4** title of daughters of peers above rank of viscount; *prefix* feminine, female; *ns* **ladybird** small reddish beetle with black spot; **l.-in waiting** lady's personal servant; **l.-killer** *coll* man

who thinks women unable
to resist his charm; **ladyship**
title of lady; *a* **ladylike**.

lag¹ *v* **lags, lagging, lagged**;
loiter; walk, move slowly; *n*
laggard loiterer.

lag² *v* wrap boiler, pipes etc to
conserve heat; *n* **lagging**.

lag³ *n sl* convict, *esp* recidivist.

lager *n* light beer; glass of this;
n **l. lout** beer-drinking
hooligan.

laggard *n* person lagging
behind.

lagoon *n* shallow salt water
channel, enclosed by reef,
sandbank or atoll.

laid *pt, pp of* **lay**.

laid-back *a coll* relaxed;
lacking in sense of urgency.

lain *pp of* **lie**.

lair *n* den; resting-place, *esp of*
wild animals.

laissez-faire *n* policy of non-
interference, *esp* by
government, allowing things
to take natural course.

lake *n* large sheet of water
enclosed by land.

lake *n* reddish pigment.

lam *v sl* beat; flog; thrash;
n **-ming**.

lama *n* Buddhist priest in
Tibet; *n* **lamasery** monastery
of lamas.

lamb *n* 1 young sheep 2 its
meat 3 *fig* gentle, innocent
child, person; *v* give birth to
lamb; *a* **lamblike** gentle; *n*
lambkin very young lamb;
term of affection.

lambast(e) *v* attack violently.

lambent *a* 1 twinkling; softly
shining 2 *fig* light and witty.

lame *a* 1 disabled, *esp* feet and
legs 2 (*fig* unconvincing; *n* **l.
duck** 1 ineffectual person 2
US polit official whose term
of office is nearly over; *v*
cripple; *n* **-ness**.

lamé *n Fr* fabric interwoven
with metallic threads.

lament *v* bewail; mourn; feel,
express deep grief; *n*
expression of deep grief;
dirge; **-ation**; *a* **-able**
deplorable.

laminate *v* roll, beat into thin
plates; cover with thin
sheets of (metal, plastic etc);
split into layers; *n* thin plate,
layer.

Lammas *n* 1st August.

lamp *n* any various devices for
giving light or therapeutic
rays; *ns* **l.-black** pigment
made from soot; **l. lighter**
lighter of street lamp; **l.-post**
post supporting street lamp;
l.-shade.

lampoon *n* venomous, abusive
personal satire; *v* satirize in
lampoon.

lamprey *n* eel-like fish, with
sucker lips.

lance *n* long, ceremonial
cavalry spear; fish-spear; *v*
pierce, cut with lance or
lancet; *ns* **l.-corporal** NCO
in army; **lancet** double-
edged pointed surgical
instrument; **lancer** mounted
soldier armed with lance; *pl*
kind of quadrille; *a*
lanceolate lance-shaped.

land *n* 1 dry solid surface of
earth 2 country; nation 3
ground; area; estate; *v* 1 put

on shore; disembark 2 set
(aircraft) down; 3 catch
(fish) 4 succeed in getting
(job); *phr vs* **land sb in** put
sb in (trouble); **land up** find
oneself (in unwanted
situation); **land with** (*esp
passive*) saddle with
responsibility; *ns* **landfall**
coming to, in sight of land;
n **landfill** practice of burying
waste in the ground; waste
buried in this way; *n* **landfill
site** site where landfill is
buried; **landlady, landlord** 1
manager or owner of rented
accommodation 2 pub
manager; **landlubber** person
unused to life at sea;
landmark 1 feature of area
easy to recognize and
orientate oneself by 2
important event; **landmine**
bomb hidden on or under
the ground; **landscape** 1
scenery of area 2 picture of
this (**l. gardening** planned
layout of garden for scenic
effect); **landslide** 1 sudden
fall of earth, rocks 2 election
win by vast majority (*n* **l.
victory**); *as* **landed** 1
owning land (*n* **l. gentry**) 2
consisting of land (*n* **l.
property**); **l. locked**
surrounded by land.

landing *n* 1 coming to dry land
from air or sea (*ns* **l. craft**
flat boat; **l. gear** aircraft
undercarriage and wheels; **l.
stage** platform for landing
passengers or cargo) 2 level
area at top of staircase 2

lane *n* 1 narrow road, street 2

regular route for shipping, aircraft 3 marked division on sports track or main road.

language n 1 speech 2 particular form of speech of nation, race, profession etc 3 any symbols, gestures expressing meaning ns **l.barrier; l.laboratory** room with audio equipment for individual or group practice in language.

languish v become languid; pine; droop from misery etc; a **languid** weak; spiritless; adv **-ly;** n **languor** want of interest; lassitude (a **-ous**).

lank a limp; long and thin; lean; a **lanky.**

lanolin n refined wool-grease.

lantern n transparent case for lamp etc; lamp-room of lighthouse; structure on dome to admit light; a **l.jawed** with long jaw and drawn face.

lanyard n 1 short cord (for securing whistle or knife) 2 short nautical rope.

lap[1] n 1 part between knees and waist of seated person 2 circuit of race-track; v **laps, lapping, lapped. 1** enfold; surround 2 complete, or have lead of, one circuit of race-track; n **l.dog** 1 small pet dog 2 person subservient to another.

lap[2] v 1 drink by scooping up movement of tongue, as animal 2 splash softly; phr v **lap up** listen eagerly to.

lap[3] n circuit of race track (n **l.counter**).

laparoscopy n med internal examination of abdomen through narrow tube.

lapel n front part of coat folded back to shoulders.

lapidary n worker in gems; a meticulous in detail.

lapis lazuli n semi-precious bright blue stone.

Lapp n member of nomadic Arctic tribe.

lapse n 1 fall; error 2 passing (of time etc.); v fall away; cease to exist.

laptop n small PC.

larboard n port side of ship.

larceny n stealing; theft.

larch n coniferous tree.

lard n refined, rendered pig fat; v 1 insert strips of fat in meat 2 enrich (style of speech) with; a **lardy.**

larder n storeroom for food.

large a great in size, number; roomy; copious; at large free; idm **by and large** in general; adv **largely** mainly. n **largesse** liberality; gift; a **l.-hearted** generous; tolerant.

largo adv mus slowly and nobly; n such music.

lariat n long, noosed string or rope.

lark[1] n singing wild bird, sky-lark.

lark[2] n jest; sport; piece of fun; v play about; jest.

larva n caterpillar, worm-like stage of butterfly, fly etc; pl **-ae;** as **larval, larviform.**

larynx n back of throat, containing vocal chords; n **laryngitis** inflammation of

the larynx.

lasagne n It flat rectangular layers of pasta cooked with layers of meat or vegetables, topped with cheese.

Lascar n East Indian sailor.

lascivious a lustful; wanton.

laser n device producing intense concentrated light beam; ns **l.beam; l.card** plastic card with printed data read by laser; **l.optics, l.technology.**

lash v 1 strike with whip 2 fig strike violently 3 fig scold fiercely 4 fasten, bind tightly; n 1 whip 2 eyelash.

lashings n pl coll plenty; extravagant quantity.

lass n young girl.

lassitude n weariness; weakness.

lasso n -os or **-oes.** rope with noose; v catch with lasso.

last[1] n shoemaker's model of foot.

last[2] a 1 final 2 previous 3 only remaining; idm **have the last laugh** be triumphant in the end; idm **on one's/its last legs** nearly dead; worn out; ns **l.post** bugle call played at military funeral; **l.rites** religious rites for person about to die; **l.straw** problem making total situation beyond endurance; **L.Supper** final meal shared by Jesus and the disciples before his arrest; **l.word** 1 final remark 2 up-to-date example of sth; pron 1 last person or thing 2 most recent person or thing; a **l.-**

ditch as a final effort to avoid defeat.

last³ v 1 continue; endure 2 suffice (for); a -ing.

latch n fastening for doors and windows; spring lock; v fasten with latch; phr vs **latch on** coll understand; **latch onto** coll 1 understand 2 grab the attention, seek out the company of; n **latchkey** key to house (**l.child** child whose parents are at work when he/she gets home from school; pl -ren).

late a behindhand; towards end; earlier than present; no longer living; comp **later**; sup **last, latest**; adv (also **lately**) recently.

latent a hidden; dormant.

lateral a at, from side; n **l.thinking** ability to find original answers to problems by abandoning strictly logical methods, by seeing unusual mental connections; adv -ly sideways.

latex n white, milky juice, secreted by plants, esp rubber tree; a bot **lactiferous** bearing latex.

lath n thin strip of wood, or other material.

lathe n machine used in turning wood, metal.

lather n 1 froth of soap and water 2 (of horse) sweat; idm **in a lather** nervously excited; v 1 form lather 2 sl beat.

Latin a of ancient Rome; of languages and races descended from this; n

member of Latin race **L.America** countries of S and Central America where Spanish or Portuguese is spoken (a -n).

latitude n 1 geog distance N and S from equator 2 freedom from restriction; scope 3 pl regions; a **latitudinal**.

latitudinarian a tolerant, esp in religious matters.

latrine n privy, esp in camp, barracks.

latter a, pron later; second of two; a **l.day** modern; adv **-ly** recently.

lattice n structure of criss-cross laths, or metal strips; window with glass crossed by lead strips; a **latticed**.

laud v praise; extol; a **-able** praise-worthy.

laugh v utter sounds expressing amusement, joy, scorn; n such sound; as **laughing**; ns **l.-gas** nitrous oxide, mild anaesthetic; **l.-matter; l.-stock** object of ridicule; **laughable** ridiculous (adv **-ably**).

launch¹ v hurl; fling; initiate; set afloat; fig embark on; phr vs **launch into** begin boldly; **launch out at** attack physically, verbally; ns **-er**.

launch² n largest boat carried by warship; large power-drive pleasure boat.

launch pad, launching pad n platform for launching rockets.

launder v 1 wash and iron (clothes) 2 make source (of

stolen money) untraceable by depositing abroad (n -ing); ns **laundress** washerwoman; **laundry** place where linen etc is laundered; clothes sent there; **launderette** place where washing machines can be used on plavment of fee.

laureate a crowned with laurels; n Poet **L.** poet appointed to Royal Household.

laurel n evergreen, glossy-leaved shrub; pl its leaves; symbol of victory, fame.

lava n molten volcanic rock.

lavatory n room with wash-basin and water-closet.

lavender n shrub with fragrant pale mauve flowers.

lavish a profuse; extravagant; abundant; v bestow; spend recklessly.

law n 1 rule imposed by authority 2 jurisprudence 3 sequence of natural processes in nature 4 sequence of causes and effects; idm **a law unto oneself** not answerable to anyone; as **l.-abiding; lawful** (adv **-ly; n -ness); lawless** (n **-ness); ns lawman; lawsuit** non-criminal case; **lawyer**.

lawn¹ n fine linen.

lawn² n stretch of close-mown grass; ns **l.-mower, l.-tennis** ball game played on grass or hard court.

lax a 1 loose 2 slack; careless 3 (of bowels) relaxed; a **-ative** having loosening effect on bowels; ns **-ity, -ness** slackness; lack of moral principles.

lay v **lays, laying, laid. 1** place horizontally; set in position **2** set out formally **3** deposit **4** produce (egg) **5** settle; *idm* **lay hold of** seize; *idm* **lay low** flatten; knock down; *idm* **lay waste** devastate; *phr vs* **lay down 1** deposit **2** specify; **lay in** put in store; **lay into** attack; **lay off 1** cease to employ **2** abandon **3** *football* pass backwards, away from goal (n **l.-off**); **lay on** provide; **lay it on** exaggerate; **lay out 1** set out; arrange (n **layout**) **2** knock unconscious; **lay up 1** keep in store **2** confine to bed; n act of laying; ns **layabout** idle person; **l.-by** side road or bay for short-term parking next to main road; **layer 1** one of several thicknesses on a surface (n **l.cake**) **2** hen which lays eggs; **l.figure** artist's model of human figure; **layman/-person/-woman** person not a professional expert, not a priest; **l.reader** lay person entitled to conduct religious services apart from special sacraments.

lay *a* not clerical or professional; n ballad; n **lay-figure** jointed figure used by artists; *fig* nonentity; **layman** one who is not expert.

layette n *Fr* outfit of clothes etc for new born child.

lazar n leper.

laze v be idle; rest oneself; *a* **lazy** indolent; n **laziness**.

lb *abbr* pound(s) (in weight).

lbw *abbr* cricket leg before wicket.

LCD *abbr* liquid crystal display (method of showing figures when electric current through liquid).

LCM *abbr* math lowest common multiple.

L-driver n *Brit* person learning to drive.

lea n meadow, open grassland.

lead[1] n **1** heavy bluish white metal element **2** piece of this used for sounding depth of water; **3** graphite (**l.pencil**); v cover, space with lead; *as* **leaded** containing lead (**l.petrol**); **leaden** heavy and dull; **l.-free** (**l.-free petrol**).

lead[2] v **leads, leading, led.** conduct; guide; act as chief; govern; be ahead; excel; *phr vs* **lead sb on** influence sb to believe or do sth wrong; **lead up to** prepare for; n **1** guidance **2** extent of advantage in competition **3** first place **4** clue to mystery **5** strap for control of dog or other animal **6** *elec* wire connecting source of power to appliance; ns **l.-in** introduction; **l.time** *comm* time needed to complete; **leader (-ship)**; *a* **leading** (ns **l.article** *Brit* editorial; **l.light** outstanding person; **l.question** question that implies the answer

expected).

leaf n **1** one of lateral growths from plant stem; flat expanded green organ of photo-synthesis **2** thin sheet **3** two pages of book etc **4** movable flap of table etc; *pl* **leaves**; *idm* **take a leaf out of sb's book** copy sb; *phr v* **leaf through** turn the pages quickly; ns **leaflet** small printed sheet of paper; n **l.mould** compost of rotted leaves; *a* **leafy** (n **-iness**).

league[1] n compact, alliance for mutual protection etc; association, group of persons, clubs etc with common interest; *idm* **in league with** working in secret with; v form alliance, league.

league[2] n *ar* distance of three miles.

leak n crack, hole through which liquid or gas passes; amount of liquid, gas that leaks; v **1** allow liquid, gas etc to pass slowly through crack **2** prematurely disclose (news etc); n **leakage** leaking; gradual escape or loss; *a* **leaky**.

lean[1] *a* thin; containing no fat; *fig* unproductive n non-fat part of meat; *a* **l.-burn** (of engine) economical on fuel.

lean[2] v **1** bend; incline; slope **2** rely on **3** prop against; *idm* **lean over backwards** make every possible effort; *phr vs* **lean on** rely on; **lean towards** be in favour of; n, *a* l.-to structure built against a wall.

leap v spring; jump (pt, pp **leaped** or **leapt**); phr v **leap at** seize eagerly; n **1** act of leaping **2** sudden increase; idm **by leaps and bounds** very fast; idm **a leap in the dark** a risk taken blindly; ns **leapfrog** game where players leap over one another in turn (v **1** play this game **2** fig take turns to go in front); **l.year** year of 366 days occurring every fourth year.

learn v **learning, learned** or **learnt**. acquire knowledge, skill; commit to memory; be taught; find out; a **learned** well-informed; erudite; ns **learner, learning** knowledge acquired by study.

lease n contract whereby land, property is rented for stated time by owner to tenant; v let, rent by lease; n **l.-back** (system of) selling property and renting it back from new owner a **leasehold** held on lease.

leash n **1** chain or strap holding dog **2** set of three dogs so held **3** thong holding hawk; v hold by leash.

least det, pron the smallest; idm **at least 1** not less than 2 **in any case; whatever happens**; idm **(not) in the least** (not) at all; adv in the smallest degree; idm **not least** especially; in particular.

leather n skin of animal

prepared by tanning; as **leathern** of, like leather; **leathery** tough; n **leatherjacket** larva of crane-fly.

leave v allow, cause to remain **2** go away **3** deposit; (pt, pp **left**); phr vs **leave off 1** cease **2** not wear; **leave out 1** omit **2** leave outside; **Leave it out!** coll Stop it!; n **1** permission **2** absence from work or duty; allowance of time for this; idm **take leave of** say goodbye to (n **l.-taking**); n **leavings** leftovers.

leaven n **1** yeast **2** fig stimulating, spiritual influence; v **1** raise with yeast **2** influence.

leaves pl of **leaf**.

lectern n reading-desk in church.

lecture n instructive discourse; admonishment; v deliver lecture; reprove n **l.hall, lecturer, lecturing** (idm **give sb a (good) lecturing** reprimand sb severely); **lectureship.**

led pt, pp of **lead**.

LED abbr light emitting diode (luminous semiconductor).

ledge n narrow shelf projecting from wall, cliff-face etc.

ledger n principal account book of business, etc; flat stone; n **l.-line 1** fishing line **2** mus additional line above or below stave.

lee n side protected from wind; a **-ward** on lee side; n **-way** leeward drift of ship; fig loss of progress.

leech n blood-sucking worm; fig usurer.

leek n vegetable like onion.

leer v glance lustfully; slyly; n such a look.

leery a coll wary; suspicious.

lees n pl sediment of wine; dregs.

left[1] (pt, pp of **leave**); ns **l.luggage office;** leftovers things, esp food remaining.

left[2] a **1** on the side of the body where the heart is **2** towards this side **3** polit tending to socialist or radical views; n **1** left side **2** polit left wing; as **l.-hand** situated on the left; **l.-handed** using left hand (n **l.-hander**); as **leftist; left-wing** polit.

leg n **1** limb supporting body **2** part of trousers, jeans etc covering this **3** support for chair, table, bed etc **4** joint of meat **5** stage of journey, of relay race etc; idm **a leg up** a boost, helping hand; idm **not have a leg to stand on** have no possible excuse; ns **legroom; l.side** cricket part of field to rear of batsman; **l.-warmer** woollen garment covering lower part of leg; **legwork** coll work that entails a lot of walking; as **legless** coll completely drunk; **leggy** having long legs.

legacy n gift, bequest by will; fig something handed down; n **legatee.**

legal a pertaining to law; lawful; ns **l.aid** subsidised

legal representation;
l.tender forms of money that must legally be accepted in payment; *adv* **-ly**; *n* **legality**; *n* **legalistic**; *v* **-ize** make legal; *n* **-ization**.

legate *n* ambassador of Pope.

legation *n* diplomatic body; chief of such body and his staff; his official residence.

legato *adv mus* smoothly, without breaks.

legend *n* **1** traditional story, myth **2** inscription, on map or medal; *a* **-ary** fabulous; mythical.

legerdemain *n Fr* conjuring trick; sleight of hand.

leggings *n pl* protective covering for legs.

leghorn *n* **1** plaited straw **2** breed of domestic fowl.

legible *a* easily read; *adv* **-ibly**; *n* **-ibility**.

legion *n* unit of ancient Roman infantry; body of troops; multitude; large organized group; *a*, *n* **legionary**.

legionnaire's disease *n* dangerous bacterial lung infection.

legislator *n* maker of laws; *v* **legislate** make laws; *a* **legislative**; *n* **legislature** legislative body.

legitimate *a* lawful; justifiable; born in wedlock; *v* make lawful; *n* **legitimacy** state of being legitimate; *vs* **legitimatize, legitimize** to legitimate.

Lego [TM] construction toy of studded interlocking

coloured plastic bricks and other shapes.

leguminous *a* pod-bearing (pea, bean etc).

leisure *n* freedom from work; free, unoccupied time; *as* **-ly** unhurried, deliberate; **leisured** having much leisure.

leitmotif *n mus* recurring theme; *fig* recurrent association of ideas.

lemming *n* small arctic rat-like animal.

lemur *n* small monkeylike animal.

lemon *n* very acid pale yellow fruit; its colour; *ns* **lemonade** drink flavoured with lemon; **l.sole** flat fish, type of plaice.

lend *v* **1** grant temporary use of **2** let out for hire, or interest **3** impart; *pt, pp* **lent**; *n* **lender**.

length *n* **1** distance from end to end **2** quality of being long **3** duration in time; extent **4** long piece of sth; *idm* **at length 1** at least **2** extensively; for a long time; *idm* **go to any/great lengths** be willing to undertake anything; *v* **lengthen** make longer; *adv* **lengthways/ -lengthwise**; *a* **lengthy**; *adv* **-thily**; *n* **-thiness**.

lenient *a* merciful; tolerant; not severe; *ns* **lenience, leniency**.

lenitive *a, n* soothing (drug).

lens *n* **1** curved disc of glass or transparent plastic which magnifies (*eg* **camera lens; contact lens**) **2** part of eye

which does this; *ns* **l.cap** cover for camera lens; **l.hood** mask for camera used facing the sun.

lent *pt, pp* of **lend**.

Lent *n* period of penance and fasting from Ash Wednesday to Easter; *a* **Lenten**.

lentil *n* dried seed of leguminous food plant.

lento *adv mus* slowly.

leonine *a* like a lion.

leopard *n* large spotted carnivore of cat tribe; *fem* **leopardess**.

leotard *n* close-fitting garment worn by dancers.

leper *n* sufferer from leprosy; *n* **leprosy** infectious chronic skin disease, also affecting tissues and nerves; *a* **leprous**.

lepidoptera *n pl* insects with four scaly wings, including moths and butterflies.

leprechaun *n* Irish sprite.

lesbian *n* female homosexual; *n* **lesbianism** homosexuality between women.

lese-majeste *n Fr* treason.

lesion *n* injury; morbid change affecting body functions.

less *a, adv* (*comp* of **little**) not so much; to a lesser degree, amount; *n* smaller amount, quantity; *prep* with deduction of; *v* **lessen** reduce; diminish.

lessee *n* one to whom lease is granted.

lessen *v* reduce.

lesser *a* **1** smaller **2** less important.

lesson *n* **1** anything learnt or

taught 2 warning example 3 portion of Scripture read in Church.

lessor n one who grants a lease.

lest conj for fear that.

let v 1 allow; permit 2 rent out (property) (pt, pp let); idm **let alone** and definitely not; idm **let/leave go** release; idm **let oneself go** behave in an uninhibited way; idm **let know** inform; phr vs **let down** 1 lower 2 deflate 3 disappoint (n letdown); **let sb in for** expose sb to (sth unpleasant); **let sb into/in on** share (a secret) with sb; **let off** 1 cause to explode 2 release 3 excuse (n let-off); **let on** tell (secret); **let out** 1 reveal 2 utter 3 release (n let-out escape l.-out clause); **let up** become less intense (n letup); n 1 letting of property; 2 tennis service touching net before landing in court; n **letting** renting out.

lethal a fatal; deadly.

lethargy a abnormal drowsiness; indifference; apathy; a **lethargic**.

letter n 1 written symbol expressing a sound of speech 2 written message 3 pl literary culture; literature; v mark with letters; a -ed 1 having education 2 marked with letters; ns **letterbomb** bomb inside an envelope; **letterbox** 1 posting box 2 slot in door for delivering mail; **letterhead** printed

heading on stationery; stationery with this; **letterpress** printing from type; **letters patent** legal document granting certain rights, or privileges.

lettuce n plant used for salads.

leucocyte n white blood corpuscle.

leucotomy n lobotomy.

leukaemia n malignant disease in which the body produces too many white blood cells.

level a horizontal; even; of same height; equable; idm **level pegging** with same score; n **l.crossing** intersection of road and railway; a **l.-headed** sensible and calm; n 1 plane surface 2 usual height 3 moral, intellectual, social standard 4 horizontal passage in mine 5 instrument for testing horizontal plane; idm **on the level** honest; v **levels, levelling, levelled.** 1 make flat 2 bring to same level 3 aim (gun); phr vs **level off/out** stop rising; **level with** coll speak frankly to; n **leveller** person seeking equality.

lever n rigid bar (usually supported at fixed point) which lifts or moves weight at one end when power is brought to bear on the other; n -age action, power of lever; v use lever.

leveret n young hare.

leviathan n 1 sea monster of the Bible 2 something very large or powerful.

levitation n power of raising solid body into air by non-physical means; v **levitate** cause to do this.

levity n frivolity; facetiousness; lightness.

levy n 1 collection of tax; sum thus collected 2 forced military enlistment; v **levies, levying, levied.** 1 impose tax etc 2 conscript (troops).

lewd a indecent; obscene; n -ness.

lexical a of words; adv -ly.

lexicon n dictionary; ns **lexicography** art, process of making dictionaries; -grapher.

liable a answerable; legally responsible; idm **liable to** 1 subject to 2 inclined to; n **liability** obligation.

liaison n 1 connection 2 co-operation 3 illicit sexual relationship; v coll **liaise** act as means of coordination with; n **l.officer** officer who acts as link between units etc.

liar n untruthful person.

lib abbr liberation.

libation n drink-offering to gods.

libel n written, printed statement likely to damage person's reputation; v **libels, libelling, libelled.** publish libel; defame character; a **libellous** defamatory; n -ness.

liberal a 1 generous 2 tolerant 3 cap member of Liberal Party.

liberal arts n college study of

the arts, humanities, natural and social sciences.

liberate v set free; ns **-ation, -ator.**

liberation theology n RC movement for more religious freedom.

libertarian a, n (person) believing in freedom of ideas; n **-ism.**

libertine n debauched, dissolute man; a dissolute.

liberty n 1 freedom 2 offensive act or remark; pl privileges, rights conferred by grant.

libido n sexual desire; a **libidinous.**

library n collection of books; place where books are kept, or may be borrowed; n **librarian.**

libretto n words of an opera or musical play pl **libretti** or **-s.**

lice pl of **louse.**

licence n 1 permission granted by authority; document granting it 2 excessive freedom; dissoluteness; **poetic l.** deviation from rules of his art by writer or artist; v **license** grant licence to; ns **licensee** holder of licence; **licentiate** one authorized to practice profession or art.

licentious a dissolute, immoral.

lichen n flowerless, moss-like plant growing on trees, rocks etc; a **lichened.**

lick v 1 pass tongue over 2 flicker round 3 sl beat; defeat; a act of licking; n **licking** sl beating, thrashing.

lid n movable cover; eyelid.

lido n open air swimming pool.

lie[1] v **lying, lay, lain.** recline, be in resting position; be situated, placed; idm **lie low** remain hidden; idm **take lying down** accept without protest; n 1 direction 2 way sth lies; (idm **the lie of the land** 1 nature, appearance of terrain 2 fig state of affairs; phr vs **lie about/around** be idle; **lie behind** be the real explanation of; ns **lie-down** siesta; **lie-in** stay in bed later than usual.

lie[2] v **lying, lied.** make false statement; n deliberate untruth; n **l.-detector** device for determining whether sb is telling a lie; ns **white lie** justifiable falsehood; **liar** one who tells lies.

liege a bound to render feudal service; n lord; sovereign; n **liegeman** vassal, subject.

lien n leg right to hold property of another until debt is paid.

lieu n Fr place; **in lieu** instead of.

lieutenant n deputy; rank below naval lieutenant-commander or army captain.

life n 1 animate existence 2 duration of this (**l.imprisonment, l.sentence**) 3 class of living beings (**animal l.**) 4 biography 5 period of usefulness 6 way of living 7 vitality; pl **lives** idm **come to life** 1 wake up 2 show enthusiasm; idm **take one's life** commit suicide; idm **take**

one's life in one's hands take dangerous risk; idm **take sb's life** kill sb; n **l.belt** worn to save person from sinking in water; **l.-blood** 1 blood essential to life 2 fig thing that gives vitality; **lifeboat**; **l.buoy** floating ring for person fallen in water to hold on to; **l.cycle** whole course of development in a living creature; **lifer** coll prisoner with life sentence; **l.expectancy**; **lifeguard** person employed to ensure safety of swimmers; **l.insurance** (also **l.assurance**); **l.jacket**; **lifeline** 1 rope for saving people's lives 2 fig sth which enables way of life, organization to survive; **l.preserver**; **l.science** biology, medicine etc; **lifespan** length of life; **l.style**; **l.support system**; **lifetime** as **lifeless** (adv **-ly**; n **-ness**); **lifelike** looking like the real thing; **lifelong**; **l.-size/-sized.**

lift v raise to higher position; take up; (of fog) disperse; phr v **lift off** avia leave the ground (n **lift-off**) n that which lifts; elevator.

ligament n band of fibrous tissue connecting bones; connecting band; n **ligature** anything which binds; thread for tying severed artery; **ling** dipthong.

light[1] a 1 not heavy 2 loose 3 friable 4 mild 5 trivial; adv in light manner; idm **make**

light of treat as unimportant; *adv* **-ly** *n* **-ness**; *as* **l.-finger** *coll* in the habit of stealing casually; **l.-headed** dizzy; unable to think clearly; **l.-hearted** cheerful; **l.-weight 1** of less than average weight **2** frivolous in attitude (n such a person); *v* **lighten** *n* **-ing**.

light[2] *n* **1** form of energy, acting on optic nerve **2** making vision possible; brightness; source of this **3** knowledge **4** aspect; *idm* **bring/come to light** reveal/be revealed; *idm* **in the light of** taking into consideration; *idm* **see the light** understand; *v* **1** set fire to **2** illuminate (*pt, pp* **lighted** or **lit**); *phr v* **light up 1** make or become bright **2** light a cigarette; *ns* **l.bulb; lighthouse** tall building with warning light to ships; **lightship; l.year** distance travelled by light in one year, approx six million million miles (*idm* **light years away** *coll* a very long way off); *a* **1** bright **2** pale (*eg* **l.brown**); *v* **lighten** give light to; become brighter; *ns* **lighter** instrument for lighting; boat for unloading goods into; **lighting** system of illumination (**l.circuit**); **lightning** electrical discharge in atmosphere seen as flash in sky; *a* **1** of lightning (n **l.conductor** wire on house wall for earthing lightning) **2** *fig* very rapid.

ligneous *a* like, made of wood; *n* **lignite** soft woody brown coal.

like[1] *a* similar; *adv* in same way; *prep* in manner of; *a* **likely** probable (n **likelihood**); *a* **like-minded** of similar views; *v* **liken** compare, *n* **likeness** resemblance; portrait; *adv* **likewise** also, moreover.

like[2] *v* be fond of; be attached to; *a* **likeable** agreeable, attractive *n* **liking**; *idm* **take a liking to** be attracted to.

lilac *n* flowering shrub; pale mauve colour.

Lilliputian *a* diminutive.

Lilo [TM] inflatable mattress.

lilt *v* sing sweetly with spirit; *n* well-marked beat or rhythm in music; swing *a* **lilting**; *adv* **-ly**.

lily *n* bulbous flowering plant *as* **l.-livered** cowardly; **l.-white 1** pure white **2** morally pure.

limb *n* **1** leg or arm; wing **2** bough of tree; *idm* **out on a limb** isolated and unsupported.

limber[1] *n* detachable part of gun-carriage.

limber[2] *a* pliable; supple; *phr v* **limber up** make supple by exercise.

limbo 1 *theology* condition, or region allotted to souls of unbaptised children **2** *fig* place for neglected and forgotten things **3** W Indian dance.

lime[1] *n* calcium oxide obtained by burning limestone; sticky substance for catching birds, birdlime); *v* dress, mix, treat with lime; *ns* **limelight** bright white light; *fig* glare of publicity; **limestone** kind of rock, calcium carbonate.

lime[2] *n* kind of tree; its round acid fruit; *ns* **lime-juice** sweetened juice of lime used as cordial.

lime[3] *n* linden tree.

limerick *n* nonsense verse of five lines.

limit *n* boundary; *idm* **be the limit** be intolerable; *idm* **off limits** US on forbidden territory; *idm* **within limits** to a moderate degree; *as* **limited; limitless** (*adv* **-ly;** *n* **-ness**) *v* restrict; curb; *n* **-ation**; *as* **-able, -ed.**

limn *v* **lit** paint; depict.

limousine *n* large, closed type of car.

limp[1] *a* flaccid; not firm; *n* **-ness.**

limp[2] *v* walk lamely; *n* lameness.

limpet *n* rock-clinging marine shell-fish.

limpid *a* **lit** clear; transparent; *n* **-ity.**

linch-pin *n* metal pin holding wheel on axle.

linctus *n* cough medicine in liquid form.

linden *n* lime-tree with yellow flowers and spade-shaped leaves.

line *n* **1** string; cord **2** very thin threadlike mark, made by pen etc **3** wrinkle **4** row **5**

mode of action 6 organized system of transport by road, air etc 7 occupation; hobby 8 lineage 9 type of goods 10 channel of telecommunication; *idm* **in line for** eligible for; *v* 1 mark with lines 2 insert lining 3 bring into line; *ns* **lineage** descent; pedigree; *ns* **1.judge** tennis person deciding whether ball has landed in court; **lineament** feature; **lineman** person repairing telephone wires or railway lines; **1.printer** comput printer; **liner** large passenger-carrying ship or aircraft; **linesman** sport person who decides if ball has gone out of play; **l.-up 1** people side-by-side standing in line 2 *sport* all those competing in an event 3 *sport* order of events planned; **lining** material used to cover inner surface; *a* **linear** of, in lines.

lineal *a* 1 in direct line of descent 2 linear.

linen *n* cloth made of flax; underclothes, bed-linen, tablecloths etc; *a* made of linen.

liner *n* 1 large passenger ship 2 thing used for lining sth (*eg* binliner) 3 thing used for making line (*eg* eye-liner).

ling¹ *n* kind of heather.

ling² *n* species of coarse sea-fish, allied to cod.

linger *v* 1 delay; loiter 2 be slow to disappear.

lingerie *n* women's underwear.

lingo *n* language or jargon, *esp* foreign.

lingua franca *n* language of communication for people of different nationalities.

linguini *n* thin flat pasta in strips.

linguist *n* expert in a language or languages; *a* **-ic**; *adv* **-ically**; *ns* **linguistics** study of nature of language and language acquisition; **linguistician** expert in this.

liniment *n* embrocation.

link *n* 1 loop, ring of chain 2 unit of measurement (7.92") 3 connection; *v* join together, with with link; connect; *ns* **linkage**; *n* **linkman/person/woman** broadcaster who coordinates items from different sources.

links *n* golf course.

linnet *n* song-bird of finch family.

linoleum *n* type of floor-covering; *n* **linocut** relief engraving on linoleum; print made from this.

linotype *n* type-setting machine which casts whole line in one piece.

linseed *n* flax seed.

lint *n* soft material for dressing wounds.

lintel *n* horizontal stone or timber bar over doorway or window.

lion *n* large powerful carnivore of cat tribe; *fig* celebrity; *fem* **lioness**; *idm* **the lion's share** the majority; *v* **lionize** treat as celebrity.

lip *n* 1 one of fleshy flaps of

tissue round mouth 2 edge; rim; 3 *coll* impertinence; *idm* **pay lip service** to show support in words but not in deed; *v* **lip-read** decipher speech when deaf by watching speaker's lip movements (*ns* **-er**, **-ing**); **lipstick** make-up for lips.

lipid *n* waxy substance in living cells.

liposuction *n* surgical removal of excess fat from under skin.

liqueur *n* Fr strong, sweetened alcoholic liquor.

liquid *n* substance between solid and gas, fluid; *a* 1 (of sounds) harmonious 2 flowing smoothly; fluid 3 easy to realize as money (*ns* **1.assets, liquidity**); *v* **liquefy** become, make liquid; melt; *n* **liquefaction**; *a* **liquescent**.

liquidate *v* 1 pay (debt) 2 wind up financial affairs and dissolve company 3 *coll* kill; *ns* **-ation, -ator** official appointed to liquidate business.

liquor *n* liquid substance, *esp* alcoholic one.

liquorice *n* black, very sweet substance extracted from root of plant of same name, used in medicine, and as sweetmeat.

lira *n* unit of currency in Italy and Turkey.

lisle *n* fine cotton thread or fabric.

lisp *v* speak with imperfect pronunciation of sibilants; *n*.

list n roll, catalogue of names, words etc; inventory; v make, write list.

list n inclination, leaning (of ship etc) towards one side; v slope; lean.

listeria n bacteria causing food poisoning.

listless a languid; apathetic.

listen v attend closely so as to hear; idm **listen in 1** listen to radio **2** eavesdrop n **-er.**

litany n prayer with responses from congregation.

literal a **1** of letters **2** based on exact words of original; accurate; word for word; adv **literally** coll absolutely.

literary a concerned with literature or writers.

literate a educated, able to read and write; n educated person; n **literacy** ability to read and write.

literati n pl fml experts on literature.

literature n writings of country or period; written works on any subject; coll any book or printed matter; a **literary** of, learned in literature.

lithe a supple; flexible; pliant; n **litheness.**

lithium n light metal.

lithography n art of printing copies from designs on prepared stone or metal plates; ns **-graph** print so made; **-grapher**; a **-graphic.**

litigate v contest at law; make subject of lawsuit; ns **litigant, litigation** a **litigious** fond of litigation.

litmus n vegetable substance

turned red by acids and blue by alkalis; n **l.-paper.**

litmus test fig use of single issue or factor as basis for judgement.

litre n metric unit of capacity (about 1 ¾ pints).

litter n **1** scattered oddments of rubbish **2** portable couch, stretcher **3** all young born at one time **4** straw etc as bedding for animals; v **1** make untidy with litter **2** give birth to.

little a small; brief; n small amount; adv **a little** slightly.

littoral a pertaining to seashore; n coastal region.

liturgy n prescribed public worship; a **-ical.**

live[1] v exist; dwell; subsist; pass one's life; n **living 1** way of life **2** livelihood; maintenance **3** church benefice; idm **live it up** have a good time; phr vs **live down** bring people to forget (one's errors, misdemeanours etc); **live together** live as if married; **live up to** be worthy of; a **living 2** carrying electric current .

live[2] a having life; vital; flaming, glowing; n **l.wire 1** wire carrying electric current **2** coll lively person **3** not pre-recorded; n **l.broadcasting;** a **lively** (n **-iness**); v **liven (up)** make more lively.

livelong a lasting throughout the day.

liver n organ secreting bile; a **liverish 1** of liver **2** irritable;

touchy n **-ness.**

livery n **1** distinctive uniform of City Company, or servants of one employer **2** food-allowance for horses; n **l.company** City of London Company; **liveryman** member of City Company; **l.stable** one where horses are boarded, or hired out.

lives pl of **life.**

livestock n farm animals.

livid a of bluish pale colour, as by bruising; sl very angry.

living a **1** alive **2** active; in use (eg **l.language**); ns **l.death** terrifying experience; **l.memory** period recalled by oldest person alive; **l.room** main room of house; n **1** livelihood **2** way of life **3** position of clergyman; his income.

lizard n four-footed reptile.

llama n woolly S American ruminant.

load n that which is carried; burden; elec amount of energy drawn from source; v place burden on, in; charge (gun); n **loadline** Plimsoll mark.

loadstone, lodestone n magnet; magnetic iron oxide.

loaf[1] n **1** mass of bread of definite size, weight **2** small cone of sugar; pl **loaves.**

loaf[2] v loiter; work lazily; n **loafer.**

loam n rich vegetable soil.

loan n something lent; act of lending; money lent; v lend.

loath, loth a unwilling;

v **loathe** detest; abhor; *n* **loathing** great disgust, repulsion; *a* **loathsome** disgusting, revolting.

loaves *pl* of **loaf**.

lob *n* high-pitched underhand ball in cricket; high ball in tennis; *v* **lobs, lobbing, lobbed.** bowl, hit shot thus.

lobby *n* 1 hall; anteroom 2 room in House of Commons were MPs and public meet 3 corridor where MPs vote; *v* **lobbies, lobbying, lobbied.** try to influence MPs (to favour particular group, interests etc); *n* **-ing** frequent lobby for such purpose; *n* **lobbyist.**

lobe *n* soft pendulous lower part of ear; rounded projecting part of liver, etc; *a* **lobed.**

lobelia *n* herbaceous plant.

lobotomy *n med* operation to remove brain tissue.

lobster *n* large edible marine crustacean.

lobworm *n* large worm used as fish bait.

local *a* of, in, confined to particular place, region, part of body; *n* 1 person belonging to district 2 *sl* public house; *ns* **locale** scene of event; **locality** position, district; *v* **localize** restrict to particular area; give local character to.

locate *v* discover, set in, particular place or position; *n* **location** position; outdoor set where scenes for film are shot.

loch *n* Scottish lake or arm of sea.

lock[1] *n* tress of hair; tuft of wool.

lock[2] *n* 1 device for closing door, safe etc, operated by key, combination 2 mechanism for firing gun 3 blockage 4 enclosure on river, canal in which boats can be moved from one level to another; *idm* **lock, stock and barrel** altogether; *v* 1 close with a lock 2 become fixed, immobile; *phr vs* **lock onto** (of missile) locate and pursue automatically; *n* **locker lockable** cupboard (*n* **l.room** *US* changing room); *ns* **lockjaw** tetanus; **locknut** nut which prevents another from being unscrewed easily; **locksmith** maker, repairer of locks; **lock up** 1 prison 2 private garage.

locket *n* small metal case for photograph etc, worn as ornament.

loco[1] *n coll* locomotive.

loco[2] *a sl* crazy.

locomotive *a* having power of moving from place to place; *n* steam, diesel, electric engine moving by its own power; *n* **locomotion** action, power of moving.

locum (tenens) *n Lat* one acting temporarily as deputy, *esp* of doctor or priest.

locus *n* 1 exact place 2 *math* line tracing path of point through space.

locust *n* destructive winged

insect; *n* **l.tree** carob tree; **l.bean** its fruit.

locution *n* mode, style of speech; phrase.

lode *n* vein of metal ore; **lodestone** see **loadstone**.

lodge *n* 1 gate-keeper's house 2 local branch, meeting place of Freemasons *v* 1 house 2 deposit 3 be embedded 4 lay (accusation, charge against) 5 occupy lodgings; *ns* **lodging** (s) room(s) let to lodger; **lodger** one who pays rent for part of another's house; **lodg(e)ment** lodging place; *mil* stable position gained by effort.

loft *n* attic; room over stable; gallery in church; *v* hit golf ball high; *a* **lofty** of great height; *fig* noble; sublime; haughty; *adv* **-ily.**

log *n* 1 unhewn piece of timber 2 apparatus for measuring ship's speed 3 daily record of ship's voyage, aircraft flight etc; 4 *abbr* logarithm; *v* **logs, logging, logged.** cut into logs; enter in log-book; *phr v* **log off/out** *comput* finish on-line operation; *ns* **logging** felling, sawing, transporting logs to river; **logger; log-book** daily record of journey **logjam** 1 immovable mass of floating logs 2 *fig* standstill in operations.

loganberry *n* hybrid fruit, cross between blackberry and raspberry.

logarithm *n* exponent of power to which invariable number must be raised to produce given number, tabulated for use in calculation.

loggerhead n blockhead; *idm* **at loggerheads** quarrelsome.

logic n art of reasoning; *a* **-al** of logic; consistent; rational; *n* **logician**.

logistics n *pl* 1 science of moving and supplying troops 2 skill in manoeuvring.

logo n **-os.** design used in emblem for an organization.

loin n (meat from) part of body between ribs and hip; *pl* **-s** dated (part of body containing) sexual organs; *n* **loincloth** cloth worn to cover this part.

loiter v linger; loaf; delay; *n* **loiterer**.

loll v 1 sit, lie lazily 2 hang out tongue.

lollipop n 1 boiled sweet on a stick 2 short piece of popular classical music; *ns* **l.lady, l.man** coll person controlling traffic to allow school-children to cross road in safety.

lollop v Brit coll walk or run in a jerky, clumsy way.

lolly n Brit 1 coll lollipop sweet or water-ice on a stick 2 sl money.

lone a solitary; isolated; *a* **-ly** feel conscious of solitude; unfrequented; *n* **-liness**; *a* **-some**.

loner n coll person who does not mix well with other people or who prefers to be

alone.

long a having length; protracted; (of series, list etc) having many items; *ns* **longhand** written script, not typed (also adv); **l.johns** (US underpants; **l.jump** (US broad jump); athletic jumping contest; **longshoreman** US docker; **l.shot** risky attempt; **l.wave** radio using range over 1000m; *adv* for a long time; *idm* **as/so long as** provided that; **no l.-onger** no more; *as* **l.-drawn-out** lengthy; tedious; **l.-life** usable for longer than normal (*n* **l.milk**); **l.-range** 1 (of forecast) looking far ahead 2 able to reach far away; **l.-sighted; l.-standing** existing for a long time already; **l.-suffering** enduring patiently; **l.term** lasting for a long time; **long-time** (**l.companion/friend**) coll homosexual partner; **longwinded** needlessly wordy and boring.

long v desire earnestly; *phr v* **long for** want very much; *n* **longing** strong desire; *a* showing such desire; *adv* **-ly**; yearning; desire.

longevity n long life.

longitude n distance in degrees, E or W from given meridian; *a* **-tudinal** of longitude; lengthwise.

long shot n 1 horse, team etc, with little chance of winning a contest 2 undertaking with little

chance of success.

loo n Brit coll lavatory.

loofah n fibrous part of tropical gourd, used as sponge.

look v 1 use eyes 2 seem to be 3 gaze, stare; *idm* **look as if** seem likely that (also coll **look like**); *phr vs* **look after** take care of; **look down on** despise; **look forward to; look into** investigate; **look out** 1 beware 2 search and find among one's belongings; *n* **look-out** 1 prospect 2 sentry 3 (bad) luck; **look to** rely on; **look up** 1 raise one's eyes 2 find and visit 3 find by consulting book; **look up to** admire; *n* 1 act of looking; glance 2 facial expression 3 appearance; *pl* **-s** person's appearance; attractiveness; *ns* **l.-alike** one of almost identical appearance; **looker** coll attractive female; **l.-in** chance to participate; **looking-glass** mirror.

loom¹ n weaving machine.

loom² v emerge indistinctly; *fig* appear important and menacing.

loon n 1 lout; fool 2 guillemot.

loop n 1 bend in cord, string etc, made by crossing ends 2 noose 3 railway line branching from main line and rejoining it farther on; *v* form loop; *n* **l. the l.** aerial manoeuvre by which aircraft describes complete vertical circle.

loophole n vertical slit in castle wall *fig* means of

evasion, or escape.

loose *a* 1 not tied; free from control 2 detached; unattached 3 not constricting; slack 4 vague 5 not compact 6 dissolute; of lax morals 7 having diarrhoea; *idm* **at a loose end** with nothing to do; *idm* **tie up the loose ends** complete the last little details; *a* **l.-leaf** having separate sheets of paper (**l.-leaf binder**); *adv* **-ly** (*n* **-ness**); *v* **loosen** (*n* **-ing**).

loot *n*, *v* plunder.

lop[1] *v* **lops, lopping, lopped.** trim, shorten by chopping (branches etc.).

lop[2] *v* hang limply; *n* **lop-ear** drooping ear; *a* **lop-sided** unevenly balanced.

lope *v* run with long, easy, bounding pace.

loquacious *a* talkative; *n* **loquacity.**

lord *n* 1 ruler; governor; master; owner 2 any peer of realm 3 the **L.** God; *idm* **lord it over** dominate; *a* **lordly** magnificent; haughty; *ns* **lordliness, lordship** power of lord; domain; title of peers.

lore *n* knowledge of special kind, often derived from tradition.

lorgnette *n* Fr eyeglasses on handle, opera-glass.

lorry *n* large, heavy, open wagon or truck used for road transport.

lose *v* losing, lost. 1 suffer loss

2 get rid of 3 fail to retain, find 4 be bereaved of 5 be defeated; *phr v* **lose out** be at a disadvantage; *n* **loser** *a* **losing** (*n* **l.battle** struggle one has no chance of winning; **l.streak** sequence of bad luck); *n* **loss** 1 act, result of losing 2 bereavement; *idm* **at a loss** (for words) unable to think of anything to do or say; *ns* **l.adjuster** employee of insurance company who assesses compensation due; **l.leader** *comm* article sold cheaply to encourage sale of other goods.

lost *pt*, *pp* of **lose**; *n* **l.cause** campaign doomed to failure; **l.property.**

lot 1 quantity 2 fate 3 item of auction; *idm* **a lot** a large quantity; *idm* **one's lot** 1 one's fate 2 *coll* all one is entitled to; *idm* **the lot** all; *idm* **lots of** a large quantity or number of; *idm* **cast/draw lots** decide fate or fortune by chance fall of die or similar marked object.

loth *a* reluctant.

lotion *n* liquid for keeping skin, hair clean, healthy.

lottery *n* gamble; competition in which prizes are allotted by chance drawing of tickets.

lotto *n* game of chance, played as bingo.

lotus *n* a kind of water lily.

loud *a* 1 producing much sound; noisy 2 boisterous; vulgar; *ns* **l.hailer** portable

device to make one's voice audible at a distance; **loudmouth** *coll* person who talks too much and without tact; **loudspeaker** equipment which amplifies volume of sound on radio or recording system; *advs* **loud, aloud, loudly** *n* **-ness**

lough *n* Irish loch.

lounge *v* recline lazily; be idle; *n* room with comfortable seats for guests in home or hotel; *ns* **l.bar** Brit more comfortable bar than public bar; **l.suit** Brit business suit with matching jacket and trousers; *n* **lounger** idler, loafer.

lour, lower *v* scowl; glare sullenly; *fig* grow dark (sky, clouds etc.).

louse *n* parasitic insect; *pl* **lice**; *a* **lousy** having lice; *sl* unpleasant; bad; *idm* **lousy with** *coll* full of; having plenty of.

lout *n* clumsy, mannerless fellow; *a* **loutish.**

louver, louvre *n* window frame with inclined boards or slats for admitting air, without rain; ventilating structure resembling this.

lovable = loveable.

love *n* 1 affection 2 charity 3 devotion 4 sexual passion 5 sweetheart 6 *tennis* no score; *idm* **make love (to)** 1 caress in an erotic way; have sex with (*n* **l.-making**) 2 (formerly) woo with words; *ns* **l.affair; l.bird** 1 small green parrot (*pl* **-s** *coll* loving couple); **l.child** child of unwedded parents; **l.match** marriage of people in love; *v* 1 be fond of; delight in 2 desire passionately, sexually 3 show deep and lasting devotion to; **lover** 1 sexual partner 2 **lover of** enthusiast for; *as* **lov(e)-able** (*adv* **-ably** *n* **-ability -ableness**) **lovely** (*n* **-iness**); **lovesick** hopelessly in love; *a,* **loving** (*n* **l.cup** wine-cup passed round and shared at banquet).

low[1] *a* 1 not high or tall 2 not intense 3 humble 4 not loud 5 vulgar; mean; sordid 6 depressed 7 inferior in order of merit or importance; *idm* **keep a low profile** contrive not to be conspicuous; *n* 1 low point 2 depression; *n, a* **L.Church** evangelical (church); *ns* **lowdown** *sl* vital information; **lowlands; l. season** less busy part of year; **l.-start mortgage** mortgage with smaller repayments in the first few years; *as* **lowbrow** simple not developed intellectually or aesthetically (*n* such a person); **l.-down** *coll* mean; **l.-key** subdued; **l.-rise; l.-spirited;** *a* **lower** 1 less high 2 inferior (*a* **l.-case** not in capitals; *n* **l.class,** *a* **l.-class**) *v* 1 make less high 2 bring down 3 reduce; *idm* **lower oneself** humble or disgrace oneself; *a* **lowly** *n* **-iness**.

low[2] *n* cry of a cow; *v* utter a sound.

lower *v* be, look threatening (*also* **lour**).

loyal *a* faithful to Crown, cause, person etc; upright; honourable; *ns* **loyalty, loyalist.**

lozenge *n* 1 diamond-shaped figure; rhombus 2 small flat medicinal tablet.

LP *abbr* long-playing record.

L-plate *n* display disc for learner driver.

LSD *abbr* lysergic acid diethylamide (dangerous hallucinatory drug) (*also sl* **acid**).

Lt *abbr* lieutenant.

Ltd *abbr* limited.

lubricate *n* make slippery, smooth with oil, grease; *ns* **lubrication, lubricant** 1 substance used to reduce friction 2 *sl* bribe; **lubricator, lubricity** 1 smoothness 2 *fig* lewdness.

lubricious *a fml* lascivious.

lucent *a* shining; bright; clear.

lucerne *n* clover-like plant, used as fodder.

lucid *a* clear; easy to understand; clear-headed; *ns* **lucidity, lucidness.**

luck *n* 1 fate; chance 2 good fortune; *a* **lucky** fortunate; *n* **l-dip** *Brit* tub with wrapped gifts to be chosen at random; **l.strike** piece of good luck; *adv* **luckily;** *a* **luckless.**

lucrative *a* profitable.

lucubrate *v* work hard, study, *esp* at night; *n* **lucubration** learned writing.

luddite *n* person opposed to new methods or technology.

ludicrous *a* absurd; ridiculous; comical.

ludo *n* simple game played with counters and dice.

lug[1] *n* ear-like projection used as handle; *n* **lughole** *Brit sl* ear; *v* **lugs, lugging, lugged.** pull, drag with effort.

lug[2] *n* common worm used as fish bait.

luggage *n* baggage, trunks, suitcases etc.

lugsail *n* oblong sail on oblique yard; *n* **lugger** small vessel with lugsails.

lugubrious *a* mournful woebegone; funereal.

lukewarm *a* tepid; *fig* lacking enthusiasm.

lull *v* 1 soothe; make quiet 2 subside; *n* temporary pause; *n* **lullaby** cradle-song; soothing sound.

lumbar *a* of, near loins; *n* **lumbago** rheumatic pain in loins, or lower part of spine.

lumber *v* 1 move clumsily, heavily 2 encumber; obstruct; *n* 1 useless odds and ends 2 sawn timber; *n* **-jack** man who fells and prepares timber for sawmill.

luminary *n* light-giving body, *esp* heavenly; *fig* distinguished, learned person; *n* **luminescence** light emitted at low temperature; *a* **luminous** 1 bright; glowing 2 *fig* clear; *n* **luminosity.**

lump *n* 1 shapeless mass 2 swelling bump; *idm* **lump in**

the throat choking sensation caused by strong emotion; *v* throw together in one mass; *idm* **lump it** *sl* put up with it; tolerate, endure it; *phr v* **lump together** treat as one; *n* **l.sum** single amount; *a* lumpy *n* -iness.

lunar *a* of, relating to moon.

lunatic *a* insane; *n* insane person; *n* **l.fringe** members of (*esp* political) group with eccentric ideas; *n* **lunacy**.

lunch *n* midday meal; (*also* **luncheon** *ns* **l.meat** cooked preserved meat *usu* served cold; **l.voucher** *Brit* ticket of certain value exchangeable for a meal (*US* **meal ticket**); *v* have lunch.

lung *n* respiratory organ in vertebrates.

lunge *n* sudden thrust, blow made with weapon; sudden movement of body; plunge; *v* make lunge.

lupin *n* garden plant with long spikes of flowers.

lupine *a* like a wolf.

lupus *n* tuberculous skin disease.

lurch *v* pitch, roll to one side; *n* sudden stagger; *idm* **leave in the lurch** leave in difficulties.

lurcher *n* dog, cross between collie and greyhound.

lure *n* bait used to recall hawk; decoy; *fig* anything which entices; *v* recall (hawk); attract.

lurid *a* **1** ghastly; sensational; crude, **2** glaring.

lurk *v* remain hidden; lie in wait.

luscious *a* delicious; excessively sweet.

lush *a* (*of grass etc*) juicy; luxuriant.

lust *n* sexual appetite; *idm* **lust for** feel excessive desire for; *as* **lustful, lusty** vigorous, powerful.

lustration *n* purificatory, expiatory ceremony.

lustre *n* **1** gloss; sheen **2** *fig* renown; glory; *a* **lustrous** shining, luminous.

lute *n* stringed musical instrument; *n* **lutanist**.

luxury *n* **1** state, mode of life of great ease and comfort **2** expensive but unnecessary thing; or *a* **luxurious** extravagant; sumptuous; *v* **luxuriate** indulge in luxury; revel in; grow profusely; *a* **luxuriant** abundant; exuberant (*n* -ance).

lyceum *n* building with lecture-halls, library etc.

lychee *n* Asiatic fruit with sweet white flesh (*also* **litchi**).

lychgate *n* gate with roof.

Lycra [*TM*] stretch material used for making tight-fitting clothes.

lying *v pr p of* **lie**[1], **lie**[2].

lying-in *n* confinement to bed for childbirth.

lymph *n* colourless fluid found in lymphatic vessels; fluid exuding from inflamed tissues; *n pl* vessels in body conveying lymph; *a* **lymphatic** of lymph; *fig*

sluggish.

lynch *v* put to death, by mob violence, without trial; *n* **l.law** rapid, summary justice.

lynx *n* fierce wildcat with short tail and tufted ears; *a* **l.eyed** keen sighted.

lyre *n* old form of harp.

lyric *n* **1** words for song **2** short emotional poem; *a* **lyric(al)** of poems expressing emotion *adv* -**ly**, *n* -**ism**.

MA *abbr* Master of Arts.

ma'am *polite form of address to a woman* (=madam).

mac *n Brit coll* mackintosh.

macabre *a* gruesome; terrible.

macadam *n* broken stone for road surfacing; *v* pave road with this.

macaroni *n* tubular form of Italian wheat pasta.

macaroon *n* small sweet cake or biscuit made of ground almonds.

macaw *n* kind of parrot.

mace[1] *n* staff of office, *esp* of mayors etc.

mace[2] *n* spice made of dried outer layer of nutmeg.

macerate *v* soften by soaking; become thin through fasting.

Mach *n* ratio of speed of aircraft etc to speed of sound.

machete *n Sp* large, heavy chopping knife.

machine *n* 1 apparatus, contrivance that applies power to perform work, or direct movement 2 organized system to carry out specific functions; *v* print, sew with machine; *ns* **m.code** *comput* binary code in which data are recorded; **m.-gun** gun firing bullets in continuous succession; **m.tool** tool which cuts, shapes: *as* **m.-made; m.-readable** that can be read by a computer; *ns* **machinery** parts of machine; system of machines; **machinist** person who makes, operates machines.

macho *a coll* exaggeratedly masculine; *n* **machismo** quality of being this.

mackerel *n* type of edible sea-fish.

mackintosh *n* rubber-coated cloth; waterproof coat made of this.

macramé *n Fr* craft-work from knotted string.

macro- *prefix* 1 long 2 large-scale.

macrobiotics *n* science of growing crops with organic fertilizers; *a* **-otic.**

macrocosm *n* the great world, the universe.

mad *a* 1 insane; irrational 2 angry 3 wildly excited 4 (*of dog*) suffering from rabies; *idm* **mad about** *coll* enthusiastic about; *ns* **madman, madness** insanity; excitement; **madcap** rash person; *v* **madden** drive mad; infuriate.

mad cow disease *n* informal name for BSE.

madam *n* formal mode of addressing women.

Madeira *n* 1 fortified dessert wine 2 plain type of cake.

Mademoiselle *n* form of address to young unmarried French woman.

Madonna *n* Virgin Mary; picture, statue of her; **M.lily** large-flowered white lily.

madrigal *n* type of part song for three or more voices.

maestro *n* eminent composer, musician or conductor.

Mafia *n* Sicilian secret criminal organization.

magazine *n* 1 store-house for ammunition, weapons etc 2 periodical containing articles, stories etc by different authors 3 cartridge chamber of repeating rifle.

magenta *n* purplish-red aniline dye; *a* of this colour.

maggot *n* grub, larva *esp* of

blow-fly; *a* **maggoty**.

magic *n* feigned superhuman control over natural forces and objects; sorcery 2 unexplained mysterious influence 3 conjuring; *n* **m.eye** photoelectric cell; *a* **-al**; *adv* **-ally**; *n* **magician** conjuror; wizard; *a* **magical**; *n* **magician** one skilled in magic; wizard; conjuror.

magistrate *n* civil official administering law; *a* **magisterial** of, pertaining to magistrates.

magma *n* molten rock below earth's crust.

magnanimous *a* of generous, noble character; incapable of pettiness, resentment; *n* **magnanimity**.

magnate *n* prominent, influential man, *esp* in finance, industry.

magnesium *n* metallic element; *n* **magnesia** alkaline compound of this used in medicine.

magnet *n* 1 piece of iron with property of attracting other iron objects 2 person or thing with the power to attract others; *a* **magnetic** (**m.field** area influenced by magnetic force; **m.north** Northern pole of axis round which Earth rotates; **m.tape** tape coated with iron oxide for audio or video recording) *adv* **-ically**; *n* **magnetism**; *v* **magnetize** *n* **magneto** small dynamo with magnet, *esp* one producing ignition spark in internal combustion

engine.

magnificent *a* splendid; of surpassing beauty, quality, generosity; *n* **-ficence**.

magnify *v* **magnifies, magnifying, magnified.** cause to appear larger, as with lens; exaggerate; *ns* **magnification; magnifying glass.**

magniloquent *a* speaking pompously; grandiose; *n* **-quence**.

magnitude *n* size; greatness; extent.

magnolia *n* flowering tree.

magnum *n* *Lat* two-quart bottle.

magpie *n* black and white bird of crow family.

magus *n* 1 Persian priest 2 magician 3 *cap* *pl* **Magi** three wise men bringing gifts to the baby Jesus.

Magyar *n* dominant race in Hungary; their language.

mahatma *n* Indian spiritual adept; one endowed with wisdom and power.

mahogany *n* reddish-brown, fine-grained, hard wood.

maid *n* 1 *dated* young, unmarried woman 2 female servant.

maiden *n* *lit* young unmarried woman; *n* **m. of honour** 1 chief bridesmaid 2 small tart with almond filling; *a* 1 virginal 2 unused 3 done or experienced for first time 4 *cricket* (of over) in which no runs are scored; *ns* **maidenhead** virginity; **maidenhood;** *a* **maidenly**

modest.

mail[1] *n* armour of interlaced metal rings or plates; *a* **mailed** wearing such armour.

mail[2] *n* postal system; letters conveyed at one time; *v* send by post; **mail order** order for goods sent by post.

mailshot *n* single mailing of publicity material to many potential customers at one time.

maim *v* cripple; mutilate.

main *a* chief; most important; leading; *n* 1 principal pipe or cable in water, sewage, electricity, or gas system; *idm* (**an eye to) the main chance** (thoughts of) making a profit; *idm* **in the main** mostly; *pl* **mains** source of water, gas, electricity (**m.adaptor** adaptor for certain electrical appliances; **m.supply**); *ns* **mainframe** large computer; **mainland** mass of land not including nearby islands (*also a*); **mainspring** 1 principal spring of watch or clock 2 main motive for action; **mainstay** chief form of support; **mainstream** dominant tendency (**m.jazz**); *vs* **mainline** inject (drug) into vein.

maintain *v* 1 cause to continue 2 keep in good condition 3 support with money 4 assert; *a* **-able**; *n* **maintenance** 1 keeping in good condition 2 payment made by absent partner, husband to support family.

maisonette n Fr small house; part of house used as flat.

maize n cereal plant.

majesty n 1 sovereignty; dignity 2 title of sovereign; a **-stic** stately, dignified.

major a 1 greater 2 more important 3 elder; n 1 person of full age 2 army rank above captain; ns **m.general** army officer above rank of brigadier; **majorette** girl in uniform marching or dancing with band; **majority** 1 greater number 2 number of votes by which one party leads in election 3 full age; **major-domo** chief steward of household.

make v makes, making, made. 1 construct; create; produce 2 prepare for use 3 earn; win 4 constitute 5 reach; attain 6 appoint 7 compel 8 estimate; calculate 9 add up to 10 complete; idm **make do** manage; idm **make good** 1 replace 2 be successful; idm **make or break** lead to complete success or total failure; phr vs **make after** pursue; **make away/off with** steal; **make out** 1 distinguish; understand 2 claim; pretend 3 write (cheque) 4 fare; **make over** 1 transfer ownership 2 convert; **make up** 1 assemble 2 compose; invent 3 apply cosmetics 4 make complete 5 be reconciled; ns **m.-believe** imagining; pretending (also a

imaginary); **m.-up** 1 cosmetics 2 combination a **m.-shift** improvised (for temporary use).

malachite n green mineral.

maladjusted a unable to adapt to demands of life or other people.

maladroit a clumsy.

malady n **-ies.** illness, esp of the mind or spirit.

malaise n Fr slight physical discomfort.

malapropism n ridiculous misuse of word.

malaria n fever transmitted by mosquito-bite.

malcontent a discontented person.

male a belonging to sex which begets offspring; ns **male chauvinism** assumption by man that he is superior to women; **m. chauvinist (pig)** such a man (also MCP); n male person or animal.

malediction n curse.

malefactor n evil-doer.

malevolence a ill-will.

malformation n deformity.

malfunction v fail to work properly; n such a failure.

malice n ill-will; spite.

malicious a spiteful.

malice n desire to hurt others; a **malicious**; adv **-ly**; n **-ness**.

malign v defame; speak evil of; a **malignant** 1 filled with ill-will 2 (of disease) likely to prove fatal; ns **malignancy**, **malignity** spite, malice.

malinger v feign illness to escape duty, work etc; n **malingerer**.

mall n, esp US street or covered area with shops.

mallard n common wild duck.

malleable a 1 capable of being hammered, pressed into shape 2 amenable; n **-ability**.

mallet n wooden-headed hammer; polo-stick; croquet-mallet.

malnourished a suffering from results of poor diet; n **-nutrition**.

malpractice n wrong-doing.

malt n dried fermented barley or other grain used in brewing; n **maltster** maker of malt.

maltreat v treat with cruelty; n **-ment**.

mama n, coll mother.

mammal n animal which suckles its young; a **mammary** pertaining to breast (**m.gland** milk gland).

mammoth n extinct type of elephant; a colossal.

man n 1 human being 2 adult male person 3 human race 4 piece used in chess, draughts etc 5 man-servant; (pl **men**); ns **man-eater** cannibal; animal that eats human flesh; **m. Friday** male assistant; **m. of straw** 1 Brit weak character 2 US imaginary opponent; **m.-of-war** armed sailing vessel; v **mans, manning, manned.** supply with men for defence, work etc; fortify; ns **manhole** hole giving access to drains, pipes etc; **manikin** dwarf; lay figure; **manliness**

manslaughter unlawful, unpremeditated homocide; *as* **manful** bold, resolute; **manlike, manly** virile; bold; **mannish** (of woman) like man.

manage *v* 1 conduct; handle 2 succeed in doing; *a* **manageable** docile; *ns* **management** 1 process of managing; administration 2 body of persons managing business; **manager** one who manages; one in charge of business etc; (*fem* **-ess**) *as* **managerial, managing**.

Mancunian *a, n* (person) of Manchester.

mandarin *n* 1 former Chinese high official 2 *a* form of spoken Chinese used by the court and officials 3 small sweet type of orange.

mandate *n* 1 command, commission to follow specified policy, *esp* given by electors to their representative 2 placing of small, backward country's affairs in care of major power; *n* **mandatary** holder of mandate; *as* **mandatory, mandated** entrusted to a mandate.

mandible *n* 1 jaw-bone 2 either part of bird's beak.

mandolin (**e**) *n* musical stringed instrument.

mandrill *n* large baboon with blue face and red rump.

mane *n* long hair on neck of horse, lion etc.

maneuver *n, v US =* **manoeuvre.**

manganese *n* metallic element.

manger *n* feeding-trough in stable etc.

mangetout *n* Fr type of pea with edible pod.

mangle *n* machine with rollers for pressing linen etc; *v* press in mangle.

mangle *v* mutilate, spoil, hack.

mango *n* **-os** or **-oes.** tropical fruit; tree bearing it.

manhandle *v* use physical force on.

manhole *n* hole in ground for access to sewers etc.

mania *n* 1 violent madness 2 *fig* obsession; craze; *a* **manic** 1 suffering from mania (*n* **m. depressive** person prone to sudden extreme changes of mood) 2 wildly excited; *n* **maniac** mad person (*a* **-al**).

manicure *n, v* care for hands and nails; *n* **-curist**.

manifest *a* obvious; undoubted; *v* make manifest; *n* list of cargo for Customs; *ns* **-ation, manifesto** public declaration of policy.

manifold *a* numerous; varied; *n* pipe with several outlets.

manipulate *v* 1 handle; manage skilfully 2 alter fraudulently; *ns* **-ation, -ator**; *a* **-ative**.

mankind *n* the human race.

manly *a* of man; virile.

manna *n* miraculous food of Israelites in wilderness; *fig* spiritual food; gum of Arabian tamarisk.

mannequin *n* live model employed to display clothes.

manner *n* way thing happens

or is done; custom; style; *pl* **-s** social behaviour; *n* **-ism** peculiarity of style; *a* **-ly** polite.

manoeuvre *n* 1 strategic movement of troops 2 clever move; *pl* **-s** mock warfare; *v* 1 manage with skilfulness 2 perform manoeuvres **manoeuvre** (US **maneuver**); *a* **manoeuvrable** (US **-verable**).

manor *n* feudal unit of land; estate, owner or lord of which retains ancient rights over land; *n* **m.-house** house of lord of manor; *a* **-ial**.

manpower *n* 1 people available for work 2 human labour.

manqué *a* Fr unfulfilled.

mansard *n* roof with two angles of slope.

mansion *n* large house.

manslaughter *n* crime of killing without intent.

mantel *n* structure round fireplace; *n* **mantelshelf, mantelpiece** shelf at top of mantel.

mantis *n* Gk predatory insect.

mantle *n* 1 loose cloak 2 incandescent mesh covering gas flame 3 *geol* part of Earth below crust; *v* cover.

mantra *n* sacred word (in Hinduism, Buddhism).

manual *a* of, done with hands; *n* 1 handbook 2 organ keyboard.

manufacture *n* process of making articles, goods etc; *v* produce goods, *esp* in large quantities; *fig* fabricate, concoct (story etc); n **manufacturer** owner of factory; person, company making goods.

manure n dung, compost used to fertilize land; v apply manure to (land).

manuscript a written by hand; n hand-written document; draft of book etc for printing.

Manx a of Isle of Man; n language of Isle of Man; **M. cat** tailless breed of cat.

many a numerous; n large number.

Maori n New Zealand aboriginal; their language.

map n 1 plane representation of earth's surface or part of this 2 chart of heavens; v **maps, mapping, mapped.** make map.

maple n tree of sycamore family; its wood.

mar v spoil; ruin.

marabou n large African stork.

maraca n Latin American instrument of shell filled with seeds to make rattling sound.

marathon n long-distance race; fig endurance competition.

marauder n roving thief; raider; v **maraud.**

marble n 1 hard kind of limestone, capable of being highly polished 2 small ball used in game; pl **-s** child's game; v stain with streaks of colour.

March n third month of year.

march v walk, proceed in steady rhythmic step, esp in military formation; n 1 act of marching 2 distance covered 3 music to accompany march; idm **give sb his/her marching orders** dismiss sb.

marchioness n wife or widow of marquis.

Mardi Gras n Shrove Tuesday (day before start of Lent); carnival on this day.

mare n female horse; **mares' tails** wispy cirrus clouds.

margarine n manufactured butter substitute.

margin n 1 edge; limit 2 extra amount beyond what is necessary 3 space round printed page; a **marginal** 1 of relatively slight importance 2 a, n polit (seat) capable of being won easily by another candidate at election; adv **marginally** by a small amount; v **marginalize** push aside, away from focus of attention (n **-ization**).

marigold n plant with yellow-orange flowers.

marijuana, marihuana n leaves of the hemp plant smoked as a drug.

marina n harbour for pleasure boats.

marinade n sauce for soaking meat, fish before cooking; meat, fish, treated this way; v soak in this way (also **marinate**).

marine a of, connected with sea or shipping; n soldier serving on warship; n **mariner** seaman, sailor.

marionette n Fr puppet moved on strings.

marital a of, pertaining to husband, marriage.

maritime a 1 connected with, situated near sea 2 having a navy, seacoast or sea-trade.

marjoram n aromatic herb.

mark[1] n 1 visible sign; symbol 2 target 3 spot; idm **make one's mark** become famous; idm **over-step the mark** behave in an unacceptable way; idm **up to the mark** fit; well; idm **wide of the mark** inaccurate; v 1 make mark 2 assign marks to (examination paper etc) 3 observe; idm **mark time** 1 not move forward 2 wait for sth to happen; idm **mark you** coll all the same; phr vs **mark down/up** reduce/increase the marks of, the price of; a **marked** clear; emphatic (adv **-ly**); ns **marker** 1 person or thing that marks 2 one who marks a score; **marking; marksman** sharpshooter.

market n 1 public gathering place for buying and selling 2 demand for goods; idm **come into the market** be offered for sale; idm **in the market for** interested in buying; idm **play the market** buy and sell stocks and shares for profit; ns **m. forces** operation of trade without government intervention; **m. garden** Brit farm where vegetables or fruit are grown for sale to markets (ns **-er -ing**); **m.-place 1** area where market is set up **2** trading activities; **m. research** survey of consumer needs and behaviour; **m. value** price that can be asked at given time; v buy, sell in, take to market; a **-able** saleable; (n **-ability**).

mark-up n proportion of increase from wholesale to retail price.

marl n limy clay soil used as fertilizer.

marline n two-ply cord; **m. spike** pointed hook for separating strands of rope to be spliced.

marmalade n jam usually made of oranges etc.

marmoset n small, bushy-tailed monkey.

maroon a brownish-crimson; n loudly detonating firework; v abandon on desert island etc; fig desert.

marquee n Fr large tent, esp one used at fêtes etc.

marquetry n inlaid wood-work.

marquis, marquess n title of nobleman between duke and earl.

marrow n **1** soft fatty substance inside bones **2** edible gourd; **marrowfat** large green pea.

marry v **marries, marrying, married. 1** take as husband or wife **2** join in marriage; n **marriage 1** state of being married n fig close union; a **marriageable.**

marsh n low-lying water-logged land; n **m. -mallow 1** marsh plant **2** sweetmeat formerly made from its root; a **marshy.**

marshal n official of royal household etc who directs ceremonies; v **marshals, marshalling, marshalled. 1** arrange in position **2** lead with ceremony; n **marshalling yard** railway yard where goods trucks are sorted into trains.

marsupial n animal which carries young in pouch, as kangaroo etc; a pertaining to pouch.

mart n **1** trading-centre **2** auction room.

marten n weasel-like animal, valued for its fur.

martial a suitable for, pertaining to war; warlike ns **m. art** fighting sport (eg judo, karate) (usu pl); **m. law** imposition of military rule (in temporary crisis).

Martian a, n (supposed inhabitant) of Mars.

martin n species of swallow; **martlet** martin; her bird without feet.

martinet n strict, pedantic disciplinarian.

Martini [TM] mixture of gin and vermouth.

martyr n **1** one who dies rather than give up faith **2** fig sufferer (from pain etc); n **martyrdom** suffering or death of martyr.

marvel n something wonderful, amazing; v

wonder; be surprised; a **marvellous** wonderful.

Marxism n theories of Karl Marx, basis for Communism; a, n **-ist.**

marzipan n paste made of ground almonds, sugar etc.

mascara n cosmetic for colouring eyelashes.

masculine a **1** relating to males **2** strong; vigorous **3** of gender denoting males; ns **-linity.**

maser n amplifier of radar and radio astronomy signals.

mash n soft pulpy mass, warm food given to animals; v beat, crush into soft pulp.

mask n covering for face; v **1** cover with mask **2** fig conceal; dissemble n **masking tape** sticky tape used by painter to cover areas not to be painted.

masochism n sexual perversion where pleasure is found in suffering physical pain and humiliation; n **masochist.**

mason n **1** stone worker **2** Freemason; a **masonic** of Freemasonry; n **masonry 1** trade of mason **2** stone-work **3** Freemasonry.

masque n verse drama with dance, music etc; n **masquerade** masked ball; v be disguised; fig assume character of.

Mass n celebration of Eucharist, esp in RC church.

mass n **1** quantity of matter in one body, lump **2** large amount, number; pl **the masses** common people; idm

masses of *coll* lots; *ns* **m. communications; m. media** way of conveying facts, ideas to wide public (*eg* TV, radio, newspapers); **m. meeting** meeting with very large audience; *v* **m. produce** produce in bulk (*n* **m. production**); *a* **massive** enormous (*adv* **-ly** *n* **-ness**).

massacre *v* slaughter indiscriminately; *n* killing of helpless persons.

massage *n* remedial treatment consisting of rubbing and kneading affected part; *v* 1 treat with massage 2 *polit* alter (figures etc) to give false impression; *n* **masseur** one who practices massage; *fem* **masseuse**.

massif *n Fr* group of mountains forming unit.

mast[1] *n* 1 pole to support ship's rigging etc 2 flagpole.

mast[2] *n* fruit of beech, oak, chestnut etc.

mastectomy *n* **-ies.** surgical removal of the breast.

master *n* 1 person having authority; head of household 2 owner 3 employer 4 captain of merchantman 5 teacher 6 expert; *ns* **m. key** key to open many different locks; **m. of ceremonies** person making announcements and introductions at big social occasion; *v* 1 overcome 2 acquire knowledge of, skill in; *as* **-ful** imperious; **masterly** showing great talent, skill; **mastermind**

clever person, *v* plan and ensure success of (difficult operation); *n* **mastery** authority; supremacy.

masticate *v* chew with teeth; *n* **-ation.**

mastiff *n* large, thickset kind of dog.

mastitis *n* inflammation of breast.

masturbate *v* stimulate one's own genital organs; *n* **-ation.**

mat *n* 1 piece of plaited straw or coconut fibre etc for wiping feet on, or covering part of floor 2 small rug 3 tangled hair; *v* **mats, matting, matted.** become tangled; *idm* **on the mat** *coll* reprimanded.

mat, matt *a* having dull surface.

matador *n Sp* man who kills bull in bull-fight.

match[1] *n* 1 thing exactly like another; person equal to another in quality, power etc 2 contest of skill, strength etc 3 marriage; eligible person; *v* 1 be equal to in contest 2 pit against in fight etc 3 marry 4 correspond; *a* **-less** peerless; unequalled; *n* **-maker** one who schemes to bring about marriages.

match[2] *n* 1 small strip of wood, tipped with combustible material 2 fuse for firing gun; *ns* **-wood** small splinters; **-box.**

mate[1] *n, v* checkmate (in chess).

mate[2] *n* 1 comrade 2 husband; wife 3 (*of animals etc*) one of

pair 4 officer in merchant ship; *v* marry; pair *esp* animals; *a* **matey** *sl* friendly.

material *n* stuff of which thing is made; fabric; cloth; *a* of matter or body; essential; important; *ns* **-ism** theory that matter is the only reality; **-ist** one engrossed in material interests; *a* **-istic**; *v* **materialize** make material; (of spirits etc) assume bodily form (*n* **-ization**); *adv* **materially** in relevant way; essentially.

maternity *n* motherhood; *a* **maternal** related through mother; motherly.

Mates [TM] type of condom.

mathematics *n pl* abstract science concerned with properties of and relations between quantities; *a* **-tical**; *n* **mathematician.**

matinée *n Fr* afternoon theatrical or musical performance; *n pl* **matins** morning service of C of E.

matriarch *n* mother as head of family or household; *n* **-archy** social system where descent is traced through female line.

matri- *prefix* (of) mother.

matricide *n* act of killing one's own mother.

matriculate *v* 1 register as student in university or college 2 pass necessary examination; *n* **-ation** act of matriculating.

matrimony *n* marriage; *a* **-monial.**

matrix *n* mould in which type

is cast; rock etc in which gems, stones etc are embedded; (*pl* **matrices**).

matron *n* 1 woman in charge of nursing and domestic staff of hospital 2 house-keeper, domestic superintendent in institution or boarding-school; 3 *lit* married woman *a* **-ly** dignified; plump.

matter *n* 1 substance of which physical object is made 2 subject of book, discussion etc. 3 affair; reason 4 pus 5 cause of complaint, trouble; *idm* **a matter of course** taken for granted; *v* 1 signify 2 discharge pus.

matting *n* floor covering of mat.

mattress *n* large cushion placed on bed, above springs and below bedclothes; similar padding with extra wires built into it.

mature *a* 1 ripe; fully developed 2 prudent; wise; *v* 1 ripen 2 complete 3 (of insurance policy etc) become due for payment; *n* **maturity**.

matutinal *a* pertaining to early morning.

maudlin *a* tearfully sentimental; self-pitying.

maul *v* beat lacerate; handle roughly.

maunder *v* talk or move aimlessly.

maundy *n* 1 ceremonial foot-washing and distribution of alms to poor people 2 royal alms given on Maundy Thursday, before Easter.

mauve *n* pale lilac, violet colour; *a* of this colour.

maverick *n* person with unorthodox ideas.

maw *n* stomach, open jaws of animal crop of bird.

maxi- *prefix* big.

maxim *n* rule of conduct; proverb.

maximum *n* greatest size, number, degree; *a* greatest *a* **maximal**; *v* **maximum** size (*n* **-ization**).

May *n* 1 fifth month 2 hawthorn blossom; **May Day** first day of May (spring festival); *n* **mayfly** ephemeral fly; imitation used in fishing.

may *v aux* expresses permission, possibility, hope; *idm* **may as well** have/has no good reason not to; *idm* **may well** probably will; *pt* **might** (no *pp*); *advs* **maybe** possibly; **mayhap** perhaps.

mayfly *n* short-lived water insect.

mayhem *n* 1 violent disorder 2 *dated or US* crime of body, as basis for damages.

mayonnaise *n Fr* sauce of egg yolk, olive oil and vinegar.

mayor *n* chief officer of city or borough; *a* **-ral**; *ns* **-ality** office, period of office of mayor; **-ress** mayor's wife.

maypole *n* pole round which people dance on May Day.

maze *n* labyrinth; network of paths, hedges or lines.

MB *abbr* Bachelor of Medicine.

MBA *n* Master of Business

Administration; university degree in business management skills.

MC *abbr* 1 master of ceremonies 2 *Brit* Military Cross 3 *US* Member of Congress.

MCP *abbr coll* male chauvinist pig.

MD *abbr* 1 Doctor of Medicine 2 Managing Director.

ME *abbr* 1 *med* myalagic encephalomyelitis 2 Middle English.

me *pron* accusative and dative case of I.

mead *n* alcoholic drink made of fermented honey.

meadow *n* grassy field; hay-field; *n* **m.-sweet** fragrant white-flowered plant.

meagre *a* 1 thin; lean 2 scanty; inadequate 3 limited.

meal *n* coarsely ground grain; *as* **mealy, mealy-mouthed** apt to mince words.

meal *n* taking of food; repast.

mean[1] *n* average; midway between two extremes; *ns* **meantime, meanwhile** intervening time.

mean[2] *a* 1 selfish; parsimonious 2 unkind 3 inferior; mediocre 4 *sport, coll* skilful 5 *dated* humble; *idm* **no mean sth** a considerable sth; *adv* **-ly**; *n* **-ness**.

mean[3] *v* meaning, meant. 1 have in mind 2 signify 3 intend 4 have meaning; *idm* **be meant to** be supposed to; *idm* **mean business** *coll* be serious in intention; *n* **-ing** 1 sense 2 importance; significance 3 intention; *a* **meaningful** (*adv* **-ly**).

means *n pl* 1 method; way 2 agent; cause 3 money; resources; *idm* **by all means** certainly; *idm* **by means of** making use of; *idm* **by no means/not by any means** not at all; *idm* **a means to an end** a way of achieving sth important; *n* **means testing** assessing sb's eligibility for monetary allowance on basis of his/her financial situation.

measles *n* infectious disease, characterized by red rash and fever; *a* **measly** *coll* parsimonious.

measure *v* 1 find the size, amount, degree etc of sth 2 be of a certain size; *idm* **measure up (to)** show the necessary qualities (for); *n* 1 system of measuring 2 unit of measurement 3 degree; amount 4 verse rhythm; rhythmical, musical unit 5 action taken for a purpose; *idm* **for good measure** as an additional item; *idm* **get the measure of** assess sb's character or capacities; *a* **measured** 1 of certain measure 2 careful; steady; *n* **-ment**; *a* **measurable** (*adv* **-ably**).

meat *n* flesh of animals used as food; *a* **meaty** *fig* substantial.

mecca *n* 1 place that attracts people with a specific interest 2 *cap* spiritual centre of Islam, birthplace of Mohammed.

mechanic *a* of machine; *n* skilled, trained workman, *esp* one working with machinery; *pl* **-s** science of motion and force; *a* **-al** concerned with, produced by machines; *fig* acting without thinking *adv* **-ally**.

mechanism *n* machinery; *n* **mechanization** making; mechanical *esp* change from manpower to machines; *v* **mechanize**; *a* **-ized**.

med *abbr* 1 medical 2 medium 3 medieval 4 *cap* Mediterranean.

medal *a* small metal disc *usu* with inscription used to mark achievement etc.; *ns* **medallion** 1 large medal 2 round panel, ornament; **medallist** one who gains medals.

meddle *v* interfere; tamper with; *a* **-some**.

media *n pl* means of mass communication (TV, radio, the press).

mediaeval, medieval *a* of, belonging to Middle Ages; *n* **-ism** cult, spirit of Middle Ages *n* **-ist**.

median *n*, *a* middle; average; **medial** in middle.

mediate *v* intervene as peacemaker; *a* through intermediary, not direct; *ns* **-ation** reconcilement; **-ator**.

medic *n coll* doctor or medical student (*also* **medico**.)

Medicaid *n US* government assistance to finance

medical care for those on low incomes.

medical *a* of medicine; of the treatment of illness *adv* **-ly**; *n* assessment of sb's physical health by examining his/her body; *ns* **medicament** medicine; **Medicare** *n US* government provision of medical care, *esp* for old people; **medication** (provision of) drugs; *as* **medicated** containing medicinal substance(s); **medicative** of medication.

medicine *n* 1 science of preventing, treating and curing disease 2 substance taken internally to treat illness; *n* **m.-man** witch-doctor; *a* **medicinal** curative *adv* **-ly**.

mediocre *a* 1 ordinary; average; of medium quality 2 second rate.

meditate *v* contemplate; ponder; *n* **-ation** concentrated thought; solemn contemplation; *a* **-ative**.

Mediterranean *a* of the Mediterranean Sea or the land round it.

medium *n* 1 that which is between extremes 2 agency; channel 3 environment 4 intermediate substance conveying force 5 one who receives messages from spirit world; (*pl* **mediums** or **media**); *a* between two extremes.

medley *n* confused, miscellaneous assortment.

meek *a* submissive; mild; humble; *adv* **-ly** *n* **-ness.**

meet[1] *a* fitting, suitable.

meet[2] *v* meeting, met. 1 encounter; come face to face 2 assemble 3 converge 4 confront 5 satisfy; fulfil; *idm* **meet half-way** reach a compromise; *phr v* **meet with** 1 be confronted by 2 experience; *n* hunt meeting; *n* **meeting** 1 encounter 2 public assembly.

mega- *prefix* 1 very big (*eg* **megadose**) 2 million (*eg* **megaton**).

megabyte *n* *comput* 2^{20} or 1,047,576 bytes (*also* **MB**).

megalith *n* huge prehistoric stone, menhir.

megalomania *n* excessive desire for power over others; *n* **megalomaniac.**

megaphone *n* funnel-shaped device used to increase volume of sound, and carry it farther.

melancholy *n* gloom; sadness; dejection; *n* **melancholia** emotional insanity accompanied by extreme depression; *a* **melancholic.**

mélange *n* *Fr* mixture.

melanoma *n* cancerous tumour of the skin.

mêlée *n* *Fr* confused fight, skirmish.

meliorate *v* improve; *n* **melioration** amendment.

mellow *a* 1 ripe; well-matured 2 grown gentle through age, experience 3 *sl* merrily drunk; *v* make, become mellow.

melodrama *n* sensational, high-flown, sentimental play; *a* **melodramatic.**

melody *n* air, tune in music; sweet agreeable sounds; *as* **melodious** tuneful, musical; **melodic** of melody.

melon *n* edible gourd with sweet juicy flesh.

melt *v* 1 make, become liquid by heat; dissolve 2 blend 3 *fig* make, become tender; *phr vs* **melt away** disappear; **melt into** become merged with; *n* **meltdown** melting and leakage of radioactivity from core of nuclear reactor; *a* **melting** 1 becoming liquid (*ns* **m. point** temperature at which solid melts; **m. pot** place where people of many nationalities live) 2 tender; affectionate; **molten**, of, like melted metal.

member *n* 1 part, limb of human or animal body 2 single part of complex whole 3 person belonging to group, society etc; *n* **membership** 1 status as member 2 total number of members of club, society etc.

membrane *n* thin, supple tissue covering or lining part of organ or body

memento *n* **-os** or **-oes.** small item that serves as a reminder of a person, place, etc.

memo *n* *coll* memorandum.

memoir *n* *Fr* biography; *pl* **-s** personal experiences and observations of writer.

memory *n* ability to remember; recollection of past events etc; period of such recollection; *n* 1 ability to remember 2 period of recollection 3 thing remembered 4 lasting impression of dead or departed person 5 *comput* place where data are stored; *n* **memorial** thing commemorating person, event etc; *a* bringing to mind; *v* **memorize** commit to memory; *a* **memorable** noteworthy; remarkable; *ns* **memorabilia** things worth remembering; **memorandum** 1 note made to aid memory 2 informal business communication 3 summary of terms of contract etc.

men *pl of* **man.**

menace *n* threat, impending danger; *v* threaten.

menagerie *n* *Fr* collection of wild animals, *esp* travelling exhibition.

mend *v* 1 repair 2 correct; improve (in health); rectify; *idm* **mend one's ways** behave better; *idm* **on the mend** recovering from illness; *n* damaged part that has been repaired, *esp* of clothes; *ns* **-er, -ing;** *n* repaired hole, patch, darn.

mendicant *n* beggar; *a* begging; *ns* **mendicancy, mendicity.**

menial *a* 1 of household servants 2 servile; mean; *n* domestic servant.

meningitis *n* *med* inflammation of membranes of brain.

meniscus n *physics* curved surface of liquid in a tube.

menopause n time in life when menstruation ceases.

menses n *pl med* passing of blood in menstruation.

menstruation n monthly discharge from womb; v **menstruate**; a **menstrual**.

mensurable a capable of being measured; n **mensuration**.

mental a 1 of, relating to mind 2 *sl* crazy, mad; ns **m. age** measure of mental ability from the average performance of people at the age specified; n **mentality** mental quality, attitude.

menthol n substance obtained from oil of peppermint.

mention v speak of; refer to; n brief reference.

mentor n counsellor; wise, prudent adviser.

menu n *Fr* list of dishes available, or to be served.

MEP *abbr* Member of the European Parliament.

mercantile a connected with trade, commercial.

mercenary a working only for payment; eager for gain; n soldier hired by foreign country.

Mercator's projection n method of depicting the world in maps as rectangular in shape by stretching the polar regions to match the equator.

mercer n dealer in fabrics, cloth; n **mercery** his trade, goods; v **mercerize** give appearance of silk to cotton fabric, by treating with chemicals.

merchant n wholesale trader *esp* with foreign countries; ns **m. bank** bank specializing in business and industrial finance; **merchandise** wares; **merchantman** ship bearing goods for trade; **m. marine, m. navy, m. ship, m. shipping.**

mercury n 1 silvery fluid metallic element; quicksilver 2 *cap* Roman messenger god 3 *cap* planet nearest sun; a **mercurial** lively; erratic.

mercy n compassion; clemency; leniency shown to offender; **mercy** *idm* **at the mercy of** having no defence against; *as* **merciful, merciless.**

mere[1] n lake.

mere[2] a only; simple; nothing but.

merge v lose identity; absorb; fade gradually into; n **merger** absorption of smaller thing by greater; combine (*esp* of commercial interests).

meridian a *Lat/Fr* relating to noon; n 1 noon 2 line of longitude passing through poles and cutting equator at right angles 3 zenith.

meringue n *Fr* cake of stiffly beaten egg whites mixed with sugar and baked in cool oven.

merit n worth; excellence; quality deserving punishment or reward; *pl* intrinsic rightness or wrongness; v deserve; a **meritorious** praiseworthy.

meritocracy n (system of government by) people with the greatest ability; country with such a system.

mermaid n fabulous creature (half woman, half fish).

merry a joyous; lively; ns **merriment, merry-go-round** round-about with hobby horses.

mesa n *US* flat-topped hill with steep sides.

mesh n one of open spaces in net; *pl* **meshes** 1 net-work 2 *fig* snares; toils, v catch in meshes; (of gear wheels) be engaged; **in mesh** in gear.

mesmerize v fascinate; completely hold the attention.

meson n type of elementary particle with mass between electron and proton.

Mesozoic a *geol* of the period lasting from about 225 to 70 million years ago.

mess n 1 muddle; disorder 2 difficult position 3 group of persons habitually eating together, *esp* in armed forces; place for this; v 1 eat thus 2 make muddle of; *idm* **mess about/around** behave in an aimless and irresponsible manner; n **mess-room.**

message n oral or written communication sent to a person; meaning; **messenger** person who delivers a message.

Messiah n Christ; promised

deliverer of the Jews.

metabolism n process of chemical changes in living organism; a **metabolic**; v **metabolize**.

metal n 1 mineral substance that is opaque, ductile, malleable and capable of conducting heat or electricity 2 broken stone for road-surfacing; as **metallic** of metal; **metalloid** resembling metal (n substance with some properties of a metal); ns **metallurgy** science and technology of metals; a **-lurgical**; n **-lurgist**; **metalwork** skilled work in metal; product from this (n **-er**).

metamorphosis n transformation; remarkable change; pl **metamorphoses**.

metaphor n figure of speech in which word is used to denote something different from its usual meaning; a **metaphorical** figurative.

metaphysics n branch of abstruse study concerned with nature and causes of being and knowledge; a **metaphysical**.

mete v (usu mete out) allot; distribute.

meteor n shooting star; fig any bright but transient object; a **-ic** like meteor; dazzling but brief (adv **-ically**); ns **meteorite** stony or metallic mass fallen from outer space; **meteorology** science of weather; **-ologist**;

a **-ological**.

meter n mechanical device for measuring quantity, volume etc.

methane n inflammable hydrocarbon gas; marsh gas; fire-damp.

methanol n methyl alcohol.

method n mode, manner of procedure; systematic, orderly arrangement; a **-ical** orderly; adv **-ically**.

Methodism n Protestant denomination founded by John Wesley.

methodology n 1 study of methods 2 set of methods (a **-ological**).

methyl n chemical basis of wood spirit; n **methyl alcohol** poisonous alcohol found in organic substances (also **wood alcohol**).

methylated spirits n alcohol used as fuel in lamps and heaters.

meticulous a over-careful about details; punctilious.

métier n Fr profession 1 occupation 2 one's line of experience.

metre n poetical rhythm; group of metrical feet; unit of length in metric system; as **metrical** of measurement of poetic metre; **metric** measuring by metres.

metronome n mus mechanical device for beating time.

metropolis n capital, chief city of country.

metropolitan a of metropolis; n bishop having authority over other bishops of

province.

mew[1] n cry of cat, gull; v utter this cry.

mew[2] v (of hawk) moult; v put (hawk) into cage; fig confine, as in cage; n pl **mews** stables, originally place where falcons were kept.

mezzanine n low storey between two higher ones.

mezzo adv mus moderately; n coll mezzo-soprano; n **m.-soprano** 1 voice between soprano and contralto 2 singer with such a voice; musical part for this.

mezzotint n (print made by) method using metal plate with smooth and rough areas to give light and shade respectively.

mg abbr milligram.

MHR abbr Member of the House of Representatives.

MHZ abbr megahertz.

MI5 n Brit (former) National Security branch of Military Intelligence to counter espionage.

MI6 n Brit (former) department of Military Intelligence that organizes espionage.

Michaelmas n festival of St Michael, 29 September; n **M. daisy** garden plant with blue, purple, pink or white blooms flowering in autumn.

mickey idm take the mickey (out of) make fun of; n **M. Finn** alcoholic drink laced with drug to induce sleep; **M. Mouse** a coll trivial;

unimportant.

micro- *prefix* **1** very small (*eg* **microorganism**) **2** one millionth (*eg* **microsecond**).

microbe *n* microscopic organism, bacterium, *esp* as cause of disease.

microbiology *n* study of minute living organisms; *a* **-ological**; *n* **-ologist**.

microchip *n* small piece of silicon or similar material marked with electric circuit.

microcomputer *n* smallest type of computer.

microcosm *n* miniature representation of sth larger.

microfiche *n* sheet of microfilm.

microfilm *n* film with minute record of large documents *v* to take photographs on such film.

microlight *n* very light miniature aircraft.

micrometer *n* instrument for measuring very small distances.

micro-organism *n* organism too small to be seen except under a microscope.

microphone *n* instrument converting sound into electrical waves for transmission to a loud speaker (*also coll* **mike**).

microprocessor *n comput* central data processing unit.

microscope *n* instrument which gives enlarged view of extremely small objects; *a* **microscopic** extremely small (*adv* **-ally**).

microwave *n* **1** very short

electromagnetic wave **2** oven which cooks food rapidly by use of microwaves (*also* **microwave oven**).

micturition *n med* urination.

mid *a* denoting middle part or position; *ns* **midday** noon; *pl* **Midlands** central England; **midnight** 12 o'clock at night; *a, adv* **midway** half way.

midden *n* dung-hill; pile of refuse.

middle *a* equidistant from extremes; halfway; *n* middle part or point; *ns m.* **age** period between youth and old age (*a* **m.-aged**; *n* **m.-aged spread** *coll* corpulence that comes in middle age); **M. Ages** period from 12th to 14th century before the Renaissance; **m. ear** cavity of central part of ear; **M. East** countries in Asia west of India (*a* **M. Eastern**) **middleman** trader, agent between producer and customer; **middle name 1** name between first name and surname **2** *coll* characteristic for which sb is well known; **m. school** school between primary and upper for pupils aged *usu* 9 to 13 or 8 to 12; **middleweight** *n* boxer of weight between welterweight and heavyweight; *as* **middle-of-the-road** supporting policy that appeals to average person and avoids any controversial or extreme

position; **middling** *a* average; mediocre.

midge *n* tiny flying, biting insect; *n* **midget** dwarf.

Midlands *n* Central parts of England.

midnight *n* 12 o'clock at night.

midriff *n* diaphragm.

midshipman *n, navy* **1** *Brit* rank below sub-lieutenant **2** *US* student training to be an officer.

midst *prep* in middle of; *n* central part.

midsummer *n* middle of summer (21st or 22nd June); *n* **Midsummer's Day** 24th of June.

midway *a, adv* half-way.

midwife *n* woman who assists women in childbirth; *n* **midwifery** science, skill of midwife; obstetrics.

might[1] *v aux* **1** expressing doubtful possibility **2** *pt of* **may**; **might have 1** could have **2** should have; ought to have.

might[2] *n* power; strength *a* **mighty**; *adv coll* very; *adv* **-ily**.

migraine *n* nervous headache.

migrate *v* move from one region to another, *esp* as certain birds etc; *a, n* **migrant**; *n* **migration** act of migrating; periodical movement of birds, fishes etc; body of individuals migrating; *a* **migratory** having habit of migration; wandering.

mike *n coll* microphone.

mild *a* **1** gentle; kind; placid **2**

temperate 3 not strong in flavour; n mildness.

mildew n parasitic fungus growing on plants; mould growing on damp food, paper etc; v affect, be affected by mildew.

mile n measure of linear distance, 1,760 yards; ns mileage 1 distance travelled 2 cost of travel per mile 3 fig possible amount of use; mileometer instrument in motor-car for recording miles travelled; milestone stone indicating distance in miles from place.

milieu n Fr -s or -x environment; social surroundings.

military a of, suitable to or performed by soldiers, or army; n army; a militant warlike, combative (n m. tendency aggressively left-wing element); ns militancy; militarism reliance on, encouragement of armed strength; militia auxiliary infantry force, called out in emergency.

milk n 1 white fluid secreted by female mammals to feed their off-spring 2 similar liquid secreted by certain plants; v 1 take milk from 2 (of cow, goat etc) give milk 3 extract money, information etc from sb by dishonest means; ns m. bar bar selling non-alcoholic drinks; m.-float electrically powered vehicle for delivering milk; m. round

route taken from house to house by milkman delivering milk; m. run coll regular ordinary journey providing service; m. shake sweet milk drink with chocolate or fruit flavour; milksop feeble effeminate man; m. tooth one of first set of baby teeth in mammals; as milk-white, milky; n Milky Way luminous belt of stars and nebulae (also the Galaxy).

mill n 1 machine for grinding grain; building containing this 2 small machine for grinding pepper, coffee etc. 3 works, factory for processing cotton, paper etc; v idm put sb through/go through the mill (cause sb to) undergo difficult or unpleasant experience; phr v mill about/around move around aimlessly in a mass of people; ns miller person who works a flour mill; millrace current of water driving millwheel; millstone 1 stone for grinding corn 2 fig burden; millwheel large wheel used to drive watermill.

millennium n Lat period of thousand years, esp that of Christ's second Advent; a millennial.

millet n small-seeded cereal grass, used as food.

milli- prefix Lat one thousandth (part of weight, measure in metric system), as milligram thousandth

part of gram; millimetre etc.

milliard n Fr 1,000 millions.

millibar n unit of pressure of 1,000 bars.

milliner n maker, seller of women's hats, ribbons, trimmings etc; n millinery milliner's business, or articles sold by milliner.

million n, pron, det 1,000 thousands; n millionaire man possessing a million pounds, dollars etc; very rich man; fem -airess; a, n, pron, det millionth.

millipede n Lat worm-like creature with many pairs of legs.

mime n 1 art of communication by use of gestures and facial expression, esp as entertainment 2 entertainer of this kind; v use this means of communicating; a mimetic; n mimeograph US dated apparatus for making copies of documents from stencil (v make copies by this method).

mimic v copy, resemble closely; ridicule by imitating speech, action; n one who mimics; n mimicry.

mimosa n genus of plants with small, fluffy yellow flowers, and sensitive leaves.

mince v cut, chop in small pieces; speak, behave affectedly; idm not mince one's words speak plainly; n finely chopped meat; n mincemeat, mixture of raisins, candied peel, suet, brandy etc; **m.-pie** small covered pie containing mincemeat.

mind n 1 intellectual faculties 2 memory 3 opinion; thought 4 intention 5 person noted for power of intellect; v 1 pay attention to 2 look after 3 object (to) 4 intend; idm **on one's mind** causing anxiety; idm **out of one's mind** insane; frenzied; v 1 look after 2 beware of 3 object (to) 4 take into account; as **m.-bending** incredible; **m.-blowing** 1 (of drugs) causing ecstasy, hallucinations etc 2 strange and exciting; **m.-boggling** coll astonishing; ns **m.-reader** person able to know another person's thoughts; **m.reading; mind's eye** imagination; **minder** person who looks after others; as **mindful** thoughtful; attentive (adv **-ly**); **mindless** thoughtless; stupid (adv **-ly**; n **-ness**).

mine[1] n 1 deep excavation from which coal, minerals (except stone) are dug 2 buildings, machinery connected with this 3 fig rich source of supply 4 tunnel under enemy position; v 1 sink mine 2 extract from mine 3 undermine; n **miner**.

mine[2] n charge of explosives detonated in container; v lay mines in sea, on land; ns **minefield** area where mines

have been laid; **minelayer** ship laying mines; **minesweeper** ship for clearing minefield.

mineral n natural, inorganic substance found in earth; anything not animal, vegetable; anything dug up by mining; a inorganic; ns **m. oil** 1 Brit petroleum or other oil of mineral origin 2 US liquid paraffin; **m. water** water with natural mineral salts taken for medicinal value or refreshment; **mineralogy** science of minerals (n **-alogist**).

minestrone n rich Italian soup of vegetables and pasta.

mingle v 1 mix; blend 2 join; combine.

mingy a coll mean.

mini n thing smaller than the usual size.

mini- prefix small; short.

miniature n, a very small (thing); v **miniaturize**; n **miniaturist** artist who specializes in small pictures.

minibus n small bus for up to 12 people.

minicab n Brit taxi that can be ordered by phone.

minicomputer n computer smaller than mainframe.

minim n mus note equal to two crotchets; ⅛th of fluid drachm; a **minimal** least possible (adv **-ly**); v **minimize** 1 reduce to smallest possible amount 2 underestimate; understate; n **minimum** smallest, least amount, lowest point

possible; pl **minima, -mums**; a least possible.

mining n extracting minerals from the earth.

minion n 1 favourite 2 subordinate.

miniscule a very tiny.

minister n 1 clergyman 2 person in charge of state department 3 diplomatic agent or representative below ambassador; v supply; help; serve; a **ministerial**; n **ministrant** acting as minister; n **ministration** service, help.

miniver n white fur; ermine.

mink n animal of weasel family; its valuable fur.

minor a less; inferior; unimportant; n person not legally of age; n **minority** 1 state of being a minor 2 smaller number.

Minotaur n fabled monster (half man, half bull).

minster n abbey church; cathedral.

minstrel n medieval singer; itinerant singer, musician.

mint[1] n place where money is legally coined; idm **make a mint** coll earn a great amount of money; v make (money); a in a new and perfect condition.

mint[2] n 1 peppermint 2 herb used to flavour meat etc; a **minty**.

minus prep, a less; deducted; subtracted; lacking; n minus sign (–).

minute[1] n 1 ⅙₀th of hour or degree 2 moment 3

memorandum; n **m. steak** thin steak that can be cooked very quickly; pl **-s** written record of meeting; v record in the minutes.

minute[2] a tiny; adv **-ly**, n **-ness**; **minutiae** small details.

miracle n marvel; abnormal event that cannot be explained; n **m. play** mystery play; a **miraculous**.

mirage n optical illusion; fig misleading delusion.

MIRAS abbr Mortgage Interest Relief at Source.

mire n mud; swampy ground; v dirty with mud.

mirror n polished surface which reflects image; fig pattern model; v reflect; **m.image** image in which left and right sides are symmetrically reversed.

mirth n 1 merriment; gladness 2 hilarity; a **mirthful**.

mis- prefix 1 forming ns bad; wrong; ill (eg **misadventure** ill luck; accident; **mischance** bad luck; **misconception** wrong understanding; **misconduct** bad behaviour, esp sexual; **misfortune, mismatch, misrule**) 2 forming ns lack of (eg **mistrust** lack of trust; **misunderstanding**) 3 forming vs and as badly; wrongly (eg vs **misapprehend** understand wrongly (n **-hension**); **misappropriate** use wrongly; **misapply, misbehave, miscalculate, miscast;**

misconceive understand wrongly (n **-conception**); **misconstrue, misdirect, misinform, misjudge, mislead, mismanage, mismatch, misquote, misread, misreport, misrepresent, misstate, mistime, misuse**; as **misguided** mistaken in judgement (adv **-ly**); **misshapen** badly formed; **misspent** spent unwisely).

misandry n hatred of men.

misanthropy n hatred of mankind and human society; ns **misanthrope, -opist** person who shows this; a **-opic**; adv **-opically**.

misc abbr miscellaneous.

miscarry v 1 go awry, astray 2 give birth prematurely; n **miscarriage** 1 premature birth in which foetus cannot survive 2 failure (of plan etc); n **m. of justice** unjust legal decision.

miscegenation n interbreeding of races, esp between black and white.

miscellaneous a mixed; consisting of various kinds; n **miscellany** medley of various kinds.

mischief n 1 harm; injury 2 immoral influence 3 troublesome conduct; a **mischievous** injurious; causing needless, thoughtless, minor damage; adv **-ly**; n **-ness**.

misconstrue v interpret wrongly; n **-struction**.

miscreant n Fr scoundrel;

villain; ruffian.

misdemeanour n misdeed; minor indictable offence.

miser n Lat one who hoards money and lives wretchedly; a **-ly** avaricious; n **-liness**.

miserable a 1 unhappy 2 squalid; wretched 3 scanty 4 pitiable; n **misery** 1 unhappiness; discomfort 2 squalor.

misfire v 1 (of gun) fire badly 2 (of plan) fail.

misfit n 1 person not well suited to job or social situation 2 badly fitting article of clothing.

misgiving n doubt; mistrust; fear.

mishap n accident; bad luck.

mishmash n coll confused mixture.

mislay v **mislaying, mislaid.** lose temporarily.

mislead v **misleading, misled.** deceive; lead astray; a **misleading** deceptive.

misnomer n wrong name; incorrect description.

misogamy n hatred of marriage; n **-gamist**.

misogyny n hatred of women; n **-gynist**.

misplace v 1 mislay 2 put in the wrong place.

Miss n title of unmarried woman, girl.

miss v 1 fail to hit, secure, meet, catch, notice 2 omit 3 feel want of; phr v **miss out** 1 omit 2 lose an opportunity; n failure to hit, secure etc; a **missing** 1 lost; mislaid 2 omitted; n **m.link**

1 thing needed to complete series 2 animal believed to have existed between apes and early man.

missile n object thrown or shot (*usu* as weapon).

mission n act of sending or being sent as representative; delegation; vocation; centre for missionary or social work; n **missionary** one sent on religious mission; a of religious missionary.

missis, missus n 1 wife 2 form of address to married woman.

missive n letter.

mist n visible watery vapour; a **misty** covered by mist; dim; obscure.

mistake v **mistaking, mistaken, mistook.** make error in understanding; identify wrongly; be in error; n error; fault.

Mister n title of address to man, written **Mr.**

mistletoe n evergreen parasitic plant.

mistral n Fr cold dry NW wind of S France.

mistress n 1 a man's secret or illicit lover 2 woman with power or control 3 female head of household 4 female teacher.

mistrust v not trust; n lack of trust; a **-ful**; adv **-fully**.

mite n 1 very small insect 2 anything very small 3 very small child.

mitigate v make less severe; alleviate; n **-ation**.

mitre n 1 headdress worn by pope, bishops etc 2 angled joint between two pieces of wood; v join with mitre.

mitt n 1 mitten 2 baseball, boxing leather glove 3 *pl sl* fists.

mitten n glove with finger and thumb ends open.

mix v 1 put together; mingle; blend 2 associate; n result of mixing; a **mixed** 1 of different sorts (ns **mixed bag** collection of varied items; **m. economy**) 2 having contradictory elements (ns **m. blessing** thing which has bad as well as good in it; **m. metaphor** ludicrous combination of two metaphors that do not go together) 3 of both sexes (**m. school**); ns **mixer** 1 person or machine for mixing 2 drink for making cocktails 3 *radio, film, TV* person or device combining two or more inputs into a single output; 4 person in a social role; **mixture** 1 combination 2 act of mixing 3 substances mixed; **mix-up** confusion.

ml abbr 1 mile 2 millilitre(s).

Mlle abbr Fr Mademoiselle.

mm abbr millimetre(s).

Mme abbr Fr Madame.

mnemonic n (phrase, rhyme etc.) helping memory.

MO abbr Medical Officer.

moan n low, mournful sound expressing pain, groan; v utter moan.

moat n defensive trench (*usu* filled with water) round castle, etc.

mob n lawless, rough crowd; rabble; excited mass of people; v **mobs, mobbing, mobbed.** jostle, attack in mob; crowd round.

mobile a a moveable; moving, changing easily; n **mobility**; v **mobilize** call up (armed forces) for service; gather resources, forces; n **-ization**.

moccasin n soft shoe (*usu* deerskin) of N American Indian.

mock v ridicule; deride; mimic; fig delude; a sham; imitation; ns **mocker; mockery** ridicule; travesty idm **make a mockery of** make appear worthless.

mocking bird n American bird of thrush family, mimic of other bird calls.

mock-up n 1 experimental model 2 lay-out of text, pictures etc before printing.

M.o.D. abbr Ministry of Defence.

modal auxiliary n verb used in front of other verb to express possibility, obligation etc (*etc* **can, may, must, shall, will**).

mod con n all mod cons all modern conveniences.

mode n method; style; fashion; a **modish** fashionable.

model n 1 pattern 2 smallscale reproduction 3 mannequin 4 one who poses for artist etc; v work into shape; act as model, pose.

modem n comput device allowing fast transmission of data to other computers over distances.

moderate *a* not going to extremes; restrained; medium; *v* make, become less extreme or violent; *n* one holding moderate views; *ns* **-ation; -ator** 1 arbitrator 2 president of Presbyterian assembly.

moderato *adv mus* at moderate speed.

modern *a* of present or recent times; up-to-date; *n* **-ism** movement expressing present day views, methods etc; *v* **modernize** make modern; adapt to present day usage (*n* **-ization**).

modest *a* 1 moderate 2 diffident; humble 3 chaste; *n* **modesty**.

modicum *n* small amount or quantity.

modify *v* qualify; alter slightly; *n* **modification**.

modulate *v* 1 regulate; adapt; vary 2 inflect (voice etc) 3 *mus* change key; *ns* **-ation; -ator**.

module *n* 1 standard part used in construction 2 part of spacecraft that can operate independently 3 unit of study that is assessed independently of other units; *a* **modular** composed of modules.

modus *n* method; style.

modus operandi *n Lat* method of working.

modus vivendi *n Lat* way of coping, of living side by side.

mogul *n* very powerful and wealthy person.

MOH *abbr* Medical Officer of Health.

moiety *n leg, lit* half-share; part.

moist *a* damp; humid; *v* **moisten; *n* moisture** dampness; condensed watery vapour.

molar *n* double grinding tooth; *a* of or relating to double grinding teeth.

molasses *n* thick dark syrup drained from raw sugar.

mold *n US* = **mould**.

mole[1] *n* 1 small furry animal that lives in underground tunnels 2 *Brit* spy working within an organization; *ns* **molehill** mound of earth left by mole when digging; **moleskin**.

mole[2] *n* dark-coloured permanent spot on skin.

molecule *n* 1 simplest unit of a chemical compound composed of two or more atoms 2 very small particle; *a* **-cular**.

molest *v* trouble; pester; accost illegally.

mollify *v* 1 pacify; appease 2 soften; *n* **mollification**.

mollusc *n* soft-bodied animal usually having hard shell (eg snail, oyster).

mollycoddle *v* pamper.

Molotov cocktail *n* homemade bomb of petrol in a bottle.

molt *v US* = **moult**.

molten *a* (of metal, rock) melted.

molto *adv mus* much; very.

moment *n* 1 brief period of time 2 importance; *a*

momentary brief; quick

momentous of great importance; *n* **momentum** impetus; increasing force.

monarch *n* sovereign; supreme ruler; *ns* **monarchy** state ruled by monarch; **-ist** supporter of monarchy.

monastery *n* house lived in by religious community; *a* **monastic** of monastery; of monks, nuns; *n* **monasticism** monastic life and system.

Monday *n* second day of week.

monetarism *n econ* theory that control of money supply creates stable economy; *n, a* **-ist**.

money *n* 1 coins; banknotes; any form of credit usable as payment 2 wealth; *idm* **make money** grow rich; *ns* **m.-bags** *coll* rich person; **m.-box** closed box with slot for keeping money; **m.-changer** person whose job is to change money from one currency to another; **m.-grubber** *coll* person greedy for money and unscrupulous about how to acquire it (*a* **m.-grubbing**); **m.-lender, m.-maker, m.-market; m.-spinner** *coll* thing which sells very well and brings a lot of profit; **m. supply** money available for spending in given economic system; *a* **moneyed** rich.

mongoose *n* **-gooses.** small Indian animal that kills snakes.

mongrel *n* animal (*esp* dog) of mixed breed; hybrid; *a* of mixed breeding or origin.

monitor *n* **1** one who warns, advises **2** school prefect **3** large lizard **4** heavy gun-boat **5** master screen in TV studio; *v* listen to foreign broadcasts; *a* **monitory**.

monk *n* member of religious order, living under vows of poverty, chastity etc.

monkey *n* **1** any of the primates (other than humans or lemurs), *esp* long-tailed **2** *coll* mischievous child; *phr v* **monkey about/around** play the fool; *ns* **m. business** mischievous behaviour; **m.-nut** peanut; **m.-puzzle tree** with long undulating branches covered with prickly spines; **m.-wrench** spanner with adjustable jaw.

mono- *prefix* single, alone.

mono *a* monophonic; *n coll* monophonic recording.

monochromatic *a* of one colour.

monochrome *n* **1** with images in black, white and shades of grey **2** using shades of one colour only.

monogamy *n* practice of marrying only one partner at a time.

monoglot *a* able to speak one language only.

monogram *n* single figure made of two or more interwoven initials.

monolingual *a* monoglot.

monolith *n* single block of stone as monument.

monologue *n* speech by single actor.

mononucleosis *n* glandular fever.

monophonic *a* using only one transmission channel.

monopoly *n* exclusive right of trading in specified commodity; *v* **monopolize** engross, enjoy to exclusion of others.

monorail *n* type of railway where train runs along single-rail elevated track.

monosodium glutamate *n* chemical compound added to preserved foods to improve the flavour.

monosyllable word of one syllable; *a* **-syllabic**.

monotheism *n* belief in only one God.

monotone *n* single, unvaried tone; *a* **monotonous** lacking in variety; dully repetitive; *n* **monotony** lack of variety; tediousness.

monotype *n* machine casting type in single letters.

Monsieur *n* form of address to French-speaking man (*pl* **Messieurs**).

Monsignor *n* form of address to senior RC priest.

monsoon *n* seasonal wind of Indian Ocean; rainy season in India.

monster *n* **1** person, animal, thing of abnormal shape or huge size **2** abnormally wicked, cruel person; *a* **monstrous 1** like a monster **2** shocking **3** hideous; *n*

monstrosity 1 freak **2** badly made, hideous object.

montage *n Fr* **1** final selection and arrangement of shots to form cinema film **2** two or more pictures imposed on single background.

month *n* one of twelve parts into which year is divided; period of moon's revolution; *a* **monthly** occurring once a month; *n* magazine published monthly.

monument *n* tombstone, building, statue etc erected as memorial; *a* **-al 1** of, serving as monument **2** massive; enormous.

mood *n ling* form of verb indicating its function.

moon *n* **1** earth's satellite **2** satellite of another planet; *idm* **ask the moon** make an unreasonable request; *idm* **once in a blue moon** very rarely or never; *idm* **over the moon** ecstatically happy; *phr v* **moon about/around** wander aimlessly and gloomily; *ns* **moonbeam** beam of moonlight; **moonlight** light of the moon (*v* do a second job as well as regular job, *usu* undeclared for income tax); **moonshine 1** moonlight **2** nonsense **3** US spirits distilled illegally; **m.-shot** launch of spacecraft to the moon; **moonstone** semi-precious stone with milky appearance; *a* **moonstruck** slightly mad.

moor *n* tract of open country, usually hilly and heather-clad; n **m.-hen** hen that lives on water.

moor v fasten, secure (ship) by cables, chains etc; n pl **-ings** place where vessel is moored; cables, buoys etc by which it is secured.

moose n large N American deer with large antlers.

mop n bundle of yarn on long handle; v **mops, mopping, mopped.** clean, wipe with mop; **mop up** fig round up, defeat.

mope v be low-spirited, depressed.

moped n small low-powered motorcycle.

moral a relating to generally accepted ideas of right and wrong; virtuous; of right conduct; n lesson taught by experience, fable; pl **-s** principles of right and wrong conduct; n **m. support** encouragement; n **morality** good moral conduct; virtue; v **moralize** draw moral lesson from, think on moral aspect; n **moralist** teacher of, writer on morals.

morale n mental state, esp regarding courage etc.

moratorium n legal authorization to delay or defer payment of debt etc.

morbid a abnormal; pathological; unwholesome.

mordant a 1 sarcastic 2 corrosive 3 (of dyeing) serving to fix colours.

more a greater in quantity, extent etc; comp of **many**,

much; adv in addition, to greater degree; adv moreover besides.

morello n dark red, bitter cherry.

mores n pl customs held to be typical of social group.

morgue n Fr mortuary.

moribund a dying; decaying.

Mormon n member of religious sect.

morn n lit morning.

morning a first part of day, from dawn until noon; ns **m.-after pill** contraceptive pill used by woman; **m. dress** clothes for man at formal day-time social occasions, including top hat with morning coat and grey trousers; **m. glory** climbing plant with trumpet shaped blue flowers; **m. sickness** nausea experienced during early weeks of pregnancy, esp in morning; **m. star** the planet Venus seen in Eastern sky before dawn.

morocco n fine, flexible leather.

moron n 1 mentally deficient person 2 sl fool.

morose a surly; sullen; gloomy.

morphia, morphine n narcotic alkaloid of opium, used to relieve pain.

morphology n 1 bio (study of) form and structure of organisms 2 ling (study of) changing forms of words according to grammatical function; a **-ological;** n **-ologist.**

morris dance n English folk

dance for men in costume.

morrow n lit next following day; tomorrow.

morse n system of telegraphic signalling, built up of dots, dashes also **Morse code.**

morsel n small piece; fragment.

mortal a 1 liable to die 2 causing death 3 unrelenting; n human being; n **m. sin** that leads to damnation unless confessed and atoned for; n **mortality** 1 condition of being subject to death 2 deathrate.

mortar n 1 vessel in which substances are pounded 2 short-barrelled cannon 3 cement of lime, sand, water for holding bricks etc together; n **mortar-board** square flat college cap.

mortgage n conveyance of property as security for debt; v convey on mortgage; fig pledge; ns **mortgagee; mortgagor.**

mortician n US undertaker.

mortify v 1 discipline by self-denial 2 humiliate 3 become gangrenous; n **mortification.**

mortise, mortice n hole cut in piece of wood into which tenon; v join by, make mortise in; n **mortise lock** one embedded in door.

mortuary a of, pertaining to death and burial; n building where corpses are kept before burial.

mosaic n pattern made by fitting together small pieces of coloured marble, stone etc.

Mosaic a of Moses.

moselle n dry white wine from Moselle area.

Moslem, Muslim n follower of the religion of Islam; a of, belonging to Islam.

mosque n Muslim temple.

mosquito n -oes or -os. biting gnat.

moss n low growing tufted plant found on moist surfaces; lichen; a **mossy** covered with moss.

most a greatest in number, quantity, degree; sup of **many, much;** idm **for the most part** mainly; idm **make the most of** use to the best advantage adv to greatest degree; adv **mostly** generally.

MOT n obligatory certificate of roadworthiness for which vehicles in Britain over a certain age are re-tested annually.

mot n Fr witty saying or remark.

motel n hotel specially designed for motorists.

moth n night-flying insect, related to butterfly; **clothes m.** whose larvae feed on woollen fabrics, furs etc; **mothball** n ball of strong-smelling substance to dispel moths from clothes; idm **in mothballs** in storage; a **m.-eaten 1** damaged by clothes-moth **2** fig shabby.

mother n **1** female parent **2** head of convent, nunnery; ns **m. country** native land; **m.-in-law** mother of wife or husband; **m.-of-pearl** iridescent lining of certain shell-fish (eg oyster, mussel); **m. superior** head of convent; **m. tongue** native language; **motherhood** state of being mother; a **motherly** n -**liness.**

motif n Fr recurrent theme, esp in music; ornamental needlework pattern.

motion n **1** movement **2** proposal put to meeting **3** gesture **4** evacuation of bowels **5** leg application for ruling; v indicate; makes gesture towards; idm **go through the motions** do in a perfunctory way, without commitment; n **m. picture** US film; a **motionless** (adv -**ly**) a **motionless** at rest; still.

motive n cause; incentive; that which influences behaviour or action; v **motivate** impel, induce; n **motivation.**

mot juste n Fr exact word or phrase.

motley a various colours; of mixed ingredients; n parti-coloured garment, esp jester's.

motocross n motorcycle racing over rough ground.

motor n that which imparts movement; machine supplying motive power; engine; v travel in motorcar; ns **motorcade** procession of cars; **m. car** Brit car; **m. cycle** (also **m. bike**) two-wheeled vehicle with engine; **m. cyclist** rider of this; **motoring** car driving; **motorist** car driver; **m. scooter** scooter; **motorway** Brit wide main road with several lanes for fast travel.

mottled a marked with irregular patches of light and dark colours.

motto n -oes or -os. short phrase expressing maxim, rule of conduct, esp on coat-of-arms.

mould[1] n furry, fungoid growth caused by dampness; a **mouldy** musty, decaying; v **moulder** crumble, decay.

mould[2] n **1** pattern, hollow shape, matrix for shaping or casting soft materials **2** fig character; v give shape to; n **moulding 1** something moulded **2** ornamental strip of wood.

moult v shed feathers, fur etc periodically; n act or time of moulting; n **moulting.**

mound n raised heap of earth, stones etc; hillock.

mount v **1** climb; ascend **2** get on horseback **3** rise; increase **4** provide frame, setting for (picture etc) **5** organize (campaign, exhibition); n **1** that on which thing is mounted; **2** gun-carriage **3** mountain; high hill.

mountain n large, lofty hill; idm **make a mountain out of a mole-hill** exaggerate the importance eg of a problem; n **mountaineer** dweller in, expert climber of mountains; a **mountainous** very high; enormous; n

mountain bike bicycle with light strong frame and thick tyres designed for riding on rough ground.

mountebank n charlatan; quack.

mourn n lament; grieve for; show sorrow; n **mourner** a **mournful**; n **mourning** 1 grief esp for death 2 clothes worn as sign of such grief 3 time these are worn.

mouse n small rodent; fig shy person (pl **mice**); v catch, hunt mice; n **mouser** cat good at catching mice.

moustache n hair on upper lip.

mouth n 1 opening in animal's head by which it eats and utters sounds 2 opening; outlet; aperture; v speak with exaggerated lip and jaw movement; n **mouthpiece** part of pipe etc held to or between lips; spokesman.

move v 1 change position of 2 set in motion 3 affect feelings 4 make formal proposal; phr vs **move on** change to sth new; **move out** leave one's accommodation; **move over** make room for sb else; n 1 movement 2 fig device 3 step 4 change of abode or place of work; a **movable**; n **movement** 1 act, fact, process of moving 2 moving part of mechanism, esp of watch 3 division of musical composition.

movie n US coll cinema film; pl **-s** cinema.

mow v **mowing, mowed** or **mown.** cut down (grass etc); fig **m. down** kill indiscriminately; n **mower** mowing machine, one who mows.

MP abbr 1 Member of Parliament 2 (member of) Military Police.

mpg abbr miles per gallon.

mph abbr miles per hour.

Mr abbr Mister (form of address to a man).

Mrs n form of address to a married woman.

Ms n form of address to a woman (married or unmarried).

MS abbr 1 manuscript 2 multiple sclerosis.

MSc abbr Master of Science.

MSS abbr manuscripts.

much n a great quantity; n great deal; adv greatly; nearly; idm **much as** although; idm **(cannot) make much of** (cannot) understand; idm **not much of** a not a good; idm **not much point** no purpose or advantage; idm **much of a muchness** very similar.

muck n 1 filth; dirt 2 manure 3 refuse; phr vs **muck about/around** Brit coll behave in a silly, inconsiderate way; waste time; **muck in** Brit coll share (accommodation, work, responsibility) equally; **muck out** clean out (excrement from stable etc); **muck up** coll 1 make dirty 2 spoil; ns **m.-raking** searching for hints of scandal so as to

spread malicious rumours; **m.-raker** a mucky 1 dirty 2 distasteful.

mucus n slimy, viscous secretion of mucous membrane; a **mucous** secreting mucus; slimy.

mud n very wet, moist earth; ns **m.-bath** 1 bath in mud for medicinal purposes 2 wet sloppy condition of sports pitch; **mudguard** curved cover above cycle wheel; **m.-pack** paste applied to face to keep skin healthy; a **muddy**; n **muddiness**.

muddle v 1 bewilder; confuse 2 bungle; n disorder; mess; confusion; phr vs **muddle along** live in a purposeless way; **muddle through** coll achieve success in spite of being poorly equipped; as **m.-headed** lacking clarity of thought (n **-ness**); muddled, muddling.

muesli n breakfast food of mixed cereals, nuts, dried fruits, etc.

muff v sport miss; bungle; n fool; blunderer.

muffin n 1 Brit round cake of yeast dough 2 US small cup-shaped sweet bread roll.

muffle v wrap with covering, for warmth or to deaden sound; n **muffler** 1 thick, warm scarf 2 US aut silencer.

mug n 1 drinking cup 2 sl face 3 simpleton; v **mugs, mugging, mugged.** sl rob with violence, in public place (ns **mugger, mugging**);

phr v **mug up** *Brit coll* study and learn quickly for a specific purpose.

muggy *a* damp; close; oppressive.

mugshot *n sl* photograph.

mugwump *n* US person trying to be neutral in politics.

mulberry *n* tree with reddish purple edible berries.

mulct *v* 1 defraud 2 fine (*also n*).

mule *n* 1 hybrid between horse and ass 2 stubborn person 3 spinning machine 4 heelless slipper; *n* **muleteer** mule driver; *a* **mulish** obstinate.

mull *v* heat (wine etc) with spices.

mullet *n* edible sea-fish.

mulligatawny *n* soup made with curry powder.

mullion *n* upright shaft, *usu* of stone, between window panes.

multi- *prefix* many; *as* **multifarious** of many kinds; **multilateral** with many participants (*adv* **-ly**); **multimedia** using several types of media; **multi-play** (of CD) providing recording as well as playback facility; **multinational** having offices, manufacturing facilities in many countries (*also n* company of this kind); **multi-task** *comput* able to carry out several diverse tasks simultaneously (*n* **-ing**); **multitrack** using tape with two or more recording tracks.

multiple *a* having many parts; *n* number which contains another number an exact number of times; *ns* **m.** **sclerosis** chronic disease of central nervous system resulting in loss of motor control, paralysis (*also* **MS**); **multiplicity** great number; *v* **multiply** 1 add (number) to itself specified number of times 2 increase in number 3 breed; (*n* **-plication**).

multitude *n* great number; crowd of people; *a* **multidinous** very numerous.

mum[1] *a* silent; *v* mime; *idm* **mum's the word** *coll* keep it secret.

mum[2] *n coll* mother.

mumble *v* speak indistinctly; mutter.

mumbo-jumbo *n* meaningless ritual or words.

mummy[1] *n* childish term for mother (*abbr* **mum**).

mummy[2] *n* embalmed body, *esp* of ancient Egyptian; *v* **mummify**; *a* **mummified**.

mumps *n pl* painful contagious disease, inflammation of parotid and salivary glands.

munch *v* crunch, chew noisily and vigorously.

mundane *a* earthly; worldly; dull.

municipal *a* belonging to affairs of boroughs, city, town; *n* **municipality** town, borough etc enjoying local government; local authority.

munitions *n pl* military stores.

mural *a* of, on wall; *n* wall-painting.

murder *n* unlawful, intentional homicide; *v* kill thus; *n* **murderer**; *fem* **murderess**; *a* **murderous** intending to murder; deadly.

murk *n* thick darkness; *a* **murky** dark; cloudy.

murmur *v* 1 make low, continuous sound 2 speak in low voice 3 grumble; *n* act, sound of murmuring.

Murphy's law *n coll* sod's law – everything that could go wrong will go wrong.

muscat *n* raisin; musky grape; *n* **muscatel** muscat; sweet wine made from it.

muscle *n* animal elastic fibrous tissue, highly contractile, by which movement is effected; *fig* bodily force, strength; *a* **muscular** of muscle 2 having well developed strong muscles (*n* **m. dystrophy** long-term illness causing wastage of muscles; *a* **muscle-bound** with muscles strained and inelastic through over-exercise.

Muse *n* 1 one of nine goddesses associated with the arts, sciences and literature; 2 *fig* **muse** poetic inspiration (*v* ponder; meditate).

museum *n* collection of natural, scientific, historical or artistic objects; building housing such collection.

mush *n* soft, pulpy mass; *a* **mushy** soft; pulpy.

mushroom *n* quick-growing edible fungus; *v* 1 *fig* grow, expand rapidly; **2** gather mushrooms; *a* of, like mushroom.

music *n* **1** art of producing rhythmic, melodious sounds **2** written or printed score of musical composition **3** *fig* pleasing sound; *n* **m.-hall** (formerly musical and comic entertainment at) variety theatre; **m.-stand** wooden or metal frame to hold printed music for player during performance; *a* **musical;** (*ns* **m. box** box with mechanism that plays music when the lid is opened; **m. chairs** party game in which players compete for chairs to sit on when the music stops.

musk *n* strong scent obtained from male musk-deer; plant with similar scent; *a* **-y;** *ns* **m.-deer** small hornless deer; **m.-ox** Arctic ox; **m.-rat** N American water rat.

Muslim *n, a* (adherent) of religion of Islam founded by Muhammad.

muslin *n* fine cotton fabric.

mussel *n* edible bivalve mollusc.

must[1] *n* new unfermented wine.

must[2] *v aux* expressing compulsion, obligation, certainty; *pt* **had to;** there is no *pp;* *n coll* an essential.

mustache *n US* = moustache.

mustang *n* American wild or semi-wild prairie horse.

mustard *n* hot, pungent powder made from pounded seeds of mustard plant, used as condiment; *n* **m. gas** poisonous irritant gas.

muster *v* assemble; summon; *n* assembly of troops etc for inspection etc.

musty *a* mouldy; stale; *n* **-iness.**

mustn't *contracted form of* must not.

mutable *a* liable to change; *n* **mutation 1** change **2** sudden genetic change.

mutatis mutandis *adv Lat* after making the appropriate changes.

mute *a* dumb; silent; *n* **1** dumb person **2** professional mourner **3** device used to soften tone or reduce sound of musical instrument; *a* **muted** muffled (sound).

mutilate *v* maim; cut off; render imperfect; *n* **mutilation.**

mutiny *n* **-ies.** revolt against authority, *esp* in armed forces; *v* **mutinies, mutinying, mutinied.** revolt; *a* **mutinous;** *n* **mutineer.**

mutt *n coll* mongrel dog.

mutter *v* speak indistinctly in low voice; grumble.

mutton *n* flesh of sheep used as food; *idm* **mutton dressed up as lamb** older person trying to appear much younger; *ns* **muttonchops** long wide sideburns (*also* **m.-chop whiskers**); **m.-head** *coll* stupid person.

mutual *a* **1** performed by joint action **2** reciprocal **3** common to both.

muzzle *n* **1** mouth and nose of animal **2** cover for these to prevent biting **3** mouth of gun; *v* **1** put muzzle on **2** impose silence on.

muzzy *a* dazed; vague; fuddled; *n* **-ness.**

MW *abbr* **1** medium wave **2** megawatt(s).

mW *abbr* milliwatt.

my *poss a* belonging to ME.

myalgic encephalomyelitis *n* viral disease affecting nervous system, with long-lasting effect of fatigue and impaired muscular control (*also* **ME** *or* **post-viral syndrome.**)

myopia *n* short-sightedness; *a* **myopic.**

myriad *n* ten thousand; endless number; *a* countless.

myrrh *n* strong-smelling resin used in perfumes and as incense.

myrtle *n* evergreen, flowering shrub.

myself *pron* **1** *emphatic form of* **I, me** *reflex form of* **I, me.**

mystery *n* **-ies. 1** something strange, secret, or inexplicable; secrecy; **2** play or story about an unexplained crime; *ns* **mystery play** medieval religious play; **mystery tour** pleasure tour to an unknown destination; *a* **mysterious;** *adv* **mysteriously.**

mystic *n* having inner, secret meanings; esoteric; *n* one who believes in attainment, through contemplation, of

inaccessible truths; *a* **-al;**
n **-ism.**

mystify *n* puzzle; bewilder; *n*
mystification.

mystique *n Fr* elusive quality
of sth much admired but not
properly understood.

myth *n* **1** fictitious story or
legend **2** imaginary person
or thing; *a* **-ical;** *n* **-ology**
collection, body of myths
concerning ancient religious
belief; *a* **-ological.**

nab v **nabs, nabbing, nabbed.** sl catch suddenly; arrest.

nadir n point opposite zenith; lowest point.

naff a Brit sl inferior; in poor taste.

nag[1] n small riding pony; horse.

nag[2] v **nags, nagging, nagged.** find fault persistently; scold; fig give constant pain.

naiad n water-nymph.

nail v 1 horny plate at end of fingers and toes 2 talon 3 metal spike for fixing things together; v fix, fasten to, with nail; phr v **nail down** force to a commitment; a **n.-biting** intensely exciting; n **n. varnish** Brit quick-drying liquid giving hard shiny finish to finger, toe nails.

naïve a Fr 1 natural; ingenuous 2 foolishly simple; n **naïveté, naïvety.**

naked a unclothed; nude; exposed; bare; without normal covering; n **-ness**.

name n 1 word by which person, thing, idea is known or called 2 lineage; family 3 reputation; v call by name; give name to; appoint; identify by name; idm **name of the game** essential purpose of activity; ns **n. day** feast day of saint after whom one was named; **namesake** person having same name as another; **name-tape** identifying tape sewn onto clothing; v **n.-drop** refer to well-known people one pretends to know in order to impress (ns **n.-dropper, n.-dropping**); a **-less** anonymous; unknown; adv **-ly**; that is to say.

nanny n child's nurse; **n. goat** female goat.

nano- prefix 1 thousand millionth part of (eg **nanometre, nanosecond**) 2 of microscopically small objects and measurements (eg **nanotechnology**).

nap[1] n downy surface of cloth; v **naps, napping, napped.** put, rise nap on.

nap[2] n short sleep; v doze; idm **be caught napping** be caught unawares.

nape n back of the neck.

napkin n small cloth used at meals to protect clothes and wipe fingers, lips; baby's nappy.

nappy n coll baby's diaper; small cloth used for nursery purposes.

narcosis n unconsciousness induced by drugs; n **narcotic** drug causing sleep, insensibility; a inducing sleep etc.

nark n 1 Brit sl police informer (also **copper's nark**) 2 Aust coll spoilsport; v Brit sl annoy; a **narky** bad-tempered.

narrate v relate; tell story of; ns **-ation, -ative** story; account; a **-ating**; n **-ator**.

narrow a of small breadth in proportion to length; v become, cause to become narrow; adv **-ly** closely; only just; a **n.-minded** prejudiced, bigoted.

nasal a of or in nose; n nasal sound (phonetics).

nasty a offensive to taste or smell; disgusting; disagreeable; n **-iness**.

natal a of, at, belonging to birth.

natation n act of swimming,

floating; *as* **natant** floating, as of plants; **natatory** pertaining to swimming.

nation *n* large group of people having common language, culture etc, and living in one area under one government; *a* **national** of, common to a nation (*n* citizen of a state); *ns* **n. debt** amount owed by country to other countries; **N. Front** extremely right-wing nationalist party; **N. Guard** US state militia; **N. Health Service** public service providing medical care in Britain (*also* **NHS**); **N. Insurance** system of compulsory contributions by employers and employees to insure against unemployment, sickness and provide pensions; **n. park** conservation area under care of the state; **n. service** compulsory military service); *adv* **-ally**; *ns* **nationalism** 1 pride in one's native country 2 political movement for independence (*n* **-ist**; *as* **-ist, -istic**); **nationality** status of belonging to a particular nation; *v* **nationalize** take under government control (*a* **-ized** *n* **-ization**); *a* **nationwide** covering the entire country.

native *a* relating to the place of one's birth; *n* person born in a place; original inhabitant.

nativity *n* birth *esp* of Christ.

NATO *abbr* North Atlantic Treaty Organization.

natter *v, n* Brit coll (have) trivial conversation.

natty *a* coll neat and smart in appearance; *adv* **-ily**.

natural *a* 1 arising from the physical world; not artificial (**n. gas**) 2 uncultivated; wild 3 normal (**n. manner**) 4 innate (**n. talent**); *ns* **n. childbirth** childbirth without use of anaesthetic; **n. history** study of plants, animals etc; **n. selection** evolutionary process in which the species that are best at adaptation tend to survive; *adv* **-ly** 1 in a natural way 2 of course; *ns* **-ism** style of art, literature that aims at presenting real life (*a* **-istic**); **-ist** person who studies natural history; *v* **naturalize** give officially changed nationality to immigrant (*a* **-ized** *n* **-ization**).

nature *n* 1 everything created (not man-made) in the world 2 *esp cap* forces controlling events in the physical world 3 character 4 primitive state (*idm* **back to/return to nature**); *idm* **call of nature** coll urgent need to defecate/urinate; *idm* **second nature** action that can be performed (as if) by instinct; *ns* **n. trail** marked route through woods, fields for observation of natural phenomena; **naturism** nudism (*a, n* **-ist**);

naturopath expert in treatment of illness by use of herbal remedies, natural dieting and natural healing (*n* **-pathy**; *a* **-pathic**).

naught *n* nothing; arithmetical symbol nought (0).

naughty *a* 1 mischievous; disobedient; badly behaved 2 immoral; *n* **-tiness**.

nausea *n* sickness; disgust; *v* **nauseate** sicken; disgust; *a* **nauseous** causing nausea; loathsome.

nautical *a* pertaining to ships, sailors, etc; *n* **n. mile** unit of distance at sea, 1,852 metres.

naval *a* of, by the navy.

nave *n* central part of church, west of chancel.

navel *n* rounded depression in abdomen, umbelicus.

navigate *v* cause to sail or travel on set course; direct ship or aircraft; *ns* **-ation** act, science of navigating; **-ator** one skilled in science of navigation; *a* **navigable**.

navvy *n* unskilled labourer.

navy *n cap* all warships of state; fleet; naval personnel; *n,a* **n. blue** (of) dark blue (colour).

Nazi *n* member of Hitler's National-Socialist party.

NB *abbr Lat* nota bene (note well).

NBC *abbr* US National Broadcasting Company.

NC *abbr* National Curriculum.

NCC *abbr* National Curriculum Council.

NCO *abbr* non-commissioned

officer.

Neanderthal man n Stone Age Man.

neapolitan a, n 1 (ice cream) in different coloured, flavoured layers 2 cap (inhabitant) of Naples.

near adv close to; not far from; a close in relationship, degree; about to come, happen; v approach; ns **N East** non-European countries of E Mediterranean; **n.miss 1** narrow avoidance of collision; narrow escape from bomb, missile 2 failure by very small amount to achieve sth; **n.thing** situation so evenly balanced that the outcome is/was unpredictable; idm (one's) **nearest and dearest** (one's) own family; idm **near by** close at hand (a **nearby**); adv **nearly** almost; as **nearside** nearest to pavement; **near-sighted** short-sighted; (n **-ness**).

neat a 1 trim; well-kept 2 skilful 3 (of utterances) apt 4 (of alcoholic liquor) pure, undiluted; n **neatness**.

nebula n luminous cloud-like patch in sky; cluster of stars; a **nebulous** 1 cloudy; misty 2 fig vague; indefinite.

NEC abbr 1 National Executive Committee 2 National Extension College.

necessary a inevitable; indispensable; requisite; obligatory; n that which is essential or indispensable; n

necessity 1 compulsion; anything inevitable because of natural law 2 poverty; want; v **necessitate** render necessary; compel; a **necessitous** poor; destitute.

neck n 1 part of body joining head to trunk 2 narrow connecting part 3 isthmus; v sl kiss and cuddle; **neckcloth** cravat; **necklace** string of jewels, gold chain etc worn round neck.

necropolis n large cemetery.

nectar n myth drink of the gods; sugary liquid produced by flowers; ns **nectary** honey-gland of flower; **nectarine** variety of peach with smooth skin.

NEDC abbr National Economic Development Council.

neé a Fr (fem) born (with the surname).

need n 1 that which is required; necessity 2 poverty; want; as **needful** necessary; **needless** unnecessary; **needy** poor; in want.

needle n 1 small sharp instrument with eye to take thread, for sewing 2 pointed end of hypodermic syringe 3 thin rod of metal, plastic etc used in knitting 4 magnetized bar of compass 5 leaf of pine or fir; v coll annoy; goad; n **-woman** skilful woman sewer; seamstress; **-work** sewing, embroidery.

ne'er-do-well n improvident

good-for-nothing.

nefarious a unlawful; wicked.

negate v deny; nullify; n **-ation** contradictions; denial.

negative a 1 expressing denial 2 lacking in positive qualities 3 phot reversing lights and shades 4 elec cathode; n word, statement which denies, refuses, forbids; v veto; disprove; n **negative equity** debt that occurs when the value of property falls below the amount of the loan that secured it.

neglect v pay no heed to; disregard; omit, fail to do; n fact of neglecting or being neglected; a **-ful**; adv **-ly**.

negligence n heedlessness; lack of care, attention; ns **negligent**; **negligible** not worth considering.

negotiate v 1 arrange, settle business matter, by discussion 2 get cash for security 3 discuss terms of peace with 4 surmount (obstacle); a **negotiable**; ns **-iation; -iator**.

neighbour n one who lives next door, or nearly so; a **neighbouring** adjacent; placed near together; n **neighbourhood** (n **n.watch** group of neighbours with mutual arrangement to protect each other's homes against criminal activities); idm **in the neighbourhood** roughly; as **neighbouring** nearby; adjacent; **neighbourly** friendly (n -iness).

neither a, pron not either; also adv, conj.

nem con adv Lat unanimously.

neo prefix new; modern.

neoclassical a of any modern style (in art, literature, music etc) influenced by classical style.

neolithic a of later Stone Age.

neologism n 1 new word, phrase 2 act of inventing word.

neon n one of inert gases occurring in atmosphere; **n.light** glowing light obtained by ionizing gas in tube or bulb.

neophyte n new convert; novice; beginner.

nephew n brother's, sister's son.

nephritis n inflammation of kidneys.

nepotism n favouritism towards one's relatives.

Neptune n god of the sea; third largest planet.

nerd n sl idiot; a -ish.

nerve n 1 cord-like fibre, bundle of fibres, carrying sensory and motor impulses from the brain to parts of body 2 courage 3 coll impudence (idm **what a nerve!**) 4 pl -s nervousness (idm **a fit of nerves**); idm **get on sb's nerves** irritate sb unbearably; idm **hit/touch a raw nerve** say sth to cause anger, anguish etc; ns **n.centre** 1 group of nerve cells 2 control centre of organization; **n.gas** gas that

paralyses central nervous system with fatal effect; as **n.-racking** terrifying; causing extreme anxiety; **nervous** 1 of the nerves (ns **n.breakdown** serious medical condition in which person is acutely depressed and exhausted; **n.system** system of nerves in living creature) 2 tensely excited 3 timid (adv -ly; n -ness); **nervy** jumpy; easily excited.

nescient a not knowing; ignorant; n **nescience** agnosticism.

nest n structure built by bird in which it lays eggs and rears young; snug shelter; v build, occupy nest; ns **n.-egg** 1 real or dummy egg left in hen's nest to stimulate laying 2 coll money saved up.

nestle v settle cosily; lie, press closely against.

nestling n young bird before it leaves nest.

net[1] n 1 meshwork of knotted, woven cord, thread etc 2 length of this used to catch anything, or for protection; v nets, netting, netted. catch in, cover with net; ns **netting** string, wire network; **netball** team game in which ball is thrown through circular net.

net[2], **nett** n free of all deductions; remaining after all necessary expenses; v yield as clear profit.

nether a lower; below.

nethermost a lowest.

nettle n plant with stinging

hairs on leaves and stalks; v irritate; vex.

network n 1 meshed structure of wire, cords etc 2 system of intersecting channels of communication (roads, railways, radio, TV) 3 system of interlinking operations (business, espionage, crime); v establish set of contacts (n -ing); **n.train** train operating service within regional network (not inter-city).

neuralgia n sharp pain along a nerve, esp in the face a **neuralgic.**

neurology n study of nerves and nervous disease; a -ological; n -ologist.

neurosis n -ses. mild mental illness that causes irrational fear or worry; a **neurotic** abnormally tense, worried, or afraid.

neuter a neither masculine nor feminine; n 1 noun, pronoun of neuter gender 2 animal deprived of sexual organs (v castrate or spay).

neutral a 1 impartial; not taking either side in dispute, esp war; 2 (of gears) disengaged; n state or subject of state taking neither side in conflict; n -ity non-participation esp in war; v -ize make, treat as neutral; counteract, make ineffectual; n -ization.

neutron n electrically uncharged atomic particle; n **n.bomb** atomic bomb causing much radiation.

never *adv* not ever; emphatic negative; *adv* **nevertheless** notwithstanding.

never-never *n Brit coll* hire-purchase.

new *a* **1** not previously existing **2** recently discovered **3** newly grown, produced; fresh **4** unfamiliar; novel; untried; *as* n.**-born**; n.**-found**; n.**-laid**; *ns* n. **blood** new members bringing new ideas, enthusiasm etc; **n. broom** *Brit* person newly appointed, eager to make important changes; **newcomer**; **n. moon** crescent moon in first days of new quarter; **newspeak** artificial language designed to distort meaning of words; **N. Testament** second part of Bible relating life and teaching of Christ and his followers; **N. World** western hemisphere; **N. Year** first few days of January; **N. Year's Day** January 1st; **N. Year's Eve** December 31st; *a* **newfangled** *coll* modern but not easy to adapt to; *adv* **newly** (*n* **newlywed** person just married, *esp pl*; *a* **-wedded**); *n* **-ness**.

news *n* information, reports of recent events; tidings; *ns* n. **agency** agency collecting news for media to use; **newsagent** seller of newspapers, periodicals (*US* n. **dealer**); **newscaster** person reading news on

radio, TV (*also* **newsreader**); n.**-hound** *coll* over-enthusiastic news reporter; n.**-letter** informal occasional letter to members of club, of organization; **newsmonger** *coll* gossip; **newspaper** daily or weekly printed publication containing news, comment, readers' letters, reviews etc; **newsprint** paper on which newspaper is printed; **newsreel** short film on current events; *a* **newsworthy** interesting enough to be reported.

newt *n* small lizard-like amphibian.

next *a, adv* nearest in order, rank, time etc; *idm* **next to** almost; *adv* **n. door** in adjacent building, house; *idm* **n. door to** close to; *n* **next-of-kin** nearest blood relative.

NHS *abbr* National Health Service.

nib *n* split pen-point; *pl* **-s** crushed cocoa beans.

nibble *v* **1** bite gently; with small bites **2** *fig* show signs of being attracted by (offer etc); *n* tentative bite.

nice *a* **1** fastidious; punctilious **2** pleasing **3** delicate; *n* **nicety** accuracy; (*pl* **-ies** subtle details).

niche *n* small recess in wall; *fig* place, scope suitable for person's work, condition etc.

nick *n* **1** notch; slit **2** *sl* police-station; *idm* **in the nick of time** only just in time; *v* **1**

cut notch in **2** *sl* steal **3** *sl* arrest.

nickel *n* hard, silvery-white metallic element.

nicker *n Brit sl* pound (in money) (*pl* = **sing**).

nickname *n* extra name given in affection or derision.

nicotine *n* oily, poisonous alkaloid in tobacco.

niece *n* brother's or sister's daughter.

nifty *a coll* **1** skilful **2** effective **3** stylish.

niggard *n* covetous, miserly person; *a* **niggardly**.

niggle *v* fret, be fussy over petty details; *a* **niggling** too fussy; small but persistent.

nigh *a, adv, prep, ar* near.

night *n* **1** period from sunset to sunrise **2** darkness; *ns* n. **blindness** inability to see in dark or dim light; **nightcap** drink before bedtime; **nightclub** late night venue for entertainment, dancing etc; **nightdress** garment worn by woman in bed (*also coll* **nightie**); **nightfall** onset of darkness after sunset; **nightingale** bird with melodious song (often noticed at night); n.**-life** entertainments at night; **nightmare 1** frightening dream **2** harrowing experience (*a* **-marish**); **nightshade** plant with poisonous berries and bell-shaped flowers; n.**-shirt** long loose garment worn in bed by man; **n. soil** human excrement taken from latrines to use as fertilizer; **n. watchman** man employed to guard building, construction site etc at night; *a, adv* **nightly** (happening) every night.

nihilism *n* systematic rejection of all religious beliefs and moral principles; violent revolutionary beliefs, doctrines etc; anarchism; *n* **-list**.

nil *n* nothing.

nimble *a* quick; agile; alert; clever.

nincompoop *n* fool.

nine *n, pron, det* cardinal number next above eight; *idm* **nine day's wonder** short-lived success; *idm* **dressed up to the nines** elaborately dressed; *as, ns, prons, dets* **ninth** ordinal number 9th part; **nineteen** nine plus ten; **nineteenth**; **ninety** nine tens; **ninetieth**; *n* **ninepins** skittles.

nip *v* **nips, nipping, nipped. 1** pinch sharply with fingers, claws **2** pinch off (buds, leaves etc) **3** (*of wind*) affect with stinging sensation; *idm* **nip sth in the bud** stop sth before it can develop; *n* **1** pinch **2** sharp keen bite of wind or frost **3** small drink; *n* **nipper** *sl* small boy; *pl* **-s** pincers; *a* **nippy 1** quick; active **2** frosty; cold.

nipple *n* **1** small protuberance at centre of breast in mammal; teat of woman's breast **2** metal or plastic device of similar shape for

lubrication of machinery.

nisi *conj leg* becoming valid after certain interval unless cause is shown for rescinding it.

nit[1] *n* egg of louse or other parasitic insect; *ns* **nit-picking** concern for little trivial details as a basis for finding fault (*a* showing such concern); **n.-picker**.

nit[2] *n* silly person (*also* **nitwit**).

nitre *n* potassium nitrate; saltpetre; *ns* **nitrate** compound of nitric acid and alkali; **nitrogen** colourless gaseous element, forming 78% of the air; *a* **nitric** (*n* **n. acid** powerful corrosive acid); *n* **nitroglycerine** explosive liquid.

no *n* refusal; negative word, vote; (*pl* **noes**); *a* not any; *adv* in no respect; none.

no. *abbr* number.

No. 10 *n Brit* Prime Minister's London house, 10 Downing Street.

nobble *v sl* **1** interfere with horse before race (by drugging or injury) **2** obtain money etc by dishonest means.

Nobel prize *n* any of the prizes founded by Alfred Bernhard, awarded annually for outstanding achievement in science, literature or promotion of peace.

noble *a* **1** famous **2** having high ideals; admirable **3** of high rank; *n* person of noble birth; *ns* **nobility** quality of being noble; body of those

with hereditary titles; **nobleman** member of nobility; peer.

nobody *pron* no person; *n* person of no account.

no-claim bonus *n* amount of reduction in insurance premium on basis of not having made any claim over a period of time.

nocturnal *n* of, in, by night; active at night.

nod *v* **nods, nodding, nodded.** bow head slightly, sharply in assent, greeting etc; droop head when drowsy; *phr v* **nod off** fall asleep; *n* act of nodding; *idm* (**have a**) **nodding acquaintance** (have) very limited knowledge.

node *n* **1** knot, joint on stem of plant **2** hard swelling on muscle **3** point of intersection; *n* **nodule** small rounded lump; *a* **nodular** of nodes; having nodules.

Noel *n* Christmas.

no-fly zone *n* area within which no aircraft are permitted to fly.

noise *n* clamour; loud sound; din; *as* **-less**; **noisy** making much noise; *n* **big noise** *sl* important person.

nomad *n* member of wandering, pastoral tribe; wanderer; *a* **-ic**.

no-man's land *n* neutral zone between two opposing forces, controlled by neither.

nom-de-plume *n Fr* writer's assumed name; pen-name.

nomenclature *n* system of

names or naming used in classifying; terminology.

nominal a 1 pertaining to name 2 existing in name only 3 inconsiderable.

nominate v name, propose person for post, office; ns **-ator; -ation; nominee** person nominated.

nominative a in the form used for grammatical subject.

non- prefix not; opposite of 1 forming as; **non-aligned** not supporting major political power; **noncommissioned** below rank of commissioned officer (n **n-officer,** also NCO); **non-specific** general (n **n-urethritis** type of venereal disease, also NSU); **non-stick** treated to prevent food sticking during cooking; **non-U** not (regarded as) typical of upper class; 2 forming ns; **non-event** event that fails to meet expectations; **nonflammable** a not burning easily; **non sequitur** statement that does not logically follow from what has gone before; **non-smoker** 1 person who never smokes 2 compartment where smoking is forbidden; **non-starter** 1 competitor that withdraws at the start of a race 2 plan that is seen to be unworkable. Many other negative compounds are not given here, where the meaning may be deduced from the simple word.

nonagenerian n person aged

between 90 and 100.

nonce n **for the n.** for the present; once only.

nonchalant a indifferent; n **nonchalance.**

noncommital a refusal to take sides, neutral; adv **-ly.**

nonconformist n dissenter esp from C of E.

nondescript a not easily classified; vague; indefinite.

none pron no one; adv in no way.

nonentity n unimportant person; non-existent thing.

nonetheless adv nevertheless, however.

nonplussed a in state of perplexity, bewilderment; taken aback.

nonsense n lack of sense; meaningless words, statement; absurdity; a **nonsensical** absurd; ridiculous; adv **-ly.**

noodle n thin flat strip of macaroni paste.

nook n corner; retreat; hiding-place.

noon n midday; twelve o'clock.

noose n loop of rope with slipknot, allowing it to be drawn tight.

nope adv coll no.

nor conj and not.

Nordic a pertaining to Germanic races of Europe, esp Scandinavian.

norm n recognized standard; pattern; type; a **-al** average; ordinary; conforming to accepted standard, type; n **-ality;** v **normalize** make

normal (n **-ization**).

normative a prescribing or conforming to a norm.

north n cardinal compass point opposite midday sun; northern parts of earth or country generally; a **to,** **from, in** north; as **northern** pertaining to north; **northerly** from, to direction of north; n **northerner** inhabitant of northern region of country.

nos abbr numbers.

nose n external organ of smell, used in breathing; any projection like a nose; idm **a nose for** an instinctive way of finding; v sniff at; idm **nose one's way** move cautiously; phr vs **nose about/around** coll try (stealthily) to satisfy one's curiosity; **nose out** coll discover; ns **nosebag** bag of food worn by horse; **nosebleed** instance of blood pouring from nose; **n.-cone** front end of rocket; v **nosedive** 1 (of aircraft) fall suddenly nose first 2 fig fall dramatically (also n such a fall); **nosegay** small bouquet; a **nosey** see **nosy** .

nosh n sl food; v sl to eat.

nostalgia n 1 home-sickness 2 longing for what is past.

nostril n one of two external orifices of nose.

nosy a coll inquisitive; **n.** **parker** person who pries into other people's business.

not adv expressing denial, negation, refusal.

notable *a* remarkable; conspicuous; *n* notable person; *adv* **-ably**; *n* **-ability** person of distinction.

notary *n* public official legally entitled to attest, certify deeds, contracts etc.

notation *n* system of symbols for representing numbers, musical notes etc.

notch *n* V-shaped cut, nick; *v* make notches in.

note *n* 1 brief informal letter or memorandum 2 brief comment on textual matter (*eg* footnote) 3 piece of paper money; printed or written promise of payment 4 single musical sound; symbol for this on paper 5 sign, hint of specified feeling (*eg* **note of anger**); *idm* **of note** famous; *idm* **take note of** pay attention to; *v* 1 observe 2 record in writing; *ns* **notebook** book of paper for making notes; **notepaper** paper for writing letters; *as* **noted** famous; *a* **n.-worthy** of interest and/or importance (*n* **-iness**).

nothing *n* not anything; zero; *adv* not at all.

notice *n* 1 announcement 2 attention 3 dismissal (of servant) 4 written warning 5 review (of play, book etc); *v* observe; here; *a* **-able** striking; easily seen; appreciable; *adv* **-ably**.

notify *v* notifies, notifying, notified. report; make known; tell officially; *a* **notifiable**; *n* **notification**.

notion *n* idea; conception; fancy; belief *n* **notional 1** imaginary 2 assumed for the purpose of discussion; theoretical (*adv* **-ly**).

notoriety *n* quality of being well-known in bad sense; *a* **notorious** commonly known in unfavourable sense.

notwithstanding *prep* in spite of; *adv*, *conj* although.

nougat *n* sweetmeat of sugar paste and nuts, fruit etc.

nought *n* nothing; symbol 0.

noughts and crosses *n* game where players compete to prevent each other from completing a row of Os or Xs.

noun *n* word used as name of person, thing, action quality; substantive.

nourish *v* feed; sustain with food 2 *fig* foster, encourage; *n* **-ment**.

nous *n* Gk intelligence; commonsense.

nova *n* star whose brilliance flares briefly.

nouveau riche *n* Fr person who makes a show of having recently acquired wealth (*pl* **nouveaux riches**).

novel *a* new; strange; unfamiliar; *n* **novelty 1** newness 2 newly-marketed knick-knack.

novel *n* fictional prose story in book form; *ns* **-ist** author of novels; **novelette** short novel or story; **novella** work of fiction longer than short story but shorter and less complex than novel.

November *n* the eleventh month.

novice *n* 1 inexperienced beginner 2 monk, nun who has not taken monastic vows; *n* **novitiate**, **novictiate** period of being a novice; apprenticeship.

now *adv* at present time; *idm* **now and again/then** occasionally; *adv* **nowadays** in these days.

no way *interj*, *adv* *sl* certainly not.

nowhere *adv* not in any place; *idm* **nowhere near 1** not at all near 2 nothing like.

nowise *adv* in no way; by no means.

noxious *a* harmful; corrupting; offensive.

NSU *abbr med* non-specific urethritis.

nth *a* last of an uncountable number; *idm* **to the nth degree** in the extreme.

nuance *n* delicate distinction in colour, meaning, feeling, tone of voice etc.

nubile *a* marriageable (of a girl).

nuclear *a* 1 of, from an atomic nucleus (*n* **n. energy** energy released by fission or fusion of nucleus) 2 producing nuclear energy (*ns* **n. fission** splitting of nucleus; **n. fusion** combining of nuclei; **n. reaction**, **n. reactor**) 3 of atomic weapons (*ns* **n. disarmament**, **n. deterrent** theory of keeping atomic weapons to discourage potential enemies from attacking; **n. war**; **n. winter** period of cold and darkness likely to follow atomic war) **4** forming a compact unit (*n* **n. family** parents and children, excluding other relatives).

nucleus *n* **nuclei** *Lat* **1** central core or kernel **2** *fig* starting point **3** core of atom.

nucleic acid *n* complex acid found in all living cells (*eg* DNA or RNA).

nude *a* naked; bare; *ns* **nudity, nudism** practice of going naked for health or religious reasons; **nudist**.

nudge *v* push slightly with elbow; *n* such touch.

nugget *n* **1** small lump of metal, *esp* of natural gold **2** small but valuable piece of information.

nuisance *n* something harmful, offensive, annoying.

nuke *a* US *sl* nuclear weapon; *v* US *sl* attack, destroy with this.

null *a* of no effect; void; **null and void** *leg* without legal force; not valid; *n* **nullity**; *v* **nullify** make useless; cancel.

numb *a* deprived of feeling *esp* through cold; *v* make numb; deaden.

number *n* **1** mathematical unit; symbol(s) representing this **2** countable amount (*eg* **a number of times**; *pl* large numbers of people) **3** issue of periodical **4** item in musical or variety show **5** *ling* category of singular or plural **6** *coll* item (described

in admiration); *idm* **have sb's number** have information to use against sb; *idm* **sb's number is up** sb is about to die; *ns* **n. one 1** most important person **2** oneself; **numberplate** plate on motor vehicle with registration number.

numeral *a* of, expressing number; *n* graphic symbol of number; *v* **numerate** count (*a* able to calculate; *n* **numeracy**); *ns* **numerati** *pl coll* financial whizz kids; **numeration 1** method or process of numbering **2** expression of numbers in words; **numerator** number above line in a numerical fraction; *as* **numerical** concerning numbers (*adv* **-ly**); **numerous** many.

nun *n* member of woman's religious order, living in convent; *n* **nunnery** community of nuns; convent.

nuptial *a* of, relating to marriage; *n pl* **-s** wedding ceremony.

nurse *n* **1** person trained to care for sick or injured **2** woman employed to look after children; *v* suckle (an infant); act as nurse to; **nurse** *n ns* **nursemaid** woman employed to look after baby or small child; **nursing** work of a medical nurse; **nursing home** home where sick or elderly people can live and be cared for.

nursery *n* **1** room designed for

small children to play in; *ns* **n. rhyme** song written for small children; **n. school** play school for children (aged 2 to 5) **2** place for rearing young plants; *n* **nurseryman** man who grows plants for sale; **nursery slope** gentle slope for inexperienced skiers.

nurture *n* nourishment; fostering care; training; *v* rear; educate.

nut[1] *n* **1** hard-shelled fruit of certain plants **2** *sl* head; testicles; *idm* **a hard nut to crack** a very stubborn person; *idm* **do one's nut** *coll* be frantically worried or furious; *idm* **off one's nut** *sl* insane; *ns* **nutcase** *sl* mad person; **nutcracker** tool for removing hard shell of nut; **nutmeg** hard fragrant seed of Indian tree; this powdered and used as spice (*v Brit coll sport* make player look foolish by passing ball between his/her legs); *a* **nuts** *sl* insane; **nutshell** (*idm* **in a nutshell** to put it concisely); *a* **nutty 1** containing nuts, food like nuts **2** *sl* insane.

nut[2] *n* hollow metal collar with internal thread to fit over bolt or screw; *idm* **nuts and bolts** basic skills or facts relating to a job.

nutrient *a* nourishing; *ns* **nutriment** nourishing food; **nutrition** process of receiving nourishment; *as* **nutritious, nutritive**

nourishing; maintaining growth.

nylon *n* synthetic plastic material with properties similar to those of silk.

nymph *n* **1** legendary maiden deity, spirit of woods, hills, rivers etc; **2** insect pupa; chrysalis.

nymphet *n coll* young and sexually attractive girl.

nymphomania *n* excessive sexual desire in women; *n* **-maniac**.

oaf *n* clumsy, awkward fellow, lout.

oak *n* type of common tree; oak timber; *a* of oak; *n* **oak-apple** fleshy excrescence on oak caused by gall-flies *a* **oaken** *lit* of oak wood.

OAP *abbr Brit* old-age pensioner (=**senior citizen**).

oar *n* long pole with flattened blade, used to propel boat; *idm* **put/shove/stick in one's oar/one's oar in** *coll* give unwanted advice; *v* row (*ns* **oarsman, oarswoman**).

oasis *n* **oases**. fertile place in desert.

oast *n* kiln for drying hops; *n* **o-house** building containing oast.

oat *n pl usu* cereal plant; its seed; *n* **oatmeal**.

oath *n* **1** solemn appeal to God or some sacred thing, as witness to truth of statement **2** curse; profanity.

OBE *abbr* Officer of (the

Order of) the British Empire.

obedience *n* submission to authority; act of obeying.

obedient *a* submissive; willing to obey.

obeisance *n* bow; formal gesture of respect etc.

obelisk *n* upright, four-sided, tapering stone pillar.

obese *a* extremely fat; corpulent; *n* **obesity**.

obey *v* carry out commands of; submit; follow rules of.

obfuscate *v* obscure; bewilder; confuse.

obiter dictum *n Lat* incidental remark (*pl* **obiter dicta**).

obituary *n* notice of death of person, often with short biography.

object[1] *n* **1** material thing **2** aim; purpose **3** *ling* noun, pronoun, noun phrase, noun clause affected by action of transitive verb or following preposition; *idm* **be no**

object be no problem; *idm* **(an/the) object of** sb/sth subjected to, likely to arouse (specified feeling or reaction); *n* **object lesson** event that serves as an example or warning; *a* **objective 1** relating to objects **2** existing outside the mind; *n* object, purpose aimed at.

object[2] *v* **1** be opposed to; feel dislike to **2** protest against; *n* **objection** (*a* **-able** liable to objection; offensive); *n* **objector**.

oblate *a* (of sphere) flattened at both ends.

oblation *n* solemn, religious offering; *n* **oblate** one dedicated to monastic life.

oblige *v* **1** compel by legal, moral force **2** do favour to; *idm* **much obliged** *fml* thank you; *n* **obligation** binding promise, contract etc; duty; indebtedness for kindness, favour etc; *a* **obligatory** compulsory; necessary to be done; *v* **obligate** bind legally, morally; *a* **obliging** helpful; courteous.

oblique *a* **1** slanting **2** *fig* not straightforward; *n* **obliquity** deviation from straight line.

obliterate *v* blot out; erase; efface; wipe out; *n* **-ation**.

oblivion *n* forgetfulness; being forgotten; *a* **oblivious** unaware; not realizing.

oblong *n, a* (rectangle) longer than broad.

obloquy *n* reproach; calumny; disgrace.

obnoxious *a* disagreeable; offensive.

oboe *n* woodwind musical instrument.

obscene *a* indecent; lewd; disgusting; *n* **obscenity**.

obscure *a* 1 dim; indistinct 2 not clear in meaning 3 unimportant; *n* **obscurity** 1 darkness 2 ambiguity 3 state of being unknown.

obsequious *a* too willing to obey; servile; ingratiating.

observe *v* 1 pay attention to; watch; consider carefully 2 comment; remark; take notice; *a* **observant** 1 attentive 2 alert; vigilant; *ns* **observance** 1 act of observing (laws etc) 2 commemoration; **observation** 1 act of noticing 2 surveillance; *pl* **-s** 1 remarks 2 critical comment on action or event etc; **observatory** building with instruments for watching stars etc; **observer** one who observes.

obsess *v* haunt, occupy mind; *a* **-ive**; *adv* **-ively**; *n* **obsession** fixed idea; exclusive preoccupation of mind.

obsidian *n* glassy, very hard volcanic rock.

obsolescence *n* state of becoming obsolete or slowly disappearing through disuse; *a* **obsolescent**.

obsolete *a* disused; out-of-date.

obstacle *n* hindrance; obstruction.

obstetrics *n pl* science of midwifery; *a* **-tric** of childbirth; *n* **-trician** specialist in midwifery.

obstinacy *n* stubborness; persistence.

obstinate *a* stubborn; persistent.

obstreperous *a* noisy; unruly; turbulent.

obstruct *v* block; hinder; impede; *ns* **-ion**; **-ionism** system of impeding Parliamentary or other business; **-ionist**; *a* **-ive** causing obstruction.

obtain *v* gain; acquire; be valid; *a* **-able** procurable.

obtrude *v* force upon; intrude; *n* **obtrusion**; *a* **obtrusive** thrusting; intrusive.

obtuse *a* blunt; (*of persons*) dull, dense; (*of angle*) greater than a right angle.

obviate *v* get rid of; make unnecessary.

obvious *a* easily seen; clear; lacking subtlety.

occasion *n* 1 point of time when some event takes place 2 cause; reason 3 special event; *idm* **on occasion** occasionally, *v* give rise to cause; *a* **occasional** 1 not all the time 2 composed for special purpose.

Occident *n* the west; Western hemisphere; *a* **occidental**.

occipital *a med* of the back of skull.

occlude *v* close, shut in or out; *n* **occlusion**; *a* **occlusive**.

occult *a* hidden; esoteric; supernatural; *ns* **-ation** eclipse; **-ism** study of supernatural.

occupancy *n* act of taking possession and residing in house etc; term of such occupation; *ns* **occupant**; **occupation** 1 possession 2 employment; *a* **occupational**; 1 of one's trade, regular employment (*ns* **o. disease, o. hazard**) 2 by physical or mental activity (*ns* **o. therapy, -apist**)

occupy *v* 1 live in, have possession of (house, land etc) (*ns* **occupant, occupier**) 2 *mil* take, keep possession of (territory) 3 take up or fill (space or time) (*a* **occupied**). 4 keep busy

occur *v* **-curring, -curred.** 1 happen 2 (be found to) exist; *idm* **occur to sb** come to sb's mind; *n* **occurrence** happening; incident.

ocean *n* one of great expanses of salt water; *pl coll* vast amount; *a* **-ic**; *ns* **-ology, -ography** branch of science concerned with oceans.

ochre *n* earthy metallic oxide of iron, used for making yellow-brown pigments.

ocker *n, a Aust sl* boorish Australian (person).

o'clock *adv* (hour) by the clock.

OCR *abbr comput* optical character reader *or* recognition.

oct-, octa-, octo- *prefix* eight.

octagon *n* plane figure with eight sides.

octave *n* eighth note above,

below any note.

octavo n size of book or page made up of sheets folded into eight.

octennial a lasting, coming every eight years.

octet, octette n group of eight.

October n tenth month of the year (eighth in old Roman calendar).

octogenarian n person aged between 80 and 90.

octopus n mollusc with eight arms bearing suckers.

ocular a of eye or sight; n **oculist** specialist in diseases of eye.

OD abbr coll overdose (also v coll take overdose).

odd a 1 not even; not divisible by two 2 not part of complete set 3 strange; unusual 4 not regular; casual 5 plus a bit more (eg fifty-odd a few more than fifty); ns **odd-ball** eccentric person (also a); **oddity** 1 strange person, thing 2 strangeness (also **oddness**); **odd man out** person, thing different from, excluded from rest of group; **oddment** sth left over; remnant; adv **oddly** 1 strangely 2 surprisingly; pl n **odds and ends** oddments.

odds n pl 1 probability of sth happening (**odds in favour of/against**) 2 (in gambling) ratio between amount of prize money and size of bet.

ode n lyric poem, with lines of varying lengths, usu addressed to a particular subject.

odometer n US mileometer.

odontology n study of teeth and their diseases.

odour n 1 smell; scent 2 fig reputation; v **odorize** perfume; as **odorous** 1 fragrant 2 coll bad smelling; **odoriferous** fragrant.

Oedipus complex n psyc (Freudian theory of) child's subconscious sexual desire for one parent and jealousy of the other.

oesophagus n part of alimentary canal leading from mouth to stomach.

oestrogen n hormone responsible for female physical characteristics.

oestrus n phase of sexual receptivity in female; heat.

of prep 1 belonging to 2 coming from 3 made from 4 containing 5 produced by 6 expressing quantity (250g of sth) 7 about; concerning 8 depicting; portraying 9 giving more precise point of reference (eg **afraid of**, **aware of**, **short of sth**).

off[1] a 1 unfriendly 2 not fresh 3 not busy (**off season**) 4 unsatisfactory (**off day**) 5 cutting off current (**off switch**).

off[2] adv 1 disconnected; detached 2 (of fuel or energy supply) not turned on 3 leaving (**just off**); 4 gone on holiday (**off for a week**), on a trip (**off to Spain**) 5 cancelled 6 emphasising completion (**finished off**); idm **off and on** sometimes;

idm on the off chance in case, perhaps; ns **off-licence** Brit shop selling alcoholic drink to take away; **off-print** reprint of selected part of publication; **off-shoot** subsidiary branch; **offspring** child (pl = sing); v **off-load** Brit get rid of; a **off-putting** disconcerting; causing distaste.

off[3] prep 1 away from 2 down from 3 not far from; idm **be/go off sb/sth** have/get dislike, no appetite for sb/sth; idm **off the cuff** impromptu (a **off-the-cuff**); idm **off the record** unofficially (a **off-the-record**); as **off-beat** unconventional (n mus beat that is not normally accented); **off-colour** 1 sickly 2 sexually improper; **off-limits** out of bounds; **off-line** comput not directly linked; not on-line; **off-peak** of, during less busy period (also adv); **off-road vehicle** n strong vehicle with four-wheel drive for use on rough ground; advs **off shore** 1 near land 2 away from land (a **offshore**); **off stage** away from view of audience (a **off-stage**); as **off-the-wall** US sl unexpected and amusing; **off-white** greyish.

offal n 1 edible internal organs of animals 2 garbage; waste matter.

offend v annoy; do wrong; ns **offence** wrong-doing; affront; **offender; offensive**

1 position of attack 2 aggression; *a* offensive 1 unpleasant 2 insulting (*adv* -ly *n* -ness) 3 attacking (*n* attack).

offer *v* 1 proffer for acceptance or refusal 2 give as sacrifice or sign of worship 3 present for sale at price 4 bid as price for 5 show signs of; *n* 1 bid 2 expression of willingness to do something, *esp* to help; *idm* on offer 1 available 2 being sold at a reduced price; *ns* offering something offered *esp* sacrifice to God; money donated; offertory collection taken in church service.

offhand *a* 1 casual (*adv* off hand without reflection) 2 disrespectful.

office *n* 1 duty; function 2 position of trust, authority 3 public, state department 4 building, room where administrative, clerical work is done 5 form of worship 6 *pl* -s kitchen etc and lavatories; *ns* officer one in command in armed forces; one who holds position of trust, authority.

official *n* one holding office *esp* in public organization; *a* having authority; *adv* -ly; *ns* officialdom 1 body of state, public officials 2 bureaucratic attitude 3 red tape; officialese pompous, obscure bureaucratic language.

officiate *v* perform duty;

preside (at); conduct Divine service.

officious *a* meddling; offering uninvited advice; overbearing *adv* -ly *n* -ness.

offing *idm* in the offing likely to appear, happen.

offset *n* 1 beginning 2 side-shoot 3 method of printing from rubber roller; *v* compensate for.

offside *n* *aut* side of vehicle furthest from pavement; *adv* *sport* in an illegal position for receiving the ball (*a* o. rule).

offspring *n* child or children; *fig* result.

oft, often *adv* many times; frequently.

ogle *v* make eyes at; look at amorously.

ogre *n* imaginary, cruel, man-eating giant.

ohm *n* unit of electrical resistance.

oil *n* viscous organic or mineral substance, insoluble in water, and inflammable; *v* lubricate with oil; take oil in as fuel; *ns* oilcake cattle food from crushed oil-containing seeds; oil-colour pigment blended with oil; oilfield area from which mineral oil is extracted; oil painting picture done with oil based paint (*idm* be no oil painting be plain or ugly); oil rig structure to allow drilling of oil from seabed; oilskin thick waterproof material; *pl* clothes from this; oil slick area of oil

spillage, *eg* from tanker, causing pollution at sea; *a* oily like oil; *fig* unctuous.

ointment *n* oily substance for healing wounds, or softening skin.

okay, O.K. *adv, a* coll all right; approved; *v* coll sanction; *n* coll agreement; sanction.

okra *n* (tropical plant with) edible green pods.

old *a* 1 having lived, existed for a long time 2 of long standing 3 former; *idm* any old *coll* emphatic any; *idm* any old how *coll* 1 carelessly; untidily 2 in a poor state of health or morale; *comp* older, elder; *sup* oldest, eldest; *n* the old old people, things; *ns* old age late stage in life (*ns* o. a. pension, -er); o. boy former student of school, college etc (old-boy network *Brit* tendency to favour old boys of one's former school etc, *esp* in making appointments); o. flame sb one was once in love with; o. guard group opposing change in organization; o. hand expert; o. maid *coll* spinster; o. master any great classical painter or painting; O. Nick *coll* the Devil; o. school traditional or conservative ideas or practices; O. Testament first part of Bible, history of the Jews and their religion; o. timer 1 old man 2 well established member; o. wives' tale old belief that one has doubts about; **O. World** Europe, Asia and Africa (*a* **old-world** not modern); *as* **old-fashioned** in style of former times; **out-of-date**; **olden** *lit* of the distant past; **olde worlde** *Brit* artificially old-fashioned in style and appearance; **old hat** *coll* out-of-date.

oleaginous *a* oily, greasy.

olfactory *a* pertaining to sense of smell.

olive *n* evergreen tree; oil-yielding fruit; *a* yellowish green; *n* **o.branch** symbol of peace.

Olympiad *n* period of four years between Olympic Games; *as* **Olympian** god-like; **Olympic, O. Games** modern revival of ancient Grecian athletic meeting.

OM *abbr Brit* (member of the) Order of Merit.

O and M *abbr* organization and method.

ombudsman *n* person officially appointed to investigate and deal with complaints made by private citizens against large organizations.

omega *n* last letter of Greek alphabet.

omelette *n Fr* beaten eggs, seasoned and fried.

omen *n* sign, portent of things to come.

ominous *a* threatening evil.

omission *n* something left out, not done.

omit *v* omits, omitting, omitted. leave out; fail to do or include.

omni- *prefix Lat* all.

omnibus *n* large passenger-carrying road vehicle, on fixed route; *a* having many uses.

omnipotent *a* all-powerful; almighty; *n* **-potence**.

omnipresent *a* present everywhere; *n* **-sence**.

omniscient *a* infinitely wise; *n* **-science**.

omnivorous *a* eating all kinds of food; *fig* assimilating everything.

on¹ *a, adv* 1 forward; ahead; further 2 in progress 3 illuminated; functioning 4 being worn 5 properly fitted, attached 6 taking place as arranged 7 appearing in public; performing 8 aboard; *idm* **be/go on about** *coll* talk tediously about; *idm* **be/go on at** nag; *idm* **not on** not acceptable or feasible; *idm* **on and off** from time to time; *idm* **on and on** continuously; *idm* **you're on** *coll* I accept your challenge.

on² *prep* 1 touching surface of; covering 2 in close proximity, adjacent to (on the corner) 3 aboard (on a bus) 4 giving day, date (on Friday 13th) 5 about (topic) 6 making habitual use of (on drugs), temporary use of (on a day ticket) 7 in a (temporary) state (on call, on duty, on heat, on vacation); *idm* **on the house** served free (by the establishment).

once *adv* 1 one time 2 formerly; *idm* **at once** 1 together 2 immediately; *idm* **once for all** without change or compromise; *idm* **once in a while** occasionally; **once more** one more time; *conj* as soon as; **once-over** (*idm* **give sb/sth the once-over** make a quick inspection of sb/sth.

oncoming *a* approaching.

one *det, n* 1 lowest cardinal number (1) 2 particular person or thing 3 the same (at one time, in one go); *idm* **all one** all the same; *idm* **at one** in agreement; *idm* **get it in one** *coll* guess immediately; *idm* **one up (on)** with an advantage (over); *pron* 1 somebody 2 anybody 3 *in giving general advice* you; we; *prons* **one another** each other; **oneself** *reflex*; *ns* **one-armed bandit** gambling machine with long handle that activates spinning wheels with symbols to line up; **one-liner** short joke; **one-night stand** play, musical etc on our, performed once only at each venue; *as* **one-off** 1 done once only 2 made uniquely (*also n*); **one-sided** unevenly balanced; favouring one side too much; **one-stop** *comm* offering full range of services, facilities as a package; **onetime** former; **one-to-one** 1 exactly corresponding 2 involving only two people (*also adv*);

one-way moving, allowing movement in one direction only (*ns* o. street, o. traffic); *n* **one-upmanship** art of winning advantage over others by using good psychology.

onerous *a* burdensome; weighty; *n* onerousness.

onion *n* strong-smelling vegetable.

on-line *a* connected to, controlled by computer (*also adv*).

onlooker *n* spectator.

only *a* single; sole; *adv* solely; exclusively; *conj* except (that); *idm* **if only** expressing frustrated wish; *idm* **only just 1** barely **2** very recently.

ono *abbr* or nearest offer.

onomatopoeia *n* formation of words by imitation of sounds associated with object named *eg* cuckoo.

onrush *n* urgent movement ahead.

onset *n* beginning; attack.

onslaught *n* violent attack.

onstream *a*, *adv* (of oil) in(to) production.

onto *prep* to and upon.

ontology *n* study of the nature of existence (*a* ontological).

onus *n* burden; responsibility.

onward *a*, *adv* forward (in space or time).

onyx *n* variety of agate.

oodles *n pl coll* abundance.

oomph *n coll* **1** energy **2** sex appeal.

ooze *n* **1** liquid mud; slime, *esp* on sea, river-bed **2** slow

trickle; *v* exude (liquid); flow slowly out.

op *abbr* **1** *coll* operation **2** *mus* opus.

opal *n* white iridescent gemstone; *a* opalescent.

opaque *n* not allowing light through; dark; obscure.

open *a* **1** not closed **2** not enclosed (o. **country**, o. **prison**) **3** without a roof; not covered over (o. **car**, o. **drain**); o. **sandwich** sandwich without top slice of bread; o. **wound** injury with broken skin) **4** not buttoned up; undone (o. **collar**, o. **neck**, o. **shirt**) **5** honest; frank (o. **character**, o. **face**) **6** not hidden (o. **quarrel**; o. **secret** fact widely known but not supposed to be) **7** for anyone to visit (o. **house**), to attend (o. **court**, o. **lecture**), to compete in (o. **race**) **8** undecided (o. **question**, o. **verdict**); unprejudiced (o. **mind**) **9** (*of position*, *vacancy*) available; to be applied for **10** (*of textiles*) loose in texture (o. **weave**) **11** (*of exhibition*, *public event*) ready for visitors **12** (*of bank account*) ready to use; *idm* **open to 1** exposed to **2** ready to accept; *as* o.-**air** outdoor; o.-**and-shut** not controversial; easily solved; o.-**cast** (of mining) close to the surface; o.-**door** (of national policy) admitting free trade from other countries; o.-**ended** without

limitations imposed beforehand; o.-**handed** generous (*adv* -ly *n* -ness); o.-**hearted** kind; sincere (*adv* -ly *n* -ness); o.-**minded** receptive to new ideas (*adv* -ly *n* -ness); o.-**plan** with few interior walls to divide up living, working space; *ns* o. **cheque** cheque not crossed and exchangeable for cash; o.-**heart surgery** *med* operation on heart with blood circulation maintained by machine; o. **letter** letter for all to read; o. **season** period of year when fish, game may legally be killed; o. **shop** place of work where union membership is optional; *n* **open space**; outdoors; *idm* **bring out into the open** make known to all; *idm* **in the open** unprotected; *v* **1** unfastened; unlock; uncover **2** make accessible **3** begin; *idm* **open fire 1** begin shooting **2** begin asking questions; *phr vs* **open into/onto** give access to; **open out 1** become wider **2** develop; **open out 1** become wider **2** develop; **open up 1** unlock **2** make accessible **3** begin business production **4** speak more frankly (*adv* -ly; *n* -ness); *n* **opening 1** gap; hole; breach **2** opportunity; favourable moment **3** job vacancy; *a* first; initial (o. **move**; o. **night** first performance at theatre).

opera *n* drama set to music,

sung to orchestral accompaniment; *a* **operatic**; *n* **operetta** short, light opera *n* **o. glasses** small binoculars used by theatre spectator.

operation *n* 1 action 2 plan; project; undertaking 3 act of surgery; *v* **operate** 1 work; cause to function 2 perform act of surgery; *a* **operative** working; valid; *n* worker; artisan; *n* **operator** one who works machine.

ophthalmic *a* pertaining to eye; *n* **opthalmology** branch of medicine concerned with eyes *n* **-ologist**.

opinion *n* 1 personal judgement (not necessarily based on facts) 2 public feeling about sth 3 professional judgment or advice; *v* **opine** utter opinion; *a* **opinionated** obstinate in beliefs etc; dogmatic.

opium *n* narcotic, intoxicant and sedative drug obtained from white poppy; *v* **opiate** mix with opium; *n* 1 drug containing opiate 2 *fig* anything that soothes or calms; *a* inducing sleep.

opponent *n* antagonist; rival.

opportune *a* seasonable; suitable; well-timed; *n* **opportunity** lucky chance; favourable occasion or time; *n* **opportunism** policy for taking advantage of circumstances; **-ist**.

oppose *v* place against; withstand; contend against; *n* **opposer**; *a* **opposite** 1 in

facing position 2 contrary in nature; *as* different as possible (*ns* **the o.**, the complete reverse, contrary of sth; **o. number** equivalent person in a different group or organization); *n* **opposition** resistance; political party opposing that in power.

oppress *v* crush; treat unjustly, cruelly; weigh heavily on, depress; *a* **-ive** 1 tyrannical; hard to bear 2 (of weather) heavy; tiring; *ns* **oppression** harshness; tyranny; **oppressor**.

opt (for) *v* choose; decide (in favour of); *phr v* **opt out** choose not to take part.

optic *a* of the eyes or eyesight (*n* **o. nerve**); 2 scientific study of vision, *esp* in relation to light; *a* **optical** (*ns* **o. character reader** *comput* device that can interpret text by identifying patterns of light and shade, *also* **OCR**; **o. fibre** thin elongated glass fibre that transmits light signals; **o. illusion** thing which is misinterpreted by the eye; **optician** 1 person who tests sight and prescribes appropriate glasses, lenses (*also* **ophthalmic o.**) 2 person who makes and sells optical instruments.

optimism *n* habit of looking at brighter side of things; doctrine that good ultimately prevails over evil; *n* **-ist** *a* **-istic**; *v* **optimize**

render as effective as possible (*n* **-ization**); *a* **optimum** best possible; most favourable (*also* **optimal**).

optimum *n Lat* best, most favourable state, condition.

option *n* 1 choice 2 privilege of buying or selling at certain price within specified time; *a* **-al** not obligatory; voluntary.

opulent *a* wealthy; abundant; luxuriant; *n* **-lence**.

opus *n Lat* work or composition *esp* in music.

or *conj* introduces alternative; offering choice.

oracle *n* 1 prophecy or answer, divinely inspired, given by ancient Greek, Roman priest 2 place, shrine where answer, often ambiguous, was given; the inspired priest; *a* **oracular** of oracle; ambiguous.

oral *a* 1 *med* of the mouth 2 spoken; not written; *n* test of this kind (*also* **o. test, o. examination**).

orange *n* large red-gold citrus fruit; tree bearing this; colour of fruit *n* **orangeade** soft drink flavoured with orange.

orang-utan *n* large reddish-coloured ape.

orator *n* eloquent, public speaker; *n* **oration** set formal speech; *a* **-ical**; *n* **oratory** eloquence, rhetoric; small private chapel.

oratorio *n* musical composition *usu* of sacred nature for solo voices, chorus and orchestra.

orb n 1 sphere; globe 2 ceremonial symbol of royalty; n **orbit** 1 path of planet or satellite round other body in space 2 fig area of influence; a **orbital** 1 of an orbit 2 passing all round outside of city (n motorway that does this).

orchard n plantation of fruit trees.

orchestra n band of musicians playing instrumental music; front part of theatre where such band plays; a **orchestral**; v **orchestrate** compose, arrange music for orchestra; n **-ration**.

orchid, orchis n kind of plant with exotic flowers.

ordain v 1 admit to holy orders 2 decree; enact, appoint.

ordeal n difficult or painful experience.

order n 1 relative position in series; sequence 2 tidiness 3 state of calm, discipline 4 command 5 request for goods, service 6 group of monks etc 7 cap group of people awarded special honour; decoration awarded to them; idm **in order** 1 tidy 2 functioning 3 permissible; idm **in order that** conj expressing purpose so that; idm **in order to** expressing purpose so as to; idm **on order** due for delivery; idm **out of order** 1 not functioning 2 not permissible; n o. **paper** programme of day's business

in committee, Parliament; v 1 command 2 request goods or service 3 arrange in organized way; phr v **order about** give sb series of instructions in a bossy way; a **-ly** tidy; law-abiding n **-liness**.

ordinal a indicating position in series; n such a number (also **ordinal number**).

ordinance n decree, regulation; religious ceremony.

ordinary a normal; usual; average; commonplace.

ordination n ceremony of ordaining priest.

ordnance n artillery; military stores, equipment, material; o. **survey** official geographical survey of Britain.

ore n metal-yielding mineral.

oregano n Mediterranean herb used to season food.

organ n 1 part of animal or plant performing particular function 2 keyboard wind instrument (US also **pipe-organ**); n o. **grinder** street musician playing barrel-organ) 3 fml organization that serves special purpose (eg o. **of government**) 4 fml means of communicating views of group (o. **of public opinion**); a **organic** 1 of the organs of the body 2 formed by living things, not from artificial chemicals (o. **fertilizer**, o. **matter**, o. **soil**) 3 (of farm produce) grown without artificial fertilizer or pesticide (o. **food**, o.

vegetables) 4 fig forming integral part of structure; developing as part of structure (adv **-ally**); ns **organic chemistry** chemistry of carbon compounds; **organism** 1 living being capable of growth and reproduction 2 system composed of interrelated elements; **organist** player of organ.

organize v arrange, group separate parts into systematic whole; make efficient; unite into society etc; **organization** act of organizing; body of persons having common purpose; n **organizer**.

orgasm n violent excitement, paroxysm, esp in sexual act.

orgy n 1 drunken revelry 2 continous round of pleasure; a **orgiastic**.

oriel n projecting bay or recessed window.

orient n (usu cap) Far East (esp China, Japan); a, n **-al** (inhabitant) of the Orient; v **orientate** 1 enable to find sense of direction; steer 2 direct attention and interest of (n **-ation**); ns **orientalist** expert in culture, languages of Orient; **orienteering** form of sport, using map and compass to find one's way across unfamiliar territory on foot.

orifice n mouth, outer opening of tube, pipe etc.

origami n Japanese art of making objects from folded

paper.

origin n source; beginning; initial cause; ancestry.

original a 1 earliest 2 new 3 creative; inventive 4 made, done for first time; n that from which copies are made; first pattern, model; eccentric person; ns **o. sin** (Christian belief in) natural wickedness of human beings; n **originality 1** creative faculty 2 novelty, v **originate** bring about; have origin in (n **-ator**).

oriole n yellow and black bird of crow family.

ornament n decoration; adornment; trinket; v decorate; embellish; a **-al**; n **-ation**.

ornate a excessively adorned.

ornithology n scientific study of birds; a **-ological**; n **-ologist**.

orphan n child who has lost one or both parents; n **orphanage** institution for care of orphans.

ortho- prefix right, correct.

orthodontics n med branch of dentistry concerned with correcting irregular formation of teeth (a **-tic**).

orthodox a 1 (of ideas, methods) generally accepted 2 (of people) conventional 3 cap belonging to Eastern group of Christian churches or to strict Jewish sect; n **-doxy 1** orthodox belief 2 state of being orthodox.

orthography n 1 (system of) spelling 2 correct

spelling; a **-graphic/ -graphical** adv **-graphically**.

orthopaedics n pl branch of surgery dealing with bone deformities; a **-paedic** pertaining to orthopaedics.

Oscar n (statuette presented as) award for best film-making, -acting etc each year; a **o. -nominated** recommended for such an award.

oscillate v swing to and fro; fluctuate between extremes.

osculate v kiss; n **-lation**; a **-atory**.

osier n species of willow, used in basket-making.

osmosis n 1 bio, chem gradual passage of liquid through porous solid matter 2 fig imperceptible process by which ideas gradually become absorbed and accepted.

osprey n sea-eagle.

ostensible a apparent; pretended.

ostentation n pretentious show of wealth etc; a **ostentatious** given to showing off; pretentious.

osteoarthritis n degeneration of cartilage in the joints, causing pain and stiffness.

osteopathy n treatment of disease by manipulation of bones; n **-path** one who practises osteopathy.

osteoarthritis n degeneration of cartilage in the joints, causing pain and stiffness.

ostracise v refuse to associate with; banish; n **ostracism**

exclusion from social group etc.

ostrich n large, flightless, African bird.

other a different; additional; not the same; pron other person or thing; adv **otherwise** differently; conj if not.

other-worldly a concerned with spiritual rather than mundane affairs.

otiose a superfluous; unnecessary.

otter n web-footed aquatic mammal.

Ottoman a Turkish; n low, padded seat without back.

OU abbr Open University.

ought v aux expressing obligation, desirability, probability.

ouija n lettered and numbered board used in seances etc.

ounce n unit of weight, sixteenth of pound avoirdupois; fig small amount.

ounce n snow-leopard; lynx.

our a belonging to us; pron **ours**; pron **ourselves** emphatic form of **we**.

oust v turn out; expel; eject.

out adv 1 away from inside 2 not at home 3 away at a distance 4 revealed 5 available for sale; published 6 no longer in power 7 no longer fashionable 8 on strike 9 unconscious 10 not acceptable; not feasible 11 extinguished 12 wrongly calculated 13 tennis (of shot) landing on wrong side of court line **14** *cricket* (of batsman) dismissed; *idm* **all out** using every effort; *idm* **out and away** by far; *idm* **out of it** excluded from taking part; *idm* **out** to determined to; *as* **o.-and-o**, thorough; **o.-of-date** no longer fashionable; **o.-of-the way** unusual; *ns* **o.-take** tray for letters ready to be sent out.

out- *prefix* **1** *forming* **v** doing better or more; surpassing (*eg* **outclass, outdo** perform better; **outfox, outmanoeuvre, outsmart, outwit** defeat by cunning; **outgrow** grow too big, old for; **outlast** endure longer than; **outlive** live longer than; **outnumber** be more numerous than; **outplay** defeat by playing better; **outrank** be of superior rank to; **outride** ride faster than; **outshine** surpass in brilliance; **outstare** manage to hold one's gaze steady longer than; **outstay** stay longer than; **outweigh** be more important than **2** *forming as, ns* isolated (*eg a* **outlaying**; **n outpost**); external (*eg a* **outside**; *n* **outpatient**); with sudden effect (*eg ns* **outbreak, outburst, outcry**).

outback *n* remote bush country of Australia.

outbreak *n* sudden start of illness, violence etc).

outburst *n* sudden eruption (of emotion).

outcast *n* rejected person.

outclass *v* surpass; excel.

outcome *n* result.

outcrop *n* part of rock stratum coming to surface; *v*.

outcry *n* protest.

outdated *a* old fashioned.

outdoor *a* of the open air *adv* **s.**

outer *a* on the outside; further from the centre; *n* **o. space** space beyond Earth's atmosphere; *a* **outermost** furthest from the centre.

outface *n* **1** outstare **2** overcome with courage.

outfield *n sport* players furthest from batsman.

outfit *n* **1** set of equipment or clothes **2** organization; working group; *v* equip, *esp* with clothes (*n* **outfitter**).

outflank *v* get the better of.

outgoing *a* **1** departing **2** ending term of office **3** extrovert; sociable; *pl* **-s** expenditure.

outhouse *n* small building separate from main one.

outing *n* excursion.

outlaw *n* fugitive not protected by the law; *v* make an outlaw; ban something by law.

outlay *n* total money invested in enterprise, spent on large or multiple purchase.

outlet *n* **1** way out for liquid, gas etc **2** means of relieving tension or emotion, of releasing energy **3** *comm* shop; trading place.

outline *n* **1** line showing shape or contour of sth **2** statement of main facts,

idea; *v* make an outline.

outlook *n* **1** view from a place **2** attitude to life **3** future prospects.

outlying *a* far from centre of city, community.

outmoded *a* old-fashioned.

outmost *a* outermost.

output *n* **1** product of physical or mental effort **2** rate of production **3** computer-processed data **4** telecommunications signal **5** tax charged on goods sent out.

outrage *n* violation; rape; violent transgression of law; *v* violate; offend against *a* **outrageous** disgraceful (*adv* **-ly**; *n* **-ness**).

outré *a Fr* exaggerated; in bad taste.

outrider *n* motor-cycle escort for celebrity.

outright *a* **1** unmistakeable (**o. winner**) **2** complete (**o. denial, o. liar**); *also adv*.

outset *n* start.

outside *n* external part; surface; extreme limit; *a* **1** external **2** unconnected **3** unlikely; *adv* out of doors; *prep* on outer side of; apart from; *n* **outsider 1** person not relating to, not accepted by social group **2** competitor with little chance of success.

outsize *a* unusually large.

outskirts *n pl* outer areas (of city, subject etc).

outsourcing *n* practice of contracting work out to companies or individuals.

outspoken *a* frank; not afraid

to say what one thinks;
adv -ly; *n* -ness.

outstanding *n* 1 remarkable 2
excellent; *adv* -ly.

outstrip *v* surpass completely.

outward *a* 1 going away
(o.journey) 2 on the outside
(o. appearances); visible (o.
sign); *adv* going away (o.
bound going away from
home; *n* O. Bound
Movement scheme to
provide adventure for young
people); *advs* -ly externally;
-s away from centre.

outwit *v* outwits, outwitting,
outwitted. deceive or defeat
by greater cunning.

outworn *a* no longer useful.

ouzo *n* strong aniseed-
flavoured spirit from Greece.

ova *pl* of ovum.

oval *a* egg-shaped, elliptical; *n*
figure of this shape.

ovary *n* female organ of
reproduction; *a* ovarian.

ovation *n* enthusiastic
welcome or applause.

oven *n* heated metal or brick
receptacle, in which food is
baked; small kiln, or
furnace; *a* o.-ready (of food)
sold in prepared state ready
for baking; **ovenware**
heatproof dishes in which
food can be baked, roasted.

over *prep* 1 above 2 across;
from one side to the other 3
beyond; more than 4 during;
throughout 5 by means of 6
because of; *adv* 1 above 2
across 3 finished 4 in excess;
n cricket sequence of six balls
from one end; *idm* all over 1

spread everywhere 2
completely finished; *idm* be
all over sb *coll* dote on sb;
idm over and above in
addition to.

over- *prefix* 1 above (as
overarm, overhand,
overhead; *v*, *n* overhang (of
rock, roof etc) project(ion)
above) 2 providing cover
(*ns* overall loose protective
coat; overcoat; overshoes
galoshes) 3 across (*vs*
overfly, overgrow, overlap,
overlay, overpass, overrun;
adv, *a* overseas) 4 indicating
superiority (*vs* overawe
inspire fear or respect in;
overcome, overpower;
overshadow cause to seem
inferior; overthrow,
overwhelm conquer
completely; *n* overlord) 5
beyond limit (*vs*
overbalance lose
equilibrium; overfill;
overrun exceed scheduled
time; overshoot pass beyond
target; oversleep; overspill
(of liquid) flow over edge;
(of population) spread
beyond city (*also n*);
overstep; *adv* overboard
over side of ship; *a* overdue
late) 6 too much (*vs*
overcharge, overcrop,
overcrowd, overdo,
overestimate, overload;
overplay exaggerate;
oversell be too enthusiastic
about; oversimplify,
overstate; *as* overbearing
dominating; overblown,
overgrown, overjoyed,

overladen, overloaded;
overmanned with too many
staff; over-sexed; over-
subscribed with too many
members or too many
orders; overweening too
arrogant; overweight;
overwrought too anxious;
adv overmuch too much);
overdraft *n* money borrowed
from bank on current
account; amount overdrawn.

overboard *adv* from a vessel
into the water; *idm* go
overboard do too much;
show too much enthusiasm.

overdraw *v* draw money
beyond the credit in one's
account; *a* -drawn.

overdrive *n* mechanism giving
higher set of gears than
usual; *idm* go into overdrive
1 use overdrive mechanism
2 start working harder than
usual.

overhaul *v* 1 check thoroughly
and rectify 2 overtake; *n*
thorough check.

overhead *a*, *adv* above one's
head; *n*, *pl* overheads *comm*
general costs of running
business (rent, electricity,
wages, etc.)

overhear *v* hear message,
conversation intended for sb
else.

overland *adv* by land, rather
than water.

overleaf *adv* on reverse side of
page.

overlook *v* 1 look out across 2
fail to see; omit by accident
3 ignore; forgive.

overly *adv* US too.

overmuch n superfluity; a, adv excessively(ly).

overnight adv, a 1 through, during the night 2 coll sudden(ly) (**o. change**).

overpass n bridge crossing motorway.

overpower v get better of, conquer.

override v disregard, nullify.

oversea(s) a, adv over, across sea; abroad; foreign.

overseer n foreman, supervisor; v **oversee** supervise.

oversight n mistake; accidental omission to do something.

overt a openly done; apparent.

overtake v 1 pass (vehicle ahead) 2 (of misfortune etc) affect suddenly.

over-the-counter a (of medicines) available for purchase without prescription.

overtime adv beyond normal working hours; n extra work of this kind; money earned from this.

overtone n 1 tinge of second colour detectable in basic colour 2 mus harmonic note; pl -s implication of more than literal meaning in what is said.

overtook pt of overtake.

overture n musical composition played at beginning of opera etc; usu pl friendly or formal approach.

overturn v 1 turn upside-down; upset 2 overthrow (regime) 3 reverse (decision).

overview n fml survey; short general description.

overwhelm v flow, cover over; overpower; engulf; a -ing irresistible.

overwrought a too excited; exhausted by emotion.

oviform a egg-shaped.

ovine a of, like sheep.

ovoid a egg-shaped.

ovulate a produce egg(s) from ovary; n -ation.

ovum n pl ova. female egg-cell; n **ovule** unfertilized seed.

owe v be indebted to; have to repay; a owing unpaid; due; conj owing to as a result of; caused by.

owl n night bird of prey; a **owlish** stupidly solemn; n **owlet** young owl.

own v 1 possess 2 admit; confess; acknowledge; a emphasises possession; **own goal** 1 sport goal scored against one's own side 2 fig action accidentally causing harm to one's own interests; ns **owner** one who possesses; **ownership** possession.

ox n castrated adult male of domestic cattle; pl **oxen**; ns **oxbow** horseshoe bend in river; **oxeye**, **oxslip** types of flowering plants.

oxide n compound of oxygen and another element; v **oxidize** unite with oxygen; make, become rusty, or dull; n **oxidation**.

oxygen n colourless, odourless gas in the atmosphere, essential to life; prefix **oxy-** of oxygen; of an oxide.

oxymoron n combination of words involving apparent contradiction (eg bitter sweet).

oyster n edible marine bivalve mollusc.

ozone n concentrated form of oxygen, with pungent smell; coll bracing sea-side air; a **ozone-friendly** not harmful to the ozone layer; n **ozone layer** layer of ozone-rich gases in the earth's atmosphere that absorbs harmful radiation from the sun.

PA *abbr* 1 personal assistant 2 public address (system).

pace *n* 1 distance covered by a single step 2 speed (of walking, running, progress, work); *idm* **keep pace with** go as fast as; *idm* **put sb through his/her paces** give sb a thorough test of ability, stamina etc; *idm* **set the pace** set a speed for others to follow; *v* walk with slow measured steps (across sth); *idm* **pace oneself** set oneself a controlled rate of progress; *phr v* **pace out** measure by counting one's strides; *n* **pacemaker** 1 person setting speed for others, example for others 2 *med* machine used to regulate heartbeats in patient with heart complaint.

pacify *v* pacifies, pacifying, pacified. make peaceful; appease; *a* **pacific** peaceable; *ns* **pacification; pacifism**

systematic opposition to war, or violence; **-ist** believer in pacifism.

pack *n* 1 bundle of things tied together for carrying 2 bag for carrying on back (*also* **backpack**) 3 paper or cardboard container for selling; packet 4 set of playing cards 5 group of hunting animals 6 *rugby* group of forwards forming a scrum 7 *coll* group of people or things with undesirable characteristic (*eg* **p. of liars, p. of lies**); *v* 1 put things into container(s) for carrying 2 fit tightly into container 3 cover or fill with protective material; *idm* **pack a punch** 1 hit hard 2 have a strong effect; *phr vs* **pack in** *coll* 1 abandon (activity) 2 crowd (*eg* spectators) into limited space 3 fit (activities) into short period of time; **pack**

off *coll* send away, *esp* quickly; **pack up** *coll* 1 finish work 2 *Brit* (of machine) fail; stop functioning; *ns* **p.-animal** animal used for carrying goods; **p.-ice** large mass of coagulated ice-floes; *a* **packed** 1 ready for journey 2 overcrowded; *n* **packer**.

package *n* 1 several things wrapped together; parcel 2 related items offered or sold as a single unit; *v* make into package, *eg* for selling; *ns* **p.deal** set of proposals for collective, not for separate negotiation; **p.holiday/tour** holiday/tour with all costs (travel, food, accommodation, insurance) combined by travel agent into single fixed price; *n* **packaging** 1 act of packing 2 packing material 3 *fig* method of presentation for selling.

pact *n* agreement, compact, covenant.

pad[1] *v* pads, padding, padded. go on foot softly; trudge along.

pad[2] *n* 1 piece of soft material to prevent jarring or chafing from movement 2 thick skin under animal's foot 3 *sport* reinforced protection for arms, legs, etc 4 block of writing-paper sheets 5 *sl* place where one lives; *v* 1 protect with pad, pads 2 fill with pads to enlarge shape of 3 extend (writing, speech) by adding superfluous material, words;

a **padded;** *n* **padding.**

paddle *n* short, broad oar without rowlock; *v* propel by paddle; walk barefoot in shallow water.

paddock *n* small grass field, or enclosure.

paddy[1] *n* field where rice is grown in water.

paddy[2] *n coll* fit of bad temper.

padlock *n* detachable lock with hinged loop to be hooked through staple etc; *v* fasten thus.

padre *n* chaplain in armed forces.

paediatrics *n pl* branch of medicine dealing with children's diseases; *n* **paediatrician.**

paedophile *n* someone who is sexually attracted to children.

paella *n* Spanish dish of rice, chicken, seafood etc.

pagan *n, a* heathen; barbarian; *n* **-ism.**

page[1] *n* boy attendant or servant; *v* try to get sb's attention, *esp* by a public address system or transmitter; *ns* **pager** radio apparatus for calling sb by coded signal; **paging** (p.service).

page[2] *n* one side of leaf of book; *v* mark page numbers.

pageant *n* splendid, imposing display in costume; series of richly costumed, historical tableaux or scenes; *n* **pageantry** gorgeous display.

paginate *v* number book pages.

pagoda *n* Oriental temple,

tapering pinnacled tower with several storeys.

paid *pt, pp of* pay; **p.-up member** member who has paid his subscription and is a full member.

pail *n* bucket; *n* **pailful.**

pain *n* bodily, mental suffering; anguish; *pl* **-s** effort; trouble; *idm* **on/under pain of sth** risking (specified penalty); *v* inflict pain on; be source of pain; *as* **painful;** (*adv* **-ly**) **painless** (*adv* **-ly** *n* **-ness**); **painstaking** (*adv* **-ly**); careful, industrious.

paint *n* colouring matter used to give colour to surface; pigment; *v* **1** colour; coat; portray with paint **2** *fig* describe vividly; *idm* **paint the town red** go out and enjoy a lively time; *ns* **painter; painting** act of colouring with paint; painted picture, *esp* hand-painted; **paintwork** area(s) decorated with paint.

pair *n* set of two similar things normally used together; mated couple of animals; *v* arrange in twos; mate; match.

paisley *n* fabric with curved designs and intricate coloured patterns.

PAL *abbr* phase alternation line (colour TV system).

pal *n sl* mate, close friend.

palace *n* residence of sovereign or bishop; large public hall; *a* **palatial** splendid, sumptuous, spacious; **palatine** with royal

privileges.

palaeolithic *a* belonging to earlier Stone Age.

palaeontology *n* scientific study of fossils.

palate *n* roof of mouth; sense of taste; *n, a* **palatable 1** good to taste **2** *fig* acceptable; *adv* **-ably;** *ns* **-ability.**

palatial *a* like, as of a palace; *adv* **-ly.**

palaver *n* conference; idle talk.

pale[1] *a* **1** whitish; wan **2** dimly coloured; not bright.

pale[2] *n* wooden stake; *n* **paling** fencing.

palette *n* small board on which colours are mixed; range of colours.

palimony *n US* money paid by court order to support former lover.

palindrome *n* word, line etc, reading same backwards and forwards.

pall[1] *n* **1** cloth spread over coffin **2** *fig* covering of smoke etc; *n* **pall-bearer** person escorting, carrying coffin.

pall[2] *v* become tedious to.

pallet *n* **1** portable platform used in storage and movement of goods by forklift **2** small, hard straw mattress.

palliate *v* mitigate; relieve without curing; excuse *a, n* **palliative** (giving) temporary relief.

pallid *a* excessively pale; *n* **pallor.**

pall-mall *n* old game,

resembling croquet.

pally *a coll* friendly.

palm *n* 1 inner surface of hand 2 tropical tree 3 leaf of this tree as symbol of victory; *v* conceal in palm; transfer by sleight of hand; *ns* **palmistry** fortune-telling from lines on palm of hand; **palmist**; **palmer** pilgrim; **palm-oil** oil from palm tree; *fig* bribe; **Palm Sunday** Sunday before Easter.

palomino *n* -os. horse of light brown, cream coat.

palpable *a* capable of being felt, touched; obvious.

palpate *v med* examine by touch.

palpitate *v* beat irregularly; flutter; throb; *n* **palpitation** throbbing; irregular, quickened action of heart.

paltry *a* trifling; petty; insignificant.

pampas *n* grassy plains of S America (**p.grass**).

pamper *v* over-indulge; cosset; coddle.

pamphlet *n* short unbound treatise; *usu* on some current topic.

pan *n* broad, shallow vessel *usu* for cooking; *v* **pans, panning, panned.** wash (gravel etc) to extract gold; *phr v* **pan out** result, turn out.

pan-, panto- *prefix* all.

panacea *n* remedy for all ills.

panache *n Fr* ostentation; swagger.

panama *n* hat made from strawlike material.

pancake *n* thin flat cake of fried batter; *v* (*of aircraft*) land flatly and abruptly.

panchromatic *a* (*of photographic film*) sensitive to light of all colours.

pancreas *n* gland secreting digestive juices and insulin.

panda *n* large black and white Himalayan bear; small bear-cat.

Panda car *n Brit* police patrol car.

pandemic *n* disease affecting whole area or community.

pandemonium *n* complete confusion; wild disorder, uproar.

pander *n* procurer; pimp; *v* act as pander; *phr v* **pander to** gratify, encourage (unworthy desires, etc).

Pandora's box *n* situation arousing curiosity and great temptation, but bringing all kinds of trouble.

p and p *abbr* postage and packing.

pane *n* single sheet of glass in window.

panel *n* 1 rectangular piece of material set into surface (of door, dress etc) 2 list of persons called for jury service 3 group of persons taking part in quiz, or game before audience; *v* **panels, panelling, panelled.** fit, ornament with panels; *n* **panelling** series of panels.

pang *n* sudden sharp pain.

panhandle *n US* narrow strip of land; *v US coll* accost (passer-by) for money.

panic *n* sudden, excessive, infectious terror, alarm; *n* **p.stations** sudden realisation of need for urgent action; *as* **p.stricken** terrified; **panicky** *coll* affected by feeling of panic.

pannier *n Fr* basket carried on back (of mule etc).

panorama *n* 1 wide, unbroken view 2 series of scenes, pictures showing historical or other views; *a* **panoramic**.

pan-pipes *n mus* instrument of reed pipes of different lengths.

pansy *n* wild or garden plant of violet family.

pant *v* gasp for breath; *phr v* **pant for** long intensely for; *n* short, laboured breath.

pantaloon *n* 1 foolish old man in pantomime 2 *ar* long tight trousers.

pantechnicon *n* furniture removal-van or store.

panther *n* leopard.

panties *n pl coll* short close-fitting knickers.

pantile *n* roofing-tile.

pantograph *n* instrument for reproducing drawing, plan etc on larger or smaller scale.

pantomime *n* 1 theatrical performance, based on legend or fairy tale, *usu* given at Christmas 2 show where words are replaced with actions and gestures.

pantry *n* room where food, plates etc are kept.

pants *n pl* 1 *Brit* underpants;

knickers 2 *US* trousers; *idm*
with one's pants down *coll*
in a state of embarrassing
unreadiness.

pap *n* soft, sloppy food; mash.

Papacy *n* office of pope;
papal system; *a* **papal**
pertaining to pope, or
papacy.

paparazzi *n pl* newspaper
photographers who follow
famous people.

papaya *n* tropical tree with
fleshy edible fruit (*also*
pawpaw *or* **custard apple**).

paper *n* 1 substance made
from pulped wood fibres,
rags etc, formed into thin
sheets for writing, drawing
etc 2 newspaper 3 set of
examination questions 4
scholarly study of topic in
form of article or lecture; *v*
cover with paper; *idm*
paper over the cracks hide
evidence of disagreement;
idm **on paper** in theory; *ns*
paperback book with thin
cardboard cover; **p.-boy/-
girl** young person
delivering newspapers;
p.chase game where
players follow trail of
pieces of paper; **p.clip**
metal clip for holding
several sheets of paper
together; **p.tiger** person
less threatening than
he/she tries to appear;
paperweight heavy object
to stop papers from
blowing away; **paperwork**
writing of reports, letters,
memos etc in an office.

papier mâché *n Fr* pulped
paper mixed with paste and
used as modelling material.

paprika *n* red, capsicum
pepper.

papyrus *n Gk* sedge-like plant;
writing material of this; *pl*
papyri manuscript written
on this.

par *n* equality of value;
nominal value (esp of
stocks, shares); *fig* normal
state of health etc.; *golf*
number of strokes reckoned
as perfect score for hole,
course; *a* **parity** equality;
analogy.

para- (**par-** before vowel or h
mute) *prefix* 1 beside;
beyond 2 contrary; wrong 3
ancillary to 4 defence
against (*eg* **parachute** *abbr*
para *also used as prefix*:
paratroop, parafoil etc).

parable *n* brief story with
moral lesson.

parabola *n* plane curve formed
by intersection of cone by
plane parallel to cone's side.

paracetamol *n* pain-killing
drug.

parachute *n* umbrella-like
apparatus used to retard
descent of falling body; *v*
leap, fall to earth using
parachute; *n* **parachutist**.

parade *n* 1 proud display 2
military review; 3 ground
where this takes place 4
promenade; *v* 1 muster; 2
march solemnly past 3
display.

paradigm *n* pattern; model 2
ling set of inflexions of a

word.

paradise *n* Garden of Eden;
heaven; place of perfect
happiness.

paradox *n* statement
apparently absurd or self-
contradictory yet really true;
a **-ical**.

paraffin *n* inflammable
hydrocarbon obtained from
wood, petroleum, shale etc.

paragon *n* model of excellence
or perfection.

paragraph *n* 1 section in prose
writing 2 short, separate
news item.

parakeet, paroquet *n* small,
long-tailed parrot.

paraldehyde *n* narcotic drug.

parallel *a* (of lines etc)
equidistant in all parts;
markedly similar; *n* 1 line
equidistant from another;
line of latitude 2
comparison; *v* compare; *n*
parallelogram four-sided
plane figure with parallel
opposite sides.

paralysis *n* **-yses.** loss of
sensation and motive power
in any part of body; *v*
paralyse 1 affect with
paralysis 2 *fig* check; render
inoperative; *n, adj* **paralytic**
(person) suffering from
paralysis.

paramedic *n* auxiliary
employee of medical service
(not doctor or nurse); *a* **-al**.

parameter *n* 1 measurable
feature or characteristic 2
usu pl limiting factor.

paramilitary *a* (of a force)
organized like, but not part

of an official army.

paramount *a* having supreme authority; pre-eminent; chief.

paramour *n Fr* illicit lover.

paranoia *n* mental disorder, accompanied by delusions of grandeur or power.

paranormal *a* not explicable by known scientific laws.

parapet *n* low wall; *mil* rampart in front of troops.

paraphernalia *n pl* miscellaneous belongings, accessories, equipment.

paraphrase *n* free rendering of any passage; free translation; *v* express in other words.

paraplegic *n* person paralysed from the waist down.

parapsychology *n* study of psychic phenomena.

paraquat [TM] very poisonous weed-killer.

parasite *n* useless hanger on; *bio* organism which lives on or within another organism; *a* **parasitic**, of, caused by parasite.

parasol *n* sunshade.

paratroops *n pl* airborne troops landed by parachute; *n* **paratrooper.**

paratyphoid *n* infectious disease resembling typhoid.

parboil *v* boil partially.

parcel *n* object, objects wrapped, *esp* in paper, to form single package; piece of land; *idm* **part and parcel of** an essential part of; *v* **parcels, parcelling, parcelled.** divide into parts; wrap up; *phr vs* **parcel out**

share out; **parcel up** wrap as a parcel.

parch *v* make, cause to become excessively dry; scorch.

parchment *n* animal skin dressed and prepared for writing on; manuscript, etc written on this.

pardon *n* forgiveness; excuse; remission of punishment; *v* forgive; grant pardon to; *a* **pardonable.**

pare *v* trim; cut away edge or surface; gradually reduce; *n* **paring** thin slice pared off.

parent *n* father or mother; *a* **parental;** *n* **parentage** ancestry, origin.

parenthesis *n* word, clause etc. inserted into sentence which is grammatically correct without it; *n pl* **parentheses** brackets () enclosing parenthesis.

parish *n* smallest local unit in civil or ecclesiastical administration; *n* **parishioner** inhabitant of parish.

parity *n* 1 equality 2 *finance* equivalent state of currencies.

park *n* 1 public garden in town 2 area of grass and trees surrounding mansion 3 country area set aside as nature reserve etc 4 place where cars etc may park; *v* 1 put car etc in car park or leave elsewhere 2 *coll* leave object in one place, *usu* temporarily; *n* **parking** act of leaving stationary vehicle (*ns* **p.-meter** machine

accepting coins to pay for limited period of parking by roadside; **p.-ticket** police notice advising motorist of fine to pay for illegal parking.

parka *n* hooded warm jacket.

Parkinson's disease *n* disease of nervous system causing severe lack of muscular control.

parky *a sl* chilly.

parlance *n* manner of speaking; words; idiom.

parley *n* conference *esp* between opponents, on peace terms; *v* discuss terms.

parliament *n* supreme legislative body of UK; representative law-making body; *a* **parliamentary;** *n* **parliamentarian** one experienced in parliamentary procedure; *hist* Roundhead.

parlour *n* 1 (formerly) sitting-room 2 in compounds (*esp* US -**parlor**) shop that provides specified goods or services (*eg* beauty-p., ice-cream-p., funeral-p.); *n* **parlour game** game played in the home, *esp* word game.

parochial *a* pertaining to parish; *fig* narrow-minded.

parody *n* -**dies. 1** mocking imitation of author's style or work 2 bad imitation, travesty; *v* **parodies, parodying, parodied.** make fun of by imitating.

parole *n Fr* word of honour, solemn pledge, *esp* given by prisoner released early or temporarily from prison.

parquet n flooring made of inlaid wooden blocks.

parr n young salmon.

parricide n murder or murderer of parent.

parrot n 1 tropical bird with hooked beak, able to imitate human speech 2 fig imitator; v repeat unthinkingly.

parse v describe (word), analyse (sentence) grammatically.

parsec n unit of astronomical distance (approx 3.26 light years).

parsimony n undue economy; stinginess; a parsimonious.

parsley n culinary herb.

parsnip n plant with edible, cream-coloured root.

parson n rector; vicar; clergyman; n **parsonage** house of parson.

part[1] n 1 portion; section; component 2 share 3 role 4 member of organism; pl -s area (eg **remote parts**); idm **look the part** have suitable appearance (for job); idm **on the part of sb** by, from sb; idm **take in good part** accept with good humour; idm **take sb's part** act in sb's defence; idm **of many parts** with many talents; ns **p. of speech** ling grammatical category of word; **p.-song** song with three or more different voice parts; adv **partly** in part.

part[2] v 1 separate; divide 2 go different ways; idm **part company (with)** be separated (from); phr v **part with** let go; relinquish; n **parting** 1 departure (n **p.shot** final remark or action made when leaving 2 line made where hair is combed in different directions.

partaker n participant; one who takes part in; v **partake** take share in; pt **partook**; pp **partaken**.

parterre n Fr level space with flower-beds.

parthenogenesis n bio reproduction without fertilization by male.

partial a 1 forming part of whole 2 biased; idm **partial to** fond of; n **partiality** bias in favour; fondness.

participate v have share in; partake; ns **participant**, **participation**.

participle n verbal adjective, having some functions of verb.

particle n 1 very small amount, part 2 minor, indeclinable part of speech.

parti-coloured a coloured in two contrasting hues.

particular a 1 distinct; separate 2 peculiar 3 specific 4 fussy; n pl -s. detailed account; specification; n **particularity**.

partisan n 1 adherent of party, cause etc 2 guerilla fighter, esp in resistance movement; a showing blind devotion.

partition n 1 division 2 minor dividing wall in house; v divide into parts, sections.

partner n 1 member of

commercial partnership 2 golf, tennis etc one who plays with another, against opponents 3 one who dances with another 4 one person of close couple; n **-ship** 1 state of being partner 2 association of two or more persons in business etc.

partook pt of partake.

partridge n game bird related to grouse.

parturition n act of giving birth.

party n 1 group of persons holding same opinions, esp in politics 2 social gathering 3 squad of soldiers etc 4 coll person; idm **be (a) party to 1** have knowledge of 2 give support to; ns **p.line 1** shared phone line 2 official policy of political party; **p.piece** well rehearsed song, poem etc that one performs when invited; **p.wall** single wall belonging to both of two adjacent rooms or properties.

PASCAL n comput programming language.

Paschal a of Passover or Easter.

pas de deux n Fr ballet dance for two.

pass v 1 go by or beyond 2 (cause to) move in specified direction 3 give (by hand) 4 sport give (by throw, kick etc) 5 transfer (money, goods) illegally 6 spend (time) 7 reach acceptable standard (in test) 8 examine and find acceptable 9 approve (law, regulation) by voting 10 utter (remark, judgement); 11 be changed (from one state to another); *idm* let pass allow; *idm* pass the buck declare sb else responsible; *idm* pass the hat round *coll* collect money; *idm* pass muster be just acceptable; *idm* pass the time of day (with) greet and have a conversation (with); *phr vs* pass away 1 die 2 disappear; pass by ignore; pass for be accepted as; pass off 1 take place 2 gradually come to an end (*idm* pass off sb/sth as sb/sth represent sb/sth falsely as sb/sth); pass on 1 move along 2 die; pass out 1 faint 2 be demobilised; pass over ignore; not select; pass up fail to take advantage of; *n* 1 narrow way between mountains 2 permit (for entry, travel etc) 3 *sport* act of giving ball etc to another player 4 acceptable standard in test or examination 5 *fencing* thrust or lunge 6 *cards* no bid; *idm* come to a pretty/sad pass reach a critical state; *a* passable; *ns* passer-by; passing 1 going past 2 end; death; *a* 1 going past 2 momentary; brief; *idm* in passing incidentally.

passage *n* 1 voyage; crossing 2 accommodation on ship 3 part of book etc referred to separately 4 means of access; *v* (*of horse*) move, cause to move sideways.

passbook *n* 1 identity document 2 building society account record of transactions.

passé *a Fr* 1 out-of-date 2 past one's best.

passenger *n* one who travels in ship, by car, train etc but does not operate it.

passim *adv Lat* throughout text.

passion *n* 1 strong feeling; enthusiasm 2 sexual desire 3 wrath 4 *cap* sufferings and death of Christ; *a* passionate violent; quick-tempered; intense; ardent; *n* passion flower large-flowered climbing plant.

passive *a* 1 inactive; offering no active resistance 2 *ling* of verb form expressing action by which grammatical subject is affected; *n* such a grammatical form (*also* passive voice); *n* p.smoking inhaling of smoke from other people's cigarettes etc; *adv* -ly; *ns* -ness, passivity.

passkey *n* 1 key given to selected people 2 key to open many locks (*also* master-key).

Passover *n* annual Jewish feast.

passport *n* official document granted to enable holder to travel abroad etc.

password *n* secret word, phrase identifying person as entitled to enter (camp, society etc); countersign.

past *a* gone by; ended; taking place in past; *n* time gone by; earlier life; *prep* beyond; after; *ns* p.participle form of verb which combines with auxiliary verbs to make perfect tenses and passive tenses.

pasta *n It* food from paste of flour, eggs and water cut into different shapes.

paste *n* 1 soft, slightly moist compound 2 adhesive compound 3 vitreous compound used for artificial gems 4 compound of finely minced food, esp meat or fish, for spreading; *v* fasten, affix with paste.

pasteboard *n* thin board made from paper sheets pasted together.

pastel *n* crayon made of powdered pigment mixed with gum, or oil; drawing in pastel; *a* delicately coloured.

pasteurization *n* sterilization (of milk etc) by heating; *v* pasteurize.

pastiche *n Fr art, lit, mus* 1 work in style of other artist, writer, composer 2 medley.

pastille *n Fr* 1 aromatic paste burnt as fumigator 2 small lozenge, often medicated.

pastime *n* recreation; amusement.

pasting *n coll* severe beating.

pastor *n* priest; minister; *a* pastoral 1 of office of pastor 2 connected with shepherds 3 (*of land*) used for pasture.

pastry *n* 1 baked paste of flour and fat 2 pie, tart etc made of this 3 small rich cream-filled cake.

pasture n grass for food of cattle; land on which cattle are grazed; v graze; n **pasturage** cattle-grazing; pasture.

pasty n small pie of meat and potatoes, baked without dish; a pale, unhealthy-looking.

pat n 1 quick light touch 2 small shaped lump of butter; v **pats, patting, patted.** tap (dog, horse etc) lightly with hand; idm **a pat on the back** (expression) of congratulation; adv without hesitation; idm **have sth off pat** know by heart.

patch n 1 piece of material used to cover, repair hole in garment etc 2 black spot worn as facial ornament 3 small plot of land; idm **a bad patch** a bad period; idm **not a patch on** not nearly as good as; v mend by means of patch; phr v **patch up** 1 repair temporarily 2 resolve (quarrel etc); a **patchy** not consistent in quality etc; adv **-ily**; n **-iness**; n **patchwork** 1 needlework of patches of different colours 2 fig medley; jumble.

pâté n Fr rich paste of finely minced meat (esp liver) or fish.

patella n Lat med knee-cap.

paten n plate, usu gold or silver, for holding bread at the Eucharist.

patent a 1 obvious 2 protected by patent; adv **-ly**

clearly; n **p.leather** very glossy usu black leather used for handbags, shoes; n licence granting sole right to make and sell invention; **letters patent** open letter issued by sovereign granting privilege etc; v secure patent.

paternal a of father, fatherly; ns **paternity** fatherhood; **paternalism** policy of controlling people by supplying their needs without giving freedom of choice; a **-istic**.

paternoster n The Lord's Prayer; eleventh bead of rosary.

path n 1 way; track; footpath 2 fig line of conduct; n **pathway** track for pedestrians.

pathetic a 1 inspiring pity 2 hopelessly ineffectual; feeble in character; adv **-ally**.

pathogen n organism causing disease.

pathology n science of diseases; a **pathological** caused by, of nature of disease; morbid; n **pathologist**.

pathos n that which evokes sympathy, sorrow or pity; a **pathetic** affecting emotions; pitiable.

patient a 1 enduring provocation or pain 2 persistent in sth; n person under medical treatment; n **patience** 1 endurance without complaint 2 card-game.

patina n 1 greenish film on old copper, bronze 2 fine gloss on old woodwork.

patio n paved area close to a house.

pâtisserie n Fr (shop selling) cakes and pastries.

patois n Fr local, provincial form of speech.

patrial n person legally entitled to live in the UK.

patriarch n father, head of family, clan etc; a **patriarchal** venerable.

patrician n member of ancient Roman nobility; one of noble birth; a of noble birth.

patricide n murder of one's own father.

patrimony n property inherited from one's father or ancestors.

patriot n one who is devoted to and loyally supports his country; n **patriotic** inspired by patriotism; n **patriotism** love of one's country.

patrol v **patrols, patrolling, patrolled.** walk regularly up and down (in); go the rounds; be on guard duty; n 1 small body of troops, police etc patrolling 2 unit of six Boy Scouts.

patron n 1 one who encourages and supports social or charitable undertaking 2 fml regular customer; ns **p.saint** saint regarded as protector of given place, activity or group of people; **patronage** special support; right of presentation to church benefice; *v* **patronize 1** encourage **2** support by being customer **3** treat condescendingly; (*a* -**zing**).

patronym *n* name derived from father, surname.

patten *n* clog; raised wooden shoe.

patter *v* **1** run with quick, light steps **2** utter, speak hurriedly; *n* **1** succession of light taps **2** speech, jargon (of thieves, conjurers, comedians etc).

pattern *n* model; shape as guide in constructing anything; sample; design.

patty *n* small pie.

paunch *n* belly; *v* remove entrails (of rabbit etc).

pauper *n* destitute person supported by charity or at public expense.

pause *n* brief stop or rest; *v* stop for a while; hesitate.

pave *v* cover surface with flat stones etc; *idm* **pave the way (for)** prepare (for); make possible; *ns* **pavement** paved walk for pedestrians; **paving 1** act of, material for laying a paved surface **2** flat smooth rectangular stone (*also* **paving stone**).

pavilion *n* **1** large tent **2** building attached to games-, sports-field **3** summer-house.

paw *n* foot of quadruped with claws; *v* scrape with forefoot; handle roughly and unnecessarily.

pawn *v* deposit article with (pawnbroker); *n* **1** loan thus raised **2** chess piece; *n*

pawnbroker one who lends money at interest on articles pledged.

pawpaw = **papaya**.

pay *v* **1** give, hand over money etc for goods or services **2** produce profit for **3** discharge (debt) **4** render; offer (**pay heed; pay respects**); *idm* **pay one's way** not rely on borrowing; *idm* **pay through the nose** pay too much; *phr vs* **pay back (1** repay (debt) **2** have revenge on; **pay for 1** pay money for **2** suffer as a result of; **pay off 1** repay (debt) **2** be worthwhile, rewarding **3** pay *sb* in order to keep silent; **pay out 1** make (big) payment **2** punish **3** unravel; *n* salary; wages (**p.packet** envelope with wages); *a* **payable** due to be paid (*pt, pp* **paid**); *ns* **payee** one to whom payment is made; **payer; payment** amount paid.

paybed *n* hospital bed paid for by occupant.

paydirt *n* US earth containing valuable mineral ore.

PAYE *abbr* **pay as you earn** (scheme for deducting income tax from earnings at source).

payee *n* person to whom payment is due.

payload *n* **1** part of ship's load for which payment is received; passengers and cargo **2** *mil* explosive power of missile, bomb etc **3** amount of equipment

carried by spacecraft.

paymaster *n* person holding money and in control.

payment *n* **1** act of paying **2** money paid.

pay-off *n* **1** pay in settlement of debt **2** deserved reward **3** climax of story.

payphone *n* public phone operated by coins.

payroll *n* **1** list of employees **2** company's total expenditure on wages.

pc *abbr* **1** per cent **2** postcard.

PC *abbr* **1** police constable **2** privy councillor **3** personal computer **4** politically correct.

PCN *abbr* personal communications network.

pcw *abbr* personal computer wordprocessor.

PE *abbr* physical education.

pea *n* leguminous climbing plant, with edible seeds enclosed in pod; *n* **peanut** ground-nut.

peace *n* calm; freedom from strife, war; tranquility; *as* **peaceable** at peace; not quarrelsome; **peaceful** free from war; calm; tranquil.

peach *n* stone-fruit with pink velvety skin; tree bearing this; *sl* pretty girl; anything very pleasant.

peach *v sl* inform against.

peacock *n* bird with brilliantly coloured fan-shaped tail; *fem* **peahen**.

peak *n* **1** pointed mountain top **2** *fig* highest point **3** projecting part of cap over brow; *v* reach high or highest point; n **p.time** TV time when largest number of viewers are watching (*a p.-time*); *a* **peaked** having peak; **peaky** having drawn, emaciated look.

peal n loud ringing of bells; set of bells tuned to each other; loud, reverberant sound; *v* ring loudly.

peanut n pea-like plant with pods that ripen underground (also groundnut); *pl* **-s** *coll* very little money.

pear n sweet juicy oval fruit; tree bearing this; **prickly pear** type of cactus; its edible fruit.

pearl n lustrous concretion found in some molluscs, *esp* pearl-oyster, and used as jewel; imitation pearl; mother-of-pearl; *fig* outstandingly fine person or thing; **p.-barley** barley with outer skin rubbed off; *a* **pearly** (n **p.gates** *coll* gates of Heaven).

peasant n countryman, rustic; n **peasantry** peasants collectively.

pease n peas; **pease-pudding** porridge of split peas.

peashooter n tube for shooting dried peas by blowing.

peat n fibrous, partly decomposed vegetable matter found in bogs; this used for fuel.

pebble n small rounded stone; **pebble-dash** small pebbles sprayed on outside walls of house; *a* **pebbly**.

pecan n N American nut, allied to walnut.

peccadillo n *Sp* slight offence; petty crime.

peck[1] n ¼ bushel; *fig* large amount.

peck[2] *v* **1** strike with beak **2** *coll* kiss hurriedly; n **1** blow of beak **2** *coll* quick kiss; *phr v* **peck at** nibble half-heartedly; n **1 pecker** pointed instrument **2** *coll* nose; *idm* **keep one's pecker up** *coll* be brave; n **pecking order** order of importance in hierarchy; **peckish** *a coll* hungry.

pectin n gelatinous substance found in some fruits.

pectoral *a* of, in connection with breast.

peculation n embezzlement; *v* **peculate** embezzle.

peculiar *a* one's own; individual; unusual; n **peculiarity** distinguishing characteristic; eccentricity; oddity; *adv* **-ly** strangely; specially.

pecuniary *a* relating to, connected with money.

pedagogue n **1** schoolmaster **2** narrow-minded teacher.

pedal n **1** lever, operated by foot, for transmitting power or movement **2** foot-lever to modify tone of piano, organ etc; *v* **pedals, pedalling, pedalled.** use pedals of organ etc; work, drive by pedals.

pedant n one who attaches exaggerated importance to minor details; one who makes tiresome display of learning; *a* **pedantic;** n

pedantry tiresome display of learning.

peddle *v* retail goods from house to house; n **pedlar** licensed itinerant vendor of small wares.

pederast n man having sexual relations with a boy; n **-asty** this practice.

pedestal n base of large column or statue.

pedestrian *a* going on foot; *fig* prosaic, uninspiring; n person on foot; walker; *v* **-ize** make accessible only to pedestrians; n **-ization**.

pediatrics n branch of medicine specializing in children; *a* **-tric;** n **-trician** children's doctor.

pedicure n chiropody; care and treatment of feet.

pedigree n genealogy; ancestry; *a* of animals bred from known stock.

pedometer n instrument recording distance walked.

pee *v coll* urinate; n *coll* **1** urine **2** act of urination.

peek n glance with half-closed eyes.

peel n skin of fruit or vegetable; *v* strip off, remove any form of covering.

peep *v* look hastily, furtively; n such a look; *ns* **peeping Tom** voyeur; **peep-show** exhibition of erotic pictures in a box seen by magnifying lens.

peer *v* look closely, gaze fixedly at.

peer n person or thing of equal merit, quality etc;

nobleman; a **peerless**
unrivalled, without equal; *ns*
peerage rank of peer; body
of peers; *fem* **peeress**.

peeve *v coll* upset; annoy; *as*
peevish fretful, irritable;
peeved *coll* annoyed; *n*
peevishness.

peg *n* wooden or metal pin,
bolt; *v* **pegs, pegging,
pegged.** fasten with pegs; fix
price etc. by regulations; *n*
off-the-peg ready made
(clothes).

pejorative *a* disparaging;
depreciatory.

pekinese *n* small Chinese dog.

pekoe *n* choice kind of black
tea.

pelagic, pelagian *a* of, in, deep
sea.

pelican *n* large, fish-eating
water bird, with food-storing
pouch beneath its beak; *n*
p.crossing pedestrian
crossing with button to
operate traffic lights.

pellet *n* small ball; small shot;
pill.

pellicle *n* thin skin;
membrane; *a* **pellicular**.

pell-mell *adv* headlong;
confusedly; *n* disordered
haste.

pellucid *a* translucent;
transparent; *fig* clear; lucid.

pelmet *n* strip of board or cloth
concealing curtain rail etc.

pelt[1] *v* throw things at; *(of rain
etc)* beat down heavily; run
quickly; *idm* **full pelt** as fast
as possible.

pelt[2] *n* raw animal skin with
fur or wool.

pelvis *n* bony girdle formed by
hipbones and sacrum; *a*
pelvic.

pen[1] *n* small enclosure for
domestic animals, fowl etc; *v*
pens, penning, penned. put
in pen; imprison; *a* **pent**
confined; repressed.

pen[2] *n* instrument for writing;
v write, put on paper; *ns*
p.friend friend by
correspondence; **p.name**
pseudonym used by writer
(*also* **nom de plume**).

penal *a* connected with
punishment, *esp* legal; *n* **p.
servitude** imprisonment
with hard labour; *n* **penalty**
legal punishment; loss,
suffering as result of folly
etc; *sport* disadvantage
imposed for breaking rule; *v*
penalize punish; handicap.

penance *n* act performed as
proof of repentance.

penchant *n* inclination;
partiality; liking.

pencil *n* instrument for writing
etc, consisting of graphite or
crayon enclosed in wood;
small brush used by painters;
v **pencils, pencilling,
pencilled.** draw, write with
pencil.

pendant *n* hanging ornament;
locket; **pendent** *a* hanging,
suspended.

pending *a* not decided,
unfinished; *prep* during;
awaiting.

pendulous *a* hanging freely;
swinging to and fro.

pendulum *n* swinging weight,
esp one regulating clock

mechanism.

penetrate *v* pierce; enter;
permeate; *fig* see through;
reach mind of; *a* **penetrable**;
penetrating piercing; shrill;
discerning; *n* **-ation** acute,
subtlety of mind.

penguin *n* flightless Antarctic
seabird.

penicillin *n* one of anti-
infective class of antibiotics,
obtained from mould.

peninsula *n* piece of land
nearly surrounded by water;
a **peninsular.**

penis *n* male sex organ.

penitence *n* sorrow for sin; *a*
penitent having sense of sin;
repentant; *n* one who
repents of sin; *n*
penitentiary reformatory;
prison.

penknife *n* small folding
pocket-knife.

penny *n* bronze coin; 100th
part of £1; *pl* **pennies,
pence;** *idm* **the penny
drops/has dropped** sb
understands/has understood;
a **penniless** poor, destitute.

pennyroyal *n* aromatic herb of
mint family.

penology *n* study of methods of
punishment and prevention
of crime.

pensile *a* hanging down,
suspended.

pension[1] *n* periodic payment
made to retired public
servants, old people etc.; *phr
v* **pension off** dismiss from
work with offer of pension; *n*
-er person receiving
pension.

pension² n Fr small private hotel.

pensive a immersed in sad thoughts; wistful.

penta- prefix five.

pentagon n plane figure with five sides; cap US Department of Defense building.

pentameter n line of verse with five metrical feet.

pentateuch n first five books of Old Testament.

pentathlon n athletic contest comprising five events.

Pentecost n Whitsunday; Jewish harvest festival.

penthouse n small house or apartment on flat roof of building.

pent up a (of emotion) not expressed.

penultimate a last but one.

penumbra n partially shaded region round complete shadow esp in eclipse; a -bral.

penury n want, destitution; a **penurious** poor; mean.

peony n shrub with large red, pink or white flowers.

people n 1 race; nation; human beings in general 2 relatives; family 3 lower classes 4 followers; servants; v populate.

PEP abbr 1 Political and Economic Policy 2 Personal and Equity Plan.

pep n coll vigour; v peps, pepping, pepped. coll **pep up** stimulate.

pepper n pungent aromatic condiment, made from dried berries of pepper plant; v sprinkle with pepper; pelt with missiles; a **p.-and-salt** speckled with brown (or black) and white; a **peppery** tasting of pepper; fig irritable.

peppercorn n dried berry of pepper plant; **p. rent** nominal rent for leasehold premises.

peppermint n 1 pungent aromatic herb of mint family 2 sweet flavoured with peppermint.

pep pill n pill containing stimulant drug.

per prep by means of; for each; advs **p. annum** each year; **p. capita** per head; **p. cent** per hundred (in percentage); **p. se** in itself.

per- prefix through; completely.

peradventure adv perhaps.

perambulate v walk up and down; walk about.

perambulator n light carriage for child, also coll **pram**.

perceive v become aware of through senses; apprehend; a **perceptible** that can be perceived; n **perception** faculty of perceiving; immediate awareness; a **perceptive** quick to notice; aware.

percentage n rate, allowance, proportion per hundred.

perch¹ n edible freshwater fish.

perch² n rod, branch for birds to roost on; measure of length, 5 ½ yds (5m); v (of birds) alight, come to rest; sit, balance on high position.

perchance adv perhaps; possibly.

percipient n perceptive.

percolate v filter, ooze, drip slowly (through); ns **percolation; percolator** coffee-pot with filter.

percussion n 1 impact; violent collision 2 musical instruments played by being struck.

perdition n damnation; ruin.

peregrinate v travel; roam about; n **-ation.**

peregrine falcon n fast bird of prey.

peremptory a imperious; dictatorial; precluding opposition, appeal etc.

perennial a lasting year after year; never failing; n plant lasting more than two years.

perestroika n reconstruction (of Soviet economy and society 1985–1991).

perfect a faultless; complete; of highest state of excellence; n verbal tense expressing complete action; v improve; make highly competent; n **perfection** state of being perfect.

perfidy n treachery; faithlessness; a **perfidious.**

perforate v pierce; penetrate; make hole(s) in; n **perforation 1** act, result, of perforating 2 holes made in paper to make tearing easy.

perforce adv by necessity.

perform v 1 accomplish; carry out 2 enact (play) in public 3 play on musical

instrument; ns **performance; performer** one who performs.

perfume n 1 pleasing smell 2 scented liquid applied to body or clothing; v impart fragrance to; ns **perfumery** place where perfumes are made or sold; **perfumer.**

perfunctory a superficial; hasty; indifferent.

perhaps adv possibly.

peri- prefix round.

perigree n point at which orbit is nearest to earth.

peril n danger; hazard; a **perilous** dangerous; risky.

perimeter n distance all round plane figure; outer edge; boundary.

period n 1 interval of time 2 era; epoch 3 phase of menstrual cycle 4 full stop (.); a characteristic of certain period of time (of furniture, dress etc); a **periodic** recurring at regular intervals (**p. table** list of chemical elements in rising order of atomic weight); a **periodical** periodic; n magazine published at regular intervals, eg weekly.

peripatetic a walking about; itinerant.

periphery n circumference; outside; outer surface.

periscope n apparatus for seeing objects above eye-level, where direct view is obstructed.

perish v die; decay; a **perishable** liable to speedy decay; n pl goods specially

liable to decay; **perished** 1 coll suffering from exposure to cold 2 (of rubber and fabrics) deteriorated in quality; no longer usable; **perishing** 1 unbearably cold 2 coll expressing annoyance with sb/sth.

peritoneum n anat membrane lining inner surface of abdomen; n **peritonitis** inflammation of peritoneum.

periwinkle n 1 trailing plant 2 small edible mollusc.

perjure v bear false witness; forswear oneself; n **perjury** deliberately false testimony under oath; crime of making false statement under oath.

perk up v regain one's health, spirits; ns **perkiness** jauntiness; **perk** coll perquisite; a **perky** cheeky; cheerful.

perm n 1 coll permutation in football pools 2 coll permanent wave (hairstyling).

permafrost n permanently frozen subsoil eg in Siberia.

permanent a continuing without change; lasting; ns **permanence** state of being permanent; **permanency** something that is permanent.

permanganate n purple salt of acid containing manganese (also **p. of potash** or **potassium p.**).

permeate v pass through; saturate; a **permeable** allowing free passage of

liquids.

permit v permits, permitting, permitted. allow; give permission to; tolerate; n warrant; licence; document giving formal permission; n **permission** leave; consent; sanction; a **permissible** allowable; **permissive** allowing unusual freedom, esp in sexual behaviour; (adv **-ly** n **-ness**).

permute v put in different order; interchange; n **permutation.**

pernicious a highly injurious; deadly; fatal.

peroration n concluding part of a speech.

peroxide n compound with maximum proportion of oxygen to other element(s), esp **hydrogen p.** colourless liquid used as bleach or antiseptic; n p. **blonde** woman who has bleached her hair with this.

perpendicular a exactly upright, vertical; n line at right angles to another line or surface.

perpetrate v commit, be guilty of; ns **perpetration; perpetrator.**

perpetual a everlasting; unceasing; constantly repeated; n perpetuity (in perpetuity for ever).

perpetuate v cause to last indefinitely; preserve from oblivion; n **perpetuation.**

perplex v puzzle; make confused; n **perplexity** bewilderment; confusion.

perquisite n profit, monetary or in kind, in addition to regular wages or salary.

perry n drink of fermented pearjuice.

persecute v harass; oppress; treat cruelly, esp on account of religious or political reasons; ns **persecution**, persecutor.

persevere v persist doggedly, patiently in attaining purpose; n **perseverance** prolonged, steadfast effort.

persimmon n US hardwood tree; its fruit, date-plum.

persist v continue in spite of opposition; remain; endure; a **persistent** obstinate; tending to recur; n **persistence** tenacity of purpose; **persistency** obstinacy.

person n 1 human being (pl **people**) 2 individual (pl **persons**) 3 ling category of pronoun or verb, eg **first p.** the one(s) speaking; **second p.** the one(s) spoken to; **third p.** any other individual(s); idm **in person** oneself, not sb acting on one's behalf; **on/about one's person** being carried with one, where one is; idm **in the person of** namely; as **personal** n 1 by, of, for a person 2 private (**p. letter**) 3 derogatory; impertinent (**p. remark**) 4 of the body (**p. hygiene**) (ns **p. assistant** secretary to manager, also **PA; p.**

column section in newspaper or magazine for private advertisements; **p. computer** desktop computer, also **PC; p. organizer** 1 looseleaf wallet with diary, addresses, business and personal information etc 2 electronic equivalent of this; **p. pronoun** ling pronoun showing person, eg I, you, he; a **personable** attractive in appearance and manner; ns **persona** character as seen by other people (**p. grata/non grata** Lat person acceptable, esp in diplomacy with foreign powers); **personage** person of importance; **personality** 1 person's qualities and character as a whole 2 (person with) lively or forceful character 3 well-known, usu popular person (n **personality cult** excessive, blind admiration for famous individual, usu entertainer or political leader.

personify v represent as person; typify, embody; n **personification**.

personnel n all members of staff; man-power.

perspective n art of depicting three-dimensional objects on plane surface; idm **in perspective** in proper relations.

Perspex [TM] strong plastic resembling glass.

perspicacious a having keen mental judgement or

understanding.

perspicuous a clearly expressed; lucid.

perspire v sweat; exude moisture through pores; n **perspiration**.

persuade v induce to think, believe; n **persuasion** creed; way of thinking; a **persuasive**.

pert a impudent; saucy.

pertain v belong to; have reference to; concern.

pertinacious a obstinate; tenacious; n **pertinacity** persistance.

pertinent a relevant; to the point.

perturb v disturb; throw into disorder, confusion; n **-ation** agitation of mind; disorder; deviation of planet from true orbit.

peruse v read through; look over; n **perusal**.

pervade v penetrate thoroughly; a **pervasive** (ns -ness, pervasion).

pervert v turn, divert from proper use; n **perversion**; a **perverse** intractable; self-willed; n **perversity**.

pervious a permeable; penetrable.

peseta n Spanish coin.

peso n unit of money in some S American countries.

pessary n contraceptive device; vaginal suppository.

pessimism n tendency to look on dark side of things; doctrine that world is essentially evil; n **-ist**; a **-istic**.

pest n 1 troublesome, vexatious or harmful person, animal or thing 2 garden parasite 3 blight, mildew etc.

pester v worry, plague esp with trivialities.

pestilence n fatal infectious, contagious disease; esp bubonic plague; as -ilent, -iliential.

pestle n instrument for pounding substances in mortar.

pet[1] n tame animal kept as object of affection; favourite, cherished child; v pets, petting, petted. treat as pet; fondle; n p. name name for a person one loves.

pet[2] n ill-humour; peevishness; a pettish sulky; fretful.

petal n one section of corolla of flowers; a petal(l)ed having petals.

petard n idm hoist with one's own petard caught in one's own trap.

peter out v coll gradually diminish.

Peters' projection n modern world map showing countries in proportional size to one another.

petit bourgeois n, a Fr (member) of lower middle class.

petite a Fr (of woman) of small, dainty build.

petit mal n Fr mild epileptic seizure.

petition n entreaty; urgent request; formal application esp one to sovereign, or court of law; v address petition to; n -er.

petrel n small black and grey seabird.

petrify v petrifies, petrifying, petrified. turn into stone; fig paralyse with fear etc.

petrochemical n any chemical derived from natural gas or oil; p. industry industry producing this.

petrodollar n US dollar earned by selling oil.

petroleum n inflammable mineral oil; n petrol spirit made from refined petroleum, used as fuel.

petrology n study of origin and structure of rocks; a petrous of, like stone.

petticoat n women's underskirt.

petty a trivial; of small worth, scale; n, a petty bourgeois = petit bourgeois; n p. cash money for small payments; p. officer naval NCO.

petulance n peevishness; irritability; a petulant.

petunia n genus of herbs with funnel-shaped purple, cerise, white, etc flowers.

pew n 1 fixed bench, used as seat in church 2 coll seat, chair.

pewter n alloy of tin and lead; vessel, plate etc made of this.

pfennig n German unit of currency $\frac{1}{100}$ of a mark.

PG abbr parental guidance (category of film for which children under 15 need to be accompanied by a parent)

PGCE abbr post-graduate certificate of education.

pH n numbered category denoting level of alkalinity.

phagocyte n white blood-corpuscle; leucocyte.

phalanx n 1 body of closely-massed soldiers 2 fig resolute group of persons.

phallus n penis; image of it used in some primitive forms of religion; a phallic.

phantasm n illusion; apparition; n phantasmagoria series of optical illusions; a phantasmagoric.

phantom n spectre; supernatural or imaginary figure; delusion.

Pharaoh n title of kings of ancient Egypt.

pharisee n self-righteous person; hyprocrite.

pharmacy n preparation and dispensing of drugs; a pharmaceutic of pharmacy; pharmacology study of drugs and medicines, n pl science of pharmacy; ns pharmacopoeia authoritatve list of drugs and directions for their use and preparation.

pharos n lighthouse; beacon.

pharynx n med cavity at back of nose and mouth opening into larynx n pharyngitis inflammation of this.

phase n stage in development; aspect of planet.

phatic communion n ling speech that conveys intent

to be sociable without any other message.

PHC *abbr* primary health care.

PhD *abbr* doctor of philosophy; (person with) higher degree of doctorate.

pheasant *n* game-bird with brilliant colouring.

phenol *n* carbolic acid.

phenomenon *n* anything perceived by senses; uncommon, remarkable event; *pl* **phenomena**; *a* **phenomenal** relating to phenomena; extraordinary.

pheromone *n bio* chemical secreted by animal, insect to attract others of species.

phial *n* small glass bottle.

phil- *prefix* loving; studying.

philander *v* make love insincerely; *n* **philanderer**.

philanthropy *n* love of mankind; benevolence; *n* **philanthropist**.

philately *n* stamp-collecting; *n* **philatelist**.

philharmonic *a* devoted to music (chiefly of societies).

philistine *n, a* (person) showing no understanding of, hostile to artistic creation, beauty or culture.

philology *n* study of linguistics.

philosophy *n* **1** theory of knowledge **2** mental balance, calmness in dealing with events, circumstances; *n* **philosopher** (**philosopher's stone** (formerly) imaginary substance supposed to be able to change other metal to gold); *a* **-sophic(al)**; *v*

-sophize indulge in philosophical theories; moralize.

phlebitis *n med* inflammation of lining of veins.

phlegm *n* **1** viscid substance secreted by mucous membranes, *esp* in nose and throat **2** apathy; indifference **3** calmness; *a* **-atic** not easily excited; sluggish.

phobia *n* morbid, irrational fear.

phoenix *n* legendary bird; unique thing *n* **p. syndrome** tendency for bankrupt businesses to start up again under new identity.

phone *n, v, a coll* telephone; *ns* **p. book** directory of numbers; **phone-in** *TV, radio* broadcast in which listeners at home are invited to give opinions, answer questions by telephone; **phone-tapping** use of electronic equipment to listen secretly to sb's telephone communications.

phoneme *n ling* single speech sound in given language.

phonetic *a of*, relating to vocal sounds; *n pl* science of vocal sounds.

phoney *a coll* sham; insincere; bogus; *n coll* insincere person; *n* **p. war** period when there is a declared state of war but no actual fighting.

phono- *prefix Gk* of sounds (*esp* vocal).

phonograph *n* obsolete instrument for recording and

reproducing sounds; *US* gramophone.

phonology *n* study of sound changes in a language.

phosphorus *n* non-metallic element emitting glow in the dark; *ns* **phosphate** salt of phosphorus acid **phosphide**, compound of phosphorous; **phosphorescence** property of emitting slight glow in dark, without heat.

photo- *prefix Gk* of light; of photography.

photo *n, v abbr* photograph.

photocopier *n* machine for making multiple photographic copies of documents; *n, v* **photocopy** (make) such a copy.

photoelectric *a* pertaining to effect of light on electrons; *n* **p. cell** device that detects, measures light (*also* **photocell**).

Photofit [TM] method of creating composite photograph of sb's face from parts of other photos.

photogenic *a* having qualities that make attractive photograph.

photograph *n* picture produced by action of light on sensitized film; *v* take photograph of; *n* **-er**; *a* **-ic** *n* **photography**.

photogravure *n* process of reproducing, by photography, an engraving.

photometer *n* instrument for measuring intensity of light.

photon *n* minute particle of

light.

photosensitive a affected by action of light.

photostat [TM] apparatus for making photographic copies; fascimile so produced; v take photostat of.

photosynthesis n (in plants) conversion of carbon dioxide and water into food by using energy from sunlight; v -thesize; a -thetic.

phrasal a of a phrase; n p. verb verb combined with preposition or adverbial particle to give new meaning.

phrase n group of words forming part to sentence; striking remark; idiomatic expression; v express in words; ns **phrase-book** book with useful phrases and expressions to assist conversation in a foreign language; **phraseology** selection of words used.

phrenology n theory that one's character, intelligence etc can be deduced from shape of skull; study of shape of skull; n -ologist.

phylloxera n vine-killing genus of aphides.

phylum n class of plants or animals.

physic n medicine; v give physic to; n **physician** one trained in medical profession, who diagnoses and treats disease, but does not operate.

physical a 1 pertaining to

matter 2 pertaining to nature and natural features of universe 3 connected with human or animal body.

physics n study of properties of matter and energy; n **physicist** one skilled in, or student of physics.

physio n coll physiotherapist.

physiognomy n 1 art of judging character from face 2 general appearance and expression of face 3 sl face.

physiology n study of functions and vital processes of living beings; n **physiologist**.

physiotherapy n remedial treatment by massage, heat, exercise etc; n **physiotherapist**.

physique n Fr physical form, structure; constitution.

piano adv mus softly; a, n soft (passage); n pianoforte; a, adv **pianissimo** very quiet(ly); n **pianist** one who plays the piano; n **pianoforte** keyboard musical instrument with strings struck by hammers.

piazza n public square, esp in Italy.

pica n largest size of type used in books, six lines to the inch (25.4mm); 12 pt size type.

picador n Sp mounted bullfighter, armed with lance.

picaresque a Fr (of literature) concerning adventures of a usu likeable rogue.

piccolo n small shrill flute.

pick[1] n tool with wooden shaft, long curved head pointed at one end and chisel-edge at other; n **pickaxe** tool for breaking ground.

pick[2] v 1 pluck; gather 2 choose; select 3 open (lock) without key 4 remove unwanted pieces from 5 nibble; idm **pick sb's brain** use sb else's knowledge; idm **pick holes in** find fault with; idm **pick a fight/quarrel etc with** purposely start a fight/quarrel with; idm **pick sb's pocket** steal from sb's pocket; phr vs **pick at** eat without interest, in small quantity; **pick off** shoot one after the other; **pick on** 1 select for special attention 2 persecute; victimize; **pick out** 1 select 2 distinguish; **pick up** 1 take by hand 2 take by transport 3 acquire or learn informally 4 make a casual acquaintance, usu with person of opposite sex 5 resume (activity) after interval 6 recover 7 find by chance; ns **p.-me-up** intake of food, drink or medicine that makes one feel better; **pick-up** 1 arm and stylus of record player 2 van or truck with low open sides 3 casual acquaintance; ns **pickings** trifles left over; dishonest profits.

pickaxe n tool with sharp points and long handle for breaking hard ground.

pickaback adv on back of

another person.

picket n 1 pointed stake 2 striker posted outside place of employment to dissuade others from working 3 *mil* patrol on special duty; v 1 fence with pickets 2 act as picket in strike.

pickle n 1 brine, vinegar etc used to preserve food 2 food so preserved 3 *coll* trouble 4 *coll* mischievous child; v preserve in pickle; a sl **pickled** drunk.

pickpocket n thief stealing directly from sb's pocket.

picky a fussy.

picnic n casual meal eaten out-of-doors; *coll* thing easily done; v **picnics**, **picnicking**, **picnicked**. go on, take picnic.

Pict n member of race formerly inhabiting Scotland.

picture n 1 painting; drawing; photograph 2 mental image 3 vivid verbal description 4 *pl* -s cinema; v make picture of; imagine; describe; *idm* **(put sb) in the picture** (make sb) clear about what is happening or being planned; a **pictorial** expressed in pictures; n journal, mainly consisting of pictures; a **picturesque** 1 like, forming striking picture 2 vivid; graphic; n **p. gallery** room, building where paintings etc are exhibited.

piddling a *coll* trivial.

pidgin n mixture of English and native tongues to be heard in some Oriental and African countries.

pie[1] n magpie; kind of woodpecker; a **piebald** irregularly marked in black and white blotches.

pie[2] n dish of meat, fruit etc, covered with pastry and baked; n **p. chart** diagram consisting of circle divided into segments to illustrate relative proportions of parts of the whole under study; a **pie-eyed** *coll* drunk.

piece n 1 bit; part 2 item 3 literary, artistic or musical composition 4 *sl* girl; v put together; join; *idm* **give sb a piece of one's mind** tell sb bluntly what you think of him/her; *idm* **go to pieces** lose control of oneself; *idm* **of a piece** similar; *idm* **pull sb to pieces** criticize in every possible way; *idm* **a piece of cake** very easy to do; *idm* **piece together** recreate; reassemble; a **piece-meal** piece by piece.

pièce de résistance n *Fr* 1 best achievement 2 event providing climax to occasion.

pied v of two contrasting colours.

pier n 1 column, mass of stone, supporting arch etc 2 projecting wharf, or landing-place; jetty.

pierce v make hole in; penetrate; stab; a **piercing** keen, sharp, penetrating.

pierrot n *Fr* pantomime character; one of troupe of seaside entertainers.

pietà n *It* image or statue of Virgin Mary and Christ crucified.

piety n devotion to God; dutiful, loyal feelings.

piffle n *sl* rubbish; nonsense.

piffling a *coll* worthless; trivial.

pig n 1 swine; hog 2 *coll* greedy, selfish person 3 oblong casting of metal; v **pig it** live in dirty, untidy way; ns **p. iron** unrefined form of iron; **p.-swill** waste food fed to pigs; **p.-tail** long single bunch of hair worn at back or 2 bunches worn on either side of head; as **piggish** greedy; stubborn; **pigheaded** stupidly obstinate; n **pigsty** 1 pen for pigs 2 very dirty room or house.

pigeon n wild or domesticated bird of dove species; as **p. chested** with rounded chest; **p.-toad** with toes pointing inwards, *idm* **sb's pigeon** sb's responsibility; n **pigeonhole** compartment for papers; v 1 store away in a pigeonhole 2 classify in a too rigid way.

pigment n substance for colouring, paint, dye; natural colour in living tissue.

pigmy n = pygmy.

pig out v pigs, pigging, pigged. *coll* to gorge oneself.

pike n 1 large freshwater fish 2 short spear; n **pikestaff** staff of pike.

pilau, pilaff n dish of meat, rice and spices.

pilchard n large-scaled fish of

herring family.

pile[1] *n* pointed beam driven into ground, bed of river etc; *n* **pile-driver** machine for driving in piles.

pile[2] *n* heap or mass; large building; *idm* **make a pile** become very rich; *idm* **make one's pile** earn enough to be comfortable for life; *v* heap up; *idm* **pile it on** (**thick**) *coll* exaggerate; *phr vs* **pile in** enter or begin in a disorderly way; **pile out** come out in a disorderly way; **pile up 1** form, be formed into a pile **2** accumulate **3** (of vehicles) crash into the back of other vehicles that have crashed (*n* **pile-up** multiple accident of this kind); **atomic p.** nuclear reactor; *v* heap up; make into pile; stack.

pile[3] *n* nap *esp* of velvet; high standing fibres of cloth.

piles *n pl* haemorrhoids in veins of lower rectum.

pilfer *v* steal small quantity; *n* **-er.**

pilgrim *n* one who visits sacred place, shrine for religious reasons; *n* **-age.**

pill *n* **1** small ball of medicinal drugs, swallowed whole **2** *sl* ball *esp* billiard ball; *n* **p.-box** small box for pills; small round concrete fort.

pillage *v* plunder; rob openly; loot; *n*.

pillar *n* slender supporting column; *idm* **pillar of** supporter of (society etc) *n* **p.-box** low, hollow pillar for posting letters in.

pillion *n* seat, cushion for another person placed behind rider (of horse, motor-cycle).

pillock *n Brit sl* fool.

pillory *n* framework with holes for neck and wrists, where offenders were secured and exposed to public ridicule; *v* punish by putting in pillory; *fig* expose to public disgrace, scorn etc.

pillow *n* cushion for head, *esp* in bed; *v* rest on, as on pillow *n* **p.-case** cover for pillow.

pilot *n* **1** one who directs course of vessels *esp* one licensed to navigate into or out of port **2** one qualified to fly aircraft **3** *fig* guide; leader; *v* act as pilot; *a* experimental; preliminary; *ns* **p. light 1** light that indicates apparatus is switched on **2** (of gas appliance) small flame that enables main flame to be relit easily; **pilotage** fee paid for pilot's service.

pimento *n* allspice; Jamaica pepper.

pimp *n* man living off earnings of prostitutes.

pimple *n* small pustule on skin; *a* pimply.

PIN *abbr banking* personal identification number.

pin[1] *ns* **pin-ball** game where balls are struck, deflected by pins and roll into holes and score points (**p. machine** mechanical version of this); **p.-cushion** (in needlework)

soft pad for holding pins ready for use; **p.-money 1** (formerly) allowance given to woman for personal needs **2** money earned to cover minor expenses; not a proper living wage; **pinprick 1** pricking with pin **2** *fig* minor inconvenience; **p.-stripe** type of dark cloth with regular pattern of thin stripes (**p. suit** suit made with this); **p.-table** table with pin-ball; **p.-up 1** photo of *usu* famous person one admires **2** such a person.

pin[2] *n* **1** short, stiff, pointed wire with head, used for fastening **2** wooden, metal peg or rivet **3** cask holding **4** ½ galls **4** *pl* **-s** *coll* legs; *v* **pins, pinning, pinned. 1** fasten, attach with pin **2** hold firmly *esp* under weight; **p. down** *fig* bind (person) to; *n* **p.-money** allowance, pocket money; *v* **pin-point** mark precisely.

pinafore *n* loose sleeveless garment.

pince-nez *n* armless eye glasses kept on nose by spring-clip.

pincers *n pl* **1** gripping tool **2** pair of sharp gripping claws (of some crustaceans).

pinch *v* **1** nip; squeeze **2** *fig* cause to become thin etc **3** *coll* steal **4** *sl* arrest; *idm* **pinch and scrape** be drastically economical; *n* **1** painful squeeze, *esp* of skin, with finger and thumb **2** as much as can be taken up between finger and thumb;

idm **at a pinch** with some difficulty; idm **if it comes to the pinch/crunch** in case of real emergency; a **pinched 1** (of face) drawn; haggard **2** miserable.

pinchbeck n zinc and copper alloy; jewellery of this; a sham.

pine 1 evergreen coniferous tree **2** pineapple.

pine v **1** languish; waste away through sorrow etc **2** long intensely (for).

pineal gland n small gland in brain.

pineapple n large, cone-shaped edible fruit; plant with spiny leaves bearing this fruit.

ping v, n (make) single high-pitched bell-like sound; n **pinger 1** device that makes such sounds as a warning **2** coll microwave oven.

ping-pong n coll table-tennis.

pink n **1** garden plant allied to carnation **2** acme; perfection **3** foxhunter's red coat; a of pale, delicate reddish colour; idm **in the pink** coll very fit; idm **tickled pink** coll delighted; ns **p.-eye** conjunctivitis; **p. gin** drink of gin with angostura bitters; v decorate (edge) with zig-zags; n **pinking shears** scissors cutting with zig-zag line.

pinkie n Scot, US little finger.

pinnacle n ornamental tapering turret; slender mountain peak; fig culminating point.

pinny n coll pinafore.

pinpoint v mark, identify precisely.

pins and needles n pricking feeling caused by flow of blood after temporary stoppage.

pint n liquid measure; half a quart; ⅛ gallon; a **p.-sized** coll (of people) very small.

pinyin n written form of Chinese using Roman alphabet.

pioneer n **1** one who is first in experiments or exploration **2** early settler in new country **3** one of party of troops preceding army on march and preparing roads etc; v take lead in; be first to introduce.

pious a devout; faithful in religious duties.

pip n **1** seed in fruit (eg apple pip) **2** short high-pitched note used as signal; bleep **3** spot on playing card **4** Brit coll star on military uniform indicating officer's rank; v **pips, pipping, pipped.** coll hit with bullet or shot; idm **pip at the post** (in a race) beat by small margin.

pipe n **1** long tube conveying water, gas etc **2** tube with small bowl at end for smoking tobacco **3** tube-shaped musical wind instruments **4** measure of wine **5** shrill voice, or bird call; v **1** play the pipe **2** make sound like pipe **3** convey by pipe **4** make tubular ornamental shapes in icing cake or on clothing;

phr vs **pipe down** coll stop talking; make less noise; **pipe up** coll begin suddenly to speak or sing; ns **p.dream** unrealistic hope; **pipeline 1** system of connected pipes for conveying oil, gas etc **2** fig channel of supply or communication; idm **in the pipeline** being prepared, processed, dealt with; to be completed or delivered soon; ns **pipe-clay** fine white clay; **piper** player on bagpipes; a **piped 1** carried by pipes **2** by radio, cable etc; (**p. music** continuous playing of recorded, not live music); n **piping 1** act of playing pipe or making such a sound **2** system of pipes for water etc; length of pipe **3** decorative trimming on garment, on cake icing etc (a high-pitched; idm **piping hot** hot to eat or drink).

pipette n Fr small graduated tube used in chemistry.

pipkin n small earthenware pot.

pippin n name for several varieties of apples.

pipsqueak n coll insignificant person.

piquant a **1** stimulating; lively **2** pleasantly sharp to taste; n **piquancy.**

pique n Fr resentment; sense of being slighted; v wound pride of.

piranha n small but dangerous carnivorous freshwater fish from S America.

pirate n **1** person illegally

plundering vessels on high seas 2 privately-owned radio transmitter operating without licence 3 one who infringes another's copyright etc; n **piracy**; a **piratical**.

pirouette n, v Fr rapid spin round on toe in dancing.

pistachio n Sp, It edible green nut.

piste n Fr ski slope.

pistil n the seed-bearing part of a flower.

pistol n small fire-arm held in one hand when fired; v shoot with pistol.

piston n 1 short cylinder within cylindrical vessel, working up and down, used to generate and apply pressure 2 sliding valve in musical instrument; n **p. rod** which connects piston to crankshaft.

pit n 1 hole in ground 2 coalmine (ns **p.-head** entrance to mine; **p.-prop** support for roof of mine) 3 hollow depression (idm **in the p. of the stomach**) 4 dram part occupied by musicians in front of stage 5 small scar on skin; hollow on surface of sth; pl **-s** aut place where racing cars are repaired or serviced during race; idm **be the pits** coll be the worst possible; v make pits in; idm **pit sb/sth against sb/sth** put sb/sth into competition with sb/sth; a **pitted** covered with small dents.

pit-a-pat adv, n (like) succession of light taps, beats.

pitch[1] n thick, dark, resinous substance obtained from coal-tar, turpentine etc; v coat with this; a **p.-black**, **p.-dark** very dark.

pitch[2] v 1 set up erect 2 hurl 3 mus set key 4 (of ship) plunge length-wise 5 fall headlong; v phr vs **pitch in** 1 join in with energy 2 contribute money; **pitch into** attack violently; a **pitched** (of roof) sloping; n **pitched battle** 1 full battle with troops in formation 2 fig polit full-scale opposition to proposal; n 1 customary position 2 act of throwing 3 cricket area between wickets 4 football, hockey etc marked area of play; n **pitchfork** fork for lifting hay etc.

pitchblende n mineral ore, mainly uranium oxide, chief source of radium.

pitcher n 1 large usu earthenware jug 2 US baseball player who throws ball at batter.

piteous a arousing pity.

pitfall n unsuspected danger or obstacle.

pith n 1 soft cellular tissue in plant stems and branches 2 fig essential part; a **pithy** 1 of, full of pith 2 fig terse, forceful.

pitiable a to be pitied (adv **-ably**; **pitiful** 1 arousing pity 2 pathetic; contemptible (adv **-ly**);

pitiless (adv **-ly** n **-ness**).

piton n Fr spike for hammering into rock to support climber.

pitta n flat oval loaf eaten esp in Middle East (also **pita** or **pitta bread**).

pittance n meagre, inadequate allowance of money.

pitter-patter n, adv (with) sound of tapping or of small footsteps.

pituitary a secreting mucus; **p. gland** ductless gland at base of brain.

pity n 1 grief, sympathy for suffering of another 2 source of disappointment, regret etc; idm **for pity's sake** coll I beg you; idm **more's the pity** coll unfortunately; v **pities, pitying, pitied**. feel pity for; as **piteous** exciting pity; **pitiable** 1 deserving pity 2 deserving contempt; **pitiless** ruthless; hard.

pivot n shaft, fixed point on which something turns; v turn as on pivot; phr v **pivot on** depend on; a **-al** 1 forming pivot 2 of essential importance.

pixel n TV single small element of picture on screen.

pixie, pixy n elf or fairy.

pizza n Italian dish of flat dough baked with topping of cheese, tomato, olives etc.

pizzazz n coll sparkle; energy

combined with glamour (*also* **bezzazz, pazzazz**).

pizzicato *a, adv mus* (played) by plucking, not with bow; *n* note or piece played this way.

pl *abbr* plural.

placard *n* public notice or advertisement, *esp* one displayed on hoarding; poster; *v* fix poster to.

placate *v* appease; pacify; conciliate; *a* **placatory**.

place *n* 1 specific position related to other people, things 2 specific situation in life 3 particular town, village, building etc 4 seat 5 unoccupied position 6 position in competition 7 position of importance; *idm* **go places** become famous or successful; *idm* **in the first/second/third place** firstly/secondly/thirdly; *idm* **out of place** 1 out of position 2 unsuitable; *idm* **put sb in his/her place** show sb that he/she is less clever or important than he/she thinks; *idm* **take place** occur; *v* 1 put into a position or situation 2 arrange 3 identify; *n* **-ment**.

placebo *n* **-os** *or* **-oes.** *med* harmless substance given (as if of medicinal value) to comfort patient.

placenta *n* mass of tissue in womb connecting foetus with mother; after-birth.

placid *a* calm; serene; unruffled; *n* **-ity**.

plagiarize *v* adopt, reproduce

as one's own the work of another; *ns* **plagiarism** act of copying without permission; **-ist**.

plague *n* 1 pestilence; serious epidemic 2 *coll* annoying person or thing; *v* vex; harass; annoy.

plaice *n* edible flat-fish.

plaid *n* cloth with tartan pattern, worn as cloak by Scottish Highlanders.

plain *a* 1 clear; obvious 2 easily understood 3 without decoration; simple 4 not beautiful; *n* tract of flat land; *ns* **p. clothes** not uniform; **p. sailing** straightforward situation, easy to handle; *a* **p.-spoken** frank; not discreet about unpleasant facts; *adv* **-ly**; *n* **-ness**.

plaint *v* statement of complaint in law court; lament; *n* **plaintiff** one who brings action in court of law; *a* **plaintive** mournful; complaining.

plait *n* 1 flattened fold, pleat 2 braid of three or more strands (of hair etc); *v* weave into plait.

plan *n* 1 drawing, diagram of structure projected on flat surface 2 map of district etc 3 mode of action; scheme; *v* **plans, planning, planned.** 1 make, draw up plan for 2 think out beforehand.

planchette *n* *Fr* small heart-shaped board on castors, used in psychic experiments.

plane[1] *n* wide-spreading tree with broad leaves.

plane[2] *n* 1 flat surface 2 carpenter's tool for smoothing wood; *v* use plane; *a* completely flat, level.

plane[3] *n* 1 *coll* aeroplane 2 wing of aircraft; *v* glide in aircraft without use of engine.

planet *n* large solid body orbiting sun or other star; *a* **-ary**; *n* **planetarium** model of solar system; building containing such model.

plangent *adj* resounding sound, resonant.

plank *n* long, flat, broad piece of sawn timber; *n* **-ing**.

plankton *n* microscopic plant and animal organisms drifting in seas, lakes etc.

plant *n* 1 vegetable organism 2 complete mechanical equipment *esp* for factory 3 *sl* hoax; swindle; *v* 1 put plant, seed etc into soil that it may grow 2 fix firmly in position 3 colonize 4 *sl* conceal (plunder) in another's possession.

plantain *n* 1 low-growing perennial herb 2 species of banana.

plantation *n* 1 collection of growing trees 2 large estate producing cotton, tobacco, sugar etc.

plaque *n* *Fr* memorial plate or wall-tablet.

plash *n* gentle splashing sound; *v* dabble in water.

plasma n 1 colourless liquid forming part of blood 2 protoplasm.

plaster n 1 medical dressing applied to wound etc. 2 mixture of lime, sand and water for coating walls etc; ns **p. cast** protective plaster mould for injured limb; **p. of Paris** white paste of gypsum that sets hard when dry; **plaster-board** prepared board for smooth, easy lining of walls and ceilings; n **plasterer**; a **plastered** sl drunk.

plastic n 1 any of several synthetic materials produced from heating of chemical compounds, moulded in solid blocks, pliable sheets or threads 2 coll credit cards; a 1 capable of being moulded 2 made of some type of plastic; ns **p. bomb** bomb containing plastic explosive; **p. explosive** explosive that can be wrapped round the object to be destroyed; **p. surgery** surgical repair of damaged tissue with tissue from other parts of body.

Plasticine [TM] coloured pliable modelling material for children.

plastron n guard to protect breast in fencing.

plate n 1 thin sheet of metal or other hard material 2 flat dish for serving or eating food from 3 collection of such dishes and cutlery in gold, silver etc 4 geol section of earth's crust (also **tectonic plate**) 5 plastic moulded to fit mouth and hold set of false teeth (also **denture**) 6 phot sheet of light sensitive glass 7 book illustration from photograph; idm **give/have sth on a plate** coll make/find sth possible to do without much effort; idm **enough/too much on one's plate** enough/too much to cope with; idm **plates of meat** coll feet; v cover with thin coating of gold, silver etc.; ns **p. glass** large thick sheets of glass, used for shop windows etc; **plater**; **plate-mark** hallmark on gold or silver; mark on engraving left by pressure of plate.

plateau n Fr elevated flat stretch of land.

platelet n tiny disc in blood that aids clotting.

platen n plate which presses paper against inked type; typewriter roller.

platform n 1 raised floor or stage 2 part of railway station where passengers enter and leave trains 3 declared polit programme, policy.

platinum n chem greyish white metal used in making jewellery; n, a **p. blonde** (woman) with very silvery blonde hair.

platitude n commonplace remark; triteness; dullness; a **-udinous**.

platonic a of, derived from Plato; **P. love** love without

sex, between man and woman.

platoon n military unit.

platter n large flat dish or plate.

platypus n duck-billed, egg-laying mammal.

plaudit n act of applauding esp by clapping; fig praise.

plausible a seeming fair or reasonable; specious; adv **-ibly**; n **-ibility**.

play v 1 (of wind, light etc) move capriciously 2 flicker; flutter 3 gamble 4 amuse oneself 5 take part in (game, sport etc) 6 perform on musical instrument 7 act part of 8 operate (video, cassette, disc player etc); idm **play ball** coll cooperate; idm **play for time** delay in the hope of gaining an advantage; idm **play into sb's hands** do sth which gives sb else an advantage over one; idm **play it/play things by ear** improvise; operate without advance plan of action; idm **play sth to play with** sth to experiment with, make use of; phr vs **play along with** coll pretend to cooperate with; **play down** make appear less important than it is; **play off (one against the other)** set in opposition (to one another); **play up** cause trouble; **play up to** try to with the favour of; n 1 stage performance 2 fun activity, esp for children 3 action in sport 4 freedom of movement; *idm* **bring into play** involve in action; make use of; *ns* **p.-back** replay of recording; **playboy** rich man living only for pleasure; **playgroup** informal school for very young children (*also* **playschool**); **playhouse 1** theatre **2** small house for children to play in; **p.-off** *sport* deciding match, *eg* for teams with equal points; **play-pen** enclosure for keeping small child safe while playing; **plaything 1** toy **2** person badly treated by another or by fate; **playwright** writer of plays; **playing card** one of set used in card games; **playing field** field designated for team sports; *v* **play-act** pretend (*n* -**ing**).

plaza *n Sp* **1** open square **2** shopping centre.

plc *abbr* public limited company.

plea *n* **1** urgent request or appeal **2** *leg* official declaration of guilt or innocence in court of law by or on behalf of defendant; **p.bargaining** practice of admitting guilt in lesser crime to avoid being charged with more serious one; *v* **plead** argue before court of law; put forward as excuse; entreat.

pleach *v* (of tree branches) interlace; intertwine.

pleasant *a* agreeable; affable; pleasing; *ns* -**ness**; **pleasantry** jocular remark,

jest.

please *v* be agreeable to; delight; gratify; impress favourably; *n* **pleasure 1** enjoyment; satisfaction **2** desire; will; *a* **pleasurable** giving pleasure.

pleat *n* variant of plait; three-fold crease in cloth; *v* form into pleats.

pleb *n coll* plebeian.

plebiscite *n* expression of public opinion by direct ballot of electorate.

plectrum *n* small thin piece of metal, horn etc used for plucking strings of guitar, zither etc.

pledge *n* **1** object given as security for repayment of loan etc **2** solemn undertaking **3** token **4** toast; *v* **1** give as security **2** promise **3** drink toast.

pleistocene *a* denoting Ice Age; *n* geological formation containing greatest number of fossils.

plenary *a* **1** full; absolute; unlimited **2** representing all sections.

plenipotentiary *a*, *n* (ambassador, envoy) having full powers.

plenitude *n* fullness; completeness.

plenty *n* prosperity; ample supply; abundance; *as* **plenteous** plentiful; **plentiful** ample; present in large quantities; *adv* -**ly**.

pleonasm *n* use of more words than necessary to convey

meaning; *a* **pleonastic**.

plethora *n* **1** superabundance **2** pathological condition due to excess of red blood corpuscles; *a* **plethoric**.

pleurisy *n* inflammation of pleura, membraneous covering of lungs.

pliable *a* **1** easily bent **2** *fig* flexible; yielding; *a* **pliant** flexible; *n* **pliancy**.

pliers *n pl* tool for gripping and cutting wire etc.

plight[1] *v* **p.one's troth** *ar* make vow of marriage.

plight[2] *n* distressing condition; awkward predicament.

Plimsoll-mark,-line mark on ships showing maximum draught allowed when loaded.

plimsolls *n pl* rubber soled canvas shoes.

plinth *n* square base to column or pedestal.

pliocene *n*, *a* (geological formation) of the Upper Tertiary period.

plod *v* **plods, plodding, plodded.** walk laboriously; *fig* work conscientiously.

plonk[1] *adv*, *n* (with) heavy sound of sth dropped; *phr v* **plonk down** drop, put down with a plonk.

plonk[2] *n*, *Brit coll* poor quality cheap wine.

plonker *n sl* idiot.

plop *adv*, *n* (with) sound of small solid object dropped into water; *v* **plops, plopping, plopped.** fall, let fall with a plop.

plot *n* **1** small piece of land **2**

conspiracy 3 series of events etc forming story of play, novel etc; v **plots, plotting, plotted.** conspire; divide into plots of land; make chart, map of; n **plotter** conspirator; one who plots course etc.

plough n implement for turning up soil; v 1 furrow 2 sl fail in exam; idm **plough (one's way) through** 1 force a way through physical obstacle 2 fig finish task with much difficulty; phr v **plough back** 1 put back into soil 2 re-invest in business (profits earned from it); ns **ploughman (ploughman's lunch** bread, cheese and pickles); **ploughshare** blade of plough.

plover n wading bird allied to lapwing.

ploy n prank; plan.

pluck v 1 pull, pick off 2 remove feathers (from bird) before cooking 3 sound by pulling and releasing strings (of instrument) with fingertips (US **pick**); idm **pluck up courage** find the willpower to overcome fear; phr vs **pluck at** snatch at; n 1 courage 2 act of plucking; a **plucky;** (adv -ily).

plug n 1 piece of rubber, plastic, wood etc used to stop up a small hole and prevent leakage 2 device with metal pins to connect electrical appliance with source of current 3 aut sparking plug 4 coll piece of

media publicity to promote sth/sb; phr v **plugs, plugging, plugged. plug away (at)** work very hard (at); n **plug-hole** Brit hole for emptying water from bath or wash-basin.

plum n tree bearing stone fruit with sweet juicy flesh; this fruit; fig best of its kind; idm **a plum job/plum of a job** excellent job.

plumage n feathers of a bird; n **plume** a feather; tuft; v dress, preen feathers.

plumb n weight, lump of lead on line used to test perpendicular (**p.line** line with weight attached); adv absolutely; v 1 test using plumb-line 2 try to comprehend; idm **plumb the depths of** reach the lowest point of; ns **plumber** person whose job is to repair water-pipes, tanks etc; **-ing** 1 system of water-pipes etc 2 work of plumber.

plummet n sounding-weight; plumb-line; v plunge headlong.

plummy a 1 full of plums 2 coll desirable 3 (of voice) sounding affected, as if with a plum in the mouth.

plump[1] a of rounded form, chubby; n **-ness.**

plump[2] v fall heavily; phr v **plump for** show strong preference for.

plunder v seize by force; loot; despoil; n booty; loot.

plunge v dive, thrust suddenly into liquid; enter with

violence; n dive; idm **take the plunge** embark on new, doubtful course of action; n **plunger** 1 vertically moving part of machine 2 suction cup on stick for clearing blocked pipes; a plunging (of neckline on woman's dress) very low-cut between the breasts.

pluperfect n, a tense expressing action already completed before past point of time.

plural n, a (form) denoting more than one; n **-ism** 1 holding more than one office at a time 2 theory that society consists of several competing but interdependent groups.

plus prep with addition of; n symbol (+) denoting addition, positive electric charge.

plush n velvet-like fabric with deeper pile.

Pluto n planet ninth in distance from Sun.

plutocracy n government by wealth, or wealthy; state ruled thus; n **plutocrat** one whose wealth makes him influential.

plutonium n artificially produced radioactive element.

pluvial a rainy; caused by rain.

ply[1] n fold, layer of cloth, wood etc; strand of wool etc; n plywood thin, cross-laminated sheets of wood.

ply[2] v plies, plying, plied. 1 wield 2 work at 3 supply excessively, in pressing manner; **p. for hire** (of taxi etc) travel to and fro; run regularly.

pm, PM *abbr Lat* post meridiem (after noon).

PM *abbr* Prime Minister.

PMT *abbr* pre-menstrual tension.

pneumatic *a* 1 worked by air-pressure 2 air-filled; *n* **p. drill** road-worker's drill worked by compressed

pneumonia *n med* inflammation of lungs.

PO *abbr* 1 post office 2 postal order.

poach[1] *v* cook eggs, without shell, in boiling water.

poach[2] *v* 1 take game or fish illegally 2 encroach on another's sphere of action; *n* **poacher** one who trespasses to take game etc.

pock *n* pustule on skin; pit, scar left by this.

pocket *n* 1 small bag or pouch in garment for carrying money etc 2 small cavity containing mineral ore 3 space where density of air causes aircraft to drop suddenly 4 small hollow; *idm* **in each other's pockets** (of friend's) always seen together; *idm* **out of pocket** having lost money (as a result of sth); *v* 1 put into one's pocket; take as profit 2 accept meekly; *a* meant for putting in pocket; miniature; *ns* **p.-book** small notebook; **p.-knife** small folding knife (*also* **pen-**

knife); **p.-money** allowance for small expenses.

pod *n* long, narrow seed-vessel of peas, beans etc.; group of whales; *v* **pods, podding, podded.** form seed-pods; shell (peas etc).

podgy *a* fat; stumpy; short.

podiatry *n US* chiropody; *n* **-trist**.

podium *n* **-s** *or* **podia.** platform for speaker.

poem *n* literary composition in metrical form, rhymed or unrhymed.

poet *n* writer of poems; *fem* **poetess; poetry** work, art of poet; **p.laureate** *Brit* official poet appointed by royal court; *as* **-ic** (*ns* **p. justice** misfortune that rightly occurs to wrongdoer; **p. licence** freedom of poet to experiment with rules of language, usage or presentation of the world); **poetical** like poetry; poetic in style or essence (*adv* **-ly**); *n* **poetaster** inferior poet, scribbler of verse.

po-faced *a* looking stupidly solemn.

poignant *a Fr* affecting with feeling of unhappiness; highly pathetic; *adv* **-ly**; *n* **poignancy**.

poinsetta *n* plant with red flower-like clusters of leaves.

point *n* 1 sharp end of sth 2 promontory 3 dot; full stop 4 unit of scoring 5 particular moment or place 6 detail in argument or statement 7 main idea, purpose 8 sign

preceding decimal (**decimal p.**); *idm* **in point of fact** actually; *idm* **make a point of** take great care to ensure; *idm* **on the point of (doing)** just about to (do); *ns* **p. duty** policeman's duty at a specific place; **p. of view** opinion; **p.-to-p.** horse race on level ground; *a*, *adv* 1 fired at close range 2 (of *question or challenge*) direct; without hesitation; *v* 1 raise forefinger (in certain direction) 2 aim 3 sharpen 4 add fresh mortar to gaps between bricks (*n* **-ing**); *phr vs* **point out** draw attention to; **point to** 1 indicate 2 suggest; *a* **pointed** tapering; *fig* satiric, critical; *n* **pointer** 1 one who, that which points, as hand of clock etc 2 indicator 3 dog trained to point muzzle towards bird, game etc; *as* **pointless** blunt; purposeless; **point-blank** (of gun) fixed directly at mark; *ns* **point-duty** duty of policeman at fixed point to direct traffic etc; **point-to-point** steeplechase.

pointillism *n* style of painting based on technique of applying minute dots of colour.

poise *n* 1 self-possession; calmness 2 equilibrium; balance; *v* 1 put in position; keep in balance 2 hover.

poison *n* any substance which when absorbed by living organism will kill or seriously harm it; *ns* **p. ivy**

climbing plant causing allergic rash when touched; **p.-pen letter** anonymous letter with malicious threats; **p. pill** tactics used in business to attempt to avert take-over; *v* I administer poison to; kill by poison 2 *fig* corrupt; pervert; *a* **poisonous; n poisoner.**

poke *v* I push, thrust into 2 jab; nudge; *idm* **poke fun at** mock; *idm* **poke one's nose into** interfere with; *phr v* **poke about/around** investigate; **n poker** rod for poking fire; card game (*ns* **p. face** solemn expression concealing sb's real feelings; **p.-work** art of making pictures on wood or leather by applying red-hot tool); *a* **poky** cramped.

polar *a* I at, near, pertaining to North, South or magnetic poles 2 having positive and negative electricity 3 *fml* (*of opposites*) complete; *ns* **p.question** *ling* question that can be answered with 'yes' or 'no'; *n* **polarity;** *v* **polarize** give polarity to; limit vibrations of light to single plane; *fig* give unity of direction to; *ns* **-ization;** **polar bear** large white Arctic bear.

Polaroid [TM] I system of photography giving prints on the spot (**P. camera, P. film**) 2 substance that polarizes light, used in making sunglasses.

pole[1] *n* I either ends of earth's

axis 2 either terminals of electric battery 3 *fig* opposite extreme.

pole[2] long rounded piece of wood; measure (5 ½ yds (5m), 30 ¼ sq.yds (25sq.m)); *idm* **poles apart** completely different in character, point of view etc; *n* **p.vault** athletic jumping contest over high bar by use of long pole; *v* propel boat by means of pole.

pole-axe *n* butcher's slaughtering axe.

pole-cat *n* small carnivore related to weasel.

polemic *a* controversial; *v* dispute, discussion.

police *n* civil administration for maintaining public order; force of men, women so organised; *v* control; *ns* **p. constable** (*also* **PC/WPC**) **policeman/-woman, p. officer** member of police force; **p. state** country where police wields political power; **p. station** headquarters of local police.

policy *n* I course of action, *esp* of government 2 political ideals of party 3 contract of insurance.

polio *n med* infection of spinal cord often causing permanent paralysis (*also* **poliomyelitis**).

polish *v* I make smooth and glossy, *esp* by rubbing 2 *fig* make elegant; refine; *n* I smoothness; glossiness 2 substance used for polishing 3 *fig* refinement; *phr vs*

polish off *coll* finish quickly; **polish up** improve to an acceptable level; *n* **polisher.**

Politburo *n* decision-making body in communist state.

polite *a* well-bred; courteous; refined; *n* **politeness.**

politic *a* I prudent; wise 2 cunning 3 opportune; *n pl* art of government; political affairs, principles, aims etc. *a* **political** of government or administration of state; *ns* **p. asylum** refuge for immigrant wishing to escape oppressive regime in own country; *n* **political correctness** avoidance of language or action that insults or offends racial or social groups; *a* **politically correct; p. economy** science concerned with production, distribution of wealth; **p. prisoner** person imprisoned for opposition to political regime; **p. science** study of political institutions and theories (*also* **politics**); **politician** one engaged in party politics; **politicking** political activity aimed at winning votes; **politico** *coll* person of influence on political scene; **politics** I activity of competing for power 2 science of government; **polity** I process of government 2 organized state system; *v* **politicize** make political.

polka *n* lively dance; music for this; *n* **p. dot** one of large round dots forming regular pattern on plain fabric.

poll[1] n 1 register of electors 2 act of voting at election 3 number of electors voting; v 1 vote 2 receive (certain number of votes); n **p. tax** tax charged on each member of community, not on property or income; **polling** act of voting (**p. booth** enclosed space where secret vote is recorded; **p. station** building where this is done); **pollster** coll person conducting opinion poll.

poll[2] v 1 remove top 2 remove horns of (cattle, etc) 3 pollard (tree).

pollen n fertilising powder on flower anther.

pollute v make foul; defile; contaminate; ns **pollutant** substance that pollutes; **pollution** act or result of polluting.

polo n ball game resembling hockey played by two teams of four players on horseback; n **p. neck** (of sweater) with high round turned-over collar (a **p. necked**).

polony n kind of sausage.

poltergeist n noisy hobgoblin or ghost.

poly- prefix Gk many; several.

polyandry n custom of having two or more husbands at same time.

polychromatic a many-coloured.

polyester n artificial fabric for making clothes.

polyethylene = polythene.

polygamy n custom of having

two or more wives at same time.

polyglot a written in, speaking, made up of, several languages; n person able to speak many languages.

polygon n multi-sided plane figure.

polygraph n device used as lie detector.

polyhedron n multi-faceted solid figure.

polymath n person expert in many subjects.

polymer n complex molecule made up of several similar ones; v **-ize**; n **-ization**.

polymorphous a found in many different forms (also **polymorphic**).

polyp n 1 sea-anemone or similar creature 2 med kind of growth.

polyphony n music with two or more independent lines of melody played or sung simultaneously; a **-phonic**.

polysyllabic a having many syllables.

polystyrene n thermoplastic material.

polytechnic a pertaining to many arts, crafts and technical sciences; n ar polytechnic school or institution.

polytheism n belief in more than one god; a **-istic**.

polythene n tough, flexible plastic material.

polyunsaturated a (of fat, oil) with chemical structure that prevents build-up of cholesterol.

polyurethane n, a resinous plastic polymer.

pomegranate n reddish, many-seeded fruit of African, Asiatic tree.

pommel, pummel n 1 knob of sword-hilt 2 rounded high front part of saddle; v **pommels, pommelling, pommelled**. strike repeatedly; pound with fists.

pom, pommy a, n Aust sl English.

pomp n splendid display; parade; pageantry; a **pompous 1** self-important 2 (of speech) florid; bombastic; n **pomposity**.

pom-pom n 1 automatic, quick-firing gun 2 small, rounded ornamental tuft of ribbon etc.

ponce n Brit 1 pimp 2 coll man acting in ostentatiously effeminate way; phr v **ponce about/around** coll 1 behave in an effeminate way 2 waste time.

poncho n **-os**. S American Sp rectangular cloak with hole for head.

pond n small lake or pool of still water.

ponder v consider; think over; muse; cogitate.

ponderous a 1 heavy; unwieldy; massive 2 dull.

pong n, v Brit coll (give off) unpleasant smell; a **-y**.

pontiff n 1 high priest 2 bishop 3 pope; n **Pontificate** dignity or office of bishop; v 1 act as bishop 2 fig speak pompously; a **pontifical**.

pontoon n 1 flat-bottomed boat or metal drum supporting temporary bridge 2 card game.

pony n 1 small horse 2 sl £25 3 small glass.

pooch n coll dog.

poodle n breed of curly haired dog.

pooh interj 1 commenting on bad smell 2 indicating scorn; v **pooh-pooh** coll reject with scorn.

pool[1] n 1 small body of still water 2 deep place in river where water is slow-flowing.

pool[2] n 1 stakes played for in various games 2 form of billiards 3 common fund 4 commercial combination 5 pl -s system for gambling on results of football matches 6 shared secretarial staff; v 1 put into common fund; amalgamate.

poop n raised deck at stern of ship.

poor a 1 having little money 2 unfortunate 3 scanty 4 unproductive; of low quality; n **p. relation** person or thing with less prestige or power than the rest; adv **-ly** badly (also a ill); a **poorly** not in good health.

pop[1] n 1 short, explosive sound 2 coll fizzy drink; v **pops, popping, popped. 1** make such sound 2 put on, into with sudden light movement; vs **p. in** coll visit unexpectedly; **p. off 1** coll go away, suddenly 2 coll die; idm **pop the question** coll

propose marriage; a **pop-eyed** with wide-open eyes.

pop[2] a coll popular; of or producing light dance music, jazz etc; n coll popular music of the day, esp for young people (also **pop music**); ns **pop art** modern art form based on ideas from commercial design; **pop group** group of pop musicians.

pop[3] abbr population.

popcorn n grains of maize heated till they burst.

pope n head of Roman Catholic church and bishop of Rome.

popgun v toy gun that pops when a cork is fired.

poplar n straight, slender, tall tree.

poplin n ribbed fabric of silk or cotton and wool.

poppadom n large round thin Indian crispbread served with curry etc (also **poppadum**).

popper n 1 press-stud 2 capsule which fires paper streamer when string is pulled.

poppy n any plant of genus Papaver.

Popsicle [TM] US ice lolly.

populace n common people, the masses.

popular a of, pertaining to populace; liked by, suited to the average person; n **popularity** quality of being popular or being generally liked; v **popularize** make popular; make familiar to

average person.

populate v furnish with inhabitants; n **population** total number of inhabitants of country, town etc; a **populous** thickly inhabited.

populist n, a (person) declaring support for interests of ordinary people (n **p. movement**).

porcelain n fine, translucent white earthenware; china-ware.

porch n projecting, covered entrance to doorway.

porcine a of, like pigs.

porcupine n rodent covered with sharp quills.

pore n minute opening esp in skin; small interstice between particles of any body; a **porous** full of pores; permeable by liquids; n **porosity.**

pore phr v **pore over** study very closely.

pork n pig's flesh as food; n **porker** pig raised for food; a **porky** fleshy; fat.

porn n coll pornography.

pornography n indecent, obscene writing, photographs etc; a **-graphic.**

porpoise n blunt-nosed marine mammal, like dolphin.

porridge n oatmeal boiled in water or milk; n **porringer** small bowl.

port[1] n 1 harbour 2 town having harbour 3 fig refuge 4 left side of ship 5 gateway 6 opening in side of ship; idm **port of call** place to be visited; v turn helm of ship to left or port side; ns **porthole** round window in side of ship; **portal** large gateway.

port[2] n strong, sweet, red wine of Portugal.

port[3] n, *comput* point for linking several pieces of equipment.

portable a capable of being carried, moved; not fixed; ns **portability; portage** carriage; transport; cost of this.

portcullis n heavy grating in castle gateway.

portend v foretell; presage; n **portent** omen *esp* of evil; marvel; a **portentous 1** ominous **2** pompous.

porter n **1** door-keeper **2** one employed to carry burden, load **3** kind of dark-brown bitter beer.

portfolio n *lt* -**os. 1** flat case for carrying papers etc **2** State ministerial office **3** list of securities owned.

portico n *lt* -**oes** or -**os.** covered colonnade or walk.

portion n **1** part; share **2** one's fate; destiny; *phr v* **portion out** share out.

portly a corpulent; stout.

portray v depict, describe vividly in words; represent on stage; ns **portrait** picture of person; **portraiture** art of portraying; **portrayal** act of portraying.

pose v **1** lay down **2** place in, assume attitude; *idm* **pose as** pretend to be; n **1** held

position **2** attitude of mind **3** pretence; n **poseur** one who assumes affected attitudes.

posh a smart, stylish, expensive-looking.

position n **1** place **2** posture **3** condition **4** situation; employment; v place in position; localize.

positive a **1** definite **2** convinced **3** absolute **4** real **5** not negative; n **1** positive degree **2** photographic print in which light and shade is not reversed **3** *elec* positive pole; anode; n **p. discrimination** deliberate favouring of underprivileged social group.

positron n positive electron.

posse n force of men a sheriff can call out to aid him; body of armed men; *sl* group of friends.

possess v **1** own **2** dominate; control; a **possessed** controlled by evil spirit; n **possession 1** act of possessing **2** ownership **3** thing owned; n **possessor**; a **possessive** selfishly domineering; indicating possession; *adv* -**ly;** n -**ness**; n possessive case or pronoun.

posset n hot milk with ale, wine, spices etc.

possible a **1** capable of existing **2** feasible **3** that may or may not happen **4** *coll* tolerable; acceptable; n **possibility.**

post[1] n **1** upright stake or pole supporting structure **2** stake

marking finishing point of race; *idm* **first past the post** *polit* of system where only the candidate receiving the most votes in each area can be elected; v fix on post or notice board.

post[2] n **1** official collection, transport and delivery of mail **2** letters, parcels etc for mailing; *idm* **catch the post** reach postbox in time for collection; **p.box** box for posting letters; **p. office 1** place for buying stamps, postal orders etc **2** *caps* organization responsible for postal services; **poste restante** *Brit* system by which traveller has letters sent to a named post office for collection when he/she arrives; v place in official box for mail; *idm* **keep sb posted** ensure sb has up-to-date information; ns **postage (p. stamp); postbag 1** postman's sack **2** total of letters received at one time; **postcard** card for sending open message without envelope; **postcode** *Brit* set of letters and numbers used as part of address to facilitate sorting of mail; **postman/-woman** person employed to deliver mail; **postmark** marking on envelope to show time and place of posting (*also* v); **postmaster/-mistress** manager(ess) of post office; a **postal** (n **p. order** voucher exchangeable for money at specified post office); *a, adv* **postfree**.

post³ *n* 1 place of duty, *eg of* a soldier 2 job; situation of employment; *v* place on duty.

post- *prefix* after; *eg* **postgraduate** *Where the meaning may be deduced from the simple word, such compounds are not given here.*

postdate *n* 1 give a later date to 2 occur at a later date than.

poster *n* large advertising notice in public place; *n* **p. paint** artist's paint with strong bright colours.

posterior *a* situated behind; *n* buttocks; rear part.

posterity *n* descendants; future generations.

postgraduate *a* of studies carried on beyond graduation.

posthaste *adv* very quickly.

posthumous *a* after death.

postmeridian *a* after midday; of or in afternoon.

postmodern *a* returning to more traditional styles in the arts, architecture etc.

post mortem *n Lat* 1 medical examination after death 2 *fig* discussion following important event.

postnatal *a* after (giving) birth.

postpone *v* defer; delay; *n* **-ment**.

postscript *n* addition to letter, written after and below signature.

post-traumatic stress disorder *n* condition of recurring stress following a traumatic event.

postulant *n* person preparing to enter religious order.

postulate *v* stipulate; take for granted.

posture *n* attitude; position, carriage of body; *v* assume affected attitude.

posy *n* 1 flower; nosegay 2 motto inscribed in ring.

pot *n* 1 rounded vessel of any material, for holding liquids etc 2 flower-pot 3 cooking vessel 4 teapot; *v* 1 put into pot 2 preserve in sealed pot; *ns* **pot-boiler** artistic or other work done simply to earn money; *n* **p. plant** plant that grows in a pot; *a* **potted**; *n* **potting** (**p. compost, p. shed**); *pl* **pots** *coll* plenty of money.

potable *a Fr* drinkable; *n* **potation**.

potash *n* crude potassium carbonate; alkali used in soap and fertilizers; *n* **potassium** malleable metallic alkaline element.

potato *n* **-oes.** cultivated plant with edible tuber.

potbelly *n coll* rounded belly.

poteen, potheen *n* illicitly distilled Irish whisky.

potent *a* 1 powerful 2 convincing 3 (*of men*) sexually vigorous; *ns* **potency** power; efficiency; **potential** 1 that which has latent power 2 possibility; *a* latent; possible; *n* **potentate** king, ruler.

pothole *n* 1 deep hole in rock, *eg* in limestone (*ns* **potholer**

person exploring one of these; **-holing**) 2 hole in road surface.

potion *n* draught; dose of medicine or poison.

potluck *n* whatever is available as food; *idm* **take potluck** accept what comes by chance.

pot-pourri *n* mixture of dried flower petals, spices etc; literary, musical medley.

potshot *n coll* quick shot without taking careful aim.

potter *v* dawdle; be busy in desultory manner.

pottery *n* earthenware; art of making it; place where it is made; *n* **potter** one who makes pottery; *n* **potter's wheel** horizontal wheel on which potter turns pots etc.

potty *a coll* 1 slightly mad 2 trivial.

pouch *n* 1 small bag, sack 2 bag in which marsupials carry young; *a* **pouched** in form of, provided with pouch.

pouffe *n Fr* large cushion for use as seat or stool.

poult *n* young chicken, turkey, pheasant; *ns* **poulterer** dealer in poultry; **poultry** domestic fowls.

poultice *n* soft mass of hot meal, mustard etc, applied to inflamed part of body; *v* apply poultice.

pounce *v* swoop down suddenly; leap on; *n* sudden swoop, movement to take something.

pound¹ n 1 measure of weight (16oz) 2 British monetary unit (100p); n **poundage** 1 percentage charged as commission on monetary transaction 2 charge of so much per pound (weight).

pound² n enclosure for straying cattle, or dogs.

pound³ v 1 reduce to pieces, powder 2 beat; thump 3 run, walk with heavy steps.

pour v 1 flow or cause to flow freely; rain heavily; move in continuous stream 2 *fig* emit copiously (words, ideas etc).

pout v thrust out lips; look sulky, displeased; n act of pouting; n **-er** breed of fancy pigeon.

poverty n 1 state of being poor 2 unproductiveness; n **p. trap** situation of earning too much to be eligible for state welfare but too little to afford one's needs in life; a **p.-stricken** very poor.

POW abbr prisoner of war.

powder n 1 solid reduced to fine, dry particles by grinding 2 drug in this form 3 gunpowder 4 cosmetic powder; v sprinkle with powder; reduce to powder; ns **p.-compact** small flat box with face powder and puff; **p.-magazine** store for gunpowder; **p.-puff** soft pad for applying face powder; **p.-room** *fml* ladies' toilet; a **powdery**.

power n 1 capacity, ability to do or act 2 strength 3 energy 4 authority 5 *math*

product of number multiplied by itself 6 *optics* magnifying capacity; *idm* **the powers that be** unknown people in power that make decisions; ns **p.-boat** fast motor boat for sport; **p. of attorney** *leg* power to make legal decisions for sb on his/her behalf; **p. plant** source of power for factory etc; **p. point** electric socket (from power rather than lighting circuit); **p.-sharing** allowing minority groups to take part in government; **p. station** electrical generating plant; **p. steering** *aut* system of steering boosted by engine power; *as* **powerful** (*adv* **-ly**; n **-ness**); **powerless** (*adv* **-ly**; n **-ness**).

pox n name for various eruptive diseases, causing pustules on skin, *esp* syphilis.

pp abbr past participle.

PR abbr 1 public relations 2 proportional representation.

practical a 1, concerning action 2 efficient 3 not theoretic 4 virtual; n **p. joke** (*usu* non-verbal) trick played on sb for fun; *adv* **-ly** 1 sensibly; 2 almost; n **-ity** realistic nature; *pl* **-ities** practical matters; a **practicable** able to be done; capable of being used (n **-ability**).

practice n 1 habitual action 2 exercise of profession 3 clients, patients collectively 4 rules of procedures in court of law; v **practise** 1 do

habitually 2 train, exercise in skill, action etc 3 pursue profession; n **practitioner** one who carries on profession *esp* medicine.

praesidium = presidium.

pragmatic a 1 concerned with practical results 2 realistic; ns **pragmatism**; **-ist**.

prairie n wide, flat, treeless grassland; ns **p.-dog** squirrel-like rodent; **p.-wolf** coyote.

praise v 1 commend highly 2 express approval of, glorify (God); n expression of approval; a **praise-worthy** commendable; laudable.

praline n sweetmeat of cooked nuts and sugar.

pram n abbr perambulator.

prance v 1 move with bounds; swagger 2 (*of horse*) spring from hind legs.

prank n mischievous trick, practical joke.

prat n Brit sl fool.

prate v chatter; prattle; talk idly.

prattle v babble; talk like child; n childish talk; n **prattler**.

prawn n edible, marine crustacean.

pray v 1 beg for, ask earnestly 2 offer prayers, *esp* to God; n **prayer** act of praying to God; prescribed form of words used; formal petition, request (n **p. wheel** drum-shaped box inscribed with prayers used by Tibetan Buddhists).

pre- prefix 1 prior to; before (eg **pre-owned**, **pre-paid**, **pre-**

war) 2 superior (*eg*
predominant, prevailing).
*Such compounds are not given
here where the meaning may
be deduced from the simple
word.*

preach *v* 1 deliver sermon 2
advocate strongly 3 exhort
morally; *n* **-er**.

preamble *n* preface; opening
part of speech etc.

prebend *n* stipend of member
of chapter of cathedral;
benefice or living in gift of
chapter; *n* **-ary** holder of
prebend; honorary canon.

precarious *a* 1 uncertain;
insecure 2 risky; dangerous;
adv **-ly**.

precaution *n* careful foresight;
measure taken beforehand
to guard against danger;
a **-ary**.

precede *v* come, be before in
time, order, rank etc; *n*
precedence; priority derived
from birth, official status
etc; *n* **precedent** 1
something that has
happened before, serving as
model for future conduct etc
2 *leg* previous judicial
decision, *esp* as guide for
present parallel case.

precept *n* rule of action or
conduct; maxim; *n*
preceptor teacher.

precinct *n* enclosure within
outer walls of building *esp* of
cathedral etc; *pl* **-s** environs,
neighbourhood.

precious *a* 1 of great value 2
beloved 3 affected; over-
refined; *adv* **-ly**; *ns* **-ness**;

preciosity affectedness.

precipice *n* sheer,
perpendicular cliff-face; *fig*
crisis; *a* **precipitous** sheer,
steep.

precipitate *v* 1 throw, hurl
down 2 cause (vapour) to
fall as rain, snow etc 3 cause
to be deposited as solid
substance; from solution; *a*
rash; impetuous; *n* **-tation** 1
undue haste 2 that which is
precipitated 3 act, process of
precipitating.

précis *n* Fr short summary of
document; abstract.

precise *a* 1 exactly defined 2
punctilious 3 definite 4
formal; *ns* **precisian**
formalist; pedant; **precision**
accuracy; exactness.

preclude *v* exclude; prevent;
make impracticable.

precocious *a* prematurely
developed; *ns* **precocity**;
-ness.

precognition *n* advance
knowledge, awareness.

preconception *n* opinion
formed beforehand without
actual knowledge.

precursor *n* forerunner;
harbinger.

predatory *a* 1 living by
plunder, robbery 2 (*of
animals*) living by preying on
others; *n* **predator**.

predecease *v* die before.

predecessor *n* 1 one who
precedes another in office,
rank etc 2 ancestor.

predestine *v* settle beforehand;
foreordain; *n* **-tination** belief
that our future lives are

controlled by God's plan
that cannot be changed.

predicament *n* unfortunate or
puzzling situation.

predicate *v* declare; affirm; *n* 1
that which is affirmed,
denied of something 2 *ling*
that which is stated about
subject of sentence; *a*
predicative.

predict *v* foretell; prophesy; *n*
prediction.

predilection *n* preference;
preconceived liking.

predominate *v* be in majority;
be chief element or factor
in; *a* **predominant**; *adv* **-ly**; *n*
predominance.

pre-eminent *a* superior to,
excelling all others; *n*
-nence.

pre-empt *v* acquire,
appropriate by anticipation;
n **-emption**; *a* **-emptive**.

preen *v* 1 (*of bird*) dress
feathers with beak 2 *fig* show
self-complacency.

prefabricate *v* construct
sections (of houses etc) for
quick assembly; *n* **prefab** *coll*
house so made.

preface *n* initial, introductory
part of book, speech etc; *v*
begin; introduce.

prefatory *a* preliminary; as a
preface.

prefect *n* 1 senior pupil in
school with authority over
others 2 official in Ancient
Rome 3 *esp cap* head of
administrative area, *eg* in
France (*n* **prefecture**
headquarters of, area under
jurisdiction of prefect).

prefer v **prefers, preferring, preferred. 1** like better **2** promote; a **-able** more to be desired; n **-ence 1** favour **2** prior claim; a **-ential** giving, receiving preference; n **-ment** advancement promotion.

prefigure v be a warning sign of.

prefix n **1** word placed before personal name **2** *ling* particle forming first part of compound word; v put as introduction.

pregnant a **1** with child; with young **2** *fig* full of meaning, ideas; n **pregnancy.**

prehistoric a pertaining to periods before recorded history; n **prehistory** prehistoric archaeology.

prejudge v judge or decide upon before hearing or enquiry.

prejudice n **1** preconceived unreasonable opinion, bias **2** *leg* injury; damage; loss; **without p.** without detraction from any claims or rights; v bias, influence person; a **prejudicial** detrimental; causing harm; injury.

prelate n church dignatory; *esp* archbishop, bishop.

preliminary a introductory; preceding; n pl **prelims** *print* pages preceding actual text.

prelude n introductory act, performance, event; v serve, act as prelude to; usher in.

premarital a before marriage.

premature a happening before

normal time; earlier than expected.

premeditated a (of crimes) planned in advance.

premenstrual a occurring because of hormonal changes before menstruation.

premier a *Fr* first in rank, degree etc; principal; n prime minister; n **premiership.**

première n *Fr* first performance.

premise n **1** assumption, proposition on which inference is based **2** *leg* introductory part of document, *esp* lease **3** *pl* **-s** building; house etc with grounds; v **premise** assume.

premium n **1** reward; bonus **2** fee paid by pupil for admission to profession **3** sum paid for insurance **4** *finance* excess of market price over par; *idm* **at a premium** highly valued; difficult to buy; *idm* **put a premium on 1** attach importance to **2** make seem important; n **p. bond** *Brit* government bond entitling holder to entry in monthly lottery.

premonition n presentiment; foreboding.

preoccupy v occupy and engross thoughts to exclusion of other things; n **preoccupation** absent-mindedness.

prepare v **1** make ready for use **2** construct **3** teach; train **4**

accustom **5** lead up to; n **preparation 1** act of preparing **2** school work, homework done before lesson; period when this is done (*abbr* **prep**); a **preparatory** serving to prepare (**p.school** school where boys, girls are prepared for public or higher school).

prepay v **prepaying, prepaid.** pay in advance.

preponderate v exceed in number, importance; n **-derance.**

preposition n part of speech, word placed before noun or pronoun, indicating its relation to another word in sentence; a **prepositional.**

prepossess v influence, *esp* favourably; a **prepossessing** attractive; n **prepossession.**

preposterous a unreasonable; absurd.

preppy n *US* **1** graduate of private preparatory school **2** young person dressed like this.

prerogative n exclusive, peculiar right or privilege.

presage n omen; portent; v foretell; give warning of.

presbyter n *Scot* church elder, minister; n **presbytery 1** church court **2** *RC* priest's house **3** E end of chancel; a, n **Presbyterian** (members) of Church governed by one order of ministers, called presbyters.

prescience n foresight; foreknowledge; a **prescient.**

prescribe v 1 ordain; dictate 2 *med* advise treatment, or use of medicine; n **prescription** 1 prescribing 2 written directions given by physician 3 medicine prescribed 4 *leg* uninterrupted possession over long period; a **prescriptive** giving exact rules about sth.

preselector n mechanism enabling gear position to be selected before changing into it.

present[1] a existing now, not absent; at present time, tense; a **p.-day** modern; n **p. participle** form of verb (ending in -ing in English) indicating simultaneous or causal relationship between two verbs; *adv* **presently** soon; n **presence** 1 being present 2 mien 3 nearness, (of danger etc); n **p. of mind** quick reaction to needs of situation.

present[2] v 1 introduce (person) formally 2 show 3 give, bestow; 4 perform n gift; a **-table** suitable for presentation; wellbred; n **-tation** 1 bestowal 2 formal gift 3 introduction, *esp* at court 4 performance.

presentiment n apprehension; foreboding.

preserve v 1 protect, save from injury, harm etc 2 prevent (food) from decaying; n 1 that which is preserved, as jam, bottled fruit etc 2 game coverts preserved for shooting 3 river etc preserved for fishing; n **preservation**; n, a **preservative** (substance) which keeps (food etc) from going bad.

preside v take control at formal meeting; superintend; ns **president** head of republic, society, college, public corporation etc; **presidency** office, tenure of president; a **presidential**.

presidium n executive committee of administration in communist countries.

press v 1 apply weight, force on; squeeze 2 exert pressure; *phr vs* **press for** ask insistently for; **press on** continue in a determined way; n 1 newspapers 2 people writing for these 3 printing machine 4 apparatus for flattening, compressing, crushing 5 crowded situation; *idm* **a bad/good press** (un)favourable reporting; *idm* **go to press** begin printing, being printed; ns **p.box** place for news reporters at sporting event; **p.conference** meeting where important person answers reporters' questions; **p.release** prepared statement for use by media. **p.-stud** small metal fastening for garment; **p.-up** type of exercise, raising the body from a prone position by pushing with the hands; *idm* **pressed for sth** short of sth; a **pressing** 1 urgent 2 insistent (n act or result of pressing); v **pressgang** force sb into service (n group which does this).

pressure n 1 act of pressing 2 *fig* compulsion; constraint 3 force exerted on surroundings by solid, liquid, gas; ns **p.-cooker** sealed pot in which food cooks quickly under steam pressure; **p.-group** organized group that seeks to promote its interests by propaganda etc; v **pressurize** 1 (of aircraft cabin) keep at constant atmospheric pressure 2 persuade forcefully; n **-ization**.

prestige n 1 good repute 2 power to influence; a designed to impress; a **-gious** highly honoured.

presto *adv, mus* very rapidly.

prestressed a (of concrete) reinforced internally with stretched steel cables.

presume v 1 take for granted; believe as probable 2 take liberties; a **presumable**; probable; n **presumption** 1 act of presuming 2 probability 3 effrontery; a **presumptive** giving reasonable grounds for belief (**heir p.** one who is heir at present) a **presumptuous** over-confident; arrogant.

presuppose v 1 assume to be true 2 imply.

pretend v 1 lay false claim to 2 feign 3 imagine oneself as;

ns **pretender** claimant to throne; **pretence 1** pretext **2** fraud; **pretension** claim; *a* **pretentious** assuming great merit or importance; conceited; snobbish.

preter- *prefix* beyond; more than.

preterite *n, a* (tense) expressing past action.

preternatural *a* beyond what is natural; supernatural.

pretext *n* reason, motive put forward to conceal real one; excuse.

pretty *a* **1** superficially attractive, pleasing, charming **2** considerable *coll* large; *idm* **a pretty penny** *coll* large sum of money; *adv* moderately; considerably; *n* **prettiness** charming personal beauty.

pretzel *n Ger* crisp salted *usu* knot shaped biscuit.

prevail *v* **1** triumph **2** be prevalent; be in use; *phr v* **prevail (up)on** persuade; *n* **prevalence** common occurrence; frequency; *a* **prevalent** widely practised; rife.

prevaricate *v* make evasive answer; quibble; *ns* **prevarication, prevaricator**.

prevent *v* guard against; hinder; stop; *n* **prevention**; *as* **-able, -ative**; *ns* **p. detention** *leg* imprisonment of sb who is thought likely to commit a crime; **p.medicine** practice of using healthy diet and exercise to prevent illness.

preview *n* advance, private showing of pictures, film etc.

previous *a* **1** prior; preceding **2** *coll* too hasty; *adv* **-ly** before.

prey *n* animal hunted by another, as food; victim; *v* **p. on, upon** kill and eat; oppress; plunder; *n* **bird of p.** one that kills and eats other birds or animals.

priapic *a* **1** phallic **2** lustful; *n* **priapism**.

price *n* **1** that which is paid or asked for anything; cost; value **2** betting odds; *v* fix price; value; *idm* **not at any price** expressing refusal not for any reason; *ns* **p.tag 1** ticket indicating price **2** *fig* price demanded; **p.war** competitive reduction of prices by rival companies to attract sales; *as* **priceless 1** very valuable **2** *coll* very amusing; **pricey** *Brit coll* dearer than normal.

prick *v* **1** pierce with sharp pointed object **2** give or experience feeling of this; *idm* **prick the bubble** destroy a falsely inflated illusion; *idm* **prick up one's ears** start to listen attentively; *phr v* **prick out** transplant seedlings; *n* **1** slight stab of pain on surface of skin **2** mark left by pricking sth; *n* **prickle** small thorn; *v* tingle as if pricked; *a* **prickly; p. heat** inflammation of sweat glands causing irritation; **p. pear** edible fruit of cactus.

pride *n* **1** high opinion of one's merits or achievements **2**

self-respect **3** too high an opinion of oneself **4** group of lions; *idm* **one's pride and joy** thing one is most proud of; *idm* **pride of place** best, most important position; *idm* **the pride of sth** the very best of sth; *phr v* **pride oneself on** feel specially proud of.

priest *n* official minister of religion; clergyman; *fem* **-ess**; *n* **priesthood**; *a* **priestly**.

prig *n* conceited, self-satisfied person; *a* **priggish**.

prim *a* **1** neat; precise **2** stiffly formal **3** easily shocked.

primacy *n* position of being first; pre-eminence; *a* **primal** first, original; *a* **prima** first (**p. donna** leading female operatic singer).

prima facie *a, adv Lat leg* based on the apparent facts.

primary *a* **1** main; fundamental **2** earliest; *n* *esp US* preliminary stage of election at which candidates are selected; *ns* **p. colour** any of the colours red, yellow or blue; **p. school 1** *Brit* school for children aged five to eleven **2** *US* grade school, *usu* for children aged six to nine; *adv* **primarily** mainly.

primate *n* archbishop; highest order of mammals, including man, monkeys etc.

prime *a* **1** chief; fundamental (**p. cost, p. concern, p.**

importance) 2 first or best in quality or rank (**p. beef; p. minister) 3** with all the typical features (**p. example**); *n* the best time of life; *ns* **p. number** any whole number that has no factors other than itself and 1; **p. time** time of day when the largest number of people watch TV; *v* **1** prepare (*eg* gun for firing, pump for pumping) **2** provide sb with essential information **3** prepare with primer before painting; *n* **primer 1** protective paint which seals wood etc before other paint is applied **2** container for explosive used to detonate bomb etc.

primeval *a* of first ages of world; prehistoric.

primitive *a* not elaborate; under-developed; old-fashioned; simple.

primogeniture *n leg* system by which title and real estate pass to eldest son on death of father.

primordial *a* of earliest origin; primeval.

primrose *n* wild plant with pale yellow flowers.

Primus (stove) [TM] small portable oil-stove for camping.

prince *n* **1** son of king, queen **2** ruler of royal status; (*fem* **princess**); *ns* **P. Charming** man representing woman's romantic ideal; **p. consort** husband of ruling queen; **P. of Darkness** the devil; *a*

princely 1 magnificent **2** very generous.

principal *a* main; *n* **1** head (of college etc) **2** sum of loan, on which interest is charged; *ns* **p. parts** main parts of verb; *adv* **-ly.**

principality *n* country ruled by a prince.

principle *n* **1** basic general truth **2** guiding rule for behaviour (*usu pl*) **3** scientific law; *idm* **in principle 1** in theory **2** in general outline; *idm* **on principle** on moral grounds; *a* **principled** morally sound.

print *n* **1** stamp **2** impression **3** printed lettering **4** photographic positive **5** printed fabric; *v* **1** impress **2** reproduce words or pictures on paper etc from inked type, plates etc **3** obtain positive photograph from **4** stamp with coloured design; *ns* **printer** one engaged in printing; **printing** process, art, style of printing; **printout** *comput* printed record of stored data.

prior *a* earlier; *n* head of religious order or house; *fem* **-ess**; *n* **priory** monastery, nunnery.

prioritize *v* give priority to.

priority *n* superiority; precedence.

prise, prize *v* raise by means of lever.

prism *n* solid figure whose bases are equal, parallel planes and whose sides are parallelograms; transparent

triangular prism for refracting light; *a* **-atic** of, like prism.

prison *n* place of captivity; gaol; *ns* **prison camp** place of detention for prisoners of war; **prisoner 1** captive (**p. of war** member of armed forces captured by enemy) **2** person in custody.

pristine *a* **1** original; primitive **2** unspoiled.

prissy *a coll* fussy; tending to overreact to anything seeming improper; *adv* **-ly**; *n* **-ness.**

private *a* **1** not public; belonging to a particular person or group (**p. performance, p. property**) **2** secret (**p. letter, p. conversation**) **3** not under state control (**p. education, p. industry**) **4** quiet; free from intruders (**p. room, p. corner**) **5** not in any official capacity (**p. visit, p. individual**); *n* lowest rank of soldier; *ns* **p. detective** detective paid to work for private individual; **p. enterprise** capitalism; **p. eye** *coll* detective; **p. parts** genitals; **p. pension** pension for which all contributions are paid by beneficiary, not by an employer; **p. sector** areas of employment not under state control; *ns* **privacy** state of being undisturbed, free from interference; **privateer** (formerly) pirate; *v* **privatize** sell (state enterprise) to

private ownership
(n **-ization**).

privation n want of necessities and comforts of life; hardship.

privet n evergreen shrub, used for garden hedges.

privilege n individual right, advantage; immunity, exemption enjoyed by some; prerogative; v grant privilege to; a **privileged** enjoying privilege; completely confidential.

privy a private; secretly knowing; n water-closet; **p. council** body of advisers appointed by sovereign; **p. purse** allowance for sovereign's personal use.

prize n 1 reward given for merit, success in competition 2 thing won in lottery, contest etc 3 that which is captured in war, esp vessel; v value, esteem highly; ns **p. fight** boxing match for money prize; **p. money** share of proceeds of sale of war prizes; money given as prize in competition etc.

PRO abbr 1 Public Records Office 2 public relations officer.

pro n coll professional.

pro- prefix -at in favour of.

proactive a showing initiative.

pro-am n, a (contest) involving amateur as well as professional contestants.

probable a likely to happen, to be true; n **probability** likelihood; likely event.

probate n proving of will; certified approved copy of will.

probation n 1 (period of) trial to decide if sb is suitable for job 2 leg system of keeping (esp young) offender out of prison under supervision; n **p. officer** person appointed to carry out such supervision; a **probationary**; n **probationer** person being given probation.

probe n 1 med instrument for exploring wound etc 2 coll investigation 3 exploratory spacecraft; v examine thoroughly.

probity n honesty; integrity.

problem n 1 question set for discussion, or solution 2 difficult situation; a **problematic(al)** doubtful; questionable.

proboscis n 1 elongated flexible snout 2 elephant's trunk 3 elongated mouth-parts of some insects.

proceed v 1 advance; go on; make progress 2 come forth, arise from 3 take legal action; n pl **-s** product; realized profit; ns **procedure** 1 mode of action 2 manner of conducting business, esp parliamentary 3 technique; **proceeding** action; pl **-s** record of transactions of society etc.

process n 1 series of continuous actions and changes 2 method of operation 3 system of manufacture 4 whole course

of legal proceedings; idm **in the process of** (doing) actually engaged, involved in (doing); n **procession** 1 body of persons marching, riding in formal order 2 act of marching forward 3 progress (a **-al**).

processor n comput microprocessor.

proclaim v announce, declare officially; make known publicly; n **proclamation**.

proclivity n inclination; tendency.

proconsul n governor of dependency or province, esp in Ancient Rome; a **-ar**; ns **-ate**, **-ship** (period of) office of proconsul.

procrastinate v delay; defer; postpone; ns **-ation; -ator**.

procreate v beget; generate; n **-ation**.

proctor n university official with disciplinary powers.

procure v 1 gain; obtain 2 leg act as pimp, pander; a **procurable** obtainable; ns **procurator** one who manages affairs for another; (**p.-fiscal** Scot local public prosecutor); **procuration**; **procurement** act of procuring; **procurer** pander; pimp.

prod n goad; poke; v **prods, prodding, prodded.** poke with pointed instrument; fig stir up; incite.

prodigal a lavish; open-handed; wasteful; improvident; n **-ity** profusion; extravagance.

prodigy n 1 extraordinarily gifted person 2 wonder; marvel 3 monstrosity; a **prodigious** huge; vast; amazing.

produce v 1 bring forward; bring forth 2 give rise to; make 3 continue 4 yield; ns **produce** that which is yielded or made, **producer; product** result of natural growth; anything manufactured; **production** act of producing, manufacturing; that which is produced; a **productive** creative; fertile; efficient; n **productivity** rate at which something is produced *esp* in industry.

prof n *coll* professor.

profane a not sacred; irreverent; pagan; v desecrate; n **profanity** blasphemous language or behaviour.

profess v 1 affirm; make public declaration of 2 practice, have as one's business 3 teach as professor; n **profession** 1 confession (of faith) 2 occupation requiring training and intellectual ability 3 body of persons following such occupation (a **-al** practising specified profession; engaged in sport or game for money; n paid player; n **-alism** position (*esp* in sport) of professional as distinguished from amateur; n **professor** university teacher of highest rank.

proffer v offer.

proficient a skilled; expert; n **proficiency**.

profile n 1 outline of side view of object, *esp* of face 2 short biographical sketch.

profit n benefit; financial gain; v benefit; ns **p. margin** difference between cost of production and selling price; **p. sharing** *comm* practice of giving workers a share in company profits; a **profitable** advantageous; lucrative; n **profiteer** one who makes exorbitant profits at expense of consumer.

profiterole n very light bun *usu* covered with chocolate and served with cream.

profligate a dissolute; depraved; recklessly extravagant; n **profligacy**.

profound a deep; very learned; n **profundity**.

profuse a abundant; prodigal. n **profusion**.

progeny n children; descendants; n **progenitor**.

progesterone n hormone which prepares uterus for pregnancy and prevents ovulation.

prognosis n **-ses. 1** act of predicting 2 *med* opinion formed as to probable future course and outcome of disease; a **-nostic** (v **-ate** foretell; predict, warn; n **-ation**).

program v, n 1 *comput* (equip with) set of instructons 2 US programme;

a **-grammable** with facility for programming; n **-grammer**.

programme n 1 printed details of performers, items etc in play, concert, broadcast etc 2 summary of things to be done 3 data for computer (US **program**); v prepare programme of work for.

progress n 1 advance; forward, onward movement 2 improvement; v 1 go forward 2 develop favourably; n **progression** 1 act of moving forward 2 *math* series of numbers each of which increase, decrease by regular law 3 *mus* succession of notes, chords; a **progressive** 1 progressing 2 advocating reform.

prohibit v forbid; prevent; n **prohibition** 1 act of forbidding 2 forbidding by law of supplying and consuming alcoholic drinks; as **prohibitive** 1 intended to prevent certain action (*also* *fml* **prohibitory**) 2 (*of cost*) too high (*adv* **-ly**).

project n plan; scheme; v 1 throw; propel 2 scheme; plan 3 jut out 4 cast (photographic image etc.) on screen; n **projectile** heavy missile, shell, bullet; **projection** 1 act or result of projecting sth 2 thing that sticks out 3 estimate for future based on available facts (n **-ist** person working cinema projector); n **projector** 1 one who plans projects **2** apparatus to project picture on screen.

prolapse *n* falling down or out of place.

proletariate *n* lowest class of society; working class, *esp* manual workers; *a* **-arian**.

proliferate *v* reproduce by budding, or rapid cell-divisions; *n* **-ation**.

prolific *a* productive; fertile; fruitful.

prolix *a* lengthy; tedious; verbose; *n* **-ity**.

prologue *n* preface to poem, play etc; introductory act or event.

prolong *v* extend, in space or time; *n* **-ation**.

prom *n coll Brit* **1** promenade **2** promenade concert.

promenade *v* stroll about for pleasure, exercise; *n* **1** such a walk **2** seaside esplanade (*coll abbr* **prom**); **p. concert** concert where some of audience (**promenaders**) walk about.

prominent *a* **1** standing, jutting out; conspicuous **2** well-known; *n* **-nence**.

promiscuous *a* indiscriminate, *esp* in sexual intercourse; *n* **-scuity**.

promise *n* **1** undertaking, assurance to do or not to do something **2** likelihood of success; *v* **1** make promise **2** give cause for hope; *n* **Promised Land** *fig* state of ideal happiness; *as* **promising** likely to develop well or achieve success etc; **promissory** containing

promise.

promontory *n* headland jutting out into sea.

promote *v* **1** raise, move to higher rank **2** assist in formation of (company, scheme etc) **3** publicize; *n* **promotion**; **promoter**.

prompt *a* done quickly; at right time; immediate; *v* help (actor etc) by suggesting forgotten words; *ns* **-er**; **-itude**.

promulgate *v* **1** put into effect **2** announce publicly; *n* **-ation**.

prone *a* **1** lying with face downwards **2** inclined; liable; *n* **-ness** inclination, tendency.

prong *n* **1** sharp pointed piece of metal; tine of fork **2** point of stag's antler.

pronoun *n* word used in place of noun; *a* **pronominal** of, like pronoun.

pronounce *v* **1** declare, utter solemnly and publicly **2** articulate, utter word, sound **3** give as expert opinion; *a* **pronounced** emphasized; strongly marked; *ns* **-ment** formal declaration; **pronunciation** way in which word, syllable etc is pronounced; articulation.

pronto *adv coll Sp* immediately.

proof *n* **1** act of proving truth of fact etc; demonstration **2** test, trial of quality, truth etc **3** standard of alcoholic strength **4** trial impression from type, plates etc; *v* **proof-read** read and correct

printed proofs (*ns* **-er**, **-ing**); *a* having standard quality of strength, hardness; *idm* **proof against** strong enough to be impenetrable, unmoved by; *v* make proof against.

prop[1] *n* support; stay; strut; *v* **props, propping, propped.** act as prop; furnish with support.

prop[2] *n dram* any portable article used on stage (*esp pl*).

prop[3] *n coll* propeller.

propaganda *n* act, method of spreading opinions, beliefs to promote a cause; views, doctrines thus spread; *n* **propagandist** zealous supporter of cause, etc.

propagate *v* **1** reproduce; have offspring **2** disseminate **3** cause to multiply by reproduction; *ns* **propagation** act, process of propagating; **propagator** one who propagates; garden frame used for propagating plants.

propel *v* **propels, propelling, propelled.** drive forward; impel; *ns* **propellant** propelling agent (*eg* explosive for rocket) (*also a,* *n* **propellent**); **propeller** (*abbr* **prop**) shaft of ship or aircraft; **propulsion**; act of driving forward; *a* **propulsive** having power of propelling; *a, n* **propellent** propelling (agent).

propensity *n* inclination, addiction; tendency.

proper *a* **1** suitable **2** peculiar;

particular 3 respectable; prim 4 one's own; **p. noun** one denoting particular person or place.

property n 1 characteristic; inherent quality, power etc 2 that which is owned; possessions (estate, land, goods, money) 4 object, costume used in play etc (*usu pl abbr* **props**).

prophet n 1 interpreter, teacher of divine will; religious leader, teacher 2 one who foretells the future; n **prophecy** prediction, foretelling of future; v **prophesy** make predictions; foretell; a **prophetic**.

prophylactic a guarding against disease or disaster; n device having this effect, *esp* condom; n **prophylaxis**.

propinquity n nearness, proximity in time, space, relationship.

propitiate v appease; conciliate; n **propitiation**; a **propitious** favourable; fortunate.

proponent n supporter; person advising in favour of sth.

proportion n 1 part or share 2 comparative relation in size, number, amount, degree 3 harmonious relation of parts in whole 4 symmetry; *pl* -s dimensions; *idm* **have sth all out of proportion, out of all proportion** attribute too much importance to some aspects of sth; a -**al** corresponding in amount, size etc (**p. representation**

polit system providing seats for each party in parliament in proportion to number of votes cast) *adv* -**ally**; **proportionate to** in due proportion to.

propose v 1 bring forward, submit for consideration 2 offer marriage 3 intend; ns **proposal** plan; offer *esp* of marriage; **proposer**; **proposition** 1 statement expressing considered opinion 2 suggestion 3 bargaining offer or proposal 4 *geom* statement of theorem or problems; v make direct proposal to sb.

propound v put forward; offer for consideration.

proprietor n owner; *fem* **proprietress**; **proprietary** 1 belonging to owner 2 made, patented, sold under exclusive ownership.

propriety n correct behaviour; appropriateness; decency.

propulsion n act of propelling or driving forward; a -**pulsive**.

pro rata *Lat a, adv fml* in proportion.

prorogue v terminate (session of parliament) without dissolution; n **prorogation**.

pros and cons n pl arguments for and against.

prosaic a matter-of-fact; unromantic; dull.

proscenium n part of stage between curtain and orchestra.

proscribe v outlaw; denounce and forbid; n **proscription**.

prose n language, spoken or written without rhyme or metre; a **prosy** dull; uninspired; n **prosiness**.

prosecute v 1 follow; pursue further 2 start legal proceedings against; ns **prosecution**; **prosecutor** one who prosecutes, *esp* in criminal court.

proselyte n convert; v -**ytize**.

prosody n art of versification; n -**odist**.

prospect n 1 wide outlook 2 something expected or thought likely 3 possible customer etc 4 *pl* -s future expectations, *esp* financial; v inspect, search for, *esp* gold etc; a future; ns **prospector** one who explores for minerals etc; **prospectus** descriptive pamphlet issued by company, school etc.

prosper v 1 excel; succeed; flourish 2 be fortunate; n -**ity** success; good fortune; a -**ous** doing well, rich; thriving.

prostate n gland accessory to male generative organs.

prosthesis n *med* artificial replacement for damaged part of body; a -**thetic**.

prostitute n person who sells their body for sexual intercourse; v *fig* put to base, dishonourable use; n -**ution**.

prostrate a 1 lying flat; prone 2 *fig* crushed; spent; utterly dejected; v 1 cast to ground 2 *fig* abase oneself; cringe; n -**ation** 1 extreme bodily exhaustion 2 extreme depression and distress.

protagonist n principal character in play etc; lead.

protect v keep safe; guard; ns **protection** 1 protecting; being protected 2 thing that protects 3 paying money to gangsters in return for not having one's business destroyed (*also* **protection racket**); money paid in this way (*also* **protection money**); **protectionism** practice of protecting home trade by taxing imported goods more heavily; a **protective** giving, wishing to give protection (*in US* condom); ns **protector** 1 one that protects 2 one appointed as regent; **protectorate** 1 rule by protector 2 state as ruled.

protégé n Fr person under patronage of another.

protein n complex organic compound of numerous amino-acids.

pro tem adv Lat temporarily.

protest v affirm; raise objection; n declaration of objection, disapproval; ns **-er**, **protestation** solemn affirmation.

Protestant a belonging to any Christian Church outside the Roman Catholic communion; n member of such church; ns **Protestantism**.

proto-, **prot-** prefix first.

protocol n 1 diplomatic etiquette 2 first draft agreement for treaty.

proton n positively charged particle in nucleus of atom.

protoplasm n basic material of which cells are composed.

prototype n original; model; pattern.

protozoone n one-celled living creature (*also* **protozoan**).

protract v lengthen; prolong; draw to scale; a **protracted** long drawn out; tedious; ns **protraction**; **protractor** instrument for measuring angles.

protrude v project; stick out; ns **protrusion**; a **protrusive** thrusting forward.

protuberant a bulging out; n **protuberance** projection; swelling.

proud a 1 feeling or displaying pride 2 arrogant 3 splendid 4 gratified 5 jutting out (*idm* **stand proud** extend above the usual surface level; *idm* **do sb proud** treat sb with great generosity).

prove v 1 establish truth of 2 turn out to be 3 test quality, accuracy; a **proven** proved.

provenance n place of origin; source.

provender n 1 fodder for cattle 2 coll food.

proverb n short, pithy, traditional saying; maxim; a **-ial** generally known.

provide v 1 procure and supply 2 equip 3 furnish with means of support.

providence n 1 fate 2 benevolent provision of God 3 foresight 4 thrift.

provident a looking ahead; farseeing; thrifty; a **-ial** lucky; merciful; beneficial.

province a 1 division of country; region 2 sphere of knowledge, thought, action etc; *pl* **-s** any part of country outside capital; a **provincial** 1 of the provinces 2 countrified; unsophisticated; n inhabitant of provinces; countryman.

proving ground n 1 place for scientific tests 2 fig opportunity for testing sth new.

provision n 1 act of providing, supplying 2 something provided, *esp pl* food 3 leg stipulation, condition; v supply with food; a **provisional** temporary, conditional.

proviso n **-os** or **-oes**. Lat condition.

provocation such as to arouse anger, sexual interest (adv **-ly**).

provoke v give rise to; stir up; make angry; incite; n **provocation**; a **provocative**.

prow n forepart of ship; bow.

prowess n 1 bravery; valour 2 skill 3 success.

prowl v go about stealthily, furtively, *esp* in search of prey, plunder; v n act of prowling; v **-er**.

proxy n 1 authority given to person to act as agent 2 person acting as agent or substitute.

prude n excessively prim, proper person; a **prudish**.

prudence n 1 careful behaviour 2 sagacity.

prudent a careful; discreet; circumspect; provident; a -ial showing prudence.

prune n dried plum.

prune v 1 cut out, shorten unwanted branches (of trees, shrubs etc) 2 fig shorten by omission.

prurient a having morbidly indecent, obscene ideas etc; n -ence.

pruritis n med severe itching.

pry v pries, prying, pried. 1 search into; peer, spy, esp with unnecessary curiosity 2 break open, as with lever.

PS abbr 1 postscript 2 police sergeant.

psalm n sacred song or hymn; ns -ist composer of psalms; **psalmody** art of singing sacred songs; **psalter** Book of Psalms, arranged for use in Prayer Book.

PSBR abbr Public Sector Borrowing Rate.

psephology n study of how people vote; n -ologist.

pseudo- prefix false; pretended; seeming. Such compounds are not given where the meaning may be deduced from the simple word.

pseud n coll false, pretentious person, esp in cultural matters.

pseudonym n fictitious name; nom-de-plume; a -ous

psittacine a pertaining to parrot tribe; n **psittacosis** contagious influenza of parrots.

psoriasis n med disease causing red, scaly patches on skin.

psych phr vs **psych sb out** coll make sb nervous; beat sb at sport by this means; **psych sb up** coll prepare sb mentally (for an ordeal).

psyche n human soul or spirit; mentality; mind; a **psychedelic** relating to a relaxed, ultra-perceptive mental state, or to drugs causing this; ns **psychiatry** treatment, cure of mental illness; **psychiatrist** one who practises this.

psychic a 1 concerned with phenomena beyond physical, natural laws 2 (seemingly) gifted with supernatural powers 3 relating to communication with the dead; adv -ally.

psycho- prefix mental; ns **p.-analysis** method of treating certain mental disorders; investigation of subconscious mind; **psycho-analyst**.

psychokinesis n ability to cause movement of objects without touching them.

psychology n branch of science studying mental processes and motives; a **psychological** 1 of or concerning the working of the mind 2 coll produced by the mind; imaginary (ns **p. moment** moment most likely to lead to success; **p. warfare** undermining the morale of the enemy by inspiring fear, political

doubts etc; n **psychologist** one who studies, practices psychology.

psychopath n person with mental disorder that can lead to sudden uncontrollable violence; a -ic.

psychosis n -oses. chronic mental disorder; a **psychotic**.

psychosomatic a caused by mental disorder.

psychotherapy n psychological treatment of illness, without drugs; n -therapist.

pt abb 1 point 2 part 3 pint.

PT abbr physical training.

PTA abbr parent-teacher association.

Pte abbr private (soldier).

PTO abbr please turn over.

ptomaine n poisonous alkaloid substance formed by putrefaction of animal or vegetable matter.

pub n coll public house; n **p. crawl** visit to many different pubs in one evening, drinking at each one.

puberty n state of sexual maturity.

pubic a of the pubes or pubis (part of the pelvic bone); (**p. hair**).

public a 1 of the community; not private (**p. building**) 2 not kept secret (**p. knowledge**); n people in general; ns **p.-address system** microphones and loudspeakers; **p. bar** Brit formerly bar in pub less comfortable than lounge bar; **p. company** company selling shares to public (*also* **public limited company** *or* **PLC**); **p. convenience** *Brit* public toilet; **p. house** building where alcoholic drinks (and sometimes food) are sold and consumed; **p. prosecutor** lawyer acting as prosecutor for the State; **p. relations 1** work of giving public good image of organization (*also* **PR**; *n* **p. relations officer** person engaged in this, *also* **PRO**) **2** relationship between organization and public; **p. school 1** *Brit* private *usu* boarding school for pupils aged 13 to 18 **2** *US* local state school; **p. sector** industries owned by the state; **p. spirit** interest in welfare of the community (*a* -ed); **p. works** building and construction carried out by the State; **publican** *n* landlord of public house **2** (in Ancient Rome) tax collector; **publication 1** making available for public to read **2** item printed for general distribution; **publicity** advertising (**publicist** person responsible for this); *v* **publicize** make known to public; *adv* **publicly**.

publicity *n* state of being generally known; advertisement; notoriety; *v* **publicize** make known to public, *esp* by advertisement.

publish *v* make generally

known; prepare and issue for sale (books, journals etc); *ns* -**er; publication**.

puce *n, a* brownish purple colour.

pucker *v* wrinkle; fall into creases; *n* crease; fold.

pudding *n* soft, cooked mixture of flour, milk, eggs etc; any solid sweet dish.

puddle *n* **1** shallow muddy pool **2** rough cement lining for ponds etc; *v* **1** apply watertight mixture to pond **2** stir molten cast iron to make it wrought iron.

pudency *n* modesty; bashfulness.

pudendum *n med* -**enda**. outer part of sexual organs, *esp* of female body.

pudgy *a coll* short and fat (*also* **podgy**).

puerile *a* childish; silly.

puff *n* **1** short blast of wind, breath etc **2** laudatory notice **3** kind of pastry; *v* blow out, send out in puff; *phr vs* **puff out 1** (cause to) swell **2** cause to be out of breath; **puff up 1** (cause to) swell **2** make conceited; *ns* **p. -adder** large poisonous viper; **puff-ball** fungus with ball-shaped spore case; **p. pastry** light flaky pastry; *a* **puffed** out of breath; *a* **puffy** swollen.

puffin *n* sea-brid with large parrot-shaped beak.

pug *n* **1** breed of dog, resembling small bull-dog **2** foot-print of wild beast; *a* **pug-nosed** snub-nosed.

pugilist *n* boxer; *a* -**ic**; *n* **pugilism**.

pugnacious *n* fond of fighting; *n* **pugnacity**.

puke *v* vomit.

pulchritude *n* beauty.

pull *v* **1** draw; tug **2** remove by pulling **3** pluck; **4** propel (by rowing); *idm* **pull a face** grimace; *idm* **pull a fast one** gain advantage by trickery; *idm* **pull one's punches** attack without vigour; *idm* **pull sb's leg** tease sb; *idm* **pull the wool over sb's eyes** conceal the truth from sb; *phr vs* **pull off 1** remove **2** achieve; **pull out** withdraw; **pull through 1** recover **2** survive **pull together** co-operate; **pull up 1** uproot **2** improve **3** stop (vehicle); *n* **1** act of pulling **2** pulling power **3** steep climb **4** power to influence; *n* **pull-in** roadside cafe.

pullet *n* young hen.

pulley *n* small grooved wheel, carring cord, used to change direction of power.

Pullman [TM] special luxury coach.

pullover *n* knitted jersey without fastening.

pulmonary *a* of lungs.

pulp *n* **1** soft, moist vegetable or animal substance; flesh of fruit or vegetable **2** mixture of cellulose fibres obtained from woodland used to make paper; *v* reduce to pulp.

pulpit *n* raised enclosed structure from which preacher delivers sermon.

pulsar n star-like object emitting radio signals.

pulse[1] n 1 throb of blood in arteries etc 2 any regular vibration or beat; v **pulsate** 1 throb; vibrate 2 fig throb with excitement, emotion etc; n -**ation**.

pulse[2] n edible seeds of leguminous plants.

pulverize v reduce to fine powder, dust or spray; fig destroy utterly; n -**ation**.

puma n large, carnivorous feline mammal; cougar.

pumice n light, porous volcanic stone.

pummel see **pommel**.

pump n device for raising water etc by suction, or for taking out and putting in air etc by piston and handle; v 1 raise 2 compress 3 take out, put in (air, liquids etc) 4 fig extract information from.

pumpernickel n Ger dark coarse rye bread.

pumpkin n edible fruit, resembling vegetable marrow.

pun n play upon words; v **puns, punning, punned.** make pun.

punch[1] n 1 blow with fist 2 tool for perforating, stamping 3 force; power; v 1 hit with fist 2 make hole with tool; ns **p. line** climax of joke or anecdote expected to produce laughter; **p. -up** Brit coll fight with fists; as **p. -drunk** 1 stupefied by repeated punching on the head 2 fig dazed; confused.

punch[2] n drink of spiced spirits or wine (usu hot).

punctilio n It, Sp being conscientious about small details.

punctilious a very exact, particular.

punctual a in good time; prompt; n -**ity**.

punctuate v divide up written or printed words by stops, commas etc; ns -**ation** commas, semi-colons etc put in writing to help make sense clear.

puncture v make hole in; prick; n small hole made by sharp point.

pundit n 1 learned Brahmin 2 very learned man.

pungent a 1 sharp; piercing 2 highly-seasoned 3 (of mode of expression) piquant; pointed.

punish v 1 inflict retribution on 2 handle roughly; as -**ing** exhausting; debilitating; -**able**, n -**ment**; a **punitive** 1 serving as punishment 2 harsh; severe.

punk n youth movement of the late 1970s, characterized by anti-Establishment attitudes, and outrageous clothes and hair-styles; a **punky**; n -**iness**.

punnet n small, flat basket for fruit.

punt[1] n flat-bottomed boat with square ends, propelled by long pole thrust against river-bed; v convey, travel in punt.

punt[2] n kick given to football dropped from hands, before it touches ground; v kick thus.

punt[3] v 1 cards lay stake against bank 2 bet, esp on horse; **punter** n 1 Brit person betting on race-horses 2 person driving punt with pole 3 coll undiscriminating consumer.

puny a weak, feeble, undersized.

pup n coll puppy.

pupa n -**ae** or -**as**. stage between larva and imago; chrysalis of insect; v **pupate** become pupa.

pupil n 1 person being taught 2 opening of iris in eye.

puppet n 1 small jointed figure, moved by strings, wire 2 fig person who is unable to act on his own; ns **p. -show**; **puppetry** art of manipulating puppets.

puppy, pup n 1 young dog 2 conceited, impudent young man; **p. -love** coll adolescent infatuation.

purblind a short-sighted.

purchase v 1 buy 2 fig obtain by effort etc 3 move by leverage; n 1 that which is bought 2 leverage; n **purchaser.**

purdah n Muslim or Hindu custom of keeping women hidden from public view; idm **go into purdah** hide oneself away.

pure a 1 clean 2 unmixed 3 not tainted 4 chaste 5 simple; adv -**ly** 1 in a chaste

manner 2 simply; only; *v*
purify make pure; *ns*
purification cleansing,
purifying; **purism** strict
adherence to correct usage
etc in language; **-ist**; **purity**
state of being pure.

purée *n Fr* soft food passed
through sieve.

purge *v* 1 cleanse; purify 2 *leg*
clear oneself of accusation
3 cause evacuation of
bowels 4 expel unwanted
members from political
party, armed forces etc; *n*
that which cleanses; *n, a*
purgative (medicine)
causing evacuation of
bowels; *n* **purgatory** 1 state
or place of torment etc,
where souls of dead are
purified 2 *fig* any such state
or place.

Puritan *n* extreme
Protestants in 16th and
17th centuries; one
holding very strict religious
and moral views; *a* **-ical**.

purl[1] *n* knitting stitch
producing ridge;
ornamental looped edging
to lace etc; *v* knit purl
stitch.

purl[2] *v* flow with gentle
murmur; babble.

purple *n* red-blue colour; *a* of
this colour; *ns* **p. heart** *coll*
heart-shaped amphetamine
pill; **P. Heart** *US* medal for
wounded soldiers; **p.
passage** section of writing
where one is constantly
made aware of the writer's
stylistic expertise.

purport *v* mean to be; seem to
signify; *n* significance;
bearing.

purpose *n* intention; aim;
design; object; *v* intend; *a* **p.
-built** made with stated
purpose in mind.

purr *v* (*of cats etc*) express
pleasure by making low
vibrating noise; *n* this
sound.

purse *n* 1 small bag, pouch for
money 2 funds 3 sum of
money offered as prize etc;
idm **hold the purse strings**
have control over spending;
v pucker, wrinkle up (lips); *n*
purser ship's officer in
charge of accounts and
passengers' requirements.

pursue *v* 1 follow closely 2
chase 3 follow to desired
end 4 continue (speaking);
n **pursuance** *idm* **in the
pursuance of** *fml* while
doing; *a* **pursuant** *idm*
pursuant to *leg* in
accordance with; *ns*
pursuer; **pursuit** 1 chasing
after; quest 2 employment;
occupation.

purvey *v* provide, supply *esp*
provisions; *n* **purveyor**.

purview *n fml* scope; range of
operation.

pus *n* yellowish matter
produced by suppuration; *a*
purulent full of, discharging
pus; septic; *n* **purulence**.

push *v* 1 use force to move
(sb/sth) away from oneself,
to another position 2 *fig*
urge very strongly 3 *coll* sell
(illegal drugs); *idm* **push**

one's luck take unwise risk;
idm **be pushed for** not have
enough (of); *phr vs* **push
around** order around in a
bullying way; **push for** make
urgent demands for; **push
off** *coll* go away; *n* 1 act of
pushing 2 concerted attack;
idm **give/get the push** *coll* 1
dismiss/be dismissed from
job 2 persuade/be persuaded
to resign 3 put an end/have
an end put to a personal
relationship; *idm* **if/when it
comes to the push** if/when
the situation becomes
urgent; *ns* **p.-bike** *Brit coll*
bicycle; **p.chair** *Brit* small
folding seat on wheels for
child (*also US* **stroller**);
pusher 1 person that pushes
2 *sl* seller of illegal drugs;
p.over 1 sth easily done 2
person easily persuaded; *as*
pushing, pushy self-
assertive; over-ambitious; *v*
push-start start (car etc) by
pushing.

pusillanimous *a* cowardly; *n*
pusillanimity.

pussy[1] *n coll* child's name for
cat (also **puss, pussycat**).

pussyfoot *v coll* act timidly,
overcautiously.

pussy willow *n* (tree with)
silky grey catkins.

pustule *n* pimple containing
pus; *a* **pustular**.

put *v* putting, put. 1 place;
locate; fix 2 express 3 throw
4 submit for judgement; *idm*
put paid to *Brit* spoil;
prevent; *idm* **not put it past
sb** suspect sb of being

capable; *idm* put it to sb challenge sb to admit or deny sth; *idm* put one's foot in it make a tactless mistake; *phr vs* put across explain (*idm* put one across sb deceive sb); put aside/by save; put back delay; put down 1 defeat 2 write down 3 humiliate (*n* p. down); put sth down to ascribe sth to; put forward suggest; put in for apply for; put off 1 delay 2 discourage 3 arouse dislike; put on 1 increase 2 provide 3 dress oneself in 4 simulate 5 deceive playfully (*n* p. -on); put out annoy; inconvenience (*idm* put oneself out make a special effort); put over explain; demonstrate (*idm* put one over on deceive); put up 1 erect 2 propose; nominate 3 accommodate 4 provide 5 offer for sale; put up with tolerate; *n* put-up job *coll* situation set up in advance to deceive sb; *a* put-upon exploited; taken advantage of.

putative *a* reputed; supposed; presumed.

putrid *a* decomposed; rotten; *v* **putrefy** make, become putrid; *n* **putrefaction** process of putrefying rotten, foul-smelling substance; *a* **putrescent** rotting; stinking (*n* -ence).

putsch *n Ger* move to overthrow government by sudden use of force.

putt *v* 1 strike golf ball gently across green 2 *athletics* throw weight (shot) from shoulder; *n* distance that ball, weight is putted; *n* **putter** golf-club used for putting.

putty *n* 1 soft cement made of linseed oil and clay 2 gem-polishing powder made of tin and lead.

puzzle *v* 1 perplex; baffle 2 try to solve; *n* 1 difficult problem 2 verbal mechanical contrivance to test ingenuity.

PVC *abbr* polyvinyl chloride (form of thermoplastic widely used in domestic articles and industry).

pygmy, pigmy *n* dwarf; *a* very small, dwarfish.

pyjamas *n pl* nightwear of jacket and trousers.

pylon *n* tall structure *usu* of steel girders, carrying electric cables etc.

pyorrhoea *n med* disease of gums; discharge of pus.

pyramid *n* 1 figure with square base and four triangular sides sloping to apex 2 Egyptian tomb of this shape; **p. selling** form of selling through chain of agents whereby least commission goes to the one who effects the sale; *a* -**al**.

pyre *n* pile of wood for burning corpse.

pyrethrum *n* species of composite plants.

Pyrex [TM] heatproof ovenware.

pyrogenic, pyrogenetic *a* productive of heat or fever.

pyromania *n* uncontrollable urge to set things on fire; *n* -**maniac** person suffering from this.

pyrometer *n* instrument for measuring high temperatures.

pyrotechnics *n pl* 1 display of fireworks 2 *fig* display of brilliant, ironical oratory.

Pyrrhic *a* **P. victory** one won at enormous and ruinous cost.

python *n* large non-venomous snake that crushes its prey.

pyx *n* 1 vessel in which Host is kept in churches 2 box at Royal Mint for specimen coins.

QC *abbr Brit* Queen's Counsel (title of barrister acting for the government).

QED *abbr Lat* quod erat demonstrandum (which was to be proved).

qua *adv* in the capacity of; as.

quack *n* cry of duck; *v* utter such sound.

quack *n* one who pretends to have skill, knowledge, *esp* in medicine; charlatan.

quad *n coll* 1 quadrangle 2 quadruplet.

quadrangle *n* 1 four-angled plane figure 2 square or rectangular court with buildings round it; *n* **quadrant** 1 quarter of circle 2 instrument for measuring angles; *n*, *a* **quadrate** square; *a* **quadratic** (*of equation*) involving square of unknown quantity.

quadraphonic *a* using four sound channels or speakers.

quadrat *n* piece of printer's type-metal used in spacing between words.

quadrilateral *n*, *a* (figure) having four sides and four angles.

quadrille *n Fr* dance for four persons; music for this.

quadruped *n* four-footed animal.

quadruple *a* fourfold; *v* multiply by four.

quadruplet *n* one of four siblings born of the same pregnancy.

quag, quagmire *n* soft, marshy, quaking ground.

quail[1] *n* small game-bird related to partridge.

quail[2] *v* cower; flinch 2 lose heart.

quaint *a* 1 attractively strange 2 odd; eccentric.

quake *v* shake; tremble; rock from side to side; *n* 1 tremor 2 *coll* earthquake.

Quaker *n* member of Christian group (Society of Friends) opposed to all forms of violence.

qualify *v* **qualifies, qualifying, qualified.** 1 obtain official qualification by study etc 2 limit (by description) 3 become competent; *a* **qualified** 1 having qualifications 2 limited; modified; *n* **qualification** 1 limiting factor 2 act of qualifying 3 proof of having passed examination; *pl* **qualifications** for relevant knowledge and experience for.

quality *n* 1 essential nature or characteristic 2 degree of value 3 high social rank; *a* **qualitative** having to do with quality.

qualm *n* 1 feeling of nausea 2 misgiving; scruple.

quandary *n* difficult perplexing situation; dilemma.

quango *abbr Brit* **-quangos.** quasi-autonomous national government organization.

quantifier *n ling* word or phrase denoting quantity (*eg* some, a few).

quantity *n* number; amount; extent; specified amount; *a* **quantitative.**

quantum *n Lat* 1 amount required 2 *physics* minimal

unit of energy (*pl* **quant**); *ns* **q. leap** sudden dramatic advance or breakthrough; **q. theory** *physics* theory that energy exists in units of a discrete kind.

quarantine *n* isolation to prevent spreading of infection; *v* put, keep in quarantine.

quark *n physics* any of the tiniest elements supposed to be distinguishable in elementary particles; soft cheese.

quarrel *n* **quarrelling, quarrelled.** angry dispute; squabble; *v* disagree; dispute; become estranged; *a* **-some**.

quarry[1] *n* person or thing that is being hunted or pursued.

quarry[2] *n* open pit from where stone, sand, etc is excavated; *v* dig, excavate from quarry.

quart *n* quarter of gallon; two pints.

quarter *n* 1 fourth part 2 area 3 clemency 4 *pl* **-s** lodgings; *v* 1 divide into quarters 2 lodge; *ns* **q. day** first day of each annual quarter when bills are due; **quarterdeck** part of ship's upper deck reserved for officers; **q. -final** stage of knockout contest involving eight competitors of whom four will go into the semi-final; **quartering** *heraldry* division of shield or emblem in it; **q. -light** *aut* small triangular window in car door; **quartermaster** 1 *army*

officer in charge of supplies 2 *navy* petty officer in charge of steering; *a* **quarterly** occurring, due each quarter of year; *n* periodical published quarterly; *ns* **quartet(te)** 1 group of four musicians 2 musical composition for four performers; **quarto** size of paper or book.

quartz *n* form of crystalline silica.

quash *v* annul; make void; suppress.

quasi *a*, *adv*, *prefix Lat* as if; in certain sense; almost.

quatercentenary *n* 400th anniversary.

quatrain *n* four-line stanza rhymed a b a b.

quaver *v* 1 tremble; shake; vibrate 2 speak tremulously; *n mus* note, time value of half crotchet; *n* **-ing** tremulous sound, *esp* made by voice.

quay *n* pier; jetty; wharf; landing-place.

queasy *a* 1 causing, feeling nausea 2 easily shocked; *n* **-iness**.

queen *n* 1 wife of king 2 female sovereign 3 court card 4 piece in chess 5 fertile female bee, wasp etc 6 female cat; *n* **q. mother** *n* king's widow; mother of ruling monarch; **the Q.'s English** standard Southern British English; **Q.'s evidence** evidence given for the State by criminal against former accomplices; *a*

queenly of or like a queen.

queer *a* 1 odd; strange; suspicious 2 slightly mad 3 unwell; **queer the pitch** spoil chances of success.

quell *v* suppress; stifle; allay; pacify.

quench *v* 1 extinguish; put out (fire) 2 slake (thirst).

querulous *a* complaining; whining.

query *n* question; interrogation mark (?); *v* question; express doubt about.

quest *n* search; *v* search for.

question *n* 1 act of asking 2 sentence requiring reply 3 point of discussion; *v* 1 ask question of 2 dispute; *idm* **out of the question** impossible; *ns* **q. -mark** punctuation mark showing end of question; **q. -master** person asking questions in a quiz; **questionnaire** list of formal questions devised to obtain information etc; *a* **questionable** 1 dubious 2 not completely honest.

queue *n* 1 line of waiting people or vehicles 2 man's pigtail; *v* line up, wait in queue; *idm* **jump the queue** go ahead of others who have been waiting longer (*v* **q.-jump** *ns* **q.-jumper, q.-jumping**).

quibble *n* play on words; *v* evade point; make puns.

quiche *n Fr* baked flan with egg, cheese and other savoury items, served hot or cold.

quick *a* 1 rapid; keen; brisk; hasty 2 living; *n* sensitive flesh below finger- or toe-nail; *v* **quicken** 1 cause to be quick 2 become faster 3 give life to 4 become living; *ns* **quicklime** unslaked lime **quicksand** very loose, wet, soft sand; **quicksilver** mercury; *as* **quickfire** in rapid succession; **quick-tempered** quick to anger; **quickwitted** reacting quickly.

quickie *n coll* sth done very quickly.

quid *n* 1 *sl* £1.00 sterling 2 chew of tobacco.

quid pro quo *n Lat* thing given in return for sth.

quiescent *a* still; calm; inactive; passive; *n* **quiescense** inactivity.

quiet *a* 1 peaceful; motionless; serene 2 monotonous; *v* **quiet, quieten** make, become quiet; *ns* **-ness, -ude.**

quietism *n* religious philosophy of calm acceptance; *n, a* **-ist.**

quietus *n* riddance; final discharge; death.

quiff *n* tuft or curl of hair over forehead.

quill *n* 1 hollow stem of bird's feather 2 long wing feather 3 spine of porcupine.

quilt *n* padded bed-cover; *v* stitch pieces of cloth together with padding between; *n* **-ing.**

quin *n coll* quintuplet.

quince *n* pear-shaped fruit with sharp flavour.

quinine *n* bitter-tasting drug.

Quinquagesima *n* Sunday before Lent.

quinquennial *a* occurring once in or lasting five years.

quintal *n* unit of weight equal to 1 100 pounds 2 100 kg.

quintessence *n* purest form of some quality; *a* **-ential.**

quintet(te) *n mus* 1 composition for five instruments or voices 2 group of five performers.

quintuplet *n* (*abbr* **quin**) one of five children born of the same pregnancy.

quip *n* **quipping, quipped.** witty remark; clever repartee.

quire *n* twentieth part of ream of paper.

quirk *n* individual trait.

quisling *n* traitor.

quit *a* **quitting, quit.** free, clear, rid of; *v* 1 leave; abandon 2 cease from; give up; retire from; *n, a* **quits** (state of) being on equal terms; *ns* **quittance** receipt, discharge; **quitter** one who abandons task in face of difficulty etc.

quite *adv* 1 to some extent; fairly (**quite good**) 2 completely (**quite right; quite finished**); *det* **quite a/an**/as intensifier (**quite an expert**); *idm* **quite a bit/a few/a lot** a considerable amount; *interj* expressing agreement.

quits *a* (after repayment) on even terms again.

quiver[1] *n* case for holding arrows.

quiver[2] *v* tremble; shake; *n* **-ing.**

quixotic *a* extravagantly generous and chivalrous.

quiz *v* **quizzing, quizzed.** 1 question closely 2 stare at inquisitively; *n* game of answering questions, or solving problems, *esp* as public entertainment; *n* **quiz-master** question-master.

quizzical *a* (of look, smile) questioning; with a hint of amused disbelief.

quod *n sl* prison.

quoin *n* 1 salient angle of building 2 corner-stone 3 wedge used for locking type in forme.

quoit *n* ring for throwing at, or over, peg; *pl* **-s** game using this.

quondam *a Lat* former.

quorate *a* (of meeting) with a quorum of members.

quorum *n* minimum number of members that must be present before meeting may proceed.

quota *n* 1 proportional share; allowance 2 amount of goods allowed to be imported during certain period.

quote *v* 1 repeat or cite something said, written by another 2 name price, give estimate; (*n* **q. mark** sign indicating beginning or end of quotation, *also* **inverted comma**).

quoth *v ar, lit* said; spoke.

quotidian *a* daily.

quotient *n* number resulting from division of one number by another.

qv *abbr Lat* quod vide (indicating cross-reference to be seen).

QWERTY *n* standard keyboard layout.

R

rabbet n groove in woodwork; v join by rabbet.

rabbi n Jewish religious minister; a rabbinical.

rabbit n 1 burrowing rodent akin to hare 2 sl unskilful player of game; beginner; n r. punch punch on back of neck; v hunt rabbits; phr v rabbit on coll talk at length.

rabble n disorderly, riotous crowd or mob; a, n r. -rousing stirring up feelings of anger and violence in a mob n r.-rouser person doing this.

rabid a 1 affected with rabies 2 furious 3 violently fanatical; n rabies infectious disease of dogs etc; canine madness.

race¹ n 1 contest of speed in running, riding, sailing etc 2 strong current of water, esp leading to water-mill 3 pl -s horse-races; v run, cause to run swiftly; compete in speed (against); ns

racecourse track for horse-races; r. meeting Brit session of horse-races lasting one or more days; racer person, animal, machine that races.

race² n 1 group of persons descended from same original stock 2 distinct variety 3 lineage; breed; ns r. relations relations between different races in the same community; racialism 1 belief that one's race is superior to others 2 unjust treatment of member(s) of a particular race (also racism); a, n racialist, racist.

rack n 1 framework to hold things (hats, baggage, letters etc) 2 medieval instrument of torture 3 mech straight bar with teeth on its edge to work with pinion; idm go to rack and ruin become delapidated; v cause great pain or distress to; idm rack one's brains make hard

effort to think; phr v rack off sl go away; n r. rent unjustly high rent (v charge such rent).

racket¹ (also racquet) n bat used in tennis; pl -s game akin to tennis played in paved, walled court.

racket² n 1 loud noise; din 2 illegal business or way of making money; n -eer one who operates illegal business.

rac(c)oon n small, carnivorous nocturnal mammal.

racy a spirited; piquant; spicy; n raciness.

radar n electronic system for direction finding and observation of distant objects, by reflection of radio waves.

raddled a coll showing effects of debauched life.

radial a arranged like the spokes of a wheel; n outer tyre with strengthening cords radial to the wheel hub (also radial/radial-ply tyre); adv -ly.

radian n geom angle formed at centre of circle by radii drawn length of each end of arc with length of one radius.

radiate v emit rays of light, heat etc; spread from centre; ns -ation emission of rays of heat, light etc); radiance brightness; brilliance; a radiant shining; displaying delight; n geom straight line assumed to rotate round fixed point; n radiator 1 that which radiates 2 device for cooling car engine **3** apparatus for heating rooms etc.

radical *a* **1** of root or origin **2** *polit* advanced; progressive **3** complete; *n* **1** number expressed as root of another **2** politician of advanced liberal views.

radicle *n* minute root of plant.

radii *pl of* radius.

radio- *prefix* of rays, of radium, of radiation.

radio *n* **1** transmission of sounds by electromagnetic waves, without wires **2** receiving apparatus (*also* **radio set** *or* **radio receiver**) **3** *the radio* (activity of) the broadcasting industry (*also* **sound radio**); *v* send (message) by radio; *ns* **r. astronomy** astronomy using radio telescope; **r. cab, r. car** cab or car equipped with radio intercom; **R. Data System** system giving finely adjusted tuning on VHF radio (*also* **RDS**); (**r. -telephone** telephone using radio waves, not cables; **r. -telescope** radio receiver used for tracking movements of bodies in space.

radioactivity *n* spontaneous disintegration and emission of gamma rays etc; *a* **radioactive**.

radiogram *n* **1** picture made by radiography **2** combined radio set and record player.

radiography *n* X-ray photography *usu* for medical

use; *n* **-pher** person qualified to do this.

radiology *n* study of X-rays and their use in medicine *n* **-ologist** specialist in this.

radiotherapy *n* treatment of disease by X-rays *n* **-therapist**.

radish *n* plant with edible, pungent root.

radium *n* rare, radioactive, metallic element.

radius *n* **radii, radiuses. 1** straight line from centre to circumference of circle **2** shorter bone of forearm; *pl*.

radix *n* number or quantity taken as basis for calculations.

raffia *n* fibre from leaves of Madagascar palm, used for tying up plants etc.

raffish *a* rakish; disreputable.

raffle *n* sale of article by means of lottery; *v* dispose of by raffle.

raft[1] *n* flat, buoyant structure of logs, planks etc.

raft[2] *US coll* large amount.

rafter *n* one of pieces of timber supporting roof.

rag[1] *n* shred, tatter of cloth; *pl* **-s** old clothes; *ns* **r. -bag** *coll* random assortment; **r. -rolling** decorating technique using rag to produce mottled effect; **r. trade** *coll* design, manufacture, selling of clothes; *a* **ragged 1** jagged; uneven **2** clothed in torn clothes; rough; *ns* **ragamuffin** ragged, dirty person or child; **ragstone**

rough blueish limestone; **ragtime** strongly syncopated music.

rag[2] *v* **ragging, ragged. 1** tease good-naturedly; play practical jokes on **2** be noisy, riotous; *n* good-natured mischievous prank, *esp* by students.

rage *n* violent anger; frenzy; fury; *v* **1** speak, act with violent anger **2** (*of storm etc*) be extremely violent, rough; *idm* **all the rage** *coll* very popular.

raglan *n* of sleeves not set into armhole.

ragoût *n Fr* highly seasoned stew of meat and vegetables.

raid *n* attack, invasion; police search on suspect premises, as low night-club etc; *v* make raid on, into; attack.

rail[1] *n* **1** horizontal wooden or metal bar; *pl* **-s** system of railway lines; *v* send by rail; *idm* **off the rails** out of control; *ns* **railing** *usu pl* fence of wooden or metal rails; **railhead** end of railway line; **railway** system of tracks for running of trains (*US* **railroad**); *v* **railroad** *coll* **1** force (sb to do sth) **2** use pressure to get proposal accepted quickly.

rail[2] *v* utter complaints against; reproach bitterly; *n* **raillery** good-humoured banter.

rain *n* condensed moisture of atmosphere falling in drops; *v* fall as rain; *fig* arrive in large numbers, in continuous succession; *idm* **come rain or shine** whatever happens; *idm* **right as rain** perfectly alright; completely fit and healthy; *v* **fall as rain**; *phr vs* **rain down** fall in abundance; **rain down on** (of abuse etc) overwhelm; *ns* **rainbow** many-coloured arc appearing in sky when sun shines through rain (*a* **r. -coloured** multicoloured; *n* **r. trout** black spotted trout with reddish stripes); **rain-check** US ticket useable later when sport event is postponed (*idm* **take a rain-check** *coll* postpone acceptance of offer or invitation); **rainfall** amount of rain falling on a given area over a given period; **r. forest** tropical wet forest; **r. gauge** instrument for measuring rainfall; *a* **rainy**; *idm* **keep/put by/save for a rainy day** save for an emergency.

raise *v* cause to rise; erect; increase amount or value of; evoke; breed, rear; increase in intensity; *idm* **raise Cain** *coll* cause trouble; *idm* **raise land** *naut* come within sight of land; *idm* **raise the roof** display great anger.

raisin *n* dried grape.

raison d'être *n Fr* reason for existence.

raj *n* (period of) British rule in India.

rake[1] *n* long handled tool with cross bar set with teeth for gathering hay, leaves etc, or for breaking, scraping ground; *v* 1 use rake 2 sweep target with fire lengthways; *phr vs* **rake in** *coll* earn or win quickly, abundantly; **rake up** *coll* 1 collect with some difficulty 2 remind about (sth better forgotten); *n* **r. -off** *coll* commission obtained dishonestly.

rake[2] *n* dissolute or immoral man; *a* **rakish** dashing; showy.

rake[3] *v* incline backwards from perpendicular; *n* (*of ship's mast, stage*) slope.

rally *v* **rallying, rallied.** 1 gather together again 2 reform after repulse etc 3 recover health, strength etc 4 revive; *phr v* **rally round** come to the rescue; *n* 1 act of rallying 2 mass-meeting 3 gathering of car-drivers etc for long competitive drive 4 *tennis* exchange of strokes.

RAM *abbr* 1 *comput* random-access memory 2 Royal Academy of Music.

ram *n* 1 adult male sheep 2 device for battering or piercing 3 hydraulic machine; *v* **ramming, rammed.** 1 collide forcibly with; crush by repeated blows; crush, cram 2 *fig* instil (ideas etc) by persistent effort.

Ramadan *n* great feast, lasting throughout 9th month of Moslem year.

ramble *v* 1 wander, walk about idly; stroll for pleasure 2 chatter, speak incoherently 3 (*of plants*) grow in long shoots; *n* casual walk; *a* **rambling** 1 wandering; poorly organized (**r. speech**) 2 irregularly shaped (**r. mansion**) 3 with long trailing shoots (**r. plant**); **rambler** one who rambles; climbing, trailing plant, *esp* rose.

rambunctious *a US* rumbustious *adv* **-ly** *n* **-ness**.

ramekin *n* small baking dish.

ramify *v* **ramifying, ramified.** spread, branch out; subdivided; *n* **ramification** branching, subdivision in complex system.

ramjet *n* type of jet aero-engine.

ramp *n* 1 inclined plane joining two level surfaces 2 *sl* swindle 3 *coll* storm of anger; rampage.

rampage *v* rage, behave turbulently; *n* wild behaviour; *as* **rampageous** violent and uncontrolled.

rampant *a* 1 flourishing without restraint (**r. disease**) 2 growing too fast and abundantly (**r. weeds**) 3 *heraldry* standing on hind leg with forelegs raised; *adv* **-ly**; *n* **rampancy**.

rampart *n* defensive mound with parapet; *fig* defence.

ramrod *n* (formerly) stick for ramming charge into muzzle-loading gun.

ramshackle *a* rickety; tumbledown; worn-out.

ran *pt of* **run**.

ranch n large American cattle farm; n **rancher**.

rancid a having offensive smell and taste esp of stale fat or oil; ns **-ity; -ness**.

rancour n deep-rooted hatred, illwill; malice; spite; a **rancorous**.

rand n S African unit of currency (pl **rand**).

R and D abbr comm research and development.

random a haphazard; made, done by chance; heedless idm **at random** in an unplanned way; r. **access** comput system allowing information to be stored or retrieved in any order (r. **access memory**) comput memory with this facility, also **RAM**); adv **-ly; n -ness**.

randy a coll lustful.

ranee, rani n Hindu queen or ruler; wife of rajah.

range n 1 line; row 2 extent; area; scope; sphere 3 distance that can be reached by weapon, vehicle etc 4 shooting area 5 cooking stove; v 1 place 2 set in rows 3 (of animals, plants etc) frequent; be found in 4 wander 5 vary within limits; ns r.**-finder** instrument for measuring distance away from target etc; **ranger** forest, or park official; rover.

rangy a tall and thin.

rank[1] n 1 line; row 2 social class, order 3 grade; class 4 pl **-s** body of soldiers; v take rank; classify; idm **rank and file** ordinary members, not

leaders; n **ranker** soldier in ranks; officer promoted from ranks.

rank[2] a 1 overgrown; coarse 2 rancid 3 flagrant.

rankle v fester; fig be remembered with bitterness, resentment; cause anger.

ransack v 1 hunt for something 2 plunder; pillage.

ransom n money, price paid for release of prisoner, or captured goods etc; v pay ransom for.

rant v speak wildly, extravagantly; use violent language; n **ranter**.

rap[1] n light, smart blow; idm **take the rap** coll be punished for sb else's wrongdoing; v **rapping, rapped**. tap, strike with quick blow.

rap[2] v sl 1 talk rapidly 2 talk rhythmically and continuously to musical accompaniment; ns **rapper, rapping**.

rapacious a greedy; grasping; avaricious; n **rapacity**.

rape[1] n plant grown as fodder for sheep; seed of this used as food for birds, and producing oil.

rape[2] v violate; ravish; assault sexually; n act of raping; n **rapist**.

rapid a swift, fast-moving; done quickly; n usu pl **-s** swift current in river owing to sudden fall in bed; a r.**-fire** in quick succession; n **-ity** speed, velocity.

rapier n light, thrusting

duelling sword.

rapport n harmony; sympathetic relationship.

rapporteur n person who investigates and reports.

rapt a carried away in body or mind; completely absorbed; intent; a **raptorial** predatory; of order of birds of prey; n **rapture** ecstasy; great delight; a **rapturous**.

rare[1] a 1 uncommon; infrequent; exceptional 2 not dense; adv **-ly** seldom; n **rarity** 1 state of being rare 2 rare object or quality.

rare[2] a (of meat) underdone.

rarebit n Welsh r. toasted cheese.

rarefy v **rarefying, rarefied**. 1 make rare or thin 2 reduce density of 3 fig refine.

raring a very eager.

rascal n 1 rogue; scamp 2 mischievous child (term of affection); a **-lly**.

rash[1] n skin eruption.

rash[2] a impetuous; spoken, done without caution or thought; n **-ness**.

rasher n thin slice of bacon or ham.

rasp n 1 coarse file 2 grating sound; v 1 file, scrape with rasp 2 grate upon (ear) 3 irritate.

raspberry n juicy, bright-red fruit growing on canes; the plant.

Rastafarian n, a (member) of Jamaican religious sect (also **Rasta**); n **-ism**.

raster n pattern of lines from which picture is formed on

TV screen.

rat n 1 small, long-tailed rodent, allied to mouse 2 *fig* cowardly traitor; *ns* **r. race** competition to succeed in business; **r. trap** *US coll* dirty, dilapidated old building, v **1 ratting, ratted.** to hunt rats 2 desert a cause etc 3 inform on someone, *a* **ratty** *sl* angry; ill-tempered.

ratafia n 1 liqueur distilled from almonds, crushed fruit kernels 2 small macaroon biscuit.

ratbag n *sl* despicable creature or person.

ratchet n set of teeth on bar or wheel, allowing motion in one direction only; n *comm* way of ensuring continous increase in profits.

rate n 1 amount, degree measured in relation to sth else 2 amount charged; *pl* **-s** local tax based on value of property; v **rate-cap** *Brit* (of government) penalise local authority that overspends by reducing rate support grant; n **rateable value** figure based on size of building as means of assessing rates to be paid; n **rate-payer** one who pays local rates.

rate v scold; take to task.

rather *adv* 1 sooner; more; slightly; preferably 2 slightly; fairly.

ratify v **ratifying, ratified.** confirm; make valid; n **ratification.**

rating n 1 act of assessing; classification 2 sailor who is

not commissioned 3 scolding; rebuke 4 *pl* **-s** order of popularity of TV programmes.

ratio n **-os** proportion; fixed numerical relations.

ratiocination n *fml* process of logical reasoning.

ration n fixed amount or allowance of food, goods; *pl* **-s** daily food allowance; v supply with, limit to certain amount.

rational a reasonable; sensible; *ns* **-ism** doctrine that reason is only source of knowledge; **-ist;** v **rationalize** give rational explanation of; n **-ization** reorganization of an industry or related group; n **rationality** reasonableness.

rationale n logical basis or reasoning for sth.

ratlines n *pl* ropes fastened across shrouds of ship, forming a rope ladder.

rattan n species of climbing palm; cane of this.

rattle v 1 give out succession of short, sharp sounds 2 move with clatter 3 talk rapidly, briskly 4 *coll* disconcert; confuse; *phr vs* **rattle on** *coll* talk fast without pausing; **rattle through** perform as quickly as possible; n 1 this sound 2 device or child's toy, making this sound 3 horny rings on rattlesnake's tail; n **rattlesnake** venomous American snake, which can rattle its tail.

raucous a hoarse; harsh-

sounding.

ravage v 1 devastate by violence 2 plunder; n *pl* **-s** destructive effect.

rave v 1 speak wildly in delirium 2 talk enthusiastically about; n *coll* praise; Acid House party; *ns* **r. review** enthusiastic review; **raver** *coll dated* person who goes to Acid House parties; young person with free and exciting life-style; **r.-up** *Brit coll* wild party; a **raving** wild and uncontrolled (n *pl* **-s** wild talk).

ravel v **ravelling, ravelled.** entangle; confuse; fray.

raven n large black bird related to crow; a jet-black.

ravening a desperately seeking food.

ravenous a voracious; famished with hunger.

ravine n deep narrow valley or gorge.

ravioli n *pl* Italian dish of small squares of pasta holding seasoned, chopped meat etc.

ravish v 1 fill with rapture 2 violate; commit rape upon; n **ravishing** delightful; entrancing.

raw a 1 uncooked; in natural state 2 crude 3 sore 4 cold; damp 5 untrained; n **r. deal** *coll* unfair treatment; n **-ness** n **rawhide** untanned hide; a **raw-bone** thin; gaunt; *idm* **in the raw 1** unprocessed 2 crude; *sl* naked.

Rawlplug [TM] small hollow tube of wood or plastic giving tight fit for screw in masonry.

ray n 1 single beam, shaft of light, heat etc 2 any one of group of radiating lines; v radiate.

ray n flat-fish, skate.

rayon n artificial silk made from cellulose.

raze v obliterate; lay level with ground; destroy.

razor n cutting instrument for shaving.

razzle n idm **on the razzle** coll out celebrating, drinking etc.

razzmatazz n coll noisy excitement, publicity.

RC abbr Roman Catholic.

RCD abbr residual current device.

Rd abbr road.

RDS abbr Radio Data System.

reactive a 1 reacting 2 chem likely to react.

re, in re prep in the matter of; concerning.

re- prefix Lat repetition; again; back. Forms compounds, these are not given where the meaning may be deduced from the simple word.

reach v 1 extend 2 touch; take with outstretched hand 3 achieve; n 1 act, power of touching 2 range 3 stretch of water, esp on river.

react v act in response to stimulus; ns **reaction** 1 response to stimulus 2 reciprocal action 3 contrary action 4 depression

following over-excitement; **reactionary** one who opposes progress and reform; a inclined to such action, retrograde.

reactor n (physics) apparatus for generating heat by nuclear fission; atomic pile.

read v 1 see and understand printed, written words, symbols etc 2 read and utter 3 learn by reading 4 (of thermometer etc) indicate; register; idm **read between the lines** understand some implied meaning; idm **read the riot act** give a strong reprimand; a **readable** easy or interesting to read; ns **reader** 1 person who reads 2 Brit high-ranking teacher of subject at university 3 elementary reading book **reading** 1 act of reading 2 extract from book 3 interpretation 4 figure shown on measuring gauge; **readership** type or number of regular readers of publication; **readout** comput printed form of data; pt, pp **read;** a **readable** that can be read; interesting, not tedious; ns **readability;** **reader** 1 student, lover of books 2 one who reads MSS submitted to publishers 3 one who reads and corrects proofs for press 4 official university lecturer 5 reading-book.

ready a prepared for use; immediately available; prompt; ns **r.money** cash;

r.-reckoner Brit tables of ready-made calculations; a **r.-made** prepared beforehand; n **readiness;** adv **readily** easily; willingly; promptly.

reagent n substance used to produce chemical change or reaction.

real a existing in fact; genuine; actual; ns **r. estate** landed property; **r. tennis** old form of tennis played indoors (also **royal tennis**); a **r.-time** comput that can handle new data and adapt existing data to this very fast; **realism** practical outlook; ability to see things as they are; attempt to depict life etc as it actually exists; **-ist;** a **-istic;** n **reality** state of being real; v **realize** 1 become aware of 2 convert into, sell for money; (ns **-ization** act of realizing); **realty** leg real estate, property.

realm n 1 kingdom 2 fig sphere; region.

realpolitik n Ger realistic policy for promoting national interests.

realtor n US estate agent.

ream[1] n 20 quires of paper, 480 or 500 sheets.

ream[2] v 1 bevel out; countersink 2 naut open for caulking; n **reamer** tool for this.

reap v 1 cut and gather (corn etc) 2 fig obtain as reward, result of action, conduct; n **reaper.**

rear[1] v 1 raise; lift up 2 bring up; educate 3 (of horse etc) stand on hind legs.

rear[2] n hind apart; part of army behind front line; position of being at back; idm **bring up the rear** be the last; v **rear-end** coll crash into the rear of another vehicle; ns **rear-admiral** lowest flag rank in Royal Navy; **rear-guard** body of troops protecting rear of army on march.

reason n 1 faculty of thinking logically 2 cause; motive 3 sanity 4 common sense; adm **within reason** not beyond reasonable limits; phr v **reason with** try to persuade by reasoned argument; a **reasonable** 1 fair 2 quite cheap adv **-ably** fairly; n **reasoning** logical process; v persuade by logical argument.

reassure v comfort; give sense of confidence; n **-surance**; a **-suring**.

rebarbative a fml fearsome; harsh.

rebate n 1 deduction; discount 2 rabbet; v cut rebate or rabbet in.

rebel v rebelling, rebelled. revolt; resent control, constraint; take up arms against; n one who rebels; n **rebellion** organized, open resistance to authority etc; a **rebellious** 1 taking part in rebellion 2 showing resistance to authority (adv **-ly** n **-ness**).

rebore v bore through (cylinder) again to regain true shape; n act, process of reboring or being rebored.

reborn a renewed in morale or religious faith.

rebound v 1 bound, spring back 2 recoil on; n act of rebounding; idm **on the rebound** 1 when bouncing back 2 when suffering from disillusion, esp in love; n **rebounder** small trampoline (n **rebounding** exercise on one of these).

rebuff n repulse; snub; check; v check; snub; defeat.

rebuke v reprove; reprimand; censure for fault; n reproof.

rebus n riddle in which names, syllables etc are represented by pictures and letters.

rebut v rebutting, rebutted. repel, check esp accusations etc; refute; n **rebuttal**.

recalcitrant a refractory; obstinately disobedient; n **recalcitrance**.

recall v 1 summon, order back 2 remember 3 restore 4 revoke; n summons to return.

recant v take back; disavow opinions, beliefs etc; n **-ation**.

recap v recapping, recapped. coll recapitulate; repeat the main points (also n).

recapitulate (coll abbr **recap**) v summarize; restate briefly; n **-lation**.

recede v 1 move back 2 slope backwards.

receipt n 1 written acknowledgement of money, goods received 2 act of receiving or getting 3 recipe 4 pl **-s** money earned in trading.

receive v 1 take, obtain (something given, sent, offered etc) 2 undergo 3 greet; welcome; allow into one's presence; n **receiver** 1 person receiving sth 2 Brit one receiving stolen goods 3 cap official appointed to collect money or administer property, eg in case of bankruptcy (**receivership** his term of office; idm **in receivership** under his control) 4 wireless receiving set 5 ear-piece of telephone.

recension n revision of text.

recent a new; fresh; modern.

receptacle n vessel; container; that which receives or contains.

reception n 1 act of receiving 2 formal act of receiving guests, clients, hotel visitors etc 3 quality of broadcasting signals received 4 desk in entrance hall of hotel or business establishment where visitors are received (also **r. desk**) 5 area adjacent to this (**r. area**); ns **receptionist** person employed to receive hotel guests, patients etc and arrange accommodation, appointments etc; **r. room** 1 living room in house 2 large hall for social functions.

receptive a able, quick to receive, esp new ideas etc;

adv **-ly** *ns* **-ness, receptivity**.
receptor *n* device for receiving signals.
recess *n* 1 cessation, suspension of business 2 alcove 3 secret place; *v* provide a recess; *a* **recessive** *bio* not evident in an offspring because of dominant effect of other gene(s).
recession *n* 1 act of receding 2 period of reduction, slackening in industry and trade.
recessional *n* hymn sung as clergy leave chancel.
recidivist *n* one who relapses into crime.
recipe *n* 1 formula, directions for making, cooking something 2 prescription.
recipient *n, a* (person, thing) that receives.
reciprocal *a* 1 felt, done in return; mutual 2 alternating; *v* **reciprocate** 1 exchange mutually 2 alternate 3 move backwards and forwards; *ns* **-ation; reciprocity**.
recitative *n mus* passage of dialogue or narrative in opera or oratorio, sung in a way that keeps rhythm of natural speech.
recite *v* repeat aloud from memory *esp* to audience; *ns* **recital** act of reciting; *mus* performance by soloist or small group, or of works of one composer; **recitation** recital of poetry or prose *usu* from memory.
reck *v ar* care.

reckless *a* heedless; careless; rash; incautious.
reckon *v* 1 count; calculate 2 *coll* think; suppose; *phr vs* **reckon in** include in one's calculation; **reckon on** rely on; base one's plans on; **reckon with/without** 1 consider important/unimportant 2 remember/fail to take into account (*idm* **to be reckoned with** meriting serious consideration as an opponent); *ns* **-er, -ing** 1 calculating 2 retribution.
reclaim *v* 1 bring back 2 demand return of 3 reform from vice etc 4 recover (land) from sea or waste state; *n* **reclaimable**; *n* **reclamation**.
recline *v* sit, lean backwards; rest; repose.
recluse *n* hermit; one who chooses to live alone in retirement; *n* **reclusion**.
recognize *v* 1 know again 2 acknowledge; admit to be true, valid; *ns* **recognition**; **recognizance** 1 obligation to fulfil some condition, undertaken before court 2 sum forfeited if party fails to meet this obligation.
recoil *v* 1 draw back 2 retreat 3 rebound 4 *fig* feel disgust, horror; *n* rebound, *esp* of gun; backward motion.
recollect *v* recall to mind; remember; *n* **-lection**.
recommend *v* represent as being suitable; advise; entrust to care of; *n* **-ation**.

recompense *v* make equal return for; reward; compensate; *n* that which is given as reward, compensation etc.
reconcile *v* 1 settle (dispute, quarrel etc) 2 bring into logical agreement 3 be resigned to; *ns* **reconciliation** restoration of friendship; act, state of being reconciled; **reconcilement**; *a* **reconciliatory**.
reconnoitre *v Fr* make preliminary survey (of enemy's position etc); explore, examine beforehand; *n* **reconnaissance** act of reconnoitring.
reconstitute *v* restore to usual state; (*eg* dried foodstuff by adding water); *n* **-tution**.
record *v* 1 write down for future information 2 store (sound) on gramophone disc or magnetic tape for subsequent reproduction; *n* 1 written account, document 2 sound recording on gramophone disc 3 best, finest achievement, *esp* in sport; *idm* **for the record** for the sake of accuracy; *idm* **off the record** *coll* unofficial(ly); confidentially; *idm* **set the record straight** correct a misunderstanding; *ns* **recorder** 1 wooden or plastic instrument of flute family 2 machine for playing recorded tape (*also* **tape recorder**) 3 *Brit* leg judge;

record player machine for playing music recorded on disc; *recording 1* act or result of putting onto disc, tape etc 2 act of making written record, *a* **recorded** 1 preserved on disc, tape or cassette; not performed live 2 written down (*n* **r. delivery** method of checking proper delivery of mail to destination by Post Office).

recount *v* 1 narrate; relate 2 count again.

recoup *v* compensate; make good (financial losses).

recourse *n* act of seeking help; application for help; *idm* **have recourse to** get help from.

recover *v* get, win back what has been lost; *a* **-able;** *n* **recovery.**

recreate *v* create, form anew; restore, revive; *n* **-ation** 1 relaxation 2 amusement; game; sport; pastime; *a* **-al.**

recriminate *v* express mutual reproach; make counter-charges; *n* **-ation** mutual abuse and reproach.

recrudesce *v* break out afresh; *n* **recrudescence;** *a* **-escent.**

recruit *n* newly enlisted member of armed forces; newly enrolled member of society etc; *v* enlist, seek to enlist (new soldiers, members etc); *n* **-ment.**

rectangle *n* right-angled parallelogram; *a* **rectangular.**

rectify *v* rectifying, rectified. 1 put right 2 purify 3 adjust 4 refine by distillation; *n* **rectification** 1 act of rectifying 2 refining 3 conversion of alternating current into direct current; *n* **rectifier.**

rectilineal, rectilinear *a* in, consisting of straight lines.

rectitude *n* moral uprightness; integrity; honesty of purpose.

recto *n Lat* right-hand page.

rector *n* C of E parish priest entitled to tithes; head of certain religious and educational institutions; *n* **rectory** rector's house.

rectum *n* **-tums** or **-ta.** *anat* lowest, terminal part of large intestine; *a* **rectal.**

recumbent *a* lying down; reclining; *n* **recumbence.**

recuperate *v* 1 recover, regain health etc 2 recover from financial losses; *n* **-ation.**

recur *v* recurring, recurred. 1 happen again 2 return to one's mind 3 *math* be repeated indefinitely; *n* **recurrence;** *a* **-rent.**

recusant *n, a* (one) refusing to obey, conform to laws etc, *esp* religious matters.

recycle *v* treat used materials from manufactured articles to make them reusable; *a* **recyclable** suitable for recycling.

red *a* 1 of colour of blood 2 (*of hair*) reddish-brown or ginger 3 *coll usu cap* Communist; *n* 1 red colour 2 *cap coll* Communist; *idm* **in the red** in debt; *ns* **r.**

admiral black and red butterfly; **r. carpet** *sport* card used by referee when sending off player for foul play or dissension; **redcoat** British soldier (18th-19th century); **R. Cross** international organization caring for the sick and wounded; **R. Ensign** flag of British Merchant Navy; **r. flag** 1 flag warning of danger 2 symbol of communism or revolution; **r. giant** enormous star cooler than white or yellow star; **redhead** person with red hair (*a* **redheaded**); **r.herring** sth irrelevant introduced as a distraction; **r. lead** red oxide of lead; **r. letter day** day made memorable by happy event; **r. light** warning light to halt traffic, to call for silence in recording studio etc; **r. light district** area frequented by prostitutes; **r. shift** *astron* increase in wavelength indicating that star is moving away from observer; **r. tape** elaborate bureaucratic rules of procedures causing unnecessary delay and inconvenience; **redwood** large conifer with reddish wood; *as* **r.-blooded** full of vigour; **redbrick** (of university) founded in 19th or early part of 20th century; **r.-handed** (*idm* **catch sb red-**

handed catch sb doing wrong); v **redden 1** make red **2** turn red; blush.

redeem v **1** buy back **2** fulfil **3** make amends for **4** ransom **5** (of God, Christ) save from damnation; ns **redeemer** one who redeems, esp **the R.** Jesus Christ; **redemption;** a **redeemable.**

redolent a fragrant; giving out sweet scent; **r. of** fig steeped in; reminiscent of; n **redolence.**

redouble v **1** double again **2** make or become more intense.

redoubt n fortified post.

redoubtable a formidable; valiant.

redound phr vs **redound on** fml recoil on; **redound to** fml add to.

redress v put right; make amends for; idm **redress the balance** make things equal again; n fml reparation; compensation.

reduce v **1** lessen; decrease **2** break down to simpler form **3** med replace dislocated joint **4** cause or become, slimmer **5** bring by force or necessity to some inferior position, state etc; n **reduction;** a **reducing.**

reductio ad absurdum n Lat way of disproving sth by taking argument to logical but absurd conclusion.

redundant a superfluous; unnecessary; n **redundancy.**

reduplicate v fml double; repeat; n **-ation.**

reed n **1** various aquatic or marsh grasses; stem of these **2** vibrating cane or metal strip of some musical instrument; a **reedy 1** full of reeds **2** harsh; piping; shrill.

reef n **1** part of sail which can be folded up to shorten sail **2** ridge of rock just below surface of water **3** lode of auriferous quartz; v reduce area (of sail) by taking in reef; ns **r.knot** double-knot that does not slip easily; **reefer 1** short close-fitting warm jacket **2** sl cigarette from cannabis (also joint).

reek n fumes; stench; v emit smoke, fumes; smell; stink.

reel n **1** small spool or bobbin round which thread is wound **2** lively Scottish dance; music for it **3** unit of length of cinema film (approx 1,000 ft, approx 328m) or of staggering; v **1** wind on reel **2** stagger sway; phr v **reel off** recite rapidly.

ref abbr **1** reference **2** coll referee.

refectory n room for meals, esp in monastery, school, etc.

refer v **referring, referred. 1** assign to **2** send to for information **3** allude **4** submit for decision; ns **reference 1** act of referring **2** testimonial **3** relation; respect; n **r.book** book designed for easy retrieval of information; n **referendum** submitting of question to electorate.

referee n **1** one to whom a thing is referred **2** umpire esp in football (coll **ref**); v act as umpire.

referent n thing to which symbol refers.

refine v **1** purify; clarify **2** make, become more elegant; ns **refinement 1** act of refining **2** culture **3** fineness of feeling, taste etc; **refinery** place where materials are refined or purified.

refit v fit new parts in; n act or result of doing this.

reflate v increase supply of money in (economy); n **-ation;** a **-ationary.**

reflect v **1** throw back, give out (light, heat etc) **2** reproduce visual image **3** think deeply **4** cast doubt on; phr v **reflect (up)on** think deeply about; idm **reflect badly/well (up)on** give bad/good impression of; ns **reflection, reflexion** act of reflecting; that which is reflected (rays of light, heat etc); reflected visual image (by mirror etc); meditation; a **reflective;** n **reflector** polished surface which reflects (rays of light etc).

reflex a directed backwards; **r. action** involuntary muscular, nervous reaction to stimulus; **r. angle** angle greater than 180° and less than 360°; a **reflexive** ling denoting action coming back on agent; **r. pronoun** one referring to subject of sentence.

reflexology n therapy using foot massage to alleviate stress in other parts of body.

reform v change for better; improve condition, by removal of abuses etc; n improvement; n **-er** person initiating social or political change.

reformation n amendment; **the R.** 16th century religious revolt.

reformatory a corrective institution for young offenders; a producing reform.

refract v deflect rays or waves from direct course; n **refraction**; a **-ive**.

refractory a 1 unmanageable; stubborn 2 med resistant to treatment; hard to cure.

refrain[1] n recurring lines, words at end of song etc.

refrain[2] v abstain; forbear; keep oneself from.

refresh v revive; invigorate; renew; provide with fresh supply; idm **refresh sb's memory** remind sb of important details; n **refresher** 1 thing that refreshes 2 further study by qualified person to bring his/her knowledge up to date (also **r. course**); a **refreshing** 1 restoring vitality 2 thirst-quenching 3 new and stimulating; adv **-ingly**; ns **-ment** 1 of refreshing, being refreshed 2 food and drink; pl **-ments** snacks.

refrigerate v freeze; keep at very low temperature; ns **-ation**; **refrigerator** machine for cooling, freezing (food etc); ice-box.

refuge n shelter; protection; sanctuary; hiding place; n **refugee** one who seeks refuge, esp in another country.

refulgent a shining; radiant; n **refulgence** brightness; splendour.

refund v repay; restore.

refurbish v renovate.

refuse v decline; reject; (of horse) be unwilling to jump; n rubbish; discarded matter; n **refusal** 1 act of refusing 2 option.

refute v reject; disprove; a **refutable**; n **refutation**.

regal a of, like king; n pl **regalia** insignia of royalty; insignia, clothes etc of a society; adv **-ly**; n **regality**.

regale v 1 feast 2 give great delight to.

regard v 1 gaze at intently 2 consider; esteem; value; n 1 look 2 esteem 3 care; attention; pl **-s** expression of goodwill; idm **with regard to** concerning; a **-less** heedless; negligent.

regatta n It race-meeting for boats or yachts.

regenerate v 1 bring new life to 2 reorganize after decay 3 recreate 4 be reformed morally; a **-ative**; n **-ation**; **-ator** device in furnace for saving fuel by heating incoming air.

regent n one who rules during absence, minority or illness of sovereign; n **regency** office or position of regent; a of, in style prevailing during regency (esp 1810-20 in England and 1715-23 in France).

reggae n type of West Indian popular music.

regicide n killer, killing of king or sovereign.

regime n system, method of government, administration.

regimen n course of treatment, esp in matters of diet, exercise etc.

regiment n military unit; fig large quantity; a **-al** of regiment; n pl uniform of particular regiment.

Regina n Brit leg the State as prosecutor.

region n 1 area, district, tract of country 2 area of body; idm **in the region on** about; a **-al**; adv **-ally**; n pl **-s** the provinces; v **regionalize** organize by regions n **-ization**.

register n 1 official record of names, events etc kept for reference 2 range of voice or musical instrument 3 moveable plate controlling airflow on stove 4 ling variety of language (formal/informal, spoken/written etc) appropriate to social situation or professional use 5 printing correct alignment; v 1 record formally 2 have one's name recorded or checked 3 enrol for sth **4** (*of machinery*) give reading or measurement; (*of measurement*) be recorded **5** (*of face*) express **6** be noted or remembered **7** send by registered post; *a* **registered** sent by special postal service with protection against loss etc (*n* **r. post**).

registrar *n* one who keeps public records (births, deaths etc); *n* **registration** act of registering (**r. number** *Brit* official code of numbers and letters for identification of motor vehicle.

registry *n* place, office where register is kept; **r.office** local registry for births, marriages and deaths.

regius *a Lat* appointed, founded by crown.

regnant *a* reigning.

regorge *v* **1** vomit **2** swallow again.

regress *n* **1** return; going back **2** relapse; *n* **-ive** falling back; *n* **regression** backward movement.

regret *v* **regretting, regretted.** be sorry for; remember with grief, sorrow; repent of; *n* grief; repentance; sorrow; *as* **-ful** feeling regret (*adv* **-ly**); **regrettable** to be regretted (*adv* **-ably**).

regular *a* **1** orderly (**r. life**) **2** normal; according to rule (**r. verb**) **3** habitual (**r. exercise**) **4** symmetrical; eve (**r. shape**) **5** unvarying (**r. pattern**) **6** permanent (**r. job**) **7** thorough (**r. check-up**) **8** *US* pleasant (**r. guy**);

n **regular** visitor, client etc; *adv* **-ly**; *n* **regularity**; *v* **regularize** (*n* **-ization**).

regulate *v* **1** put in order **2** control by law make clock etc **3** work correctly; *ns* **-ation** act of regulating; rule; order; **regulator** lever of watch etc; *a* **regulatory**.

regurgitate *v* **1** flow, gush back; bring up again (swallowed food etc); *n* **-ation**.

rehabilitate *v* restore normal capacity; reinstate; *n* **-ation**.

rehash *v* rearrange old literary material, and produce under new title.

rehearse *v* perform, practise (play, piece of music etc) in private, before public performance; *n* **rehearsal**.

Reich *n* former German state.

reify *v* treat as real, concrete.

reign *n* rule, supreme power of sovereign; period of ruler's reign; *n* **r.of terror** period of violence and murder on a large scale; *v* rule as monarch; be supreme; predominate.

reimburse *v* refund; compensate by payment; *n* **-ment**.

rein *n* leather strap fastened to bit for leading, holding horse; *fig* that which restrains; *v* hold in, control with reins; *idm* **give rein to** allow full play to; *idm* **keep a tight rein on** control very strictly.

reincarnation *n* return of soul to earth, after death, in fresh form; *v* **reincarnate** cause to

be reborn in other form.

reindeer *n* large, domesticated deer of northern regions; **r.moss** grey arctic lichen.

reinforce *v* **1** *mil* strengthen with additional troops, supplies etc **2** strengthen (fabric etc) by increasing thickness etc; *ns* **-ment**; **reinforced concrete** concrete strengthened by steel bars embedded in it.

reinstate *v* restore to former state, position; *n* **reinstatement**.

reiterate *v* repeat many times; *n* **-ation** repetition.

reject *v* discard as imperfect, valueless, useless; refuse to accept; disallow; *n* that which is rejected; *n* **rejection** refusal.

rejig *v* **rejigging, rejigged.** *coll* reorganize.

rejoice *v* to make, be glad; feel, express joy; delight; *n pl* **-s** outward expression of joy, festivities.

rejoin *v* **1** join again **2** make answer; *n* **rejoinder** retort; answer to a reply.

rejuvenate *v* renew youth of; become young again; *n* **-ation**.

relapse *v* **1** fall back into former bad state **2** become ill again; (*also n*).

relate *v* narrate; *phr v* **relate to 1** have connection with **2** refer (to) **3** belong to same family as; *phr v* **relate to 1** connect, be connected with **2** *coll* show sympathy towards; *a* **related 1**

connected 2 of the same kind.

relation n 1 connection by blood, marriage 2 connection between things 3 narration; n pl -s links between people, groups of people (**international rs; sexual rs** sexual intercourse); n **relationship** 1 connection 2 friendship or other mutual link between people.

relative n member of same family; a comparative; not absolute; idm **relative to** 1 referring to 2 compared with; ns **r.clause** ling clause performing adjectival function relating to noun or pronoun; **r.pronoun** ling pronoun who, which or that used to relate relative clause to sth in main clause; **relativism** theory that there can be no objective standards of truth (n, a -ist); **relativity** 1 fact or state of being relative 2 Einstein's theory based on principle that time and space are inseparable.

relax n loosen; slacken; make, become less rigid, tense; unbend; become less severe; n -ation act of relaxing; slackening of strain, tension etc; recreation.

relay n 1 team of men, horses or dogs etc replacing tired ones 2 broadcast sent from one station to another; v 1 pass on (information) 2 transmit from relay station 3

to lay again; **r.race** race between teams, each member running part of distance and handing baton to next runner.

release v give up; set free; discharge; n 1 liberation 2 formal discharge 3 catch releasing mechanism.

relegate v send, dismiss to inferior position; transfer; n -ation.

relent v become less hard, severe, stern or obstinate; a -less pitiless; inexorable (adv -ly).

relevant a bearing on point at issue; pertinent; applicable; n -ance.

reliable a dependable; trustworthy; adv -ably; ns **reliability; reliance on** 1 trust in 2 dependence on; a **reliant on** dependent on.

relic n object surviving from past, esp one associated with saint; memento.

relief n 1 alleviation of pain, anxiety etc 2 help for people in distress 3 coll sexual gratification 4 release from duty 5 person relieving another from spell of duty 6 Brit legitimate allowance against taxable income 7 supplementary bus, train provided to meet unusual demand 8 method of decoration or design which stands out above surface (**r.map** map showing hills, valleys etc either by shading or by raised moulding); v **relieve** 1 bring relief to 2

take over duty from 3 lessen (the effect of); idm **relieve oneself** coll urinate or defecate; idm **relieve one's feelings** release one's emotion by shouting, weeping, violent action; phr v **relieve sb of sth** 1 take sth esp, burden from sb 2 coll rob sb of sth; a **relieved** freed from anxiety.

religion n belief in and worship of God or gods; as **religious** 1 pertaining to religion 2 devout, pious 3 fig conscientious; **religiose** sanctimonious (n -osity).

relinquish v abandon; surrender; let go.

relish n 1 enjoyment of food 2 fig zest; enthusiasm 3 spicy sauce for flavouring food; v enjoy.

relocate v move to new place, esp of work or residence; n -ation.

reluctant a unwilling, disinclined; difficult to treat; n **reluctance**.

rely phr v relying, relied. rely on depend on; trust; a **reliable** dependable; trustworthy; ns **reliability; reliance** ground of trust or confidence; a **reliant** confident; trusting.

REM abbr rapid eye movement (occurring while dreaming).

remain v stay, be left behind; persist; stay, continue in same place; n pl -s what is left or survives; relics; dead body; n **remainder** 1 remaining persons or things **2** quantity left after subtraction **3** copies of books etc unsold in publisher's stock; *v* offer unsold books etc at reduced prices.

remand *v* send back, *esp* into custody; *n* **r. home** institution for young delinquents.

remark *v* **1** take notice of; observe **2** utter comment; *n* observation; comment; *a* **-able** noticeable; unusual; *adv* **-ably.**

remedy *n* **-ies. 1** substance, treatment which cures disease etc **2** action or method tending to mitigate an evil or wrong; *v* **remedying, remedied.** put right; *as* **remediable** that can be remedied; **remedial 1** providing remedy (**r.action**) **2** backward; needing special education (**r. pupil**) **3** provided for backward pupils (**r. class, r. education**).

remember *v* call to mind; retain in memory; have in mind; *n* **remembrance 1** memory **2** keepsake; souvenir; (**R. Day** Sunday nearest to 11th November when British people hold services of remembrance for those who died in the 1st and 2nd World Wars).

remind *v* put in mind of, cause to remember; *n* **reminder** that which reminds.

reminisce *v* talk, *usu* with enjoyment, about past

memories; *n* **reminiscence** recollection; *pl* **-s** memoirs; *a* **-miniscent of** tending to remind one of; similar to.

remiss *a* negligent; careless.

remit *v* **remitting, remitted. 1** forgo, give up in whole or part **2** send back; transmit; *a* **remissible**; *ns* **remission** abatement; pardon; **remittance** sending of money; sum of money sent as payment or allowance.

remnant *n* **1** remaining fragment **2** short length of fabric, oddment.

remonstrate *v* protest; expostulate, plead, with; *n* **remonstrance.**

remorse *n* repentance; regret, *as* **-ful**; **-less** ruthless; pitiless; relentless; (*adv* **-ly**; *n* **-ness**).

remote *a* **1** far away **2** aloof; distant; *n* **r.control** device for controlling machine, weapon etc from distance by radio waves.

remove *v* **1** take, carry (thing) away, off; withdraw **2** erase **3** relieve of office, rank etc **4** move from one place to another, *esp* residence; *idm* (**at) one remove/two removes from** with a certain degree of distance from; *n* **removal** act of removing of furniture from house.

remunerate *v* pay; compensate; *n* **-ation;** *a* **-ative** profitable.

Renaissance *n* rebirth; revival, *esp* **the R.** revival of art and learning in 14th–16th

centuries.

renal *a* of the kidneys.

renascent *a* reviving; springing into fresh life.

rend *v* **rending, rent.** tear apart; split; *fig* cause anguish to.

render *v* **1** give in return; tender **2** depict by art **3** interpret **4** put on first coat of plaster etc; *n* **-ing** version; interpretation; **rendition** interpretation; performance.

rendezvous *n* Fr **1** meeting-place fixed beforehand **2** popular, general resort.

renegade *n* apostate; deserter; turncoat.

renege *v* break promise (*also* **renegue**).

renew *v* **1** restore to original condition or state of freshness **2** begin again **3** prolong, extend existence or validity of **4** grow again; *n* **renewal** revival; restoration; *as* **-able; -ing** regenerating; quickening.

rennet *n* preparation (*usu* from membrane of calf's stomach) used to curdle milk, and in cheese-making.

renounce *v* **1** formally give up, disclaim **2** repudiate **3** not to follow suit at cards; *n* **renunciation.**

renovate *v* restore to good condition; renew; repair; *ns* **-ation; -ator** one who renovates.

renown *n* fame; celebrity; *a* **-ed** famous.

rent *n* payment made for use of house, land etc; *n* **r. boy** *Brit* coll young male prostitute; v occupy (house etc) for payment; hire out; let; n **rental** amount payable as rent.

rep n coll abbr representative; n coll abbr repertory theatre.

repair[1] v mend; set right; compensate for; n act or result of mending; as **reparable, repairable**; n **reparation** redress, amends.

repair[2] phr v repair to have recourse to; frequent.

repartee n readiness in making witty reply or retort.

repast n meal; feast.

repatriate v send back, return to native country; n -**iation**.

repay v repaying, repaid. 1 pay back, refund (money) 2 make return for; reward; n -**ment**.

repeal v revoke; abrogate; annul (law etc); n revocation.

repeat v 1 say again, reiterate; recite 2 do again; reproduce 3 recur; n **repetition** thing repeated, esp programme or order for goods; adv -**edly** over and over again; n **repeater** 1 person or thing that repeats 2 watch that strikes hours 3 repeating fire-arm; n **repetition** act of repeating; recital; recitation; a **repetitive** tending to repeat.

repel v repelling, repelled. drive back; spurn; rouse dislike, disgust in; n **repellence**; a **repellent** disgusting; revolting; n that

which repels (insects etc).

repent v feel penitence, regret for deed or omission; a **repentant**; n repentance.

repercussion n 1 rebound; recoil 2 fig indirect effect, consequence usu pl.

repertory n store; stock; n **repertoire** stock of songs, plays that person or company can perform; n **repertory theatre** theatre with permanent company, depending on constant change of plays.

repetition n act of repeating; as **repetitious; repetitive** containing excessive repetition (adv -**ly**; n -**ness**).

repine v fret; complain; be discontented.

replace v put back; supersede; substitute for; n **replacement**.

replenish v fill up again; restock; n **replenishment**.

replete a well-filled; sated; gorged; n **repletion** surfeit.

replica n duplicate, copy of anything; esp, of work of art, done by the artist himself.

reply v, replying, replied. n answer in speech or writing.

report v 1 state formally 2 make official complaint about 3 present oneself for duty or service; n 1 objective account 2 rumour 3 sound of explosion; n **reportage** (style of) news reporting on media; a **reported** alleged (n **r. speech** indirect speech; adv -**ly** according to reports); n

reporter.

repose v place; rest; idm **repose hope/trust in** place one's hope/trust in; n act of reposing; n **repository** place where things may be deposited, stored; warehouse.

repossess v retake possession of (mortgaged property, hire-purchase goods etc) when borrower has not kept up payments; n **repossession**.

reprehend v rebuke; censure; blame; a **reprehensible** not good; deserving reproof.

represent v 1 depict by painting etc 2 symbolize 3 be an example of, the result of 4 act on behalf of 5 act as substitute for; n **representation** 1 act of representing, being represented 2 picture or other art form which depicts sb/sth (a -**al** giving realistic, life-like image); pl idm **make representations** to protest to; a **representative** 1 typical 2 of elected members (n 1 person elected to represent group 2 agent of firm, esp as travelling salesman).

repress v suppress; put down; curb; check; overcome; n **repression** suppression; restraint; psyc result of mental conflict; a **repressive** cruel and harsh (adv -**ly** n -**ness**).

reprieve v cancel or defer punishment esp, death sentence; give respite (to); n cancellation or suspension of criminal sentence; respite.

reprimand v rebuke, censure severely; n severe reproof.

reprisal n retaliation.

reprise n mus repeat.

reproach v scold; upbraid; charge with some fault; n rebuke; thing bringing disgrace etc; idm **beyond reproach** perfect; a **-ful**; (adv **-ly**).

reprobate a, n depraved (person); (one) without honour or principles.

reproduce v 1 become parent of 2 produce afresh 3 repeat 4 present again; n **-duction** 1 process of reproducing 2 copy; facsimile; a **-ductive** pertaining to, used in, reproduction; fertile.

reprography n copying of printed, written material (eg by photography).

reprove v chide; rebuke; n reproof.

reptile n cold-blooded, air-breathing vertebrate, which crawls, as snake, lizard etc; fig sly person; a **reptilian**.

republic n State having no monarch and governed by representatives elected by people; a, n **republican** (person) in favour of such a system (n **-ism**); n cap member of US Republican Party.

repudiate v reject; disown, disclaim; n **-ation**.

repugnant a distasteful; offensive; n **-ance** dislike; aversion.

repulse v 1 drive, beat back 2 fig snub; rebuff; n **repulsion** aversion; dislike; disgust; a **repulsive** loathsome; repellent.

repute n good or bad name; reputation; idm **of repute** of good reputation; as **reputable** of good repute; held in esteem; **reputed** considered; believed; thought of as; n **reputation** opinion commonly held of person or thing.

request n act of asking for something; petition; n **r.stop** bus stop where driver does not stop unless requested to; v ask for; demand politely.

requiem n dirge; RC mass for the dead.

require v 1 ask, claim as right; command 2 need; want; n **-ment** 1 need 2 condition; provision.

requisite n, a (something) needed, essential.

requisition n formal demand or request; v demand supply of.

requite v 1 reciprocate (love) 2 avenge (injury).

rerun v, n (give) repeat of film or TV show, or of any planned operation.

reschedule v postpone repayment of (loan) or interest on (it).

rescind v cancel; make void; n **rescission** act of rescinding.

rescript n offical order.

rescue v save from danger, injury etc; n **-er**.

research n diligent search and

investigation esp with view to gaining new knowledge etc; n **-er**.

resection n surgical removal of part of body.

resemble v be like; have qualities, features in common with; n **resemblance**.

resent v feel and show displeasure, irritation at; regard as offensive; n **-ment**; a **-ful**; adv **-fully**.

reserve v 1 keep, hold back; keep for specific person or use 2 order in advance; n 1 that which is reserved 2 fig aloofness; self-restraint 3 part of army only called up in emergency; n **reservation** 1 act of reserving 2 unexpressed doubt 3 tract of land reserved for use of natives, or for preservation of animals; a **reserved** not showing feelings.

reservist n, a (soldier) serving in reserve force.

reservoir n 1 large storage tank or artificial lake for water supply of town etc 2 any receptacle holding liquids 3 fig reserve supply.

reset v 1 set again; 2 change reading (eg on clock).

reshuffle n, v (make) changes in people holding positions of responsibility.

reside v dwell in permanently or for long time; ns **residence** abode, habitual dwelling; **residency** official residence of British Government agent in semi-

dependent State; *a, n*
resident (one) dwelling
permanently in given place;
a **residential** of part of town
etc mainly of residences.

residual current device (*also*
RDC) sensitive cut-out
device to prevent
overloading of electrical
system.

residue *n* remainder, what is
left; *as* **residual, residuary.**

resign *v* give up or back; retire
from office etc; abandon;
idm **resign sb to sth** get sb to
accept sth; *n* **-ation 1** act of
resigning office etc **2**
submission to will of God; *a*
resigned content to endure;
uncomplaining.

resilient *a* capable of returning
to original shape, state; *n*
resilience 1 elasticity **2**
recuperative power.

resin *n* sticky substance
secreted by most plants, *esp*
pines, firs.

resist *v* withstand; oppose; *n*
resistance 1 act of resistance
2 organized armed
opposition by civilians in
occupied country **3** *elec*
opposition of conductor to
flow of electricity; (*passive*
r. non-violent act done as
protest against abuse etc); *as*
resistant; resistless
inevitable.

resolute *a* firm; steadfast;
determined; *adv* **-ly;**
n **-ution 1** firm intention **2**
vote or decision of public
assembly or legislative body
3 analysis.

resolve *v* **1** separate
component parts of **2** make
clear **3** decide; firmly intend
4 form by vote or resolution;
n determination; firmness of
purpose; *as* **resolvable**
capable of being resolved; *n,
a* **resolvent** (substance) that
can disperse, dissolve.

resonant *a* **1** echoing;
resounding; sonorous
(**r.note, r.voice**) **2**
producing prolonged
vibration or echo
(**r.building, r.cave**); *n*
resonance 1 quality of being
resonant **2** sound caused by
vibrations of same
wavelength from another
body; *v* **resonate** be
resonant; *n* **-ator** device that
produces or adds resonance.

resort *phr v* **resort to** have
recourse to; frequent; use as
means; *n* frequently-visited
place, *esp* for holidays etc;
recourse.

resound *v* **1** ring with
prolonged sound; echo **2** be
loud and clear; *a* **resounding**
1 loud and clear **2**
outstanding (**r.success**) (*adv*
-ly).

resource *n* inventiveness, skill
in adapting thing to one's
purpose; *pl* **-s** means of
support; stock that can be
drawn on; *a* **resourceful.**

respect *v* pay heed to; hold in
esteem; treat as binding; *n* **1**
attention; esteem **2** special
aspect, point; reference; *idm*
with respect to about;
concerning; *a* **respectable**

estimable; decent; moderate;
passable; *n* **respectability;** *as*
respectful deferential;
respective of each
individually (*adv* **-ly** taken
separately in the order
mentioned).

respire *v* breathe; *ns*
respiration; respirator
apparatus worn over mouth
and nose to protect lungs
from fumes, gas etc; *a*
respiratory pertaining to
breathing.

respite *n* temporary rest from
work, effort, duty, pain etc;
pause; reprieve.

resplendent *a* gorgeously
bright; brilliant;
magnificent; splendid;
n **-ence.**

respond *v* **1** reply, make
answer **2** act as result of
another's action **3** react *usu*
in good sense; *ns* **respondent**
one who answers, *esp* to
lawsuit for divorce; **response**
answer; reaction to stimulus;
a **responsive** sympathetic;
readily reacting to stimulus;
(*adv* **-ly;** *n* **-ness**).

responsible *a* **1** legally, morally
answerable for actions etc;
capable of assuming
responsibility **2** of good
credit, repute etc; *n* **-ibility**
moral obligation, liability,
duty; charge; state of being
answerable.

rest[1] *n* **1** cessation of activity
or movement **2** repose **3**
support; prop **4** pause; *idm*
**put/set sb's mind at rest/at
ease** reassure sb; *idm* **lay sb**

to rest bury sb; *v* 1 (let) take repose; stop working for a while 2 lean; support; *idm* **rest assured (that)** be confident (that); *idm* **rest one's case** *leg* have no further argument to present; *phr vs* **rest on** 1 (of gaze) be turned towards 2 (of argument) depend on; **rest with** be the responsibility of; *ns* **r.-home** convalescent home, *esp* for old people; **r. room** *US coll* public lavatory; *as* **restful** (*adv* **-ly**, *n* **-ness**); **restless** (*adv* **-ly**, *n* **-ness**).

rest[2] *n* what is left; residue; others; *v* remain in (specified state or condition).

restaurant *n* place where meals can be bought and eaten; *n* **restaurateur** restaurant-keeper.

restauration *n* 1 running of restaurants 2 provision of restaurant food.

restitution *n* reparation; act of giving back something that has been taken or lost; *v* **restitute**.

restive *a* restless; fidgety; stubborn; impatient of control; *adv* **-ly**; *n* **-ness**.

restore *v* 1 bring back to former place, state etc; reinstate 2 renovate; repair 3 give back; *n* **restoration** act of restoring, *cap* **The R.** return of Charles II to his kingdom; *n, a* **restorative** (medicine, treatment) restoring health etc.

restrain *v* 1 check; control 2 confine legally; *a* **restrained** calm; controlled (*adv* **-ly**); *n* **restraint** 1 control of emotions 2 limitation 3 confinement.

restrict *v* impose limits on; limit by law; *n* **restriction** limitation; law, regulation that restricts; *a* **restrictive** (*n* **r. practice** *Brit* 1 agreement contrary to public interest 2 *esp pl* set of rules applied by union or pressure group impeding efficient operation of industry.

result *v* happen, follow as consequence; have as natural effect; *phr v* **result in** end in; *n* consequence; outcome; (in games) final score; *a* **resultant** arising as result.

resume *v* assume, occupy again; begin again; summarize; *n Fr* **resumé** summary; *n* **resumption** starting again; resuming.

resurge *v* rise again; *n* **resurgence**; *a* **resurgent**.

resurrection *n* rising again, *cap* **the R.** rising of Christ from the tomb; *v* **resurrect** restore to life; resuscitate; use once more.

resuscitate *v* restore to life, consciousness, activity; *n* **-tation**.

retail *n* sale in small quantities to consumer; *a* concerned with such sale; *adv* by retail; *v* sell by retail; repeat (gossip, news etc); *ns*. **r. park** landscaped area with

shops; **r. politics** electioneering by traditional methods of addressing meetings, speaking face-to-face; *n* **-er**.

retain *v* 1 hold 2 keep control of 3 engage services of 4 remember; *n* **-er** 1 fee to retain services of barrister 2 dependant, follower.

retaliate *v* pay back in kind; take vengeance; *n* **-iation** return of like for like; reprisals; *a* **-atory**.

retard *v* 1 delay, make slow or late 2 reduce speed or rate; *a* **retarded** slow in physical development; *n* **-ation**.

retch *v* try to vomit, strain as in vomiting.

retd *abbr* retired.

retention *n* 1 act of retaining 2 memory (**powers of r.**) *a* **retentive** having good memory (*n* **-ness**).

reticent *a* reserved in speech; uncommunicative; secretive; *n* **reticence**.

retina *n* sensitive layer of nerve fibres at back of eye.

retinue *n* suite, train of retainers, attendants.

retire *v* withdraw; give up profession, occupation etc; go to bed; *a* **retired** private, secluded; having withdrawn from active life, business etc; *n* **-ment**; *a* **retiring** shy, unobtrusive.

retort *v* answer sharply; repay in kind; reply with counter-charge; *n* sharp, witty reply; glass vessel with long, bent back used in chemistry, distilling etc.

retouch v touch up; add finishing touches to (photograph etc).

retrace v 1 go over again 2 recall; a **retraceable**.

retract v draw back; disavow, recant; as **retractable**; **retractile** that can be retracted; ns **retraction** recantation; **retractor** muscle which draws back; surgical instrument.

retread v walk over or along again; put new tread on (tyre); n used tyre given new tread.

retreat v retire; move, cause to move backwards; n act of retreating; military signal to retire; secluded, quiet, private place.

retrench v cut down, esp expenditure; curtail, lessen; n **-ment**.

retribution n punishment for evil deeds; fitting recompense.

retrieve v search for and fetch; regain; make good; atone; ns **retrieval**; **retriever** kind of dog trained to retrieve shot game; a **retrievable**.

retro- prefix backwards in place, time etc.

retroactive a having validity from an earlier date.

retrocession n act of yielding, granting back; movement backwards; v **retrocede** move backwards; retire; a **-cessive**.

retroflex a 1 bending backwards 2 ling pronounced

with tip of tongue curled back.

retrograde a moving, going backwards; deteriorating; n **retrogression**.

retro-rocket n rocket used to slow down spacecraft or reverse direction.

retrospect n mental review of past; a **-ive** referring to past; n **-ion**.

retsina n Greek wine flavoured with resin.

return v 1 go, come back 2 give, send back 3 elect to parliament or council; idm **return a verdict** leg (of jury) give considered opinion; n 1 act of returning 2 official report 3 esp pl profit 4 ticket for two-way journey (also **r.ticket**) 5 ticket for theatre, concert etc returned before performance for re-sale; idm **by return (of post)** by the next post; idm **many happy returns (of the day)** expressing greetings happy birthday; idm **in return (for)** in exchange (for); ns **r.match** second match between two opponents or teams; **returning officer** official appointed to organize and ensure fair conduct of election and declare result.

reunion n 1 joining; being joined together again 2 social gathering for former associates, friends etc.

rev n coll revolution (of engine); v revving, revved. increase speed of engine; phr

v **rev up** run engine fast to check smoothness of running before engaging gear.

Rev abbr Reverend.

revalue v give new higher value to; n **-ation**.

revamp v coll renew; give a new appearance to.

reveal v make known or visible; divulge; n **revelation**.

revel v revelling, revelled. feast; carouse; phr v **revel in** enjoy; n pl rejoicing; merrymaking; ns **reveller**; **revelry** unrestrained merrymaking.

revelation n 1 uncovering of secret 2 fact disclosed in a surprising or dramatic way.

revenant n ghost; apparition.

revenge v avenge; make retaliation for; n vindictiveness; vengeance; (sport, cards etc) return game; a **-ful**; adv **-fully**.

revenue n total income, esp of State; **Inland R.** government department dealing with collection of national revenue.

reverberate v echo, resound; throw back, reflect (sound etc); n **-ation**.

revere v venerate; regard with great or religious respect; n **reverence** feeling of awe and admiration; deference; as **reverend** worthy to be revered (**R. Mother** mother superior of convent); **reverent, reverential** showing reverence (adv **-ly**).

reverie n Fr 1 day-dream; dreamy contemplation 2 musical composition reflecting this state of mind.

revers n lapel; part of garment turned back.

reverse v 1 turn upside down 2 cause to go backwards 3 cancel; annul; idm **reverse the charges** make telephone call paid for by recipient; n 1 what is contrary, opposite 2 less important side 3 set-back; defeat; financial loss; a contrary; opposite; ns **reversal** act of reversing; state of being reversed; **reversion** leg return of estate to grantor or his heirs at expiry of grant; bio return to ancestral type; a **reversionary** leg of, pertaining to reversion; n **reverse gear** mechanism causing backward motion.

revert v pass back legally to grantor; phr v **revert to 1** go back to (former state) 2 refer to again.

revet v cover, face (surface) with stone etc to strengthen; n **-ment** protective covering.

review v 1 recall to mind in detail 2 inspect formally, officially 3 write critical notice of book etc; n 1 revision 2 formal inspection, esp of armed forces 3 written criticism of book etc 4 periodical with critical articles and discussion of current events; n **reviewer**.

revile v abuse; bitterly reproach; n **reviler**.

revise v look over and amend; n **revision** act of revising; something that has been revised; n **-ism** questioning of basic political beliefs, esp Marxist (n, a **-ist**).

revive v come, bring back to life, consciousness, health etc; ns **revival** rebirth, esp of religious fervour; **revivalist** organizer of, or preacher at, revival meeting.

revoke v 1 annul 2 cards fail to follow suit, although possible to do so; a **revocable**; n **revocation** act of revoking, esp leg repeal, annulment.

revolt v 1 rebel 2 disgust; n rebellion; a **revolting** repulsive; disgusting; n **revulsion** marked repugnance.

revolve v 1 go round; rotate 2 move, occur in cycles; phr v **revolve around** have as main concern; n **revolution** 1 complete rotation or turning round 2 complete overthrow of political system; a **revolutionary** of, causing, radical change of outlook, methods etc; n person taking part in revolution; v **revolutionize** make fundamental changes in.

revolver n pistol with revolving magazine.

revue n theatrical entertainment, with songs, sketches, dancing etc.

reward v repay, recompense for service, conduct etc; n that which is given in return for goods received, or for return of lost articles etc; a **rewarding** satisfying.

Rex n leg the State as prosecutor in trial (when king is ruling).

rhapsody n 1 highly emotional, enthusiastic utterance 2 emotional musical composition; idm **go into rhapsodies** be very enthusiastic; a **rhapsodic**; phr v **rhapsodize about/over** express eager approval of.

rhea n large flightless bird of S America.

rheostat n instrument for regulating value or resistance in electrical circuit.

rhesus n small long-tailed monkey; **rhesus factor** med substance in blood causing harm to Rhesus-positive new-born baby if mother is Rhesus-negative (also **Rh. factor**).

rhetoric n art of oratory; flowery, high-sounding language; a **-al 1** showing rhetoric 2 uttered for effect, not for a response (**r. question**); adv **-ally**.

rheumatism n name of various diseases attended with painful inflammation of joints and muscles; as **rheumatic** (n **r. fever** severe disease that can cause damage to heart, esp in children); **rheumatoid** (n **r. arthritis** long-term disease causing inflammation of joints).

Rh factor *see* **rhesus factor.**

rhino *n coll* rhinoceros.

rhinoceros *n* large, thick-skinned, tropical quadruped, with one or two horns on nose.

rhizome *n bot* root-like stem of plants growing underground.

rhodium *n* hard, greyish-white metal resembling platinum.

rhododendron *n* evergreen, flowering shrub.

rhombus *n* equilateral parallelogram with two acute and two obtuse angles; *a, n* **rhomboid.**

rhubarb *n* perennial garden herb, with thick pink stalks which are cooked and eaten as fruit; *coll* non-sense; squabble.

rhyme, rime *n* close similarity of sound in words or final syllables, *esp* at ends of lines of verse; *idm* **with no/without rhyme or reason** without sense; *v* make rhymes.

rhythm *n* regular increase and decrease of sounds, movements; pleasant rise and fall *esp* of words, musical sounds; *ns* **r. and blues** popular music based on blues (*also* **R and B**); **r. method** method of contraception based on study of menstrual cycle; *a* **-ic;** **-ical;** *adv* **-ically.**

rib *n* one of bones curving forward from spine, and enclosing thorax, curved timber or framework of boat;

n **r. cage** structure of ribs; *v* **ribbing, ribbed.** furnish with ribs; *coll* tease.

ribald *a* coarse; irreverent; scurrilous; *n* **ribaldry** coarse, indecent joking.

ribbon, riband *n* narrow woven strip of silk, satin etc; *fig* long, narrow strip; *n* **r. development** act of building single row of houses, factories etc. along each side of main road.

riboflavin *n* vitamin B2, found in liver, fish, milk, green vegetables etc.

ribozyme *n* enzyme made from genetic material RNA, able to cut down molecules at specific points.

Richter scale *n* scale measuring intensity of seismic activity.

rice *n* cereal plant grown on marshy or flooded ground in tropical climates; seeds of this plant used as food; *n* **r.-paper** edible paper used for packing sweets etc.

rich *n* **1** wealthy **2** abundant **3** costly **4** (*of food*) very fatty, sweet or highly seasoned **5** (*of colours, sound*) full, deep intense; *idm* **that's (a bit) rich 1** amusing **2** ridiculous; *n* **the r.** wealthy people; *n pl* **riches** wealth; abundance.

rick *n* stack of corn, hay, thatched for storing in open.

rickets *n* deficiency disease of children, marked by deformation of bones; *a* **rickety** suffering from rickets; shaky, tottering.

rickshaw *n* light, two-wheeled, Oriental carriage drawn by man.

ricotta *n* Italian cottage cheese from sheep's milk.

rid *v* **ridding, ridded.** free, deliver from; clear away; *pt and pp* **rid;** *idm* **be rid of** be free of; *idm* **get rid of** dispose of; *phr v* **rid sb of sth** set sb free of sth; *n* **riddance** act of getting rid; **good r.** welcome relief from unwelcome, unwanted person or thing.

riddle[1] *n* **1** enigma **2** puzzling question *esp* with pun **3** puzzling thing or person.

riddle[2] *n* large meshed sieve; *v* sift by means of riddle; make many holes in; *phr v* **riddle with 1** pierce with many holes **2** filled with (negative feelings).

ride *v* **riding, rode, ridden. 1** go on horseback **2** travel in, be carried by any vehicle **3** (*of ship*) float, lie at anchor; *idm* **let things ride** take no action; *idm* **ride high** enjoy success; *idm* **ride roughshod over** treat harshly, with contempt or without sensitivity; *idm* **riding for a fall** likely to meet with disaster; *phr v* **ride out** manage to survive; **ride up** (*of clothing*) work its way upwards, out of place; *n* **1** journey by vehicle on horse or other animal **2** apparatus in fairground for carrying people, *esp* with quick or violent motion **3** session on one of these; *idm* **come for**

the ride be a spectator, not a participant; *idm* **take sb for a ride** cheat sb; *n* **rider 1** one who rides **2** supplementary clause to document or verdict; *as* **riderless; riding** used for riding.

ridge *n* **1** long raised strip **2** elongated summit of mountain etc **3** line where two slopes of roof meet **4** elevated part between furrows; *v* form ridges.

ridiculous *a* absurd; preposterous; foolish; *v* **ridicule** make fun of; deride; *n* mockery; derision.

Riding *n* one of three administrative divisions of Yorkshire.

Riesling *n Ger* medium-dry white wine.

rife *a* prevalent; frequent; common.

riff *n* (in jazz) repeated phrase.

riffle *v* shuffle (cards) from two halves of pack against pressure of thumbs; *phr v* **riffle through** turn pages of (book etc) rapidly.

rifle *v* **1** search and rob **2** furnish gun barrel with spiral grooves; *n* type of firearm; *n* **rifling** spiral grooves in gun barrel; plundering.

rift *n* **1** opening; crack; split **2** *fig* serious disagreement between friends, colleagues etc *n* **r. valley** steep-sided valley formed by land subsidence.

rig[1] *v* (*of ship*) fit out with spars, ropes etc; *phr vs* **rig out** equip with clothes (*n* **r.-out**); **rig up** arrange hastily, *esp* in makeshift way; *n* way ship's masts and sails are arranged; style of dress; *n* **rigging** complete system of ship's ropes, sails, spars etc.

rig[2] *v* rigging, rigged. manipulate dishonestly; arrange by underhand means; *n* dishonest dealing (also **rigging**).

right *a* **1** morally good; just **2** correct **3** on side of body further from heart **4** in a healthy state **5** proper **6** *coll* absolute; *v* **1** put right **2** set straight or upright; *n* **1** moral goodness; justice **2** moral claim **3** *esp pl* what one is entitled to by law **4** right side **5** political parties opposed to socialism; *idm* **by rights** according to justice; *idm* **within one's rights** with legal justification; *idm* **in one's own right** by one's own authority; *idm* **in the right** morally justified; *ns* **r. angle** *geom* angle of 90°; **r. of way 1** (right to walk on) road or path over private land **2** priority over vehicles coming from other directions; *as* **righteous 1** morally good **2** justifiable (*adv* **-ly** *n* **-ness**); **r.-hand** on the right (*n* **r.-hand man** valued helper); **r.-handed** using the right hand (*n* **r.-hander** person doing this); **rightist** *polit* of the

right (*n* such a person); **r.-minded** with sound principles, views; *adv* **1** towards the right side **2** directly **3** completely **4** correctly **5** certainly; *idm* **right away** immediately; *v* **1** put right **2** set straight; restore to correct position; *adv* **-ly** *n* **-ness**.

rigid *a* **1** stiff; inflexible **2** stern; severe; *adv* **-ly** *n* **-ity**.

rigmarole *n* long, rambling, incoherent string of words.

rigor *n* shivering, with sense of chill; **r. mortis** stiffening of body after death.

rigour *n* severity; inflexibility; austerity; harshness; *a* **rigorous**.

rile *v* make angry; annoy; irritate.

rim *n* **1** edge; margin; brim **2** outer part of wheel.

rime *n* hoar-frost; *a* **rimy**.

rind *n* **1** peel; bark; crust **2** tough outer layer of bacon, cheese.

ring[1] *n* **1** line enclosing round space **2** flat circular object with large hole in middle **3** hoop of gold, silver etc for finger **4** area within roped square for boxing etc **5** coil; *v* put ring around; put identifying ring or tag on (bird's leg etc); *idm* **run rings round sb** *coll* to be greatly superior to sb; *ns* **r. binder** binder with metal rings for loose sheets of paper; **ring-leader** leader of group of wrongdoers; **ringlet** loosely hanging curl of hair;

r. mains main domestic electrical circuit; ringmaster director of circus performance; r.-pull metal ring for opening can of drink; r. road Brit road which by-passes centre of town; ringside area close to boxing ring (idm have a ringside seat have good view of action); ringworm disease causing red patches on skin.

ring² v 1 ringing, rang, rung. cause (bell) to sound 2 (of bell) sound 3 call by phone 4 be filled with (ringing) sound; pt rang; pp rung; n sound of ringing; telephone call; idm ring a bell remind sb of sth; idm ring the changes vary one's actions; phr vs ring off end telephone conversation suddenly; ring out resound loudly; ring up 1 record (prices) on cash register 2 call by phone 3 raise (curtain in theatre); n ringer.

rink n 1 sheet of ice for skating or curling 2 floor for roller skating 3 one of divisions of bowling green.

rinse v wash in clean water; n act of rinsing; hair-dye.

riot n 1 disturbance of public peace; tumult 2 fig unrestrained profusion; idm run riot get out of control; v take part in riot; ns r. police; rioter; rioting; a riotous wild and disorderly (adv -ly n -ness).

RIP abbr Lat requiescat in pace (rest in peace).

rip v ripping, ripped. cut; slit; slash, tear with violence; n rent, tear; idm let sth rip coll take away all restraints; phr v rip off 1 tear off 2 coll defraud by overcharging (n r.-off) 3 sl steal; a r.-roaring 1 wild and noisy 2 (of success) resounding; ns rip-cord cord to open parachute; rip-tide tide causing violent currents.

rip n 1 worn-out, useless horse 2 reprobate.

ripe a 1 ready to harvest as food etc 2 fully matured, developed 3 ready for specific use; v ripen grow, become ripe; mature.

riposte n 1 quick return lunge or thrust in fencing 2 fig quick retort.

ripple v form, flow in, small slight waves; n 1 slight wave 2 light, soft sound 3 ruffling of surface.

ripsaw n hand-saw with coarse, narrow-set teeth.

rise v rising, rose, risen. 1 ascend; stand up; get up 2 increase in value, price 3 appear above horizon (of sun, moon etc); idm rise to the occasion show oneself capable of success when challenged; n 1 increase 2 move towards situation of greater power 3 Brit increase in salary, wages 4 slope upwards; idm give rise to lead to; n riser upright face of step, between two treads;

person or thing that rises; n rising uprising; revolt (r. damp moisture rising from ground within walls of house; r. generation young people growing up); adv (of age) almost.

risk n 1 possibility, likelihood of danger 2 amount covered by insurance; idm at risk exposed to danger; idm at one's own risk agreeing to bear the cost of any loss or damage; v 1 expose to danger 2 hazard 3 accept the possibility of; a risky hazardous (adv -ily n -iness).

risotto n It dish of rice with meat, vegetables etc.

risqué a Fr verging on, tending towards impropriety.

rissole n ball, cake of minced meat, fish etc, fried in egg and breadcrumbs.

rite n solemn act usu religious ceremony; n r. of passage ceremony in some societies marking stage of change (eg puberty); a ritual of rites; n system of religious or magical ceremonies; book of prescribed ceremonies; n ritualism practice of, and insistence on, ritual.

ritzy a coll glamorous.

rival n one who competes against another for success, favour etc; v rivalling, rivalled. vie with, equal, be comparable to; n rivalry close approach to equality in merit etc; keen competition.

rive v split, tear apart; pt rived; pp riven.

river n large body of water flowing in natural channel to sea; plentiful flow.

rivet n bolt or pin for fastening metal plates; v 1 fasten with rivets 2 fig hold attention of; n **riveter;** a **riveting** coll very interesting.

riviera n stretch of coast with fashionable resorts.

rivulet n small stream, brook.

RN abbr Royal Navy.

RNA abbr chem ribonucleic acid (acid carrying genetic information in cells).

roach[1] n freshwater fish.

roach[2] n 1 coll cockroach 2 sl butt of reefer.

road n 1 track with surface prepared for use by vehicles, esp as means of communication between places; highway 2 direction; route 3 fig mode, line of action by which aim is attained; ns **r.-block** barricade across road; **r.-hog** reckless or selfish driver; **r.-house** roadside inn; **roadie** organizer of tour for pop group; **r. safety** prevention of road accidents; **r. sense** awareness of dangers on roads and how to avoid accidents; **r. show** entertainment by company on tour; **roadstead** sheltered water for ships near shore; **roadster** open sports car; **r. tax** tax paid by owners of motor vehicles; **roadway** part of road between pavements; **r.-works** (site of) repair or building of

road; a **roadworthy** in safe enough condition to be driven; n **-iness.**

roam v wander; ramble aimlessly n **roam-a-phone** portable telephone.

roan n, a (horse, dog) of bay, sorrel, chestnut mingled with white, grey; of mixed reddish colour.

roar n loud, deep, resonant sound; bellow; burst of laughter; v make such sound.

roast v 1 cook in hot oven, bake 2 make, be very hot; n roasted joint of meat etc; n animal, bird suitable for roasting.

rob v **robbing, robbed.** steal; plunder; deprive of unlawfully; ns **robber; robbery.**

robe n long, loose garment; (esp in pl) official, ceremonial dress; v dress; put on robe.

robin n small, brown, singing bird with red breast.

robot n 1 mechanical man 2 fig one who works mechanically with unthinking efficiency n **robotics** use of robots in industry.

robust a strong; sound; healthy; vigorous; n **robustness.**

rock[1] n 1 mass of hard mineral matter 2 crag; boulder 3 hard sweetmeat; idm **on the rocks** 1 (of drink) with ice cubes 2 (of marriage etc) likely to fail ns **r.bottom** the

lowest point; **r. cake** small hard fruit cake; **r. crystal** pure natural quartz; **r. salt** common salt mined in crystal form; n **rockery** mound of earth and rocks, where rock plants are grown; a **rocky** full of, made of rocks.

rock[2] v sway, move from side to side; shake violently; idm **rock the boat** coll upset finely balanced situation; ns **r. and roll** style of pop music originating in the 1950s; **rocker** curved base of rocking chair, of object that rocks; idm **off one's rocker** coll insane; **rocking chair** chair with rockers; **rocking horse** wooden horse mounted on rockers as child's toy; a **rocky** unsteady.

rocket n 1 projectile driven through space by explosion produced in it 2 large jet-powered missile 3 explosive firework, used for signalling, display or carrying life-line 4 coll reprimand; v 1 rise straight upwards 2 fig increase sharply (in price etc).

rococo a (of furniture, architecture) florid; flamboyantly ornamented in style of 17th and 18th century; n this style.

rod n 1 slender piece of wood; long, light, pole of metal, wood etc; wand; cane 2 fig corporal punishment 3 measure of length, 5 ½ yds

(5m).

rode pt of **ride.**

rodent a gnawing; n gnawing animal, as rat.

rodeo n rounding-up of cattle on ranch; display of skill in rounding up cattle.

roe[1] n small species of deer.

roe[2] n mass of fish eggs.

roebuck n male roe-deer.

Rogation days n three days preceding Ascension Day.

roger interj rad all right; understood.

rogue n 1 scoundrel; rascal; criminal; dishonest person 2 mischievous child or person 3 savage, wild beast, living apart from herd; n **rogues' gallery** set of pictures of criminals or villains; a **roguish** arch; mischievous; n **roguery.**

role n part played by actor; specific function or action ns **r. model** person representing ideal to be imitated **r.-playing** taking part in imaginary situation for practice.

roll v 1 move round and round; turn like wheel 2 (of ship) wallow 3 form into ball or cylinder 4 pass roller over something to flatten it 5 wrap round on itself; phr vs **roll in** arrive in large numbers; **roll on** (of time) pass by (a **roll-on roll-off** of ferry big enough for vehicles to drive on and off); **roll out** 1 unroll 2 (of pastry) spread out flat; **roll up** coll 1 arrive 2 come and

be entertained; n 1 packet, bundle formed by folding into cylindrical shape 2 small rounded loaf, bun, rissole 3 cylindrical mass 4 list of names 5 swaying motion; ns **r. call** calling of names to check absentees; **roller** 1 long powerful sea wave 2 cylindrical object for smoothing, flattening (ns **r. coaster** amusement park railway with track that rises and falls, twists and turns sharply; **r. skate** skate on wheels (v ride on this); **r. towel** towel in one continuous loop on roller; a **rolling** (ns **r. mill** factory where metal is rolled into bars; **r. pin** cylindrical object for flattening pastry; **r. stock** carriages, wagons etc of railway; **r. stone** person with no fixed home, no responsibilities).

rollmop n pickled herring.

roly-poly a coll fat and round.

ROM abbr comput read only memory.

Roman a of Rome; ns **R. candle** firework that shoots coloured balls of flame; **R. Catholic** member of branch of Christian church headed by the Pope; **R. nose** large curved nose; **R. numeral** any of the symbols used by Ancient Romans as numbers.

romance n 1 sentimental, adventurous novel 2 happy love-affair 3 medieval tale of chivalry 4 glamorous charm,

atmosphere; v invent fanciful stories; exaggerate.

Romance a (of language) derived from Latin.

Romanesque a of architectural style developed from 9th century AD, using rounded arches.

Romansch n language spoken in E Switzerland.

romantic a 1 connected with romance 2 (of literature etc) seeking to rouse personal feelings, expressing sentiment and imaginative episodes etc 3 emotional; n **-ism** (in literature and art) emphasis on feelings rather than objective realism; v **-ize** make seem more romantic than in reality.

romany n gipsy; gipsy language.

Romeo n romantic male lover.

romp v play noisily; idm **romp home** win easily; phr v **romp through** finish easily; n wild, noisy game.

rompers n pl one-piece garment for babies.

rondo n musical composition with principal theme repeated after each subordinate one.

röntgen rays n pl X-rays.

rood n crucifix esp one over junction of nave and choir; **r. screen** one separating nave from chancel.

roof n **-fs.** outer covering over top of building; **roof of mouth** palate; v put roof on; idm **raise the roof** express loud indignation; ns **r.**

garden garden on flat roof; **r. rack** luggage rack on roof of car.

rook[1] n bird of crow family; v cheat, swindle; n **rookery 1** colony of rooks **2** fig crowded tenement building.

rook[2] n piece in chess, castle.

rookie US newly recruited soldier or policeman.

room n **1** space **2** separate apartment in a building **3** scope; opportunity; n **r. service** serving of food, drink etc in hotel room; n pl **-s** lodgingings; a **roomy** large spacious.

roost n perch for birds at night; v sleep on perch; n **rooster** domestic cock.

root n **1** source; origin **2** downward-growing part of plant **3** essential element **4** basic element of word **5** factor of quantity which gives that quantity when multiplied by itself; v implant roots firmly; be firmly established, esp by development of roots; idm **root and branch** completely; phr vs **root for** support enthusiastically; **root out** get rid of; n **r. beer** US sweet fizzy drink from roots and herbs; n pl **roots** (one's sense of belonging to) one's place of upbringing; a **rootless** (n **-ness**).

rope n thick cord; idm **give sb plenty of rope** give sb freedom of action; idm **know the ropes** have previous experience; v tie with rope;

phr vs **rope in 1** bind with rope **2** persuade to take part; **rope off** separate by ropes; a **ropey** Brit coll of poor quality (also **ropy**); n **ropiness**.

Roquefort n French cheese of goats' and ewes' milk.

Rorschach test n psyc test based on interpretation of random shapes made by inkblots on paper.

rose n **1** any of genus Rosa; flower of this **2** perforated nozzle **3** pinkish colour **4** method of cutting gems; idm **a bed of roses** easy and comfortable; idm **not all roses** not all easy and straightforward; n **rosary 1** rose-garden **2** string of beads used by RCs to count prayers; a **roseate** rose-coloured; ns **rosette** rose-shaped bunch of ribbon etc; **rosewood** dark-coloured fragrant wood used in cabinet making; a **rosy 1** pink; flushed **2** fig favourable; optimistic.

rosemary n evergreen fragrant flowering bush.

roster n list showing rotation of duty etc; list of names.

rostrum n platform; pulpit.

rot v rotting, rotted. decompose naturally; n **1** decay **2** fungus disease of timber, plants etc; **3** coll nonsense; a **rotten 4** decomposed **5** coll deplorably bad **6** unwell.

rota n roster; round of duties; tribunal in RC Church.

rotary a turning like wheel; v **rotate** revolve round axis; follow regular succession; n **rotation** act of rotating; recurrence; a **rotatory**; ns **Rotary Club** one of international association of business men's clubs; **Rotarian** member of such; **rotary engine** one turning like wheel.

Rotavator [TM] machine for breaking up heavy soil before gardening.

rote n **by rote** by heart, from memory.

rotgut n coll cheap strong alcohol.

rotor n rotating part of machine, esp of helicopter.

Rottweiler n large powerful type of guard dog.

rotund a round; plump; ns **-ity**; **rotunda** circular building.

rouble n Russian coin.

rouge n **1** red cosmetic used to colour cheeks and lips **2** silver polish; v colour with rouge.

rough a **1** uneven; not smooth (**r. surface**) **2** stormy; violent (**r. sea; r. weather**) **3** boisterous (**r. play**) **4** unrefined (**r. appearance; r. manners; r. diet**) **5** not precise (**r. calculation; r. estimate; r. figure**) **6** unfair; harsh (**r. justice**); idm **rough and ready** simple; without refinement; adv without comfort or amenities (**live/sleep r.**); n golf areas with unmown grass; idm **take the rough with the**

smooth accept that problems are bound to arise; *idm* **rough it** live simple life without comforts; *ns* **r.-and-tumble** boisterous play or fighting; **r.diamond** kind but unrefined person; **roughhouse** brawl; **roughneck 1** rowdy person **2** oilrig worker; **r. paper** cheap paper for draft work or notes; *a* **r.-hewn** (*of wood, stone*) cut roughly; *v* **roughen** make rough; *adv* **roughly** approximately; *n* **-ness**.

roulette *n Fr* game of chance, played with revolving wheel and ball.

round *a* **1** spherical; circular; curved **4** approximate **3** plump **4** blunt; outspoken; *n* **1** circle **2** thing round in shape **3** fixed circuit **4** type of song **5** complete slice of bread as in sandwich **6** single shot from rifle **7** series of actions, duties etc **8** game (*of golf*) **9** singe bout (*in boxing etc*); *ns* **r. robin** letter signed by many people in turn; **r. trip** journey to a place and back; *adv* **1** in circular motion **2** converging on central point **3** to a variety of places **4** to a place nearby; *idm* **round about** approximately; *prep* **1** with circular movement about **2** surrounding **3** to various parts of **4** near; *v* **1** go round **2** make round; *phr vs* **round down** reduce to nearest whole unit or

number; **round off** finish; **round on** turn and attack; **round up 1** increase to nearest whole number or unit **2** gather together; *n* **-ness**.

roundabout *n* **1** fair-ground machine on which people can ride in regular circular motion **2** (*at road junctions*) raised circular area round which traffic must follow specified direction; *a* indirect.

roundelay *n* song with refrain.

rounders *n* children's game similar to baseball.

Roundhead *n* supporter of Parliament in English Civil War.

rouse *v* wake up; cause to rise; stimulate; excite to action.

rout *n* **1** rabble; mob **2** overwhelming defeat; *v* defeat, put to flight; drag out by force.

route *n* road; way; *mil* order to march; *n* **r. march** long march as part of military training (*also v*).

routine *n* customary actions; regular procedure; boringly automatic procedure.

roux *n Fr* blend of melted fat, flour as base for sauce.

rove *v* wander at random; *ns* **rover** one who wanders; **roving commission** authority to travel in carrying out one's duties.

row[1] *n* number of things or persons in straight line.

row[2] *v* propel (boat) by oars; transport by rowing; *n* act of

rowing; trip in rowing boat.

row[3] *n* disturbance; dispute; quarrel; *v* quarrel; brawl.

rowan *n* mountain ash (tree).

rowdy *a* disorderly; noisy; rough; *n* hooligan.

rowel *n* small spiked wheel on spur.

rowlock *n* forked support in boat serving as leverage for oar.

royal *a* pertaining to, patronized by, king or queen; majestic; *n* member of the royal family; *adv* - **ly**, *ns* **r. assent** *Brit* king's/queen's formal agreement to passing of new law; **r. blue** deep rich blue colour; **r. jelly** substance with which worker bees nourish queen bee; *ns* **royalist** supporter of monarchy; **royalty 1** state of being royal **2** royal persons collectively **3** percentage paid to author by publisher **4** payment to owner of land for right to exploit it **5** or to inventor for use of his invention.

rpm *abbr* revolutions per minute.

RSA *abbr* Royal Society of Arts.

repetitive strain or **stress injury** *n* muscle injury caused by repetitive work, *esp* keyboarding.

RSI *abbr* repetitive strain or stress injury.

RSVP *abbr Fr* répondez s'il vous plaît (please reply).

rub *v* **rubbing, rubbed. 1** apply friction to **2** abrade, make sore 3 become frayed, worn by friction; *idm* **rub it in** keep referring to fact that causes embarrassment to sb; *idm* **rub salt in the wound** add further to sb's suffering; *idm* **rub shoulders with** *coll* meet (famous person) socially as if on equal terms; *idm* **rub up the wrong way** *coll* cause offence to; *phr vs* **rub down** 1 dry by rubbing 2 smooth by rubbing; **rub off** remove, be removed from surface by rubbing; **rub off on** have influence on (through example); *n* **rubbing** impression of relief picture made by laying paper over and rubbing with crayon or charcoal.

rubato *adv mus* with varying speed for effect.

rubber[1] *n* 1 elastic substance from sap of rubber tree 2 *Brit* eraser made from this 3 *US coll* condom; *ns* **r. band** loop of rubber for keeping things firmly bundled together (*also* **elastic band**); **r. cheque** *coll* cheque which 'bounces' (*ie* is refused by bank through lack of money in account); **rubberneck** *US coll* 1 tourist 2 inquisitive person; **r. plant** house-plant with large thick leaves; **r.-stamp** stamp with lettering or figures for printing (*v* give official approval without questioning anything); *a* **rubbery**.

rubber[2] *n* series of odd number of games; two out of three

games won.

rubbish *n* 1 refuse, waste material 2 nonsense; *v coll* discredit; *a* **-y** valueless.

rubble *n* 1 broken, crushed pieces of stone 2 builders' rubbish.

rubella *n* German measles.

rubicund *a* reddish; ruddy.

ruble = **rouble**.

rubric *n* 1 instruction, chapter-heading printed, written distinctively *esp* in red 2 liturgical direction.

ruby *n* deep red, transparent, precious stone; its colour; *a* of this colour.

ruche *n Fr* pleated trimming for dress etc.

ruck *n* 1 ordinary, commonplace things or people 2 *Brit rugby* loose scrum; *phr v* **ruck up** go into creases.

rucksack *n* bag, knapsack strapped on back.

ruckus *n US coll* rumpus.

rudd *n* fresh water fish, red eye.

rudder *n* steering device at stern of boat, or tail of aircraft.

ruddy *a* of fresh, red colour; rosy.

rude *a* 1 primitive; rough; crude 2 uncivil; insulting.

rudiment *n* 1 beginning; first principle 2 slight trace; vestige 3 basic elementary facts of subject; *a* **rudimentary** in undeveloped, unformed state; vestigial.

rue[1] *n* small, perennial herb

with bitter leaves.

rue[2] *v* grieve for; regret; repent of; *a* **rueful** sorry; dejected.

ruff[1] *n* 1 starched frilled collar 2 bird allied to sandpiper, *fem* **reeve**; *v* **ruffle** gathered or pleated frill, *v* 1 make uneven, untidy 2 upset; disconcert.

ruff[2] *v* trump at cards; *n* act of trumping.

ruffian *n* rough, violent, lawless person; bully.

rug *n* thick, woollen wrap; coverlet; floor-mat, *esp* with long pile.

rugby *n* form of football, played with oval ball which may be carried in hands; *also coll* **rugger**.

rugged *a* 1 rough and rocky 2 robust and strong.

rugger *n coll* rugby football.

ruin *n* state of decay, collapse; destruction; cause of ruin; *pl* **-s** remains of buildings etc; *v* 1 reduce to ruins; spoil 2 impoverish; *n* **-ation**; *a* **-ous** tending to cause financial ruin; wasteful; likely to cause destruction.

rule *n* 1 principle, line of conduct 2 government 3 *pl* **-s** regulations of society, game etc 4 custom 5 graduated metal or wooden bar for measuring; *idm* **as a rule** normally; *v* 1 govern; give judicial decision 2 draw straight lines; *idm* **rule the roost** be in charge; *phr v* **rule out** 1 regard as impossible 2 render impossible; *n* **r. of thumb** rough type of calculation; *ns* **ruler 1** governor; sovereign **2** instrument for measuring, or drawing straight lines; **ruling** official decision or pronouncement.

rum[1] *a coll* odd; peculiar; queer.

rum[2] *n* alcoholic spirit distilled from sugar-cane.

rumba, rhumba *n* dance of Cuban origin.

rumble *v* **1** make low, continuous, rolling noise, as of thunder, or heavy cart etc **2** *Brit* detect (deception or secret).

rumbustious *a* noisy and cheerful; *adv* **-ly**; *n* **-ness**.

ruminate *v* chew cud; *fig* mediate, think deeply over, *ns* **-ation** act of chewing cud; *fig* deep thought; **ruminant** animal which chews cud; *a* thoughtful.

rummage *v* grope about; turn over roughly; search thoroughly; *n* **1** ransacking **2** jumble.

rummy *n* card-game.

rumour *n* gossip; hearsay; story; statement without basis.

rump *n* **1** buttocks **2** *fig* last, inferior part.

rumple *v* crease; wrinkle; crush.

rumpus *n* noisy disturbance; confusion.

run *v* **1** move along on foot, more swiftly than walking; flee; compete in race **2** flow **3** melt **4** manage; *pt* **ran**; *phr vs* **run across** meet by

chance; **run down 1** knock down with vehicle **2** pursue and catch **3** (of clockwork) lose power and slow down **4** criticise in negative way; **run into** meet by chance; **run off** print (multiple copies); **run out 1** leave by running **2** (of supply) be used up; **run out of** have none left; **run out on** desert; **run over 1** overflow **2** knock down with vehicle; **run through 1** repeat for practice **2** check over **3** pierce with sword; **run to** be enough, have enough for; **run up 1** raise **2** make quickly **3** incur; accumulate (debt); **run up against** be confronted by; *n* **1** act of running **2** continuous sequence **3** animal enclosure **4** unit of score in cricket; *idm* **on the run** trying to escape, *esp* from justice; *idm* **have a run for one's money 1** have satisfaction for what one has paid **2** be in a competitive situation; *ns* **r.-about** small car; **r.-around** *sl* evasive behaviour; **r.-down** *coll* brief report; **r.-in** *coll* **1** time leading to event **2** *US* quarrel; **r.-through 1** review **2** rehearsal; **r.-up** period leading to event; **runway** strip of ground for landing and take-off of aircraft; *as* **runaway 1** having escaped **2** out of control; **run-down 1** dilapidated **2** in poor health; **runny 1** more liquid than usual **2** producing mucus.

runner *n* **1** person who runs **2** smooth or tubular plate making movement of sledge etc more efficient **3** mat covering lino **4** long, fast-growing shoot of plant **5** smuggler; *ns* **r. bean** bean with long edible pod; **r.-up** next one after the winner(s) of contest, **running** *n* **1** act or sport of running **2** operation or management of sth; *idm* **in/out of the running** having some chance/no chance of success; *idm* **make the running** give the necessary lead or momentum make sth work; *a* **1** flowing (**r.** water) **2** continuous (**r.** commentary) **3** performed while running (**r.** jump; *idm* **take a running jump** *coll* blunt expression of refusal to unacceptable proposal) **4** exuding pus (**r.** sore) **5** incurred in running sth (**r.** costs); *idm* **in running order** working properly; *adv* in succession; *ns* **r. mate** *US polit* partner with whom one hopes to be jointly elected for office; **r. repairs** minor repairs; **r. total** total that is continually revised as each new item is added.

rune *n* angular character of Teutonic alphabet; magic sign.

rung[1] *n* cross-bar of ladder, or chair. **rung**[2] *pt* of **ring**.

runnel *n* gutter; small rivulet.

runt *n* **1** weakest animal *usu* lastborn of litter **2** *sl* small disagreeable person.

rupee *n* Indian coin.

rupture *n* 1 breaking; split 2 hernia; *v* 1 burst; break 2 produce hernia.

rural *a* of country; rustic.

ruse *n* stratagem; trick.

rush[1] *n* aquatic herb, stems of which are used for basket-making etc.

rush[2] *v* move with violent rapidity; take by storm; enter hastily; *n* impetuous forward movement; sudden increase; eagerness to obtain; *n* **r. hour** busiest time of day for travelling.

rushes *n pl cinema* first printing of film.

rusk *n* piece of crisp baked bread or biscuit.

russet *a* of reddish-brown; *n* this colour; homespun fabric; kind of apple.

Russian *n* 1 language of Russia 2 person whose native language is this; *a* of Russia, its culture, people or language; **R. roulette** dangerous game of chance where player fires revolver containing bullet in only one chamber at his own head.

Russo- *prefix* of Russia.

rust *n* 1 reddish-brown coating produced on iron etc by oxidation 2 disease of plants, caused by fungus.

rustic *a* of country life or people; rural; unsophisticated; *n* **rusticity**; *v* **rusticate** 1 send down temporarily from University 2 live country life; *n* **rustication**.

rustle *v* 1 emit soft, whispering sound as of dry leaves 2 steal cattle (*n* **rustler**); *phr v* **rustle up** provide, *esp* at short notice.

rut[1] *n* wheel-track; groove; *idm* **in a rut** leading a boring, meaningless existence; *a* **rutted** full of ruts.

rut[2] *n* sexual excitement, *esp* of deer; *v* **rutting, rutted.** be affected with rut.

ruthless *a* pitiless; merciless; cruel.

rye *n* cereal plant, grain used for fodder and bread; **rye whisky** distilled from rye grains; *n* **rye-grass** grass grown for fodder.

Sabbath *n* day of rest and worship, observed by Jews on Saturday and Christians on Sunday; *ns* **Sabbatarian** strict observer of Sunday; **sabbatical year** one allowed to some university staff, teachers etc, as working holiday; *a* **sabbatical** of or like Sabbath.

sable *n* small Arctic carnivore, having valuable dark brown fur; *a* black.

sabot *n* wooden shoe.

sabotage *n* deliberate damage to industrial plant, materials etc by strikers or spies, *n* **saboteur.**

sabre *n* curved cavalry sword; *n* **s.-rattling** trying to intimidate sb by threat of attack.

sac *n* membraneous bog or pouch in animal or vegetable body.

saccharine(e) *n* very sweet white substance from coal-tar; *a fig* too sweet, sentimental.

sacerdotal *a* priestly.

sachet *n* small soft bag for holding handkerchiefs or scented powder etc.

sack[1] *n* **1** large rectangular bag of strong, coarse fabric **2** loose waistless dress; *ns* **sackcloth** coarse cloth for making sacks (**s. and ashes** sign of mourning or repentance); **sacking** pieces(s) of this.

sack[2] *v* dismiss from post; *n idm* **give/get the sack** dismiss/be dismissed.

sack[3] *v* destroy (city) in war; *n* act of doing this.

sack[4] *n* dry, white wine.

sackbut *n* old musical instrument.

sacrament *n* **1** one of solemn religious ceremonies of Christian Church, *esp* Eucharist **2** any sacred, solemn obligation **3** *cap* bread and wine taken at Communion.

sacred *a* holy, dedicated to God, a god; set apart; inviolable *n* **s. cow** person or thing felt to be beyond criticism; *n* **-ness.**

sacrifice *n* **1** making offering to God or deity **2** thing offered **3** giving up (sth valued) for sake of someone else; *v* offer as sacrifice; give up (sth valued); *a* **-ficial.**

sacrilege *n* violation of something sacred; *a* **sacrilegious** profane.

sacristy *n* room in church for keeping ceremonial things.

sacrosanct *a* protected from harm or change by being sacred or very important.

sacrum *n anat* bone at lower end of spine, formed by five fused vertebrae.

sad *a* sorrowful; mournful; lamentable; *v* **sadden** made sad; *n* **sadness.**

saddle *n* **1** rider's seat on horse, bicycle etc **2** part of animal's back **3** mountain ridge **4** joint of mutton or venison; *idm* **in the saddle** in control; *v* put saddle on (horse etc); *phr v* **saddle with** burden with (duty, responsibility).

saddler *n* maker of saddles; *n* **saddlery** trade, shop of goods sold by saddler.

sadism *n* **1** sexual perversion marked by cruelty **2** love of inflicting pain; *n* **sadist** (*a* **-ic**)

sadomasochism *n* (sexual) gratification from inflicting pain on oneself and/or others; n -ist.

s.a.e. abbr stamped and addressed envelope.

safari n hunting, shooting or photographic expedition, esp in Africa; ns **s. park** large park where wild animals living in natural habitat can be observed by tourists; **s. jacket** light linen jacket with belt and breast pockets.

safe a 1 free from danger 2 not causing danger 3 not threatened; n strong metal box with lock for keeping valuable objects or documents secure; ns **s. conduct** official protection when travelling; **s.-deposit box** box for storing objects safely, esp at a bank; **safeguard** means of protection (v protect); adv **safely**; n **-ness**.

safe sex n sex in which steps are taken to prevent the spread of sexually transmitted diseases, esp AIDS.

safety n condition of being safe; ns **s. catch** lock to prevent gun from being fired accidentally; **s. glass** glass which does not splinter when broken; **s. match** match which can only be ignited on special material; **s. net 1** net to save people who fall from a height 2 fig safeguard; **s. pin 1** pin with protective guard over sharp end 2 pin to prevent premature detonation (of

grenade etc); **s. valve 1** valve that releases pressure (in machine) if it becomes dangerously high **2** fig means of releasing dangerous emotion.

saffron n variety of orange-yellow crocus; dye and flavouring substance from this; a of this colour.

sag v sagging, sagged. sink, droop downwards in middle; buckle; fig become low-spirited; (fig of prices) drop in value.

saga n ancient Norse prose epic; long novel or series about family or group; romantic tale of adventure and heroism.

sagacious a shrewd, keenly intelligent; n **sagacity** sound judgement; quality resembling reason in lower animals.

sage a wise; serious; characterized by sagacity; n person of great wisdom.

sage n shrubby aromatic herb, used in cooking.

sago n edible starchy pith of certain Malayan palms.

sail n 1 piece of canvas etc arranged to catch wind, to drive ship, esp sailing vessel **2** voyage on ship **3** various sail-like objects (eg revolving part of windmill etc); idm **set sail** begin journey at sea; v travel across water; start sea trip; navigate; ns **sailboard** shaped board with sail for windsurfing; **sailcloth** thick

canvas for making sails, tents etc; **sailing 1** sport of riding, racing in yacht, dinghy etc **2** regular voyage on water; (time of) departure for this; **sailor** member of ship's crew (**bad/good s.** person liable/not liable to be seasick).

saint n 1 one recognised and venerated as holy etc by Christian Church **2** title of canonized person; a **sainted** venerated, regarded as saint; n **saintliness** piety, holiness of life.

sake n 1 cause **2** benefit **3** purpose; idm **for the sake of** in order to please, benefit, obtain.

saké n Japanese drink made from fermented rice.

salaam n ceremonial bow; Eastern mode of greeting; v make salaam.

salacious a lewd; lecherous; n **salacity**.

salad n 1 dish of raw, or cold cooked vegetables or fruit **2** lettuce; ns **s. days** age of youth and immaturity.

salami n highly seasoned Italian sausage.

salary n fixed payment for work (usu non-manual) made at regular intervals of month or more; a **salaried**.

sale n act of selling; auction; offering of goods for sale, esp at reduced prices; ns **salesman** one engaged in selling; **salesmanship** business skill of salesman.

salient *a* projecting; prominent; *n* body of troops projecting from main line.

saline *a* metallic, alkaline salt; *n* **salinity** saltness.

saliva *n* fluid secreted in mouth to aid digestion; *a* **salivary**.

sallow[1] *n* species of willow.

sallow[2] *a* having sickly, yellow colour.

sally *n* 1 quick repartee 2 sudden but brief attack; *phr v* **sallying**, **sallied**. **sally forth** set out (on campaign).

salmon *n* large edible silvery fish, with pink flesh; *n* **s.-trout** seatrout.

salmonella *n* bacteria causing food poisoning.

salon *n* reception room; private reception of people notable in the arts; annual exhibition of pictures.

saloon *n* 1 large reception room 2 main cabin in passenger ship 3 more expensive bar in public house with comfortable furnishing (*also* **s.bar**) 4 public room for specific use (*eg* hairdressing, billiards etc) 5 closed car without partition between driver and passengers.

salsify *n* long tapering root vegetable.

salt *n* 1 chemical substance (sodium chloride) used to season and preserve food 2 any of compounds formed by replacing hydrogen of acid, by metal 3 wit; pungency; *idm* **the salt of the earth**

admirable person/people; *idm* **with a pinch of salt** with scepticism; *v* 1 flavour with salt 2 cover (roads) with salt to prevent ice forming; *phr v* **salt away** save (money) secretly, dishonestly; *ns* old s. sailor; **s.-cellar** small receptacle for salt at table; **s.-lick** 1 place where animals lick salt 2 block of salt for animals; **s.-pan** hollow where salt collects after evaporation of salt water; *a* **salty**; *n* **-iness**.

SALT *abbr* Strategic Arms Limitation Talks.

saltpetre *n chem* white powder used in making gunpowder, matches etc.

salubrious *a* healthy; beneficial; promoting health.

salutary *a* wholesome; having good effect.

salute *v* 1 greet, acknowledge by words or customary gesture 2 perform military salute; *n* 1 greeting 2 *mil* formal gesture made by hand to superior; *n* **salutation** act of saluting, usually by spoken or written words.

salvage *n* 1 saving, rescue of ship, cargo etc from shipwreck, fire etc 2 reward for this act 3 ship, cargo etc, so saved 4 saving goods from fire etc 5 property so rescued 6 saving and utilization of waste material; *v* save from shipwreck, fire, destruction.

salvation *n* fact or state of being saved; *n* **S. Army**

missionary Christian organization.

salve *n* healing, soothing ointment.

salvia *n* herbaceous plant of culinary, medicinal use.

sal volatile *n* alcoholic aromatic preparation of ammonia.

SAM *n abbr* surface-to-air missile.

Samaritan *n* inhabitant of Samaria; helpful, charitable person; *pl* **-s** organization available by telephone to help people in despair.

samba *n* dance of Brazilian origin.

same *a* 1 identical; unchanged 2 aforesaid 3 monotonous; **all the same** after all; nevertheless; *n* **sameness**.

samizdat *n* underground organization in former USSR, publishing literature that had been officially banned.

samosa *n* triangular pastry snack filled with spicy meat or vegetables (of Indian origin).

sampan *n* light, flat-bottomed Chinese river boat.

samphire *n* edible plant used in pickles, found in coastal areas.

sample *n* specimen, example; *v* test quality of; take sample; *n* **sampler** piece of embroidery, needlework.

sanatorium *n* hospital, *esp* one for treatment of tuberculosis; *pl* **-ia** *or* **-iums**.

sanctify *v* purify from sin;

regard as holy; *ns* **sanctity** saintliness; inviolability.

sanctimonious *a* making outward show of piety; *adv* **-ly**; *n* **-ness** hypocritical piety.

sanction *n* 1 authorization; consent 2 measure taken to compel nation to obey international law 3 justification; *v* permit; allow; approve.

sanctuary *n* holy place; place of refuge for fugitives from justice; *n* **sanctum** any private or inviolate retreat.

sand *n* fine, dry, gritty substance; mass of this found on seashore and in deserts etc; *pl* **-s** area of sand or sandbank; *idm* **the sands of time** time available for getting something done; *ns* **sandbag** sand-filled sack used in protecting wall (*v* 1 protect with these 2 hit with sandbag); **sandbank** shoal of sand in river or sea; **s. bar** sandbank barring estuary or harbour-mouth; **sandpaper** paper coated with abrasive material for smoothing wood etc (*v* rub with this); **sandpiper** wading bird with long thin bill; **sandshoe** light shoe for beach wear; **sandstone** soft porous type of rock formed from compressed sand; **s. yacht** wheeled vehicle with sail driven by wind power; *v* **sandblast** clean by firing jet of sand at (*n* **-er** machine for doing this); *a* **sandy** of sand

or colour of sand (*n* **-iness**).

sandal *n* open shoe consisting of sole secured by straps.

sandalwood *n* hard, yellowish sweet-scented wood of E Indian tree.

sandwich *n* two slices of bread with meat, cheese or other filling between them; *v* insert between two other things; squeeze in; *ns* **s. boards** pair of boards carried on front and back of person to advertise sth; **s. course** *Brit* type of training in which periods of work in business alternate with periods of academic study.

sane *a* 1 sound in mind; mentally normal 2 sensible; rational, *n* **sanity**.

sang *pt of* sing.

sang-froid *n Fr* coolness; presence of mind; composure.

sangria *n* Spanish drink of red wine containing fruit juice, lemonade etc.

sanguine *a* 1 ruddy; florid 2 hopeful; optimistic; *a* **sanguinary** bloody; bloodthirsty; accompanied by bloodshed; *adv* **-ly** hopefully, confidently.

sanitary *a* hygienic; having to do with health and cleanliness; *n* **s. towel** absorbent pad worn by women during menstruation; *v* **sanitize** 1 make hygienic 2 *fig* make less offensive; *n* **sanitation** 1 public hygiene 2 system of drainage, disposal of sewage,

ventilation and pure water supply.

sank *pt of* **sink.**

sans-culotte *n Fr* extremist revolutionary.

Sanskrit, Sanscrit *n* ancient language of Hindus.

Santa Claus *n* man with white beard and red clothes believed to distribute toys to children at Christmas (*also* **Father Christmas**).

sap[1] *n* 1 juice, fluid circulating in plant tissue 2 *fig* vigour; vitality; *v* **sapping, sapped.** *fig* weaken; drain away strength of.

sap[2] *n mil* covered trench; *v mil* construct these; undermine; *n* **sapper** member of Royal Engineers.

sapient *a* wise; shrewd; knowing; *n* **sapience**.

saponaceous *a* containing soap, soapy; *fig* unctuous.

Sapphic *a* of Sappho, Greek poetess; kind of verse.

sapphire *n* deep blue translucent precious stone.

Saracen *n* Muslim at time of Crusades.

sarcasm *n* bitter, ironic remark; sneer; mocking taunt, intended to wound; *a* **sarcastic**.

sard *n* semi-precious stone, variety of chalcedony.

sardine *n* small fish of herring family, usually preserved in oil; *idm* **packed like sardines** packed close together.

sardonic *a* bitter; sneering; scornful.

sardonyx *n* semi-precious

stone of layers of red sard and white chalcedony.

sarge n coll sergeant.

sari, saree n robe worn by Hindu women.

sarky a coll sarcastic.

sarong n principal garment of Malay men and women.

sarsaparilla n species of smilax; its dried root used medicinally.

sarsen n large block of hard sandstone, as used in Stonehenge.

sartorial a pertaining to trade and work of tailor.

SAS abbr Brit Special Air Service (commando force).

sash[1] n ornamental scarf worn over shoulder, or round waist.

sash[2] n one of two sliding frames holding glass of window.

sassy a US coll saucy, insolent.

sat pt, pp of **sit**.

Satan n the Devil; a **satanic(al)** fiendish, malignant, wicked; n **satanism** devil worship (n, a **-ist**)

satchel n bag for school books.

sate v satisfy; gratify to the full; glut surfeit.

sateen n glossy, imitation satin, cotton fabric.

satellite n 1 hanger-on 2 planet revolving round another 3 projectile in orbit round the earth; n **s. dish** concave disc used as aerial for receiving satellite TV; **s. television** TV relayed by satellite in space to any part

of Earth.

satiate v 1 satisfy 2 dull, cloy by over-indulgence; ns **satiety** feeling of having had too much; **satiation**.

satin n soft silk fabric with glossy surface; n **satinwood** fine, hard yellowish wood used in cabinet-making.

satire n 1 holding up of human follies, vices to ridicule 2 literary work of this nature 3 bitter contempt, directed against hypocrisies of society; a **satiric(al)**; n **satirist** writer of satires; v **satirize** make object of satire.

satisfy v **satisfying, satisfied.** 1 gratify 2 suffice for 3 comply with discharge (debt) 4 set doubts at rest; n **satisfaction**; a **satisfactory** (adv **-ily**).

satsuma n small citrus fruit like mandarin orange.

saturate v 1 soak thoroughly 2 chem cause substance to combine completely 3 fig be steeped in, affected by; n **-ation** act, result of saturating (**s. point** stage at which greatest amount of something has been absorbed).

saturated fat n fat found in meat and dairy products, thought to be harmful to health in large quantities.

Saturday n seventh day of week.

Saturn n 1 Roman god 2 large planet surrounded by rings; a **saturnine** gloomy, glowering, morose; n

saturnalia revelry; orgy.

satyr n 1 woodland deity (half beast, half man) 2 lecherous man.

sauce n 1 spiced or flavoured liquid used to add to taste of food; gravy 2 coll impudence; ns **saucepan** cooking pot; **s.-boat** small vessel for serving sauce at table; a **saucy** 1 impertinent 2 (of clothes) jaunty 3 sexually provocative (a **-ily** n **-iness**)

saucer n shallow dish put under a cup.

sauerkraut n Ger chopped raw cabbage fermented in brine.

sauna n 1 room heated with brazier to obtain hot dry atmosphere 2 period of relaxation in this, followed by ice-cold bath or shower.

saunter v walk slowly; stroll; n leisurely walk.

sausage n minced, seasoned meat packed into skin or thin membrane; n **s. roll** cylinder of pastry baked with sausage meat filling.

sauté a Fr lightly, quickly fried.

Sauterne n light, sweet white French wine.

savage a wild; uncivilized; fierce; cruel; brutal; v bite and worry ferociously; n **savagery**.

savanna n prairie; extensive grassy treeless plain.

savant n Fr man of learning; scholar.

save v 1 rescue 2 preserve untouched for future use 3 guard against; prevent need

of 4 put by (money); *idm*
save face avoid
embarrassment (*a face-
saving*); *idm* **save one's
bacon/neck/skin** *coll* escape
from death or serious crisis;
idm **save one's breath** not
bother to say sth which will
be ignored; *ns* **-er** person
who saves money; **saving**
amount saved (*prep* except;
n **s. grace** good
characteristic that
compensates for all the bad
ones); *n pl* **-s** money saved
(*n* **s. bank**).

saveloy *n* highly seasoned,
dried sausage.

saviour *n* one who redeems;
cap Jesus Christ.

savoir faire *n Fr* ability to
know how to behave in any
situation.

savour *n* 1 taste; flavour 2 *fig*
slight trace; *v* 1 have
particular flavour 2 enjoy
taste of; *phr v* **savour of**
suggest presence of; *a*
savoury tasty; appetizing; *n*
light tasty dish, flavoured
with salt, cheese etc.

savoy *n* kind of cabbage with
curled leaves.

savvy *v sl* understand; *n*
common sense.

saw[1] *pt of* see.

saw[2] *n* maxim; traditional
saying.

saw[3] *n* tool with toothed edge,
for cutting wood etc; *v*
sawing, sawed, sawn or
sawed. 1 cut with saw 2 *fig*
make to and fro movement,
as of sawing; *ns* **sawdust**

small particles of wood made
by sawing; **s.-horse** frame to
hold article being sawed;
sawmill (factory with)
machine that saws timber
into planks.

Saxon *n, a* (member) of
Germanic people settling in
Britain from 5th century
AD.

saxophone, saxhorn *n* reeded
brass wind instrument with
many keys or valves.

say *v* utter, express in words;
state; report; be of opinion;
pt, pp said; *idm* **go without
saying** be obvious; *n*
expressed opinion;
opportunity of stating it; *idm*
have one's say (have chance
to) express one's view; *n*
saying proverb; adage;
maxim.

scab *n* 1 dry crust which forms
over wound in healing 2
skin disease 3 plant disease
4 *coll* blackleg.

scabbard *n* sheath for sword or
dagger.

scabies *n* contagious itching
skin disease.

scabious *n* herbaceous plant
having round cushion-like
mauve flowers.

scabrous *a* 1 having rough
surface 2 scurfy 3
controversial 4 indecent.

scaffold *n* 1 temporary
structure of poles and planks
to support workmen 2
gallows; *n* **-ing** collective
term for planks and poles
used as scaffold, *esp* by
builders.

scald *v* 1 injure tissues of body
with hot liquid, steam 2
heat almost to boiling point;
n burn caused by hot liquid,
steam etc.

scale[1] *n* 1 one of hard, thin
flakes covering fish and
reptiles 2 any flaky deposit
in boilers, kettles etc; *v* 1
clear scales from 2 flake off.

scale[2] *n* one of two pans of
balance; *pl* weighing-
machine; *v* be weighed.

scale[3] *n mus* 1 series of
graduated notes, *esp* in
octave 2 system of grading
by size, rank, amount, degree
etc 3 ratio of size; *v* 1 climb
up; clamber up 2 increase,
reduce according to fixed
ratio.

scalene *a* (of triangle) having
unequal sides.

scallop *n* edible bivalve
mollusc; *pl* series of curves,
like edge of scallop shell,
used as ornamental edging; *v*
ornament (dress) with
scallops.

scallywag *n* rogue; scamp.

scalp *n* skin and hair on top of
head; *v* strip, cut scalp off.

scalpel *n* small, slender surgical
knife.

scam *n coll* scheme for
swindling people.

scamp *n* rogue; rascal.

scamper *v* 1 run about gaily;
caper 2 run off hastily.

scampi *n pl* (dish of) large
prawns.

scan *v* **scanning, scanned. 1**
look closely at; examine 2
med obtain image(s) of

(parts of) body with scanner 3 (*of searchlight*) pass across several times 4 read quickly to find certain things 5 analyse (*verse*) metrically 6 (*of verse*) have metrical pattern; *n* act of scanning; *n* **scanner** *med* apparatus for examining the body by producing images from many angles (*ns* **body s., head s.**); *n* **scansion**.

scandal *n* damaging, malicious or idle talk, act or thing that brings disgrace on reputation; *v* **-ize** arouse indignation in; shock feelings of; *a* **-ous**; *n* **scandalmonger** one who spreads scandal.

scant *a* small, inadequate in amount; *a* **-y** insufficient, meagre.

scapegoat *n* one who takes blame, or is punished, for faults of others.

scapula *n* shoulder-blade; *pl* **-lae, -las**; *a* **scapular** (*of* scapula); *n* short cloak worn by monks of certain religious orders.

scar *n* mark left by wound, burn or sore, after healing; *v* **scarring, scarred.** mark, heal with scar; *a* **scarred**.

scar, scaur *n* craggy, precipitous part of mountainside.

scarce *a* not plentiful; rare; infrequent; uncommon; *idm* **make oneself scarce** hide away (to avoid trouble); *adv* **-ly** not quite; only just; *n* **scarcity** deficiency of

supply; rarity.

scare *v* startle; frighten; *n* ill-founded alarm; widespread fear; *n* **scarecrow** 1 dummy figure used to scare birds from crops 2 badly dressed person.

scarf *n* **-arfs or arves.** long piece of material worn round neck; loose neckerchief; *pl* **scarves** or **scarfs.**

scarify *v* **scarifying, scarified.** 1 scratch, cut (skin) 2 break, loosen surface (of soil) 3 *fig* lacerate feelings of; *ns* **scarification; scarifier** agricultural implement.

scarlet *n* 1 brilliant, vivid red 2 cloth, clothing of this colour *esp* robes of High Court Judges etc; *a* of this colour; *ns* **s. fever** infectious disease, accompanied by high temperature and red rash; **s. pimpernel** small red flower; **s. woman** prostitute.

scarp *n* steep slope or face below rampart or hill; escarpment.

scarper *v Brit sl* run away.

scat[1] *v coll* leave quickly.

scat[2] *n* improvise wordless jazz singing.

scatheless *a* unharmed; uninjured; *a* **scathing** 1 damaging 2 (*of remarks, comments etc*) cutting, bitter.

scatter *v* 1 sprinkle; spread over 2 be dispersed 3 drive off in disorder; *n* **scatterbrain** flighty, thoughtless person.

scatty *a coll* crazy.

scavenge *v* 1 feed on dead flesh of other animals 2 search among refuse for usable objects; *ns* **-enger, -enging.**

scenario *n It* 1 written outline of action, scenes etc for film, play etc 2 imagined sequence of coming events.

scene *n* 1 place of action 2 background for fictional events, as in play etc 3 *coll* outburst of anger etc 4 view 5 sub-division of play within an act; *idm* **behind the scenes** 1 behind the stage 2 in secret; *idm* **make a scene** make a great fuss; have an emotional outburst; *idm* **on the scene** present; *idm* **set the scene** make everything ready; *n* **scenery** painted scenes in theatre; landscape; woods, hills etc collectively as view; *a* **scenic** theatrical; picturesque; pertaining to natural scenery.

scent *v* 1 smell 2 track by smell 3 make fragrant; *n* 1 odour; pleasant smell 2 liquid perfume.

sceptic *n* one who refuses to accept statement without positive proof; agnostic; *a* **-al;** *n* **-ism**.

sceptre *n* ornamental rod carried as symbol of sovereignty; *a* **sceptred** wielding royal power.

schedule *n* 1 written or printed list 2 tabulated statement 3 timetable; *v* set out, put into, form of schedule; *idm* **on schedule**

on time; a **scheduled 1** planned for a certain time **2** regular.

schema n diagram (pl **schemata**); a **schematic** shown by diagrammatic representation (a -**ally**); v **schematize 1** simplify **2** organize schematically (n -**ization**).

scheme n **1** plan; design; project; enterprise **2** outline; synopsis; v **1** plan as scheme **2** plot dishonestly; intrigue; n **schemer** one who schemes, esp in bad sense.

scherzo n mus lively, playful movement or passage.

schism n division in organized body or society, esp in Church.

schist n type of crystalline rock.

schizophrenia n psychosis or mental disorder marked by split personality etc; as **schizophrenic; schizoid** tending towards schizophrenia.

schmaltz n coll excessive sentimentality in art, music etc; a -**y**.

schmuck n US coll fool.

schnapps n Ger strong alcoholic drink.

scholar n **1** school pupil **2** learned person **3** holder of scholarship; a -**ly**; n -**liness**; n **scholarship 1** quality of learned person **2** grant of money to scholar; a **scholastic 1** of school, scholars **2** academic (n -**ism**).

school[1] n **1** place of education for children **2** (period of life in) attendance at such a place **3** teaching establishment of specified kind (**s. of art**) **4** university department (**law s.**) **5** group of artists, composers, writers sharing common ideas, methods **6** coll experience valued for learning sth (**s. of life**); idm **school of thought** people sharing common ideas; v train; educate; discipline (n -**ing**); ns **schoolmarm** coll domineering woman with old-fashioned ideas; **schoolmaster/mistress/teacher; schoolmate** fellow pupil.

school[2] n large shoal of fish; shoal of whales or porpoises.

schooner n **1** fore-and-aft rigged vessel with two or more masts **2** large glass (for beer, sherry etc).

science n **1** systematized knowledge of natural or physical phenomena; investigation of this; knowledge or skill based on study, experience and practice; ns **s. fiction** stories of imaginary events set in future, esp involving space or time travel; **s. park** area designated for companies working on new technological developments; a **scientific** based on principles and methods of science; systematic; objective; n **scientist** one learned, trained in natural science.

scientology n religious movement believing in self-awareness and reincarnation, but no supreme being.

scintillate v **1** sparkle; twinkle **2** fig be witty and brilliant in conversation; ns **scintilla 1** spark **2** fig particle; atom; **scintillation** act of sparkling.

scion n slip for grafting; young member of family, descendant.

scissors n pl **1** cutting instrument of two blades pivoted together **2** style of high jumping **3** wrestling hold **4** movement in Rugby football.

sclerosis n med hardening of body tissue.

scoff[1] n taunt; expression of contempt, derision; v jeer at; mock.

scoff[2] v coll eat greedily and quickly.

scold v reprove angrily, noisily; find fault with; n nagging woman.

sconce n **1** metal bracket candlestick on wall **2** socket of candlestick **3** earthwork; v entrench.

scone n small, round cake.

scoop n **1** article for ladling, dipping, or shovelling **2** tool for hollowing out **3** sl unexpected and profitable piece of luck **4** journalism exclusive news item; v **1** ladle, shovel out **2** hollow out **3** sl obtain as profit, before others.

scoot v coll run quickly; run away; n **scooter 1** low-powered motorcycle with small wheels **2** child's toy.

scope n **1** range of activity **2** extent of view **3** area **4** outlet.

scorch v burn superficially (of plants etc); dry up; wither; n **scorched earth policy** tactic of devastating one's own land to leave nothing for an invading army.

score n **1** notch, mark drawn or scratched **2** reckoning **3** number of points made in game **4** set of 20 persons, or objects **5** (pl indefinite, large number) **6** printed, written copy of orchestral music; idm **on that score** as far as that is concerned; idm **pay/settle an old score** have revenge; v **1** notch **2** cross out **3** record, make points in game **4** fig gain advantage; phr vs **score off/over** make appear foolish; **score out/through** draw line through; delete; n **scoreboard** board showing points scored; n **scorer** one who keeps or makes score in game.

scorn n contempt; disdainful state of mind; v feel, show contempt of; treat with derision; a **-ful** full of contempt.

scorpion n small arachnid insect with sting in tail and lobster-like claws.

scot n tax; rate; a **scot-free** free from payment; unpunished; unhurt.

Scot n native of Scotland; as **Scotch** contracted form of Scottish (n whisky from Scotland; ns **S. egg** hard boiled egg coated with sausage meat; **S. mist** very fine drizzle); **Scottish (S. highlands)**; ns **Scotsman/woman; Scotland Yard** head office of criminal investigation department in London.

scotch v **1** crush, render harmless **2** thwart; hinder; n wedge to prevent wheel etc from slipping.

scoundrel n blackguard; rogue; a **-ly**.

scour v **1** clean and polish by friction **2** search thoroughly **3** wash away by rapid flow of water **4** get rid of; free from.

scourge n **1** whip; lash **2** affliction; pest; v **1** flog; chastise **2** oppress.

Scouse n, a person from Liverpool.

scout n **1** member of organization founded by Lord Baden-Powell to train boys in ideas of survival, initiative and community service **2** soldier sent to reconnoitre **3** person sent out to look for people with talent; ns **s. car** armoured vehicle; scouting activity of being a scout; **scoutmaster** leader of scout group.

scowl v frown; look sullen, angry; n sullen, angry frown.

scrabble v scratch; scramble about; n **1** scrawl **2** cap [TM] word-building board game.

scrag n bony end of neck of mutton; a **scraggy** skinny; thin; lean; v wring or tackle neck.

scram v coll go away at once.

scramble v **1** clamber, climb using arms and legs **2** struggle roughly with **3** cook eggs beaten with butter, until partly solid; n **1** act of scrambling **2** rough hill climb in motor-cycle racing **3** disorderly proceeding.

scrap n **1** small detached piece **2** waste material **3** pl odds and ends of waste food **4** coll fight; v **scrapping, scapped. 1** break up **2** dispose of as useless; coll fight; ns **s. book** book with plain pages for pasting in press-cuttings etc; **s. heap** pile of waste material (idm **on the scrap heap** of no further use); **s. metal** metal for melting down and re-using; **s. paper** (US **scratch paper**) used paper for making rough notes.

scrape v graze, abrade surface with sharp edge; clean thus; scratch; phr vs **scrape along** coll manage with difficulty; **scrape through** pass test with difficulty; **scrape together/up** collect or obtain with difficulty; n act, sound of scraping, coll awkward predicament; n **scraper** instrument for scraping.

scratch v **1** leave slight mark on skin or surface with claws, or anything pointed **2**

fig withdraw from game, competition etc; *idm* **scratch the surface** begin dealing with (problem) without progressing far; *n* **1** wound or mark made by scratching **2** zero, par, in games scored by numerical points; *idm* **up to scratch** satisfactory; *a* arranged at short notice, impromptu.

scratch card *n* purchased game ticket on which surface is scratched away to reveal numbers.

scrawl *v* write, draw hastily; scribble; *n* shapeless, untidy handwriting etc.

scrawny *a* thin and scraggy.

scream *v* utter shrill, piercing cry; laugh wildly and shrilly; *n* shriek, shrill cry.

screech *v* utter shrill harsh cry; *n* scream.

screed *n* long tedious speech or letter.

screen *n* **1** structure giving shelter from heat, cold, wind, or concealing something **2** large white surface on which cinema films, photographic slides are projected **3** coarse sieve; *v* **1** shelter, protect with screen **2** conceal **3** project (film etc) **4** examine (person) for political motives **5** riddle, sift (*esp* coal) *ns* **screenplay** script for film; **s. test** test of sb's suitability for part in film.

screw *n* **1** cylindrical piece of metal with spiral groove running round it and used

as fastening **2** ship's propeller **3** action of twisting, turning **4** *sl* wages etc; *idm* **put the screws on** use forceful method to persuade; *v* **1** fasten with screw(s) **2** *fig* extort; *phr vs* **screw off** remove by turning; **screw on** fasten by turning; **screw up 1** twist (paper etc) into a ball **2** fasten with screw(s) **3** distort (one's face) in a grimace **4** *sl* handle badly (*idm* **screw up one's courage** overcome one's fears; *idm* **all screwed up** *coll* tense and anxious), *n* **screw-driver** chisel-shaped tool for turning screws.

scribble *v* write carelessly, illegibly; make meaningless marks with pencil etc; *n* something scribbled.

scribe *n* writer; author; *v* mark with scriber; *n* **scriber** tool for marking lines on stone etc.

scrimmage *n* scuffle; confused struggle.

scrimp *v* make small; be niggardly; *a* **scrimpy** scanty.

scrip *n* share-, or stock-certificate.

script *n* **1** handwriting **2** text of play, film etc.

scripture *n* sacred writings; the Bible.

scroll *n* **1** roll of parchment or paper **2** ornamental spiral or curved design.

scrooge *n* miserly person.

scrotum *n* pouch of skin containing testicles.

scrounge *v sl* cadge; pilfer; *n* **scrounger** cadger.

scrub *n* brushwood; land covered with such; *a* **scrubby** insignificant; undersized; inferior, *esp* of sports team.

scrub *v* **scrubbing, scrubbed. 1** clean by hard rubbing, *esp* with brush and water **2** *sl* cancel; *n* act of scrubbing; *ns* **scrubbing-brush** hard stiff brush; **scrubber** one who scrubs.

scruff *n* **1** nape of neck **2** *Brit coll* untidy person.

scrummage *n* scrimmage; *abbr* **-scrum** struggle between opposing forwards in Rugby football, with ball on ground between them; *n* **scrum-half** player who puts ball into scrum, etc.

scrumptious *n coll* delicious.

scrumpy *n Brit* strong dry cider.

scrunch *v* **1** crush; crumple **2** chew noisily; (*n* noise of this).

scruple *n* **1** small weight, 20 grains **2** doubt, hesitation about proposed action **3** conscientious objection; *a* **scrupulous** punctilious; conscientious; meticulous; *n* **scrupulousness**.

scrutiny *n* searching look; careful, official examination (of voting papers etc); *n* **scrutineer** examiner, *esp* of ballot papers; *v* **scrutinize** examine carefully, look into closely.

scud v **scudding, scudded.** move quickly; n type of missile.

scuff v scratch (shoes) by dragging feet; a **scuffed** (of shoes) roughened or grazed.

scuffle v struggle; push roughly; n confused struggle.

scull n light, one-handed oar; v propel, move (boat) by means of scull(s).

scullery n room off kitchen, where rough work and cleaning of pots etc is done; ns **scullery-maid; scullion** ar boy who cleans dishes etc.

sculpture n art of carving or chiselling stone, wood etc to form figures in relief or solid; example of this art; v represent by sculpture; n **sculptor** artist who models in clay, carves wood or stone figures; fem **sculptress.**

scum n froth or other floating matter on liquid; waste part of anything; fig lowest, most degraded people; a **scummy.**

scurf n thin flakes of dried skin on scalp; dandruff; a **scurfy.**

scurrilous a coarsely abusive; n **scurrility.**

scurry v run; hurry; scuttle.

scurvy n disease of malnutrition, due to lack of fresh vegetable food; a 1 mean; low; contemptible 2 scurfy.

scuttle[1] n receptacle for holding coal, in a room.

scuttle[2] v run away hurriedly; bolt.

scuttle[3] n covered hole in deck of ship, or in wall, roof etc; v make holes in ship, to sink it.

scythe n tool for mowing, with long curved blade set at right angles to handle; v cut with scythe; mow.

SDI abbr Strategic Defence Initiative (US plan for destroying enemy missiles in space).

sea n 1 mass of salt water covering much of earth's surface 2 particular named area of this 3 large plain on surface of moon 4 fig large expanse of sth; pl **-s** condition of sea as caused by the weather; idm **all at sea** coll confused; ns **s. anemone** sea animal with many tentacles resembling a flower; **seaboard** coastal area of country; **s. change** gradual, but complete change; **s.-cow** type of marine mammal; **s.-dog** experienced sailor; **seafood** fish and other edible sea creatures; **s. front** area above beach at seaside resort; **seagull** gull; **s.-horse** small fish with horse-like head; **s. legs** ability to walk around on moving ship without being sea-sick; **s. lion** large seal; **seaman** sailor, esp one with skill in handling ship; **s. mile** nautical mile; **seaplane** aircraft able to land on the sea; **seascape** picture of sea; **seaside** Brit (holiday resort on) coast; **s. urchin** small sea creature with prickly shell; **seaweed** any form of plant life growing in the sea; as **seafaring** travelling by sea (n seafarer); **seaworthy** fit for a sea voyage (n **- iness**).

SEAC abbr School Examinations and Assessment Council.

seal[1] n marine, amphibious fish-eating mammal with flippers; v hunt seals; ns **sealer** ship or man hunting seals; **sealskin** fur of seals.

seal[2] n 1 piece of metal etc with engraved design for stamping on wax 2 disc of wax thus stamped as authentication of a document or for security 3 any substance used to fill a crack or gap preventing leakage of gas, air, water, oil etc 4 decorative sticker, esp sold in aid of charity; idm **seal of approval** formal approval; idm **set the seal on 1** finish 2 confirm; make certain; v 1 fix seal on (document) 2 stick down (envelope) 3 close securely (to prevent leakage) 4 coat with protective, esp waterproof substance 5 settle (agreement) 6 decide (fate); phr v **seal off** close securely to prevent entry or exit; ns **sealed unit** mechanical part that is sealed to prevent damage from outside; **sealing wax** hard-setting wax for sealing documents or letters.

seam n 1 join between two edges (of cloth, or planks) 2 thin layer; vein; stratum; v join by sewing together; mark with furrows, wrinkles; a **-less**; n **seamstress**, **sempstress** needlewoman; a **seamy** showing rough side of life.

séance n Fr meeting of spiritualists.

sear v dry up; scorch burn surface of; brand; a **-ing** 1 (of pain) burning 2 fig provoking strong emotion.

search v go through and examine closely; scan; reconnoitre; idm **search me** coll I don't know; idm **search one's conscience/heart** think honestly about one's motives; n act of searching; a **-ing** 1 penetrating (s. **look**) 2 severely testing (s. **question**); ns **searcher** person who searches; **searchlight** powerful beam of light for scanning area in darkness; s.-**party** group of people sent to search for missing person.

season n 1 one of four divisions of the year (spring, summer, autumn, winter) 2 period of year associated with specific activity (**mating s.**), with availability of something (**soft fruit s.**), with more or less of sth (**high/low s.**); idm **in season** 1 easily available now 2 (of female animal) ready to mate 3 in the most popular

holiday months 4 in the period when hunting is permitted; idm **out of season** not in season; v 1 give extra flavour to by adding salt, pepper, spice etc 2 (of wood) make or become fit for use by gradual drying out to avoid warping; ns **seasoning** flavouring added to food; **season (ticket)** ticket valid for any number of times' use within a specified period (**weekly/monthly/quarterly/annual s.**); as **seasonable** appropriate to the time of year; **seasonal** varying with the seasons (adv **-ly**); **seasoned** fig with plenty of experience.

seat n 1 anything made to sit on 2 right to sit (as in Parliament, theatre etc) 3 way of sitting, esp when horse-riding 4 buttocks 5 locality of trouble, disease etc 6 large house, esp in country; v 1 make sit down 2 provide with seating accommodation.

sebaceous a fatty; s. **glands** sweat-glands, or glands of hair follicles.

sec abbr second.

secant n reciprocal of cosine of angle.

secateurs n pl Fr pruning shears.

secede v withdraw voluntarily from federation etc; n **secession** act of seceding.

seclude v shut up, keep apart from others; a **secluded**

remote, withdrawn, esp of place; n **seclusion**.

second[1] n 1 sixtieth part of one minute 2 coll brief space of time.

second[2] det 1 2nd (ordinal number of two); next after first (also adv, pron) 2 inferior; n 1 helper of boxer or duellist 2 second-class university degree 3 second gear (of vehicle) 4 pl imperfect goods sold with a reduction; as s. **best** not as good as best; s.-**class** 1 inferior in quality to first-class 2 (of travel, accommodation) standard class 3 regarded as socially inferior; s.-**hand** 1 previously owned, used by sb else 2 (of information) obtained indirectly (also adv); s.-**rate** of inferior quality; s.-**string** sport as substitute for regular player; ns s. **chamber** upper house in parliament (eg Brit House of Lords) s. **childhood** dotage; s. **coming** return of Jesus Christ on Day of Judgement; s. **cousin** (child of) parent's cousin; s. **nature** sth done easily through force of habit; s. **sight** ability to foresee the future or know what is happening elsewhere; s. **thought** change of opinion; s. **wind** fresh burst of energy in activity after first onset of tiredness; v s.-**guess** US coll 1 make retrospective criticism of 2 forecast 3 guess better than.

second³ support (proposal or nominee for post); n **-er** supporter.

second⁴ Brit fml transfer from normal to other duties, usu for stated period; n **-ment**.

secondary a 1 following what is first or primary (s. education, s. school) 2 less important than primary (s. consideration, s. motive) 3 dependent on, caused by what is primary (s. infection); ns s. picket picket not directly involved in dispute (n s. picketing); adv **-ily**.

secret a 1 hidden, meant to be kept from common knowledge 2 mysterious; clandestine 3 remote; secluded; n thing kept secret; n **secrecy** ability, fidelity in keeping secret; a **secretive** unduly reticent; furtive; n **secretiveness**.

secretary n 1 one employed to deal with correspondence, keep records, and generally act in confidential manner 2 head of state department; a **secretarial**; n **secretariat** body of secretaries; building occupied by secretarial staff; n **s.-bird** long-legged S African bird, resembling heron.

secrete v 1 hide, conceal 2 (of gland etc) collect and distribute material from blood as secretion; n **secretion** process of collecting substances from blood for use of body or expulsion as excreta; a **secretory** secreting.

sect n group holding minority views in religion; religious denomination; a **sectarian** characteristic of sect; n **sectary** member of sect.

section n 1 act of cutting 2 severed part 3 any separate, distinct part of anything 4 smallest military unit 5 drawing of an object cut vertically; a **-al**.

sector n 1 portion of circle enclosed by two radii and arc which they cut off 2 mil part of fortified front or position.

secular a 1 worldly; not ecclesiastical 2 age-long; persistent; v **secularize** transfer from ecclesiastical to civil ownership or use etc; make secular.

secure a 1 free from care 2 made safe 3 firm; stable 4 certain; v 1 make safe 2 ensure; make certain 3 fasten, firmly 4 get hold of; n **security** safety; protection; safeguard; guarantee; pl **-s** bonds, title-deeds, share certificates etc; ns s. feature device that makes theft difficult; s. system system of burglar alarm devices for property.

sedan n covered chair carried on two poles; large closed motor-car.

sedate a calm; staid, decorous; adv **-ly**; n **-ness**.

sedative a allaying anxiety; soothing; n sedative drug; n **sedation** act of administering sedative drug.

sedentary a sitting; requiring little bodily exertion.

sedge n coarse, perennial, grasslike plants, growing in marshy ground; n s.-**warbler** summer migrant bird.

sediment n matter which settles at bottom of liquid; dregs.

sedition n offence against State authority, not amounting to treason; public commotion, riot; a **seditious**.

seduce v 1 corrupt; lead astray 2 induce (sb) to have intercourse; 3 charm; entice; n **seduction**; a **seductive** alluring; attractive; persuasive.

sedulous a diligent; assiduous; careful; painstaking; n **sedulity**.

see¹ v seeing, saw, seen. 1 have power of eyesight 2 perceive with the eyes 3 look at 4 understand 5 imagine; visualize 6 verify 7 meet 8 interview 9 spend time with 10 experience 11 bear witness to 12 consider possibility; idm (one must) be seeing things (one must) be suffering from illusions; idm see fit to decide to; idm see red become angry; idm see you (around) coll goodbye for now; idm see sb somewhere escort sb somewhere; idm see the light reach a state of understanding; *idm* (**I'll**) **see you in court** *coll* I'll sue you; *phr vs* **see about 1** think about 2 deal with; **see off 1** escort to place of departure 2 chase away; **see out 1** escort to the exit 2 endure to the end of; **see over/round** inspect (place); **see through 1** not be deceived by 2 ensure completion of 3 help and support (in difficult times); **see to** attend to (*idm* **see to it that** ensure that); *conj* **seeing that** because.

see[2] *n* diocese, office, jurisdiction of bishop.

seed *n* 1 fertilized reproductive germs of flowering plants; one grain of this 2 sperm, milt etc 3 *fig* offspring 4 seeded player; *idm* **go/run to seed 1** (of plant) produce seeds 2 *fig* lose efficiency; become shabby; *v* 1 form seed 2 remove seed 3 arrange draw for lawn-tennis or other tournament so that best players, or those of same nationality do not meet in early rounds; *n* **seedling** young plant raised from seed; *a* **seedy** 1 run to seed 2 *coll* shabby 3 *coll* out of sorts.

seek *v* seeking, sought. search for; want.

seem *v* look like; give one impression; appear to be; *as* **-ing** ostensible; apparent; **seemly** decent; proper; appropriate.

seen *pp* of **see**.

seep *v* trickle through slowly; percolate; leak *n* **seepage** slow seeping through.

seer *n* prophet.

seersucker *n* lightweight, puckered, cotton fabric.

see-saw *n* 1 children's play apparatus, plank resting on central support, child sitting on each end, moving up and down alternately 2 any motion as this; *v* move up and down.

seethe *v* boil, bubble up; *fig* be violently agitated by.

segment *n* section, portion cut or marked off; *v* divide into parts *n* **-ation**.

segregate *v* separate from main body; isolate; *n* **-ation**.

seigneur *n* *Fr* formerly feudal lord.

seismic *a* pertaining to earthquakes; *ns* **seismograph** instrument for recording earth tremors; **seismology** science of earthquakes.

seize *v* 1 grasp, take by force 2 grasp rapidly with mind; *phr v* **seize up**; (of machinery etc) stick, bind, esp from overheating or undue friction; *n* **seizure** 1 forcible taking 2 sudden attack of illness, esp stroke or fit.

seldom *adv* rarely; not often.

select *v* pick out; choose; *a* chosen; exclusive; fastidious; *a* **selective** having power of selection, able to discriminate; *ns* **selection** act of selecting; collection of samples; **selector**; **selectivity** ability to

discriminate.

selenium *n* non-metallic element used in photoelectric cells.

self *n* person's own identity, and individual character; personality; ego; essential quality, inmost nature of anything; *pl* **selves**.

self- *prefix* expressing reflexive action to, by, for oneself; automatic; acting upon agent. *Such compounds are not given here where the meaning may be deduced from the simple word.*

self-addressed *a* addressed for return to sender.

self-absorbed *a* only concerned with one's own interests.

self-assured *a* self-confident.

self-centred *a* preoccupied with one's own affairs or personality.

self-confident *a* sure of oneself and one's ability; *adv* **-ly**; *n* **-fidence**.

self-conscious *a* easily embarrassed, shy.

self-contained *a* compact or complete within itself; of reserved personality.

self-denial *n* voluntary abstention from pleasures.

self-determination *n* right, power of race, nation to decide on its own form of government.

self-devotion *n* giving up one's time to cause etc.

self-effacing *a* keeping oneself from being noticed.

self-employed *a* earning

money directly from one's own business; not being employed by another.

self-evident a clearly so; not needing explanation; adv **-ly.**

self-fulfilling a happening, likely to happen simply because it has been predicted.

self-importance n conceited, pompous manner; exaggerated idea of own importance.

self-possessed a composed; having presence of mind.

self-raising a (of flour) containing agent to cause dough to rise and swell.

self-reliant a independent; n **-ance.**

self-respect n proper regard for one's own character etc.

self-righteous a too sure of one's own goodness; adv **-ly** n **-ness.**

selfsame a identical.

self-satisfied a conceited.

self-service a (of stores etc) where customers serve themselves.

self-seeking a acting only for one's own advantage.

self-styled a using title for oneself without having the right to do so.

self-sufficient a able to supply all one's needs for existence without help from elsewhere; n **-ency.**

self-will n obstinacy; being headstrong.

sell v 1 give, dispose of in return for money 2 be sold 3

deal in 4 persuade people to buy 5 persuade people that sth is good; pt, pp **sold;** idm **be sold on** coll be enthusiastic about; idm **be sold out (of)** have sold all available; idm **sell one's soul** be ready to do anything for money, power etc; idm **sell so down the river** betray sb; idm **sell short 1** sell at less than true value **2** not recognize the value of **3** deceive; phr vs **sell off** dispose of by selling, esp at reduced price; **sell out 1** sell one's whole supply **2** be all sold (n **sell-out** entertainment for which all tickets are sold) **3** betray, esp for money (n **sell-out**); **sell up** sell one's entire possessions, one's house or business; n coll deception; poor bargain (idm **hard/soft sell** aggressive/discreetly persuasive way of selling); ns **sell-by date** date marked on perishable product as last acceptable date for selling; **seller** (**seller's market** situation where demand for sth is greater than supply, and higher prices can be asked).

Sellotape [TM] Brit cellulose or plastic sticky tape (usu transparent) dispensed from a roll.

selvedge, selvage n edge of cloth woven to prevent ravelling.

seltzer n fizzy mineral water.

selves pl of **self.**

semantics n pl branch of linguistic study dealing with development of meaning of words.

semaphore n 1 post with two movable arms worked by levers, for signalling 2 signalling by use of person's arms and flags; code used for such signals; v signal thus.

semblance n appearance; similitude; outward show.

semen n spermatic fluid of male animal.

semester n university term of six months.

semi- prefix partly, half.

semi n coll semi-detached house.

semibreve n musical note equal to two minims or four crotchets.

semicircle n half-circle; a **semi-circular.**

semicolon n punctuation mark (;).

semiconductor n substance that conducts electricity under certain conditions.

semi-detached a (of house) having another joined to it on one side.

semi-final n round before the final.

seminal a 1 capable of developing 2 original, important and influential 3 containing semen.

seminar n meeting for discussion; conference.

seminary n college for training (esp RC) priests.

semiology n study of signs and symbols; a **-logical** n **-logist.**

semiquaver n musical note half length of quaver.

Semite n member of racial group including Jews, Arabs; Jew; a **Semitic** pertaining to Semites and their languages.

semitone n musical half-tone.

semolina n ground grains of wheat, used in making macaroni.

senate n 1 ancient Roman legislative assembly 2 upper legislative council of State (as of USA); academic governing body of university; n **senator**; a **-torial**; n **s. house** building where senate meets.

send v 1 cause to go, be conveyed 2 dispatch 3 sl rouse to ecstasy; pt, pp sent; idm **send crazy/mad** cause to become crazy/mad; idm **send to Coventry** refuse to speak to; phr vs **send down** 1 coll send to prison 2 Brit expel from university; **send for** 1 order 2 request to come; **send off** 1 post 2 sport dismiss from field of play (n **sending-off**) 3 accompany with good wishes (n **send-off** expression of good wishes at start of sth); **send up** 1 make mockery of (n **send-up**) 2 US coll send to prison; n **sender**.

senescent a growing old; n **-ence**.

senile a showing weakness and decay of mental faculties, due to old age **senile dementia**; n mental deterioration in old age, resulting in memory loss; n **senility**.

senior a older, of higher degree, rank, position; n older person; superior n **s. citizen** person beyond age of retirement; n **seniority**.

senna n dried leaves of pea-like plant used as laxative.

sesor n (title of) Spanish man; fem **sesora** married Spanish woman; **sesorita** unmarried Spanish woman, girl.

sensation n effect felt by senses; state of excitement; event, person etc causing such state of mind; a **sensational** arousing, tending to arouse, great interest, curiosity etc; n **sensationalism** crude, melodramatic presentation of news items, esp sex and violence.

sense n 1 any of five faculties by which one perceives the world around (sight, hearing, taste, smell, touch) 2 practical wisdom 3 understanding (of sth); ability to judge 4 meaning 5 feeling (about sth) 6 purpose 7 pl ability to think; idm **bring/come to one's senses** (cause to) stop acting foolishly; idm **make sense** be intelligible; idm **make sense (out of)** understand; idm **sense of occasion** 1 special atmosphere created by event 2 awareness of how to behave; **sixth sense** ability to know things that one has neither seen nor heard

directly; v become aware of; feel; detect; as **senseless** 1 unconscious 2 foolish;

sensible 1 conscious 2 wise (adv **-ibly**) 3 sensible of aware of; n **sensibility** delicate feeling about style, correctness etc (pl **-ies** capacity for being shocked easily).

sensitive a 1 feeling acutely; keenly perceptive 2 easily distressed 3 reacting quickly to slight changes; n **sensitiveness** state of being sensitive; **sensitivity** degree of sensitiveness; v **sensitize** phot make sensitive to light.

sensor n device for detecting presence of heat, sound, smoke etc; a **sensory** of the physical senses.

sensual a 1 pertaining to body senses 2 lustful; voluptuous; ns **sensuality** proneness to sexual indulgence; **sensualism** sexual indulgence; a **sensuous** pertaining to, based on bodily senses.

sent pt, pp of send.

sentence n 1 judgement, decision of court, declaring punishment to be inflicted on criminal 2 combination of words which convey complete meaning; v condemn.

sententious a full of maxims; uttering trite, pompous expressions.

sentient a having sense or feeling.

sentiment n 1 tender emotion;

tendency to be influenced more by emotion than reason 2 verbal expression of feeling; *a* **sentimental** arising from sentiment, rather than logical motives; foolishly emotional; *ns* **sentimentalist** one affected by or working up sentiment; **sentimentality** tendency to be sentimental; sloppy.

sentinel *n* one who keeps watch; sentry.

sentry *n* armed military guard.

separate *v* divide; cut up, off; come, go apart; part; *a* 1 divided; distinct physically 2 isolated; kept apart; *a* **separable;** *ns* **-ation** 1 act, process of separating 2 in law, formal arrangement when married couple live apart, without divorce; **-ator** that which separates; device for separating cream from milk.

separatism *n* policy of keeping a religious or political group separate and independent; *a, n* **-ist**.

sepia *n* dark brown pigment, made from ink of cuttle fish; *a* of this colour.

September *n* 9th month.

septennial *a* lasting, occuring every seven years.

septet(te) *n* music for, group of, seven instruments or voices.

septic *a* of, caused by blood-poisoning or putrefaction; **s. tank** underground tank where sewage is dispersed through action of bacteria;

ns **sepsis** infection of blood by micro-organisms; **septicaemia** blood-poisoning; **septuagenarian** *a* aged between 70 and 80; *n* person so aged.

Septuagesima *n* third Sunday before Lent.

sepulchre *n* tomb; burial vault; *a* **sepulchral** 1 of pertaining to grave, burial or dead; funereal 2 (*of voice etc*) deep; hollow; *n* **sepulture** burial.

sequel *n* 1 consequence 2 account, story of later events.

sequent *a* following; *n* **sequence** order in which events, objects follow; series; succession **sequential** *a* in sequence; *adv* **-ly**.

sequester *v* set apart; isolate; *v* **sequestrate** confiscate; *leg* take (property) by process of law and divert income to meet claims against owner; *n* **sequestration**.

sequin *n* ornamental disc or spangle; old Venetian gold coin.

seraph *n* one of highest orders of angels; *pl* **seraphim;** *a* **seraphic** angelic.

Serbo-Croat *n* Slavonic language of Yugoslavia.

serenade *n* music sung or played at night (*esp* by lover) beneath lady's window); nocturne; *v* sing serenade to.

serendipity *n* faculty of finding valuable or interesting

things by chance.

serene *a* 1 calm; placid 2 unclouded *n* serenity.

serf *n* feudal labourer; slave; *n* **serfdom**.

serge *n* hard-wearing, twilled woollen cloth.

sergeant, serjeant *n* NCO in army; police officer; **s.-at-arms** ceremonial official of Parliament; **sergeant-major** senior NCO of regiment etc.

serial *a* of, forming series; **s. number** identifying number of item in series; *n* story, novel etc published in successive instalments; *v* **-ize** arrange in series; publish, produce as serial.

serial killer person who commits a series of murders, *usu* in the same way.

series *n* 1 sequence 2 set; succession 3 linear, end-to-end arrangement.

serif *n* short thin line at top or bottom of letters.

serious *a* 1 solemn; meant in earnest, genuine 2 grave; critical.

sermon *n* discourse on moral and religious subjects forming part of church service; *v* **-ize** preach, *esp* tediously.

serpent *n* 1 snake 2 malevolent person 3 obsolete wind instrument.

SERPS *abbr* State Earnings Related Pension Scheme.

serrated *a* having notches like teeth of saw; *n* **serration**.

serried *a* in compact order; closely packed.

serum n watery fluid remaining after coagulation of blood; such fluid prepared by culture for use in inoculation.

serval n African wildcat.

servant n one employed in domestic service to another.

serve v 1 work for; perform duty for 2 wait upon (with food) 3 satisfy 4 undergo (prison sentence) 5 deliver (writ) 6 (tennis etc) deliver ball to opponent, by striking it 7 be useful for.

service n 1 (performance of) official duty 2 help given 3 fig work done by machine 4 public organization or department 5 organized system of transport or communication 6 satisfying of needs of clients; money given in recognition of this 7 maintenance (eg of machinery) 8 set of crockery, cutlery etc 9 ceremony of religious worship 10 tennis, squash method of putting ball into play; ns **s. area** area near to motorway with petrol station, shop, restaurant etc; **s. charge** sum added to basic bill for element of service; **serviceman/woman** person serving in armed forces; **s. road** minor road alongside main road for access to shops, houses etc; **s. station** garage for petrol and car maintenance; a **-able** usable; useful; ns **servicing** maintenance; **serving**

portion of food.

serviette n Fr table-napkin.

servile a 1 pertaining to slaves, slavery 2 cringing; obsequious; n **servility**.

servitude n slavery; bondage.

servo-mechanism n device controlling larger mechanism.

sesame n annual E Indian herb, with seeds yielding oil.

sesquipedalian a consisting of very long words.

session n 1 formal assembly or meeting 2 period during which legislative body sits, esp Parliament; continuous series of such meetings.

set v setting, setted. 1 put; arrange in position 2 cause to be in specified state 3 cause to begin 4 adjust 5 fix 6 establish 7 present (task, problem) to be dealt with 8 (cause to) become solid 9 compose music for (words to be sung) 10 (of sun, moon etc) go below horizon 11 (of current, tide) flow in stated direction; idm **be all set** be ready; idm **set free** liberate; phr vs **set about 1** begin 2 attack; **set aside 1** abandon 2 keep, save for later; **set back 1** place further to the rear 2 delay (n **set-back**) 3 incur a cost of; **set down 1** write down 2 let (passenger) get off; **set forth 1** begin journey 2 fml present (in detail); **set in** (of weather, disease) begin and become established; **set off 1** depart 2 cause to explode 3 initiate

4 make appear better by contrast; **set on** (cause to) attack; **set out 1** depart 2 arrange in order; **set out to** begin with intention to; **set to** begin eagerly (n **set-to** argument or fight); **set up 1** erect 2 prepare 3 establish; organize (n **set-up** arrangement; organization) 4 coll restore to good health 5 coll equip with necessary resources 6 sl con or frame; a 1 fixed (**s. price**) 2 prescribed (**s. books**) 3 inflexible (**s. attitude**); idm **be all set** to be quite ready; idm **be set on** be determined about; n 1 complete group 2 radio or TV receiver 3 arrangement of scenery on stage or for filming 4 tennis specified number of games; subdivision of match 5 group identified by social class; ns **s. piece** sequence of action executed according to plan; work of art of traditional type; n **setting** act, process of setting; background; that in which gems are set.

setsquare n flat triangular plate with one right-angled corner for geometrical drawing etc.

sett n badger's burrow.

settee n sofa; couch.

setter n breed of dog trained to point at game.

settle n wooden bench with high back and arms; v 1 arrange; establish 2 make firm or quiet 3 decide on 4

endow legally 5 end
(dispute) 6 subside 7 pay 8
become clear 9 take up
abode; *phr vs* **settle down** 1
subside 2 make a home 3
begin to lead a quiet life 4
form a regular pattern of
work; **settle for** agree to
accept; **settle in** get used to
new home, job etc; **settle on**
agree on; decide on; **settle
up** pay what one owes; *a*
settled 1 calm 2 established;
ns **settlement** 1 movement
of people to new habitat 2
small newly-built village 3
agreement 4 gift of money 5
payment of required sum;
settler colonist.

seven *n, pron, det* cardinal
number next above six; *ns,
as, dets* **seventh** ordinal
number; seventh part; *idm*
(be in) seventh heaven (be
in) state of bliss; **seventeen**
seven plus ten; **seventeenth;
seventy** seven tens;
seventieth; *n* **seven-year
itch** feeling of restlessness
after seven years of marriage.

sever *v* separate; cut off;
divide; *n* **severance** (**s. pay**
money paid to worker
dismissed through no fault
of his/hers).

several *a* 1 separate; distinct 2
more than two; not many;
adv **-ly** apart from others.

severe *a* 1 harsh; strict 2
rigorous 3 intense 4 austere
5 violent; *n* **severity.**

sevruga *n* species of sturgeon.

sew *v* sewing, sewed, sewn or
sewed. fasten, work with

needle and thread; *phr v* sew
up 1 repair by sewing 2 *fig*
conclude satisfactorily; *n*
sewing needlework.

sewage *n* waste matter, excreta
etc carried away in sewers;
ns **sewer** underground
conduit or drain for carrying
off sewage; **sewerage** public
drainage.

sex *n* 1 fact or quality of being
male or female 2
physiological difference
between male and female 3
coll sexual intercourse; *ns* **s.
appeal** power of sexual
attraction; *n* **sex offender**
person who has committed a
sexual crime; *n* **sex offence**
sexual crime; **s. object**
person considered
interesting only for sexual
attraction; **s. organ** organ of
reproduction; *ns* **sexism**
discriminatory treatment of
one sex by the other (*a* **-ist**);
sexology study of sexual
behaviour (*n* **-ologist**); *a*
sexual (**s. intercourse** act of
intimacy by joining sex
organs of male and female)
adv **-ly;** *a* **-ity;** *a* **sexy.**

Sexagesima *n* second Sunday
before Lent.

sexennial *a* lasting, happening
once in, six years.

sextet(te) *n* group of six
instruments or players;
music for this group.

sexton *n* man employed by
church as caretaker,
gravedigger etc.

sextuplet *n* any of six children
born of the same pregnancy.

SF *abbr* science fiction.

sforzando *a, adv, n mus* (note)
played with initial force.

shabby *a* 1 wearing old, worn
out clothes 2 well worn 3
mean; squalid 4 shameful; *n*
-iness.

shack *n* hut; shanty; *phr v*
shack up *sl* live together as
if married.

shackle *n* strong metal link; *pl*
-s fetters; chains; *v* fasten
with shackles; *fig* hamper.

shad *n* edible marine fish of
herring family.

shade *n* 1 partial darkness;
shadow 2 depth of colour 3
something which gives
shelter, protection from
light 4 spirit, ghost 5 slight
amount, degree; *idm* **put in
the shade** outshine; cause to
seem inferior; *pl* **-s** *coll*
sunglasses; *idm* **shades of**
a reminder of; *v* 1 darken;
screen from light 2 represent
light and shade in drawing;
a **shady** 1 affording,
standing in shade 2 *coll*
disreputable.

shadow *n* 1 patch of shade 2
person who follows closely 3
phantom 4 indistinct,
imperfect image 5 very
slight amount or degree; *v* 1
cast shadow over 2 follow
closely, *esp* as detective or
bodyguard; *v* **s.-box** practise
movements of boxing
without an opponent
(*n* **-ing**); *a* **shadowy**
unsubstantial; dim.

shaft *n* 1 handle; stem 2 arrow
3 beam (of light) 4 vertical

opening to mine etc **5** ventilating channel **6** pl **-s** poles between which horse is harnessed **7** revolving rod transmitting power.

shag[1] n **1** long-napped cloth **2** fine-cut tobacco; a **shaggy** rough; unkempt (n **-iness**); n **shaggy-dog story** long rambling joke with pointless ending.

shag[2] n small crested cormorant.

shagpile n (of carpet) long soft pile.

shagreen n kind of untanned leather; sharkskin.

Shah n former ruler of Persia.

shake v **shaking, shook, shaken. 1** tremble; vibrate **2** totter **3** agitate **4** cause emotional shock to **5** make insecure; (pt **shook,** pp **shaken**) idm **shake hands (with sb)** grasp sb's right hand in greeting; idm **shake (hands) on it** join right hands in agreement with sb; phr vs **shake down 1** sleep in improvised bedding **2** settle down **3** US coll search thoroughly **4** US coll extort money from (n **shakedown 1** extortion **2** shakeout); **shake off 1** elude **2** get rid of **3** remove by shaking; **shake out 1** open out by shaking **2** dispose of unprofitable elements (n **shakeout** process of firms going out of business in a recession); **shake up 1** mix by shaking **2** rouse from apathy **3** reorganize

fundamentally (n **shake-up**); ns **shaker** container for shaking (eg cocktail); pl **shakes** coll shaking of body through fear, disease etc (idm **in two shakes** very soon; idm **no great shakes** not much good); a **shaky** insecure; unsteady.

shale n clay rock formation, which flakes easily.

shall v aux used to denote promise, obligation, intention, command, futurity; pt **should**; no pp.

shallot n kind of onion.

shallow a **1** not deep **2** (of thought, feeling etc) superficial; trivial; n esp pl shallow place in body of water.

sham n imposture; counterfeit, faked article; imitation; v pretend; imitate.

shamble v walk with stumbling, shuffling gait.

shambles n pl **1** slaughter-house; butcher's stall **2** fig place of bloodshed, carnage **3** coll muddle.

shambolic a Brit coll totally disorganized.

shame n **1** emotion of regret and contrition, caused by consciousness of guilt, dishonour etc **2** disgrace **3** coll unfair happening; hard luck; v **1** make ashamed **2** bring shame, disgrace on; as **shame-faced** ashamed of oneself; **shameful** outrageous; disgraceful; **shameless 1** impudent; brazen **2** immodest.

shammy n coll chamois-leather (also **shammy leather**).

shampoo v wash (hair) with shampoo; wash carpet, car etc with special preparations; n special preparation for washing hair, carpet, etc.

shamrock n trefoil plant, probably wood-sorrel, taken as national emblem of Ireland.

shandy n beer mixed with lemonade or ginger-beer.

shank n **1** lower leg; shin **2** handle; shaft; stem.

shank's pony a walking.

shan't contracted form of shall not.

shantung n tussore silk; natural Chinese silk.

shanty[1] n small hut; temporary wooden building.

shanty[2], **chanty** n sailor's song.

shantytown n poor residential area consisting of rough improvised huts.

shape n external form or appearance; pattern, mould; v form, fashion; assume shape; as **shapely** well proportioned; **shapeless**.

shard n broken fragment of pottery.

share[1] n **1** portion **2** part played in action **3** one of equal portions into which capital of joint-stock company is divided; v give, allot, take a share; n **shareholder**.

share[2] n blade of plough.

sharecropper n US farmer

paying part of rent in produce.

shark n one of large group of voracious sea-fishes; fig rapacious, grasping swindler.

sharp a 1 having keen edge, piercing point 2 clearly seen 3 intense 4 shrill 5 alert; brisk 6 clever but dishonest; n mus note raised semitone in pitch; v **sharpen** whet edge or point; fig make keen; ns **sharp end** area where most difficulty is found; ns **sharper** one who cheats, esp at cards; **sharpness, s. practice** methods that are dishonest without being illegal; as **sharp-set** hungry; **sharp-witted** very quick and intelligent; n **sharpshooter** skilled marksman.

shatter v break in fragments; smash; fig cause to crumble.

shave v shaving, shaved, shaved or shaven. cut off (hair) with razor; pare; graze; n 1 act of shaving 2 fig narrow escape; ns **shaver** 1 person or thing that shaves 2 coll youngster, esp young boy; **shaving** thin slice, esp of wood.

Shavian a after, in manner of George Bernard Shaw.

shawl n large square of fabric worn round shoulders, or for wrapping babies in.

she fem nom pron (3rd pers sing) female person etc just referred to; a female.

sheaf n bundle of things tied together esp cut corn stalks; pl **sheaves**.

shear v shearing, sheared, sheared or shorn. 1 clip, remove (fleece) from 2 cut off by one stroke; n pl **shears** large cutting implement with blades like scissors; n **shearer** one who shears, esp sheep.

sheath n 1 close-fitting cover (eg for sharp weapon) 2 condom; v **sheathe** cover with sheath.

shebang n idm **the whole shebang** coll everything.

shed[1] n wooden hut; outhouse; shelter for cattle, tools etc.

shed[2] v 1 cast off; emit; moult 2 cause to flow; pt, pp **shed**; idm **shed blood** cause death or injury; idm **shed/cast/throw light on** help to explain.

she'd contracted form of 1 she had 2 she would.

sheen n gloss; lustre; a **sheeny**.

sheep n pl **sheep.** ruminant mammal with woolly coat and edible flesh; a **sheepish** bashful; ns **sheepcote** shelter for sheep; **s.-dip** liquid insecticide used to preserve wool and kill vermin.

sheer a 1 clear; unmixed 2 perpendicular 3 (of fabric) transparent; phr v **sheer away/off** turn suddenly in another direction.

sheet n 1 large piece of fabric used to cover bed 2 broad, piece of any thin material 3 thin flat piece of metal 4 rope fastened to sail; n **s.-anchor** 1 large emergency anchor 2 fig person, thing which can be relied on; n **sheeting** (material for making) sheets.

sheikh n Arab chieftain; Muslim title of respect.

shelf n 1 horizontal projecting board on wall etc 2 horizontal ledge of rock etc 3 reef; pl **shelves**; idm **on the shelf** 1 left aside as no longer useful 2 beyond the age when one is likely to get married; n **s.-life** length of time a product can remain on sale before it deteriorates.

shell n 1 hard outer covering of animal or vegetable object 2 explosive projectile 3 framework 4 ruined building with only walls standing; n idm **go into/come out of one's shell** behave/stop behaving in a shy, retiring manner; v 1 remove shell from (nut, pea etc) 2 bombard with shells; phr v **shell out** coll pay out, esp unwillingly; n **shellfish** edible marine mollusc or crustacean; n **shell-shock** functional nervous disorder, caused by experience of bursting shells etc (a **-ed** 1 suffering from this 2 fig dazed).

she'll contracted form of she will.

shellac n coloured resin used in varnishes, sealing wax etc; v coat with shellac.

shelter n protection; cover; screen; place of refuge; v 1 give, afford cover to; protect 2 seek safety.

shelve v 1 put on shelves 2 fig postpone; abandon 3 slope gently.

shelves pl of **shelf**.

shelving n (structure of) shelves; a sloping.

shenanigans n pl coll 1 mischief 2 deception.

shepherd n one who tends sheep; fig minister of religion; **the Good S.** Christ; fem **shepherdess**; n **shepherd's pie** baked dish of minced meat covered with mashed potato (also **cottage pie**).

sherbet n Eastern drink of fruit juice etc; effervescent drink; powder for making this.

sherd = **shard**.

sheriff n 1 county official (formerly representing Crown) 2 chief judge of Scottish county 3 (in USA) chief officer enforcing law, order in county.

Sherpa n member of Tibetan people noted as mountaineers.

sherry n type of Spanish wine.

she's contracted form of she is.

shield n piece of protective armour carried on arm; that which serves as protection or defence; v protect; guard; screen.

shift v 1 (cause to) change

position 2 remove 3 coll move fast; idm **shift for oneself** look after oneself; idm **shift one's ground** change basis of argument; n 1 change in position or direction 2 (period of work allocated to) team of workers interchanging with other teams 3 trick for avoiding a problem 4 woman's straight narrow dress; ns **s. key** typewriter key giving access to upper case letters; **s. stick** US gear level; a **shiftless** lazy (n -ness); **shifty** evasive, dishonest; furtive.

Shiite n Muslim follower of Ali.

shilling n former British silver coin worth 12 old pence or 5 new (decimal) pence.

shilly-shally n indecision; needless delay; v hesitate; waver.

shimmer v shine with faint light; n faint, tremulous light; glimmer.

shin n front of lower leg; v **shinning, shinned.** climb, swarm up by using legs and arms.

shindy, shindig n 1 coll noisy party 2 disturbance.

shine v 1 emit, reflect light 2 sparkle 3 excel 4 show great intelligence; pt, pp **shone**; v polish; brilliance; idm **take a shine to** coll begin to like; a **shiny**.

shingle[1] n 1 wooden tile for roofing, outside walls etc 2

woman's short hair-style; v 1 cover with shingles 2 cut hair in shingle.

shingle[2] n coarse rounded stones, pebbles found on seashore.

shingles n acute inflammatory disease of nerve endings.

Shinto n national religion of Japan.

shinty n game like hockey.

ship n large sea-going vessel; v **shipping, shipped. 1** send (goods etc) by ship 2 embark, serve in ship; idm **when one's ship comes home** when one becomes rich and successful; v **send by ship**; idm **ship oars** remove oars from water; idm **ship water** let in water over the side; idm **on shipboard** on board ship; ns **s. biscuit** hard coarse biscuit; **shipper** person sending shipment; **shipping** 1 ships 2 transporting by ship; **shipmate** sb travelling/working on same ship; **shipment** (act of sending) cargo; **shipwreck** destruction of ship by storm, collision etc (a -ed); **shipwright** builder of ships; **shipyard** place where ships are built; a **shipshape** in good order.

shire n county pl rural counties of England.

shirk v evade, refuse to face (danger, duty etc); n **shirker.**

shirt n sleeved garment, worn

under jacket.

shirty *a coll* angry.

shish kebab *n* pieces of meat cooked on skewers.

shiver *v* splinter, break in pieces.

shiver *v* tremble, shake with cold or fear; *n* shudder, quivering movement; *a* **shivery** inclined to shiver.

shoal *n* 1 large mass of fish swimming together 2 submerged sandbank; *v* 1 form shoal 2 become shallow.

shock¹ *n* 1 violent jolt, collision 2 feeling of horror, surprise, disgust etc 3 that which causes such feeling 4 discharge of electric current through body 5 upset of nervous system and vital functions of body following accident, operation etc; *v* cause, produce shock; *ns* **s. absorber** device fitted to vehicle to reduce effects of jolting and vibration; **s. therapy** method of treating mental illness by electric shocks, drugs etc; **s.-troops** troops trained for assault tasks; **s. wave** 1 air pressure wave in wake of ultrasonic aircraft 2 *fig* public reaction to spread of bad news; *n* **shocker** *coll* sensational novel, film etc; *a* **shocking** 1 distressing 2 disgusting (*adv* **-ly**) 3 *coll* very bad.

shock² *n* 1 group, pile of sheaves of corn 2 mass of hair.

shoddy *n* cheap material

made of waste or old woollen cloth; anything made of cheap inferior material; cheap and nasty.

shoe *n* 1 covering for foot 2 metal rim, or plate, nailed to hoof of horse 3 part of brake which presses on rim of wheel; *v* protect, furnish with shoes; *pt*, *pp* **shod**; *ns* **shoelace** string for securing shoe; **shoestring** *idm* **on a shoestring** with very little money.

shone *pt*, *pp* of **shine**.

shoo *interj* used, *esp* to animals go away.

shook *pt* of **shake**.

shoot *v* 1 move suddenly and rapidly; dart 2 fire (missile) 3 kill or wound with bullet, arrow etc 4 project, hurl rapidly 5 take (pictures) with movie or video camera 6 *football* kick directly towards goal; *idm* **shoot one's mouth off** *coll* talk indiscreetly; *idm* **shoot be/get shot of** *coll* be/get rid of; *phr vs* **shoot down** 1 cause to fall by shooting 2 *fig* discredit; **shoot up** 1 grow rapidly 2 wound by shooting 3 *sl* inject (drug) into vein; *n* 1 act of shooting 2 sprout 3 shooting-party; *idm* **the whole (bang) shoot** *coll* everything; *a*, *n* **-ing** (*ns* **s.-gallery** enclosed space where one can practise shooting at targets; **s. star** burning meteor seen as bright streak in sky (*also* **falling star**);

s.-stick pointed stick with folding handle to make small improvised seat.

shop *n* 1 place where goods are retailed 2 workshop 3 *fig* one's business etc; *idm* **talk shop** discuss one's work on a social occasion; *v* **shopping, shopped.** 1 visit shops to buy goods; 2 *sl* betray; *phr v* **shop around** compare goods and prices in shops before buying; *ns* **s.-assistant** person who serves in shop; **s.-floor** 1 production area in factory 2 workers; shopkeeper owner of small shop; shopper; **shopping** 1 act of buying 2 goods bought; **s.-steward** trade union elected representative of workers; *v* **shoplift** steal from shop (*ns* **-er**, **-ing**); *a* **shop-soiled** dirty or slightly damaged from being kept in shop for a long time.

shore *n* land at edge of sea or lake.

short *a* 1 brief; not tall; scanty 2 concise 3 abrupt 4 deficient; reduced 5 friable; *idm* **short of** 1 lacking in; having insufficient of 2 failing to reach; *idm* **be short with** be impatient with; *idm* **give short shrift to** pass over quickly without fair consideration; *adv* **stop short** stop suddenly; *n* 1 *elec* **short circuit** 2 *coll* strong alcoholic drink; *pl* **-s** 1 short trousers 2 US short underpants; as **s.-haul** (of air flight) over a quite short distance; **s.-lived** not lasting long; **s.-range** covering a short distance or time; **s.-sighted 1** not able to see distant objects clearly **2** not thinking of the future (adv -ly; n -ness); **s.-term** for the near future only; v **s.-change 1** give back less than the correct amount **2** fig treat unfairly; ns **shortage** lack; **shortbread** crumbly sweet biscuit; **s. circuit** elec bypassing of normal circuit through faulty insulation or loose connection (v **s.-circuit**; also fig); **shortcoming** failing; **s. cut** quick way; **shortfall** deficit; **shorthand** system for quick writing; **s.-list** Brit preliminary selection of applicants from whom an appointment for a post is to be made (v select for such a list); **short-term** a relating to the immediate future; **short-termism** planning based only on short-term benefits; **s. wave** radio broadcasting on waves of under 60 m; adv **shortly 1** soon **2** briefly.

shot[1] pt, pp of **shoot**.

shot[2] a woven so as to change colour, according to angle of light.

shot[3] n **1** small lead pellet in cartridge **2** act of firing **3** noise of this **4** attempt; try **5** sl injection, injected dose, esp of drug; **big s.** important

person; **s. in the dark** random guess.

should modal v (pt or conditional of **shall**) **1** ought to **2** were to **3** 1st person was going to; neg **should not** (contracted form **shouldn't**).

shoulder n **1** part of body to which arm or foreleg is attached **2** edge of land bordering road; v put on one's shoulder; fig undertake responsibility for; **shoulder-blade** shoulder bone.

shout n loud outcry; v utter with loud voice.

shove v, n push.

shovel n broad spade, used for lifting earth etc; v lift, move with shovel.

show v **showing, showed, shown** or **showed. 1** expose to view **2** demonstrate **3** guide **4** exhibit **5** appear; phr v **show off 1** show to best effect **2** try to impress others by talk or behaviour (n **show-off** person who does this); **show up 1** arrive **2** embarrass **3** reveal the bad side of; n **1** performance; entertainment **2** display **3** ostentation **4** indication **5** effort; ns **s. business** work of people in theatre, cinema etc; **s.-case** set of shelves in glass case for displaying articles; **s.-down** final settlement of a dispute; **showgirl** girl who sings and dances in musicals; **s. jumping** sport in which horses are ridden to jump

over obstacles; **showing 1** act of showing **2** proof of quality; **showman 1** organizer of public entertainments **2** person skilled in self-promotion (n **-ship**); **s.-piece** excellent example of sth; a **showy** ostentatious; (too) bright etc (adv -ily; n -iness); make display of one's attainments, abilities etc; **s. up** expose, reveal bad side of.

showbiz n coll show business.

shower n **1** short fall of rain **2** copious discharge (of missiles) **3** shower-bath; v **1** fall as shower **2** give out abundantly **3** take shower; **s.-bath** ablutionary device where water falls in shower from overhead; a **-y** with frequent rain-showers.

shown pt, pp of **show**.

shrank pt of **shrink**.

shrapnel n shell filled with bullets or pieces of metal which scatter on bursting; piece of such metal.

shred n tattered fragment; strip; v **shredding, shredded.** tear into shreds.

shrew n mouselike carnivorous mammal; bad tempered woman; a **-ish** nagging.

shrewd a astute; sharp-witted; piercing; n **-ness.**

shriek v, n screech; scream.

shrike n butcher-bird, bird of prey.

shrill a piercing, high-pitched in tone.

shrimp n small edible, long-tailed crustacean; fig small person; v fish for, catch shrimps.

shrine n sacred place, chapel etc, associated with saint; casket containing holy relics; fig something held sacred in memory; v **enshrine**.

shrink v **shrinking, shrank** or **shrunk, shrunk** or **shrunken. 1** contract; diminish **2** recoil; retreat; flinch; pt **shrank;** phr v **shrink away/back (from) 1** flinch **2** retreat (from); **shrink from** doing be reluctant to do; n coll psychiatrist or psychoanalyst; v **s.-wrap** wrap in tight-fitting plastic film to exclude air; ns **shrinkage** act of or degree of shrinking; **shrinking violet** timid, shy person.

shrive n give absolution to; pt **shrove;** pp **shriven.**

shrivel v **shrivelling, shrivelled.** curl, roll up; wither.

shroud n cloth wound round corpse; fig covering; pl ropes from masthead; v wrap in shroud; hide, cover, veil.

Shrovetide n three days before Lent; **Shrove Tuesday** day before Ash Wednesday.

shrub[1] n low-growing bushy, woody plant; n **shrubbery** plantation of shrubs.

shrub[2] n drink of sweetened fruit juice with rum.

shrug v **shrugging, shrugged.** lift and draw up shoulders slightly, as sign of doubt etc;

phr v **shrug off** make light of; n shrugging.

shrunk(en) a contracted; shrivelled; reduced.

shucks interj US coll expressing regret.

shudder v quake, tremble violently; feel aversion, be disgusted at; n shuddering.

shuffle v **1** move feet without lifting them **2** speak, act evasively **3** mix cards up; n shuffling; n **shuffler.**

shufti n dated Brit coll look.

shun v **shunning, shunned.** avoid; keep clear of.

shunt v turn, switch (train) to side line; fig push to one side.

shush interj requesting silence.

shut v close; lock up; imprison; exclude; pt, pp **shut;** n **shutter 1** hinged window screen **2** device in camera for screening lens.

shut-eye n coll sleep.

shuttle n **1** weaver's instrument for carrying weft **2** sliding thread holder in sewing machine; v move regularly back and forwards between two places; ns **s. diplomacy** international negotiation through diplomats who travel back and forth; **s. service** regular transport service back and forth between two places.

shuttle-cock n feathered, weighted cork, used in badminton or battledore.

shy[1] a **shyer, shyest. 1** timid **2** reserved **3** easily frightened; phr vs **shy at** turn away in

fear; **shy away from** avoid.

shy[2] n v **shying, shied.** coll fling, throw; n act of throwing; pl **shies.**

shyster n US coll unscrupulous person, esp lawyer.

Siamese n pl, a (people) of Thailand; ns **S. cat** cat with short pale brown fur and blue eyes; **S. twin** either of two twins whose bodies are joined at birth.

sibilant n, a (consonant) uttered with hissing sound.

sibling n brother or sister.

sibyl n **1** wise woman; soothsayer **2** witch; a **sibylline** oracular.

sic adv Latin thus (indicating that previous word is intended as written).

sick a **1** ill **2** fig (of humour) macabre; idm **be sick 1** be unwell **2** vomit; idm **be sick (to death) of** be angry, fed up disgusted with; idm **feel sick/want to be sick** suffer from nausea; idm coll **make sb sick** disgust sb; idm **sick as a parrot** Brit coll disgusted; idm **sick at heart** very unhappy; phr v **sick up** vomit; n **1** vomit **2 the s. people** who are ill; ns **s.-bay** room for nursing those that are ill; **s.-leave** permission to be away from work because of illness; **s.-pay** money paid to employee while ill; v **sicken 1** become ill **2** disgust (a -ing; adv -ingly); a **sickly 1** often ill **2** unhealthy looking **3** showing or causing distaste (n -iness); n **sickness** illness (**s. benefit** money paid by State when illness causes long absence from work).

sickle n reaping hook; n **s.-cell anaemia** severe hereditary type of anaemia.

side n 1 external or internal surface 2 area 3 space that is to right or left 4 edge, margin 5 team 6 group 7 area between ribs and hip in human body 8 line of descent through one parent 9 sl arrogance; conceit; v support (person, party etc); idm **on the side** as additional, esp dishonest activity; phr v **side with** support; act or speak in favour of; ns **sideboard** cupboard for crockery, glasses etc (pl -s hair grown in front of man's ears; also **sideburns**); **s.-car** small passenger cabin attached to motorcycle; **s. effect** secondary effect; **s. issue** not the main issue; **sidekick** esp US coll companion or assistant; **sidelight** 1 small lamp at front of vehicle 2 additional minor fact; **sideline** 1 secondary activity 2 secondary line of goods 3 sport line marking limit of play (v put out of action; idm **on the sidelines** not directly involved) **sideshow** amusement stall at fairground or circus; **sideslip** skid; **sidesman** assistant to churchwarden; **s.-stroke** swimming stroke performed

on one side; **s.-swipe** US 1 indirect blow 2 fig critical remark; **sidewalk** US pavement; as **sidelong** directed sideways; **sidesplitting** coll very funny; advs **sideways** to the side; **sideways** moving or turned towards one side; vs **s.-track** divert sb from his/her purpose.

sidereal a relating to, measured by apparent motion of stars.

sidle v move, walk sideways in cringing, fawning manner; phr v **sidle up** walk nervously towards.

SIDS abbr sudden infant death syndrome; cot death.

siege n besieging of fort or town.

sienna n brownish-yellow earthy pigment.

sierra n Sp mountain chain with jagged ridges.

siesta n short rest, sleep in early afternoon.

sieve n framework of mesh or net for sifting; v pass through sieve, sift.

sift v pass through sieve or riddle; separate coarse from fine particles; examine carefully; sprinkle; n **sifter**.

sigh v utter long audible breath; express grief, fatigue etc by this act; **s.** for long for; lament; n act, sound of, sighing.

sight n 1 faculty of seeing; vision 2 that which is seen 3 device (on gun etc.) for helping vision 4 view; spectacle; idm **a sight for**

sore eyes sb/sth one is delighted to see; idm **be in sight of** be near to; idm **a (damn) sight** (+comp) coll very much; idm **adjust/raise/lower one's sights** be more/less ambitious; idm **set one's sights on** aim to have or do; idm **take sight** take aim; v manage to see (of distant object) (n -ing); v **s.-read** mus be able to perform at first reading (ns **-er, -ing**); ns **s.-screen** cricket moveable white screen enabling batsmen to see ball more clearly; **s.-seer/seeing** tourist visitor/visiting; as **sighted/sightless** able/unable to see.

sign n indication, token, symbol which conveys meaning; visible mark; agreed word, gesture expressing meaning; omen; v 1 write one's name on 2 ratify 3 indicate by word or gesture; phr vs **sign away** formally give up by signing document; **sign for** acknowledge receipt by signing; **sign in/out** indicate arrival/departure by signing; **sign off** 1 end letter with signature 2 stop work 3 end broadcast; **sign on** 1 register one's name for activity 2 register as unemployed 3 enlist in armed forces; **sign up** enrol; ns **s. language** method of communication by gestures, **signpost** post with signs showing direction, distance (*v* provide with/indicate with signposts).

signal *n* message conveyed to distance; indication, warning of something else; apparatus whereby message is conveyed; *v* **signalling, signalled.** make signal to; send, notify by signals; *a* remarkable; conspicuous (*adv* **-ly**); *ns* **s. box** building with control system for railway points and signals; *v* **signalize** make conspicuous.

signatory *n* representative of party or state who signs document, treaty etc.

signature *n* person's name written by himself; **s. tune** one associated with programme or performer on radio etc.

signet *n* small seal.

significant *a* meaningful; noteworthy; suggesting covert meaning; *ns* **significance** import; meaning; **signification** exact meaning or implication.

signify *v* **signifying, signified. 1** mean; imply **2** matter; be of importance.

Signor *n* title for Italian man; *fem* **Signora** (*married*) **Signorita** (*unmarried*).

Sikh *n* member of military sect in Punjab.

silence *n* absence of noise or sound; refraining from speech; *v* **1** cause to be silent **2** *fig* put to shame; *a* silent; *n* **silencer** device for reducing, muffling noise of

machinery or firearms.

silhouette *n* **1** portrait in outline or profile, cut from black paper, or done in solid black, against white background **2** outline, profile, of object seen as dark against light background; *v* show up in outline.

silica *n* hard, white mineral; *n* **silicate** salt of silicic acid; *as* **silicic** pertaining to silica; **siliceous** flinty; *n* **silicon** non-metallic element, one of principal constituents of earth's surface; *n* **s. chip** microchip of silicon used in making integrated circuit. **silicone** *n* one of various compounds of silicon and hydrocarbon, used in lubricants, polishes etc.

silk *n* fine filament produced by pupae of certain moths; thread, fabric made from this; *as* **silken** made of, like silk; **silky** glossy, fine, soft to touch; *ns* **silkiness**; **silkworm** silk-producing caterpillar.

sill *n* **1** horizontal block or slab at base of window or door **2** slab of igneous rock between sedimentary layers.

silly *a* foolish; trivial; weak-minded; *n* **s. season** summer period when newspapers have little of importance to report; *n* **silliness**.

silo *n* pit, tower for fodder or grain; *n* **silage** cattle fodder partly fermented and stored.

silt *n* mud etc deposited by

water; *v* **silt up** become choked, blocked with silt.

silvan, sylvan *a* of woods, forests; rural.

silver *n* **1** white precious metal element **2** objects made of, plated with this **3** coins of silver or similar metal; *a* **1** made of, resembling silver **2** *fig* shining; lustrous **3** (*of* sound) ringing; clear; soft; *v* coat with silver; *ns* **s. birch** birch with silvery-white bark; **s.-fish** small, flattish wingless insect found *esp* in damp, dark parts of houses; **s. paper** paper with shiny metallic coating; **s. plate** metal coated with silver (*a* **s.-plated**); **silverside** *Brit* cut of beef from top of leg; **silversmith** person making or selling articles in silver; **s. wedding** 25th anniversary of wedding; *a* **silvery**.

simian *a* of, like apes.

similar *a* like; resembling; *n* **-ity** likeness; resemblance.

simile *n* figure of speech in which one thing is directly compared to another.

similitude *n* comparison; likeness; similarity.

simmer *v* **1** boil gently; be just below boiling point **2** *coll* be in condition of suppressed rage or excitement; *n* state of simmering.

simper *v* smile affectedly; smirk; *also n*.

simple *a* **1** clear; intelligible **2** easy **3** austere **4** ingenuous; credulous; foolish **5** not complex or compound; *n*

herbal medicine;
a s.-minded showing lack of intelligence; *ns* simpleton foolish, weak-minded person; simplicity quality state of being; simple; *v* simplify make less complicated or easier *n* simplification; simplistic treating complex matter as if it were simple (*adv* -ally).

simulate *v* imitate; pretend to be, have or feel; *a* -ated artificial; *ns* -ation (s. game game in which real life activities, relationships are simulated as educational exercise); -ator device for simulating real conditions.

simultaneous *a* occurring at same time; *adv* -ly *n* -ness.

sin *n* 1 transgression of divine law, moral code 2 any offence in general; vice; iniquity; *v* sinning, sinned. be sinful; commit sin; *a* -ful *n* sinner; (*n* -ness).

since *adv* from then until now; ago; *prep* after; succeeding; *conj* because; seeing that.

sincere *a* genuine; honest; true; free from deceit or pretence; *n* sincerity.

sine *n* perpendicular drawn from one extremity of arc to diameter drawn through other extremity; ratio of this perpendicular to radius of circle.

sinecure *n* paid office or work with few or no duties.

sine die *adv* *leg* *Lat* without fixed date.

sine qua non *n* *Lat* essential thing.

sinew *n* 1 tendon 2 *pl* -s muscles 3 *fig* (of war) money and material resources; *a* sinewy muscular.

sing *v* singing, sang, sung. 1 utter musical notes 2 (*of birds*) utter natural cries 3 *fig* rejoice; *ns* singer; singing.

singe *v* singeing, singed. burn superficially; scorch; *n* slight burn.

single *a* 1 one only; not double 2 separate 3 unmarried 4 for one person 5 valid for one-way journey; *phr v* single out select for special attention; *n* 1 one-way ticket 2 *coll* record with one song on each side; *pl* -s tennis match between two players; *as* s.-breasted (of jacket) with one row of buttons; s.-handed unaided (*adv* -ly); s.-minded with one clear purpose in mind (*adv* -ly *n* -ness); *n*, *adv* s. file in a line one behind the other; *adv* -ly; *n* singleton sth without a pair.

singlet *n* undervest.

singsong *n* *Brit* informal occasion when songs are sung; *a* with repeated rising and falling intonation (*n* such speech).

singular *a* 1 of, relating to one person or thing 2 remarkable, unusual, eminent; *adv* singularly oddly; outstandingly; *n* singularity.

sinister *a* 1 evil; ominous; malevolent 2 *her* on left hand side.

sink *v* 1 be, become, submerged in liquid 2 subside; become lower (in value, degree, health etc) 3 penetrate deeply 4 excavate; *pt* sank; *pp* sunk; *phr v* sink in become fully understood; *a* -ing (s. feeling *coll* feeling of fear or helplessness; *n* kitchen basin; s. fund one formed by setting apart yearly sums of money to pay off liability.

Sino- *prefix* Chinese.

sinology *n* study of Chinese language and culture; *n* -ologist.

sinuous *a* a curving, bending; snaky, undulating; *n* sinuousity.

sinus *n* med cavity in tissue or bone, *esp* in facial bone; *n* sinusitis inflammation of nasal sinus.

sip *v* sipping, sipped. drink in very small quantities; *n* very small mouthful of liquid.

siphon *n* bent tube used for transferring liquid from one level to lower one; bottle with tap at top, through which aerated water is forced by gas pressure; *v* draw off by siphon (*occasionally* syphon.)

sir *n* term of respect for man; title of knight or baronet.

sire *n* form of address to monarch; male parent, *esp* of horse, dog; *v* beget, be sire of.

siren *n* 1 mythological sea-nymph 2 *fig* alluring woman

3 loud warning hooter or signal.

sirloin n upper part of loin of beef.

sirocco n hot Mediterranean wind.

sisal n fibre of American agave, used for rope-making.

sissy n coll effeminate boy or man.

sister n 1 daughter, woman, born of same parents 2 nun 3 nurse in charge of ward; a closely related, of same type; a -ly; n **sisterhood** community of nuns etc; **sister-in-law** sister of husband of wife; wife of brother.

sit v 1 rest on buttocks or haunches 2 take one's place in assembly 3 pose for portrait 4 fit, hang well 5 (of birds) remain on eggs 6 undergo examination; pt, pp **sat**; idm be sitting pretty coll be in a secure position idm **sit tight** remain where one is; phr vs **sit back** relax and do nothing; **sit in** occupy (premises) in protest (n **sit-in**); **sit in for** be a substitute for; **sit in on** be present at; **sit on** 1 delay action concerning 2 be a member of; **sit up** 1 raise oneself to a sitting position 2 not go to bed until late 3 fig suddenly show interest; n period of sitting; ns **sitdown** form of strike within an institution; **sitter** 1 artist's model 2 bird that does not fly away 3 baby-sitter; **sitting** 1 session

of parliament, committee etc 2 serving of meal 3 period spent in sedentary occupation, esp as model for artist, photographer etc (ns **s. duck** sb easy to take advantage of; **s. room** esp Brit living-room; **s. tenant** person who occupies rented or leased accommodation).

sitar n type of Indian lute.

sitcom n coll situation comedy.

site n ground; situation; local position.

situate(d) a placed, having particular site; n **situation** place; employment; state of affairs; in a **s. comedy** TV or radio series of programmes with characters that appear in different comic situations.

six n, pron, dey cardinal number one above five; idm **at sixes and sevens** coll confused; n **s.-shooter** revolver with six bullet chambers; a, n, det **sixth** ordinal number after fifth (ns **s. form** Brit years 12 and 13 in secondary school; **s. former** member of this; **s. sense** facility for knowing things without evidence from any of the five senses; n **sixpence** silver coin worth six old pennies, two and half decimal pence; ns, as **sixteen** six and ten; **sixteenth**; **sixty** six times ten; **sixtieth**.

size[1] n standard measure of length, weight, quantity; magnitude; fixed dimension; v arrange according to size;

idm **cut sb down to size** make sb realize he/she is not as good as he/she thought; phr v **size up** assess and form opinion of.

size[2] n thin glue used to glaze and stiffen paper, etc; v apply size to.

sizzle v make hissing noise; n hissing, spluttering sound, esp in frying.

skate[1] n edible flat fish of ray family.

skate[2] n 1 one of pair of steel blades, attached to boot, for gliding over ice 2 roller-skate; v move on skates; n **skateboard** narrow board on wheels for standing and riding on (ns **-er, -ing**).

skedaddle v sl run away, clear out; n hasty flight.

skein n 1 quantity of coiled and knotted yarn (of cotton, silk etc) 2 flock of wild geese in flight.

skeleton n 1 bony framework of human or animal body; such bones preserved in their natural position 2 coll very thin person 3 outline; draft 4 framework; idm **skeleton in the cupboard** embarrassing fact from one's past that one prefers to keep secret; ns **s. key** that opens many different locks; **s. service** minimal service much reduced from normal; a **skeletal** pertaining to, attached to skeleton.

skeptic n US = sceptic.

sketch n 1 rough drawing serving as study for finished

picture 2 rough draft 3 short play; *v* make sketch of; *a* **sketchy** depicted in outline; unfinished, inadequate.

skew-whiff *a coll* askew.

skewer *n* thin pointed pin of wood or metal for keeping piece of meat in shape; *v* pierce or fasten with skewer.

ski *n* long wooden runner, fastened to foot, for moving over snow; *v* **skiing, skied.** use skis for travelling over snow; *n* **skier** one who skis *ns* **ski-bob** cycle-like vehicle for racing on snow (*ns* **-bobber, -bobbing**); **ski-lift** apparatus for carrying skiers uphill; **ski run** slope for skiing on.

skid *n* drag fixed to wheel, to reduce speed; *v* **skidding, skidded.** (of vehicle) slip sideways out of control *fig* slip and fall; *ns* **skid-lid** crash-helmet; **skid-pan** slippery area where motorists may practise skid-control.

skid row *n US* slum area frequented by vagrants.

skiff *n* small rowing, sculling boat.

skiffle *n* jazz folk-music; *n* **s. group** musical group using guitar and improvised percussion instruments.

skill *n* deftness, manual dexterity; cleverness; ingenuity; *as* **skilled** skilful; expert; trained in some specific trade etc; **skilful** clever, dextrous.

skillet *n US* frying pan.

skim *v* **skimming, skimmed. 1** remove scum, fat or other substance from surface of liquid 2 pass lightly over *fig* read through (book) rapidly and perfunctorily.

skimmed milk *n* milk from which the cream has been removed.

skimp *v* stint; supply in too small an amount; do carelessly; *a* **skimpy** meagre; fitting too tightly.

skin *n* outer covering of anything, as of human or animal body, fruit etc; *v* **skinning, skinned.** remove skin of; *idm* **by the skin of one's teeth** only just; *n* **skinner** dealer in pelts and hides; *as* **skinny** thin; **s.-tight** very close fitting; *ns* **s.-flint** miser; **s.-diving** under-water swimming with oxygen cylinders but no diving suit.

skint *a Brit coll* with no money.

skip *v* **skipping, skipped. 1** leap lightly; gambol 2 jump on spot, while rope passes underneath one 3 *coll* decamp; bolt 4 omit, pass rapidly over in reading.

skipper *n* captain of ship; *coll* captain of team; *v* act as skipper.

skirl *n* shrill, piercing sound of bagpipes.

skirmish *n* fight between small groups of soldiers etc; *fig* brief, slight contest or argument; *v* engage in skirmish.

skirt *n* 1 woman's garment hanging below waist 2 flank of beef 3 outlying part; *v* border, go round; *n* **-ing** board running round bottom of walls of room.

skit *n* light, satirical, humorous sketch or burlesque; *a* **skittish** playful; lively; frolicsome.

skitter *v* move rapidly, lightly.

skittles *n pl* game of ninepins.

skive *Brit coll* avoid work.

skivvy *n* low-paid female servant; *v* work in this way.

skulduggery *n coll* trickery; devious behaviour.

skulk *v* lurk in concealment; sneak away; *n* **-er.**

skull *n* bony case containing brain of animals; *n* **s. cap** close-fitting cap.

skunk *n* 1 small, carnivorous N American mammal emitting offensive odour when attacked 2 *coll* contemptible person.

sky *n* upper part of earth's atmosphere; *fig* heaven *pl* **skies;** *v* throw, hit (ball) high up; *a* of a colour of blue, cloudless sky; *ns* **s.-diving** sport involving free-fall from aircraft before using parachute (**s.-diver** person doing this); **skylight** window in roof or ceiling; **skyline** line in sky formed by buildings, trees etc on horizon; **skyscraper** very tall city building; *as, advs* **s.-high** very high; **skyward(s)** upward(s); *vs* **skyjack** hijack aircraft;

skylark play around; frolic; **s.-rocket** (of prices) rise very sharply.

skylark n common bird, noted for its song and soaring flight.

slab n thick, squarish piece.

slack[1] a 1 sluggish; loose; relaxed 2 lazy 3 not busy; **s. water** period when tide is neither rising nor falling; n anything left slack or loose; n pl **slacks** loose sports trousers; v 1 sag 2 be idle, lazy; v **slacken** abate; diminish; reduce (speed).

slack[2], **slag** n dross or refuse of coal or smelted metal.

slain pp of **slay**.

slake v 1 quench; allay 2 mix (lime) with water.

slalom n 1 ski-race down zig-zag course 2 any similar race, eg with canoes.

slam v **slamming, slammed.** shut, close with bang; put down noisily; n loud bang or noise; **grand s.** cards taking of all tricks in one deal.

slander n leg malicious, false spoken statement; v utter such statement; a **-ous**; n **slanderer**.

slang n colloquial word, phrase not recognized as suitable for serious usage; v scold, abuse violently.

slant v slope; incline from perpendicular; n 1 slope 2 coll point of view; adv **slantwise** obliquely.

slap v **slapping, slapped.** smack, strike smartly with

open hand; n such blow; idm **slapbang** coll exactly; as **slapdash** careless and hasty; **slaphappy** carefree and irresponsible; **s.-up** Brit coll (of meals) lavish; n **slapstick** rough knockabout farce or comedy.

slash v 1 gash; make cuts or slits in; lash violently at 2 reduce (prices) abruptly; n 1 long cut; slit 2 act of slashing.

slat n thin narrow strip of wood or metal; a **slatted**.

slate n hard, grey, shaly rock which splits easily into thin layers; piece of this used for roofing, or writing upon; idm **on the slate** on credit; v 1 cover with slates 2 US propose (for office) 3 Brit coll criticize severely (n -ing) ns **slating** rebuke, severe criticism; **slateclub** club whose members pay weekly subscriptions, which are repaid at specified time.

slattern n slut; a **slatternly** untidy, dirty, sluttish.

slaughter n 1 butchering of animals for food 2 needless killing (of humans, animals) in large numbers; v 1 kill animals for meat 2 kill needlessly, massacre; n **slaughterhouse** abattoir; place where animals are butchered for market.

slave n 1 one held in bondage to another; drudge 2 one dominated by desire,

passion or devoted to cause, principle; v work like slave; ns **s. driver** person who forces one to work hard; **slavery** bondage; serfdom; drudgery; a **slavish** servile; n **slaver** person, ship engaged in slave trade.

slaver v 1 let saliva run from mouth 2 fig flatter.

Slavic a of the Slavs (also **Slavonic**).

slay v fml or US **slaying, slew, slain.** kill; n **slayer** killer.

sleaze n dishonest or immoral behaviour, esp among public figures.

sleazy a coll sordid; dirty-looking.

sledge, sled n vehicle on runners, for sliding on snow; toboggan; v travel, convey by sledge.

sledge-hammer n heavy hammer with long handle.

sleek a glossy; smooth; oily.

sleep n 1 natural unconscious state recurring regularly in man and animals; period during which one sleeps 2 fig lethargy 3 death; v 1 slumber; take rest by sleeping 2 coll provide beds for; pt, pp **slept**; idm **lose no sleep over** not worry about; idm **put to sleep** kill by merciful means; v 1 take rest by sleep 2 provide sleeping accommodation for; pt, pp **slept**; **sleep in** remain in bed late in the morning; **sleep off** dispose of (bad effect of sth) by sleep;

sleep on sth postpone decision on sth till next day; **sleepover** n children's party at which guests stay the night; n **sleeper 1** person who sleeps **2** wooden beam supporting railway track; a **sleeping** (ns **s. bag** bag for sleeping in, usu lined for warmth; **s. car** railway coach with sleeping accommodation; **s. partner** non-working partner with shares in a company; **s.-pill** pill with drug to make sleep easier; **s. policeman** coll road hump for reducing speed of traffic; **s. sickness** serious tropical disease causing great lethargy); a **sleepy** (adv -**ily** n -**iness**).

sleet n mixture of rain and snow falling together; v fall as sleet.

sleeve n **1** part of garment which covers arm **2** tubular case or cover enclosing smaller tube or rod; decorative outer cover of book, record etc; idm **up one's sleeve** in reserve (secretly); v furnish with sleeves; ns **sleeve-link**, **cuff-link**; **sleeve valve** sliding valve; as **sleeved**; **sleeveless**.

sleigh n sledge.

sleight n dexterity; cunning; **s. of hand** conjuring trick, esp by substitution.

slender a thin; slight; scanty.

slept pt, pp of **sleep**.

sleuth n detective; v track by scent; n **sleuth hound** bloodhound.

slew[1] pt of **slay**.

slew[2] v swing round suddenly, out of control.

slice n **1** flat, thin piece; cross-section **2** broad serving implement **3** slicing stroke, esp in ball games; v **1** cut in slices **3** hit ball so that it turns away.

slick a **1** smooth; sleek **2** coll glib; persuasive but not always honest (adv -**ly**; n -**ness**); v make smooth or glossy; n area of split oil floating on water; n **slicker 1** slick person **2** US raincoat.

slide v **1** slip, glide easily, down or off **2** fig pass over lightly **3** propel, push, thrust along slowly; pt, pp **slid**; idm **let sth slide** coll let unsatisfactory situation remain or deteriorate even further; n **1** act of sliding **2** strip of smooth ice **3** shoot **4** frame of glass or card holding picture for projection, or object to be examined under microscope; n **s.-rule** mathematical instrument for rapid calculations; **sliding-scale** schedule for raising, lowering taxes, wages etc. in agreement with fluctuations in cost of living etc.

slight a **1** slim; slender **2** mild; trivial; idm (**not**) **in the slightest** (not) at all; v **slimming**. **slimmed**. neglect; disregard; n act, utterance of disrespect; humiliation.

slim a slender; slight; reverse

of stout, thick; v make thin; reduce weight by diet etc; adv -**ly** n -**ness**; n, a **slimming** reducing one's weight (**s. exercises** exercises to promote this); n **slimmer** person doing this (also comp a less fat); a **slimline 1** giving slim appearance **2** not fattening.

slime n **1** soft wet dirt; liquid mud **2** moisture secreted by snails etc; a **slimy 1** like smeared with, slime, slime **2** fig fawning; servile.

sling n **1** loop of leather etc for hurling stones or other missiles **2** strip of cloth supporting injured limb **3** rope, band etc for hoisting weights; v throw, suspend by sling; pt, pp **slung**; v idm **sling one's hook** Brit sl go away; idm **sling mud at** say damaging or libellous things about; phr v **sling out** throw out forcibly; n **s.-shot** US catapult.

slink v move furtively, secretively; pt, pp **slunk**.

slip v **slipping, slipped. 1** slide **2** miss one's footing **3** pass rapidly **4** release (dog) **5** escape from **6** give birth to prematurely; idm **let slip 1** lose (opportunity) **2** make known by inadvertent remark; n **1** act of slipping **2** error of judgement **3** moral lapse **4** loose cover for pillow **5** petticoat **6** cutting for grafting **7** narrow strip (of paper etc) **8** thin mixture of clay and water for making pottery **9** young sole or plaice; *idm* **slip of a girl** very small, slim girl; *idm* **give sb the slip** escape from or elude sb; *ns* **s.-knot** knot that slides or comes undone easily; **s.-on** (shoe) shoe that slips on easily; **s.-over** garment that slips easily over the head; **slippage** (degree of) slipping; **slipped disc** displacement of cartilage disc between two vertebrae, *usu* causing great pain; **s.-road** access road, *eg* to motorway; **s.-stream 1** air vacuum that forms behind fast moving vehicle **2** air propelled backwards by aircraft engines; **s.-up** *coll* mistake; **slipway** hard slope for launching or beaching of ship; *as* **slippery 1** smooth and difficult to keep a firm hold of **2** elusive (*n* **-iness**); **slipshod** done without much care and attention; **slippy** fast; quick moving.

slipper *n* soft indoor shoe.

slit *v* **slitting, slit.** cut open, make incision in; *n* narrow opening, incision.

slither *v* slip and slide slowly along or down.

sliver *n* small, narrow piece, cut, torn on anything; splinter.

slob *n sl* fool, lout.

slobber *v* **1** allow saliva to run out of mouth; dribble **2** *fig* show sentimental affection for; *n* dribbling saliva; *fig* sentimentality.

sloe *n* bluish-black fruit of black-thorn; **sloe gin** liqueur of sloes steeped in gin.

slog *v* **slogging, slogged.** work hard and persistently; hit hard (*esp* at cricket).

slogan *n* catchword or phrase used in advertising etc; Highland war-cry.

sloop *n* single-masted sailing vessel; small warship.

slop *v* **slopping, slopped.** spill; be spilt; overflow; *phr v* **slop about/around 1** play around in mud, water etc **2** move about idly, purposelessly; *n pl* dirty water, liquid waste; soft food for invalids *in* **s. basin** small receptacle for dregs of tea or coffee.

slope *n* inclined direction or surface; steepness; *v* be, have inclined (in) surface; *phr v* **slope off** *Brit coll* absent oneself; leave with job incomplete.

sloppy *a* **1** wet and messy **2** careless in one's work **3** maudlin; sentimental; *adv* **-ily;** *n* **-iness.**

slosh *v* **1** (*of liquid*) move noisily; splash **2** *Brit coll* hit; *a* **-ed** *coll* drunk.

slot *n* **1** narrow slit; aperture, *esp* for insertion of coins; **2** space in programmes; *v* **slotting, slotted.** make slot(s) in; *phr v* **slot in(to)** fit neatly, closely (into).

sloth *n* **1** indolence; laziness **2** sluggish S American mammal; *a* **slothful** lazy; inactive.

slouch *n* careless, clumsy, slovenly gait; *v* walk thus; *n* **slouch hat** soft hat with turned down brim.

slough[1] *n* swamp, bog.

slough[2] *n* cast-off skin of snake; *phr v* **slough off 1** (*of snake*) shed skin **2** get rid of sth unwanted.

sloven *n* lazy, dirty and untidy person; **slovenly** *a* untidy in appearance; careless; slipshod; *n* **slovenliness.**

slow *a* **1** moving at low rate of speed; taking longer than usual; behind correct time **2** not alert; stupid; inactive; *v* reduce speed; *ns* **-ness; slowcoach** person slow in acting, thinking etc; *adv* **-ly.**

slow-worm *n* blind-worm, limbless lizard.

sludge *n* thick, greasy mud; slush; any slimy deposit.

slug *n* **1** land snail with no shell **2** small bullet for airgun etc **3** *print* line of type-metal used for spacing; **4** mouthful of alcoholic drink; *v* **slugging, slugged.** hit hard; slog; *a* **sluggish** slow; inactive; lazy; (*n* **-ness**).

sluice *n* flood-gate *coll* brisk wash with water; *v* **1** provide with sluices **2** *coll* wash down with, splash water over.

slum *n* dilapidated, squalid street or area, *usu* overcrowded; *v* **slumming, slummed.** visit slums; deliberately experience poorer conditions than usual.

slumber v sleep; *fig* lie dormant; n sleep.

slump n sudden fall in prices, value etc; v fall in price, demand; financial depression; *fig* decline in esteem.

slur v **slurring, slurred.** pass lightly over; pronounce indistinctly; *mus* sing, play legato; n act of slurring; stain; stigma.

slurp v drink noisily; n noise caused by this.

slurry n mixture of mud, clay etc with water.

slush n liquid, soft mud; melting snow; *coll* sickly sentiment; drivel; n **s. fund** money reserved secretly for dishonest use.

sly a cunning; underhand; not frank; artful; *idm* **on the sly** secretly; (*adv* **-ly** **-ness**).

smack[1] n taste, trace of; suggestion of; *phr* v **smack of** 1 taste of; 2 be suggestive of.

smack[2] n smart explosive sound (of lips); crack of whip; slap; v make such sound; *adv* 1 sudden, 2 exactly.

small a 1 little; very young 2 trivial, unimportant; petty; paltry; *ns* **smallness; small-arms** revolvers and rifles; **small** feel ashamed; *idm* **cost a small fortune** *coll* cost a lot of money; n narrow part of back; *ns* **s.-arms** revolvers and rifles; **s. beer** *coll* sb/sth of very little importance; **s. change** coins; **s. fry**

insignificant person; **s.-holding** small plot of agricultural land or farm; **s. hours** *pl* hours after midnight; **smallpox** acute infectious and contagious disease leaving scars on skin; **s. print** detailed terms of a legal contract; **s. screen** *coll* TV; **s. talk** trivial conversation used as a means of socializing; as **s.-minded** petty and mean; **s.-scale** limited in size or extent; **s.-time** unimportant; n **smallness.**

smarmy a *coll* ingratiatingly polite; flattering.

smart a 1 sharp; forcible; brisk; alert; clever 2 well-dressed; fashionable; n **s. alec** *coll* know-all; v 1 feel sore and painful 2 feel hurt, resentful; n sharp pain.

smart card n credit or debit card with built-in microprocessor to record information on transactions.

smarten v make, give spruce appearance to; a **smartly** fashionably; quickly; n **smartness.**

smash v 1 break to pieces; shatter; hit violently 2 defeat utterly; ruin, *esp* financially; n 1 violent shattering 2 bankruptcy; ruin 3 violent collision of vehicles; n **smash-hit** *coll* highly popular song, film etc; a **smashing** devastating; *coll* outstanding; delightful.

smattering n slight, superficial knowledge of subject.

smear n 1 stain, mark made by contact with oily, greasy substance 2 *coll* malicious rumour; n **s. test** for screening against cervical cancer; v mark with smear; damage by rumour.

smell v **smelling, smelt** or **smelled.** 1 perceive, inhale, emit odour 2 stink 3 *fig* track; discover; *idm* **smell a rat** *coll* suspect sth is wrong n odour; scent; act of smelling.

smelt[1] n small edible silvery fish.

smelt[2] v extract metal from ore, by heat.

smidgin n *coll* tiny amount.

smile v 1 curve, part lips in expression of pleasure, amusement 2 *fig* be favourable to; n act of smiling; facial expression showing happiness, affection, amusement.

smirch v dirty; stain; disgrace.

smirk v simper in self-satisfied manner; n conceited; knowing smile.

smite v **smiting, smote, smitten.** wound; afflict; affect strongly, *esp* with love, fear.

smith n worker in metal; n **smithy** smith's workshop; forge.

smithereens n *idm* **in(to) smithereens** in(to) tiny pieces.

smitten *pp* of **smite**; smitten (with) 1 suddenly in love (with) 2 deeply affected by.

smock n loose outer protective

garment, formerly worn by shepherds; *v* adorn with honeycomb needlework; *n* -ing.

smog *n* dense mixture of smoke and fog.

smoke *n* fine particles, emitted by burning matter; *idm* **go up in smoke** *coll* 1 be burnt to nothing 2 be a complete failure; *ns* **s.-screen** 1 smoke used to hide military operation 2 attempt to conceal one's real intentions; **s.-stack** funnel; chimney; *v* 1 emit smoke 2 inhale and expel smoke from burning tobacco 3 cure (fish etc) by exposing to wood-smoke; *phr v* **smoke out** force out of hiding (*eg* by use of smoke); *ns* **-er**, **-ing**; *a* **smoky** (*n* **-iness**).

smolder *US* = **smoulder**.

smooch *v coll* cuddle and kiss.

smooth *a* polished; even; level; calm; soothing; unruffled; *adv* **-ly**; *n* **-ness** *v* make smooth.

smorgasbord *n* Swedish buffet of savoury dishes.

smote *pt of* **smite**.

smother *v* 1 suffocate 2 cover thickly 3 suppress.

smoulder *v* burn slowly without flame.

smudge *n* smear; blur; blot; *v* make smudge.

smug *a* complacent; prudish; prim; *adv* **-ly**; *n* **-ness**.

smuggle *v* 1 import or export (goods) without payment of customs duties 2 convey secretly; *n* **smuggler**.

smut *n* 1 particle of soot, dirt, etc 2 parasitic fungus 3 obscene talk, writing etc; *a* **-ty**.

snack *n* hasty, light meal; *n* **snack-bar** bar in restaurant where snacks are served; café.

snaffle *n* light bit for horse; *v sl* steal, pinch.

snag *n* 1 tree-stump, *esp* in river bed 2 *fig* unexpected obstacle 3 run or catch in stocking.

snail *n* shell-bearing, slow-moving mollusc, leaving slimy trail; *fig* slow-moving person.

snake *n* scaly limbless reptile, serpent; *idm* **snake in the grass** false friend *a* **snaky** of, like snakes; winding; *v* move like snake; twist; wind.

snap *v* **snapping, snapped.** 1 break suddenly with sharp sound 2 open or close with sharp sound 3 speak sharply; *idm* **snap to it** *coll* move quickly into action; *idm* **snap out of it** *coll* throw off bad mood; *phr v* **snap at** 1 try to catch in the mouth by snapping one's jaws 2 speak sharply to; **snap up** seize or buy quickly; *n* 1 act or sound of snapping 2 informal photo 3 card game; *interj* *showing recognition that two things are identical*; *a* sudden (**s. judgement**); *a* **snappy** 1 hasty 2 impatient; irritable 3 *coll* stylish (*adv* **-ily**; *n* **-iness**).

snapdragon *n coll* antirrhinum.

snapper *n* tropical fish.

snare *n* device for catching birds, animals etc; *n* **s. drum** drum with snares, *ie* loose strings that produce rattling effect; *v* catch in snare.

snarl *v* growl threateningly; *phr v* **snarl up** (*n* facial expression, sound made in snarling; **snarl-up** (*n* confusion of traffic; traffic jam).

snatch *v* seize, make quick grab at; *n* 1 act of snatching 2 disconnected fragment, portion.

snazzy *a coll* stylishly attractive (*adv* **-ily**; *n* **-iness**).

sneak *v* 1 move, creep furtively 2 *sl* inform against; *n* mean, furtive person; tell-tale; *ns* **s. preview** opportunity to view before official public opening or premiere; **s. thief** thief who takes small items without using violence; *a* **sneaky** (*adv* **-ily**; *n* **-iness**).

sneer *v* smile, speak scornfully; *n* act of sneering.

sneeze *v* eject air through nostrils with sudden involuntary noise and spasm; *n* **sneezing**.

snick *n* small cut, notch; *v* cut thus.

snicker *v* laugh furtively, slyly; neigh; *n* such sound.

snide *a* implying criticism in an indirect, unpleasant way;

sneering.

sniff v inhale audibly through nose; *phr vs* **sniff out** *coll* find out (sb/sth secret); **sniff at** express scorn etc by sniffing; n **-er.**

sniffle v sniff repeatedly; n 1 slight cold 2 sniffing sound.

snigger n unpleasant surreptitious laugh; v laugh in this way.

snip v **snipping, snipped.** cut, clip with scissors, shears; n 1 short, quick cut 2 *sl* profitable bargain; n **snippet** small piece.

snipe n bird of plover family; v shoot at enemy from cover; n **sniper.**

snitch v *coll* 1 inform on 2 steal.

snivel v **snivelling, snivelled.** whine, whimper peevishly; sniff repeatedly; n **snivel.**

snob n one who pretends to be better than he is; one who puts exaggerated importance on rank, wealth etc; n **snobbery;** a **snobbish.**

snood n cover for hair.

snooker n game combining pool and pyramids played on billiard table.

snoop v *sl* pry; peer into.

snooty a *coll* showing a superior unfriendly attitude.

snooze v take short, light nap; doze; n.

snore v breathe heavily, noisily when asleep; n act, sound of snoring.

snorkel n breathing tube for underwater swimmers; v use

this.

snort v make loud noise by drawing air through nostrils; n.

snot n *sl* mucus from nose.

snotty-nosed a snooty.

snout n projecting nose of animal.

snow n 1 frozen vapour falling as flakes from sky 2 *sl* powdered cocaine; v fall as snow; *idm* **snow under** overwhelm; *ns* **snowdrift** deep mass of snow driven by wind; a **snowy** covered with snow; inclined to snow; n **snowball** snow pressed into hard ball; something growing bigger; v play with snowballs; increase in size rapidly; *ns* **snowdrop** early spring flower; **snowplough** 1 apparatus for clearing snow 2 skier's method of stopping by pointing feet inwards; **snowshoe** racquet-shaped frame attached to foot for travelling across snow.

snub v **snubbing, snubbed.** rebuff by sneering remark; slight; insult; n **snubbing;** n **snub nose** one turned up at end.

snuck *US pt, pp* of **sneak.**

snuff n powdered tobacco for sniffing up nose; v put out (candle); *idm* **snuff it** *coll* die; *phr v* **snuff out** 1 extinguish 2 put an end to.

snuffle n 1 sniffing noise; v 1 make this noise 2 talk through the nose.

snug a warm; cosy; trim; n

snuggle nestle, lie close to; cuddle.

so *adv* 1 in such manner; thus 2 to such extent; *conj* 1 therefore 2 **so (that)** in order that; *conj* **so as to** in order to; *idm* **or so** approximately; *idm* **so long!** *coll* goodbye; n **so-and-so** 1 unnamed person 2 annoying person; a **so-called** called thus, but without justification.

soak v steep; drench; wet thoroughly; *phr v* **soak up** absorb; n 1 act of soaking 2 *coll* drunkard; *as* **-ed, -ing** very wet; n soaking.

soap n compound of fatty acid and base which cleans and washes; n **s.box** improvised stand for public speaking; *idm* **get on one's soapbox** express one's opinions like a public speaker; **s. opera** serialized drama on radio, TV about everyday life; **soapstone** soft type of stone used in making ornaments; a **soapy** (n **-iness.**)

soar v fly high; *fig* rise to heights of imagination etc; n **soaring.**

sob v **sobbing, sobbed.** weep noisily; catch breath in weeping; n **sobbing;** n **sob stuff** *coll* exaggerated pathos or sentimentality.

sober a 1 temperate; moderate 2 quiet in colour 3 not drunk; v make, become sober; n **sobriety** state of being sober.

soccer n coll abbr Association football.

sociable a companionable; affable; n **-ability**.

social a relating to society; gregarious; sociable; ns **s. climber** person seeking acceptance by higher social class; **s. democrat** person believing in gradual move towards socialism by democratic means (n **s. democracy** this person's theory); **s. science** one of group of subjects dealing with study of society; **s. security** state money paid to unemployed, sick and other people in need; **s. service** local services dealing with public welfare, health, education etc; **s. work** work in giving aid to people in trouble or need (n **-er**); n **socialite** member of high society.

socialism n political movement advocating public ownership of means of production, distribution and exchange; n **-ist** member of socialist party.

socialize v 1 mix with other people socially (n **-izer**) 2 adapt to society (n **-ization**).

society n 1 organized community of mutually dependent individuals 2 companionship 3 association; club; group 4 fashionable people

collectively.

socioeconomic a relating to both social and economic aspects.

sociology n social science.

sociopath n psychopath.

sock[1] n short stocking; inner sole of shoe; idm **pull one's socks up** coll start to do better; idm **sock it to them** coll speak forcefully.

sock[2] v coll hit; thrash.

socket n hollow, recess into which something fits.

sod n flat piece of turf; n **Sod's law** coll apparent tendency for things to turn out always to one's disadvantage.

soda n any of various sodium compounds; coll soda-water; n **s. fountain** US place where soft drinks are served, n **soda-water** aerated water.

sodden a 1 soaked; saturated 2 fig heavy; stupid.

sodium n metallic alkaline element n **s. bicarbonate** white alkaline salt used in baking powder.

sofa n long padded couch with back and arms.

soft a 1 not hard; smooth 2 flabby; gentle 3 not loud 4 feeble-minded; (adv **-ly**; n **-ness**); **s. drink** non-alcoholic drink; ns **s. copy** comput information in memory or on screen; **s. currency** econ currency not convertible into gold etc; **s. landing** spacecraft landing without damage; **s. option**

easier course of action; **s. palate** soft rear part of roof of mouth; **s. pedal** piano pedal for muting sound of notes (v **s.-pedal**) coll make seem of less importance); **s. sell** using gentle persuasion to sell; **s. soap** coll flattery (v **s.-soap**); **s. spot** fond feeling; **s. target** mil personnel unarmed or without power of retaliation; **s. touch** person easy to persuade or deceive; as **s.-hearted** kind; easily persuaded to sympathize (adv **-ly** n **-ness**); **s.-spoken** with gentle voice; v **soften** make soft; phr v **soften up** 1 weaken 2 render unable to resist; ns **-ener**, **-ening**.

softball n game similar to baseball.

softie, softy n physically weak or sentimental person.

software n comput programs that operate computer.

softwood n wood from coniferous trees that cuts easily.

soggy a soaked with water, sodden.

soigné a Fr elegant.

soil[1] n surface earth; land; country.

soil[2] v make, become dirty; tarnish, sully.

soirée n Fr evening party, esp with entertainment.

sojourn v stay for a time; n short visit; n **sojourner**.

solace n consolation; v comfort

in distress.

solar *a* pertaining to sun; *ns* **s. cell** device for converting sunlight into electrical energy; **s. panel** unit composed of several solar cells; *v* **solarize** expose to action of sun; *ns* **solar plexus** network of nerves in pit of stomach; **solar system** system of planets, comets, asteroids etc which revolve round the sun.

solarium *n* 1 glass-walled place giving maximum exposure to sunlight 2 bed with lamps for giving artificial sun-tan (*pl* **-ia** *or* **-iums**).

sold *pt, pp of* **sell**.

solder *n* fusible metal alloy used for joining metal; *v* join with this; *n* **soldering-iron**.

soldier *n* one enlisted in army; *v* serve as soldier; *n* **soldiery** soldiers collectively.

sole[1] *n* 1 under surface of foot; under part of shoe etc 2 edible marine flat-fish; *v* (*of shoes etc*) fit with (new) sole.

sole[2] *a* one and only; single.

solecism *n* 1 grammatical error 2 social mistake.

solemn *a* serious; formal; grave; deliberate; *n* **solemnity**; *v* **solemnize** perform with legal formalities; make solemn; *n* **-ization**.

sol-fa *n mus* system giving name to each note of scale, applicable to any key (*also* **tonic sol-fa**).

solicit *v* 1 request earnestly 2 accost (person) for immoral purpose; *ns* **-ation**; *n* **solicitor** lawyer; *a* **solicitous** eager; anxious; *n* **solicitude** anxiety; concern.

solid *a* 1 not liquid or gaseous 2 compact; not hollow 3 financially sound 4 unanimous; *n* solid body of three dimensions; *a* **s.-state** *elec* using transistors *n* **solidity**; *v* **solidity** make, become solid; *ns* **solidification**; **solidarity** unanimity.

solidus *n* oblique stroke.

soliloquy *n* talking to oneself; monologue not addressed to anyone; *v* **soliloquize**.

solipsism *n* theory that one can only have knowledge of oneself (*n* **-ist**; *a* **-istic**.)

solitary *a* alone; single; lonely; *n* **solitude** state of being alone; loneliness; *n* **solitaire** 1 single gem set on its own 2 card game for one.

solo *n mus* **-os**. 1 composition for single instrument or voice 2 *fig* display, performance by one person 3 card game like whist; *n* **soloist**; *a* **solo** alone; unaccompanied.

solstice *n* time of year when sun reaches point furthest N or S of equator.

solve *v* work out; find answer to; *as* **soluble** capable of being dissolved in liquid; **solvable** able to be solved; *ns* **solubility**; **solution** answer to problem; liquid containing dissolved solid; *a* **solvent** able to pay all debts;

n substance that can dissolve something (*n* **s. abuse** glue-sniffing); *n* **solvency** ability to pay debts.

somatic *a* of the body.

sombre *a* dark, gloomy.

sombrero *n* *Sp* **-os**. wide-brimmed hat.

some *pron* certain number, not specified; *a* unspecified (person, thing, number) *coll* remarkable; great; *n* **somebody**; *adv* **somehow** by means still unknown; *n* **something** thing not clearly defined; *idm* **something of a** rather a; *a* **sometime** formerly; *advs* **sometimes** now and then; occasionally; **somewhat** rather; **somewhere** in unspecified place.

someplace *adv* US somewhere.

somersault *v* turn, fall head over heels; *n*.

somnambulist *n* sleep-walker; *n* **-ism**.

somnolent *a* sleepy; drowsy; *n* **-ence**.

son *n* male child; *n* **son-in-law** daughter's husband.

sonar *n* apparatus used in locating underwater objects.

sonata *n* musical composition in several movements; *n* **sonatina** short sonata.

son et lumière *n* *Fr* outdoor spectacle with music and special flood-lighting to present the history of a place dramatically.

song *n* musical utterance by human voice, or by birds;

idm **for a song** very cheaply;
idm **song and dance** *coll*
unnecessary fuss; *n* **songster**
singer; *esp* singing-bird.

sonic *a* of sound; *ns* **s. bang, s.
boom** sound of shock waves
set up by aircraft flying
through sound barrier.

sonnet *n* short poem of
fourteen lines.

sonny *n* friendly way of
addressing a young boy.

sonorous *a* deep, resonant.

soon *adv* in short time; early;
readily; immediately.

soot *n* black flaky substance
produced by burning matter;
a **sooty**; *v* cover with soot.

soothe *v* appease; make calm;
allay pains etc.

soothsayer *n* prophet; diviner.

sop *n* 1 bread dipped in liquid
2 *fig* concession; bribe; *a*
soppy *sl* soft; sloppy; *coll*
weakly sentimental; *v* **sop
up** absorb (liquid).

sophist *n* plausible reasoner,
quibbler; *ns* **sophism**
fallacious argument;
sophistry clever but false
argument; *v* **sophisticate**
deprive of naturalness;
corrupt (*a* **-ated** worldly-
wise; artificial; (engine etc)
having latest refinements; *n*
-ation).

sophomore *n* second-year
student at American
university.

soporific *n, a* (drug) causing
sleep.

sopping *a* very wet.

soppy *a Brit* 1 sentimental 2
foolish (*adv* **-ily**; *n* **-iness**).

soprano *n* **-os.** person with
highest singing voice;
musical part for this.

sorbet *n Fr* water-ice flavoured
with fruit.

sorcerer *n* wizard, magician; *n*
sorcery witchcraft;
enchantment.

sordid *a* mean; ignoble;
squalid; obscene; *n* **-ness**.

sore *a* painful; affronted;
grieved; *n* boil; ulcer; *n*
s.point painful memory; *adv*
-ly very greatly; grievously; *n*
-ness.

sorghum *n* cereal grown in
tropical countries.

sorority *n US* society of female
students.

sorrel *n* herb with reddish-
brown acrid tasting leaves; *a*
of this colour.

sorrow *n* grief; mental pain;
regret; *v* grieve, mourn;
a **-ful.**

sorry *a* 1 regretful; gloomy 2
mean; poor.

sort *n* a class; kind; *idm* **of sorts**
of inferior quality; *idm* **out
of sorts** *coll* unwell; *idm* **sort
of** *coll* rather; *v* arrange,
select in groups; *v* put in
order; *phr v* **sort out** 1
separate from others 2 *Brit*
deal with in *n* **sorter.**

sortie *n Fr* sudden attack by
besieged troops.

SOS *n* international signal of
distress.

so-so *a coll* neither good nor
bad; mediocre.

sotto voce *adv* in an
undertone.

sou *n* coin of minimal value.

soufflé *n Fr* light dish made
with beaten whites of egg.

sought *pt, pp* of **seek**; *a* **s.-after**
wanted; popular.

soul *n* 1 spiritual, non-material
part in man; part thought to
be immortal 2 human being
3 quality of decency and
sincerity 4 essence (of
quality) 5 *coll* quality of
Black American culture, *esp*
music; *ns* **s. brother/sister**
black man/woman (as
referred to by other black
people); **s. mate** person with
whom one has deep
understanding; **s.-searching**
critical analysis of one's own
motives; *as* **s.-destroying**
tedious; **soulful** showing
deep feeling (*adv* **-ly**;
n **-ness**); **soulless** without
emotion; cruel; impersonal
(*adv* **-ly**; *n* **-ness**).

sound[1] *n* what is heard; noise;
v emit, cause to emit noise;
seem; *phr v* **sound off**
express feelings with forte; *n*
sound-barrier moment
when aircraft's speed equals
that of sound-waves.

sound[2] *a* 1 healthy; in good
condition 2 logical 3
reliable; strong; *adv* **-ly**
thoroughly.

sound[3] *v* measure depth of
(water); plunge to bottom;
phr v **sound out** ascertain
views of; test with
stethoscope; *n* strait;
channel; *n pl* **soundings**
depth of water taken with
lead; **sound bite** *n* short
extract from an interview, eg

419

with a politician quoted in the media; n **sounding board** means of testing opinion.

soup n thick or clear liquid food made from meat or vegetables; *idm* **in the soup** *coll* in trouble; *phr v* **soup up** *coll* increase the power of.

soupçon n Fr a little bit.

sour a 1 acid; rancid; fermented 2 (*of soil*) poor; damp 3 morose; *idm* **sour grapes** belittling what one cannot have because one cannot have it; v make, become sour; n **-ness**.

source n 1 spring 2 starting-point; origin.

souse v pickle; soak with water; a **soused** pickled; *sl* very drunk.

south n cardinal point opposite N; region in this direction; a, adv **southerly** towards south; as **southerly** towards, coming from south; **southern** pertaining to south; ns **sou'wester** waterproof hat.

southpaw n left-handed boxer.

souvenir n keepsake; memento.

sovereign n 1 monarch, supreme ruler 2 British gold coin worth £1; a supreme; efficacious; effectual; n **sovereignty** supreme power or rule.

soviet n political unit of former USSR; council of workers, soldiers etc; **S. Union** bolshevik state of Russia and its satellites

(1917–1991).

sow n fully grown female pig.

sow v scatter, cast seed on ground; *pt* **sowed**; *pp* **sown** or **sowed**; n **sower**.

soy = **soya**; n **soy sauce** dark brown sauce from soya beans.

soya n species of oil-yielding bean; **s. flour** flour made from ground soya beans.

sozzled a *sl* drunk.

spa n 1 mineral spring 2 health resort having mineral spring.

space n 1 area; distance 2 period of time 3 region beyond Earth's atmosphere 4 room; empty place; v place at intervals apart; *phr v* **space out** leave plenty of room between; as **spaced out** *coll* stupefied (as by drugs); ns **spacecraft**, **spaceship** vehicle designed for travel outside Earth's atmosphere; **spaceman** *coll* astronaut; **s. shuttle** vehicle travelling back and forth between space and space station; **s. station** large satellite base from which space research can be carried out; **spacious** extensive, roomy.

spade n digging tool with flat blade; card of suit of spades; **spade work** preliminary work.

spaghetti n It pasta in the form of long strings.

span n 1 distance between tip of thumb and little finger, when fully extended;

approx. 9" 2 full extent 3 space between supports of bridge 4 extreme breadth, *esp* of birds or aircraft across wings; v **spanning, spanned.** measure with hand; stretch across, over.

spangle n small disc of brilliant metal, used as ornament.

Spaniard n Spanish person.

spaniel n breed of sporting dog with long drooping ears and silky hair.

Spanish n, a (language) of Spain.

spank v slap with open hand; move briskly; n **-ing** series of slaps, as punishment; a brisk, rapid; n **spanker** fast horse; fore-and-aft sail on mizzen mast.

spanner n tool for tightening or loosening nuts and bolts; *idm* **spanner in the works** sabotage.

spar[1] n pole used as mast.

spar[2] n kind of crystalline mineral.

spar[3] v **sparring, sparred.** practise boxing blows; contest in friendly manner; n **sparring partner** one against whom boxer practises.

spare a 1 meagre; lean, thin 2 additional; extra; in reserve; *idm* **go spare** *coll* be very angry; n spare part for machine, *esp* motorcar; v 1 refrain from killing etc; show mercy 2 do without; give away.

spark n 1 glowing particle thrown off by burning

substance; brief flash of light accompanying electric discharge 2 *fig* vitality; life; *v* emit sparks; *phr v* **spark off** ignite; cause; **sparking plug** device for securing electric ignition in internal combustion engine.

sparkle *v* glitter; effervesce; *n* brilliance; gaiety, wit; *n* **sparkler 1** *coll* diamond **2** small hand-held firework; *a* **sparkling 1** scintillating **2** intellectually brilliant **3** (*of wine*) effervescent.

sparrow *n* small common brown bird; **s.-hawk** small hawk.

sparse *a* thinly scattered; scanty; *adv* **-ly**; *n* **-ness**.

spartan *a* austere; hardy; unflinching.

spasm *n* sudden violent, involuntary muscular contraction; *a* **spasmodic** jerky; intermittent (*adv* **-ally**).

spastic *a* suffering from lack of muscular control, due to congenital brain damage; *n* person suffering from such damage.

spat *n* short gaiter.

spate *n* sudden flood of river after rain; *fig* excessive amount.

spatial *a* pertaining to space.

spatter *v* splash drops on; *n* shower, sprinkling.

spatula *n* blunt, broad-bladed knife used for mixing paint, and in cooking.

spawn *n* eggs of fish, frogs etc; offspring; *v* **1** (*of fish etc*) lay eggs **2** *fig* generate in mass.

spay *v* remove ovaries of (female animal).

speak *v* speaking, spoke, spoken. **1** utter words; convey meaning **2** give speech, lecture etc; converse; *n* **speaker** one who delivers, speech, lecture etc; *cap* presiding officer in House of Commons.

speakeasy *n* esp US place for illegal sale of alcohol.

spear *n* long-shafted weapon with pointed head; *v* pierce, catch with spear.

spearmint *n* common garden mint.

spec *idm* **on spec** *Brit* as a gamble.

special *a* particular; exceptional; not for public, general use; for specific purpose; distinctive; *ns* **s. school** school for handicapped children; **s. licence** licence allowing marriage at short notice without usual requirements of notification etc; **s. pleading** argument based on biased representation of facts; *n* **-ist** one who devotes himself to a particular branch of science, art or profession; *v* **-ize** make special; limit; particularize; *ns* **-ization, speciality** special product, distinctive feature etc.

specie *n* coined money.

species *n* pl **species.** class; group; sort, kind.

specific *a* **1** characteristic of species **2** definite; **3** *med* of or for particular disease (*n* such a remedy); *adv* **-ally**; *n* **s. gravity** ratio of density of substance to that of water; *n* pl **-s** particular details; *v* **specify** state definitely, precisely; *n* **specification** detailed description or statement.

specimen *n* representative example or sample; *coll* odd person.

specious *a* plausible.

speck *n* small spot, mark; *v* **speckle** mark, be marked with small spots; *a* **speckless** spotless.

spectacle *n* show; display; *pl* pair of optical lenses in frame; *a* **spectacular** impressive, remarkable; *n* **spectator** onlooker.

spectre *n* ghost; apparition; *a* **spectral.**

spectrum *n* series of bands of coloured light formed when beam has passed through prism; *pl* **spectra**; *n* **spectroscope** instrument for analysing spectra.

speculate *v* form theory about; invest in uncertain security; *n* **speculator**; *a* **speculative** given to guessing; risky; *n* **speculation.**

sped *pt, pp* of **speed.**

speech *n* **1** act, faculty of speaking; language **2** formal public discourse; *n* **s. synthesizer** computerized device for generating oral messages in imitation of human speech; *v* **speechify**

make long, tedious speeches; *a* **speechless** dumb; at loss for words.

speed *n* swiftness; velocity; *v* **speeding, sped** or **speeded.** move quickly; drive (vehicle) at high speed; *ns* **s. hump** raised surface across width of road causing traffic to move very slowly; **s. limit** maximum legal speed; **s. trap** section of road where police monitor speed of traffic by radar; *v* 1 (cause to) move quickly 2 exceed speed limit (*n* -**ing**); *phr v* **speed up** go faster; *ns* **speedometer** instrument to show speed of vehicle; **speedway** motor-cycle racing track; *a* **speedy** rapid; prompt.

speedwell *n* flowering herb.

spell[1] *n* 1 magic formula 2 fascination; *as* **spellbinding** fascinating; **spellbound** entranced.

spell[2] *n* bout, short period of activity.

spell[3] *v* **spelling, spelt** or **spelled.** say or write letter by letter; *phr v* **spell out** explain in more detail; *n* **spelling** way in which word is spelt.

spelter *n* zinc.

spend *v* pay out; expend; wear out, exhaust; *pt, pp* **spent**; *n* **spend-thrift** one who squanders; wasteful person.

sperm *n* 1 male fertilizing fluid (*also* **semen**) 2 single male reproductive cell (*also* **spermatozoon**); *ns* **s. bank** place where supplies of

sperm are kept for later use in artificial insemination; **spermicide** substance that kills sperm (*a* -**cidal**).

spermaceti *n* white, waxy substance obtained from head of sperm-whale; *n* **sperm-whale** large whale.

sphere *n* 1 ball; globe 2 scope; range; status; *ns* **spherical**; *n* **spheroid** nearly spherical body.

sphincter *n anat* ring of muscle that contracts to close an orifice (*eg* anal sphincter).

Sphinx *n* fabulous human-headed lion; Egyptian statue of this; *fig* inscrutable person.

spice *n* aromatic pungent vegetable seasoning; *fig* that which adds interest or excitement; *a* **spicy**.

spick and span *a* bright, fresh, tidy.

spider *n* small eight-legged animal, which spins web to catch prey; *a* **spidery**.

spiel *n coll* long voluble speech intended to create an impression.

spigot *n* plug for stopping air hole in cask.

spike *n* 1 sharp pointed piece of metal, wood etc 2 ear (of corn etc); *pl* -**s** athlete's running shoes; *v* 1 impale 2 *coll* make (drink) strong by adding alcohol to it 3 prevent (news article) being printed; *idm* **spike sb's guns** make sb's plans ineffective; *a* **spiky** (*n* -**ness**).

spill[1] *n* splinter, strip of paper, or wood used as taper.

spill[2] *v* **spilling, spilt**, or **spilled.** (*of liquid*) flow, be upset, out of vessel; (*of persons*) fall from vehicle etc; *idm* **spill the beans** *coll* reveal a secret (by accident or intentionally); *n* fall.

spin *v* **spinning, spun.** twist (wool etc into thread); whirl; (*of spiders etc*) exude filament for web; *n* act of spinning; twist; whirl; **spin doctor** person who puts a positive slant on events on behalf of a political party or politician; *idm* **in a flat spin** in complete panic or confusion; *phr v* **spin out** prolong; *ns* **s.-off** additional indirect benefit; **spinner**; **spinning (s.wheel** household machine for spinning wool into thread); *ns* **spinning** act of making web; process of forming thread; **spinneret** silk-spinning organ of silkworm, spider etc.

spina bifida *n med* malformation of spine which leaves spinal cord partly exposed.

spinach *n* garden vegetable with edible leaves.

spinal *a* of the spine; *n* **s.cord** thick cluster of nerves enclosed within the spine.

spindle *n* rod, axis on which anything rotates; *a* **spindly** long and slender.

spine *n* backbone; thin, sharp thorn, or growth on animal;

back of book; as **s.chilling** terrifying; **spineless** 1 without backbone 2 *fig* weak; cowardly (*adv* -**ly**; *n* -**ness**); **spiny** prickly.

spinet *n Fr* keyboard instrument.

spinney *n* small wood.

spinster *n* unmarried woman.

spire *n* pointed part of steeple.

spiral *a* winding constantly about centre, like thread of screw; *n* spiral curve.

spirit *n* 1 person's mind or feelings; soul 2 soul separated from the body (as after death); ghost 3 life force 4 temper; emotion 5 courage 6 liveliness 7 characteristic quality of sth 8 intended meaning 9 distilled alcohol for industrial use 10 *usu pl* distilled alcohol as a drink 11 *pl* -**s** state of morale; 11 **s.level** tool used by builder for checking whether surfaces are level; *as* -**ed** lively (*adv* -**ly** *n* -**ness**); *phr v* **spirit away** remove secretly; *as* **spiritual** pertaining to soul or spirit, not material; **spiritless** listless, apathetic; *ns* **spiritualism** belief that spirits of dead can communicate with living; (*n, a* -**ist**); *a* **spirituous** alcoholic.

spit *n* sharp rod for roasting meat on; sandy point projecting into sea; *v* thrust through.

spit *v* **spitting, spat.** eject saliva; *n* saliva; *ns* **spittle**

saliva; **spittoon** vessel to spit into.

spite *n* malice; *v* act maliciously towards; *prep* **in spite of** notwithstanding; *a* **spiteful**.

spitting image *n* exact likeness.

spiv *n* one who makes living by dishonest, but not criminal means.

splash *v* 1 scatter (liquid) on 2 fall in drops on; *phr v* **splash down** (of spacecraft) fall into the sea (*n* **splashdown**); *n* 1 sound of, result of splashing 2 impressive effect; *a* **splashy** flamboyant; showy.

splatter *v* 1 splash noisily 2 cover with splashes.

splay *v* slant; dislocate (joint); *n* slanting edge; *a* **s.-footed** having flat, turned-out feet.

spleen *n* ductless gland in abdomen; *fig* ill-humour; *a* **splenetic**.

splendid *a* magnificent; illustrious; *coll* excellent; *n* **splendour** brilliance; magnificence.

splice *v* join by interweaving strands; join (wood) by overlapping; *coll* marry.

splint *n* rigid piece of wood etc, *esp* when keeping fractured bone in place; *v* support with splint; *n* **splinter** small, sharp broken off piece of wood, glass etc; *n* **s.group** group separated from main body; *v* break into fragments.

split *v* **splitting, split.** 1 divide

lengthways 2 divide into parts 3 share; *idm* **split hairs** argue over very small differences; *n* cleft, tear (in fabric).

splodge *n* irregular blob of liquid (*eg* paint) landing on or applied to a surface in a random way; (*a* -**y**).

splosh *v* make loud splashing sound; *n* this sound.

splotch = **splodge.**

splurge *n* ostentation; *v* make vulgar display.

splutter *v* spit slightly while speaking; utter indistinctly.

spoil *v* **spoiling, spoilt** or **spoiled.** 1 injure; damage; deteriorate 2 cause to become badly-behaved, selfish etc by over-indulgence; *idm* **spoiling for** eager for; *idm* **be spoilt for choice** have a wide range of options; *n pl* -**s** 1 booty; stolen goods 2 profits; *n* **spoil-sport** one who prevents others from enjoying themselves.

spoke[1] *n* radial bar of wheel; *n* **spokeshave** kind of plane.

spoke[2] *pt*, **spoken** *pp* of **speak.**

spokesperson *n* person chosen to represent views of group (*also* **spokesman** *pl* -**men**, **spokeswoman** *pl* -**women**).

spolation *n* robbery with violence; act of spoiling.

sponge *n* 1 marine animal whose fibrous skeleton is used to absorb liquids, or for cleaning 2 light cake; *v* clean with sponge; *phr v* **sponge off/on sb** live at sb's expense (n **sponger**); ns s. **bag** (usu waterproof) bag for holding toiletries; s. **cake** very light cake; a **spongy** soft but resilient; having texture of sponge.

sponsor n guarantor; patron; godparent.

spontaneous a (of persons) voluntary; self-acting, or self-originated; n **spontaneity**.

spoof n, v hoax; n amusing untrue copy.

spook n ghost, wraith.

spooky a coll ghostly; mysteriously frightening.

spool n reel, bobbin.

spoon n implement consisting of shallow bowl on handle, used in cooking and conveying food to mouth etc; v use, lift with, spoon; sl make love; v s.**-feed** 1 feed (baby) with spoon 2 fig teach in a way that requires no thinking from pupils.

spoonerism n ridiculous error resulting from accidental exchange of sounds (eg 'share of poohs' instead of 'pair of shoes').

spoor n track of wild animal.

sporadic a scattered; occurring in single cases.

spore n minute reproductive organism, of flowerless plant, or as in bacteria.

sporran n leather pouch worn in front of kilt.

sport n 1 physical activity, esp outdoor, for exercise or amusement 2 particular form of this; game with set

rules 3 fun 4 coll fairminded person with sense of fun; pl Brit athletics meeting; as **sporting** 1 relating to sport 2 fond of sport 3 fair and generous (adv **-ly**); **sportive** playful (adv **-ly**; n **-ness**); ns **sports car** low fast car; **sportsman** (pl **-men**; n **-manship** respect for fairness in competing); **sportswoman** (pl **-women**); a **sporty** 1 fond of, good at sport 2 attractive to see.

spot n 1 small mark, esp if round; pimple 2 small place; fig moral blemish; idm **hot spot** uncomfortable or dangerous situation; idm **in a (bit of a) (tight) spot** coll in a difficult situation; idm **put sb on the spot** 1 force sb to act 2 cause sb embarrassment; ns s.**check** random check without warning; v **spotting, spotted**. mark with spot; coll see; catch sight of; **spotlight** strong beam of light able to be focused on one spot (v illuminate with spotlight; coll draw attention to); as **spotted** decorated with spots; **spotless** 1 without blemish 2 perfectly clean (adv **-ly**; n **-ness**); **spotty** with pimples (n **-ness**).

spouse n husband or wife.

spout v gush, pour out; n projecting lip or spout for pouring liquid; gushing jet of liquid, water; idm **up the spout** 1 coll ruined 2 sl pregnant.

sprain v, n twist or wrench (of muscles, tendons, etc).

sprat n small edible fish.

sprawl v lie, be stretched out awkwardly; straggle.

spray[1] n sprig, twig with smaller branches or flowers.

spray[2] n fine droplets of liquid; wind-blown particles of sea-water; atomizer; device for spraying; v squirt, treat, with spray; become spray; n **sprayer** device for spraying.

spread v cover (surface) with; stretch out, extend in all directions; become widely diffused, circulated; pt, pp **spread**; n 1 extent 2 increase 3 feast; a s.**-eagled** lying with arms and legs stretched wide; n **spreadsheet** comput program for displaying rows of figures, esp in accounting.

spree n frolic; drinking or spending bout.

sprig n small twig; small nail; scion; a **sprigged** ornamented with spray-like design.

sprightly a lively, brisk; n **sprightliness**.

spring v 1 leap 2 pounce 3 bubble, gush forth 4 sprout up; pt **sprang**; pp **sprung**; n 1 source; well 2 first season of year 3 recoil 4 piece of coiled resilient metal etc 5 leap; idm **spring a leak** (of container) begin to let liquid escape; phr vs **spring from** originate from; **spring sth on sb** surprise sb with sth; n 1 season after winter 2

424

natural source of running water 3 coiled or bent length of resilient metal 4 elasticity 5 act of springing; ns **springboard 1** flexible board used for diving 2 *fig* starting point; **s. onion** small onion eaten raw in salad; **s. roll** Chinese pancake; **s.tide** strong tide occurring at time of full or new moon; *v* **s.-clean** clean (house etc) very thoroughly; *a* **springy** elastic; *n* **springer** variety of spaniel.

springbok *n* S African gazelle.

sprinkle *v* scatter in small drops; strew; *ns* **sprinkler; sprinkling** small quantity of drops, particles; few scattered people or objects.

sprint *v* run at full speed for short distance; *n* such run; *n* **-er**.

sprite *n* fairy; elf.

sprocket *n* projecting tooth on wheel for engaging chain.

sprout *v* put forth shoots, begin to grow; *n* young shoot; *n pl* **Brussels sprouts** vegetable like miniature cabbages.

spruce[1] *n* type of coniferous tree; *a* smart and neat in dress.

spruce[2] *a* clean and neat (*adv* **-ly** *n* **-ness**); *phr v* **spruce up** make (oneself) clean, neat.

sprung *pp* of **spring**.

spry *a* nimble, agile; alert; (*adv* **-ly**; *n* **-ness**).

spud *n* small spade for digging up weeds etc; *sl* potato.

spume *n*, *v* foam; froth.

spun *pt*, *pp* of **spin**.

spunk *n coll* courage

spur *n* **1** pricking wheel fixed on horseman's heel, for urging on horse 2 pointed projection on cock's leg 3 projecting ridge or part of mountain range 4 stimulus; *idm* **on the spur of the moment** without forethought; *v* **spurring, spurred**. prick with spurs; urge; ride hard.

spurious *a* not genuine; false; sham.

spurn *v* reject scornfully; repel.

spurt *n* jet; short vigorous effort, *esp* in race; *v* gush out suddenly; make sudden brief effort (to increase speed etc).

sputnik *n* (Russian) satellite.

sputter *v* make series of spitting noises.

sputum *n* saliva; spittle.

spy *n* agent employed to obtain secret information; *v* **spying, spied**. act as spy; catch sight of; *n* **spy-glass** small hand telescope.

sq *abbr* square.

squabble *n* petty quarrel; *v* quarrel, bicker.

squad *n* small group of people working together, *esp mil.*

squadron *n* **1** body of cavalry 2 group of warships.

squalid *a* foul; dingy; sordid; mean; *n* **squalor**.

squall *n* **1** harsh, shrill shriek 2 brief, violent storm; *v* scream; *a* **squally** gusty.

squander *v* spend, use

wastefully.

square *n* **1** rectangle with sides of equal length 2 open space of similar shape in a town 3 product of number multiplied by itself 4 *coll* very conventional person; *a* **1** of the shape of a square 2 tidy; arranged straight 3 fair and honest 4 of units used to measure area (*eg* **square metres**) 5 having gained equal points in contest 6 having settled all debts (mutually); *v* **1** give square shape to 2 divide into squares 3 multiply (number) by itself 4 make even 5 get cooperation of, *esp* by bribery 6 settle debt; *phr v* **square up to** confront (challenging situation) with determination; *ns* **s. dance** dance for four couples; **s. meal** *coll* meal that satisfies hunger; **s. one** the beginning; **s. rig** way of setting sails on old ships (*a* **s. rigged**); **s. root** number which when squared gives specified number; *adv* **-ly**; *n* **-ness**; *as* **squared** covered with squares; **squarish** roughly square in shape.

squash *v* crush, press flat; *coll* snub; *n* **1** drink of crushed fruit 2 pulpy mass 3 game for two, played with rackets and soft ball in walled court 4 packed crowd.

squat *v* **squatting, squatted**. sit on heels; *a* short and thick; *n* **squatter** illegal settler in unoccupied house or land.

squaw n N American Indian wife.

squawk n loud, harsh cry; v utter such cry.

squeak v utter weak, thin cry of fright etc; make high, grating noise, as of unoiled hinge; n such noise.

squeal v utter shrill prolonged cry; sl betray secrets; n long shrill cry.

squeamish a easily nauseated; over sensitive.

squeegee n rubber broom for cleaning wet floors.

squeeze v press; wring; extort; extract; n act of squeezing.

squelch v produce sucking, gurgling sound; n such sound.

squib n small hissing firework.

squid n cuttle-fish.

squidgy a Brit coll soft and pulpy.

squiffy a Brit coll slightly drunk.

squiggle v wriggle; squirm; n twisty illegible writing.

squint v look in different directions with each eye; n this eye affection, strabismus; coll glance.

squire n county landowner; formerly, attendant on knight; man escorting woman; v escort woman.

squirearchy n landowners as political or social force.

squirm v, n wriggle; writhe.

squirrel n small bushy-tailed rodent.

squirt v eject, be forced out, in jet; n jet (of liquid); syringe.

Sr abbr Senior.

SRN abbr state registered nurse.

SS 1 Saints 2 steamship 3 Schutzstaffel (Hitler's secret police force).

ssh interj be quiet.

St abbr Saint.

stab v stabbing, stabbed. pierce with pointed weapon; n wound so inflicted; idm **have a stab (at)** coll make an attempt (at); idm **stab in the back** act of betrayal; a **stabbing** (of pain) sharp (n act of stabbing).

stabilize v make stable; restore to equilibrium; ns **stabilization, stabilizer** device for keeping ship, aircraft etc. in equilibrium.

stable a firmly fixed; not easily upset; resolute; n **stability** steadiness, firmness.

stable n building where horses are kept; v put in stable.

staccato a mus with each note played in sharply detached manner.

stack n 1 large heap, esp of hay, straw 2 neat pile 3 tall chimney 4 rack with shelves for books; pl -s coll large amount; v pile up in orderly way.

stadium n -iums or -ia. open-air arena for athletics etc.

staff n tall pole; organized body of workers; servants of one employer; mus five lines on which notes are written (also **stave**); pl **staffs, staves**.

stag n male deer; a coll for men only, as **s.party**.

stage n 1 raised floor or platform in theatre 2 fig scene of action 3 fixed stopping place (of bus etc) 4 point of development; ns **s.-coach** (formerly) horse-drawn public vehicle; **s.door** theatre back entrance used by actors and staff; **s. fright** nervousness felt when appearing in public; **s. left/right** left/right from actor's point of view. **s. manager** person responsible for arranging stage sets, properties etc (v **s. manage**); **s. whisper** loud whisper intended for audience to hear; a **s.-struck** ambitious to become actor; v 1 put (play) on stage 2 cause to happen, esp to create effect; n **staging** 1 production of drama, opera etc 2 scaffolding.

stagger v walk, move unsteadily; reel; shock; prevent from coinciding; n unsteady gait; n pl disease of horses and cattle.

stagnant a 1 (of water) not flowing; stale; unhealthy 2 fig sluggish; not making progress; v **stagnate** be or become stagnant (n -ation).

stagy a theatrical; exaggerated; adv **-ily**; n **-iness**.

staid a sedate; sober; steady; n **staidness**.

stain v discolour, impart colour deliberately; soil; blemish; n spot, blemish; n **stained glass** colour glass for decorative windows; a

stainless 1 free from stains **2** resistant to rust (n **s.steel**).

stairs n pl series of steps usu in building; ns **staircase, stairway** structure enclosing stairs; flight of stairs.

stake n **1** pointed stick or post **2** prize **3** money wagered **4** financial interest **5** share; idm **at stake** at risk; v wager, risk; mark with posts etc; idm **stake a claim** claim ownership; phr v **stake out 1** declare special interest in **2** coll (of police) watch secretly (n **s.-out**).

stalactite n tapering lime formation hanging from roof of cave etc; n **stalagmite** similar formation rising from floor.

stale a **1** not fresh **2** fig out of practice **3** tired by too much work.

stalemate n **1** chess position in which neither player can win **2** fig deadlock.

stalk[1] v stem of plant.

stalk[2] v walk in stiff, dignified way; pursue (prey, game etc) stealthily; ns **stalker; stalking-horse** horse used as cover by hunter; fig pretext.

stall n **1** division in stable etc **2** booth in market for sale of goods **3** front seat in theatre etc **4** seat in chancel; v unintentionally stop (engine); (of aircraft) lose flying speed.

stallion n uncastrated male horse.

stalwart a strong; brave; unflinching.

stamen n pollen-bearing male organ of flower.

stamina n power of endurance; vigour; vitality.

stammer v speak hesitantly, with repetition of speech sounds; stutter; n this speech defect; n **stammerer**.

stamp v **1** put foot down heavily **2** affix postage stamp **3** impress mark on; phr v **stamp out** fig destroy utterly; n **1** act of stamping **2** imprinted mark, or instrument making it **3** gummed label printed with device as evidence of postage paid **4** class; character; n **stamping ground** favourite haunt.

stampede n sudden frightened rush, esp of cattle; crowd etc; v flee in panic; cause to stampede.

stance n attitude in standing, esp when about to strike ball in golf etc.

stanch v US = **staunch**.

stand v standing, stood. **1** be in, move to upright position **2** be on one's feet **3** be in a certain position, condition **4** remain in force **5** endure; tolerate **6** pay for; treat sb else to **7** Brit become candidate for election; idm **stand a chance** have some hope or prospect; idm **stand on one's own feet** be independent; idm **stand to reason** be clear to any sensible person; phr vs **stand against sb** cause prejudice against sb; **stand back**

refrain from taking part; **stand by 1** remain loyal to **2** be ready to act (n **standby** reserve); idm **on standby 1** ready for action **2** waiting for a cancellation (**s.ticket** ticket available if a cancellation occurs) **3** take no part; **stand down 1** resign **2** leg leave witness box; **stand for 1** represent **2** be strongly in favour of; support **3** tolerate; **stand in (for sb)** be a substitute (for sb) (n **s.-in**); **stand out 1** be clearly seen **2** be different in quality; **stand up** (of evidence) be convincing; **stand sb up** fail to keep a date with sb; **stand up for** support; **stand up to** resist; n **standing** a erect; lasting; ns **standpoint** position, repute; point of view; **standstill** complete cessation of progress etc.

standard n flag; fixed rule; quality; approved model; ns **s.-bearer 1** person carrying standard **2** leader; **s. lamp** lamp with tall base; **s.of living** level of material comfort and wealth; v -ize make so as to conform with single standard (n -ization).

standing n **1** rank **2** reputation; idm **of long standing** well established; n **s. order** Brit order for bank to make regular payments from one account to another; **standoffish** a unfriendly; adv -ly; n -ness.

stank pt of **stink**.

stannary n tin-mine; a of, pertaining to tin-mines.

stanza n group of verse-lines.

staple n 1 U-shaped piece of metal with pointed ends, for fastening 2 paper-fastener 3 principal commodity 4 chief raw material 5 thread, fibre of wool, cotton; a leading, principal; v fasten with staple; grade (wool etc); n **stapler** grader of wool etc; machine for wire-stitching paper etc.

star n 1 luminous heavenly body 2 figure, device resembling apparent shape of star 3 popular actor etc; leading player; 4 asterisk (*); ns **s.chamber** powerful, secret court; **s.dust** dreamy, romantic fantasy; **s.-gazer 1** coll person interested in astronomy 2 dreamy, unrealistic person (n **s.gazing**); **s.sign** any one of 12 signs of the zodiac; **s.turn** item in entertainment causing greatest attraction; **s.wars** coll SDI; as **s.-crossed** ill-fated; **s.studded** with any famous performers; v **starring, starred. 1** play a main role 2 mark with stars; ns **stardom** state of being famous actor; **starfish** flat star-shaped fish; **starlet** young actress; a **starry** full of stars (a **s.-eyed** enthusiastic, but unrealistic).

starboard n right-hand side of ship, looking forward; a of, on this side.

starch n 1 carbohydrates, main food element in vegetables 2 white soluble powder mixed with water for stiffening linen etc; v make stiff thus; a **starchy** containing starch; stiff, formal.

stare v look, gaze at intently, fixedly; n prolonged intent look.

stark a stiff; rigid; absolute; utter; adv absolutely.

starkers a coll completely naked.

starling n glossy black gregarious bird.

start v begin; set going; move with jerk; n sudden jerk; beginning; advantage in contest; n **-er** signaller for race to start; idm **for starters** to begin with.

startle v alarm; shock; surprise.

starve v die, suffer, from lack of food; suffer from cold; ns **starveling** thin, underfed person or thing; **starvation**.

stash v coll hide; store away (also n).

state n 1 condition; rank; position 2 nation and its government; self-governing division of country 3 pomp; v state express in words; as **state-of-the-art** using most modern technology; **stateless** having no citizenship of any country (n **-ness**); ns **statecraft** skill in handling State affairs; **S.Department** US government department of foreign affairs; **s.room** ceremonial reception room; a **stated** previously

determined, fixed.

stately a dignified; imposing (n **-iness**); n s. **home** large house or estate, usu of historical interest, open to public.

statement n 1 formal declaration (oral or written) 2 summary of financial transactions, showing present state of account.

statesman n person skilled in management of State affairs; wise leader (pl **-men**); a **-like**; n **-ship**.

static a stationary; n atmospheric interference on radio or TV; **s.electricity** electricity that accumulates in an object; n pl **statics** branch of physics concerned with bodies at rest and balance of forces.

station n 1 place, position where train stops or is placed 2 walk in life; employment; occupation; v place in specific spot; ns **stationmaster** person in charge of railway station; **s.wagon** US estate car; a **-ary** at rest; not moving; not changing.

stationery n writing materials, pens, paper, ink etc; n **stationer** dealer in writing materials.

statistics n pl systematic collection and arrangement of numerical facts; study of these; n **statistician** one skilled in dealing with statistics; a **statistic(al)**.

statue n carved or moulded

figure of human or animal etc; n **statuary** statues collectively; a **statuesque** having dignity or serenity of statue.

stature n bodily, height, size.

status n 1 legal or social standing 2 high social position; ns **s. quo** present or original state of affairs; **s. symbol** possession believed to give proof of one's high social standing.

statute n law made by Parliament; a **statutory** depending on, enacted by statute.

staunch, stanch v stop flow (of blood); a trustworthy; loyal; adv **-ly** n **-ness**.

stave n curved wooden strip forming part of cask; stanza; mus staff; v pt, pp **stove** or **staved** phr vs **stave in** smash a hole in; **stave off** keep away with a struggle.

stay v 1 check 2 remain in place as visitor etc 3 last out 4 pause; idm **stay put** remain in place; idm **stay the course** persevere to the end; n rest, visit; leg suspension of proceedings, restraint; n **staying power** stamina.

stay n prop; strut; rope supporting mast etc; pl corsets; v support, sustain.

St Bernard n big powerful dog used in mountain rescue.

std abbr standard.

STD abbr 1 subscriber trunk dialling (automatic telephone dialling to all parts of the world) 2

sexually transmitted disease.

stead n place; service; in (one's **stead** in place of; in good **stead** be of good service; n **steading** farmstead.

steady a firm; regular; sober; reliable; v make, become steady; a **steadfast** unwavering; resolute; n **steadiness**.

steak n thick slice of meat, esp beef, or fish; n **s. tartare** raw minced steak.

steal v **stealing, stole, stolen.** rob; thieve; move furtively, silently; idm **steal a march on sb** anticipate sb by acting first; idm **steal the show** do sth to attract admiration that should have gone to sb else; n **stealth** secret, furtive action; a **-y.**

steam n water-vapour; v cook, treat with steam; give off steam; move by steam power; idm **run out of steam** lose impetus; become exhausted; idm **under one's own steam** by one's own effort; a, ns **steam-engine** one worked or propelled by steam; **steamer** utensil for cooking with steam; steamship; **s.-roller** 1 heavy roller for levelling roads 2 fig massive force (v use forceful means to overcome opposition to proposal); as **steamed-up** coll angry; **steaming** 1 very hot 2 coll very angry; (n form of robbery by armed gang passing through train and demanding money of

passengers); **steamy** 1 full of steam 2 coll erotic.

steed n poetic horse.

steel n iron containing carbon; tool, weapon of steel; ns **s. band** W Indian band of steel drums made from empty oil containers; **s. wool** pad of steel strands used as scourer; a **steely.**

steep[1] a 1 sharply inclined 2 coll exorbitant 3 incredible.

steep[2] v soak, saturate; fig imbue.

steeple n tall tapering structure on church; ns **steeplechase** cross-country horse race; **steeplejack** man employed to repair, clean steeples, tall chimneys etc.

steer[1] v guide, direct course of (car, ship, etc); aim one's course; idm **steer clear (of)** keep well away (from); ns **steerage** cheapest form of travel by sea; **steering** 1 mechanism for controlling direction of travel (**s. wheel**) 2 ability to steer.

steer[2] n young ox, bullock.

stellar a of stars.

stem[1] n 1 stalk; trunk 2 part of word to which inflexional endings are added; phr v **stemming, stemmed. stem from** be a result of.

stem[2] v check flow of; resist.

sten gun n type of machine gun.

stench n offensive smell.

stencil n thin plate of metal etc perforated with design, or letters; pattern, design produced by applying colouring matter through holes of stencil plate; *v* decorate, make copy of, by using stencil.

stenography *n* shorthand writing; *n* **-grapher**.

step *v* **stepping, stepped.** lift and set down foot; walk; *n* 1 act of stepping 2 sound, mark made by foot 3 gait 4 pace 5 procedure 6 stair 7 *fig* degree, stage; *pl* **-s** portable ladder with hinged prop; *idm* **in/out of step** 1 moving one's feet in/out of line with the rest of the group; *idm* **step by step** gradually *idm* **step on it!** *coll* go faster; *idm* **step out of line** fail to conform with accepted rule of behaviour; *phr vs* **step aside** make way for sb else; **step down** resign; **step in** intervene; **step up** 1 approach 2 increase; *n* **stepping-stone** 1 stone laid on bed of river enabling one to cross on foot 2 *fig* stage in progress towards objective.

stepchild *n* child of husband or wife by previous marriage; *ns* **stepfather; stepmother.**

steppe *n* broad, open, treeless plain.

stereophonic *a* (of sound) giving effect of coming from many directions.

stereoscope *n* optical instrument producing illusion of relief and distance by presenting two different images of same subject, one to each eye.

stereotype *n* 1 fixed set of

ideas or expectations about a certain type of person or thing (*a stereotypical; adv* **-ly**) 2 metal plate cast from mould of set-up type; *a* **-typed** 1 repeated without variation 2 printed from stereotype.

sterile *a* barren; unproductive; *n* **sterility**; *v* **sterilize** make incapable of reproduction; destroy bacteria; *ns* **sterilization** act, process of sterilizing; **sterilizer.**

sterling *a* in British money; genuine, pure; *fig* dependable.

stern *a* severe; strict; *n* **sternness.**

stern *n* after part of ship; rump of animal.

sternum *n* **-nums** or **-na** breast bone.

steroid *n chem* any one of group of soluble organic compounds having strong effect on development of body.

stertorous *a* breathing loudly, as with sound of snoring.

stet *n* direction to printer, on proof, to cancel correction made.

stethoscope *n* instrument for listening to action of heart or lungs.

stevedore *n* one who stows and unloads cargoes at docks.

stew *v* cook slowly in closed vessel; *n* food so cooked; *coll* agitated condition.

steward *n* 1 salaried manager of large household or estate 2 catering manager of club

etc 3 waiter, attendant on ship's, aircraft's passengers 4 official helping to organize race-meeting, etc; *fem* **-ess**.

stick[1] *v* 1 thrust into, stab 2 attach; adhere 3 *coll* bear bravely 4 come to a stop; *pt*, *pp* **stuck**; *idm* **stick one's neck out** *coll* take a big risk; *idm* **stick to one's guns** refuse to be deterred by any opposition; *phr vs* **stick around** linger; **stick by/with** remain loyal to; **stick out** (cause to) protrude (*idm* **stick it out** *coll* persevere); **stick out for** *coll* insist on; **stick to** 1 adhere to 2 refuse to change; **stick up** 1 attach for display (*eg* on a wall) 2 project upwards 3 *coll* threaten with gun etc (*n* **s.-up** *coll* armed robbery); **stick up for** defend; *ns* **sticker** 1 adhesive label 2 *coll* persevering person; **stick-in-the-mud** *coll* person without enterprise; one who resists change; *a* **sticky** 1 glue-like; adhesive 2 *coll* difficult (*n* **-iness**)

stick *n* slender rod of wood or other substance; *idm* **a lot of stick** *coll* severe criticism.

stickleback *n* small fish with spiny dorsal fin.

stickler *n* one who insists on trivial points of procedure.

sticks *n pl* **the s.** rural area far from any big city.

stiff *a* rigid; not easily moving; thick; formal; difficult; *idm* **stiff upper lip** ability not to show fear or any other emotion when in pain, danger etc; v **stiffen** make, become, stiff; n **stiffness**; a **stiffnecked** obstinate.

stifle v smother.

stigma n **-mas** or **-mata**. 1 moral reproach 2 *bot* part of pistil receiving pollen; v **stigmatize** mark out (something discreditable); n **stigmatism**.

stile n steps, rail for climbing hedge or fence.

stiletto n **-os**. small dagger; small pointed boring instrument; n **s. heel** thin high heel of woman's shoe.

still[1] a 1 motionless; silent 2 (of wine) not sparkling; v calm; quieten; n **-ness**; as **stilly** quiet; **stillborn** born dead; n **s. life** picture of inanimate objects.

still[2] n apparatus for distilling; n **s.-room** store room for liquors, preserves etc.

stilt n (usu pl) pole with foot rests, for raising walker above ground; wading bird; a **-ed** stiff in manner.

Stilton n strong-flavoured English cheese with blue veins.

stimulus n anything which excites action; incentive; pl **stimuli**; v **stimulate** rouse up; urge, incite; n, a **stimulant** (drink, drug etc) producing temporary increase of energy; n **stimulation**.

sting n sharp, pointed defensive, offensive organ of

insect, reptile etc; sharp pain caused by sting; v thrust sting into; cause, feel sharp pain; pt, pp **stung**.

stingy a mean; niggardly; n **stinginess**.

stink v **stinking, stank**, or **stunk, stunk.** give out bad smell; n **stench**; offensive smell.

stint v grudge; be niggardly with; n limitation.

stipend n salary, esp of clergyman; a **-iary** salaried (n **s. magistrate** one appointed by State).

stipple v paint, engrave in dots; n this method.

stipulate v make conditions in bargain; insist on; n **stipulation** proviso.

stir v **stirring, stirred.** set in motion; mix round and round with spoon etc; rouse, excite; phr v **stir up** provoke; n mental excitement, esp public.

stirrup v metal hoop hung by strap from saddle for supporting foot of rider; ns **s.-cup** farewell drink of wine; **s.-pump** small portable water pump.

stitch n movement of needle in sewing; result of such movement; sharp pain in side; idm **in stitches** laughing uncontrollably; v sew.

stoat n animal of weasel family.

stock n 1 supply 2 goods available for sale 3 juice saved from food preparation for use in making soup,

sauces etc 4 farm animals (also **livestock**) 5 lineage of family 6 capital of corporation or company 7 thick part of tree trunk or stem of plant 8 sweet-smelling flower; pl **-s** 1 framework to support ship under repair 2 (formerly) wooden frame in which to place criminals on public display by immobilizing their arms and legs; idm **take stock (of)** consider well before making a decision; v keep supplies of; a 1 constantly available 2 habitually produced 3 commonplace; ns **s. car** car that is modified for use in racing; **S. Exchange** place for trading in stocks and shares; **s.-in-trade** 1 standard equipment for an occupation 2 fig standard behaviour or words of an individual; **s.-market** (business done at) stock exchange; **s.-taking** 1 checking of stock 2 review of progress; ns **stockbroker** person trading in stocks and shares on behalf of clients; **stockholder** owner of stocks and shares; **stockist** Brit person who keeps supplies of certain goods; **stockjobber** member of Stock Exchange that deals with stockbrokers; **stockman** man looking after livestock; **stockpile** large supply accumulated for future use (v accumulate); **stockyard** yard where animals are kept prior to sale or slaughter.

stockade n barrier, wooden fence for defence.

stockinet n elasticated fabric used for underwear and for bandages.

stocking n close-fitting covering for leg and foot; n **s.-filler** small gift to put in Christmas stocking.

stocky a short, solid in appearance; n -**iness**.

stodgy a heavy; indigestible; dull.

stoic n person of rigid calm, fortitude; a **stoic(al)**, impassive; n **stoicism**.

stoke v fill with fuel; idm **stoke up** coll eat plenty; n **stoker** person tending furnace; fireman.

stole[1] pt of **steal**; pp **stolen**.

stole[2] n long, narrow wrap of fur etc worn about shoulders; narrow strip of cloth or silk worn by priests.

stolid a impassive; lacking animation or action; adv -**ly**; n -**ity**.

stomach n 1 sac in abdomen in which food is digested; abdomen 2 fig liking; wish; v 1 eat without falling ill 2 fig tolerate; n **s. pump** apparatus for emptying stomach quickly; a **stomachic** pertaining to stomach; n digestive medicine.

stomp v walk heavily.

stone n 1 fairly small piece of rock 2 gem 3 hard seed-case in certain fruits 4 hard

deposits formed in kidneys, bladder etc 5 measure of weight, 14 lbs (6.350kgs); v throw stones at; remove stone from fruit; idm **stone's throw** a very short distance; ns **S. Age** early period of history when stone tools were used; **stonemason** person who prepares stone for use in building; **stoneware** pottery from clay containing flint as **stone-blind/dead/deaf** completely blind/dead/deaf; **stoned** coll 1 blind drunk 2 under influence of drugs; **stony** 1 full of stones 2 fig hard and cruel 2 (of silence) complete (a **s. broke** Brit coll penniless); v **stonewall** 1 cause obstruction and delay without making any positive contribution 2 cricket bat defensively (ns -**er**, -**ing**).

stood pt, pp of **stand**.

stooge n one who is butt of comedian's jokes; coll dupe; butt; vs **s. around** wander about purposelessly, idly.

stool n 1 backless seat 2 footstool 3 matter evacuated from bowels.

stoolpigeon n coll person used as decoy by police to trap criminal.

stoop v 1 bend forwards or down 2 be round-shouldered 3 condescend 4 (of hawk) swoop; phr v **stoop to (doing sth)** lower one's moral standards by (doing sth); n position of stooping.

stop v stopping, stopped. 1

cease, cause to cease motion 2 prevent 3 close opening 4 discontinue 5 stay; remain; n 1 act of stopping 2 any device for altering pitch of note 3 peg, block 4 punctuation mark; idm **pull out all the stops** coll use all one's resources to achieve sth; ns **stopcock** valve or tap; **stopgap** temporary substitute; **stopover** short stay in middle of journey; **stoppage** 1 cessation of work 2 deduction from pay 3 blockage; **stopper** plug, esp for bottle; **s. press** late news; **s. watch** with split second start-stop facility for timing races.

store n 1 reserve supply, stock 2 warehouse 3 large general shop; v accumulate and keep supplies etc; hold storage room for; ns **storage** act of storing, being stored; **storage battery** accumulator; **s. heater** one using stored electrical heat.

storey n horizontal division, floor of building.

stork n large wading bird.

storm n violent atmospheric disturbance; tempest; idm **take by storm** 1 overcome by sudden attack 2 fig win enthusiastic approval of; n **s. trooper** Nazi militia man; v assault; fig express rage, scold; a **stormy** tempestuous; passionate.

story n spoken or written narrative; tale; account; coll truth; n **storyteller** 1 reciter,

writer of stories 2 *coll* liar.
stout *a* 1 durable; resolute 2
fat; *n* strong dark beer; *a*
stouthearted *lit* brave (*adv* -
ly *n* -**ness**); *n* **stoutness**.
stove *n* cooker; apparatus for
heating.
stow *v* pack away; fill (hold)
with goods; *phr v* **stow
away** hide on board ship or plane
in hope of having free
journey (*n* **stowaway** person
doing this); *n* **stowage**
(room for) stowing.
straddle *v* spread legs wide;
bestride.
straggle *v* loiter, be apart from
main group; *a* **straggly**; *n*
straggler.
straight *a* 1 not bent or
crooked; *lit*, *fig* upright 2 in
order 3 (of spirits) neat; *n*
straight stretch of road, river
etc; *cards* sequence; *adv* 1 in
a straight line 2 directly; *idm*
go straight give up life of
crime; *idm* **keep to the
straight and narrow** *coll*
lead an honest life; *advs*
straightaway immediately;
s. up *Brit coll* honestly; *a*
straight-forward 1 simple 2
frank and honest (*adv* -**ly**;
n -**ness**); *v* **straighten** make
straight or tidy; *phr v*
straighten out remove
difficulties from.
strain[1] *v* 1 make taut 2 over-
exert; over-tax 3 wrench by
too sudden effort; *n* 1
tautness 2 severe physical or
mental effort 3 *fig* tune 4 *lit*
tune; *a* **strained** showing
nervous fatigue, forced.

strain[2] *n* breed; stock;
ancestry.
strainer *n* sieve; colander; *v*
filter.
strait *a* 1 *ar* narrow; strict; *n*
narrow channel of water
between two seas 2 (often
pl) difficult position; *as*
straitened impoverished, in
financial difficulty;
straitlaced austere, strict; *n*
strait-jacket coat to confine
arms of violent lunatics etc.
strand[1] *n* shore; *v* run aground;
leave, be left helpless,
destitute.
strand[2] *n* single thread of
wool, fibre, rope etc; lock of
hair.
strange *a* unfamiliar; unusual;
foreign; singular; *ns* -**ness**;
-**er** unknown person;
foreigner.
strangle *v* kill by compressing
windpipe; throttle; *ns*
stranglehold powerful
control that prevents action;
strangulation act or result of
strangling.
strap *n* strip of leather or metal
for fastening; *v* **strapping,
strapped.** fasten with strap;
beat with strap; *a* **strapping**
tall, well-made; *n* **s.-hanger**
standing passenger in train
etc who holds on to strap to
steady himself.
strata *pl* of **stratum**.
stratagem *n* trick, plan for
deceiving enemy, opponent;
ns **strategy** art of military
manoeuvring; *fig* battle of
wits; **strategist;** *a*
strategic(al).

stratify *v* arrange in strata; *n*
stratification.
stratosphere *n* upper
atmospheric layer beginning
approx 9.7 km (6 miles)
above earth's surface.
stratum *n pl* **strata** 1 *geol* layer
2 *fig* social division, class.
straw *n* dry cut stalks of corn;
idm **the last straw** new
development that makes an
already difficult situation
quite intolerable; *ns*
strawberry plant bearing red
sweet juicy fruit (*n* **s. mark**
red birthmark); **strawboard**
cardboard made from straw;
s. poll unofficial survey of
public opinion.
stray *v* wander; lose one's way;
a strayed; occasional; *n* lost
animal or child.
streak *n* 1 long line; stripe 2
(of lightning) flash; *v* 1 mark
with streaks 2 *coll* rush
quickly past (*n* -**er** person
running naked in public); *a*
-**y**.
stream *n* body of flowing water
or other liquid; rivulet;
brook; *idm* **on stream** in
operation or production; *v* 1
flow, run with liquid 2 fly
out, float on air; *n* **streamer**
ribbon, flag to fly in air.
streamlined *a* of curved shape,
offering minimum resistance
to water or air.
street *n* road in town or village
with buildings on both sides;
idm **up one's street**
connected with one's special
interests; *idm* **streets ahead**
greatly superior;

ns **s.-credibility** convincing knowledge of current fashion among urban youth (also coll **s.-cred**); **streetwalker** prostitute; a **streetwise** coll quick-witted enough to survive in a tough urban environment.

strength n power; intensity; quality of being strong; force; idm **on the strength of** on the basis of; using the advantage of; v **strengthen** make stronger.

strenuous a energetic; unremitting.

stress n 1 strain 2 emphasis 3 intense pressure 4 mech force exerted on solid body; v 1 emphasize 2 accent 3 subject to mechanical stress; as **stressed out** coll exhausted by stress; **stressful** causing stress (n **-ness**).

stretch v extend; be elastic; reach out; exert to utmost; idm **stretch a point** coll make special concession; idm **stretch one's legs** take exercise by walking; n **stretcher** one who, that which stretches; light framework for carrying disabled person.

strew v scatter, spread on surface; pt **strewed**; pp **strewn** or **strewed**.

striated a marked in stripes; n **-ation**.

stricken a affected by grief, illness, terror etc.

strict a exact; inflexible; stern; rigorous; ns **strictness**; **stricture** 1 med contraction

of duct or vessel 2 fig severe criticism.

stride v striding, strode, stridden. walk with long steps; cross over with one long step; n single step or its length; idm **make strides** make fast progress; idm **take sth in one's stride** manage a difficult situation without any problem.

strident a harsh; shrill; grating.

stridulate v (of insects) make high-pitched sound by friction of limbs etc; n **-lation**.

strife n conflict; discord.

strike v stricking, struck. 1 hit; collide; aim, deliver blow 2 (of clock) sound time 3 affect 4 ignite 5 take down (tent, flag etc) 6 make (coin, medal) 7 stop work to enforce demand; pt **struck**; idm **strike a balance** reach a compromise; idm **strike a chord** remind sb of sth; idm **strike a note of** express feeling of; idm **strike camp** prepare to leave camp by taking down tents; idm **strike while the iron is hot** make use of opportunity; phr vs **strike off** remove (person's name) from list; **strike out** move in a determined way (idm **strike out on one's own** coll begin to be independent); **strike up** 1 initiate (friendship) 2 begin playing (music); n 1 refusal to work 2 attack, esp aerial 3 discovery of mineral deposit, eg oil; n **-er**; **-ing** 1

noteworthy 2 attractive to look at (adv **-ly**; idm **within striking distance** nearby); a **strikebound** affected by strike; **s.-breaking** refusing to go on strike (n **s.-breaker**); n stoppage of work; n **striker** person who is on strike; anything that strikes sth; a **striking** noteworthy.

string n cord, twine; series of objects, chain; (of musical instrument) cord of catgut, wire; pt, pp **strung**; pl **-s** (players of) stringed instruments in orchestra; idm **strings attached** special conditions; v 1 attach string to 2 thread onto string 3 tie with string 4 remove stringy fibres from (pt, pp **strung**); idm **highly strung** very sensitive and excitable; phr vs **string along** 1 coll keep company for a while 2 persuade by deception; **string out**; **string up** hang; n **s. bean** US runner bean; as **stringed** furnished with strings; **stringy** fibrous (n **-iness**).

stringent a strict; rigid; binding; n **stringency** severity.

strip v stripping, stripped. 1 remove clothing 2 take away property; phr v **strip down** (of machine) remove detachable parts before cleaning, repairing; n 1 act of stripping 2 long thin piece (of fabric, wood etc) torn off; idm **tear sb off a**

strip/a strip off sb *coll* reprimand sb; *ns* **s. cartoon** comic story in pictures; **s.-lighting** (method of lighting with) long fluorescent tube; **s.-tease** type of night-club entertainment where performer undresses slowly in front of spectators (*n* **stripper** person who does this).

stripe *n* narrow mark, band; chevron worn as symbol of military rank.

strive *v* try earnestly; fight; contend; *pt* **strove**; *pp* **striven.**

strobe (light) *n* light that flashes on and off rapidly; *n* **stroboscope** instrument that produces such light (*a* **-scopic**).

strode *pt of* **stride.**

stroke *n* 1 blow 2 line made by single movement of pen, brush etc 3 single movement of hands or hand-operated instrument (as in swimming, cricket etc) 4 rower in stern setting rate 5 sudden attack of illness; *v* 1 pass hand lightly over, caress 2 row stroke in boat.

stroll *v* take short leisurely walk; saunter; *n.*

strong *a* powerful; tough; healthy; affecting senses acutely; *idm* **be strong on** be good at; *ns* **s.-box** secure box for keeping valuables; **stronghold** 1 fort 2 *fig* place where specified activity is

strongly supported; **s. language** swearing and cursing; **s. point** thing in which one is especially skilled; **s. room** room in bank with strong walls, doors etc for storage of valuables; *as* **s.-arm** using violence; **s.-minded** very determined (*adv* **-ly**; *n* **-ness**).

strontium *n* soft silver-white heavy metal; **strontium 90** dangerous radio-active form of this found in fall-out from nuclear explosion.

strop *n* leather strap for putting edge on razor; *v* **stropping, stropped.** apply strop to razor.

strophe *n* one of the units of several lines of which a poem consists (*also* **stanza, verse**).

stroppy *a Brit coll* quarrelsome; rebellious.

strove *pt of* **strive.**

struck *pt, pp of* **strike.**

structure *n* 1 formation; construction 2 that which is made up of many parts 3 building; *a* **structural.**

strudel *n Ger* cake of fruit covered with puff pastry.

struggle *v* fight; grapple with; make strenuous effort; move convulsively; *n* contest; violent tussle.

strum *v* **strumming, strummed.** play noisily, idly or badly on stringed instrument.

strung *pt, pp of* **string.**

strut *n* 1 prop; stay 2 affected,

pompous gait; *v* **strutting, strutted.** support with struts; swagger.

stub *n* tree-stump; end part, remnant (of cigarette, pencil etc); *v* **stubbing, stubbed.** hit one's toe accidentally on something; *phr v* **stub out** extinguish (cigarette); *a* **stubby** short and thick.

stubble *n* short stalks of corn etc left in ground after reaping; short growth of hair.

stubborn *a* resolute; unyielding; obstinate; pig-headed; *n* **-ness.**

stucco *n It* fine plaster for coating walls.

stuck *pt, pp of* **stick**; *a* **stuck-up** conceited.

stud[1] *n* large headed projecting nail or peg; double headed button for cuff or collar of shirt; *v* **studding, studded.** set, decorate with studs.

stud[2] *n* 1 number of horses kept for breeding, hunting etc 2 *coll* man regarded as sexually active, virile; *ns* **s.-book** register of pedigree of thoroughbred horses etc; **s.-farm** place for breeding horses.

student *n* person studying at university, college, evening class etc 2 person with specified interest (**student of sth**).

studio *n* work-room of artist, photographer etc; room or premises where films are made or radio broadcasts are transmitted.

study v **studying, studied.**
learn systematically; analyse;
show concern for; n **1**
subject studied **2**
experimental painting,
sketch **3** room in which to
study; a **studied**
premeditated.

studious a **1** fond of study **2**
careful (adv **-ly** n **-ness**).

stuff n **1** substance; material **2**
textile fabric **3** fig nonsense;
idm **do one's stuff** coll show
what one can do; v **1** fill **2**
put stuffing inside **3** fill skin
of (dead animal for
preservation) **4** eat greedily;
idm **get stuffed!** sl expressing
rejection, extreme scorn; phr v
stuff up block; n **stuffed
shirt** coll boring, pompous
person; n **stuffing** filling;
savoury seasoning used
inside bird, meat; a **stuffy 1**
lacking ventilation **2** coll too
formal.

stultify v make a fool of; make
ineffectual; n **-fication.**

stumble v trip up; falter; **s.
across, on**, come upon by
chance; n **stumbling-block**
impediment; obstacle.

stump n **1** stub; remainder;
remnant **2** cricket sticks of
wicket v **1** walk noisily **2**
cricket put batsman out by
striking bails off wicket; phr
v **stump up** coll pay out; a **-y**
short, thickset.

stun v **stunning, stunned. 1**
knock senseless **2** shock;
amaze; a **stunning**, causing
loss of senses; coll excellent;
very beautiful; (adv **-ly**); n

stunner coll very attractive
person.

stung pt, pp of **sting.**

stunk pp of **stink.**

stunt[1] v **1** coll spectacular feat
or display, esp involving
danger **2** sensational
newspaper article etc.

stunt[2] v check growth of; a
stunted undersized;
retarded.

stupefy v **stupifying,
stupified. 1** make stupid;
dull **2** amaze; n
stupefaction.

stupendous a astonishing;
extra-ordinary; adv **-ly.**

stupid a slow-witted; dull;
lacking intelligence; adv **-ly;**
n **-ity.**

stupor n dazed condition;
torpor; mental dullness.

sturdy a robust; vigorous; well-
developed; n **-iness.**

sturgeon n large fish from
which caviare and isinglass
are obtained.

stutter v speak with hesitation
and repetitions; stammer; n
speech-defect.

sty[1] n pen for pigs; fig filthy
place.

sty[2] stye n inflamed swelling
on eyelid.

style n **1** manner of doing,
expressing **2** deportment **3**
sort; variety **4** correct mode
of address **5** manner; v
designate; idm **in style** in an
elegant way; a **stylish**
fashionable (adv **-ly;**
n **-stylist 1** person who aims
at good style, esp in writing
2 one who styles clothes,

hair etc; v **stylize** treat in
fixed, conventional style
(a **-ized;** n **-ization**).

stylus n **-uses. 1** sharp needle
fitted to pick-up of record
player, reproducing sound
from groove of record **2**
sharp instrument for writing,
esp in ancient times.

styptic n, a (preparation)
which stops bleeding.

Styrofoam [TM] US
polystyrene.

suave a Fr bland; urbane;
affable; adv **-ly;** n **-ness;** n
suavity.

sub- prefix forming ns, as and vs
1 under **2** almost **3** smaller
than; less than **4** inferior. A
compound may not be listed if
the meaning can easily be
deduced from the basic word.

sub n coll **1** submarine **2**
substitute **3** subscription **4**
Brit payment of wages
in advance; v **subbing,
subbed.** give part payment
of wages in advance.

subaltern n commissioned
officer in army below rank of
captain.

subaqua a of underwater sport.

subconscious a not fully
realized by mind; n (psycho-
analysis) part of mind
outside personal awareness
of individual.

subcontract v arrange
subsidiary contracts with
workers for all or part of a
big job for which one has
signed the main contract.

subculture n (behaviour of)
particular group in society.

subcutaneous *a* under the skin.

subdivide *v* divide further into smaller units.

subdue *v* overcome.

subedit *v* check and correct details of text before sending to printer (*ns* **-editor, -editing**).

subject *n* 1 thing being considered, discussed; topic 2 branch of learning 3 *ling* (word or phrase referring to) thing or person doing action of verb 4 person being experimented on 5 citizen of a state; *a* 1 under sb's political control; **subject to** 1 exposed to 2 liable to 3 depending on (specified conditions); *v* 1 bring under political control; *phr v* **subject sb** *to* cause sb to undergo; *n* **subjection** act of bringing, or state of being, under control; *a* **subjective** 1 existing in the mind; not objective 2 based on personal feeling (*adv* **-ly**; *n* **subjectivity**).

subjoin *v* add later.

sub judice *a Lat leg* not for public comment while being considered in a court of law.

subjugate *v* conquer; force under control; *n* **subjugation**.

subjunctive *n ling* mood of verb expressing wish, possibility; *a* of, in, that mood.

sublease, sublet *v* re-lease or re-let to another person or persons property on which one has taken a lease or letting.

sublet *v* let to another, property of which one is tenant.

sublimate *v* 1 refine; purify by heating from solid to vapour and restoring solidity 2 *psyc* express undesirable impulses in more socially desirable form; *n* sublimated substance; *n* **-ation** act of sublimation.

sublime *a* majestic; exalted; awe-inspiring; *ns* **sublimity; -ness**.

subliminal *a* at a level where the ordinary senses are not aware; *adv* **-ly**.

submarine *a* below surface of sea; *n* ship designed to remain, travel, under water for long period; *n* **submariner** seaman serving in submarine.

submerge *v* plunge, cause to go, beneath surface of water; *n* **submersion**.

submersible *n, a* (craft) which can be submerged.

submit *v* **submitting, submitted**. 1 surrender 2 suggest, put forward for consideration etc; *n* **submission**; *a* **submissive** resigned, docile.

subnormal *a* 1 below normal 2 inferior in intelligence.

subordinate *a* inferior in rank or importance; dependent upon; *n* **-ation**.

suborn *v* bribe, induce to commit crime; *n* **-er**.

subplot *n* secondary, less important plot (*eg* in play)

subpoena *n leg* writ summoning person to attend court; *v* serve with such writ.

subscribe *v* 1 pay regularly (*eg* contribution to club, instalment to magazine) 2 **s. to** *fig* be in favour of; *ns* **subscriber; subscription** 1 act of subscribing 2 amount of money regularly paid for membership etc.

subsequent *a* later, following as result; *adv* **-ly** *n* **subsequence**.

subservient *a* submissive, servile; *n* **subservience; -viency**.

subside *v* settle, sink down; diminish, abate; *n* **subsidence**.

subsidy *n* grant of money by State; *v* **subsidize** give, support by subsidy; *a* **subsidiary** additional; auxiliary; secondary.

subsist *v* sustain life; continue in being; *n* **-tence** means of supporting life.

subsoil *n* level of soil below the surface.

subsonic *a* of less than speed of sound.

substance *n* 1 matter; material 2 essential, most important elements or parts 3 portion of solid 4 considerable wealth (*n* **-ity**; *v* **substantiate** give reality to; prove, establish truth (*n* **-ation**); *a* **substantive** having real existence; *ling* expressing existence; *n* noun.

substation n place where electric power is relayed from main power station to other places.

substitute n person, thing taking place of another; deputy; v put, use in place of another; n **-tution**.

substratum n underlying layer; basis; pl **-ta, -tums**.

subsume v fml include.

subtend v geom be opposite to.

subterfuge n equivocation; means of evasion.

subterranean, -eous a situated, existing underground.

subtitle n explanatory second title (v add subtitle to); pl **-s** visual translation of dialogue in foreign film.

subtle a 1 elusive 2 discriminating 3 ingenious 4 cunning; n **subtlety**.

subtotal n part total combining with others to make grand total.

subtract v take away; deduct; n **subtraction**.

sub-tropical a between temperate and tropical zones.

suburb n outlying part of town or city; a **-an**.

suburbia n (architecture and lifestyle of) city suburbs.

subvention n fml subsidy.

subvert v try to undermine the power of; a **subversive**; adv **-ly**; ns **-ness**; **subversion** act of subverting.

subway n underground passage; US underground railway.

succeed v 1 follow; come after 2 follow (as heir) 3 accomplish purpose; n **success** fortunate accomplishment, attainment of desired object, or result; triumph; a **successful**; n **succession** 1 act or right of following in office, rank etc 2 series of things, events; a **successive** consecutive; n **successor** one who follows another in office etc; heir.

succinct a concisely expressed; terse.

succour v, n help, aid in difficulty or distress.

succulent a juicy; full of sap; n **succulence**.

succumb v 1 yield; give way 2 cease to exist.

such a of that, of similar kind, degree or quality specified, implied; a **suchlike** similar.

suck v 1 draw (liquid) into mouth 2 dissolve in mouth; phr v **suck up to** coll flatter in order to win favour, n **sucker** 1 organ appliance adhering by suction 2 sl gullible person 3 bot shoot from subterranean stem.

suckle v feed (young) with milk from breast; n **suckling** unweaned baby or young animal.

sucrose n form of sugar in sugarcane and sugar-beet.

suction n act of sucking; creation of partial vacuum causing body to adhere to, or enter, something under atmospheric pressure.

sudden a done, occurring unexpectedly; abrupt; adv **-ly**; n **-ness**.

suds n pl froth of soap and water, lather.

sue v 1 bring, take legal action against 2 beg; plead.

suede n Fr leather with a velvety nap on one side.

suet n solid fatty tissue round kidneys etc of oxen, sheep etc.

suffer v 1 undergo; tolerate 2 be injured; be punished; ns **sufferer**; **sufferance** toleration; idm on **sufferance** with reluctant consent.

suffice v be enough, adequate; a **sufficient**; n **sufficiency** adequate supply.

suffix n letter or syllable added to end of word.

suffocate v deprive of air, stifle; kill by depriving of air; smother; n **suffocation**.

suffrage n vote, right to vote, esp at elections; n **suffragette** woman who campaigned for right of women to vote in elections.

suffuse v (of fluid, colour etc) spread over, flood, cover; n **suffusion**.

sugar n 1 sweet, crystalline vegetable substance; 2 sl money; v sweeten with sugar 3 fig flatter; disguise unpleasantness of; ns **s.-beet** variety of beetroot yielding sugar; **s.-cane** tall grass from whose juice sugar is obtained; **s. daddy** older man who spoils a young woman with generous gifts in return for sexual favours; *a* **sugary**.

suggest *v* imply; put forward, present for consideration; *as* **-ible** easy to influence (*n* **-ibility**); **-ive 1** evoking association of ideas **2** provoking indecent thoughts (*adv* **-ly**; *n* **-ness**); *n* **suggestion 1** proposal **2** hint **3** *psych* process of persuading sb to accept an idea, *esp* under hypnosis.

suicide *n* **1** act of killing oneself **2** one who intentionally kills himself; *a* **suicidal**.

suit *n* **1** action at law **2** set of clothes worn together; *esp* man's outer clothes **3** one of four sets in pack of cards; *v* **1** satisfy **2** match **3** please **4** be convenient; *a* **suited 1** appropriate **2** compatible; *idm* **suit oneself** do as one wishes; *n* **suiting** material for making suits, *n* **suitcase** portable flat oblong travelling case.

suitable *a* convenient; proper; becoming; *n* **suitability**.

suite *n Fr* **1** band of retainers **2** complete set (as of rooms, furniture etc).

suitor *n* petitioner; wooer.

sulk *v* resentful and unsociable; *a* **sulky** (*adv* **-ily**; *n* **-iness**); *n pl* **sulks**, sulky mood.

sullen *a* ill-tempered; morose; surly.

sully *v* **sullying, sullied.** stain; defile; tarnish.

sulphate *n* salt of sulphuric acid.

sulphide *n chem* compound of sulphur with other element.

sulphonamide *n* type of antibiotic.

sulphur *n* pale yellow, inflammable, non-metallic element; *n* **s. dioxide** colourless gas with choking smell; *as* **sulphurous**, **-ic** (*n* **s. acid** very strong corrosive acid).

sultan *n* Mohammedan prince or king; *ns* **sultana** sultan's wife; kind of raisin; **sultanate** (state under) rule of sultan.

sultry *a* **1** (*of weather*) hot and close **2** showing strong sexual desire; (*adv* **-ily**; *n* **-iness**).

sum *n* amount; total; *phr v* **summing, summed. sum up 1** summarize **2** (*of judge*) review and comment on evidence.

summary *a*, *n* carried out without delay; brief statement or abridgement of chief points (of document, speech etc); *v* **summarize** present briefly and concisely; *n* **summation** reckoning up.

summer *n* warmest season of year; *v* spend summer; *a* **summery**; *ns* **summerhouse** small garden building for sitting in in warm weather; **s. school** short teaching course given in summer holiday period; **s. time** *Brit* period when clocks are put one hour ahead in summer.

summit *n* **1** top; peak **2** *coll* political conference between heads of States.

summon *v* **1** send for **2** leg order to attend court **3** *fig* muster (quality in oneself); *phr v* **summon up** evoke, *n* **summons** call; notice to appear before judge or magistrate.

sumptuary *a* relating to expenditure.

sumptuous *a* lavish; splendid; costly; *n* **sumptuousness**.

sun *n* **1** luminous heavenly body round which earth and other planets rotate **2** chief source of light and heat in solar system **3** direct rays of sun; *v* exposed to, bask in, sun's rays; *v* **sunbathe** lie in the sun in order to have a suntan (*ns* **-bather -bathing**) *as* **s.-baked 1** very sunny **2** hardened by the sun; **s.-drenched** very sunny; *ns* **sunbeam** ray of sunshine; **sunbed** couch for lying under sunlamp; **s.-blind** awning protecting against strong sunlight; **sundial** device with pointer that shows time by movement of shadow across dial; **sunflower** large flower with yellow petals and seeds containing edible oil; **s.-glasses** spectacles with dark lenses for protecting eyes from strong light **s.-lamp** lamp for giving artificial sun-tan by ultra-violet rays (*also* **s.-ray lamp**); (**s. lounge** room with large window panels to admit sunlight; **sunrise** time when sun rises at start of dray; **s. roof 1** retractable panel in roof of car, coach etc **2** flat house roof for sunbathing (*n* **s. industry** new, expanding industry); **sunset 1** time when sun sets at end of day **2** view or picture of sky at this time; **sunspot 1** *astron* dark area on sun's surface **2** *coll* holiday place where sun usually shines; **sunstroke** illness caused by too much exposure to sun; **s.-tan** browning of skin from exposure to sun (*a* **s.-tanned**); **s.-trap** warm, sunny place sheltered from wind; **s.-worship 1** worship of sun as god **2** *fig coll* (show off) addiction to sunbathing (*n* **s.-worshipper**); *a* **sunless**.

sundae *n* ice-cream with crushed fruit and nuts.

Sunday *n* first day of week.

sunder *v* put apart; sever.

sundry *a* several, of indefinite number; *n pl* **sundries** unspecified odds and ends.

sup *v* supping, supped. **1** take by sips **2** take supper.

sung *pp of* **sing**.

sunk *pp of* **sink**.

sunken *a* **1** fallen to the bottom of the sea **2** on a lower level **3** (of cheeks, eyes etc) hollow.

super- *prefix; forms compounds with meaning of* above, *in* excess. *Such words are not given when the meaning may be deduced from the simple word.*

super (*a coll*) marvellous; superb.

superannuate *v* pension off; dismiss on account of old age; *a* **-ated 1** too old to work **2** old-fashioned; **-ation 1** pension paid after retirement **2** contributions towards this paid regularly into a fund, *n* **superannuation** payment, pension given on retirement.

superb *a* splendid; magnificent.

supercharge *v* charge, fill to excess; *n* **supercharger** device to increase petrol mixture in cylinders of motor engine; *a* **-ed**.

supercilious *a* disdainful; haughty; *n* **-ness**.

superconductivity *n physics* property of certain metals that allows electricity to be conducted easily at very low temperatures; *n* **superconductor** such a metal.

superego *n psyc* the conscience.

superficial *a* of, on surface; shallow.

superfluous *a* more than necessary; redundant.

supergrass *n Brit* person able to give police detailed information about activities of criminals.

superhuman *a* of more than can be expected of ordinary man.

superimpose *v* put sth on top

of sth so that both can be seen (or heard) together.

superintend *v* direct; control; oversee; supervise; *ns* **-ent** manager; police officer above inspector; **-ence**.

superior *a* **1** higher in position, rank, grade **2** upper; *idm* superior to; not affected or biased by; **-ity** (**s. complex** *psyc* aggressively self-satisfied attitude).

superlative *a* of, in highest degree of excellence, or quality; *n ling* superlative degree of adjective or adverb.

superman *n* hypothetical being possessing supreme physical and mental powers.

supermarket *n* large self-service store.

supernatural *a* not explicable by known laws of nature.

supernumerary *n*, *a* (person, thing) in excess of normal number; extra.

superphosphate *n* acid phosphate; fertilizer.

superpower *n* very large, powerful nation.

supersede *v* replace; supplant.

supersonic *a* moving faster than speed of sound; of sound-waves of too high frequency to be audible to human ear.

superstar *n coll* entertainer, *esp* sportsperson, with outstanding skill and reputation.

superstition *n* irrational belief in charms, omens, etc; dread of supernatural; *a* superstitious.

superstructure n 1 part of building above ground or of ship above main deck 2 institutions arising from an economic system.

supervene v happen as consequence, or in addition; n -**vention**.

supervise v oversee; inspect; control; direct; ns **supervisor** (a -**visory**); **supervision**.

superwoman n woman of outstanding physical and mental talents.

supine a lying on back, face upwards; inactive; n Lat verbal noun.

supper n last meal of day; a -**less**.

supplant v take place of, oust, esp by fraud, craft etc.

supple a pliant; flexible; docile; amenable; n -**ness**; adv **supply**.

supplement n 1 something added to fill need 2 separable part of newspaper etc; v add to; supply deficiency; a **supplementary** extra; additional (n s. **benefit** Brit money paid regularly by State to help poor people to live).

supplicate v pray for; ask for humbly; ns -**ation** entreaty; **suppliant** petitioner; a beseeching.

supply v **supplying, supplied.** 1 provide (sth to/for sb) 2 equip (sb with sth); n 1 amount available 2 (system for) providing; idm **in short**

supply difficult to obtain; idm (**a matter/question of**) supply **and demand** the effect on prices of relating the amount available on the market to the amount needed; pl **supplies** everyday provisions; n **supplier**.

support v 1 hold, prop up 2 maintain; assist; n act, state of being supported; that which helps, supports; n -**er** 1 person loyal to a team, political party etc 2 person devoted to an activity, principle etc; as -**able** tolerable; -**ing** giving support (s. **part/role** not a leading role); -**ive** ready to offer encouragement, help (adv -**ly** n -**ness**).

suppose v 1 assume 2 surmise; v imagine; imperative used to imply a question what if ? or a suggestion would you like (me/us) to ?; idm be **supposed to** be required, expected to; a **supposed** believed to be (adv -**ly**); conj supposing what if; n **supposition** hypothesis; guess.

suppository n soluble medicinal stick inserted in rectum or vagina.

suppress v 1 subdue, crush by force 2 prevent publication of; ban; n -**ion** n -**or** 1 person who suppresses 2 device that prevents electrical interference to TV, radio etc.

suppurate v produce pus; n **suppuration**.

supra- prefix above, higher than; beyond.

supranational a going beyond national boundaries n -**ism** n, a -**ist**.

supreme a highest, superior in rank, power, jurisdiction etc; utmost; ns **supremacy** 1 superiority 2 dominance; -**acist** person believing in racial, national superiority of any kind.

surcharge n extra charge; v demand extra payment.

surd n, a math irrational (quantity).

sure a certain; reliable; undoubted; adv, interj coll certainly; willingly; idm be **sure to** coll don't forget to; idm **make sure** 1 verify; be certain 2 guarantee; idm **for sure** certainly; idm **sure enough** as one would expect; as s.-**fire** certain to happen or succeed; s.-**footed** able to walk, climb without fear of falling (n -**ness**); n **surety** 1 one who makes himself responsible for another's good conduct 2 money laid down as pledge of person's good behaviour.

surf n foam of breaking waves; n **surfboard** board used in sport of surfing.

surface n exterior; outside; top; visible side; a superficial; v 1 come to surface of water 2 emerge from hiding; be found after being missing; ns s. **mail** post sent by land and sea (not by air); s. **tension**

property of liquids that they form an apparent film on the surface.

surfeit n excess, esp in feeding; satiety; repletion; v overindulge.

surge v (of waves, water) swell; rise powerfully; n 1 act of singing 2 sudden rush of electric current in circuit.

surgeon n medical practitioner who performs operations; n **surgery** 1 treatment of disease and injuries by operation or manipulation 2 doctor's consulting room; a **surgical**.

surly a sullen; gloomy, churlish; n **surliness**.

surmise v guess; conclude; infer; n conjecture; inference.

surmount v overcome (difficulty); be placed over top of; a **-able**.

surname n hereditary family name transmitted in male line.

surpass v go beyond, excel in degree, quality etc; a **-ing** excelling all others; matchless.

surplice n loose white vestment worn by clergy and choristers.

surplus n excess quantity; a forming amount over and above what is required.

surprise v come upon unexpectedly; shock; startle; astonish; n astonishment; something unexpected.

surrealism n movement in art or literature that believes in expressing dream-like effects and irrational fantasies; n, a **-ist**.

surrender v give up under pressure or voluntarily; hand over; submit; n act of surrendering.

surreptitious a stealthy; clandestine; furtive.

surrogate n substitute; deputy, esp of bishop; n **surrogate mother** woman who bears a child for another woman.

surround v encircle; be, come all round; n pl **surroundings** material environment; circumstances.

surtax n additional tax on high incomes.

surveillance n Fr constant watch, observation.

survey v 1 look over; review 2 inspect and assess value of (house etc) 3 measure, map (area of land); n record of result of surveying; n **surveyor**.

survive v 1 outlive 2 continue to live or exist; n **survivor** 1 one left alive when others are dead 2 one who does not give in to adversity.

sus v Brit sl discover; find out truth about (also **suss**); phr v **sus out** Brit sl investigate carefully and secretly.

susceptible a highly sensitive; accessible; n **-ibility**.

suspect v 1 believe or imagine to be true 2 doubt; mistrust 3 believe guilty; a rousing suspicion; n suspected person.

suspend v hang up; postpone; defer; debar, prohibit temporarily; n pl **suspenders** device for holding up stockings or socks.

suspense n state of anxious uncertainty; n **suspension** state of being suspended (in various senses) (**s. bridge** bridge hung from cables supported by towers on piers).

suspicion n 1 act of suspecting 2 feeling of doubt, mistrust 3 slight trace; a **suspicious** (adv **-ly**; n **-ness**).

suss see **sus**.

sustain v 1 support; hold up 2 undergo; ns **sustenance** nourishment; maintenance.

suture n 1 act, process of sewing up wound 2 thread, wire used for this 3 anat articulation of bones of skull; v join with suture.

suzerain n Fr feudal law; State with sovereignty over another; n **suzerainty**.

svelte a slender; graceful; willowy.

swab n 1 mop 2 med absorbent pad; v **swabbing, swabbed**. clean; wash out with swab.

swaddle v swathe; bundle up; n pl **swaddling-clothes -bands** strip of cloth formerly wrapped round baby.

swag n sl booty; plunder; hanging wreath or festoon.

swagger v strut; show off; bear oneself jauntily; n such gait or manner.

swain n lit country lad; lover; admirer.

swallow[1] n migratory bird with

long, pointed wings and forked tail; *n* **s.-tail** kind of butterfly or humming bird; dress-coat.

swallow[2] *v* 1 make (food, drink etc) pass down gullet 2 put up with (insult) 3 believe implicitly 4 overwhelm; *n* act of swallowing food etc.

swam *pt of* **swim**.

swamp *n* marsh; bog; *v* cover with water; *fig* overwhelm; *a* swampy.

swan *n* large, long-necked aquatic bird; *n* **s.-song** 1 fabled song of dying swan 2 *fig* last work, utterance of actor, writer etc; *n* **swannery** place where swans are kept.

swank *v coll* behave, talk boastfully; *n* 1 such talk or behaviour 2 person who does this; *a* **-y** 1 boastful 2 (of clothes, possessions) showy or fashionable.

swap, swop *v* **swapping, swapped.** exchange, barter.

swarm[1] *n* large mass of insects, *esp* cluster of bees with queen; crowd; *v* 1 (of bees) leave hive with queen 2 gather in large numbers.

swarm[2] *v* climb (rope etc) by clasping with hands and legs.

swarthy *a* dark-complexioned.

swastika *n* hooked cross, used as a badge by Nazi Party.

swat *v* **swatting, swatted.** crush; squash (insect etc).

swatch *n* sample of cloth.

swathe *v* cover, wrap with bandage or cloth.

sway *v* swing, cause to swing unsteadily; move; influence; *n* swaying motion; influence; power.

swear *v* **swearing, swore, sworn.** 1 promise on oath 2 cause to take an oath 3 curse; *phr vs* **swear by** have great faith in; **swear in** cause to take oath in court or on taking political office.

sweat *n* 1 moisture exuded by pores of skin 2 hard labour 3 great anxiety; *idm* **no sweat** *coll* (it causes) no great difficulty; *v* 1 exude sweat 2 (cause to) work hard for low wages 3 suffer great anxiety; *idm* **sweat blood** *coll* work abnormally hard; *idm* **sweat it out** endure (in discomfort) to the end; *ns* **s.-band** strip of material worn to absorb sweat; **s.-shirt** long-sleeved sweater *usu* of cotton; **s.-shop** place where people work hard for low wages; **sweated labour** hard work for small reward; **sweater** thick woollen jersey.

Swede *n* 1 native of Sweden 2 kind of turnip.

sweep *v* **sweeping, swept.** 1 clean with brush, broom 2 move in stately manner 3 form wide curve 4 drive, move violently away; *idm* **sweep sb off his/her feet** overwhelm sb with feelings of love, admiration; *idm* **sweep the board** be completely successful; win all the prizes; *idm* **sweep under the carpet** try to hide (sth that causes embarassment); *phr v* **sweep aside** ignore completely; *n* 1 act of sweeping 2 wide curve or curving movement 3 person who cleans chimneys 4 *fig* range 5 *coll* sweepstake; *ns* **sweeper** 1 machine for cleaning carpets 2 person who sweeps 3 *football* player giving extra support to defenders; **sweepstake** form of gambling in which winner takes all money staked; *a* **sweeping** 1 extensive 2 too generalized (*n pl* **-s** collected dust)

sweet *a* 1 tasting like sugar 2 pure 3 fragrant 4 melodious 5 agreeable 6 gentle; *n* dessert; sweetmeat; *ns* **sweetbread** pancreas of calf or lamb served as meat; **s.-briar/brier** wild rose; eglantine; **s.corn** type of maize with sweet grain; **sweetheart** (term of endearment for) person one loves; **sweetmeat** *ar* item of confectionery; **s. pea** climbing plant with colourful sweet-smelling flowers; **s. potato** tropical plant with yellow edible roots; **s. talk** *US coll* flattery used to persuade (*v* **s.-talk**); **s. tooth** love for sweet things; **s. william** biennial plant with clusters of sweet-smelling flowers; *adv* **-ly** *n* **-ness**; *v* **sweeten** 1 make sweet 2 *coll* bribe (*ns* **-er**, **-ing**).

swell v **swelling, swelled, swollen** or **swelled.** expand; be elated; increase in size; n 1 act of swelling 2 succession of unbroken waves 3 coll smartly-dressed person; a coll excellent; fine.

swelter v suffer discomfort from heat; a -**ing.**

swept pt, pp of **sweep**; as **s.-back** 1 with front edge angled backwards 2 (of hair) brushed backwards.

swerve v swing round; deviate from course; deflect; n.

swift a rapid; quick; speedy; adv -**ly;** n -**ness;** n bird like swallow.

swig v **swigging, swigged.** to drink a liquid in large mouthfulls.

swill v coll drink usu large mouthful (esp from bottle); n such a mouthful.

swill v 1 rinse; wash out with water 2 drink greedily; n liquid pig food.

swim v **swimming, swam, swum.** 1 move through water by movement of limbs, fins etc 2 feel dizzy 3 be flooded; idm **swim with the tide** copy what others do; n spell of swimming; idm **in/out of the swim** familiar/unfamiliar with what is happening in the world; ns **swimmer; swimming** (ns **s. bath** Brit public swimming pool; **s. costume** one-piece garment for swimming (also **bathing-costume/suit); s. pool** artificial indoor or outdoor pool for swimming; **s.-trunks** shorts for swimming); adv **swimmingly** coll smoothly; pleasantly.

swindle v cheat, defraud; ns **swindler; swindling.**

swine n pig; coll unpleasant person; pl **swine.**

swing v **swinging, swung.** 1 move to and fro, esp as suspended body 2 turn on hinge or pivot 3 coll be hanged; idm **swing into action** begin to act quickly; idm **swing for it** coll be hanged; idm **swing the lead** dated Brit coll avoid work by pretending to be ill; idm **go with a swing** coll be a great success; n 1 act of swinging 2 seat for children to swing on for amusement 3 sudden change or reversal 4 type of jazz with strong regular beat, popular in 1930s and 1940s; idm **in full swing** operating at its peak; idm **get into the swing (of)** coll become adapted (to); idm **(it's all) swings and roundabouts** any gains are matched by corresponding losses (or vice versa); ns **s.bridge** bridge that pivots to allow passage of ships; a **swinging** modern and lively.

swipe v strike with powerful blow; coll steal.

swirl v whirl about; form eddies; n such motion.

swish v pass, cut through air with hissing sound; move with such sound; n swishing sound, or movement.

Swiss a of Switzerland; n **S.roll** cylindrical roll of spongecake with jam, cream or chocolate filling.

switch n 1 device for interrupting or diverting electrical current in a circuit 2 sudden change 3 substitution 4 slender, flexible twig or rod 5 piece of false hair; v 1 change 2 exchange; transfer; phr vs **switch off/on** 1 turn off/on (electrical device) 2 coll cease/begin to show interest; ns **switch-back** 1 road or track with hairpin bends 2 big dipper; **s.-blade** US flick-knife; **switchboard** control centre for manual operation of telephone system.

swivel n link consisting of ring and shank, allowing two parts to revolve independently; v turn on swivel.

swiz n Brit coll situation in which one feels cheated.

swizzle n US frothy mixed drink.

swollen pp of **swell;** a **s.-headed** conceited.

swoon v, n (have) fainting fit.

swoop v descend steeply through air like hawk; n act of swooping; sudden attack.

swop see **swap.**

sword n weapon with long sharp blade fixed in hilt; n **s.-fish** fish with long, sharp upper jaw **s.-play** fighting with swords; **swordsman** man skilled in using sword (n -**manship** this skill).

swore *pt* of **swear**.

sworn *pp* of **swear**; *a* 1 (of statement) made under oath 2 (of friend or enemy) long-established; confirmed by pledge.

swot *v* **swotting, swotted**. *coll* study hard; *n* one who studies hard.

swum *pp* of **swim**.

swung *pt, pp* of **swing**.

sybarite *n* one who is fond of luxurious comfort; *a* **sybaritic**.

sycamore *n* tree allied to maple.

syllable *n* division of word, as unit of pronunciation; *a* **syllabic**.

syllabus *n* programme; list of subjects.

sylph *n* sprite; *a* **sylphlike** slender and graceful.

sylvan *a* of, in woods; rustic.

symbiosis *n bio* condition of living things which depend on each other for survival; *a* **symbiotic**.

symbol *n* sign; anything representing or typifying something; *a* **symbolic**; *v* **symbolize**; *n* **symbolism** represented by symbols.

symmetry *n* balance of arrangement between two sides; *a* **symmetrical** duly proportioned; harmonious.

sympathy *n* fellow-feeling; sharing of emotion, interest etc; compassion; *a* **-pathetic**; *v* **-pathize**.

symphony *n* 1 harmony of sounds 2 *mus* sonata or composition for full orchestra; *a* **-phonic**.

symptom *n* outward sign; change in body indicating presence or development of disease; *a* **-atic**.

synagogue *n* religious congregation of Jews; Jewish place of worship.

synchro- *prefix* at the same time; operating together; *n* **synchromesh** *aut* gearbox system facilitating smooth changing between gears (*also a*); *v* **synchronize** 1 make agree in time 2 (cause to) happen at same time (*n* **-ization**); *a* **synchronized** (*ns* **s.swimming** sport where swimmers aim to perform complex movements in complete synchronization.

syncopate *v* 1 shorten word by omitting medial sound 2 *mus* begin (note) on normally unaccented beat; *n* **syncopation**.

syndicate *n* body of persons, combining for some enterprise.

syndrome *n* combination of various symptoms of disease.

synod *n* Church council; convention.

synonym *n* word with same meaning as another; *a* **synonymous**.

synopsis *n* **-opses.** summary; outline.

syntax *n ling* sentence structure.

synthesis *n* **-theses.** combination; putting together; *a* **-thetic** artificial; *v* **synthesize** make by synthesis; combine into a whole *n* **-sizer** electronic keyboard instrument with facility for producing and sustaining a variety of instrumental sounds and rhythmic effects.

syphilis *n* contagious venereal disease; *a* **-litic**.

syphon see **siphon**.

syringe *n* instrument for drawing in liquid by piston and ejecting it in jet; spray, cleanse with syringe.

syrup *n* thick solution obtained in refining of sugar; *a* **syrupy**.

system *n* plan, scheme for organizing, classifying objects; complex whole; *a* **-atic**.

systemic *a* affecting entire organism.

systems analysis *n* analysis of management requirements in a form which can be programmed to a computer; *n* **s.analyst** specialist in this.

tab n 1 small flap or strip of cloth, paper etc attached to larger object 2 US bill; *idm* **keep tabs on** *coll* keep under observation.

Tabasco [TM] hot spicy sauce.

tabby n striped cat.

tabernacle n 1 tent of Israelites 2 dissenting place of worship 3 small chest on altar to contain Host.

table n 1 piece of furniture consisting of flat board supported by legs 2 set of facts, figures etc arranged in lines, or columns; *idm* **turn the tables** reverse situation to one's advantage; *ns* **t. d'hôte** meal at fixed price; **t. talk** conversation during meal; **t. tennis** game like tennis played with wooden bats and hollow plastic ball on table with net (*also* **ping-pong**); **tablespoon** large spoon for serving food; **tableware** crockery and cutlery. *v* enter into list etc; submit for discussion etc.

tableau n *Fr* group of motionless, costumed persons posed to represent well-known picture, scene etc; *pl* **tableaux**.

tablet n 1 small flat slab 2 small flat medicinal pill or sweet.

tabloid n 1 [TM] medicinal tablet 2 *fig* small, condensed, sensational newspaper; *a* concentrated; brief.

taboo n setting apart as sacred, certain persons or things; ban; restraint; *v* prohibit, forbid by taboo.

tabor n small drum.

tabulate v arrange (words, figures) in a table; *n* **-ation;** *a* **tabular.**

tachograph n device that records vehicle's speed and distance.

tachometer n device for measuring speed.

tacit a implied, inferred by silence; *a* **taciturn** speaking little; *n* **taciturnity.**

tack n 1 small broad-headed nail 2 long temporary stitch 3 rope fastening corner of sail 4 ship's course 5 *fig* course of action 6 *sl* food; *v* 1 fasten with tacks 2 sew loosely 3 change course obliquely.

tackle n equipment; apparatus for moving, *esp* raising weights; *v* grip; grapple with.

tacky a sticky; of poor quality.

taco n Mexican flat bread that can be filled.

tact n skill in dealing with people, situations; natural perception of what is right and fitting; *as* **tactful;** **tactless** accidentally offensive.

tactic n means of achieving sth; *pl* **-s** *mil* art of deploying troops, weapons etc; *a* **tactical** 1 of tactics 2 with calculated intent (*adv* **-ly**); *n* **tactician** person expert in tactics.

tactile a of, relating to sense of touch; tangible.

tadpole n young frog or toad, having gills and tail.

taffeta n *Fr* stiff fabric or silk, or wool.

Taffy n *coll* nickname for Welshman.

tag n 1 projecting flap, end 2 metal point of boot lace 3 hanging label 4 cliché; *v* **tags, tagging, tagged.** label; *phr vs* **tag along (with)** *coll* follow closely (behind): **tag on** *coll* add.

tagliatelle *n It* pasta strips.

tail *n* 1 prolonged extension of animal's spine; anything resembling this; hindmost, rear part of anything 2 *coll* follower; pursuer 3 *pl* -s tailcoat 4 *pl* reverse side of coin; *v* follow (person) closely; *phr v* **tail away/off** become smaller, less numerous, weaker; *ns* **tailback** long line of obstructed traffic; **t.board** flap at rear of vehicle to make loading and unloading easier; **t.-coat** formal evening dinner jacket; **t.-end** very end; **t.-gate** 1 tail-board 2 rear door of hatchback (*v US coll* follow closely behind); **t.-light** red light at rear of vehicle; **tailpipe** car exhaust pipe; **t.-spin** *avia* uncontrolled spiral dive; **t.-wind** wind blowing from behind; *a* -**less**.

tailor *n* one who makes or sells outer clothing, *esp* men's; *v* work as tailor; *fig* adapt for special purpose; *a* **t.-made** individually made; precisely made for specific need.

taint *n* stain; trace of decay; disgrace; *v* stain slightly; become infected.

take *v* 1 seize; get possession of 2 accept 3 carry 4 conduct 5 accommodate 6 receive into 7 use (transport) 8 tolerate 9 need (time) 10 imbibe 11 be effective 12 earn 13 record (on film, tape); *pt*

took; *pp* taken; *idm* **take it** presume; *idm* **be taken aback** be astonished; *idm* **be taken ill** fall ill; *idm* **take it easy** *coll* relax; *idm* **take place** happen; *idm* **take sides** show a bias; *phr vs* **take after** look or behave like (parent etc); **take apart** 1 dismantle 2 *coll* vandalize; **take away** 1 subtract 2 remove 3 carry (food) away from premises (*a, n* t. away) (*of* such food); **take in** 1 provide accommodation for 2 include 3 reduce size of (clothes) 4 deceive 5 understand properly; **take off** 1 remove 2 leave unexpectedly 3 leave the ground 4 mimic (*n* t. off 1 departure of aircraft 2 mimicry; *idm* **take time/a day/week etc off** have holiday of stated length) **take on** 1 accept a challenge from 2 start to employ 3 accept (work etc) 4 *coll* have an emotional outburst; **take out** 1 extract 2 escort (socially) 3 obtain by official agreement 4 *US* take away (*n* t.out); (*idm* **take sb out of himself** cause sb to forget worries; *idm* **take it out of sb** exhaust sb; *idm* **take it out/things out on sb** *coll* make sb suffer for one's bad feelings; **take over** 1 gain control (of) 2 assume responsibility (for) (*n* t.-over); **take to** 1 like instantly 2 begin doing regularly 3 escape to (*idm*

take to one's heels run away); **take up** 1 pick up 2 begin to practise or study 3 occupy (time/space) 4 accept (offer) (*n* t.-up rate rate at which sth is accepted); **take sth up with sb** ask sb, complain to sb about sth; *ns* **t.-home pay** amount of pay after deduction of tax etc; **taker** person accepting offer or challenge; **takings** money received from selling goods, performing in public etc.

talc *n* magnesium silicate; *n* **talcum** powdered talc; toilet powder.

tale *n* story, account; rumour; narrative.

talent *n* marked aptitude; special faculty; *a* **talented** gifted.

talisman *n* charm, amulet; object regarded as having magic powers.

talk *v* 1 speak; utter in speech 2 converse 3 discuss; *phr vs* **talk down to** speak in a condescending way to; **talk sb into/out of** persuade sb to do/not to do; **talk sb round** talk until one persuades sb to change his/her mind; *n* 1 conversation 2 informal lecture 3 words of no special meaning 4 characteristic speech; *idm* **the talk of** subject of gossip for; *pl* -s formal discussion *esp* political; *n* -**er**; *as* **talkative** fond of talking (*n* -**ness**); **talking** capable of speech (*ns* **t.point** subject of discussion; **t.-to** reprimand).

tall *a* above average in stature; lofty; *sl* difficult to believe; untrue; *ns* **t. order** *coll* unreasonable request; **t. story** story difficult to believe.

tallboy *n* high chest of drawers.

tallow *n* melted-down animal fat.

tally *n* notched rod to count by; *v* **tallies, tallying, tallied.** account by tally; agree, correspond exactly.

Talmud *n* written record of Jewish law and tradition.

talon *n* claw.

tamarind *n* (fruit or wood of) tropical evergreen tree.

tamarisk *n* evergreen shrub.

tambour *n* 1 bass-drum 2 embroidery frame; *n* **tambourine** small shallow drum fitted with tinkling discs.

tame *a* 1 not wild 2 subdued 3 *fig* dull; *v* make tame; *n* **tamer.**

Tamil *n* member of mixed Dravidian and Caucasoid people of S India and Sri Lanka.

tamp *phr v* **tamp down** ram down tightly.

tamper *phr v* **tamper with** 1 interfere with 2 alter fraudulently.

tampon *n* internal protection used during menstruation.

tan[1] *n* bark of oak bruised to extract tannic acid; *a* of yellowish-brown; *v* **tans, tanning, tanned.** 1 make

into leather 2 make become brown *esp* by sunburn 3 *coll* flog; *n* **tanner** one who tans; *n* **tannery** place where hides are tanned.

tan[2] *abbr* tangent.

tandem *n* bicycle for two riders; *idm Lat* **in tandem** (working) in close cooperation.

tandoori *n* food cooked by Indian method in clay oven.

tang *n* 1 projecting spike 2 strong flavour or smell 3 kind of seaweed.

tangent *a* touching, but not cutting; *n* line touching curve at one point; *n idm* **fly/go off at a tangent** *fig* suddenly change direction; *a* **tangential.**

tangerine *n* small, sweet, thin-skinned orange.

tangible *a* capable of being touched; *fig* clearly defined in mind, practical.

tangle *v* form confused mass, intertwine; **t. with** *coll* come into conflict with; *n* intricate knot; disorder.

tango *n* **-os.** type of S American dance; music for this; *v* dance tango.

tank *n* 1 receptacle for storing liquids, oil or gas 2 heavy armoured vehicle with tracked wheels and guns; *ns* **tanker** ship, lorry carrying oil, liquid fuel in bulk; **t.-engine** locomotive carrying its own water and fuel.

tankard *n* large beer mug.

tanner *n Brit coll* formerly

coin worth six pence.

tannic *a* of, obtained from tan; *n* **t.acid;** *n* **tannin** astringent substance; tannic acid.

tannoy [TM] loud-speaker public address system.

tantalize *v* torment by repeated renewal of hope and disappointment; tease; *n* **tantalus** stand for decanters, with locking device.

tantamount *a* equal in value or effect; equivalent.

tantrum *n* fit, outburst of violent temper.

Taoism *n* religion of Ancient China.

tap[1] *n* 1 device with turning valve or screw for controlling flow of liquid from pipe, cask etc 2 instrument for cutting internal screw-threads; *idm* **on tap** available for immediate use; *v* **taps, tapping, tapped.** 1 fit tap in 2 draw off (liquid) 3 listen in deliberately to (telephone conversation); *ns* **tap-root** long tapering root of plant; **tapster** one who draws beer.

tap[2] *v* strike lightly; *n* light blow; sound of this; *n* **t. dance** dance with special shoes that make rhythm audible.

tape *n* 1 long narrow band of fabric, paper etc 2 (spool holding) length of magnetic tape; recording on this; *v* 1 fasten with tape 2 record on tape; *idm* **have sth taped** *coll* be totally familiar with, in control of sth; *ns* **t. deck**

tape recording component of hi-fi system; **t.-measure** flexible strip of fabric or metal for measuring lengths; **t.-recorder** apparatus for recording on magnetic tape; **tapeworm** parasitic flat worm living in intestine of animals, humans.

taper n thin candle; v narrow gradually to point at one end.

tapestry n fabric with designs worked in wool by hand; a **-tried** hung with tapestry.

tapioca n starchy food obtained from dried manioc.

tappet n short rod transmitting motion intermittently.

tar[1] n thick black viscous liquid distilled from coal etc; v **tars, tarring, tarred.** cover, treat with tar.

tar[2] n coll sailor.

taramasalata n Greek appetizer of paste from fish roe.

tarantula n large venomous spider.

tardy n slow; late; reluctant; adv **-ily;** n **-iness.**

tare[1] n common vetch; weed.

tare[2] n weight of unladen goods vehicle; allowance made for this.

target n 1 object of attack (military, verbal etc) 2 round board marked in circles, to be shot at; butt.

tariff n list of duties on imports and exports; list of charges.

tarmac n mixture of tar and macadam used as road-

surfacing material.

tarn n smoorland or mountain lake.

tarnish v 1 spoil brightness of by exposure to air etc 2 fig stain; sully; n loss of lustre.

tarot n set of special cards used by fortune-teller.

tarpaulin n water-proof canvas treated with tar.

tarragon n aromatic herb used for flavouring.

tarry v linger; stay in a place.

tart[1] a sour; sharp; acid.

tart[2] n open, or covered fruit pie; n **tartlet** small tart.

tart[3] phr v **tart up** embellish in a cheap way, esp in order to conceal blemishes; a **tarty;** adv **-ily;** n **-iness.**

tartan n woollen fabric woven in various coloured checks, each pattern belonging to a Highland clan.

tartar n 1 incrustation forming on teeth 2 deposit formed in wine vats 3 cap native of Tartary 4 fig violent person; n **t. sauce** type of mayonnaise with capers, herbs etc; a **-ic (t. acid)** acid found in juice of fruit etc.

task n piece, amount of work imposed or undertaken; idm **take to task** reprove; ns **task-force** military, police unit detailed for specific operation; **task-master** exacting master; overseer.

tassel n knotted bunch of silk or other threads, used as ornament.

taste v 1 test, perceive flavour

of 2 have particular flavour of; n 1 faculty of experiencing flavours on tongue 2 small portion of food or drink 3 discernment; tact; idm **a/some taste for 1** tendency towards 2 liking for; n **t. bud** cells of tongue sensitive to taste; as **tasteful** showing refinement; in good taste; **tasteless** insipid; tactless; **tasty** pleasant to taste; savoury.

tat n Brit sl worthless rubbish.

ta-ta interj esp Brit goodbye.

tatting n lace-like trimming of looped and knotted threads; v **tat** make tatting.

tatter n rag; torn fragment.

tattle v gossip; indiscreet talk.

tattoo[1] n 1 military pageant or spectacle 2 drum-beat or bugle-call of recall 3 knocking.

tattoo[2] v mark (skin) by pricking and inserting indelible pigments; n mark so made.

taunt v reproach sarcastically, contemptuously; n jeer; gibe.

taut a stretched tightly; tense; a **-ly;** n **-ness;** v tauten make tight.

tautology n unnecessary repetition of same idea in different words; a **tautological.**

tavern n inn; public house.

tawdry a showy; flashy; gaudy; cheap; n **tawdriness.**

tawny a of light, brownish yellow colour.

tax n 1 compulsory duty or levy imposed on income,

goods etc 2 strain; *v* 1 impose tax on 2 lay heavy burden on; *idm* **tax sb's brains** set sb challenging mental task; *a* **t.-deductible** recognized as an allowance against tax; *ns* **t. haven** country with low tax rate; **t. return** statement of income for tax authorities; **t. shelter** method of legally avoiding tax on some income; *n* **taxation** act of levying tax; *a* **taxable**; *n* **taxpayer**.

taxi *n* taxi-cab, car for public hire; *v* **taxies, taxiing** *or* **taxying, taxied.** (*of aircraft*) run along ground under own power before take-off, or after landing; **t. -meter** instrument recording fare due for mileage covered; **t. rank** place where taxis wait for customers.

taxidermy *n* art of preparing and stuffing animal skins; *n* **-dermist.**

TB *abbr med* tuberculosis.

T-bone *n* thick beefsteak with T-shaped bone.

tea *n* 1 dried leaves of tea-plant, infused to make drink 2 light afternoon meal; *ns* **teabag** paper sachet with enough tealeaves for one or two cups of tea; **t.cake** large currant bun for toasting and serving with butter; **t.chest** large wooden crate for exporting tea; **t. cosy** cover to keep teapot warm; **t. garden** 1 tea plantation 2 cafe which serves refreshments outdoors;

t.-rose scented China rose; **t. towel** cloth for drying wet cutlery and crockery.

teach *v* **teaching, taught.** instruct; train; impart knowledge; *ns* **t.-in** meeting at which knowledge and opinion on subject of interest are exchanged; *n* **teacher** one who instructs; schoolmaster, -mistress; **teaching** 1 job of teacher 2 *esp pl* doctrine of religious leader.

teak *n* Indian tree with very hard wood.

teal *n* kind of small wild duck.

team *n* number of animals harnessed together; number of persons working, acting, playing together; *phr v* **t.up with** *coll* work in harmony; match; *ns* **teamster** *US* truck-driver **t.work** combined effort.

teapot *n* container with spout for serving tea.

tear[1] *n* single drop of saline fluid coming from eye; *as* **tearful** shedding tears;sad; **tearless**; *ns* **tear-drop**; **tear-gas** irritant poison-gas, causing abnormal watering of eyes; *n* **t.-jerker** story or film likely to provoke tears.

tear[2] *v* **tearing, tore, torn.** 1 pull apart; be torn; rend 2 rush; *idm* **be torn between** be unable to decide between; *phr vs* **tear down** 1 pull down; destroy 2 run fast; **tear up** 1 tear to pieces 2 run fast; *n* torn hole; *n* **tearaway** *Brit coll* riotous,

uncontrolled, *usu* young person.

tease *v* 1 tear apart fibres of 2 worry 3 bait; poke fun at; *n* one who torments; *a* **t.-er** difficult question; *a* **teasing** harassing.

teaspoon *n* small spoon.

teat *n* nipple of female mammal's breast; nipple of feeding bottle.

TEC *abbr* Training and Enterprise Council

technical *a* pertaining to industrial or mechanical arts; peculiar to some specific branch of science or art; not understandable by laymen; *n* **t. college** college with emphasis on practical subjects; *ns* **-ity** state of being technical; technical term; detail of procedure; **technique** method of execution or performance; skill in methods of special art etc; **technician** one skilled in mechanical art.

technocracy *n* 1 control of country's resources by technical experts 2 country where this occurs; *n* **technocrat** scientific expert in favour of technocracy; *a* **-cratic.**

technology *n* science of industrial and mechanical arts; **technologist**; *a* **-ological** (*adv* **-ly**).

tectonic *a* pertaining to art of building; relating to structure of earth; *n pl* **-s** art of functional designing combined with artistic merit.

teddy *n* soft toy bear (*also* **t.bear**); **t. boy** (in 1950s) any young man identifying with group of rebels wearing Edwardian clothes.

tedium *n* weariness; boredom; *a* **tedious** dull, long and boring (*adv* **-ly**; *n* **-ness**).

tee *n* 1 small peg off which golf ball is first played at each hole 2 *quoits* mark aimed at; *phr vs* **tee off** golf drive ball from tee; **tee up** golf place (ball) on tee.

teem *v* rain heavily; *phr v* **teem with** abound with.

teens *n pl* age between 13–20; *n* **teenager** adolescent between 13–20.

teeny-bopper *n* young person, *esp* girl following current trends in pop fashion.

teeny (**weeny**) *a coll* very tiny.

tee shirt = t-shirt.

teeter *v* move or stand unsteadily.

teeth *pl* of **tooth**.

teethe *v* develop or cut teeth; *n* **-ing** process of (baby) growing teeth (*n* **t. troubles** *fig* problems in early stages of using sth).

teetotal *a* of, observing total abstinence from intoxicants; *n* **-(l)er**.

TEFL *abbr* teaching of English as a foreign language.

Teflon [TM] substance used on surface of non-stick pans.

tele- *prefix* at or over a distance; from far off.

telecast *v* broadcast on TV.

telecommunications *n pl*

communication of messages over distances, *esp* by telephone and radio.

telegraph *n* electrical apparatus for transmitting messages to a distance; *n* **t. pole** pole supporting telephone wires; *v* communicate by telegraph; *ns* **-er**, **-ist**; *a* **-ic**; *ns* **telegraphy** art, process of communicating by telegraph; **telegram** message sent by telegraph.

telegraphese *n* written style using as few words as possible.

telekinesis *n* ability to cause objects to move by power of mind.

telemarketing *n* selling by telephone (*also* **telesales**).

telemeter *n* instrument that takes measurements and sends results by radio; *n* **-metry** collection of information in this way.

teleology *n* belief that all things and events are planned for a purpose; *a* **-logical**.

telepathy *n* thought transference; *a* **-pathic**.

telephone *n* instrument for transmitting conversation over a distance; *v* use, communicate by, telephone *ns* **telephony** telephonic communication; **telephonist** one who works a telephone; *a* **-phonic**.

telephoto *abbr* **telephotography** photograph(ing) of distant

objects through magnifying; **t. lens**.

teleprinter *n* machine for handling telex messages.

Teleprompter [TM] device used on TV to present script to presenter while he/she looks into the camera.

telescope *n* optical instrument for viewing magnified images of distant objects; *v* close, slide together as parts of telescope; compress forcibly; *a* **telescopic**.

teletext *n* TV system of information presented as written text.

television *n* transmission of visible moving images by electro-magnetic waves; viewing of such; *v* **televise** transmit by television.

telex *n* (written message sent by) system of satellite and telephone communication; *v* send (to sb) by telex.

tell *v* **telling**, **told**. 1 narrate; divulge 2 order; command 3 be of importance 4 inform; *idm* **all told** counting every one; *phr vs* **tell against** be counted to the disadvantage of; **tell off** reprimand; **tell on** 1 have harmful effect on 2 *coll* (*esp* used by children) inform against; *n* **teller** narrator, bank-clerk who pays out money; *a* **telling** impressive; *n* **tell-tale** sneak; *a* revealing.

tellurian *a* pertaining to earth; *n* **tellurium** rare, brittle, non-metallic element; *a* **telluric**.

telly n coll television.

temerity n rashness; audacity; great boldness.

temp n coll person in temporary employment; v coll work as a temp.

temper v 1 harden (metal, glass etc) 2 moderate; knead and moisten clay; n 1 degree of hardness (of steel etc) 2 frame of mind 3 angry mood.

temperament n natural disposition; emotional mood; a -al unreliable; unstable; liable to strong changes of mood.

temperate a moderate and restrained; not extreme; n temperance 1 abstinence, esp from alcohol 2 moderation.

temperature, n degree of heat or cold in atmosphere or body; idm have a temperature be feverish.

tempest n violent storm; fig violent emotion; a -uous stormy; violently excited.

template = templet.

temple[1] n building, place of worship.

temple[2] n flat part of head on either side of forehead.

templet, template n mould, pattern, used as guide in shaping.

tempo n degree of speed; rate; pace.

temporal a 1 pertaining to, limited by time 2 secular; a temporary lasting short time; not permanent.

temporize v try to avoid making decision; be evasive.

tempt v try to persuade esp to evil; excite desire in; ns -ter; -tation act of tempting; attraction; inducement.

ten n, pron, det cardinal number next after nine; 10.

tenable a capable of being held, defended; (of opinions etc) logical.

tenacious a holding fast; unyielding; retentive; n tenacity.

tenant n one who holds land or house etc on rent or lease; ns tenancy; tenantry body of tenants.

tench n fresh-water fish.

tend[1] v take care of; watch over; n tender 1 one who tends 2 small ship in attendance on larger one 3 fuel and water carrier attached to locomotive.

tend[2] v have inclination; move in certain direction; n tendency inclination; bent; trend; a tendentious not impartial.

tender[1] v offer; make estimate; n 1 offer made to carry out work etc at fixed price 2 money offered in settlement of claim etc.

tender[2] a 1 delicate; sensitive to pain; easily injured 2 kind; loving; a t. hearted disposed to show sympathy to others; kind; ns tenderness; tenderfoot newcomer; novice.

tender[3] n 1 container for coal and water attached to steam locomotive 2 small ship in attendance on larger one.

tenderize v make (sinewy meat) more tender.

tenderloin n cut of pork, beef between sirloin and ribs.

tendon n sinew attaching muscle to bone.

tendril n 1 slender coiling stem in climbing plants 2 curl of hair.

tenement n house, dwelling divided into separate apartments.

tenet n opinion, belief held as true.

tenner n coll ten pounds.

tennis n game for two or four players, in which ball is struck over net with rackets.

tenon n tongue cut on end of piece of wood to fit into mortise; n t. saw.

tenor n 1 singing voice between baritone and alto; singer with this range.

tenpin n skittle used in tenpin bowling; n t. bowling game like ninepins with one extra skittle.

tense[1] n modification of verb to show time of action.

tense[2] a taut; stretched tight; a tensile capable of being stretched; n tension 1 act, process of stretching, tightening 2 emotional strain 3 elec voltage.

tent n portable canvas shelter supported by pole(s).

tentacle n long, slender, flexible organ of feeling; feeler.

tentative a experimental; provisional.

tenter n frame for stretching cloth; **t.hook** hooked nail used in stretching cloth; **on t.hooks** in state of anxiety, suspense.

tenth a, n, pron, det ordinal number of ten; next after ninth.

tenuous a 1 thin; fine; flimsy 2 too subtle; n **tenuity**.

tenure n act of, manner of holding land, office etc.

tepid a lukewarm; fig showing little interest etc.

tequila n Mexican strong alcoholic drink.

tercentenary n three hundredth anniversary.

tergiversation n shuffling; evasive conduct; vacillation.

term n 1 limit esp of time; fixed, limited period 2 period when courts sit, schools are open etc 3 word used in any special art, science 4 pl -s conditions (of contract etc) 5 pl personal relations; v designate; call.

terminal n 1 (passenger building at) airport or end station of rail, bus or coach line 2 place of connection to electric circuit 3 comput apparatus for input to and output from central computer; a of, near the end (adv -ly); n t. disease incurable illness that will cause death.

terminate v bring, come to an end; n -ation conclusion; ending.

terminology n system of special, or technical terms; a

-ogical.

terminus n -ni or -nuses. 1 station at end of railway line etc 2 final point reached.

termite n one of order of destructive insects; so-called white ant.

terms n pl conditions of agreement or sale; idm come to terms reach agreement; idm come to terms with learn to accept (sth unpleasant); idm (buy/have) on terms comm (buy/have) on credit (with repayment agreement); idm on good/bad/etc terms (with) having a good/bad/etc relationship (with).

tern n sea-bird of gull family.

terpsichorean a pertaining to dancing.

terrace n raised level platform of earth etc; row of end-to-end houses; v build up, cut, into form of terrace a **terraced** arranged in terraces (n t. house house forming part of terrace).

terracotta n It hard unglazed reddish-brown pottery.

terra firma n Lat solid, dry land.

terrain n Fr tract of land.

terrapin n edible fresh-water turtle.

terrarium n -iums or terraria. 1 container for growing plants 2 enclosure for animals.

terrestrial a earthly; of, living on dry land.

terrible a 1 fearful 2 coll very bad; adv -ibly 1 badly 2 coll

very.

terrier n 1 one of several breeds of dogs 2 document setting out extent, rights etc in land.

terrific a 1 awe-inspiring; enormous 2 coll wonderful; excellent; adv -ally extremely.

terrify v fill with terror; as -ified, -ifying.

territory n region; district ruled by State or ruler; a **territorial** of territory; n **Territorial Army** force of volunteers, serving for home defence.

terror n extreme fear; v **terrorize** intimidate with threats of violence; n, a **terrorist** (person) using violence for political ends; n -ism.

terrycloth n thick cotton cloth for making towelling.

terse a concise; curt, abrupt in speech; n **terseness**.

tertiary a of third rank or order; n geological era; a **tertian** (fever) recurring every third day.

Terylene [TM] type of synthetic fibre from polyester (US Dacron).

TES abbr Times Educational Supplement.

TESOL abbr teaching English to speakers of other languages.

test n method adopted to try or prove knowledge of; critical, searching examination; idm put to the test test the quality of sb/sth; v 1 prove the quality, extent, reliability of 2 try by examination; *phr v* **test for** ascertain the presence or absence of (*eg* mineral deposit, disease) by testing; *ns* **t. case** lawsuit which establishes precedent; **t. match** one of series of international matches, *usu* cricket or rugby; **t. tube** small tubular container used in scientific experiments (*n* **t. baby** baby conceived by artificial insemination, *esp* in vitro fertilization); *v* **t.-drive** take on trial drive before deciding whether to purchase.

testament *n* 1 one of two major divisions of Bible 2 *leg* will; *a* **-ary**.

testate *a* having left a valid will; *ns* **testacy** state of being testate; **testator**; *fem* **testatrix**.

testicle *n* sperm-secreting gland in male animals.

TESSA *abbr* tax-exempt special savings account.

testify *v* **testifies, testifying, testified.** bear witness; give evidence; *ns* **testimony** solemn statement; evidence; **testimonial** document setting forth person's character, ability etc; tribute given in token of esteem.

testis *n anat* **testes.** testicle.

testosterone *n* hormone controlling development of secondary characteristics in males.

testy *a* irritable; irascible.

tetanus *n* lock-jaw; violent muscular contraction.

tetchy *a* irritable; bad-tempered; *adv* **-ily**; *n* **-iness**.

tête-à-tête *n Fr* private talk, meeting; *a* confidential.

tether *v* fasten, tie up with rope; *n* rope, chain for fastening grazing animal.

tetragon *n* figure with four sides and four angles.

Teutonic *a* of German language or ancestry.

text *n* 1 original words of author 2 verse, short-passage of Scriptures 3 main part of book etc; *n* **textbook** instruction manual (*a* 1 typical 2 exactly as required); *a* **textual** of, based on, text; literal.

textile *a* woven; *n* woven fabric.

texture *n* 1 quality, structure of fabric 2 degree of coarseness, fineness etc as felt by touch.

thalidomide *n* drug formerly used in pregnancy, but now banned owing to risk of producing deformed babies.

than *prep* used after comp as and *advs* before *ns* and *prons*; *conj* used after comp as and *advs* before clauses.

thank *v* express gratitude to; *n pl* **thanks** words of gratitude; *idm* **thanks to** because of; *interj* **t. you** expressing gratitude (*n* such an expression); *as* **thankful** grateful (*adv* **-ly** *n* **-ness**); **thankless** unlikely to bring show of gratitude (*n* **-ness**); *n* **thanksgiving** 1 expression

of thanks, *esp* to God 2 *cap* US national holiday in late November (*also* **T. Day**).

that *dem pron* thing, person just mentioned, or pointed out; more remote thing or person; *pl* **those**; *idm* **that's that** *coll* there is no more to be said; *rel pron* person who, thing which; *dem a* of person, thing just mentioned etc; *conj* introduces noun, or adverbial clause.

thatch *v* cover (roof, rick etc) with reeds, straw etc; *n* **thatch, thatching** straw, reeds etc used to cover roof etc.

thaw *v* 1 (*of snow etc*) melt; 2 *fig* become more friendly or genial; *n* 1 melting 2 *fig* detente.

the *definite art* indicating particular person or thing.

theatre *n* 1 place where plays are performed; scene of important events or actions 2 room in hospital where operations are performed 3 drama; dramatic works collectively; *a* **theatrical** 1 pertaining to theatre 2 showy 3 affected, insincere (*adv* **-ly** *n* **-ity**).

thee *pron, lit, ar* objective case of **thou**.

theft *n* act of stealing.

their *poss a* of **them**; *poss pron* belonging to them.

theism *n* belief in personal God, capable of revealing Himself; *n* **theist**.

them *pron* objective case of

they; those persons or things; *pron* **themselves** emphatic and reflexive form; *idm* **by themselves** (they) alone.

theme *n* 1 recurrent or important idea in talk or writing 2 *mus* brief recurring melody; *n* **t. park** open-air enclosure with entertainments based on a single idea or subject.

then *adv* 1 at that time 2 next 3 that being so; therefore; *n* that time.

thence *adv ar* 1 from that place 2 for that reason; therefore **thenceforth** from that time on (*also* **thenceforward**).

theocracy *n* government by guidance from God; *a* **-cratic**.

theodolite *n* surveying instrument for measuring angles.

theology *n* systematic study of religion and foundations of belief; *a* **theological**; *n* **theologian** student, authority on theology.

theorem *n* proposition to be established by reasoning.

theoretician *n* person developing theory rather than practical aspects of subject; *a* **theoretical** based on theory; speculative (*adv* **-ly**); *n* **theorist** unpractical person; *v* **theorize** form, put forward theories.

theory *n* 1 supposition to explain group of

phenomena; underlying principles of body of facts 2 opinion.

theosophy *n* mystic form of religious thought aiming at direct contact between individual soul and divine principle; *n* **theosophist**.

therapeutic *a* 1 of, for healing 2 promoting better health or mental state; *pl* **-s** branch of medicine concerned with curing disease.

therapy *n* curative treatment; *suffix* as in psycho-therapy *n* **therapist**.

there *adv* in that place; *idm* **all there** 1 completely sane 2 intelligent; *idm* **there there!** used to comfort a child; *idm* **there you are** 1 used when giving sth to sb 2 used to reassure sb, to demonstrate sth; *idm* **there you go** 1 used when giving sth to sb who is going 2 criticising, *esp* habitual, action or expression one disapproves of; *adv* **thereabouts** 1 approximately 2 in that vicinity; **thereafter** *fml* always after that; **thereby** by this means; **therefore** for this reason; **thereof** *leg* of it, them; **thereupon** *fml* immediately.

therm *n* unit of heat; *a* **thermal**, of, by heat; *n* vertical rising hot-air current; *a* **thermic**.

thermion *n* ion emitted by incandescent body; *a* **thermionic**; *n* **t. valve** system of electrodes in glass

vacuum.

thermo- *prefix* of, by heat.

thermodynamics *n* branch of science dealing with relation between thermal and mechanical energy.

thermometer *n* instrument for measuring temperature; *a* **thermometric**.

thermoplastic *n*, *a* (substance) which becomes soft and plastic when heated.

thermos *n* [TM] vacuum flask.

thermosetting *a* becoming hard after being heated and moulded.

thermostat *n* device for regulating temperature automatically.

thesaurus *n* treasury, *esp* lexicon of words grouped by meaning, not alphabetically.

these *pron pl* of **this**.

thesis *n* **theses**. proposition; essay, treatise written for purposes of university degree.

thespian *a* of acting; *n* actor.

they *pron* third person pl nom.

they'd *contracted form of* 1 they had 2 they would.

they'll *contracted form of* they will.

they're *contracted form of* they are.

they've *contracted form of* they have.

thick *a* 1 of great distance between surfaces 2 (*of liquid*) not flowing easily 3 closely spaced 4 opaque 5 *Brit sl* stupid; *adv* (**-ly**); *idm* **be thick with sb** *coll* habitually associate with sb; *idm* **thick**

and fast coll very frequently; idm **thick with** covered, filled with; idm **through thick and thin** despite all hardship; ns **t. ear** smack on the ear; swollen ear; **t. head** headache; a **thickhead** coll stupid person; (a **-ed**; n **-edness**); a **t.-skinned** insensitive to pain or criticism; v **-en**; n, a **-ening**; n **-ness** 1 state of being thick 2 layer; **thicket** dense growth of shrubs, trees; a **thickset** short; broadly-built.

thief n one who steals; pl **thieves**; v **thieve** steal; a **thievish**.

thigh n thick upper part of leg.

thimble n small cap for protecting finger when sewing.

thin a reverse of thick; slender; •sparse; loosely packed; v make, become thin; idm **thin end of the wedge** minor event likely to lead to sth more serious; idm **thin on the ground** scarce; n **t. air** (idm **into thin air** completely out of sight and impossible to find); a **t.-skinned** easily offended; adv **-ly**; n **-ness**; n **thinner** liquid used to dilute paint.

thine poss pron lit, ar 2nd person sing of thou.

thing n any object, material or immaterial; idm **have a thing about** coll have strong like or dislike for; idm **make a thing of** treat as important; pl **-s** 1 personal possessions 2 general situation.

think v 1 use one's mind; ponder 2 reflect 3 believe; imagine 4 deliberate; pt, pp **thought**; idm **think better of** decide against; phr vs **think out/through** plan in detail; idm **think over** consider carefully; **think up** invent; n **t.-tank** group of experts meeting to advise on national problems.

third det, pron ordinal number of three; next after second; n third part; ns **t. degree** prolonged questioning, esp with torture; **t. party** person or body other than those involved in a relationship or contract; **t. person** form of verb or pronoun used for someone other than the speaker/writer or addressee; **T. World** underdeveloped countries; a **t.-rate** of poor quality.

thirst n 1 craving for liquid 2 fig strong desire; v suffer thirst; a **thirsty**.

thirteen n, pron, det cardinal number three and ten; 13 (n, a, pron, det **thirteenth** ordinal number 13th).

thirty n three times ten; 30; a, n pron, det **thirtieth** ordinal number 30th.

this dem a, pron **these**. denotes thing, person near, just mentioned.

thistle n prickly-leaved flowering plant n **thistledown** seed-bearing fluff from head of thistle.

thither adv ar to, towards that direction, stage, result.

thong n narrow strip of leather, strap.

thorax n part of body between neck and abdomen; a **thoracic**.

thorn n prickle, spine on plant; idm **thorn in one's flesh** persistent cause of annoyance; a **thorny**.

thorough a complete, absolute; a **thoroughbred** pure-bred; n purebred animal; n **thoroughfare** road for public traffic; a **thoroughgoing** 1 complete 2 conscientious.

thorp (e) n hamlet village.

those pron pl of that.

thou pron lit, ar 2nd pers. sing. nom. of you.

though conj in spite of; although; conj **as though** as if.

thought pt, pp of think; n 1 idea; impression 2 act of thinking; careful consideration 3 intention 4 regard; as **-ful** (adv **-ly**; n **-ness**); **-less** (adv **-ly**; n **-ness**).

thousand n, pron, det cardinal number, ten hundreds; 1,000; pl **-s** a large number a, n, det **thousandth** ordinal number 1,000th.

thrash v 1 beat; flog 2 thresh; phr v **thrash out** fig clear up (problem etc.) by discussion.

thread n fine cord used for sewing; yarn; spiral groove cut in screw; v put thread into (needle etc.); idm **thread one's way through** make one's way through patiently in spite of difficulty; *a* **-bare** very worn.

threat *n* statement of intention to injure, punish etc; menace; *v* **-en** utter threats; menace (*a* **-ing** foreshadowing disaster, etc).

three *n, pron, det* cardinal number, one more than two; 3; *a* **t-dimensional** with length, width and height (also **three-D**); *ns* **t.-legged race** race in which each competitor has one leg tied to leg of partner; **t.-line whip** order from political party to elected members to vote on important bill in parliament; **t.-quarter (back)** rugby player positioned between half and full-back; **t. R's** reading, writing and arithmetic; basic educational skills.

thresh *v* separate grain of corn from chaff by beating.

threshold *n* stone or plank below door, at entrance to house etc; (*fig*) beginning.

threw *pt* of **throw**.

thrice *adv lit, ar* three times.

thrift *n* 1 frugality; economy 2 genus of plant, sea-pink.

thrift *n* 1 economy with money; frugality 2 seashore or alpine plant (also **sea-pink**); *a* **-y** frugal; *adv* **-ily**; *n* **-iness.**

thrill *v* stir emotions of; vibrate, tingle; *n* intense emotional stirring; exciting event; *n* **thriller** book or film of exciting, usu crime story *a* **thrilling** exciting.

thrive *v* **thriving, thrived** or

throve, thrived or **thriven.** grow well; prosper.

throat *n* front part of neck; gullet; wind pipe; *a* **throaty** hoarse, guttural.

throb *v* **throbs, throbbing, throbbed.** beat, pulsate strongly; *n* beat, palpitation (of heart etc.).

throe *n* pang; brief agony; **in the throes of** struggling with, coming to grips with (some difficulty).

thrombosis *n med* clotting of blood in blood vessel.

throne *n* seat of state, *esp* of king; *v* enthrone.

throng *n* crowd; large number of people; *v* crowd.

throttle *n* 1 valve in engine regulating flow of steam, gas etc 2 *coll* throat; *v* 1 reduce flow of steam etc 2 strangle.

through *prep* 1 from one end 2 by means of; 3 across *adv* from end to end; *a* 1 unobstructed 2 *coll* finished 3 going all the way without changes; *adv, prep* **throughout** right through; in every particular; **t. and t.** completely; **be t. with** have done with.

throughput *n* quantity of work or material produced in given time.

throughway, thruway *n US* wide road carrying fast traffic.

throw *v* **throwing, threw, thrown.** 1 hurl; fling 2 dislodge (from saddle) 3 form (pottery) on wheel; *idm* **throw a fit/tantrum/wobbly**

coll have sudden outburst of anger; *idm* **throw in one's lot with** join (*usu* with some misgivings); *idm* **throw one's weight about** behave in a bossy manner; *idm* **throw in the towel** *coll* admit failure or defeat; *phr vs* **throw in** add without extra charge; **throw off** 1 escape from 2 resist (illness); **throw open** give free access to; **throw over** end relationship with; **throw together** *coll* construct hastily; **throw up** 1 abandon (job) 2 bring to light 3 *coll* vomit; *n* 1 act of throwing 2 distance thrown; **t.away** 1 expendable 2 (of remark) casual; *n* **t.back** example of regression.

thrum *n* ends of thread of warp on loom after web is cut; loose thread; *pl* waste yarn; *v* **thrums, thrumming, thrummed.** drum, strum or repeat monotonously.

thrush[1] *n* one of varieties of songbirds.

thrush[2] *n* fungal infection of mouth, throat and vagina.

thrust *v* **thrusting, thrust.** 1 push; lunge; stab in with violent action 2 *fig* obtrude oneself; *n* onset with pointed weapon; lunge.

thud *n* dull, sound as of heavy body falling on ground; *v* **thuds, thudding, thudded.** make such sound.

thug *n* murderous ruffian; robber; *n* **thuggery** *a* **thuggish.**

thumb *n* short thick inner

finger of hand; **rule of t.** rough and ready way of doing anything; *idm* **thumb all thumbs** clumsy; *idm* **thumb one's nose at** *coll* show contempt for; *idm* **thumbs up/down** sign of approval/disapproval; *idm* **under sb's thumb** ruled by sb; *idm* **thumb a lift** obtain lift from passing motorist; *ns* **t.-nail** nail of thumb (**t. sketch** very small portrait); **thumbscrew** former instrument of torture; **t.-tack** *US* drawing pin; *v* make dirty (pages of book etc) by handling.

thump *v* strike with heavy blow; *n* such blow, or sound of it; *a* **-ing** *coll* very big.

thunder *n* **1** loud rumbling sound following flash of lightning **2** any such noise (as of applause etc); *v* **1** emit thunder **2** utter with loud, powerful voice; *ns* **thunderbolt 1** flash of lighting **2** *fig* startling news or event; **thunderclap** single crash of thunder; *as* **thunderstruck** deeply and suddenly shocked; **thundery** oppressive.

Thursday *n* fifth day of week.

thus *adv lit, ar* in this way; accordingly; *idm* **thus far** until this moment or point.

thwack *v*, *n* whack.

thwart *v* oppose; hinder; obstruct; *n* seat for oarsman in boat.

thy *poss pron lit, ar* of **thee**; *pron* **thyself** emphatic form of **thou**.

thyme *n* pungent, aromatic herb used in cooking.

thyroid *n* large endocrine gland in neck of vertebrates; *a* of thyroid; **t. cartilage** Adam's apple.

tiara *n* jewelled coronet worn by women; triple crown of pope.

tibia *n* shin-bone; *pl* **-biae**, or **-bias**; *a* **tibial**.

tic *n* convulsive twitching of facial muscles.

tick[1] *n* blood-sucking parasite.

tick[2] *n* outer covering of mattress, pillow etc; *n* **ticking** coarse strong material for this.

tick[3] *n* **1** slight clicking, tapping noise, as of clock **2** mark (✓) indicating that sth has been checked, *esp* for correctness **3** *Brit coll* moment; *v* **1** make sound of tick **2** mark with symbol ✓ *idm* **make sb tick** *coll* cause sb to behave as he/she does; *phr vs* **tick off 1** check (items on list) by marking with ✓ **2** reprimand; **tick over 1** *aut* (of engine) idle **2** continue working in routine way; *n*, *a* **-ing** (of) sequence of ticks; *n* **t.-tack-toe** *US* = *Brit* noughts and crosses.

tick[4] *n coll* credit.

ticker *n coll* heart; *n* **t. tape** *esp US* **1** paper from teleprinter **2** such paper thrown in streets to greet well-known person (**t.-tape parade**).

ticket *n* **1** marked card or paper entitling holder to admission, travel, view etc **2** label; *v* mark with ticket; label.

tickle *v* **1** itch; tingle **2** amuse; please; *n* irritation of superficial nerves; *a* **ticklish 1** sensitive to tickling **2** difficult to deal with.

tiddler *n Brit* tiny fish.

tiddly *a Brit coll* slightly drunk.

tiddlywinks *n* game in which flat circular discs are flipped into a cup.

tide *n* **1** ebb and flow of surface of sea **2** *fig* trend; tendency **3** *ar* period; season; *phr v* **tide over** help through difficult period; *a* **tidal** (*n* **t. wave** massive wave of great destructive power); *n* **tideway** tidal part of river or channel affected by tidal current.

tidings *n pl* news.

tidy *a* **1** trim; neat; orderly **2** *coll* fairly large; *v* **tidies**, **tidying, tidied.** put in order.

tie *v* **tying, tied. 1** fasten with rope etc form into knot **2** (in games etc) make equal score; *phr vs* **tie down 1** restrict **2** force to make a clear statement or decision; **tie in** be connected with, consistent with; **tie up 1** bind **2** invest (money) and make it unavailable for immediate use **3** cause obstruction to (work, negotiations etc) (*n* **tie-up 1** link; partnership **2** *US* halt to progress); *n* neck-tie; connecting piece; moral obligation; equality of scores in contest; n **t.-breaker** means of finding winner from contestants with equal scores (*also* **tiebreak**); v **t.-dye** make varied patterns on fabric by tying parts together (n -**ing**); a **tied** (ns **t. cottage** cottage with tenancy for employee paying rent to employer; **t. house** pub obliged to sell only products of brewery that owns or rents it).

tier n 1 row; rank 2 several rows placed one above the other.

tiff n trifling dispute; passing quarrel.

tiger n large, carnivorous Asiatic mammal, having tawny back with black stripes; *fem* **tigress**.

tight a 1 firm; compact; taut 2 cramped 3 *coll* stingy 4 *sl* drunk; n pl close fitting garment covering legs and lower part of body; **tight** *as* **t.fisted** stingy (n -**ness**); **t.-lipped** 1 with lips pressed close together 2 refusing to speak; ns **tightrope** rope stretched horizontally for sb to walk along as acrobatic feat; v **tighten** make, become tighter.

tile n flat cake of baked clay used for roofing; one of finer clay, plastic etc. for inside use; *idm* (**out**) **on the tiles** indulging in wild, *usu* drunken pleasure v cover with tiles; a **tiled**.

till[1] *prep* up to time of; *conj* to time that.

till[2] n small drawer or box where cash is kept.

till[3] v cultivate (ground) n **tillage** *ar* cultivation of land.

tiller n lever to move rudder of boat.

tilt[1] v slope; slant; tip up; n slope; slant.

tilt[2] v take part in medieval contest with lances; *phr* v **tilt at**; attack, criticize; n 1 tournament 2 thrust in tilting; **at full t.** with great speed, or force.

timber n 1 wood cut and prepared for building 2 trees; v furnish with timber; cover with trees; a **timbered** built of or with timber n **timberline** treeline.

timbre n quality of sound of different musical instruments or voices.

timbrel n small drum.

time n 1 concept of past, present and future 2 hour 3 period taken or required for an action 4 period of life or history 5 moment; occasion 6 opportunity 7 experience related to an occasion (good/bad time); *idm* **behind the times** out-of-date; *idm* **do time** *sl* be in prison; *idm* **in time** 1 not too late 2 after some time has passed; *idm* **on time** punctual(ly); *idm* **take one's time** make no attempt to hurry; *as* **t. and motion** regarding efficient methods of working; **t.-honoured** accepted as good by tradition; **t.-lapse** *phot* running together

sequence of still shots giving impression of long process speeded up; **timeworn** 1 very old 2 worn or damaged by long use; ns **t. bomb** bomb set to explode at given moment; **t. capsule** sealed container with objects and documents to inform people in the future about life in present time; **t. exposure** *phot* (picture taken with) exposure of more than one second; **timekeeper** person recording time taken; **t.-lag** period elapsing between two events; **timepiece** watch or clock; **t. server** person adapting principles to suit occasion, fashion (a, n **t.serving**); **t.-sharing** 1 shared access to computer by several users 2 shared ownership or renting of property, with contract allowing limited period of use (eg for annual holiday) (a **t.-share**); **timetable** 1 (list of) times for public transport 2 (list of) times for lessons, lectures etc 3 (plan of) timing for business operation (v plan sequence of events; n **timetabling**); **t. zone** any one of the earth's zones within which time is standardized for each hour of the day; **timer** device or person that measures time; a **timeless** 1 never ending 2 unchanging (adv -**ly** n -**ness**); **timely** well-timed; opportune (n -**liness**); n **timing** choosing of appropriate moment.

timid *a* shy; easily frightened; *n* -**ity**.

timorous *a fml* timid; apprehensive (*adv* -**ly**; *n* -**ness**).

tin *n* 1 white malleable metal 2 container made of tin or tinned iron 3 *sl* money; *v* **tins, tinning, tinned. 1** coat with tin 2 preserve in tin container; *ns* **tinfoil** thin flexible metallic sheet; **t. god** *coll* person with exaggerated sense of self-importance; **t. hat** metal helmet worn by soldiers; **t. opener** tool for opening tin can; *a* **t.-pot** worthless, but pretentious; **t.-tack** short iron nail coated with tin; *a* **tinny** (*of sound*) shrill; (*of food*) metallic tasting.

tincture *v* 1 tinge, shade of colour 2 medicinal solution; *v* tinge; affect slightly.

tinder *n* inflammable material formerly used to catch spark from flint and steel; *n* **t. box** 1 (formerly) box holding materials for fire-lighting 2 *fig* situation full of danger.

tinge *v* colour, flavour slightly; *n* slight trace.

tingle *v* 1 feel prickling or stinging sensation; smart 2 vibrate; *n* such sensation.

tinker *n* mender, *esp* itinerant, of pots and pans; *v* mend, patch *esp* clumsily.

tinkle *v* give out series of light sounds like small bell; cause to do this; *n* this action or sound.

tinnitus *n med* hearing disorder causing ringing sound.

tinsel *n* 1 glittering material made of thin strips of metal, used for decoration 2 anything sham or showy.

tint *v* colour; tinge; *v* dye; give colour to.

tintinnabulation *n* ringing of bells.

tiny *a* very small; minute.

tip *n* 1 slender or pointed end of anything 2 useful hint 3 small sum of money given to waiter etc. for service 4 private information 5 rubbish dump; **tip** *n idm* **on the tip of one's tongue** almost ready to say but momentarily gone from one's memory; *v* **tips, tipping, tipped. 1** tilt; pour; upset 2 lean over; be tilted 3 give tip to; *idm* **tip the balance/scale** be a deciding factor; *idm* **tip sb the wink** *coll* pass on secret information to sb; *phr v* **tip off** *coll* give advance, *esp* secret warning (*n* **t.-off**); *a* **t.top** *coll* excellent.

tipple *v* take strong drink frequently; *n* **tippler**.

tipster *n* person giving advice on likely results of (*esp* horse, dog) races.

tipsy *a* drunk; mildly intoxicated.

tiptoe *v* **tiptoes, tiptoeing, tiptoed.** walk on toes; walk softly.

tiptop *a* 1 highest point 2 *coll* first-rate.

tire, tyre *n* rim of metal, rubber etc round wheel.

tire *v* make or become weary or fatigued; *as* **tired 1** needing rest, sleep 2 lacking in inspiration (*idm* **tired of** having lost patience with; fed up with; *adv* -**ly** *n* -**ness**); tiring.

tiresome *a* 1 annoying 2 tedious; *adv* -**ly**; *n* -**ness**.

tiro, tyro *n* beginner; novice.

tissue *n* 1 structural material of body of animals or plants 2 light woven fabric; *n* **tissue-paper** very thin wrapping paper.

tit *n* any of various small, brightly-coloured birds; **t. for tat** retaliation.

titan *n* person of great strength, intellect.

titanic *a* 1 huge; gigantic 2 containing titanium.

titanium *n* rare, grey-coloured metallic element.

titbit *n* choice morsel; *fig* spicy item of news.

titchy *a coll* tiny.

tithe *n* tenth part, *esp* of profit from land, produce etc paid to church.

titillate *v* tickle; stimulate; pleasurably; *n* -**lation**.

titivate *v* 1 smarten up oneself 2 adorn; *n* -**ation**.

title *n* 1 name, heading of book, picture etc 2 appellation of distinction or honour 3 name showing rank, occupation etc 4 admitted right or claim; *a* **titled** having title of nobility; n **t.-deed** legal document establishing ownership, *esp* of land etc.

titmouse n small bird, allied to nuthatch.

titter v utter quiet laugh; giggle; n such laugh.

tittle-tattle n gossip; *also* v.

titular a having title but no real power.

tizzy n *coll* state of nervous excitement.

T-junction n T-shaped road junction.

TLS *abbr* Times Literary Supplement.

TNT *abbr* trinitrotoluene (powerful explosive).

to *prep* 1 towards; as far as 2 expressing comparison, contrast 3 introducing infinitive mood of verb, indirect object; *adv*, into normal, desired position etc; *adv* **to and fro** backwards and forwards.

toad n amphibian like large frog; ns **toadstool** any fleshy fungus other than mushroom; *esp* if poisonous; **toady** servile flatterer; v act thus; n **toad-in-the-hole** meat (*usu* sausage) baked in batter.

toast v 1 make crisp and brown by heat; warm at fire 2 drink health of; n 1 slice of bread browned by heat 2 proposal to drink health of 3 person toasted; n **toast-master** announcer of toasts at banquet.

tobacco n plant whose leaves are used for smoking; its

prepared and dried leaves; n **tobacconist** one who sells tobacco etc.

toboggan n sledge for sliding down snowy slopes; v **toboggans, tobogganing, tobogganed.** use, slide on toboggan.

toccata n musical composition for keyboard instrument.

tocsin n bell sounded to give alarm.

tod n fox; *idm* **on one's tod** alone.

today n this day; *adv* on this day; at present time.

toddle v 1 walk unsteadily, as small child 2 *coll* stroll; n **toddler** young child just starting to walk.

toddy n drink of spirits, lemon and hot water.

to-do n *coll* fuss and bother.

toe n one of five digits of foot; v touch with toes; *idm* **on one's toes** alert and ready; *idm* **toe the line** conform; obey orders.

toffee n sweetmeat made of boiled sugar with butter.

tofu n bean curd.

toga n loose flowing robe of ancient Romans.

together *adv* 1 in company 2 happening at same time, place, etc; *idm* **together with** as well as; *idm* **get it together** have everything under control; a sl *esp US* well-organized; n **-ness.**

toggle n short metal or wooden pin fixed through loop (of rope etc) to secure it; small wooden bar used

instead of button.

togs n *sl* clothes; dress.

toil n severe labour; exacting work; v work hard; labour; *as* **toilsome** wearying; **toilworn** (of hands, face etc) hard and tired.

toilet n 1 process, style of dressing 2 lavatory; ns **t.-paper** paper for cleaning oneself in a lavatory; **t.-roll** roll of toilet paper; **t. water** scented water; dilute form of perfume; **toiletries** articles used for personal cleanliness etc.

token n symbol; evidence; coin, disc or voucher.

tokenism n half-hearted form of positive discrimination to create good impression.

tolerate v put up with; n **-ation;** *as* **tolerable** fairly good; bearable; **tolerant** forbearing; broadminded; n **tolerance.**

toll[1] n tax, duty paid for use of road etc.

toll[2] v cause (bell) to ring slowly at regular intervals, *esp* at funeral.

tomahawk n light hatchet used by N American Indians in war or hunting.

tomato n **-oes.** plant with bright red or yellow edible fruit.

tomb n grave; vault; n **stone** memorial stone on grave.

tombola n kind of lottery.

tomboy n romping boyish girl.

tomcat n male cat.

tome n volume; large book.

tomfoolery n foolish behaviour; silliness.

tommy-gun n short-barrelled submachine gun.

tomorrow adv on, during day after this; n day after today.

tom-tom n primitive African or Oriental drum.

ton n 1 measure of weight, 2,240 lbs; 2 unit of ship's carrying capacity; pl -s very large amount (also adv); n **tonnage** freight-carrying capacity of ship; ships collectively.

tonality n 1 (creation of music having) sense of key 2 tonal quality.

tone n 1 musical sound 2 pitch of voice 3 shade of colour 4 prevailing mood 5 vigour; v give tone to phr vs **tone down** make less forceful; **tone in** (cause to) harmonize; **tone up** make more prominent; as **tonal** 1 of tone 2 mus of tonality; **t.-deaf** unable to distinguish between notes of different musical pitch; n **t. poem** mus orchestral piece evoking poetic idea, person, legend etc.

tongs n pl large pincers.

tongue n 1 fleshy muscular organ in mouth; chief organ of taste, speech, etc 2 language; speech 3 anything resembling tongue in shape; idm (with) **tongue in cheek** insincerely (a **t.-in-cheek**); a **t.-tied** unable to speak; n **t.-twister** phrase difficult to pronounce, esp quickly.

tonic a (of tones, sounds) invigorating; n 1 medicine invigorates 2 tonic water 3 mus key note; **t. water** carbonated mineral water flavoured with quinine.

tonight n this night; night after today; adv on, during this night.

tonnage n cargo capacity of ship, expressed in tons.

tonne n measure of weight equal to 1,000 kilograms.

tonsil n gland at the back of the throat; n **tonsilitis** infection of tonsils.

too adv 1 in addition; as well 2 excessively; idm **only too** very.

took pt of take.

tool n 1 implement; instrument; appliance used in mechanical operations 2 fig cats-paw; puppet; v shape, mark with tool.

toot n sound of horn or trumpet; v make this sound.

tooth n teeth. 1 one of hard growths inside jaws of vertebrates 2 various pointed tooth-shaped objects 3 prong 4 cog; **tooth** idm **tooth and nail** very fiercely; idm **get one's teeth into** work at in a concentrated way; idm **in the teeth of** in spite of; idm **set sb's teeth on edge** (of sharp taste, sound) give sb unpleasant sensation; as **toothless** without teeth; **toothsome** coll tasty; **toothy** exposing one's teeth; ns **toothbrush/gel/paste**

brush/gel/paste for cleaning teeth; **toothpick** small pointed stick for removing food from between teeth; v furnish (wheel, comb etc) with teeth.

tootle v coll play wind instrument casually; phr v **tootle along/by/past** coll drive along/by/past in leisurely way.

top[1] n 1 highest part; summit 2 highest rank, degree 3 highest in merit; idm **be on top of** be able to cope with; idm **get on top of sb** coll be too much for sb; idm **on top of the world** coll very happy; idm **over the top** Brit coll beyond what is considered proper or reasonable; v **tops, topping, topped.** 1 be higher, better than 2 provide top for; idm **top the bill** play leading role; phr vs **top off** coll finish; **top up** replenish; ns **t. brass** coll high-ranking military officers; **t. dog** person in most powerful position; **t. hat** man's formal tall cylindrical black or grey hat; **topspin** spinning action causing ball to shoot forward as it hits the ground; as **t.-flight** of high quality; **t.-notch** coll of the best; **t.-secret** highly confidential; a **-less** with breasts uncovered.

top[2] n small spinning toy.

topaz n semi-precious stone usually yellowish.

tope v drink frequently and

excessively; n **toper**.

topiary n art of cutting living shrubs, trees into shapes of animals, birds etc; n **-arist**.

topic n subject of thought or discussion; a **-al** connected with subject of current interest.

topography n systematic description of place etc; detailed features of district; n **grapher**; a **-graphical**.

topper n coll top hat.

topping n decoration on top, esp garnish on food.

topple v fall over; overbalance.

topsy-turvy a upset; upside-down.

torch portable light or flame; n **torchlight** light shed by torches.

tore pt of **tear**.

toreador n Sp bull-fighter.

torment n suffering; anguish of mind or body; v **torture**; annoy; tease; harass; n **-tor**.

tornado n **-oes** or **-os**. violent, destructive localized storm; hurricane.

torpedo n **-oes**. self-propelled underwater missile used for destroying shipping; **t. fish** electric ray; v attack, destroy with torpedo.

torpid a sluggish; dull; apathetic; ns **-ity** state of being torpid; **torpor** numbness; dullness; inactivity of mind.

torque n 1 twisted necklace or chain 2 mech twisting force or movement.

torrent n 1 violently rushing stream 2 fig rush of words; a

-ial flowing, falling with great violence.

torrid a 1 (of climate) very hot and dry 2 passionate; **t. zone** that between tropics.

torsion n act of twisting; state of being twisted.

torso n **-sos**. 1 trunk of human body 2 limbless, headless statue.

tort n leg injurious, harmful act against which civil action can be brought.

tortilla n Mexican flat bread.

tortoise n reptile with complete scaly covering for body; n **tortoise-shell** mottled brown shell of tortoise, polished and used commercially; a.

tortuous a 1 twisting; winding 2 (of mind, aims etc) devious.

torture n 1 deliberate infliction of severe pain 2 great mental anguish; v subject to torture; n **torturer**.

Tory n, a (member) of British Conservative party.

toss v 1 throw up; fling; pitch 2 be flung, thrown; **t. for** spin coin to decide (choice etc); n act of tossing; n **t.-up** uncertain situation.

tot n 1 tiny child 2 small quantity esp of drink; dram.

tot up v **tots, totting, totted**. add up.

total n whole amount; complete number; a entire; complete; v **totals, totalling, totalled**. 1 add up 2 amount to as whole; n **-ity** entirety; **totalizator** automatic

betting machine on racecourse etc.

totalitarian a applied to State run by dictator or single political party, allowing no opposition or other political representation.

totem n tribal symbol or emblem; n **t. pole** post supporting them.

totter v 1 walk unsteadily 2 (of building etc) be about to fall.

toucan n large billed S American bird.

touch v 1 put hand on; make physical contact with; reach; 2 move to pity etc 3 coll try to borrow money from; n 1 act of touching 2 sense of feeling 3 characteristic method of technique 4 children's game; idm **touch wood** expressing hope of avoiding bad luck; phr vs **touch down** land (n **touchdown**); **touch off** cause (eg violence) to begin; **touch on/upon** mention briefly; **touch up 1** make minor improvements to 2 sl touch in a sexually provocative manner; a **t.-and-go** risky; uncertain; ns **touchline** line along longer side of football pitch; **t. paper** paper slow-burning fuse of firework; **touchstone** sth used to measure standard; v **t.-type** type without looking at keyboard; a **touchy** easily offended; (adv **-ily** n **-iness**).

touché interj Fr acknowledging a hit in fencing or the

aptness of a remark against
oneself.

tough *a* **1** strong; firm **2** not
brittle **3** sturdy **4** ruthless **5**
needing effort to chew; *n sl*
hooligan; criminal; ruffianly
man; *n* **toughness**; *v*
toughen.

toupee *n Fr* artificial tuft or
front of hair; wig.

tour *n* **1** journey round district
2 excursion **3** series of visits
to different places; *v* make
tour; travel; *ns* **-ist** one who
travels for pleasure; **-ism**
business of organizing,
operating tours, and catering
for tourists.

tour de force *n Fr* highly
skilful achievement.

tournament *n* **1** medieval
contest between mounted
knights **2** *games* contest of
skill *usu* for championship.

tourniquet *n Fr* device or
bandage used to stop arterial
bleeding.

tousle *v* make untidy; rumple;
ruffle.

tout *v* importune, pester in
order to sell; *n* one who acts
thus; tipster; one who sells
tickets unofficially outside a
heavily-booked event.

tow *v* pull along (vehicle etc)
by rope; *n* act of towing or
being towed; *idm* **in tow**
following closely behind;
idm **on tow** being towed.

toward *a* imminent, at hand;
prep **towards, toward** in
direction of.

towel *n* cloth used for drying
(skin, china etc) after

washing; *v* dry, rub with
towel; *n* **towelling** absorbent
cloth for making towels.

tower *n* **1** tall strong structure
often forming part of church
or other building **2** fortress;
v rise, stand very high; *ns* **t.
block** *Brit* tall block of flats,
offices; **t. of strength** person
that can be relied on for
moral support.

town *n* group of houses and
other buildings, larger than
village; *idm* **go to town**
behave freely, in an
uninhibited way; *idm* **(out)
on the town** (out) enjoying
places of entertainment, *esp*
at night; *ns* **t. clerk** official
responsible for records of
British town or city; **t. crier**
person making public
announcements; **t. hall**
public building,
headquarters of local
government. *n* **township**
town and surrounding area
forming municipality.

towpath *n* path along bank of
river or canal.

toxic *a* pertaining to, caused
by **toxaemic** poison; *ns*
toxaemia blood-poisoning;
toxicology study of poisons
and their effects; **toxin**
poisonous organic substance.

toxophily *n* archery; *n*
toxophilite lover of archery.

toy *n* **1** plaything **2** trifle;
bauble; *v* trifle with; *phr v*
toy with 1 consider without
serious thought **2** handle in
an aimless way; *n* **t. boy**
young man with whom older

woman has amorous
relationship.

trace *n* **1** one of two straps by
which vehicle is drawn by
horse **2** visible signs left by
anything **3** slight tinge; *n* **t.
element** any chemical
element found only in
minute quantities in an
organism, but essential to its
healthy development; *v* **1**
follow course, track of **2**
draw, copy exactly *esp* by use
of tracing-paper; *ns* **tracer
bullet (shell)** one which
leaves visible trail; **tracery**
intricate decorative pattern
of lines; **tracing** traced copy
of drawing; (**t. paper** thin,
transparent paper on which
tracings are made).

trachea *n* -**eae.** *anat* wind-pipe.

track *n* **1** mark, marks left by
passing animal, person,
vehicle **2** unofficial (rough)
path **3** railway line **4** *US*
railway platform **5** course for
racing **6** rail that supports
sth moving (*eg* curtains) **7**
mus any of the sections that
make up the contents of a
record, cassette or compact
disc **8** continuous belt
covering wheels of tank,
bulldozer etc; *idm* **keep/lose
track of** manage/not
manage to have up-to-date
information about; *idm*
make tracks (for) *coll* leave
(for); go on one's way; *idm*
on the right/wrong track
thinking of the right/wrong
kind of answer, solution; *v* **1**
follow the track of **2** (*of*

camera) move while filming; *phr vs* **track down** find by tracking, searching; *a* **-ed** having tracks; *ns* **t. and field** *esp US* athletics; **tracker** person tracking wild animals (**t. dog** dog used by police to track down criminal); **t. event** sport athletic running contest; tracking *aut* alignment of car wheels (**t. station** place where movement of satellites, missiles etc can be observed by radar, radio); **t. record** past record of achievement; **t. suit** loose-fitting suit worn for warmth when training for sport.

tract *n* 1 expanse of country 2 *anat* system of related organs.

tract *n* pamphlet; treatise.

tractable *a* 1 easily managed 2 docile 3 easily wrought.

traction *n* 1 act, process of drawing along 2 *med* artificial stretching of spine etc; *ns* **t. engine** steam engine for drawing loads along road; **tractor** motor vehicle for drawing plough etc.

trad *n coll* traditional, jazz (*also* **trad jazz**).

trade *n* 1 commerce; buying and selling 2 those engaged in trade; *v* traffic; buy and sell; barter; *idm* **do good/bad trade** be successful/ unsuccessful in business; *v* 1 buy and sell goods 2 barter 3 exchange; *phr vs* **trade in** offer in part exchange for

sth new (*n* **t.-in**); **trade off** sth (against sth) sacrifice sth as compromise in return for sth beneficial (*n* **t.-off**); **trade on** take advantage of; *ns* **trader, trading; t. gap** difference between value of imports and exports; **t. mark** 1 official design of manufacturer 2 *fig* characteristic thing by which one can be identified; **t. name** 1 name given by manufacturer to identify brand 2 name by which person, firm is known for business purposes; **tradesperson/man/woman** 1 shopkeeper 2 trader calling at people's homes; **t. union** organization that protects interests of workers if in conflict with employers (*ns* **t. unionism, -ist**); **t. wind** strong steady wind blowing towards the Equator.

tradition *n* 1 belief, custom, law etc handed down verbally from one generation to another 2 unwritten history; *a* **-al** (*n* **-ism**; *n*, *a* **-ist**; *adv* **-ly**).

traduce *v* slander.

traffic *n* 1 passing to and fro of vehicles etc in street 2 body of vehicles using street 3 trade; *v* **-ficking, -ficked.** trade; *ns* **trafficker** person trading, *esp* in sth illicit or immoral; **t. jam** congested state of traffic in which vehicles come to a standstill; **t. light** light that controls flow of traffic automatically;

t. warden person appointed to monitor illegal parking of vehicles and to report offenders to police.

tragedy *n* 1 very sad event, calamity, *esp* one causing death 2 drama dealing with human misfortunes and sorrows; *a* **tragic** 1 of, like tragedy 2 fatal; disastrous *adv*; *ns* **tragedian** tragic actor; *fem* **tragedienne; tragi-comedy** play with both tragic and comic scenes.

trail *v* 1 drag along ground 2 follow track of; shadow; *n* 1 track or trace 2 rough ill-defined road; *n* **trailer** 1 expert in following trail 2 vehicle towed by another one 3 advertisement of forthcoming film etc.

train *v* 1 educate; instruct 2 (*of plants etc*) cause to grow in certain way 3 aim (gun) 4 *sport* follow course of physical exercise, dieting etc; *n* 1 series of railway coaches etc drawn by locomotive 2 trailing part of dress 3 retinue 4 line of gunpowder to mine etc; *ns* **trainee** one who is being trained in certain skill etc; **training** 1 process of educating 2 art of preparing persons for athletic contests or horses for racing.

traipse, trapse *v* walk around aimlessly.

trait *n* characteristic feature.

traitor *n* 1 one who is guilty of treason 2 one who betrays a trust (*fem* **traitress**); *a* **-ous**

treacherous.

trajectory n path of object fired or thrown through air.

tram n 1 public vehicle running on rails on road 2 truck used in coalmines; n **tram-car**.

trammel n 1 kind of fish-net 2 shackle; pl **-s** thing that impedes freedom of movement or action; v **trammels, trammelling, trammelled.** confine; restrict; hinder.

tramp v 1 walk, tread heavily 2 travel as vagabond 3 travel on foot; n 1 act of tramping 2 long walk 3 homeless vagrant 4 cargo vessel; v **trample** tread under foot.

trampoline n frame with sheet of strong fabric stretched by springs where people can jump, rebound and perform gymnastic exercises; v perform on this; n **-lining.**

trance n 1 state of suspended consciousness 2 ecstasy; rapture.

tranny n coll transistor radio.

tranquil a calm; serene; peaceful; unruffled; n **tranquility;** v tranquilize make calm (n **-izer** sedative).

trans- prefix across; through; beyond. Compounds, where the meaning is obvious, are not given here.

transact v to carry through (negotiations etc); n **-ion** piece of business; pl proceedings.

transcend v go beyond; surpass; a **transcendent** surpassing.

transcendental a going beyond normal human knowledge or understanding (**t. meditation** form of meditation used by Hindus); n **-ism;** n, a **-ist.**

transcribe v copy out; write out (notes) in full.

transcript n written or printed version of oral speech, n **-ion** 1 act of transcribing 2 transcript.

transducer n device for converting electrical into mechanical energy.

transept n part of cruciform church which crosses main nave.

transfer v **transfers, transferring, transferred.** move, convey from one person or place to another; n 1 act of transferring; conveyance 2 design etc transferred from one surface to another by heat pressure etc; a **-able;** n **-ference.**

transfigure v 1 alter appearance of 2 idealize; glorify, n **-figuration.**

transfix v 1 impale 2 fig root to the spot.

transform v change shape, character, nature of; ns **-ation; -er** mechanical device in electricity for changing voltage of alternating current.

transfuse v transfer (blood) from veins of one person or animal to another;

n **-fusion.**

transgress v 1 exceed, violate (law) 2 sin; ns **-gression; -gressor.**

transient a fleeting; brief; momentary; n **transience.**

transistor n small electrical device used in place of thermionic valve, small portable radio containing this.

transitory a of short duration; adv **-ily;** n **-iness.**

transit n passage; crossing; n **transition** change from one place to another (a **-al**); as **-ive** (of verb) requiring direct object; **-ory** not lasting.

translate v 1 render into another language 2 transfer (bishop) from one see to another; ns **-lator; -lation.**

transliterate v render in script of another alphabet; n **-ation.**

translucent a letting light pass through.

transmigration n (after death) transfer of soul to a different body (human or animal).

transmit v **transmits, transmitting, transmitted.** 1 pass on 2 hand down (by heredity etc) 3 communicate; ns **-mitter** 1 one who transmits 2 apparatus for sending out radio waves; **transmission** act of transmitting; that which is transmitted.

transmogrify v change appearance in a surprising, esp grotesque way;

n -ification.

transmute *n* change into sth different (*n* -**mutation**).

transparent *a* 1 permitting passage of light 2 *fig* clear; obvious; *ns* -**ence**; -**ency** 1 quality of being transparent 2 picture on transparent material, visible when lit from behind.

transpire *v* 1 exhale as vapour 2 become known 3 *coll* happen.

transplant *v* 1 dig up (plant) and replant elsewhere 2 *med* remove (healthy organ, tissue) and graft elsewhere; *n* -**ation**.

transponder *n* radio, radar apparatus sending signal in response to one received.

transport *v* 1 carry, convey from one place to another 2 enrapture; *n* 1 act, method of conveying persons, goods 2 vehicle, ship, etc. so used.

transpose *v* 1 change order of 2 *mus* put into different key; *ns* **transposal; transposition**.

transputer *n* very powerful computer microchip.

transsexual *n* 1 person who feels he/she belongs to the opposite sex.

transubstantiation *n* change of substance or essence, *esp* RC belief that bread and water changes into the substance of body and blood of Christ at the Eucharist.

transverse *a* cross-wise; at right angles.

transvestism *n* seeking of sexual pleasure from wearing

clothes usually associated with opposite sex; *n* **transvestite** person who does this.

trap *n* 1 device for catching, snaring animals etc; pit-fall 2 two-wheeled carriage 3 device to prevent gas, foul air, etc escaping; *v* **traps, trapping, trapped.** 1 snare 2 *fig* deceive by cunning; *ns* **t.-door** hinged door in floor, ceiling etc; **trapper** one who traps animals for their fur.

trappings *n pl* equipment; ornaments; one's belongings.

trapeze *n* swinging horizontal bar for gymnastic and acrobatic use.

trapezium *n* quadrilateral figure with only two sides parallel.

trapezoid *n* quadrilateral with no parallel sides (US **trapezium**); *a* -**al**.

trash *n* 1 rubbish; useless matter 2 worthless person; *a* **trashy** cheap; shoddy.

trashcan *n* US dustbin.

trauma *n* 1 injury 2 emotional injury caused by shock etc; *a* **traumatic** (*adv* -**ally**); *v* **traumatize.**

travel *v* **travels, travelling, travelled.** move along; make journey; *n* **t. agent** person who takes responsibility for making all travel arrangements and reservations; *n pl* -**s** 1 journeys 2 tour, *esp* abroad; *ns* **traveller** one who travels; one who travels to obtain business orders, often

commercial t.; *a* **travelled** experienced in travelling; *n* **traveller's cheque** cheque issued by bank to client for use abroad.

traverse *v* 1 pass, lie across 2 swivel; *n* 1 ledge etc crossing rockface horizontally 2 sideways movement (of gun).

travesty *n* parody; ridiculous distortion; *v* make, be travesty of.

trawl *n* open-mouthed fishing net drawn along sea-bottom; *v* fish with one; *n* **trawler** fishing vessel using trawl.

tray *n* flat board, slab of wood, metal etc, with rim, for carrying things.

treachery *n* betrayal; perfidy; breach of trust; *a* **treacherous** disloyal; unreliable; dangerous.

treacle *n* thick syrup obtained from unrefined sugar, molasses; *a* **treacly.**

tread *v* 1 walk; step; set foot on 2 press; crush (eg grapes) 3 (+*adv*) *fig* speak, act, proceed in specified way; *pt* **trod**, *pp* **trodden** or **trod**; *idm* **tread on air** feel happy, carefree; *idm* **tread water** remain afloat by moving one's legs; *n* manner, sound of walking; part of tyre in contact with ground; top surface of step; *ns* **treadle** lever worked by foot; **treadmill** cylinder turned by treading on steps fixed to rim; *fig* monotonous routine.

treason *n* violation by subject

of allegiance to sovereign or state; *as* **reasonable; treasonous.**

treasure *n* stored up valuables; money; riches; *v* store, regard; *as* valuable; cherish; *ns* **treasurer** person in charge of funds of club, society etc; **treasury 1** department of state, collecting and controlling public money and taxation **2** place for storing treasure; **treasure-trove** unclaimed treasure.

treat *v* **1** behave towards, use **2** seal with chemically **3** pay expenses of **4** negotiate; *n* **1** pleasurable event **2** entertaining; *n* **treatment 1** act, mode of, treating, attempting to cure **2** manner of artistic handling.

treatise *n* systematic written account of something.

treaty *n* agreement, contract entered into between states etc.

treble *a* **1** threefold **2** high pitched; *n* treble part of voice; *v* increase threefold.

tree *n* **1** large perennial plant having woody trunk **2** cobbler's last; **family t.** diagram showing descent from common ancestor; *ns* **t. fern** large tropical fern with tree-like stem; **t. line** line of latitude or height above sea-level beyond which trees will not grow; *a* **treeless** (*n* **-ness**).

trefoil *n* **1** plant whose leaf has three lobes *eg* clover **2** *arch*

carved three-lobed ornament.

trek *v* make journey; travel; migrate; *n* long journey.

trellis *n* lattice, structure of crossed wooden strips.

tremble *v* shiver; quake; *n* tremor; quiver; involuntary shaking.

tremendous *a* **1** vast; amazing; awe-inspiring **2** *coll* very exciting; *adv* **-ly** extremely.

tremolo *n* quivering effect in playing or singing.

tremor *n* **1** shaking **2** qualm **3** thrill.

tremulous 1 shaky; trembling **2** timid; fearful.

trench *n* long opening, furrow, cut or dug in earth; *v* cut trench or groove in.

trenchant *a* keen; incisive; biting; *adv* **-ly**; *n* **trenchancy.**

trend *n* **1** course; direction **2** *fig* general tendency **3** fashion; *n* **t.-setter** person leading the way in fashion; *a, n* **t.-setting** *a* trendy in latest fashions.

trepidation *n* state of alarm; nervous fluster.

trespass *n* **1** go unlawfully on another's land **2** commit an offence; *phr v* **trespass on** take unfair advantage of; *n* act of trespassing; offence; injury; *n* **trespasser.**

tress *n* lock of hair; *pl* hair of head.

trestle *n* framework of board supported by wooden legs.

tri- *prefix* three.

triad *n* group of three.

trial *n* **1** act of trying, testing **2** adversity **3** source of irritation **4** judicial inquiry; *idm* **stand trial** be tried in court; *idm* **trial and error** experimental method of solving problem by learning from mistakes.

triangle *n* figure with three angles; musical instrument; *a* **triangular.**

triangulation *n* method of calculating position or distance by use of triangles.

triathlon *n* contest in running, swimming and cycling.

tribe *n* social unit; class; group; *a* **tribal**; *n* **tribesman** member of tribe.

tribulation *n* grief; affliction; mental distress.

tribunal *n* court of justice; special court of enquiry.

tribute *n* **1** tax, payment made by one state to another **2** act performed; words uttered as sign of respect, esteem, affection for; *a* **tributary 1** paying tribute **2** auxiliary; *n* stream flowing into larger one.

trice *n* instant; brief space of time.

triceps *n* large muscle at back of upper arm (*pl* **triceps** or **tricepses**).

trichology *n* study of hair growth and associated problems; *n* **-ologist.**

trick *n* **1** deception; swindle **2** illusion; pranks **3** mannerism **4** cards played in one round; *v* cheat; deceive; *idm* **do the trick** achieve one's aim; v **t.-or-treat** US (of children) threaten to play tricks on people who will not give a treat (eg sweet) on Hallowe'en. n **trickery, trickster** a **tricky** shifty; ingenious.

trickle v flow slowly; n thin flow.

tricolour n national flag with three stripes of different colours.

tricycle n three-wheeled cycle.

trident n three-pronged fork.

tried pt, pp of **try**; a well tested.

triennial a happening every three years.

trier n person who tries.

trifle n 1 small, insignificant thing of no value 2 sweet dish of sponge-cake, wine and cream etc; idm **a trifle** coll a little bit; phr v **trifle with** treat casually, without respect; a **trifling** trivial.

trigger n catch that releases spring, esp to fire gun; phr v **trigger off** initiate large scale process by small act; a **t.-happy** too eager to use unnecessary violence.

trigonometry n branch of mathematics dealing with relationship between sides and angles of triangles.

trilateral a having three sides.

trilby n soft felt hat.

trill v sing, with vibrating sound; warble; n such singing.

trillion n 1 Brit one million million million 2 US one million million; pl **-s** a very large number.

trilogy n series of three connected literary or musical works.

trim v **trims, trimming, trimmed**. 1 prune 2 decorate (garment etc) 3 adjust balance of (ship, aircraft etc); a neat; tidy; in good order; v, n 1 act of trimming 2 decorative finish (eg on car bodywork); idm **in (good) trim** in good condition; physically fit; n **-ming** decorative addition (pl **-s 1** pieces trimmed off 2 usual extras).

trimaran n boat with three parallel hulls.

trinity n 1 the three divine persons of Godhead 2 state of being threefold.

trinket n bauble; worthless trifle.

trio n **-os**. group of three; music for three voices or instruments.

trip v **trips, tripping, tripped**. 1 stumble; make false step 2 skip; dance; v phr v **trip up** make a mistake; n 1 short journey 2 act of tripping 3 sl sensations experienced from taking hallucinatory drug; n **tripper** holiday-maker esp day excursionist.

tripartite a of, in three parts.

tripe n 1 stomach of ruminant animal, prepared as food 2 coll nonsense; rubbish.

triple a threefold; v increase threefold; ns **t. jump** athletic contest of hop, step and jump; **triplet** three of a kind; as **triplex** threefold;

triplicate made in three identical copies; n one of three identical copies.

tripod n three-legged stand, support etc.

tripos n examination for Honours degree at Cambridge.

tripwire n stretched wire that activates alarm or other device when tripped accidentally.

trisect v geom divide into three equal parts.

trite a banal; commonplace.

Triton n minor sea-god.

triturate v grind to powder, pulverize; n **-ation**.

triumph n 1 victory; success; exultation 2 processional entry of victorious ancient Roman general; v achieve success; prevail; exult; as **-al; -ant**.

triumvir n member of triumvirate ruling group of three such men.

trivet n three-legged stand for pot or kettle.

trivia n pl things of little or no importance.

trivial a 1 of minimal importance 2 ordinary; v **- ize;** n **-ity**.

trochee n metrical foot of two syllables, one long, one short.

trod pt, pp of **tread**.

trodden pp of **tread**.

troglodyte n 1 cave-dweller 2 common wren.

Trojan n 1 inhabitant of Troy 2 person of courage and endurance.

troll v fish by trailing bait *esp* behind boat; sing cheerfully.

troll n legendary Scandinavian goblin, giant or dwarf.

trolley n 1 light low cart or wheeled platform, pushed by hand 2 truck on rails 3 metal arm conveying current from overhead wires to tramcar; **t. bus** bus powered by overhead electric cable.

trollop n slovenly disreputable woman.

trombone n powerful brass wind-instrument with sliding tube; n **-bonist** trombone player.

troop n number of people; subdivision of cavalry squadron; *pl* soldiers; v move as troop; crowd; n **-er** cavalry soldier.

trope n figure of speech.

trophy n token of victory; prize.

tropic n one of two parallels of latitude 23° 28' N and S of equator; *pl* hot regions of earth between these parallels; a **-al** extremely hot; growing occurring in tropics.

trot v trots, trotting, trotted. (*of horse etc*) move rapidly but not at gallop; run easily with short steps; n rapid pace of horse etc; quick walk; *idm* **on the trot** consecutively; continuously; *phr v* **trot out** repeat in an unoriginal way.

troth n *lit* fidelity; word of honour.

Trotskyist a, n (follower) of the ideas of Leon Trotsky.

trotter n pig's foot.

troubadour n French medieval poet.

trouble v 1 disturb; afflict 2 agitate; worry; n 1 agitation 2 difficulty 3 disturbance; *ns* **t.maker** person who causes trouble; **t.shooter** person who helps to solve mechanical problems or to settle disputes; *as* **troublous** disturbed; **troublesome** annoying; unruly.

trough n 1 long narrow container for food or water for animals 2 narrow channel between waves.

trounce v beat; defeat; censure.

troupe n *Fr* band of actors; touring company.

trouper n performer of long experience.

trousers n *pl* two-legged outer garment, enclosing legs from waist to ankles.

trousseau n *Fr* bride's outfit.

trout n edible fresh-water fish.

trowel n small flat-bladed took for spreading mortar; small hollow-bladed tool for lifting, planting plants.

troy n system of weights used for gold, silver, etc.

truant n person who stays away from school, work etc, without permission; a shirking school or duty **truant** *phr v* **play truant** be a truant.

truce n temporary agreement to stop fighting; respite.

truck n 1 open railway-wagon 2 lorry 3 barrow; *idm* **have no truck with** refuse to consider or have dealings with; n **t. farm** US market garden.

truckle v cringe; *phr v* **truckle to** fawn on; submit to.

truckle-bed n low bed, *esp* on wheels, which fits under a higher one.

truculent a aggressive; fierce; violent; n **truculence**.

trudge v walk wearily, with effort; n long tedious walk.

true a in accordance with fact; accurate; genuine; correct; *idm* **out of true** not properly balanced, aligned or shaped; *as* **t.-blue** totally loyal; **t.-life** based on real events and people; *ns* **t.love** sweetheart; **t. north** north according to earth's axis; *ns* **truism** statement of something obviously true; *adv* **truly** really; loyally; sincerely; n **true bill** bill of indictment endorsed by grand jury.

truffle n 1 edible fungus, growing below ground 2 small *usu* rum flavoured chocolate cake.

trump n card of suit temporarily ranking above others; *idm* **come up/turn up trumps** *coll* (unexpectedly) do the right thing; *phr v* **trump up** *coll* invent (excuse, accusation); a **trumped up** fabricated; concocted; n **t. card 1** card of suit that is trumps 2 *fig* way of gaining advantage; v take trick with trump.

trumpery *a* showy; rubbishy; worthless.

trumpet *n* 1 metal wind instrument 2 funnel; *v* sound on trumpet; *fig* proclaim, announce widely; *n* **-er** trumpet player.

truncate *v* cut off; lop.

truncheon *n* short thick staff or cudgel, baton of office.

trundle *v* cause to roll along; move on wheels.

trunk *n* 1 stem of tree 2 person's body not including head or limbs 3 main body or line (of railways, telephones etc) 4 large suit-case 5 long flexible snout of elephant etc; *ns* **t. call** *Brit* long distance telephone call; **t. line** main line of communication between large towns; **t. road** important main road; *pl* **trunks** man's swimming shorts.

truss *v* bind, tie up, tie wings (of fowl etc) before cooking; *n* 1 bundle (of hay etc) 2 cluster of blossom 3 surgical support for ruptured organ 4 framework of beams etc supporting roof etc.

trust *n* 1 confidence; faith 2 group of persons administering fund 3 responsibility 4 property held for another; *v* have faith in; rely on; *idm* **on trust** without further enquiry 2 on credit; *phr v* **trust in** *fml* believe, have faith in; *ns* **trustee** one

legally holding property in trust for another (*n* **-ship**); **t. fund** money under control of a trust; *as* **trustful** confiding; **trusting** willing to trust other people; **trustworthy** deserving to be trusted; **trusty** *fml* dependable.

truth *n* quality, state of being true; honesty; sincerity *a* **truthful** (*adv* **-ly** *n* **-ness**).

try *v* tries, trying, tried. 1 test; attempt 2 conduct judicial inquiry into 3 purify, refine (metals); *phr vs* **try on 1** put on (garment) to see if size, colour etc are right 2 *coll* behave in an unreasonable way to see if this will be tolerated (*n* **t.-on**); **try out** test by experience; *n* attempt (Rugby football) touch-down; *as* **tried** proved, reliable; **trying** provoking; painful; wearisome.

tsar *n* formerly emperor of Russia; *fem* **tsarina**.

tsetse fly *n* African fly which conveys parasite of sleeping-sickness.

T-shirt casual shirt with short sleeves shaped like T.

T-square *n* ruler shaped like T.

tub *n* 1 wooden vessel, often shaped like half barrel; *coll* 2 bath 3 boat used for rowing practice; *v coll* bathe, take bath (**t.-thumper** person doing this).

tuba *n* large brass wind instrument with low sound.

tube *n* long, hollow cylinder;

pipe; underground electric railway; *a* **tubular** shaped like tube; *n* **tubing** series of pipes; piece of tube.

tuber *n* swollen part of underground stem; containing buds, eg potato; *a* **tuberous** producing, growing from tubers.

tuberculosis *n* infectious disease causing growth of small nodules at affected part, caused by tubercles.

tuberose *n* bulbous garden plant like lily, having spikes of fragrant flowers.

TUC *abbr* Trades Union Congress (*Brit* association of trade unions).

tuck *v* gather up; fold; be folded up; press together; *phr vs* **tuck in/into** 1 push end in, so that it is neatly hidden 2 *coll* eat heartily; **tuck up** make comfortable in bed; *ns* 1 stitched fold 2 *sl* sweets, cakes; **t.-shop** school sweet shop; **tucker** *Aust sl* food; *v* *US* **tucker (out)** exhaust, tire out.

Tudor *a* pertaining to, made in age of Tudor monarchy.

Tuesday *n* third day of week.

tuft *n* bunch, bundle *esp* of grass, hair etc.

tug *v* tugs, tugging, tugged. pull violently; *n* 1 act of tugging 2 small boat for towing; *ns* **t. of love** *Brit coll* dispute between separated parents over custody of their child; **t. of war** contest of strength between two teams pulling in different directions on same rope.

tuition n teaching; instruction.

tulip n bulbous plant of lily family; n **t.-tree** tree allied to magnolia.

tulle n Fr soft fine silky material.

tumble v 1 fall down; stumble 2 turn somersaults 3 upset 4 rumple; phr vs **tumble down** collapse (a **tumbledown** in ruins); **tumble** to coll realize the truth about; n fall; somersault; ns **t. drier** machine with rotating drum for drying clothes **tumbler** 1 acrobat 2 part of lock moved by key 3 drinking glass without stem or foot.

tumid a swollen; enlarged.

tummy n coll stomach.

tumour n abnormal mass of growing body tissue; a **-ous**.

tumult n uproar; disturbance; a **-uous** noisy; greatly agitated.

tumulus n **-li.** ancient burial mound or barrow.

tun n large cask for storing, fermenting beer and wine; formerly measure of liquid 252 galls.

tuna n large sea fish with dark flesh.

tundra n frozen desert of N Russia and Siberia.

tune n 1 air; melody 2 harmony 3 correctness of pitch; idm **change one's t.** fig speak, act very differently; idm **in/out of tune** 1 at correct musical pitch 2 in agreement; idm **to the tune of** 1 using the music of 2 coll to the total sum of; v adjust

to correct pitch; adjust radio etc to receive programmes on certain wave length; phr v **tune in** turn on radio or adjust controls to particular wavelength; as **-ful** melodious (adv **-ly** n **-ness**); **-less** (adv **-ly** n **-ness**); n

tuner 1 person who tunes instrument 2 device for selecting radio signal of particular frequency.

tungsten n greyish white metallic element, wolfram.

tunic n military surcoat; loose belted knee length garment.

tuning n act of getting in tune; n **t.-fork** pronged piece of steel that resonates when struck to help check tuning of other instrument(s).

tunnel n 1 underground passage esp one for railway 2 burrow (of mole, etc); n **t. vision** 1 sight defect from which sufferer can only see straight ahead 2 fig tendency to see only one aspect of a question; v **tunnels, tunnelling, tunnelled.** make tunnel through.

tunny n tuna.

turban n Oriental head-covering made by coiling long strip of cloth round head.

turbid a muddy; opaque; fig confused etc; adv **-ly**; ns **-ity; -ness.**

turbine n motor driven by jets of steam, water etc playing on blades.

turbocharger n compressor device in internal

combustion engine that makes it more powerful.

turbo-jet n, a (engine) using exhaust gas to drive turbine.

turbot n large edible flat seafish.

turbulent a riotous; unruly; disorderly; n **-lence.**

turd n taboo 1 lump of excrement 2 sl contemptible person.

tureen n deep, lidded dish for soup.

turf n **-fs** or **-ves.** area of earth covered by grass; sod; peat; **the t.** horse racing; phr v **turf out** coll turn out roughly.

turgid a swollen; inflated; pompous; n **-ity.**

turkey n large, domestic fowl of pheasant family, used as food; idm **talk turkey** coll esp US speak openly and negotiate seriously.

Turkish a pertaining to Turkey, the Turks; n **T. bath** hot air or steam bath; **T. delight** sweetmeat of flavoured gelatine coated in sugar.

turmeric n aromatic plant of ginger family used as medicine, dye and condiment.

turmoil n agitation; uproar; confusion; tumult.

turn v 1 move round an axis; rotate 2 move in different direction 3 move to reverse side 4 cause to move in specified direction; aim 5 look round 6 curve away 7 (cause to) become 8 fold 9 go sour **10** pass (in time or age); idm **turn a blind eye/deaf ear** pretend not to see/hear; idm **turn a phrase** express cleverly; idm **turn one's head** make one conceited; idm **turn one's stomach** make one feel sick; idm **turn up one's nose at** reject as inferior; phr vs **turn down 1** (turn controls to) reduce (heat, noise, etc) **2** refuse (request); **turn in 1** fold inwards **2** coll surrender **3** coll go to bed **4** hand in; **turn off 1** cause to stop operating **2** cause to lose interest, esp sexual (n **t.-off 1** road branching off main road **2** sth which bores or disgusts one); **turn on 1** cause to start operating **2** attack without warning **3** depend on **4** sl arouse with excitement, esp sexual (n **t.-on**); **turn out 1** empty **2** extinguish **3** expel **4** happen **5** appear at public event **6** produce (n **t.-out 1** number of people attending **2** act of emptying, tidying **3** way of dressing); **turn over 1** move to next page **2** ponder **3** (of engine) idle **4** do trade (n **turnover 1** amount of business done or rate of selling **2** changes in staff **3** small pie); **turn up 1** arrive **2** find or be found **3** fold upwards, esp to shorten garment **4** raise in heat, volume etc by turning

controls (n **t.-up 1** turned end of trouser leg **2** unhoped for good fortune); n **1** act of turning **2** change of direction **3** rightful time or opportunity **4** move from one period or condition to another **5** attack of illness **6** short theatrical performance; idm **give sb a turn** shock sb; idm **a good/bad turn** a kind/mean action; idm **in turn 1** in rightful order **2** one after the other; idm **on the turn 1** starting to change **2** turning sour; idm **out of turn 1** before one's proper time **2** in a tactless way; idm **(done) to a turn** (cooked) exactly right; ns **turnabout** change of direction; **turncoat** disloyal person; **turnkey** jailer (a ready for use and occupation); **turnpike** toll gate; **t.round** time taken to unload and reload before return journey; **turnstile** revolving gate to control admission, eg to sports event; **t.table** (machine that drives) revolving flat surface for playing records; ns **turner** person working at a lathe; **turning** corner, curve or branch in road (n **t. point** time when most important change occurs).

turnip n plant with large white globular edible root.

turpentine n liquid solvent, distilled from resin of pine trees.

turpitude n depravity, infamy.

turquoise n semi-precious greenish-blue stone; this colour.

turret n small tower; revolving armoured tank for guns in warship tank or aircraft.

turtle n marine tortoise; edible species of this; idm **turn turtle** (of ship) turn over.

turtle-dove n wild dove.

turtle-neck n (sweater with) high close-fitting neck-band.

turves pl of **turf**.

tusk n long pointed tooth in some animals, as elephants etc; n **tusker** animal with fully developed tusks.

tussle n scuffle; rough struggle; v engage in rough struggle.

tussock n clump of grass; tuft.

tut interj expressing annoyance or disapproval.

tutelage n stage of acting as guardian, or being under guardianship.

tutor n teacher, private instructor, a -ial.

tutti-frutti n Italian ice-cream containing small bits of fruit.

tutu n -us short, full, ballet skirt.

tuxedo n US dinner jacket (also **tux**).

TV abbr television.

twaddle n empty, foolish talk; nonsense.

twain n, a lit, ar two.

twang n **1** nasal speech **2** vibrating metallic sound; v pluck strings of musical instrument.

tweak n, v nip; pinch.

twee *a* excessively dainty or sentimental.

tweed *a*, *n* (made from) Scottish woollen cloth; *pl* **-s** suit of tweed; tweed clothes; *a* **-y 1** like or made of tweed **2** behaving in a hearty way typifying rich country people.

tweet *v*, *n* chirp.

tweezers *n pl* small pair of pincers.

twelfth *det*, *pron* ordinal number of twelve; next after eleventh; **T.-night** evening of 6th January.

twelve *n*, *a* cardinal number one above eleven; 12.

twenty *n*, *pron*, *det* cardinal number, twice ten; 20; *a* **twentieth** ordinal number 20th.

twerp *n Brit sl* fool.

twice *adv* two times.

twiddle *v* twirl; twist.

twig[1] *n* small branch; shoot.

twig[2] *v* **twigs, twigging, twigged.** *coll* understand.

twilight *n* **1** (fading light at) time after sunset before complete darkness **2** *fig* declining years (of life, career); **t. sleep** state of induced semi-unconsciousness, to lessen pains of childbirth; *a* **twilit** lit by twilight.

twill *n* diagonally ribbed fabric; *a* **twilled.**

twin *n* one of two persons, animals born at one birth; *a* **1** double **2** closely connected; resembling; *n* **t. bed** one of pair of single beds in one room (*a* **t.-bedded** of such a room); *v* **1** link, match closely **2** establish special offical relationship between (places in different countries); *ns* **t. town** such a town; **t. set** *Brit* woman's matching jumper and cardigan; *a* **twinned;** *n* **twinning.**

twine *v* twist, coil round; *n* strong string.

twinge *n* sudden, sharp, shooting pain; pang.

twinkle *v* flash, sparkle intermittently; (*of eyes*) show sudden gleam of mirth; *n* **twinkling** intermittent sparkle; brief moment.

twirl *v* turn or twist quickly; spin round.

twist *v* **1** twine; wind round **2** act dishonestly **3** make, become spiral; *idm* **twist sb's arm** use physical or moral pressure to persuade sb; *idm* **twist sb round one's little finger** be able to get from sb anything one wants; *n* **1** act of twisting **2** spiral **3** bend **4** hand of thread **5** unexpected turn of events; *n* **-er** *coll* **1** swindler **2** *US* tornado **3** difficult puzzle; *a* **twisty** winding.

twit *v* **twits, twitting, twitted.** taunt *n Brit coll* fool.

twitch *v* pluck, pull jerkily; *n* spasmodic movement of body; *a* **-y** showing signs of nervousness; *adv* **-ily;** *n* **-iness;** *n* **twitcher 1** one who twitches **2** *coll* keen birdwatcher.

twitter *v*, *n* (*of birds*) chirp intermittently; *idm* **all of a twitter** *coll* nervously excited.

twixt *prep lit*, *ar* between.

two *n*, *pron*, *det* cardinal number next above one (2); pair; *as* **t.-bits** *US* petty; **t.-faced** insincere; **t.-handed 1** using two hands **2** needing two people; **twopenny** costing two pence (*a* **t.-halfpenny** trivial; cheap); **t.-way** moving, communicating in both directions; *ns* **twosome 1** couple **2** game for two; **t.-step** (music for) lively ballroom dance; *v* **t.-time** deceive (*n* **t.-timer**).

tycoon *n coll* powerful business man.

tympanum *n* ear-drum.

type *n* **1** class; group; kind; variety; example **2** *print* block of wood, metal with letter or symbol on surface **3** set of type; **in t.** set up ready for printing; *v* **1** classify **2** print with typewriter; *vs* **t.-cast** (repeatedly) give actor/actress role that corresponds with his/her natural character; **t.-set** for printing (*ns* **t.-setter, -setting**); *ns* **t.-face** style of lettering for printing; **typescript** typed draft of book etc; **typewriter** writing machine with keys to make individual letters and signs; **typist** personal able to type; *a* **t.-written.**

typhoid *n med* infectious

enteric fever; *n* **typhus**
contagious fever.

typhoon *n* violent whirlwind,
hurricane.

typical *a* true to type;
characteristic; *v* **typify**
-fying, -fied. serve as type or
model of.

typography *n* art of style of
printing; *a* **typographical;** *n*
typographer.

tyrant *n* **1** despotic; harsh;
unjust ruler **2** one who
forces his will on others
cruelly, oppressively; *a*
tyrannical; *v* **tyrannize** rule,
exert authority harshly; *n*
tyranny despotism.

tyre *n* *Brit* covering for rim of
wheel, *usu* of inflated,
reinforced rubber for
absorbing shocks (*US* **tire**).

ubiquitous *a* present, existing everywhere; *n* **ubiquity**.

udder *n* external milk gland of cow etc.

UDI *abbr* unilateral declaration of independence.

UFO *abbr* unidentified flying object.

ugh *interj* expressing disgust, horror.

ugly *a* 1 unpleasant to look at; hideous 2 hostile; threatening; *n* **u. duckling** person who at first seems unattractive, unpromising, but changes into someone beautiful or admirable; *n* **-ness**.

UHF *abbr rad* ultra-high frequency.

UHT *abbr (of dairy products)* ultra heat treated.

UK *abbr* United Kingdom (Great Britain and N Ireland).

ukase *n* Russian decree; any aribitrary order.

ukulele *n* small four-stringed musical instrument, like guitar.

ulcer *n* 1 open sore, discharging pus, on skin or mucous membrane 2 *fig* corrupting influence; *v* **-ate** (*usu* in *pp* as *a*) infect with ulcer; *n* **-ation**; *a* **-ous**.

ullage *n* amount by which cask, bottle is short of being full.

ulna *n* **ulnae** inner bone of forearm; *a* **ulnar**.

ulterior *a* 1 later in time 2 lying on farther side 3 *(of motive etc)* undisclosed.

ultimate *a* furthest; final; last; fundamental; *n* **ultimatum** final demand, terms offered by person or power; *adv* **ultimo** *(abbr* **ult**) in preceding month.

ultra- *prefix* beyond in space; beyond what is normal; excessively.

ultra-high frequency *a (of*

radio waves) over 300 million hertz.

ultramarine *n* bright blue pigment; *a* of this colour; overseas.

ultra-red *a* rays of spectrum below red; infra-red.

ultra-short *a* **rad** of waves below ten metres.

ultrasonic *a (of sounds)* beyond limit of human hearing; *n* **ultrasound**.

ultrasound *n* pressure waves with frequency above 20,000 hertz (hz).

ultra-violet *a* of electromagnetic waves between visible violet and X-rays.

ululate *v* howl; screech; wail; *n* **-lation**.

umber *n* brown earthy pigment.

umbilicus *n anat* navel; *a* **-ilical** of, near navel; *n* **u. cord** 1 structure joining foetus to placenta 2 tube, cable linking spaceship with astronaut outside.

umbrage *n* feeling of resentment or injury; *idm* **take umbrage** be offended.

umbrella *n* 1 folding circular shade or cover, for protection against rain or sun 2 agency or group that coordinates work of other groups in an organization.

umpire *n* person chosen to judge, decide doubtful point, or enforce rules in game; *v* act as umpire.

umpteen *det, pron coll* an indefinite large number of.

UN see **uno.**

un- *prefix* expressing negation before simple words or reversal of action before verbs. *Such words are not given when the meaning may be deduced easily.*

unable *a* not having ability, opportunity or permission.

unaccountable *a* inexplicable; not responsible.

unadopted *a* (*of road*) not maintained by local authority.

unaffected *a* 1 not touched or influenced 2 not pretentious; simple.

unanimous *a* being of one mind; agreeing; *n* **unanimity.**

unassuming *a* modest; unpresuming.

unattached *a* 1 not joined 2 not belonging to group 3 not married, engaged or committed to relationship.

unavailing *a* ineffectual; useless.

unaware *n* ignorant; not noticing; *adv* **-s** without warning; inadvertently.

unbalance *v* 1 throw off balance 2 affect the mental stability of; *a* **-anced** 1 unevenly arranged 2 insane.

unbeknown to *adv* without it being known by.

unbelief *n* lack of (*esp* religious) faith; *n* **-liever;** *as* **-lieving** 1 lacking faith 2 sceptical; **-lievable** incredible (*adv* **-ly**).

unbend *v* 1 straighten 2 behave less formally; *a* **-ing**

not yielding; stubborn.

unbidden *adv* 1 uninvited 2 voluntarily.

unbosom *v* **u. oneself** share one's personal secrets.

unbowed *a fml* not defeated.

unbridled *a* uncontrolled; extravagant.

uncalled-for *a* not necessary, desirable or deserved.

uncanny *a* weird; mysterious.

uncate *a* hooked; *a* **unciform** hook-shaped.

unceremonious *a* 1 informal 2 discourteous (*adv* **-ly**).

uncharitable *a* (*of attitude, comment*) unkind; harsh.

uncharted *a* 1 not marked on map 2 *fig* unexplored.

uncle *n* 1 brother of father or mother 2 husband of aunt 3 *sl* pawnbroker; *n* **U. Sam** *n coll* (people or government of) USA.

unconscionable *a* unscrupulous; excessive.

unconscious *a* not knowing; involuntary; insensible; *n* the subconscious; *adv* **-ly;** *n* **-ness.**

unconsidered *a* 1 spoken thoughtlessly 2 unimportant.

uncouple *v* separate.

uncouth *a* awkward; unrefined in manner.

uncover *v* 1 remove cover from 2 find out (truth).

uncrowned *a* 1 not officially appointed; **u. king of** person widely recognized as the best.

unction *n* 1 anointing with oil 2 *fig* fervour, *esp* religious 3

suavity; gush; **Extreme U.** sacrament given to dying; *a* **unctuous** 1 greasy; oily 2 *fig* smug; gushing.

undaunted *a* bold; intrepid; not frightened.

under *prep* 1 beneath; below 2 ruled, protected by 3 working for 4 subject to; in the process of 5 less than; *idm* **under age** less than legal age; *idm* **under the counter** (*of trade*) illegally (a **u.-the-counter**); *adv* 1 below 2 less; *idm* **down under** *coll* in the antipodes.

under- *prefix* lower; inferior; insufficiently; beneath. *Such words are not given when the meaning may be deduced easily.*

underact *v* act with less force than is needed.

underarm *a, adv sport* with the hand below shoulder level.

underbrush *n esp US* undergrowth.

undercarriage *n* wheels on which aircraft lands; framework for these.

undercharge *v* charge too little.

undercoat *n* coat of paint applied before top coat.

undercover *a* acting secretly, *esp* as spy.

undercut *v comm* charge less than (competitor).

underdeveloped not fully developed; *n* **u. country** country where economic potential (*eg* in industry) has not been fully exploited.

underdog *n* person regarded as

weaker or likely to lose.

undergo v **undergoing, underwent, undergone.** experience.

undergraduate n member of university who has not yet taken first degree.

underground a below surface of earth; secret; idm **go underground** fig hide from limelight; n 1 underground railway 2 secret resistance movement.

undergrowth n bushes and other low plants, esp growing among trees.

underhand a 1 (of bowling, tennis) with arm lower than shoulder 2 sly.

underlay n material laid under carpet.

underline v 1 mark (word etc) with line underneath 2 fig emphasize.

underling n subordinate.

undermentioned a, n (sb/sth) named below.

undermine v wear away by erosion etc; fig weaken, injure by secret means.

underneath adv beneath; below.

underpants n pl garment worn underneath trousers.

underpass n tunnel or covered cutting taking one road under another.

underpin v support.

underplay v 1 underact 2 give too little importance to.

underscore v underline.

undersell v 1 sell too cheaply 2 undervalue.

understand v 1 comprehend 2

assume; infer 3 learn; be informed of; (pt, pp -**stood**); n -**ing** comprehension; sympathy; a -**able**; adv -**ably**.

understate v 1 say sth is less than it is 2 show strong feeling ironically by less strong expression; n -**ment**.

understudy v learn part (of actor etc) in order to deputize for him, if necessary; n.

undersubscribed a not supported by enough participants.

undertake v **undertaking, undertook, undertaken.** enter upon; promise; pledge oneself; n **undertaker** one who undertakes; one whose business is to arrange funerals; n -**taking** an enterprise; guarantee.

undertone n 1 low voice 2 esp pl concealed meaning.

undertow n undercurrent of wave breaking on shore.

underwear n clothes worn beneath others.

underwent pt of undergo.

underworld n criminals as social group; place of departed spirits.

underwrite v 1 insure shipping 2 undertake to buy, take up shares not brought by public.

undies n coll women's underwear.

undo v **undoing, undid, undone. 1** reverse 2 ruin 3 cancel 4 unfasten; n **undoing** cause, source of ruin; unfastening; a **undone**

1 untied 2 ruined 3 not done.

undoubted a acknowledged as certain; adv -**ly**.

undue a excessive; improper.

undulate v rise and fall like waves; n -**ation**.

undying a everlasting.

unearth v dig up; discover.

uneasy a (of person) anxious; (of situation) worrying adv -**ily**; ns **unease, uneasiness** apprehension.

unemployed a without a job; n **unemployment** state of having no job.

unerring a reliably accurate; adv -**ily**.

UNESCO abbr United Nations Educational Scientific and Cultural Organization.

unexceptionable a beyond criticism or objection.

unfailing a 1 constant 2 totally reliable; adv -**ly**.

unfeeling a insensitive; cruel; adv -**ly**.

unfit a not healthy, suitable or capable (n -**ness**); as **unfitted** unsuited; **unfitting** inappropriate.

unflappable a always able to keep calm in a crisis.

unfold v 1 open out from folded state 2 be revealed.

unfortunate a 1 unlucky 2 regrettable 3 awkward; adv -**ly**.

unfounded a without justification.

unfrock v dismiss from holy orders (also **defrock**).

ungainly a awkward; clumsy.

ungrounded *a* false; unjustified.

ungulate *n, a* (animal) which has hoofs.

unhand *v lit* release from hold with hand.

unheard-of *a* very unusual; unprecedented.

unholy *a* 1 wicked 2 *coll* terrible; dreadful; *n* **u. alliance** grouping of those that are normally opposed to one another for a common evil purpose.

uni- *prefix* one; single.

unicameral *a* with only one legislative chamber.

UNICEF *abbr* United Nations (formerly International) Children's (formerly Emergency) Fund.

unicorn *n* fabulous animal like horse with one horn in middle of forehead.

uniform *a* not changing; similar in every way; *n* distinctive dress worn by members of organized body; *a* **-ed** wearing uniform; *adv* **-ly** evenly; *n* **-ity** sameness.

unify *v* unifying, unified. cause to be one, combine; *n* unification.

unilateral *a* one-sided; *adv* **-ly**; *n* **-ism**; *a, n* **-ist**.

unimpeachable *a* that cannot be doubted.

union *n* act of uniting or being united; federation; trade union; *a* of a trade union; *n* **U. Jack** national flag of UK; *v* **-ize** organize into, (cause to) become member of trade

union (*n* **-ization**); *n* **ism** *a*, *n* **-ist**.

unique *a* having no like or equal; unparalleled *adv* **-ly** *n* **-ness**.

unisex *a* of style suited to both men and women.

unison *n* harmony; concord; *mus* identity of pitch.

unit *n* 1 single complete thing 2 group of people or things forming complete whole 3 least whole number; *n* **u.trust** company that invests in other companies on behalf of members to whom it pays dividends.

unite *v* to join into one; associate; combine; cause to adhere; *n* **unity** state of being unit; agreement of aims, interests etc; harmony, amity; *a* **united** joined; in alliance (*ns* **U. Kingdom** *see* UK; **U. Nations** *see* UNO **U. States** *see* USA.

universe *n* whole system of created things viewed as whole; the cosmos; *a* **universal** relating to all things or men (*adv* **-ly** *n* **-ity**).

university *n* institution for higher education, empowered to confer degrees; members collectively, governing body of such institution.

unkempt *a* of untidy appearance.

unknown *a* not known; *n* **u. quantity** 1 *math* unknown number represented by symbol x, y etc. 2 *fig* sb/sth

whose true qualities are yet to be discovered.

unleash *v* release from control.

unless *conj* if not; except that.

unlettered *a fml* 1 unable to read 2 not well educated.

unloose *v* untie; set loose (*also* **unloosen**).

unnerve *v* take away (sb's) confidence; frighten; *a* **unnerving** (*adv* **-ly**).

unnumbered *a* 1 not marked with a number 2 countless.

UNO *abbr* United Nations Organization (international organization working for world peace; *also* **UN**).

unpick *v* remove (stitches from).

unplaced *a* 1 not one of the first three in race or contest 2 not accepted on course 3 having no accommodation.

unprintable *a* too offensive to publish in print.

unqualified *a* 1 with no qualifications 2 absolute.

unremitting *a* persistent; *adv* **-ly**.

unrequited *a* (*esp* of love) not reciprocated.

unrest *n* state of dissatisfaction; expression of this.

unruly *a* disorderly; ungovernable.

unsightly *a* ugly; *n* **-iness**.

unspeakable *a* too bad to mention; outrageous (*adv* **-ably**).

unstinting *a* given freely (*adv* **-ly**).

unstuck *a* not held by glue; *idm* **come unstuck** 1 fall apart 2 *fig coll* fail.

unstudied *a* natural.

until *prep* so far as; up to; *conj* up to time when.

untimely *a* before time; at an unsuitable time (*n* **-iness**).

unto *prep lit, ar* to.

untold *a* 1 not told 2 very great; excessive.

untouchable *a* 1 that cannot be touched, reached, equalled 2 of lowest Hindu caste (*n* such a person).

untoward *a* inconvenient; unlucky; awkward.

untrammelled *a US* able to develop freely.

unutterable *a* too great to be put in words; inexpressible; *adv* **-ably**.

unvarnished *a* plain; without embellishment.

unversed in *a* having no skill or experience of.

unwarranted *a* not justified.

unwell *a* ill; not well.

unwieldy *a* too large to be carried or moved easily; too complicated to be managed or controlled easily.

unwind *v* 1 unravel 2 (cause to) relax.

unwitting *a* unintentional; *adv* **-ly**.

up *adv, prep* 1 to, at higher or better position 2 to, in the north, 3 to, at university 4 out of bed 5 in phrasal verb denoting finality, completion (**finish up, eat up**) 6 on, at the top (of) 7 at the far end (of); *prep* **up to** as far as; until; *idm* **up against** facing (opposition,

difficulty); *idm* **up and about** out of bed and moving; *idm* **up for 1** on trial for 2 being considered for; *idm* **up front** (of money) in advance before delivery; *idm* **be up to** 1 be busy doing or planning 2 be capable of 3 be the responsibility of; *idm* **be well up in/on** have good knowledge of; *idm* **on the up-and-up** making good progress; *as* **up-and-coming** new and promising; **up-market** *comm* of better quality; more expensive.

upbeat *n mus* unaccented beat; *a coll* cheerful.

upbraid *v* censure; reproach; scold.

upbringing *n* way in which a child is educated and disciplined.

upcoming *a* imminent.

update *v* revise; bring up to date; *n* revision.

upend *v* turn upside down.

upfront *a* frank and direct.

upgrade *v* raise status of; put higher price on.

upheaval *n* violent disturbance.

upheld *pt, pp* of **uphold.**

uphill *a* ascending; *fig* difficult.

uphold *v* **upholding, upheld.** support; maintain.

upholster *v* 1 furnish (room) with carpets, curtains etc 2 stuff and cover chairs etc.; *ns* **-sterer** one who repairs covers chairs etc or sells such goods; **-stery** trade of upholsterer; goods supplied by him.

upkeep *n* (cost of) maintenance.

upland *n* (often *pl*) higher ground of region.

uplift *v* lift up, raise *esp* spiritually or culturally.

upon *prep* on.

upper *a* higher; nearer the top; *n* top part of shoe; *n, a* **u. case** capital (letters); *ns* **u. class** titled class; aristocracy (*a* **U.-class**); **u.hand** control; *adv* **uppermost** in highest position; on top.

upper-cut *n* upward blow to chin.

uppity *a* snobbish, arrogant (*also* **uppish**).

upright *a* 1 erect 2 *fig* honest; just; *n* upright post, beam, support etc.

uprising *n* rebellion or revolt.

uproar *n* noisy tumult; clamour; *a* **-ious** noisy, rowdy (*adv* **-ly**; *n* **-ness**).

upset *v* 1 knock, turn over 2 distress, annoy; *n* state of disorder; cause of distress; *coll* quarrel.

upshot *n* result, consequence.

upstairs *a, adv* on, to higher floor; *n* upper floor.

upstanding *a* 1 strong and vigorous 2 honest; *idm* **be upstanding** *fml* stand (when drinking a toast).

upstart *n* one who has risen suddenly to high position or wealth etc.

upsurge *n* sudden increase.

uptake *n* rate of acceptance, absorption; *idm* **quick/slow on the uptake** quick/slow to understand.

uptight a anxious and inhibited.

up-to-date a 1 modern 2 having all the latest news, developments.

uptown a, adv US in, of or to residential area of city.

upturn n improvement in business or fortune; a -ed turned upside-down.

upward a going higher; adv **upwards** to higher position; prep **upwards** of more than; a **upwardly-mobile** able to, seeking to improve one's wealth and social status.

uranium n white metallic radioactive element.

Uranus n planet 7th in distance from the Sun.

urban a pertaining to town; v -ize change from rural to urban condition; n -ization.

urbane a courteous; affable; refined; n **urbanity**.

urchin n mischievous, roguish boy.

urge v 1 drive, push forward 2 exhort insistently; a **urgent** requiring immediate attention; highly important; n -ency.

uric a of or from urine.

urine n fluid secreted by kidneys; a **uric** of urine; v **urinate** pass urine; n **urinal** place for urinating.

urn n large lidded, metal vessel for serving tea or coffee; rounded vase for ashes of dead.

us pron objective case of **we**.

US, USA abbr United States (of America).

usage n 1 way of using 2 way of speaking 3 custom.

use n 1 act of employing anything 2 advantage; purpose served; utility 3 habit; custom; usage; v 1 employ 2 consume 3 behave toward 4 avail oneself of; idm **make use of** take advantage of; use; idm **of use** useful; idm **put to good use** use profitably; phr v **use up** exhaust supply of; as **us(e)able** fit for use; **used** not new; **used to** familiar with; accustomed to; **useful** of practical use (adv -ly; n -ness); **useless** (adv -ly; n -ness); n **user** (n u.code comput secret code used by user; a **u.-friendly** technology designed for easy use by any user).

usher n 1 official in charge of entrance to court etc 2 person showing people to seats and ensuring orderly behaviour in cinema, theatre etc (fem **-ette** usu in cinema); v escort (sb) in specified direction; idm **usher in** fig mark beginning of.

USSR abbr (formerly) Union of Soviet Socialist Republics.

usual a commonplace; habitual; adv **usually** generally; as a rule.

usufruct n right to use and profits of another's property without damage to it or waste.

usurp v take possession of without right or by force; n **usurper**.

usury n lending of money at excessive interest; n **usurer** extortionate money-lender.

utensil n vessel, container for domestic use; any tool or implement for particular purpose.

uterus n womb.

utilitarian a 1 serving material or practical ends 2 based on belief in action that benefits the largest possible number of people (n -ism).

utility n 1 usefulness 2 useful thing; pl **utilities** public services, as supplying of water, gas, electricity etc; v **utilize** put to use, make profitable use of (n -ization).

utmost a most extreme; to greatest, highest degree; n most possible.

Utopia n imaginary State with ideally perfect social and political system; a **utopian** ideally perfect but impracticable.

utter[1] a complete; total; absolute; adv -ly.

utter[2] v produce audibly with voice; say; express by word of mouth, or in writing; n **utterance** act of speaking; spoken words.

uttermost a farthest out; n **utmost**.

U-turn n 1 turn by vehicle to go in opposite direction 2 politics complete reversal of policy.

uxorious a excessively devoted to one's wife.

vacant *a* empty; unoccupied; *fig* empty-headed; *n* **vacancy** vacant post; gap.

vacate *v* waver in mind; resign from; quit; *n* **-ation** act of vacating; fixed holiday period.

vaccinate *v* inoculate with vaccine; *ns* **-ation; vaccine** preparation of virus (*esp* of cowpox) used as inoculation against disease.

vacillate *v* waver in mind; hesitate, be undecided; *n* **-lation** indecision, hesitation.

vacuous *a* stupid; expressionless; *adv* **-ly;** *n* **vacuity** lack of ideas, interest etc.

vacuum *n* 1 space empty or devoid of all matter or content 2 space from which air has been partially exhausted; *a* **v.-packed** enclosed in plastic with air removed; *ns* **v. cleaner** apparatus for removing dirt etc by suction; **v. flask** vessel with two walls separated by vacuum, used to keep liquids at constant temperature; **v. pump** pump for extracting air or gas.

vagabond *a* wandering; having no fixed abode; *n* tramp, vagrant; *coll* rascal.

vagary *n* caprice; whim; freak.

vagina *n* female genital passage; *a* **vaginal.**

vagrant *a* 1 wandering; nomadic 2 *fig* roving; wayward; *n* tramp; *n* **vagrancy.**

vague *a* 1 indefinite; blurred 2 absent-minded 3 not clearly expressed.

vain *a* 1 fruitless; futile 2 conceited; self-satisfied.

vainglorious *a* inordinately proud or boastful; *adv* **-ly;** *n* **-ness.**

valance *n* short curtain above window or in space between bed and floor.

vale *n* valley.

valediction *n* farewell; *a* **valedictory;** *n* farewell oration.

valence, valency *n* *chem* combining power of atom or substance.

valentine *n* sweetheart chosen on 14 February; card or gift sent on that day.

valerian *n* perennial herb; its root as medicine.

valet *n* *Fr* manservant who looks after his master's clothes etc; *v* act as valet.

valetudinarian *n, a* (person) in poor health; (one) unduly engrossed by state of health.

valiant *a* brave; courageous; heroic; *adv* **-ly.**

valid *a* having legal force; well founded; *n* **-ity** soundness; legal force; *v* **-ate** make valid; *n* **-ation.**

valise *n* *Fr* small travelling-bag.

Valium [TM] drug diazepam used as tranquilizer.

Valkyrie *n* *myth* one of 12 war-goddesses, who led the slain to Valhalla.

valley *n* tract of land lying between hills; large river-basin.

valour *n* (*US* = **valor**) bravery; *a* **-ous;** *adv* **-ously.**

value *n* 1 worth 2 purchasing power 3 precise meaning, force 4 relative proportion of light and shade in picture 5 duration of note in music; *pl* **-s** principles (**sense of v.** appreciation of what is good or bad); ns **v. added tax** tax on increased value at each stage of manufacture of product (*also* **VAT**); **v. judgement** estimate of worth based on personal impression rather than objective facts; *v* estimate worth of; appraise; esteem, rate highly; *a* **valuable** costly; of great worth; very useful; *n usu pl* valuable objects, goods etc; *n* **valuation** estimated worth; *a* **valueless**; *n* **valuer**.

valve n device which regulates flow of air, liquid, gas etc. through opening, pipe etc; *a* **valvular** of, like, affecting valves.

vamp[1] n front upper part of footwear; improvised musical accompaniment; *v mus* improvise.

vamp[2] n v woman seeking deliberately to entice men.

vampire n myth corpse that revives itself by sucking human blood; *fig* ruthless blackmailer or money-lender; ns **vampire bat** American blood-sucking bat.

van[1] n covered goods vehicle.

van[2] n leading part of army, fleet, procession; *idm* **in the van** leading the way.

vanadium n rare metallic element used in alloys.

vandal n person who wilfully damages or destroys beautiful things in art or nature, or items of public or private property; *v* **-ize**

damage in this way; *n* **-ism**.

vane n weathercock; blade of propeller; sight of quadrant or surveying instrument; web of feather.

vanguard n 1 leading part of army or fleet 2 leaders of political, social movement or fashion.

vanilla n kind of orchid; its pods used for flavouring.

vanish v disappear; cease to exist; become invisible; *n* **vanishing point** point in perspective drawing where receding parallel lines appear to meet.

vanity n conceit; futility; worthlessness.

vanquish v conquer; subdue; be victorious; *n* **vanquisher**.

vantage n advantage (tennis) first point after deuce; *v* **v. point** favourable position.

vapid a insipid; lifeless; *n* **vapidity**.

vapour n substance in gaseous state; steam, mist; *fig* freak of fancy; *v* **vaporize** convert into or pass off in vapour; *a* **vaporous**; *n* **vaporizer** atomizer.

variable a changing; liable to change; not constant; *n* 1 thing that can be changed, substituted 2 *math* (symbol for) unspecified value; *adv* **-ably**; *n* **-ability**.

variance n **at variance (with)** in conflict (with).

variant a, n different, alternative (version or form).

variation n 1 degree of varying

2 variant 3 one of set of stylistic elaborations on musical, literary theme.

varicose a (of veins) abnormally swollen.

varied a 1 of different kinds 2 showing change of type.

variegate v mark with different colours; *a* **-gated** parti-coloured; streaked; *n* **-gation**.

variety n 1 diversity; varied assortment 2 kind; type; group; *a* **various** 1 of several different kinds 2 some 3 *coll* many.

variform a found in various forms.

varnish n gum or resin dissolved in spirit, applied to surface to make it shiny; *v* apply varnish to; *phr v* **varnish over** cover up (sth inferior, dishonest etc).

vary v varying, varied. change; alter; modify; become different.

vascular a containing, concerning vessels conveying fluid in plants and animals.

vase n ornamental container for flowers; similar ornament as architectural feature.

vasectomy n operation to remove sperm-duct from male.

Vaseline [TM] soft petroleum jelly.

vassal n feudal tenant; dependant.

vast a very extensive; huge; *coll* great; *n* **-ness**; *adv* **-ly** *coll* extremely.

vat n large cask or tub.

VAT abbr value added tax.

Vatican n 1 palace of pope in Rome 2 fig papacy; papal authority etc.

vault[1] n 1 arched roof; arched cellar 2 strongroom.

vault[2] v leap, spring over, esp with support of hands or pole; n such leap or jump.

vaunt v boast, brag about.

VC abbr Victoria Cross (award for valour in war).

VCR abbr video cassette recorder.

VD abbr venereal disease.

VDU abbr visual display unit (computer screen).

veal n flesh of calf, used for food.

vector n 1 animal transmitting parasites 2 maths magnitude having direction 3 course of aircraft.

veer v shift; change in direction; position; fig change (opinion etc).

veg n Brit coll vegetables.

vegan n person with diet of strictly vegetable produce.

vegeburger n burger of vegetables with no meat.

vegetable a pertaining to, concerning, composed of plants or plant life; n plant, esp edible one; n **vegetarian** one who does not eat meat.

vegetate v live dull monotonous life; n -ation plant growth and development; plants collectively.

vehement a passionate; impetuous; adv -ly n

vehemence.

vehicle n means of conveyance usu on wheels; means, medium of expression etc.; a **vehicular**.

veil n covering for face or head; fig that which conceals; v cover with veil; conceal; idm **take the veil** become a nun; a **-ed** 1 covered by veil 2 fig with implied meaning.

vein n 1 blood-vessel conveying blood to heart 2 veinlike marking 3 crack 4 layer or fissure containing metallic ore 5 fig mood; disposition; a **venous** of veins.

Velcro [TM] fastener of fabric strips that stick when pressed together.

vellum n parchment of calf-skin used for book-binding or manuscripts.

velocity n speed, rapidity of motion; rate of motion.

velours, velour n Fr soft velvety material.

velvet n 1 silk fabric with soft thick pile or nap on one side 2 fig soft downy surface; a **velvety** like velvet; n **velveteen** imitation velvet made of cotton.

venal a corruptible; mercenary; influenced by hope of reward; n -ity.

vend v sell; ns **vendor**; **vending machine** automatic selling machine.

vendetta n It hereditary blood-feud.

veneer v 1 thin layer of fine

wood laid over inferior kind 2 fig superficial polish concealing defects; v cover with veneer.

venerable a worthy of deep respect; v **venerate** revere; respect; worship; n -ation.

venereal a pertaining, due, to sexual intercourse; n v. disease (also VD).

Venetian blind n one made of horizontal movable slats.

vengeance n revenge; infliction of punishment for wrong done; idm **with a vengeance** coll much more than is normal or desirable; a **vengeful** filled with, caused by desire for revenge (adv -ly n -ness).

venial a pardonable; trivial.

venison n deer's flesh, as food.

venom n 1 poison secreted by snake etc 2 fig spite; bitter words; a **-ous** poisonous; spiteful.

venous a 1 of veins 2 (of blood) in veins.

vent n slit, hole, outlet; v pour forth; utter; idm **give vent to** express openly; idm **vent one's anger/feelings etc on** find target for one's anger/feelings etc in.

ventilate v 1 supply with fresh air 2 aerate 3 fig discuss freely; ns **-ator**; **-ation**.

ventricle n cavity in organ of body, esp main pumping chamber of heart; a **-tricular**.

ventriloquist n one who can speak and throw his voice without apparent movement

of lips; *a* **-loquial**;
n **-loquism**.

venture *n* risky course of action; financial speculation; *v* expose to risk or danger; dare to go etc; presume to put forward; *n* **v. capital** money provided for investment in new business; *a* **-some** (*n* **-ness**).

venue *n Fr leg* 1 place fixed for trial 2 *fig* meeting-place 3 any place where an organized gathering takes place, *esp* pop concert, public meeting.

Venus *n* 1 Roman goddess of beauty and love 2 planet second nearest to sun 3 beautiful woman.

veracious *a* truthful; true; *n* **veracity**.

veranda(h) *n* open portico outside house.

verb *n* part of speech expression action, existence in present, past, or future; *a* **-al** pertaining to words; literal; spoken, not written; *ns* **v. diarrhoea** *coll* inability to stop talking; *v.* **noun** noun derived from verb + -ing; *v* **-ize** express in words (*n* **-ization**); *advs* **-ly** by word of mouth.

verbatim *a, adv* (recorded) in exactly the same words.

verbena *n* genus of fragrant herbaceous plants.

verbiage *n Fr* use of too many words.

verbose *a* using too many words; *adv* **-osely**; *n* **-osity**.

verdant *a* green, as of fresh young grass, foliage etc; *fig* youthful; *n* **verdure** green vegetation.

verdict *n* finding; decision of jury; opinion, judgement.

verdigris *n* greenish blue deposit formed on copper or brass.

verge *n* edge; brink; *idm* **on the verge of** very close to; *phr v* **verge on** approach; border on.

verger *n* bearer of wand of office, *esp* C of E; church caretaker.

verify *v* **verifying, verified.** prove; confirm; authenticate; *a* **verifiable**; *n* **verification**.

verily *adv* truly; in truth.

verisimilitude *n* appearance of truth; likelihood.

veritable *a* real; genuine; true; actual; *adv* **-ly**.

vermicelli *n It* thin, worm-like kind of macaroni.

vermiculite *n* expanded form of mica used in insulation.

vermiform *a* worm-shaped; *n* **vermicide** preparation for killing worms.

vermilion *a, n* (of) brilliant red colour.

vermin *n* destructive, harmful animals (*usu* small) collectively; *a* **-ous** infested with vermin.

vermouth *n Fr* fortified white wine flavoured with wormwood etc.

vernacular *a* of native, commonly spoken language; *n* 1 native dialect 2 strong language.

vernal *a* of spring.

veronica *n* genus of flowering herbs.

verruca *n* infectious wart of the foot.

versatile *a* adaptable; changeable; fickle; many-sided; *n* **versatility**.

verse *n* 1 sub-division of poem or chapter of Bible 2 poetry; *a* **versed** (**in**) skilled (in); *v* **versify** tell in verse; compose verses; *n* **versification**.

version *n* 1 translation 2 personal account, statement.

verso *n Lat* left hand or reverse of page of book; reverse of coin, medal.

versus *prep* (*abbr* **v.**) *Lat* against.

vertebra *n* **-brae.** one of joints of spine; *a* **-brate** having backbone; *n* **vertebrate** animal; *a* **-bral** of vertebrae.

vertex *n* **vertices.** summit; zenith; *a* **vertical**; overhead; perpendicular; *adv* **-ly**.

vertigo *n* giddiness; *a* **vertiginous**.

verve *n* vigour; liveliness of spirit.

very *a* actual; real; *adv* exceedingly; absolutely.

vespers *n pl* evensong.

vessel *n* 1 any hollow article or receptacle; ship 2 duct for blood, fluid, sap etc of animal or plant body.

vest *n* 1 undergarment worn on upper part of body 2 waistcoat; *v* endow; confer right, power etc; *phr v* **vest in/with sb** confer (legal right or power) on sb; *idm* **have a vested interest (in)** be likely to benefit from; *n* **vestment** ceremonial garment worn by clergy.

vestal *a* of Roman goddess Vesta; *n* **v. virgin** female servant of temple dedicated to Vesta.

vestibule *n* ante-chamber; lobby.

vestige *n* visible trace or mark; rudimentary survival of organ, etc); *a* **vestigial**.

vestry *n* room in church where vestments and Communion vessels are kept, and parish meetings are held.

vet *n coll abbr* of **veterinary (surgeon)**; *v* **vetting, vetted**. *coll* examine critically.

veteran *n* one with long experience *esp* in fighting services.

veterinary *a* of, concerned with diseases of animals; *n* **v. surgeon** one trained to treat sick animals.

veto *n* **-oes**. *Lat* constitutional right to reject an enactment, or act of administration; absolute prohibition; *v* **vetoing, vetoed**. forbid; exercise veto against.

vex *v* irritate; cause worry to; *n* **-ation** mental distress; worry; *a* **vexatious; vexed** angry; annoyed (*n* **v. question** difficult problem leading to much argument).

VHF *abbr rad* very high frequency.

via *adv* by way of; calling at.

viable *a* capable of

maintaining separate existence; practicable; *n* **viability**.

viaduct *n* long, high bridge carrying railway, road etc over valley.

vial, phial *n* small glass bottle.

vibes *n pl coll* 1 vibraphone 2 vibrations; mental effect (on sb created by sb else).

vibrant *a* 1 throbbing; resonant 2 (of colour) bright and exciting 3 (of people) full of vigour; *n* **vibrancy**.

vibraphone *n* instrument like xylophone, but with metal bars and electric resonators.

vibrate *v* move rapidly to and fro; quiver; oscillate; *n* **-ation**.

vibrato *n mus* resonance given by singing or playing with slight undulation of pitch.

vibrator *n* electrical device that makes vibrations *esp* used in massage.

vicar *n* clergyman in charge of parish; *n* **vicarage** house of vicar.

vicarious *a* acting as substitute; done, felt on behalf of another; *adv* **-ly**.

vice[1] *n* defect; fault; wickedness; immoral conduct; depravity.

vice[2] *n* device for holding, gripping an object in given position.

vice- *prefix* forms compounds with meaning of second to; in place of. *Such compounds are not given where the meaning may be deduced from the simple word.*

vice-chancellor *n* (in UK) administrative head of university.

viceroy *n* one who rules as representative of sovereign; *fem* **vicereine** wife of viceroy; *a* **viceregal**; *n* **viceroyalty**.

vice versa *adv Lat* conversely.

vicinity *n* nearness; neighbourhood.

vicious *a* 1 malicious 2 depraved 3 harmful; dangerous; *n* **v. circle** cycle of bad events each causing the next to go on recurring; **v. spiral** continuous alternate rise (*eg* in prices and wages, each stimulating the other).

vicissitudes *n pl Fr* ups-and-downs of life.

victim *n* 1 human being or animal offered as sacrifice 2 one who suffers through no fault of his own; *v* **victimize** make to suffer, penalize *esp* unjustly; *n* **victimization**.

victor *n* conqueror; winner; *n* **victory** conquest; act of winning; *a* **victorious** triumphant; winning.

Victorian *a* 1 of the time of Queen Victoria (1837–1901) (*n* person of this time) 2 (*of moral attitude*) based on principles of self-control, respectability and thrift.

victual (*n usual pl*) food; *v* supply, take in stores, food; *n* **victualler** supplier of victuals (**licensed v.** publican licensed to sell alcoholic liquor).

video a (for recording, reproducing) televised pictures; n -**os**. 1 videotape recording 2 machine for recording and replaying this; v **videoing, videoed**. make video recording of; ns v. **cassette recorder** machine for recording video (also **video (recorder)** abbr **VCR**); v. **clip** short video extract from film etc; **videodisc** disc for video recording; v. **nasty** coll video film with disturbing scenes of sex, violence; **videotape** magnetic tape for recording moving pictures and sound (v record in this way).

vie v **vying, vied**. strive with; rival; content with.

view n 1 act of seeing; sight 2 scene 3 picture, photograph of scenery etc 4 opinion; v look at; consider; hold specified opinion; idm **in view** of because of; considering; idm **on view** being exhibited; idm **take a dim/poor view** of regard with strong disapproval; idm **with a view to** with the hope, intention of; ns v.-**finder** part of camera showing area to be photographed; **viewpoint** point of view; opinion; **viewer** 1 one who watches 2 device for looking at photographic slides.

vigil n act of keeping watch (esp on sick-bed) or of praying all night; eve of feast-day; a -**ant** watchful;

alert; (adv -**ly**); ns -**ance** watchfulness; **vigilante** member of self-appointed group seeking to prevent crime by unofficial means.

vignette n Fr small delicate illustration in book; fig short wordsketch.

vigour n strength, potency; vitality; a -**ous** strong; active; forceful (adv -**ly**).

Viking n Scandinavian pirate in 8th–11th centuries.

vile a depraved; shameful; atrocious; adv -**ly**; n -**ness**; v **vilify** speak ill of; slander; n **vilification**.

villa n smallish suburban house; country house esp in Italy or south of France.

village n small rural community with cottages, shops, church etc; n **villager**.

villain n scoundrel; a -**ous** wicked; vile; adv -**ly**; n **villainy**.

villein n feudal serf.

vim n coll energy; vigour.

vinaigrette n Fr 1 bottle for smelling-salts 2 salad dressing.

vindicate v establish truth or merit of; prove innocence of; ns **vindication; vindicator**.

vindictive a revengeful; punitive; adv -**ly**; n -**ness**.

vine n climbing plant with tendrils, esp one bearing grapes; ns -**yard** grape vine plantation; **vinery** hot-house for growing grapes.

vinous a of, like wine.

vintage n 1 gathering of grapes

for wine-making 2 yield of wine grapes in given year 3 fig date, as criterion of quality; n **vintner** wine merchant.

vinegar n acid liquid got from fermented wine, beer etc; a -**y** very sour, acid; fig bitter, spiteful.

vinyl n any of various tough flexible plastics, eg PVC.

viol n medieval instrument like violin.

viola[1] n genus of plants including pansy, violet etc.

viola[2] n stringed instrument slightly larger and lower pitched than violin.

violate v desecrate; rape; infringe; ns -**ation** act of, thing which violates; -**ator**.

violent a forcible; boisterous; passionate; using, showing great physical strength; adv -**ly** n **violence**.

violet n 1 plant of viola species 2 bluish-purple colour; a of this colour.

violin n fiddle; small four-stringed musical instrument; n -**ist** player of violin.

VIP abbr very important person.

viper n venomous snake, adder.

viral a of or caused by virus.

virgin n one who has never had sexual intercourse; a 1 being a virgin; chaste; undefiled 2 (of land) never before cultivated; a **virginal** of, like virgin; pure; fresh; unsullied; (n kind of spinet); n **virginity** state of being a virgin; maidenhead.

Virginia creeper n climbing plant with leaves that turn scarlet in autumn.

viridescence n greenness; verdure; freshness; youthful vitality; a **viridescent**.

virile a manly; not impotent; n **virility** masculinity; sexual potency in men.

virology n study of viruses and diseases caused by them; a **-ological**; n **-ologist**.

virtual a in effect but not in name; adv **-ly** to all intent and purposes.

virtual reality n environment simulated by computer software in which a user can interact as if it were the real world.

virtue n 1 integrity 2 female chastity 3 moral excellence; merit; idm **by virtue of** thanks to; as a result of; a **virtuous** morally good; chaste (adv **-ly** n **-ness**).

virtuoso n **-sos** or **-si.** one with high degree of technical skill in one of fine arts esp in music; n **-osity**.

virulent a 1 (of disease or poison) powerful and deadly 2 fml bitterly hostile; adv **-ly** n **virulence**.

virus n **-ses.** one of minute parasitic organisms causing infectious diseases (eg common cold, flu, AIDS); such a disease.

visa n endorsement on passport; v endorse passport with visa.

Visacard [TM] type of credit card, usable for shopping, travel etc in many parts of the world.

vis-à-vis adv, prep Fr opposite, facing.

viscid a glutinous; sticky; a **viscous** sticky; semi-fluid; n **viscosity**.

viscose n form of cellulose used in making artificial silk.

viscount n rank of nobility immediately below earl; fem **-ess**.

viscous a sticky; semi-fluid but not runny; n **viscosity**.

vise US = Brit **vice**[2].

visible a perceptible; apparent to the eye; n **-bility** 1 state, quality of being visible 2 degree of atmospheric clarity esp in navigation.

vision n 1 sight 2 intuition 3 something seen 4 apparition or phantom; a **-ary** impracticable; unreal; (n impractical idealist).

visit v go to see; call upon socially; inspect; phr v **visit on** ar inflict on; **visit with** US coll talk with; v temporary stay; social or professional call; ns **visitor**; **visitation** 1 official, formal visit 2 calamity.

visor, vizor n movable front part of helmet.

vista n Sp, It 1 distant view esp if seen through avenue of trees etc 2 mental prospect of past events etc.

visual a of sight; n **v. aid** picture, film, OHP or video used as teaching aid; **v. display unit** screen used

with computer (abbr **VDU**); adv **-ly** v **-ize** form a mental picture of (n **-ization**).

vital a 1 essential to life 2 lively, animated 3 necessary to some object or purpose; n **v. statistics** 1 statistics regarding population changes 2 Brit coll woman's bust, waist and hip measurements; n **vitality** capacity to live; vigour; v **-ize** make alive; give animation to.

vitamin n one of organic substances present in food, essential for preventing deficiency diseases.

vitiate v destroy force of; taint; leg invalidate; n **vitiation**.

viticulture n Lat cultivation of grape-vines.

vitreous a pertaining to glass; glassy; transparent; v **vitrify** convert, become converted, into glass; n **vitrifaction;** a **vitriform** glass like.

vitriol n sulphuric acid; fig biting sarcasm; a **-lic**.

vituperate v abuse loudly; scold violently; n **-ation;** a **-ative**.

vivacity n liveliness; gaiety; sprightliness; a **vivacious**.

vivarium n place where living animals are kept in natural surroundings.

viva-voce adv Lat by word of mouth; n oral examination.

vivid a 1 (of colour) brilliant; intense 2 animated; graphic; adv **-ly** n **-ness**.

viviparous a bringing forth young alive and capable of

independent life.

vivisection n operating or experimenting on living animals.

vixen n female fox; *fig* spiteful woman.

V-neck n neckline of dress, sweater etc shaped like V; a -**ed**.

vocabulary n 1 stock of words used by person 2 alphabetical list of words and their meanings.

vocal a of voice; uttered by voice; adv -**ly**; v -**ize** (n -**ization**); n -**ist** singer.

vocation n 1 profession; occupation 2 divine call to spiritual or religious life; a -**al** (adv -**ly**).

vociferate v shout; bawl, utter loud cries; n -**ation**; a **vociferous** noisy.

vodka n Russian spirit distilled from rye.

vogue n Fr prevailing fashion, custom etc; popularity.

voice n 1 sound produced by organs of speech 2 quality of such sound 3 wish, desire expressed as vote; v give utterance to, express; n **v.-over** TV, *film* voice of unseen person; a -**less** 1 mute 2 without speaking aloud 3 *ling* without vibrating vocal cords (adv -**ly** n -**ness**).

void a empty; lacking; legally invalid; n empty space; vacuum; v excrete from body; nullify.

voile n Fr thin cotton, woollen or silken material.

volatile a evaporating quickly; changeable; lively but unstable; n -**tility**; v -**tilize** render, become volatile; evaporate.

vol-au-vent n Fr light raised pie of puff pastry.

volcano n -**oes.** mountain formed by eruption of molten lava, ashes etc through opening in earth's crust; a **volcanic** of, like volcano; *fig* acting with sudden violence.

vole n mouse-like rodent.

volition n act or faculty of willing; choosing.

volley n 1 number of missiles thrown or shot at once 2 *fig* torrent of words etc 3 (tennis etc) striking of ball before it touches ground; v fire, hit volley; n **v. ball** hand ball game played over high net.

volt n unit of electromotive force; ns -**age** ; such force measured in units; -**meter** instrument for measuring electromotive force.

volte-face n Fr reversal of opinion or direction.

voluble a fluent in speech; talkative; adv -**bly**; n -**bility**.

volume n 1 book 2 mass, bulk, size in cubic units 3 intensity of sound; a **voluminous** bulky; abundant (adv -**ly** n -**ness**).

voluntary a 1 acting without compulsion 2 made, done freely; 3 given, supported by private donations; adv -**ily**; n organ music before or after

church service.

volunteer n one who offers services of own free will; *esp* in armed forces; v offer freely.

voluptuous a 1 fond of, addicted to sensual pleasure 2 shapely and sexually attractive; adv -**ly**; n -**ness**; n **voluptuary** one addicted to luxurious sensual pleasures.

vomit v discharge from stomach through mouth; n that which has been vomited.

voodoo n form of witchcraft practised by W Indians.

voracious a greedy; ravenous; n **voracity**.

vortex n **vortices.** whirlpool; whirling mass; *fig* anything which engulfs; a **vortical**.

votary n one vowed to service of a god, devotee of a cause etc; *fem* **votaress**; a **votive** given, offered to fulfil vow.

vote n formal expression of one's wish, opinion etc; right to vote at elections etc.; v 1 give vote 2 *coll* suggest; n **voter**.

vouch v; *phr* v **vouch for** guarantee; be responsible for; n **voucher** document confirming fact or authenticity of something; ticket acting as substitute for cash; v **vouchsafe** condescend to grant.

vow n solemn pledge, promise *esp* to God; v promise faithfully.

vowel n speech-sound produced by unhindered

passage of breath through mouth; letter representing such sound.

voyage n journey, *esp* long one, by water; v travel, make a journey, by water; n **voyager**.

voyeur n *Fr* one who enjoys seeing sexual objects or acts; n **-ism**.

vs *abbr* versus.

vulcanize v treat (rubber) by sulphur, under heat; ns **vulcanite** hard substance so made; **vulcanization**.

vulgar a 1 (*of person*) uncouth; ill-mannered 2 (*of taste*) unrefined 3 (*of humour*) likely to offend; obscene; n **v. fraction** one with numerator above denominator (*also* **simple fraction**); adv **-ly**; ns **-ism** rude or obscene expression; **-ity** coarseness; lack of refinement; bad taste; v **-ize** (n **-ization**).

Vulgate n 4th century Latin translation of Bible.

vulnerable a 1 capable, of being, liable to be, wounded, attacked etc 2 open to criticism 3 easily hurt 4 *bridge* having won one game towards rubber; n **-ability**.

vulpine a 1 pertaining to foxes 2 sly; crafty.

vulture n 1 large carrion-eating bird of prey 2 *fig* rapacious extortioner.

vulva n *anat* external opening of female genitals.

vying *pr, p of* **vie**.

wacky *a esp US* crazy; zany; *n* **-iness**.

wad *n* small pad of fibrous material; compact bundle of paper, *esp* bank notes; *v* pack, press, etc with wad; *n* **wadding** soft material used for stuffing etc.

waddle *v* walk heavily with swaying motion, like duck; *n* this gait.

wade *v* walk through water, mud, etc; *phr vs* **wade in** begin with determination; **wade into** attack with vigour; **wade through** read through (sth long and tedious); *n* **wader** one that wades (*pl* long waterproof boots).

wadi, wady *n* dried-up desert watercourse.

wafer *n* 1 light thin biscuit 2 small round disc of special bread eaten at Communion service; *a* **w.-thin** very thin.

waffle[1] *n* thin crisp cake of batter.

waffle[2] *v Brit coll* talk or write lengthily in a meaningless way.

waft *v* carry lightly and smoothly through air or over water; *n* breath of wind; faint odour, whiff.

wag *v* **wagging, wagged.** move or shake up and down or from side to side; as of dog's tail; *n* humorous, joking person; *a* **waggish** comical, droll (*adv* **-ly**; *n* **-ness**).

wage *n* payment for labour; *n* **w.-claim** demand by workers for specified increase in wages; **w.freeze** government policy which requires employees not to agree to any wage increases for a specified period; *v* carry on (war).

wager *n*, *v* bet.

waggle *v* wag; *a* **waggly**.

wagon *n* four-wheeled vehicle for heavy loads (*Brit* also

waggon); *w.lit Fr* railway sleeping car; *ns* **wag(g)oner** driver of wagon; **wag(g)onette** four-wheeled open carriage with facing seats.

wagtail *n* small long-tailed bird.

waif *n* homeless, straying person or animal; *fig* neglected child.

wail *v* howl; lament; *n* cry of grief.

wain *n Lit* wagon or cart; *n* **wainwright** builder of wagons.

wainscot *n* wooden panelling on walls of room.

waist *n* 1 part of body between ribs and hip-bone 2 narrowed middle part of some objects 3 middle part of ship's upper deck; *ns* **waistband** strip of fabric enclosing waist at top of trousers, skirt etc; **waistcoat** sleeveless garment worn under jacket; **waistline** measurement round waist; narrow part of garment at the waist.

wait *v* await; defer action; serve and hand dishes at table; *phr v* **wait on 1** serve food to **2** act as servant to (*idm* **wait on sb hand and foot** be very subservient to); *n* act of waiting; *pl* **-s** Christmas carol singers; *n* **waiter** person serving in restaurant (*fem* **waitress**); *a* **waiting** (*ns* **w.list** list of people waiting their turn; **w.room** room where one waits to be attended to; *idm* **(play) a waiting game** (use) tactic of delay.

waive *v* relinquish (claim etc); forgo; *n* **waiver** legal renunciation.

wake[1] *v* **waking, woke, woken.** rouse from sleep; stir up, excite; *idm* **wake the dead** cause great disturbance (with noise); *phr v* **wake up** to realize; *v* **waken** wake up; rouse; *as* **wakeful** vigilant (*n* -**ness**) **waking** when one is awake.

wake[2] *n* track left in water by ship; *idm* **in the w. of** following as consequence of; close behind.

wake[3] *n* meeting to lament dead person before burial.

walk *v* move along on foot at moderate pace; cause to go at walk; *n* act of walking; gait; journey on foot, *esp* for pleasure, exercise; *idm* **walk of life** job or sphere of activity; *phr vs* **walk into 1** *coll* obtain (job) easily 2 fall into (trouble, danger etc) through lack of vigilance; **walk away/off with** *coll* 1 remove by theft 2 win with ease; **walk on 1** continue walking 2 go on stage (*n* **w.- on part** *theatre* small non-speaking part; **walk out 1** leave suddenly without further comment 2 go on strike (*n* **w.-out**); **walk out on** abandon; **walk over 1** traverse on foot 2 *coll* treat with contempt (*idm* **walk all over,** *esp* in sport defeat

easily; *n* **walkover** easy victory; *ns* **walkabout 1** *Aust* time of wandering into the bush by Aborigine 2 informal walk by famous person among ordinary people; **walker; walkie-talkie** portable radio receiver/transmitter; **walking** (*ns* **w.papers** *US* marching orders; **w.-stick** stick to support person walking; **walkway** passage for walking along.

Walkman [*TM*] personal stereo.

wall *n* 1 upright structure of brick, stone etc forming part of building or room, or as fence 2 *fig* barrier 3 *bio* outer surface of cell or organ; *idm* **go to the wall** fail; *idm* **go up the wall** *coll* be furious; *phr vs* **wall off** separate with wall; **wall up** enclose by walls; *ns* **wallbars** bars for exercising fixed to wall; **wallpaper** decorative paper for interior walls of house; *v* decorate with this; *as* **walled** having wall(s); **wall-to-wall** covering whole floor area.

wallflower *n* 1 perennial plant 2 *coll* girl who has no partners at dance.

wallaby *n* species of small kangaroo.

wallet *n* 1 flat leather case or pocket book 2 small bag or case for tools.

wall-eyed *a* having eye(s) with whitish iris; squinting.

Walloon *a, n* French-speaking Belgian.

wallop *v* beat severely; thrash; *n sl* beer; *n* **walloping** thrashing; beating; *a coll* large size.

wallow *v* roll about in water, mud etc; *fig* revel in.

Wall Street *n* 1 centre of American business world 2 *coll* the American money market.

wally *n* *Brit coll* foolish person.

walnut *n* 1 edible nut with crimpled surface 2 tree bearing this 3 decorative hardwood used in cabinet making.

walrus *n* large amphibious mammal.

waltz *n* dance in triple time, performed by couple; *v* dance waltz; whirl, twirl round; *phr v* **waltz off with** *coll* run away with.

wan *a* pale; sickly; livid.

wand *n* long, slender rod.

wander *v* 1 roam; ramble; stray 2 be delirious; be absent-minded; *ns* **wanderer; wanderlust** urge to travel.

wane *v* diminish in amount, intensity, power.

wangle *v* *coll* use irregular means to obtain something; *n coll* something obtained by guile or dishonesty.

wank *n* lazy, ineffectual person.

want *v* lack; desire; *n* deficiency; need.

wanton *a* capricious; unchecked; purposeless; loose, dissolute; *v* frolic without restraint.

wapiti *n* N American elk.

war *n* armed conflict between nations; hostility; *v* contend, fight; *idm* **in the wars** *coll* (showing signs of) having been injured; *ns* **w.clouds** signs that war is imminent; **w.cry 1** *sth* shouted in battle **2** *coll* slogan, *esp* political; **w.-game 1** tactical game with models of troops, weapons etc **2** military training exercise; **w.horse 1** (formerly) horse used in battle **2** *fig* seasoned campaigner in war, politics etc; **w.-paint 1** body make-up used by N American Indian warriors **2** *coll* cosmetics; *a* **warlike** martial; bellicose.

warble *v* sing with trills, as bird; *n* **warbler** genus of small wild singing birds.

ward *n* **1** action of watching or guarding **2** minor under care of guardian **3** division of city **4** section of hospital, prison etc; *pl* ridges, notches in key or lock; *v* guard; *phr v* **ward off** defend oneself against; *ns* **warder** *fem* **wardress** prison officer; **warden** governor; person having authority; **wardrobe** cupboard in which clothes are kept; stock of clothes; **wardroom** naval officers' messroom.

ware¹ *n* articles for sale collectively; manufactured articles, *esp* pottery; *pl* -**s** goods; merchandise; *n* **w.-house** storehouse for goods; *v* store; place in warehouse.

ware² *v coll* guard against; avoid.

warfare *n* (fighting in) war.

warlock *n* wizard; sorcerer.

warm *a* **1** moderately hot **2** affectionate; ardent **3** (of colour) suggesting warmth; *v* make, become warm; *idm* **keep sb's seat warm** reserve seat for sb (by occupying it); *idm* **make things warm/hot for** punish or reprimand severely; *phr vs* **warm to** begin to like; **warm up 1** make or become warmer **2** prepare for more energetic activity; *as* **w.-blooded 1** having constantly warm body temperature **2** *fig* passionate; **w.-hearted** kind (*n* -**ness**); *n* **warming** (**w.pan** pan formerly filled with hot coals for warming a bed); *n* **warmth 1** mild heat **2** *fig* cordiality **3** anger.

warmonger *n* person that likes to provoke war.

warn *v* caution; admonish; be a signal to; *n* -**ing** notice, hint of possible danger, consequences etc; premonition; notice to terminate employment.

warp *v* twist distort; become twisted; *n* threads running lengthwise in fabric; rope; distortion in timber caused by contraction.

warpath *idm* **on the warpath** in fighting mood.

warrant *n* authority; document that authorizes; *v* justify; guarantee; *n* **w. officer** *Brit* *mil* highest rank of non-commissioned officer; *n* **warranty** justification; guarantee.

warren *n* ground honeycombed by rabbit-burrows.

warrior *n lit* fighter.

warship *n* naval vessel used in war.

wart *n* small hard growth on surface of skin; *n* **w.-hog** large wild African pig with tusks.

wary *a* cautious; prudent; vigilant.

was *1st, 3rd* person *sing pt of* be.

wash *v* **1** clean with water or other liquid **2** wash oneself **3** (of sea, river etc) flow over, across, past, against or cause to move in specified direction; *idm* (**not**) **wash with sb** *coll* (not) be accepted as an excuse by sb; *idm* **wash one's dirty linen (in public)** discuss unpleasant personal affairs publicly; *idm* **wash one's hands of** refuse to have further interest in or responsibility for; *phr vs* **wash away** (of water) carry elsewhere; **wash down 1** clean (dirty surface) with water **2** facilitate swallowing of (food, medicine) by drinking; **wash out 1** (of dirt) be removed by washing **2** clean inside of **3** (of rain) cause to be cancelled (*n* **w.-out** *coll* failure); **wash over sb** *coll* fail to stir sb emotionally; **wash up 1** *Brit* wash oneself 2 *US* wash face and hands 3 (of sea) bring to shore; *n* 1 act of washing 2 load of clothes etc (to be) washed 3 waves made by passing boat etc 4 painting, thin brushing on of very diluted colour; *ns* w.-basin bowl for washing hands etc (*also* w.-hand basin; *US* w.-bowl); w. leather (piece of) chamois leather for cleaning windows etc; washroom *US coll* lavatory; w.-stand (formerly) bedroom table with jug and basin for washing; w.-tub wooden tub for washing clothes etc; *as* washed-out 1 faded 2 exhausted; washed-up *coll* defeated by failure; *ns* washing 1 act of washing clothes etc (to be) washed (*ns* w.-line line for drying washed clothes; w.-machine/-powder machine/powder for washing clothes; w.-up *Brit* (act of washing) dishes, cutlery etc left dirty after meal; washerwoman (formerly) woman who washes clothes etc; *a* washy 1 pale 2 watery 3 insipid.

wasn't *contracted form of* was not.

wasp *a* waspish (*n* -ness).

wasp *n* stinging insect; *as* -ish spiteful; biting; w.-waisted having very slender waist.

waste *v* 1 use extravagantly or uselessly 2 devastate 3 cause to shrink 4 lose strength; become emaciated; *a*

desolate; useless; *n* 1 desert 2 extravagant, unnecessary expenditure 3 refuse; *phr v* waste away become weak and thin; *ns* w. disposal unit sink attachment for shredding and washing away waste vegetable matter; w.-paper used paper (w.-(paper) basket receptacle for waste paper; w.-pipe pipe carrying used water to drain; *n* wastage amount lost by waste; loss; *a* wasteful extravagant; *ns* wasteland 1 barren or desolate area 2 *fig* unproductive situation in life.

watch *v* 1 remain awake and alert 2 observe; *idm* watch it/watch one's step be careful; *phr vs* watch (out) for look out for; watch out (for) beware; watch over guard and protect; *n* 1 small, portable clock, *usu* worn on wrist (*ns* watchmaker; watchmender) 2 act of watching 3 person, group of people employed to watch or protect sth (*ns* w.-dog 1 dog that guards sth 2 *fig* person or group acting to protect people's rights; watchman person employed to protect property at night); *a* watchful vigilant; observant; *ns* watcher observer; watching brief brief of lawyer to advise client not directly involved in case; watchword slogan expressing one's principles and beliefs.

water *n* 1 transparent, tasteless liquid for drinking (oxide of hydrogen) 2 body of water (sea, river, lake etc) 3 liquid secretion of animal body, *eg* urine 4 quality (of diamond, sapphire etc); *pl* -s 1 sea, river, lake (coastal/inland w.) 2 fluid surrounding foetus in womb; *idm* (not) hold water (not) be credible or logical; *idm* make/pass water urinate; *idm* take the waters have medicinal water at spa; *v* 1 pour water on (plants, land) 2 supply with drinking water 3 produce tears or saliva; *phr v* water down 1 dilute 2 reduce strength of; *ns* w. bed bed with water-filled mattress; w. biscuit plain hard unsweetened biscuit; w. butt barrel for collecting rainwater; w. cannon apparatus used in riot control; w. closet lavatory (*abbr* WC); w. ice sorbet; w. lily floating pond plant with large round leaves; w. meadow meadow near river liable to become flooded; w. pistol toy gun that shoots water; w. polo ball game with goalposts for two competing teams of swimmers; w. softener device or chemical for softening hard water; w. table underground water level; w. wings pair of floats to help people learning to swim; *a* watery.

watercolour *n* (picture painted

with) paint made to be mixed with water.

watercourse n (channel of) stream, river etc.

watercress n strong-flavoured cress grown in water.

watered silk n glossy silk fabric with wavy markings.

waterfall n cascade of water.

waterfront n quayside.

waterhole n pool at which animals drink.

watering n act of pouring on or supplying water; a exuding tears, saliva; ns **w. can** vessel for sprinkling water on plants; **w. hole** 1 waterhole 2 pub or bar; **w. place** 1 spa 2 waterhole.

waterlogged a saturated, soaked with water.

Waterloo idm **meet one's Waterloo** be finally defeated.

watermark n faint design in paper.

waterproof a, n (garment) proof against water.

watershed n 1 geog ridge of high land on either side of which streams and rivers flow in opposite directions 2 fig moment of important change in life or career.

waterspout n column of water drawn up from the sea by strong cyclone.

watertight a tightly fitting to ensure exclusion of water; fig flawless, unassailable.

waterworks n pl 1 place from where public water supply is controlled 2 coll person's urinary system; idm **turn on the waterworks** coll weeps.

watt n unit of electrical power.

wattle n 1 fencing of plaited twigs and wicker 2 fleshy lobe on neck of turkey 3 Australian acacia.

wave v 1 move to and fro in air; undulate 2 greet by raising and moving hand 3 (of hair) arrange in undulations; phr v **wave aside** reject without consideration; n 1 act of, gesture of waving 2 swelling ridge on surface of water 3 (of specified activity) sudden, temporary increase 4 form of each vibration of light, sound etc 5 curve of line of hair; ns **waveband** rad specified range of wavelengths; **wavelength** rad 1 distance between two waves 2 signal using particular frequency (idm **on the same wavelength** having a mutual understanding); **wavelet** ripple; a **wavy**.

waver v fluctuate; hesitate; yield, give way.

wax[1] v increase in size, (chiefly of moon).

wax[2] n solid insoluble substance, non-greasy and melting at low temperature, used for candles, models, sealing etc.; secretion of ear, bees; a **waxy**; n **waxwork** wax model of person (pl exhibition of wax models of famous people); **waxbill**, **waxwing** kinds of small birds.

way n 1 road; path; track 2 direction 3 distance 4 manner 5 means; method 6 point of view; respect; pl **-s** habits; customs; idm **by the way** incidentally; idm **by way of** 1 going past, through 2 as a form of; idm **get in the way (of)** impede; idm **get into the way of** acquire habit of; idm **get/have one's own way** do or get what one wants irrespective of other considerations; idm **give way** collapse; idm **give way (to)** 1 yield (to) 2 wait for (other traffic to go first) 3 be superseded (by); idm **go out of one's way** make a special effort; idm **have a way with** one have pleasant, persuasive personality; idm **make one's way** progress; idm **make way (for)** 1 allow to pass 2 give scope to; idm **no way** coll interj expressing strong denial or refusal; idm **out of the way** conveniently absent (a **out-of-the-way** unusual) idm **under way** 1 moving 2 happening; a **w.-out** coll bizarre; unorthodox; n **wayside** side of road or path; n **wayfarer** traveller; v **wayward** perverse, wilful; n **way-bill** list of passengers and goods.

WC n lavatory.

we pron 1st pers pl nom of I.

weak a lacking strength; frail; irresolute; insipid; faint; a **w.-kneed** feeble; cowardly; a **weakly** not robust; v

weaken make, become weaker; *ns* **weakling** person or animal lacking strength; **weakness**.

weal[1] *n* mark left on flesh by blow from lash etc.

weal[2] *n* well-being; welfare.

weald *n* open country once wooded.

wealth *n* abundance; profusion; riches; *a* **wealthy** rich; *n* **wealthiness**.

wean *v* accustom to food other than mother's milk; *phr v* **wean sb (away) from** help sb by gradual process to give up.

weapon *n* any object used for attack or defence.

wear *v* **wearing, wore, worn.** 1 to be clothed in; bear 2 diminish 3 be reduced by use 4 withstand usage 5 *coll* tolerate; *phr vs* **wear down** weaken; **wear off** become less intense, less effective; **wear on** (of time) pass slowly, tediously; **wear out** 1 exhaust 2 make or become unserviceable; *n* 1 act of wearing 2 clothes 3 damage from usage 4 lasting quality.

weary *a* 1 tired 2 bored by; tedious; *v* 1 tire 2 become bored by; *a* **-ily** *n* **-iness**; *a* **wearisome** tiresome; tedious.

weasel *n* carnivorous animal resembling ferret; *phr v* **weasel out (of)** *coll esp US* avoid fulfilling duty or promise; *in* **w. word** evasive form of expression.

weather *n* general atmospheric

conditions; *v* 1 expose to action of weather, season 2 show effect of such exposure 3 come safely through; *idm* **keep a weather eye open** be watchful; *idm* **under the weather** slightly ill or depressed; *ns* **w.-board(ing)** board(s) on outside wall or door to protect house from wind and rain; **weathercock** weathervane shaped like cockerel; **w. forecast** description of expected weather; **weatherman** *coll* weather forecaster; meteorologist; **w.-ship/-station** ship/station for monitoring weather; **w.-vane** device on top of building pointing to where wind is coming from; *as* **w.-beaten** having rough, sunburnt skin; showing effects of exposure; *a* **weatherproof** able to keep out wind and rain (*n* **-ing** material that serves this purpose).

weave *v* **weaving, wove** or **weaved, woven** or **weaved.** form (threads) into web or fabric by intertwining; plait; wind in and out; *ns* **weaver**; **weaving** act of doing this; fabric so made.

web *n* 1 something woven; net; cobweb spun by spider 2 membrane between digits of aquatic bird, frog etc; *as* **webbed** having skin between toes to assist swimming; **w.-footed** with webbed feet; *n* **webbing**

strong woven fabric used to make straps etc.

wed *v* **wedding, wedded.** 1 marry 2 *fig* unite.

we'd *contracted form of* 1 we had 2 we would.

wedding *ns* **w. breakfast** meal to celebrate wedding; **w. ring** ring worn as sign of being married.

wedge *n* V-shaped piece of wood, metal etc; *v* make, become firm with wedge; split with wedge; fix immovably; *idm* **thin end of the wedge** slight, unimportant action having considerable results.

Wedgwood *n* [P] fine earthenware; **W. blue** soft powdery blue.

wedlock *n* *fml* state of being married; *idm* **born out of wedlock** born to unmarried parents.

Wednesday *n* fourth day of week.

wee *a* very small; tiny; *n, v sl* urine, urinate.

weed *n* wild plant, *esp* one which tends to choke cultivated ones; *v* free (ground) from weeds; *phr v* **weed out** select for rejection; *n* **w.-killer** chemical for killing weeds; *a* **weedy** 1 full of weeds 2 lanky.

week *n* period of seven days, *esp* from Sunday to Saturday; *ns* **weekday** any day except Sunday; **week-end** from Friday or Saturday until Monday; *a, adv* **weekly**

once a week.

ween v ar suppose.

weeny a coll very tiny.

weep v shed tears; (of trees etc) droop gracefully; pt, pp wept.

weevil n small beetle harmful to corn etc.

weigh v bear down vs **weigh down** burden; **weigh in** 1 be weighed before contest or race 2 coll join in (discussion, argument, fight); **weigh up** consider (by balancing facts, arguments); n **weighbridge** machine for weighing loaded vehicles.

weight n 1 heaviness of sth 2 sth heavy 3 piece of metal used as standard for weighing other things 4 importance; idm **a weight off one's mind** a cause of anxiety removed; ns **w.-lifting** contest in lifting heavy weights (**w.-lifter** person doing this); **w.-watcher** person trying to lose weight by dieting etc; as **weightless** (n -ness); **weighty** 1 heavy 2 serious.

weir n river-dam.

weird a eerie; uncanny; adv -ly; n -ness; n **weirdo** coll eccentric person.

welcome a causing gladness; free to use or enjoy; n cordial greeting on arrival; v greet.

weld v 1 unite (hot metal) by fusion or pressure 2 fig unite; n **welder**.

welfare n 1 well-being;

comfort, health and happiness 2 social care for well-being of individuals, families etc (ns **w. work**; **w. worker**); 3 US money paid by State to those in need (Brit **social security**); n **w. state** (country with) system of social, medical, financial etc help for those in need.

well[1] a 1 in good health 2 favourable 3 satisfactory; comp **better**, sup **best**; adv 1 in a good way 2 skilfully 3 thoroughly 4 easily; idm **as well** 1 also 2 equally well (prep **as well as** in addition to); idm **well out of** coll lucky not to be involved in; idm **well up in** well informed about; as **well-adjusted** at ease in society; **w.-advised** sensible; **w.-appointed** well equipped; **w.-connected** related to or friendly with influential people; **w.-done** thoroughly cooked; **w.-heeled** rich; **w.-lined** coll full of money or food; **w.-mannered** polite; **w.-off** 1 rich 2 fortunate; **w.-oiled** coll drunk; **w.-rounded** 1 pleasantly plump 2 mature and pleasant 3 (of education) wide-ranging; **w.-to-do** rich; **w.-tried** known from experience to be reliable.

well[2] n 1 shaft sunk to obtain water or oil 2 natural spring 3 liftshaft; deep enclosed space in building; n **w.-spring** (constant) source; v spring; gush.

wellingtons n pl waterproof boots up to knee.

Welsh a of Wales, its people or language; n **W. rabbit** (**rarebit**) toasted cheese.

welsh, welch v sl (of bookmaker) fail to pay a gambling debt or fulfil an obligation; n **welsher, welcher**.

welt n 1 strip fixed to shoe to strengthen join between sole and upper 2 ribbed edging to top of sock etc 3 weal; v 1 provide with welt 2 coll thrash.

welter v wallow; tumble; n tumult; disorder.

welter-weight n 1 boxer weighing between 135 and 147 lbs (65.3–66.5kg) 2 extra weight carried by racehorse.

wen n sebaceous cyst on skin.

wench n young woman.

wend v **w. one's way** proceed slowly on journey.

Wendy house n Brit model house in which children can play.

went pt of go.

wept pt, pp of weep.

were pt of be.

we're contracted form of we are.

werewolf n myth person changed into wolf.

west n 1 direction of setting sun 2 one of four points of compass 3 usu cap capitalist as opposed to Communist countries; America and Europe as opposed to Asia; a pertaining to the west; situated in or facing west;

idm **go west** *dated coll* be ruined; lost; *as* **westerly**; **western** (n film of cowboy life in US; *v* **-ize** adapt to lifestyle of US and Europe; *n* **-ization**) **westward** towards the west (*adv* **-s**); *n*, *a* **W Indian** of W Indies.

wet *a* **wetter, wettest. 1** covered, saturated, moistened with liquid **2** rainy; *v* **wetting, wetted.** make wet; *n* moisture; rain; *ns* **w. blanket** *coll* spoilsport; *ns* **w. dream** erotic dream resulting in emission of semen; **w. nurse** woman employed to feed another's baby (*v* **cosset**); **w. suit** rubberised body garment to keep swimmer warm.

we've *contracted form of* **we have.**

whack *v* hit, slap sharply, noisily, *esp* with stick; *n* such blow; *coll* due share; *a* **-ing** *coll* huge (in beating).

whale *n* huge aquatic mammal; *idm* **have a whale of a time** *coll* enjoy oneself a lot; *ns* **whalebone** thin, horny substance growing in upper jaw of some whales; **whaler** man, ship engaged in hunting whales; *v* **whale** hunt whales; *n* **whaling.**

wham *n coll* (sound of) heavy blow; *v* **whammed, whamming.** hit violently.

wharf *n* berth where ships tie up, load and unload; *ns* **-age** dues for use of wharf; **-inger** wharf owner or manager.

what *pron* that, those which; which thing? how much? *a* which? of which kind? how much, how great; *idm* **what with** because of.

what(so)ever *pron*, *a* anything at all; no matter which; emphatic form of **what.**

whatnot *n* shelved display-case for ornaments etc.

wheat *n* cereal plant; edible grain, ground into flour; *ns* **wheatgerm** part of wheat kernel rich in vitamins; **wheatmeal** brown flour from wheat; *a* **wheaten** made from wheat.

wheedle *v* coax; cajole.

wheel *n* circular frame with spokes or solid disc, revolving round axle; *v* **1** move on wheels **2** cause (line of men) to turn as on pivot; *idm* **wheels within wheels** secret network of influences; *idm* **wheel and deal** *coll esp* US negotiate in cunning, unscrupulous way (*n* **wheeler-dealer**); *ns* **wheelbarrow** small one-wheeled cart; **wheelbase** distance between front and rear wheels; **wheelchair** mobile chair for invalids; **w. clamp** device for immobilizing illegally parked car; **wheelhouse** enclosed space on deck for housing helmsman, wheel, compass etc; **wheelwright** one who makes and repairs wheels and wheeled vehicles.

wheelie *n coll* trick of riding bike, motorbike with front wheel raised.

wheeze *v* breathe with audible friction; *v* **1** noisy breathing **2** *coll* trick, joke; *a* **wheezy.**

whelk *n* edible marine mollusc.

whelp *n* puppy; cub of lion, tiger etc; ill-bred youth; *v* bring forth young.

when *adv* at what time? how soon? *conj* on the occasion that; at the time that; *adv*, *conj* **whenever** as soon as; as often as.

whence *adv*, *conj* from where.

where *adv*, *conj* to, at, or in which place or part? *adv* **whereabouts** in what place? *n* locality; situation; *conj* **whereas** in view of the fact that; but on the contrary; while; *advs* **wherever 1** in, to, at, any place **2** no matter where **wherefore** why? for which reason.

wherry *n* light row-boat; broad heavy barge.

whereby *a fml* by means of which.

whereupon *conj* (immediately) after which.

wherewithal *n* resources; money needed.

whet *v* **whetting, whetted.** sharpen; stimulate, excite (appetite, curiosity); *n* **whetstone** stone for sharpening knives etc.

whether *pron ar* which of two; *conj* expressing doubt, alternative possibility.

whey *n* watery part of milk separated from curd.

which *a* what person or thing?

pron the thing(s) that; what person, thing?

whichever *det, pron* 1 the one which 2 no matter which.

whiff *v* puff; emit slight unpleasant smell; *n* 1 puff; breath; slight gust 2 small cigar.

while *n* space of time; period; *conj* as long as; during; *phr v* **while away** pass (time) idly; *conj* **whilst** while.

whim(sy) *n* passing fancy; caprice; *a* **whimsical** capricious; quaint; *n* **whimsicality**.

whimper *n* feeble, fretful cry; *v* cry thus.

whine *n* high-pitched noise (in motors) or long-drawn thin wail; *v* cry or emit this.

whinge *v* *coll* complain in a whining manner.

whinny *v* (of horse) neigh gently; *n* such sound.

whip *v* whipping, whipped. 1 strike with lash 2 whisk (eggs, cream) 3 *coll* defeat, overcome 4 move fast and suddenly; *n* 1 lash attached to handle 2 MP who ensures presence of his party members at voting time 3 hunt servant in charge of hounds; *phr v* **whip up** 1 stir up (feelings) 2 quickly enlist (support); *ns* **whipcord** 1 thin strong cord 2 ribbed cloth; **w.hand** firm control; **whiplash** 1 blow from whip 2 sudden violent jerk to head and neck as in *eg* road accident; **w.-round** *Brit* improvised collection of

money by group; **whipper-snapper** impudent person; small boy; **whipping boy** scapegoat.

whippet *n* small, cross-bred dog like greyhound.

whir(r) *v* whirring, whirred. revolve, move with rapid buzzing sound; *n* this sound.

whirl *v* rotate; spin rapidly on axis; *n* 1 rapid rotation 2 bewilderment; *idm* **give sth a whirl** *coll* try sth; *idm* **in a whirl** bewildered; *ns* **whirligig** spinning toy; merry-go-round; **-pool** rapid circular eddy; **-wind** column of rapidly rotating air.

whisk *v* 1 sweep lightly, briskly 2 twitch; beat lightly; *phr v* **whisk off** carry away suddenly; *n* 1 light, stiff brush 2 instrument for beating eggs etc.

whisker *n* one of long bristles growing from side of animal's mouth; *pl* **-s** hair growing on man's face; *idm* **within a whisker (of)** *coll* very near (to).

whisky *n* alcoholic liquor distilled from malted grain, *esp* barley; **whiskey** Irish whisky.

whisper *v* speak in low voice; *fig* tell as secret; *n* such speech.

whist *n* card game for two pairs of players.

whistle *v* 1 produce shrill piping sound from wind instrument or through pursed-up lips 2 (of *bird, missile etc*) make shrill sound

3 summon by whistle; *n* 1 shrill, piercing sound 2 device, instrument producing such sound; *n* **w.-stop** brief visit by politician in election campaign (**w.-stop tour**); *n* **whistler**.

Whit *n* Whitsun.

white *a* 1 colourless 2 of colour of unstained snow 3 of fair complexion; of Caucasian race 4 *fig* honourable, sincere; *n* 1 white pigment 2 white of egg 3 white man; *pl* **-s** white sports clothes; *ns* **w. ant** termite; **w. corpuscle** blood cell that resists infection; **w. dwarf** hot, dense star; **w. elephant** sth useless; **w. flag** sign of surrender; **w. heat** temperature at and above which metal glows white (*a* **w.-hot**); **w. hope** *coll* person expected to be sure of success; **W. House** official home in Washington DC of US President; **w. knight** person, organization that saves business company from takeover by investing money in it; **w. lie** trivial lie, *esp* one that avoids hurt to sb; **w. noise** jumbled noise made up of many frequencies; **w. paper** Government paper on policy; **w. slave** woman forced to become prostitute, *usu* abroad; **w. spirit** form of petroleum used as paint solvent or cleaner; *as* **w.-collar** of office work; working in an office; **w.-tie**

(of social occasion) when men wear tails and white bow ties; v **whiten** make, become white; n **-ness**; a **whitish**.

whitebait n type of small fish.

Whitehall n (London street containing many offices of) British Government and Civil Service.

whitewash n 1 white liquid for wall decor 2 fig attempt to conceal fault or error; v 1 cover with whitewash 2 try to make (sth bad) seem good.

whiting n edible sea fish.

whither adv 1 to what place or purpose? 2 to whatever place, or purpose.

Whitsun(tide) n weekend that includes Whit Sunday (seventh after Easter).

whittle v 1 shape, pare (wood) with knife 2 fig reduce gradually.

whiz(z) n buzzing sound; v **whizzing, whizzed.** move very quickly; make buzzing sound; n **w.kid** person who very quickly becomes successful.

who pron (obj **whom** poss **whose**) which or what person? that person who; pron **who(so)ever** anyone (at all) who.

WHO abbr World Health Organization.

whoa interj used to stop horse moving.

whodunit a coll detective story.

whoever pron 1 no matter who 2 anyone at all.

whole a 1 intact 2 entire; complete; n complete sum, amount; entirety; adv **wholly** idm **on the whole** mostly; generally; idm **go the whole hog** do sth to the limit, esp for pleasure; as **w.-hearted** without doubt or restraint; unqualified (adv **-ly**; n **-ness**); ns **w.food** unrefined food free from additives (a **w.-food**); **w.note** mus semi-breve; **w.number** math number without fraction; integer; n, a **wholemeal** (of) flour made from whole unrefined grain of wheat etc; as **wholesale** 1 of selling goods in bulk to retailers (also adv; n **wholesaler**) 2 fig complete; **wholesome** 1 (of food) good for health 2 (of people) looking healthy and morally sound.

whom pron fml object form of who.

whoop n loud cry or yell; noise peculiar to whooping-cough; v utter such sound; idm **whoop it up** coll have a good time; ns **whooping-cough** infectious respiratory disease; **whoopee** coll exclamation of joy.

whoops interj used after mistake or clumsy action.

whoosh n noise of rushing wind etc.

whop v **whopping, whopped.** beat severely; **whopper** n coll 1 big thing 2 big lie; a **whopping** coll big.

whore n prostitute.

whorl n circular group of petals, leaves etc; single coil of spiral.

whose det, pron of who; of which.

whosoever = whoever.

why adv for what reason? because of which; interj expressing surprise; n cause of reason for something; idm **whys and wherefores** explanations.

WI abbr 1 Women's Institute 2 West Indies.

wick n length of thread in candle or oil lamp, which burns until wax or oil is consumed; idm **get on sb's wick** Brit coll irritate sb.

wicked a 1 evil; vicious; depraved 2 coll mischievous; n **wickedness**.

wicker n, a (fabric) made of interwoven osiers etc; a, n **wickerwork** (made of) plaited wickers.

wicket n 1 small gate or door in larger one 2 set of three cricket stumps and bails 3 cricket pitch.

wide a broad; far-reaching; spacious; vast; of extensive scope, range; n ball bowled past wicket out of reach of batsman; idm **wide of the mark** badly mistaken; as **w.-eyed** 1 with eyes wide open 2 gullible; **w.-ranging** extending in many directions; **widespread** extended over a large area; n **w.boy** dated Brit coll shrewd, unscrupulous person in business; adv **-ly**; v **widen** (n

-ing).

widow n woman whose husband has died; masc **-er**; v make widow of.

width n distance from side to side.

wield v handle; make use of (implement, weapon etc) control.

wife n married woman; pl **wives**; a **wifely**.

wig n artificial hair for head; a **wigged**.

wigging n sl severe scolding.

wiggle v move quickly from side to side; wriggle.

wigwam n N American Indian's conical tent.

wild a 1 w. animal not domesticated 2 w. plant uncultivated 3 uncivilized (w. tribe) 4 uncontrolled (w. behaviour) 5 stormy (w. night) 6 irrational (w. guess); idm be/go wild (at) coll be/become angry (with); idm beyond one's wildest dreams better than one could ever have hoped; idm run wild go out of control; ns the w. natural habitat (pl -s remote area); wild card 1 card usable as equal in value to others 2 fig secret advantage, eg in business; wildfowl game bird(s); w.-goose chase useless search; a wildcat reckless (w.scheme; w.strike unofficial strike); adv -ly; n -ness.

wildebeest n large African antelope (pl same or -s).

wilderness a desert; desolate expanse of land, water; idm

in(to) the wilderness out of active, esp political, life.

wildfire n phosphorescent light; idm like wildfire very rapidly.

wile n (usu pl) ruse, cunning stratagem; a wily crafty; artful.

wilful a stubborn; capricious; premeditated; n wilfulness.

will v aux forms moods and tenses expressing future, intention, resolve etc; pt **would**.

will n 1 faculty of deciding what one will do; volition 2 wish 3 document making disposition of property after death; idm at will at any time one wishes; idm with a will with enthusiasm; v 1 wish 2 leave as bequest; a **willing** ready, eager to help (adv -ly; n -ness).

willies n pl coll nervous feeling.

will-o'-the-wisp n 1 phosphorescent light over marshy ground 2 fig elusive person or thing.

willow n 1 genus of trees, yielding osiers; this wood 2 coll cricket bat; n w.pattern traditional blue and white oriental design, esp for china (also a); a willowy slender; graceful.

willy-nilly adv whether one will or not; inevitably.

wilt v (of plants) fade; droop; wither.

wily a full of wiles; cunning (n -iness).

wimp n coll weak, ineffectual person; a -ish (n -ness).

win v winning, won. 1 gain, achieve by effort 2 obtain as prize 3 prevail; phr v win over/round gain favour of by persuasion; win through success with difficulty; n victory, success, esp in contest.

wince v shrink away; flinch; n involuntary recoil.

winceyette n soft warm fabric used to make nightwear.

winch n machine for hoisting, windlass; crank used as handle.

wind[1] n 1 air in rapid motion 2 breath 3 flatulence; idm break wind expel air from bowels; idm get wind of hear about by chance; idm get/have the wind up coll become/be scared; idm in the wind likely to happen soon; idm put the wind up coll scare; idm take the wind out of sb's sails coll disconcert, destroy sb's advantage; ns w.-break line of trees etc giving shelter from the wind; w.-cheater anorak; windfall 1 fruit blown off tree 2 fig piece of unexpected good fortune; w.-instrument mus instrument played by blowing (brass, woodwind); wind-jammer large sailing vessel; wind-mill mill, water-pump driven by force of wind; windscreen front window of vehicle (w. wiper rotating arm with rubber blade that keeps windscreen clear of rain etc); w.-sock canvas tube flown from mast to show wind direction; **windsurfer 1** flat board with keel and sail **2** person using this (*v* **windsurf**; *n* **windsurfing**); **w.tunnel** tunnel along which air is forced at speed to test aircraft; *a* **w.-swept 1** exposed to strong wind **2** (*of* hair) untidy; *n, a, adv* **windward** (of, on, to) the side from which the wind blows; *a* **windy 1** bringing much wind **2** exposed to wind **3** *Brit coll* nervous; scared (*adv* **-ily** *n* **-iness**).

wind² *v* **winding, wound. 1** turn, meander **2** tighten (watch spring) by turning **3** make into ball **4** twine; *phr vs* **wind down 1** lower by winding **2** (*of machinery*) go slow and **3** *coll* relax after stress etc; **wind up 1** finished **2** *coll* arrive finally **3** *coll* tease or provoke *n* **windlass** apparatus for hoisting or hauling.

window *n* opening in wall, roof, vehicle etc to admit light, air etc *usu* filled by glass panes; *ns* **w.-dressing** art of arranging goods in shop window; *fig* attractive presentation; **w.-sill** ledge under window.

Windows [TM] *n* computer operating system which several programs can be run simultaneously using different parts of the screen.

wine *n* fermented grape juice; *v* entertain (person) to wine;

drink wine.

wing *n* **1** limb by which bird, insect etc flies **2** projecting part of aircraft's structure by which it is supported in air **3** side, flank **4** side projection from building etc **5** group of three RAF squadrons; *v* **1** fly (over or through) **2** wound in wing **3** *fig* disable *idm* **take wing 1** fly away **2** become active; *idm* **under the wing of** protected, helped; *pl* **-s** theatre hidden area at sides of stage (*idm* **in the wings 1** waiting to come on stage **2** *fig* ready to become involved); *ns* **w.-chair** high-backed chair with projecting arms; **w.-commander** RAF officer next in rank below squadron leader; **w.-nut** nut with flanges for easier turning with finger and thumb; **w.-span** distance between tips of wings; *as* **-ed; -less**; *n* **winger** person playing on left or right wing.

wink *v* open and close eye rapidly; blink; *phr v* **wink at** *coll* connive at; *n* act of winking.

winkle *n* edible shellfish, periwinkle; *phr v* **winkle out** *coll* obtain with difficulty, *esp* information.

winner *n* **1** person who wins **2** winning stroke or move, **winning** *a* **1** bringing victory **2** pleasantly persuasive; *adv* **-ly**; *n pl* **-s** money won.

winnow *v* separate grain from husks by fanning; *fig* sort out

good from bad.

wino *n* **-os.** *coll* alcoholic, *esp* wine drinker.

winter *n* coldest season of year; *v* spend winter in; tend animals, plants during winter. *a* **wintry 1** of, like winter; cold; snowy **2** *fig* frigid.

wipe *v* **1** clean, dry by rubbing with cloth etc **2** check validity of (credit card) by passing through machine; *idm* **wipe the floor with** *coll* defeat utterly; humiliate; *idm* **wipe the slate (clean)** *coll* forget all past debts or offences; *phr vs* **wipe off 1** clean by wiping **2** *coll* fig remove; **wipe out** eliminate; *n* **wiper**.

wire *n* **1** fine-drawn slender flexible thread of metal **2** *coll* telegram; *idm* **get one's wires crossed** *coll* have misunderstanding with sb; *v* **1** fasten with wire **2** equip or connect with electric wiring **3** telegraph; *a* **w.-haired** having short stiff hair; *ns* **w.-tapping** using secret connection to overhear sb's telephone conversations; **wiring** connection or system of wires; *a* **wiry** like wire; tough and flexible (*n* **-iness**).

wireless *n* transmission of sound by electro-magnetic waves; *coll* radio set; *a* pertaining to radio or broadcasting.

wise[1] *a* 1 prudent; sagacious 2 having knowledge, intelligence; *idm* **be/get wise to** *coll* be/become aware of (sth important); *phr v* **wise up** *US coll* (be) inform(ed); *n* **w. guy** *coll* person who gives impression of being very knowledgeable; *ns* **wisdom** sagacity, sound judgement; **w. tooth** one cut during adult years.

wise[2] *n* way; manner; fashion.

wisecrack *n coll* smart remark; witticism.

wish *v* have desire; long for; *n* desire; expression of desire, *esp* order, request; *phr v* **wish sb/sth on sb** *coll* pass sb/sth (unwanted) on to sb; *n* **w. fulfilment** *psyc* means of gratifying subconscious desire in fact or through fantasy; *a* **wishful** expressing desire or hope (**w. thinking** belief based on unrealistic desire); *n* **wishbone** forked breast bone of chicken, turkey etc, often split by pulling between two people, of whom recipient of larger piece may make a secret wish.

wishy-washy *a coll* weak; insipid (*n* **-iness**).

wisp *n* small bunch of straw etc; thin, straggly lock of hair.

wistaria, wisteria *n* climbing plant with blue flowers.

wistful *a* yearning; sadly pensive.

wit *n* 1 ability to express sth with clever, humorous words 2 person able to do this 3 *esp pl* mental capacity; quick understanding; *idm* **at one's wits end** too desperate and anxious to know what to do next; *idm* **have keep one's wits about one** be alert and ready to act; *idm* **to wit** leg, lit that is; *as* **witless** foolish; **witty** cleverly amusing; *n* **witticism** witty remark; *adv* **wittingly** knowingly; deliberately.

witch *n* sorceress; hag; crone; *ns* **witchcraft** magic; **w.-doctor** medicine man in primitive tribe; **witchery** fascination; **w.-hunt** 1 hunt to destroy witches 2 *fig* campaign to persecute those with unorthodox views on morality, politics etc.

witch-hazel, wych-hazel *n* N American shrub whose bark yields astringent medicinal substance.

with *prep* against; in company of; beside; possessed of; by means of; *adv* **withal** besides, moreover.

withdraw *v* **-drawing, -draw, -drawn.** 1 draw, take back 2 retire; not take part.

wither *v* fade; decay; grow feebler; *fig* snub; *a* **-ing** severe; contemptuous (**w. look;** *adv* **-ly**).

withhold *v* **-holding, -held.** keep back; refuse to bestow.

within *prep, adv* in, inside; *adv* **without** outside; *prep* lacking.

withstand *v* **-standing, -stood.** resist.

witless *a* foolish (*n* **-ness**).

witness *n* 1 testimony; corroboration; 2 one who gives evidence; person or thing furnishing proof; *v* see; attest; testify *n* **w. box** area in court where witness stands (*US* **w. stand**).

witter *v Brit coll* complain endlessly about trivial matters; *ns* **-er; -ing.**

witticism *n* witty remark.

wives *pl of* **wife.**

wizard *n* 1 sorcerer; magician 2 *fig* expert; ingenious person; *a sl* marvellous.

wizened *a* shrivelled; dried up.

WO *abbr* warrant officer.

wobble *v* move, sway unsteadily; *n* oscillation; unsteady movement.

woe *n* cause of sorrow; misfortune; *as* **woebegone** mournful; doleful; **woeful** sorrowful; pitiful (*adv* **-ly**).

wok *n* deep curved pan used in Chinese cookery.

woke *pt*, **woken** *pp of* **wake.**

wold *n* expanse of high open country.

wolf *n* 1 large wild carnivorous animal of dog family 2 man who pursues women mainly for sex; *pl* **wolves**; *idm* **wolf in sheep's clothing** person seemingly innocent but having secret evil intentions; *ns* **w. cub** 1 young wolf 2 junior boy scout; **wolfhound** large hunting dog; *n, v* **w. whistle** (give) loud whistle to seek attention of sexually attractive female.

wolverine n small carnivorous animal; its fur.

woman n adult human female; female sex; pl **women**; ns **-hood** condition of being a woman; **-kind** women in general; as **-ly** having good qualities of woman; **-ish** effeminate v **-ize** (of man) have affairs with many different women (ns **-izer**; **-izing**).

womb n female organ in which embryo develops.

wombat n small bear-like Australian wild animal.

won pt, pp of **win**.

wonder n 1 prodigy; marvel 2 emotion, feeling of awe, excited by marvellous object, person etc; v be amazed; be curious about; as **-ful** amazing; marvellous (adv **-ly**); **wondrous** inspiring wonder (adv **-ly**); n **wonderment** 1 astonishment 2 deep admiration.

wonky a sl wobbly; hesitant; not well.

wont a accustomed; n usual practice.

won't contracted form of will not.

woo v court, seek to win love of; n **-er** suitor.

wood n tract of tree-covered land; solid substance of trees; timber; idm **out of the wood(s)** coll Brit free from danger, problems; as **-ed** covered with trees; **wooden** 1 made of wood 2 fig stiff; inhibited (n **w. spoon** Brit

notional prize for coming last in competition); **woody** 1 wooded 2 like wood, a, n **woodland**.

woodcock n woodland game bird with long straight beak.

woodcut n engraving on wood block; print from this.

woodlouse n small insect (pl **woodlice**).

woodman n forester.

woodpecker n bird that pecks holes in trees.

woodwind n musical instruments usu made of wood and played by being blown.

woodwork n carpentry; wooden part of structure.

woodworm n 1 larva that eats wood 2 holes in wood made by this.

woof[1] n, interj, v coll (sound of dog's bark).

woof[2] n threads crossing warp in woven fabric.

wool n fleece, coat of sheep, angora goat, alpaca etc.; n, a **woollen** (cloth) made of wool; n, a **woolly** (garment, jersey) made of wool; (n **-iness**; **w.-headed** not thinking clearly); ns **w.-gathering** letting the mind wander instead of concentrating; **woolsack** 1 bale of wool 2 Lord Chancellor's seat in House of Lords.

woozy a coll 1 dizzy, eg from drinking alcohol 2 mentally confused (adv **-ily**; n **-iness**).

word n 1 simplest element of speech; unit of language

serving as name of object etc 2 brief speech; message; promise; v express in words; idm **have a word (in sb's ear)** coll speak privately (to sb); idm **have words (with)** quarrel (with); idm **(not) in so many words** (not) using exactly these words but implying them; idm **put words into sb's mouth** coll 1 tell sb what to say 2 claim falsely that sb said sth; idm **word for word** using exactly the same words; as **w.-blind** dyslexic (n **-ness**); **w.-perfect** recalling every word perfectly; n **w. processor** computerized keyboard with programs and VDU for editing text etc (also **PCW**); v **w.-process** edit in this way (n **-ing**); a **wordy** verbose (adv **-ily**; n **-iness**).

word-blind a unable to spell; dyslexic.

work n 1 bodily, intellectual labour 2 occupation 3 product of labour or artistic activity; pl **-s** 1 factory 2 mechanism 3 coll everything; idm **all in a day's work** nothing abnormal; easy to cope with; idm **have one's work cut out** find it difficult in the time available; idm **give sb the works** 1 give sb full treatment 2 tell sb everything 3 treat sb harshly; v 1 do one's job 2 do activity needing effort 3 (make) function 4 produce (effect) 5 manipulate 6 gradually move or turn to specified position or condition; *idm* **work to rule** (of industrial action) do only what is legally required (*n* **w.-to-rule**); *phr vs* **work off** reduce by working; **work out 1** calculate **2** develop **3** decide **4** *coll* do physical exercise (*n* **w.-out**); **work out at** (of calculation) prove to be; **work up 1** develop by stages **2** arouse **3** make nervous, excited; *a* **-able** able to be arranged, achieved, used; *n* **-er**.

workaday *a* ordinary; routine.

workaholic *n* person unhealthily obsessed with work.

workbench *n* table where mechanic, craftsman etc works.

workbook *n* supplementary book with practice exercises.

workforce *n* total number of workers.

workhorse *n* **1** useful machine **2** sb doing routine jobs.

workhouse *n* home for paupers.

working *n* functioning; way in which process works; worked area of mine *pl* **-s** way in which sth operates; *idm* **in (full) working order** functioning properly; *a* **1** of, at, for work **2** used at, spent in work; *ns* **w. capital** money used for running costs of business; **w. class** proletariat (*a* **w.-class**); **w. knowledge** sufficient practical knowledge to put to some

use; **w. party 1** group appointed to investigate and report on special area of concern **2** group of manual workers.

workload *n* amount of work expected from machine or employee in specified time.

workman *n* manual labourer; *a* **-like** of or like a good workman; *n* **-ship** (result of) skilful working.

workout *n* concentrated spell of physical exercise.

workshop *n* **1** room or building where goods are made or repaired **2** group meeting where members exchange ideas and develop skills, methods, projects etc.

work-shy *a* reluctant to work; avoiding work.

worktop *n* flat surface for preparing food etc (also **work-surface**).

world *n* **1** the universe **2** the earth **3** mankind **4** category of specified living creatures **5** sphere of human activity; *idm* **a world of difference** a great deal of difference; *idm* **be/mean the world to** *coll* be very precious to; *idm* **do the world of good** *coll* benefit greatly; *idm* **for all the world as if/like** *coll* just as if/like; *idm* **out of this world** *coll* wonderful; *idm* **worlds apart** *coll* totally different; *as* **w.-class** among the best in the world; **w.-famous** well-known everywhere; **w.-weary** tired of life; **w.-wide** found, happening in all parts

of the world (*also adv*); *ns* **w.-beater** sb/sth better than all others; **w.-power** powerful nation; **w. view 1** attitude to life **2** philosophy; **w. war** war involving many major countries; *a* **worldly 1** experienced in the ways of society **2** regarding human affairs as more important than religious life; materialistic (*n* **-iness**; **w.-wise** shrewd in handling of human affairs).

world-wide web *n* body of data stored in computers world-wide, accessible using the Internet.

worm *n* **1** long invertebrate; earthworm; grub; maggot **2** spiral thread of screw **3** *fig* weak, obsequious person; *v* wriggle, edge along slowly; *idm* **worm one's way into** gain (affection, trust) by flattery etc, *usu* in order to deceive; *phr v* **worm out** extract (secret information) by cunning questions; *n* **worm's-eye view** view from below, from inferior position; *a* **w. -eaten 1** full of worm holes **2** *fig* old.

wormwood *n* aromatic bitter herb; *fig* bitterness.

worn *pt, pp* of **wear**; *a* **1** much used **2** threadbare (**w.-out 1** exhausted **2** too worn to be usable any longer).

worrisome *a* **1** anxious **2** causing anxiety (*adv* **-ly**).

worry *v* **worrying, worried. 1** (cause to) be anxious **2** pester; harass **3** (*esp* of dog) seize and shake; n **1** anxiety **2** cause of this; as **worried** (adv **-ly**); **worrying** (adv **-ly**).

worse a comp of **bad**; v **worsen** make, grow worse; deteriorate.

worship v **worshipping**, **worshipped**; revere, adore as God; idolize; adore; a **-ful**; n **worshipper**.

worst a sup of **bad**.

worsted a, n (made of) woollen yarn.

wort n liquid from malt used in beer-making.

worth a having specified value; deserving of; n merit; material value; idm **for all one's worth** with maximum effort; idm **for what it's worth** although it's probably not of much value; idm **be worth it 1** be of use **2** be of the value claimed; idm **worth one's salt** competent; idm **worth (one's) while** profitable (for one); as **-less** (n **-ness**); **-while** sufficiently rewarding.

worthy a **1** virtuous **2** deserving; n eminent person (adv **-ily**; n **-iness**).

would pt of **will**; a **w.-be** aspiring (usu in vain).

wouldn't contracted form of would not.

wound[1] n cut, hole or tear in skin or tissue of body; v inflict such injury on; hurt (feelings of).

wound[2] pt, pp of **wind**; a **w.-up** intensely excited or anxious.

wove pt, **woven** pp of **weave**.

wow[1] interj expressing surprise; n coll great success; v US sl impress.

wow[2] n mus variation in pitch from irregularity in playing speed of tape or disc.

WPC abbr woman police constable.

wpm abbr words per minute.

wrangle v quarrel; dispute angrily; n noisy quarrel; n **wrangler** one who argues thus.

wrap v **wrapping**, **wrapped**. fold round; cover (person, thing) in (folding material or garment); phr v **wrap up 1** put on warm clothes **2** complete (task, agreement) **3** make obscure (by using difficult words) (idm **wrapped-up in** coll engrossed in); n garment covering woman's shoulders; idm **under wraps** coll being kept secret; ns **wrapper** protective outer covering (esp for goods on sale or sent by post); **wrapping** material, used to cover or wrap sth (**w. paper** paper for wrapping parcel or gift)

wrath n anger; a **-ful**; adv **-ly**; n **-ness**.

wreak v give vent to (anger etc); exact (vengeance).

wreath n circle of intertwined leaves or flowers; garland; wisp of smoke; v **wreathe** twist, wind into wreath; surround; wind round.

wreck n destruction, esp of ship by wind and waves; ship fast on rocks; ruin;

broken remains of structure; v cause wreck of; ns **-age; -er** one who engineers wreck.

wren n species of small songbird.

wrench n **1** violent twist **2** adjustable spanner to turn nuts **3** fig grief felt at separation; v twist; seize forcibly.

wrest v tear away, take by force.

wrestle v grapple with and try to throw opponent; fig strive with (difficulties etc); n **wrestler**.

wretch n miserable unfortunate person; a **-ed** miserable, unhappy; squalid (adv **-ly**; n **-ness**).

wriggle n squirming, twisting movement; v move thus.

wring v **wringing, wrung**. twist; squeeze out moisture; idm **wringing wet** very wet; n **-er** machine for wringing clothes.

wrinkle n **1** small crease, fold, esp of skin **2** coll useful hint; v make wrinkles in; pucker; a **-kly**.

wrist n joint between forearm and hand.

writ n leg document issued in sovereign's name giving instructions to do or refrain from doing, something; **Holy W.** the Bible; idm **writ large** lit on a larger scale.

write v **writing, wrote, written. 1** mark paper etc with symbols representing words or sounds **2** compose (letter for sending; work for publication etc) 3 complete (cheque) in words and figures with signature; *phr vs* **write down** record in writing; **write off** acknowledge as irretrievable or irreparable (*n* **w. -off**) 2 treat (debt) as no longer existing; **write off (for)** send written request (for); **write out** write in full; **write up** give full written account of (*n* **w. -up** report or review); *ns* **writer**; **writing** 1 act of writing (*a* of or for writing) 2 written symbols; handwriting 3 form of written expression (*pl* literary works).

writhe *v* twist, contort body about (in pain etc.); be distorted.

written *pp of* **write**.

wrong *a* 1 wicked 2 incorrect 3 mistaken in opinion etc 4 unsuitable; *idm* **go wrong** 1 miscalculate; make errors 2 stop functioning properly 3 become difficult, troublesome; *n* 1 that which is wrong 2 harmful act; *idm* **in the wrong** responsible for error; blameworthy; *v* do wrong to; *ns* **-doer; -doing;** *v* **w. -foot** *esp sport* put at disadvantage by change of tactics; *a* **wrongful** unjust or illegal (*adv* **-ly;** *n* **-ness**); **w.-headed** obstinately holding mistaken opinion; misguided (*adv* **-ly;** *n* **-ness**).

wrote *pt of* **write**.

wrought *a* worked; **w. iron** iron hammered, beaten into

shape.

wrung *pt, pp of* **wring**.

wry *a* 1 twisted 2 *fig* ironical; expressing distaste; (*adv* **-ly;** *n* **-ness**); *n* **wryneck** bird related to woodpecker; *a* **wry-necked** with deformed, twisted neck.

X *n math* unknown quantity; *fig* any person, anything unknown.

xen-, xeno- *prefix* relating to hospitality; external, foreign.

xenon *n* inert, heavy gas present in air.

xenophobia *n* irrational hate or fear of foreigners, strangers.

xer(o)- *prefix* dry; dryness.

Xerography *n* [TM] photo-copying process.

xerophilous *a* able to thrive in conditions of drought; *n* **xerophyte** drought-loving plant.

xerox [TM] **1** dry process for making multiple photocopies **2** photocopy thus made; *v* produce photocopy by this method; *n* **x. machine.**

Xmas *n coll* Christmas.

X-rated *a* (*of film, video*) classified as unsuitable for young people under 18 years of age; *n* **X-rating.**

X-ray *n* **1** *usu pl* electromagnetic short wave radiation capable of penetrating matter **2** photograph taken with this **3** medical examination by this method; *v* take such a photograph or examine by this method.

xyl(o)- *prefix* wood, pertaining to wood.

xylograph *n* wood-engraving; *n* **-grapher;** *a* **-graphic.**

xyloid *a* of, like wood.

xylophone *n* musical percussion instrument of graduated wooden bars, which vibrate when struck.

yacht n light sailing vessel used for racing or pleasure-cruising; n **-sman** owner or sailor of yacht.

yack, yak v sl talk noisily and continuously on trivial matters (also **yak**); n sl chat; ns **-ing; yackety-yack** sl incessant chatter (also **yakkety-yak**).

yak1 n long-haired ox of Central Asia.

yam n fleshy edible root of tropical climbing plant; sweet potato.

yammer v coll talk incessantly in complaining manner; n **-ing**.

yang n (in Chinese philosophy) active male principle.

yank v coll pull sharply, jerk; n sharp tug.

yankee n inhabitant of New England states; coll American.

yap n bark of small dog; v yapping, yapped. yelp, bark; coll chatter.

yard1 n unit of length, 36 ins; long spar supporting sail; n **yardstick** yard-measure; fig standard of comparison.

yard2 n 1 enclosed space, often paved, adjoining building 2 enclosure for some specific purpose.

yarn n continuous thread of twisted fibres (of wool, cotton etc); coll tale, chat; v tell a yarn; talk at length.

yarrow n white-flowered perennial herb.

yashmak n veil worn by Mohammedan women.

yawn v 1 open mouth widely and breathe in involuntarily 2 fig open wide; gape; n act of yawning, esp arising from boredom, sleepiness.

ye pron lit, ar pl of thou.

yea interj, n yes; affirmative statement.

year n period of time taken by earth to revolve once round sun; unit of time, 365 ¼ days; idm **put years on** coll make feel much older; idm **the year dot** Brit coll a very long time ago; n **y.-book** book of information revised each year; a **y.-long** lasting all year; n **yearling** animal one year old; a **yearly** every year; adv annually.

yearn v desire earnestly; feel tender longing towards; n **yearning.**

yeast n fungoid substance used as ferment in brewing, bread-making etc; a **yeasty** frothy, fermenting.

yell v cry loudly and sharply; n loud piercing cry.

yellow a 1 of colour between green and orange in spectrum 2 similar to colour of gold, lemons etc 3 sl cowardly; n this colour; ns **y. fever** serious infectious tropical disease; **y.-hammer** yellow feathered bird; **Y. Pages** telephone directory arranged under categories of business etc; **y. press** newspapers trading on sensationalism; v turn yellow, esp with age (as **-ed**); **-ing**).

yelp v give short sharp bark of pain or anger; n such cry.

yen n 1 Japanese dollar 2 sl intense desire, urge.

yeoman n hist small landowner cultivating his own land; **y. service** effective assistance; n **yeomanry** yeomen collectively; territorial volunteer cavalry force recruited mainly from country districts.

yes *interj* expressing affirmation, consent; is that so?; *n* **yes-man** one who weakly agrees with his leader's opinions.

yesterday *n* day before today; *pl* **-s** past times, former days.

yesteryear *n lit* recent past.

yet *adv* until now; now; besides; *conj* nevertheless, but still; *idm* **as yet** so far; until now.

yeti *n* hairy man-like creature believed to live in Himalayan mountains (*also* **Abominable Snowman**).

yew *n* evergreen coniferous tree; its wood.

Y-fronts *n Brit* type of underpants with Y-shaped front panel.

YHA *abbr* Youth Hostels Association.

Yiddish *n* mixed dialect of German, Hebrew and Slavonic, used by Jews in Europe and America.

yield *v* 1 produce, return as food 2 bring in (as financial return) 3 concede; give up; 4 be amenable (to treatment); *n* amount produced; result, profit, return; *a* **-ing** 1 flexible 2 easily persuaded.

yin *n* (in Chinese philosophy) inactive female principle.

yippee *interj* shout of delight.

YMCA *abbr* Young Men's Christian Association.

yob *n Brit* aggressive, ill-mannered youth (*also* **yobbo**).

yodel *v* **yodelling, yodelled.** warble, changing rapidly from natural voice to falsetto; *n* wordless, song or cry in this style.

yoga *n* Hindu system of meditation, controlling the body and mind; *n* **yogi** one who practices yoga.

yoghurt, yogurt *n* thick milk preparation, fermented by bacterial action.

yoke *n* 1 cross-piece shaped to fit necks of draught-animals, to which plough etc may be attached 2 part of garment cut to fit shoulders 3 *fig* authority; dominion; *v* harness with yoke; *fig* unite.

yokel *n* countryman; rustic.

yolk *n* yellow central part of egg.

yon *a lit* that, those over there; *a ar* **yonder** over there; *adv* in that direction.

yonks *n Brit coll* very long time.

Yorkshire pudding *n* baked batter eaten with roast beef.

you *pron* 2nd pers sing, pl) 1 person(s) lately spoken to 2 one, anyone.

you'd *contracted form of* 1 you had 2 you would.

you'll *contracted form of* you will.

you're *contracted form of* you are.

young *a* in early stages of life; not yet old; immature; inexperienced; *n* offspring; *n* **-ster** child, *esp* boy.

your *a* belonging to you; *pron* **yours** *poss of* you *idm* **yours truly** 1 formally polite phrase for ending letter 2 *coll* myself; *pron* **yourself** emphatic form of **you** (*pl* **yourselves**) *idm* **(all) by yourself** 1 alone 2 unaided; *idm* **(keep/have etc) to yourself** (keep/have) as exclusively for you or as a secret.

youth *n* early life; state of being young; young man; young people; *a* **-ful** (*n* **-ness**).

you've *contracted form of* you have.

yowl *v, n* (make) loud wailing cry.

yo-yo [TM] **-os.** toy consisting of double disc with groove between that runs up and down on a string.

YTS *abbr* youth training scheme.

yucca *n* tall plant with white bell-like flowers.

yuck *interj sl* expressing disgust; *a* **-y** *sl* disgusting (*also* **yukky**).

Yule *n* Christmas season or festival; **Yuletide** Christmas time.

yuppie, yuppy *n coll* ambitious young person in well-paid professional or business job; *a* typical of such people and their life-style (*also* **yuppish**).

YWCA *abbr* Young Women's Christian Association.

Z

zany a crazy (adv -ly; n -ness); n 1 clown 2 idiot, fool.

zap v zapping, zapped. coll 1 move suddenly with great force 2 attack with destructive force; a zappy lively and vigorous.

zeal n enthusiasm; earnest (adv -ly; n -ness); a zealous full of zeal; n zealot fanatic.

zebra n striped African quadruped; n z. crossing black and white pedestrian-crossing in street.

Zen a, n (of) Japanese Buddhist sect seeking truth through meditation.

zenith n point of heavens directly overhead; fig highest point, climax; acme.

zephyr n 1 West wind; 2 lit gentle breeze 3 very thin fine woollen fabric.

zeppelin n German dirigible airship used in World War I.

zero n 1 figure 0; nought 2 starting point in scale of measurement 3 fig lowest point; phr v zero in on 1 aim (missile etc) at 2 fig direct one's attention to; a forming z.-hour exact time at which important operation (esp mil) is due to begin.

zest n 1 keenness; gusto; ardour 2 relish; flavouring; a -ful (adv -ly).

zigzag n line having repeated sharp bends in alternate directions; a forming zigzag; adv with such course; v zigzagging, zigzagged. move in such course.

zillion det, n, pron extremely large number.

zimmer frame [TM] n metal walking frame.

zinc n bluish-white metallic element.

zinco, zincograph n design in relief on zinc plate; print made from this.

zinnia n annual plant of aster family.

Zion n hill in Jerusalem; fig City of Jerusalem; religious system of Jews; Christianity; n Zionism political and military movement that established independent Jewish state of Israel.

zip n 1 device for fastening with two rows of interlocking teeth, opened by sliding grip 2 light whizzing sound 3 coll energy, vigour; v zipping, zipped. fasten with zip-fastener; whizz ns z. code US numerical postcode; zipper US zip (fastener); a zippy coll fast.

zither v flat, stringed musical instrument.

zits n pl sl spots.

zodiac n imaginary belt in heavens, divided into twelve sections or signs, within which moon, sun and chief planets have their paths; a -al.

zombie n 1 corpse revived and controlled by witchcraft in W Indian voodoo 2 coll one who acts mechanically, without feeling or intelligence; as -ish; -like.

zone n belt, band; one of five regions of earth differentiated by climate; specified area, region; a zonal; n zoning designated areas of town etc.

zonked a sl 1 exhausted 2 drunk or drugged.

zoo n park where wild animals are kept and exhibited.

zoolite n fossil animal.

zoology n scientific study of animals; n **-logist;** a **-logical** of, for zoology (n **z. gardens** place where wild animals are kept for exhibition), ns **zoo-dynamics** animal physiology; **zoogeography** study of distribution of animals on surface of earth.

zoom v **1** compel aircraft to ascend rapidly at sharp angle **2** fig rise sharply in price; n **zoom** zooming; n **z. lens** camera lens allowing quick focus change, making distant subject suddenly seem much closer.

zoophyte n plant-like animal, eg sea-anemone.

zucchini n sing or pl US courgette(s).

Zulu n member, language of Bantu people of S Africa.

zygote n fertilized ovum.

zymotic a (of diseases) induced by propagation of living germs.